Mastering
Mac OS X v10.4 Tiger

Mastering™
Mac® OS X v10.4 Tiger
Fourth Edition

Todd Stauffer & Kirk McElhearn

SYBEX®

San Francisco   London

Publisher: Joel Fugazzotto
Acquisitions and Developmental Editor: Mariann Barsolo
Production Editor: Leslie E.H. Light
Technical Editor: James Bucanek
Copyeditors: Sarah Lemaire and Kathy Grider Carlyle
Compositor: Maureen Forys, Happenstance Type-O-Rama
Proofreaders: Nancy Riddiough, Candace English, James Brook
Indexer: Ted Laux
Book Designer: Maureen Forys, Happenstance Type-O-Rama
Cover Designer: Design Site
Cover Illustrator/Photographer: Jack T. Myers, Design Site

For Mom.
— T.S.

Acknowledgments

Todd would like to thank the people who helped make previous editions of the book possible, including Ellen Dendy, Diane Lowery, Elizabeth Campbell, Jim Gabbert, Joe Webb, Marilyn Smith, David Read, Fred Terry, Marty Cortinas, Lori Newman, and Maureen Forys. He'd also like to thank Chris Pepper and Dan Nolen for the chapters they contributed to the original edition of this book.

Thanks to the editorial team of Joel Fugazzotto, Mariann Barsolo, and Leslie Light for their kind management on the project. Thanks also to technical editor James Bucanek, whose detailed verification of every feature and function kept us on our toes, and copy editors Sarah Lemaire and Kathy Grider Carlyle, who dotted all the *I*s and crossed every *T*. And our thanks to Apple, Inc., and Mac OS senior product manager Mike Shebanek for answering frantic questions and offering valuable insight from Apple.

We'd be remiss in not thanking Studio B's David Rogelberg, Neil Salkind for helping us secure the opportunity to write this book—even if it was last century when we first started down this particular road. Thanks as always to the rest of the Studio B staff, particularly Laura Lewin, Renee Midrack, Katrina Bevan, and Sherry Rogelberg, for the diligence that keeps us (and scores of other authors) fed and clothed.

Finally, personal thanks from Todd to Donna Ladd for putting up with his bailing out of social plans at the last minute so that he could work on some of the tough parts of this book—particularly during the gruesome final weeks. He's grateful for her patience, and he promises that we won't revise this book again until the memory of the all-nighters this one produced has faded, at least somewhat.

Kirk would like to personally thank Todd for giving him an opportunity to work with him again on this project. He would also like to thank all the readers whose questions keep him on his toes. And thanks, as always, to Marie-France, for her everyday help, and Perceval for being a budding Mac fanatic.

Contents at a Glance

Contents

Introduction

Mac OS X 10.4, dubbed "Tiger" as both its development code name and in some marketing materials, is a good example of an operating system that's starting to really mature and blossom. We've watched Mac OS X for over five years now, and we're persistently amazed at what Apple is able to do and accomplish toward both making the Mac experience better and incorporating some of the latest computer science in a way that advances the way we work with computers. With Mac OS X 10.4, we're getting both sides of that coin, with incremental improvements in things like an updated Mail program and increased capabilities for iChat AV, as well as all-new systems for extending the computing experience, such as the Spotlight search engine and Automator, which offers a new way for everyday Mac users to automate repetitive tasks.

Those advances are part of what made *Mastering Mac OS X v.10.4 Tiger* a fun book to update. We think you'll find valuable information, occasional wisdom, and some plain old decent advice for making the transition to Mac OS X version 10.4—and then making the most of the experience once you've made that transition.

This latest release of Mac OS X is focused on improving productivity and efficiency via updates to Mail, iChat, and Safari, and by integrating Spotlight-style searches and automation into a number of applications. In many cases, Apple has added "smart folders" and other items that automate the process of searching and filtering within applications or for your entire system. Spotlight in particular is interesting because it can change the way you work on your Mac, enabling you to search the content of a variety of documents and files—everything from PDFs to e-mail messages—meaning you can spend a little less time searching for and managing your files in folders and subfolders. And the new Dashboard feature is not only fun to play with, but it offers quick access to small applications (called "widgets") that you can use to be more productive in your work—dictionary, time, weather, flight lookups, and the potential to add tons of third-party widgets to extend its capabilities.

Mac OS X version 10.4 improves performance considerably, takes advantage of Mac hardware (such as the PowerPC G4 and G5 processors and the graphics accelerator circuitry in many Mac models), and goes further down the road of incorporating core technologies for multimedia and excellence in technologies that support creators and users. In particular, Mac OS X 10.4 offers support for advanced 64-bit applications (which may be slow coming, but represent something new on the horizon) as well as core improvements such as QuickTime 7.

Mac OS X is interesting even if you're accustomed to other operating systems, because it offers impressive new capabilities and compatibilities. Mac OS X can participate in a Windows or Unix-based network of computers, and it offers a host of Internet and file-sharing services and tools. Mac OS X ultimately is based on Unix-like FreeBSD, making it a familiar environment for users of

Unix- and Linux-based operating systems who would like the opportunity to run Mac applications such as Microsoft Office, Adobe Photoshop, and Apple's Final Cut Pro alongside open-source Unix-based applications, compilers, utilities, graphical applications, server enhancements, and so on.

Mac OS X offers even more new and interesting technologies that are worth exploring for users of any OS, including Bonjour, .Mac and synchronization support, Bluetooth support, network-based Address Book updates, improvements to iCal, and many others. It's built to be faster, more capable, and a little bit more mature and sophisticated than its previous incarnations.

If you're just now moving to Mac OS X, it may require some transition time, particularly for users familiar with Mac OS 9 and earlier versions. (See Appendix B for some tips.) Mac OS X offers a different filesystem, also based on the FreeBSD operating system, which can take a little getting used to. It offers some wonderful new bells, whistles, and honest-to-goodness productivity enhancements. And it offers a glimpse into a whole new world—Unix and Unix-like operating systems—that most Mac users have never encountered but will enjoy exploring. However, some Classic Mac users and users of other operating systems occasionally will find the newness of Mac OS X frustrating.

Once you grow familiar with this new OS—hopefully *Mastering Mac OS X v10.4 Tiger* will help—you won't want to go back.

What This Book Covers

Mastering Mac OS X v10.4 Tiger is designed to be a comprehensive look at Apple's latest release of Mac OS X, and it is aimed particularly at users who are interested in advancing their knowledge beyond the basics to intermediate or even advanced user status. If you'd like to apply your knowledge of early versions of the Mac OS or Microsoft Windows (or even Unix and Linux variants) to this exciting new OS, you've come to the right place. From the fundamentals of the interface to the depths of the Darwin command line (and Unix-like syntax), you'll find that *Mastering Mac OS X v10.4 Tiger* covers most of the topics you need to know to exploit your Mac as a workstation, either as a stand-alone computer or in a networked environment.

Mastering Mac OS X v10.4 Tiger is organized as a reference, with parts and chapters divided into topic areas. While you may find it useful to read straight through the text, you certainly don't have to. Once you've mastered the basics, you can move directly to a particular chapter to see topics such as:

◆ Burning data CDs from the Finder (Chapter 3)

◆ Working with Dashboard (Chapter 4)

◆ Customizing the desktop and your home folder (Chapter 5)

◆ Finding anything on your Mac with Spotlight (Chapter 6)

◆ Setting up a network or local printer (Chapter 7)

◆ Managing a multi-user Mac OS X system (Chapter 9)

◆ Working with Safari, using .Mac, dealing with downloaded files, and using Sherlock (Chapter 11)

◆ Using the improved and expanded Mail application, including its ability to filter and automate mail filing (Chapter 12)

◆ Viewing and exporting QuickTime movies (Chapter 13)

◆ Working with iTunes, digital audio, and the iPod (Chapter 14)

◆ Managing all your personal information, with Address Book, iCal and iSync (Chapter 16)

◆ Setting up an Ethernet or AirPort network connection (Chapter 18)

◆ Running Windows applications or Unix applications and sharing cross-platform documents (Chapter 20)

◆ Learning to use Automator and AppleScript (Chapter 21)

◆ Getting around on the command line via the Terminal applications (Chapter 22)

◆ Installing and working with command-line applications (Chapter 23)

◆ Configuring and tweaking the Apache web server (Chapter 24)

◆ Maintaining your hard disk and data (Chapter 26)

◆ Troubleshooting Mac OS X (Chapters 27, 28, and 29)

Here's a quick look at each of the sections of the book:

◆ In Part 1, "The Mac OS X Basics," you'll begin with the fundamentals of the operating system that make Mac OS X unique, focusing in many cases on the differences between Mac OS X, Mac OS X Server, and earlier versions, particularly from the user's point of view. You'll see how to customize the Finder, how to work with native and Classic applications, and how to access the help and search components of Mac OS X. This section also shows you how to customize your personal Mac OS X workspace, how to set up a printer and print to it, how to create and work with PDF documents, and how to manage your Mac as its administrator. You'll also look at some of the applications and utilities included with Mac OS X.

◆ In Part 2, "On the Internet," you'll delve into Internet setup for individual Macs or a network of Macs, and you'll see Mac OS X's built-in Mail client, as well as other Internet clients and applications. In this edition, this discussion includes a look at Apple's sophisticated Internet tools, such as .Mac and iChat AV, as well as a look at the fundamental improvements in Mail 2.0 and the enhanced security features available in the Network settings. This section also takes a look at a number of third-party solutions, such as the variety of web browsers and FTP applications that are available for Mac OS X.

◆ Part 3, "Audio, Video, and Your Personal Information," focuses on Mac OS X's capability to deal with visual and audio files, technologies, and applications, including QuickTime and movies, iTunes, MP3 audio, speech, handwriting recognition, and speech recognition. Chapter 15 takes a look at digital images and how you can use the Mac's various photo-focused applications, including iPhoto, to create, view, and manipulate those images. Chapter 16 rounds things out with a look at Address Book, iCal and the technologies that Mac OS X offers for synchronizing your personal data.

◆ Part 4, "Networking, Connectivity, and Portables" starts with a look at the multitude of ways you can log in to and use existing servers, whether on your local network or over the Internet. Then you'll see how to create your own Ethernet or wireless network and how to share files over it. Chapter 19 discusses issues that relate particularly to users of portable Mac models such as the iBook and PowerBook, and Chapter 20 takes a look at the different ways you can use Mac OS X to be "cross-platform," including support for Windows and Unix documents, file sharing and, in some cases, running applications meant for another OS.

◆ Part 5, "Advanced Mac OS X Topics," dives beneath the graphical OS, introducing you to the most advanced parts of Mac OS X—scripting, the command line, and the built-in server applications. You'll learn the basics of the Automator application and the AppleScript language, get an in-depth introduction to the Darwin command line, and learn about the specifics of using and working with the Apache and FTP servers built into Mac OS X.

◆ Part 6, "Hardware, Troubleshooting, and Maintenance," rounds out the book with five chapters on setup and troubleshooting, including coverage of peripherals, application troubleshooting, system-level diagnostics, and file maintenance. Chapter 29 ends the section with common Mac OS X problems and their solutions.

After that, you'll find three appendices—Appendix A helps you get Mac OS X installed (if Mac OS X didn't come preinstalled on your Mac and/or you're installing a new version), Appendix B will prove helpful if you're an experienced user of the Classic Mac OS who would like a quick explanation of the differences and changes you'll encounter in Mac OS X, and Appendix C covers the many applications included with Mac OS X.

Conventions Used in This Book

This book uses some conventions and special formatting to easily communicate different commands, ideas, and concepts. Here's a look at some of the formats you'll encounter:

◆ Items in *italic* generally are terms being introduced and defined. In some other cases, italics also are used for variables or placeholders (as in *you@youraccount*.com) that suggest information you need to know or enter to work with a particular feature or application.

◆ Items in **boldface** generally are commands or text you can type, while lines of programming code, filenames, Internet addresses, and command-line entries appear in a `monospaced` font.

◆ Menu commands use a right-facing arrow to suggest the menu you should select, followed by the command. For instance, File ➢ Open means to click the File menu in the menu bar at the top of the screen and then click the Open command.

◆ Keyboard shortcuts often include special symbols and a plus sign (+) between them, such as Control+click or Shift+Tab. With the special Apple Command key, you'll see entries such as ⌘P, which means press the Command key (with the Apple logo on it) and the letter "P" to invoke the command. With keyboard shortcuts, you need to press all of the keys indicated simultaneously and then release them together.

Aside from these formatting conventions, you'll come across a few special callout boxes within the body of the text itself. These boxes are designed to focus your attention on particular issues, depending on the type of box:

NOTE   Notes are designed to give you additional information about the current topic or to offer additional insight or definitions. Notes also are used sometimes as cross-references to other topics and chapters.

TIP   Tips help you perform the current task faster or give you some other option for working with the current topic. You can ignore a Tip without risking trouble, but hopefully you'll enjoy them all.

WARNING   Warnings definitely are not to be ignored. In most cases, we'll issue a Warning only if you could damage files, erase disks, or otherwise perform an irreversible task that you might want to think about twice.

Along with these callouts, you'll also find sidebars throughout the text that are designed to give you more information related to the current discussion. Again, sidebars often can be ignored, but they may offer interesting or helpful advice for going deeper into a particular topic.

Finally, you'll encounter one special little graphic in this edition of *Mastering Mac OS X*—the "Tiger" icon. This is just a little hint to let you know that you're reading about a feature that's new in Mac OS X 10.4.

Extras and Contact Info

Mac OS X is a constantly moving target—as the first five or so years of its release have proven—and this book is printed and bound. That doesn't mean it can't breathe, however. For additional information as it becomes available, as well as answers to frequently asked questions (FAQs) and any errata that this book generates, you can visit Sybex's site at www.sybex.com for official updates, addenda, and other information (search for 4401, which is part of the book's ISBN).

In addition, you can visit the website Todd created to support this book at www.masteringmacosx.com/ He maintains important links on that page, including a link to his website's public discussion forum, where you can ask questions and find answers to questions about Macs, Mac OS X, and so on. Please look there before writing Todd directly, because you're likely to get answers more quickly.

Kirk's website, Kirkville (www.mcelhearn.com), presents information about Macs, iPods, iTunes, music, books and more. You can find out about all of Kirk's books, and read some of his musings on these subjects.

If you don't find the answer you need after visiting those websites, please feel free to send us an e-mail message at todd@masteringmacosx.com. Include a detailed subject line with your e-mail, indicating whether or not your question is an immediate priority. It can take a while (sometimes weeks) to reply to every e-mail, but we'll do our best. Thanks for your patience, and thanks for choosing *Mastering Mac OS X v10.4 Tiger*.

Part 1

The Mac OS X Basics

In this section, you will learn how to:

- ◆ Compare Mac OS X to other Mac versions
- ◆ Work with files and folders in the Finder
- ◆ Personalize your Mac
- ◆ Get help and search for items
- ◆ Print and fax files
- ◆ Set permissions and add users

Chapter 1

What Is Mac OS X and What's New?

An operating system (OS) is a set of computer instructions that enables the computer to interact with the user and any peripheral devices such as printers, disk drives, and monitors. More to the point, the OS is what gives your computer a great deal of its "personality." The OS determines the look of windows and icons and other controls on your screen. It's used for managing your files and applications and documents. It's the underlying technology for all sorts of tasks, from printing to playing back onscreen video to connecting to other computers over a wireless network or via the Internet.

Apple's flagship OS is Mac OS X, now in its fifth major iteration, Mac OS X 10.4 "Tiger." Mac OS X is Apple's twenty-first-century operating system—both metaphorically and in terms of its timeline—bringing a number of interesting tools and capabilities to Mac users while taking advantage of the continued hardware advances that Apple has made with its various models of Macintosh computers.

In this chapter, you'll learn how Mac OS X came to be, what its outstanding features are, and how you can use your existing Mac applications with OS X. You'll also learn about the changes that have been made since Mac OS X was first introduced, particularly those that have occurred at the various milestone releases since Mac OS X was brought to market.

In this chapter:

- ◆ What Is Mac OS X?
- ◆ Mac OS X Features
- ◆ Mac OS X and Applications
- ◆ Classic Compatibility
- ◆ What Changed in Mac OS X Versions 10.1 Through 10.3?
- ◆ What's New in Version 10.4?

What Is Mac OS X?

For years, the Mac OS (or the Macintosh "system" software, as it used to be called) has been considered the cutting edge of interface design and user friendliness.

The Mac OS, as innovative as it was when introduced in 1984, has long been in need of a major overhaul in order to make it fully "modern"—it should be as stable and capable as today's computer scientists and programmers can make it. Although the Mac OS has been updated year after year, those updates were hampered somewhat by the original Mac OS design—a design that didn't foresee every innovation in OS thinking. Since those innovations tended to be quick in coming—what seems impossible today becomes necessary within months, sometimes—the Mac OS in the late 1990s was consistently restricted by limitations that meant the Mac OS wasn't taking advantage of the latest advances in computer and software design.

To solve this problem, Apple opted to essentially do away with the foundation of the existing Mac OS and move on to different technology. While some of the cues, interface elements, and tools of the new Mac OS X are similar to what is known now as the "Classic" Mac OS, many of those features have changed dramatically. And what has changed even more is the technological foundation of the Mac OS.

Mac OS X is based on much of the technology that Apple acquired when it bought NeXT Software, a company launched and run by Steve Jobs from the mid-1980s until 1997. NeXT Software sold an operating system called OpenStep, based on its earlier NeXTStep, which in turn was based on FreeBSD, a Unix-like, open-source operating system. OpenStep was a very modern operating system, featuring many of the advantages that Apple wanted the Mac OS to sport.

There was still a lot of work to do, though. OpenStep was designed to run on Intel-compatible chips and ran applications that weren't very Mac-like in their interface design. Although OpenStep offered a very attractive graphical interface for applications, it also had a dark side: a Unix command line even more intimidating than the arcane DOS commands that run underneath Microsoft Windows (see Figure 1.1).

Porting the OpenStep underpinnings to run on Macintosh hardware was a challenge for Apple. On top of that, Apple spent even more time making the Mac OS X interface similar to the existing Classic Mac interface, while updating and improving it. Throughout this process, Mac OS X was engineered to support most existing Mac OS 9–based applications. Finally, it needed to be better than the previous operating system both in terms of its underlying technology and the features that it offered. That has been Apple's goal with Mac OS X since it was introduced as version 10.0—improving it and making it truly an indispensable upgrade in the computing experience.

NOTE   Watching Mac OS X gain respect in the computing community, particularly among developers and...well, computer geeks, has been interesting. It turns out the Mac OS X offers something that some people have wanted for a long time—a Unix-based operating system that offers a wide array of commercial applications and a user-friendly interface. It has surprised some industry watchers that this "buzzword-compliant" OS has been supplied by Apple under the guise of the Macintosh, which has historically been considered something of a "toy" computer by outsiders. (Its popularity in high-end creative and corporate tasks belies the notion that the Macintosh has ever been a toy.) Mac OS X offers nearly all the advantages of an open-source Unix-based operating system, with most of the advantages of the Macintosh's existing base of quality applications, developer support, and ease-of-use advantages.

Mac OS X Features

Mac OS X was designed to address performance shortcomings in the Classic Mac OS with the following features: preemptive multitasking, memory protection, dynamic RAM allocation, and a microkernel-based design. With these four fundamental changes, Mac OS X is a more modern, less errorprone operating system than its predecessors. In addition, Mac OS X improves on two technologies that have a limited implementation in Mac OS 9: multithreading and symmetrical processing.

FIGURE 1.1
The Unix command line, shown in Mac OS X's Terminal window

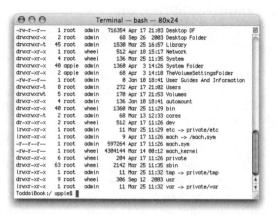

Perhaps more noticeably, Mac OS X also offers a new interface that builds on many of the strengths of Mac OS 9 while incorporating other theories and elements from OpenStep, Linux, and even Microsoft Windows. The result is a visually pleasing interface—called Aqua—that makes it easier to navigate a network, work on the Internet, and manage multiple open applications and documents. Beyond that, Apple is incorporating even newer technologies like Spotlight—which can search the contents of files on your drive and return smart results from keyword searches—to extend Mac OS X into spaces where no widely used operating system has yet been.

What this means for the user is that Mac OS X is a user-friendly operating system that's also very powerful, taking full advantage of modern Macintosh hardware. Mac OS X is useful for a wide variety of tasks, including professional graphics and layout, 3D design and video editing, file sharing, and specialized Internet tasks such as serving QuickTime streaming media. Mac OS X is also perfectly well suited to the home or small office user, assuming that the user's consumer-level hardware can handle Mac OS X's requirements. Mac OS X is a consumer OS as well as a business one—it ships as the default operating system on all new Apple Macintosh computers, including the consumer-focused iMac, eMac, and iBook offerings. It's both a heavy-duty operating system, more capable and stable than the Classic Mac OS, and at the same time a "friendly" OS that offers typical users a pleasing experience for daily computing.

That's what Mac OS X is capable of. Let's take a look at some behind-the-scenes features that make Mac OS X what it is and enable it to take on heavy-duty computing tasks.

NOTE   Throughout this book, we'll refer to "Mac OS 9," the "Classic Mac OS" and, occasionally, a specific version, such as Mac OS 9.2.2. While it may seem confusing, there's good reason to do this. We refer to "Mac OS 9" when we mean it generically but don't intend to include earlier versions (such as Mac OS 8, 8.5, and so on) in the discussion. For instance, Mac OS 9 introduced certain changes to networking that are similar to some offerings in Mac OS X but weren't present in some earlier Mac OS versions. When we mean to include the entire gamut of earlier Mac OS versions, we'll refer to the "Classic Mac OS," as in "unlike the Classic Mac OS, Mac OS X cannot work with serial-based printers." Finally, we'll refer specifically to a Mac OS 9 version number when discussing a particular compatibility issue.

Preemptive Multitasking

Although the Classic Mac OS had basic *cooperative* multitasking capabilities (which allowed more than one application to be running at a time) since Mac System 7 in the early 1990s, the Classic Mac OS was never updated to embrace the fully modern *preemptive* multitasking approach that Mac OS X offers.

In cooperative multitasking, it's up to each individual application to determine how much of the processor's attention it deserves and how much of that attention it's willing to give over to other applications. This system works well when all applications behave. A poorly written application or one that's experiencing errors can get in the way of this multitasking system, making the entire OS less reliable or causing it to hang or freeze, thus forcing you to restart the Mac and possibly lose unsaved data.

With preemptive multitasking, Mac OS X is responsible for telling applications how much time they can get from the processor and how much time other applications get. Working as a traffic cop, Mac OS X can keep an errant application from affecting others that are running at the same time. In practical terms, this limits the number of freezes or endless-loop crashes that you'll have in Mac OS X versus the Classic Mac OS.

Memory Protection

One of the major reasons for an application crash is the accidental processing of garbage input—data that the application isn't expecting and doesn't know how to handle. With any operating system, each launched application generally is assigned a certain amount of RAM (system memory); that application then can decide how to use the RAM, including where to put its data and instructions. If one application were to put bad data into a RAM location that belongs to another application, the second application might experience errors or crashes when it tries to read that spurious data.

Memory protection in Mac OS X makes it impossible for one application to overwrite another's memory locations. This isn't exactly a common occurrence in Mac OS 9, but it's possible, resulting in a less stable system. With memory protection, Mac OS X can keep one crashing application from bringing down other applications, because Mac OS X doesn't allow one application to write to another's memory space. The upshot is a fairly dramatic decrease in the number of application crashes in Mac OS X versus the Classic Mac OS, as well as the virtual elimination of a common problem in earlier Mac OS versions in which one application can cause another to crash. Even if an application encounters an error in Mac OS X, you can almost always continue computing in other applications without fear that they, too, will soon crash.

Dynamic RAM Allocation

Users of previous Mac OS versions know that each application gets a fixed allocation of RAM when the application is started. It's a range that's determined by a setting in the application's Get Info dialog box. (You can see this dialog box in Mac OS 9 by selecting an application icon and choosing File ➤ Get Info from the Finder's menu, as shown in Figure 1.2.) This fixed RAM allocation system, though, is wasteful because RAM assigned to an open application—even if that RAM isn't being used—is reserved and can't be used by another application.

Unfortunately, many Classic Mac crashes and problems arise from having the Get Info memory settings too low. Even though the Classic Mac OS may have more RAM at its disposal, it will give an application only as much RAM as it requests when the application is launched. If the Get Info setting is too low and the application runs out of memory, there isn't much that can be done by the operating system. Instead, the user has to quit the application, open the Get Info dialog box, and manually increase the memory allocation. Upon relaunch, the application has access to more RAM.

FIGURE 1.2

The Memory panel of
the Get Info dialog box
(for Microsoft Excel) in
Mac OS 9

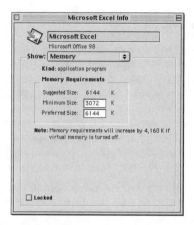

Because of its dynamic RAM-allocation approach, Mac OS X is in charge of dealing with RAM requests from applications. When you launch an application, it will ask for as much RAM as it needs. If that RAM is available, Mac OS X will hand it over. If the application needs more because of additional documents or temporary tasks or for other reasons, it can ask for more, and Mac OS X can hand some over. If the application isn't using all that it has been allocated, it can free up that RAM on-the-fly, and the Mac OS can assign the RAM to another application that needs it.

This technology results in more stability for the system and less hassle for the user than was true in the Classic Mac OS: with RAM allocation out of your hands, you can simply launch applications and let Mac OS X figure out how best to allocate memory for those applications.

Multithreading

Another advanced OS feature is *multithreading,* which allows individual applications to create more than one *process*. For instance, a word processing application might create a thread that's designed to print one document while another thread enables the user to edit a second document. In this way, a multithreaded application can be more responsive to user input, with multiple threads within that application accomplishing tasks simultaneously.

Although both Mac OS 9 and Mac OS X offer multithreading, Mac OS X is designed from the ground up to support it, while multithreading support in Mac OS 9 is grafted onto the OS. Not all applications written for Mac OS 9 are multithreaded, for instance, because the approach just isn't as pervasive. Applications written directly for Mac OS X use multithreading as a matter of course.

As Mac OS X has matured, more and more of its included applications and system-level components have been rewritten for multithreading, including such vital applications as the Finder (the main file management utility). This, along with other improvements and optimizations, has helped Mac OS X versions become better performers over time, even on the same equipment.

Symmetrical Multiprocessing

Mac OS X supports Macintosh computers that feature more than one processor (called *multiprocessor systems*). Although Macintosh systems have been capable of dealing with multiple processors in the past, it has always been on an application-by-application basis. (For instance, Adobe Photoshop, a favorite of Macintosh power users, offers a plug-in that supports multiprocessing in the Classic Mac OS.) With Mac OS X, the support is built right into the operating system, meaning all tasks and processes can take advantage of multiple processors.

WHAT IS MAC OS X SERVER?

By now, you're probably clear on what Mac OS X is, but you also may have heard of Mac OS X *Server* and wondered about the differences. Actually, they're reasonably similar—Mac OS X Server is the same operating system with more bundled applications that focus on managing a network of computers and/or an Internet presence. Mac OS X Server is more expensive, too, because it's designed to be a hub for the activity generated by a workgroup of Mac OS X and Mac OS 9 (and Mac OS 8) computers. One Macintosh running Mac OS X Server can serve files, manage the printing, and even serve content to Internet users, all from the same machine. Mac OS X Server can be bought separately and run on most modern Mac hardware, although it's best suited to the Power Mac G4 Server or Apple's high-end, rack-mounted server computer, called Xserve (www.apple.com/xserve/).

Mac OS X Server is essentially a package of server applications and utilities that run on top of Mac OS X. The basic underpinnings—the Mach kernel, the "modern" OS capabilities, and many of the interface elements—are the same for both Mac OS X and Mac OS X Server. Although Mac OS X includes some server applications and utilities in its own right, Mac OS X Server extends those capabilities with high-end add-ons, including these:

QuickTime Streaming Server and Broadcaster   QuickTime 4 and higher versions support streaming media—movies and audio clips that play as they arrive, instead of waiting for an entire download before playing. The QuickTime Streaming Server software built into Mac OS X Server enables you to webcast such streaming media, making them available to many people at once. QuickTime Broadcaster works with Streaming Server to enable you to broadcast live events over the Web.

WebObjects and Internet Serving   This is another technology brought to Apple from NeXT Software. WebObjects is a network (usually Internet) application development and serving environment, making it easier to create full-fledged e-commerce solutions such as online stores. (For instance, Apple's online store is built and served using WebObjects.) Mac OS X Server includes Apache and SSL security, plus additional servers such as an e-mail server and support for PHP and MySQL server applications. Mac OS X Server also includes an e-mail server, FTP server, QuickTime Streaming Server, and others.

NetBoot and NetInstall   NetBoot allows Mac OS X Server to boot client machines—iMacs, Power Macs, PowerBooks, and others—directly from a server instead of from that computer's internal hard disk. This feature makes it easier to standardize computers and control them from a central location. It also makes it easier for your personal files to follow you around, because you can boot a client computer with your password and then gain access to all your files and custom settings. NetInstall makes it possible for you to install applications on multiple networked Mac clients at the same time.

File and Printer Sharing   Mac OS X Server can offer file sharing between the server and Macs using typical AppleShare protocols, over either AppleTalk or TCP/IP-based networks. Like AppleShare IP servers, a Mac OS X Server computer can store files and transfer them from the main server to workstations that are logged into the server. Mac OS X Server also can serve files to Windows clients and manage network print queues.

Because the OS has control over managing the processors in a multiprocessor Mac, different tasks and threads can be assigned to different processors. This makes the machine more capable and more responsive overall because more processors are at work, and therefore things happen more efficiently. Symmetrical multiprocessing takes this concept even further: you can assign processes and threads *within one application* to different processors, which makes individual applications more responsive as well.

Although multiprocessing hasn't been a hallmark of Apple's hardware designs in past decades, that changed somewhat in the summer of 2000 with the introduction of dual-processor Power Macintosh G4 models. Although the dual processors are only somewhat useful when running Mac OS 9 (as mentioned, individual applications such as Photoshop must specifically support multiprocessing), Mac OS X takes full advantage of multiple processors automatically. Since then, the trend toward multiprocessor Power Macintosh models has continued, with more and more of Apple's most powerful desktop computers sporting multiple processors now and in the future.

Microkernel Architecture

At the heart of all of Mac OS X's improvements is a *microkernel*—a small mini-OS that works between the Mac OS interface and the physical Macintosh hardware. This microkernel provides a level of abstraction between the hardware and software; in this way, most of Mac OS X isn't written for a particular piece of hardware, as Mac OS 9 is. That makes the OS more stable and reliable. It also makes it more *portable*, leaving open the possibility that Mac OS X (and later versions) could run on processors other than Motorola's (or IBM's) PowerPC processor, which is the processor type currently shipped in every Macintosh.

The microkernel, called Mach 3.0, is also the traffic cop that manages many of the other features already mentioned: preemptive multitasking, multithreading, and multiprocessing.

Other Innovations

Besides the basic system advances that Mac OS X offers over earlier Mac OS versions, it also sports a number of new features. These range from advantages brought on by the Unix underpinnings to new features that have been written specifically for Mac OS X. Let's take a look at a quick list, although we'll be exploring these features throughout the book:

Finder and Interface Mac OS X sports a new Finder, based on the browser interface that was used in NeXT Software's operating systems, including OpenStep. The Mac OS X Finder offers a unique way to browse not only files on your Mac's hard disk but also those that exist over a network—whether it's a local network in your organization or disks and volumes that are available to you via the Internet. The Finder works hand-in-hand with a revamped interface (called *Aqua* by Apple) that offers a simpler, more animated look and feel. The OS also features a new Dock for managing applications and open documents, as well as the System Preferences application, menu behavior, menu bar icons, and many other changes.

Graphics Architecture Called *Quartz*, the graphics architecture is based in part on Adobe's Portable Document Format (PDF). PDF technology enables computers to create documents that can be transmitted to other users and displayed or printed correctly, even if those users don't have the same printer, fonts, or other features as the computer where the document was created. Basing the underlying graphics system on this technology makes it easier for Mac OS X applications to share documents among multiple computers. Likewise, the graphics architecture builds in some sophisticated visual effects such as the transparency and text smoothing that's used throughout the Mac OS X interface. In Mac OS X 10.2 and higher, Apple's *Quartz Extreme* technology allows the OS to take advantage of the advanced graphics processors that are installed in modern Macs, enabling the OS's elements to display more quickly and with more sophisticated graphical effects.

Integrated E-Mail Client Mac OS X offers Mail, an e-mail client included with the Mac OS that offers full support for various types of email accounts, including .Mac accounts using Apple's subscription services, as well as standard POP accounts available from your ISP or IMAP account that you might use in an organizational setting. It also supports system-level technologies, such as adding PDF graphics to e-mail messages and searching your e-mail with Mac OS X's built-in search engine. In Mac OS X 10.4, Mail has been completely updated and is given the Mail 2.0 moniker.

QuickTime Apple's multimedia architecture, QuickTime, is a fundamental part of the operating system, making its capabilities available to any application that wants to use them. That gives applications the capability to work easily with images, video, and audio, while translating between file formats and generally working some impressive multimedia magic. Even the Finder, Dock, and other parts of the Mac OS can quickly preview images and multimedia presentations to help you manage your "digital hub" tasks, such as working with photos, editing video, and managing music files.

NOTE "Digital hub" is Apple's name for its marketing and product development strategy to encourage the use of Macintosh computers as the hub for a variety of digital lifestyle devices such as digital cameras and camcorders, MP3 music players, and personal digital assistants.

Multiuser Support Mac OS X requires a login name and password, enabling multiple users each to access a unique desktop, store personal documents and applications, and manage their own Internet connections. Log in with your username, and all your personal preferences are preserved, while your documents and personal applications are secure from other users.

Advanced Networking Features Because it's based on TCP/IP, the networking protocol used over the Internet, Mac OS X features a number of networking features, including the capability to network and share files (in various ways) over the Internet. One of these is Apple's AirPort technology, which enables wireless connections between your Macs.

The Classic Environment With support for Classic Macintosh applications, Mac OS X is able to run almost any application that's compatible with Mac OS 9. Although these applications aren't given access to full Mac OS X features (such as preemptive multitasking and protected memory), they can be run at the same time that other Mac OS X applications run. This enables you to use older applications that don't offer Mac OS X upgrades or that you can't afford to upgrade for one reason or another. The Classic environment has proven to be very useful for users who are transitioning to Mac OS X but haven't yet replaced all their older applications. (Also, because Mac OS X is very new, it's taken a while for all vendors to offer *native* Mac OS X versions of their popular applications.) As time wears on, the Classic environment will be less and less important. For now, however, it can still be critical, at least under some circumstances.

Mac OS X and Applications

You'll encounter five different types of applications that Mac OS X can run. Which you choose can affect the performance of not only that one application but also your entire Mac OS X system. You need to know the types:

Mac OS X Applications These applications are written specifically for the "Cocoa" native portion of Mac OS X. They require no special emulation, and they run directly on top of Mac OS X without modification. Best of all, they take full advantage of multitasking, multithreading, multiprocessor support, and memory protection. An example of these applications is the Mail application included with Mac OS X; it was written from scratch to support Mac OS X.

Mac OS "Carbon" Applications   These applications also are native to Mac OS X, and they can pretty much take full advantage of the modern OS underpinnings. They may be a little more limited in their full performance potential because the Carbon libraries are a stopgap measure for Mac OS 9 developers who want their applications to run effectively in both Mac OS 9 and Mac OS X. That said, there's nothing wrong with running a Carbon application every day, all day, if you like. AppleWorks 6.*x*—an "office" application included with many consumer Mac models—is an example of a "carbonized" application.

Mac OS Classic Applications   These applications are designed to run only in Mac OS 9. Thanks to Mac OS X's capability to run a Mac OS 9 environment as an individual process, these applications also can be run in your workspace. This is fine on occasion, but relying on Classic applications for all your computing needs is not recommended. If you have a lot of Classic applications, you should consider sticking with Mac OS 9, at least until you've upgraded to Carbon applications. (See the next section of this chapter for more on the Classic environment.)

Java Applications   These are applications designed to run on any computer that supports the Java programming language. Mac OS X features an impressive Java interpreter. In general, it's okay to run these applications, although they might not have full access to all the features of the Mac OS. These applications, because of their one-size-fits-all approach, tend to be more limited in both capabilities and scope, but they are usually useful smaller applications that can perform their designed tasks well. (See Chapter 20, "Mac OS X and Other Platforms," for more on Java applications.)

Command-Line Applications   Although its use is discouraged by Apple, the fact remains that Mac OS X has a command-line interface (accessed most often through the Terminal application), and it's relatively easy to write and port applications that run from the command line without a standard Mac graphical interface. If you encounter such an application and wish to run it, you'll definitely need Mac OS X because it's the only Mac OS that supports such applications. (The Terminal and command-line applications will be discussed specifically in Chapter 22, "Terminal and the Command Line," and Chapter 23, "Command-Line Applications and Magic.")

Classic Compatibility

Fortunately, using Mac OS X doesn't mean you have to leave behind your critical Mac OS 9 applications, if you still have any. That's because Mac OS X can run a process that emulates the Mac OS 9 environment, enabling you to use applications that run specifically on Mac OS 9 (see Figure 1.3). Whenever you launch a Classic application (one that isn't designed to run natively in Mac OS X), the operating system will attempt to launch it in the Classic compatibility environment and will launch the environment itself if it isn't already running. If the application works in the Classic environment, you'll be able to use it side by side with other Mac OS X applications. The menu bar and windows will look slightly different, but that's the only obvious difference.

There are less obvious differences, however. The support for Mac OS 9 applications in Mac OS X has its limitations because Mac OS X runs the entire Mac OS 9 Classic environment as a single process, as though it were just another Mac OS X application. In other words, individual Mac OS 9 applications are susceptible to crashes, freezes, and so on, thanks to the lack of memory protection and pre-emptive multitasking *within* the Classic environment.

FIGURE 1.3
Mac OS 9 (the Classic
environment) starting
up on a Mac OS X system

Other Mac OS X applications continue to enjoy those features, so if the Classic environment does crash, it shouldn't affect the rest of the Mac OS X system. Instead, you'll be able to kill the Classic process and start over again if you like. However, that's the reason you shouldn't rely on multiple Mac OS 9 applications on a day-to-day basis if you're going to run Mac OS X. Aside from the potential for crashes, the Classic environment can be taxing on a Mac OS X system, causing sluggishness.

How about other machines in the office? Mac OS X and Mac OS 9 can work together in harmony on different machines. Because both support Apple File Services file sharing and AppleTalk printer sharing, Mac OS X and Mac OS 9 can coexist nicely on the same network. Even if you have older Macintosh computers sharing a network with your Mac OS X machine, you should have no problem using them together.

What Changed in Mac OS X Versions 10.1 Through 10.3?

Released in the fall of 2001, Mac OS X version 10.1 was considered by many (the suggestion was made even by Steve Jobs, CEO of Apple, Inc.) to be the first truly full-featured release of Mac OS X. This was the one that was deemed ready for prime time, with fewer hang-ups and problems than it had innovations and improvements. External devices worked better, new applications flourished, user interface improvements were made, and so on.

Perhaps the key improvement that Mac OS X version 10.1 offered over its predecessors was performance. While the earlier versions of Mac OS X were slow on anything but the latest G3 and G4 processors, Mac OS X version 10.1 worked well even on midrange iMacs and PowerBooks. In particular, applications tended to launch much more quickly, and windows were redrawn and moved around on the screen in real time. In fact, Mac OS X version 10.1 tended to be much more responsive in multitasking situations—playing a song and a QuickTime movie and checking your email all at the same time—than earlier versions of Mac OS X.

Aside from performance, Mac OS X offered a few other improvements:

◆ New *menu bar icons*, which enabled you to change basic settings without opening System Preferences or accessing a Dock Extra. Menu bar icons made it easier to change system preferences—volume, display settings, networking settings, and so on—by adding small menus to the top of the display near the clock in the top-right corner, by default.

◆ Improvements to the Finder window, including longer filenames, resizable columns, and more options on the toolbar; there also were more options to customize the Finder's desktop and how it handled removable disks.

◆ The capability to burn a data CD from the Finder, as well as to burn an audio CD from within iTunes, Apple's free music-management application for MP3 and CD audio.

◆ Changes to the Dock, including the capability to customize some of its characteristics, such as positioning it on the left or right side of the display.

◆ New or improved System Preference panes, including more General options and new keyboard, universal access, international, and other options.

◆ Networking improvements, including more support for AppleTalk, better support and configuration of AirPort Base Stations, and a rearranged Sharing pane.

◆ The (rudimentary) capability to connect to Microsoft Windows file servers.

◆ Changes to iDisk (Apple's online storage space made available to .Mac subscribers), including technology to keep it from complaining and disconnecting all the time.

◆ The capability to play DVD movies on Macintosh models that support DVD playback.

◆ Improved AppleScript support and support for remote Apple events.

◆ Changes in security, additional printer drivers, changes to the Disk Utility application, improvements to Disk Copy, and many more miscellaneous advances.

Mac OS X version 10.2 was another exciting milestone for the Mac OS, if only because of the numerous new features and capabilities it brought to the table. While it's certainly true that many portions of the operating system were tweaked— again, including performance and responsiveness—what prompted Apple to give Mac OS X version 10.2 a new, hefty price tag (for most buyers, whether they were upgrading from Mac OS 9 or Mac OS X, the price for version 10.2 was a full U.S. $129) was a slew of new and mostly impressive features:

Enhanced Applications What most users recognized about Mac OS X version 10.2 were the improvements made to the applications included with the operating system. Apple beefed up offerings such as Apple Mail, which sported new features, including a junk-mail-blocking feature; iChat for text-based chatting with friends and family; and Sherlock, which offered a slightly new twist on browsing the Web, with topic-focused *channels* that cull information from various websites.

New Personal Management Applications   Version 10.2 also sported a new Address Book, designed to be a central location for people-based information such as physical addresses, phone numbers, and e-mail addresses. Around the same time that Apple released Mac OS X 10.2, it finished iCal, a calendar/date book application, and iSync, an application that synchronizes data from iCal and Address Book between different Macs or between a Mac and portable devices, such as a compatible cell phone or a personal digital assistant.

Input Technologies   For users with physical challenges, Mac OS X 10.2 offered improved Universal Access features (Chapter 5, "Personalizing Mac OS X"), comprising a number of improvements over previous Mac OS X versions, such as the capability to magnify portions of the screen, to have text read aloud, and to alter certain keyboard or mouse commands for slower, one-handed, or more precise use. Version 10.2 also included Inkwell, a new OS-level technology designed to make handwriting recognition available to applications, so that you can write your input on a special input device (a graphics tablet) and have it turned into computer text.

QuickTime 6 and Quartz Extreme   Apple's QuickTime (Chapter 13, "Video Playback and Editing") multimedia technology was updated to support MPEG-4, a new standard for video that offers high-quality, highly compressed streams of video that is particularly well designed to work over the Internet. When coupled with certain video circuitry, Quartz Extreme (Chapter 25, "Peripherals, Internal Upgrades, and Disks") increases the performance of the display of certain 2D and 3D video and graphics on the screen. It essentially off-loads some of the processor-intensive visual tricks and features used to make the Mac OS X interface (and its native applications) so, well, pretty.

Networking   Version 10.2 offered some interesting updates in its networking capabilities, including the introduction of Rendezvous, a technology that makes networking setup a "zero configuration" proposition. (In Mac OS X 10.4, this technology has been renamed Bonjour.) It also added considerable networking compatibility with Microsoft Windows, including support for accessing Windows-based computers or acting as a server for Windows users, so that you can share files back and forth on a local network. New to 10.2 was support for more secure forms of the File Transfer Protocol (FTP) and a new application for visually accessing a Mac over a network, called Remote Desktop.

Miscellany   The miscellaneous improvements are too extensive to cover completely. Version 10.2 focused on adding considerable security options to the OS, including an Internet firewall (Chapter 10, "Configuring Internet Access"), a more easily understood password-management application, an improved Finder (Chapter 3, "The Finder"), and a new Find application for locating files (Chapter 6, "Getting Help and Searching Your Files"). Version 10.2 was the first to support Bluetooth (Chapter 25) for wireless peripherals and communications and offered increased support for digital cameras and scanners, a revamped Print Center, and much, much more.

NOTE   Mac OS X 10.2 was code-named "Jaguar" during its development, and that code name became popular. If you remember seeing Jaguar-print icons and marketing material, that's why. Apple carried the theme through to the final product. Since then, each of its Mac OS X updates has been "cat" themed, with Mac OS X 10.4 maintaining the "Tiger" from code word to final product.

With Mac OS X version 10.3, the OS began to look like it had been around for a while. This version had both major differences (in terms of how the OS looks and feels to the average user) and many, many subtle updates as well. While we won't cover them all here, some of the key improvements included:

Finder Updates The Finder window in Mac OS X 10.3 sported a new brushed-metal look and rearranged toolbars. It also included the Sidebar, where you can find your Mac's disks and short-cuts to the folders you most often access. The Finder window also integrated a universal search capability. It also brought the ability to assign AppleScripts to folders (called Folder Actions) and colorful Labels for folders, two features that were in the Classic Mac OS but absent from Mac OS X until 10.3.

Exposé One of the more amazing new features in Mac OS X 10.3 was Exposé, which makes it easier to focus on the windows from a particular application—the Mac OS darkens other parts of the screen in order to highlight certain windows. By pressing one key, you can make all your windows small enough so that you can mouse over each one to select it (see Figure 1.4).

FIGURE 1.4
Exposé offers some cool ways to handle multiple open windows.

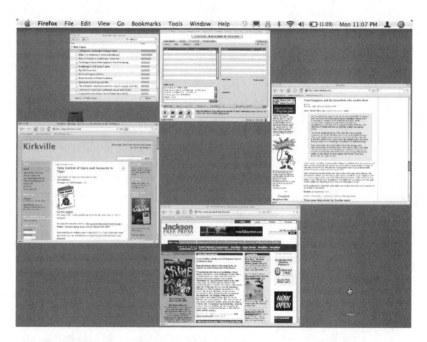

Fast User Switching While all versions of Mac OS X have included multiple user accounts as a fundamental part of the experience, Mac OS X 10.3 added a twist: Fast User Switching, allowing users to switch between their accounts *without* logging out of one and logging in to the other. That means you can quickly switch to your own settings, applications, and folders without waiting for someone else's applications and documents to close first. The feature also included a whiz-bang rotating-screen animation that shows the OS changing from one user to another.

File Vault and Secure Deletion Mac OS X 10.3 introduced the File Vault technology (Chapter 5), which allows each user to encrypt their personal files automatically so that others who gain access to the hard disk can't access the data, even if they get around the login security of the OS.

Mac OS X 10.3 also added secure file deletion through a new command in the Finder, called Secure Empty Trash (see Chapter 3).

Fonts, Printing, and Faxing   The way you select and manage printers changed in version 10.3, as did Font Book (see Chapter 7), which lets you preview, group, and manage fonts. This version also added faxing as a completely new feature, enabling you to send faxes from the Print dialog box in most applications.

iDisk and iChat AV   Version 10.3 was the first to allow you to place a "permanent" copy of your remote iDisk on your Mac's desktop; this enables you to move files back and forth more readily than in the past. Your iDisk is then synchronized when you have an Internet connection. iChat AV (Audio Visual), introduced with version 10.2, added audio-visual features, so that instead of simply typing messages back and forth, you can use the application (and online service, via .Mac) for audio chat. iChat AV can also work with Apple's iSight video camera for long-distance video conferencing over the Internet.

Miscellany   A number of other features were updated in version 10.3, from the Mail application's speed and search capabilities to Address Book's ability to print labels for envelopes or to print a copy of your contacts. Version 10.3 offered more sophisticated tools for dealing with PDFs, compatibility with Windows virtual private networks, and a number of enhancements for Mac users who want to use Unix-based applications and networking. It made it even easier to browse for connected servers in a networking environment, and Windows file-sharing servers show up right next to Macs.

What's New in Version 10.4?

Mac OS X 10.4 simply continues to build on the foundation that took shape in Mac OS X 10.1 and 10.2 and really matured in 10.3. Now, version 10.4 adds some new features and fun accessories, and it's starting to change the way—fundamentally—that we work with our computers and files.

Spotlight   Perhaps nothing else demonstrates the shift in how Mac users will be managing files in the future than Spotlight does—it literally allows you to search within documents, wherever they reside on your computer, in folder, in applications, and so on. Using keywords, you can search and find saved documents regardless of whether they are word processing files, PDFs, e-mail messages, or stored web pages. Spotlight is also extremely fast, and it suggests a file-management approach where you do a little less "filing" of your computer documents and more searching.

Dashboard   Building on Exposé technology, the Dashboard gives you one-button access to an overlay of interesting "applets" or small applications that gather information from the Web or enable you to perform quick calculations. Old Mac hands might remember the desk accessories from the early Mac OS; Dashboard brings back the spirit of desk accessories in a fully modern way (see Figure 1.5).

Automator   Building on its AppleScript technology and moving toward more "easy automation," the Automator enables you to create "workflows" between your applications, so that you can make your Mac perform redundant tasks automatically.

Safari RSS   The Safari web browser has been improved with a variety of features including a new privacy mode, parental controls, and faster browsing. The biggest new feature is extensive support of RSS (Real Simple Syndication), which enables you to view headlines on sites around the Web, so that you can quickly see what's new on your favorite sites without clicking into them.

.Mac Sync   Mac OS X 10.4 owners who have a .Mac subscription can use the service to synchronize a lot of different information among two or more Macs, including appointments, contacts, web bookmarks, Mail accounts, and more. Just by enabling the feature on your various Internet-connected Macs, you'll find that when you sit down to work, you've got synchronized data at your fingertips.

FIGURE 1.5
Dashboard gives you quick access to small applications.

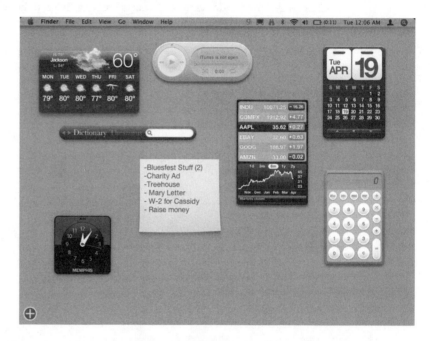

Beyond all these there are, of course, miscellaneous updates and improvements. Apple says there are over 200 improvements, ranging from the completely updated Mail 2.0 application to the improvements in speed and quality in QuickTime movie playback and iChat AV video conferencing. Some of the unsung heroes include burnable folders (gather files and burn them to disc quickly), smart folders (which use keywords to gather file aliases into the folders for easy access), image slideshows in the Finder, and even new logs and archives when you send faxes electronically.

And some other changes aren't exactly additions, but they're worth noting. Rendezvous technology, for instance, has been renamed Bonjour—you may still see Rendezvous mentioned in third-party literature and even on printer and networking hardware boxes—they're the same exact thing, just with a name change. And Apple no longer includes new versions of iPhoto, iMovie, and iDVD with Mac OS X, having separated them out into their retail iLife package. You can still get free updates to iTunes (because it helps Apple sells songs via the Music Store), and you'll get incremental updates to any iLife applications already installed on your Mac. But just be aware that simply running the Mac OS X 10.4 updater on your Mac won't update those applications to their latest versions; you'll need to make an additional purchase in most cases.

What's Next?

Mac OS X is new and exciting; the latest versions are even more so. Mac OS X takes the friendliness of the Classic Mac OS and transforms it with powerful and sophisticated underpinning, making it a truly modern operating system. Versions 10.1 through10.3 added considerable benefit to the original in the form of improved capabilities and completely new features and applications. Now, in version 10.4, tons of new features, tweaks to the way Mac OS X works, and overall improvements make it an impressive upgrade.

In Chapter 2, "The Fundamentals of Mac OS X," you'll learn the basics of Mac OS X's interface, including the Finder, the Dock, and the way individual items—icons, windows, buttons, and controls—look and work.

Chapter 2

The Fundamentals of Mac OS X

Mac OS X's Unix-like underpinnings make it, technologically, a very different beast from pre–OS X releases. Mac OS X's interface—the very way you relate as a user to the Mac OS—changed dramatically in Mac OS X. From each window's appearance to the way icons work, Mac OS X is different not only from previous Mac OS versions but from most other operating systems that came before it.

The Mac OS X interface is colorful and attractive and is both simple for novice users and powerful for advanced users. If you're making the move from Mac OS 9 or an earlier version, or if you've switched from Windows, you may have an adjustment period ahead of you. Once you're familiar with Mac OS X, though, we think you'll find that it's a pretty effective way to use your Mac.

If you've updated from Panther (Mac OS X 10.3), you won't find much of a difference in the fundamentals. While Panther introduced new Finder windows with a sidebar, Tiger doesn't make any changes in this area: the sidebar is still there, and the basics of the Finder are pretty much the same. However, if you skipped Panther and have updated from Jaguar (Mac OS X 10.2) or an earlier version of Mac OS X, you'll need to get used to some new ways of working with the Finder.

In this chapter, you'll look at the fundamental components of the Mac OS X interface and how to interact with them. If you're used to other graphical operating systems, much of this will be very familiar—feel free to skim for differences. If you're a new computer user or you haven't worked with a newer operating system in the past few years, you may want to read a bit more closely. You'll see how to log in to Mac OS X (which isn't always necessary) and how to get around on the desktop. You'll see how Mac OS X windows and menus work, and you'll be introduced to Mac OS X's Apple menu. You'll also learn how to work with some of the special elements of the Mac OS X interface, including the Dock and the menu extras.

In this chapter:

- ◆ Startup and Login

- ◆ Getting around the Mac OS

- ◆ Working with Menus, the Menu Bar, and Menu Extras

- ◆ Working with Icons

- ◆ Working with Windows

- ◆ The Dock

- ◆ The Apple Menu: Shut Down, Log Out, and Preferences

- ◆ Switching Users

Startup and Login

When you start or restart your Mac, you'll see the Mac OS go through its startup process. Startup begins with the Apple logo icon, which pops up to let you know that the Mac has powered up successfully and has found a valid version of the Mac OS. After that, the Mac OS X screen appears. During startup, Mac OS X loads system components from the disk and configures hardware components and peripherals according to the preferences you've set (or the default preferences). You'll see small messages below the Mac OS X image that show you what's being loaded and configured. Meanwhile, the progress bar creeps across the screen, giving you some indication of how much longer the startup process will take.

When the startup process is finished, you'll see one of two things: either the login window or, if your Mac isn't configured for multiple users, you'll see the Mac OS X desktop. By default, Mac OS X automatically logs in the original user (the one you first created using Mac OS X Setup Assistant after installing Mac OS X), so the desktop displays immediately. If your Mac has been configured for multiple users, however, you'll need to log in before you can see the desktop.

NOTE   Mac OS X isn't configured for multiple users by default, so if you've recently installed it or if you simply haven't added any new users, you won't see the login window at startup. Instead, you'll be logged in automatically, since you're the only user configured on that Mac. Displaying the login window and creating multiple user accounts is discussed in Chapter 9, "Being the Administrator: Permissions, Settings, and Adding Users."

In the login window, select your username and enter your password for the system. With the mouse, click your username in the list and type your password in the Password entry box; then press Return or click the Log In button.

NOTE   In some cases, you may need to type your username. This is an optional security precaution you can enable, so that a potential user needs to know a valid username and the password for that username.

If your login is successful, the login window will disappear and the desktop will begin to load. If the login fails, you may have mistyped your password or username. In that case, the login window will appear to vibrate (almost as if it's shaking its head "no"), and the entry fields will be cleared. Reenter your username and password; if you've forgotten either of them, you'll need to contact your system administrator or log in as an administrator and reset your password. (For more on administrator accounts, see the sidebar "Logging In: User and Administrator Accounts." For resetting passwords, see Chapter 9 and Chapter 29, "Typical Problems and Solutions.")

The login window also enables you to restart or shut down the Mac using the Restart and Shut Down buttons or put your Mac to sleep by clicking the Sleep button. Restarting shuts down the Mac OS and restarts the computer without cutting power to its internals. Shut Down not only shuts down the Mac OS, it also turns off the computer. Sleeping puts your Mac into low power mode but does not turn it off. To start up again, press the Mac's power button or the power key on the Mac's keyboard. For more on shutting down your Mac and putting it to sleep, see "The Apple Menu: Shut Down, Log Out, and Preferences" later in this chapter.

NOTE   The login window can be reconfigured quite a bit using various options that can be set in the System Preferences application, so if you don't see something described here, that's not a problem. Setting preferences for the login window is discussed in Chapter 9.

LOGGING IN: USER AND ADMINISTRATOR ACCOUNTS

Mac OS X uses a concept that most Unix users consider old hat but that Mac users have only really discovered since the advent of Mac OS X. (Mac OS 9 had a Multiple User feature, but it wasn't as restrictive as what Mac OS X uses.)

Max OS X is designed from the ground up to be a multiuser environment; since Mac OS X is built on a Unix foundation, this is natural. Each individual user account gets its own settings and a distinct "home" folder on the Mac for storing documents and installing applications. (We'll go a little deeper into the home folder concept in Chapter 5, "Personalizing Mac OS X.") In fact, even if you have only one user on your Mac, you'll still have your own home folder that you can use for storing your personal documents, application preferences, and even personal fonts or printer drivers.

Mac OS X also differentiates between two types of users: regular users and administrators. When you first install Mac OS X and create your initial personal account, you're actually creating an administrator account—one that has quite a bit of power within Mac OS X.

When you are logged in to Mac OS X using an administrator account, you can install applications for all users and make system-level changes in the System Preferences application. If you subsequently create regular user (non-administrator) accounts, users of those accounts will be able to make changes only within their own personal folders, thus ensuring that important system files and settings won't get changed or deleted. (Likewise, these regular accounts have limited access to the Mac when they're logged in over a network or via the Internet, making your Mac a bit more secure from the outside world.) If you want, you can also create additional administrator accounts so that trusted users can have access to settings and special folders.

There's another account that's even more powerful than an administrator account—the root account. The root account is disabled by default in Mac OS X, but it can be activated using the instructions given in Chapter 28, "Solving System-Level Problems." Although you probably won't often find a reason to use the root account, it can be useful for troubleshooting and for some more advanced networking and configuration tasks.

Getting around the Mac OS

When you log in to your Mac, your personal workspace is loaded. Your workspace consists of your desktop, your home folder (where your personal files and folders are stored), and the settings and appearance options you've chosen, including such things as your desktop background and any files or folders you have on the desktop.

As mentioned earlier, Mac OS X is a multiuser operating system, meaning that it is designed from the ground up to deal with more than one user. One of the manifestations of this is that each user has a personalized workspace. When another user logs in under a different username, he will see his own workspace, which has different folders, documents, and settings associated with it. In fact, every user's workspace is unique.

After you've logged into your user account (which, as mentioned, can happen automatically), the first thing you'll see is the *desktop*. The desktop is the pattern or color behind everything else that's shown on the screen. In a way, the desktop is like the top of an actual desk in the real world—it's where you'll spread out your work, access your files, and open your documents. On the desktop, you'll see icons and windows, as well as menus, which appear in the *menu bar* at the top of the desktop.

NOTE   Of course, if you've used a modern graphical operating system at all, you're probably already familiar with windows, icons, and menus. In that case, skim this entire section just to catch up on the differences between Mac OS X's interface and the elements you're used to in the earlier Mac OS, Microsoft Windows, or a Unix-based graphical user interface (GUI).

Open a menu, and you'll see the various commands available to you for managing files, formatting your work, or otherwise getting things done in the active application. (We'll discuss menus in depth in the following section, "Working with Menus and the Menu Bar.")

Icons are the small pictures, usually labeled, that are familiar to users of most any modern graphical operating system. The icons you see in Mac OS X represent items you can work with on the desktop (or, as you'll see later, in Finder windows). If you're used to Mac OS 9 or Windows, you'll notice that Mac OS X's icons are set to a larger size by default. The size of the icons can be customized, but the larger icons are designed to be discernible at higher screen resolutions; a typical 17-inch monitor, running at a resolution of 1024 × 768 pixels, shows Mac OS X icons well. (Dealing with icons—particularly the unique ways that Mac OS X handles them—is discussed in the section "Working with Icons," later in this chapter.)

Windows are areas on the screen where you view information or get work done. As with other graphical operating systems, you can stack windows on top of one other, move them around the screen, or move them to the Dock using the Minimize button for safekeeping until you want to work with them again. The unique qualities of Mac OS X's windows are discussed in greater detail in the section "Working with Windows," later in this chapter. Shown here is the Finder window in Mac OS X 10.4.

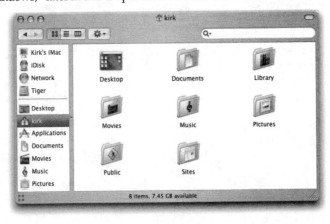

You'll also see the Dock on the desktop, by default. The *Dock* is a multipurpose region of the workspace that enables you to manage your applications, windows, and Trash. We'll cover using and customizing the Dock in depth later in this chapter, in the section "The Dock."

Working with Menus and the Menu Bar

The menu bar holds individual menus that you open to reveal the different commands that are available to you at a particular moment. The menu bar in Mac OS X is similar to the menu bar in earlier Mac OS versions, and it's central to the way the Macintosh has worked for years. If you're more familiar with Microsoft Windows or other graphical operating systems, the main difference is that the Mac menu bar is always at the top of the screen, as opposed to appearing at the top of individual windows, as it does in Windows. When you change to a new application in the Mac OS, the menu bar's contents change to show menus available from that application, but its location doesn't move.

Every application you use has its own menus that appear in the menu bar when that application is active. Most applications also feature File, Edit, and Help menus, but otherwise the menus can vary widely, depending on the tasks and tools available within a given application.

NOTE   Along with these menus comes one standard menu that's always on the menu bar, called the Apple menu. Also, each application will always have its own Application menu, which will appear right next to the Apple menu and in bold type. We'll discuss the Apple menu in the section "The Apple Menu: Shut Down, Log Out, and Preferences" and the Application menu in Chapter 4, "Using Applications."

Each word that appears in the menu bar is the title of a different menu; you'll also find menus that are represented with an icon such as those at the right of the menu bar.

To open a menu, click once on one of the menu titles or icons; the menu displays and stays open until you click again. Then you can move the mouse up and down on the open menu to select menu commands. Selected items are highlighted as you roll the mouse over them. In some cases you'll highlight a menu item that in turn reveals another menu that pops out to the right. These are called *submenus*. A menu that contains a sub-menu has a right-facing triangle after its name.

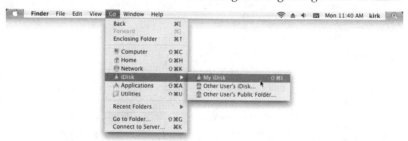

To invoke a particular command, click the mouse button again while that menu item is highlighted. Whatever action is associated with that menu command is activated. If you don't want to invoke a command, simply click the menu's name again or click somewhere outside of the menu (on a blank portion of the menu bar, a window, the desktop, and so on). Also, while the menu is open, you can move the mouse pointer to another menu's name, and that menu will open, closing the previous one. For instance, while the File menu is open, if you move the mouse pointer over to the Edit menu, it will open, and the File menu will close.

NOTE If you prefer, you can click a menu title and hold the mouse button down to open that menu, then drag the mouse to the command you want to select. When you release the mouse button while pointing to a menu command, that command is invoked. (Since this is the way menu selection worked in Mac OS versions prior to Mac OS X, the behavior has been left in for the comfort of those familiar with it.)

As you work with menus, you may notice that some menu commands will appear dimmed. (The gray text is much lighter than the black text of most menu commands and is more difficult to see.) A *dimmed* menu command is simply one that cannot be selected because it's not available or applicable for the current context. For instance, the Save command in a word processor's File menu will be dimmed if there are no changes (no typing or editing has occurred) in the document that can be saved to disk.

You'll also notice that many menu commands have letters and symbols associated with them in the menu, usually placed near the menu's right edge. The symbols in those keyboard commands represent the modifier keys you'll find on the Mac's keyboard:

- The cloverleaf (⌘) symbol represents the Command (Apple) key.

- The up arrow (⇧) represents the Shift key.

- The caret (^) symbol represents the Control key.

- The (⌥) symbol represents the Option or Alt key.

These keys are used in combination with other keys to create shortcuts that enable you to perform basic commands without using the mouse or opening menus. For the most part, these shortcuts help you perform tasks more quickly. For instance, ⌘Q is used in most applications to quit that application. As you can see, keyboard shortcuts are associated with particular applications, including the Finder. We'll discuss some keyboard shortcuts specific to the Finder in Chapter 3, "The Finder;" likewise, you'll see references to keyboard shortcuts throughout the book.

TIP You'll also find that some menu commands have an ellipsis (...) after the name. The ellipsis is there simply to let you know that selecting that command will open a new window, usually a dialog box where you'll make choices or select settings.

Menu Extras

Mac OS X includes another special class of items that appear on the menu bar, called, cleverly enough, *menu extras*. Aside from their appearance, these items work just like menus in that you click them to view their contents and make a choice, such as setting a preference or accessing an internal setting. For instance, you'll see a Volume menu extra by default, which you can use to quickly alter the volume level for your Mac's audio speakers.

NOTE Mac OS 9 users will note that menu extras are comparable to Control Strip items; Microsoft Windows users will find them very similar to the System Tray on the Taskbar near the clock.

What else can menu extras do? You'll see one menu extra that shows the day and time. PowerBook and iBook users will see a battery level indicator on their menu bar. If you use a modem to connect to the Internet, you can enable an option that displays modem status on the menu bar. If you change your Mac's display settings often, you can add a menu extra that lets you do that. A lot of these menu extras are turned on using options in the System Preferences application, which is discussed in Chapter 5. In some other cases, you'll find that you can add menu extras using a third-party application—that's discussed in Chapter 5, too. We'll discuss turning on and using menu extras throughout the book in the chapters that are relevant to their functions.

There's one additional menu extra—or is it simply a menu icon? The Spotlight menu, at the far right of the menu bar, is visible at all times, just like the Apple menu. If you click this icon, a text field displays; when you want to search for files on your computer, enter your search string here. Spotlight is one of the most powerful new features in Mac OS X 10.4; we talk about it in detail in Chapter 6, "Getting Help and Searching Your Files."

Contextual Menus

In most applications, on the desktop and in Finder windows, you can hold down the Control key and click the mouse button to bring up a *contextual menu* (Apple also calls these *shortcut menus* in the Mac OS X Help). This menu responds to the context of the item or area you're clicking and offers only relevant menu commands. For instance, Control+clicking on the desktop displays menu items such as New Folder, Get Info, and Change Desktop Background; Control+clicking a file in a Finder window gives you options such as Open, Move to Trash, and Duplicate. (See Figure 2.1. In this example, the Desktop icon in a home folder is the target.)

TIP If you have a USB-based mouse that has two (or more) buttons, most Mac OS X–native applications, including the Finder, will automatically recognize the second mouse button as a Control+click operation, making it easier to access contextual menus. In fact, the Finder and many applications will even recognize the scroll wheel if your mouse is so equipped.

FIGURE 2.1
Control+clicking brings up a contextual menu containing items relevant to the item or area that was clicked.

Working with Icons

Mac OS X provides icons to help you manage your files—both the documents you create and the applications you use to create them. You'll create folders to organize files, and you'll access disk icons to store them and move them around. Icons are also an essential part of many Mac OS X applications, including Mail, the Finder, System Preferences, and others that Apple includes with the OS. Icons also appear on toolbars, where they're used for quick access to application commands. This section gives a brief look at the types of icons you'll encounter and the different ways they can be activated and manipulated using the mouse and keyboard.

NOTE The Finder—the application that always launches when your Mac starts up—can be considered an "icon management" utility. It's the main application you'll use to move icons around, create folders for your icons, and so on. We mention that here because you'll see a few references to the Finder in this chapter, even though it's covered in depth in Chapter 3. If you're new to the Mac, the Finder is similar to the File Manager or Windows Explorer in various versions of Microsoft Windows or similar file-and-folder browsing programs in other operating systems.

Types of Icons

In any graphical operating system, icons are usually designed to help you see immediately what sort of item you're dealing with, so the icon's picture should give you a strong clue to what an item is. This is true in Mac OS X, which uses some visual clues to let you know what sort of icon you're dealing with.

Two major types of icons are used for organizing and storing other icons: disks and folders.

Disk icons appear on the desktop when removable disks or network disks are recognized and *mounted* by the Mac OS. CD-ROM and DVD-ROM icons, for instance, appear on the desktop when you insert them in the Mac's CD-ROM or DVD-ROM drive. Folder icons represent directories on your hard disk or on network disks. Folders are used to store and organize other items (all of which are also represented by icons), including document, application, and system files. (Though you can choose which of these types of icons you want the Finder to display on the desktop. See Chapter 3 for more on these Finder preferences.)

Document icons generally look like a piece of paper with a curled corner or a variation on that theme. These icons represent application files (such as a Word document) and often look quite a bit like the application that created them or the application with which they are associated. Documents can also be files used by the Mac OS itself, including fonts, preference files, and other items stored in the main System or Library folders on your hard disk.

Application icons represent specific software applications and are generally the most creative because the applications' authors are free to make these icons look the way they want them to look. Their images are usually designed to hint at what the application does, which can be seen in the following examples.

An alias icon represents an empty file that points to another file. You can use aliases for convenience, to access files that are stored elsewhere. An alias icon generally looks like the item it points to—disks, folders, documents, applications, or system components—but you know it's an alias because the icon includes a small a curvy arrow.

For the most part, system icons in Mac OS X aren't that unique—almost all of them are document icons or some variation. Occasionally you'll find one that looks like a Lego brick or something similar, suggesting it's a plug-in or a component. In early Mac OS versions, system icons were more distinct because they were more accessible to the user. (This is particularly true of control panels and system extensions, which could be installed or uninstalled by the user.) In Mac OS X, true "system-level" files aren't as easily accessed and tend to have generic icons, whereas some of the system-level icons you can access and work with are a little more creative (like the "plug-in" icon that's shown here).

Aside from these standard types of icons you'll encounter when managing files (that is, in the Finder), you'll also see icons in the toolbar of many of your Mac OS X applications. In those cases, the icons can look like whatever the programmer desires. Generally, these toolbar icons will have a name under the icon to make it clear what that icon's function is. And, unlike standard icons, you'll generally just click a toolbar icon once to activate it.

Selecting and Activating Icons

As you probably know, in any modern operating system, icons are small representations of items stored on your computer—files, folders, tools—and the mouse is your "virtual hand" for picking up and moving those items around on your desktop. The ability to work with icons using the mouse goes well beyond the metaphor; you'll see that icons can be selected, activated, and otherwise manipulated in many different ways within Mac OS X. Some of those methods differ slightly from the behavior found in other operating systems.

Selecting icons   You select a single icon the way you select anything else with the mouse—move your mouse so the pointer is touching the icon you want to select, then click the mouse button once. The icon will usually become highlighted, enabling you to work with it. (For instance, you can select a command from one of the available menus. If an icon is highlighted, that icon will be affected by the menu command.)

In certain situations, such as when you're viewing the desktop or a Finder window, you can also select icons by pressing the Tab key or the arrow keys. You also can select an icon in a Finder window by typing the first few letters of its name quickly.

NOTE   Icons becomed darkened, and their names highlighted to show that they've been selected.

Dragging icons   If you click an item and continue to hold down the mouse button, you can drag that item elsewhere on the screen. (This is particularly true of windows and icons, although other items can also be dragged around.) When you get to where you'd like the item to be, release the mouse button to drop the item—hence the phrase *drag and drop*. In document windows, dragging often will highlight the words or sentences quickly as you pass the mouse pointer over them.

NOTE   Mac OS X offers many opportunities for dragging and dropping throughout the interface; for instance, you can pick up an icon and drag and drop it onto the Trash icon in the Dock to designate it for deletion. Likewise, you can drag and drop a document icon onto a program icon to open and work with the document using that program.

Selecting multiple icons   Need to select more than one icon? If the icons are contiguous, you can select them by dragging a box around them (click the mouse, hold down the mouse button, and drag the mouse to create the box). When you release the mouse button, all the icons within the selection box will be highlighted. You can now move them as a group (dragging one of the items will drag all the selected items), and any commands you invoke will affect every icon.

Selecting noncontiguous icons   If the multiple icons you want to select aren't next to one another so that they can be easily selected by dragging a selection box, you have another option. If you select icons while holding down the Shift key or the ⌘ key, each new item is added to your selection, and previously selected items remain selected. (Usually when you click a new item, a previously selected item becomes unhighlighted.) To select multiple items, simply click each one while holding down the Shift or ⌘ key (see Figure 2.2). You can then move the highlighted icons or issue a command that will affect all of them while leaving others alone.

Activating icons   If you double-click an icon, in most cases you'll activate that item. If the icon represents a program, the program will launch. If the icon represents a document, that document's program will open and the document will be displayed. (Note that items on the Dock and on toolbars are activated with a single click.)

TIP   Clicking text in a typical Mac OS X document window works a bit differently. Double-clicking text will generally select an entire word. Triple-clicking often selects entire sentences or paragraphs. Occasionally an application will support a quadruple-click (four quick clicks in a row) to select a large group of text—a paragraph or a page.

You can also activate a selected icon by pressing the ⌘O keys. (It might seem to make sense to press Enter to activate an icon, but doing so highlights the name of an icon so that you can edit it.)

In addition to the basic behaviors, you'll find that Mac OS X offers some modifier keys that work in conjunction with the mouse to perform different tasks. Many of these depend on the context in which you're using the mouse; for instance, while dragging items in Finder windows, you can use the drag modifiers to determine the result of the drag. Here are some of those modifiers:

Shift+click   Holding down the Shift key while clicking an item in a window will select all items *between* the currently highlighted item and the item you Shift+click, if those items are arranged in a list or column. (With regular icons, Shift+click works just like ⌘click.) In an alphabetized list of animals, if you had previously clicked Aardvark (so that it's highlighted) and you now Shift+click Zebra, all the names between would become highlighted.

NOTE   This would also work in a text document if you click once at the start of a paragraph and then Shift+click at the end of it. Note, however, that in other areas this wouldn't be appropriate, such as windows full of icons that don't really have a "start" and "end." Shift+click acts just like ⌘click.

Option+drag   In Finder windows or on the desktop, you can hold down the Option key and drag an icon (or a group of icons, if you have selected more than one) to copy or duplicate that item. (Chapter 3 contains more information on the duplicate function, since it's one of the Finder application's responsibilities.) This is done to keep from simply moving the icon, which is the default behavior in most cases. When you Option+drag in this way, the mouse pointer gains a plus (+) sign to suggest that a duplicate command will be given.

FIGURE 2.2
You select a group of individual icons by using the Shift or ⌘ key while clicking.

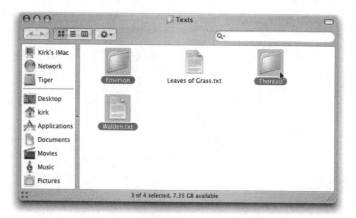

TIP   When you drag an item from one disk to another, you'll see the plus sign (+) regardless of whether you press Option while dragging, because Mac OS X's default behavior is to copy between disks. You can choose to *move* the file, however, by holding down ⌘ as you drag. Chapter 3 contains more information on copying (and duplicating) versus moving files.

Option+⌘+drag   If you modify an Option+drag by tossing in the ⌘ key, you'll create an alias instead of a duplicate when you drop the item. When this function is active, the mouse pointer includes a small, curly arrow.

NOTE   Aliases are discussed in depth in Chapter 3.

Working with Windows

Most of the work you'll accomplish in Mac OS X will take place in document windows. When you interact with the Mac OS itself (whether you're setting preferences and options or responding to queries by the OS), you'll do that within windows, too. Windows come in a variety of shapes and sizes. Likewise, the typical Mac OS X window has a number of controls you'll encounter, some of which differ from previous Mac OS versions and those of other graphical operating systems.

Parts of a Mac OS X Window

Let's begin by looking at the different parts of a standard window. Then you'll see the other, more specialized types of windows you may encounter.

The top of a typical document window looks like Figure 2.3. Although windows vary in the type of information presented within them, they all have these basic controls.

FIGURE 2.3
The parts of a
regular window

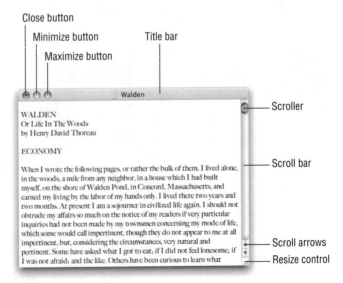

Here are the different parts of the window and how to work with them:

Close button   Click the red Close button to close the window. If the window contains items that have not yet been saved, clicking the Close button will bring up the Save dialog box (if appropriate), or it will automatically save the changes you've made in the window. If the current document has unsaved changes, the red Close button has a little black dot in its center.

Minimize button   Click the yellow Minimize button to send the open window to the Dock. This removes it from the screen (usually with a fancy animation) and places it on the Dock as an open item. To see the window again, you simply click the item on the Dock, and it will return to its last location on-screen.

TIP   In most applications, you can use keyboard shortcuts to close and minimize open windows. To close the window, press ⌘W (you may be prompted to save the document's changes). To minimize a document window to the Dock, press ⌘M. Also, for a completely useless (but fun) little effect, hold down the Shift key while clicking the Minimize button in a document window to see the document minimize to the Dock in really slow motion.

Zoom button   The green Zoom button is used to enlarge the window so that it becomes large enough to show as much of its content as possible. Clicking Zoom will often expand a window to the default large size set by the application. (In some applications, holding down the Option key while clicking the Zoom button will cause the window to fill your entire screen.) Click the button again to return the window to its previous size. In some applications, such as iTunes, clicking the Zoom button changes the window to a reduced version, one where you have access to main controls but little else. In this case, click the button again to return the window to its normal size.

TIP   When your mouse gets near the Close, Minimize, and Maximize buttons, a symbol will appear on each of them: X (for Close), – (for Minimize), and + (for Maximize). This feature is meant to assist users who cannot discern the colors of the buttons.

Title bar   The title bar appears at the top of the window, displaying the name of the window. You can click and drag the title bar to move the window around on the screen. You can also (by default) double-click the title bar to minimize the window, sending it to the Dock.

NOTE   In many windows, including Finder windows, the title bar's icon (the one right next to the name of the window) is actually active. Often you can click that icon, hold down the mouse button, and drag it to a new location, such as onto the desktop, to a new folder in the Finder, or even to somewhere else in the window. It doesn't work in every window, but it's common in web browsers, e-mail applications, and other places where you can drag items to organize them.

Scroll bars   The scroll bars can appear on the right side and bottom of the window, but only when there's information in the window that currently cannot be displayed. When the scroll bars are active, they show the scroll arrows and scroll controls to indicate that more information is contained in the window.

TIP   By default, you can click within an active scroll bar (other than on the scroller) to scroll quickly through the contents of a window. This behavior is governed by a preference setting accessible via the System Preferences application. See Chapter 5 for details.

Scroller   The scrollers are a bit difficult to describe—one of these little boxes, blobs, or thingies appears on each active scroll bar if the contents of the window are not displayed completely. You can drag the scroller up and down (or left and right) on the scroll bar to display information in the window. The scroller in a given scroll bar will change size to indicate how much more information is not displayed in the window: the larger the scroller, the higher the portion of information you can currently see. If you have a very large document, for instance, the scroller will appear smaller and thus take up only a small portion of the scroll bar.

Scroll arrows   The scroll arrows appear in active scroll bars. You can use them to scroll through the contents of the window. Simply click the arrow that points in the direction you'd like to scroll.

TIP   Scroll arrows are sometimes at each end of the scroll bar, and sometimes both arrows are grouped at the bottom of the scroll bar, depending on a setting in the Appearance pane of the System Preferences application. See Chapter 5 for more on System Preferences.

Resize control   You can use the resize control, the little square ribbed part at the bottom right of the window, to drag the window to a larger or smaller size. Simply point at the resize control, click and hold, and then drag to change the size of the window.

Which and how many of these controls you see depends on a number of factors, including the size of the document and the type of contents being displayed. Likewise, not all windows will offer all of these controls. For instance, dialog boxes qualify as windows, but they don't usually offer scroll bars or resize areas.

Types of Windows

When the Mac OS needs more information from you, you'll see a dialog box or a dialog sheet; when it needs to communicate something to you, you'll see an alert. Likewise, you'll see windows when you attempt to save or open documents and when you open folders in the Finder and elsewhere.

This section takes a look at the different types of windows (aside from the regular windows discussed in the previous section) you'll encounter.

DIALOG BOXES AND SHEETS

Dialog boxes are windows that are designed to receive information from you. These will often have check boxes, radio controls, menus, entry areas, and sliders.

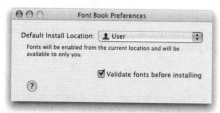

In dialog boxes, you'll also encounter a variety of buttons that enable you to dismiss or alter settings in the dialog box. For instance, if the dialog box has a Cancel button, you can click it to close the dialog box without making any choices or changes. If the dialog box has an OK button as in Figure 2.4, click it to accept whatever information is presented or to move on to another task. Some dialog boxes have an Apply button that enables you to apply changes you've made without dismissing (closing) the dialog box. (Some will have neither, in which case you use the Close button.)

You'll find other buttons in dialog boxes as well, most of which are designed to help you deal with the questions or contents within the dialog box. You may see buttons marked Yes, No, Save, Open, Use Default Settings, Revert, and others. These will all make sense in the context of the dialog box's purpose.

In Mac OS X, many dialog boxes have Close, Minimize, and Maximize title bar buttons. You can use these buttons as you would in any other window. Clicking the Close button in a dialog box's title bar is the same as clicking Cancel.

Dialog boxes can be modal or modeless. A *modeless* dialog box enables you to continue working in the active application's other windows; a *modal* dialog box requires that you deal with the dialog box before you can continue working in the application or the document. (However, you can always switch to a different application.)

Some modal dialog boxes in Mac OS X are actually a part of the document window they relate to (see Figure 2.4). In fact, such a dialog box tends to appear by popping down from the title bar in an animated little entrance, almost as if it were a window shade pulled by a string. Apple calls these modal dialog boxes *dialog sheets* or simply *sheets*. This trick makes it very clear which window needs to be dealt with and why work is being blocked in that document. In those cases, you can still switch to other documents in the application or even use the menu commands in that application—a change from earlier Mac OS versions, thanks to the threaded nature of processes within Mac OS X applications.

FIGURE 2.4

Certain types of dialog boxes, called sheets, "pop down" from the title bar of the document window.

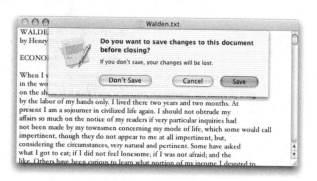

NOTE   Application developers can choose whether they want to implement a dialog box as a dialog sheet, so you may find that they're a bit inconsistent. (For instance, sometimes the Save As dialog will be a box, sometimes a sheet.)

A dialog sheet works just like a dialog box. Make your choices or selections, then click OK, Save, or whatever button is made available to you. If you want to dismiss the dialog box without doing anything in it, click Cancel; it should pop back up into the title bar.

ALERTS

An alert is a special type of dialog box that is designed specifically to tell you when something is happening in an application or part of the Mac OS that requires your attention. Most of the time, these will be error messages, although they may be messages telling you something else important or asking you to switch to another open application or process. Most alerts simply have an OK button; click it to dismiss the alert once you've read it.

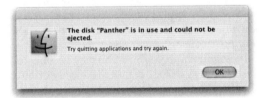

PALETTES

Generally, palettes are floating windows designed to hold tools that you need for working in the current application. Mac OS X also features many different types of *inspectors*, which are floating palettes designed to offer information about items in the Finder or in an application.

One of the significant features governing palette windows is that they always stay "on top," meaning other windows can't cover them up. A palette usually will have only a Close button, a Minimize button (in some cases), and a title bar. (It may appear to have a Maximize button as well, but that button isn't active in a palette window.)

Layering Windows

When you have just one window open, you'll always be able to see its controls and manipulate it—move it, minimize it, close it—immediately. If you have more than one window open, the windows overlap. The window in the *foreground* maintains its detail, but windows in the *background* lose some of their characteristics—for instance, scroll bars lose their color, and the title bar becomes dimmed, as shown in Figure 2.5.

The foreground window is the *active* window. To make another window active, click it once. If the window that you click is in the current application, that window simply switches to the foreground, and the previous window is moved behind it. If you click a background window that belongs to a different application, that application's menu bar will also appear as the window comes to the foreground. However, this behavior is a little different than in earlier Mac OS versions, because in Mac OS X, only one window—the one you clicked—from a background application comes to the foreground. There's more information on that in Chapter 4.

TIP Want to move a background window without making it active? Hold down the Command (⌘) key and drag the window to move it around while it remains in the background.

FIGURE 2.5
Background windows don't show as much detail and color as the active window.

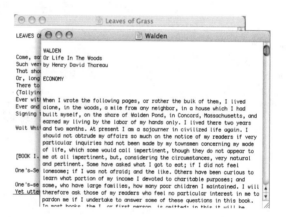

Controls within Windows

As mentioned earlier, the typical window has features—buttons, title bars, scroll controls—that enable you to manipulate them on-screen and view their contents. Within windows of all types, however, you'll see a number of different controls that are actually used to make choices and enter data. Besides typing documents and invoking menu commands, the controls you find in windows are the primary way you'll interact with your Mac and its programs. Figures 2.6 and 2.7 show most of these controls.

Here's what each control enables you to do:

Tabs Tabs are used to enable more than one screen of choices to appear in a single window. A tab makes it possible to group similar choices so that one huge window with scores of choices isn't necessary. Click a tab to view its grouping of controls and options.

Check box Click the check box to place a check mark, which turns on that option. If there's already a check mark in the check box, click the box to remove the check mark, thus turning off the option.

FIGURE 2.6
Some of the controls you'll find in Mac windows

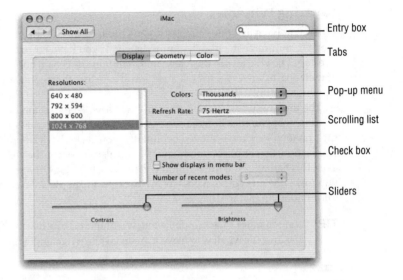

— Entry box
— Tabs
— Pop-up menu
— Scrolling list
— Check box
— Sliders

FIGURE 2.7
Some additional controls you'll encounter in Mac windows

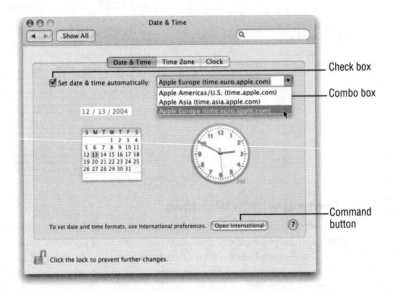

— Check box
— Combo box
— Command button

Pop-up menu   Click the menu to open it and reveal its options; click again to select one of the options.

Radio buttons   Use these controls to select one of several options presented. They're a little like presets on a radio, in that they allow you to make only one choice from a number of options.

Slider   Drag the selector along the slider to configure the setting. (Note in the earlier Figure 2.6 that sliders can vary slightly. The slider on the right has a small line representing the default setting, which the slider control will "snap" to as you bring it close.)

Command button   Click the button to put the command into action. In some windows, this command will be OK for accepting an action or Cancel for stopping an action. Often you'll also find that these buttons toggle between Start and Stop or between On and Off.

Entry box   Click in the entry box to place the insertion point, then enter information by typing.

Combo box   A combo box works exactly like an entry box except that it also gives you the option of selecting a preset entry from a pop-up menu.

Scrolling list   Select an item from the list using the mouse, or if the list is too long to display completely, using the scroll arrows or scroller. In many scrolling lists you can hold down the ⌘ key to select more than one option or the Shift key to select a range of options.

Disclosure triangle   Click the triangle to reveal additional information (which will cause the triangle to point downward). If the triangle's information is already revealed, click the triangle again to hide the additional information.

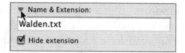

Toolbar   Some Mac OS X windows offer a toolbar that enables you to access different commands or options quickly. The Mail application and Finder all have toolbars; some of them have only a couple of icons, such as the default Finder window; others have many icons, such as Mail. You also can customize most of these toolbars by dragging icons to and from them.

The Dock

Another fundamental element of the Mac interface is the Dock, Mac OS X's interesting little beast—part launcher, part task manager, and part information center. If you're accustomed to Mac OS 9, you'll find that the Dock replaces many traditional Mac OS elements, including the original Applications menu (used for switching between applications) and the Launcher. Microsoft Windows users will see some similarities to the Taskbar at the bottom of the Windows screen. Even Unix and Linux users will see similarities if you use KDE, Gnome, or a similar graphical user interface. However, nothing in all of computing is quite like the Dock.

Actually, that's not totally fair. The Dock is based on a similar task-switching interface that was originally a hallmark of the NeXTStep/OpenStep interface, which was the precursor of much of the technology in Mac OS X. That said, the Dock's mission has been enlarged in Mac OS X, making it different from all other task-switchers.

The Dock offers an innovative and simplified approach to the tasks it accomplishes: launching often-used items, switching between applications, and managing open windows. The Dock may seem too simple at first glance, but that doesn't attest to its full power (see Figure 2.8).

FIGURE 2.8
The Dock is a deceptively
simple-looking part of
the Mac OS X interface.

By default, the Dock appears at the bottom of the screen with a number of preinstalled icons. The default icons include the Finder, Mail, System Preferences, Safari, iTunes, and iChat, among others. You'll also find Trash on the Dock, and if someone else configured your Mac, you may find icons for other applications there—your word processors, web browsers, terminal emulators, or anything else you need to access quickly.

The Dock is designed to show you four different things:

Application aliases   Besides the aliases placed on the Dock by default, any application's icon can be dragged to the Dock, which creates an icon for that application that can be clicked for convenient launching. In fact, a few applications will install their own icons on the Dock when you run their installer programs.

Applications currently running   Whether or not an application's alias is on the Dock already, its icon will appear there after it has been launched. That makes it possible to monitor and switch between all your running applications using the Dock interface.

Document or folder aliases   You can also place aliases to documents on the Dock, or, for that matter, aliases to folders. When clicked, a document alias will launch the original document and its associated application; a folder alias will open that folder in a Finder window.

Minimized document windows   When you minimize a document window within an application, it will appear separately on the Dock, making it easier for you to return immediately to that document. Note, by the way, that *document window* is defined loosely here; any window within a running application that has its own Minimize button will appear on the Dock if you click that button. (For instance, some applications offer dialog boxes that you can minimize to the Dock.) Minimized windows always go to the right-hand section of the Dock, between the vertical divider and the Trash icon.

NOTE   Microsoft Windows users and Unix/Linux users (especially those who have used KDE or an OpenStep–like window manager) may find the Dock easy to get used to. In some ways, the Dock is similar to the Windows Taskbar, especially when it comes to managing open applications and documents.

On the Dock is a small, vertical dividing line that visually separates the application side of the Dock from the document side. On the left side of that line is where the icons for application aliases and running applications are found; on the right side of the Dock is where document aliases and minimized document windows appear. Application icons can't appear in the document space and vice versa. Trash, which is really just a special folder icon, always appears on the far-right side of the Dock.

Using the Dock

One of the Dock's primary purposes is its role as a launcher. By default, you can launch an application on the Dock by pointing to its icon and clicking once. When you click, you'll see the icon bounce up and down (unless you've changed a setting in the Dock's preferences) to indicate that the application is starting up. After a few seconds, you should see the application's menu appear at the top of the screen.

NOTE   One reason you can classify the Dock as a launcher is that it interprets one click, not two, as a command to launch applications or documents. If an item is already active, though, the Dock will simply switch to that application or document.

Once you have an application running, you can use the Dock to switch to and from that application. Simply click once on a running application's icon; that application comes to the front, and you can begin to work in it.

Want to switch to an application while simultaneously hiding all others? Hold down ⌘Option while clicking the application's icon on the Dock.

How do you know if an application is running? Actually, a closer look at the Dock reveals a couple of indicators that are important to using it effectively (see Figure 2.9).

Running indicator   If an application has been launched and is running, you'll see a small arrow beneath its icon. This indicator is there to let you know that the application has already been launched. If you click that icon, you'll switch to the application.

Mouseover names   Pass the mouse over the icons on the Dock, and the names of the items will appear immediately above their icons. Although it's not always possible to determine what an item is simply from its icon, the combination of icon and name should give you a good idea.

TIP   You can use the keyboard to switch between open applications: ⌘Tab will take you from left to right along the running applications on the Dock, and ⌘Shift+Tab will take you through them from right to left. When you do this, the Finder displays a huge graphic in the center of your screen showing the icons of the active applications. Also, when switching like this, the Dock switches first to the last active application so you can switch back and forth between two applications easily, even if you have several open. Just press ⌘Tab until you get to the application you want to switch to and release the keys. Now, to return to the previous application (no matter where it is on the Dock), press ⌘Tab again—that application is the first one to which you'll be switched. Pretty handy.

Dock icons feature one more little trick: Each of them offers menu commands that pop up directly over the item's icon. Click and hold the mouse button on an icon to see the menu commands that are available to you. Every icon has a menu; active applications can be quit from their icons, active document windows can be selected, and so on. Some applications go much further: You can use the iTunes Dock menu to control iTunes, skipping songs, pausing, playing, etc. It also shows you the name and artist of the currently playing song.

FIGURE 2.9
You have to look closely at the Dock to see all its features.

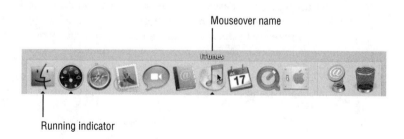

Mouseover name

Running indicator

Finally, it's important to note that many Dock icons are *active*—they can change to show you different bits of information. This can be great for quickly learning about a change in status without switching to that application or utility. For instance, the Mail icon can include a small number (when the Mail application is running) that tells you how many new messages are waiting for you. Or when you launch iCal, its icon changes to show the current date. Many applications' icons will bounce in the Dock to get your attention when something new or important has happened. Even the Printer Setup Utility icon is active, showing an animated page being printed (as well as the page number currently in the printer) so that you can check printer status quickly.

TIP   In Mac OS X version 10.2 and above, application icons sometimes include a small exclamation point when that application isn't responding. That usually means the application has encountered trouble and needs to be restarted or, perhaps, quit using the Force Quit command.

Minimizing Windows to the Dock

Aside from launching items and switching between them, the Dock also helps you manage your minimized windows. When you're working with a document or application window and you click the Minimize button, the window disappears from the screen and moves to the Dock—at least, that's what appears to happen. Once on the Dock, a minimized window will generally look like a smaller version of itself—in many cases along with a small icon that shows what application that window is from. (A Finder window is shown below.) Note that minimized windows always appear on the right side of the Dock's dividing line.

All you're doing is getting the window out of your way so that you can use the main portion of your display for something else. These minimized window icons can be active, but that depends on the application. For instance, if a QuickTime movie was playing before you minimized it, it will continue, and you'll be able to see the movie playing (and hear sound, if you were hearing sound before you minimized the movie) on the Dock icon.

Notice that as you pass your mouse over the minimized window, its name appears above its title—which can be handy if you have multiple minimized windows that look very similar.

If you're ready to work with the window again, click it once in the Dock; it will spring back to its previous location in the main portion of your display.

NOTE   You can do a lot more with the Dock, including use it as a drag-and-drop target, as you'll see in Chapter 4, and customize it, which we'll cover in Chapter 5.

The Apple Menu: Shut Down, Log Out, and Preferences

Perhaps the most recognizable menu on your Mac is the Apple menu, which is always on the far-left side of the menu bar in Mac OS X and displays as a blue Apple icon against a white background. The Apple menu is a convenient way to access a few commands and shortcuts from wherever you happen to be working on your Mac. Instead of requiring you to switch back to the Finder to perform some important task, the Apple menu is always in the upper-left corner, ready to be selected regardless of the application you're using.

The Apple menu is where you'll go to put your Mac to sleep, restart it, shut it down, or log out of your user account. It also offers a quick way to access the System Preferences, some recent items (applications, documents and servers), and lets you change some settings quickly (see Figure 2.10).

NOTE   If you're familiar with Microsoft Windows, you'll find that the Apple menu offers some of the features of the Start menu in Windows but is much simpler. The Apple menu gives you access to Sleep, Restart, Shut Down, and Log Out commands, as does the Start menu. Also, you can quickly access recent items and preferences. (The Control Panel in Windows is the equivalent of the System Preferences application in Mac OS X.) The similarities end there, because the Apple menu isn't really intended as a launcher for applications and system commands as the Start menu is.

Top of the Menu

Open the Apple menu, and you'll immediately see three very specific commands: About This Mac, Software Update, and Get Mac OS X Software. They do very different things. The About This Mac command opens a small window that tells you the current version of Mac OS X, the amount of RAM you have installed in your Mac, the type of processor that's installed, as well as the name of the startup disk. If you click More Info, you'll open the Apple System Profiler, which gives a more detailed report on your Mac, its hardware and its software. To dismiss the About This Mac window, click its Close button.

The Software Update command opens the Software Update application, where you can check for updates to Mac OS X or other Apple programs included with it (including programs like iTunes, iChat, etc.).

The Mac OS X Software command will launch your web browser and (if you're connected to the Internet or set up to connect automatically) load a special website that Apple has designed to help you locate and download software and software updates for Mac OS X.

FIGURE 2.10
The Mac OS X
Apple menu

Preferences

The Apple menu gives you quick access to a number of preference settings, including fast ways to launch the System Preferences application and to change some basic Dock behaviors. Open the Apple menu, and you'll see the following commands:

System Preferences   Select this command to launch the System Preferences application, where you can make basic decisions about how your Mac will operate and behave. (System Preferences is discussed in Chapters 5, 9, and elsewhere.)

Dock ➢ Turn Hiding On/Off   This option toggles Dock Hiding, which causes the Dock to disappear at the bottom of the screen. When you point the mouse at the bottom of the screen (and wait a second), the Dock pops back up for you to use.

Dock ➢ Turn Magnification On/Off   This option toggles on Dock magnification, so that icons in the Dock are magnified when you point to them with the mouse.

Dock ➢ Position On   Use this option to decide if the Dock will appear on the left, bottom, or right side of your display. By default, the Dock is shown on the bottom, but some users prefer placing it elsewhere. (We'll discuss some possibilities in Chapter 5.)

Dock ➢ Dock Preferences   Select this option to launch the Dock pane of the System Preferences application quickly.

Location   The Location menu is used to change between different saved *location sets* of Network and Internet settings. Locations are discussed in Chapter 19, "PowerBooks, iBooks, and Mac OS X."

Recent Items

The Recent Items menu enables you quickly to access the applications, documents, and servers that you've worked with most recently. You'll find that this is handy; for instance, when you start working for the day, you'll often want to open an application and document that you were working with the previous afternoon. If it's one of the most recent applications or documents, you should be able to find it in this menu, thus avoiding a hunt through your home folder or hard disk.

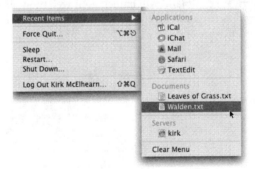

If you want to clear the Recent Items menu so that none of the items on it are there the next time you check, select Clear Menu from the menu. Any new applications and documents you launch will appear on the freshly cleared Recent Items menu.

NOTE   You can customize the number of items in the Recent Items menu via the General pane of the System Preferences application. See Chapter 5 for details.

Force Quit

The Force Quit command launches the Force Quit window, which you can use to cause an errant application to shut down immediately. You should do this only when the application in question has frozen or hung, because the Force Quit command causes that application to quit immediately without saving any changed data. Another way to access the Force Quit window is by pressing ⌘Option+Escape. See Chapter 27, "Fixing Applications and Managing Classic," for more on using Force Quit.

Sleep

The Sleep command is used to put your Mac into the special Sleep mode. Sleep is a low-power mode that keeps power trickling to some of the components, including system memory. Anything you're working on (such as open documents and applications) can be left active while the Mac is in Sleep mode. When you wake the Mac up (by pressing a key or the spacebar or clicking the mouse), your open documents and applications will appear on the screen almost immediately, and you will be ready to begin working again. (You should still save changes in your documents before invoking Sleep, however, just in case the computer loses power or encounters a major error while you're gone.)

NOTE If you're using a PowerBook or iBook, Sleep mode is invoked automatically if you close the screen while the Mac is still operating. (On some Mac models, you'll then see a pulsating indicator light that almost suggests that the Mac is "snoring" as it sleeps. It's cute.) On the latest portable models, opening the screen will automatically wake the Mac from Sleep mode. (On some others you may need to press a key.) Most modern Power Macintosh and iMac models can be put into Sleep mode by pressing the power button on Mac. (Don't hold the power button down too long, however, because that may reset the Mac.) The power button on your keyboard, if you have one, will bring up a special dialog box where you can select Sleep with the mouse.

The advantages of the Sleep command are pretty obvious. The Mac uses very little power while sleeping, but you can get back to work quickly when you wake up the Mac. The major disadvantage, however, is that Sleep mode leaves your personal account signed in to Mac OS X. If you walk away from your Mac, others have access to your personal files, settings, and home folder simply by pressing a key on the keyboard. If that's a risk you don't want to take—perhaps because your Mac is in a high-traffic area and you have sensitive files—it's best to log out.

TIP As you'll see in Appendix C, "Mac OS X Applications," you can set your personal keychain to lock itself when your Mac enters Sleep mode. This can help secure your private passwords if other people gain access to your Mac after it has been put into Sleep mode.

Restart

The Restart command in the Apple menu is used to shut down Mac OS X and immediately send the Mac through the startup process again, without actually powering down your hardware. When you choose this command, all open applications are told to shut down by the Mac OS; in all cases, you should be given the opportunity to save any changed data in your applications. Then the Mac OS will go through its own shutdown process. When it's done, the Mac will immediately start up again (complete with the startup chime).

Restarting is useful when you've installed a driver or a utility application that requires the Mac to go through its startup phase in order to be recognized. It's also useful if you want to boot from a different startup disk (such as if you have a Mac that can still boot with Mac OS 9) that you've selected from the Startup Disk pane in the System Preferences application.

If you have Fast User Switching turned on (explained in the section "Switching Users" later in this chapter), or another user is logged in when you shut down your Mac, a dialog displays warning you of this.

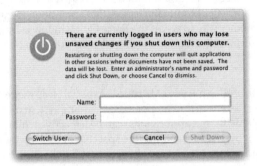

You can also restart your Mac from the login screen. Choose Log Out from the Apple menu, and you'll see the login screen. Then, click the Restart button to restart your Mac.

Shut Down

If you'll be gone for a while and you don't need your Mac running, you can choose Apple ➤ Shut Down, or select Apple ➤ Log Out and then click Shut Down. In either case, applications and documents will be closed. Then, after you're logged out, the Mac OS will shut itself down and then shut down your Mac. To power the Mac back up, press its power key or power button, depending on the model.

As for when you restart your Mac, if you have Fast User Switching turned on or another user is logged in when you shut down your Mac, a dialog box appears warning you of this.

You must enter an administrator's name and password to shut down your Mac. Bear in mind that other users may not have saved their documents, so if you have doubts, it's best to check with them and have them switch to their active sessions to make sure their files are saved. You can click Switch User, shown on the previous graphic, to switch to another user's account and make sure they've saved all their work.

The advantages of shutting down Mac OS X are that the computer won't use any electricity, and no one will be able to access it while you're away. Although it may be common to shut down Macs used as home or office workstations, Macs used as servers or lab machines are likely to be shut down much less often.

NOTE   You may occasionally have trouble when shutting down your Mac, because some applications can block the shutdown process. Most of the time this happens when an application needs to know whether or not you want to save changes in a document. If you take too long to respond, the shutdown process may *time out*, meaning it stops because too much time has gone by without activity. If you're having trouble shutting down, check your applications to make sure any open documents are saved (see Chapter 4) and that you don't have open dialog boxes or other pending issues. If you still have trouble, you may be encountering an application that needs to be forced to quit; see Chapter 27 for details on the Force Quit command.

Log Out

The Log Out command shuts down all your active applications and documents. If you have unsaved changes to any documents, you'll be asked if you want to save them. After any such documents are saved and all open applications are successfully closed, you're logged out. The Mac OS makes a note of the fact that you're no longer using the Mac and returns to the Login window discussed at the beginning of this chapter, as well as in Chapter 9. Another user can then log in.

You don't have to shut down the Mac after logging out. It will automatically go into a power-saving mode after a few minutes of inactivity. If you do want to shut down, though, simply click the Shut Down button. You can also restart the Mac if desired. Some application installations and preferences require that the Mac be restarted before they can take effect.

Switching Users

There may be times when you are working on your Mac and someone else absolutely *has to* do something on their account. Perhaps you have separate accounts on a home Mac for different family members, or a shared Mac in an office may have different accounts for each employee. In Mac OS X 10.3 or higher, if you have Fast User Switching turned on (see Chapter 9), you can switch to another user account without logging out. You can switch users at any time, without quitting your applications or even saving your documents (though you *should* save your documents before switching users, just in case).

Fast User Switching is invoked from a special menu at the right of the menu bar. If this function is turned on, you'll see either your name or an icon as the header on a menu to the right of the clock. (You can choose how you want this menu to display in the Accounts preferences; see Chapter 9 for more on these options.)

Click this menu to see a list of users who have accounts on your Mac. Those users currently logged in have an orange check icon before their names. To switch to another user, select their name in the menu; the Login window displays for that user, asking them to enter their password. When they type their password and press Return, a new session opens with their settings and preferences, keeping the first user's session open in the background. (And, if your Mac has a fast enough video card, a 3D cube rotates as the sessions switch; it's a cool effect that is pure eye-candy, but it will impress your Windows-using friends.)

When you want to switch back, select the other username in the menu, enter their password, and press Return. The other user's session displays exactly as it was before the switch.

You can use Fast User Switching to switch between several sessions created for different employees, family members, or students. Each session is personal, provides the user with their files in their home folder, and lets them work according to their authorizations. (In fact, you can have multiple user accounts for yourself if you find them helpful; in producing this book, Todd found it handy to have one user account that was used for producing the screenshots—the desktop was kept uncluttered and so forth—and another used for other projects and tests, such as video editing and installing shareware.)

You can also select Login Window from the user menu. This allows you to exit your session without logging out and provides a login window so any other user can log in; you don't need to choose a specific user from the user menu.

Note that changing users with Fast User Switching is not the same as logging out. When a new user logs in using this method, the previous user's session is still open, and any active applications remain active. For example, if you are downloading files in your session and switch users this way, the files will continue to download. But some programs will stop working; iChat will log out of any active accounts, and iTunes will stop playing music.

What's Next?

Those are the fundamentals of the Mac OS X interface—how to get around, how to select things, and how some of the key elements of Mac OS X work. In Chapter 3, you'll learn more about the Finder, including how to create, move, and duplicate items; how to use and customize Finder windows; how to create and work with aliases; and even how to burn recordable data CDs and DVDs from within the Finder interface.

Chapter 3

The Finder

After you log in to Mac OS X, you're presented with your workspace, where you'll access applications, save documents, and manage files. As a user on a Mac OS X system, you get your own home folder, which is given the same name as your username; it holds Documents, Desktop, and Public folders, among others. The home folder also stores your personal preferences, which is why it's possible for your desktop, application preferences, Internet bookmarks, and more to be different from those of another user who logs in to the same Mac.

Central to your workspace experience is the Finder, Apple's file and folder management program. The Finder, by default, is launched immediately after you log in to your Mac (if your Mac logs in automatically, the Finder is loaded after the Mac has started up), and it runs the entire time you're working with your Mac. You'll use it to launch documents and applications, to access files, and to store and manage your documents, applications, and other computer files in the folders and on the disk volumes that your Mac can access.

In this chapter, you'll get a quick introduction to the Finder. Then you'll see how to work within Finder windows and change their settings, as well as how to use the Finder's special Go menu to quickly access certain folders and disks. After that, it's on to working with icons in the Finder—copying, moving, and getting information about items and using labels to flag your files and folders. You'll also learn how to use the Finder to create CDs and how to use the Trash to delete items. Finally, we'll quickly cover the Finder Preferences to give you a sense of some of the customizable Finder behavior.

In this chapter:

- ◆ Working with the Finder
- ◆ The Go Menu
- ◆ Working with Icons
- ◆ Using Smart Folders
- ◆ The Trash
- ◆ Finder Preferences
- ◆ Burning Data CDs

Working with the Finder

The Finder is a program that Mac OS X always loads when you log in to your account. You can't quit the Finder as you can quit most applications. It's a permanent fixture in your workspace, designed to help you access and manage your files, folders, and applications. Even while you work in other programs, the Finder is in the background, waiting to help you manage the workspace. Just click the desktop color or pattern behind your open windows or click the Finder icon in the Dock, and you're returned immediately to the Finder.

When you switch to the Finder, its windows display your disks, folders, and files. Here you can create, rename, and delete folders, and you can move items between folders. Using menu commands in the Finder, you can duplicate items, create aliases, and get additional information about items.

Most of all, the Finder is designed to help you manage your personal files and folders while enabling you to access other resources connected to your computer, including external hard drives, removable media, and network volumes.

If you're an experienced Macintosh user, you might know that the Mac OS has offered a Finder since the operating system's debut in the mid-1980s. However, starting with the first versions of Mac OS X, Apple completely updated the Finder application, based in part on some of the technology Apple acquired in OpenStep. But beyond that lineage, there is little resemblance between today's Finder windows and those of yore. The Mac OS X Finder window features a toolbar across the top with buttons for performing common actions—for example, Back and Forward buttons that work a little like a web browser's Back button, and an Action button that enables you to perform certain actions according to what type of item is selected. It also has a sidebar, where you see some of your most common folders and to which you can add other folders. You'll see all of these elements—including a good bit about customizing the Finder window and the way you view items in it—in this chapter.

The Mac OS X Hierarchy

Mac OS X, because of its Unix-like, multiuser underpinnings, requires a rigid structure in the way it organizes files and applications. All users of the Mac OS X system—even if only one user account exists—have their own places on the hard drive (or on a network, in some configurations) where documents, preference files, e-mail mailboxes, personal applications, and many other interesting tidbits are stored. This home folder bears the name of the user and is accessible to each user when they log in.

This organization segments the Mac OS X filesystem into folders and files that a user should work in, and into other folders and files that are best left completely alone. The exact location and format of certain files are necessary for Mac OS X to operate correctly. Therefore, a regular user account is allowed access only to certain parts of the filesystem.

This structure also makes it possible for certain shortcuts to enable you to use the Finder to move quickly to your documents, applications, and home directory. We'll explain more about that later in this chapter.

For starters, though, we need to look at the Mac OS X filesystem hierarchy. Figure 3.1 shows the basics of a typical Mac OS X folder hierarchy.

FIGURE 3.1
Hierarchy of the folders in Mac OS X

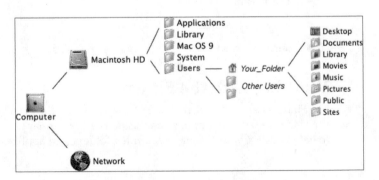

The most basic level of the filesystem is the Computer, which you can access by clicking the Computer icon in the Finder Sidebar. This icon bears the name of your Mac; this is usually *Your-Name*'s Computer, but you can change it in the Sharing pane of the System Preferences. (See Chapter 18, "Building a Network and Sharing Files.") When you do so, you'll see your hard drive(s), any mounted removable media (such as CD-ROMs or Zip disks), and Network disks (via file sharing, including an iDisk, if you have one) that the computer has to offer.

If you click the icon in the Sidebar for the main startup disk where Mac OS X is installed, you'll see four basic folders: Applications, Library, System, and Users. (You may also see a Mac OS 9 System Folder and an Applications (Mac OS 9) folder, if you installed Mac OS X over Mac OS 9, or if you still have a System Folder on your Mac to run the Classic environment.) The Library folder holds a number of application-related settings and system files, including fonts, preferences, and logs for your applications. The System folder holds the hierarchy of folders and files used to get Mac OS X up and running. (If you're the administrator for your Mac OS X machine or network, you'll dig deeper into the Library and System folders, as discussed in Chapter 9, "Being the Administrator: Permissions, Settings, and Adding Users," and later chapters.)

The Applications folder is designed to hold applications accessible by all users on your Mac. You'll find a number of applications already installed there after installing Mac OS X. To learn more about installing new applications in the Applications folder, see Chapter 9.

Within the Users folder, you'll find the home folder for each individual user, where a person can store their documents, personal applications, and program settings or data such as mailboxes and downloaded files. Users (aside from an administrator) cannot change or move the contents of another user's home folder.

THE LINGO OF HIERARCHY AND PATHS

Files on Mac OS X disks generally are stored hierarchically, meaning you'll have folders that include subfolders that include subfolders and so on. The enclosed folders are called *child folders*, and the enclosing folders are called *parent folders*.

An example might be your home folder in Mac OS X. The folder is given the same name as your short username, and (by default) it has the subfolders (child folders) Documents, Library, and Public, among others. The parent folder for these subfolders is your home folder.

Likewise, your home folder has a parent folder called Users. The Users folder's parent is the root folder on the hard disk, which is usually represented by a hard disk icon when viewed in a Finder window. (The root folder may be called Macintosh HD, or, if you have renamed your hard disk, it may have another name.)

This series of relationships creates a path in the hierarchical storage system on your Mac. Suppose your home folder is named bobby. The path is represented as /Users/bobby/ in Unix-style notation. Note that in Unix-style notation, the first slash is used to represent the root level of the hard disk, and the trailing slash isn't required if you're typing it in Terminal or elsewhere. So, an example like /Users/bobby would work, but Users/bobby/ is incorrect. (We'll cover this more in the section "The Go Menu," later in this chapter.)

In Mac OS X, the hierarchy extends all the way back to the computer that you're working on, as represented by the Computer icon in the toolbar of each Finder window. Selecting the Computer icon shows you the disks connected to that computer. At the Computer level, you'll also see a Network icon, which can be used to browse any items connected to your Mac via a network connection.

Within each home folder, you'll find other folders—Documents, Library, Public, and others. Although it isn't mandatory to store documents in the Documents folder (you can store them anywhere within your home folder), you'll find that doing so can be convenient because Finder windows can offer quick-access icons in their Sidebars to take you directly to Documents and the other folders.

The Finder Window

Finder windows are receptacles for files and folders. Each window displays the contents of a folder, or, if you are at the root level of your hard disk, the highest level of folders on the disk. When you double-click a folder, the Finder window changes to show you its contents. You can continue double-clicking down the folder and file hierarchy to find the files, folders, or applications you want to work with.

Mac OS X offers a streamlined way of accessing folders from the Finder window sidebars (see Figure 3.2). The Finder window helps you move quickly to different parts of a large filesystem—one with many folders and subfolders where items may be hiding. Likewise, the Finder window makes it easy to see networked disks and volumes.

The Finder's Sidebar, the section at the left of the default Finder window, contains icons to give you quick access to commonly used folders. These include icons to your home folder and some of its subfolders, but you can add your own icons here. We'll look at using the sidebar later in this chapter.

The Finder window offers three different views—Column, Icon, and List. How you view the Finder window may be a matter of personal preference, but you might discover that certain views are more productive than others for certain tasks.

FIGURE 3.2

The Finder window, by default, shows icons in a single window.

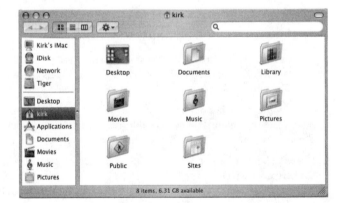

Opening a Finder Window

To open a Finder window, select File ➤ New Finder Window in the Finder's menu or press ⌘N. A Finder window appears. If you already have a Finder window open, a second Finder window will open.

You can open as many Finder windows at a time as you like. Opening more than one Finder window is one way to copy and move files between folders (more on that later, in the section "Working with Icons"), though the Sidebar helps by giving you access to folders you use often. You can then close Finder windows by clicking their Close buttons or by selecting a window and choosing File ➤ Close Window from the Finder menu or pressing ⌘W.

TIP   You can use the Window menu in the Finder to switch between different Finder windows quickly. Also, remember that you can click a Finder window's Minimize button if you'd like to place it out of the way on the Dock.

Browsing in the Finder Window

By default, the Finder window opens in Icon view, meaning the window is filled with the current folder's icons. If you've just logged in, you're probably looking at the icons in your home folder, as illustrated in Figure 3.2.

You can treat these icons as you would any icons in windows or on the desktop, as described in Chapter 2, "The Fundamentals of Mac OS X." You can single-click an icon to select it, drag-select multiple items, and so on. You double-click a document or application to launch it, and you double-click a folder to view its contents.

Double-clicking a folder doesn't open a new Finder window; instead, the entire Finder window changes to show that folder's contents. If you'd prefer to open a new window with the folder's content shown, hold down the ⌘ key while double-clicking the folder icon.

TIP   You can change the way windows open in the Finder when you double-click a folder icon. For details, see the section "Changing Finder Window Behavior," later in this chapter.

You might notice that the Finder window in this view works a little like a web browser. When you double-click a folder icon, you'll go forward to that folder's contents, similar to when you click a link in a web-browsing application. To move back, click the Back button—the left-facing arrow.

At the top of the Finder window, you'll see the name of the folder currently being viewed. This title bar also hides a secret capability: If you hold down the ⌘ key and click the folder name, you'll see a pop-up menu that enables you to select any of the parent folders of the current folder.

TIP   It's also worth noting that the small folder icon next to the folder name in the title bar is an active element. You can drag that folder icon to the desktop or to another Finder window if you'd like to move the entire folder to another location on your hard disk (or copy it to another disk). You also can drag the icon to the Dock if you'd like to add the folder you're currently viewing as a Dock icon.

The Finder Window Sidebar

One of the most useful features of the Finder is the *Sidebar*, the pane at the left of the Finder window. The Sidebar provides a bird's eye view of your computer, in the top section, showing (by default) the Computer icon, the Network icon, and your hard disk(s), as well as any removable media, such as CDs or DVDs. In the bottom section, it contains icons that give you shortcuts to the folders you use most.

You can change the contents of both parts of the Sidebar. Display of the top section, which contains disks and volumes, is controlled by the Finder Preferences; we'll discuss those in the section, "Finder Preferences," later in this chapter. As for the bottom section of the Sidebar, you can change its contents by dragging icons into or out of it. Icons in the Sidebar are like aliases; if you drag a folder from the Sidebar, you won't lose or delete that folder. Just drag a folder icon outside of the Sidebar to remove it.

You can add frequently used files and folders to the Sidebar, and you can add application icons, but ideally, you should use the Dock for applications. To add a file or folder to the Sidebar, just navigate to a window containing the folder and then drag its icon into the Sidebar. You'll be able to position it wherever you want; the Sidebar icons are not maintained in any special order, and you can use the positioning guide to place it where you want.

TIP To add any item to the Sidebar quickly, just click it once to select it and press ⌘T.

WARNING Be careful when adding icons to the Sidebar—if you don't place your icon *in* the Sidebar (which is indicated by the appearance of the small dividing line), you might accidentally move it into one of the folders whose icons are in the Sidebar.

To access the contents of any of the folders in the Sidebar, just click them—this displays their contents in the right-side section of the Finder window. To move files into any of these folders, just drag them onto the Sidebar icons. This is an easy way to organize files without having to navigate into your folders and subfolders.

The Sidebar is dynamic and changes the size of its contents to fit in the available space. It will keep shrinking the size of its icons and text until it reaches a minimum (it won't shrink the text to anything smaller than 12 points), after which it will display a scroll bar.

You can resize the width of the Sidebar by dragging the divider that separates the Sidebar from the rest of the Finder window. If you want, you can make it just wide enough to show only the icons and not the text labels for their contents.

Finally, if you want to remove the Sidebar entirely, just drag the separator all the way to the left of the Finder window, or double-click the separator. You'll no longer see the Sidebar, but it will still be there; you can drag the separator back to the right, or double-click it again, if you want to display it again.

TIP As you'll see in Chapter 4, "Using Applications," the Sidebar also has a direct relationship to Open and Save dialog boxes; folders that you add in the Sidebar can be quickly accessed in those dialog boxes as well.

The Finder Window Toolbar

At the top of the Mac OS X Finder window is a row of buttons, arranged in what's called a *toolbar*. These buttons, such as the View button or the Action button, provide quick access to different Finder functions. Figure 3.3 shows these icons.

FIGURE 3.3
The Finder window's toolbar

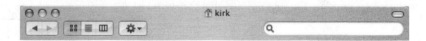

Users of early versions of Mac OS X might be surprised that there are so few buttons in this toolbar. Since the Sidebar is the standard receptacle for folder and file shortcuts, the only buttons available in the Finder toolbar are those that provide Finder functions. By default, these are the Back and Forward buttons, the View buttons, and the Action button at the left.

The first two are self-explanatory. The three small View buttons enable you to change the way you view the window. From left to right, they're the Icon, List, and Columns View buttons.

The Action button provides contextual functions according to what is selected in the Finder. This offers similar functions to those displayed when clicking an item while holding down the Control key, or when clicking with the right mouse button on mice that have more than one button.

TIP   You can customize the toolbar to show some other functions that you'd prefer to have quick access to. See the section "Customizing the Finder Toolbar," later in this chapter.

WHERE HAVE FAVORITES GONE?

If you used Favorites in early versions of Mac OS X, you'll be surprised to find them absent from the Finder; Apple removed them from Mac OS X 10.3 (Panther). Favorites were simply aliases that were stored in a special folder—your Favorites folder—that was accessible from the Finder's Go menu and from Open and Save dialogs.

Apple's idea is that the Finder Sidebar replaces Favorites. This may be the case, if you don't have many of them, but if you used a lot of favorites to easily access folders, you might be disappointed.

However, if you install Mac OS X 10.4 over Mac OS X 10.2 or earlier, you'll find a Favorites folder in your Finder Sidebar. This folder is the same Favorites folder you had under the previous Mac OS X; it is stored in the /Library folder of your home folder. You can use this folder from the Sidebar, and you can even add your own favorites to it by creating aliases and placing them in this folder. And, if you want access to these favorites from Open and Save dialogs, this Favorites folder will display in the Sidebar of these dialogs.

The Favorites function is no longer present, but the idea is similar. You'll need to adjust to this new way of working with your favorites, but they won't be lost.

The Status Bar

In a Finder window, you'll see some statistics and information that tell you a little about the folder you're viewing and the disk that the folder is stored on. At the bottom of the window, you'll see the *status bar*, which tells you how many items are in the current folder and how much space remains on the current disk.

11 items, 808.6 MB available

At the far left of the status bar, you'll see a small icon if you don't have write permission in the current folder. Each user account has certain permissions that enable different levels of access to folders on local or networked disks. For instance, only administrator accounts have the capability to change files (or *write* files) within certain system-level folders such as the Applications and Library folders. As a regular user, you'll have the capability to write files to your personal folders, execute files from public folders (such as the Shared folder inside the Users folder), and read files from some others.

If you see an icon that looks like a pencil with a line through it, you don't have *write* permission for the folder (or the folder is on read-only media, such as a CD). You can't change its contents or alter anything within it. While you can open and view documents in that folder (meaning you have *read* permission), you can't change those documents unless you use a Save As command to save a copy of the document to a folder for which you have write privileges. However, if you can open the folder and see items in it, you do have read permission—you can launch applications or view documents in the folder. (In some cases, such as the Drop Box folder found in other users' Public folders, you won't be able to open the folder and view its contents—that's a folder to which you do not have read permission.) If you can open the folder, and you don't see a pencil icon with a line through it, then you have both read and write permissions.

NOTE The Mac OS long called the settings for read and write status "privileges," although it's more common to call them "permissions" in the Unix world. Starting in Mac OS X 10.2, Apple began calling them "permissions" in settings and dialog boxes. The two terms are basically synonymous.

See Chapter 4 for more on the Save As command and Chapter 5, "Personalizing Mac OS X," for more on setting permissions for your personal folders.

Using Column View

Column view is a sleek and powerful way to peer into your Mac's mounted disks and navigate their contents. Column view, in a nutshell, enables you to see and think of the disk as hierarchical. Instead of moving back and forth one folder at a time by double-clicking icons and opening and closing windows, you can use the Finder window to see three, four, or five levels of the folder hierarchy at once. All you have to do is select View ➤ As Columns or click the Columns button in the Finder window's toolbar. Figure 3.4 shows the Finder in Column view.

TIP The number of columns you can see in Column view depends in part on your display's resolution. The higher the resolution, the more columns you'll be able to see in a Finder window. Chapter 5 discusses changing display resolution.

FIGURE 3.4
In Column view, you get a better view of the hierarchy of folders.

In Column view, clicking the Computer icon in the Sidebar sets the first column to show any disks connected to your Mac, both internally and externally, including any active removable disks (such as a Zip disk or a CD-ROM) and any network volumes that are mounted on your Mac. Then, if you click a disk icon, for instance, all the subfolders on that disk appear in the next column to the right. If you click once on one of the subfolders, its items appear in the next column, and so on.

NOTE   Column view is even more compelling when working with folders in the Sidebar. Since the Sidebar is always a column, regardless of the Finder view you use, it makes Column view more natural to use.

To select a disk, folder, application, or document, click it once in *any* of the columns. In the next column to the right, you'll see either the folder's contents or, in the case of files or applications, some information about that item (see Figure 3.5). In some cases, text files, PDF files, images, or QuickTime-compatible files can show a preview of themselves right in the Finder window.

To view a different disk or folder, you can select a folder, disk, or item in any of the visible columns. Doing so changes your location on the disk, revealing the contents or information of the item selected. This can take some getting used to because clicking in earlier columns (those to the left) will completely change what appears in later columns (those to the right). If you're looking at your home folder, for instance, and go back a few columns and click the main System folder, the entire character of the Finder window will change, showing you the contents of the System folder.

FIGURE 3.5
For items other than folders, you can view a little information or even a preview.

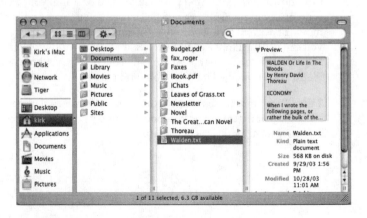

If you have quite a few columns open (because you've dug deep into a particular folder hierarchy), you'll notice a scroll bar and arrows running across the bottom of the window. You can scroll to see previous columns.

If you'd like to see more columns in the window, drag the resize box (at the bottom-right corner of the window) to make the Finder window larger. The larger the Finder window, the more columns you can see. You can also resize columns in Column view within a Finder window. That makes it possible for you to decide how much of an item's name will appear. At the bottom of each column are drag marks; click and drag them to the left or right to resize a single column, or hold down the Option key while clicking and dragging to resize all columns.

As with Icon view, you can use all the icons in the Finder window's Sidebar (Home, Applications, and so on) to move directly to your home, `Documents`, or `Applications` folder simply by clicking the corresponding icons. Likewise, you can use the Back button to move backward through the choices you made to get to where you are. If you clicked your home folder and then clicked the `Sites` folder, clicking the Back button will return you to your home folder.

Changing to List View

Another view you can use in the Finder window is List view, which you can set by choosing View ➢ As List. List view replaces the columns or icons of the default view with a listing of the items on a particular disk or in a folder, as shown in Figure 3.6. List view is generally best suited to folders that include many, many files—usually documents—about which you'd like the most information possible. List view can be sorted by name, date modified, size, or other variables that other views can't be sorted by. (The view can be sorted by only one variable at a time.) You then can find files more easily and quickly.

If you double-click a subfolder while in List view, the window switches to a view of the subfolder's contents. Using the Back button returns you to the parent folder. As with the Icon and Column views, you can hold down the ⌘ key while double-clicking a folder icon to open a second Finder window containing the subfolder's contents.

FIGURE 3.6
List view shows the contents of a disk or folder with columns of information.

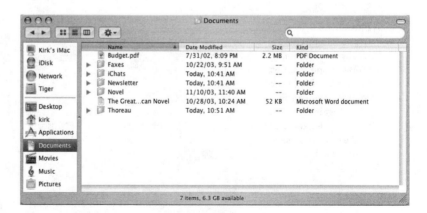

List view's greatest strength is probably its capability to show more than one folder's contents at a time. Click the disclosure triangle next to a folder in the list, and that folder will reveal its contents. Notice that the subfolders list is indented somewhat to show at a glance that it's a subfolder (see Figure 3.7).

List view is pretty flexible in its presentation of subfolders. For instance, you can have more than one subfolder revealed, as shown in Figure 3.7. Further, subfolders needn't have the same parent in order to be revealed—you can see subfolders within other subfolders as long as you have enough space on the screen to reveal them. If you run out of screen space, you can use the up and down scroll arrows to see more folders and files in the hierarchy.

TIP Want to move an item from a revealed subfolder to its parent folder that's currently displayed in the Finder window's List view? Just select the item you want to move and drag it onto the window's icon in the Finder window title bar (if there is only one level of hierarchy visible below this folder). When you release the mouse button, the item will pop right into that folder.

List view windows can be sorted in many ways. Click any of the column heads (Name, Date Modified, Size, or Kind), and you'll see the list sorted by that column's criterion. If you'd like to change the order of the sort, simply click the column's name again and the sort order will change (see Figure 3.8).

FIGURE 3.7
Clicking disclosure triangles enables you to see the contents of a folder and a subfolder simultaneously.

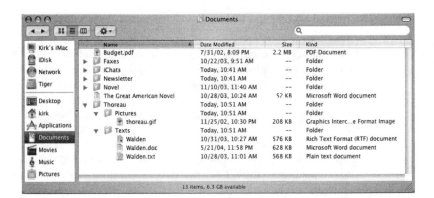

FIGURE 3.8
Click a column title to sort by that column. (This example is sorted by Date Modified.) The column name can be clicked again to change the sort order, indicated by the small triangle in the column heading.

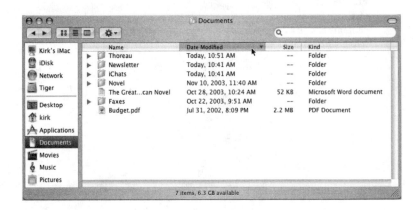

You can change the width of the columns by placing your mouse pointer on the line that divides two columns. The mouse pointer changes to a line with arrows pointing left and right. Click and hold the mouse button and then drag to resize the column. Release the mouse button when you're happy with the width of the column.

To change the order of columns, point at a column name and then click and hold the mouse button to drag that column to another part of the window. When you drop the column name, that column is placed in that spot, and other columns are reordered accordingly.

TIP   One nice trick in List view is to move directly to an item in the list using the keyboard. How? Just start typing the first few characters of its name. If you have a folder named Memos that you want to select, just start typing **mem**, and the selection will jump to folders with those letters. Although this is most effective when List view is sorted alphabetically, it works regardless of the sort order. (The trick works in Icon and Column view, too.) In fact, even if you are in List view and have several levels of hierarchy visible, pressing Tab will move to the next item alphabetically, no matter where it is in the hierarchy; Shift+Tab will move to the previous item alphabetically.

Arranging Icons (in Icon View)

If the icons in a Finder window have become a bit haphazard, you can clean them up easily. Select the window you want to organize (you don't need to select the icons) and then choose View ➢ Clean Up. The icons will be placed on a grid and separated by a minimum distance to make them easier to view (see Figure 3.9).

FIGURE 3.9
On the top, a messy Finder window; on the bottom, it's all cleaned up.

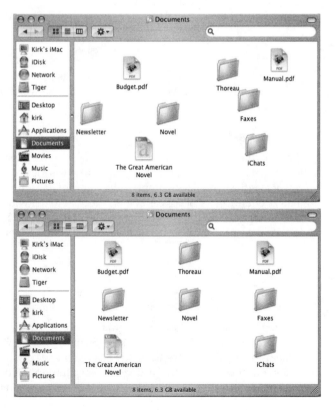

You also can choose to arrange icons according to one of several criteria, if you'd like. Select the window you want to arrange and then choose View ➤ Arrange by Name, for example. The icons will be cleaned up (again, by an invisible grid that keeps the icons a certain distance apart) and alphabetized. You can arrange icons by Name, Date Modified, Date Created, Size, Kind, or Label.

View Options

As you've seen, the Finder window offers a number of methods for viewing and arranging the contents of a folder. To help get a handle on all these different view options and behaviors, the Finder application offers a command that enables you to set some basic preferences for how folders look and behave.

Mac OS X can store preferences for folders individually. You may have already noticed that one folder can be set to List view while another is set to Icon view, for instance, and each time you return to a folder, its most recently set view is displayed. (With Column view, however, once you set the Finder window to view columns, it stays that way.) Likewise, you can set both global preferences for how List view and Icon view windows will look and individual preferences for each window.

You can set the viewing preferences in the View Options palette. With the Finder active, select View ➤ Show View Options from the menu.

In any View Options window (the window will actually be named for the folder that you're altering), you can change either the settings for that window or the settings for All Windows. These represent the *scope* of the settings—will your changes simply affect the current window or all windows set to this View type? For instance, will you change the size of the icons only in this window or in all windows that are also set to View ➤ As Icon?

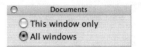

Once you've chosen the scope of your settings, you can begin to make your selections. The options you see are based on the configuration of the current window; if the window is in List view, you'll see those options; if it's in Icon view or Column view, you'll see the corresponding options.

ICON VIEW SETTINGS

If you're choosing the options for Icon view, you have five settings: Icon Size, Text Size, Label Position, Icon Behavior, and Background. Figure 3.10 shows the entire window.

For Icon Size, you'll see a simple slider control. Drag the selector back and forth on the slider to change the size of the icons that appear in this particular folder window. Similarly, the Text Size menu can be used to select the size of the text that's used to label icons. The Label Position radio buttons can be used to place the label text either below the icons or to the right of the icons, as shown here:

In the Icon Behavior section, you have four options that you can toggle on and off:

Snap to Grid Select this option to force icons into a grid-based alignment whenever you drop them in the window. When you have Snap to Grid on, you can override this option when moving items by holding down the ⌘ key before you release the mouse button; this lets you place items and not snap them to the grid. If you have this option off, you can always move items and place them on the grid by holding the ⌘ key as you move them.

FIGURE 3.10
The settings options
for Icon view

Show Item Info   When selected, information about an item will appear along with the item's label. For folders, you'll see the number of items in the folder; for disks (or volumes), you'll see the volume's size and amount of free space. For graphics, you may see the size of the images in pixels; and for music and movies, the length of the songs or videos.

Show Icon Preview   Turning on this option will cause the window to change the icon of images and other multimedia files from a generic document image to a small preview of the actual image or multimedia file, if possible. The only reason to keep this off is that it can slow down the viewing of a folder on older Macs.

Keep Arranged By   This option places icons in a grid alignment and automatically arranges the window by the criterion you select in the pop-up menu. Your choices for arranging the window are by name (alphabetically), by the creation or modification date, by the size of the file or folder, by the kind of item, and by the item's label. It's a good idea to keep your icons arranged; it has the advantage of making a specific file or folder easy to find at a glance (especially if you have them arranged by name) and aligns them more neatly in the window.

In the Background section, you have three options:

White   Choose this option if you don't want any special background for the folder.

Color   When you select Color, a small button appears. Click the button to show the Color Palette, which enables you to choose the background color. (See Chapter 4 for more on the Color Palette.)

Picture   Choosing Picture brings the Select button to the screen. Click Select, and an Open dialog box appears, enabling you to locate an image file that you'd like to use as the background of the folder. You then locate the appropriate file and click OK in the Open dialog box. Your selected image will appear as the background in the current folder.

NOTE   Interestingly, not all images will work as background images, because the Finder doesn't necessarily tile images in folder windows the same way it does for your desktop. If it looks like a background image doesn't work, it could be because it's a small image that is supposed to be tiled but isn't. Try a different image, preferably one that is 1024×768 pixels or larger so that it will fill the entire folder window (depending on your Mac's resolution settings; see Chapter 5).

LIST VIEW SETTINGS

If you're choosing the options for a folder that's in List view, you'll have some settings that are different from those in Icon view, including what columns will appear and how the date and size of items will be shown. Figure 3.11 shows the View Options dialog box for List view.

At the top of the window, you can choose between two different icon sizes for the icons that appear in List mode. Then, in the Text Size menu, you can choose the size of the text in the list.

You can also use the check boxes to make choices:

Show Columns Choose each column that you'd like to see in List view by placing a check mark next to its entry.

Use Relative Dates Select this option to enable date entries that are relative to the current date, as in "Yesterday, 9:16 P.M.," as opposed to month, day, and year.

Calculate All Sizes Turn this option on, and folder sizes (for subfolders in the window) will be calculated and displayed. Displaying folder size can slow down your computer, which spends a lot of time adding up the sizes of files, which is why you can turn it off.

FIGURE 3.11

The View Options dialog box for a folder in List view shows options different from those for Icon view.

COLUMN VIEW SETTINGS

If you're choosing the settings for a window that's in Column view, the options are very limited. You can choose the text size for items in the columns and whether or not icons should appear in the columns. You also can turn on the preview column behavior, if you prefer that previews of items not appear in the Column view.

Customizing the Finder Toolbar

If you're upgrading from Mac OS X 10.2 or earlier, you'll find that, while you can still add icons to the toolbar, it's much easier and more practical to place them in the Sidebar. The Sidebar lets you view the contents of icons quickly, since they display in the current Finder window.

Dragging Items to the Toolbar

The easiest way to customize the toolbar is simply to drag items to it from either the desktop or from the Finder window itself. This enables you to add a document or application that you'd like to be able to launch with a single click, or that you'd like to be able to access at all times. Since the Sidebar is designed for folder icons, the toolbar is best for other items, such as applications or files. To add an item, simply drag it to the toolbar area.

When you drag an item to the toolbar, you must insert it between two other items. In the default Finder toolbar, there is a flexible space between the Action button and the Search field. If you try to drag an item onto this space, it won't go into the toolbar. You must drag it just to the right of the Action button, or to the left of the search field, or between two other buttons. When you've got the icon in the right location, your cursor changes and shows a plus (+) sign to indicate that it can be moved.

What this essentially does is place an *alias* to the item on the toolbar. You haven't moved the item anywhere—it still resides in the same place on your hard disk as it did before. But you now have an easy click or drag-and-drop target, which can add a bit of convenience. If you put applications on the toolbar, they become omnipresent drag-and-drop targets, accessible from every Finder window. If you have an application that you're often dragging items to—the StuffIt Expander application, TextEdit, or Preview, for instance—it might be nice to have the application right there on the toolbar. Of course, you can drag and drop to the Dock as well—so you can avoid cluttering up your Finder window toolbar with icons.

If you want to remove an item from the toolbar, simply hold down the Command (⌘) key and drag it from the toolbar to somewhere else on the screen (for instance, the desktop area). As long as you don't drop the item back in the toolbar area, it will disappear from view when you release the mouse button. Nothing will be deleted—only the icon will be gone.

CUSTOMIZING THE TOOLBAR

Besides dragging items to the toolbar, you also can go in for more wholesale changes. Select View ➤ Customize Toolbar, and a sheet displays showing the icons and buttons you can add to the toolbar, as shown in Figure 3.12.

Now you can drag any of these items up onto the toolbar to add them. Note that the icons represent only functions that you can carry out with the Finder: You can add an Eject button for ejecting disks, a Burn button to burn CDs or DVDs, a Path button for navigating parent folders, and even a separator line to help organize the toolbar. You also can drag items already on the toolbar to other locations—for instance, put the View buttons on the right side or rearrange the items that are already on the toolbar.

Here's a fully customized example:

> **TIP**   If you add more items to the toolbar than can be shown (or if you subsequently change the size of a Finder window), a small double arrow appears on the right side of the toolbar; you can click that arrow to access the items that aren't shown on the shrunken toolbar.

The Customize screen also offers a small pop-up menu in the bottom-left corner, where you can choose how you'd like the tools in the toolbar to appear. By default, only icons display. You also can choose Icon & Text or Text Only if you want. Icon & Text takes up more space, both vertically and horizontally (at least for icons whose names are longer than the icons are wide). Text Only saves space vertically but may use more horizontal space. Finally, check Use Small Size if you'd like to squeeze a few extra buttons onto the toolbar.

> **TIP**   You can cycle through the different toolbar views by holding down the ⌘ key and clicking the Hide Toolbar button at the top right of any Finder window. This is a good way to see which view you like best.

FIGURE 3.12
All-out customizing of the toolbar happens on this sheet.

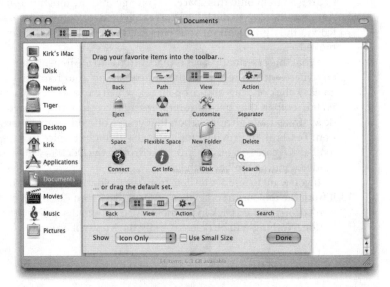

When you've finished customizing, click the Done button. You'll be returned to the Finder window, now complete with your new toolbar. If you want the standard toolbar back, just drag the default set from the bottom of the Customize screen up to the toolbar area, and it will replace any custom icons you've added.

CHANGING FINDER WINDOW BEHAVIOR

If you don't like the toolbar, and especially don't like the Finder's brushed metal windows with the Sidebar, you can remove these two elements and, in the process, change the way Mac OS X's Finder windows act.

At the top right of every Finder window is a small oval button. Click it once, and the Finder toolbar disappears. (You also can select View ➤ Hide Toolbar.) The result is a plain window that can still be viewed in Icon, Columns, or List view.

There's one other important thing to note about this window. Double-clicking a folder inside it will now open that folder in a *new* window—one that still doesn't have a toolbar.

TIP   When you're in this mode, you can hold down the Option key while double-clicking a folder if you'd like the parent folder's window to disappear when the new folder's window appears. (This reduces folder clutter, and it's a holdover from older Mac OS versions.)

To return the Finder window to its default behavior, click the oval button again or select View ➤ Show Toolbar. The normal Mac OS X Finder window will return in all its glory.

The Go Menu

The Finder offers a menu that lets you quickly access folders at any of a number of key locations on your Mac: the Go menu. If you're used to Microsoft Windows, you'll see that the Go menu has some similarities to the Start menu (see Figure 3.13).

FIGURE 3.13
The Go menu in action

Hidden within the Go menu are a few important and disparate tasks such as these:

Folder Presets   The Go menu includes commands that give you quick access to your main folders. Select Go ➤ Home, for instance, and the frontmost Finder window (if one isn't open, a new window will appear) will switch to a view of your home folder. (You also can get to the home folder by pressing Shift+⌘H anywhere within the Finder application.) Other options include Computer (Shift+⌘C), Applications (Shift+⌘A), the Network icon (Shift+⌘K), and the Utilities folder (Shift+⌘U).

iDisk   Choose the iDisk preset and then its submenu to open your iDisk (assuming you have an active Internet connection and a Mac.com account) based on the settings in the Internet pane of the System Preferences application. (See Chapter 11, "The Web, Online Security, .Mac, Sherlock, and iChat," for more on iDisk.) The iDisk submenu also lets you access another user's iDisk or another user's iDisk Public folder.

Recent Folders   When you select a recently used folder in the Recent Folders menu (Go ➤ Recent Folders), you move directly to it. Once selected, that folder's contents are displayed in the frontmost Finder window.

Connect to Server   Choosing Go ➤ Connect to Server or pressing ⌘K opens the Connect to Server window, which enables you to connect to shared network volumes available on your network. (You'll read more about this in Chapter 17, "Accessing Network Volumes.")

Go to Folder   When you select Go ➤ Go to Folder or press Shift+⌘G, the Go to Folder dialog sheet appears in the frontmost Finder window, where you can type a *path statement* to a particular folder. A path statement describes the entire hierarchy of a folder's location on the hard drive. Enter this statement and click Go, and the frontmost Finder window will change to that folder if it's found (see Figure 3.14).

Interestingly, the Go to Folder dialog sheet enables Unix-like command syntax to creep into the Finder. This is quite convenient if you know what you're doing.

You've seen in this chapter that a hierarchy of folders exists on your disks, and digging into them creates a path, which is shown in the Icon bar. The path has an equivalent in the text-based, Unix-like underbelly of Mac OS X. Essentially, each folder name is separated by a slash (/), with another slash at the beginning to represent the "root" of a disk. For instance, say you want to open your Mac hard disk's Users folder and then the Shared folder. The text-based shorthand in Figure 3.14 would take you directly to that folder (in the frontmost Finder window) when you click Go.

FIGURE 3.14
The Go to Folder dialog

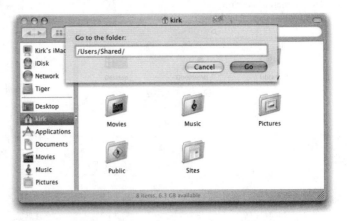

TIP   You can use two special shortcuts in the Go to Folder entry box. The first is that leading forward slash (/) already mentioned. Enter it by itself and press Return, and you're taken immediately to your Mac's root folder on the startup disk. The other is the tilde (˜). Enter it and press Return to be taken immediately to your home folder. You can build on the tilde if you like, as in ˜/Documents/ Newsletters to get to folders within your home folder.

Working with Icons

Once you've figured out the Finder and the many options for its windows, you're ready to do more than just look through your disks and folders. Using the menu commands in the Finder (or keyboard combinations in conjunction with the mouse), you can create folders, duplicate items, and move items between folders. We'll also discuss some other Finder commands such as creating smart folders and burn folders, using the Info window to get information about an item, and using the Add to Favorites command. Also, we'll dig into the Trash, so to speak, and see how to delete your files.

Creating a Folder

Before creating a folder, you must first decide where to put that folder. Begin by selecting the disk or parent folder where you'd like the new folder to appear. In a Finder window, click the parent folder once in a Columns view or double-click it to open it in an Icon or List view.

Then select File ➤ New Folder or press ⌘Shift+N. The new folder appears with its name highlighted, ready for editing. Type in the folder's name. When you've finished typing the name, press Return or click once outside the text area. Once named, the folder may jump to another location in the Finder window if you've previously chosen to arrange the folders by name, date modified, or some other criterion.

Creating a Smart Folder

Mac OS X 10.4 offers a new type of folder: the smart folder. If you're familiar with iTunes' smart play-lists or iPhoto's smart albums, you'll immediately understand the concept behind smart folders. If you're not familiar with these items, you'll understand quickly.

Start by creating a new smart folder: Select File ➤ New Smart Folder (or press ⌘Option+N). A New Smart Folder window opens.

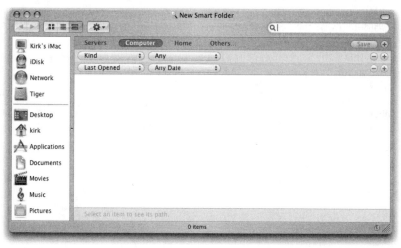

The smart folder works like a live search among your folders, disks, and even network volumes. It matches one or several criteria, allowing you, in essence, to save a preset search and access its results—which are always up to date—with a single click.

Start by selecting the location for the search: At the top of the smart folder window, you have several choices: Servers (network volumes that are currently mounted on your computer), Computer (all disks and removable media available, but not network volumes), Home (your home folder), and Others. If you select Others, you'll be able to choose specific folders or volumes by adding them to the Search In window and selecting them.

The smart folder window shows two search criteria: The first is set to Kind and Any, and the second is set to Last Opened and Any Date. You can change these criteria to build your search.

Let's look at a simple example: Leave the first criterion as Kind, and, from the second menu on that line, select PDF. You'll immediately see a list of all the PDF files on your computer.

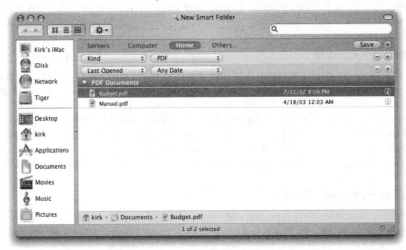

Click one of the items in the results and you'll see its file path at the bottom of the window; double-click one of the items to open it.

Now that you have searched for all your PDF documents, you may want to save this search as a smart folder so you can access it again at any time. To do this, click the Save button near the top of the window. Name your smart folder (for example, PDF Files) and select a location to save it. (By default, this is the Saved Searches folder, but you can store it wherever you want). Finally, you can choose to add this folder to the Sidebar so you can access this search again with a single click. Click Save.

TIP We'll look more closely at searching for files in Finder windows, with smart folders, and with Spotlight, in Chapter 6, "Getting Help and Searching Your Files."

Creating a Burn Folder

Another new type of folder available in Mac OS X 10.4 is the Burn folder. This is a special type of folder that has a Burn button in its window. You can add items to this folder—files, folders, photos, music files, etc.—then simply click the Burn button to start burning a CD or DVD.

Select File ➤ New Burn Folder, and a new folder is created in the current window, or on the Desktop if that is active. This folder has a special icon to show you what it is:

Burn Folder

You can change its name to whatever is convenient: `Backup`, `My Music Files`, `Photos to Burn`, and so on.

When you add items to this folder, you'll see that the original items aren't copied; Mac OS X creates aliases to the original files so you don't use up extra disk space with these folders. If you want to copy the actual file, to burn as it is (so any changes made to the file later aren't reflected in the burned copy), hold down the Option key when you drag it into the Burn Folder.

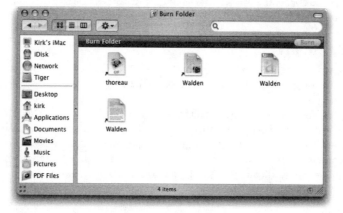

When you're ready to burn a CD or DVD with the contents of this folder, just click the Burn button. Insert a blank disk and follow the instructions as Mac OS X guides you through the process. See "Burning a Data CD or DVD" later in this chapter for more on burning CDs and DVDs.

Renaming Items

You can rename items, folders, and even disks, depending on the account you're using and your access permissions. For instance, ordinary users can easily rename items and folders within their home folders. However, only a user with administrative permission can change folder names for most folders on the system (not that you'd necessarily want to, because renaming some system folders can cause trouble).

To rename an item for which you have write permission, select the item in a Finder window. Click once on the name (not the icon) of the item and then press the Return or Enter key. The name of the item becomes highlighted, and you can type a new name or use the arrow and delete keys to edit it.

Items can just as easily be renamed in List view or Columns view. The process is the same—click the name (not the icon), press Return or Enter, then edit to taste.

NOTE   Item names can be up to 255 characters long and shouldn't begin with a period (.), nor should they contain colons (:). Note that names longer than about 31 characters, however, may be difficult to work with if you're using the Classic environment.

When you're naming or renaming documents and applications in Mac OS X, be careful to maintain the filename extension that ends the name of the file. The extension is usually three or four letters after a period, and it tells the Mac OS what type of file it is—a document associated with a particular application. We'll discuss extensions in more depth in Chapter 4.

WARNING   Although you'll see the importance of filename extensions in Chapter 4, it's worth noting here that you should never add a filename extension to a *folder's* name. Doing so could cause it to no longer look or act the way a folder should. (You can rename such a folder without the extension, however, and it will revert to folder-like behavior.)

Duplicating Items

Duplicating an item creates a separate copy of the item. Once created, the duplicate can be used separately from the original. If you duplicate a document, for instance, you have a separate copy of the document that you can edit and save.

To duplicate an item, highlight it in a Finder window or on the desktop. Then choose File ➢ Duplicate or press ⌘D. A new, identical item appears, with the word copy appended to the end of the name (unless it has a file extension showing, in which case the word copy is added before the extension). Two items can't have the same name if they're stored in the same folder—hence the appendage. You can then rename the duplicate, if desired, or move it to another location.

Moving Items

You can move items between Finder windows or, in many cases, between a Finder window and the desktop area. Moving an item means you simply change its location from one folder to another on the same disk. After a successful move operation, the document will no longer be available in its original location, which is what makes it distinct from duplicating.

You can move files and folders from one Finder window to another Finder window or between folders in Column or List view. To move an item, simply drag it from one window to another or from one part of a Column or List window to another. (See Figures 3.15 and 3.16.) Note that when you hover over the destination window, it jumps to the foreground after a few seconds.

When you're moving an item, avoid dropping it on another program icon; doing so may launch both of the items. (As detailed in Chapter 4, you can open a document for editing by dropping the document's icon on an application icon.) However, you can drop items on a folder icon; the action will store that item within the folder. In any view (List, Icon, or Column), a folder becomes highlighted if you drag an item to it. If you release the mouse button while the folder is highlighted, the item will be stored within that folder.

FIGURE 3.15

Moving items from one Finder window to another Finder window

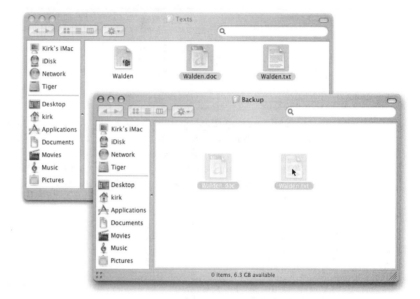

FIGURE 3.16

Moving from one folder to another in Columns view (The document Walden.txt is being dragged from the Texts folder to the Texts Backup folder.)

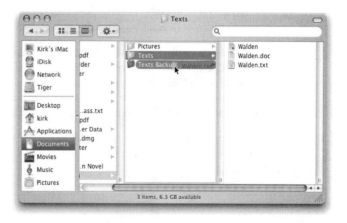

You can also move items from any folder into one of the folders displayed in the Sidebar. Just drag the item from its window onto one of the folder icons in the Sidebar, and the file is moved, just as if you dragged it into a folder directly.

Copying Items

The two methods just described enable you to create a copy of an item and move it to a new folder. Using the Duplicate command and a move, you could place a copy of an existing item in a new folder.

Of course, the Mac OS can make it easier for you. If you'd like to copy an item using a simple mouse movement, you can. Simply perform a drag-and-drop while simultaneously holding down the Option key. You'll see the mouse pointer change so that it includes a plus sign (+), which is the indicator that a copy is in progress.

In this drag-and-drop method, the word copy isn't appended to the duplicate item's name, unless you release the item in the same location. In that case, the Finder treats the drag as a duplication. Since two items can have the same name in different folders, it isn't necessary to change the name.

The plus sign also appears when you're dragging items from one disk to another, because the Mac OS won't allow a move between two disks. It requires that you copy between disks.

TIP   You can do this in another way, too. Select a file or folder or a group of icons and choose Edit ➢ Copy or press ⌘C. That copies the items. Navigate to the folder where you'd like the files to appear— do that by selecting the folder in Columns view or by double-clicking the folder to open it in Icon or List view. (You also can click the desktop once to select it if that's where you'd like the files.) Now, choose Edit ➢ Paste or press ⌘V. The items are copied to the new location.

If you're copying reasonably large files or folders with a number of items in them, you may see a dialog box. The Progress dialog box tells you how many items are being copied and approximately how much time is remaining.

The Progress indicator also may include an alert message if you need to attend to something before the copy can take place. For instance, you may see an alert if an item or folder has the same name as the item or folder you're attempting to copy. (You need to decide whether to overwrite that item or folder or return to the original and rename it before copying.) You may also encounter an alert if you don't have the correct file permissions for copying items to or from a location you're working with.

Using Spring-Loaded Folders

Sometimes you'll find that it's inconvenient to open both the original and target folders before you can copy or move any item by dragging the mouse. For instance, if you wanted to move an item from your home folder to the main Library folder, you might think you'd need to open both folders in separate windows before you could drag from one to the other.

You can get around this by using spring-loaded folders. With this feature, you can pick up an item and drag it to a folder; wait for a second or so, and the folder will "spring" open, showing you what's inside. If you want to open another folder, you just drag the item to the new folder and wait a second, and that folder will spring open. You can continue to dig until you get to the folder where you want the file to be; release the mouse button, and the file will be copied or moved. Once you get the hang of it, it's a neat feature.

NOTE By default, spring-loaded folders in icon view windows open in the same Finder window. To change this and have each folder open a new window, or to turn spring-loaded folders on and off, you'll need to make a change in the Finder preferences, discussed toward the end of this chapter.

You should experiment with the spring-loaded folders feature because it works under many different circumstances. It will open folders in Column view and folders that you've dragged to a Finder Window toolbar. It doesn't work with folder icons in the Dock, however.

If you've sprung yourself into a few layers of folders and decide not to complete the action, simply move the item away from the folders you've opened or press the Escape key, and your window will return to its original folder, or any additional open folder windows will close automatically, depending on your settings. The same thing occurs if you drag your item or items onto the menu bar. (Don't drop the item you're dragging carelessly, however—if you decide not to move it, you'll need to drop it back in the folder from whence it came.)

Using Undo

Mac OS X has great support in the Finder for the Undo feature, meaning you can quickly fix any mousing or other mistakes, as long as you catch them in time. If you copy an item to the wrong folder or move something to the Trash accidentally or even rename the wrong item, choose Edit ➤ Undo in the Finder or press ⌘Z. The Finder only has one level of Undo, so after you've undone something, the command changes to Edit ➤ Redo, meaning, essentially, "undo the Undo."

Using Labels

The Mac OS X 10.4 Finder offers a useful organizational feature called *labels,* which allows you to apply color labels to any file, folder, or application. These labels show as color highlighting on the files' names, and they display in all three views: Icon, List, or Column.

To apply a label to a file, select the file in any view, then click the Action button in the Finder window toolbar and select the label color you want from the Action menu. (You can also hold down the Control key or click your right mouse button if you have one, and select the label color from the contextual menu, or you can select the File menu and choose the label from the bottom of this menu.)

This results in a colored highlighting of the file in the Finder, which is different in each of the three views.

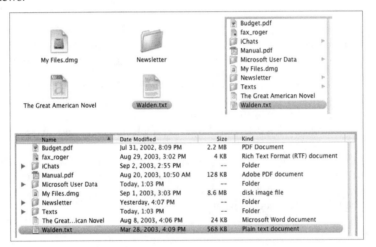

Labels are useful for several reasons. First, they highlight files or folders. You could have a folder containing several subfolders, such as folders for a specific project that show the status of their contents. A red folder could contain files in progress, a yellow folder files to be approved, and a green one files that have been finished. The same goes for files: You can set colors that correspond to their status, size, type, or whatever you want.

Another reason to use labels is to find files you have flagged. You can use the Finder's Find function (discussed in the next section and more thoroughly in Chapter 6) to look for only files with a certain label, or only unlabeled files.

Finally, as you saw earlier in this chapter, you can arrange icons in Icon view windows by a number of criteria, including labels; you can sort files in List view by the same criteria. If you choose to display the Label column in List view, you can sort your files by their labels.

Later in this chapter, in the "Finder Preferences" section, you'll see how to change the names of your labels to use your own, custom names.

Searching for Items

In addition to smart folders, discussed earlier in this chapter, Mac OS X has an extensive search utility that is explained in Chapter 6. It also has a quick and handy search capability built right into the Finder window that you're sure to find handy every once in a while.

To use the search box, simply enter a few letters and press Return; the Finder window will reconfigure and show you all items that include those letters in their names (see Figure 3.17).

FIGURE 3.17

Viewing results after searching via the Finder window toolbar

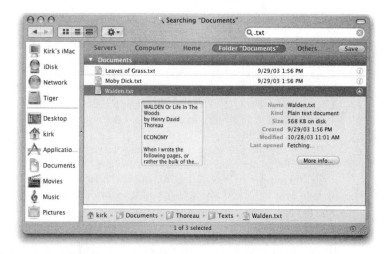

The resulting window is reconfigured into a Search Results window. This window probably looks familiar; it's almost the same as the smart folder window. In fact, if you click the Save button, you can save this search as a smart folder.

Select an item in the list, and you'll see its path in the bottom pane of the window; if you find the item you want, you can drag and drop it to copy it, move it, and so forth. Clicking the "i" icon to the right of any item displays more information about the item, as shown in Figure 3.17. Here, you see additional information for a text file, including a preview that shows the first few lines of text. (See Chapter 6 for more on the Search Results window.)

It's important to know that this search box will search for letter matches in subfolders of the folder that you're viewing as well as the folder itself. For example, if you're viewing your home folder, entering some letters will search your home folder and all subfolders—the Documents folder, Music folder, Pictures folder, and so forth. You can choose from several locations, including Servers, Computer, Home, the current folder (this is the Documents folder in Figure 3.17) and others.

NOTE Want your regular Finder window back? You can close the Search Results window and open another Finder window, or, even easier, just click the Back button in the window's toolbar or choose Go ➢ Back, or simply click the × at the right of the search field.

Getting Info about Items

The Finder includes a component called the Info window, which enables you to learn more about items. The Info window lets you look at an item's information and statistics. Via the Info window, you also can set privileges for an item, determining who can access it and under what circumstances.

GENERAL INFORMATION

To see an item's information, select it in the Finder and choose File ➤ Get Info (you also can press ⌘I or Control+click the item and choose Get Info from the context menu). You'll see the General screen, shown in Figure 3.18. Unlike earlier versions of Mac OS X, version 10.2 and higher offer you the option of opening multiple Get Info windows—just select different objects and choose the File ➤ Get Info command again. To see different portions of the Get Info window, simply click the disclosure triangle(s) next to the item(s) you want to see.

If you're viewing the information for a folder, you can click the Locked option to lock it. Locked folders have special characteristics: If you drag a locked folder to a different location, the Finder copies it, and the copy is locked. You can't drag a locked folder to the Trash. And you can't add items to it, though you can drag items from it (and, as for the folder itself, the Finder treats this as a copy). However, the folder can be unlocked and moved or renamed by other users with write privileges for the parent folder.

When you're viewing the Info window for a document, you'll see both a Locked option and a Stationery Pad option. A locked document can't be thrown away, but it also can't be edited by applications. When loaded in an application, the locked document will be *read-only*, meaning the application can't save edits to the file.

If you turn on the Stationery Pad check box, the file becomes Mac OS Stationery—a template for documents, as opposed to a document itself.

If you happen to be viewing information on a Carbon application (one that is capable of running in both Mac OS X and Mac OS 9), you'll see another check box on the General Information screen: Open in the Classic Environment. When this option is turned on, the application will be launched as a Classic application instead of as a native Mac OS X application.

TIP The Info window offers a hidden capability. Select the icon next to the name of the item—whether it's a folder, a file, or even a disk—and it becomes highlighted. You can then use the Edit ➤ Copy command to copy that icon. You also can use the Edit ➤ Paste command to replace that icon with the contents of Mac OS X's clipboard. These Edit commands enable you to change the look of an item's icon by first copying an item elsewhere (for instance, copying a downloaded custom icon out of an Info window or copying an altered icon graphic from a graphical application) and then pasting that copied icon in the Info window. If you want to customize your folder icons, you can download thousands of icons from InterfaceLIFT (http://interfacelift.com/icons-mac/).

FIGURE 3.18
The Info window shows general information about items you select in the Finder—it can be particularly handy for getting statistics about your hard disks.

SPOTLIGHT COMMENTS

The Spotlight Comments section of the Info window is an area where you can add your own comments that Spotlight uses when searching for items on your Mac. For more on using Spotlight, see Chapter 6.

GENERAL

The General section shows general information about the selected item. Back in Figure 3.18, you can see that for a hard disk, this shows the capacity, format, amount of spaced used, as well as the created and modified dates. You can also set a label in this part of the Info window. If you select a file, folder, or application, this section shows the complete path of the item as well.

NAME & EXTENSION

Open the Name & Extension disclosure triangle, and you'll be able to rename the item or hide the file's extension, if it has one. It's best not to change a filename's extension unless you know what you're doing. (See Chapter 4 for details about filename extensions.)

OPENS WITH

You'll see this disclosure triangle only when you're viewing a document. Reveal these controls if you'd like to select an application (or a different application) to associate with a particular document.

MORE INFO

Some files show additional information here: graphics files that QuickTime can decode, such as TIFF, JPG, GIF, PICT, etc., show the size of the files and pixels and the color space. PDF files show the number of pages, the size of the pages in pixels, the encoding software (whether the PDF was made with Mac OS X or Acrobat, for example), and more. Music files show a number of additional items, including the name of the song, album, genre, author, composer and more. This information is the metadata that Spotlight uses to allow you to search for files by information other than file names and contents.

PREVIEW

Click the Preview triangle to see a preview of the selected document. Images or multimedia files will appear in *thumbnail* view (a smaller version of the original that lets you see its contents quickly) in the Info window. Text-based documents will show some of the text in the document if the Info window is capable of rendering it. If you select an audio file or movie, you'll be able to listen or view the file from this section. Otherwise, you'll likely see a big version of the file's icon.

LANGUAGES

When you're viewing the Info window for an application, you may see a Languages disclosure triangle. Click it to view a listing of associated language localizations that you can turn on and off if desired. You can also remove language files for a specific application by selecting one or several languages and clicking Remove.

PLUG-INS

Some applications offer a Plug-Ins section in the Info window. If this is the case, you can activate or deactivate plug-ins for the program.

MEMORY

If you're viewing information for a Classic application, you may see the Memory disclosure triangle. Here you can set the minimum of preferred memory partitions for the application—see Chapter 27, "Fixing Applications and Managing Classic," for details.

OWNERSHIP & PERMISSIONS

In the Info window's Show menu, you can select Ownership & Permissions to choose the privileges for that item. Permissions determine who can access a particular folder or file in a multiuser and networked environment.

Setting permissions to secure your personal files is discussed in more detail in Chapter 5, and setting permissions as an administrator is covered in Chapter 10, "Configuring Internet Access."

Ejecting Disks

Another type of icon we haven't discussed much is the disk icon, which appears whenever you insert a removable disk into a drive that's attached to your Mac. That includes CDs or DVDs that you place in your Mac's built-in disk drive, as well as other disks you may have for removable drives connected via FireWire, SCSI, USB, or some other technology. (Disk icons also appear whenever you mount a *disk image* file, as discussed in Chapter 11.) You can use these icons to access the folders and files stored on the external disk, just as you would use the icon for your main hard disk. (Likewise, by default, hard disk icons representing your internal hard disk(s) also appear on the desktop.)

When you've finished working with a removable disk, there are several ways you can eject it from its drive so that you can work with another disk. Switch to the Finder, select the disk's icon (either in the Sidebar of a Finder window, if your Finder preferences are set to show removable media there, or in the `Computer` folder in a Finder window, or on the desktop). If you select the disk in the Sidebar of a Finder window, just click the small arrow icon next to it. If you select it in a folder or on the Desktop, choose File ➤ Eject or Control+click on the icon and choose Eject from the context menu. That should cause the disk's icon to disappear from the desktop and the disk to pop out of its drive or otherwise disengage.

If you want to eject a CD or DVD, you can use the keyboard; just press and hold F12. You'll see a triangle graphic on your screen (the Eject symbol), and the disc will eject. Make sure you hold down the F12 key for a second; if you press it and let go of it, that activates Dashboard. If you have a full-size keyboard, you may have an Eject key; just press that key once to eject an optical disc or close the drive's drawer, if it has one. (See Chapter 4 for more on Dashboard.)

Finally, there is one other way to eject any kind of disk: Drag the disk's icon to the Trash icon in the Dock. This may seem disconcerting at first, but I promise that you won't be deleting anything on the disk; in fact, the Trash icon changes to show you that you'll be ejecting the disk from your computer. Drop the disk's icon on the Trash icon, and it will disappear from the desktop and pop out of its drive (if it's a removable disk).

NOTE   You also can eject hard disks, which you should do if you plan to disconnect a hard disk that's connected via FireWire or USB; if you don't, you may damage the disk's structure and lose data. (You'll need to make sure nothing on that disk is open or being used before you can eject it.) Eject the disk's icon and then unplug the external drive; that way, you can be sure the drive isn't in use when it's disconnected. Apple warns against ejecting internal disks, however. Although Mac OS X won't allow you to eject your startup disk, you sometimes can eject volumes that are partitions on the startup disk, as long as they are not being used by any applications.

Burning a Data CD or DVD

All new Macs come with optical drives: these drives can read CDs and DVDs and can either burn CDs or both CDs and DVDs (if you have a SuperDrive). To burn a CD or DVD on your Mac, you'll need a blank disc; this can be a rewriteable disc (a CD-RW or DVD-RW) or a write-once disc (a CD-R or DVD-R). Rewritable discs are good for backups, since you can reuse them; CD-R and DVD-R discs are good for archives or for sending files to others.

While new Macs contain CD or DVD burners, you may also be able to use an external drive if it is supported—see Apple's website (`www.apple.com/macosx/upgrade/storage.html`) for a complete list of supported drives.

NOTE   The process is called "burning" because the CD-RW drive is changing the dye layer on the CD's data side, using a laser to "burn" changes into the layer to represent data. This is different from commercial CDs, which are "pressed" to create physical (if microscopic) *pits* and *lands* on the surface of the CD. CD-RW discs use a crystalline layer instead of a dye layer; this material can be turned opaque and then "reset" to clear again, enabling you to reuse the disc.

When you insert a blank recordable disc into a compatible drive, you'll see a dialog box asking you what you'd like to do. In the Action menu, choose Open Finder, and then click OK. (Turn on the Make This Action the Default option if you'd like to skip this dialog box in the future.) An icon for that disc will appear on the desktop.

NOTE   If you don't see a dialog box and instead iTunes or another application launches, it's because of a setting in the System Preferences. Open the CDs & DVDs pane in System Preferences and set the When You Insert a Blank CD option to open the Finder.

If you double-click the CD or DVD icon on the Desktop, you'll see that it looks like a Burn Folder (discussed earlier in this chapter). The procedure for adding items to this folder is the same as for Burn Folders; this folder contains a Burn button at the top, below the Search field, and there is a graphical Burn icon next to the disc's name in the Sidebar.

WARNING   You need to be very careful how you work with files you copy to a blank optical disc. When you copy a folder, for example, you are actually placing an alias of that folder on the disc, and it is the Finder that copies the folder and its contents when you burn the disc. However, this folder alias acts just as other aliases do: double-click it and it opens the *original* folder. You may think you can copy a folder to a blank CD or DVD, then remove the items that you *don't* want to copy from it, but if you do this, you'll be deleting the originals. The best way to add items to an optical disc is individually; if you add folders, make sure you want to copy everything they contain.

Even though it looks like your files are copied, you're not out of the woods yet. When you're ready to burn the disc, you can do one of the following:

♦ Drag the disc icon to the Trash in the Dock. (You'll see the Trash icon turn into a Burn icon.)

♦ Click the Burn icon next to the CD icon in the Finder Sidebar (if you have the Finder preference set to show CDs and DVDs).

♦ Select the disc icon and then choose File ➤ Burn Disc.

♦ Click the Burn button at the top of the window, just below the toolbar.

When you do any of those things, the burner will go into action. You'll see a dialog box showing the progress as the disc is prepared, burned, and then verified. Once verified, the disc will be ready to use.

If you change your mind and decide not to burn the disc, drag it to the Trash and click Eject in the dialog that displays.

There is another way to burn optical discs in Mac OS X. You saw earlier in this chapter that you can create a special Burn folder. If you have done this, just double-click the Burn folder you have created, and then click the Burn button at the top of the window.

You should be aware that, unlike some disc-burning software, the Finder can't burn multiple *sessions* to a single disc. (However, Disk Utility can burn multiple sessions; see Chapter 25, "Peripherals, Internal Upgrades, and Disks," for more on Disk Utility.) Once the disc is burned, it's finalized. In the case of a write-once disk (CD-R or DVD-R), you're stuck with it. If you have a CD-RW or DVD-RW disc, you can erase it (or *format* it) and start over. You'll erase the disc using the Disk Utility application.

The Trash

The Trash is unique among the icons you'll find in Mac OS X: It's always there on the Dock, it has a very specific task, and it can't be removed. It's also the main way that you'll delete items in the Mac OS.

To delete an item, drag it from the desktop or from a Finder window and drop it on the Trash icon. You'll see the Trash icon change; as you're hovering over it, it darkens a bit. When you release the mouse button, you've "thrown away" the item. Once you've dropped the item on the Trash icon, you'll see the icon change so that wadded-up paper appears in the picture of a trash can. This tells you that there are items in the Trash.

TIP   In the Finder, you also can move items to the Trash by selecting an icon and pressing ⌘Delete on the keyboard, or selecting Move to Trash from the Action menu in the Finder toolbar. You can also move an item to the Trash by Control+clicking the item and choosing Move to Trash from the context menu or from the Finder's File menu.

Not all items are deleted immediately when you drag them to the Trash, although some are, such as items on network volumes. For the most part, items remain in the Trash until you empty the Trash using a special command in the Finder. If an item is to be deleted immediately, however, you'll see a warning alert box that reminds you that the item will be deleted immediately.

Because most items stay in the Trash, it's possible to open the Trash and retrieve items you've thrown in there. (Fortunately, there are no coffee grounds or eggshells in this particular trash can.) To open the Trash, click its icon in the Dock. A window appears, showing you the items that have been dragged and dropped on the Trash previously, as shown in Figure 3.19.

To retrieve items, simply drag them out of the Trash window to the desktop or to another open Finder window. (You'll find that some items can't be dragged directly to the desktop from the Trash—you'll need to drag them to an open Finder window instead.)

To delete items in the Trash permanently, you'll *empty* the trash. Items deleted in this way can't be retrieved through the Finder and might be gone for good. (Some disk utilities can recover deleted files in an emergency, but otherwise they can't be retrieved easily.) You should think carefully and be sure before you empty the Trash.

To delete items in the Trash, choose Finder ➤ Empty Trash. (If you're not currently working in the Finder, you'll need to switch to it by clicking once on the desktop area or the Finder icon on the Dock.) You'll see an alert box warning you that emptying the Trash is permanent. If you're sure you want to proceed, click the OK button. The items in the Trash will be deleted.

TIP   If you'd like to skip the warning alert box, you can hold down the Option key while selecting Finder ➤ Empty Trash. Also, you can use the keyboard sequence Shift+⌘Delete to empty the Trash while the Finder is active.

If you have sensitive documents on your Mac and want to make sure they are deleted permanently— when you delete files normally they *can* be recovered by special file-recovery programs—select Finder ➤ Secure Empty Trash. This not only deletes the files, but overwrites them several times so it is impossible to recover them. This deletion process will take much longer than normal, since the Finder overwrites the files several times. It's a good idea to use this to delete any personal files on your computer if you plan to sell or otherwise dispose of it.

NOTE   Disk Utility now has an Erase Free Space function, which allows you to securely delete all the free space or your hard disk or any removable media. See Chapter 26, "Hard Disk Care, File Security, and Maintenance," for more on using Disk Utility.

FIGURE 3.19
Opening the Trash reveals items that have been tossed there.

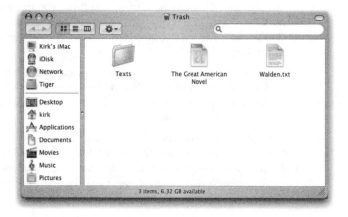

Finder Preferences

You can modify some characteristics of the Finder application, the background desktop, and the Finder window through the Finder Preferences dialog box. To open this dialog box, switch to the Finder application and then select Finder ➤ Preferences (see Figure 3.20). Even if you've been using versions of Mac OS X prior to version 10.2, you'll find this dialog box has some significant differences.

In the Finder Preferences dialog box, you'll see four icons at the top of the window, each corresponding to different sets of preferences: General, Labels, Sidebar, and Advanced.

FIGURE 3.20

The Finder Preferences dialog box

General Preferences

These preferences control the way many general Finder functions act, such as what is displayed on the desktop and how windows open.

Show These Items on the Desktop This section lets you choose which types of items display on the desktop. If you check Hard Disks, all hard disks attached to the Mac at startup will also appear on the desktop. Also, any hard disks you turn on after startup will display on the desktop. If you check CDs, DVDs, and iPods, these items, as well as other removable media, will appear on the desktop. And if you check Connected Servers, any network servers you are connected to will show on the desktop.

If you don't check any of these options, you can still view these items by clicking the Computer icon in a Finder window's Sidebar, or by selecting Go ➤ Computer in the Finder. Some of these items will also display in the top of the Sidebar; see the Sidebar Preferences section below for settings on what to display there.

New Finder Windows Open You can choose to have a new Finder window (when you select File ➤ New in the Finder) open to either your home folder, the main Computer level where all attached disks are visible, your Documents folder, the Computer level of your startup disk (which shows all currently available disks and volumes), a specific disk or volume, or your iDisk, if you have one. You can also select Other to set new Finder windows to open to any other folder of your choice.

Always Open Folders in a New Window   Turn on this option, and you can force Mac OS X to work like the Classic Mac OS, disregarding the state of the Hide Toolbar button. Double-clicking a folder will *always* open it in a new window if you have this option checked.

Open New Windows in Column View   If you like Column view (and there's a lot to like about it), you can turn on this option, which will keep you from having to switch to Column view after opening a folder that's been set to a different view. It's a convenience.

Spring-Loaded Folders and Windows   Turn on this option if you want to use the spring-loaded folders feature; if it's on, you can use the Delay slider to decide how long the Mac OS should wait while you point at a folder before that folder springs open.

Label Preferences

The Labels tab lets you set names for Finder labels. You can't change the colors, but you can use any names you want for them. By default, their names correspond to their colors, such as Red, Blue, Gray, and so on. Change them to names that fit the way you work, such as Pending, Finalized, Personal Files, or anything else, by typing new names in their text fields.

Sidebar Preferences

If you click the Sidebar icon, you can choose which items to display in the Sidebar of Finder windows. This window shows items in two sections: The top section corresponds to the top part of the Sidebar, which contains such items as hard disks, removable media, and connected servers, and the bottom section corresponds to the bottom part of the Sidebar, where you can drag your own files and folders.

Check or uncheck the items in this list to adjust the way you want to use the Sidebar. If you drag any of these items out of the Sidebar in a Finder window, you'll find that they become unchecked here.

Advanced Preferences

Finally, the Advanced preferences give you a few additional options for how the Finder works:

Show All File Extensions   This is turned off by default because Mac OS X is designed to hide file-name extensions (for example, `.jpg` or `.doc`). If you'd prefer to see filename extensions, turn on this item.

NOTE   Should you view extensions? It depends on what makes you comfortable. Mac users have long eschewed filename extensions as a clunky way to determine a file's true nature. However, the cross-platform world that we live in, particularly on the Internet, requires that files you share with Windows and other Unix users include those extensions—particular for Microsoft Word documents (.doc), graphics files (.jpg, .gif, or .tif), and even QuickTime movies (.mov or .qt). If you find you're sharing files with others often, it's a good idea to get used to seeing and including those filename extensions when you're creating files.

Show Warning before Emptying the Trash   This option enables you to turn off the default warning Are You Sure? if you don't want to see it when emptying the Trash.

When you're done with the Finder Preferences dialog box, click its Close button to dismiss it.

What's Next?

In this chapter, you saw how the Mac OS X Finder enables you to manage your icons, how to customize its display, and how to burn CDs with the Finder. In Chapter 4, you'll learn how to launch applications, open and save documents, and use some of the basic commands that you'll encounter in most native and Classic Mac OS applications you use.

Chapter 4

Using Applications

In Chapter 2, "The Fundamentals of Mac OS X," you saw the basic elements that the Mac OS uses to create an interface for applications; in Chapter 3, "The Finder," you saw a special application—the Finder—that's used to manage your disks, folders, and files. Your ultimate goal with Mac OS X, of course, will be to get tasks—other than just managing files—accomplished. You'll get those things done in *application* programs, which are computer programs that you apply toward some task or goal. Most often, you'll use applications to create, edit, and save documents. Documents are so central to the operation of your Mac that dealing with them—in particular, opening and saving them—is built into the OS, with standard Open and Save dialog boxes and sheets made available to application programs by the Mac OS.

In this chapter, you'll see the different ways you can launch applications in Mac OS X and what the standard methods are for opening and saving documents to your disks. You'll learn some of the basic controls found in most *native* Mac OS X applications, including menus, commands, and dialogs that are common to all applications written specifically for Mac OS X. You'll discover a new family of mini-applications, or *widgets*, and Dashboard, the tool that lets you work with them. Finally, you'll take a look at the Classic environment, which enables you to run *Classic* Mac applications (those designed for Mac OS 9 and earlier versions), and you'll see the issues and trade-offs involved in using such applications.

In this chapter:

◆ Launching an Application or Document

◆ Opening and Saving Documents

◆ Working with Applications

◆ Switching Applications and Windows

◆ Using Dashboard and Widgets

◆ Running Classic Mac Applications

Launching an Application or Document

An application such as Microsoft Word, Apple Mail, or Adobe Photoshop needs to be launched before you can work with it. When you launch an application, you're telling the Mac OS that you want to use that application's tools. The Mac OS responds by reserving a portion of system memory for the application and loading portions of that application from the hard disk into this memory. The application then begins running, often showing you a "splash screen" that tells you the application's version number and gives credit to the programmers; a native Mac OS X application then places the application's menu commands on the menu bar, representing the *Application menu:*

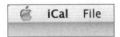

There are two primary ways to launch an application: directly or by launching an associated document. If you're going to work with a particular document, it's more convenient to launch the document. You'll launch an application directly if you want to create a new document or if the application isn't designed to work with documents.

Launching an Application Directly

If you'd like to launch an application directly, you'll generally do that in one of four ways:

Launch the application by icon. In a Finder window or on the desktop, locate the application's icon and double-click it with the mouse. You also can select the icon and choose File ➤ Open or press ⌘O.

Launch the application by alias. If you come across an alias to the application on the desktop or in a Finder window, you can double-click that alias, or you can select the alias and choose File ➤ Open or press ⌘O.

Launch the application's icon in the dock. When you single-click a Dock icon that represents an application, that application is launched if it isn't already running. (If it is already running, then selecting it on the Dock will make that application and all its windows active, bringing it to the foreground.) Once launched, the Dock icon may bounce up and down to show that the application is in the process of loading.

Select the application via the apple menu. If you've used the application recently, you can relaunch it by selecting it from the Apple menu's Recent Items menu.

Using any of these methods should result in the application launching and appearing on your screen. If you launch an alias, you may run into trouble if the alias can't locate the original application (see Chapter 3).

NOTE If you attempt to launch an application that's already running, you will most likely be switched to that application. Very few applications will open more than one *instance* of themselves.

Once the application opens, you will generally see one of four things:

◆ In many applications that work with a main window, such as Mail, iCal, or iTunes, and with most utilities, you'll see that window display. If you open a web browser, you'll see a browser window, which will open to your home page.

◆ Some applications may display a screen allowing you to choose the type of document you want to open. This occurs with AppleWorks and with Microsoft Office applications (Word, Excel, or PowerPoint), though there is usually a preference setting to prevent this screen from displaying.

◆ Some other applications will display a blank document. This is the case with programs such as TextEdit or other word processors, though in many cases you can change this in the program's preferences and have no document open on launch.

◆ Finally, some programs display nothing. They'll show their menu bar, and perhaps some palettes or toolbars, but will not display a document window. This is often the case with graphics applications, such as Photoshop or Illustrator, though you can usually set preferences to open documents of a given size or format automatically.

Launching a Document

If you have a particular document you'd like to work with, you can launch the document itself, and its associated application will launch along with it. Mac OS X attempts to keep track of the application that created a document and associates the document with that application. Ideally, that means you can launch the document and the application will also be launched, instead of launching the application first and then loading the document. In practice, you don't always want to launch a document using its associated application. Also, sometimes the association breaks down, or you might be working with documents that weren't created on your Mac. The Mac OS gives you four basic ways to launch a document directly:

Double-click the document or an alias to the document.   This will launch the document and the application the Mac OS believes to be associated with the document type. It won't always launch the correct application (or it may not launch the application you want), but you can change that behavior as detailed in the next section, "How Mac OS X Recognizes Documents."

NOTE   If you launch a document that happens to be associated with a Classic application—even if you have a native application that's capable of dealing with the document—Mac OS X may attempt to load the Classic environment and launch the Classic application. If that's not what you want, see the next section "How Mac OS X Recognizes Documents" to learn how to change the application a document is associated with.

Select the document from the Recent Items menu.   If the document has been used recently, it may also appear on the Recent Items menu in the Apple menu, where you can select it to launch it again.

Drop the document icon on an application icon.   You can drag a document icon to an application icon to launch it. Only certain applications can accept dragged documents; when you hover over the application icon with the document icon, you should see the application icon become highlighted. If it does, then the application will accept the dragged document and attempt to display it. If the application does not become highlighted, then it can't open that document (or at least it doesn't recognize it as a document that it can open).

Drop the document icon on an application's Dock icon.   If you've added the application to the Dock, you can drag a document to the application and drop it on its icon. The application will launch and attempt to display the document. The real power in using the Dock, however, comes from the fact that you can drag and drop documents to applications that are *currently running*. Because running applications also appear in the Dock, they can be drag-and-drop targets, too, as shown in Figure 4.1. That can be a convenient way to launch documents in an application they're not associated with; for instance, if you have an HTML document that's associated with Safari, but you'd prefer to launch it in TextEdit (so that you can edit it instead of view it), you can drag the document to the TextEdit icon.

FIGURE 4.1
The application's icon will become highlighted to signify that it can accept the dragged-and-dropped document.

TIP Dragging a document to a running application's Dock icon is also a convenient way to work with documents that came from other computing platforms. For instance, while an application such as Adobe Photoshop or GraphicConverter can read a Microsoft Windows BMP image file, double-clicking the image file often won't launch the proper application. Instead, dragging the image file to the application's Dock icon (or an icon in the Finder) will cause it to open in that application.

MANAGING MULTIPLE APPLICATIONS

You've already seen that Mac OS X is a powerful operating system that enables you to *multitask,* or run multiple applications, in a very efficient way. The manifestation of that multitasking is the Dock, where you can switch between running applications.

If you've launched one application, you can launch another just as you did the first. Switch to the Finder (click the desktop background, in a Finder window or on the Finder icon in the Dock) and double-click the second application, double-click a new document, or use any of the other methods to launch another application.

You can run as many applications as your Mac's system memory will allow. Each application requires a certain minimum amount of memory (determined by the application itself) to be active, so each application takes away from the total available system memory. Applications request memory as needed, and the Mac OS can assign that RAM dynamically. However, you still have a finite amount of RAM, and each new application requires a certain portion of it. Once the Mac OS reaches a certain limit, your Mac will slow down considerably. Because Mac OS X makes extensive use of *virtual memory* (a scheme that allows the hard disk to be used as a temporary memory-swapping location), the more applications you have open (and the more demanding those applications are), the more the Mac OS will have to access the hard disk. The hard disk is much slower than RAM, so those accesses tend to bog down the system, especially as you switch between applications.

If you notice a slowdown and you have quite a few applications open, try quitting one or two of them to see if your Mac speeds up. If quitting the applications speeds things up—but you like the idea of having that many applications active at once—then your Macintosh is a prime candidate for a RAM upgrade. And since, at press time, RAM prices remain relatively low, the best thing you can do for your Mac and for your productivity is buy more RAM; in fact, for many Mac models (such as iMacs, iBooks, or PowerBooks), the best advice we can give is to buy as much RAM as you can afford, and as your Mac can hold.

Also, some applications have a Recent Items menu or submenu that works like the Apple menu's Recent Items submenu. For example, Microsoft Word displays a number of recently used documents at the bottom of its File menu and AppleWorks has an Open Recent menu at the bottom of its File menu.

Which approach you use is up to you and the circumstances. You'll often find that the most convenient way to start working on a document is to double-click it. If it launches the correct application, that's certainly the most efficient approach. If the document is associated with the wrong application, though, that can be frustrating. Fortunately, you can change that association, as described in the following two sections.

How Mac OS X Recognizes Documents

Mac OS X uses two different methods to determine how a document is associated with a particular application. The first method is simple—it's the three- or four-letter *filename extension* on the end of a document's name. (While file extensions are generally three or four letters long, they can be much longer; there is no limit.) A file with .html or .htm as its filename extension is assumed to be an HTML document. If Apple hasn't kept track of the true creator of that document, then it will associate that document with the default application it has stored for .html—in many cases, that would be Apple's Safari web browser.

The other method is a little more devilish. Mac OS X actually tracks some *meta* information about your files—in particular, a creator code and a type code—and stores it in a special catalog entry for the file. (*Metadata* is commonly defined as "data about data.") This data is generated when a Macintosh application is used to create a document, which is why you're more likely to see odd icons and filename extensions when you copy a file from a disk or download it from the Internet. In those cases, the metadata isn't in your Mac's database.

What's interesting about these methods is that they can sometimes get a little convoluted. For instance, changing a filename extension can actually change the type of file that the Mac OS believes a file to be. (Change the name of a file from mydoc.doc to mydoc.tif, and the Mac OS will believe that the file is a TIFF image instead of a Microsoft Word document—but only if that Word document wasn't originally created on your Mac.) Also, you can have two different files—even in the same folder—that have the same filename extension, but that are actually associated with different applications.

Budget.pdf   Manual.pdf

The solution to the first issue—that renaming a file changes its file type—is to *not do it*. Indeed, the Finder will prompt you with a warning message if you attempt to change the filename extension, just to remind you that it is rarely necessary. A Word document (.doc) is not a TIFF image (.tif or .tiff), and applications that attempt to open it as such will encounter errors. If you subsequently forget what type of document it was to begin with, you'll need to do some spelunking (such as opening the document in a raw text editor or a troubleshooting application) to find its type before you can work with the document again.

NOTE   One utility program you can use to change type and creator information is Super Get Info from Bare Bones Software (`www.barebones.com`). This program can display the type and creator code of a document that was created on a Macintosh and let you set them to different codes. Super Get Info also has slightly more sophisticated tools than the regular Show Info command for changing document associations, which is discussed in the next section.

In the case of the second issue—a document that's associated with the wrong application—you can do something about that more easily, as described in the next section.

Changing a Document Association

Sometimes a document won't be associated with the correct application, or in some cases, it won't be associated with any application at all. (As mentioned already, this is often true because the document has been transmitted—via disk or Internet—from another computer.) If that's the case, you can associate the document with an application manually. Doing so will enable you to open the document with the selected application in the future.

You set a document association using the Info window in the Finder. Select the document in the Finder and choose File ➤ Get Info or press ⌘I. The Info window appears. Select the disclosure triangle next to Open With, as shown in Figure 4.2.

To associate the document with an application, you use the pop-up menu that appears in the Info window. Click the menu once to see a list of the applications that Mac OS X believes might work for this document type.

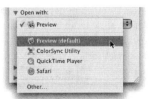

If the application you want to associate with this document doesn't appear on the menu, you can select Other. You'll see the Choose Other Application dialog box (which acts just like a standard Open dialog box), which enables you to select the application you'd like to use. Highlight the application in the dialog box and click Add. (If you can't highlight the application you want to use, select All Applications from the Enable menu at the top of the dialog box.)

When the Add Application dialog box closes, you're returned to the Info window. If your goal was simply to launch this document in the new application, then close the Info window and you're done. Now, double-clicking the document will launch it within the application you selected.

If you'd prefer that *all* documents like this one be changed to the new application association, click the Change All button in the Info window. This causes all documents of that same type created by the same application to be associated with the new application.

FIGURE 4.2

The Info window can be used to associate a document with a particular application.

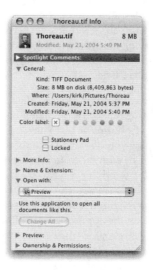

NOTE In our experience, after you click the Change All button, not every icon on your Mac will change to reflect the new setting, even if these files will launch in the new application. For instance, if you use the Change All button when viewing a PDF document, to force all PDFs to launch in the third-party PDF viewer Adobe Acrobat, you may still see some PDF documents that display an icon that looks like Apple's built-in PDF viewer, Preview. Double-clicking such a document, however, most likely will launch the document in Acrobat. If the icon really bugs you, open the Info window, click the Open With disclosure triangle, click the pop-up menu, and reselect the application you want to use with this document. The new document icon should pop into place. Restarting your Mac should also fix this.

Opening and Saving Documents

When launched directly, some applications will create a new document. If a new document is what you want, you can begin working in it—typing, drawing with the mouse, selecting items, or doing whatever the application is designed to do. (As noted in the section "Saving a Changed Document," later in this chapter, it's a good idea to save a document soon after you begin working in it.) If you encounter an application that doesn't create a document automatically, look for a File ➤ New or File ➤ New Document command. (In most applications you also can press ⌘N to create a new document.)

In Mac OS X, you'll encounter two distinct types of Open and Save dialog boxes, because the Mac OS supports diverse types of applications. The "native" dialog boxes are those that appear when you're working with applications that run directly on top of Mac OS X—the Carbon and Cocoa applications. You'll encounter the other type of dialog box when working with Classic applications; we'll cover that type in the section "Running Classic Mac Applications," later in this chapter.

Opening an Existing Document

If you have an application in which you'd like to edit an existing document, you'll use the application's Open command. In nearly all applications, that's File ➤ Open. (In most applications you also can press ⌘O.) What you see next depends on the type of application you're using.

NOTE Mac OS X allows you to switch to a different application even if an Open dialog box is currently on the screen. In earlier Mac OS versions, Open dialog boxes are often (although not always) *modal*, requiring you to finish using the box before you can access another application. In Mac OS X, however, you can switch to a different application and then switch back to finish working with the Open dialog box, if desired.

If your Open dialog box looks similar to that in Figure 4.3, your application is using the native Mac OS X–style dialog boxes. These dialog boxes tend to be a bit simpler to use, especially if you're a fan of the Finder's Columns or List view.

The first thing you'll notice about this dialog box is that it looks a lot like a default Finder window: It has the Sidebar, with the same icons as in the Finder, and it displays, by default, in Columns view. At the top of the window, you can see the familiar toolbar buttons to go Back and Forward and to change views, but here you can only choose between Columns and List view. The Open dialog box also has a Search field, where you can search for specific documents.

Depending on the application, you'll see one or two pop-up menus at the top of the Open dialog box. The navigation menu (the one on the same line as the toolbar buttons) is a quick navigation tool for moving directly to folders higher up in your filesystem or to recently used folders. As you can see at the top of this menu, the current folder is shown with its parents below it. You can select any of these folders to move to them. Also, if you've recently visited another folder in an Open dialog box (or a Finder window), you'll see that folder listed in the bottom part of this menu so that you can return to it quickly.

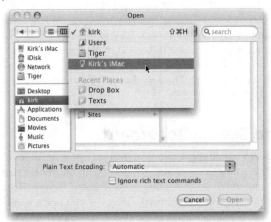

The Enable menu (which doesn't always appear) is used to restrict the types of files that are presented in the dialog box. For instance, an application can show only the documents that work with that application, helping to cut down the clutter. Select an option in the Enable menu if you'd like to pare down the files that are displayed in the dialog box.

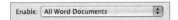

FIGURE 4.3
The Mac OS X Open
dialog box

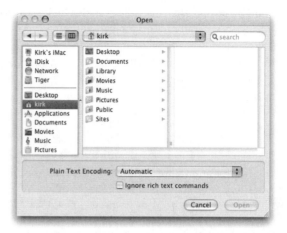

The rest of the dialog box works almost exactly like the Finder's Column view. In the leftmost column, the Sidebar, select a folder or volume to view. That folder's listing appears in the next column to the right, where you can select another folder or an item. Keep selecting folders until you've found the item you want to open and then click Open. (Don't forget about the scroll bar at the bottom of the columns area—that's what you'll use to go up in the hierarchy to the root folder of your disk, or to select other disks connected to your Mac or via a network connection.)

You can also choose List view for the Open window, if you prefer, which displays the right-side part of the dialog box like a Finder List view window. As in the Finder, you can click the disclosure triangles to see the contents of any folder and select their files.

And if you don't like the Sidebar in this dialog box, you can drag it out of the way by clicking and dragging its separator to the position you prefer—you can remove it entirely, or you can leave, for example, just the icons visible without their names.

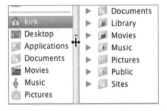

Each application stores settings for this dialog box individually, so if you change the display in one application, those changes won't apply to others. If you want to change the default (Columns view with the Sidebar) for all your programs, you'll need to do it in each of your applications.

You can also use the Search field in the Open dialog box to look for files; with Mac OS X 10.4's lightning-fast search capabilities, you may find it quicker to type a few letters of a document's name in this field than to navigate through folders and subfolders.

The Open dialog box switches to a different view as you type in the Search field, and almost instantly starts displaying results (if it finds any). You'll see that the search results look a lot like searches you make in Finder windows (as explained in Chapter 3); you can choose from different locations, such as Computer, your home folder, or the currently selected folder, and you can filter the results by choosing one of these locations.

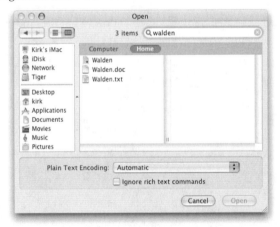

At the bottom of the Open dialog box, you'll find an area where applications may add their own options to the dialog box, allowing you to make choices specific to that application. You'll find pop-up menus, check boxes, and other controls here, depending on the application. For instance, Microsoft Word gives you the option of loading a document as a copy of the original or in read-only format so that it can't be edited.

TIP You can use the toolbar buttons or the keyboard to move around in an Open dialog box. Click the Back or Forward button to go to folders you have already visited. Press the Tab key to move to different elements (such as the menus or entry boxes), and press Shift+Tab to move back to a previous element. Use the arrow keys to move up and down in a list, and press the right and left arrow keys to move to the next column or previous column, respectively, in the file listing area. Also, if you think the Open dialog box is too small, just drag the bottom-right corner to make it as large as you want.

To select a document in the Open dialog box, you have several options:

♦ You can click with the mouse cursor. In Column view, you can click folders to display their contents and click their subfolders to navigate, finally selecting the file you want to open; or in List view, you can navigate through folders by clicking their disclosure triangles.

♦ You can use the arrow keys to move around in either section of the dialog box and use the Tab key to switch from the Sidebar to the column or list section. In the right side of the window, when in Columns view, pressing the right arrow key when a folder is selected moves you into that folder, and pressing the left arrow key moves you up to its parent folder.

♦ Finally, you can type the first letter or letters of a file or folder to move to it more quickly, both in the Sidebar or in the columns or list section of the dialog box.

When you've found the file you want to open, you can double-click it to open it, or you can select it and click Open (or press Return) to open the document. Click Cancel if you want to dismiss the dialog box without opening a file.

TIP You can select multiple documents in the Open dialog box if you'd like to open more than one file at a time. Hold down the ⌘ key to select noncontiguous documents or hold down the Shift key to select a range of documents. When you click Open, the application will attempt to open all of those items.

Saving a Changed Document

Whether you've created a new document or you're editing an existing one, you should save that document almost immediately after making any changes and continue to save often. Saving a document writes the content of the document to the hard disk or other disk that you're using for storage, saving it for future use. Saving regularly also provides security in case of a system failure or application crash.

With Mac OS X, you'll see two different types of Save dialog, depending on how the application has been designed. In most cases you'll see a *dialog sheet*—a Save dialog box that's connected to the document you're working on. In other applications, you'll see a more typical dialog box that's similar to the Open dialog box. Most of the time, you can display these dialog boxes by selecting File ≻ Save or File ≻ Save As from the application's menu bar.

TIP You can also press ⌘S in most applications to invoke the Save command. Some applications enable Shift+⌘S for the Save As command.

Mac OS X's native Save dialog box is a slightly different animal from the Open dialog boxes you've seen. The first time you invoke the Save command, you'll see a dialog sheet. Instead of popping up like any of the others you've seen so far, this one opens up in an animated way from the window's title bar, as shown in Figure 4.4.

FIGURE 4.4
Saving with the Mac OS
X Save dialog sheet

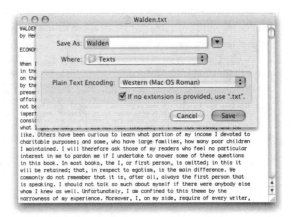

There's a good reason for taking the dialog sheet approach: it makes it absolutely clear which window's contents you're about to save. Simply enter a document name (filename) and choose a destination folder from the Where menu. The Where menu corresponds to the Sidebar in the Open dialog box. It contains all the volumes and folders in your Finder Sidebar, as well as Recent Places, folders, and volumes you've used recently.

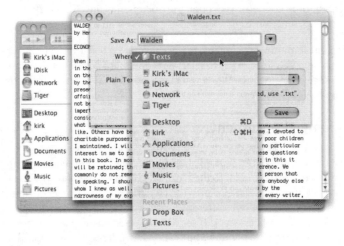

You don't see the destination folder where you want to save the file? In that case, click the down-arrow button. That reveals the rest of the dialog box, which you'll notice is similar to the Mac OS X Open dialog box. You can use the columns to navigate to the destination folder (see Figure 4.5), or you can choose List view by clicking the List View toolbar button. You can also use the Search field to type a few letters of the name of the folder you're looking for.

TIP   As with the Open dialog box, you can use the keyboard to maneuver in the Save dialog. Press Tab and Shift+Tab to cycle back and forth between the different elements (lists, entry boxes) in the dialog, then use the arrow keys to select items in the file listing area.

FIGURE 4.5
Once you've clicked the
down-arrow button,
the full dialog sheet is
revealed.

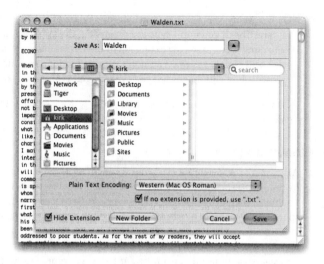

TIP   The Save dialog sheet enables you to create a new subfolder for storing the document. Select the folder (for instance, Documents) in which you'd like to create the new subfolder. Now, click New Folder. In the small dialog box, enter a name for the folder and click Create. The folder is created and automatically opened so that you can save your document in it.

Enter a filename in the Save As entry box. The filename may contain up to 255 characters and should not, in most cases, include a three-letter extension code; instead, the application you're using will likely add this on its own. In some cases, such as with TextEdit, shown in Figure 4.5, adding this extension is an option.

In general, it's best not to begin filenames with non-alphanumeric characters, and you *must* avoid starting a filename with a period (.) or a hyphen (-). You may use a hyphen in the middle of a name; in fact, Mac OS X will automatically change any slashes (/) to hyphens if you try to type them. Slashes are strictly disallowed because they're used to indicate folders in Unix-style path statements.

TIP   The Save dialog sheet, by default, gives you the option in some cases to hide the filename extension. This doesn't mean it isn't there—only that the Mac OS won't display it in dialogs or in the Finder. If you transfer the file elsewhere (such as via an e-mail application) or you view it in certain applications (including Classic applications), you'll see that extension. This corresponds to the Info window's capability to hide and show individual extensions, as discussed in Chapter 3.

Although a filename can be up to 255 characters in most native applications, it's best to limit the number to 31 if you'll be working with the file in both Mac OS X and Mac OS 9, or if you intend to send the file to someone who uses an older Mac OS version. Older Mac OS versions (and some Classic and Carbon applications) are limited to working with filenames of 31 characters or less, and some applications won't display the entire filename, if it's more than 31 characters, in their window title bars. Also, shorter filenames are usually easier to read in Finder windows and on the desktop. In fact, for best results when moving files over the Internet and from one OS to another, the shorter the filename, the better.

NOTE   Many Mac OS X applications are aware of the filename extension issue and do something interesting: If you don't type the extension, the application may assume you want it hidden (that you don't want to see the extension in the Finder and so on). If you type the extension, the application will simply assume you don't want it hidden. Nothing changes—the extension will be there regardless of whether or not you type it—but typing it makes it visible automatically.

Once you've entered a filename, press Return or click the Save button. Your document will be saved. If you decide not to save, click the Cancel button.

Saving Again

After you've saved your document for the first time, you're still not done with the Save command. Instead, you should save your work at regular intervals while you're working in the application. As you type, edit, draw, or otherwise work with a document, you'll want to save any changes you make so that, in case of an application crash or a computer failure, you'll still have all your recent changes.

To save as you work, simply select File ➤ Save or press ⌘S. After you've named the file for the first time, this command no longer brings up the Save dialog box. Instead, it simply saves the changes you've made to the file, updating it to the current state of the edited document.

Save As Command

If you're working in a named document and you'd like to save it using a different name or save it to a different folder or disk, choose the File ➤ Save As command instead of the Save command. This instructs the application to display the Save dialog box, even though you've already given the file a name. You can select a new name or a new folder in which to store the document. When you've named it and pressed Return, the new copy is saved.

Note that using the Save As command does two things. First, any changes you've made since you last saved the original document will not appear in the original document, only in the new copy. For instance, if you saved a document called Letter, typed the words Dear Mom, immediately chose the Save As command, and saved a new document called Mom Letter, then the words Dear Mom would show up only in the document Mom Letter, not in the document called Letter.

Second, the Save As command leaves the *newly named* document open in the application for editing, not the previous document you were working in. When you use Save As, the original document you were working in is still available on the disk, but you're no longer editing it. Instead, you're editing the copy you just created. (Though using Save As with a new document is the same as using Save; there is no other original copy of the document.)

NOTE   What do you do if you want to save changes in the current document and then change the document's name? Take the steps one at a time. First, choose File ➤ Save to update the current document's file. Then, choose File ➤ Save As to give the file a new name and begin editing the new file.

Saving by Closing

If you've been working in a document that either has never been saved or has changes that haven't been saved, you'll see a small dot in the window's Close button. This is one indication that you have changes that need to be saved.

Clicking the Close button (or pressing ⌘W to close the window) causes a dialog sheet to appear (again, animated from "under" the title bar), asking if you want to save changes. If you do, click Save.

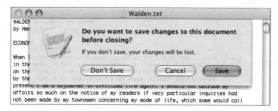

If you've saved the document previously, any changes are saved automatically, and the document window closes. If the document is still untitled, the Save dialog sheet appears, enabling you to name the document and determine where it will be stored.

Switching Applications and Windows

You'll generally be working with several applications at a time; in fact, unless you are only moving files around in the Finder, you'll always have more than one application running: the Finder and whatever other program you are using.

Mac OS X gives you several ways to switch among applications and windows, using either the keyboard or the mouse.

Once you have multiple applications running, you can use the Dock to switch between them by clicking their icons, as discussed in Chapter 2. Just click the icon of the program you want to switch to.

You can also use the keyboard to switch applications: Just press ⌘Tab and ⌘Shift+Tab to cycle forward and backward, respectively, through all running applications.

Switching windows is a different animal, though; when you switch to a different application, all its windows come to the front. One way to go directly to the window you want is to switch to the program you want to use and then select a window from its Window menu; all programs that can work with multiple windows have this menu.

Another way to access a specific window is to click and hold a program's Dock icon. The menu that appears shows, among other things, a list of windows available. Just select the one you want to use, and it will come to the front.

Mac OS X has an intriguingly deviant way of working with document windows, one that may be disconcerting for those familiar with other operating systems. Imagine this scenario: You're writing a report in TextEdit, and you decide to switch to Safari to view a website. (In this scenario, Safari is already running and has multiple windows open.)

If you switch to Safari by selecting its icon in the Dock, all of the Safari windows come to the foreground, most likely obscuring your TextEdit document window as it slips into the background. (The TextEdit document window doesn't disappear, minimize, or hide, but you probably can't see it.)

TIP   You can hide the foreground application when you select another application's icon in the Dock: hold down the Option key while clicking the Dock icon. You can also hide the foreground application by holding down the Option key and clicking another application's window; this switches to the other application and hides the foreground application's windows at the same time.

Besides clicking the Safari icon in the Dock, there's another way to bring a Safari window forward: click part of that window directly. If you can see one of Safari's windows behind your TextEdit document window and you click it, the Safari window will come to the foreground, and Safari's menus will take over the menu bar.

Interestingly, however, *only* that clicked Safari window will appear on top of the TextEdit window—the other open Safari windows will remain in the background. This is also the behavior if you select a window from a program's Dock icon menu.

But there's a much more powerful way to access specific windows in Mac OS X: it's called Exposé.

Switching Applications and Windows with Exposé

Since every application you use has at least one window, and sometimes several, and since you probably use several applications at a time, you can sometimes get confused by all those windows. The Dock, discussed earlier in this chapter, certainly helps you by allowing you to switch among applications, bringing only their windows to the front. But sometimes you want to switch among windows in one application, or you want to have an idea which windows are available in all your applications. That's where Exposé comes in.

Exposé gives you a bird's-eye view of your windows and to help you switch among applications and windows. Exposé allows you to very quickly move active windows and see items behind them, but it can also be used as an application switcher and as a fairly sophisticated way to help you juggle multiple tasks with only limited screen space in which to manage those tasks.

If you tend to work in more than one application at once—as many of us do all the time—your screen probably looks a little something like this:

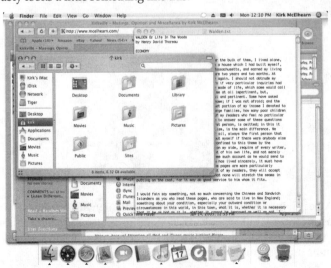

This graphic shows a screen with two Finder windows open, as well as a window for Safari, another for TextEdit, one for iTunes that is barely visible, and a Mail window hidden by the others. If you were working in a conventional way, you would need to either choose the Hide Applications command or use the Dock to move around and see windows from different applications. (Also, if a portion of a background window was peeking around the edge of an active window, you might click it to bring it forward.)

Using Exposé, however, you get a different way to view your open windows. By either pointing the mouse in the corner of a screen or pressing a special function key, you can get Mac OS X to turn your windows into thumbnails and rearrange them on the screen so they can be viewed and selected in a unique way.

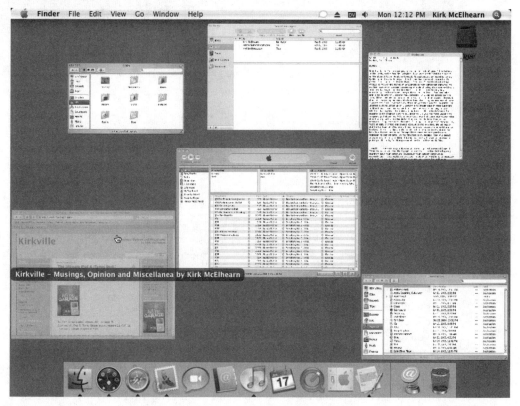

TIP Pressing the Exposé hotkey to show all windows (this is F9 by default, but you can change this in the Exposé pane of System Preferences) shrinks all your windows so you can see miniature versions of them. Move your mouse cursor over any window to see its name—this may be the application name, if the application only has one window, or the name of the current folder, if it is a Finder window, or the name of the document displayed in the window. To switch to any of these windows, just click its miniature image. When using Exposé to display all windows, only those applications that are not hidden are displayed. If you have hidden an application and its windows by pressing ⌘H, they remain hidden when you invoke Exposé.

Exposé can also let you see only the windows of the active application. For example, here's what happens when the Finder is active and three windows are open, and you press F10 (the default hotkey to show all the windows of the current application):

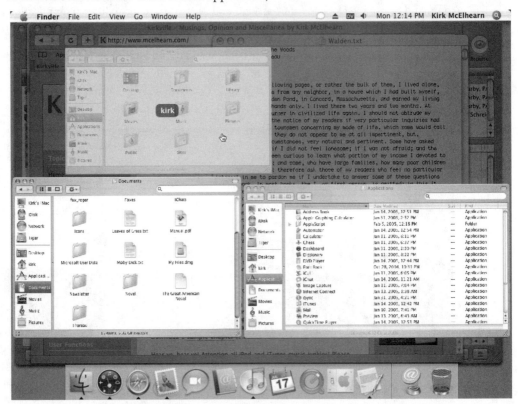

As with the previous example, you just move the mouse cursor over a window to see its name and then click to bring that window to the front.

If you ever want to return to the normal view, with windows layered, you can just click any of the dark gray part of your screen, click anywhere in the menu bar, or press the Escape key.

Exposé has one other view that can be useful for people who use the desktop as a receptacle for their files or for accessing hard disk icons or mounted network volumes. If you press the F11 key (which you can change in the Exposé preferences), all your windows move out of the way and you see the desktop.

You can now access any items on your desktop easily and return to the previous view by clicking anywhere in the dark gray border around your desktop.

NOTE   Another way to return to the previous view—of the active application or of all windows—is to press the same hotkey you pressed to get to the Exposé view. If you pressed F9 to see all your windows, press F9 again to return to a normal view. You can also cycle through Exposé views by pressing the different hotkeys without returning to the normal view.

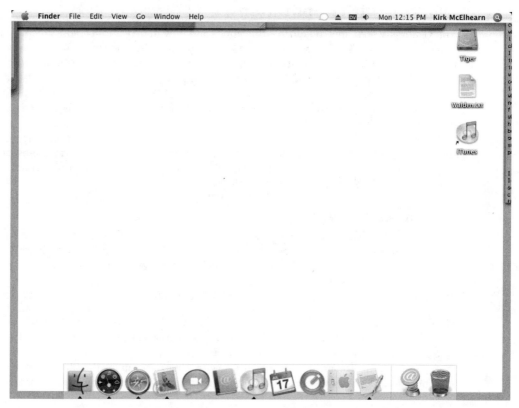

To change the way you invoke Exposé, go to the Dashboard & Exposé pane in System Preferences. (We'll look at Dashboard later in this chapter.) You'll see two sections:

Active Screen Corners   This section lets you choose to invoke Exposé's three views by moving your cursor into one of your screen corners. You can set any of the four corners to the three Exposé views, and you can also choose to invoke Dashboard and start or disable your screensaver in any of the corners.

Keyboard and Mouse Shortcuts   You can choose here which hotkeys you use to invoke Exposé and Dashboard. You can leave the defaults, which are in the left-hand column of pop-up menus—F9, F10, and F11 for Exposé and F12 for Dashboard—or you can set your own hotkeys, using modifier keys such as the ⌘, Shift, or other keys. You can also choose to have just one modifier key (for example, the right ⌘ key, the command key to the right side of the space bar) invoke Exposé. If you choose a key like this, Exposé is invoked when you press that key, and releasing the key returns your screen to a normal view, so you won't need to click anywhere to do so. The right-hand column of pop-up menus lets you set mouse actions to invoke Exposé and Dashboard. If you have a two- or three-button mouse, you can set these additional buttons to invoke Exposé or Dashboard.

Working with Applications

You've already seen how to launch applications and how to save and load documents within your applications. Now let's move on to some standard features you're likely to encounter in Mac OS X applications. Since these applications use special *application programming interfaces (APIs)* that are built into the Mac OS, you can be reasonably assured that many Mac OS X applications will use these dialog boxes or similar controls with a minimum of alterations. Nevertheless, some application developers will create their own controls, and some controls, such as print dialogs, can be altered by the printer manufacturer's driver software.

What are we talking about here? Specifically, the special commands that appear in the Application menu, along with the Print, Page Setup, Colors, Font, Special Characters, and Spelling dialog boxes and palettes, are all standard offerings in Mac OS X that application developers can and often do use, particularly in Cocoa (fully native) applications.

The Application Menu

As mentioned in Chapter 2 and elsewhere in this book, every application has its own Application menu that appears on the left side of the menu bar (just to the right of the Apple menu) at the top of the screen. The name or icon of the menu changes according to the application that's currently active. In each Application menu, you'll find some commands that are specific to that application, including the About command, the Services menu, the Hide/Show commands, and the Quit command.

NOTE   Because the Application menu changes for each application, you'll notice that whenever we tell you to access a command in the Application menu, it will be in the form *Application menu* ➢ *command*. In those references, *Application menu* is simply a placeholder for whatever the current application's Application menu is named. Likewise, some commands will include the name of the application, such as Quit Word or Hide Word; in the text, we'll often just call those commands Quit and Hide.

ABOUT COMMAND

The *Application menu* ➢ About command is present in all applications. It's used to tell you something about the application, generally by showing you a splash screen. On this screen you'll see the name of the application, the version number, and usually some information about the programmers (or company) who created the application. This screen may also show a serial number, or other information you need for technical support, and may have a URL for the developer's website. Most About windows have a Close button that you can click; in some cases, the About window may be a dialog box that includes an OK button that you can click when you've finished learning about the application.

SERVICES MENU

In the Application menu of most programs (including the Finder), you'll find a Services menu. The Services concept is an interesting one, offering a unique way for applications to communicate with one another. This special menu is designed to enable you to access the commands of other applications from within the current application, even if those other applications aren't currently running. When you choose a command from the Services menu, you feed data from the current application to another application for processing. You usually have to select or highlight something in the current application before the commands in the Services menu will become active.

For instance, by default you can access commands from the Stickies application via the Services menu of almost any other Mac OS X application. If you highlight some text and choose *Application menu* ➤ Services ➤ Make New Sticky Note, the selected text will then be opened in a new note in Stickies, which will open if it is not already active.

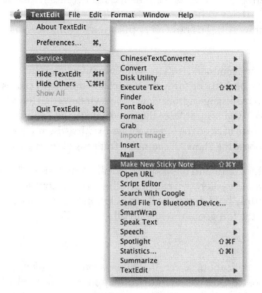

As you can see in the previous graphic, Mac OS X 10.4 offers many commands in the Services menu, and these are just the commands available from Apple software that Tiger installs by default. Third-party applications may also add commands to the Services menu. You don't need to do anything for applications to add commands to this menu; Mac OS X discovers them automatically, if an application has a service available, and adds them to the menu.

For example, Apple Mail offers commands in the Services menu that enable you to highlight text and send it to an e-mail recipient from within the current application. You can use the Reformat service to reformat text; you can use the Search with Google service to search for the selected text on Google; and you can use the Spotlight service to use Spotlight to search for the selected text on your computer.

Just remember that you usually need to highlight or choose something in the current application, such as an image or a selection of text, before a command in the Services menu will become active. (Some Services commands will deal with an entire window or document, but not many.)

NOTE The problem with Services is that not enough applications implement them, including some that we think really should, such as most Microsoft applications. Also, accessing the Services menu takes one click too many. It would be more practical if a separate Services menu were directly in the menu bar. Rather, you have to go to a submenu and, in many cases, another application submenu, to access them. (However, many services offer keyboard shortcuts, giving you quick access to their functions.) Services are an interesting and useful offering, so check your Services menu every once in a while to see if there's a time-saver in there you've overlooked.

HIDE AND SHOW COMMANDS

The Application menu also holds some other commands that you'll use to manage your applications: the Hide, Hide Others, and Show All commands. These commands can be used to remove the windows of an application from the visible screen quickly (Hide), to hide the windows of all other background applications (Hide Others), or to show all windows for all currently running applications in the background (Show All). To show an application's window(s) again, select the application's icon on the Dock.

NOTE   Using the Hide command isn't the same as minimizing windows. Instead of placing individual windows on the Dock in icon form, the Hide command simply causes the application's menu bar and all its windows to disappear from view—even windows that have been minimized to the Dock. They're still active—you just can't see them, even if you use Exposé to view your applications and windows. To get them back on the screen, either switch to the application (using the Dock or a similar method) or choose the Show All command from any other application's Application menu.

Note that the Hide command has a keyboard shortcut—press ⌘H to hide the current application. Likewise, as mentioned earlier, you can hide other applications as you switch to a particular application in the Dock. Simply hold down the ⌘ and Option keys while clicking a Dock icon, and that application will come to the foreground while all others are hidden.

QUIT COMMAND

To quit the current application, select *Application menu* ➢ Quit. (You can also press ⌘Q in nearly any application to invoke the Quit command.) Most applications will display dialog boxes if you have any unsaved changes in open documents. Choose whether or not to save changes. Then those documents will be closed, and the application will terminate, handing its portion of memory back to the Mac OS.

Page Setup and Print

Before you print for the first time in any Mac OS X application (or any time you change some basic settings), you should open the Page Setup dialog sheet. Select File ➢ Page Setup to see this standard dialog sheet, which offers a few basic options (see Figure 4.6).

At the top of the Page Setup dialog sheet, you'll see the Settings menu, where you can choose Page Attributes to see the basic options for a page or choose Summary to see a summary of your current selections.

In the Format For menu, select the printer whose options you want to change. All printers currently installed via the Printer Setup Utility (see Chapter 7, "Printing and Faxing in Mac OS X") are available in this menu.

If you've selected Page Attributes in the Settings menu and you've chosen a printer in the Format For menu, you can now select the type of paper you'll be printing to from the Paper Size menu. Then click the button that represents the orientation you'd like the printer to use when printing to the paper. Finally, you can enter a percentage at which you'd like the page to be printed—for instance, entering **90** results in the page being scaled and printed at 90 percent of its actual size.

Once you've left the Page Setup dialog sheet (by clicking OK), you can head to the Print dialog sheet to print the document. With the document active on your screen, select File ➢ Print from the application's menu. That brings up the Print dialog sheet.

FIGURE 4.6
The Page Setup
dialog sheet

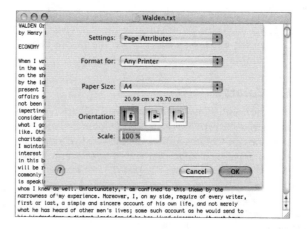

NOTE Some applications will launch a Print dialog box instead of a dialog sheet, but they'll look almost identical. (Whether or not it's a dialog box or dialog sheet is up to the application, but the look of the Print dialog itself is controlled by the Mac OS and the printer's driver software.)

From the Printer menu at the top of the dialog sheet, you can choose the printer you'd like to use. Once you've made that selection, the dialog sheet may reconfigure itself slightly for that printer; in most cases, the items that change are the options available in the unlabeled pop-up menu, which by default shows Copies & Pages, as shown in Figure 4.7. (In some cases, the dialog box may change more drastically when you select a different printer, because some printers have their own dialog box routines that stray from the Mac OS X standard.)

FIGURE 4.7
The standard Mac OS X
Print dialog sheet

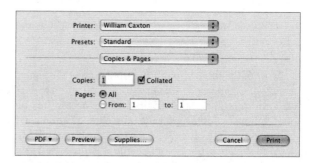

For basic printing, simply enter the number of copies you'd like to print, whether to collate the copies, and the range of pages within your document that you'd like to print. If desired, you can pull down the options menu (it doesn't have a label, but it's the menu that defaults to Copies & Pages) to see other options for your particular printer. For instance, depending on the printer model, you might be able to choose different quality levels, different graphics printing options, or the option to print more than one document page per sheet of paper.

Once you've set your options, click the Preview button to see a full-screen representation of the printed output, click the Print button to send the document to the printer and begin the printing process, or click the PDF button to save your document as a PDF file or send it as a fax.

NOTE Printing and faxing are discussed in much more detail in Chapter 7 and Chapter 8, "PDFs, Fonts, and Color," which include information on setting up printers and installing driver software. Chapter 7 also takes a closer look at the options in the Print dialog and the options available when sending faxes.

The Colors Palette

At some point, many applications will call upon you to choose colors for use within your documents, so the Mac OS provides a standard Colors palette. Actually, "Colors palette" has two meanings: not only does the Colors window enable you to choose from a "palette" of color choices, it's also officially a floating *palette window* that will appear over other windows in the application (see Figure 4.8).

FIGURE 4.8
The Colors palette, showing the Color Wheel tool

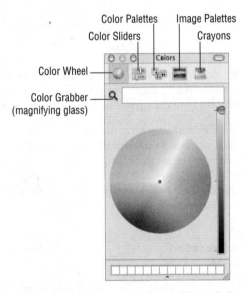

Most of the time, you'll bring up the palette by selecting a Colors or Show Colors menu command—the command will vary from application to application. In text editors that use standard Mac OS X controls (such as TextEdit), you can access the Colors palette under Format ➤ Font ➤ Show Colors. Obviously, fonts aren't the only elements that can be colorful, so you'll find the Colors palette popping up fairly often. It's easy to use, although it offers some interesting and complex options.

At first glance, the Colors palette is simple: You select an item (text, image, shape) in your application and then invoke the Colors palette. Then, you choose a color. What's a bit more complicated is how you pick the colors. You've got a number of ways to accomplish that:

Magnifying glass One way to choose a color that may not be immediately obvious is to click the small magnifying glass icon and then click with that magnifying glass anywhere on the screen. When you click, whatever color is under the magnifying glass will become the selected color in the Colors palette. This is a great way to match exactly another color in an image, document, or any other open window on your screen.

Color wheel The Color wheel allows you to pick a color simply by clicking it with the mouse. Once the color is selected, you can use the slider control on the right side of the window to darken or lighten the color.

Color sliders   Click the Color Sliders button, and a pop-up menu appears representing the different ways to select a color. These are the grayscale, RGB (red-green-blue), CMYK (cyan-magenta-yellow-black), and HSB (hue-saturation-brightness) controls. Using the Color sliders is the easiest way to get exact color mixtures using common numbering schemes.

Color palettes   Here, you can select an exact color by its name or other label. By default, you can access system colors and Apple colors, but you can also customize the name by pulling down the List menu and choosing Open. That makes it possible to add other lists (for instance, Pantone colors) that are appropriate for your project. (You'll likely find that professional graphics applications and utilities will add lists that are compatible with this portion of the Colors palette.)

Image palettes   By default, this button leads to a Spectrum tool, which simply allows you to select a color using the mouse. However, other images can be loaded into the control by selecting the Palette menu and choosing the New from File option. Once it is loaded, you can use a custom palette created for your project, for web development, and so on.

TIP   Actually, the Image Palettes tool can be used to load *any* QuickTime-compatible image and choose colors from it. This can be very handy if you're trying to match the colors in an existing image. When you choose New from File, simply locate an image file (TIFF, JPEG, PICT, and others) in the Open dialog box. It will appear in the Colors palette, enabling you to choose colors from within the image.

Crayons   This tool enables you to choose colors using an approach familiar to most anyone who has been through grade school—a "box" of crayons. Simply point to a color and click it to select it as the color you want to use.

TIP   At the top of each of these palettes is a wide box where your selected color appears. You can drag that color to one of the series of smaller boxes you'll find across the bottom of the palette to save that color as a favorite color. Later, you can get to the favorite colors more quickly—simply click a color in one of the small squares. It's a handy way to store your favorite colors for quick access while you're working. And if one row of boxes isn't enough, grab the bottom of the Colors palette with your mouse cursor and drag it downward to add more rows for your favorites.

The Font Panel

Many applications also include the Font panel, which enables you to preview and fine-tune your selection of fonts in the documents that you create and edit. You'll usually find the panel under Format ➣ Font ➣ Show Fonts or a similar command. This panel is shown in Figure 4.9.

FIGURE 4.9
The Font panel gives you a standard window for choosing fonts.

Changes to your selected font are made on the fly in your document windows. Select a new family, typeface, or size, and you'll immediately see it reflected in any highlighted text on your document page.

CHOOSING A FONT

Choosing a font is actually fairly simple. Begin by selecting a collection (you'll likely choose All Fonts unless you've created collections in the past) and then choose a font family. That will display a list of typefaces you can choose from. After selecting the typeface, you can choose the point size of the font, or you can enter a size in the small entry box that's above the scrolling list of sizes.

Collections is a Mac OS X term. Collections enable you to organize fonts in sets, making them easy to manage. In fact, the Mac OS separates its own fonts into some collections, which enable you to view a subset of the overall number of installed fonts on your Mac. Figure 4.9 (displayed earlier) shows the Classic collection, for instance.

The Family column shows *font families*, which are groups of typefaces with the same basic design—for instance, Helvetica or Times. The *typefaces* within those families (selectable in the Typeface column) are individual fonts that use the font family's characteristics—for instance, Helvetica Oblique (italic) or Helvetica Bold Oblique (bold italic).

After you've selected the font you want to use, you can select Add to Favorites from the small menu at the bottom of the panel or simply click the panel's Close button. That will close the window, and you can get back to editing.

NOTE   Fonts, the Font panel, and font technology are discussed in more detail in Chapter 8.

USING FAVORITE FONTS

If you've been adding fonts to your Favorites collection by clicking the Action button at the bottom of the Font panel and choosing Add to Favorites, you can access them by selecting the Favorites collection in the Collections column of the Fonts panel. You'll see a list of your favorite fonts, enabling you to select quickly.

Special Characters

The fonts you use in Mac OS X have much more than just letters, numbers, and punctuation. You may be familiar with some of the special characters available, but there are literally hundreds of them in most Mac OS X fonts. These include math symbols, arrows, currency symbols, accented characters, and much more.

Most Mac OS X applications—including the Finder—let you access the Character palette by selecting Edit ➤ Special Characters. (You can also access this palette from the Input menu; this menu extra displays if you have more than one keyboard active in the Input Menu tab of the International preferences, or if you check Character palette in these preferences.) This palette shows a list of categories to the left and, for each category, a set of characters to the right.

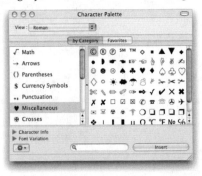

When you need to insert a special character, open this palette, select the category, and then find the character you want to use. You can either double-click this character or click the Insert button—this inserts the character at the current cursor location in your active window.

If you use certain characters often—say you need the copyright symbol a lot—you can add it to your Favorites by clicking the Action button (the one with the gear) and selecting Add to Favorites. When you need to use it again, click the Favorites tab to display the characters you've added and insert it as explained in the previous paragraph.

If you want to see the variants available for a specific character in all the fonts installed on your Mac, select the character and click the Font Variation disclosure triangle.

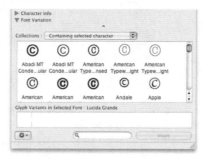

This shows how the character looks in every font you can use, and for some fonts, it shows additional variants.

Checking Spelling

The Check Spelling tools are also common across many Mac OS X applications, allowing the most basic programs to include a spell-checking feature. This also is handy because when an application uses the built-in Spelling dialog box, you have access to your personal dictionary, which you may have trained to understand the spelling of new words.

In applications that support the Spelling dialog box (again, Apple's TextEdit is a good example), there are three special commands in the Edit menu:

In the Spelling dialog box, click the Find Next button to find the first word that the application has noted as misspelled. The panel offers its guesses for the word's actual spelling in the Guess scrolling list. If you see the correct spelling, select it in the list and click the Correct button.

◆ Edit ➤ Spelling ➤ Check Spelling As You Type causes misspelled words to appear in the document window with a red underline. This helps you notice immediately and at a glance if you've misspelled something. If you Control+click a word, a contextual menu displays a list of possible corrections.

◆ The Edit ➤ Spelling ➤ Check Spelling command is used only if you don't have the As You Type option turned on. Check Spelling causes the next misspelled word in the document (after the insertion point) to be highlighted. The misspelled word won't stay highlighted when you resume typing. (This option is designed for people who are annoyed by the colorful underlining created by the Check Spelling As You Type option.)

◆ Of course, just the highlighting of misspelled words may not help, which is why the Mac OS offers the Spelling dialog box. If you don't know how to spell a word, you can consult the dialog box. Select Edit ➤ Spelling ➤ Spelling, and the Spelling dialog box appears (see Figure 4.10).

FIGURE 4.10

The Spelling dialog box

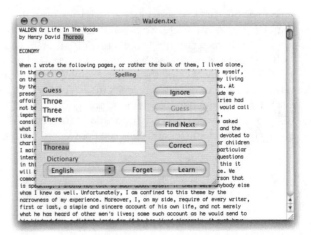

You also can correct the word yourself by editing the misspelled word in the entry box just below the Guess list. Then click the Correct button to change the spelling in your document.

After you've corrected the word, or if you simply intend to ignore it, click Find Next again. The Spelling panel will move on to the next word. When no more words are found, the Spelling panel can't find any more words that it believes are misspelled.

At the bottom of the panel, you'll find the dictionary controls. In the pop-up menu, you can select from the different languages and language dialect dictionaries, if you have more than one installed on your Mac. The Learn and Forget buttons are used to add words to or remove words from the dictionary, respectively.

If the Spelling panel comes across a word that you know is spelled correctly, click the Learn button. (For instance, the dictionary doesn't know the word *eMac* even if you've typed it correctly.) Doing so adds that word to the dictionary.

If you add a word that actually is not spelled correctly—or if you notice that the Spelling panel seems to pass over an incorrectly spelled word—you can do something about that. In the Spelling panel, enter the word in the entry box below the Guess menu and click the Forget button. That particular word will be "forgotten" by the dictionary and in the future will be flagged with a red underline when it's spell-checked.

Using Dashboard

One of the new features in Tiger is Dashboard, a combination of Exposé and, for those who recall older versions of Mac OS X, desk accessories. Dashboard uses *widgets,* which are tiny applications, each dedicated to a single, specific task. Dashboard lets you access a group of widgets with a single keypress or mouse click, providing these discrete functions whenever you need them.

Apple describes widgets as "useful mini applications that help you do everyday tasks." While many of them are "mini" applications, others are linked to full-featured programs and provide simpler or quicker interfaces to them. For example, the Address Book widget lets you access all your contact information that is stored in the main Address Book application; the Dictionary widget is a simpler version of the Dictionary application.

Dashboard uses an Exposé–like means of presentation; when you press the default Dashboard keyboard shortcut—F12—your display darkens and Dashboard widgets appear over your workspace (see Figure 4.11). You can work with these widgets—entering text, clicking buttons, or selecting menus—without your other windows getting in the way.

FIGURE 4.11
A half-dozen Dashboard widgets on display

Figure 4.11 shows six widgets: Stocks, Weather, and Calculator, and then below that, Dictionary, iTunes, and Unit Converter. Mac OS X comes with more than a dozen widgets, including Stickies, World Clock, and a Tile Game, which may bring back memories to those who have used the Mac for a long time.

To view all the widgets available, click the + icon at the lower left of the screen after invoking Dashboard. This moves your workspace up and displays the Widget bar. This "perforated metal" bar that resembles the front of Apple's G5 computers displays all the widgets you can use. Arrow icons at each end of the Widget bar let you switch to different screens. Depending on your display resolution, you may see just one screen or two, but if you install more widgets (you can get more by clicking the More Widgets button above the Widget bar), you may have many screens of icons.

TIP At press time, only Apple's default widgets were available, but there is no doubt that many third-party developers will be providing both freeware and shareware widgets as soon as possible. Dashboard has the potential to become a very lively "platform" for developers, since Apple has released a software developer kit (SDK) for it. The More Widgets button above the Widget bar takes you to Apple's Dashboard page, but you'll also find other widgets on websites such as MacUpdate (www.macupdate.com) and Version Tracker (www.versiontracker.com).

As you saw earlier, the default Dashboard shortcut is F12; press it once to display widgets, and press it again or click anywhere other than on a widget to hide them. You can use this shortcut, or you can change to another key combination (see the section "Switching Applications and Windows with Exposé" earlier in this chapter). You can also set an active corner to access your widgets, or simply click the Dashboard icon in the Dock. If you don't see the Dashboard icon in the Dock, you can drag it to the Dock from its location in the Applications folder.

If you want to open a widget, display the Widget bar and click a widget to move it on-screen. To close a widget, click the X icon at the top left corner of the widget; if you don't see this icon, hold down the Option key to display it.

Using widgets is generally simple; their interface is uncluttered, and, since they usually have just a single function, you most often type text in a field, click a button, or select information from menus.

One example of a simple widget is the iTunes widget. You can open iTunes, if it is not already running, by clicking the Play button. This button then allows you to play or pause your music, and the Next and Previous buttons let you skip ahead or back one song at a time; if you drag the click wheel (the ring around the control buttons), you can change the volume.

Some widgets, such as Weather and Stocks, allow you to customize the data they display. These widgets show a small i icon at the bottom right of their windows; click that icon to access the configuration section of the widget.

With the Weather widget, you type a city, state, or ZIP code to specify what weather information you want. After you've entered this information, click Done to return to the main window of the Weather widget and see the current temperature and weather conditions.

Other widgets offer more options. The Unit Converter widget lets you select from several types of conversions from the Convert menu (weight, temperature, area, etc.) and then select the units you want to convert from two other pop-up menus.

The Flight Tracker widget lets you select departure and arrival city, and, if you know them, the airline and flight number to find out about flights, departure and arrival times, and flight status.

As for the other widgets, try them out and discover what they do. You can also check the Mac OS X help to find out about specific widgets and how they work.

Running Classic Mac Applications

While Mac OS X is designed to run best with applications written specifically for it (native applications), it offers a compatibility mode that allows it to run some applications designed for Mac OS 9. In fact, Mac OS X is capable of running five different types of applications:

Native applications   A native Mac OS X application, also called a Cocoa application, runs directly within the Mac OS X environment. When you double-click the application, Mac OS X creates a memory partition for it, loads its menu bar, and presents you with the application.

Hybrid applications   These applications, also called Carbon applications, are designed to run in either Mac OS 9 or Mac OS X. These applications run the same way as native Mac OS X applications, except that they also can run within the Classic environment. You'll notice that these applications can behave a bit differently from Cocoa applications, for instance, sometimes displaying a slightly different Save dialog box instead of a Save sheet that's attached to the document's toolbar.

Java applications   Applications written in Sun Microsystems' Java language can be compiled to work in a *virtual machine* environment that is built into Mac OS X. The idea behind the Java virtual machine is that such applications can run on any computer platform that supports Java, instead of being written specifically for Mac OS X or, say, Microsoft Windows. In practice, there aren't as many Java applications available as you might think, because the virtual machine environment is often a bit more limited in capabilities than a native operating system environment is. (For that reason, Java applications tend to look different from Mac applications.) Still, we'll cover using Java applications in Chapter 20, "Mac OS X and Other Platforms."

Command-line applications   These are programs and commands that you can run from Terminal, the application that gives you access to the Unix underpinnings of Mac OS X. While you generally run these commands and programs through Terminal or a similar terminal program, Mac OS X runs many of these programs behind the scenes to do its everyday tasks. We look at using the command line in Chapter 22, "Terminal and the Command Line."

Classic applications   Classic applications are those designed to run exclusively in Mac OS 9. (Such an application may have been written initially for an older version of the Mac OS, but it needs to be fully compatible with the latest version of Mac OS 9 to work in the Classic environment.) Although Classic applications appear to run from within Mac OS X, the truth is that an entire Mac OS 9 environment—the Classic environment—is launched first in its own Mac OS X process, and then the Classic application launches within the Classic environment. Classic applications are easy to spot because they use different menu fonts, dialog boxes, and window controls that are reminiscent of earlier Mac OS versions.

Although native applications are the best to choose in terms of performance and reliability, hybrid applications also run efficiently and productively within the Mac OS X environment. And they have the advantage of being able to run in Mac OS 9 and Mac OS X environments simultaneously.

Even though Mac OS X has become mature, and most applications are available in Mac OS X versions, some people still use older applications in the Classic environment. One notable example is FrameMaker, Adobe's document-creation program, which has not been updated for Mac OS X, and may never be.

Classic applications are less efficient than the other types in that they don't take full advantage of Mac OS X. The Classic environment also requires quite a bit of RAM (after all, an entire instance of Mac OS 9 is launched along with the Classic application), and the Classic environment can be responsible for system-wide slowdowns. Because of that, we recommend that you work with native Mac OS X applications whenever possible. If it's not possible, though, Mac OS X can launch Classic applications in two ways: either double-click the Classic application to load the application and the Classic environment or launch the Classic environment first via the System Preferences application or from the Classic menu in the menu bar, if you have this displayed (see the graphic on the next page), and then launch the Classic application at your leisure.

TIP Because Carbon applications, by definition, can run in both Mac OS 9 and Mac OS X, you have the option from within Mac OS X to launch a Carbon application in either the native environment or the Classic environment. To access this option, select a Carbon application in a Finder window and use the File ➤ Get Info command. In the Info window, note that there's an option on the General screen, Open in the Classic Environment, that you can turn on by clicking to place a check mark. Once turned on, this application will run as though it were a Classic application the next time it's launched.

The Classic Environment

You can launch the Classic environment in one of three ways. The first way is to simply launch a Classic application, following any of the steps discussed in the section "Launching an Application or Document," earlier in this chapter. (In fact, we guarantee you'll do this every so often without thinking about it, particularly if you have a mix of native and Classic applications on your hard disk.) When a Classic application is launched, the Mac OS automatically loads the Classic environment. In essence, the Mac OS is loading a "transparent" version of Mac OS 9. Instead of switching between Mac OS 9 and Mac OS X, you'll continue to do all your work within Mac OS X. The transparent Mac OS 9 code, however, sits in the background and makes it possible for the Classic application to run correctly and appear—as much as is possible—to be just another application.

When a Classic application is first launched, you'll need to wait for a minute or two while the transparent Classic environment is launched if it wasn't already running. The indication of this process is a small window and a progress bar, which shows you the Mac OS 9 transparent environment being launched.

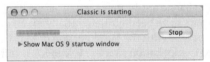

The Classic window includes a disclosure triangle, which you can click to reveal the startup screen for the version of Mac OS 9 your Mac is using for the Classic environment (see Figure 4.12). You can also click the Stop button in the window to stop the launching of the Classic environment.

NOTE As noted elsewhere, you'll need an up-to-date version of Mac OS 9 to work as the Classic environment in Mac OS X—Mac OS X 10.3 requires Mac OS 9.2 or higher if you want to run Classic applications. See Appendix A, "Getting Installed and Set Up," for details on installing Mac OS 9 and Mac OS X.

Another way to launch the Classic environment is from within the Classic pane of the System Preferences application. There you'll find options that enable you to launch the Classic environment at any time by clicking the Start button. You can also opt to have Classic start up whenever you log in to your Mac. The main reason for launching Classic from the System Preferences application is to avoid waiting for the environment to load whenever you want to use a Classic application. The disadvantage of this method is that it leaves the Classic environment open in the background, where it can use precious system memory and sometimes slow down your Mac's overall performance.

FIGURE 4.12
The Classic environment
window appears when
you launch a Classic
application.

One important option in the Classic preference pane is Show Classic Status in Menu Bar. If you check this, a Classic icon displays in your menu bar at all times. Click this icon to access the Classic Status menu.

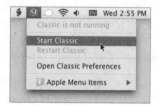

You can start Classic from this menu—which is much easier than going to System Preferences— and, if it's running, you can shut Classic down from here. You can tell at a glance if Classic is running: the icon is grayed out if Classic is off, and it is darker when Classic is running. You can also open the Classic preferences from this menu, and you can even access Apple Menu Items in your Classic System folder. This is a great way to open Classic applications directly, since you can select Recent Applications and choose one of the applications you use often.

Once launched, the Classic environment can be used to run more than one Classic application at a time. Simply locate a Classic application and double-click it in the Finder. The application launches, appears in the Dock, and will seem to work much like a native application. There are some differences, but they're more cosmetic than functional. You may notice different dialog boxes, different window controls, and a few different conventions used by the Classic Mac environment. For instance, you'll notice that dragging the window of a Classic application shows only the outline of the window while it's dragged; dragging a window in Mac OS X shows the entire window as it's dragged.

If you started the Classic environment by launching a Classic application, you won't need to shut down the Classic environment specifically; it automatically shuts down a certain amount of time after you quit the last Classic application. (You can set this option on the Advanced tab of the Classic pane in System Preferences.) If necessary, you can quit the Classic environment, especially if a Classic application has crashed or has become unresponsive.

You can shut down and restart Classic from the Classic menu, if you have it displayed in your menu bar.

And you can shut down (Stop) and restart the Classic environment from the Classic pane of the System Preferences application. If you do this, make sure the Start/Stop tab is selected and then click either the Stop button or the Restart button.

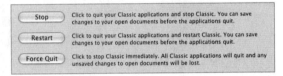

You can also force-quit the Classic environment from this preference pane, which is something you cannot do from the Classic menu.

Restarting is the same as shutting down, except that Classic starts backup immediately after shutting down successfully. This is useful if you're having intermittent problems in the Classic environment or if a Classic application has just crashed or encountered an error. Unlike Mac OS X's native applications, a problem with one Classic application can cause other Classic applications to exhibit problems (or even crash and quit), so after any sort of Classic crash, it's a good idea to restart the Classic environment.

Note that you can also use the Force Quit command in the Classic pane or on the Apple menu to shut down the Classic environment. This command can be used when the Restart and Shut Down commands don't appear to be effective, particularly after a crash within the Classic environment. This is a choice of last resort, however, because you'll lose unsaved data in any open Classic applications.

NOTE If you start the Classic environment from the Classic pane in the System Preferences application, then you *do* need to shut it down specifically. Again, you can shut it down by clicking Stop in the Classic pane or by selecting Stop Classic from the Classic menu. The environment is also shut down automatically when you log out of your account.

Since Mac OS X is designed for multiple users, each user may want to use Classic differently. When you launch Classic as described previously, the Classic environment uses preferences and settings from the Classic System Folder. This can be an annoyance if each user changes these settings for their own way of working and then finds those settings different the next time they run Classic if another user has changed the settings back again.

On the Advanced tab of the Classic preference pane, you can check Use Mac OS 9 Preferences from Your Home. This creates a special Classic preference file in your home folder, so any settings you change to the Classic environment remain the next time you start up Classic. Each user can then have their own customized Classic environment.

The Application and Apple Menus

Aside from the look and feel of many of the windows and menu items, two other obvious vestiges of earlier Mac OS versions appear when you're running a Classic application: the Classic version of the Application menu and the Apple menu. If you're familiar with Mac OS 9, you'll recognize these menus right away.

The Classic Apple menu (see Figure 4.13), which appears on the far left (the same place where the Mac OS X Apple menu appears), is a repository of aliases and shortcuts to many Mac OS 9 applications, control panels, and tools. It's different from the Mac OS X Apple menu, which is more limited. In fact, many of those control panels can be accessed and their values changed, with the results affecting only the Classic environment. For instance, you can use the Internet control panel, accessible from Apple ➢ Control Panels, to change default Internet settings for Internet applications that run in the Classic environment.

FIGURE 4.13

The Classic Apple menu, accessible when a Classic application is frontmost

You'll find that the Classic Apple menu offers some other quick-access options, such as Recent Applications, Recent Documents, and Recent Servers. Each option holds (by default) the 10 items you've most recently accessed in that category. In many cases, even items you've accessed outside the Classic environment show up in these menus. Remember, you can access the contents of the Apple menu from the Classic menu in the Mac OS X environment. Click the Classic menu and select Apple Menu Items to see the contents of your Classic Apple menu.

TIP   As with Mac OS 9, you can open the Apple Menu Items folder, located inside the active System folder (the one you're using for the Classic environment), to see the items that are slated to appear on the Apple menu. If you copy items (or aliases) into that folder or remove items from it, they'll appear on or disappear from the Apple menu, respectively.

On the other side of the Classic menu bar, you'll see the Mac OS 9 version of the Application menu. This menu is somewhat similar to the Application menu that appears on the left side in native Mac OS X applications. Like the Mac OS X Application menu, the Classic Application menu has the name of the current application (or its icon), and the menu enables you to hide the current application (using the Hide Application command) or hide all other applications that are running (using the Hide Others command).

In other ways, though, the Classic Application menu (see Figure 4.14) is different because it's really the precursor to the Dock's application-switching capability. Open the menu and select one of the applications listed, and you're switched to that application, just as though you had selected the application in the Dock.

FIGURE 4.14
The Classic Application
menu is really an appli-
cation switcher—sort of
a precursor to the Dock.

Classic's Application Dialog Boxes

Besides the different look and feel and the additional menu items, the Classic environment also offers slightly different dialog boxes within Classic applications. If you're familiar with Mac OS 9, these Classic dialog boxes won't pose much of a challenge to you. If you're new to the Mac with Mac OS X, however, you may begin to find the proliferation of different-looking dialog boxes and applications a bit troublesome. Don't worry—although they look different, for the most part they are similar to dialog boxes in Mac OS X's native applications. In this section, we'll take a quick look at some of the differences.

WARNING   It's important to note that some Classic dialogs will enable you to see files you normally don't see in native dialogs, such as hidden preference and database files used by the Mac OS
for various purposes. For instance, you can sometimes use Classic dialog boxes to view hidden files
using the convention of a period (.) at the beginning of the hidden file's name. (This is particularly
true of older Classic applications that haven't been updated since the advent of Mac OS X.) You
should avoid opening, editing, or saving these files (unless you're working with them), because they
may affect your Mac's capability to function.

CLASSIC'S OPEN DIALOG BOXES

Although most Open and Save dialog boxes in native Mac OS X applications (those that employ either Carbon or Cocoa technology) use the Columns or List view interface discussed earlier in this chapter, Classic applications continue to use dialog boxes that look exactly like their Mac OS 9 counterparts. These dialog boxes can vary somewhat, since the Mac OS has a few different interfaces available to programmers. (As the Mac OS engineers have improved the Open and Close dialog box templates, they've left older types available in order to retain compatibility with older applications.)

One of the more common types is called Navigation Services, and it's the dialog box interface that you'll see in more recent versions of Classic applications. If you're working in a Classic application and select File ➤ Open, there's a good chance you'll see either the standard Mac OS Open dialog box shown in Figure 4.15 or the Navigation Services Open dialog box shown in Figure 4.16.

FIGURE 4.15

The standard Mac OS 9
Open dialog box

FIGURE 4.16

The Navigation Services
Open dialog box

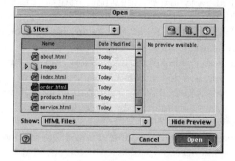

NOTE Why "Navigation Services"? When Apple was updating the Mac OS to Mac OS 8.5, it introduced this new type of dialog box, designed to improve the way you access files in future Mac applications. At the time, these dialogs were called Navigation Services to differentiate them from the earlier style of dialog box, as well as to underscore the fact that they offered a lot more flexibility for accessing files. Except when you're working in the Classic environment, though, it's a moot point, because Mac OS X introduces its own style of Open and Save dialog boxes based on the Finder window's Columns or List view.

The standard Open dialog box is fairly straightforward—you locate a file in the hierarchy of folders, select the file, and click Open to open it. (You also can double-click the filename in the list of files.) To move back to a parent folder, you can use the pop-up menu at the top of the dialog box.

The Navigation Services dialog box isn't very different, although it does offer a bit more flexibility. Within the dialog box, you can click the disclosure triangle to reveal a subfolder's contents. The other major differences are the small menu buttons at the top-right corner of the dialog box. From left to right, these are the Shortcuts, Favorites, and Recent menus.

In the Classic environment, these buttons vary in their usefulness. Click the Shortcuts button, and you'll bring up a menu that shows you the main hard-disk volumes, removable drives, and network drives that are connected to your Mac. Select one of the volumes in this menu, and it's displayed in the dialog box immediately.

The Favorites menu includes an Add to Favorites command that enables you to select an item in the dialog box and select the command. When you next open the Favorites menu, you'll see that Favorite. On the far right, the Recent menu can be used to access items and folders that you've selected recently in this or another Navigation Services dialog box. Note, however, that these Recent and Favorites menus don't have any relationship to the same menus and commands in the Mac OS X and the Finder; if you add an item to the Favorites here, it isn't added to the Favorites you can access via the Go menu in the Finder.

TIP   Need to see more files or folders? You can drag the Navigation Services Open dialog box to make it larger, using the resize control at the bottom-right corner of the window. You can't resize a regular Mac OS 9 Open or Save dialog box, however.

You may also see a Show pop-up menu (there's one in Figure 4.16) in some Open dialog boxes, which allows you to choose what sort of documents you'd like to see in the Open dialog box. You can use this menu if you're not seeing the document you want (in that case, you might choose Show Readable Documents or Show All Documents), or you can use the menu to limit the number of items you're seeing in the Open dialog box.

Some dialog boxes include a Show Preview button, which enables you to view a small preview of image and text documents. Click the Show Preview button to see the preview pane. Now, when you select a document that has a compatible format (image, Internet, and some text files), you'll see a preview of that document in the Open dialog box. (If you're seeing the Preview pane, you can click Hide Preview to get rid of it.)

Once you find the document you'd like to open, select it so that it's highlighted and click Open. If the document is compatible with your application, the document should load in that application and appear on-screen.

TIP   In the Navigation Services dialog box, you can hold down the Shift key to select multiple items in the Open dialog box. Then, when you click Open, all of the selected items will open in the application (assuming the application can open those items).

If you don't find the document you want, or if you'd like to dismiss the dialog box for some other reason, click Cancel.

CLASSIC'S SAVE DIALOG BOXES

The first time you save your document from within a Classic application, you'll see one of two Save dialog boxes—either the standard Mac OS 9 Save dialog box (see Figure 4.17) or the Navigation Services Save dialog box (see Figure 4.18).

FIGURE 4.17
The Save dialog box
in many early Classic
applications

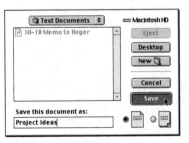

FIGURE 4.18

The Navigation Services
Save dialog box

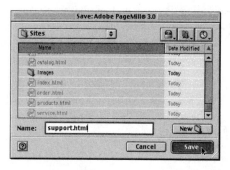

Again, the standard Save dialog box is fairly straightforward, and the Navigation Services dialog box has a few additional options that make the dialog work like the List view in a Finder window. Using the tools in the dialog box, locate the folder where you'd like to store your document. When you find the folder, give the file a name in the Name entry box.

When saving in the Classic environment, you're limited to 31 characters for filenames. In general, it's best not to begin filenames with non-alphanumeric characters, and you should avoid starting with a period (.) or a slash (/). (You can actually get away with the slash, and Mac OS X compensates by displaying the name with a colon at the command-line level. It's probably best to avoid the slash, because the slash is used to represent folders in Unix-style path statements.)

NOTE   Because most Classic applications don't append a three-letter file extension to your documents, in some cases you may opt to add one yourself, particularly if you intend to send that document over the Internet or use it later with a native Mac OS X application. This is particularly true if the document you're creating is being saved in a standard, cross-platform format, such as a plain text (.txt), Rich Text (.rtf), or Word (.doc) file, or in an image-file format such as TIFF (.tif), GIF (.gif), or JPEG (.jpg). Check though—some applications add them, others don't.

You also might find application-specific options below the Name entry box. Many applications, for instance, allow you to choose a format for your document if that application supports more than one document format. Likewise, you'll usually find a New Folder button, which you can use to create, within your selected folder, a new subfolder where you can save your document.

When you've entered the filename and made your optional choices, press Return or click the Save button. Your document will be saved.

If you choose a filename that already exists in the selected folder, an alert box will appear, asking if you want to replace the existing document with the one you're saving. If you do, click Replace. Otherwise, click Cancel and either rename the file you're saving or choose a different location.

CLASSIC PRINTING

Whenever you attempt to print from within a Classic application, the Classic environment will again present you with dialog boxes that look a little different from those you're accustomed to. In fact, before you can print at all from a Classic application, you'll need to configure a printer from within the Classic environment's Chooser. (This is discussed in detail in Chapter 7.) Once you have the printer configured, you can access the Page Setup and Print commands from within a Classic application.

Select File ➢ Page Setup from within a Classic application, and you'll see a Page Setup dialog box that looks somewhat like Figure 4.19. In this dialog box you can select the basics that were discussed previously in the section "Page Setup and Print" earlier in this chapter. These include page attributes such as the paper type to print to, the orientation of the final printed output (whether the page should be printed vertically or horizontally for wider output), and the percentage at which the final printout should be scaled. You may also find that the Options pop-up menu (which defaults to Page Attributes) hides some other option screens, including options specific to the selected printer.

FIGURE 4.19

The Page Setup dialog box from a Classic application

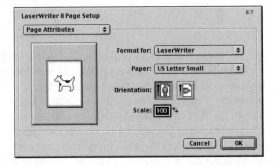

Once you have the Page Setup dialog conquered, you can select File ➢ Print to bring up the Print dialog box. This one, unlike the native Mac OS X Print dialog box, may be dramatically different, depending on the printer that has been selected; many printers have different driver software and hence different Print dialog boxes. Figure 4.20 shows a fairly common Classic Print dialog box—it's the dialog box that's based on the LaserWriter 8 driver. This is the printer driver used by many Post-Script-compatible printers, even if the printers aren't manufactured by Apple.

FIGURE 4.20

The Print dialog box for a LaserWriter-compatible printer

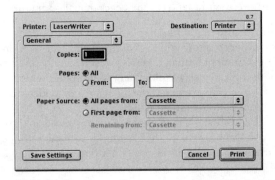

At its most basic, the Print dialog box enables you to enter the number of copies you want to print and which document pages you want to send to the printer. You can also select the paper source if your printer has multiple paper trays or loading options.

In the untitled options pop-up menu (by default, it has the name General), you may have many, many more options to choose from, depending again on the printer driver you're using. For Laser-Writer-compatible printers, options include the capability to select when to print a document, how color matching will work, whether to print a coverage page, and how many document pages will be printed on each sheet of paper.

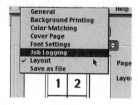

Once you've made all your selections, you're ready to print. If you'd like to save the settings changes you made for use in future printing sessions, click the Save Settings button. The driver will reflect those settings the next time you print from a Classic application. To print, click the Print button. Your print job is sent to the printer.

In many cases, PrintMonitor (another Classic application—see Figure 4.21) will be launched when you send a document to the printer. PrintMonitor enables you to manage your print jobs. Select the name of a print job (if you have more than one) and click Cancel Printing to clear that document from PrintMonitor and temporarily stop printing. You can select a print job and click Set Print Time to schedule that job for a later date. When all documents have finished printing, PrintMonitor quits on its own. (It will also quit if you shut down or restart the Classic environment, after it asks whether you'd prefer to print documents before shutting down or saving the documents until the next Classic session.)

FIGURE 4.21
PrintMonitor enables you to manage print jobs in the Classic environment.

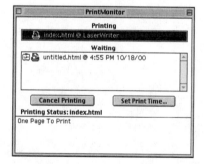

What's Next?

In this chapter you saw how to launch and work with applications and documents, both in Mac OS X and within the Classic environment. In the next chapter, we'll dig into using Mac OS X and personalizing Mac OS X for your own use. You'll learn to work with your home folder and its subfolders, set permissions for others to access your files, customize the interface, and set personal preferences. You'll also get some advice for setting up and using Mac OS X more efficiently and some tidbits for tweaking Mac OS X and making it work the way you want it to.

Chapter 5

Personalizing Mac OS X

When you start up your Mac, you may or may not see a login screen that asks for your username and password. If you're just beginning to use Mac OS X in a home or small-office setting, your Mac may have only one user—the user account you created when you first configured Mac OS X using the Setup Assistant. That user account is an administrative user, and, by default, the account is logged in to your Mac automatically whenever you start up the computer. (You can change this, as explained in Chapter 9, "Being the Administrator: Permissions, Settings, and Adding Users.")

If you do see a login screen, and your system administrator (or whoever has administrative responsibilities for your Mac) has given you a username and password, you may be a "regular" user on a multiuser Mac. You'll have a home folder and access to your personal documents, but your capability to alter other files on the Mac will be limited. This is as opposed to an administrative (Admin) user, who can alter system settings as well as personal settings. (It's easy to give a user Admin capabilities—again, this is discussed in Chapter 9.)

Mac OS X is designed, ultimately, to support multiple users, each with his or her own personal username and password. This multiuser approach is useful for two reasons. First, it allows different users to have completely different preferences and to maintain a personal workspace that's separate from other users' workspaces. Second, these user accounts prevent users from gaining access to the entire Mac's filesystem, so that only special administrator accounts can change important system files.

Mac OS X has a rigid, hierarchical system of folders and files that aren't supposed to be moved much. The structure implemented by Mac OS X is good, because it allows multiple users to log in to the computer and gain access to their own personal space on the Mac OS X system. Once logged in, you'll have access to your own files and preferences, as you've seen in previous chapters.

You'll also have your own home folder, where you can store documents, install applications, and otherwise organize your presence. If your Mac is connected to a network, you can use your login to access other resources elsewhere.

NOTE   This chapter discusses working on your Mac as an individual user—it's tailored to an examination of issues that affect all users. We'll examine some of the issues that involve making your Mac environment your own, as a user. If you are an administrator for your Mac (either as the primary user for a home machine or as the dedicated administrator in an office environment), see Chapter 9 for more on creating individual user accounts for the people who need to use or access your Mac. Chapter 9 also explains the responsibilities that an administrator has on a Mac OS X machine.

In this chapter:

◆ Working from Home

◆ Managing Permissions

◆ Personalizing Your Workspace

◆ Using the Finder Effectively

◆ Fast User Switching

◆ Setting User Preferences

Working from Home

For day-to-day work, your base of operations in Mac OS X is your home folder, which gives you a location on the Mac OS X system to store files and control other users' access to them. Also, the home folder enables you to store preferences and applications that make your workspace unique.

You can access your home folder quickly by clicking the Home icon in the Finder window sidebar or by selecting Go ➢ Home in the Finder's menu. The home folder is named for your username and is stored in the Users folder on your Mac.

Inside the home folder, you'll find four important folders: the Desktop folder, Library folder, Public folder, and Sites folder (see Figure 5.1). You'll also see some other folders available for convenience (and for working with Apple's applications such as iMovie, iTunes, and iPhoto): the Documents, Movies, Music, and Pictures folders.

NOTE　You can't rename your home folder, although you're free to create folders within your home folder and name them as you please. (You could create an Applications folder and a Games folder, for instance, to store programs that you don't necessarily need to share with other users on the Mac.) You shouldn't rename, move, or delete the existing folders within your personal folder (such as Desktop or Library), because the Mac OS and your applications require them as named.

FIGURE 5.1
A sample home folder

Your *Desktop* Folder

The Desktop folder contains the items that appear on your desktop—the background behind Finder windows and other applications. If an item is placed in this folder, it will appear on the desktop. It may seem a bit redundant to have both this folder and the actual desktop area, but the Desktop folder is there for a reason. It's an easy way to access desktop items quickly from within an Open or Save dialog box. For instance, if you need to open an item that's on your desktop from an Open dialog box, simply click the Desktop folder in the sidebar or press ⌘D and select the item.

As you saw in Chapter 4, "Using Applications," there is an Exposé shortcut that displays your Desktop with a single keystroke. By default, press F11 to move all your open windows out of the way and view your desktop; you can access any of the files and folders on your Desktop. Press F11 again to return your windows to their previous locations.

Your *Documents* Folder

You can store documents anywhere that you'd like in your home folder—again, the Documents folder is there simply as a convenience. Using the Documents icon in the Finder window sidebar, you can quickly maneuver to your Documents folder.

Store all your documents in your Documents folder, and you'll also make it easier to back up your Mac—you'll know where all your documents are at all times. You can create as many subfolders inside your Documents folder as you want to organize your files. You'll find that some applications, such as iChat, AppleWorks, and Microsoft Office, create folders here as the default location to store files. You can also store documents on your desktop, if you want, in which case you'd need to back up both the Documents folder and the Desktop folder. In fact, it's clearly a good idea to back up your entire home folder at least occasionally.

The Documents folder, by default, is also designed so that only you can read and write to that folder; other users, when logged in to the Mac, won't be able to see items you place in the Documents folder. This is an important distinction from your home folder, which does allow other users of your Mac to see items immediately inside it. (See the section "Managing Permissions," later in this chapter, for more details on read and write permissions.)

NOTE Similar to the Documents folder are the Movies, Pictures, and Music folders. These can be used in any way you'd like to store such files, although they're also used automatically by iMovie, iPhoto, and iTunes, respectively, for storing the files those applications create. If you use one or more of those applications and wonder where the files are stored, check those folders first.

Your *Public* Folder

Mac OS X creates a folder in your home folder called the Public folder, which is used for a very specific purpose. If you'd like to share files with others who have access to your Mac OS X computer, drag those items to your Public folder. By default, the contents of your Public folder are available to any user who is logged in to your Mac, either via a direct user account or over a network connection.

You'll also find that you can access the Public folders that are in other users' home folders, even if you can't access their other folders and files. Any user can read and copy the files that appear in another user's Public folder, but you cannot copy files *into* another user's Public folder. All Public folders have another special folder inside them—the Drop Box folder (see Figure 5.2). Although you can't open the Drop Box folder of another user (because you don't have read permission for it), you can drop items onto the Drop Box folder to copy them there. If you drop a file into another user's Drop Box folder, only that user will be able to see and access the file.

FIGURE 5.2
A Drop Box folder
appears inside each
user's Public folder.

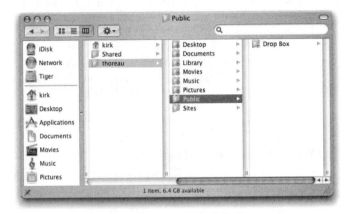

NOTE You also can see in Figure 5.2 how permissions work: The folders with the minus signs on them tell Kirk that his account doesn't have access to folders in the thoreau home folder. If you're not that user, you can't open them, read files from them, or write files to them. We'll cover more on permissions in the section "Managing Permissions."

Your *Library* Folder

Your personal Library folder isn't really for day-to-day use, but it's worthwhile to know what's in there. The Library folder holds general preferences, data files, and other settings files required by your applications. Remember, whenever you launch an application—even if it's in the main Applications folder on the hard disk—you get your own preferences and settings for that application. Those preferences files are stored, predictably enough, in the Preferences folder inside your Library folder.

Besides preferences and data files, you'll find some other interesting subfolders within your Library folder. For instance, the Fonts folder is a repository for any personal fonts you want to install. Once installed, these fonts will be available in the applications that you use, but they won't appear in other users' Font panels. This can be convenient if you like to work with certain fonts but don't want (or don't have permission) to install them in the main Library folder on your Mac's hard disk.

The Application Support folder is where you'll find special data and temporary files stored by some of your applications. The Mail folder inside your Library folder holds information about your different POP or IMAP accounts. (See Chapter 12, "Managing E-Mail," for more on the Mail application and checking e-mail accounts.) The Mailboxes folder, inside your Mail folder, is where all of your sorted mail is stored.

What's most interesting about the Mail folder is how easy it makes it to back up your e-mail. Just copy the Mail folder to a removable disk or otherwise put this folder into your regular backup rotation (see Chapter 26, "Hard Disk Care, File Security, and Maintenance"). If you ever need to restore your e-mail files, you just copy the backup folders back into your Library folder.

The *Sites* Folder

The Sites folder is where you can store HTML documents and images for your own personal website. If web sharing is turned on, others can access your website via a web browser, using a combination of the Mac's hostname, domain, and your username, as in http://www.mycompany.com/~thoreau/ or http://192.168.1.3/~thoreau/. Turning on web sharing and making websites available via your Mac is discussed in Chapter 24, "Web Serving, FTP Serving, and Net Security."

Managing Permissions

Mac OS X uses *permissions* to determine which users may read or write to files within different folders on your Mac. Whenever a user (whether a local user or one accessing your Mac over a network) attempts to access a particular folder on the Mac OS X system, the OS takes a look at the permissions allowed by the owner of that folder. If all users have permission to access the folder or, more likely, if the user is an administrator and you've given the administrator group permission to access the folder, the OS will let the user access the folder.

In most cases, you may never need to worry about permissions. If you are the only user on your Mac, you'll never need to change permissions, although you may need to know about them if you are troubleshooting system problems. (See Chapter 29 for more on permissions and troubleshooting.) Conversely, if you work in an environment where your Mac is managed by an administrator, you probably won't be allowed to change any permissions; that's generally the administrator's job.

But if your Mac is accessible to other users and you are the administrator—either a home Mac with several users or a Mac in a small business—you'll need to understand the concept behind permissions.

WARNING   If another administrative user restarts your Mac into Mac OS 9 using the Startup Disk pane of System Preferences, that user will have access to all your files; permission settings in Mac OS X don't restrict users in Mac OS 9. (There also are ways to access files as the superuser using the Terminal command line, as discussed in Chapter 22, "Terminal and the Command Line," and Chapter 28, "Solving System-Level Problems.") Realize that storing files with certain permissions isn't completely secure and private, particularly if other users have administrator access on your Mac. To secure files, you need to encrypt them, as discussed in chapter.

You are the owner of your home folder and any subfolders you create within it—so you alone determine who gets access to them. Using the Show Info command in the Finder, you can set four access levels for any or all of your folders:

◆ With *Read Only* access, a user can open the files or documents within a folder but cannot save documents in that folder, copy files to it, rename it, or delete files in it. Read access also makes it possible for other users to launch applications or open and view files that you've stored in your file folders.

◆ With *Write Only* access, also called *Drop Box*, the user can save and copy items into the folder but cannot see or open items already in the folder.

◆ With *Read & Write* access, the user has full access to the folder.

◆ A fourth option, *No Access*, means the user does not have permission to access the folder at all.

To set permissions for one of your folders, select it in a Finder window and choose File ➢ Get Info or press ⌘I. In the Info window, click the disclosure triangle labeled Ownership & Permissions, and you'll see the permissions options (see Figure 5.3). You'll need to click the padlock icon to unlock the options. You'll then be able to set the permissions for the owner, permissions for a particular group, and permissions for others (meaning all other users, regardless of their group status).

FIGURE 5.3

The Permissions options for a folder in Kirk's home folder

Most likely, you won't want to change the permissions for the owner of the folder, because that's you. However, you *can*; click the menu and select a different privilege level.

In the Group section, you can change both the group and the permissions for that group. By default, the group is you again—but you can change that to the Admin group, for instance, if you'd like to give others who have Admin status access to this folder. (In fact, the group may already be set to Staff or Wheel if you've installed Mac OS X 10.4 over an earlier version of the OS.)

NOTE   You can change Owner or Group, if desired, although doing so generally isn't necessary. To change them, click the padlock icon to authenticate (you may need to enter an administrator's username and password). If you aren't an administrator, you can't change the Group setting, even for your own files and folders.

Besides setting permissions for the owner and the group, you also can do so for everybody else on the system. For instance, you may want everyone on the system to be able to read files but only administrators to have read and write access. You can set up that scenario (or other similar scenarios) by selecting the Read Only level for the Others entry. Just open its Permissions portion of the Info window and select that level.

WARNING   When you set a level for Others, it applies to anyone with access to the system. It's generally wise to not assign full read and write access to Others, because limiting permissions will keep your files (and your Mac OS X system) more secure from mischief or mistakes.

Finally, once you've chosen permissions for a folder, you may decide that you want all items and subfolders of the folder to have the same permissions. Instead of setting them individually, you can click the Apply to Enclosed Items button to copy the same privilege settings to all the folders enclosed by the current folder.

WARNING   Think carefully before clicking the Apply to Enclosed Items button, because previously set subfolder permissions will be negated.

When you've finished setting permissions, click the Info window's Close button. Your changes will then be made, and new permissions will be set.

The *Shared* Folder

Mac OS X offers another special folder that any user, regardless of account type, can access. The Shared folder inside the main Users folder is designed to allow all users on the Mac to access files that should be made public. For instance, if you have created a particular memo or report that all users of this Mac should be able to access, you can store that document in the Shared folder. Other users then can read the document and save any changes they make to the Shared folder, if desired.

You'll find other uses for the Shared folder, too. Todd stores MP3 music files in the Shared folder so that different users on his Macs who decide to launch iTunes can access them. Also, when he downloads a third-party application, game, or utility program, he often puts it in a Downloads folder that he's created within the Shared folder so that others can access it without needing to spend the time downloading that item again.

It's important to note the permissions that are assigned to items you move to, or create within, the Shared folder. In most cases, you (as owner) will have read and write permissions, while all other users will have read-only permissions. This is often okay, but sometimes you may want to change the permissions for items you save in the Shared folder so that other users have read and write permissions. This is particularly true if you've created a folder within the Shared folder; if you don't change the permissions to read and write for Others, those other users will not be able to save items within that folder.

Installing Personal Applications

Mac OS X lets you install applications for your personal use within your home folder. Doing so is useful when an application won't be of interest to the other users on your Mac, or when you don't have an administrator's account, which would allow you to install system-wide applications. Generally, applications are installed in the main Applications folder so that they will be available to all users. (If that's your goal, see Chapter 9.) In more controlled environments, such as computer labs and work settings, installing personal applications in the home folder can be a convenience.

If you are the only user of your Mac, you may not find it all that useful to install personal applications in your home folder. Certain situations may still lend themselves to that type of installation—for instance, if you have a financial program that you don't want the kids to launch and play with from their own personal accounts.

NOTE   Remember, other users can still launch applications in your home folder or a subfolder if those users have read access to the folder.

To install an application, you'll need to find and launch the program's installer. If the program is on a CD or other removable media, it should be easy to install. Simply skip down to the "Installer Applications" section. If the application is one that you've downloaded from the Internet, you'll first need to unarchive the downloaded file.

OPENING ARCHIVES

Most applications that you download for Mac OS X will be in one of two forms. The StuffIt archive file is a common file format that's been carried over from the Classic Mac OS; "unstuffing" this sort of archive is done using the StuffIt Expander application, which you can download from www .stuffit.com. The other type of archive, which is becoming increasingly common on Mac OS X, is a Zip archive. This form of compression is now prevalent because it is built into the Mac OS X Finder. You can expand this type of archive by simply double-clicking its file.

An *archive* is a file that's created for storage or transfer of a group of files or an application and its associated support files. Archives are often created from entire folders or folder hierarchies and can include many different files. Using a special application, all the folders and files are turned into a single archive file to make them easier to track, name, and transmit over the Internet or a similar network.

NOTE   Files, including archives, often will be compressed before they're transmitted over the Internet. Using a sophisticated algorithm, the compression tool is able to remove redundant information from the file, making it smaller but unusable until it is expanded again. See Chapter 11, "The Web, Online Security, .Mac, Sherlock, and iChat," for more on downloading and dealing with compressed files.

You generally can tell how an archive has been stored by its filename extension. A StuffIt archive (which is both archived and compressed) will have a .sit filename extension. Zip archives have .zip extensions. Other possible archive formats you may see include TAR archives compressed with GZIP with a .gz (or sometimes .tgz or .tar.gz) extension, and TAR archives not compressed with GZIP with a .tar extension. GZIP files, regardless of whether they've been archived with TAR, may have a .z extension. Thus, if an archive has been compressed, you'll likely see a filename extension such as .sit, .zip, .tar, .gz, .z, or .tgz.

Certain types of Zip files can be decompressed automatically by the Finder in Mac OS X. Simply double-click the archive to decompress it. These archives have a .zip extension and icon:

Archive.zip

The easiest way to decompress any of the non-Zip types of compressed files is simply to double-click the files. If you see an icon with a zipper on it, like the Zip archive in the preceding graphic, this means that Mac OS X can decompress the file on its own. For other types of files, if you have installed Stuffit Expander, double-clicking should open the Stuffit Expander application and decompress the file automatically. Once the file is expanded, you'll probably see one of three formats:

◆ The full application (which you simply double-click to begin using)

◆ A disk image (which you can double-click to mount)

◆ An installer application

A disk image is a file that acts like a removable disk. When you double-click the image file, a disk icon appears on your desktop. This disk icon works just like a removable disk such as an Iomega Zip disk or a CD. (You also unmount a disk image icon in the same way: drag the disk icon to the Trash.

Note, however, that dragging the disk image *file*—the one with the .img or .dmg extension—to the Trash will place the file in the Trash for deletion.)

Once the disk icon is mounted, double-click the disk icon, and you'll see its contents in a Finder window, as shown in Figure 5.4.

FIGURE 5.4

After you double-click a disk image file (the file with the .dmg extension), a disk icon appears, along with the image's contents, in a Finder window.

Some disk images simply contain files and folders, but others may also contain graphics and text. If the contents of the disk image include an installer application, double-click the installer. Often, though, the disk image will simply contain a full version of the application (and any other necessary files) that you can drag to your home folder or a subfolder within your home folder. Once the application is installed, it's ready to run.

NOTE   Working with and even creating disk images is covered in more depth in Chapter 26.

INSTALLER APPLICATIONS

If you have an application that installs itself with an installer application, you can begin simply by double-clicking the installer. There are a few different types of installers. An installer package will most likely end with the filename extension .pkg or .mpkg, and, when double-clicked, it will launch Mac OS X's built-in Installer application. (This installer is commonly used with Mac OS X–only applications built in the Cocoa environment.)

Click the Install button, and the installer will step you through the process. You'll select a destination folder (most likely the Applications subfolder of your home folder) and otherwise customize the installation. Once the installation is completed, you should be able to access the new application by double-clicking it in your home folder or using any of the other methods described in Chapter 4.

Some applications use third-party installers, such as the Installer Vise application. This is often the case for Carbon applications that can be installed for either Mac OS 9 or Mac OS X. If you see such an installer, shown in Figure 5.5, be aware that you have the option of selecting a destination for the installation. After you choose what you want to install and then click Install, you're prompted to select a location for the application. Some other types of installers may have an Install Location menu or button that allows you to select a location for the application.

FIGURE 5.5
Third-party installer applications are used with some programs.

When the installer is finished, a new Finder window should appear, showing you the installed application. Double-click its icon to begin working with it.

Personalizing Your Workspace

This section takes a look at some of the options you have for the different ways that you can work with Mac OS X. In particular, it focuses on some of the technologies offered by the Finder and other interface elements that are optional—you don't have to work with them, but it's worthwhile to see their real power. We'd also like to discuss briefly some other tools for customizing the interface and making Mac OS X work they way you want it to.

Using Aliases

Once you begin working with applications and documents, you'll be able to more fully appreciate the power of *aliases*, those special icons that we've only hinted at so far. Aliases are essentially "empty" files—little more than icons, really—that the Mac OS uses to reference another item.

Aliases enable you to access a particular file from more than one place in the hierarchy of your folders. If you'd like to have an icon for accessing a particular document or folder from the desktop, you can create an alias there. If you want to create a folder for a particular project and be able to easily get at the necessary applications and documents in the same folder for convenience, you can employ aliases (see Figure 5.6).

FIGURE 5.6
You can create a project folder that mixes in aliases for documents, folders, and applications.

Consider the example in Figure 5.6. You wouldn't want to *move* the QuickTime Player to the project folder because you're likely to want to use it for other projects. Also, moving applications around in Mac OS X can sometimes keep them from working properly. You can use aliases in your own folders to represent those items. When you launch the alias, it finds the original item and executes it for you.

Aliases offer another advantage. When you delete an alias, you're simply deleting the alias file, not the original document. You can delete aliases without worrying about accidentally deleting important folders, documents, or applications.

TIP   You can create an alias of an item located elsewhere on a network. When you double-click the alias, the network connection will be accessed, if possible. If the connection isn't available, you'll see a dialog box that enables you to log in to the network volume to access the item. An alias offers a quick and convenient way to access often-used items stored on a network volume.

CREATING AN ALIAS

If you've read Chapter 3, "The Finder," you know how to create a duplicate. Creating an alias is really no different—except for the Finder command. To create an alias, simply select the item you'd like to create an alias of and then choose File ➤ Make Alias from the Finder menu or press ⌘L.

By default, the alias will include the word *alias* at the end of its name to differentiate it from the original file. (Remember, files must have unique filenames if they're stored in the same folder.) The alias icon will also include a small curving arrow. The name of the alias will be highlighted so that you can immediately type in a new name, if desired. You can move, duplicate, or copy the alias to any other folder or disk where you have access permissions.

You also can create an alias by holding down modifier keys as you drag an item to a new folder. When you drag an icon while holding down the Option and ⌘ keys, you're indicating to the Mac OS that you don't intend to copy or move the item but you do intend to create an alias. While you're holding down the modifier keys, you'll see a small curved arrow as part of the mouse pointer to indicate that you're creating an alias.

When you release the mouse button, the alias is created in the folder to which you've dragged the item. The alias will not have the word alias appended to its name because you are creating it in a location different from the original file. However, it will have a small curved arrow as part of its icon.

TIP   After an alias is created, you can rename it without affecting the link to the original. If you make an alias of the file Walden and change the name of the alias to Leaves of Grass, double-clicking the alias will still launch Walden.

LOCATING THE ORIGINAL

The Finder includes a command that makes it easy to locate the original file that an alias is pointing to. Select the alias and choose File ➤ Show Original in the Finder or press ⌘R. The original item's parent folder will open, and the original item will appear on-screen in the frontmost Finder window.

SELECTING A NEW ORIGINAL

Although you can select a new original for an alias at any time, the main reason for doing so is a *broken* alias. An alias can break—that is, it no longer is able to locate the original—for a variety of reasons: the original was deleted, the alias was moved to a network disk, the original was on a removable disk that's no longer available, or the permissions for a folder changed.

If an alias stops working, it's conceivable that you could fix it. Select the alias and choose File ➤ Get Info. In the Info window, click the General triangle and then click the Select New Original button. (The button's label doesn't seem to strike the Apple engineers as a paradox, so that's its name. See Figure 5.7.) The Select New Original dialog box then appears.

FIGURE 5.7
The Info window enables you to select a "new" original file for a broken alias.

In the Select New Original dialog box, locate the file that you want the alias to point to. Once you've selected that item, click the Choose button. The alias will launch that new item (even if it's the *old* item that you've managed to track down) whenever it's double-clicked.

Customizing the Dock

The Dock is one of the main tools you use to manage applications in Mac OS X. It is a multipurpose tool—part launcher, part application switcher, and part window manager. To get the most out of the Dock, you can customize it, deciding how much to allow the Dock to get in your way, where to position it, and so on.

SETTING THE DOCK'S PREFERENCES

The more icons you have on the Dock—of any variety—the more it gets filled up. As it fills, it reaches toward the ends of the screen, and when it gets there, the icons start to get smaller. This can eventually make the icons hard to read.

The solution is in the Dock Preferences dialog box. Choose Dock ➤ Dock Preferences from the Apple menu in the top-left corner of your screen. This launches the System Preferences application and displays the Dock options, shown in Figure 5.8.

FIGURE 5.8

The Dock options in the System Preferences application

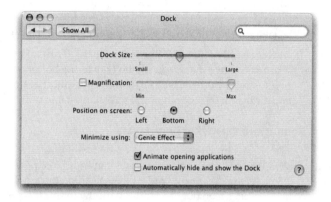

Now you'll see a few settings that relate to the Dock:

Dock Size Use the slider to change the size of the Dock, sliding between Small and Large. Note that you can make the Dock only as large as will currently fit, given the number of icons on the Dock. (Once you have enough icons to fill the screen, the icons automatically become smaller to accommodate more.)

TIP You can also change the size of the Dock using only the mouse. Point the mouse to the dividing line between the application side and the document side of the Dock. The pointer should change to a two-sided arrow. Hold down the mouse button and drag the mouse upward to make the Dock bigger, or drag it downward to make the Dock smaller. Likewise, you can access the rest of these Dock settings by Control+clicking (or right-clicking, if you have a two-button mouse) on the Dock's dividing line and choosing items from the pop-up menu.

Magnification Turn this on (by clicking its check box), and an interesting thing happens: as you run the mouse pointer along the Dock, each icon will be magnified so that you can see it more easily. This feature makes it possible for you to have more items on the Dock than you can see comfortably; when you mouse-over the icons, their true purposes will be revealed. Notice also that if the Magnification slider is set the same as the Dock Size slider, there's no magnification until the Dock fills with icons and begins to shrink them to accommodate them all.

Position on Screen Choose whether you'd like the Dock to appear at the bottom of the screen or on the left or right side.

Minimize Using Choose the graphical behavior for items that you want to minimize to the Dock. The Genie effect is really just for looks, and the Scale effect is less processor intensive and should speed up the apparent operation of your Mac just a little bit.

Animate Opening Applications If this option is on, application icons will seem to bounce up and down as they're starting up, to indicate that they've been launched successfully. You can turn off this behavior if you find it distracting or annoying or if you feel it slows your Mac down slightly.

Automatically Hide and Show the Dock Turn on this option, and the Dock will appear only when you move the mouse all the way to the bottom of the screen. When you pull the mouse pointer away from the bottom (to move it around in applications or documents), the Dock will disappear below the bottom of the screen, invisible until you move the mouse to the bottom again.

ADDING AND REMOVING DOCK ITEMS

The Dock isn't much use to you as a launcher if you can't make your own decisions as to what items you want to put there. Of course, you can—and it's quite simple.

If you have a document, folder, or application that you'd like to add as an icon on the Dock, simply drag that item's icon out of a Finder window (or off the desktop) and down to the Dock. (Remember that applications go to the left of the dividing line and documents and folders go to the right. When you've dragged the icon to the Dock, you should notice some space open up; it's showing you where the icon for this item will appear if you release the mouse button. (Notice also in the following graphic that the original Dictionary icon is still in its Finder window, suggesting that the application itself hasn't been moved or altered.)

You can drag the item to different locations on the Dock if you'd prefer that it appear in another place. Once you've found your chosen spot, release the mouse button, and an icon for that item is created.

By doing this, you're simply creating an alias to the document, folder, or application. It isn't *moved* to the Dock, so the original item will still be stored in your folder in the same place it was before you dragged its icon to the Dock.

Once you've got an alias on the Dock, you can drag it around on the Dock to change its location, or you can remove it altogether. To move an item, point to it with the mouse and then click and drag it left or right on the Dock until you find the location you like.

Another way to add an application icon to the Dock is to do so when the application is running. If this is the case, click the application icon and hold your mouse button down; a menu displays. Select Keep in Dock to add that icon to the Dock, even after you quit the application. Note that this menu offers other options:

◆ Open at Login, which adds the application to your Login Items

◆ Show in Finder, which opens a Finder window showing the location of the application

◆ Hide, which hides the application's window(s)

◆ Quit, which quits the application

To remove an icon, simply drag it up and off the Dock. With the icon hovering over the desktop, release the mouse button. You'll see a small, animated puff of smoke, and the Mac plays a sound to show that the icon is now gone from the Dock. This doesn't erase or otherwise alter the original file or folder; it simply lets you know in a cute way that the alias has been removed from the Dock.

CHANGING FOLDER (AND DISK) ICONS

If you add a folder or disk to the Dock, you'll notice that it's just a plain folder icon; the folder can be tough to differentiate if, for instance, you add another folder. They'll look the exact same in most cases. (The obvious exceptions are the folders inside your home folder, some of which have special icons.) The trick is to give the folder a unique icon to make it stand out on the Dock. You can do that by cutting and pasting a new icon into the General area of the folder's Info window. Copy a suitable image to the clipboard and then highlight the folder's icon in its Info window and paste the image using the Edit ➢ Paste command.

You can create your own folder icons (make them 128 pixels by 128 pixels so that they scale nicely), or you can download them from various locations, including popular websites such as The Iconfactory (www.iconfactory.com), Icons.cx (www.icons.cx), and InterfaceLIFT (http://interfacelift.com/icons-mac/).

Adding Menu Bar Icons

Mac OS X uses menu bar icons for some of its preferences to offer quick-access menus that are handily situated on the menu bar that's always at the top of the screen. Most of these menu bar icons are Apple-created icons that are added via panes in the System Preferences application, but some third-party applications and preferences panes add menu bar icons as well.

Most of the menu bar icons available in Mac OS X can be turned on and off from the different panes of the System Preferences application. These include such icons as a volume menu, a display menu, an eject icon, and, for iBooks and Powerbooks, a battery icon. In addition, some applications use menu bar icons: Apple's iChat gives you a quick-access icon, and many third-party programs do as well.

In most cases, you'll turn these icons on by clicking check boxes in preferences panes; this is the case, for example, with the displays menu: check Show Displays in Menu Bar in the Displays preferences pane to activate this menu bar icon.

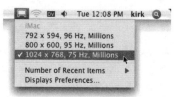

Some menu bar icons may be added by third-party applications. In most cases, these icons are optional; the program's preferences generally allow you to display or remove the icon.

With most menu bar icons, including Apple's, you can hold down the ⌘ key and drag them off of the menu bar (or rearrange them) if you no longer need to see them. To reinstate an icon, simply do so the way you would have in the first place—activate the menu bar icon in System Preferences or launch the appropriate application.

Using Finder Effectively

As you're working in the Finder, no doubt you'll come to appreciate some of its finer points. The Finder in Mac OS X provides many ways to work with your files, including the Finder window sidebar, where you can add commonly used folders, and the different Finder views. (The Finder views are described in Chapter 3.)

Here are some tips that may help you get the most out of the Finder and help you work more productively:

Use Column view   It may seem more comfortable at first to use the standard approach to digging through folders and opening windows to get to things, and fortunately the Finder allows this. You can use Icon view all the time, either opening folders in the same window or opening them in new windows by checking the Always Open Folders in a New Window option in Finder Preferences. However, the Column view is very powerful, and we recommend that you try it out for a while. One trick is to use Column view in conjunction with at least two Finder windows (even if one is uses Icon view) on the screen at once (see Figure 5.9). If you do this, you'll find it's easy to navigate quickly to almost any part of your hard disk (or attached volumes) and move files around quickly.

FIGURE 5.9
Using Column view and at least two windows, you'll be able to navigate quickly and move files around easily.

Move (or hide) the Dock By default, the Dock appears at the bottom of the screen and is always visible. Unfortunately, it ends up hiding a lot of windows' bottom controls because of that placement and the fact that Apple has made the Dock so that items can be placed "below" it. (In many operating systems that have something similar to the Dock, such as the Taskbar in Windows, it's a fixed part of the bottom of the display that can't overlap document windows.) One solution is to try putting the Dock on one of side of the screen or the other (see Figure 5.10). You also can use the Dock Hiding option (Apple menu ➤ Dock ➤ Turn Hiding On) to hide the Dock when it's not in use.

FIGURE 5.10

Placing the Dock on the side of your display can make it a convenient drag-and-drop target and keep it from overlapping the bottoms of windows.

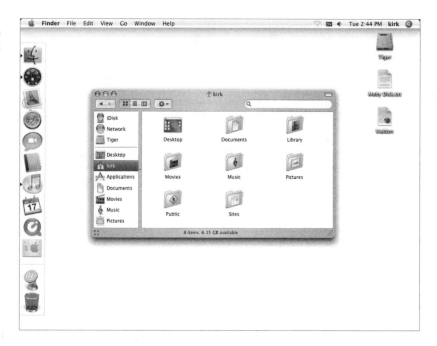

NOTE With the Finder window Sidebar, you may find you don't mind turning off the Finder's ability to place mounted disks and CDs on the desktop. Choose Finder ➤ Preferences and click the General icon to select which items will appear on the desktop.

Maximize the Dock Not everyone will agree with this one, but Todd likes to drag the Dock out to its maximum size, even if that makes the icons a little large. Why? Because it anchors the Finder and Trash icons on either side of the screen, so that as you launch or quit applications, those icons don't move around too much. (They'll get smaller and larger, but they won't move from the edge.) Your hand can get used to where those items are located, and you may find yourself moving the mouse to a spot where they aren't anymore, after you've developed some muscle memory. If the Dock is full size at all times, that muscle memory will prove a bit more useful. (You can also use some third-party utilities, such as TinkerTool—www.bresink.de/osx—to anchor the Dock to the left or right side of the screen.)

Add to your Sidebar Mac OS X enables you to drag folders from a Finder window to the Sidebar, adding them instantly as toolbar items. You can then single-click that folder to see it immediately or drag items to that folder's icon to store them in that folder. We find this incredibly convenient for quickly accessing the projects we're working on. When a project is over, we simply drag the icon off the toolbar. Here's how a folder looks as it's being added:

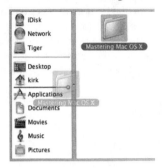

You can also select a folder and press ⌘T to add it to the Sidebar. If you do this, it gets added to the bottom of the Sidebar, but you can move it to the position where you'd like to keep it.

Learn Finder keyboard shortcuts   One of the best ways to save time is to use your hands instead of your mouse. When you keep your hands on the keyboard, you can work faster, and you'll also keep your wrists and shoulders in better shape—constantly moving from keyboard to mouse to keyboard to mouse gives your tendons and muscles a workout and may contribute to repetitive stress injury. The Finder offers a plethora of keyboard shortcuts, most of which are shown in the various Finder menus. Start with this one to save lots of time: When you want to move files to the Trash, select the files and then press ⌘Delete. This is much faster than selecting files and dragging them to the Trash. When you want to delete the Trash, just press ⌘Shift+Delete. For more keyboard shortcuts (to open new windows, create new folders, create aliases, and even go to different folders quickly), check the Finder menus.

Fast User Switching

If you have more than one user account on your Mac, Fast User Switching allows you to switch between user accounts without first logging out. This is a great feature for Macs that have multiple users—a family setting comes to mind—although this could work well in an office environment, too.

Say you're at home working on a word processing document, but you decide to stand and stretch for a few minutes away from the Mac. Meanwhile, a family member wants to check her mail. She can sit down, quickly switch to her account, and check her mail, and then she can log out or let you switch back to your account. All this happens without you closing all your applications and logging out first—that's what makes this feature so cool.

Enabling Fast User Switching is easy. If you've created multiple user accounts (see Chapter 9), then you can enable Fast User Switching from the Accounts pane in System Preferences; click the Login Options button (at the bottom of the list of users) and then turn on the Enable Fast User Switching option.

A dialog sheet appears, warning you to enable this only if you trust the other users of your Mac. If that's the case, click OK. Choose one of three options to indicate how you want usernames to display:

♦ Name, which displays the user's full name in the menu bar; this can take up a lot of space.

♦ Short Name, which displays just the short username.

♦ Icon, which displays a silhouette icon, not indicating which user is logged in at any given time.

The first thing you'll notice on your Mac's screen is that your account name has been added to the menu bar at the top. That's the Fast User Switching menu. Whenever you want to log in a new user or switch to a different account, simply select that user—or the Login Window option—from this menu:

Now, if this user is not currently logged in, you'll see a login window that enables you to enter a password. If you enter the password successfully, you'll be treated to a dramatic animation on-screen—the entire desktop turns into a cube and rotates one turn to reveal the new user's desktop. After a few seconds, that user is ready to compute using his or her own desktop, files, and preferences.

To switch back, simply choose another name in the Fast User Switching menu or, if you're done with a particular account, choose Log Out from the Apple menu. When you're returned to the login window, you'll see a small check mark next to any users who are still logged in to the Mac.

WARNING   It's important to save any critical work before allowing the Mac to switch to another user. If another user decides to restart the Mac while your session is still open—and that user is an administrator—you could lose changes in your open documents if that user goes ahead with the restart.

TIP   Fast User Switching can be handy for one person, too, because it enables you to switch quickly to the Login Window, thus securing the computer if you get up to walk around.

Setting User Preferences

Another aspect of managing your personal workspace is setting preferences that affect it. The System Preferences application, one could argue, is somewhat poorly named because it offers options that affect both the entire system (including all users—to be set from an administrator's account) and your personal workspace. We'll talk about that second category here. (Chapter 9 describes how to use administrator preferences.)

To set the preferences in System Preferences, launch the application. The quickest way is to select System Preferences from the Apple menu. Most likely, a System Preferences icon is already on your Dock, waiting to be single-clicked. If you don't find it there, System Preferences can be found in the main Applications folder. When it's launched, you'll see the main System Preferences window (see Figure 5.11).

FIGURE 5.11
The System Preferences
window

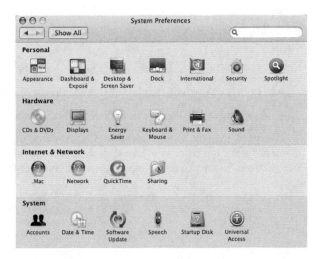

The System Preferences window contains several groups of icons, each of which represents what Mac OS X calls a *pane*, which is used to change different settings. When you click a given pane's icon, the window changes to show that pane and allow you to make choices.

The only part of the window that doesn't change is the toolbar at the top, which includes the Show All icon, Back and Forward buttons, and a Search field. If you're looking for specific settings, and you don't know which pane they appear in, type a few letters of an appropriate word in the Search field. As you type, a list displays showing the different tasks available, and "spotlights" highlight the different icons; the brightest icon represents the selected text in the search results. You can move through this list by using the up and down arrow keys; as you do so, the different preferences panes highlight according to your current selection.

TIP You can view the panes in the System Preferences window in two different ways. Choose View ➢ Organize by Categories to see the default view or choose View ➢ Organize Alphabetically to see the panes listed in alphabetical order.

Administrator Settings

Note that not every item enables you to edit the settings. In some cases, settings can be changed only by an account with administrator permissions. In those panes, you'll see a small padlock icon that indicates that you can't edit items in the window. The Preferences screens that are disabled for user editing are Accounts, Date & Time, Energy Saver, Network, Sharing, and the Startup Disk pane.

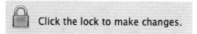

If you know the administrator's password or your account has administrator permissions, however, you can edit these items. Simply click the padlock icon and enter an administrator's account name and password. Then click OK. If Mac OS X recognizes the login as a valid administrator's account, you'll be able to edit those options. (System administrator settings are covered in Chapter 9.)

User Settings

If you're logged in to a regular (non-administrator) user account, you can still work in a number of System Preferences panes, and those preferences will affect only your personal workspace. Among the Mac OS Preferences panes you can control are .Mac, Accounts, Appearance, CDs & DVDs, Classic, Desktop & Screen Saver, Displays, Dock, Exposé, International, Keyboard & Mouse, QuickTime, Security, Sound, Speech, and Universal Access. We will cover some of these panes in more depth in later chapters; however, we'll take a brief look at them here (in alphabetical order).

.MAC

The .Mac pane is used to enter your .Mac account name and password if you have them, which enables the Mac OS to access your iDisk, Mac.com e-mail account, and other .Mac items automatically. You can also use this preferences pane to set iSync settings, so you can synchronize some of your Mac's data with another Mac. See Chapter 11 for more on using .Mac.

ACCOUNTS

While you can't create accounts or access other users' accounts without an administrator's password, you can make changes to your own account in the Accounts pane. Here's a look at the options:

◆ Select the Password tab to change your full name, password, or password hint; you can also edit your Address Book card from this tab.

◆ On the Picture tab, you can select a new picture or click the Edit button to edit the current picture and/or load one from disk.

◆ On the Login Items tab, you can select and manage the items that start up automatically whenever you log in to this account.

Login items are files or applications that open each time you log in to your account. To add items that launch automatically when you log in, click the Add (+) button. This displays an Open dialog box where you can locate and select applications that you want to run at the beginning of your sessions. (You also can drag and drop applications or documents from Finder windows into this list, if desired.)

Using the check boxes, you can determine whether or not each item should be hidden when it launches. (Items in the list will always launch until they're removed, but you can opt to have them launch in the background, hidden from view, until you select them in the Dock.) These items can be applications or utilities (such as Stickies) that you like to be greeted with every time you log in to your Mac, as shown in Figure 5.12.

FIGURE 5.12
After adding some items to the Login Items pane, you can click their check boxes to hide them at login.

To remove an item from the list, select it and click the delete button (–). That item won't launch when you sign in to your account. Note that some applications—including drivers for mice, keyboards or scanners—may install their own login items. In Figure 5.12, you see the iTunesHelper application, a background program installed by iTunes. Make sure not to remove any such login items; doing so may prevent certain programs from working correctly. If you're not sure where a specific login item comes from, move your pointer over its name; a tooltip displays showing you the path of the item.

APPEARANCE

The Appearance pane enables you to choose appearance and behavior options for Mac OS X's windows and menus. At the top of the panel you can select Appearance. By default, the color choices are Blue and Graphite.

The Blue appearance settings cause scroll bars and buttons to appear blue (or aqua) in color, whereas the Graphite appearance tones that down to a more subtle gray. Graphite is deemed better for graphic artists and designers whose judgment of colors in photo, multimedia, or page-design programs may be affected by the additional color that the aqua scheme adds to windows and scroll bars. You can also choose a personalized Highlight color for how the selection area in menus and applications will look.

In the middle of the pane are options to customize the appearance of scroll arrows in your windows and to customize the behavior of scroll bars. In addition, you can choose to use smooth scrolling (a different type of scrolling in text and browser windows) and choose whether a double-click on a window's title bar minimizes the window, sending it into the Dock.

Below that you can choose the number of recent items that should appear in the corresponding menus within the Apple menu. At the bottom of the pane, you can customize the behavior of font smoothing by selecting a scheme in the Font Smoothing Type menu and choosing the size at which font smoothing should be turned off.

NOTE　Font smoothing is a technology that's used to make text on your Mac's display look more like the smooth text you'd find in a magazine or on a printed page. It can have the effect of looking blurry, however, so if you're having trouble reading items on the screen, consider changing the font-smoothing setting.

CDs & DVDs

On this pane you can choose a series of behaviors that answer the question, "What happens when a disc is inserted in the Mac?" Because Mac OS X offers a variety of different disc reading, burning, and playing applications, you can use the items in this pane to decide which one will be used in a given circumstance. Simply select one of the options in the menu next to each scenario (When You Insert a Blank CD, When You Insert a Music CD, and so on). Note that some of the options are the default Apple applications for that type of disc, while others give you the opportunity to launch an AppleScript script or a third-party application. See Chapter 3 for more on burning CDs in the Finder and Chapter 26 for more on burning CDs from Disk Utility.

CLASSIC

The Classic pane enables you to select the disk volume (from the Select a Startup Volume list) to be used for starting up the Classic Mac OS environment. (Mac OS X uses Classic to run older Macintosh applications; you won't see this preferences pane if you don't have a Classic System Folder installed. See Chapter 4 for details.) You can also determine whether or not Classic should be started up when you log in. If you choose to turn on Start Classic When You Log In, the Classic environment will launch and operate in the background once you log in, leaving less of your system RAM available for Mac OS X native applications. The advantage of background operation is that you won't encounter any delays when starting up an application that requires Classic; the disadvantage of leaving Classic running in the background is that your entire Mac may run much more slowly when Classic is active, particularly if you don't have a great deal of RAM installed.

You also can start, restart, and force-quit the Classic environment from within the Classic pane; these and the Advanced options are covered in more depth in Chapter 27, "Fixing Applications and Managing Classic."

DASHBOARD & EXPOSÉ

This preferences pane lets you select screen corners and keyboard and mouse shortcuts to invoke Dashboard and Exposé. Both of these technologies, and the settings in this preferences pane, are discussed in Chapter 4.

DESKTOP & SCREEN SAVER

This pane covers two areas and has two tabs. The Desktop tab is where you can choose the appearance of the desktop area. First, choose a collection from the left side of the screen and then click the color swatch or image that you'd like to use. Apple provides a number of desktop images, such as those in the Nature, Plants, and Black & White folders, but you can also select from iPhoto albums if you use iPhoto. (This program is not included with Mac OS X; it is part of iLife and is included with new Macs, or is available for purchase separately.)

To use your own image, either drag it from the desktop to the image area at the top of the screen and drop it or select the Choose Folder command to view an Open dialog box that you can use to locate a folder of pictures.

Note also the Change Picture option; turn it on, and you can choose an interval to automatically rotate the images that appear on the desktop.

The Screen Saver tab enables you to set options for Mac OS X's built-in screensaver. In theory, a screensaver prevents a monitor from burning in a particular screen image that appears on the screen for too long. (You may have seen the effect on older ATM displays at your bank.) Modern CRT and LCD screens don't suffer from burn-in, so screensavers are really designed more for entertainment and, in the case of Mac OS X, for additional password security.

On the Screen Saver tab, select the screensaver you want to use from the list. The item Pictures Folder is a special case—it will use images you place in your personal Pictures folder (inside your home folder) to create a custom screensaver. You can also select Choose Folder if you want to select a folder of images.

NOTE   One of the new screensavers in Mac OS X 10.4 is the iTunes Artwork screensaver. If you use iTunes, and any of your music has album art, this screensaver displays the album art on your screen.

Once you've selected a screensaver, you can click the Options button to see any settings for a particular screensaver module, and you can click the Test button to see a module in action. You'll also see a slider that enables you to set how much idle time should pass (without the keyboard or mouse being touched) before the screensaver starts.

NOTE   There is an option to turn on password security for your Mac's screensaver; this is located in the Security pane.

How do you activate the screensaver? Aside from waiting the amount of time specified on the Activation tab, you can use a hot corner for the screensaver. Click the Hot Corners button and then choose a behavior for each corner of your screen using the menus. (Note that they also include Exposé commands, which work using hot corners as well.) Now, whenever you move the mouse pointer to a Start Screen Saver corner of the screen (and leave it there for a second), the screensaver will launch into action immediately. If you place the mouse in a Disable Screen Saver corner, then it won't come on even after the allotted idle time has passed.

DISPLAYS

The Displays pane enables you to choose the resolution for the Mac's display. Using the Display tab in this pane (see Figure 5.13), you can choose your own resolution, color, and refresh rate settings.

FIGURE 5.13
Changing your display's settings in the Display pane

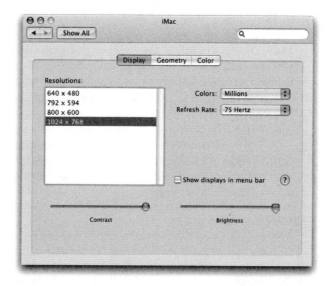

Before changing these settings, however, be sure you know what your monitor can handle. Here's a quick discussion:

Resolutions   In the Resolutions scrolling list, you can select the resolution at which you'd like the screen displayed. Resolution is measured in pixels wide by pixels high, with a pixel representing a single dot, or *picture element*, on the screen. Switching to a larger resolution enables you to see more items on the screen at one time (often described as more *screen real estate*), but it makes each item—icons, text, and so forth—appear smaller. Larger monitors are suited to larger resolutions (for instance, 20-inch monitors look good at 1024×768 or 1152×870), but you should choose a level that's comfortable for your personal viewing.

TIP   Choosing a very high resolution may limit the number of colors you can choose in the Colors menu and lower the maximum refresh rate you can choose in the Refresh Rate menu. If you'd prefer to see more colors (for instance, you'd like to choose millions of colors, but you can't) or a higher refresh rate, try lowering your resolution.

Colors   The Colors menu enables you to determine the overall color *palette* available to applications and the Mac OS. By this, we mean the number of *potential* colors available for displaying images on the screen. The more colors, the crisper and "truer" the images, especially with photographs and movies.

Refresh Rate   The Refresh Rate menu enables you to choose the number of times per second that a CRT display is updated or refreshed. The more often the display is refreshed, the clearer the overall screen image will appear. If your screen appears to flicker, you might do well to select a higher refresh rate if one is supported. (Note that Refresh Rate is not an option if you have an LCD flat-panel display connected to your Mac.)

WARNING   Selecting an unsupported resolution or refresh rate for your monitor could damage the monitor. For best results, leave the Show Modes Recommended by Display option turned on unless you're sure that an unrecommended option will work correctly.

Show Displays in Menu Bar   Turn on this option if you'd like to see a menu bar icon that enables you to switch between resolutions and color depths quickly. Use the Number of Recent Modes menu to set how many recent resolution choices will appear in that menu.

If your display is an Apple-branded model (or you're using a Mac with a built-in display such as an iMac, iBook, or PowerBook), you may see other options in the Displays pane. In addition, some monitors let you choose from a rotate angle: you can choose 90-degree increments. This allows you to rotate a monitor between portrait and landscape view.

At the bottom of the Display tab, you may see one or two sliders: a Contrast control and a Brightness control. You can use these sliders to change contrast and brightness for the monitor. (Our general monitor advice: Bump the contrast all the way up to maximum, but slide the brightness back a bit from the maximum setting until things look good. A very high brightness setting can wear out your monitor over time.)

You may also see a Geometry tab, which you can select to change the exact position and shape of the image on your screen. Select one of the radio buttons and then use the on-screen buttons to change the height, width, pin cushion, shape, and so on. If you mess things up and don't like the shape of your display's picture, click the Factory Defaults button.

NOTE   You also may see a Color tab, which is used for calibrating your monitor's ColorSync profile. This process is discussed in Chapter 8, "PDFs, Fonts, and Color."

Mac OS X can support more than one monitor connected to the same computer. If you have two Mac OS X–compatible video cards installed in your Mac and two monitors connected, on each monitor you'll see Display options where you can change each screen's resolution, color, and refresh settings.

NOTE   Some PowerBook G3 and all PowerBook G4 models can support dual monitors. If you connect a monitor to the PowerBook's external VGA port, you may be able to configure both displays separately, particularly with newer models. Older PowerBook G3 models only mirror output to a second monitor (such as for presentations), which doesn't require additional setup. (iMac DV and later iMac and iBook models also can mirror video output.)

If Mac OS X detects two or more compatible displays and display circuits, you'll also see a new option: on the "main" screen (the one with the System Preferences window on it), there will be an Arrangement tab in the Displays pane. Select that tab, and you'll see an interface that shows representations of both (or all) of your screens. By dragging the screens around, you can determine which screen will have the menu bar (making it the startup and main screen) and which screen will be on which "side," as far as the mouse pointer is concerned. Once you have the screens arranged properly, you should be able to move the mouse naturally from one screen to the other as though you were dealing with one very wide display.

NOTE Are the screen representations on the Arrange tab different sizes? If so, the difference simply indicates that each monitor is running at a different resolution—for instance, one at 800 × 600 and one at 1024 × 768. If you can, switch them to the same resolution for best results.

DOCK

The Dock pane is where you customize the appearance and behavior of the Dock; it's discussed earlier in this chapter, in the section "Setting the Dock's Preferences."

INTERNATIONAL

The International pane holds a number of options for determining how your Mac deals with languages, dates, times, and numbers. You can set the keyboard mapping from within this panel so that international keyboards (non–U.S. English keyboards) map keystrokes to the appropriate letters.

Mac OS X offers built-in support for multiple languages, allowing users around the world to use the Mac OS in their native language without having to install any additional software or language kits. Click the Language tab in the International panel, and you're given the opportunity to choose a preferred language for application menus and dialog boxes. For instance, native French speakers might choose to drag Français above English in the Languages list box so that applications that support both French and English display the French commands and text, but applications that don't support French show their English-language commands and text. Figure 5.14 shows an example in which French is selected as the primary language.

FIGURE 5.14
With French moved to the top of the Languages list box, most commands and items are changed to French.

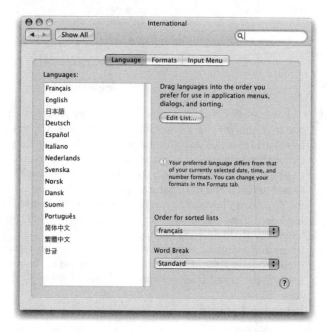

NOTE   You need to log out and log back in before changes to your language options take effect, especially to see changes in the Finder. Changes in other applications may occur immediately after
you've made the setting change. Note that you'll only be able to use these language texts if you've
installed them. If not, you can run the Mac OS X installer and customize your installation, selecting
to install the language files you want. See Appendix A, "Getting Installed and Set Up," for more on
installing Mac OS X.

The Formats tab can be used to set preferences for how you'd like dates and times to be represented on-screen and in applications. The Formats tab has a pop-up menu in which you can select a
particular predetermined region. This is the easiest way to switch to the generally accepted settings
for your area of the world.

Once you've chosen a region, you can tweak the settings yourself if you want. For instance, if you
prefer a different month/day/year ordering, click the Customize button in the Dates area and make
those changes. For different separators between hours and minutes, select the Customize button in
the Times area and change settings there.

Finally, the Input Menu tab allows you to enable more than one keyboard layout or input method
so that you can configure Mac OS X to work with your particular keyboard or nonstandard input
device (such as a Dvorak keyboard layout). Place a check mark next to the items that you want to use.
A new menu item called the Keyboard menu (but labeled only with the flag or icon of the current keyboard layout) will then appear as a permanent fixture on the Mac OS X menu bar. You will then be
able to switch between different keyboard layouts at any time.

For more detailed options on keyboard layout behavior on the Input Menu tab, click the Options
button. Using the check boxes, you can determine which keyboard shortcut will switch the available
keyboard layouts. You also can choose whether or not changing to a different keyboard layout will
automatically change you to an international font layout.

The Input Menu options in the International pane offer two other useful options. You can choose
to add to this menu the Character palette, which lets you find obscure characters and symbols, and
the Keyboard Viewer. You can turn on these options and then access them via the menu bar icon. The
Keyboard Viewer is handy because it shows you what results when you hold down keyboard combinations—hold down ⌘ and Option while the Keyboard Viewer is open, for instance, and all of the
letters and numbers on that keyboard will change to show what would result when you hold down
those modifier keys and press another key on the keyboard. It can be very handy for figuring our how
to type special and international characters on the typical U.S. keyboard, for instance.

KEYBOARD & MOUSE

On the Keyboard tab, you can select some basic options for how your Mac responds when you press
a key. Move the slider below Key Repeat Rate to determine how quickly a key will repeat if you hold
it down. Move the slider below Delay Until Repeat to determine how long the Mac OS will wait while

you hold down a key before it goes into repeat mode. Once a key starts repeating, the character you've pressed repeats on-screen without requiring you to lift your finger.

Select the Mouse tab to change the way your mouse behaves. Three sliders appear:

◆ Move the Tracking Speed slider to change how quickly your mouse moves across the screen.

◆ Move the Double-Click Speed slider to determine how much time can pass between the two clicks of a double-click and still have the Mac OS recognize it as such (instead of as two single-clicks). You can use the small test area to try your double-clicking prowess.

◆ Set the Scrolling Speed, if you have a mouse with a scroll wheel, which adjusts the speed at which the scroll wheel makes pages move up and down.

In addition, you can choose a primary mouse button: If you're right-handed, you'll probably want to choose Left; if you're left-handed, choose Right. The primary mouse button, on a multi-button mouse, is the one that sends a single click. The other button sends a Control+click, displaying contextual menus in some applications (such as the Finder).

NOTE   If you've got a PowerBook or iBook you'll see a Trackpad tab instead of the Mouse tab. It offers options for how the trackpad responds to different input, such as tapping the trackpad for clicking and dragging.

If you have a Bluetooth-enabled Mac and a Bluetooth wireless keyboard and/or mouse, you can access their settings on this tab. Click the Set Up New Device button to launch the Bluetooth Setup Assistant. (See Chapter 25, "Peripherals, Internal Upgrades, and Disks," for details.)

On the Keyboard Shortcuts tab, you can set keyboard shortcuts for a number of predefined system functions, such as Screen Shots, Universal Access, the Dictionary, Spotlight, and more. You can also set keyboard shortcuts for just about any menu command in just about any application.

To create a new keyboard shortcut, click the plus (+) icon. A sheet displays; select an application from the Application menu. If you don't find the application you want in the menu, select Other and navigate until you find it. Next, in the Menu Title field, type the *exact* name of the command you want to add. If this contains an ellipsis (...), make sure you include that. Finally, type the shortcut you want to use in the Keyboard Shortcut field. Figure 5.15 shows the results of adding a shortcut to the Finder's Clean Up command (located in the View menu), which tidies up icons in a window or on the Desktop.

TIP   When Full Keyboard Access is turned on (there's an option at the bottom of the screen), you can use arrow keys, the Tab key, and others to access items in lists, dialog boxes, and so on.

FIGURE 5.15
Setting a custom keyboard shortcut to the Finder's Clean Up command.

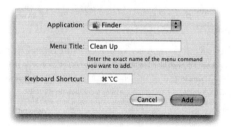

QuickTime

The QuickTime pane enables you to set certain options concerning how movies are played in your web browser (on the Plug-In tab), what connection speed QuickTime should report to distant Quick-Time servers (on the Connection tab), and what keys you have enabled to access secured QuickTime content (on the Media Keys tab). QuickTime settings are discussed in detail in Chapter 13, "Video Playback and Editing."

Security

The Security pane allows you to set up FileVault encryption, as discussed in Chapter 26. At the bottom of the Security pane is the Require Password to Wake This Computer from Sleep or Screen Saver option. Choose this option to ensure that your Mac is secure even if you get up and walk away from it. It works in conjunction with the screensaver (Desktop & Screen Saver pane) and Energy Saver (which requires an Admin password), where you can automate the screensaver and sleep functions, respectively. (Other security options require an Admin password.)

Software Update

The Software Update pane is used to configure the Software Update service that can be used to update the Mac OS and your Apple-written applications automatically. See Chapter 25 for more on Software Update.

Sound

Open the Sound pane to change the sound settings on your Mac. Here's what you can set on the Sound Effects tab:

Alert Sound   From the scrolling list, choose the alert sound you'd like.

Alert Volume   The Sound pane has a separate control for the volume at which alerts (error or other attention-getting tones) play.

Play User Interface Sound Effects   Turn off this option if the sound effects in Mac OS X version 10.2 and higher are annoying to you.

Play Feedback When Volume Keys Are Pressed   Turn on this option if you want to hear a tone when you press the volume up and down keys on your keyboard.

Output Volume   Set the volume using the speaker-icon slider. Volume is increased as you move the slider to the right. Note also the Mute option, which you can turn on to mute the speaker volume.

Show Volume in Menu Bar   Turn this option on to see the Volume menu bar item.

The Sound pane also has two other tabs: Output and Input. Switch to the Output tab to select the speakers or connection you'd like to use for playing sounds. You can use the left/right slider under the volume slider to change the balance between two speakers. On the Input tab, you can select the device that should be used for sound input as well as the input volume (gain). The Input Level meter will show a reaction if the input device can detect sounds or speech.

SPEECH

The Speech pane enables you to select a few options for the Text to Speech and Speech Recognition technologies. On the Default Voice tab, you can select a voice that you'd like your Mac to use when it talks; Fred, Bruce, Kathy, and Victoria are the most human-like, but the others are fun to listen to. Once you've selected a voice, you can choose the rate at which it speaks (certain speeds can sound more natural) using the Rate slider; click the Play button to hear a sample. On the Spoken User Interface tab, you can choose what items (if any) you'd like spoken aloud as you're working with your Mac, including alert text and text that is under your mouse pointer (when assistive features are turned on).

The Speech Recognition tab gets a bit more complex, so it's best left for Chapter 14, "Audio, iTunes, and the iPod," where Text to Speech is also discussed in more depth.

SPOTLIGHT

Spotlight, Apple's new search technology, is discussed in depth in Chapter 6, "Getting Help and Searching Your Files."

UNIVERSAL ACCESS

Mac OS X contains many assistive features that can be configured via the Universal Access pane. The pane itself has four tabs, each of which offers options to assist with a different physical challenge:

Seeing   If you have trouble seeing items on the screen, there are three options you can enable:

◆   Use VoiceOver to have your Mac speak to you.

◆   Turn on the zooming feature, which zooms items you point at.

◆   Switch the screen to white-on-black to invert the entire screen image.

Hearing   On the Hearing tab, you can cause the screen to flash instead of playing an audible beep.

Keyboard   On the Keyboard tab, you can activate Sticky Keys (you can also enable a shortcut: press the Shift key five times), which enables you to press keyboard combinations (such as ⌘Shift+3) in sequence instead of all at once. The Slow Keys option will cause the computer to wait between the time that a keypress occurs and when it's accepted to avoid problems with pressing the key for too long and causing repeated characters to appear.

Mouse   On the Mouse tab, you can turn on the Mouse Keys feature, which enables you to use the numeric keypad on the keyboard to move the mouse pointer instead of a physical mouse. (You can also enable a shortcut: press the Option key five times.)

At the bottom of the Universal Access pane is an option to enable access for assistive devices.

What's Next?

In this chapter, you saw a number of options associated with working in your own home folder and setting preferences that govern your personal workspace. In Chapter 6, you'll be introduced to the various help systems built into and included with Mac OS X, including the Help Viewer. And you'll learn about the Mac OS's new search technology called Spotlight, and you'll learn how to use smart folders to call up searches whenever you want.

Chapter 6

Getting Help and Searching Your Files

One thing that computer users eventually encounter is the need to find things. On your Mac, you'll probably need to find files and get additional help for Mac OS X or for specific applications. Mac OS X has powerful technologies for both of these tasks. First, Spotlight, Apple's new search technology, is available across the board. Not only can you search for files, their contents and metadata from the Finder, but other applications can leverage this technology. (One example is Mail, which uses Spotlight technology to search for messages and their contents.) In addition, the Finder offers powerful smart folders, which allow you to save searches and let you use a multi-criteria Find tool to zero in on the files you want.

When you need help, the built-in Help Viewer uses a standard web-like interface and HTML-based help documents, making it familiar to most users and developers. You'll be able to browse Help and search for keywords. And Mac OS X and some applications even use the Help Viewer to access the Internet to get the latest information.

In this chapter, you'll look at the Help Viewer, Spotlight, and Find, as well as see other ways to get help on your Mac and for your applications.

In this chapter:

◆ Viewing Help Documents

◆ Help in Classic Applications

◆ Finding with Find

◆ Building Complex Searches

◆ Searching with Spotlight

Viewing Help Documents

Mac OS X uses the built-in Help Viewer application to provide access to help files, both for the operating system and for applications. Apple's applications all have help files that open in Help Viewer, and many (though not all) third-party applications use this Help system as well. It's a one-stop shop for finding out about both the Mac OS and applications written for Mac OS X.

NOTE   In previous Mac OS versions, a number of different ways existed to get help. If you've used the Mac OS in the past, you may be familiar with Balloon Help and earlier types of help systems, such as the Apple Guide system. In fact, you still might encounter those systems occasionally in a Classic application (see the section "Help in Classic Applications" later in this chapter).

The Help Viewer works in a way that's very similar to a web browser, so if you've surfed the Web, you'll be reasonably comfortable with the Help Viewer interface. Figure 6.1 shows the Help Viewer.

FIGURE 6.1
The Help Viewer window

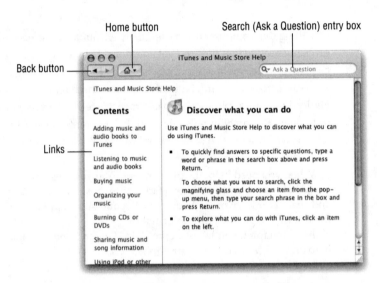

The Help Viewer features instructional text, images, and illustrations to help you understand the concepts it is teaching. It has links that work just like hyperlinks in a web browser. Click a link once, and you're taken to a related article, or the Help Viewer automatically locates documents on the selected topic. (In some cases, the Help Viewer will download a help document from a special Apple server on the Internet, but most of the time documents are stored on your Mac's hard disk.) Other links activate AppleScripts, which are used to cause other applications to open automatically or to choose settings in the Mac OS for you.

Also like a web browser, the Help Viewer has Back and Forward buttons (in the top-left corner) to enable you to move back and forth between previously accessed screens. Next to the Back and Forward buttons, the Help Viewer has a Home button that takes you to the home page for the application whose Help you're browsing. If you select the Library menu, you can select from each of the Help systems installed on your Mac and go to the main page of the Help for any of these applications. You can also access different help files by clicking and holding the Home button and selecting an application from the menu that displays; this is the same list that shows in the Library menu.

At the top of the Help Viewer window is the Ask a Question entry box, in which you can enter keywords to search Help documents. Once your keywords are entered, press the Return key to initiate the search. (We'll have more on searching in the section "Help by Keyword" later in this chapter.)

Accessing the Help Viewer

The Mac OS has a fairly simple, straightforward Help system, and you can access it in quite a number of ways. The Finder and most other applications written specifically for Mac OS X include a Help menu, where you'll find at least one Help command. In most cases, the command name includes the name of the application (for instance, Mail Help in the Mail application). In the Finder, the command is Help ➢ Mac Help. In the QuickTime Player application, the command is Help ➢ QuickTime Player Help.

TIP In Mac OS X 10.2 and higher, you can press the Help key on extended keyboards to get help in some applications. You can also press ⌘? (⌘Shift+/) to get Help, both in the Finder and in many applications.

Another way to access the Help Viewer is through the Help button, located in many different places throughout the interface, including Print dialog boxes and settings windows. What's more, these quick links are usually *contextual*, meaning the link takes you directly to a help topic of interest, not just a general index of help topics. The Help button should be obvious—it's a small, round button with a question mark inside it.

When you have the Help Viewer open, you can switch and view the help for another application, as long as that application has installed a standard Mac OS X help file. Select the Library menu, or click and hold the Home button, and choose the application whose help you want to view.

Help by Topic

In some cases, such as when you click a ? button in an application, accessing the Help Viewer takes you directly to a page that discusses the topic that you're seeking. In other cases, though, you may want to browse a particular application's help or look through a number of different articles to learn more about a procedure or feature. You would then start at the top level of an application's help topics and click a topic link to view related help documents.

Most applications that use the Help Viewer have a main page that includes topic listings on one side of the screen (see Figure 6.2). In the case of Apple's own Help documents, these links are to the main sections of the Help file. As you can see in Figure 6.2, these often include special Contents, What's New?, Learn About, and Solving Problems links; some help files include a Browse link as well.

The Solving Problems section for these help files is like a Frequently Asked Questions list, containing entries for the most common questions and problems that arise.

Some applications' help files have a different kind of main page, with links that are actually built-in search phrases; when you click one of the links, some predetermined search keywords are plugged into the Help Viewer's search box. With some third-party applications, the Help screen may open to a more involved list than Apple generally uses. These lists help you see most of the available help topics all at once.

Articles that match the search criteria appear on a results listing page, enabling you to click to view an article that looks interesting. You may also see a More Results link at the bottom of the results listing. Click that link, and you'll see another series of help articles that may be of interest. If you click one of the results listings, more than likely you'll view the help document in the Help Viewer window immediately.

FIGURE 6.2
Many applications have
a main page with links to
the main sections.

As you're browsing, you can use the Back button to return to a previous screen. The Home button takes you to the main page of the current application's Help, and you can switch to another program's Help by selecting it from the Library menu.

NOTE Some of the applications included with Mac OS X—including Finder and many of the Mac OS X utilities—have help documents stored within the Mac Help document. (In other words, you may not see individual listings for them in the Help Viewer like you can see help for Mail, TextEdit, iTunes, and so on.) Access the Mac Help system to learn more about the included applications, or select the Help command within these individual programs to go directly to their help sections in the Help Viewer.

Help by Keyword

If you know what you want help with, and you'd prefer not to browse for it, you can search for it directly. Open the Help system for a particular application using one of the methods described in the section "Accessing the Help Viewer" earlier in this chapter. At the top of the Help Viewer, enter a keyword or two that describes the topic on which you'd like help. If you enter more than one keyword, separate the words with just a space and then press Return to begin the search.

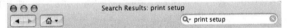

You can also choose whether you want to search in the currently active help file or in all available help files by clicking the triangle next to the magnifying glass and selecting one of these options.

After you press Return, you'll see a results page listing the help documents that the Help Viewer found. If you click one of the titles in the top pane of the window, you can then click the Show button to display the full help document (or, as noted previously, it will cause that help document to be downloaded from Apple's Internet Help server). You'll also notice, as shown in Figure 6.3, a "relevance" system in the Rank column; that's Help Viewer's way of showing you how relevant it thinks each article is to your search. The more relevant the document is according to Help Viewer, the longer the relevance bar.

FIGURE 6.3
A results listing page in
the Help Viewer

If you don't see a document that helps you, it can alter your search a bit. One way to do that is to use special symbols to create *Boolean* search phrases. A Boolean search phrase is made up of keywords and the words `and`, `or`, or `not`. For instance, `Printer and USB` is a Boolean search phrase that will find pages with both the words `Printer` and `USB`. `Printer or USB` would find pages that include either of the two terms. `Printer not USB` would locate pages that include `Printer` but don't include `USB`.

In the Help Viewer, these phrases must be put together with symbols instead of `and`, `or`, and `not`. The plus sign (+) stands for `and`, an exclamation point (!) stands for `not`, and a vertical line (|) stands for `or`. For example, the following tells Help Viewer to search for documents that have the word `Printer` but not the word `USB`:

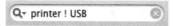

You can also use parentheses to enclose parts of the Boolean phrase. The following tells Help Viewer to search for documents that include either `Printer` or `Scanner` but not `USB`:

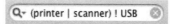

Also, it's worth noting that, by default, words entered without Boolean symbols are always assumed to be "or" searches, meaning you don't need to enter the "or" symbol if you're simply typing two or three keywords.

TIP   You can also enter "natural-language" queries in the search box, such as `How do I install a USB printer?` or `How can I find a friend on the Internet?` As far as we can tell, natural phrasing offers no advantage over targeted keywords (such as `USB + printer` or `search + Internet`), but you can try it as another approach to brainstorming your keywords.

In some cases, the Help Viewer will display a series of support articles at the bottom of the results list. These are indicated by the red and white "first aid" icon before them. When you click Show to view the article, your Mac connects to the Internet to download that article and display it in the Help Viewer. These articles all come from Apple's support site (`www.apple.com/support`), but you may find that searching for them and viewing them in the Help Viewer can be easier than using a web browser.

Help Documents Links

Whether you've arrived at a Help document by browsing or searching with keywords, once you're there, you'll sometimes see some specific types of links. Here's what they do:

Next   Not too many pages have a Next link, but those that do offer it so that you can see a second page of explanations. These links also appear in results listings when there are additional articles that result from a search.

See Also   This link will often take you to a revised search that results in documents that are topically similar to the one you're reading.

Go   Sometimes this one is called Go to the Web Site. Most of the Go links you find in Apple Help are links to external websites that offer more information on the topic at hand. (Help Viewer doesn't display these documents. Instead, it will prompt your default web browser to retrieve them.)

Open This For Me   This link uses AppleScript to open a particular application or utility. In some of Apple's own help documents, for instance, these links will sometimes launch a particular System Preferences pane, enabling you to alter the setting discussed in the help article quickly.

Of course, third-party application authors are welcome to put other links in their documents or to give them slightly different names. Most of them, at a minimum, differentiate between links to external documents on the Internet and links back to the table of contents, index, or search results within the Help Viewer itself.

Installing Help Documents

In most cases, the Mac OS installer or application installers should install help documents for you. If for some reason you have a help document that hasn't been properly installed, you can install it in one of two places.

Help documents for the entire Mac OS X system (all users) are stored in the main `Library` folder in the `Help` subfolder, which is located in the `Documentation` folder. (That's the `/Library/Documentation/Help` folder.) If you have a valid Help Viewer system file (with the filename extension `.help`), you can drag that file to this folder. The next time you launch the Help Viewer, the new help file will be recognized and accessible via the Help Center drawer.

You also have a personal `Documentation` folder (inside the `Library` folder in your home folder) where you'll find the subfolder `Help`. If desired, you can install Help system files there, where they can be accessed only by you when your user account is logged in. Other users will not be able to see the Help system you've installed. (This may be your only option, by the way, if you aren't logged in to an administrator's account.)

Other Documentation Systems

Although the Help Viewer is the main retrieval system for getting help in the Mac OS, you'll find documentation in other forms and formats as well. The most common type is probably the Read Me file, which usually is included in any new application's folder.

The Read Me file can vary from a simple document telling you a little about the program or programmer to a complex set of instructions, bug alerts, and other issues that have to do with the application. Read Me files are usually plain-text files that can be read in TextEdit, although they may also be RTF (Rich Text Format, which TextEdit can also display) or PDF documents (display these in Preview, Adobe Acrobat Reader, or another PDF-capable application).

NOTE PDF stands for Portable Document Format, a special document format designed to display documents in a standard way on multiple computer platforms. Creating and working with PDF documents is discussed in Chapter 8, "PDFs, Fonts, and Color."

Applications aren't limited strictly to the Apple Help system for their own help documents, so it's also possible that you'll find help documents stored in an application's folder in PDF format or RTF format. Either type of file can be printed out and used as a hard-copy manual (see Figure 6.4).

Of course, application developers are free to write their own Help systems or, in some cases, use updated versions of older Mac OS Help systems; many application developers (especially those who develop Internet applications such as web browsers and e-mail programs) opt for HTML-based Help systems that use a web browser instead of the Help Viewer.

FIGURE 6.4

Here's a user's manual in PDF format.

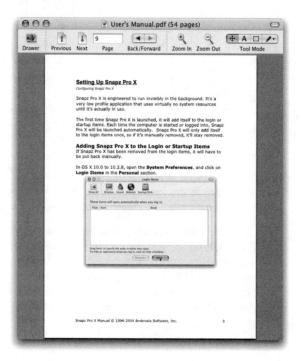

TIP Working in the Terminal application? Commands and programs in the Unix-like environment of Terminal have their own help system, called "man" (manual) pages. Type **man** *command*, where *command* is the name of the command (or command-line program) you're trying to learn more about. See Chapter 22, "Terminal and the Command Line," for details on using Terminal.

Help in Classic Applications

Classic applications don't have access to the Mac OS X Help Viewer and don't place their help documentation within its control. Instead, you'll use the Help system in Mac OS 9, which is similar in many ways to Help Viewer. It's like a web browser, using links and the Back, Home, and Forward buttons to get around.

To access a Classic application's Help system, pull down its Help menu and select the Help command. The application name will precede Help (for instance, QuickTime Help). Figure 6.5 shows a sample of the Help system used by Classic applications.

FIGURE 6.5

The Classic Help Viewer

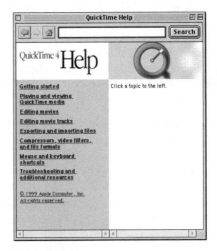

NOTE Increasingly, at least with Apple's applications, selecting *Application* Help from the Help menu in a Classic application will bring up the Mac OS X native Help Viewer. In third-party applications, however, you'll still see the Classic Help Viewer.

Aside from the Help command, you might encounter some other types of earlier Mac OS Help systems. The Apple Guide system, for instance, was a popular way to add help to Mac OS applications in the mid 1990s. If you're using Classic applications written during that time (or a Classic application that hasn't had its Help system updated, since the Apple Guide will still work in Mac OS 9 and the Classic environment), you may see a Guide entry in the Classic application's Help menu. Select that entry, and you'll see the Guide window, as shown in Figure 6.6.

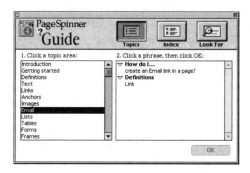

The Apple Guide system was a bit more complex than the current Help Viewer approach. Although some of the controls work like a web browser, the Guide is a more active help system. Using AppleScript and other technologies, it guides you through basic tasks, working a little more like the Setup Assistant that helps you configure Mac OS X after an installation. (Assistants and wizards are also popular in productivity applications such as Microsoft Office or AppleWorks.)

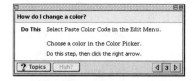

If you encounter a Guide, simply walk through the suggested steps using the arrow buttons. You'll notice in some cases that the Guide will perform tasks automatically for you. You'll also find that the main Topics window offers an Index view and a search view (via the Look For button), enabling you to move quickly to any topic that interests you.

NOTE   Apple Guide is a nice system for help. It fell out of favor with Apple primarily because it's hard for application developers to implement (at least, harder than HTML pages or the Help Viewer approach). Therefore, it wasn't used by nearly as many developers as had been hoped.

While working in Classic applications, you'll likely encounter at least one other type of standard help—the venerable Balloon Help. It was Apple's first real help system for the Mac and, although limited in scope, it was fairly effective during its time. (It still is, at least in Classic applications. A Balloon Help feature doesn't exist in Mac OS X, although some programs offer similar functions.)

Balloon Help works by being turned on and off. Select Help ➢ Show Balloons from the menu of a Classic application, and you've turned on Balloon Help. Then move the mouse over a button, command, or portion of a window that you don't understand. If a Balloon Help resource was written for that item, a small, cartoon-like balloon pops up to tell you about the item.

Perhaps the most persistent complaint about Balloon Help is that, when it's switched on, balloons pop up continuously as you work (or any time you move the mouse to an item with a Balloon Help resource). Most folks turn off Balloon Help after they've learned what they need to know. Select Help ➤ Hide Balloons to turn off the feature.

Finally, as with applications native to OS X, Classic applications can have help systems written or implemented by application developers. For instance, Figure 6.7 shows Adobe PageMill 3.0's Help system, which uses QuickHelp, a popular third-party help system that was also used by Classic versions of Palm Desktop and earlier AppleWorks and ClarisWorks implementations. If you encounter such a system, just hold your breath and dive in. In most cases, it will resemble a web browser or be reasonably similar to the Help Viewer, so it should make sense almost immediately.

FIGURE 6.7
A Classic application can have its own help system, generally similar to a web browser interface.

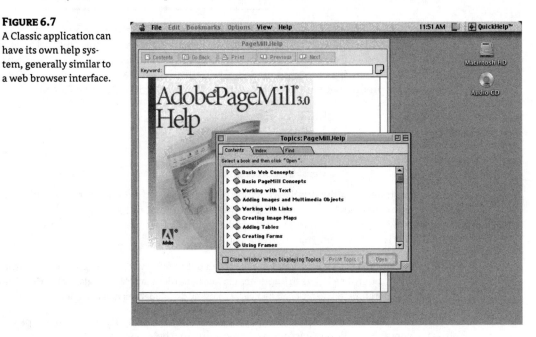

Finding Files

One of the biggest innovations in Mac OS X 10.4 is Spotlight, a system-wide technology that indexes your files according to their names, contents, and metadata, and allows you to find them incredibly fast. Spotlight is built into the heart of Mac OS X, and other applications can leverage this technology to search for content within their own files. The Finder naturally uses Spotlight for its searches, as does Mail, which uses Spotlight to search for e-mail messages in your mailboxes. Spotlight is also present in the System Preferences, Address Book, and the Help Viewer.

Since there are so many files on your Mac, finding the right ones when you need them is essential. Not only does Spotlight offer a quick, convenient search bar to look for files, but you can also search from Finder window toolbars, and you can use the same technology to run complex, multi-criteria searches from Finder windows.

This section will look at all three of these ways of searching for files, starting with the Finder window toolbar, then the Finder's Find function, and finally Spotlight's search bar. You'll see that these are three sides of the same coin, as it were, and the same techniques apply to all three ways of searching for files and their content.

Using the Finder Toolbar's Search Field

Finder windows contain, by default, a search field at the right side of their toolbar. This search field lets you quickly find files or folders anywhere on your computer. You can remove this search field if you want; see Chapter 3, "The Finder," for more on customizing the Finder toolbar.

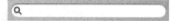

To use the search field, type in a keyword or part of a filename or folder name; that name is matched against files and folders, and matches are displayed. By default, the search field looks for files and folders on local disks, or on your entire computer .

Searching from the Finder toolbar's search field is fast—in fact, it's so fast that the Finder begins displaying the results before you even finish typing your keyword. Since Spotlight indexes file and folder names, searching from the Finder toolbar involves merely sorting the contents of a database.

NOTE We'll use the term Spotlight in several locations in the rest of this chapter because this is the underlying technology that the Finder and its Find feature use to search for files or their content.

As you can see in Figure 6.8, the Finder window splits into three parts:

◆ To the left is the Sidebar, with its icons according to your Finder preferences.

◆ The right side of the window has two panes, similar to many e-mail programs.

◆ The top pane lists the search results, and when you click a result, the small bottom pane shows the path to that file or folder.

FIGURE 6.8

When you select a result from the search list, the Finder displays its path at the bottom of the window.

The Finder returns a list of files of different types and organizes them by category: It displays folders, images, PDF documents, HTML documents, music, movies, and much more. The Finder only displays the top five of each category; if more files are found, an X More link displays at the bottom of the category, where X is the number of additional results. Click this link, which may say 25 More, to see all the results.

If you run a search with the Computer option (which is the default), the Finder looks in local disks and network volumes. Since files on these volumes may be changed after you run a search, you can search again by clicking the Search Again button at the bottom-right corner of the window.

As you can see in Figure 6.8, there is a small button bar at the top of the search results list. The buttons here let you refine your search; you can click Servers if you want to run your search again only on network volumes that are currently available. Click Home to limit the search to files in your home folder, or click Others to choose one or several other folders or volumes. If you click the Others button, a sheet displays where you can add folders or volumes either by dragging them from the Finder or by clicking the + button and adding specific items.

The Save button in the button bar lets you turn your query into a smart folder. Chapter 3 discussed smart folders; here, you don't need to select File ➢ New Smart Folder, but rather click the Save button to store the search criteria you used. When you do this, you are prompted for a name for the smart folder and a location to save it, and you can choose whether or not you want to save it in the Sidebar.

To the right of each filename in the search results is an Info icon (the small *i* in a circle). If you click this, the Finder shows you more information about the file. This is the same information you see in Columns View in the Preview column; it tells you the filename, the kind of file, the size, creation, and modification dates, and when it was last opened. It also shows, for some types of files, a preview of the file's contents; this works for many graphics files, plain-text files, PDFs, movies, music files, and others.

If you click the More Info button, the Finder opens the standard Info window, the window that displays when you select a file then select File ➢ Get Info, or press ⌘I.

It's important to note that when you search for files in this manner, the Finder not only returns search results for files whose names contain your keywords, but *any* files that contain your keywords *anywhere* in the filename, the file's contents, or even its metadata. For example, if I search for Bill Evans on my Mac, the Finder returns not only folders with that name, but also music files where Bill Evans is listed as the artist or composer.

NOTE   We'll look more closely at metadata later in this chapter when we examine the Spotlight feature.

At the far right of the button bar that you see in Figure 6.8 is a + icon. If you click this icon, you can refine your search by adding additional criteria. Since this functions the same as multi-criteria searches using the Find tool, we'll look at this in the next section.

Using the Find Tool

In previous versions of Mac OS X, there were two different ways to search for files in the Finder: using the search field in the Finder window toolbar, as described previously, and using the Find tool, which you accessed by pressing ⌘F. In Tiger, as you have seen, the Finder window search field contains new powers, bringing multi-criteria searches to what before was simply a quick search function.

The Find tool still exists—sort of. If you press ⌘F in the Finder, the currently active window changes its display to become a New Search window. The search field becomes active, the button bar displays, with Servers, Computer, or Home selected (The Finder remembers the last search location you used; if you have not searched before, it selects Computer), and two search criteria display: Kind=Any and Last Opened=Any Date. (The button bar also adds the currently active folder to the list of search areas, if this folder is not Computer or your home folder.)

You search the same way as you do from the Finder search field; in fact, the only difference is the way you invoke this window and the fact that it displays, by default, two criteria. While searching from the Finder search field is convenient, you're less likely to use that basic search function for power searching. Understanding the flexibility and precision of multi-criteria searches lets you find anything on your Mac.

Mac OS X maintains various criteria about each file and folder on your hard disk and attached volumes. For each item, these include the date it was created, the date it was modified, and the size of the file or the amount of storage space it requires on disk. These items (along with a few dozen others, thanks to the Spotlight technology) can all be turned into search criteria if you choose to customize your search.

As you saw previously, invoking the Find tool by pressing ⌘F displays two criteria by default; if you're interested in refining a search you began from the Finder search field, click the + icon at the right of the button bar to add criteria. This adds a new line to the list of criteria; Find sets this new criterion automatically, but you can choose a different one by selecting it from the criterion menu, the one at the left.

NOTE   You don't have to remove a criterion line if you don't want to use it—simply don't make any choices on that line. Some of the menu-based criteria have options such as No Value or All that you can choose if you don't want that criterion to affect the results.

The first two criteria in that menu—Kind and Last Opened—correspond to two of the most common types of searches you may want to perform (other than for specific filenames). Each of these criteria lets you then choose specific information from the second menus. For the Kind criterion, you can choose

◆ Any (the default choice)

◆ Images

◆ Text

◆ PDF

◆ Movies

◆ Music

◆ Documents

◆ Presentations

◆ Folders

◆ Applications

◆ Others

If none of the preset choices fits your search, select Others to display a combo box with dozens of choices. These include, for example,

◆ Address Book Person Data

◆ Aliases

◆ C Source Files

◆ HTML Documents

◆ Specific types of audio files (MP3, AAC, AIFF)

◆ QuickTime Movies

◆ Safari Bookmarks

TIP   Do you want to be able to access your Safari bookmarks from the Finder? Search for Kind=Others and select Safari Bookmark from the combo box. Don't add any other criteria; this finds *all* your bookmarks, which are stored as special metadata. Click the Save button in the search window button bar to save this as a smart folder and add it to the Sidebar. You'll then be able to double-click any of these bookmarks from this folder to open Safari to the pages you visit most often.

The more creativity you need to find a file, the more useful these additional criteria can be. Also, the ability to combine criteria is where these search options really shine. The following is a quick look at each of the options and a sense of what you can do with them.

Kind   This lets you search for common and less common types of files.

Last Opened   This entry lets you narrow down your search to files that you have opened within a certain amount of time (This Week, This Month) or on an exact date. This is different from the Last Modified criterion.

Last Modified   While Last Opened lets you look for files according to when you have viewed them, Last Modified searches by the date you have last made and saved a change to a file. The Mac OS also keeps track of the date when any file, folder, or volume is modified, so you can base your search on that date. Thus, you can limit a search to the files most recently worked with, or you can search for files that haven't been modified in quite some time. The option is very useful for backup or archiving purposes. It can also be useful for finding lost files. For instance, if you've forgotten a filename you created last week, you could search for a document that was modified within the past week that includes certain keywords in its contents.

Created   Search for files or volumes created on, after, or before a certain date or within a range of dates.

Keywords   This entry lets you enter keywords, which can be defined in files in many ways. These keywords can either be metadata for files or keywords defined, for example, in HTML files as META CONTENT tags. When Spotlight indexes your hard disk(s), it ferrets out any such keywords. You can enter a keyword in the combo box or click the arrow to select from available keywords (which is a good way to find out exactly what Spotlight has picked up).

Color Label   If you use labels to organize your files, you can use a specific label as a search criterion. You can search for files that have or don't have a specific label, or look for files with any labels or with no labels (by clicking the ×, which means no labels). If you want to search for any of several labels, click one color, then hold down ⌘ and click others to add them to the search criteria.

Name   This entry is useful for customizing the standard filename search. Choose from Contains, Begins With, Ends With, and Is.

Contents   This option lets you look for the text inside your documents. For instance, suppose you're looking for a memo that you addressed to Nancy. To find it, you could turn on Name and enter **Memo**, and then turn on Content and enter **Nancy** as the keyword. Find will search diligently for a file with Memo in the name and Nancy in its contents.

Size   Search for files that take up more (select Is Greater Than) or less (select Is Less Than) than a certain amount of storage space, in kilobytes.

Other   If you thought that the above criteria were sufficient, you've only scratched the surface. Again, the breadth and depth of Spotlight technology give you an astounding number of search criteria; Apple only puts the most common criteria in the menu and includes more than one hundred others in the Other window. Select Other and then scroll through the list to find one that can be useful. (It's a good idea to familiarize yourself with some of these other criteria so you know how powerful your searches can be.) For example, the following graphic shows a complex search for music files, looking for the name of the album, the composer of the songs, the genre, and duration.

Some of these other criteria are worth noting, because they allow you to search for files that you might not find otherwise.

Visibility This option enables you to find items that have been marked as Invisible (so that they don't appear in Finder windows) via a third-party utility application or a command in the Terminal. Choose Visible Items to search for items that are visible or choose Invisible Items to find hidden items. Choosing both Visible and Invisible Items searches for all files, whether or not they are visible. In Mac OS X, files or folders that begin with a period (.) are invisible by default. If you'd like to make a file or folder invisible, you can use the Terminal application to do so by renaming the file with a period.

Type This lets you search for files that are a specific type. You need to know the four-character code for different file types. Some examples are JPEG, TEXT, APPL (for applications), or WDBN (for Microsoft Word documents).

Creator As with Type, the creator code is a four-character code for the application that created the documents you're looking for. Some examples are ttxt for TextEdit, TVOD for Quick-Time files, or CARO for Acrobat Reader files. The type and creator together form a signature for files.

Spotlight Searches

One of the most powerful new features in Mac OS X is Spotlight. As mentioned earlier in this chapter, this is a system-wide search technology that Mac OS X can use in the Finder or in specific applications to search for files by their names or their content.

Spotlight is fast. To try it out, click the Spotlight icon in the menu bar (the blue magnifying glass icon), or press ⌘Spacebar, and enter a word in the field that displays.

You'll see that Spotlight starts returning hits even before you've finished typing your text. The results are listed by type: You may see a Top Hit, the one that Spotlight thinks is the closest to your search string, followed by categories such as Documents, Folders, Mail Messages, PDF Documents, Movies, Music, Contacts, and more.

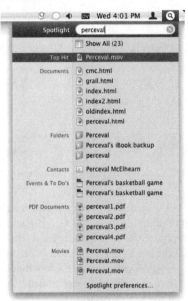

NOTE How does Spotlight work so fast? Well, it's not searching your files when you ask it to; it indexes your files in the background, adding new files, changing its database according to their content, and removing files you've deleted. For this reason, after you install Tiger or if you add a new hard disk, Spotlight will not be available until it has indexed all your files. (You'll see a white dot inside the magnifying glass, indicating that indexing is in progress; clicking the Spotlight icon shows you the amount of time remaining for indexing.)

You can click an item in the Spotlight results menu, or, if you want to see more information about the files or if there are too many files to display in the menu, click Show All to open the Spotlight window, as illustrated in Figure 6.9.

TIP To search directly in the Spotlight window, press ⌘Option+Spacebar. You can change this keyboard shortcut if you like; see "Spotlight Preferences" later in this section.

The Spotlight window displays five items in each category. If a category contains more than that, you can click the X More link; for example, if Spotlight finds 20 documents, the top five are displayed, and the link says 15 More. You can return to the top-five display by clicking Show Top 5.

FIGURE 6.9
The Spotlight window lets you access more information about the files found by your search.

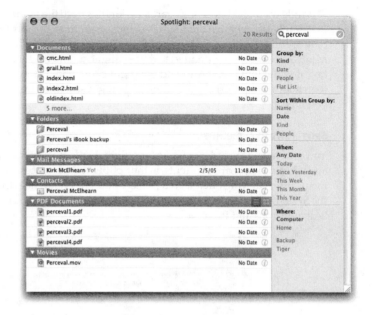

TIP To clear the Spotlight search field and any results in the Spotlight menu or window, just press the Escape key.

You can get more information about any of the files by clicking the i icon. Just as for searches in the Finder toolbar search field, this displays as much information as is available for the item: its file path, size, and a preview for certain files (graphics, movies, music, text files, PDFs), as well as any metadata that Spotlight has stored. Some categories allow you to view their results in icon form: this is the case for images and PDF files. Click the Icon View icon to change the display. Click the List View icon to return to List View.

You can even view images returned by a Spotlight search in a slide show: Click the arrow icon, to the left of the list view icon, to start a slide show. This displays the images at five-second intervals. If you move the cursor, a toolbar displays at the bottom of the window; you can use this to skip ahead or back, pause or resume the slide show, display an "index sheet," a kind of exposé window showing all the images that you can click to open, zoom images to fit the screen, and close the slide show.

You can further refine the display in the Spotlight window by clicking the various links in the right-hand column. You can choose to group the results in different ways (by type, date, people, or in a flat list, where no categories are displayed). You can sort in the groups by name, date, kind, or people. You can narrow down the dates of the files, and you can select different locations such as Computer, Home, or any specific volumes or disks you have.

While we looked closely at searching for files from the Finder and using multiple criteria, it's likely that you'll discover that Spotlight is sufficient for most of your searches, and that Finder searches are only useful for multicriteria searches. Spotlight searches for filenames, content, and metadata, as well as any keywords you've added to the Spotlight comments for files or folders. (See Chapter 3 for more on using the Info window to add Spotlight comments.) However, Spotlight does not allow you to search for multiple criteria; running a Spotlight search on multiple words looks for any of the words you type.

SPOTLIGHT PREFERENCES

You can change the order in which Spotlight displays its search results, as well as the Spotlight menu and window keyboard shortcuts, in the Spotlight Preferences. You can access these from the Spotlight menu, after carrying out a search (select Spotlight Preferences from the bottom of the menu), or from the System Preferences application (click the Spotlight icon). This preference pane contains two tabs: Search Results and Privacy.

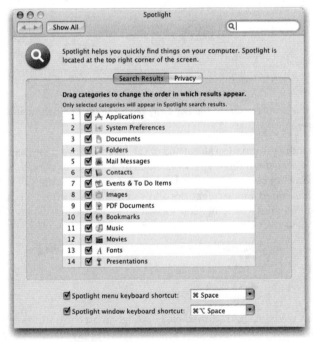

The Search Results tab lets you change the order of search categories; when the Spotlight menu or window displays search results, they are grouped by the categories in this list and presented in the order shown in this preference pane. Drag the categories to a different order to put the most important ones at the top of the list. You can also choose to turn off Spotlight search results for selected categories. You might, for example, never want to search for music files or fonts from Spotlight. Turning them off will result in fewer hits, but will limit the hits to the files you might actually want to find, especially if, for example, you have a large music library, where Spotlight will find many song files because of the metadata these files contain.

The Search Results tab also lets you set the Spotlight menu and window keyboard shortcuts. By default, ⌘Spacebar opens the Spotlight menu and ⌘Option+Spacebar opens the Spotlight window. You may especially want to change these shortcuts if you use application launchers such as Launch-Bar, QuickSilver, or Butler, which may, by default, use the same keyboard shortcuts.

NOTE   Since Spotlight lets you search for applications and launch them quickly, you may find that it is a great way to launch programs and files. There are several application launchers that give you quick access to both applications and other files. In general, you press a keyboard shortcut, type a few letters, select the application, and press Enter or Return to launch it. Three of these programs offer this application launch feature, together with myriad other features: LaunchBar (www.obdev.at/products/launchbar/), Quicksilver (quicksilver.blacktree.com/), and Butler (www.petermaurer.de/butler/). If you already use one of these applications, you know how much they enhance your productivity; if you've never tried them, you owe it to yourself to check them out.

The Privacy tab of this preferences pane lets you choose specific folders or volumes that Spotlight will ignore. Add folders, disks, or volumes to the list by dragging them from the Finder or by clicking the + button and selecting them. Why would you want Spotlight to ignore certain locations? If you have, say, an external hard disk or a partition that you use for backups, you probably don't want Spotlight to search that volume; you'll end up with double results (your original files and their backups) and may open and modify files that you don't intend to change. You may also want to add folders that contain specific files that you don't want indexed for other reasons. Say you have a lot of text files, source code files, or other documents that you won't want to find. Telling Spotlight to ignore them can make your searching easier. You can always use the standard Find function to search these specific folders if you need to.

What's Next?

In this chapter, you learned how to access Mac OS X's Help system, and you saw how to search local disks and folders using Find and Spotlight. In the next chapter, you'll learn the basics of printing in Mac OS X, including setting up your printer, using the standard Print dialog boxes, printing from the Classic environment, and troubleshooting.

Chapter 7

Printing and Faxing in Mac OS X

Mac OS X relies in most cases on a sophisticated printing engine for both simple and complex printing tasks. With the right driver software and connection cables, you easily can add a basic ink-jet or laser printer to your individual Mac. If you have a workgroup of Macs and PCs, you can add a network printer that multiple computers can access. You can even share a printer on a home network, giving access to any kind of printer to all your Macs. How you go about doing this depends on both your printer and your printing needs.

How your printer works also depends in large part on the *printer driver* software that you use. The driver software tells the Mac OS how to communicate with the printer, including options and preferences that enable you to configure the printer's unique capabilities. Mac OS X has become more widely accepted, and printer drivers have been written and rewritten to support a variety of printers. Mac OS X itself also comes with some basic drivers for popular printers, so even if your printer manufacturer hasn't released a Mac OS X–compatible driver, in many cases you'll at least have some basic printing functionality.

In Mac OS X versions 10.3 and 10.4, printers are set up and managed using the Printer Setup Utility, found in the Utilities folder inside the main Applications folder. If you're familiar with earlier versions of the Mac OS, you'll notice that the Printer Setup Utility incorporates the functionality of both the Chooser and the PrintMonitor (or, with later Mac OS 9 and earlier Mac OS X versions, the desktop printer icons and/or the Print Center). That is, you both set up *and* manage your printer with the Printer Setup Utility.

The truth is that printing in Mac OS X has been constantly evolving since version 10.0, with each major iteration bringing new features and, in some cases, restoring features that used to be part of the Classic Mac OS. Additionally, since Mac OS X 10.2, the underlying print spooler is based on CUPS (Common Unix Printing System), which is good technology for complex print jobs. In Mac OS X 10.3, printer-sharing features were added and the Printer Setup Utility was overhauled; in Mac OS X 10.4, browsing for connected printers that your Mac can access is easier than it has ever been.

When it comes to printing your documents, the overall process should be familiar, regardless of the operating system you're used to. In all your applications (at least those that support printing), you'll find a Page Setup dialog box and a Print dialog box, where you can configure options for how your final document will look. When you send a document for printing, the Quartz engine in Mac OS X actually creates a PDF, which results in great-looking output that's also reasonably uniform from printer to printer. Plus, it negates some compatibility issues that have affected Macs in the past with respect to printing and printers.

Mac OS X also includes built-in fax software, so you can send a fax as easily as you print documents. You can use your Mac to receive faxes, and you can set it to automatically save, print, or send by e-mail your incoming faxes. You can also share a fax across a network, so if one of your Macs has a modem that's connected to a phone line, anyone on your network will be able to send faxes through it.

We'll examine all of these in this chapter, along with the basics of the Preview feature, which enables you to see your document on-screen before it's printed. Also, you'll see how to configure certain compatible printers for printing from the Classic environment.

In Chapter 8, "PDFs, Fonts, and Color," you'll see some advanced issues related to printing documents, including creating PDFs, installing and customizing fonts, and dealing with color and color matching in Mac OS X.

In this chapter:

◆ Connecting and Configuring a Printer

◆ Printing Your Documents

◆ Managing Print Jobs

◆ Printing from Classic

◆ Sending and Receiving Faxes

WHAT PRINTERS DOES MAC OS X SUPPORT?

The easiest printers to use with Mac OS X are PostScript-compatible printers that connect via either Universal Serial Bus (USB) or Ethernet. (FireWire also is a possibility with Mac OS X, although there aren't many FireWire-based printers available.) Mac OS X supports most PostScript printers right out of the box, with only minor tweaks necessary (for instance, a PostScript Printer Description [PPD] file specific to the printer can be handy) to get a good deal of functionality from the printer. These aren't the only printers supported—just the easiest.

The next easiest type of printer to use with Mac OS X is a USB-based laser or ink-jet printer that uses Printer Control Language (PCL) as the basis of its print engine. PCL is the most popular printer language for Windows-compatible printers, and it has become very popular with the latest USB-equipped Mac printer models. Nearly all USB-based ink-jet and many USB-based laser printers marketed for the Macintosh use PCL to print the page (particularly the lower-cost models). The only real issue this creates for Mac users is the necessity of installing a PCL printer driver so the Mac can talk to the printer. (As mentioned, Mac OS X includes some basic drivers that may enable you to print to popular ink-jet models; for more sophisticated feature support, you'll rely on the manufacturer of the printer for drivers.) This is true for Mac OS 9 and earlier, as well as for Mac OS X.

If you have an older printer that doesn't have a USB or Ethernet port but is PostScript-compatible, you may still be able to adapt it for use with your Mac and OS X. For instance, some PostScript-based LocalTalk printers that can be used with beige Power Macintosh G3 models can't be used with Mac OS X because a LocalTalk connection isn't supported in Mac OS X. In that case, you can get an Ethernet-to-LocalTalk adapter, such as AsantéTalk (`www.asante.com/products/productsLvl3/AsanteTalk.asp`). You'll then be able to access the printer as if it were an Ethernet printer.

Mac OS X doesn't support printers aimed at older Macs that use the discontinued Mac serial port. Likewise, older printer models that use *QuickDraw* technology aren't supported by Mac OS X. These include a number of printers made by Apple in the past, including the ImageWriter, Personal LaserWriter (some models), and StyleWriter models.

Connecting and Configuring a Printer

Mac OS X supports two basic types of printers: PostScript printers and non-PostScript printers. To recognize a printer, Mac OS X must have printer driver software installed so the Mac OS can locate and communicate with that printer.

Most PostScript printers are easy to configure, partly because the Mac OS already has a PostScript printer driver built into it. First you connect a PostScript printer to your Mac (or to a network that your Mac can also access), and then you open the Printer Setup Utility and look for the printer. Once a printer is recognized by the Printer Setup Utility, it can be assigned a PostScript Printer Description (PPD), which tells the built-in PostScript driver what makes this particular printer different from other Post-Script printers. You'll then see different options in the Page Setup and Print dialog boxes for that printer, thanks to the PPD.

Other printers are different because the Mac OS includes only basic non-PostScript drivers for a limited number of printers. For these printers, which often are ink-jet printers and some low-end lasers that use the PCL printer language instead of PostScript, you'll have to install a printer driver first in order to use all the features of that printer. Once the driver is installed, you can open the Printer Setup Utility and locate the printer. You won't have to assign a PPD to that printer, though, because the driver tells the Mac OS what's unique about that printer, and it will be reflected in the Page Setup and Print dialog boxes.

Installing Drivers and PPDs

The first issue for any printer is to make sure you have the right software to get the printer and Mac OS X to communicate. For PostScript printers, this generally means a PPD from the printer manufacturer. (If you have an Apple PostScript printer, Apple includes PPDs for most models.) You then install the PPD file either by running the manufacturer's installer application or by copying the PPD to the PPDs folder in the main `Library` folder. This folder (shown in Figure 7.1) is found at `/Library/Printers/PPDs/`on your main startup disk.

NOTE   Installing PPDs and printer drivers requires an administrator account because the software must be written to the main `Library` folder (so that all users can use the drivers and PPDs). However, your personal `Library` folder also has a `Printers` folder in which you can install drivers and PPDs for local printers if you don't have access to the administrator account. Those printer drivers will be available only when you're signed in to your account.

If your printer requires a driver, you'll almost certainly install it using an installer application made available by the printer's manufacturer—in most cases, the best plan is to check the manufacturer's website, or visit Apple's Mac OS X download page (`www.apple.com/downloads/macosx/`) to check up on new drivers.

Otherwise, you'll find the printer drivers on the disk that came with your printer or on the printer manufacturer's website. Once you've found it, launch the installer and enable it to install the printer driver (see Figure 7.2); it may require authentication, depending on how it goes about the installation.

NOTE   It's not uncommon for printers to have their own third-party installers and, in some cases, setup assistants or other tools that help you configure the printer. So, don't be surprised if you see installers that don't look exactly like Figure 7.2.

FIGURE 7.1
The PPDs folder,
where PPD files for
your PostScript
printers are installed

FIGURE 7.2
Running the printer
driver installation
application for a
non-PostScript
laser printer

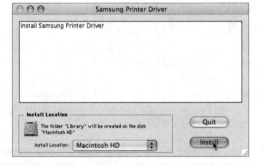

Printer drivers are stored in the folder /Library/Printers/, generally in their own folders or folders named for the printer manufacturer. In some cases, you'll notice that drivers have been preinstalled by Apple for some printers, such as popular Canon, HP, and Lexmark printers. If you don't find these drivers, you may have chosen not to install them when installing Mac OS X. Use your installation CD to do a custom installation, and install any of the drivers that you need.

Once your printer driver or PPD is installed, you can physically connect the printer to your Mac or network, if it isn't already connected. Then you can launch the Printer Setup Utility and begin configuring the printer.

Types of Printer Connections

It goes without saying that to get your printer configured, you'll have to know how it connects to your Mac. The way your printer is connected has a direct bearing on how the Printer Setup Utility accesses the printer. Here's a look at the options:

USB If a printer offers a USB connection, you'll connect that printer directly to your Mac via a USB port on the side of the Mac or on a USB hub. USB devices are hot-pluggable, so you should be able to connect your printer to your Mac at any time. USB-based printers can be either PostScript printers or non-PostScript. PostScript printers require a PPD, and non-PostScript printers require special driver software. With those items installed, open the Printer Setup Utility, and the printer should be accessible.

You can also connect your USB printer to an AirPort Base Station, if your Base Station model has a USB port. If this is the case, you'll be able to share your printer directly from the AirPort Base Station, rather than sharing it from your Mac.

NOTE   Mac OS X (starting with Mac OS X 10.2) offers the ability to share USB printers over a network; if you have a valid network connection, you can turn on Printer Sharing in the Sharing pane in System Preferences on the Mac where the USB printer is configured. In the Printer Setup Utility of other Macs connected to that network, you'll see an entry for that printer appear automatically, where it can be used as if it were a USB printer connected directly and configured solely for your Mac. (Note that you may need to install a printer driver on the networked Macs as well as the Mac that's connected directly to the printer.)

AppleTalk   An AppleTalk printer usually is connected to your Mac via Ethernet. The printer can be plugged directly into your Mac's Ethernet port using an Ethernet crossover cable, or the printer can be connected to an Ethernet hub to which your Mac is also connected. If you have the printer connected to an Ethernet hub, there's the added advantage that the printer is now available for all Macs on that network (indeed, all computers on the network, if they're compatible with the printer). For an AppleTalk-based printer connection to work correctly, you must turn on AppleTalk in the Network pane of the System Preferences application (see Figure 7.3) of each Mac that will access the printer. Most AppleTalk-based printers also are PostScript printers, so they don't require special driver software.

NOTE   If the printer is connected to an Ethernet hub that is also connected to an AirPort Base Station or similar wireless router, you can access the printer from your AirPort-enabled Mac as well. (In the Network pane of System Preferences, select AirPort from the Configure menu, and then use the AppleTalk tab to turn on AppleTalk access over the AirPort connection.) Likewise, you'll find special "bridge" devices that connect LocalTalk-based PostScript printers to Ethernet ports and networks offered by companies such as Asanté, discussed earlier in the sidebar "What Printers Does Mac OS X Support?"

Line Printer (LPR)   Mac OS X also can support a line printer (LPR) connection, which is a TCP/IP-based connection to a network printer that's generally connected via Ethernet. (Apple calls this *IP Printing*.) Some printers can act as line printers on their own, while others require a printer server to manage their spool files. If your printer supports an LPR connection, you'll need to know the IP address of the printer and whether or not it requires that you use a local spool. The advantage of this setup, if your printer supports it, is that you don't have to enable AppleTalk in order to print.

Directory Services   Under some circumstances, you may want to choose Directory Services—particularly if you're running Mac OS X Server on your network, which uses Directory Services to communicate the location and details of printers and other devices.

Bluetooth   If you have a printer that connects via Bluetooth, the setup is similar to USB—with the exception that your Mac will need to scan for and locate the wireless signal to and from your Mac. If your Mac is already configured for Bluetooth, this shouldn't be much of a problem.

FIGURE 7.3

You'll need to turn on AppleTalk for the port that will be used to access an AppleTalk-based printer over your local network.

Bonjour *Bonjour* (formerly Rendezvous) is Apple's name for the ZeroConf specification, which is technology that essentially enables printers to show up automatically on a network with no configuration, so your printer may say that it's ZeroConf or Bonjour/Rendezvous-compatible. If you have such a printer, you shouldn't actually need to configure it—your Mac will detect it whenever it connects to the network where that printer resides. That's what's automatic (and rather cool) about Bonjour.

With software installed and the printer connected, you're ready to move on to the Printer Setup Utility and configure the printer.

NOTE In general, printer drivers written for Mac OS X conform to what we're saying here—you install the driver or PPD and then access it via the built-in connection types discussed in this section. However, we have worked with printer installers that use slightly different drivers or enable you to access the printer in different ways. If you have an entry in your Printer List or Printer Browser that specifies the name or manufacturer of your printer, for instance (instead of the connection type), then choose that entry to connect to your printer.

Configuring in the Printer Setup Utility

The Printer Setup Utility is a catchall utility in Mac OS X that performs two different major tasks with regard to printing: printer setup and printer management. In previous Mac OS versions (including the Classic environment), setting up a printer was handled in the Chooser, and managing print jobs was done either in the PrintMonitor or via a desktop printer icon. In Mac OS X, all of that management is done through the Printer Setup Utility, although since Mac OS X 10.3, desktop printers are again available, and you can use these to manage print jobs on individual printers.

NOTE Desktop printing isn't possible in the Classic environment, but if you boot into Mac OS 9, you can access your printer (if you have a driver installed) via a desktop printer icon. However, you can use the PrintMonitor in the Classic environment, as you'll see later in this chapter.

ADD A PRINTER

We'll focus on managing print jobs later in this chapter; for now, it's time to configure the printer. If you've connected the printer to your Mac (or your network of Macs) and installed the proper drivers or PPD files, you're ready to launch the Printer Setup Utility. Do so by double-clicking its icon in the Utilities subfolder of the main Applications folder.

TIP   You can also launch the Printer Setup Utility from the Print & Fax pane in System Preferences. Click the Printing tab, and then click the Printer Setup button (it's inactive unless you've added a printer already). In fact, the Printing tab can be used to add new printers, which you can do by clicking the plus (+) icon beneath the list of printers; that immediately launches the Printer Setup Utility. You can also select a printer and click the minus (-) icon to delete the printer immediately, without accessing the Printer Setup Utility.

If you haven't set up a printer previously, the first thing you'll see is a dialog box asking if you'd like to set up a printer.

Click the Add button, and a new dialog window, called the Printer Browser, appears (see Figure 7.4). Once the window is opened and active, you should see a list of all printers that are currently accessible to your Mac. When you find the one that you want to configure, select it in the list.

The next step is to give the printer a name and enter a location. (Both of these entries are optional, but they can help you to locate and differentiate printers if you have quite a few at your disposal, particularly in an office or computer lab environment.) Choose the printer manufacturer in the Print Using menu, and choose the specific printer model if you can find it. With those selections made, click Add.

FIGURE 7.4
Using the Printer Browser window to select a shared printer

If you don't see your printer right away, click the More Printers button. This pops up a *dialog sheet*, which allows you to select the *type* of connection (AppleTalk, Bluetooth, or Windows Printing) you're using for your printer from the pop-up menu. You may also see entries for some specific printers if you've installed specific printer drivers.

Once you've selected the type of connection, any recognized printers will appear in the listing. How you select the printer depends on the type of connection:

AppleTalk　If you've chosen AppleTalk from the menu, you'll see any printers that are currently connected to your Mac via AppleTalk, including any printers found on the local network. If you have multiple AppleTalk zones, you'll see a second pop-up menu from which you can select the zone where you'd like to look for the printer. (Printers can be placed in different zones using AppleTalk routers. Selecting the correct zone makes it easier for you to avoid using an AppleTalk printer that isn't convenient—on another floor or in another building within your company. If you have a home or small-office network, however, you most likely don't need to worry about AppleTalk zones.) Once that zone is selected, you should see the printer. Select it, and the Printer Model menu comes alive. You can either leave it on Auto Select or open the menu and choose the manufacturer of your printer. (This is where you select the PPD you installed, if you installed one. If not—and your printer isn't listed in the menu—you might want to select a compatible printer or the Generic entry.) When you select the manufacturer, you'll see a list of possible model matches; select your model and click Add.

NOTE　In the list of printer models, you may see some entries that say CUPS+Gimp-Print v4.2.5, or something similar. Gimp-Print drivers are additional printer drivers available with Mac OS X that support older printers, and for which the manufacturer does not provide updated drivers. Gimp-Print (http://gimp-print.sourceforge.net) is an open source project that develops drivers for hundreds of printers, and these drivers are installed by default with Mac OS X. If you perform a custom install, you can choose to not install them, if you're sure you won't need them. You should only use one of the Gimp-Print drivers if there is no other driver for your printer.

TIP　In the Printer Model menu, near the top, is an Other command. Select it if your printer manufacturer or model isn't listed but you've downloaded a PPD for your printer. You'll see an Open dialog box that will enable you to locate the PPD file and add that description.

Bluetooth　If you have a printer that connects via Bluetooth, select Bluetooth from the top menu and the dialog will reconfigure somewhat. If the Bluetooth printer is within reach, it should appear in the list. If it doesn't, click Scan to see if rescanning the area causes it to appear. If so, select it, then choose a printer driver from the Printer Model menu, if appropriate. (Some printers will be recognized immediately via Bluetooth and won't require that you select the model.) Click Add to add the printer to your Printer List.

Windows Printing　If you'd like to print to a printer that's being shared by a Windows PC or server, the solution is to select Windows Printing from the menu. Another menu appears, where you can choose the workgroup or network neighborhood where the printer can be found over on the Windows side of things. Make your selection, choose a printer model if necessary, and click Add.

Printer Specific　If you've installed printer drivers that are specific to your printer, you may see other options in the menu, such as Epson FireWire or Canon BJ Network, which can be used to attach to those types of printers.

Now, if the printer has been selected via the More Printers dialog sheet and you've clicked Add, then it should be available in the Printer Browser. Select it and click Add again.

IP PRINTING

There's one other type of printing via the Printer Browser that we haven't covered. At the top of the Printer Browser window is the icon IP Printer; click it if you'd like to set up to print to a networked printer over IP instead of AppleTalk or Rendezvous. Then you'll take some steps to configure the IP printer (see Figure 7.5):

1. If you choose IP Printer, the printer isn't automatically recognized. Select the protocol from the first pop-up menu; the selection you make depends on what your printer supports.

2. Next, enter the printer's IP number in the Address entry box. (If the printer or print server has its own host and domain name, such as `printer1.mac-upgrade.com`, you can enter that instead.)

3. If the remote printer or print server has its own queue, leave the Queue entry box blank. If you want a local queue, enter the name of a queue in the Queue entry box.

4. At the bottom of the window, you can enter a Name and Location; these entries are optional, but they can help you identify the printer if you have several you can access.

5. Finally, select the driver or printer model of the printer from the Printer Using menu, and then choose the model name of the printer. (If the model isn't listed and the printer is PostScript, you can choose LaserWriter or Generic for basic functionality.) Click Add to add the printer. (In some cases, you'll see another quick dialog that asks you to specific any installed options on your printer; do so and click Continue.)

TIP   Suggestions for AppleTalk-based PostScript printers also apply to most IP-based PostScript printers. Refer to those notes and tips earlier in this chapter.

FIGURE 7.5
Adding an IP printer
using the Printer
Browser

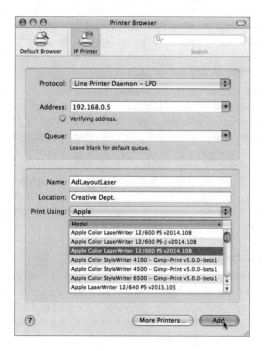

MANAGING THE PRINTER LIST

Once you've added a printer, you're returned to the Printer List, where you can see all the printers to which your Mac has access. Double-click a printer, and you'll see that printer's queue, where you can manage individual print jobs. (More on the printer queue in the section "Managing Print Jobs," later in this chapter.)

The Printer List enables you to select a default printer—the printer that's selected automatically when you or your users attempt to print a document. (It's also the printer used by applications that have a Print One Copy command or a similar command that bypasses the Print dialog box.) In the Printer List, the default is indicated by a bold font.

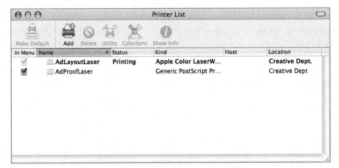

To change the default, select a new printer's name in the Printer List and choose Printers ➢ Make Default from the Printer Setup Utility's menu bar or click the Make Default button in the Printer List toolbar. The selected printer will become the default.

To delete a printer, select that printer in the Printer List and click the Delete button. The printer is immediately deleted unless it has active print jobs. If you attempt to delete a printer while it has active jobs, you'll see an error message, and you'll need to wait until the printer is finished printing; you can cancel active print jobs before deleting the printer.

PRINTER SETUP

Many printers won't require additional setup, but some more sophisticated PostScript and other laser printers may offer additional options. To see if that is the case, select your printer in the Printer List and choose Printers ➢ Show Info, or click the Show Info button in the toolbar. In the Info window, you'll see the printer's name and location or other information. (You also can rename the printer in the Printer Name entry box if you want.) From the pop-up menu, you have two other options—Printer Model and Installable Options. Choose Printer Model if you want to change the PPD associated with this printer.

Choose Installable Options if you want to let Mac OS X know that you have customized your printers with one or more options (see Figure 7.6). For instance, you may have options to choose additional paper cassettes or inform Mac OS X that the printer has upgraded memory. When you're finished with configuration, click Apply Changes.

CREATING A DESKTOP PRINTER

After you have added your printer to the Printer List using the Printer Setup Utility, you can manage your print jobs with this utility (see "Managing Print Jobs"), or you can create a *desktop printer* to make printing and managing jobs easier. A desktop printer is a kind of alias to your printer that offers some special features. (It is, in fact, just an alias to a file located in /Library/Printers inside your home folder.) To create a desktop printer, select your printer in the Printer List, then select Printers ➢ Create Desktop Printer. You'll see a Save dialog asking you where to save this desktop printer. You'll probably want to save it on your desktop, but you can save it anywhere you want. You can also create several desktop printers and put them in different locations, such as your `Documents` folder or other frequently used folders.

TIP   With some printers, you can select Printers ➢ Configure Printer to dig into that printer's special configuration options, such as commands that enable you to calibrate the printer, print a test page, and so on. Select a printer in the Printer List; if this menu item is active (if it is not grayed out), then you should be able to select it and make changes to that printer's settings. You'll also find some of those sorts of commands right on the Printers menu, allowing you to, for instance, print a test page.

TIP   If you want easy access to a desktop printer, drag its icon into the Dock, so you can use it without having to switch to the Finder.

FIGURE 7.6
Installable Options in the
Printer Info window

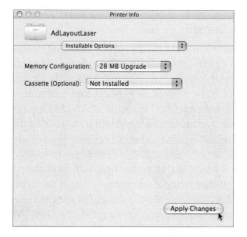

SUPPLY LEVELS

Added in Mac OS X 10.4, the Supply Levels command is an interesting addition—with the latest printers, you can check to see how they're doing on toner and so on. And whether or not the printer's supply levels are recognized, clicking the Supplies button that appears in the Supply Levels dialog sheet takes you to the Apple Store, where you can buy ink and toner for Mac-compatible products. To try this out, select your printer in the Printer List and then choose Printers ➢ Supply Levels.

POOL PRINTERS

This addition in Mac OS X 10.4 is very interesting for workgroup environments. The Pool Printers command allows you to build a collection of your printers so that when one is busy another one can be used to print your document. This can be handy in a work environment where you have a few different printers set up in close proximity and you'd like to simply print to the one that's least busy at any given moment.

To pool printers together, first select them in the Printer List, then choose Printers ➤ Pool Printers. In the dialog box that appears, drag the printers around to select which has priority, then give the printer pool a unique name and click Add. Now, that grouping of printers will appear in the Printer List. In the future, you can select it as a "printer" in your applications, allowing you to print to the pooled printers and, hopefully, get your document a bit more quickly.

Printing Your Documents

Once you have your printer or printers installed and recognized by the Printer Setup Utility, you're ready to move on to printing from your applications. This is a two-step process. The first step, Page Setup, is where you'll select some overall options for how you'd like to print to your printer; specifically, you'll choose the type of paper and the orientation of the output. Then, every time you print a document, you'll use the Print dialog box (or, in some cases, a Print dialog sheet interface that pops out of the document window's title bar) to configure the individual print job, including settings such as the number of copies, page range, and printer-specific options.

Page Setup

The first time you visit an application, and occasionally after that, you'll want to visit the Page Setup dialog box by selecting File ➤ Page Setup. This dialog box (or a dialog sheet in some applications, such as TextEdit, shown in Figure 7.7) offers basic options that govern how documents within that application will be printed. In general, these include the paper size you plan to print to, the orientation of the printed page, and the scale at which the page will be printed.

Note the Format For menu in the Page Setup dialog sheet. This menu enables you to select the printer for which you'd like to select Page Setup attributes. It enables you to choose from among printers that you've already added in the Printer Setup Utility. You also can choose Any Printer in the Format For menu if you'd like all your printers to have the same basic Page Setup settings.

At the top of the Page Setup dialog is the Settings menu, which enables you to switch between the different panels of information in the window. (By default, the menu reads Page Attributes.) To switch between different setup options, select an item from this menu. By default, you'll likely see only Page Attributes and an option called Save As Default, which enables you to save any of the changes that you end up making to the items we're discussing here. (Depending on the printer driver or PPD you've installed, however, you may see additional options in the Settings menu.)

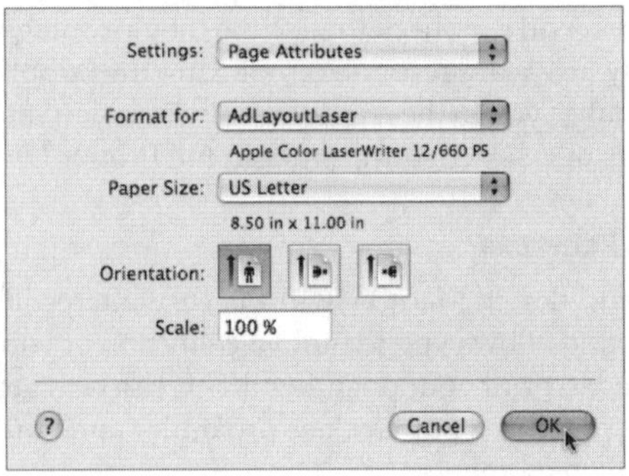

FIGURE 7.7
The Page Setup dialog sheet enables you to set Page Setup options for each application.

With Page Attributes selected, you can set a few different parameters:

Format For   Choose the printer for which you're making choices.

Paper Size   Select the size of paper that the application should be prepared to encounter in the printer. (You'll also have to load that paper and tell the printer, in the Print dialog box, where to find that particular type of paper, if necessary.) The standard settings include US Letter, US Legal, international paper sizes, and standard envelope sizes. Note that different printer drivers and PPDs will change these options to any other specific paper sizes that are supported by that printer.

TIP   If you don't see the size you need, choose Manage Custom Sizes. Click the plus (+) icon and give the new size a name, then enter a Page Size and Printer Margins. Click OK to save the Page Size.

Orientation   Orientation refers to how the document should be printed on the page. The default option is Portrait, which prints a page that is longer than it is wide—the typical orientation. Click the middle button for Landscape, which prints a page that's wider than it is long (ideal for ledger books or other columnar output). The third button sets the printer to print in Reverse Landscape, which simply flips the Landscape output by 180 degrees.

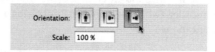

Scale   Enter a number in the Scale entry box that represents the percentage of the original size at which you want to print the document. A document that's larger than your selected paper size, for instance, might be printed at 75 percent or smaller in order to fit on the page.

Once you've set your options, you can select Save As Default from the Settings menu if you'd like to store these settings for future print jobs. If everything looks right, click OK in Page Setup to set your choices and dismiss the dialog sheet.

NOTE   As mentioned, each application's Page Setup dialog box is a separate entity. You should select Page Setup in each of your applications to make document setup choices whenever necessary.

Print

When you've set up a printer, configured it, and made your choices in Page Setup, you're ready to print. Printing is accomplished via the Print dialog box, which you access in nearly all applications by choosing File ➤ Print or pressing ⌘P. (You'll also find that many applications with icon-based toolbars offer a Print icon that you can click to open the Print dialog box.) When you've selected the Print command, you'll see either the Print dialog box or the Print dialog sheet (see Figure 7.8), which pops out from the document window's title bar.

Mac OS X offers this standard Print dialog box/sheet interface element to application developers and those who develop drivers for printers. In almost all cases, you'll find that the dialog box works in a standard fashion, with typical settings located in familiar places. At the same time, though, programmers can extend the Print dialog so that you can access the special features of the application's printing capability as well as the built-in special features of the printer.

FIGURE 7.8

The Print dialog sheet, which appears in native Mac OS X applications

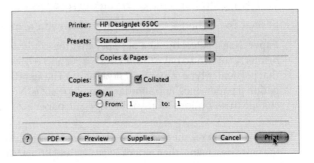

NOTE As we said, you'll see this print dialog in *almost* all cases. Some printer manufacturers (particularly those of non-PostScript ink-jet printers) will offer their own print dialogs that are slightly different from this one. Generally, they will look similar and offer similar options, but if your particular printer driver has a unique look to its Print dialog box, take a moment to get acquainted with it and, perhaps, compare similarities and differences to the Print dialog items shown in this section. (Note also that some applications will offer their own Print dialog boxes, particularly high-end publishing and graphics applications.)

To begin, note one nice feature: the capability to select the printer you want to use from within the Print menu. Instead of heading back to the Printer Setup Utility or some other application to activate a printer, you simply can select it in the Print dialog box. You do so by selecting the desired printer in the Printer pop-up menu:

Also in the Printer menu, you can select Edit Printer List if you don't see the printer you'd like to choose. When you select Edit Printer List, the Printer Setup Utility application is launched and brought to the front so that you can configure or add more printers.

TIP In Mac OS X 10.4, you can change the behavior of the Printer menu in the Print dialog box via the Print & Fax pane in System Preferences. On the Printing tab in that pane, you can choose whether the Printer menu automatically shows the printer that was most recently used or the default printer. (In that same preference pane, you can also determine which printer will be the default.)

Below the Printer menu is the Preset menu, where you can access previously saved sets of Print dialog settings. As you'll see, you can change a host of settings in the Print dialog box (number of copies, quality settings, special layout options) and then save those settings with a particular name by choosing Save As from the Preset menu. Then, you can access that set of choices in the Presets menu, making it quick and easy to change from one set of choices to another.

The next menu is the untitled panel menu, which shows the default Copies & Pages selection. This pop-up menu is used to access both the standard and optional panels of printer options. Here's a quick look at the standard options available in most Print dialog boxes:

Copies & Pages   In the Copies & Pages panel, enter in the Copies entry box the number of copies of this document you'd like printed. If you'd like those copies collated (so that all pages of the first copy are printed in their entirety before the next copy is printed), turn on the Collated option. Then, for the Pages option, select either All or From. If you select From, enter the range of pages in the current document that you'd like to have printed. (The range is inclusive, so if you want the last page that prints to be page 7, for instance, then enter **7** in the second entry box.)

Layout   In the Layout panel, choose how many document pages should appear on a single sheet of paper and, if more than one, in what order they should be printed. (You may find it useful to print more than one page at a time on a piece of paper, either to create a "thumbnail" representation of a longer document or to conserve paper for drafts or notes that you're printing for your own use.) In the Pages Per Sheet menu, choose the number of document pages you want to print on each printed sheet of paper. Then select the icon that represents the layout direction you'd like those multiple pages to take on each page—this is the flow of document pages on the printed piece of paper. Finally, from the Border menu, select the type of line you want to separate each document page that appears on the printed sheet.

Output Options   Many printers will include an Output Options panel in which you can choose to save the print job as a file instead of sending it to the printer. Turn on the Save As File option, and you'll be able to access a format—PDF, PostScript, or a third-party option if one is installed. Note that you also can save a document as a PDF using the PDF button at the bottom of the Print dialog sheet. The Output Options panel is a holdover from earlier printer drivers when PDF wasn't as prominent as it is in Mac OS X, but it's also handy for special circumstances, particularly when you specifically need to save the document in PostScript format, not PDF.

Scheduler   This panel lets you choose when you want to print your document. You can select Now, to print right away; At, to set a specific time; or On Hold, so your print job is created and spooled but not launched. You'll then need to go into the Printer Setup Utility and open your printer, by double-clicking it in the Printer List, to start the job. If you have created a desktop printer, you can access your printer's management functions directly by double-clicking this desktop printer icon. If a job is On Hold, select it in the printer dialog, and then click the Resume button in the toolbar when you want to print it. You can also set a priority for your print job, so the most urgent documents get printed first. This is useful if you are sharing a printer on a network, and many jobs get sent to the printer. Jobs with higher priorities will be handled first.

Paper Handling   This panel lets you choose how you want the pages of your document printed. You can choose Reverse Page Order to have the document printed from last page to first. This is practical if your pages come out face up; you won't need to reorder them after they have printed. You can also choose to print All Pages, Odd Numbered Pages, or Even Numbered Pages. The Odd and Even options let you create two-sided documents: you first print the odd pages, then you place the printed pages back in your paper drawer and print the even pages.

ColorSync   The ColorSync panel lets you access special color features, such as choosing a Color Conversion or a Quartz Filter. You can choose from a number of preset filters or create your own. See Chapter 8 for more on using ColorSync.

Paper Feed   Standard on many printers, especially workgroup laser printers, this is a panel that enables you to select the cassette or tray from which the paper should be retrieved when you print. In the Feed Page From menu, you can choose a tray from which the paper for this print job should be loaded. In some cases, you also may have a First Page From option, which enables you to select the first page from one tray (or the manual feed) and the remaining pages from a different tray.

Quality Or Print Modes   Many ink-jet printers offer a Quality or Print Modes panel, where you can select the quality setting for printed output. In most cases, you'll simply select from options such as Draft, Normal, and Fine. You also may be able to select paper types (normal or photo paper) so the printer knows how densely to print pages and images.

Error Handling   For PostScript printers, you can determine how PostScript errors are reported—either they're ignored or a report is generated. You also can tell the printer how to handle an out-of-paper error, either by switching to another cassette or by displaying an alert message.

Application-Specific   The application you're printing from has the option of adding panels to your Print dialog box, enabling you to select from options the application developer wants to specify. For instance, a particular application may offer you options such as printing only part of the document (text but not images), printing documents in a particular sequence, setting an internal quality level, and so forth. If an application offers such choices, you'll likely see a menu item in the panel menu with the application's name. (For Safari, for instance, options include printing web page information in the header and footer and whether or not Safari should print the background images and colors of pages.)

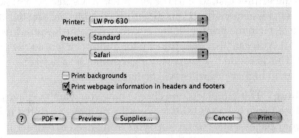

Summary   Select this panel to see a listing of all the options as you've set them so far.

Have you made all your choices? If so, you have several options left. You can click the Print button, which sends the print job to the Printer Setup Utility. You then can move on to the section "Managing Print Jobs," assuming you feel the need to manage this print job. (If you don't, just move on to other tasks as your document prints in the background.)

Before you click the Print button, however, you also have the option of clicking the Preview button, which causes your document to appear in a preview window (see Figure 7.9). In fact, it appears in a new window in the Preview application.

TIP Before clicking Preview, you should use the Presets ➤ Save As option to save any changes you've made to the settings in the Print dialog box up to this point. You also can choose Presets ➤ Save if you'd like to update the current settings with any changes you've made in the Print dialog box. When you preview a document, the Print dialog sheet is closed, and any changes you've made to settings will be lost if you haven't saved them.

If the preview looks good, you can use the Print button at the bottom of the Preview application window to immediately print the document. If you don't like how it looks, click Cancel and you can switch back to your application to make changes.

TIP When you check the Soft Proof check box, Mac OS X will use ColorSync technology to attempt to make the preview look more like your final printed output based on the printer's color capabilities. (If your printer is black-and-white only, the images will change to reflect that, too.)

FIGURE 7.9
Previewing your document before printing

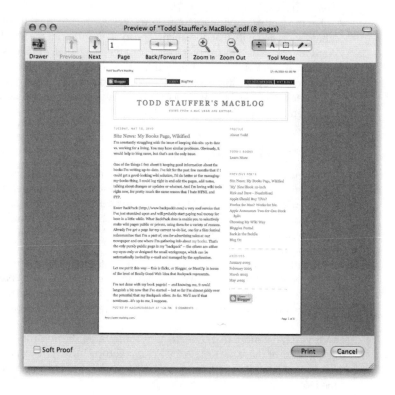

Another option available in the Print dialog is the PDF button, which hides the Save As PDF command. This creates a PDF file that you can send to others, on any platform, so they can view the document just as you see it on-screen. If you click this, you'll see a Save dialog prompting you to name your PDF file. See Chapter 8 for more on creating and working with PDF documents. Note that the PDF button is also used for sending faxes, as we'll discuss later in this chapter.

PRINTING WITH A DESKTOP PRINTER

We showed you earlier how to create a desktop printer. This icon lets you access print job management easily (see the next section). But it also offers a useful feature: you can drag files onto the desktop printer to print them. If you want to print a file, just drag its icon onto your desktop printer, and the print job will begin.

This works in two different ways. For some files (such as plain-text files, RTF files, and PDF files) or graphic files (such as GIFs, TIFFs, and JPEGs), the print job begins immediately. You'll see the desktop printer icon bounce once or twice in the Dock and then quit. The print job is launched, and you don't need to do anything else. If you want to manage the print job, double-click the desktop printer to see its current jobs. (See the next section for more on managing print jobs with a desktop printer.)

For most other application formats, dragging a file document onto a desktop printer tells the application associated with that document type to open and print the file. If, for example, you drag a Microsoft Word file onto a desktop printer icon, Word will open (if it is not already running) and open its print dialog for that file. You'll need to choose any options you want, then click Print.

You can drag multiple icons onto a desktop printer—each one will work in one of the two ways mentioned previously. If your icons are different formats, some will print right away, and others will open their applications.

Managing Print Jobs

Once you've sent a document to the printer, management of that document is taken over by the Printer Setup Utility. The Printer Setup Utility enables you to manage each printer's *queue*, the lineup of documents waiting to be printed. If you need to change the order of documents as they print, halt the printing of a document, or suspend printing to a particular printer, you'll do that from within your printer's queue window (which you can access via the Printer Setup Utility or in some other way, such as via a desktop printer).

The Printer Setup Utility isn't launched automatically when you print, but your printer's helper application is, which is used to display your printer's queue. We'll look at that a bit more later in this section, including creating a desktop printer to quickly access that queue. Putting a link to your desktop printer in the Dock can be extremely convenient, particularly if you only have one printer.

If you have more than one printer, though, you'll find the Printer Setup Utility useful for managing them at the same time—the Printer Setup Utility is located in the Utilities folder inside the Applications folder. (If you print often, you'll probably want to drag the Printer Setup Utility to the Dock to create a Dock icon for it.)

The Printer Setup Utility's Printer List shows you immediately if items are printing by displaying each printer's status in the Status column.

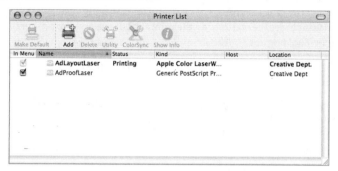

If all is going well, the status of your selected printer will be shown as Printing; if the printer's queue has been stopped, the status could be Stopped; if there's a problem with the printer, the status will be Error. In the Printer List, you can select a printer and use the Printer Setup Utility's Printers menu to stop the queue (Printers ➤ Stop Jobs, if items are currently printing) or start it again (Printers ➤ Start Jobs).

The Document Queue

To open a particular printer's queue (thereby revealing all the currently printing and waiting documents), double-click the printer in the Printer List or select a printer and choose the Printers ➤ Show Jobs command. That printer's queue appears, as shown in Figure 7.10.

At the top of the printer queue window (each window's actual title is the name of the printer, as you can see in Figure 7.10), you'll see the name of the currently printing document. Beneath that is the status area, where you'll be able to determine at what point the printer is in the process—sending data, processing the job, and so on. If the printer reports an error (it's out of paper, there's a paper jam, and so on), you'll see that in the status area as well.

FIGURE 7.10

Managing documents in the printer's queue

NOTE You can also access the queue window by double-clicking your desktop printer icon, if you have created one. Or you can click the icon for your printer that displays in the Dock when your job starts printing. The Printer Setup Utility is useful for managing print jobs if you have more than one printer and want to see the status of all the printers, but the desktop printer is a more direct way to manage individual printers.

In the job list, you'll see each print job as it has been added to this printer's queue. Using the job list, you can manage each print job:

◆ Select a job, and you can click the Hold button (or select Jobs ≻ Hold Job) to keep that job from printing. Other jobs behind it will take priority and move up in the job list. After you hold a job, you can resume printing it by selecting it in the job list and clicking Resume (or selecting Jobs ≻ Resume Job).

TIP You can use the Jobs ≻ Resume Job on Page command if you'd like to choose a particular page number for it to begin printing.

◆ To remove a job from the queue, select it in the job list and click Delete (or select Jobs ≻ Delete Job). You can select multiple jobs by holding down the ⌘ key while clicking them.

In Mac OS X 10.4, you can access the Completed tab to see jobs that have been printed (or failed to print) and to get a sense of when that happened. The list is handy for knowing what has printed successfully and what hasn't. Note that you can clear that list by choosing Jobs ≻ Clear Completed Job List.

The Desktop Printer

For a little easier access to a particular printer's queue, you can create a desktop printer. That gives you an alias that, when clicked, launches the printer's queue window immediately, even if there's nothing currently printing.

To create a desktop printer, select a printer in the Printer List and choose Printers ≻ Create Desktop Printer. A dialog sheet appears asking you to give the desktop printer a name (you can leave it the same if desired) and enabling you to choose a destination for saving it. (That's right—a desktop printer doesn't have to be on the desktop.) When you've made those choices, click Save.

You can also drag a printer directly from the Printer List to your desktop (or another folder in the Finder) to create a desktop printer icon. In that case, you won't be asked if you want to rename it.

Once the icon is on the desktop, you can move it elsewhere—the Dock, for instance. Then, launch the icon and the queue window for that printer will appear.

Printing from Classic

Printing in Classic applications in Mac OS X is different from printing in Cocoa and Carbon (that is, native-running) applications. For one, printing from Classic is a little more limited. Although most AppleTalk-compatible PostScript printers will enable you to print from Classic, other printers may be touch-and-go because the Classic environment doesn't access printers directly.

In some cases, a printer driver (such as the driver for an ink-jet printer) that works for printing in Mac OS 9 doesn't necessarily work for printing in the Classic environment. For printers that do work, you'll need to configure the Classic environment to use them.

With others—particularly USB-connected PCL printers—you may need to configure the printer driver separately within the Classic environment and print to it. In fact, many ink-jet printers install two sets of drivers—one for Mac OS X and one for Classic—but support printing from within the Classic environment.

Otherwise, you'll find that the Page Setup and Print dialog boxes for PostScript printers are similar to their Mac OS X counterparts in the Classic environment. Dialog boxes for USB-based printers are a bit different, as you'll see later in this section.

NOTE As mentioned earlier, Mac OS X (and available drivers and technology) doesn't support printing to serial port printers that use the older QuickDraw language for printing. To use such a printer, you'll need to boot into Mac OS 9.

The Chooser

In order to print from Classic applications, you need to access the Classic Chooser application. To do so, launch any Classic application. Once Classic is launched, open the Apple menu (on the Classic menu bar) and select Chooser. The Chooser appears (see Figure 7.11).

TIP You also can launch the Chooser directly by opening the System Folder that you use for Classic, then opening the Apple Menu Items folder. Inside, you'll find the Chooser icon. Double-click the Chooser icon to launch the Classic environment and the Chooser application. You can also get to the classic Apple menu via the Classic status menu bar icon, which is discussed in Chapter 27, "Fixing Applications and Managing Classic."

On the left side of the Chooser, you'll see icons that, in most cases, represent printer drivers. If you haven't installed any additional printer drivers for the Classic environment, you'll see only the Laser-Writer 8 driver. When you select an active printer driver, the right side of the window will light up with either a list of compatible printers or a port you can choose in order to access that printer.

Support for non-PostScript printers in Mac OS X varies from manufacturer to manufacturer. If your printer manufacturer supports printing from Classic, you need to download drivers from the manufacturer's website and run an installer application. Depending on the driver's installer, you may need to boot into Mac OS 9 (don't forget to select the System Folder that you use for Classic, if you have more than one Mac OS 9 System Folder installed) and then run the installer you've downloaded. (Some of the latest installers we've worked with will install Classic drivers at the same time as they install Mac OS X drivers, without requiring that you boot into Mac OS 9.)

FIGURE 7.11

The Chooser is where you set up a printer for Classic printing.

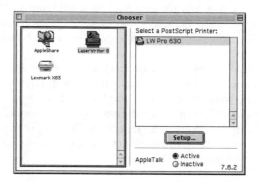

Once the driver is installed, open the Chooser and configure the printer by selecting its driver on the left side and the printer connection on the right. You might even want to test the printer by printing from an application in Mac OS 9. Then, boot back into Mac OS X to configure the printer in the Classic environment.

If you've installed an ink-jet driver that can work from the Classic environment, select it from the left side of the Chooser window. On the right side of the window, you'll see the connection options—most likely a USB icon and a printer name. Select that connection and click the Configure button to configure the printer.

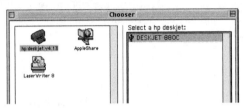

For PostScript printers, select the LaserWriter 8 icon, as shown previously in Figure 7.11. Now, the right side should change to a listing of recognized PostScript printers. (If you don't see the printers, you may not have AppleTalk turned on. Click the On button in the AppleTalk portion of the Chooser window. If that doesn't work, make sure the printer is on.)

Select the printer you want to use, and then click the Setup button. You'll see a small status window. If you have the option, click either Auto Setup (which will automatically configure the printer) or Select PPD. In the Select the PostScript Printer Description File dialog box, locate the name of the printer you're using and click Select. If you don't see the exact printer, you can choose LaserWriter for basic functionality.

NOTE   PPD files for the Classic environment are stored in the System Folder that you use for the Classic environment. If you installed Mac OS X over Mac OS 9, you'll find those PPDs in /System Folder/Extensions/Printer Descriptions/.

Once you've set up the printer, click the Close box in the top-left corner of the Chooser window to close it (or select File ➢ Quit). The Chooser closes, and you're ready to print.

Classic Page Setup

Choose File ➢ Page Setup in any Classic application, and you'll see the printer's Page Setup dialog box. In the Classic environment, both the Page Setup and Print dialog boxes vary much more widely than they do in Mac OS X. In some cases, the Classic versions of these dialog boxes offer more options than do the native Mac OS X counterparts. Figure 7.12 shows a typical Page Setup dialog box for a PostScript printer.

The first thing you might notice about Page Setup in the Classic environment is that the dialog box is completely *modal*—you can't move it or do anything else at all (in the Classic environment) while the dialog box is on the screen. This is how dialog boxes often work in Mac OS 9 and earlier versions, and it's one of the reasons for the development of modeless dialog boxes and dialog sheets in Mac OS X. Within the Classic environment, you'll need to complete your work in the dialog box before you can do anything else. (If you want to use the Dock to switch to another Mac OS X application, though, you can do that.)

FIGURE 7.12

Page Setup in the
Classic environment

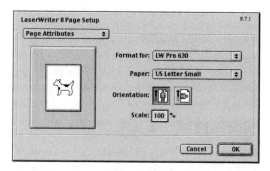

Like the Page Setup dialog in Mac OS X, the Classic Page Setup dialog box offers different panels that are accessed via an untitled pop-up menu. By default, you'll see the Page Attributes options, where you can select which printer you're formatting for (in the Format For menu), what size paper you're printing to (in the Paper menu), the orientation, and whether or not documents should be scaled before they're printed.

Unlike the native Mac OS X Page Setup dialog, you'll find another option in most LaserWriter 8–based Classic Page Setup dialog boxes: PostScript Options. Select PostScript Options from the pop-up menu, and you'll see a slew of choices you can turn on to affect how items print on your PostScript printer.

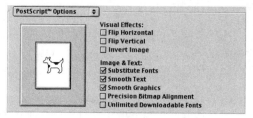

Once you've made your choices in the Page Setup dialog, click OK to dismiss it. Now you're ready to print.

Classic Print Dialog for PostScript Printers

Printing to PostScript printers in Classic is similar to printing in the native Mac OS X Print dialog box, partly because they share the same approach to using PPD files (at least, for PostScript printers). Choose File ➤ Print in a Classic application or press ⌘P to bring up the Print dialog box, shown in Figure 7.13.

FIGURE 7.13

The Classic Print
dialog box

Like the native Mac OS X Print dialog box, the Classic version has quite a few options available from the unlabeled pop-up menu (by default, it's called General), especially when you're dealing with PostScript printers. Some of them are similar: General (similar to Copies & Pages) offers settings for the number of copies to print, the range of pages to print, and the paper sources. Layout is another familiar option in which you choose how many document pages will print on each sheet of paper.

You'll also find some other panels that vary somewhat from the Print dialog box in native Mac OS X applications. Here are some of those, which you can select from the unlabeled pop-up menu:

Background Printing This panel lets you decide whether or not the document will print in the background, enabling you to continue your work in the application. In Mac OS X, this isn't an option; documents are always printed in the background. In Classic, a document will print more quickly if it prints in the foreground, but you'll get control of the application more quickly if it prints in the background. If you elect to print the document in the background, you also can choose to have it print at a particular time or priority level.

Color Matching Here you can select whether or not you want the document to print in color (assuming that's an option with your printer) and if so, what ColorSync profile to use. (More on ColorSync in Chapter 8.)

Cover Page On this panel, you can choose whether or not a cover page (that offers details on the print job) should print before or after your document prints.

Font Settings Here you can decide on certain options regarding fonts and PostScript printing. Annotate Font Keys means that comments are added to PostScript output. In the Font Download-ing section, you can choose which type of font should be downloaded to the printer, whether or not fonts should be downloaded if needed, and whether they should be turned into a special type of font called a *hinted Type 42* font.

NOTE Type 42 fonts are TrueType fonts that are converted to this special format for printing on PostScript printers that recognize Type 42 fonts. The quality is better but not always as compatible with PostScript interpreters.

Job Logging This panel has two sections. In the top section, you can determine what happens in case of a PostScript error: nothing, a screen report, or a detailed report. In the Job Documentation section, you can determine whether a full copy of the PostScript file will be saved (Generate Job Copy) or just a log entry (Generate Job Log). If you choose one of these options, you then can choose the Job Documentation Folder on the right side of the panel.

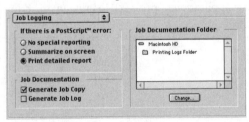

Paper Handling You can choose how the printer responds when it's out of paper.

Save As File By default, you can save a PostScript print job as a file—either as a job file or as an Encapsulated PostScript (EPS) document. If you've installed Acrobat software, you also can save print jobs as PDF files. In the Save As File section, select the options for saving to the particular file type you're interested in creating.

NOTE   The Save As File options come into play only if you choose File from the Destination menu in the top-right corner of the Print dialog box. Selecting File changes the Print button (in the lower-right corner of the Print dialog box) to a Save button, telling you that you'll be saving a file instead of printing it when you click the button.

Application Specific   As with the Mac OS X Print dialog, you'll find that some applications will add their own entries in this menu. Select it and make choices as warranted—these will be options that the application provides for altering the printing process or the printed document in some way.

Your particular printer (or more specifically, the PPD file) may offer special settings such as Imaging Options and Printer Specific Options. Consult your printer's manual and make your choices in those panels, if they're available.

At the bottom-left corner of the Print dialog box, you can click the Save Settings button to save the current settings and assign them as the defaults. (You can't create a special Custom set of options as you can in native Mac OS X Print dialog boxes.)

Finally, when you're ready to print, click the Print button. You'll see a status window appear while your document is sent either to the printer (if you're printing in the foreground) or to a spool file (if you're printing in the background). For foreground printing, you'll wait until the entire document is sent to the printer; for a long document, it can be many minutes, depending on the speed of your printer and the number of print jobs that the printer or print server is trying to manage.

Classic Print Dialog for Non-PostScript Printers

If you've installed a non-PostScript printer that supports access from the Classic environment, you'll find that the Print dialog box for your printer is likely very different from anything you've seen in this chapter. That's because non-PostScript printer drivers in Mac OS 9 and before (and, hence, the Classic environment) create a Print dialog box completely on their own, for the most part eschewing any standard Mac OS interface element. (As mentioned, this is possible but more rare in the native Mac OS X environment.) That means that each printer's Print dialog box can be very different from another (see Figure 7.14).

NOTE   You'll find that the Page Setup dialog box for non-PostScript printers also varies from model to model. In most cases, though, the options are very similar to those offered in standard Page Setup dialog boxes.

Although they are different, you'll find that these print dialog boxes are familiar enough to get the job done. You'll find copies, paper type, print quality, layout, color, and other choices. Make your selections and click the OK or Print button to begin printing.

TIP   Getting errors when printing to ink-jet printers from the Classic environment? One solution (according to postings in Apple's online help forums) appears to be to increase the memory allocation for the PrintMonitor application, which is located in the Extensions folder inside the Mac OS 9 System Folder. Highlight the PrintMonitor icon and select File ➤ Get Info. Choose Memory from the Show menu. Set the Minimum Size to at least 300KB. Click the Close button in the Show window, and then try printing again.

Changing Printers in Classic

Some Print dialog boxes in the Classic environment will enable you to choose between different Post-Script printers as long as they all use the LaserWriter 8 driver. Those printers will appear in the Printer menu in the Print dialog box, enabling you to send a particular print job to a particular printer.

If you're switching between PostScript and non-PostScript printers, though, you'll need to choose a different printer before you invoke the Print command. You'll do that by returning to the Chooser and selecting the new printer. Then, open Page Setup in the application and make any settings changes that are necessary. (In fact, you should open the Page Setup dialog box in any Classic applications that were running at the time you changed the printer, so that the applications can be made aware of the changes.) Finally, invoke the Print command to print a document using the newly chosen printer.

Managing Background Printing

For background printing from Classic applications, wait until all pages are sent to the spool file; then you have control over your application again. You'll notice, however, that even background printing doesn't add the job in the Printer Setup Utility. Instead, you won't really see any progress indicators regarding your print job—at least, not by default. If you encounter an error, you'll likely see a floating alert box that you can dismiss by clicking its Close box.

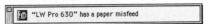

The other way to check progress is by switching to the PrintMonitor, using Classic's Application menu at the top-right corner of the screen. (You can see this menu only when a Classic application is active.) Select PrintMonitor, and you're switched to the PrintMonitor, where you can see the current printer's queue (see Figure 7.15).

You can stop the currently printing document by selecting that document and clicking Cancel Printing or choosing File ➢ Stop Printing. Select a print job in the Waiting area to delete it (click Remove from List) or to set a certain time when it should print (Set Print Time). To close the PrintMonitor, click its Close box or select File ➢ Close, or you can simply wait until all queued documents have printed, when PrintMonitor will close itself.

TIP The PrintMonitor has a File ➢ Preferences command that you can use to change the way Print-Monitor behaves.

FIGURE 7.15
The Classic
environment's
PrintMonitor

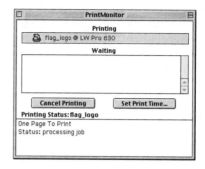

Sending and Receiving Faxes

Mac OS X 10.3 and higher includes built-in fax software so you can send and receive faxes with your Mac. Unlike previous versions of Mac OS, you don't need any third-party software for these tasks. Sending a fax with Mac OS X is as easy as printing a document; receiving faxes is simple too (assuming your Mac has a built-in modem or a fully compatible external model), since your Mac can handle everything. All you need to send and receive faxes with your Mac is a modem that's plugged into a working phone jack.

Using your Mac to send and receive faxes saves paper; you don't need to print them out before sending them, and you may find it sufficient to read your incoming faxes on-screen. Receiving faxes on your Mac also lets you organize them more easily, because you receive them as electronic documents that can be easily archived.

Sending Faxes

Sending a fax is just like printing a document. As you saw previously in this chapter, when you select File ➤ Print, the Print dialog has a PDF button, which offers the command Fax PDF. Adjust any settings you want in this dialog, such as Copies & Pages, Layout, and so forth. Then, instead of clicking Print, click the Fax button. This displays a Fax sheet, where you enter the necessary information to send your fax.

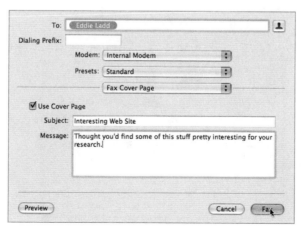

In the To field, enter a name and phone number, or just a phone number. You can click the Address Book button to the right of this field to display a list of your contacts from which you can select. Enter a subject, if you wish, and a dialing prefix (such as 9 for an outside line), if necessary, and then select a modem. (In most cases, this will be Internal Modem, unless you have an external modem or use a shared modem on another Mac.)

The Presets menu functions in the same way as for printing, enabling you to save sets of preferences; see the section "Printing Your Documents," earlier in the chapter.

The untitled menu offers the same options as for printing, with three exceptions:

Fax Cover Page   This panel lets you use a cover page and enter text if you wish. Check Cover Page and in the text field type the text you want to be displayed on this page. All you get here is a simple, text-only cover page, unlike some fax software that offers graphical choices as well.

Modem   This panel gives you options for using your modem. You can use Tone or Pulse dialing, turn the sound On or Off, and choose Wait for Dial Tone before Dialing.

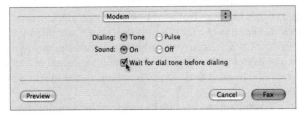

Printer Features   This section lets you choose from two resolutions for your faxes: High (200dpi) or Low (100dpi). High-resolution faxes take longer to send, but they are more readable.

Once you have made all your choices, just click Fax to send the fax. You'll see the Fax icon appear in the Dock as the fax is sent. If you want to monitor the fax as it is sent, click this icon; you'll see an interface that is the same as for a printer.

Managing Faxes

When you send a fax, the fax icon, which represents your modem, displays in the Dock. You can click this icon to see the progress of your fax—this is similar to what you see when you click your printer icon and check its jobs.

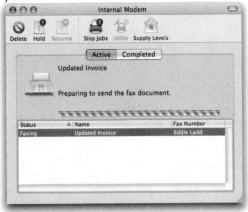

You can manage faxes the same way you manage print jobs: click a fax in the job list to select it, then click Hold to pause the job, Resume to restart it, or Delete to delete it. Click the Stop Jobs button to stop sending faxes, and click Start Jobs to send again.

Also, if you have several faxes in the queue, you can reorder them by dragging them in the list—the top line goes next.

Receiving Faxes

Sure, it's easy to send faxes, but it's also a breeze to receive faxes on your Mac. In addition to receiving faxes, your Mac enables you to choose from several options for post-processing these faxes. You configure fax reception by opening the Print & Fax pane of System Preferences and choosing the Faxing tab (see Figure 7.16).

To be able to receive faxes, you must first check Receive Faxes on This Computer. Then enter your fax number and select how many rings before your Mac answers. Next, choose from the following options:

Save To   Choose a folder to hold your saved faxes. Even if you choose to print or e-mail them, it's a good idea to save them as well. Select a folder from the list, such as Shared Faxes, which is accessible to all users (it's located in /Users/Shared), or select another folder by choosing Other Folder.

Email To   You can e-mail a fax automatically to yourself or any other user. Click the Address Book icon and select a name and e-mail address.

Print On Printer   If you want your faxes to be printed immediately, select a printer from the pop-up menu.

When you receive a fax, it is saved as a PDF file that you can view or print using Preview or Adobe Acrobat Reader. This is practical, since you don't need any special application to view, print, or archive faxes. Just move them where you want like any other type of file; even send them to others by e-mail.

FIGURE 7.16
The Faxing tab in the Print & Fax preference pane is where you'll select options for receiving faxes.

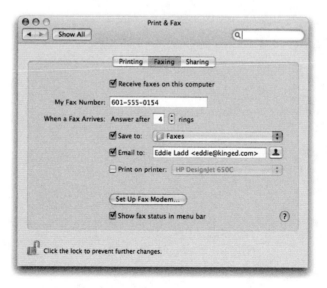

NOTE One problem with receiving faxes using Apple's built-in tools is that they don't make you aware that the faxes have arrived. Indeed, if you don't choose to have faxes e-mailed or printed, you may not know that they are waiting on your computer. One way to solve this problem is to use an AppleScript that alerts you when something has been added to your faxes folder—which is something that's actually easy to do. See Chapter 21, "Automator and AppleScript," for more on using Folder Actions and the Add New Item Alert script that comes with your Mac.

What's Next?

In this chapter, you saw the basics of setting up a printer, configuring it in the Printer Setup Utility, and managing print jobs in that printer's queue. You also saw the Page Setup and Print dialog boxes in Mac OS X and the Classic environment, as well as the Chooser and PrintMonitor in the Classic environment. And you saw how to send and receive faxes with Mac OS X. In the next chapter, we'll move on to advanced printing and imaging issues, including saving print jobs as PDF documents, installing and managing fonts, and dealing with ColorSync, Apple's color-matching technology.

Chapter 8

PDFs, Fonts, and Color

Chapter 7, "Printing and Faxing in Mac OS X," covered installing your printer, selecting drivers, and printing and faxing from your applications and from within the Classic environment. In this chapter, you'll see some of the more advanced issues that augment Mac OS X's sophisticated printing capabilities.

Because of Mac OS X's advanced Quartz engine, you'll find that your Mac is very capable when it comes to one advanced printing issue in particular: creating Portable Document Format (PDF) files. In fact, the Print Preview function is based on the PDF concept, enabling you to view pages exactly as they'll appear once printed. Mac OS X goes a step further by allowing you to save that previewed document as a PDF file. The resulting file can then be viewed later in Preview or transmitted to others, who will be able to view or print the file on their computers in applications such as Adobe Acrobat Reader, either on Macs or on Windows PCs.

Mac OS X also has a practical approach to managing fonts. You can install fonts while applications are running, and those applications, in some cases, are automatically updated so that they can use the fonts. As with many other aspects of Mac OS X, you can manage fonts at both the system and user levels, so individual users can have their own fonts, if desired. Most Mac OS X applications have access to the special Font panel, and FontBook, which can be customized so that collections of fonts can be managed on the fly. Also, Mac OS X includes FontSync technology, which you can use to help synchronize your fonts between two or more Macs.

Finally, Mac OS X incorporates ColorSync, a technology that enables you to create device-independent color schemes so that colors on your screen look like the colors in your printed documents.

In this chapter:

- ◆ Previewing and Creating PDFs
- ◆ Working with Fonts
- ◆ Organizing Fonts
- ◆ Fonts in the Classic Environment
- ◆ Working with ColorSync

Previewing and Creating PDFs

One of the tangible benefits of Mac OS X's Quartz graphics environment is strong support for the Portable Document Format (PDF) throughout the Mac OS. What PDF does is enable you to create documents that include fonts and layout information that can then be used on other computers or even other computing platforms. This may not seem like a big deal, but suppose, for instance, that you create a document in TextEdit, like the one shown in Figure 8.1. If you send that file as a Rich Text document, what your recipients see will vary widely. Other Mac OS X users, of course, will see something similar to what you've created; but on other computing platforms, the results may be quite different. If you happen to use fonts that the remote user doesn't have, your document will change even more (see Figure 8.2).

What Mac OS X includes, however, is a built-in capability that enables you to create PDF documents from nearly any Mac OS X application that supports printing. Because a PDF file maintains the layout of your document and even embeds special fonts, your recipients will see a document that's nearly (if not completely) identical to the document you created (see Figure 8.3).

As you can see from Figure 8.3, saving directly to PDF is a powerful feature. First, it enables you to save documents so that the vast majority of computer users can see your file. Second, it doesn't require a special application to do the saving, as PDF creation required in the past. Any application that can print in Mac OS X can create PDF documents. Third, saving to PDF makes it possible for others to print out your document from their computers and have it look exactly as you intended it to look. That makes for a printer-independent, platform-independent document that you can shoot across the Internet to, say, your prepress shop, your printer, your boss, or a client.

FIGURE 8.1
Here's a document I've created in TextEdit.

FIGURE 8.2

Here's that document saved as an RTF (Rich Text Format) file and viewed on a Mac OS 9 machine.

FIGURE 8.3

Here's the document saved as a PDF (Portable Document Format) file and viewed in Adobe Acrobat Viewer on a Mac OS 9 machine.

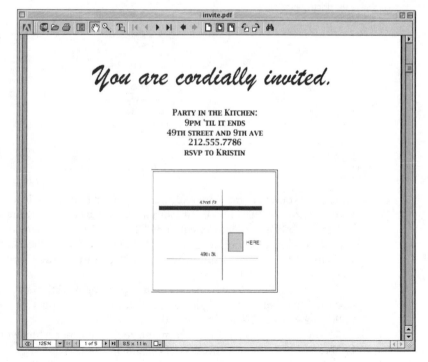

Creating a PDF

To create a PDF, you first build your document in a Mac OS X application. You can't create PDFs from Classic applications unless those applications are specifically designed for creating PDFs (such as Adobe Acrobat Distiller). In Mac OS X, you don't need a special application to create PDFs.

Once you've put together the document you'd like to save as a PDF, you should open the Print dialog box by selecting File ➤ Print or pressing ⌘P. In the Print dialog box, click the PDF button and select Save as PDF from the pop-up menu.

A standard Save dialog (or sheet) appears, as shown in Figure 8.4. Give the PDF a name and choose a location where you'd like to save the file. (Note that you can also toggle the Hide Extension option to hide or show the .pdf filename extension.) Choose Save; the file will be saved to that location, and the dialog box will disappear.

TIP   When transferring PDF documents to other users, make sure you keep the filename extension .pdf intact so that other computing platforms will know what type of document they're dealing with.

FIGURE 8.4
The Save to File dialog lets you save the document as a PDF file.

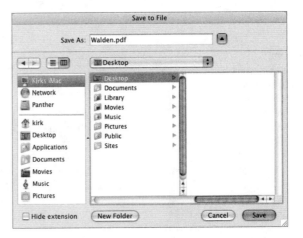

The PDF button in the Print dialog gives you other options. In addition to saving a file as a PDF, you can also save a file in PostScript format, choose to fax a PDF, compress a PDF to save size, encrypt a PDF, save a PDF to iPhoto, or edit the PDF menu. The Edit Menu option gives you a powerful new way of working with your documents by adding *workflows* to the menu. Using Automator, described in Chapter 21, "Automator and AppleScript," you can save a series of actions using filters and other commands as a workflow.

If you select Edit Menu, you can add any printing workflows you have created with Automator, so you can then apply them with a single click. Just click the plus (+) icon and select a workflow to add to this menu. Click OK to close the Edit PDF Menu dialog.

The next time you access the PDF menu, you'll see your custom workflows in the menu, and you'll be able to select them to process your documents quickly.

There's another way you can save files as PDF documents that gives you different options, such as applying filters or password-protecting your PDFs. After displaying the Print dialog as explained previously, click the Preview button. This creates a PDF document that then opens in the Preview application. Select File ➤ Save As, and a Save As sheet displays.

Choose a location to save your file and a name for the file, and you'll then be able to apply a Quartz filter (a preset filter that Mac OS X's Quartz graphics engine can use). To apply a filter, just select one from the Quartz Filter pop-up menu. The filters include changes in tone, lightness, and a file-size reduction filter that helps optimize your PDFs.

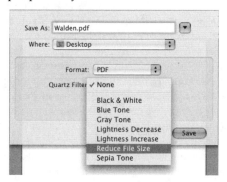

If you want to password-protect a PDF file, click Encrypt in the Save dialog. When you click Save, Preview asks you to enter and confirm a password. You'll need to remember this password, since no one will be able to view the file without it. When you double-click a password-protected PDF, Preview opens and displays a Password field before it shows the document.

NOTE What about that paperless office that people have been predicting for years? Well, we'll probably never get there, but with Mac OS X's built-in PDF support, you can get closer. Many people save files as PDFs for reference and store scans of paper documents so they can have them on their computers for easier access. Also, with Spotlight's ability to search in PDF files, you may find it useful to start saving PDFs of many of your documents—Spotlight can search in other files as well, of course, but if your scanner driver uses optical character recognition (OCR) software to import your documents with their text intact, you'll be able to easily search for those tidbits you need among your invoices, bills, and records.

Printing PDFs

The ability to save your print preview documents has another level of usefulness. It's possible to save documents in such a way that you're creating a "printed image" of sorts; the PDF stands in as an electronic version of the printed document. This means two things: First, you can create a "paperless archive" of documents in PDF format, so you can view the documents later without printing them. For instance, you can archive a group of PDF documents to a CD; those documents can be retrieved later and viewed easily, even on other computing platforms.

Second, you can defer printing a document by saving it as a PDF. Then it can be printed at a later date, on a different printer, or even transferred to some other computer or output center for printing.

How do you print a PDF? From within Mac OS X, you simply locate the saved PDF and double-click it to launch the document in Preview. (Or launch Preview and use the File ➤ Open command to locate the PDF document.) With the document open, choose File ➤ Print. Now you can make choices in the Print dialog box just as you normally would; the quality of the printed PDF page should be no different from the quality of the same page printed directly from the original application.

NOTE If your PDFs launch in Adobe Acrobat, you should be able to print them from there without any trouble, too. For more on associating documents and applications, see Chapter 4, "Using Applications."

You should recognize that this system of printing PDF documents isn't quite magic. You will sometimes encounter quality problems, particularly if you attempt to print the same document on different printers. The reason for this is simple—the preview was created by the original application with particular settings in the Page Setup dialog box. For instance, if you created the document originally with a LaserWriter printer selected in Page Setup and the Print dialog sheet, and you subsequently print the resulting PDF to an ink-jet printer, you may have trouble getting the margins and sizing to work. In some cases, accessing Page Setup in the Preview application can help. In other situations, however, you need to have saved the original preview document with the specific Page Setup and Print dialog settings for the ultimate target printer, preferably using a driver for that printer (see Chapter 7).

Also note that you may not always get best results when a document created by saving a file as a PDF is printed in Adobe Acrobat Reader. Apple notes that Acrobat Reader will exhibit trouble at times if you attempt to print from its preview function. (For instance, if you're viewing a document in Acrobat, then you choose the Preview button in *its* Print dialog box, you're essentially creating a PDF of a PDF, which can affect quality.) If that's the case, simply use the Print command within Acrobat Reader, and the output will be optimal.

NOTE PDFs can be saved in such a way that they can't be printed, or can only be printed at low resolution; if you find that your efforts to print a PDF are frustrated by the PDF viewer that you're using, it's possible that printing is locked for some reason.

Working with Fonts

Another aspect of creating documents and printing from the Mac OS is dealing with *fonts*, files that describe a typeface and set of attributes that make up printed and on-screen characters. Common typefaces are Times New Roman, Arial, and Helvetica; combine those typefaces with attributes such as size, pitch, and spacing, and you've come up with a font.

As far as the Mac OS is concerned, fonts are special files that you install in particular folders. Mac OS X is capable of dealing with several different types of fonts, including PostScript Type 1, TrueType, OpenType, and Multiple Master. Here's a quick look at each type:

Type 1 PostScript Type 1 was the original *outline font* technology, developed by Adobe Systems. Outline fonts can be scaled to different sizes when they're printed. In fact, PostScript fonts were originally designed as printer fonts and couldn't be displayed on computer screens without some additional software. PostScript Type 1 fonts can be used easily both on-screen and for printed output.

TrueType TrueType is a technology that Apple and Microsoft created together in the late 1980s as a competitor to Adobe's PostScript. TrueType has become enormously popular for all but the most professional uses of fonts; in publishing, PostScript still reigns supreme. Many of the fonts that come with Mac OS X are TrueType fonts.

OpenType OpenType is a more recent technology that has been developed by—who else?—Adobe and Microsoft. Although OpenType fonts aren't specifically Apple technology, Apple supports them within Mac OS X. They're as easy to work with as TrueType fonts, but OpenType is really a superset of TrueType and PostScript Type 1 fonts—an OpenType font can contain either type or font data or both. OpenType fonts are also particularly downloadable (especially in applications such as web

---

CREATING HIGH-QUALITY PDFS

While you can create PDF files from just about any document (as long as its application has a Print function) in Mac OS X, these PDFs won't be as high quality as those created with Adobe Acrobat (www.adobe.com). Acrobat—the full version, not Acrobat Reader—has advanced features and functions that give you total control over the way your PDFs are created. These include image compression (to make graphic-laden documents smaller), font embedding (to include the fonts you use in the final PDF, which ensures that its display is as close as possible to the original), and a choice of resolutions, including print-quality resolution. If you need to create PDFs often and want higher quality than what Mac OS X can create, Adobe Acrobat is what you need.

---

browsers), so this technology is an exciting new approach to fonts. If you have OpenType fonts, you can install them easily in Mac OS X.

Multiple Master   Another Adobe innovation, Multiple Master fonts were created to allow designers to tweak font parameters such as size and weight to create custom styles called *instances*. Mac OS X can work with Multiple Master fonts that have been created with third-party tools.

Apple uses a font rendering engine called *Apple Type Services*. Along with support for TrueType, OpenType, Multiple Master and Type 1 fonts, Apple Type Services provides advanced font display and printing, including anti-aliasing, so your fonts always look smooth, and high-quality scaling, so fonts appear clean at any size.

Installing and Using Fonts

Mac OS X offers a number of different folders in which fonts can be installed for particular purposes. When a font is correctly installed, it becomes immediately available to open applications; you don't have to quit all your applications before they will be able to access the new fonts.

Mac OS X has three distinct places where fonts can be stored, with a fourth location possible. If you're installing new fonts, you'll want to pick the correct location. Here's a look at the locations:

/System/Library/Fonts/   Fonts stored in this location are required by the Mac OS to display information on the screen. In this folder, you'll also find the default fonts that are installed with Mac OS X, including some familiar typefaces (to users of previous Mac versions) such as New York, Times, and Chicago.

/Library/Fonts/   In the root-level Library folder, you can install fonts that are made available to all users on this Mac. This folder can accept any type of font, and all applications can use fonts from this folder.

~/Library/Fonts/   In the Library folder inside each user's home folder (~), there's a Fonts folder where you can install and keep personal fonts. These fonts are not available to others on your Mac; they're active only when you are logged in.

NOTE   There's another location where fonts can be stored for use in Mac OS X applications—the Fonts folder inside the Mac OS 9 System Folder. Mac OS X automatically adds any compatible fonts in the Classic Fonts folder to the Font panel for use in Mac OS X applications. Plus, those fonts also are made available to Classic applications, as discussed in the section "Fonts in the Classic Environment" later in this chapter.

If your Mac is set up on a properly configured network (one that is administered from a Mac OS X Server computer or a similarly capable server), you also may find that your system administrator has installed fonts in a special `Fonts` folder inside the network hierarchy at `/Network/Library/Fonts/`. These fonts are made available to your entire network of Macs and, in general, cannot be altered by users (or even administrator-level users, in most cases). For personal fonts or fonts on your local Mac, you'll use the main `Library` folder or your personal `Library` folder inside your home folder.

To install fonts, you can simply drag them to one of the directories described previously. This is good to know if you have lots of fonts to install at once, such as if you buy a CD-ROM containing hundreds of fonts. However, the easiest way to install a font file in Mac OS X is simply to double-click a font file. This opens FontBook—Apple's font-management application—and displays a small window with a preview of the font, as you can see in Figure 8.5.

FIGURE 8.5
A preview window
for a new font

Click the Install Font button to install the font into your `/Library/Fonts` folder. FontBook then opens with the new font displayed. By default, FontBook installs new fonts in your personal `Fonts` folder, but you can change this in the FontBook preferences. Select FontBook ➢ Preferences and select Computer as the default install location. Once you've installed a new font, it's recognized immediately, so you can start using it without quitting and restarting your applications.

In an application (such as TextEdit) that offers text-editing tools, select Format ➢ Font ➢ Show Fonts (or, in some applications, Format ➢ Fonts or Format ➢ Font Panel) so that the Font panel is revealed. Check the Font panel to see if the new font is available. If the font doesn't appear, it's possible that you've either installed an unrecognized font type or installed a font that's already installed in a different font folder (in which case you can access the font, but the Font panel doesn't change).

The easiest way to remove a font is to use FontBook. We'll talk about this in the next section.

Using FontBook

FontBook is a program that lets you

◆ Manage fonts

◆ Create font collections

◆ Enable, disable, and remove fonts

◆ Get more information about your fonts

This program, located in your Applications folder, has a three-column interface, much like a Finder window.

FontBook displays collections, fonts, and font previews. There are a number of preset collections in the left column, and you can add your own. Click any of the fonts in the Font column to see a preview of that font in the right section of the window. You can select from three choices in the Preview menu: Sample, shown in the preceding graphic, which gives just the basic characters of the font; Repertoire, which shows all the font's characters in their ASCII order; and Custom, where you can choose which characters to display by typing the ones you want to see.

One useful feature in FontBook is the ability to enable and disable individual fonts or font collections. If you disable any fonts, they won't be available for you to use in your applications, but disabling some of them can make your font menus easier to deal with. Just select a collection or a font and then click the Disable button. To enable a font or collection that you have disabled, select it and click the Enable button.

To remove a font, select the font in FontBook and then select File ➤ Remove [*font name*]. This deletes the font and moves it to the Trash. However, in most cases, you probably won't want to do delete a font permanently, because fonts are expensive! Make sure you have a backup of the font or the original installation CD on which the font came.

You can also add and remove fonts manually, dragging them into Fonts folders, as you've seen previously, or dragging them from their current Fonts folder location to another folder. In fact, this is one way to manage your fonts per project, if desired. You can move fonts into and out of the font folders at any time, including entire groups of fonts that you use for particular projects. To delete a font, drag it to the Trash.

WARNING   If you remove a font that's currently used on text in a document, any text that uses that font will either change to a more generic font or, in some cases, disappear from the document window.

In most cases, if you're dragging fonts back and forth, the best plan is to drag them into and out of your personal Fonts folder (~/Library/Fonts/) instead of the main /Library/Fonts/ folder. That way, if you leave the fonts installed (or remove any), other users on the system (if there are other users) won't be perplexed by a changing set of fonts in their applications. Plus, if you move a font out of its Fonts folder and then open a document that uses that font, the document will no longer have access to that font—a situation that may frustrate other users on your Mac.

TIP If you find that you spend a fair amount of time managing your fonts, or if your work requires strong font management, you might want to consider a third-party application. Extensis Font Reserve and Suitcase (www.extensis.com) enable you to activate different groups of fonts, learn low-level details about your fonts, and troubleshoot fonts that appear to be corrupt.

FONT COLLECTIONS

Collections of fonts enable you to whittle down the list of fonts to something a bit more manageable. FontBook lets you create new collections that are task specific, such as a group of fonts you use for editing web pages or a group of fonts you want to use on a particular project.

To create or edit a collection, click the plus (+) button below the Collection column in FontBook. Highlight the collection's name (it's something like New-0) and edit it as desired, pressing Return when you're done (see Figure 8.6). If subsequently you decide to rename the collection, highlight the collection name, click the Rename button, edit the name with your keyboard, and press Return when you're done.

FIGURE 8.6

Creating a new font collection

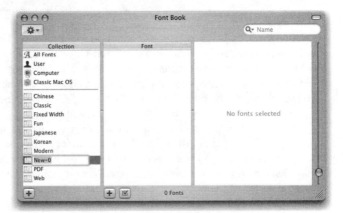

The new collection will appear, by default, with no font families installed. To add fonts to your collection, click one of the other collections to display their fonts, or click All Fonts to see all the fonts available. Click the font you want to add to your collection, in the Family column, and drag it onto the name of your collection in the Collections column. This moves the selected font family into the Family list for the new collection. Continue selecting families by dragging them onto your collection until you've added all the families you want to that particular collection.

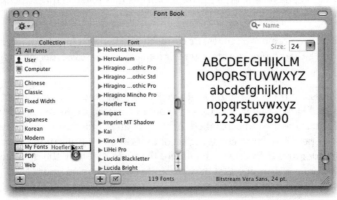

FONTSYNC: FONT PROFILES

Mac OS X 10.2 and higher include a capability that's been present in earlier versions of the Classic Mac OS—FontSync. FontSync, put simply, enables you to create a profile of the fonts that are on your Macintosh and compare them to other Macs, so as to ensure that you're working with the same fonts in a production environment. This can be particularly helpful when you're having trouble getting a document to look exactly as it should on two different Macs, even if the Macs seem to have identical fonts installed. That's because FontSync compares not just the names of fonts, but rather the entire contents of fonts to make sure they're utterly identical—something you can't always know simply by looking at the fonts in their folders.

The manifestation of FontSync is two AppleScript scripts found in the `FontSync Scripts` folder inside the `Scripts` folder inside the main `Library` folder. The first of these scripts, `Create FontSync Profile.scpt`, is designed to create a profile document that includes all relevant information about the fonts on the Macintosh on which it's run. Then the script prompts you to name a profile document and, using a Save dialog box, select a location for it to be stored.

The second script, `Match FontSync Profile.scpt`, can be used to match a FontSync document that was created on another computer (or on this Mac at a different time) to the current state of the active fonts on this Mac. If it finds a discrepancy, it makes a note in its log file. That way, you can quickly determine what's different between two different Macs (or the same Mac over time) and correct the problem by installing the appropriate font(s).

FontSync technology also can be scripted from within AppleScript if you'd like a script to access its routines and automate some processes. To learn more about it, locate the file `/System/Library/ScriptingAdditions/FontSyncScripting` and drag it to the AppleScript Script Editor's icon. When you drop it, the Script Editor will open the AppleScript dictionary for FontSync. (See Chapter 21 for more on AppleScript.)

The new collection doesn't affect any other collections—that is, when you move a font from the All Families list to the Family list, you're not taking that font away from any other collection. You can have as many collections as you want because they're designed to be a convenient way for you to view your fonts in different groupings. When you've finished creating the collection, you can select fonts from it easily by clicking its name in the Collections column. Once you select a collection, you'll see a subset of all currently available fonts, making it easier to see the exact fonts you need to work with.

TIP When you create a font collection, it's stored in a new folder inside your personal `Library` folder called `FontCollections`, in a file with a `.collection` filename extension. If you like, you can share that font collection file with others. Just drop copies of the file in other users' `Drop Box` folders and tell those users to copy the font collection file to their own `Library` folders, creating a `FontCollections` folder if necessary. Now, when users open their own Font panels, the collection you've created will be available to them. (Note that if you've enabled the Root account and you know the password, you can log in as root and copy the font collection file to your users' `Library` folders on your own.)

TWEAKING YOUR COLLECTIONS WITH THE FONT PANEL

After you've created font collections with FontBook, you can use the Font panel, available in Cocoa applications such as TextEdit, to tweak the way fonts display. By default, you can use either a slider or a text field to select font sizes. For the former, move the slider up or down to change the font size;

for the latter, enter the exact size (or select it in the list next to the slider) if you know what size you want. You can turn either or both of these options off, if you'd like. But you can also customize the default sizes that will appear when you're selecting fonts, for example. Choose Edit Sizes from the Action menu at the bottom of the Font panel. This displays a sheet showing the font size options. To add a size to the fixed list, enter it in the New Size box and click the plus (+) button. To remove a size from the list, highlight it and click the minus (-) button.

You can choose here whether you wish to remove the slider or font size field from the Font Panel. Uncheck either of these options if you wish. (If you uncheck both, however, you won't be able to choose font sizes.) Click Done, and the Font panel will show the controls you've selected.

Fonts in the Classic Environment

Once again, the dual nature of Mac OS X means that the Classic environment has a slightly different approach to how it works with fonts. Fortunately, it isn't an overwhelmingly different system—at least, as long as you don't plan to tax Classic's capabilities with high-end design and layout applications—but it's different enough that it needs to be covered separately.

The Classic environment uses its own Fonts folder for all fonts to which Classic applications have access. That folder is inside the Classic environment's System Folder, which you'll find at the root level of whatever volume you used for your Mac OS 9 installation (see Figure 8.7).

NOTE   As mentioned earlier, Mac OS X can use fonts that are installed in the Mac OS 9 System Folder for the Classic environment. That road isn't two-way, however. The Classic environment can use only fonts that are installed in the Classic System Folder; it can't use fonts installed elsewhere in the Mac OS X /System or /Library/System hierarchy.

The Classic environment supports bitmapped, TrueType, and PostScript Type 1 fonts, although installation is a little different than in Mac OS X. Here's a look at each:

Bitmapped (fixed-width)   These fonts generally look and print well in only one point size; that point size is usually part of the font's name. If you happen to encounter a bitmapped font in a Classic application, you'll notice that many Classic applications will tell you which point size is supported by outlining that point size in the application's font size menu.

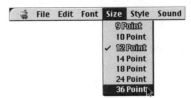

NOTE   Bitmapped fonts are a bit archaic, but they're important for one particular instance in the Classic environment: You must have at least one bitmapped version of any PostScript font you have installed on your Mac if you want to see and choose that PostScript font in your Classic applications.

TrueType   TrueType fonts can be installed either individually or in a special type of folder called a *font suitcase*, as mentioned in the earlier section, "Installing and Using Fonts." A font suitcase can hold any number of TrueType (or, for that matter, fixed-size) fonts, and these suitcases are useful for getting around an interesting limitation in Mac OS 9 (and the Classic environment): you can't have more than 128 items in the Fonts folder at once. The solution is to place multiple fonts within a font suitcase and then copy that suitcase file to the Fonts folder. Note that the easiest way to see font suitcases is to dual-boot into Mac OS 9 and manage them from within Mac OS 9's Finder instead of trying to use Mac OS X's Finder, which doesn't properly recognize font suitcases (see Figure 8.8).

NOTE   A font suitcase isn't much more than a special type of folder that can hold multiple fonts. It's really just designed to be sort of "see-through" so that the fonts it holds are counted by the system as though they were directly installed in the Fonts folder. That notwithstanding, there isn't a convenient way to create a font suitcase; the only solution is to boot into Mac OS 9, duplicate an existing one (File ➢ Duplicate in the Mac OS 9 Finder), and clear out its contents and rename the suitcase. Note, also, that the name of the suitcase isn't important; all the valid font files inside that suitcase will appear in the font menus of your Classic applications.

FIGURE 8.7
The Fonts folder inside the Mac OS 9 System Folder is where fonts reside for Classic applications.

FIGURE 8.8
In Mac OS 9, you can see the font suitcases and open them as though they were folders.

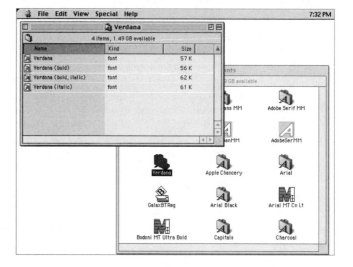

PostScript   PostScript fonts can be installed directly in the `Fonts` folder in order to make them available to Classic applications. (Indeed, PostScript fonts should not be stored in font suitcases.) However, PostScript fonts are a special case in Mac OS 9 and earlier: In order to display a PostScript font on the screen, Mac OS 9 must have available to it either a bitmapped font or a TrueType font of the same typeface. The reason for this is simple: Mac OS 9 (and hence the Classic environment) doesn't have a built-in rasterizer. Instead of displaying the PostScript font, Mac OS 9 attempts to compensate by displaying a bitmapped or TrueType font instead. (Mac OS X *does* have a built-in rasterizer, which is why it doesn't have to jump through these hoops to display PostScript fonts.)

> **TIP**   There's another solution to the problem of getting PostScript fonts to appear on-screen: install a third-party rasterizer. One such rasterizer for Mac OS 9 (and hence the Classic environment) is the Adobe Type Manager Lite utility, which you can download directly from Adobe (www.adobe.com). Once installed, PostScript fonts can be used on-screen from within your Classic applications (as well as when you dual-boot into Mac OS 9). Note that version 4.6.1 (or higher) of Adobe Type Manager Lite is recommended for the best compatibility; older versions of ATM don't work properly in the Classic environment.

Whenever you install or remove fonts, you need to quit all active Classic applications and relaunch them before the fonts will be recognized in those applications.

How do you install the fonts? Using Mac OS X Finder windows, it's possible to drag and drop font files and suitcases to the `Fonts` folder inside the Mac OS 9 `System Folder`. The problem is that the Mac OS X Finder application doesn't really recognize the differences between the different types of font files and suitcases. The easiest way to add or change fonts in the Classic environment is to reboot your Mac into Mac OS 9. Once there, you can see and work with font suitcases with relative ease. When you return to Mac OS X, the Classic environment will work as expected with your new fonts.

> **TIP**   In Mac OS 9, you can double-click individual font files (TrueType and bitmapped only) to display a little window that shows what the font looks like.

Working with ColorSync

One problem for users of any operating system is matching colors on the screen to colors from input and output devices. Different devices—monitors, printers, scanners—view colors in different ways, from the method used (such as RGB and CMYK) to the range, or *gamut,* of colors that the device can deal with. Most computer monitors use red-green-blue (RGB) color information to create the image on the screen. On the other hand, printers use cyan-magenta-yellow-black (CMYK) to create colors, and printers can vary significantly in the range of colors supported due to the variety of printer types (ink-jet, laser, dye sublimation, and so on).

In Mac OS X, this problem is solved by ColorSync, Apple's color-matching technology. ColorSync uses color *profiles* for the devices connected to your Mac. Once a profile for a particular device is known, your Mac (and any ColorSync-compatible applications that you use) has a good idea of how that device deals with color, making it easier for ColorSync (and applications that support ColorSync) to match the color from two or more devices. The result: What you see on the screen matches the scanned input or printed output you're trying to create.

We'll take a look at the default ColorSync settings in this section. You'll also see how to calibrate your Mac's monitor using the color calibration tool in the Display pane of System Preferences. As for the individual profiles for your devices—those are generally installed when you install the software for the device, or you may be able to download them from the manufacturer's website. Once installed, ColorSync will register the device and note its color characteristics.

NOTE   Inside the main `Library` folder on your startup disk is the `ColorSync` folder, where profiles are stored. There, you'll also find a `Scripts` folder, which includes a number of AppleScripts that are useful for various ColorSync-related tasks—including getting information about documents with embedded ColorSync information or automatically changing your display for different calibration scenarios. Most of the scripts are "droplet" scripts that accept a dragged document. Also, dragging one of the scripts to the Script Editor icon (in the `AppleScript` folder inside the main `Applications` folder) will enable you to open the script and read its comments, where the functionality of the script is better explained.

Choosing Default Profiles

When an application is ColorSync aware, it often will embed ColorSync data within documents themselves. When you install a device—a printer, a scanner—it should also install its ColorSync profile so that your Mac has a sense of its color capabilities and calibrations. That's what enables it to maintain color fidelity from the computer display all the way to the printed page.

When you're creating a new document or working with one that doesn't have color information already specified, default settings can be assigned by ColorSync according to the selections you make in ColorSync Utility, found in `/Applications/Utilities`. Open this program and click the Devices icon. Select your device, such as a display, to see the current profile (see Figure 8.9). You can change this profile by clicking the arrow button and selecting Other. This shows you the available profiles. Choose the appropriate profile and click Open. To return to the factory profile, if any, select Set to Factory.

In most cases, you can stick with the default; if you're supposed to be working with other settings, you'll know it because they need to be created by your applications or otherwise installed in the folder `/Library/ColorSync/Profiles/`.

FIGURE 8.9
Set a profile for
your display.

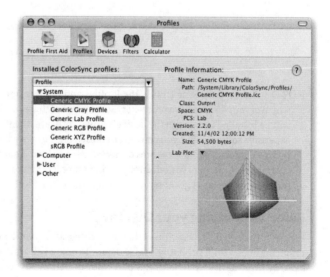

You probably won't need to change these unless you're in a production environment and you know what you want to set them to. For most users, the limited number of devices that you've connected to your Mac should be adequately served by the default settings. Then, in your applications you can choose profiles as necessary—for instance, the Image Capture application allows you to select a profile for a digital camera, so that the profile is used to manage the color of images captured from that camera.

REPAIRING PROFILES

If you have installed a profile that doesn't appear in the ColorSync pane or your applications, it may be damaged; ColorSync profiles can become corrupted fairly easily through normal use, and the corruption is something that Apple has identified as often following an easily repaired pattern. Click the Profile First Aid button to have ColorSync Utility quickly check for problems (see Figure 8.10). If you find any, click the Repair button to repair those profiles.

FIGURE 8.10
ColorSync Utility is used to repair corrupt ColorSync profiles.

> **NOTE**   Also in ColorSync Utility, the Profiles and Devices buttons can be used to dig in and find out which of your devices have profiles created and what those profiles look like. In most cases, the profiles will be installed along with the device's driver software; if not, then creating profiles tends to require expensive software. But you can look in these panes to see what profiles you have installed and what registered ColorSync devices are connected to your Mac. The Filters button lets you set up and apply custom color filters to your documents and graphics. You can use these filters to change color tones, increase or decrease lightness, and even optimize PDF files.

Color-Calibrating your Display

Whether or not you're a serious graphics professional using your Mac for extraordinary color-matched undertakings, you'll probably find it useful to color-calibrate your Mac's display. Display calibration is a pretty important step to getting good color matching, even for simple output to a color ink-jet printer. It's also a way of making your display look better; some displays, by default are too blue or too red. If you calibrate your display, your colors will look better on-screen, and your computing experience will be improved. In Mac OS X, ColorSync technology is always active, so you'll find that a calibrated display will better match the output sent to your color printer (or the output received from your color scanner) than will an uncalibrated display.

Fortunately, calibrating is easy. You'll need to launch the Displays pane of the System Preferences application and click the Color tab. Select a prebuilt Display Profile from the list or click the Calibrate button to launch the Display Calibrator assistant.

> **NOTE** If you're calibrating a PowerBook or an LCD display, you won't see all of these steps. If you select the Expert Mode option, you'll see more than these steps, but the Display Calibrator Assistant will walk you through them.

Here are the steps for monitor calibration:

1. Begin with the Introduction screen, where you can read about the steps. If you're a color publishing professional (or you know a little something about monitor technology), you might want to turn on the Expert Mode option toward the bottom of the screen. To move on, click Continue.

2. On the Display Adjustments screen, you'll see instructions regarding the setting of Contrast and Brightness for your monitor so that the image appears as described. With third-party monitors, you'll set Contrast and Brightness manually. If you have an Apple-branded monitor (or an integrated display), you'll see sliders that enable you to set Contrast (top) and Brightness (bottom) right on the screen. Set Contrast to the highest setting and then move the brightness up to the point where you see the circle, but a solid-colored background. Click Continue when you're done.

> **NOTE** If you're using the Expert Mode, you'll see a series of screens that aren't described here—you drag various lines and points around in order to set a native gamma for your monitor. These extra tests are to get your calibration as correct as possible. The more exact your gamma settings are, the more exact the color reproduction on your display will be as compared to your printouts.

FIGURE 8.11
Selecting a target white
point for your display

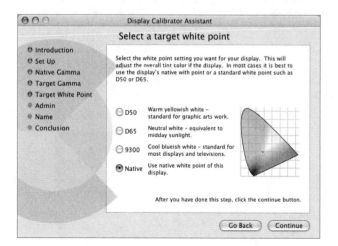

3. On the Native Gamma page, move the slider around so that the Apple logo shape seems to disappear into the background (see Figure 8.11). If you chose Expert Mode on the Introduction screen, you'll see five different colors to blend. When you're done, click Continue.

4. On the Target Gamma page, select the gamma setting at which you'd like your monitor to be set. Regular options are simply Standard and Television. Television is good for testing websites; you can see how images will appear on PCs. Standard Gamma is generally recommended only if you're working with a high-end graphics application that manages its own gamma settings. (Expert Mode users will see a slider that enables you to pick a more exact gamma number.) Click Continue to move to the next screen.

5. On the Target White Point page (see Figure 8.12), you'll select the white point setting for your monitor; in essence, you're choosing a color temperature for white, which will determine how all other colors appear. D50 (5,000 degrees Kelvin) is the standard white point for matching internal lighting, so it's often chosen by graphics professionals, particularly for photo manipulation. Higher color temperatures give your display a brighter effect overall but may lead to less accurate color choices in your applications for printed output—but more accurate for web or TV output. (Expert Mode users see a slider that enables you to choose an exact color temperature.) When you're done, click Continue.

6. Now, type a name for the profile in the entry box and click the Create button to create the profile.

That's it—the profile is created and added to the list that appears on the Color tab in the Display pane of the System Preferences application, as well as in the ColorSync pane, where it can be selected when you're creating a workflow. With a calibrated monitor, what you see on-screen should match what you see as color printed output, particularly when you're working with ColorSync-aware applications and devices.

FIGURE 8.12
To choose the native gamma, move the slider until the Apple logo blends fully into the background.

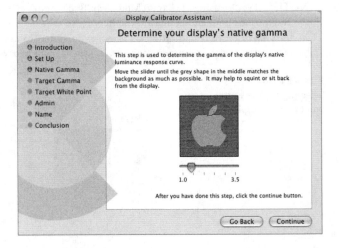

What's Next?

This chapter discussed advanced printing topics, including creating PDF documents, installing and managing fonts, and working with ColorSync. In the next chapter, you'll find out about the tasks performed by and tools used by the Mac OS X administrator, including creating users, managing system files, and setting system-wide preferences.

Chapter 9

Being the Administrator: Permissions, Settings, and Adding Users

Mac OS X can appear at first to be a mild-mannered operating system for home users. Don't be fooled. The fact is, Mac OS X is designed from the ground up as a multiuser operating system, and when you first set up Mac OS X and choose a username, the Mac OS endows that user account with administrator capabilities. However, it sets the account so that it logs in automatically, masking the multiuser heart of the operating system.

Many functions rely on the creation of multiple user accounts. One reason to create multiple user accounts is to give each user of your Mac a different desktop, preference settings, and home folder for storing files. Mac OS X's reliance on the multiuser system goes deeper than that. For instance, you'll use the same approach to create network users who access your Mac remotely via FTP, secure Telnet, or similar network services.

This multiuser approach requires extra vigilance if you're the person who manages the system. In Mac OS X, the administrator account is required for a number of tasks, including the creation of user accounts, the installation of applications for all users, and some fairly regular maintenance tasks. If you've installed Mac OS X or configured a new Mac OS X installation, you are the administrator. We'll discuss some of these tasks throughout the book; issues ranging from networking to disk maintenance have components that require an administrator's intervention.

NOTE Have you been given a "regular" user account on your Mac, perhaps as a computer lab, organizational, or corporate setting? In that case, you may want to stick with the user-focused preferences discussed in Chapter 5, "Personalizing Mac OS X." Realize that you won't be able to make many of the changes to Internet, networking, and other settings discussed throughout the rest of this book. (You still may find this chapter interesting, though.) Instead, you'll need to discuss them with your Mac administrator. Throughout the book we'll make the distinction between tasks that can be performed using a regular account and those that require an administrator's password.

In this chapter we want to talk about the administrator account itself, along with special issues that require you to log in using an administrator's account. Then we'll look at the process of creating user accounts, determining which users have access to certain files and folders, managing hard disks and resources, installing applications, and setting system-level preferences. We'll also look at ways you can limit users' access to specific applications; this is designed as a parental control system for children, but you may want to use it for some employees if you use your Mac in an office environment, or for general users in a lab environment.

Even if you're the only person who uses your Mac, you might want to take a quick look at this chapter, because it will set the groundwork for discussions in other chapters (on networking, printing, peripherals, installations) that require some knowledge of an administrator's responsibilities and privileges. And you'll see a discussion of system-level preference settings that are relevant regardless of the number of users on your Mac.

In this chapter:

♦ The Administrator Basics

♦ Administrative Folder Privileges

♦ Creating and Editing Users

♦ Setting Parental Controls

♦ Installing Applications

♦ System-Level Preference Settings

The Administrator Basics

When you first install Mac OS X (or the first time you turn on a Mac that has Mac OS X preinstalled), the Setup Assistant asks you to create an initial user account. That account is automatically given administrator responsibilities and permissions, which means that you can write to many of the main folders on your Mac's hard disk, such as the Applications and Library folders. Likewise, you can set many of the system-level preferences in the System Preferences application without first entering an administrator's password—those panes are automatically "unlocked."

NOTE   As discussed in Chapter 5, *permissions* (also called "privileges") are the rights a particular user account has to read or alter files and folders. Throughout this section, we'll refer to the administrator's permissions as "write" permissions or a particular folder as "writable" by the Admin group. That means that items within can be copied, created, or changed as well as deleted. When users don't have write permissions, they can only read or launch the items in a folder; they can't change them or add to them.

As we'll see in the section "Creating and Editing Users," other user accounts can also have administrative (Admin) access, making it possible for others to install applications or drivers and make system-level preference changes. We'll see many of those options later in this chapter.

The extra power granted to Admin users means that such users should take care to avoid leaving their accounts logged in on a Mac that sees a lot of traffic—such as in an organizational, corporate, or Mac lab setting. One solution is to turn on the password features of the Security pane in the System Preferences application so that if you do get up, your password will be required to unlock the screensaver. It's best to remember to keep your Admin password well hidden and to log out of an Admin account whenever you'll be leaving a Mac that others could access; the file permissions of an Admin account could allow a neophyte or reckless user to damage applications, drivers, and settings. If you have Fast User Switching activated, you can switch to the Login Window when leaving your computer. We'll discuss Fast User Switching later in this chapter.

For the record, an Admin account is different from the *Root* account, or what is often called the *superuser* account in Unix circles. The Root account has universal permissions—it can change any file on your Mac with no warnings, and with no questions asked. It can also access hidden files and folders, and it can make changes to any preferences setting. By default, however, the Root account is disabled in Mac OS X. Although this isn't customary in most Unix distributions, it was deemed wise by Apple's engineers, who apparently decided that beginner and intermediate Mac users should be shielded from the Root account at all costs. After all, one false move (renaming or deleting the wrong file in the System hierarchy, for instance) could render your Mac useless.

In general, there isn't much reason to use the Root account, even as an advanced user; Admin accounts have enough power and permissions to perform most of the tasks you need to accomplish. In some cases, you may need to re-enable the Root account to do some very low-level troubleshooting, as well as some system administration tasks that are discussed in the final chapters of this book. Enabling the Root account is discussed in Chapter 28, "Solving System-Level Problems." In this chapter, though, we'll stick to discussing the Admin accounts.

WHY HAVE MULTIPLE USER ACCOUNTS?

For many users, the notion of multiple user accounts may seem a bit foreign. After all, if you (or you and a family member or two) are the only user(s) of your Mac, there may not seem to be much reason to create multiple users. In reality, though, your Mac already has multiple users created, and you may come up with a variety of reasons to create more users, particularly if you allow anyone else to access your Mac remotely via a network or the Internet.

First, let's start with the existing user accounts. When you installed or set up Mac OS X, you created the first one—your named administrator-level account. That account has access to many of the Mac's folders and can perform most of the system-level tasks you'll ever need to attempt, but it isn't the only account. Mac OS X has a number of underlying user accounts that are used by the Mac OS and components for various reasons. For instance, the www account is used to launch processes related to the Apache web server included with your Mac OS X installation. The Root account also works in the background with a number of system-level processes, even if it hasn't been enabled for login.

Beyond those, you'll need to create user accounts for the following reasons:

◆ *Multiple local users.* If you want to have more than one user on the same physical Mac, you'll create user accounts. Each user account has its own home folder, preferences, and personal settings, such as the Displays setting, e-mail defaults, and Internet bookmarks. Also, users can be designated regular users rather than administrative users, giving them less power over the Mac's system-level settings. Finally, multiple user accounts enable individual users to keep files or folders private (or at least inaccessible or unalterable by other users). The Fast User Switching feature makes this even handier, as you can simply sit down at the Mac, switch to your account, and instantly access your own settings and documents, without the current user having to close their session.

◆ *Network users.* If you plan to allow users to connect to your Mac over a local network (other than for web sharing), you'll need to create accounts for those users. Mac OS X works with the same user mechanism for local user accounts as it does for network user accounts. However, users without accounts can access your Mac as a guest, which gives them read access to each user's Public and Sites folders, and write access to the user's Drop Box, located in the Public folder.

◆ *Remote users.* Users who connect to your Mac via FTP, secure FTP, Telnet, SSH, password-protected websites, or similar Internet protocols will need user accounts in order to sign in (in most cases). Those user accounts are the same ones you create for the other types of users specified here.

◆ *Server users.* At the high end, you may occasionally find that you need to create a user account that isn't for an actual human user, but instead is for a server process of some kind. For instance, some installations of the MySQL database require (or encourage) the creation of a special user account that's specifically employed by the server. You may come across this in a number of different situations, often to make the server more secure (that is, to keep it from running as root or within an existing administrator's account).

You'll get used to the idea of multiple user accounts quickly—in fact, you may come up with other reasons, such as creating user accounts for testing, gaming, or programming or any time you'd like to change a whole set of preferences easily and quickly by simply logging out and logging back in as a different user. In fact, Kirk uses a different user account to manage music for his second iPod; since iTunes doesn't allow you to set up multiple libraries, it's simple to create a new library in a separate user account, switch to that account, and synch the iPod.

In any case, it's a good idea from a security viewpoint to log out of your Admin account and log in to a regular user account to perform typical desktop tasks. As an administrator you may find that the very next user account you create is a regular user account for yourself.

Administrative Folder Permissions

One of the issues discussed in Chapter 5 is the idea of read and write permissions and how you can change them within user folders. The rest of the folders throughout the Mac OS X system are also defined in some ways by which user accounts have permissions to access the folders. The most important folders, for instance, can be changed (written to) only by the Root account and by certain installers and utility applications that can be given Root account permissions. (However, administrators can make changes to all folders eventually, either by authenticating or by using the sudo command in Terminal.)

The second level of importance goes to any user with administrative rights. Once you are made a member of the Admin group, you can change many basic system-level settings, folders, and files. (Adding a user to the Admin group is discussed in the section "Creating and Editing Users," later in this chapter.)

Let's take a look at the various root-level folders to get an idea of who has access to what.

Root-Level Folders

In Chapter 3, "The Finder," we discussed the basics of the Mac OS X file system, including a quick look at the root-level folders that appear in a standard Mac OS X system: the Applications folder, Users folder, Library folder, System folder, and Mac OS 9 System Folder, if you have one. Don't let the term *root-level* fool you, by the way. This use of "root" doesn't mean "Root account" but rather that these folders are the top level of folders on a typical Mac OS X startup disk. In Mac OS X's path parlance, these would be represented as /Applications and /Library, for instance. The initial slash (/) is referred to as the *root level* of the disk.

In both Chapter 3 and Chapter 5, you'll find a lot of information about the Users folder (and particularly, each user's home folder), where most users' account permissions enable them to alter and affect the makeup of their individual folders. The other folders on the Mac, however, tend to be writeable only by Admin accounts (see Figure 9.1).

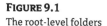

FIGURE 9.1
The root-level folders

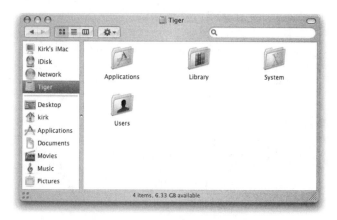

WARNING The Admin account grants you the power to rename some important folders, which you should avoid doing. Don't rename root-level folders or subfolders within them, such as those in the Library hierarchy or the Utilities folder inside the Applications folder. Doing so can adversely affect your applications and even the Mac OS itself.

The Applications folder is where you, as an administrator, can install applications for all users on the Mac to use. While regular users can only read and launch applications in this main Applications folder, an Admin account can install, move, or delete applications in this folder.

Any Admin account can read files in the System folder and can also write to it, delete items from it, or move items to it. If you want to carry out an action on files in this folder, and you have an Admin account, just go ahead with want you want to do. For example, if you want to copy a file to the System folder, copy the file normally. You'll be asked to authenticate by entering your password, and the file will be copied.

Mac OS X is designed so that the System folder should be accessed and altered very rarely, since many of the system settings and drivers for Mac OS X reside in the root-level Library folder, not the System folder. Ideally, only Apple installers, updaters, and some third-party utility applications should access the System folder, though if you are an administrator and need to make changes to any of these files, you can. Just be careful. (That's not to say you aren't occasionally encouraged to delve into the System folder—but only very rarely for troubleshooting tasks as discussed in Part 6 of this book, "Hardware, Troubleshooting, and Maintenance.")

The Library folder at the root level is the main repository of system-level preferences and settings files for applications, including items like fonts, ColorSync profiles, and system-level Help files. Likewise, you'll access subfolders inside the Library folder that store preferences, settings, and plug-ins or other support files for system-level applications and even server programs. The root-level Library folder and its subfolders are writable by anyone with an Admin account.

WARNING By default, all users have read and write permissions for the Mac OS 9 System Folder, if you have one, and only the Root account can change this. If you've enabled the Root account, it may seem tempting to limit permissions to the Mac OS 9 System Folder, but doing so could affect your users' ability to run applications in the Classic environment. A user must have read and write permissions for the Mac OS 9 System Folder for the Classic environment to launch. (Note that the only major visual differences between the Mac OS 9 System Folder and the Mac OS X System folder are the folders' icons and the inclusion of the word Folder as part of the name in Mac OS 9's case.)

Determining Permissions

So, by default, the Admin-level accounts can write to the Applications folder, the System folder, and the Library folder. The implications of this may be obvious: Admin-level users have the permissions they need to install system-level applications (those that all users on a particular Mac can access) and even to troubleshoot the support files of applications in the Library folder.

If you want to see this for yourself, select one of the folders (such as Applications, Library, or System) and use the File ➢ Get Info (or ⌘I) command to view that folder's attributes. In the Info window, click the Ownership & Permissions disclosure triangle and then click the Details triangle. You'll see the permissions for the folder. As shown in Figure 9.2, the System account has ownership of the Applications folder (along with read and write permissions). Because the account used to view the Applications folder in Figure 9.2 isn't the Root account, the permissions can't be changed. The Admin group also has read and write permissions, while all other users have only read permissions (making it possible for them to launch applications but not alter the folder's contents).

FIGURE 9.2

The permissions associated with the root-level Applications folder

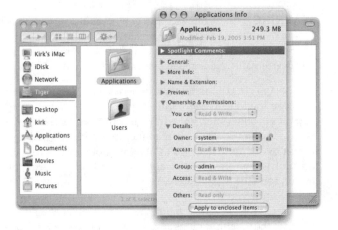

Users' Home Folders

Users' home folders actually work a little differently from the other folders because they aren't owned by the System account; a home folder is owned by the individual user, who is free to set permissions, as discussed in Chapter 5. That means that even Admin-level users generally have only read access to a user's home folder and no access to their subfolders, except for the Public and Sites folders, unless that user has specifically given the Admin group or wheel group read and write access.

NOTE If you aren't familiar with Mac OS X's home folder concept, see Chapter 5 for an explanation.

For the Users folder itself, the Admin group has read and write permission (see Figure 9.3). Administrators can access the Users folder and even create new folders inside it (though this is not a good idea), but they cannot change the contents of other users' home folders. (Admin users, like all others, can actually read any user's home folder to get to their Public and Drop Box folders; we'll discuss these folders in a moment.) But Admin users can manage user accounts, even deleting them and their home folders, from the Accounts pane in the System Preferences application, as you'll see in the section "Creating and Editing Users," later in this chapter.

You should also note that within the Users folder, the Shared folder has a different permissions profile by default. The Shared folder grants read and write permissions to everyone, making it a safe place for users to copy files that all other users should be able to access freely.

Likewise, each user has a Public folder (inside his or her home folder), where everyone, regardless of account type, has read permission. Inside that folder is a Drop Box folder, where everyone has write permission but *not* read permission. That makes it possible, for example, for a user to send a file to Gwen by placing it in her Drop Box folder, while prohibiting users other than Gwen from seeing (and launching or copying) what has been placed in that folder.

FIGURE 9.3
The Permissions settings
for the Users folder

Volume Permissions

If you have additional disks or volumes (other than the startup disk) attached to your Mac, you also might want to check the permissions set for those volumes. By default, the root level of attached disks can have wide-open permissions. If you highlight a disk icon and select File ➢ Get Info in the Finder, you may find that all users have read and write permissions. If that's okay with you, you can leave the settings that way; otherwise, you may want to change the permissions for that disk so that the volume is read-only or offers no access to some or all users.

If you prefer that users have access only to certain parts of an attached volume, you can dig into the volume and assign permissions to individual folders. Set the Others setting to Read & Write for those folders, setting the rest of the folders to Read Only or None.

You may notice that folders created on external volumes will sometimes have Unknown as the group instead of the Admin or wheel group. If you want to assign a folder on the volume so that administrative users have different access permissions from regular users, you can do this in the Info window.

You'll also notice that the Info window for some external volumes includes another option, Ignore Ownership on This Volume. This allows you to use an entire disk or volume as a shared space; all users, regardless of the type of account they have, will be able to access files and folders on such a volume. However, if they copy any files that they own onto the volume, these files will no longer be protected by their original permissions. Think of a volume like this as a receptacle for files where permissions don't matter. This is the best way, for example, to provide shared access to music files, photos, or videos that all members of a household want to access, or to provide access to archives or other shared documents in a company.

There's a flip side to the Ignore Ownership option, as well. In some cases, an external disk may not appear to recognize the changes that you make to permissions, particularly an external USB or FireWire hard disk. This is because the Mac OS is set up to ignore privilege settings on external drives that can be easily "ejected," such as FireWire and USB drives, the assumption being that many people use these drives as if they were huge removable drives, connecting them to different Macs at different times. If you have an external hard disk that you'd like to make a more permanent addition to your Mac, and you'd like to assign permissions on that disk, open the Info window for that disk and turn *off* the Ignore Ownership option.

Creating and Editing Users

Admin accounts are the only accounts that can create (add) and edit users on the system. To add users to a particular Mac, launch the System Preferences application and then choose the Accounts pane (see Figure 9.4).

If you're currently logged in to a regular user account, you'll need to *authenticate* as an Admin user by entering a username and password for an account that has Admin status. Then you can edit or add a user.

To do so, click the padlock icon toward the bottom of the window. In the dialog box that appears, enter your username and password (if you have Admin status). If your username, password, and Admin status are recognized, the padlock icon will change from locked to unlocked.

Now you're ready to add, edit, or delete a user account from the Mac OS X system.

Creating a User

Once you have full access to the Accounts pane, you can add a user by clicking the plus (+) button below the user account list. Doing so displays a sheet that lets you enter a username, short name, and password. Figure 9.5 shows the Accounts pane and the new user sheet.

WARNING   Apple warns that you shouldn't use root for Short Name when creating a user. If you need to enable the Root account, do so using the instructions in Chapter 23, "Command-Line Applications and Magic" and Chapter 28.

FIGURE 9.4
The Accounts pane enables you to create and edit users for a Mac.

FIGURE 9.5
Entering information for a new user

Here are the items you should fill in to create a new user. First you enter the user's name and password in the New User sheet, then you enter other information on three tabs: Password, Picture, Login Items, and Parental Controls. (For information on using the Login Items tab, see Chapter 5.)

New User sheet   The New User sheet lets you enter a username, password, and password hint.

Name   In the Name entry box, enter the full name (first and last) of your user.

Short Name   In the Short Name box, enter the username you'd like to assign to this user, assuming you don't like the default that Mac OS X assigns. Note that a user can use either the name or the short name to sign in to Mac OS X. The short name doesn't actually have to be short.

While older versions of Mac OS X had an eight-character limit on this name, Mac OS X 10.3 and later let you use short names of up to 256 characters. Some applications, however, may not work with longer short names, so it's best to keep them relatively short. The short name can be used in any applications that require a shorter username (especially FTP, Telnet, or other applications used to access the Mac from a different computer).

Password tab   Enter the user's password. Remember that passwords are case sensitive. If you want to check the security of your selected password, click the key icon next to the password field. This opens the Password Assistant window, which gives you an idea of whether your password is good enough for a secure environment.

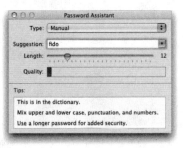

The Password Assistant examines the password you have entered in the Password field (if any), and its quality bar shows how good it thinks the password is. The Password Assistant will tell you why it considers a password to be insecure; for example, a word in the dictionary could be discovered by a brute-force attack that simply tries every dictionary word until it finds the right one. The length of a password is important, since the difficulty in discovering it increases exponentially with every additional character. Finally, using uppercase and lowercase letters, numbers, and punctuation increases the complexity and makes it much harder for anyone to figure out the password.

You can allow the Password Assistant to suggest passwords if you want. Click the Type menu and select one of the choices:

- Memorable, which creates a password containing a combination of real words and other characters
- Letters & Numbers, which gives a suggestion with a combination of alphanumeric characters
- Numbers Only, for those who want passwords containing only digits
- Random, which is a truly random selection of letters, numbers, and punctuation
- FIPS-181 compliant, a U.S. government system for generating passwords

Finally, you can move the Length slider to adjust the length of the password, from 8 to 31 characters. Though we challenge any reader to remember a random 31-character password...

This is all moot if you have a Mac at home, of course. Just use whatever password you want. In fact, you may even want to leave blank passwords for family members, if you don't need privacy for their accounts (though you shouldn't use a blank password for an administrator account). And bear in mind that even the best password only prevents a user from accessing your files in "normal" conditions; anyone with a Mac OS X installation CD can reset the administrator password, obtaining access to all the files on your Mac. See Chapter 26, "Hard Disk Care, File Security, and Maintenance," for more on security issues with Mac OS X.

Verify   Retype the user's password to verify that it was typed correctly the first time.

Password Hint   This optional entry box enables you to enter a hint to help the user remember the password. A hint can be dangerous because it might reveal the password or help others guess it. The hint should definitely not be a code that could be broken by rearranging letters or numbers.

Allow User to Administer This Computer   Selecting this option places the user in the Admin group. As noted in the section earlier in this chapter, "Administrative Folder Permissions," this gives that user the ability to install applications and alter settings in the root-level Library folder.

Picture tab   When you add a new user account, Mac OS X applies a picture by default. This picture is displayed next to the user's name on the Login screen (under certain circumstances) and in the user menu that you can select from the menu bar if you have Fast User Switching turned on. If you want to change this picture, click the Picture tab. You can choose from one of the Apple Pictures shown on the tab or add your own. To change the picture, click Edit and then click Choose in the Images window or drag a picture into this window.

NOTE   If you opt to use your own image for Picture, the file should be in a standard QuickTime-compatible format, such as JPEG, GIF, TIFF, or PICT, among others. Ideally, the image should be roughly square. For a perfect fit, the image should be 128 pixels by 128 pixels. The default images are stored in the folder /Library/User Pictures/, if you'd like to add to them.

PLAYING WITH PASSWORDS

There's an interesting issue when it comes to assigning passwords in Mac OS X. Generally, you want to encourage two things about passwords—that they be as long as possible and that they be as difficult to guess as possible. You should encourage your users to create passwords that are at least eight characters long with nonwords, numbers, and text, such as h8m4y5s9. (Remember that passwords are case sensitive.)

One of the easiest ways to generate such passwords is to use the first letters (and mnemonic numbers) of a phrase, poem, or something similar that's familiar to you, but not readily identifiable with you, such as 4sa7yao4, which would work for "Four score and seven years ago, our forefathers...." Also, remember to use unique passwords for every login or account you create, both on your Mac and elsewhere.

Note that Mac OS X will allow you to create a user account that doesn't have a password, making that account easy to sign in to and work with. This isn't recommended, especially in any organizational setting or in any situation where your Mac is connected directly to the Internet. (Even over a modem-based Internet connection, this could be insecure, allowing others access to your Mac.) If for some reason you do want to do this, simply leave the Password and Verify entry boxes blank. (We'd absolutely recommend *not* giving this account administrator permissions.) When that user logs in, no password will be required.

FIGURE 9.6
The Parental Controls
tab enables you to
control a user's access.

Parental Controls tab If you've created a regular user (this won't work with Admin users), you can limit the user's access to various portions of the Mac OS or to applications on the Parental Controls tab (see Figure 9.6).

You set parental controls by application. There are five applications available: Mail, Finder & System, iChat, Safari, and Dictionary.

Mail controls To set controls for Mail, check the box next to the Mail icon and click Configure; a sheet displays where you can add e-mail addresses that the user can exchange mail with. This is a whitelist; e-mail from other users requires permission. When a user attempts to send a message to a user not on the whitelist, they see a dialog asking if they want to ask permission to send that message. The message is stored in the Drafts folder until the administrator grants permission for the message. Set the address for permission messages in this sheet. Note that these permission messages only function if the user receiving the permission request is also using Mac OS X 10.4 and Mail.

Finder & System controls If you check Finder & System and then click Configure, a sheet displays giving you options to limit user access to the Finder. You have two choices: Some Limits and Simple Finder.

◆ Some Limits—In this section, you can toggle on and off some of the Finder-based tasks that the user can perform; by default, all these tasks are set to off. For instance, you can allow or deny access to the System Preferences, though regular users normally modify some of these preferences. You can turn off the Modify the Dock option to keep the user from changing the mix of items on the Dock (if you'd like a standard appearance, such as for a computer lab or classroom setting). You can leave off the Burn CDs or DVDs option if you don't want users to copy items on your publicly situated Mac. You can choose whether you want a user to be able to administer printers, and also choose to allow supporting programs to run for the user. This latter choice controls whether certain applications can call on other programs for their tasks.

◆ If you check This User Can Only Use These Applications, you can limit a user to a specific set of applications—this is particularly useful for public Macs, but it also can be useful for classrooms, households with kids, or other settings. With the option enabled, use the disclosure triangles to see particular items and turn them on or off; you can get very specific about the applications, the utilities, and even the Classic applications that a user is allowed to access.

◆ Simple Finder—If you turn on this option, users won't see the full Finder when they log in; instead, they will see only a limited subset of the commands that are made available by the Finder—the Sleep and Log Out commands and the capability to launch documents, launch a limited number of applications, and throw out personal items. As the administrator, you can choose the applications available to users via the Show These Applications in "My Applications" Folder option, which is the same as the This User Can Only Use These Applications option discussed in the preceding paragraph.

iChat controls   Check the box next to the iChat icon and then click Configure to see the iChat control sheet. You can add names that the user is allowed to chat with. If the user attempts to chat with others, or if others try to chat with them, the chat sessions will be blocked.

Safari controls   If you want to limit which websites a user can access, check Safari and then click Configure. This tells you to log in as that user and launch Safari to add sites that the user can access. When you launch Safari, you'll be limited by parental controls to only a handful of sites (those which Apple includes as default bookmarks). For other sites, the user will see a web page saying Safari is Limited by Parental Controls. To add a website that has been blocked, click the Add Website button; this requires that an administrator enter their name and password, but when they do, the user is allowed to add this site to their bookmarks bar.

An easier way to set up websites for Safari is to go to the Safari preferences (Safari ➤ Preferences), click the Security tab, and uncheck Enable Parental Controls. Add bookmarks to sites you want to allow and then check Enable Parental Controls again. Note that you can only add sites to the bookmarks bar; no Bookmarks menu displays if parental controls are activated. If you need to add a lot of websites, it is best to make folders in the bookmarks bar. (See Chapter 11, "The Web, Online Security, .Mac, Sherlock, and iChat," for more on using Safari.)

Dictionary controls   If you check the box next to the Dictionary icon, this "prevents this user from viewing certain words, such as some profanity." To each their own.

Parental controls provide a great deal of control and flexibility for a variety of situations; they're for more than just parents. They are particularly useful when quite a few people use a Mac in a high-traffic area. You can create accounts that don't have as much freedom to launch particular applications or to change the appearance of the Mac. You even can limit or cut off access to the System Preferences application, the `Utilities` folder, or particular applications (such as games and Internet applications) if it makes sense for your circumstances.

Login Options

The Accounts pane has another section we haven't touched on yet—the Login Options section. To access this, click the Login Options button below the list of users. This displays several options for logging in and switching users.

When you first install Mac OS X, it configures itself to automatically log in to the primary account you create using the Setup Assistant. If you want the login window to display each time you start up your Mac, you can turn off automatic login (after creating another user account) by clicking to remove the check next to Automatically Log In As. You can also change the automatic login account by selecting one of the user accounts from the pop-up menu after this option. If you set a different account for automatic login, you'll need to enter the user's password in a sheet that displays.

The Display Login Window As options enable you to either show a list of users or force users to type their usernames without any prompting. The first option is more convenient for users, but the second option is more secure because the users have to know both their valid username and their password.

You also can turn on the option to hide the Restart and Shut Down buttons in the Login window if you'd like to prevent users from restarting or shutting down the Mac. This can keep the machine somewhat more secure, especially in a computer lab setting, because it makes it more difficult for a user to boot the Mac into an earlier Mac OS version or to use a system CD.

If you check Show Input Menu in Login Window, users will be able to switch keyboards; this resolves a problem with prior versions of Mac OS X where the login window would only accept typing using the last applied keyboard layout. This is very useful if users work with different keyboard layouts, such as Dvorak or layouts set to different languages.

The Use VoiceOver at Login Window option tells Mac OS X to use VoiceOver, its speech technology for visually impaired users, when the login window displays.

Checking Show Password Hints allows the login window to display password hints if a user erroneously enters their password three times. The hint displays below the Password field in the login window.

Finally, you can turn on Fast User Switching, which lets users log out and other users log in without shutting down their sessions. With Fast User Switching, you can work in one account, and if other users need to use the same Mac, they can switch to their accounts without shutting down the applications you're using. This makes it quicker to switch accounts when multiple users need to access the Mac, or when you need a special account for testing purposes. See Chapter 2, "The Fundamentals of Mac OS X," for more on Fast User Switching.

ENSURING TOTAL SECURITY FOR YOUR MAC

Why is allowing users to restart or shut down a Mac a security risk? If a user restarts the Mac, inserts a CD-ROM with a valid System folder on it, and presses the C key on the keyboard, the Mac will start up from that CD-ROM and give the user some direct access to files on the Mac. This is especially true if the CD holds a copy of Mac OS 9 (for Macs sold before 2003, and for some models sold in that year) or even some Linux operating systems. (The Gentoo distribution, www.gentoo.org, available for PowerPC computers, has a type of startup CD called a *live CD* that you can boot from.)

Likewise, if you restart while holding down the Option key on a dual-boot Mac OS X system, the Mac can be restarted in Mac OS 9, again giving the user access to other users' document files as well as portions of the Mac OS X System folder. (Mac OS 9, when viewing a Mac OS X disk, doesn't adhere to the existing permissions settings, making it possible for any user to see, copy, and alter existing files all over the disk.) Disabling the Restart and Shut Down buttons makes it harder to restart the Mac from the login window, although the Restart and Shut Down commands are still active when a user is logged in.

If your users are in a high-traffic area, then for increased security, make sure you remind them to log out when they've finished working. (To enhance security even more, this option can be used in conjunction with the Open Firmware Password utility discussed in Chapter 26.)

Editing a User

Once a user account has been created, you can return to the Accounts pane to edit the user's information, giving you the opportunity to rename the user, change the user's password, or alter the user's Admin status. To do so, you may need to enter the administrator's password by clicking the locked padlock icon. (If the icon appears unlocked, then you're ready to edit.)

You can only edit users who aren't currently logged in—if you have Fast User Switching on, and other users are logged in without being active, you can't make any changes to their accounts. Highlight the user in the Accounts pane and edit the portions of the user's profile that you'd like to change, including the long name, password, or Admin status.

NOTE Although these entries are the same as those you use to create a new user, note that Mac OS X doesn't allow you to change the short name of a user in the Edit User window. If your user requires another username, you'll need to create a new user account and move that person's personal files to the new user folder.

Removing a User

Although removing a user isn't in any way more difficult than adding or editing a user, it's not something you'll want to do hastily. When you delete a user, the contents of their home folder are archived as a disk image, if you so choose, and the original folder is removed. The files are intact, but the user's settings, preferences, and any Library additions (personal fonts or printers, for example) will need to be reinstalled. It's best, therefore, to remove users only when you're fairly sure they won't be accessing your system in the future.

NOTE You can restore a user, but it's a more complicated task, requiring use of NetInfo Manager or the Terminal application. See Chapter 28 for an explanation of restoring a user with these tools.

To remove a user, simply select that user in the Users list and click the minus (–) button. You'll then see an alert box asking if you really want to delete the user. Click OK if that's what you want. Once you've deleted the user, the account will no longer appear in the Users pane. The user's home folder will be deleted, but those files will be stored in a newly created disk image file, found in the Deleted Users folder. Double-clicking the file will mount it, making the user's home folder available in the Finder.

If you're sure you don't want to keep the user's home folder, click Delete Immediately in the confirmation dialog box. The account and home folder will be deleted right away, meaning all user files and documents associated with that account will be gone.

You can't reinstate the user, but you can re-create the user by clicking New User in the Accounts pane and walking through the steps of creating the user. After the user is re-created, and only if you deleted them and kept their home folder, you can copy the deleted account's disk image from the Deleted Users folder to the user's new Drop Box folder (or otherwise make the disk image available to the user). The user can now access old files and place them elsewhere in the new home folder.

Installing Applications

Why is the installation of applications considered an administrative function? It isn't unless you want those applications to be available to more than one user. Any users can install applications in their home folders, as is detailed in Chapter 5.

To install applications that all users of the Mac OS X system can use requires that you have the correct permissions—you need to be able to write files to the Applications folder (or another folder outside your home hierarchy). To do that, you'll need to log in to an account with Admin status. You can then install applications in one of two ways:

◆ You can drag applications (or folders that include applications) to the Applications folder.

◆ You can use an installer application to install the applications.

Installing by Dragging

If you've logged in using an Admin account, one way to install an application is to drag its file to the Applications folder. You can also drag a folder that contains an application to the Applications folder. Because the Admin group has the correct permissions for writing to the Applications folder, anything you drag to the folder will be placed there, such as the application shown in Figure 9.7. Such applications become available to all users on the Mac, because all user accounts have read access to the Applications folder.

NOTE   This drag-to-install feature works often with Mac OS X applications because Mac OS X uses a special file called a *package*, which is actually a type of folder. A package includes many different files that make up the content and resources of an application, but the actual .app package icon itself is double-clickable, making it appear to be a single computer file. These tend to be the easiest type of Mac OS X applications to work with, but not the only ones, which is why you'll find different ways to install Mac OS X applications.

So, where do you find these applications—waiting around to be dragged to the Applications folder? Some applications that you buy online or in a computer store are installed this way, dragged directly from the mounted CD. In other cases—particularly when you download an application or utility via the Internet—you'll find that applications are stored as *disk images*, a special type of archive that appears to mount on the desktop like a removable disk.

FIGURE 9.7
Here's an application being dragged from a mounted disk image to the Applications folder.

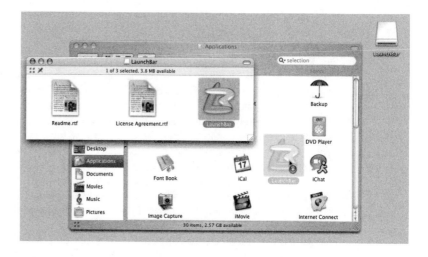

When you double-click the disk image file (which will usually have an `.img` or `.dmg` filename extension), you'll see the file "mount" on the desktop as though it were a disk. Then, if you double-click the disk icon, the application or an application installer will appear in the disk's Finder window. Note that if you've set the Finder application so that it doesn't mount removable disks on the desktop (in the Finder ≻ Preferences dialog box), you'll see the mounted disk image after clicking the Computer button in a Finder window.

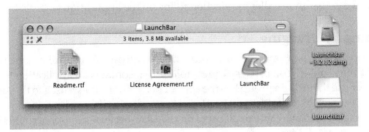

NOTE   See Chapter 26 for more on using disk images.

In many cases, the mounted disk image will reveal the application itself, which you then simply drag to the `Applications` folder (or to another folder, if desired) on your hard disk. If you're logged in to an administrator account, you'll successfully drag that application to the `Applications` folder, and it will be made available to all users.

NOTE   An administrative user has the freedom to copy applications to other folders on the root level of the hard disk or even to create folders (such as `Games` or `Demos` or `Graphic Apps`) and drag items to those folders. Note, however, that doing so may require you to change privilege levels so that other administrators can change the folder (you'll need to change the group permissions to Read & Write). Also, remember that the `Applications` folder is reached easily through the Finder window's toolbar and Go menu, which makes it a good default location for most applications you install.

If you drag an application's folder to the `Applications` folder, it's also a good idea to create an alias to the actual application if you plan to store it in that folder. The alias makes it easier for users to find and double-click the application icon without wandering into the application's folder and subfolders. Remember that the alias and the folder will need to have slightly different names, because no two items in the same folder (in this case, the `Applications` folder) may have the same name.

Problematic permissions are another thing to watch out for when dragging applications around. When you're dragging an application from your home folder to the `Applications` folder to relocate it there, you'll probably need to change the permissions for the application (or the application's folder, if relevant). For instance, open the Info window for a particular application or folder and make sure Others is set to read-only permissions; otherwise, some of your users may not be able to launch the application. If you are setting permissions for a folder, you should also copy those permissions to all enclosed folders using the Apply to Enclosed Items command in the Ownership & Permissions portion of the Info window. (In some cases you may need to set an application's folder to Read & Write for Others, particularly if there's a subfolder in that folder where the application needs to store temporary files.)

That said, if you'd like to set an application or application folder so that only Admin users (those in the Admin group) can access the application, that's possible and might be useful if you have certain applications that only Admin-level users should access. (Note that you must be an administrator to change this setting.) Select the application's or application folder's icon, choose File ➤ Get Info in the Finder, and click the Ownership & Permissions disclosure triangle. Now, set the permissions so that only the wheel or Admin group (whichever is listed) has read and write permissions, and the Others entry is set to None.

WARNING   While you can move some applications to different places, it's a good idea to leave most of them in the Applications folder. This is especially the case for Apple applications such as Mail, Safari, iCal, and even those applications not included with Mac OS X, such as the components of iLife or iWork. When you use the Software Update preference pane to install updates for these applications, the updates may not be made correctly if these applications are not in the standard location.

Installing via an Installer Application

What if you don't encounter a draggable application for installation? The next most likely thing you'll encounter is a specialized installer application of some kind: either the Package Installer written by Apple (and described in the next section) or a third-party installation application. Just about all applications use Apple's Installer application for this, but you may encounter third-party installers occasionally. Some of these installers, such as Apple's Installer, require you to authenticate with an Admin password, while others will allow you to install applications into the Applications folder only if you're already logged in to an administrator account.

Using the Installer

If the result of decompressing or mounting a disk image is not a draggable application (or a folder in which the application is stored) or a third-party installer application, it's possible that it's a package file (especially if it has a .pkg filename extension). When you double-click the package archive file, the Apple Installer will open. In many cases, the Installer will require a password just before installing the software (see Figure 9.8). If your user account has Admin status, you can enter your own account name and password. Generally, the Installer is used when an application will be installing items in other parts of your Mac OS X installation—for instance, when it's installing driver software in the System folder.

FIGURE 9.8
Here Kirk is trying to install an application that requires an administrator password.

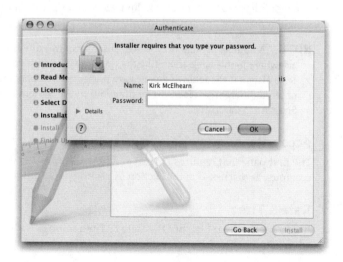

WARNING Bear in mind that authenticating the Installer is a potential security risk. It's possible that the package you're installing could do harm—purposefully or accidentally—to system-level files in the main System folder, Library folder, or elsewhere on your Mac. You should authenticate the Installer only when you're dealing with packages from Apple or from other reliable third-party application developers.

When you launch the installer, you'll see Read Me and License pages in some cases (particularly Apple installers), which you should read, and click Continue or Agree to move on. Then, you're ready to begin the installation process. The installer will walk you through the process of selecting a destination (the volume where you'd like the application installed) and customizing the installation, if you have that option. (Some installations don't allow customized installation.) If the Customize button is available, click it. You'll see options that enable you to select which parts of the application you'd like to install and which parts you'd like to skip.

When you've made your choices, click the Install button. The installer will now ask you to enter your administrator password, as shown in Figure 9.8. The installation will take place, with a progress indicator crawling across the screen to prove it. When the installation is complete, you'll be asked if you'd like to quit the installer or, in some cases, restart your Mac. Click the appropriate choice.

System-Level Preference Settings

Chapter 5 explained in detail the settings via the System Preferences application that regular users have access to, enabling them to customize their personal Mac OS X environment. Along with those settings come a few others that can be accessed only by users who belong to the Admin group. These particular settings affect the Mac at a system level—the disk it starts up from, its networking settings, the file-sharing services it runs, and others. Although some of these will be explained in depth in later chapters, let's take a quick look here at the settings that require an administrator's password.

To access these preferences, launch the System Preferences application by clicking its icon in the Dock, selecting its entry in the Apple menu, or double-clicking its icon in the Applications folder. Then you'll see all the System Preferences panes, including those that I'm discussing here: Accounts, Date & Time, Energy Saver, Network, Print & Fax, Security, Sharing, and Startup Disk. By default, you won't have to authenticate as long as you're signed into an Admin account; if you're signed into a regular account, you'll need to authenticate with a valid Admin username and password.

NOTE A number of other utility applications require authentication, and most of them are covered elsewhere in this book, including the NetInfo Manager (Chapter 28) and Disk Utility (Chapter 26). Note also that the following panes are presented in alphabetical order, even though they can be ordered differently (according to function) in the System Preferences application using View ➤ Show All in Categories.

Accounts

The first pane that requires Admin access—Accounts—is where you create, edit, and delete user accounts, as discussed in the section "Creating and Editing Users," earlier in this chapter.

Date & Time

It may seem odd at first, but the Date & Time settings within the Mac OS can be altered only by an administrator. The reason for this is simple: Many parts of the Mac OS and some applications rely heavily on the clock and calendar being correct; if they are changed, it can affect everything from automated tasks to the way e-mail is received and sorted. Because of this, and the fact that Date & Time offers some Internet-related settings, these preferences are padlocked away for non-administrative users.

The Date & Time pane offers three different tabs: Date & Time, Time Zone, and Clock. Once unlocked, the Date & Time tab can be used to select Today's Date (by clicking on the calendar interface) and the Current Time (using the up and down arrows next to the digital time readout). Note that these can't be set if Set Date & Time Automatically has been checked.

If you do check Set Date & Time Automatically, your Mac does this by connecting to a network time server. These are special computers that are synchronized to atomic clocks in an effort to make an exact standard time available on the Internet. Select a particular NTP time server from the combo box or enter one of your own. The time will be checked periodically to make sure it's correct.

Note that you can set Date & Time formats by clicking the Open International button at the bottom of this pane. These are user-dependent settings, which explains why you go to a different pane to set them. See Chapter 5 for more on Date & Time formats.

On the Time Zone tab, you can select your current locale and time zone, which include special areas of differentiation. For instance, choose a time zone near the eastern coast of the U.S., and you can individually select U.S.A.—Indianapolis from the pop-up menu, which tells your Mac to note the differences in that locale's observation of daylight savings time. Obviously, you can also choose the country where your Mac is located to force its clock to follow national timekeeping guidelines.

On the Clock tab, accessible to non-administrators, you can determine whether or not you want the menu bar clock (in the top-right corner of the Mac's screen) to be displayed, and you can also set some options for how it's displayed. You can even choose to have a voice tell you what time it is, on the hour, the half-hour, or the quarter-hour.

Energy Saver

In the Energy Saver pane, you can set how long the Mac should wait while it's inactive before it automatically enters Sleep mode. To set this, use the slider control to choose the amount of time, in minutes, before an idle Mac will put itself into Sleep mode.

You also can set separate timings for turning off the display by using the slider (where applicable) to set a time limit. Note that the display sleep time limit must be *less than* the main Sleep setting because there's no point in having the display enter Sleep mode *after* the entire Mac (including the display) has entered Sleep mode!

You can also check Put the Hard Disk(s) to Sleep When Possible, if you want your hard disk to spin down when you're inactive.

The Schedule button displays a sheet that lets you set your Mac to start up or shut down at a specific time every day, on certain days of the week, on weekdays, or on weekends. You can even use your Mac as an alarm clock—its startup chime is certainly loud enough to wake you up.

The Energy Saver pane also has an Options tab (depending on your Mac model), which you can click to see several options. One wakes your Mac from Sleep mode when an incoming call is detected by the modem (for accepting a remote access connection or an incoming fax), or for Ethernet network administrator access, and another can restart the Mac automatically after a power failure. You can also choose to allow the power button to put your Mac to sleep—if you check this option, just press the power button once to put your computer to sleep. PowerBooks and iBooks also have a Show Battery Status in Menu Bar option that enables you to turn on and off the battery menu bar icon. Each one is a check box; click in the box to turn the option on or off.

Network

The Network pane offers extensive administrator-only controls that govern how the Mac will behave on both a local network and the Internet via Ethernet, modem, or other interfaces, such as AirPort wireless networking, that you may have installed. You assign TCP/IP (Transmission Control Protocol/Internet Protocol) characteristics on the TCP/IP tab and basic AppleTalk settings on the AppleTalk tab. All these options and settings are discussed extensively in Chapter 10, "Configuring Internet Access," and Chapter 18, "Building a Network and Sharing Files," but if you already have an awareness of how TCP/IP and AppleTalk work, you can open the Network pane and begin changing things.

Print & Fax

The Print & Fax pane lets you choose default options for printers and for faxing. On the Printing tab, you can add printers by clicking the plus (+) icon to open the Printer Setup Utility. (See Chapter 7, "Printing and Faxing in Mac OS X," to find out more about adding printers.) You can also choose the default printer and paper size.

The Faxing tab lets you choose whether you want to receive faxes on your Mac. To do this, its modem must be connected to a phone jack with a modem cable. When you receive faxes, you can have your Mac do one of several things: It can save the fax to a selected folder, e-mail it to you or to someone else, or print it immediately. You can also choose to turn on a menu icon that displays fax status.

The Sharing tab lets you turn on Printer Sharing, which allows other users on your network to share your printer. (Note that you can also control Printer Sharing from the Sharing preference pane.) You can also turn on Fax Sharing, allowing other Macs on your network to send faxes through your computer.

Security

The Security pane lets you turn on or off certain Mac OS X security features. You control FileVault here—this is a function that protects your home folder and all its documents by encrypting them. Chapter 5 tells you more about FileVault.

You can also turn on other security options: You can choose to require a password when you wake your Mac from sleep or after a screensaver has displayed; you can disable automatic login; you can require a password to access all secure system preferences (overriding the default, which does not ask for a password if you have logged in with an administrative account); and you can set your Mac to log out after a certain period of inactivity. Finally, you can choose to use secure virtual memory. This feature encrypts the data that your Mac shunts into virtual memory files (which are written to your hard disk), so that even after you turn off your Mac, no one can access the traces that remain. This slows down your computer's operation, so you'll only want to use this setting if you're in an environment where such security is essential.

All the settings in this pane affect the entire computer, with the exception of FileVault, which only activates encryption for the current account.

Sharing

Like the other preference panes presented in this chapter, the Sharing pane requires an Admin account for changes to be made. Here you can specify a number of different settings, including whether or not file sharing is turned on (making it possible for others to access this Mac via Apple File Services). You can also turn on web sharing, FTP access, and remote login (SSH) access. All these options are discussed later in this book, in Chapter 17, "Accessing Network Volumes," and Chapter 18.

Startup Disk

In the Startup Disk pane, you can choose which disk (or which System folder, if you have multiple folders on a particular disk) should be used to start up the Mac. This pane primarily enables you to dual-boot between Mac OS 9 and Mac OS X installations by choosing the appropriate folder or volume (see Figure 9.9), if your Mac is capable of booting in Mac OS 9. If your local network supports NetBoot, you may also have the choice of selecting a network volume, giving you the capability to boot a Macintosh from a network server.

FIGURE 9.9

The Startup Disk preferences pane

To change startup disks, all you have to do is select the startup folder you'd like to use from the pane. You have two choices: Click the Restart button in the pane or simply close the Startup Disk pane. If you click the Restart button, a dialog sheet will appear, asking you to confirm your desire to restart the Mac. Click Save and Restart if you'd like to begin the restart process immediately. If you opt to close the Startup Disk pane (or to quit System Preferences), your new startup disk selection will still be remembered, but it won't be implemented until you've restarted the Mac from the Apple menu or login menu or after a shutdown command. In other words, you can do some other computing first before the Mac will restart using the selected disk.

Why would you choose different startup disks? If you have various Mac OS installations on your Mac, you may find it useful to switch between them on occasion. You can also use the Startup Disk control panel to start up from a CD-ROM or similar removable disk that has a valid Mac OS System folder on it. And if you choose the Target Disk Mode option, you can start the computer in a way that it functions as an external hard disk. After you start it in target disk mode, you can connect it to another Mac to transfer files. This is especially useful when you buy a new Mac and want to transfer your files from your old computer.

What's Next?

In this chapter you saw some of the tools and responsibilities for administrator accounts. In Chapter 10, you'll move on to issues involving the Internet, including a close-up look at how to connect to the Internet under various circumstances, the secrets of Mac OS X's Network pane, wireless Internet access, and how to troubleshoot your Internet connection.

Part 2

On the Internet

In this section, you will learn how to:
- Configure Internet access
- Explore the Web securely
- Use Sherlock
- Chat and videoconference with iChat AV
- Send, receive, and manage e-mail

Chapter 10

Configuring Internet Access

Mac OS X is an operating system completely at home on the Internet, with its web-like Help system, the Safari web browser, the Sherlock information application, and Software Update technology, which can regularly check for updates to Mac OS X and Apple's applications. In addition, of course, a host of web browsers, e-mail applications, chat applications, the optional .Mac service, and others are available that can access the Internet. Mac OS X can easily serve files on the Internet, too. Unless you have a drop-dead security reason for keeping your Mac totally off the Internet, getting Internet access is probably one of your top priorities and it's easily accomplished with Mac OS X.

How you access the Internet depends on the type of connection you've secured and paid for via an Internet service provider. That will determine, in part, the *port* that you'll be using for your Internet connection—a modem, the Ethernet port, or an AirPort (or similar) wireless connection.

If you have a modem and a dial-up Internet connection, you'll configure it in the Network pane of the System Preferences application, and you'll use the Internet Connect application that's included with Mac OS X to manage the connection.

If you have a cable modem or DSL (digital subscriber line) connection—fairly common ways to connect from homes and small offices these days—you'll also configure them using the Network pane in the System Preferences application. (For some DSL implementations, you'll also use the Internet Connect application, with which you can initiate some PPP-over-Ethernet connections. More on that later in this chapter.)

Finally, if you're on a local area network (LAN)—either wired, wireless, or a combination of technologies—that has direct access to the Internet, you needn't do much more than simply tweak your network settings so that you can access Internet sites. However, you may need to add special hardware or software if you have a small LAN (in your home or small office) that needs Internet access to all its computers.

Once you're connected, you can move on to a discussion of Internet access from within the Classic environment (what will and won't work and what to do about it). Finally, this chapter will look at basic Internet security and what you can do to keep your Mac or group of Macs secure while you surf.

In this chapter:

◆ Dial-Up Internet Access

◆ High-Speed Connections

◆ Internet Security and Firewalls

Dial-Up Internet Access

If your Mac has a modem and you want to use the modem for Internet access, you'll make some settings in the Network pane of System Preferences, and you'll use the Internet Connect application (or its menu bar icon menu) to initiate your connection. Before you can do that, though, you'll need an Internet service provider (ISP) that offers PPP access and either dynamic or static IP addressing service (either will work). *PPP* stands for Point-to-Point Protocol, and it's the standard way to create a TCP/IP connection over a phone line. The Mac OS X application called Internet Connect does just that—it initiates the connection over the phone line, making it possible for you to run Internet applications over a modem-based Internet connection.

NOTE   TCP/IP stands for Transmission Control Protocol/Internet Protocol, which is the basic language of the Internet. In order to get you on the Internet, your Mac must create a network connection to an ISP's server via TCP/IP. That can happen via a modem, or as you'll see in later sections, the connection can be made over a cable wire or a DSL phone connection. Once you have a TCP/IP connection active, you're ready to use Internet applications such as web browsers and e-mail programs.

If you're familiar with PPP connections in earlier Mac OS versions, you might also be interested to know that with Mac OS X you can store TCP/IP settings for your modem and other ports that are used for networking, such as Ethernet or AirPort. Even if you're using TCP/IP for file sharing over Ethernet, for instance, you don't have to change the TCP/IP settings to use a modem for Internet access; Mac OS X can remember different settings for your different ports, and TCP/IP can be active on multiple ports at once. When you use the Internet Connect application to initiate your modem connection, it will use the proper settings—if you subsequently set up a different type of TCP/IP connection (such as a cable modem), Mac OS X does a good job of automatically using the appropriate TCP/IP settings. (More on that in the section "Active Ports and Creating New Configurations," later in this chapter.

 Want to take the easy way out? In the latest versions of Mac OS X, a button appears in the Network pane called the Assist Me button. Click it to launch the Network Setup Assistant, which will walk you through most typical Internet access scenarios. Also, Mac OS X 10.4 includes a feature that pops up a window if you haven't yet configured Internet access; you can click the Assist Me button in that window to get some help, or click Continue to close the window and set up the modem connection yourself.)

Setting Up Your Modem and TCP/IP

For Internet access over a modem, your first step is to configure TCP/IP and other settings for your modem connection. You'll need all of the information your ISP has given you regarding the connection, which you'll usually receive when you first establish service with the ISP. That information should include the following:

◆ How to configure or automatically retrieve the proper settings for your modem. (Most connections will use the Using PPP setting to retrieve certain TCP/IP settings automatically, but others may require you to choose Manually.)

◆ Your username (or account name), password, and one or more phone number(s) for the ISP.

◆ Any special addresses needed, such as a Domain Name Server entry or proxy server addresses.

◆ Any recommended settings, particularly those that have been tested with Mac OS X.

When you have these items available, you'll be ready to configure your modem for Internet access in the Network pane.

Launch System Preferences and select the Network icon. Choose your modem's entry from the Show menu (most likely Internal Modem, although you may see other entries if you have an external USB or PC card–based modem) in the Network pane, or double-click the modem's entry in the Network Status list (see Figure 10.1). You'll see the PPP, TCP/IP, Proxies, and Modem tabs (shown in Figure 10.2), which you can use to set up your modem-based Internet connection.

NOTE   Don't see your modem in the Show menu or on the Network Status screen? By default, Mac OS X shows all of the modems, Ethernet ports, and similar networking devices that it finds attached to the Mac. So, it's possible that your modem simply isn't recognized. (If it's an external modem, make sure its power is turned on.) If you're dealing with an internal modem, it's possible that the port is turned off. See the section "Active Ports and Creating New Configurations" for more on turning ports on and off.

THE PPP TAB

The first tab you'll see once you've selected the modem is the PPP tab. On that tab's screen, you'll see entry boxes for setting up the connection information for your PPP dial-up account. You'll enter the phone number, account name, and password, among other items (see Figure 10.2).

Here's an explanation of the information you'll enter on the PPP tab:

Service Provider   This is the name of your ISP. It isn't mandatory, but it can be helpful for identifying this setup if you have more than one dial-up account.

Account Name   Enter the username for your Internet account as assigned by the ISP.

FIGURE 10.1
Opening the
modem connection
in Mac OS X 10.4

FIGURE 10.2

The PPP tab of the Network pane when configuring a modem connection

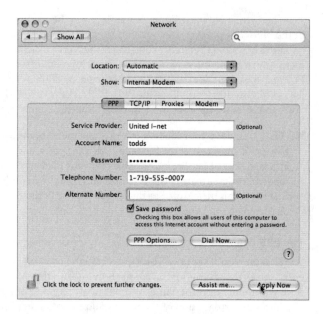

Password This is the password for your Internet account. (Note the Save Password check box that you can turn on so that the password is remembered every time you sign on. Otherwise, you'll have to enter it each time you connect to the Internet via Internet Connect.)

Telephone Number What number will you be calling to initiate the Internet connection? On the PPP tab, you'll enter everything that needs to be dialed for the connection, including the number 1 for long distance and an area code where necessary.

TIP Need to dial special codes or numbers? A comma will cause your modem to pause so that you can enter special numbers, then it will continue dialing. For instance, if you're calling from a hotel room and need to dial 9 for an outside line, you could enter **9,555-1234** or **9,,1-800-555-6450** as the phone number. Your modem would pause after each comma to allow the phone system to catch up with the dialing; more than one comma lengthens the pause. In fact, you could even enter something like **1010555,,1-212-555-0345** if you needed to enter a special long-distance code first. Also, you can enter special codes to disable the Call Waiting feature on your phone line. In most places in the U.S., that's *70, which you could enter as ***70,555-1234**.

Alternate Number If your ISP offers another number that you'd like to specify as a backup in case the first number fails to connect, you can enter one here. This number will be dialed if a connection using the first number doesn't succeed.

The PPP tab also offers a special PPP Options button, which you can click to see a dialog sheet that offers advanced PPP options. At the top of the dialog sheet are the session options. Most of them are self-explanatory; you can elect to have a prompt appear after a certain amount of idle time, and you can automate the disconnect process. One important setting is Connect Automatically When Needed. By default, this option is turned off, but having it turned on can be handy. If you'd prefer to have your

Mac automatically dial its modem whenever you access an Internet application (Mail, Safari, Sherlock's channels, and so on), check this option.

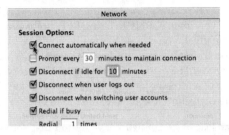

At the bottom of the dialog sheet, you'll see advanced options, most of which you shouldn't have to alter unless your ISP or a technical support representative suggests it. Just know that the options are found by clicking the PPP Options button on the PPP tab of the Network pane.

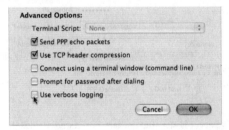

One of these settings, Use Verbose Logging, may be of interest to you, particularly if you're having trouble with your Internet connection. When turned on, the Internet Connect log records more information than the default setting. You can see the log in the Internet Connect application by selecting Window ➤ Connection Log.

Another that may be useful under certain (relatively rare) circumstances is the Connect Using Terminal Window option, which enables you to initiate your PPP connection using a command-line interface. It's fairly unlikely that you'd need to do this in a setting where you're using a commercial ISP, but you may find it useful for connecting to the Internet through your company, university, organization, or perhaps when traveling. If this option is turned on, you'll see a terminal window after your modem dials and a remote computer responds and initiates a PPP connection. The terminal window enables you to communicate with the ISP's server. Log in and activate the connection using whatever command-line PPP command you've been told to issue. The terminal window should disappear, and you're ready to work in your graphical Internet applications.

The Prompt for Password option can be used if you'd prefer to enter your password for a connection after your Mac has already attempted to connect. (You'll also need to turn off the option Save Password on the PPP tab back in the Network pane if you'd like to be prompted for the password.)

When you've finished changing options, click OK in the dialog sheet. Now you're ready to move on to the TCP/IP tab.

NOTE   You may be able to connect immediately to your ISP if it uses standard PPP to assign a dynamic IP address. If that's the case, just click Dial Now to get the connection started.

THE TCP/IP TAB

If necessary, you can select the TCP/IP tab so that you can tell the Network pane how your Mac is supposed to configure its TCP/IP addresses and settings. If you're working with a dial-up connection, then it's extremely likely that you'll set TCP/IP to Using PPP, unless you have a fixed IP address, in which case you might use Manually. If you choose Manually, you'll need to enter some numbers in the entry boxes. In most cases, you'll simply enter an IP address—Mac OS X assumes that the other numbers (Subnet Mask and Router) will be made available by the ISP's server computer. Also, if your ISP tells you to, you should enter IP addresses for your DNS servers in the Domain Name Servers entry box; press Return to separate each entry if you have more than one.

NOTE   The TCP/IP tab features a Configure IPv6 button that you can click if your ISP or system administrator tells you to manually configure an IPv6 address for your connection. IPv6 addresses aren't common yet, but are gaining in popularity.

THE PROXIES TAB

Proxy servers are intermediary servers that are used to either increase performance or filter the sites that are available to your Mac. For instance, a company might use proxy servers to intercept web requests and determine whether a requested website has already been viewed by someone else in the company and is thus available in a cached version on a local server. The site can then be sent to your Mac more quickly. Likewise, a company, organization, school, or parents of school-age children might use proxy servers to disallow access to unapproved web or FTP sites.

NOTE   Because a proxy server is an intermediary between you and the Web, by definition it often will have the side effect of making you more "anonymous" on the Web. That's because the proxy server is actually the one requesting content from the web servers that you surf to, meaning that the web server believes the request is coming from the proxy server. Indeed, a fairly common use of proxy servers is specifically to enable you to surf the Web with some level of privacy or anonymity. In addition to privacy, proxy servers can also be used to block advertisements, manage cookies, and do similar tasks, including content filtering (block ads, censor content, etc.). To explore proxies more, see http://directory.google.com/Top/Computers/Internet/Proxying_and_Filtering/ for some related sites. Also, see Chapter 11, "The Web, Online Security, .Mac, Sherlock, and iChat," for a more in-depth look at web privacy and security.

Few dial-up connections use proxy servers, but if your connection is one of them, you can set those proxy servers on the Proxies tab. Click the check box next to the server type, and then enter an address in that server's entry box. Proxy servers can also have a unique port number, which you should enter in the Port entry box on that server's row.

If you have particular hosts and domains that should bypass the proxy server, enter those in the entry box at the bottom of the tab's screen, separating them by pressing Return.

NOTE   Why bypass your proxy server? Sometimes a host that you want to access will not work with a proxy server. For instance, some sites require a direct connection for password authorization, while others have multimedia services that won't work correctly through a proxy server.

THE MODEM TAB

Before you can dial out and create your Internet connection, you may need to tell the Network pane a little something about your modem. (If you're dealing with an internal Apple modem, it's often automatically configured.) You configure your modem by selecting the Modem tab (see Figure 10.3). Here's a look at the options:

Modem Use the Modem pop-up menu to choose the type of modem that's installed in (or external to) your Mac. If you don't have one of the specific models listed, you can choose Hayes Compatible to get basic modem capabilities. (If you have an external modem from a third party, and you don't see its name in this list, you may need to install that modem's Mac OS X driver using an installer made available by the manufacturer.)

NOTE Modem configuration files are stored in the Modem Scripts folder inside the main Library folder on your hard disk. If you don't have Admin privileges, you can store a modem configuration file in the Modem Scripts folder inside your personal Library folder, located inside your home folder.

Enable Error Correction And Compression In Modem You'll usually want to have this option turned on because it will result in a more efficient Internet connection. However, if you're experiencing trouble connecting to your ISP or staying connected, turning this off will sometimes result in a more stable, albeit slower, connection.

Wait For Dial Tone Before Dialing This option causes the modem to attempt to detect a dial tone on the line before it begins dialing the ISP's number. Having this option turned on isn't mandatory, and turning it on can cause the modem to be confused by "stutter-tone" features such as phone company voicemail. It can be used to detect when the phone line isn't working or when it is in use (for instance, when someone is talking on another extension) and to stop the modem from dialing.

FIGURE 10.3
The Modem tab in
the Network pane

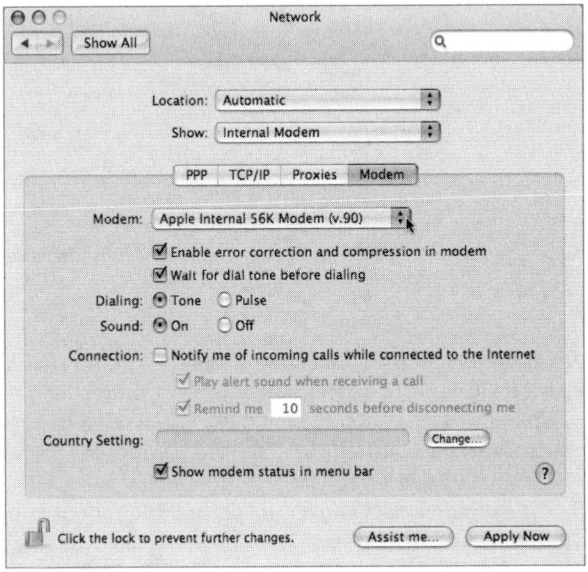

Dialing Select Tone or Pulse, depending on the type of phone line to which you've connected the modem. (Pulse is used only for rotary-service lines that don't support touch-tone dialing. Few of these are left, although you may still have one in a rural area.)

Sound Select On if you'd like to hear the internal modem's connection tones through your Mac's speaker. (External modems generally have their own speakers.)

Connection This setting allows you to be notified of incoming calls that your Mac's modem detects while you're online. Turn the option on, and you'll activate the two options below it, which enable you to tweak the responses you'll get from your Mac when an incoming call is detected.

Show Modem Status In Menu Bar This option activates your modem's menu bar icon, which can then be used to initiate your connection and switch between your modems if you have more than one. See more on the menu bar icon in the next section, "Making the Connection."

Country Setting You also may see a country listed in the Country Setting box; if it's the wrong country for where you are currently, you can choose a different country by clicking the Change button and changing your current location on the Time Zone map in the Date & Time pane.

Once you've made these choices, you've finished configuring your modem in the Network pane. Click Apply Now in the Network pane and close the System Preferences application. You're ready to move on to Internet Connect to establish your connection.

Making the Connection

If you've entered all the preferences and settings for your PPP service and modem in the Network pane, you're ready to connect to the Internet. Verify that your phone line is connected to your modem and then open the Internet Connect application, which is located in your main Applications folder. (You can also launch Internet Connect by clicking the Dial Now button on the PPP tab of the Network pane.)

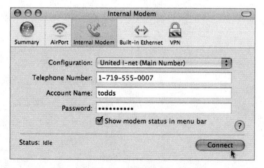

Establishing the connection is easy. With Internal Modem selected at the top of the window, click the Connect button in the Internet Connect window. Internet Connect will dial your modem, displaying a small status line to tell you what's happening. Once your PPP server has been contacted and the connection established, you'll see the window reconfigure slightly to display connection statistics.

The window tells you a number of things about your connection, including small indicator bars that show activity (the Send and Receive bars), the length of time you've been connected for this session, and your current IP address. (The IP address won't change if you have a fixed IP address, but it will change if you have a dynamic address.)

The Internet Connect window includes a Configuration menu that you can use for different dialing scenarios. For instance, if you have more than one ISP, or if you'd like to add a different number for your current ISP, you can choose Edit Configurations from the Configuration menu. A dialog sheet appears where you can add a configuration—click the Add (+) button—and enter a different phone number, or even a different username and password.

Once you've got multiple configurations, you can select among them in the Internet Connect window before dialing—this is handy in situations where the TCP/IP and other settings remain the same, but you simply want to dial a different phone number or log in using a different account.

NOTE   You can quit the Internet Connect application, and your PPP connection will remain up and running until it times out (either due to a setting in PPP Options or because many ISPs will disconnect the connection after a certain amount of inactivity) or until you relaunch Internet Connect and disconnect.

Of course, Internet Connect isn't the only way that you can initiate a connection. The modem menu bar icon, if enabled, is a convenient way to initiate (and cancel) connections quickly without first needing to open Internet Connect. Simply click the modem menu bar icon to view its menu and then choose Connect.

The modem should dial and attempt to connect to your ISP. (As it dials, you'll see the menu icon become animated to indicate that it's trying to connect.) If it succeeds, the message at the top of the menu will change to reflect that you're connected, and the command in the menu will change to Disconnect. Note also that the modem menu bar icon is a convenient way to launch Internet Connect quickly.

TIP   If you didn't activate the modem menu bar icon in the Network pane, the Internet Connect application gives you another opportunity to do so. You may find the menu bar icon more convenient once the novelty of the Internet Connect application has worn off.

Disconnecting from PPP

To disconnect your PPP session, click the Disconnect button in the Internet Connect window. You'll see the Disconnecting status indicator momentarily; then you'll see the full PPP window, and the status will indicate Idle.

You can also disconnect by selecting the modem menu bar icon and choosing Disconnect from its menu.

Note that logging out of your Mac OS X account does not necessarily disconnect the Internet connection—it will remain up and running for as long as your ISP allows an inactive connection to stay connected. (This is one of the options in the PPP Options dialog sheet that you can access from the PPP tab of the Network pane.) Another user can log in and immediately begin using Internet applications, if desired. The connection is terminated, however, if you shut down or restart your Mac.

Troubleshooting Your Dial-Up Connection

The most common problem with modem connections is the status of the phone line that connects to your modem: is the modem plugged in to your Mac and to the phone jack? Seems like a silly question, we know, but it is probably the likeliest culprit. Once you've cleared that particular hurdle, the next problem is probably a connection issue.

Dials Correctly But Won't Connect   Sometimes your modem simply won't connect to the remote receiving modem. If it sounds as if the Mac is dialing correctly and the other side of the connection is being picked up by a computer (with the tell-tale squeals and whirs), but your connection keeps encountering errors, you've likely come up against one of three problems: your modem isn't configured properly, your account information is wrong, or your phone line suffers from too much background noise or interference for a stable connection.

Modem configuration is the problem to hope for, because a bad phone line generally requires contacting your phone company and having them come out for a maintenance check. If you hear a lot of noise (background static, whirs, pops, and so on) when you're talking on the phone, or if you happen to know your phone box is a nest of frayed cables—or an actual nest of birds—a call to the phone company is in order.

For configuration problems, dig back into the Network pane of System Preferences. Begin by ensuring that the modem in question is selected in the Show menu, then select the Modem tab. Make sure you've selected the proper modem script in the Modem pop-up menu. If you don't see the exact modem brand and model that you have, you may need to install a new modem script file in the /Library/Modem Scripts folder on your hard disk. You can also open the Connection log in Internet Connect (Window ➢ Connection Log) to see if you can find any clues as to what Internet Connect thinks is the problem.

If your problem is a modem that won't connect to the remote modem—or it connects but won't seem to hold the connection—the culprit could be your Enable Error Corrections and Compression in Modem setting. Oddly, either setting—on or off—can contribute to errors in different situations. Sometimes a remote modem will connect more willingly when this option is turned off; sometimes a connection will be more error prone if the option is turned off. In any case, toggling it on and off is something to experiment with if you're having trouble. You might also try a different number, if your ISP provides them—sometimes you'll even have better luck with dial-up numbers that are listed as slower than your modem (for instance, those for 28.8kbps connections).

Modem Isn't Detecting A Dial Tone And Dialing Out   Also on the Modem tab is another possible culprit—your modem won't properly detect a dial tone and dial out. If you know for a fact that your phone line is properly plugged in to the modem and an active telephone port, deselect the Wait for Dial Tone before Dialing option. A modem's capability to detect a dial tone can sometimes be thrown off by different phone systems and such things as the stutter dial tone used by some voicemail systems.

Modem Connects But Then Immediately Disconnects   Your username and password may be incorrect. Check them again and make sure they're correct. You also should make sure your settings on the TCP/IP tab of the Network pane are correct—if you've set the wrong option in the Configure menu, your ISP may not be able to connect you properly, even though the modems are communicating successfully.

Intermittently Kicked Off The Internet   If you're tossed off the Internet intermittently, you should start on the PPP tab. Click PPP Options and make sure your Disconnect If Idle setting isn't set abnormally low. You also can disable this option completely. Note also that the advanced options in the PPP Options dialog sheet can be helpful for some troubleshooting. Occasionally turning off Use TCP Header Compression will help a flaky connection. You can also get kicked off if your modem detects a call-waiting tone; on the Modem tab of the Network pane, turn on the Connection options to see if Call Waiting is an issue. You can disable Call Waiting in most parts of the U.S. by adding *70, (include the comma) in front of your ISP's phone number.

Slow Internet Surfing   If you have slowdowns only when you're surfing the Net, it may be a result of a bad DNS server entry on the TCP/IP tab, or the DNS server you're relying on may not be reliable. That's particularly true if, for instance, you wait a long time after entering a URL in your web browser with no results and then suddenly the page appears at regular speed. (This could also indicate that the connection has gone down and is being redialed.) Also, if you can connect to some services but not others—for instance, you can retrieve e-mail but can't access websites—there's a good chance your DNS server setting is misconfigured, or the DNS server is not responding.

Modem Not Recognized At All   What do you do if your modem isn't being recognized at all? If it's an external modem, you can try turning it on and off or unplugging it and plugging it back in (if it's a USB modem). USB devices are recognized when plugged in, so perhaps Mac OS X will note the modem and place it on the Network pane's Show menu once it's recognized. (If not, you may get an error message telling you that you need a new driver.)

High-Speed Connections

More and more people are moving from modem-based Internet connections to *broadband* connections, which is simply a catchword for any Internet connection that has reasonably high speed. Technologies for such high-speed connections include DSL technologies, cable modem technologies, and direct connections such as frame relay or T1 and T3 connections. Phone companies (and ISPs working in conjunction with phone companies) commonly provide DSL, while cable TV companies provide cable Internet connections. Other types of connections (T1, T3, and frame relay) are commonly found in businesses or large organizations that can afford the dedicated lines and hardware required to complete the connections.

NOTE   Another type of subscription technology, ISDN (Integrated Services Digital Network), is still common in some locales in the United States and remains very popular in Europe and elsewhere. ISDN is somewhat similar to DSL service, although it's slower (in most implementations) and requires additional hardware and software. Both provide Internet access over phone lines; however, ISDN requires that a special digital phone line be installed, while DSL offers a high-speed Internet connection over your existing phone line. Phone companies and most consumers prefer DSL, but ISDN remains the only option in some areas, especially rural areas in the U.S. (Some rural areas are now getting special DSL technologies, and that may be the wave of the future for many areas that currently lack broadband, as a lot of innovation has been put toward extending the reach of DSL.)

Most of these high-speed technologies are "always on" Internet connections that are really just a form of wide area networking. Just as you can use TCP/IP settings to configure a local area network (LAN) of Macs and PCs (as discussed in Chapter 18, "Building a Network and Sharing Files"), you can also use TCP/IP settings—and the correct boxes and wiring—to access computers at your phone company, cable company, or ISP. This creates the high-speed connection, making it possible for you to launch and use Internet applications such as web browsers and e-mail programs to access Internet servers.

Exactly how you set up Mac OS X for high-speed access depends on the type of service you have and how it's implemented. In some cases, your approach to completing an Internet connection may be very similar to completing a modem dial-up connection, using special settings in the Network pane and the Internet Connect application. This is especially true if your Internet connection requires a PPP-over-Ethernet connection (PPPoE), which is common for many DSL implementations. Some ISDN connections also require the Internet Connect application, particularly those that are set up with the Using PPP setting on the TCP/IP tab. If your connection requires PPPoE, you'll need to follow the special setup instructions in the section "PPPoE Connections," later in this chapter, to get up and running on your connection.

NOTE Cable, ISDN, and DSL hardware devices are often called "modems," even though they don't *technically* modulate and demodulate, as phone line modems do. (Cable modems are a bit more like phone modems than DSL and ISDN modems, which are nothing like phone modems. Say that three times fast.) They're called modems simply because it's a convenient marketing term meant to suggest "a small box that gets you on the Internet."

In other cases, setup is as simple as entering an IP address for your router in the Network pane of the System Preferences application. Most cable modems, for instance, don't require special setup or a dial-up application such as Internet Connect, but they do require particular TCP/IP settings in the Network pane of the System Preferences application.

NOTE Do you want to use your Ethernet port for Internet access—but you already have a LAN connection that is using the Ethernet port? This presents an interesting problem. An Ethernet port can be used for only one connection—using one set of addresses and so forth—at any given time. If you have such a LAN and your Mac has only one Ethernet port, then changing your TCP/IP settings to access the Internet (via a cable modem, for instance) could mean interrupting your ability to share files on your LAN. The solution is to either install a second Ethernet adapter to be used exclusively for the Internet connection or install a *router*, which is a device that can send Internet data to all computers on your LAN. The router makes it possible for your Mac to access both local network volumes and the Internet at the same time.

Direct Ethernet Connections

If you have a direct connection to the Internet via your Ethernet port—T1, T3, or a similar connection that's made available over your local network—configuration should be fairly simple. Open System Preferences, click the Network icon, and select an Ethernet port from the Network pane's Show menu or double-click it in the Network Status listing; then click the TCP/IP tab in the Network pane. (You may select either the Built-in Ethernet port or another Ethernet port if you have an internal Ethernet card installed and you want to use it for Internet access.) At this point, you may need to click the padlock icon and enter an administrator's username and password in order to edit these settings. (This step isn't necessary if you're logged in to an administrator account.) Now you're ready to edit the TCP/IP settings (see Figure 10.4).

NOTE The instructions for a direct Ethernet connection are generally true for cable modem connections, too; in both cases, these Ethernet-based connections don't require any type of initialization along the lines of a PPPoE connection. Most of the time you can connect to your cable modem via an Ethernet cable and then set that Ethernet port to Using DHCP on its TCP/IP tab. If the cable modem is working correctly, that's often all you need to get up and running.

FIGURE 10.4

TCP/IP settings for
an Ethernet port

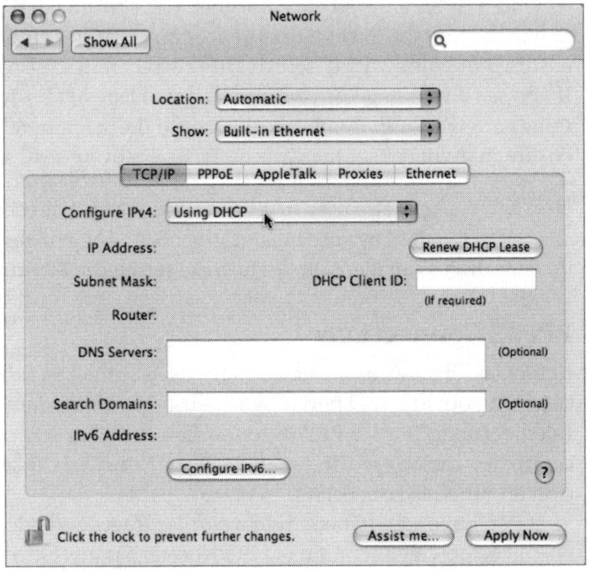

For the next step, configure TCP/IP according to your ISP's instructions. How you do that can vary, depending on your ISP (or your system administrator, if you're configuring this Mac in an organizational setting):

◆ If your ISP or administrator uses DHCP to assign IP addresses, select Using DHCP from the Configure IPv4 menu. Then move down to the Domain Name Servers entry box and enter the DNS address(es) for your connection if your ISP requires this. (If not, you can leave this entry box blank.)

◆ If your ISP or administrator requires you to enter the TCP/IP configuration manually, choose Manually from the Configure IPv4 menu. Enter an IP address, subnet mask, router, and other information as required by the ISP. For manual settings, the router address is important to get right because it tells your Mac where to locate the router device that will feed it TCP/IP data.

NOTE   If you can't seem to select Using DHCP, it may be because PPP over Ethernet is turned on. Click the PPPoE tab and turn off PPPoE. Having PPP over Ethernet turned on limits your ability to choose DHCP in the TCP/IP pane because the PPPoE protocol can't use a DHCP server to retrieve an address—by definition PPPoE uses a PPP server to retrieve a dynamic address.

◆ Your ISP or administrator may offer a hybrid approach—you're supposed to enter your IP address manually, but your other settings are retrieved from a DHCP server. If that's the case, select Manually Using DHCP with Manual IP Address and then enter an IP address in the IP Address entry box. Again, in this instance you can enter DNS server addresses if required by your ISP.

◆ Finally, your ISP or administrator may require you to use a BootP server to retrieve your IP settings. To do so, select Using BootP from the Configure IPv4 menu. This is more common in computer lab situations, particular if some of the computers in the lab are "diskless" workstations using the NetBoot feature of Mac OS X Server (www.apple.com/macosx/server/).

Once you've entered your settings, you should click the Apply Now button on the Network pane and then close the System Preferences application. Now you can launch an Internet application to ensure that your TCP/IP settings are correct and the broadband connection is functioning correctly. If you see a web page or you find that you can successfully download your e-mail, it's likely that things are working. If not, dive back into the documentation from your ISP or administrator and ensure that you've set the various TCP/IP addresses correctly.

NOTE   You may also need to set proxy servers for a direct connection to the Internet, particularly if they're required by your organization. See "The Proxies Tab" section earlier in this chapter. The same discussion there applies to proxy settings in Ethernet-based connections.

PPPoE Connections

PPP-over-Ethernet, as the name suggests, is similar to a dial-up modem connection, except that it takes place via your Ethernet port instead of using your modem and phone lines. Unlike some Ethernet-based Internet connections, a PPPoE connection isn't "always on," but must be initiated before the Internet connection can be used. In a manner of speaking, you're setting up your Mac to "dial out" to the ISP, but over an Ethernet connection.

If you have a DSL modem or a similar Internet device that uses PPPoE protocols, you have some special setup considerations in the Network pane. Once those settings are made, you'll then use the Internet Connect application to complete your PPPoE connection.

THE PPPoE TAB

Begin by selecting your Ethernet port from the Show menu in the Network pane. If you have multiple Ethernet ports, select the port that's connected to your Internet modem or gateway device.

NOTE   Turning on PPPoE automatically changes your TCP/IP setting (on the TCP/IP tab) to Using PPP (on the TCP/IP tab). Again, if you're using this Ethernet port for a LAN connection, you cannot also use it for a PPPoE connection because you can't successfully "dial out" over an Ethernet port that's already configured for a local network. You'll need to either install a second Ethernet adapter card (if your Mac will support one) or add an Internet router, discussed in Chapter 18. If you install a router, note that you'll likely use it to configure your PPPoE connection, not the Network pane.

To configure PPPoE, you'll skip the TCP/IP tab and go straight to the PPPoE tab (see Figure 10.5). At the top of the tab's screen, you'll see the option Connect Using PPPoE. Click the check box to turn on that option. The Service Provider entry box is optional—you can enter your ISP's name if you'd like. The PPPoE Service Name box is reserved, however; enter something in that box only if your ISP instructs you to.

Then, in the Account Name entry box, enter the account name that your ISP assigned to you; in the Password box, enter the password you were assigned. If you'd like to save this password (so that you don't have to enter it later in the Internet Connect application), turn on the Save Password option.

The PPPoE tab offers a PPPoE Options button (you'll only see it when PPPoE is turned on). Click this button, and a dialog sheet with two sets of options will appear: Session Options and Advanced Options. In Session Options, you can choose how often your Mac will remind you that you're connected and how much idle time will elapse before your Mac automatically disconnects you. You can also select if the Mac will disconnect as you log out of your account. By default, the option Connect

Automatically When Needed is turned off, but you may want to turn it on. This enables your Mac to initiate the PPPoE connection whenever you launch an Internet request (checking your e-mail in Mail, Safari, or a channel in Sherlock) if the connection isn't already active.

In Advanced Options, you can turn off Send PPP Echo Packets if your ISP suggests this, and you can turn on Use Verbose Logging if you'd like more detailed logging of your connections. (This log can be accessed via the Internet Connect application by choosing Window ➤ Connection Log.) When you're done in the dialog sheet, click OK.

NOTE   You may need to switch back to the TCP/IP tab to add domain name servers if your ISP requires you to enter them manually. Also, if your Internet connection requires proxy servers, use the Proxies tab as discussed in the section "Setting Up Your Modem and TCP/IP," earlier in this chapter.

Finally, if you'd like to access your PPPoE connection via a menu bar icon, turn on the option Show PPPoE Status in Menu Bar. Doing so turns on the small Ethernet icon in the menu bar that you can use to launch the connection and access status, as discussed next.

MAKING THE CONNECTION

Once you've entered your PPPoE settings in the Network pane, you can switch to the Internet Connect application to initiate the connection. Launch Internet Connect (it's in the main `Applications` folder) and select your Ethernet port from the Configuration menu. Now you can simply click the Connect button to initiate the connection. If your DSL (or similar) modem is turned on and properly connected to your Mac, you should quickly see the status line indicate a connection; also, the Internet Connect window will change to show Send and Receive indicators, as well as the length of time connected and the current IP address.

FIGURE 10.5
The PPPoE tab is where you'll configure your PPPoE account information.

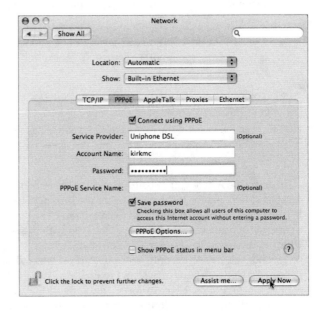

If you'd like to see more information about your connection, or if you need to enter your password, click the triangle button next to the Configuration menu. That opens up the Internet Connect window to reveal your username, password entry box, and other details.

To disconnect, simply click the Disconnect button. You should see the status line return to Idle.

If you enabled the PPPoE Status icon discussed in the previous section, you can also use it to connect and disconnect from the Internet; likewise, you can check the status of your connection in the menu.

AirPort-Based Internet Connections

If your Mac is configured with an AirPort card or otherwise has AirPort connectivity built in, you may be able to access the Internet wirelessly. There are multiple scenarios for Internet over AirPort, although most of them require an AirPort Base Station (or a similar wireless router). Here's a quick list of the possibilities:

◆ The AirPort Base Station has a modem, which you can dial from any AirPort-enabled Mac, thus connecting to the Internet.

◆ The AirPort Base Station (or AirPort Express router) has an Ethernet port, which can be connected to a broadband modem. The Base Station is a router, so it can initiate a PPPoE connection if necessary, or it can simply route Internet data from an "always on" connection to your AirPort-enabled Macs.

◆ The AirPort Base Station can act as a node on an existing Ethernet network, accepting routed Internet data from another source. If your wired LAN has access, your AirPort network can have access, too.

◆ You can share an Internet connection from one AirPort-enabled Mac to another.

NOTE Later versions of the AirPort Base Station include two Ethernet ports, meaning the AirPort Base Station can act as a stand-alone Internet router that sends Internet packets to both wired and wireless machines. See Chapter 18 for details.

In each case where you're using an AirPort Base Station or Airport Express router, you'll need to do at least two, maybe three things. (For the Internet Sharing solution, see the section "Internet and Personal File Sharing Together" in Chapter 18.) First, you need to configure the AirPort Base Station so that it can connect to the Internet. Doing so with the AirPort Setup Assistant and AirPort Admin Utility is discussed in Chapter 25, "Peripherals, Internal Upgrades, and Disks."

Second, you'll need to configure your AirPort-enabled Mac to connect to the Base Station. That's done in the Network pane of System Preferences. With the Network pane open, select AirPort from the Show menu (or double-click AirPort in the Network Status list). On the TCP/IP tab, you'll likely choose Using DHCP from the Configure menu unless you've specifically set up your AirPort network to use manually selected IP addresses, in which case you'll choose Using DHCP with Manual Address.

(Again, see Chapters 18 and 25 for a discussion on setting up the AirPort Base Station.) You may also need to enter a DNS server on the TCP/IP tab, although AirPort networks tend to provide the DNS automatically.

With the TCP/IP settings made, click the AirPort tab. Here you can select your Mac's default AirPort behavior from the By Default, Join menu—select Automatic if you want to join the strongest network or choose Preferred Networks. If the latter, then you can choose the network from the Network menu and enter a password if necessary. (If you don't enter a password, you'll be prompted for it.) You also may want to turn on the AirPort status menu bar icon.

NOTE If you turn on the AirPort status menu bar icon, you can use it to select your active AirPort network, check status, and even turn off your AirPort card when you're not using it. (That's a good idea, particularly in a portable, because it consumes power even when it isn't connected to a network.)

Now, to connect to the Internet via AirPort, you first need to connect to the AirPort network. Open Internet Connect and choose the AirPort button at the top of the window. If the Network menu says No Network Selected, you should select a network from that menu. When you select a network, you may be asked for a password. If the password is accepted, you'll see Base Station ID and Signal Level for that network appear in the Internet Connect window.

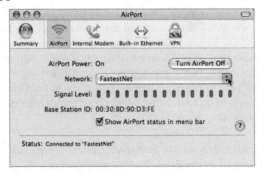

At the very bottom of the window, you'll see the controls for connecting to and disconnecting from the Internet if your connection is via modem or PPPoE. If you're not currently connected to the Internet (meaning you have a dial-up or PPPoE connection), click the Connect button; if you're connected and want to disconnect, click the Disconnect button. Now, with the connection up and running, you should be able to begin surfing the Web, checking your e-mail, and so forth.

NOTE If you don't see buttons at the bottom of the Internet Connect window, it may mean that your wireless Internet connection is handled by a wireless router or similar non-Apple device that doesn't give you control over the connection, or that the connection isn't the type that can be connected and disconnected.

Also note that if the AirPort Base Station is configured to access the Internet directly or automatically, it will connect when you attempt to access an Internet service.

Troubleshooting Broadband Connections

The fact that Mac OS X has all of the networking hooks built in, including direct support for technologies such as PPPoE (which used to be the exclusive domain of third-party dialer software), means that broadband connections generally are less troublesome, particularly from the computer's side of the equation. That's not to say you won't have trouble with your broadband modem, cable, connection, service, or the customer service at your phone or cable company. Thank goodness (for us, at least) those issues are outside the scope of this book.

On your Mac, however, there are a few problems that may occasionally cause a broadband connection to hiccup. (This assumes that you've made sure the correct cables are plugged in to the correct ports, all of your modems and other devices such as AirPort Base Stations are turned on, and you've connected to the Internet if that's required of your connection.) Let's look at those basic solutions here briefly:

Do You Need A DNS Entry?   It may not always be clear from your ISP's documentation, but you may need a valid DNS server in order to access websites and other Internet resources. If you notice that your connection otherwise seems valid—for instance, if Internet Connect is reporting a connection and you can even access your e-mail—but you can't seem to load web pages or access FTP sites, the culprit is likely the DNS address. Check your ISP's documentation again to see what DNS address you should enter on the TCP/IP tab of the Network pane. Or, if you suspect that your DNS entries are bad, you can delete them and see if your Mac is able to get its DNS information from its DHCP or PPP server connection.

Do You Need A Router Entry?   If you've specified Manually as your method of configuration on the TCP/IP tab of the Network pane—most likely in a situation where you connect to the Internet via your local network—then you must enter not only an IP address, a subnet mask, and a DNS server address, but also a router address. This entry is often misunderstood. You need to enter the address of the router that is used to send Internet packets over your LAN; otherwise, your Mac doesn't know what device to ask for Internet access. Often the router is at the .1 address of your internal IP addressing scheme (such as 192.168.1.1), but not always. If you're not sure, and you didn't set up the router yourself, consult with your administrator. (Also, see Chapter 18 for more on routing Internet data to a LAN.)

TIP   In your ISP's documentation, the router address will sometimes be referred to as a gateway address, so look for that if you're not finding the router address.

Are Your Proxy Server Settings Correct?   Proxy servers can cause problems—the most likely being that you don't always remember you're using a proxy server. If you've set up a proxy server entry on the Proxies tab in the Network pane and access used to work but doesn't now, the proxy server may be temporarily or permanently unavailable.

Have You Restarted?   Most changes to Mac OS X settings in the Network pane don't require a restart. Occasionally, however, a restart is a good idea if your Mac needs to capture a new address or setting from an external device. For instance, if you're having trouble with a cable modem or DSL modem that you turn off and on again, the solution is generally to first make sure the settings are correct in the Network pane. Then shut down your Mac, and turn off the broadband modem for a few minutes (so it clears out any settings held in short-term memory) or otherwise "hard" reset the device. Now, start it up and let it acquire a connection. When it does, restart your Mac and let it talk to the broadband device anew—hopefully, the device and your Mac will interact as expected.

> ### TESTING YOUR CONNECTION WITH NETWORK UTILITY
>
> You think you may have an active connection, but certain things aren't working. It might help to test. You can test your connection using Mac OS X's built-in Network Utility, which is included in the `Utilities` folder inside the `Applications` folder. Network Utility gives you access to `ping`, `traceroute`, `nslookup`, and other Internet-related commands that are commonly used to test connections.
>
> Click the Ping tab, for instance, to see if you can successfully contact outside servers. Enter **www.apple.com** in the entry boxes at the top of the Ping tab's screen, then click Ping to begin pinging. If you see repeated lines that say *xx bytes from*, that means your connection is working. You can also use `ping` with inside servers (those on your LAN) to see if Internet-type services are working on your internal network.
>
> Likewise, you can use `lookup` to make sure your DNS server addresses are correct. Choose the Lookup tab, enter an Internet server address in the entry box at the top of the window, and click Lookup. After a moment, you should see an entry that shows you the IP address for the domain name you entered. If you don't, you may need to jump back into the Network pane and change the DNS server addresses so that they're valid.
>
> Experiment with the other tabs in Network Utility. The Whois tab offers tools for looking up and showing you a particular domain's registration details. Finger looks up a particular e-mail address to see if it has a `finger` record attached to it (which gives personal info about that person). Traceroute traces the route of a packet of data from your computer to a remote computer, showing you all the Internet points through which the packet passes. For more on Network Utility, see Chapters 19 and 29.

TCP/IP in the Classic Environment

For the most part, you can access the Internet within the Classic environment without any trouble. The idea is to treat the Classic environment as if it were simply another Mac OS X application such as a web browser. If you need to connect to the Internet using a Classic application, you'll want to establish your Internet connection first, particularly if you don't have an "always-on" Internet connection and you use Internet Connect (or a menu bar icon) to initiate your connections. Once the Internet connection is established, you should be able to launch the Classic application and begin accessing online resources.

If you have a direct connection to the Internet, including a broadband connection like DSL or a cable modem, using Internet applications within Classic is even easier. Once TCP/IP is properly set up in the Network pane of System Preferences and you've successfully accessed the Internet from Mac OS X, launch a Classic Internet application and test your connection from within the Classic environment.

This system works because the TCP/IP control panel in Mac OS 9 has been modified to work in a Classic configuration, where the panel receives TCP/IP settings directly from Mac OS X. (In versions prior to 10.2, you can view this control panel by launching a Classic application and then choosing Control Panels ➤ TCP/IP from the Classic Apple menu. In later versions it isn't accessible.) By default, you can't alter any of these settings because they're set by Mac OS X. You should avoid changing this configuration, for instance, by using File ➤ Configurations in the TCP/IP control panel's menu.

Classic applications can't work directly with your Mac's modem, so modem-based applications such as America Online can't be run from within the Classic environment. You should upgrade your Classic applications to the native Mac OS X version if they need to access the modem.

TIP   Although it is outside the scope of this book, you shouldn't have trouble understanding modem-based Internet connections from within Mac OS 9, if your Mac supports the option of booting directly into Mac OS 9. It's similar to the discussion in the section "Dial-Up Internet Access," earlier in this chapter, except you'll use different control panels for settings instead of using the Network pane. Use the TCP/IP control panel (Apple menu ➤ Control Panels ➤ TCP/IP) to select PPP and configure it for your connection—it's somewhat similar to the options you'll see in the Network pane. Use the Modem control panel (Apple menu ➤ Control Panels ➤ Modem) to choose your modem's script and make volume, pulse/tone, and other settings. Then use the Remote Access control panel (Apple menu ➤ Control Panels ➤ Remote Access), which is similar to Internet Connect, to enter an account name, password, and phone number to dial your ISP and initiate the connection.

Active Ports and Creating New Configurations

So far in this chapter, you've seen the basics of connecting your Mac to the Internet. In this section, let's dig a little further into the Network pane and look at Mac OS X's capability to store multiple configurations for any of your ports and something called *multihoming*—OS X's capability to access multiple network connections simultaneously. This means you can have multiple connections configured at once, and the OS will use those that connect successfully. The upshot is that you don't necessarily have to reconfigure your ports when you want to use a different network connection or Internet access method.

NOTE   We're saying "network connection" because these configurations cover both Internet connections and local area network connections. See Chapter 18 for details on the networking side of things.

SETTING YOUR PORT ORDER

Mac OS X puts items in the Show menu of the Network pane automatically by detecting those items and doing its best to assign driver software to them. When that happens, they're placed on the Show menu where they can be selected, configured, and so forth as you've seen in this chapter. Each port gets one set of configuration settings.

Select Network Port Configurations from the Show menu, however, and you can do a little more with these ports. Using this interface (see Figure 10.6), you can add configurations for your existing Internet ports. You can then turn those configurations on and off as desired, or you can leave them active but put them in the order in which they should be attempted.

Let's start with the multihoming concept first. The Network Port Configurations screen enables you to choose the order in which your Mac will attempt to use the ports for the connection when an Internet application requests Internet data. For instance, you can tell your Mac to check for an Ethernet-based connection when you launch a web browser window or perform a task such as checking your e-mail, then check for an AirPort connection if the Ethernet connection doesn't work, and so on. Simply drag the ports around on the Active Ports screen to rearrange them, thus choosing the order of their priority.

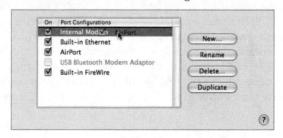

FIGURE 10.6

Select Network Port Configurations from the Show menu in the Network pane, and you can add port configurations.

If you have a modem-based Internet connection, that can be part of the multihoming hierarchy as well. In most cases, we'd recommend putting the modem at the bottom of the list. That way, if other, higher-speed connections are unavailable, you could try the modem. You might also want to access the PPP Options for the modem (on the Modem tab when you access the modem in the Network pane of System Preferences) and turn on the option Connect Automatically When Needed. That way, the modem can be dialed automatically if other connection types aren't available. If you have multiple Ethernet ports, a Bluetooth connection, or even an IrDA connection of some kind (available on some PowerBooks—see Chapter 19, "PowerBooks, iBooks, and Mac OS X"), those can be part of the mix, too.

By prioritizing your connections, you can better automate the process of getting on the Internet under different circumstances. This means you can just let your Mac check for the most efficient or most desired network connection first and then settle for the next-best one if the first one fails.

Managing the order of your ports is also useful, however, in situations where you move around with your Mac. Suppose you have an Ethernet-based connection at work, an AirPort connection in the organization's office where you volunteer, and a PPP-based phone connection to the Internet at home. Set Ethernet first, then AirPort, then Internal Modem. Then, wherever you are, you'll be able to connect to the Internet; the Mac will attempt to connect to each of those in turn until it settles on one that works.

We're not saying this is the most efficient way to set it up, but it will work, and it's a cool technology. The most efficient way would probably be to configure different *locations*, which you also can do via the Network pane. We've put the discussion of Location Manager in the chapter on portables (Chapter 19) because it's most often used with portables; however, if you have a desktop Mac or iMac that you move around a bit, the Location Manager will work just as well for you, too.

CREATING AND MANAGING NEW CONFIGURATIONS

Aside from the order of your ports, the Network Port Configurations screen gives you the ability to create new ports. Why do this? One reason is so that you can quickly turn different configurations on and off. For instance, by default you can have only one configuration for Built-in Ethernet. But suppose you want two settings—one that retrieves an IP address via DHCP and another that sets the IP address manually.

If that's the case, you could go into the Network pane and type the changes every time you want to alter them, or you could create a new configuration and turn the two on and off as necessary.

The other reason to do this is another take on multihoming—you could create two different configurations for the same port and leave them both on. For instance, you could create a second configuration for your Ethernet port, designed to connect to the Internet using a different method than the first configuration. With both of them active, the first configuration will be attempted first; if it fails, the second configuration will kick in.

To create a new port configuration, you can either click the New button or highlight an existing port and click Duplicate. If you do the latter, a dialog sheet appears asking you to name the port, and then the port appears in the list; if you click New, a dialog sheet appears in which you can type a name for the new configuration. Then you can select the port you'll be configuring from the Port menu.

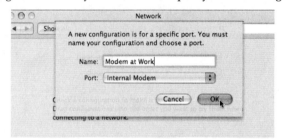

With the new port configuration duplicated or created, you can edit the configuration by selecting it in the Show menu and running through the various tabs in the Network pane.

When you're done making all the configuration choices, you can return to the Active Ports screen. Drag the port names around to rearrange them. To turn off one of them (because you don't want the Mac to connect with that configuration), remove the check from the check box next to that port's listing. To turn it back on, place a check in its check box. Click Apply Now or close the Network pane, and you're ready to use your new settings.

Internet Security and Firewalls

The last thing we'd like to discuss in this chapter is Internet security, particularly as it concerns your network or modem connection to the Internet. In this discussion, we'll assume that you're interested in security for one Mac at a time that connects directly to the Internet via a modem or broadband connection. Internet security is certainly also a concern when you're talking about Internet access via a local area network, but it's a touch more complex and deserves its own discussion, which is in Chapter 18.

NOTE   With AirPort, you can use this discussion if you want to secure your personal Mac, or see Chapters 18 and 25 for discussion specific to secure access and surfing with AirPort.

Internet Connection Security Issues

Whenever you connect to the Internet, you're placing your Mac on the Internet right along with hundreds of millions of other computers. That means your Mac, conceivably, could be accessed by those computers. As you might be aware, some computers are *servers*, designed to make data available, and others are *clients*, like yours, designed to locate, download, and display (or otherwise use) the data being served.

The problem is that there's a fine line between being a server and a client—all it takes is running server software to make your Mac a server. That server software is built into Mac OS X, so it's even possible to be an accidental server. Whenever your Mac is online with an IP address, it can be accessed—or at least others can attempt to access it—using that address. If a malicious user finds any holes or vulnerabilities in the front that you present to the Internet, it's possible that your data could be accessed or a virus or worm could be placed on your Mac—it's not overwhelmingly likely, but possible.

In fact, there are instances of unsuspecting users (mostly Microsoft Windows, but some others) whose computers are used as unauthorized servers for nefarious purposes or as unwitting pipelines for hiding another user's true identity. (In other words, a hacker type could use the unsuspecting Internet user's IP address to mask his own.) Mac OS X opens the Macintosh up to a greater possibility of these vulnerabilities and others because it's based on Unix, which has been the domain of sophisticated Internet programmers (and hackers) for decades. (The Classic Mac OS was largely invulnerable because it wasn't designed with many different points of entry on the Internet, and its market share made it unattractive to authors of Trojan horses, viruses, and worms.)

At the same time, Unix security experts are vigilant, so many of the holes that are found in Unix system and server software get plugged fast. What concerns us, however, is how vulnerable your Mac is to an attack or intrusion of some kind. There are a couple of basic circumstances that dictate how vulnerable your Mac is.

Static IP Addresses   With most dial-up Internet connections, you're given a new IP address with every connection. That means your IP address doesn't stay the same, making you slightly less vulnerable to someone looking for an easy online target. That said, the longer you stay connected to the Internet in a given session, the longer that IP address remains static. Also, many broadband modems request and receive the same IP address over and over again, even via PPPoE connections. And, with a broadband connection, it's more likely that you'll leave the connection (and your Mac) running for many hours or days at a time. Unless you specifically want a server on the Internet, changing your IP address frequently (by signing off or requesting dynamic service from your ISP) is a good idea.

NOTE   It might seem unlikely that someone could locate your computer in the vast sea of IP addresses on the Internet—but remember that there are *automated* methods of searching for valid IP addresses, and they're pretty darned sophisticated. The more time your Mac spends online with the same IP address, the more likely it is to be checked out or "sniffed" for possible vulnerabilities.

Servers   Mac OS X has a number of different servers that you can enable easily—File Sharing, Web Sharing, FTP, Remote Login, and Remote Apple Events, among others. All of these run over TCP/IP, and all can be accessible to the Internet simply if *they're turned on while you're surfing!* The moment you access the Internet (via Internet Connect or a direct connection) with File Sharing turned on, you've made it possible for someone to attempt to access your computer remotely. If you have user accounts created in the Users pane that have names or passwords that are easily guessed (or no passwords at all), it's possible for someone you don't know to gain access to your Mac. Indeed, File Sharing, by default, lets guest users access the `Public` folders of your users and lets them copy files to the user's Drop Box. If a file has a virus attached and your user launches it, it could infect the user's files or even his `System` files, depending on the user's privileges.

NOTE   See Chapter 18 for more on File Sharing.

Open Ports   Servers are made available on different *ports*, many of which are well known (such as port 80, which is where most web server applications make a connection available to web browsers). The more ports you have open, the more potential vulnerabilities. For instance, turning on Apple File

Sharing over IP can be handy for sharing files on your local network, but if your Mac has a direct connection to the Internet, then turning on File Sharing opens ports that could be detected by someone on the Internet. If a port scan detects those ports, it gives a hacker an excuse to start trying to connect to your Mac. This is particularly true if you don't have a firewall of some sort set up for your Mac and/or your network.

NOTE Another example to think about is a program like Limewire, which some people use for file sharing and for downloading files. Recognize that, by default, Limewire will *share* some of your Mac's files on the Internet if you don't read its instructions carefully, which may also be a vulnerability.

Broadband Technologies The last circumstance we'll cover is the approach that the ISP takes to security. If your ISP places you behind a firewall or a router of some kind, you might be less vulnerable. The ISP may also offer proxy server settings that mask your IP address or otherwise make you a bit less easy to pinpoint. The design of some ISPs' networks, however, may leave you open to access from other members of the service—for instance, some cable loops are designed in such a way that File Sharing, if turned on, could be easily accessed by other people who share your ISP—in fact, your Mac might even show up in their Connect to Server windows automatically. (See Chapter 18 for more on that issue.)

NOTE Most ISPs tend to assume that you'd like some level of direct access to your IP address so that others can access your Mac directly—even someone with a dial-up connection. That's useful if you'd like to allow someone you know to log in to your Mac remotely, or if you'd like to make your Mac available as a web server or even an Internet game server for a few friends or others. Likewise, the proliferation and popularity of peer-to-peer networking solutions (those that make any computer on the Internet a potential server—in the vein popularized by Napster) mean many users don't want their IP address hidden from the Internet. So, most likely your Mac can be reached publicly if you're directly connected to an online service, even if your IP address only stays the same for the duration of each connection to your ISP. If that's the case, it means the security is up to you. (Actually some ISPs block the outside world from accessing certain types of services on your Mac such as FTP, Web server and so on. Check with your ISP's user policy to find out if they block your ability to serve data via FTP and/or HTTP or if you need a special account—often a business account—in order to run servers from your connection.)

What's the solution? For an Internet connection that serves your entire network, you may want some sophisticated hardware. (Again, we'll discuss that in Chapter 18.) For an individual Mac connecting directly to the Internet, the best solution is to run firewall software directly on your Mac. (That's in conjunction with virus-checking software, discussed in Chapters 12, "Managing E-Mail," and 26, "Hard Disk Care, File Security, and Maintenance.") Firewall software is used to note access to particular services and ports, to block particular activity, and to log (or sometimes alert you to) anything that seems suspicious. We recommend firewall software for your Macs that spend time online.

NOTE Make sure you stay on top of security issues that are reported by the Mac media such as Todd's site (www.maseringmacosx.com) and specialized sites such as SecureMac (www.securemac.com). Visit the website of your firewall software manufacturer regularly for updates and advice. The toughest thing about Internet security is understanding the different ports, why they're there, and how much you should worry about them.

Firewalls for Mac OS X

There's good news and bad news about firewall software and Mac OS X. The good news is that a firewall is actually built into Mac OS X and you can access it from the Sharing pane of System Preferences. The bad news is that Apple's interface isn't quite as full-featured as the actual firewall is. There are solutions, however—one is a good shareware firewall and the other two are commercial options you might consider purchasing.

As is the tradition with both Mac and Unix software, the shareware solutions such as Firewalk X are great programs written and updated by individuals. Of the commercial options, NetBarrier X is easy to use and offers commercial-level support, while Norton's Personal Firewall is the most expensive but also the "household name" option.

WARNING   Don't forget about your built-in or third-party firewall! The point of a firewall is to block various types of Internet-related network traffic. That's what it does. If it's configured badly, it may block traffic that you don't want blocked, but you may not be completely aware of it. In other words, if you're having trouble accessing a particular service, website, or e-mail account or even viewing images on a web page, it's possible that it has to do with your firewall, if it's active. Remember to test the settings in the firewall application if you have trouble online or on your local network.

THE FIREWALL TAB

Launch the Sharing pane of System Preferences, and you'll see the Firewall tab, where you can turn on the firewall that's built into Mac OS X and make some choices about it. (By default, it's turned off.) This firewall offers basic functionality—when you turn it on, it blocks all access attempts to your Mac except for those that you specifically allow in the Allow list. You do that by placing a check mark next to the ports (and services) that you'd like to use. (Note that you can turn on only services that are actually running on your Mac, which you turn on via the Services tab.)

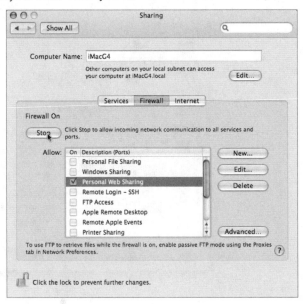

Once you've turned on the services that you want to use, click the Start button. The firewall is started, and your Mac is now protected from attempts to access those services that aren't turned on.

If you don't see a service that you'd like to use, click the New button. A dialog sheet will appear in which you can select from a number of additional port names and port numbers. You also can select Other in the Port Name menu and specify a different port number and a description of the service. Click OK in the dialog sheet, and the port is added to your Allow list.

Why is this limited? For one thing, it doesn't enable you to differentiate between traffic that happens locally and traffic over the Internet. Secondly, many of the other firewall solutions offer additional features, such as the capability to create different configurations for different networking ports or to notice when sensitive information (credit card numbers, ID numbers) are being requested from your Mac and block those requests if they appear to be unauthorized. The built-in firewall is a very adequate solution that will work for many of us; you can dig in further and look at some of the third-party solutions in this section if you're interested in more options.

DOORSTOP X FIREWALL

www.opendoor.com/

Shareware

Instead of using the Mac's built-in firewall code, DoorStop X Firewall offers its own firewall code and interface in the form of a utility application. DoorStop X Firewall places its main focus on the Internet ports to be blocked, but does so in a user-friendly way that makes it clear what Internet services on your Mac are associated with the particular ports that you're managing.

DoorStop X Firewall offers basic customization options—you can deny or allow all access for a particular service, or you can get specific about the addresses that can access a particular service. (Likewise, you can explicitly deny certain addresses from accessing your service.) In addition, DoorStop X Firewall offers an extensive list of built-in ports and services that you can add by clicking the New button under the Services window.

FIGURE 10.7

DoorStop X Firewall offers user-friendly, advanced features if you're looking for a firewall.

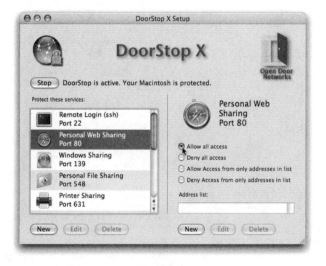

If you're interested in digging into Firewalk's capabilities, an HTML User's Manual is included with the distribution, which we recommend you read. Also, you may be interested to know that the authors of DoorStop are Mac Internet Security experts, having written a book on the subject that's also available via their website.

NetBarrier X3

www.intego.com/

Commercial application, approximately $60, 30-day trial download available

NetBarrier X3 is more expensive, more graphically pleasing, and a bit friendlier for beginner users (see Figure 10.8) than the shareware applications you'll encounter. Designed to make sense to the relatively inexperienced user, NetBarrier X3 doesn't rely on Mac OS X's firewall capabilities, but rather runs as a fully independent firewall application. It also incorporates some other features, including antivandal features (it alerts you to certain types of scans and access attempts while enabling you to stop certain IP addresses and allow others) and Privacy features, which include the capability to protect certain data, filter banner ads out of your Internet browser, and manage some fundamental web privacy issues such as web cookies, browser caches, and history files, as well as some global variable settings (your computer brand and browser and the last site you visited).

Once launched, the NetBarrier firewall is always working in the background until you turn it off—the application need not be active. To change settings or actively monitor the firewall, however, you can launch the interface and leave it on-screen. The NetBarrier X3 interface splits into four basic functions—Firewall, Antivandal, Privacy, and Monitoring. Here's a synopsis of what can be done in each section of the program:

Firewall The Firewall screen has three tabs—General, Log, and Trojans. On the General tab, you'll set up the various rules for your firewall—you can choose either a default set of rules (No Restrictions, Client Only, and so forth) or Customized, which enables you to create individual rules and add them to the list. Rules are applied in the order that they appear in the window, so you're free to drag them around if necessary.

TIP Interested in one of the default settings? Point to each with your mouse to see a pop-up description. The descriptions do a good job of making each default's purpose more clear.

On the Log tab, you can view a log of all recent access to your Mac that has been noted by the firewall—it keeps track of everything, including access to e-mail servers, web servers, and so on. Check a box to see that box's log information. You can also export a log by clicking Export, and you can clear the log by clicking the Clear button. The Name Resolution option is useful if you'd like to see the DNS names of servers that are being accessed instead of their IP addresses. The Log window can be shown separately, if desired; choose Window ➤ Show Log Window. Also, when viewing the log, you can Control+click a particular entry to see contextual commands about that item.

The Trojans tab lets you block malicious Trojan horses that may get installed on your Mac. NetBarrier detects them by spotting activity on specific ports that these Trojan horses use. Trojan horses can be installed on your computer by rogue applications and can send data out of your computer, or they can let a hacker take control of or alter your computer from a distance. This said, there are not many Trojan horses that affect Macs.

FIGURE 10.8
NetBarrier X3 is one commercial entrant, offering a great feature set.

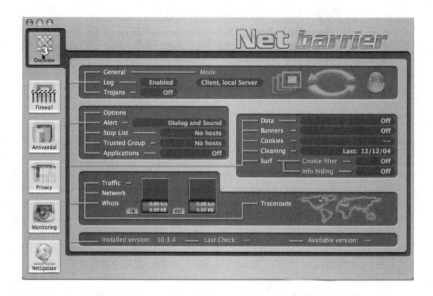

NOTE The NetBarrier X3 preferences dialog box (NetBarrier X ➤ Preferences) includes an option that enables you to automatically export your log files for long-term keeping. Click the Log icon and then use the radio buttons to determine how often the logs should be exported and where they should be stored. These logs can be used to analyze potential intrusions or—perhaps more paternalistically—to see what sites you and other users have visited on your Mac.

Antivandal On the Antivandal screen, you'll see five different tabs: Options, Alerts, Stop List, Trusted Group, and Applications. In Options, you choose the antivandal steps that you want the software to take; in most cases, you can turn on all of them, although you may not want Ping Replies enabled, and you may have other reasons to disable some of these options. On the Alerts tab, you can set options for the type of alerts, the sound, and whether or not an e-mail should be sent when an alert is set off. On the Stop List tab, you can see a list of intruders that have activated alerts and their IP addresses. On the Trusted Group tab, you'll see a list of IP addresses you've added to the list, as well as buttons that enable you to add or edit those entries. These are IP addresses that will not generate an alert even if they attempt something (such as a ping command) that would normally set off the Antivandal options. (The firewall rules still apply to these users.) On the Applications tab, you can choose whether NetBarrier monitors an application's request to connect to other computers over the network. You can have an alert displayed each time this occurs, so you can see which applications are accessing the network, and you can block or allow network access for any individual application.

Privacy The Privacy screen offers options that aren't really firewall features but are more like outgoing filters. The Data tab enables you to enter certain secure data (credit card numbers, Social Security number) that is not allowed to leave your computer. NetBarrier looks at the data as it leaves; this keeps others from being able to copy text documents that have that data element in them (a credit card number, for instance) but doesn't block encrypted entries in your web browser used for e-commerce. On the Banner tab, you can block ad banners—when it detects an ad, NetBarrier X will turn it into a transparency graphic. Note that this works only if the ad has certain obvious keys in its URL path (such as /ads/ or /banner/), but you can add to those attributes. The Cookies tab lets you manage, edit, and delete cookies individually. The Cleaning tab lets you easily delete all the cookies, cache files, and history files for all your browsers. Finally, on the Surf tab, you'll see controls for managing web cookies globally and some of the general information that your web browser makes available to web server computers.

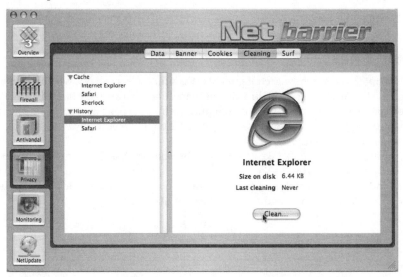

Monitoring On the Monitoring screen, you're given a few different options for viewing your web traffic and information about your various network connections. On the Traffic tab, you can see gauges showing how much information is going in and out over various services. The Network tab shows the currently open ports and gives you a sense of why ports are being opened or accessed. The Whois tab enables you to look up a particular web domain to see who has registered it. And the Traceroute tab lets you run a traceroute, which shows you all the servers between your computer and a remote network address.

NetBarrier X appears to be a well-written program that takes advantage of the Mac interface and offers some interesting bells and whistles along with its simple-to-understand firewall capabilities. If you're looking for a firewall application that is as user-friendly as possible, you'll pay for the polish, but it might be worth it.

NORTON PERSONAL FIREWALL

www.symantec.com/
Commercial application, around $70, demonstration version available
Under the familiar Norton brand, Symantec offers Personal Firewall as a stand-alone application or in conjunction with virus protection and personal privacy software in the Norton Internet Security bundle. Personal Firewall offers a very simple interface and relatively few options for configuration, offering features that are very similar to the firewall that's built into Mac OS X. To enable and disable it, use the button at the top of its window.

Personal Firewall goes beyond the built-in firewall in that it enables you to specify that certain addresses can access services on your Mac—for instance, you could allow access to your Mac for file sharing but limit that access to certain addresses or ranges of addresses. To do so, select a service and choose one of the Allow or Deny options. If you choose to allow or deny from certain addresses, click the New button (under the Allow Addresses window) to add addresses to the list. Those addresses are now on the list and will be allowed or denied access to the service, depending on the option you've chosen.

NOTE Norton Internet Security is discussed in more detail in Chapters 11 and 12.

What's Next?

In this chapter, you saw how to configure Mac OS X for Internet access, whether you're using a modem and phone line or a higher-speed broadband connection. You also saw how to use Internet applications in the Classic environment and how to configure the Internet pane with common Internet addresses and preferences. Then you saw how to secure your Mac on the Internet, including a look at a few different firewall software options.

In the next chapter, you'll take a look at web browsers in Mac OS X, including a number of different options for browsing. You'll also read a discussion on surfing the Web securely, maintaining passwords, and protecting your privacy online. Also, you'll be introduced to .Mac, Apple's suite of online applications designed to extend the usefulness of Mac OS X.

Chapter 11

The Web, Online Security, .Mac, Sherlock, and iChat

As you might expect from a modern operating system, Mac OS X is built for retrieving information online. Not only is it relatively easy to set up your Mac for Internet access, but the OS includes a full suite of built-in applications designed specifically for the Internet.

Mac OS X comes with Safari, a powerful, full-featured web browser. Safari handles all your web-browsing needs, with tabbed browsing, Google searches from its toolbar, powerful bookmark-management tools, and RSS feed viewing. (If you don't know what some of these features are, read on to find out!) But some people prefer using other browsers, and we'll look at a couple of other candidates, such as Firefox and OmniWeb, that have interesting features that make them serious contenders.

While you're surfing the Web, you should consider some security and privacy issues, not the least of which is dealing with your passwords and personal information. In this chapter we'll discuss using your Mac OS X keychain with websites, and you'll see a more general discussion of security issues and products to deal with cookies, web caches, and other browser-related issues. You'll also read about the preference settings that make the different Mac browsers unique and a discussion of web plug-ins and helper applications.

Working together with Mac OS X and your web browser, Apple offers .Mac, a group of online applications designed for use by Mac OS X users who subscribe to the .Mac service. The .Mac suite includes online storage (a personal space on the Internet for you to store and swap files), a Mac.com e-mail address, and HomePage, which enables you to create your own web page without extensive knowledge of HTML or web-development tools.

You'll learn about Sherlock's web-searching and channel-display features, giving it the capability not only to locate items on the Web, but to repurpose and display web-based data in the Sherlock window itself, making it easy (and kind of enjoyable) to access all sorts of data.

Finally, you'll be introduced to iChat AV, Apple's chat and audio/video conferencing utility. Not only is it useful for chatting with friends and colleagues, but it also can be used for peer-to-peer file sharing and, via Bonjour, for an easily configured local network chat and files solution.

In this chapter:

◆ Web Browser Basics

◆ Web Security, Passwords, and Privacy

◆ Apple's .Mac tools

◆ Internet Channels with Sherlock

◆ Using iChat AV

Web Browser Basics

Mac OS X includes Apple's web browser, Safari, a program based on open-source code from the KDE project. (KDE is a graphical desktop environment for Unix workstations, similar in function to Microsoft Windows or the Aqua environment in Mac OS X.) The KDE project has certain technologies, including the cross-platform KHTML library, that underlie its Konquerer file and web browser, which Apple was able to use as a jumping-off point for developing a stand-alone web browser that's both very fast and largely compliant with web standards. That compliance is important, because it's made Safari easier for Mac users to adopt in lieu of Internet Explorer.

> **NOTE**   Part of the way that open-source software works is that Apple can freely use aspects of other open-source technologies but must publish what they change and make those changes available. Apple does that through its Developer website. Apple calls the technology behind Safari *WebCore*. You can find out more about this at `http://developer.apple.com/darwin/projects/webcore/index.html`.

Web browsing is easy: start up your Internet connection (if you have a connection, such as a PPP or PPPoE connection, that requires a startup) and launch your browser. Safari appears as an icon on the Dock by default; if you've installed a different browser, you can double-click its icon in the `Applications` folder (or wherever you installed it).

Once launched, most web browsers will display the home page that's configured in the browser's internal preferences settings. If you haven't changed the default home page, what you're likely looking at is the Apple Start page, which offers news, weather, sports, and lots of other information that is constantly updated. Every time you open a new window in your web browser, it will default to the home page.

Getting around on a web page is fairly simple—you click underlined hyperlinks within the text, which causes a new web page to be accessed and displayed in the browser window. You'll also find that images on the web page can also be links, so clicking them loads a new page in the browser.

> **NOTE**   When you're viewing a web page, each hypertext link has a URL (Uniform Resource Locator) associated with it. When you click the link, that URL is fed to the browser, which then begins the process of locating the document and downloading it to your Mac so that the document can be displayed in the browser window. You don't have to click a link to access a particular URL—you also can enter one directly. You do so in the Address box toward the top of the Safari window or the similar address bar that you'll find in any web browser. Enter a URL and then press Return or click the Go button to access that web document.

> **NOTE**   So, how does a URL work? A URL can have three parts. It starts with a *protocol*, such as `http://` or `ftp://` that tells the browser what type of server it's connecting to. (`http` is used for a web server.) Then, there's a *server address*—this is the name or IP number of a web server computer, such as `www.apple.com` or `192.168.0.2`. Finally, there's a *document path*, such as `index.html` or `products/catalog/056.html`. Taken together, they compose a URL, as in `http://www.apple.com/index.html`.

When you're using most web browsers, they give away the fact that you're pointing the mouse at a link. When the mouse pointer turns into a pointing hand icon (the index finger is extended on the little hand icon), that means that the item is "clickable." Click the mouse button once to load the associated web page.

Safari offers you a few different ways to modify that clicking behavior for opening new pages. Hold down the Command (⌘) key while clicking a link (or an image), and the resulting web page will be displayed in a new window. Hold down the Control key while clicking a link (or use the right mouse button if you have a two-button mouse), and a context menu appears that offers you a number of different choices regarding that link.

These options include

◆ Open Link in New Window, which does the same thing as Command+clicking the link.

◆ Download Linked File, which downloads the linked web page; instead of displaying it in a browser window, it's saved to your Mac. If the link is to a file, such as a graphic, an installer, or other file, this downloads the file.

◆ Add Link to Bookmarks, which adds the selected link to Safari's Bookmarks menu, as discussed in the section "Managing Bookmarks," later in this chapter.

◆ Copy Link, which copies the web address of that link to the Mac's clipboard, enabling you to paste it into another document or program.

But Safari (and other web browsers; see "Using Other Browsers" later in this chapter) also offers *tabbed browsing*, which is a way to open multiple browser windows in tabs, as opposed to opening them in different windows. This allows you to more easily work in multiple windows, even having one web page load while you're looking at another one.

To use tabbed browsing, you need to turn it on. Select Safari ➤ Preferences and then click the Tabs icon. If you check Enable Tabbed Browsing, the shortcuts shown in the preferences will allow you to work with tabs.

Here's how it works:

◆ To open a link in a new tab behind the current tab, hold down the Command (⌘) key and click.

◆ To open a link in a new tab and display it in front of other tabs, press ⌘+Shift+click.

◆ To open a link in a new *window* behind the current window, press ⌘+Option+click.

◆ To open a link in a new window and bring it to the front, press ⌘+Option+Shift+click.

You'll also see these options in the contextual menu that displays when you Control+click a link.

That can be a bit confusing, but you'll find that tabs are very practical. For example, say you've searched for something on Google and want to check some of the results pages. Instead of clicking a link, checking the page, and then using the Back button to come back to the Google page, just open each link you want to view in a new tab.

If you check Always Show Tab Bar in the Tabs preferences, Safari will display even a single window as a tab; this can be less disconcerting than having the current window shift down on the screen a few pixels when you open a second tab. Try it and you'll see the difference. (Also try checking the Set New Tabs as They Are Created option, which inverts the effect of the Shift key in the above shortcuts.)

The tab bar (see Figure 11.1) shows part or all of the window's title. To switch from one tab to another, just click anywhere on the tab you want to view. Or, to switch from the keyboard, press ⌘+Shift+Arrow, using either the left arrow or right arrow button to cycle to the left or to the right through your different tabs.

FIGURE 11.1
Safari with three
tabs open

Common Browser Commands

At the top of the Safari window you'll find the toolbar, where a number of commands can be accessed quickly. Many of these are standard items found in most web browsers, and they include navigation buttons, an address field, and a search field. Here's a look at the basic toolbar:

What do these buttons do? Here's a quick look:

Back   The Back button enables you to return quickly to the previously visited page. Click and hold the mouse button on the Back button, and you'll see a menu of recently visited pages.

Forward   If you've just clicked Back, you can then click Forward, which returns you to a page from which you've gone back. (The button isn't always active.)

Stop/Refresh   The third button in the previous graphic is either the Stop or Refresh button, depending on whether a web page has loaded completely. If the current web page is still in the process of downloading to your Mac, you can click the Stop button (this displays as an X icon) to stop it from finishing. Your browser will display as much of the page as it managed to download. The refresh button (the circular arrow shown in the previous graphic) causes the current page to be reloaded. This is useful if it didn't load completely the first time, or if the page is updated frequently (as are many commercial news sites) and you want to see the latest version.

Add Bookmark   The + button lets you add a bookmark for the current page. See "Managing Bookmarks" later in this chapter for more on working with bookmarks.

In addition to these default buttons, the toolbar contains two fields:

◆   The Address Field is where you enter a URL.

◆   The Search field lets you type keywords and press Return to run a Google search. This is very practical since you don't even have to go to the Google website first; just enter your keywords and press Return.

NOTE   There's another way to run Google searches from Safari. Select any text—one word or several—on a web page, press the Control key, and click the mouse on the selected text. Choose Search in Google, and Safari will go to the Google site and search for your text.

In addition to the default buttons that Safari displays, you can add others by selecting the View menu and then Customize Address Bar. This displays buttons for other useful functions: You can add a Home button that takes you to your home page; two Text Size buttons, to increase or decrease the size of text on web pages; or add a Print button if you print a lot from Safari.

SAVING, SENDING, AND PRINTING WEB PAGES

While most of your work on the Web will be viewing pages yourself, you may want to save web pages to view again later, send web pages to friends or colleagues, or print web pages. Safari offers ways to do all three of these:

Saving a web page   You can save a web page in two ways. You can either save the source of the page, which is the HTML code in the web page (which includes any text but not graphics), or you can save a *web archive*, a special file that saves all the contents of the page: the source, text, and graphics or other multimedia elements. Select File ➤ Save As and then from the Format menu, select either of these. Saving a file as a web archive means that you can see the page again at any time, exactly as it was when you saved it.

Sending a web page   You can send either an entire web page, or simply a link to it, by selecting File ➤ Mail Contents of This Page or File ➤ Mail Link to This Page. The former opens a new message in your e-mail program containing the contents of the page as an HTML message, and the latter opens a new message simply with the link. If you want, you could also send a web archive, saved as described in the preceding paragraph, as an attachment to an e-mail message.

Printing a web page   You can print any web page, though bear in mind that it may not look exactly as you see it in Safari; some web page elements don't print correctly. Select File ➤ Print and then print like any other document. You can also create a PDF file from a web page like this; see Chapter 8, "PDFs, Fonts, and Color," for more on printing and PDFs.

Managing Bookmarks

As you surf the Web, you'll probably come across pages that you'd like to revisit in the future. Instead of forcing you to write down each URL that you deem worthy of tracking, Safari lets you save bookmarks, and you can store and manage the addresses to websites you want to revisit. Bookmarks make it easy to store a web page's URL so that you can access the site again easily at a later date. To save a bookmark in Safari, you either choose Bookmarks ➤ Add Bookmark from the Safari menu or click the Add Bookmark button (the plus sign) in the toolbar. When you do, a small dialog sheet appears in which you can enter a name for the bookmark. And then, in the pop-up menu, select the location where you'd like the bookmark to be stored.

By default, Safari offers to store your bookmarks in the Bookmarks Bar. This is the thin bar below the toolbar where you see a few preset bookmarks. This is fine for some bookmarks, but if you add more than a handful, you'll run out of room. (You can access the ones that don't fit by clicking the arrows at the right end of the Bookmarks Bar and selecting one.) Also, if you add bookmarks to this bar, think of shortening their names so you can fit more bookmarks.

The other choice is to click the pop-up menu and select Bookmarks Menu or select one of the folders that appear in the pop-up menu. (These folders are *bookmark collections*; they don't display in the Bookmarks menu, though it's easy to add them to it.) It's easier to organize less commonly used bookmarks in this menu and to keep only those bookmarks you use often in the Bookmarks Bar.

After you add a bookmark to your bookmark menu or to the Bookmarks Bar, selecting it from the menu or clicking it on the bar loads the page in your web browser.

You'll probably find that, after a while, you have a lot of bookmarks. When you get to that point, it's time to start organizing and managing them so you can find what you want more easily. Safari offers a special window (shown in Figure 11.2) where you can organize your bookmarks and manage bookmark collections, add folders to the Bookmarks menu or Bookmarks Bar, and more.

FIGURE 11.2

Safari's Bookmarks window, where you manage bookmarks, edit bookmarks, and create and sort bookmark collections

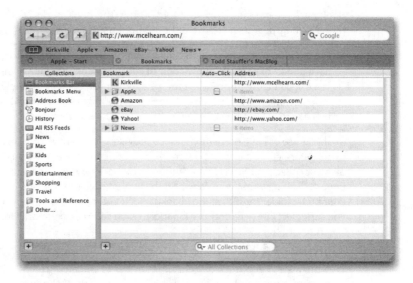

To view this window, click the book icon at the far left of the Bookmarks Bar or select Bookmarks ➣ Show All Bookmarks. Think of this window as the nerve center for your bookmarks. After you've saved dozens of bookmarks, this is where you go to put them in some semblance of order.

TIP   Can't find a bookmark? Use the search field at the bottom of the Bookmarks window. Enter a word or string of characters that you're sure is in the bookmark and then press Enter or Return. You can also use this to search your history; see the next section for more on working with your history.

As you can see in Figure 11.2, this window shows two panes: At the left, the sidebar contains bookmark collections; the right side shows the contents of the selected collection. Click one of them to see your bookmarks. Figure 11.2 shows the Bookmarks Bar. You can drag these bookmarks to reorder them, select any of them and press Delete to remove them, or move bookmarks into folders. The Bookmarks Bar contains two folders by default: Apple and News. If you click the disclosure triangle next to one of these folders, you'll see the individual bookmarks it contains.

TIP   Using folders on the Bookmarks Bar is a great way to provide quick access to bookmarks yet not fill up the Bookmarks Bar. Think about creating folders there for the categories of bookmarks you use most.

To create a new folder in a collection, click the + icon at the bottom of the window, below the Collections list. Enter a name for it and then drag other bookmarks into the folder. The check box in the Auto-Click column (this only applies to folders in the Bookmarks Bar) gives this folder special powers. If you check this, you'll see that the folder name in the Bookmarks Bar no longer contains an arrow next to it, but a small square. Click the name of the folder, and all the bookmarks it contains open in tabs. This is very practical if you want to check, say, a half-dozen news sites every day; rather than open each one individually, you can check them all with a single click.

When you're editing bookmarks, you can drag a bookmark to any of the folders that appear in the Collections list; drop the bookmark on the folder icon to store it inside that folder. Folders in the Collections list are accessible from the Bookmarks window, but if you want to add a folder to the

Bookmarks menu, just drag that folder on to the Bookmarks Menu icon in the Collections list. The folder will appear as a submenu in the Bookmarks menu.

NOTE   Other special items in the Collections list include Address Book, which displays any URLs you have added to contact information in Address Book; Bonjour, which displays any devices that you can configure from a web browser and that use Bonjour technology to indicate their presence on a network; History, which we'll look at in the next section; and All RSS Feeds, which is discussed in the section "Reading RSS Feeds with Safari" later in this chapter.

If you use or have used another web browser, you may already have stored bookmarks for that program. Safari lets you import bookmarks from other browsers so you can add them to your Bookmarks menu or collections. Select File ➤ Import Bookmarks and then navigate to the bookmarks file you want to import. (You may first need to export the bookmarks from the other browser; if you can't do this, search your home folder for files named bookmarks if you're not sure where to find the file you want.) Likewise, you can select File ➤ Export Bookmarks to save Safari's bookmarks for use with another program.

Viewing and Managing Your History

Web browsers keep track of a certain number of the most recent web pages you've visited or other items you've accessed via the browser in a feature that's known as the *history*. Safari presents a History menu that contains basic commands (Back, Forward, Home), recently viewed pages, and a series of submenus for other pages you've viewed recently. If you've viewed a lot of web pages today, you'll see the 20 most recent pages in the menu, and, below that, submenus for different days; if you've viewed more than 20 pages today, you'll see a submenu for Earlier Today; you'll also see other submenus for the past 7 days.

You can also view your history in the Bookmarks window; as you saw earlier, History appears in the Collection list. You can view pages and access them by double-clicking in this window. And if you decide you want to save one of these pages as a bookmark, you can drag it to the Bookmarks menu or to a folder from this window as well.

TIP   Safari has a very cool history-related feature called *SnapBack*. This enables you to define a particular page in your history that you can "snap back" to at any point, even if you've surfed three or four pages away from that SnapBack page. By default, search results pages are turned into SnapBack pages by Safari, so that you can access them by choosing History ➤ Search Results SnapBack. To define the current page as a SnapBack page, choose History ➤ Mark Page for SnapBack. Now you can choose History ➤ Page SnapBack to return to this page instantly.

If you ever want to clear Safari's history (so that sites you've visited are no longer tracked), you can delete those files without harming your browser's capability to function. At the bottom of the History menu, you'll see Clear History. Select this to remove all the History entries, but be aware that you cannot undo this action.

NOTE   The history function is often used by web browsers to enable the Back button in the browser—when you click Back, you're actually going up one level in the history log. That's one reason why you may want to clear the history—if you've used a public Mac to access a webmail service, bank account, or other such information, clearing the history is a good idea, so that others can't use the Back button to go to the pages you've seen. Likewise, clearing the cache helps remove personal info from the hard disk; see the section "Web Security, Passwords, and Privacy," later in this chapter, for more on transferring personal information securely.

Downloading Files

Sometimes you'll be able to click a hyperlink and download a file to your Mac; this is a file that isn't necessarily designed for reading by a web browser or an associated application. Instead, most such downloads are either document files or application archives that you can then use to install an application on your Mac. It might even be a Mac update that you download from Apple. (As mentioned earlier, you also can download any link by clicking and holding on the link until a context menu appears, then selecting Download Linked File.)

TIP You can set the default folder where downloads will appear on the General tab of Safari's preferences. That can be handy if you're sick of seeing your downloads appear on the desktop. (If you use another browser, look for a downloads option in the its Preferences dialog box.)

When you click a link to a downloadable file in Safari, that file appears in the Downloads window, which pops up automatically. (If you don't see it, select Window ➢ Downloads.)

Safari's Downloads window shows the name of the file, the size (or amount downloaded), the download speed, and a progress bar while the download is going on. You can stop downloading any file by clicking the X icon to the right of the progress bar in this window. If you do this, the icon changes to an orange circular arrow (like Safari's Reload button); click this icon to restart the download. In some cases the download will continue where it left off, but in other cases the download will start over. If you don't recall where your files are being downloaded, click the magnifying glass icon to have a Finder window open showing the file.

By default, downloads remain in the Downloads window until you remove them manually (by clicking the Clear button at the bottom of the window). You can change this behavior from the General tab of Safari's preferences; select the Remove Download List Items menu and choose from Manually, When Safari Quits, and Upon Successful Download.

NOTE What do you do once the file is downloaded? See Chapter 12, "Managing E-Mail," for a discussion on decompressing file archives, and see Chapter 5, "Personalizing Mac OS X," and Chapter 9, "Being the Administrator: Permissions, Settings, and Adding Users," for information on installing applications.

NOTE If you download a lot of files with Safari or with another web browser, you may find it useful to use a special program to manage downloads. One such program, Speed Download (www.yazsoft.com) interfaces perfectly with Safari and offers two modes of operation: an automatic mode, where it activates and handles downloads for any links you click in Safari, and a manual mode, where you can use a contextual menu item, when you Control+click a link, to start the download with Speed Download. This program offers many other features, such as a download queue, so that not all your files are downloaded at once, upload management, bandwidth controls, and much more.

Internet Shortcuts

With most Internet applications, including most web browsers, you can drag a URL to the desktop (or to a Finder window) to create a shortcut file to that URL.

Double-clicking the shortcut will launch that URL in your browser window (or if you've used another type of Internet application, the shortcut will launch in that application).

With Safari, you can drag many things to get a shortcut like this. You can select a URL in the address bar and drag it; in this case, the shortcut's name shows the URL. If you click the icon to the left of the URL, the shortcut displays the name of the web page. You can drag a link, in which case the shortcut's name is the link text. You can even drag a graphic that links to another page; as with text links, the shortcut is named after the link. You can also drag a link out of the Bookmarks window onto the desktop to create a shortcut.

TIP You also can drag URLs directly to the Dock, where they will be represented by an icon that looks like an @ symbol attached to a coiled spring. If you hold your cursor over one of these icons, the name displays above the Dock.

In other web browsers, you generally can drag any icons that appear in the title bar of the page or an icon that appears next to the site's address in the address bar. Likewise, many browsers will let you drag a bookmark from the Bookmarks window pane to the desktop or Dock.

Reading RSS Feeds with Safari

If you check a lot of websites regularly, especially news sites and blogs, you've probably encountered RSS feeds. RSS (an abbreviation for Really Simple Syndication) is a technology that lets you download the headlines and some (or all) of the text of an article and lets you get this information automatically.

Safari comes with a number of RSS feeds already bookmarked, so you can discover this technology easily. You can view them by selecting these bookmarks; for example, in the default Safari Bookmarks Bar you'll see a folder named `Apple`. Select one of these bookmarks such as Apple Hot News. As you can see in Figure 11.3, the window changes from the usual web page display to one that shows headlines, dates, and the beginnings of articles.

You can view an entire article by clicking the Read More link or search for articles by typing keywords in the search field in the right-hand column. You can also modify the way articles are displayed. The Article Length slider lets you adjust how much text displays (though some RSS feeds only display headlines); click one of the Sort By links to change the sort order; click a link under Recent Articles to choose whether you want to see all articles, or only those posted within a certain time period. The Source section gives you a link to the web page whose RSS feed you're seeing, and the Actions section includes a Mail Link to This Page link, which opens a new message in your e-mail program containing a link to this page so you can send it to a friend.

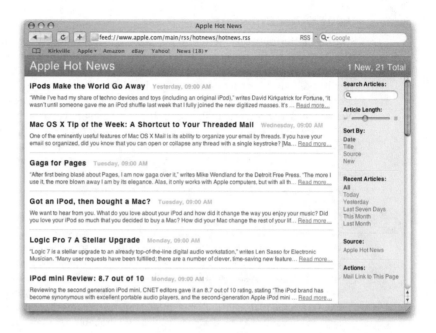

FIGURE 11.3

Apple Hot News as an RSS feed

NOTE Both the authors of this book have their own blogs, and you can check out their content using RSS. Todd's site is MacBlog (www.macblog.com), and Kirk's site is Kirkville (www.mcelhearn.com). You can check out Todd's site for information on Macs and Mac OS X, and Kirk's site talks about Mac OS X, the iPod and iTunes, and more.

If you want to add an RSS bookmark to a site, look for a link on the site's main page that says either RSS or XML. If you click this link, Safari opens the RSS feed in a window similar to Figure 11.3, and you can click the Add Bookmark link in the Actions section at the right of the window. You'll see an RSS button at the right of the Address Bar; if you click this button, the page display toggles to the normal page; click it again and it returns to the RSS article display.

NOTE You may already be a regular RSS browser, and you may use a program designed specifically for displaying RSS feeds. If this is the case, you can set the default RSS reader in Safari's preferences. Click the RSS tab and select a new Default RSS Reader. A couple of excellent programs that offer more features for RSS reading than Safari, include NetNewsWire (available in pro and lite versions; www.ranchero.com), NewsFire (www.newsfirerss.com), and PulpFiction (http://freshlysqueezedsoftware.com/products/pulpfiction/). If you use the Firefox browser (see later in this chapter for more on Firefox), you can use the Sage plug-in (http://sage.mozdev.org/) to provide RSS functionality in the browser.

Safari's RSS preferences (Safari ➤ Preferences, RSS tab) let you adjust how RSS articles are updated and displayed. You can set an update frequency, set a color for new articles (to make them stand out better), and have old articles removed after a set time, from one day to never.

Using Other Browsers

Safari is not the only browser out there. In fact, Safari was only introduced with Panther, Mac OS X 10.3. At that time, the browser market was very different than it is now. Microsoft's Internet Explorer was bundled with Mac OS X, and other browsers such as Netscape, OmniWeb, Opera, iCab, and Mozilla were the alternatives. Recently, the Mozilla-based Firefox has been released for Mac, and OmniWeb has seen a substantial upgrade. While Opera and iCab are still out there, Firefox and Omni-Web are the two browsers to look at if, for some reason, you don't want to use Safari.

You can still use Internet Explorer (`www.microsoft.com/mac/`), and in some cases you may need to. Some corporate servers, and some secure sites such as banks, may not work with Safari. (Though the most recent versions of Safari are compatible with just about every site we use.) Other contenders include Firefox (`www.mozilla.org`), OmniWeb from Omni Group (`www.omnigroup.com`), iCab for Mac OS X (`www.icab.de`), and Opera (`www.opera.com`).

NOTE   Should you use another browser? For most users, Safari is everything they need. But there are some reasons to check out other browsers. Firefox is free, small, fast, and very extensible. If you like to customize your tools, Firefox is for you—it lets you set your own theme and add dozens of extensions that bring new features to your web browsing and make you more productive. OmniWeb gives you built-in ad-blocking, RSS feeds, and an innovative interface that displays tabs as thumbnails in a drawer. If you're a web designer, its HTML Source Editor is a tool you may not be able to live without. Opera and iCab have their own interesting feature sets that could make them useful to you. In any case, if you are a web designer, you should probably use them all to make sure your sites look good in every possible browser.

If you elect to install another web browser, however, you'll need to use Safari to set it as the default web browser. Open Safari's preferences, click the General icon, and select your browser from the Default Web Browser menu.

Browser Plug-Ins and Helper Applications

Web browsers are good at handling some types of data—certain text formats and a few graphic image formats—but they're not designed to deal with some other types of data, such as QuickTime movies, Macromedia Flash animations, and RealPlayer streaming audio and video. Still, some browsers manage to handle these things very well. How? They use plug-ins or helper applications.

PLUG-INS

A *plug-in* is a special snippet of a computer code that a web browser can use to extend its knowledge of how to work with and play back certain types of data. When the browser encounters a particular command (the EMBED or OBJECT command, to be exact), it looks for the plug-in that's being requested by that command. If it finds it, it gives part of the browser window to the plug-in so that the data can be displayed within the web page.

One example of this is the QuickTime plug-in, which is a part of Mac OS X. (That's why QuickTime movies can play back in a web browser even though, as we just mentioned, web browsers generally don't have the technical know-how to display them on its own.) QuickTime movies can be embedded in web pages by web developers so that they appear as part of the page itself (see Figure 11.4). A Macromedia Flash Player plug-in is also included with Safari and can be downloaded for other web browsers.

FIGURE 11.4
Here's a web page with
a QuickTime movie
embedded in it.

For multimedia files other than QuickTime movies and Flash animations, you'll need to download and install the appropriate plug-in file. These files are stored in /Library/Internet Plug-Ins/ on the main level of the Mac's disk. If you have a plug-in that you'd like Internet Explorer to work with, drag it to this folder and then restart Internet Explorer (or direct the plug-in's installer application to this folder, if necessary).

NOTE   If your user account doesn't have Admin privileges, you can store plug-ins in the ~/Library/ Internet Plug-Ins/ folder located inside your home folder.

If you need to set preferences for a plug-in, it probably will enable you to do so through a context menu. Click and hold the mouse button on an image that's created by a plug-in (on the QuickTime movie or Flash animation, for instance).

HELPER APPLICATIONS

A helper application isn't really anything particularly special—it's simply an application that can deal with a downloaded document or media file that a web browser can't. Some helper applications are helper applications as their sole function—for instance, some multimedia players are designed for the sole purpose of being helpers. Others, though, just happen to be able to accept a document that a web browser passes on to it. For instance, the QuickTime Player, Windows Media Player, and even Microsoft Word can act as helper applications. If the application can accept and display a file that the web browser passes to it, that application qualifies as a helper.

This usually is not a pressing issue—if your browser tells you that it can't display a particular document, you may need to download an application that can. In fact, the browser (or the web page you're viewing) may suggest where you can download the helper application via a dialog box or new browser window.

Where this gets a little messy is when you need to specify helper applications. Occasionally you'll want to dig into your browser's Preference dialog box and set or change the helper applications that are being used. You'll generally do this by altering the MIME settings in your browser's preferences. MIME stands for Multipurpose Internet Mail Extension, and it's a method by which multimedia data can be identified over the Internet.

TIP See www.hunnysoft.com/mime/ for information on different MIME types and other helpful hints.

Safari doesn't let you set MIME types, and, in most cases, you'll never need to. If you do, you might want to check out Monkeyfood Software's free More Internet preference pane (www.monkeyfood .com/software/moreInternet/), which gives you control over the most obscure MIME types.

Web Security, Passwords, and Privacy

Chapter 10, "Configuring Internet Access," discusses securing your Internet connection and your Mac against possible intrusion by other users on the Internet. In this section, the security we're talking about is more along the lines of securing the information you're sending to others—in particular, things such as credit card numbers and passwords. You also may want to consider privacy part of that equation, including the things that a remote site can learn about you, how web browser *cookies* work, and how to select and manage your passwords.

The most important security measure on the Web is the easiest one—keep your eyes open. Watch your browser's alert boxes carefully and never send personal or private information via the Web when you're suspicious of either the security of the remote site, the truth of its claims, or the necessity of the information. It *is* possible for data to be intercepted online, and it's possible for credit card numbers and passwords to be "sniffed" when connections aren't secure. However, a little careful consideration will take you most of the way to a secure surfing experience.

NOTE When you're browsing at home, you probably don't need to worry too much about security. But if you're at work, in an Internet café, in a library, or any other public location, be careful about entering any personal information. After all, the computer you use will probably store that information, and a hacker, or even another user, could get a hold of it. Safari offers *private browsing*, where the program does not store any private information on the computer you're using. Simply select Safari ➤ Private Browsing to turn this on. Safari displays a dialog explaining what type of information is not stored (history, Google searches, downloads, AutoFill, etc.) Another reason to use a Mac when you want to surf the Web.

Securing Data

Safari, like all other web browsers, supports Secure Sockets Layer (SSL) technology, which encrypts data in your browser before it's sent to the target website. This is the technology that's used for secure transactions such as e-commerce order taking. Most of today's browsers will warn you when you're sending personal data over a connection that is not secure—a nonsecure connection is one to a regular web server (using the http:// protocol) instead of a secure web server (using the https:// protocol). Generally, it's easy to tell when you're connected to a secure server—most web browsers use a padlock icon at some location in their window. In the following example, Safari's icon is shown; it's at the top right of the window. Other browsers may also display text in the status area, such as "Connection is secure RC4-128," meaning a 128-bit encrypted connection has been made.

NOTE Secure connections aren't only for credit card transactions. More and more sites are enabling secure connections for simple password entries—for instance, Yahoo! Mail (http:// mail.yahoo.com/) offers a secure connection for entering your password. Keep an eye out for secure server options and use them whenever possible, particularly if you're being asked for information—identifying numbers, addresses, account numbers—that you wouldn't want overheard in the checkout line at a local store.

Secure connections work like this: When you sign into a secure web server (one running the `https://` protocol), the site presents a *security certificate*, which the web browser checks for authenticity. The certificates are made available by trusted sources—companies such as Verisign (`www.verisign.com`), Baltimore CyberTrust (`www.baltimore.com/`), and others. These certificates vouch that the site at a particular domain is the company that it claims to be—the certificate source has confirmed the organization's or individual's identity. If the certificate presented doesn't match the URL you've accessed, you'll see an alert message from your browser. Sometimes when a certificate has expired (or when the date on your Mac is set to something many years off from the current date, thus causing the browser to believe that the certificate has expired), you'll also see a warning.

WARNING You should visually check the URL to ensure that it says `https://` for the protocol and that the URL shown matches the company you're accessing. Some sites will place a "Secure Connection" message or graphic image on the *web page*, but that's not a 100 percent indicator that the connection is actually secure. Make sure your browser confirms the secure connection with its padlock (or similar) icon and the `https://` protocol.

Once a site is authenticated, the next step for a secure connection is *encryption*. While you're connected to a secure server, any data that you send to the server will be scrambled using a sophisticated algorithm (40-bit security is good; 128-bit security would require an exceptional amount of time and computing power to break). The magic of this is that the website's security certificate is a *public encryption key*—in essence, you're encrypting your data with half of the website's "password." Only the other half of that password combination—the half that they keep private—can decrypt your communication. So, ideally, what you send to the site can be read only by that site *even if* it's intercepted by a third party.

Unlike encryption in e-mail (see Chapter 12), this encryption doesn't take a hands-on effort on your part. Your browser will automatically encrypt data that you enter into HTML forms; the target web server will automatically decrypt the information when it arrives. To you, the transaction will look normal, except for the `https://` protocol and the padlock that you verified before sending—right?

WARNING Beware of phishing! This technique is used by nefarious scammers who send you e-mails telling you to go to a website and reenter your account and/or credit card information. When you click the link, which may look legitimate, a web page appears that looks like the real page for eBay, PayPal, or a bank. But you'll actually be on a different server, perhaps located in some poorly policed island nation. If you enter your credit card information, the scammers will be able to empty your bank account. To ensure that you are on the correct site, check the URL. But, in any case, no legitimate company will ever send you an e-mail asking you to enter this information. So don't give it away. If you want to find out more about phishing, see the Anti-Phishing Working Group (`www.antiphishing.org/`), which contains a list of recent phishing attacks.

Securing Passwords

Increasingly, the world of the Web relies on passwords. You'll find that sites of all sorts request or require that you log in with a username and/or password. Frequently, a site requires a user account simply to keep track of aggregate visitor stats or to keep a log of visitors who contribute to a site via a comments link or an online forum. In other cases, passwords are required to access e-commerce tools for buying or selling items online. Of course, passwords and user accounts are required to access highly personal information such as credit card accounts, online banking information, and maybe the private areas of the organizational or corporate websites you visit.

Keeping up with these passwords is rarely fun—usually it runs a gamut from being a pain to being a nightmare. If your solution is the simplest one—use only one password for all the sites and keep it memorable, such as your birthday or anniversary—then you're making a mistake that's almost worse than having no passwords at all.

The appropriate way to choose and use a password (you'll see this in other parts of this book as well) is to

◆ Have a different password for each website account you create.

◆ Make the password nonsensical and devoid of meaning that could be guessed because of its discoverable significance to you.

◆ Change each password frequently.

It turns out that only six people in the world have the memories capable of managing all their passwords mentally, and they're all in Las Vegas counting cards at the blackjack tables. For the rest of us, the solution is some sort of system for managing passwords.

Apple has one system built in—the keychain—that's a good option for web passwords. What it does, essentially, is store all of your web passwords (along with other important and personal information) in an encrypted database that's saved on your Mac's hard disk. When you log in to your Mac, your keychain (by default) is unlocked using your account password. With the keychain unlocked, you can open it directly to see what a given password is (by launching the Keychain Access application in the `Utilities` folder inside the main `Applications` folder on your hard disk) or, in some cases, your web browser can access the keychain directly. When it does that, either it will pop open a dialog box asking for your permission to retrieve the stored password or it will simply go and get it—depending, again, on the preferences you've set in the Keychain Access application.

The only real downside to the keychain is that you have to stay on top of it—particularly if the security of your Mac's physical location is also an issue. When you log out of your Mac account, your keychain is secured; likewise, you can set your keychain to lock itself when you put your Mac to sleep or after a certain number of minutes without being accessed. If your keychain happens to be open and unlocked when someone else comes along and sits at your Mac, that person will be able to access your passwords—which wouldn't happen if you had a good enough memory to count cards.

NOTE See Chapter 16, "Managing Contacts, Appointments, and Your Personal Info," for the specifics on creating and managing your keychain. It's a good system once you understand it and grow accustomed to it.

OK, so let's say you want to use your keychain to manage passwords. How does it work? If you have a keychain-aware web browser such as Safari, you can add passwords directly from within the browser. That's the easiest way. The other method is manual—it's discussed in Chapter 16. In essence, the manual method simply allows you to create a keychain item that can then be accessed whenever your keychain is unlocked—you can double-click the item, which allows you to view your username and password and refresh your memory.

As mentioned, the cooler method is to create a keychain item directly from within your browser. In nearly all cases, tracking a password works only when the website uses a server-based password query (an authorization dialog box or dialog sheet) for the password. If you enter a password directly on the page, you can store the password in your keychain automatically.

To use this with Safari for usernames and passwords, you have to turn on an option. Go to the Safari preferences and click the AutoFill tab. Check User Names and Passwords to allow Safari to both remember and autofill these items. When you're in a situation that enables you to save the password to your keychain, you'll know it. In Safari, you'll see a dialog that asks if you want to save the username and password to your keychain. Choose Yes to add the username and password to the keychain, Not Now to tell Safari to not add it but to ask again next time, or Never for this Website, in which case Safari won't ask again.

When you return to that password-protected site, the browser *should* attempt to access your keychain in order to gain access to the site. If not, you can open Keychain Access to view your password for the site; once you're viewing the entry in Keychain Access, you can click the Go There button to have your default browser open the site in a new window and attempt to access the password-protected area.

If you ever want to remove usernames and passwords that have been stored by Safari, go back to the AutoFill tab in the preferences and click the Edit button next to User Names and Passwords. In the sheet that displays, select the website for which you want to remove this information and click Remove. To delete everything that Safari has stored in your keychain, click Remove All.

WARNING   If you elect in your web travels to store usernames and passwords for sites that have their entry boxes embedded in the web page (via a Remember Me check box or similar), you're probably storing that username and password in a cookie. (More on cookies in the next section.) When you do this, there's no way to secure your browser from accessing those sites (short of deleting your cookies) if another user gains access to your Mac and user account. The best solution: Always log out (Apple Menu ➤ Log Out) if you leave your Mac and don't want others to have access to passwords or other items stored by your browser. Likewise, you should consider turning on password protection when your Mac's screensaver turns on and when your Mac sleeps, as discussed in Chapter 5.

Securing Browser Loopholes

With most any web browser, there will be security holes, and there will be security patches. Fortunately (at least, for us Mac users), many of the security holes are exploited in Microsoft Windows versions of the major web browsers (because they have the dominant market share and, hence, more people attempting to crack them), and many of the problems skip over the Mac. That said, Mac OS X's Unix roots open it up to a larger share of that market and make it a sibling of operating systems that are often pounded by security professionals and hackers alike.

The major web browsers—Safari, Firefox, and OmniWeb—will be hacked, tested, and fixed on a fairly regular basis because they're developed and distributed widely. Opera and iCab, along with any others that come along for Mac OS X, won't get as much testing by fire, but they will likely be shepherded carefully by their programmers. In any case, with any browser, stay on top of any bug fixes and security releases so that you can take advantage of any security issues that have been solved. Download and install every new version you can. If you notice odd behavior from your browser (for instance, you're accessing a website, you click something, and suddenly you're viewing someone's hard disk), report the behavior as a bug to the browser's authors.

TIP   Many browsers will automatically check for new versions of themselves; you can generally adjust the frequency of update checks in the program's preferences. Updates to Safari are made available automatically via Apple's Software Update feature.

In the meantime, there's another security consideration: Java. When Java support is enabled in your browser, it introduces possible (although minimal) security risks via your browser. You may want to disable Java or, if that's not practical, limit it. Safari and the other browsers discussed in this chapter have various levels of limitations for Java—most allow you to make very specific choices about Java security, such as turning on Java.

TIP   Some security experts recommend disabling plug-ins (such as QuickTime and Flash) for the most bulletproof web-surfing machines. Personally, Kirk likes both Flash and QuickTime and leaves them on. If you want to hedge your bets, then stick to those two plug-ins (and perhaps any others that you need to get paying work done) and use helper applications instead of plug-ins whenever possible for other multimedia or rich documents.

Dealing with Cookies

One of the focal points of web privacy issues, at least in past years, has been the web cookie. "Cookie" was originally Netscape's name for a small piece of data that could be stored by a website via a visitor's web browser. (We think they meant "cookie crumbs," or something Hansel and Gretel-ish like that, but the name *cookie* stuck.) As a general security precaution, web browsers aren't allowed to respond to a remote request to save items to disk, except in the very limited case of cookies. This enables a little bit of identifying data to be stored (usually in your Preferences folder, in a special cookies file), but it doesn't grant a remote web server the capability to save files directly to your disk, thus avoiding (theoretically) the possibility that a virus or other malignant program could squeeze through.

NOTE   All in all, cookies are only mildly disconcerting, and they're occasionally useful. They make some people uncomfortable because they happen behind the scenes. If that's the case for you, use your browser to turn on notification options.

When users, the media, and others first learned about the potential for tracking, however, there was some outrage because websites can use the cookies to track your activities on that site—indeed that's what they're for. Generally, when you access an e-commerce site (or some content sites), you'll receive a cookie from the server. The web server then uses that cookie to track you as you move around on the site—to keep tabs on what items you order, what preferences you've set, and so forth.

Of course, clever web programmers have figured out how to get cookies to bend to their will—they'll track exactly what pages you're viewing and try to push other appealing products on you. (That's how some online retailers—Amazon.com comes to mind—perform some of their somewhat Orwellian-seeming marketing, just in case you're curious.) Once stored on your hard disk, cookies can maintain a record of the sites you've visited (and often other personal information). If you're interested in knowing when a website requests a cookie, you can dig a little deeper into cookie management.

In all Mac OS X browsers you'll find cookies preferences in the Preferences dialog box. In fact, they all have a clearly marked Cookies option (in Safari, click the Security icon in Preferences; in Firefox, go to the Privacy preferences). Look for an "Ask Me Every Time" option in Firefox; Safari only lets you choose between always allowing cookies, never allowing them, or only from sites you expressly navigate to. In Firefox, if you choose to have the program ask you for each cookie, you'll be able to choose which sites' cookies to accept and which to decline. If you don't feel that a site should be tracking your movements—or it seems to benefit the site more than it benefits you—then decline the cookie and surf on. If you encounter errors, enable cookies for that site or leave the site.

In most browsers, you also can dig into the Cookies or Security screen in the Preferences dialog box and see what sites have left cookies in the past. If you see a site you no longer visit or a site that you don't think should be tracking you, delete it. Check out your other options—some browsers enable you to expire cookies after a certain amount of time; others will always reject cookies that aren't configured properly. Most browsers allow you to delete all cookies if you want to surf with no sites tracking your previous movements.

NOTE   Tools used for web security and privacy—those that sweep up browser caches, history, and so on—often have options for cleaning out cookies. See the sidebar "Web Privacy Tools" in the next section for more info.

Web Privacy

You've already seen the steps you can take to keep your data secure on the Internet and to manage your web certificates and cookies to authenticate sites and control what information they track about you—to a certain extent.

Other web privacy issues include a few other tidbits of information that web servers can learn about you, as well as some information that your web browser stores on your hard disk about you and the sites you visit. If you're interested in privacy issues, you may want to look into both aspects.

On the web side of things, we're talking about some basic *variables* that websites can access about your browser. If it wants to, a website can learn, at a minimum, the IP address and the web browser type and model that your Mac appears to be using and the URL of the web page that you were on before you visited the new site. This is generally done for programming reasons—if a scripted page can know what browser you're using, then the script can serve you a more compatible page. If a site supports only Microsoft Windows, then that site can check your browser type and then decline to allow you to access the site so that it doesn't mess up or crash your browser.

Some browsers will block these requests if you want or reroute them or give an answer you choose. In particular, browsers that aren't Windows browsers (like Internet Explorer) will often enable you to fool a web server into believing that they are IE, so that the website won't attempt to kick you out as an incompatible browser. For instance, if you use Firefox, you can download an extension called User Agent Switcher (`www.chrispederick.com/work/firefox/useragentswitcher/`) that lets you choose from a number of different browsers such as Internet Explorer, Netscape, and Opera (Windows versions). Safari doesn't offer browser masquerading or any similar privacy settings.

The flip side of web privacy is the stuff that's stored on your Mac about your web-surfing sessions. Every browser stores history, bookmarks (or favorites), and cache files that leave a record of your

WEB PRIVACY TOOLS

A few companies offer web privacy and security tools for Mac OS X—some of them bundled together, some as separate applications. For instance, Norton, mentioned in Chapter 24 for its Norton Personal Firewall software (www.symantec.com/sabu/nis/npf_mac/index.html), also sells a bundle called Norton Internet Security, which includes Personal Firewall, Norton AntiVirus, Norton Privacy Control (blocks personal data from being downloaded and blocks web ads), and iClean, from Allume, which can be used for removing cookies, cache files, and web history logs. iClean is also available directly from Aladdin Systems (www.allume.com). Intego's NetBarrier, also discussed in Chapter 24, offers fairly extensive web privacy features; Intego also offers an Internet Security Barrier suite.

session, and some browsers also store passwords, e-mail account information, and other data. Those areas include

Browser cache   The browser cache is a folder of files or a database file where pages, images, applets, and other data are stored from your web-surfing sessions. The cache is used to make return visits to the same pages happen more quickly—if you return to a page that's in your cache, it loads more quickly from your hard disk than from the Internet. Most browsers have a command that enables you to flush or delete the browser cache, thus purging it of all pages, images, and information you've viewed or sent during a session. Check the Advanced or Cache settings in the browser's Preferences dialog box.

NOTE   Safari has a convenient Safari ➢ Empty Cache command for quick cleanup. In Firefox, you have to go into the Privacy preferences, and OmniWeb has a Flush Cache command in its OmniWeb menu. Other browsers offer similar commands.

History   Most browsers track two types of history—a global history and a *local* or browser history. The local history is used to track the URLs where a particular window has been (for the Back button as well as for other history access points, depending on the browser). The global history, if tracked, stores the location of all sites that a browser has accessed over a specified amount of time or up to a certain number of sites. Again, each browser enables you to set your history limits in its respective Preferences dialog box, and most browsers will also enable you to click a button and clear your history. In Firefox this is in the Privacy preferences; both OmniWeb and Safari let you clear the history globally, with a History ➢ Clear History command, or by web page, from Safari's Bookmarks window or OmniWeb's History ➢ Show History command, History tracking is also what makes "auto completion" typing work in most browsers. Some browsers track this separately, with Preferences entries to match, if you'd like to turn it on or off.

Images and ads   Some browsers (and third-party firewalls) will block images with certain pathnames that are giveaways that they're advertisements. Others will block images that aren't on the same server as the web document you're accessing. This can cut down on the clutter that you see in the browser window and, in some cases, it can cut down on the pop-up advertising windows that appear. (Disabling JavaScript often can also accomplish that, if you feel it's more important than being able to access some of JavaScript's finer qualities.) Another thing some browsers and firewalls can block effectively is a scheme whereby advertising companies (and some others) use small, one-pixel images (or "clear images" or "pixel tags") on pages to access their cookie on your computer and note when you visit a site that uses that advertising company's (or megaconglomerate's) services. In other words, they track you across their sites or their clients' sites to learn more about your habits or other (usually broad demographic) information. If you don't like that idea, you can turn off image display altogether (which all browsers support) or turn on the blocking of advertising-like URLs and images.

NOTE Of the browsers discussed, OmniWeb offers ad-blocking features, and Firefox lets you manage ad-blocking through a powerful extension, Adblock (`http://adblock.mozdev.org/`). Safari offers the option of blocking pop-up windows by choosing Safari ➢ Block Pop Up Windows, which can go a little way toward cutting down on annoying ads.

Apple's .Mac Tools

One of the tricks that Apple uses to lure and keep Mac users buying Macintosh computers and Mac OS upgrades is extending the Mac OS out onto the Internet itself. It does that via .Mac, a subscription suite of Internet applications that work either via a web browser or directly within the Mac OS and its applications to offer some interesting, if not unique, services to Mac users.

For $99 a year, you get a Mac.com e-mail address, an iDisk, on online virtual network volume where you can store files and make them available to others, 250MB of online disk space (that you split between your e-mail account and your iDisk), HomePage, where you can create your own web pages using web-based templates, free software, including Apple's Backup and McAfee's Virex, and additional freebies throughout the year. The .Mac service is useful if you're using Mac OS X to its fullest—you can back up to your iDisk, you can use iCal to publish your calendar—there's tons of stuff to play with. If you already have extensive Internet services and solutions, however, it may not be worth the expense.

You can use some or all of Apple's .Mac tools, depending on your level of interest. These are all Internet-based applications, enabling you to perform some Internet-based tasks easily from your Mac. Here's a quick look at the tools that Apple offers.

E-mail and webmail   You can use .Mac to create your own e-mail account within the `Mac.com` domain, proclaiming to one and all that you are a Mac user. You access the Mac.com e-mail from your own e-mail application (such as the Mail application), making it easy to work with. The .Mac service also offers a webmail tool that enables you to access your Mac.com account from any browser, as well as access a POP e-mail account from the Web when you're on the road.

iDisk   The iDisk tool gives you an area (250MB, by default, which you split with your Mac.com mailbox) on Apple's Internet servers where you can store files remotely. This is great for transferring documents from one Mac to another, accessing files while you're traveling, or simply backing up files to a secure location away from your home. (That way, if your computer got destroyed, some of your data could still be secure, which might be more important and valuable than the computer itself.) It's also a great way to provide large files to others; you can put files in the `Public` folder on your iDisk, and anyone can download them from a web page.

HomePage   If you want to create your own personal web page but don't want to learn a lot about HTML and web publishing, that's easily accomplished with the HomePage tool. Plus, HomePage helps you create web pages that display images, QuickTime movies (such as those created with Apple's iMovie), and other multimedia files you've created on your Mac.

NOTE   Apple offers a free .Mac tool, called iCards, that enables you to send Internet-based greeting cards. It's easy to walk through and available to anyone, even non-Mac users, so it isn't explained here. (Unlike the other tools, it doesn't require you to subscribe and log in before you can use it.)

Address Book and bookmarks   .Mac can work with iSync to synchronize your Address Book contacts to an online version of Address Book so that you can access your contacts from the road. Likewise, .Mac can create a web-based window of your bookmarks, which makes it easier to access your favorite sites from computers that aren't yours—according to Apple, the Bookmarks window works great in all sorts of web browsers. In Tiger, Apple has expanded the ability to synch data to other applications: You can also synch keychains, mail account information, mail rules, signatures, and smart mailboxes. We'll look more closely at synching data with .Mac in Chapter 16.

If you haven't already signed up for .Mac (you are given one opportunity when you first install Mac OS X), you can do so via the Web. Visit www.mac.com and click the Free Trial or Join Now link on the screen. (You also can begin this process by clicking the Sign Up button on the .Mac tab of the Internet pane in the System Preferences application.) On the signup screen, select the option to create a new account. (Currently the button says Sign Up, but the ever-changing Web could see that altered in the future.)

Once you've created your account, you can sign in at any time at www.mac.com. Enter your username and password in the Member Sign In section of the screen and then click the Submit button. If you've entered your information correctly, you'll see the main .Mac screen, where you can select the tool you want to work with.

TIP   You may find it convenient to add your .Mac information to the .Mac pane of the System Preferences application. With the .Mac pane open, click the .Mac tab. Now, enter your username and password. This makes it possible for you to use .Mac tools automatically in a number of situations, including the option to choose your iDisk in the Finder's Go menu and in Open and Save dialog boxes.

Mac.com E-Mail

The Mac.com e-mail tool is really two different things—it's an e-mail account and a webmail application. If you've successfully signed in to a new .Mac account, you have a Mac.com address automatically: *username*@mac.com. All you have to do to begin sending and receiving e-mail from that account is to add it in your e-mail application. (Chapter 12 explains how to create a new account in the Mail application.)

The webmail tool enables you to access your .Mac e-mail from any web browser, which can be handy when you're not near your own Mac. Just head to http://www.mac.com and click the Mail icon on the main .Mac screen. You'll be asked to log in—enter your member name and password and then click Enter. That gives you access to the webmail application, which, you'll notice, bears a resemblance to the Apple Mail application (see Figure 11.5).

If you plan to use Mac.com e-mail with your own e-mail application, all you need to know to set up your e-mail account are a few simple items. If you enter your .Mac username and password in the .Mac preferences in System Preferences, Apple's Mail application will use these to automatically set up a new .Mac e-mail account (see Chapter 12):

E-Mail address   *username*@mac.com—for example, steve@mac.com. The *username* portion is the member name you use to sign in to your .Mac account.

FIGURE 11.5
.Mac Mail gives you access to your Mac.com account via nearly any web browser.

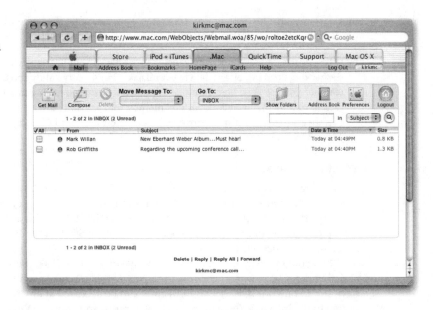

Account name *username*. Again, it's the same member name you use to sign in to .Mac.

Mail password The same password you use to sign in to .Mac.

POP server `mail.mac.com`.

SMTP server For this one, use the SMTP server offered by the ISP that gives you access to the Internet.

The .Mac preferences give you other options for dealing with your Mac.com mail—for instance, you'll see an option that enables you to forward your Mac.com mail to another account. You can also set an auto reply, which notes messages received and sends an automatic reply to the senders, usually to let them know that you're out of town or otherwise not responding to e-mail for some length of time. You'll still be able to retrieve your e-mail and reply personally when you return. And you can check other POP e-mail accounts on the Web, which is practical when you're traveling and don't have your Mac with you.

iDisk

The iDisk gives you an area on Apple's web servers where you can store (after you've signed and paid for your subscription) up to 250MB of files. (Remember, you split this between your .Mac e-mail account and your iDisk. Set this in your .Mac account settings from the .Mac website.) In addition, you can purchase additional space.

The advantage of online storage is twofold: First, you can access it from any compatible Mac, regardless of where you are; you can even access it from a Windows computer if you download the iDisk Utility for Windows XP, available from the iDisk page on the .Mac website. Second, your iDisk is an extra layer of backup safety for important data, enabling you to store documents offsite in case something catastrophic happens to your Mac. If Todd's office went up in flames, for instance, he could still access some of the important work documents that he tends to store on his iDisk. To him, that data is worth more than the computer, and it may be the same for you if you use your Mac at work or use it for important household or organizational tasks.

NOTE With a .Mac account, Apple includes the Backup application, which enables you to automate the backing up of important data to your iDisk. That's a very handy app to implement, regardless of whether you use your Mac for office or personal business; having that backup will save you from reconstructing financial data, letters, memos, and anything else you elect to back up, if your Mac ever meets with failure or catastrophe. See Chapter 26, "Hard Disk Care, File Security, and Mainte-nance," for more on using Backup.

SYNCHING AN IDISK

You can log in to iDisk in a few different ways. The first way is to set up your .Mac account informa-tion in the .Mac preference pane of System Preferences. Your iDisk appears in the Finder window sidebars; to mount it, just click its icon. By default, iDisk synching is turned off. You can turn it on from the iDisk tab of the .Mac preferences pane; click Start and then click either Automatically or Manually for synchronizing.

When you do this, your Mac creates a local copy of the iDisk; this copy is like a clone of the iDisk, and it works in both ways. (The first time you do this can take a while, depending on how much you have stored on your iDisk.) This local copy can be accessed at any time, whether or not you're con-nected to the Internet. You can freely copy items to and from it. When you're connected again to the Internet, the contents of the iDisk can be synchronized either automatically or manually.

To synchronize manually, click the synchronize button that's next to your iDisk icon in the Finder window. If you choose manual synchronizing, you can synchronize your iDisk by clicking the icon to the right of the iDisk in the Finder window Sidebar. If you choose automatic synching, this occurs whenever you change anything on your local iDisk, or whenever your Mac detects that there are changes to the contents of the iDisk on Apple's servers.

Automatic synching is totally transparent; you may notice network activity, especially if you have limited bandwidth—your other Internet access may be slowed down. But the iDisk compares the con-tents of the remote iDisk and the local disk and copies any files that differ.

Whether your iDisk works this way is up to you—it's pretty convenient, because it makes iDisk much more responsive than it often is via other methods. The one caveat is that, unlike the direct-access methods, using your desktop iDisk means there's a delay between the time that you copy data to the iDisk icon on your desktop and the time it actually gets placed online. In most cases, this may not be a problem, but if you often move your portable around, or if you have a tendency to shut off your Internet access or only be online during certain intervals, you may want to synchronize your iDisk manually whenever you copy items to it.

TIP Don't want to work with a local copy of your iDisk? Open the .Mac pane in System Preferences and click Stop in the iDisk synching section.

USING YOUR iDISK

Your iDisk, regardless of how it's mounted on your desktop, works like any network or removable disk volume: just drag and drop items from Finder windows to the folders in the iDisk. You'll notice that you can drag files only to the folders on the iDisk—you can't save items on the main level. Also, you can create folders only within the folders—you can't add a new subfolder at the main level.

When you drag a file to one of the folders, you may notice something else about your iDisk: it can be slow. This is especially true if you have a modem-based or other low-bandwidth Internet connection. This is simply a fact of online life—your iDisk is just like any other server on the Internet, and your capability to copy files to and from it depends completely on the speed of your Internet connection.

When you're copying files to your iDisk, it's also important to consider which folder you're copying to. Your iDisk offers individual folders for very particular types of files, depending on what you plan to do with them:

Documents   Use this folder to store your personal documents for backup or for accessing from a different Mac.

Music   Place AIFF and MP3 music files in this folder for use with iTunes and the HomePage tool.

Movies   Place QuickTime movies in this folder for use with the HomePage tool.

Pictures   Place image files (generally in JPEG or GIF format) in this folder for use with Home-Page, iCards, and other graphical .Mac tools. (The HomePage tool, for instance, can use images placed in the Pictures folder to create online photo galleries.)

Public   Place files in this folder that you want to share with others on the Internet. Anyone with Mac OS 9 or higher, or with Windows XP and the iDisk Utility for Windows XP, who knows your .Mac member name can access your Public folder and download files from it or upload files to it.

NOTE   Actually, users of other operating systems can access files in your Public folder via a web browser. If you're interested only in making files available for download, you can use the HomePage tool to create a page for downloads accessible to any web user. (See the main iDisk page within the .Mac website for more details.) You can also limit access to and password-protect your Public folder using the iDisk screen in the .Mac pane of System Preferences.

Sites   The files and folders for the websites you create using HomePage are stored here. If you find the HomePage tools limiting and you know a little something about HTML, you can edit these files from this folder.

UPSTREAM VERSUS DOWNSTREAM SPEEDS

Many broadband connections, especially DSL and cable modems for home users, can have two speeds: *upstream* and *downstream*. The downstream speed is usually faster, and it's the one you'll encounter more often, while downloading web pages, images, files, and anything else you might be accessing on the Internet. The upstream speed is the speed of your connection when you're *sending* files.

Depending on your type of connection, your uploading speed might be considerably slower than your downloading speed, because ISPs assume that, in general, users send much less data to the Internet than they receive from the Internet. If the slow upstream speed is too much to bear, you might discuss higher speeds with your ISP. There may be a more expensive option that improves speeds in both directions.

If you're just storing files online, use the Documents folder; if you're going to be making your files available to others, use the Public folder. In other cases, copy files to the appropriate folder for use with other .Mac tools, such as HomePage and iCards.

NOTE   Apple can add folders to your iDisk at any time, sometimes just to help you organize things and at other times to add new features. For instance, the Software folder is a special folder that's not really on your iDisk—it's an alias to a repository of shareware and freeware archives that Apple has stored on its servers. You can use this folder to access both Apple software updates and popular third-party applications. Just drag them to your desktop, home folder, or another folder on your disk, and they're downloaded from Apple's servers.

Bookmarks, Contacts, and Calendars

As you'll see in Chapter 16, you can automatically or manually synchronize much of your personal info to your .Mac account. This allows you to then synch it to another Mac (say from your desktop Mac at the office to your PowerBook), but also to access much of this information from the .Mac website. This allows you to

◆ Work on the road, using your Address Book contacts to send e-mail messages to any of your contacts from any web browser.

◆ Access your Safari bookmarks from any browser.

◆ Access and share your iCal calendars on the Web.

BOOKMARKS

When you synch your Safari bookmarks to your .Mac account (as explained in Chapter 16), you can access them from the .Mac website. Click Bookmarks and then click Open Bookmarks. A narrow window opens showing all your Safari bookmarks. You can work with these just as you do with Safari; access any of your favorite sites from any computer, even running Windows or Linux.

You can also use this Bookmarks window as a control center for .Mac. Click its Mail button to access your e-mail, and click Address Book to access your contacts.

CONTACTS

If you synch your contacts from Address Book to the .Mac website, you can use them to send e-mail messages from the .Mac webmail page. This means you can always have the e-mail addresses you need handy, even when you don't have your Mac with you. Click the Address Book icon on the .Mac website, and a window opens showing your contacts. You can scroll through your contacts, edit them, send e-mail to them, and even create new contacts from this window, which are then synched back to your Mac.

CALENDARS

Just as you can use iCal to manage your appointments and tasks, you can use it on the Web to ensure that no matter where you are you can access your schedule. All you need to do is publish your calendars to the Web and check the URL that iCal presents after you publish the calendar. You can then either use the published calendar to check your schedule when you're on the road or provide the link to a friend or colleague so that they can keep up with your schedule. If they have a Mac as well, they can subscribe to your calendar and view it directly in their copy of iCal. See Chapter 16 for more on using iCal and publishing calendars.

HomePage

The HomePage tool enables you to create your own web page (or a site consisting of multiple pages) using some easy-to-learn editing tools. HomePage offers basic templates that you step through, typing text and adding images and QuickTime movies that you've stored in the appropriate folders on your iDisk. To begin using HomePage, click the HomePage link at the top of the main .Mac screen.

A full discussion of the HomePage tool is beyond the scope of this book, but it's easy enough to use. On the main HomePage screen, select the type of page you want to create in the Create a Page section; options range from photo albums and iMovie "theater" screens to résumés, classroom pages, and team sports newsletters. Once you've selected a theme, HomePage will walk you through the process of entering information and selecting multimedia files that you've uploaded to your iDisk in the `Movies` or `Pictures` folder.

Once created, your web page is stored in the `Sites` folder on your iDisk, and you (and others) will access your web page at `http://homepage.mac.com/`*username*`/`, where *username* is your exact .Mac member name. Typing **`http://homepage.mac.com/steve/`** into a web browser, for instance, brings up Steve Jobs' page.

NOTE   If you happen to know a little HTML, you can create your own web pages and upload them to your `Sites` folder on your iDisk. Click the Advanced tab on the HomePage page and then select one of these pages to add to your .Mac website.

You can choose from a full range of templates, including pages for photo albums, file sharing (using files you place in your `Public` folder), site menu pages, iMovie pages (using movies you place in your `Movies` folder), newsletters, résumés, invitations, and more.

Internet Channels with Sherlock

Another Internet tool that Apple provides with Mac OS X is Sherlock. Originally (back in the pre-OS X days), Sherlock was a high-powered find tool, used for searching for files on your Mac. Apple then redesigned it to become a sort of browser that can search for and display a variety of information (see Figure 11.6).

FIGURE 11.6
The Sherlock channels

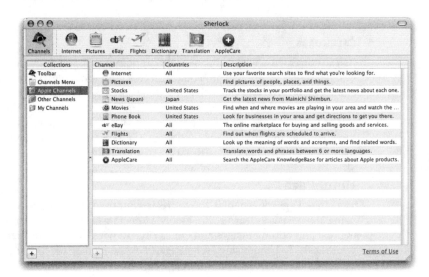

Internet Searching

You can use Sherlock to search the Internet for keywords, much as you might use Google. You can also use it to access the channel-based content—each channel returns specialized types of data. In most channels, you'll have an entry box or other controls (menus, check boxes) that you'll use to select criteria or to search for something in particular. Once you put the search in motion, you'll get responses, with the window configured to show you that information in an optimum way.

NOTE To use Sherlock, you need to be connected to the Internet. (In some cases, accessing Sherlock's Internet capabilities will cause your Mac to attempt to connect.) If you're not sure how to connect to the Internet yet, see Chapter 10 for details.

Click the Internet channel icon, and you'll see a fairly plain-looking screen. In the Topic or Description entry box, enter keywords or a description of the web documents you'd like to find. Then, click the Magnifying Glass icon.

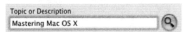

The search will be put into motion, and results will appear in the Web Sites list beneath the keyword entry box. The results are listed by relevance—the more often the keywords come up and the closer they are to one another, the more relevant Sherlock believes a particular result is. Once you have a results list, you can click it to see it in Sherlock's bottom pane. If you want to see more, drag the pane upwards to increase the size of the display. If you want to see an entry in your default web browser, double-click it.

The only disadvantage to using Sherlock's Internet channel is the type of search engines it uses. This channel cannot replace a Google search in Safari or another web browser. However, the search engines in this channel are more theme-based search engines, so while you won't find as many hits for your searches, they'll be much more useful.

Using Channels

Internet searches aren't even half the fun. Select another of the channels, and you'll be able to see a much more creative presentation of the data being retrieved from the Web. In most cases, you'll be asked to enter some sort of data—on the Movies channel, you'll be asked for your zip code so that Sherlock can retrieve local movies; on the Stocks page, you'll be asked for ticker symbols.

Beyond just retrieving information about local movies or stock prices, Sherlock tends to do more. On the Movies page, it will show you information about the theater you choose (distance and address), the current movie times, and details about the movie you're considering, including a synopsis and, in some cases, a poster and even a QuickTime movie clip. On the Stocks page (see Figure 11.7), you'll get stock quotes, recent news about the company, and access to various charts, including intraday activity.

FIGURE 11.7

Viewing stocks in Sherlock

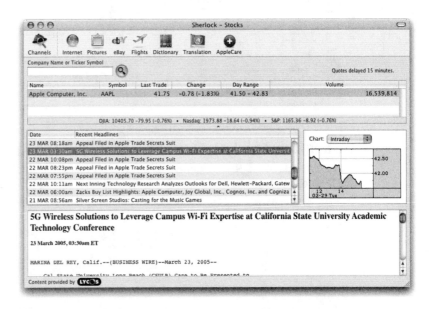

On the eBay channel, you can get a fairly comprehensive interface for searching for products on the popular personal auction site, including a quick look at the product image and description and the opportunity to track the auction with the click of a button. (You'll have to sign into eBay via a web browser to do any bidding or posting.)

One thing that's nice about Sherlock is the fact that you can switch back and forth between channels and not lose your most recent search—if you're looking at an item on the eBay channel and you switch to the Internet channel to search for something quickly, you can switch back to eBay and see your latest entries and results.

One especially useful channel is the AppleCare channel. This lets you search Apple's knowledge base for help, specifications, or information about your Mac, Mac OS X, your iPod, or more. Not only does Sherlock return many results for your searches, but you can view each of the documents in the program's bottom pane, saving you a lot of clicks in your browser. You may find this to be the best place to start when you're looking for advanced help for your Mac.

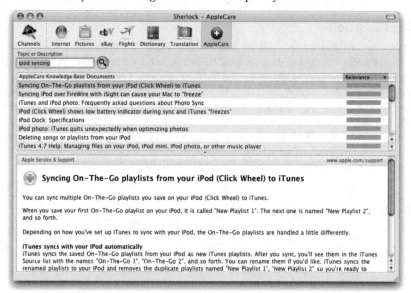

Customizing Sherlock Channels

On the left side of the Sherlock interface is a Collections pane, similar to the pane you see in iTunes and iPhoto, where you can manage different playlists, photo albums, and so on. In Sherlock, this pane is used to manage collections of Sherlock channels.

In the Collections pane, you'll find some default entries, including the Toolbar, Apple Channels, and Other Channels. You can use the Toolbar collection to manage the icons that appear at the top of the Sherlock window; click the Toolbar icon to see those icons and then use drag-and-drop to rearrange them or to drag others to the Toolbar icon to add them to the Toolbar.

The Apple Channels collection includes those that Apple has created for Sherlock; the Other Channels collection is a repository of third-party Sherlock channels. Again, you can drag the icons between collections or drag a particular channel icon to the Toolbar icon to add it to the Sherlock toolbar.

You can also create your own collections by clicking the small add (+) button at the bottom of the Collections pane. A blank folder appears, enabling you to name it. You can then drag channels to that folder from other channels as you please.

How about adding new channels? When you're on the Web, you'll occasionally come across a site that has built its own Sherlock channel. In most cases, the web page will have a link that enables you to instantly add the channel to Sherlock. When you do, you'll see a small dialog sheet that asks where you'd like to add the channel; make a selection and click OK.

TIP Sherlock Channels (www.sherlockchannels.info) is a fun place to begin your quest for new Sherlock channels. Also note that Apple can add third-party channels to the Other Channels collection at any time.

Using iChat AV

Our final foray into Internet and network applications in this chapter looks at iChat, a powerful little program that's useful not only for chatting online but also for sharing files. Beyond that, iChat AV offers Voice over IP (VoIP) and teleconferencing capabilities, even allowing chats with multiple people. You can hold audio chats with up to 10 participants, and video chats with up to four people. iChat is a great way to communicate over the Internet using a variety of methods. It can work with the AIM (America Online Instant Messaging) service as well as with .Mac usernames—or you can use iChat locally, on your Bonjour-enabled network, both for chatting and for file sharing.

NOTE Bonjour (formerly known as Rendezvous) is Mac OS X's auto-configuring TCP/IP technology that makes it possible for Macs and Bonjour-enabled devices (and applications) to find one another on a network connection. See Chapter 18, "Building a Network and Sharing Files," for more details.

When you first launch iChat, you'll see a dialog box asking you to enter your first and last name and the type of connection you want (AIM or .Mac). If you have an AOL, AIM, or .Mac screen name, choose your service type and enter the username and password below it. If you don't have one of those accounts, you can either sign up for .Mac using the button that's available or sign up at www.aol.com for a free AIM screen name. If you already have an Apple ID (a Mac.com address), and you entered it when you set up your Mac, it will already be entered on this screen. Finally, if you don't want to use online chat at all, just click Continue

Next, you'll see a screen asking if you want to use Jabber instant messaging. This is a protocol often used on corporate networks. If you use Jabber, check Use Jabber Instant Messaging and enter your account name and password. If not, just click Continue to skip to the next screen.

You'll then be asked if you want to set up Bonjour chat. Check Use Bonjour Messaging if you're planning to use iChat locally. Don't worry if you're not sure yet; you can always turn these options on or off later. Click Continue.

Next, the Set Up iChat AV screen appears. If you have a compatible camera connected to your Mac, you'll see that camera's image in the setup window, and you'll see a small indicator at the bottom of that screen that shows the audio pickup levels. If you don't have a camera, you'll still see the audio pickup levels in the window, which indicate to you that you have a microphone live and that it can hear you speak. (If you don't see the little green bars appear as you speak, then you may need to make sure your Mac has a microphone, the microphone is active, and nothing is plugged in that can interfere with it.

NOTE Once you've gotten into iChat, you can use the iChat ➤ Preferences command to fine-tune your AV options.

Chatting (by Typing) Online

To chat online, begin in the Buddy List, which appears when you launch iChat. In the Buddy List window, click the small plus sign to add a buddy. (You also can choose Buddies ➤ Add a Buddy.) You can click New Person to add a person to the list, or you can select an existing entry from your Address Book. Once you have a person in your Buddy List, iChat will track that person to see when he is online and available. When he is, his entry in the Buddy List will be full color; when a buddy is not available, the entry will be dimmed.

When a buddy is available, you'll see what type of availability they have. If you only see their name and icon (either a photo or a default globe icon for a Mac.com address, or an AOL running man icon for an AIM address), then you can only use text chats with them. If you also see a green icon that looks like a phone, then you can audio chat with them; if you see a green icon that looks like a camera, then the buddy have video chat capabilities as well.

To start a text chat, double-click a buddy's name to open up an Instant Message window. Type a message in the entry box at the bottom of the screen and press Return. The user will be contacted with your initial message and asked if he wants to join the chat. If he responds, you'll see his response in the chat window.

TIP   Is the cartoon styling too cute for you? Choose View ➤ Show As Text to get rid of the balloons. You also can experiment with other view options, such as View ➤ Show Names and View ➤ Set Chat Background. With those choices, you should be able to fit your style. You also can open Preferences (iChat ➤ Preferences) and choose Messages to change the colors; choose the Actions tab to set iChat's responses to certain events.

Now you can chat back and forth. In the Instant Message window, type your entries in the entry box at the bottom. You can highlight text and press ⌘+B to make the text you type bold or press ⌘+I to make text italic. You also can add an emoticon (a "smiley") by clicking the Smiley Face icon and choosing the emotion you'd like to communicate. The emoticon appears at the insertion point when chosen. Press Return to send your text message.

If you'd like to chat with someone who is not on your Buddy List, you can do that, too. Choose File ➤ New Chat with Person. In the Instant Message window that appears, you'll see a dialog sheet—enter the screen name or .Mac name of the person with whom you would like to chat. Then type an introductory message in the entry box and press Return. If the person is available and responds, you'll see the response in the window.

You can even hold text chats (as well as audio and video chats; see later in this section) with more than one person at a time. Select File ➤ New Chat and a new Chat window opens with a drawer to the side. Click the + icon to add a user from your Buddy List or select Other to add other users. Each user sees all the messages sent in the chat, a bit like a chat room.

NOTE   If you want quick access to your buddies without switching to iChat, and without accessing the Buddy List and Bonjour windows, go to iChat's preferences, click the General tab, and then check Show Status in menu bar. This puts a little iChat balloon in the menu bar; click this to change your status or to select a buddy to start a chat. You can switch between AIM and Bonjour buddies from this menu, so you may never need to use the buddy windows again.

Don't want to receive messages for a while? In the Buddy List, click the word Available that appears under your name; it's a menu in which you can choose a different state—Away, Offline, Current iTunes Track (this displays the song you're listening to and updates as iTunes changes), or a custom entry. When you choose Custom, you can type the message that will be shown to others who try to contact you. Choose Offline if you want to sign off of the service but leave iChat open.

NOTE   You can select iChat ➤ Preferences to tweak a number of settings, including whether or not you want to accept chat requests from people who aren't on your Buddy List.

Bonjour Chatting

If your Mac is connected to a LAN with other Macs running Mac OS X 10.2 or higher, you can use iChat's Bonjour messaging feature. Essentially, it enables you to chat with people on your network without requiring any special setup or servers—just launch iChat on two or more of your Macs, and they should automatically find one another. You'll see the other person's name (the full name entered at setup) in the Bonjour window in iChat.

Double-click a name in the Bonjour window, and you can open up an Instant Message window—type your message and press Return to send it. If your recipient is available, the reply will appear in the window beneath your message.

iChat File Sharing

One thing we really like about iChat is the ability to send files to other users when you're connected via Bonjour or over the Internet—this works with both .Mac and AIM accounts. This is a sort of a live version of sending an e-mail attachment, and it can be great for collaborating with colleagues or simply transferring files across a local network.

If you have a file you'd like to send to someone you're chatting with, simply drag the file to the text area where you're typing your message or drag it to that person's name in your Buddy List. When you do that, a dialog box appears asking you to confirm—click Send if you really want to send the file.

The recipient will see the name of the file and a link. When the recipient clicks that link, the file will be transferred. It works the other way, too—if the other party sends you a file, click the link, and it will be downloaded to your desktop.

You also can send the file without first initiating a connection—and you can do it in one of three ways:

♦ Control+click the recipient's name in the Bonjour list or the Buddy List and choose Send File from the context menu. In the Open dialog box that appears, locate the file and click Open.

♦ Select the recipient in the list and choose Buddies ➢ Send File. In the Open dialog box that appears, locate the file and click Open.

♦ Drag the file to the recipient's name in the Bonjour or Buddy List window. In this case, you'll be asked to confirm that you want to send the file via a dialog box.

In all of these cases, the action will cause an Incoming File Request window to pop up on the recipient's computer, asking if she would like to accept the downloaded file.

Audio and Video Chatting

If you're working with iChat and you have a broadband Internet connection, you've got the next generation of "chatting" at your disposal—you can have an audio chat or a video conference using the software. Not only can you talk to and see someone else, but you can carry out audio conferences with up to nine other people and video conferences with up to three others.

Nothing else really needs to be set up in terms of your iChat account—if you both use iChat, you can initiate an audio chat as long as you have the right equipment attached to your Mac. If your Mac has a built-in microphone and speakers, you can use them; otherwise you'll need to install a microphone and speakers or purchase a computer headset that's compatible with your Mac. (Shop carefully, as some Mac models do not include a sound-in port; if you have such a Mac, you'll need to get a USB-based computer headset.)

NOTE Apple says that users of 56Kbps modems can manage audio conferencing, while broadband connections (DSL, cable modem, ISDN, and so on) are recommended for video conferencing. In our experience, broadband is helpful for audio chats as well.

You'll know you're set up for an audio chat because your own name in your Buddy and/or Rendezvous List will show the audio chat (telephone handset) icon. Likewise, anyone with whom you can have a chat will also have an icon.

To initiate an audio chat, click the other user's audio chat icon. You'll see an audio chat window pop up with that user's name and an audio indicator that shows you if your microphone appears to be working. Adjust your volume and wait to see if the other person accepts the chat.

If you're on the receiving end of an audio chat invitation, you'll get a window that asks you to respond to the request:

♦ Click Accept to attempt an audio conference.

♦ Click Text Reply if you'd prefer to type a response.

♦ Click Decline if you don't want to chat at all.

For video conferencing, the steps are pretty much the same—if both you and a buddy have video cameras set up, you'll see small camera icons next to your names. To initiate a video conference, simply click the video icon next to that person's name. If they accept, you'll be able to see and hear one another in a video conference—iChat gives you a large window in which you can see the other person and a smaller window you can use to see yourself.

iChat shows you whether your users are able to carry out audio or video conferences, either one-to-one or in groups. The following icons show you the different possibilities: at the top are audio and video icons; below are the same icons for users with the ability to handle multiple conferences.

To get a group conference going, select all the buddies you want to add to the chat and then click the audio or video button at the bottom of the Buddy List. When you hold an audio conference, each user sees all the other users' names and sees level indicators for them. When you hold a video conference, each user sees all the other users live.

You'll need to consider both processor power and bandwidth, however, if you want to use audio or video conferencing with multiple buddies. Apple states that you need a G5 Mac, a 1GHz single processor G4, or a dual-processor 800MHz G4 or faster for a multi-person video conference. You also need a broadband Internet connection. If you're hosting the video conference, you need either the G5 or dual 1GIIz G4.

For audio conferences, it's a bit easier. The number of users you can talk with depends on your processor: if you have an 800MHz G4, you can talk with up to three other people. If you have a 1.2MHz G4, you can have a 10-person audio conference.

NOTE iChat has the Connection Doctor (under the Audio menu), which can be used to help you determine why you're having trouble with your iChat audio or video conferencing. Remember that every bit of bandwidth helps—Ethernet can be more reliable than AirPort for these types of connections, for instance.

What's Next?

In this chapter, you were introduced to Safari, Apple's web browser, and a few other web browsers that are available for Mac OS X. You saw how to configure Mac OS X so that any of them could be your default browser. You then learned about some of the web browser basics—and how each browser handles them. You saw a brief discussion of URLs, how to work with bookmarks, favorites, and history, how to install and use plug-ins or helper applications, and how to configure some of the preferences available to you in each browser.

Beyond the browsing basics, you learned about Internet security and privacy, including a primer on choosing passwords and using your Mac OS X keychain to store and retrieve important passwords. You also learned about some of the security pitfalls of using a web browser, as well as how to enable the privacy features available in various web browsers.

Next up was a brief introduction to .Mac services, Apple's subscription-based online suite of utilities that give you a presence on the Internet. The .Mac service includes online storage (iDisk), a web page-building component (HomePage), and Mac.com e-mail (which is also discussed in Chapter 12), along with a host of other features. You then saw a discussion of Sherlock's capability to search the Internet and specific Internet sites for web pages, people, news headlines, or products to buy, and finally, Apple's iChat, which lets you carry out text, audio, and video chats over the Internet or a local network.

In the next chapter, you'll learn about e-mail using Apple's Mail program, setting up accounts, sending and receiving e-mail, and Mail's junk mail filtering, rules, and smart mailboxes.

## Chapter 12

Managing E-Mail

Mac OS X features a built-in mail client called Mail, which enables you to access Internet e-mail in a sophisticated way. Mail offers a number of features for managing, storing, and searching through all the e-mail you receive. Although it's included with Mac OS X, it's not the only option you have, and you might want to consider a different application if you find that Mac OS X's Mail doesn't suit your needs. In this chapter, we'll cover some third-party applications briefly.

Mail enables you to deal with multiple accounts, including Post Office Protocol (POP) and Internet Message Access Protocol (IMAP) accounts and even Microsoft Exchange accounts. The IMAP support includes Apple's own Mac.com accounts, which enables you to store your mail on a mail server, downloading messages only when you need to read them. You also can create automatic filters and set advanced preferences to automate the retrieval and filing of incoming messages. With any e-mail program, including Mail, you should consider the security of your e-mail messages and how to avoid receiving and activating viruses via e-mail. We'll discuss this subject at the end of this chapter.

In this chapter:

◆ Choosing an E-Mail Application

◆ The Mail Basics

◆ Managing Your E-Mail

◆ Advanced Sending and Attachments

◆ Creating and Editing Mail Accounts

◆ E-Mail Security and Virus Avoidance

Choosing an E-Mail Application

Mail has evolved quite a bit from the e-mail application that was originally included with NeXTStep and OpenStep, the operating systems that Steve Jobs' Next, Inc., created before the company was bought by Apple. For the most part, those operating systems were designed for an audience of scientists and programmers, and some of Mail's heritage in that area remains. But these's days it's an attractive and versatile program, with only the occassional odd quirk that shows its heritage. It integrates well with Address Book, iChat, and other Apple applications; it's free, it's powerful, and it's definitely worth trying if you haven't already.

If you—for some reason—prefer Microsoft software, you have an option for a native Mac OS X application in Entourage (www.microsoft.com/mac/), which can be purchased separately or as part of Microsoft's Mac Office package. Entourage is an application that wears many hats—an e-mail application, an address book, a calendar, a tasks manager, and a notepad. It can synchronize with Palm OS devices, for instance, negating the need for the Palm Desktop software. It's a very capable and useful program, but it is expensive when compared to other solutions.

Thunderbird is the latest release from the Mozilla project, which is an open-source consortium using what was original Netscape Navigator code. Thunderbird is a great little e-mail application, complete with a fully Mac OS X-enabled interface, Junk mail management, built-in support for e-mail encryption, and the ability to filter e-mail as it comes in. Thunderbird also has the ability to display and work with RSS (Real Simple Syndication) formatted documents for quickly reading blogs and news headlines from within the e-mail application.

Eudora (`www.eudora.com`) is the venerable grandaddy of Mac e-mail clients, updated for Mac OS X. Eudora offers one version of the software, but with three different modes: a free "lite" version of the software with fewer features; a full-featured, ad-based version that's free; and a version with all the features and no ads if you pay the registration fee, for currently around $50. The application uses a multiwindow approach to create an interface that many users appreciate, with some similarities to Mail (or, to be timeline-sensitive, Mail has similarities to Eudora). Eudora offers some advanced features, too, including:

◆ Built in "emoticons"

◆ A ScamWatch feature that watches for e-mails that disguise their URLs

◆ The capability to detect the "mood" of a message (Eudora will warn you when it believes a message might be offensive).

◆ The capability to manage multiple user personalities easily

◆ An interesting technology called Eudora Sharing Protocol (ESP) that uses a peer-to-peer file-sharing protocol to automatically sync files in a special folder on your Mac and on the computers of other Eudora users.

MailSmith, from Barebones Software (`www.barebones.com`, around $100) offers an e-mail client that's worthy of the makers of BBEdit text editor software—it's heavy on the capability to search and manipulate the text of incoming e-mail messages. For instance, you can easily clean up and rewrap messy messages. MailSmith is a scripter/programmer's e-mail application that can create very advanced filters and AppleScript add-ons. It also features integration with SpamSieve (a service that cuts down on junk e-mail messages), support for PGP 8 (for encrypting e-mail), and the ability to import mail messages from many popular Mac OS X and Classic Mac applications.

Another popular commercial alternative is PowerMail (`www.ctmdev.com/`, about $60), designed to be compact and fast. PowerMail takes advantage of Mac OS technologies, in particular AppleScript, multithreading, memory protection, and the text-searching engine that makes it easy to search the content of messages quickly. PowerMail's goal, in general, is to make it easy to manage a lot of e-mail messages with quick searching, straightforward filing, and a very Finder-like interface that doesn't have a steep learning curve.

NOTE If you opt for a different e-mail application, you should find that setting up e-mail accounts and basic operations are similar and, hopefully, that the rest of this chapter is somewhat useful.

The Mail Basics

To get much done with Mail, you need to set up your Internet e-mail accounts. Mail can handle three different types of accounts easily: POP, IMAP, and Mac.com, the account that's included with a .Mac membership. Here's a look at the different account types:

◆ A *POP* (Post Office Protocol) mail account is the standard, offline approach to e-mail. When you access your POP e-mail account, you download to your Mac all messages from an e-mail server that's designed to receive messages from others. Once downloaded, the messages are processed by Mail and displayed in the Inbox. By default, e-mail is left on the server computer until it's deleted manually, but you can change the default so that the mail is deleted from the server immediately after you've accessed it. The mail server computer can be on your network (perhaps running on another Mac OS X or Mac OS X Server machine), or your Internet service provider may manage it.

◆ With an *IMAP* (Internet Message Access Protocol) account, more of your e-mail storage and access is done on the server. Instead of immediately downloading incoming messages to Mail, you view the message titles, search them, and organize them while they're still on the server. This way, you can maintain your e-mail on a remote server and access all your mail—even mail that has been read, categorized, and stored in folders—in any IMAP client. If you have such an account, you can use Mail to access it. (You can also, if you decide to, download and archive messages to folders in Mail that are stored on your Mac's hard disk.)

◆ Mac.com accounts, in fact, are IMAP accounts, at least when configured automatically by Mac OS X and Mail. If you'd like a Mac.com account, you'll need to sign up for the .Mac subscription service, as described in Chapter 11, "The Web, Online Security, .Mac, Sherlock, and iChat." You can then use your Mac.com e-mail address together with Mail to read, reply to, and manage your mail. (Note that unlike with some corporate and institutional IMAP accounts, you need to download and file your Mac.com e-mail in separate folders, called mailboxes, in the Mail application. That's because you have a limited amount of storage space you can use on Apple's servers. Messages left in your Inbox still can be accessed from other IMAP clients or other computers, as desired.)

TIP   When configured as an IMAP account, there's another advantage to using Mac.com e-mail—you can access it online via Apple's Webmail application. Launch a web browser and visit `http://webmail.mac.com/`, where you can access Apple's online interface to Mac.com accounts.

Note that POP is an offline solution (you download your e-mail and read it at your leisure), whereas IMAP is an online solution—you have to be connected to the server to access and manage your mail. Although a POP account is probably the more convenient choice for modem-based users, anyone with an "always-on" Internet connection (such as a LAN-based connection, a service such as DSL, or a cable modem) might at least consider an IMAP account, assuming your ISP or administrator can provide one. The main advantage of IMAP is that you can access the account from different locations and different computers because both new and saved messages are left on the server.

NOTE   Mail also supports Exchange accounts (accounts that connect to a Microsoft Exchange server). Microsoft Exchange servers are popular in many corporate and educational environments, so Mail supports them directly.

POP and IMAP Account Information

Most e-mail accounts you'll manage in Mail are either POP or IMAP accounts. If you're not sure whether you have POP or IMAP, ask your Internet service provider or your system administrator. Once you know, you'll just need some additional information, which you enter at setup. Here's the information you'll need to get from your ISP or system administrator:

Incoming Mail Server Address   This is the mail server's name or address. In most cases, it will be in a form such as mail.*mynamedserver*.net, pop.*mynamedserver*.com, or imap.*mynamedserver*.com.

Username or Account ID   You'll need to know the username you've been assigned for your e-mail account.

Password   You'll need to enter the password that's been assigned to your mail account.

Outgoing Mail Server Address   This is the server address for outgoing messages, often called a Simple Mail Transport Protocol (SMTP) server address. The address is often (though not always) different from the address of your incoming mail server; sometimes it's in the form smtp.*mynamedserver*.net. It may also be in the form smtp.*myserviceprovider*.net if you're accessing an e-mail account that isn't managed by your ISP. For instance, if you're accessing your office POP account, but you're currently on the road using your Earthlink account to access the Internet, you'll use Earthlink's SMTP server instead of your office's SMTP server.

Creating Your First Account

Before you can get started with Mail, you have to enter information for at least one e-mail account. If your only e-mail account is a Mac.com account, you'll need to configure it in the .Mac pane; the Mail Setup window doesn't give you the option of easily creating a Mac.com account. (See Chapter 11 for more on .Mac.)

If you want to set up Mail with something other than a .Mac account (and you've never configured Mail before), you'll likely see the Welcome to Mail dialog box on-screen when you launch Mail for the first time (see Figure 12.1). This dialog box is designed to make your setup as easy as possible the first time around if you have a standard POP or IMAP account.

Here's how to create the account:

1. First, realize that it can be helpful to sign on to the Internet (if you need to use Internet Connect or a similar launcher for your Internet connection) before launching Mail. When you've finished entering your e-mail information, Mail will attempt to connect to your account and immediately download any waiting e-mail. If you're not connected, you may get an error message.

2. If you haven't already launched Mail, do so by clicking its icon in the Dock or double-clicking its icon in the Applications folder. The Welcome to Mail dialog box will appear if you haven't previously set up an e-mail account. Enter your name in the Your Name entry box.

3. Begin by choosing the type of account you want to create. Select .Mac, POP, IMAP or Exchange from the Account Type menu.

NOTE   If you choose .Mac, all you need to do is enter your Mac.com username and password. Click Continue, and everything else will be set up automatically.

FIGURE 12.1

Setting up your first e-mail account

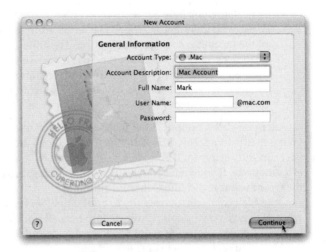

4. With your account type chosen, you'll see space for a description and your full name. Enter those, noting that the description can be anything you want it to be—"Mark@Work," "Josie's Home Account," or whatever. Then, in the e-mail Address entry box, type the e-mail address you're going to use for this account. Note that this is the address that others will use to send you e-mail (for instance, you@yourcompany.com, even if you sign in to the account using an address such as accountname@yourserviceprovider.net or something similar).

NOTE In some cases, your *actual* e-mail address is different from the e-mail address you give out to friends and family. For instance, you might have an e-mail address such as bob@macblog.com, even though your actual e-mail account is bob@macblog.com. In the New Account dialog box, the e-mail Address entry box is for your public e-mail address.

Click Continue to move to the next step.

5. In the Incoming Mail Server entry box, type the address for your incoming mail server specified by your ISP. This is sometimes different from the server that you use for receiving e-mail. (For instance, you may send outgoing mail via your cable modem or DSL provider, even though you download your e-mail from a corporate server.)

6. In the User Name entry box, enter your account ID or username for accessing the mail server. This may be different from your e-mail address. For instance, you might have an account for which your username is bob@macblog.com, even though you receive mail at the address bob@macblog.com.

7. In the Password section, enter your mail account password.

8. Click Continue to move to the next step. (If you're setting up an Exchange account, enter your webmail server first, then click Continue.) In the Incoming Mail Security section, choose the regular Password entry unless your ISP recommends a different scheme for the password management. Click Continue again.

9. In the Outgoing Mail Server (SMTP) entry box, enter the address of the SMTP server you want to use with this account. The SMTP server address is often (but not always) different from that of the incoming mail server. If your ISP requires (or allows) it, you can click the Use Authentication option to enter a name and password for your SMTP server, which allows you to send your e-mail through outgoing servers that require passwords. Click Continue; if you've opted for security, you'll be asked what type; Password usually works, unless your ISP specifies a different approach.

After you click Continue, Mail will automatically attempt to connect to the Internet and verify your e-mail settings. If you use Internet Connect for a modem-based connection and that connection isn't currently active (or if you otherwise don't yet have a working Internet connection), you'll get an error message. If you know your Mail account settings are correct and you'd like to continue despite the error message, click the Continue button.

Once Mail connects successfully to your e-mail server you'll see the Account Summary screen, which will give you the opportunity to import mail from other programs (click the Import Mailboxes button) or create another account (click the Create Another Account button).

When you're done importing and setting up, click Continue, and then click Done. Mail will connect to your e-mail server(s) and download your incoming e-mail (if you have a POP account and any e-mail is waiting for you) or otherwise open your account for access (if you have an IMAP or .Mac account). Then you'll see Mail's viewer window, with your Inbox displayed. If your main interest is simply accessing one or a few Internet e-mail accounts, you're done.

TIP   If you need further configuration, want to add more e-mail accounts, or have special settings or circumstances for your e-mail, see the section "Creating or Editing an Account," later in this chapter.

Accessing Your E-Mail

Once you've set up your initial Internet account(s), you're ready to begin reading and replying to incoming e-mail. In this section, you'll see a quick overview of how to read messages, reply to them, and compose new messages. If you've worked with Internet e-mail applications in the past, you can probably skip this section and move straight to the section "Managing Your E-Mail," where we'll detail the unique features in the Mail application. For now, though, we'll cover just the quick basics.

RETRIEVING YOUR MAIL

By default, Mail automatically checks (and for POP accounts, downloads) your mail every 5 minutes, as long as it is running. While active, it also updates the Mail icon in the Dock so that you can quickly see whether you have new messages. (The number in the red circle represents how many new messages are in your Inbox.)

Automatic checking is convenient for some, but it can be something of a problem if you have a dial-up connection to the Internet, so you may want to change the setting. (See the section "General Options," later in this chapter.)

If you've turned off the automatic option or if you'd simply prefer to check manually, all you have to do is click the Get Mail button at the top of the viewer window. You'll see a spinning indicator in the account list, next to your active POP accounts, or a sundial-type icon showing that messages are being checked in your .Mac accounts.

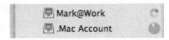

If you have new messages, you'll see them in the message list at the top of the viewer window.

TIP If you'd prefer, you also can select Window ➤ Activity Viewer to display the Activity Viewer window. The Activity Viewer will give you a more exact sense of what's going on as your mail is being checked and downloaded.

READING INCOMING MAIL

As mentioned earlier, immediately after you enter information about your e-mail account, Mail will bring up the viewer window (see Figure 12.2) and display your Inbox, along with any messages that have been received. Reading messages in this interface is very simple. All you have to do is click an e-mail in the top pane of the window (the *message list*). The bottom pane of the window (the *message area*) displays the text of the selected message. On the left (by default) is the *mailbox list*, where the Inbox and personal mailbox folders are stored. If you can't see new messages, make sure the Inbox mailbox is selected. (If you have more than one account, make sure that either the one marked Inbox is selected—so that you can see all your messages—or that the correct inbox is selected for the account you want to view.)

You also can double-click a message in the message list to view it in a separate window. When you've finished viewing the message, you can click one of the buttons in the message's toolbar (Delete, Reply, Reply All, Forward, or Print), or if you're done reading it, you can click the Close button in the window to close the message.

NOTE You can customize how e-mail looks in the message area. Select Mail ➤ Preferences, and you'll see the Mail Preferences dialog box. Select the Viewing icon to see options for viewing, including how much header detail (the details of the To, From, and routing information for the message) should appear, via the Show Header Detail menu. You also can choose to have an icon appear if a message comes from a "buddy" who is available for chatting via iChat, and you can make other choices. Click the Fonts & Colors icon if you'd like to change the fonts and sizes used for the message list and message area.

While viewing a message, you can perform another little trick: you can add the sender of the message to your Address Book. This can be convenient for finding and sending messages to that person later. To add a sender to your Address Book, highlight the message in the viewer window or double-click the message to view it in its own window. Select Message ➤ Add Sender to Address Book. The user's name and e-mail address will be stored in the Address Book for retrieval later. (Chapter 16, "Managing Contacts, Appointments, and Personal Info," discusses the Address Book in detail.)

FIGURE 12.2

The viewer window shows your incoming mail and the text of the selected message.

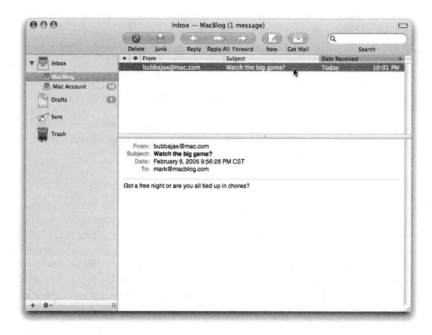

REPLYING TO A MESSAGE

You can reply to an incoming e-mail message by selecting it in the list and clicking the Reply button. A new window appears where you compose your response. Notice that the window already has the recipient's e-mail address filled in for you. Simply type your reply above the quoted portion of the message that appears in the message area (see Figure 12.3).

FIGURE 12.3

Replying to a message

NOTE If the original message was sent to other recipients besides you, you can send your reply to all of them if desired. You can do so in two ways. In the viewer window, select the message in the message list and click the Reply All button instead of clicking Reply. If you've already clicked Reply, you get another chance—another Reply All button is at the top of the reply composition window. Click that button, and any additional recipients of the e-mail message will be added to the Cc line.

By typing an e-mail address on the Cc line, you can send a courtesy copy of an e-mail to another user. (In fact, receiving a courtesy copy is the same as receiving a regular e-mail except that the recipient's address appears on the Cc line.)

Once you've finished typing your reply, click the Send button (it looks like a paper airplane) to send the e-mail reply. If you're connected to the Internet, the message will be sent immediately. If you aren't connected to the Internet, see the later section "Sending Your Message" for details on what happens.

FORWARDING A MESSAGE

If you're reading a message that you want to send to someone who didn't see it the first time, select the message in the viewer window and then click the Forward button. Doing so creates a message with the content of the original plus the line "Begin forwarded message." The To address line is blank for you to fill in the e-mail address for the person to whom you're forwarding the message. (As with a reply, you can use the Cc line for additional addresses, separated by commas, if desired.) Once you've entered all the addresses (and you've typed a note in the message area, if desired), you can click the Send icon (the paper airplane) to send the message.

REDIRECTING A MESSAGE

The Redirect command is somewhat similar to the Forward command, but with a twist. As with Forward, it sends a message that you've received to another recipient. Unlike Forward, it does so without making it clear that it has come from you. For instance, if you received a message from Steve and you forward it to your friend Karen, it will appear to have come from you with a subject line that begins Fwd:. If you redirect the message, however, it will still appear to have come from Steve, and it will have the regular message and subject line.

To redirect a message, highlight it in the viewer window and choose Message ➢ Redirect from the menu. Enter the e-mail address of the person to whom you'd like the message redirected and click Send.

TIP The Message ➢ Bounce command can be used in a similar way, but this causes the message to return to the sender in a way that looks like it was rejected by your mail server application. See "Bouncing a Message" later in this chapter.

CREATING A NEW MESSAGE

Creating a new message is just as easy as working with a reply. Choose File ➢ New Message or click the New button (it looks like a pencil and paper) in the viewer window, and a New Message window appears (see Figure 12.4). Enter an Internet e-mail address on the To line and a subject for your message on the Subject line. (Note that once you enter a subject, the name of the window changes from New Message to whatever you've typed as the subject of the message.) If you'd like to send a courtesy copy to another user (or multiple users, separated by commas), you can enter e-mail addresses on the Cc line.

FIGURE 12.4
Composing a new
message

Enter the text of your message in the message area. When you're done, you can click the Send button to send the message on its way.

SENDING YOUR MESSAGE

A new message, a reply, and a forward all get sent the same way—you click Send in the composition window. Unlike some other e-mail applications, Mail doesn't have an option that enables you to "send later"—at least, not from the composition window. If you aren't currently connected to the Internet, you can still compose and mark messages for sending; when you click Send in a new message or reply composition window, the message is simply moved to the Out mailbox. There it will wait until you're connected to the Internet again; when it is able to connect, it will send the queued outgoing messages.

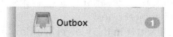

If you'd prefer that messages wait in the Out mailbox before sending them even while you're connected to the Internet, choose Mailbox ➢ Online Status ➢ Go Offline from the menu. Now, when you click the Send button in a new message or reply composition window, messages will queue in the Out mailbox until you choose Mailbox ➢ Online Status ➢ Go Online, at which point the messages will be sent.

Once the message is sent, a copy of it is stored in the Sent mailbox, found in the mailbox list. In the Mailbox list, click the Sent icon to see items you've sent to others.

SAVING A MESSAGE

If you haven't finished composing a message or a reply and you'd like to save it for later, you can do so easily. With the composition window frontmost, select File ➢ Save As Draft from the Mail menu or press ⌘S. The message, in its current state, is saved to the Drafts mailbox, accessible in the mailbox list.

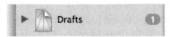

Once the message is saved, you can close the composition window if you've finished working on the message for now, or you can continue typing. Note that, in this case, the Save As Draft feature can be used to save an e-mail as you're working on it, just in case Mail crashes or you get distracted and accidentally close the message. If you've used Save As Draft, even if you continue working on the message, you'll only lose changes since the last Save operation.

If you've closed the composition window and subsequently want to work on the saved message, you can return to the message by selecting the Drafts mailbox and double-clicking the message. Then edit the message and click Send to send it as usual.

Managing Your E-Mail

Once the e-mail starts pouring in, you'll probably want to manage it more effectively. You can do that by filing the messages in different *mailboxes* (Mail's word for folders) that you create. Mail allows you to customize how you view items in your mailboxes, including the Inbox mailbox that appears on-screen when you access your account. We'll focus on the tools for managing e-mail in the second part of this section.

The Inbox

A good deal of your time in Mail will be spent in the Inbox mailbox of your POP or IMAP account. It's there that you'll see new messages in the message list, as well as those that you haven't yet filed or deleted.

If you're not viewing the Inbox mailbox in the viewer window, you can switch to it by heading to the mailbox list and then selecting the Inbox icon that you'd like to use. If you have more than one e-mail account configured in Mail, each has its own separate Inbox mailbox, which you can access by first clicking the disclosure triangle next to the Inbox icon.

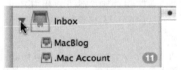

This is a very useful feature—Mail enables you to view each e-mail account as a separate Inbox mailbox by clicking the disclosure triangle and selecting one of the accounts listed. If you'd prefer to view e-mail messages sent to all your accounts at once, you can also click the In icon itself. The listing will include all of the messages you've received.

CUSTOMIZING THE TOOLBAR

Many basic commands can be accessed via the toolbar in the viewer window. Some of these commands have been covered already in the section "Accessing Your E-Mail," and the rest of them will be discussed in more detail in this section.

If you'd like, you can customize the toolbar in a way that might seem familiar if you've done any customization in Finder windows—it's the same drag-and-drop system. Choose View ➤ Customize Toolbar, and a large dialog sheet pops out from the viewer window's title bar. To customize the toolbar, drag items from the dialog sheet to the toolbar. You also can drag the separator to the toolbar, and you can drag items around on the toolbar to rearrange them.

If you'd like to return the toolbar to its original set, drag the default set of icons at the bottom of the dialog sheet to the toolbar.

In the Show menu at the bottom of the dialog sheet, you can choose whether the toolbar buttons should appear as icons, text, or both. When you've finished customizing, click the Done button to dismiss the dialog sheet.

THE MESSAGE LIST

The message list in Mail offers quite a bit of information about each e-mail message. A new message shows a small bullet at the far left of the listing (in the Status column), which tells you that the message is unread. The indicator likely means that you've *never* read the message, but it may also mean that the message has been *marked* as unread, as I'll discuss in the section "Marking and Deleting Messages." For now, though, assume that a bullet at the leftmost edge simply tells you the message has not been read.

To the right of the read indicator, you'll see the Buddy Availability column, and then you'll see the name of the sender of the message. If the sender has entered a name in his e-mail program, you'll usually see the sender's full name. (You may also see their full name if you have a card in your Address Book that corresponds to their e-mail address.) If he hasn't entered a name in his e-mail program, you'll see the sender's e-mail address.

Next, you'll see the subject of the message, which the sender entered when composing the message. To the right of the subject is the approximate date and time that the message was sent.

Aside from these columns, you can display a few optional columns if you want. Select View ➤ Columns, and you'll see a menu of optional columns you can turn on and off in the viewer window, including these:

◆ View ➤ Columns ➤ Attachments adds a column that shows whether or not an incoming message has an attachment. If the message has an attachment, a small paperclip icon appears in this column.

◆ View ➤ Columns ➤ Buddy Availability works in conjunction with iChat to let you know if the sender of the message is available on the AIM or .Mac service. (See Chapter 11 for more on iChat.)

◆ View ➤ Columns ➤ Date Received and View ➤ Columns ➤ Date Sent should be fairly self-explanatory. Date Received is the date and time when you download the message from the server; Date Sent is the date and time that the sender sent the message. (Note that these times can be somewhat inaccurate, depending on the sender's own computer clock, the ISP's server clock, and so forth.)

♦ View ➤ Columns ➤ Flags displays a column that shows when a message has been flagged via the Message ➤ Mark As Flagged command. This is useful for noting a message that you want to remember to deal with later.

♦ View ➤ Columns ➤ Mailbox displays the location of the message, which can be useful when you're viewing the main In mailbox and have multiple accounts.

♦ View ➤ Columns ➤ Number displays a message's number. Each incoming message is numbered by Mail; you can, therefore, view your messages in the order they were downloaded. The download order can sometimes be different from the date-and-time order because the date represents when the message was sent (it may have been sent from a different time zone, or it may have taken longer than another message to arrive at your mail server computer).

♦ View ➤ Columns ➤ Size displays a column that shows the amount of disk space each message consumes.

♦ View ➤ Columns ➤ To offers a column that might not seem useful at first—it shows you the To recipients of your messages. However, it can be useful to see if a message was addressed directly to you or if you're a Cc (or Bcc) recipient, particularly when you're trying to decide if a message is an advertisement, a hoax, or a message otherwise sent to a group of recipients.

SORTING THE MESSAGE LIST

With all these different criteria available in the message list, you may find reason to sort the display using one of them. After all, it would be nice to view the list differently at different times. You might want to view in order of date sent, for instance, or view messages sorted alphabetically by the name of the sender.

It's easy enough to do. Simply click a column title in the message list, and you'll see the list re-sorted according to that column's entries.

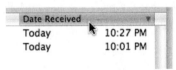

To reverse the order of the sort, just click the column title again. For instance, if you want to see names from Z to A or dates from the past to the present, you can click the column title to reverse the sort order. You'll see a small triangle in the active column title. It's pointing up when the sort order is reversed.

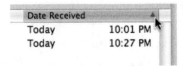

This is useful not only for dates and alphabetical lists; clicking to change the sort order in the Status (read or unread) column, for instance, can bring all of your unread messages to the top of the message list, making them easier to scroll through quickly and file away or delete. The same is true for the Attachment and Flagged columns.

The same sorting commands appear in the View ➤ Sort By menu, if you'd prefer to use a menu command. In the Sort By menu, select the type of sort you'd like to perform—Attachments, Color, Date Received, Flags, Size, and so on. You can't change the sort order via the menu; however, you'll have to click the column heading.

Marking and Deleting Messages

Aside from different ways to view messages in the viewer window, Mail also has a number of commands that let you change the status of the messages. When you select a message to view it, for instance, you're automatically changing that message to a *read* status. You can change that, though, if you'd like to mark it *unread* so that it appears with a bullet point and is considered not yet read by the program. You also can change the status when it comes to deleting and undeleting messages, as shown in this section.

TIP If you hold down the Control key and click a message in the message list (or click the right mouse button on some third-party, two-button USB mice), you'll see a context menu that enables you to delete a message or mark that message as read, as described next. In fact, the menu gives you quick access to all of the commands that are available in the Message menu plus a few from the View menu.

READ/UNREAD

You mark a message as read by selecting it in the message list. (Mail doesn't actually watch you to see if you're reading the message, because it trusts you.) Simply selecting the message with the mouse or using the keyboard arrow keys to select it will mark it read—its new-message bullet disappears and the message becomes "read." (That means it won't show up with other unread messages when you select View ➤ Sort By ➤ Message Status, for instance.)

If you'd like to change a particular message back to unread status, select it and choose Message ➤ Mark ➤ As Unread. The message will then have new message status again, meaning the bullet reappears and the message will appear again if the Hide Read command is invoked.

DELETE/UNDELETE

There are a few different ways to delete messages. The default behavior is to move a deleted message to the Trash mailbox folder. All you have to do is select a message in the message list and press the Delete key or choose Edit ➤ Delete. The selected message is moved to the Trash mailbox folder, where you can forget about it. If you decide you want the message back, select the Trash mailbox, and then drag the deleted message back to the In mailbox. After a message has been in the Trash mailbox for a week, it is deleted permanently.

You can change this default setting for each of your e-mail accounts:

1. Select Mail ➤ Preferences. In the Mail Preferences window, select the Accounts icon.

2. Select the account you'd like to alter, and click the Mailbox Behaviors tab.

3. Locate the Trash preferences, and choose the length of time that messages should be in the Trash before they're deleted from the Erase Deleted Message When menu. (Note that you can

choose Never if you'd prefer to delete them manually by choosing Mailbox ➢ Erase Deleted Messages.)

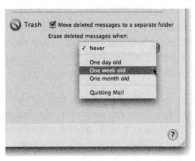

If you turn off the Move Deleted Mail to a Separate Folder option (that is, remove the check from the check box), you'll get a different behavior. Instead of moving to another folder, the deleted messages will simply be marked as deleted and hidden from view. These messages will then wait around until you choose to have them permanently deleted.

NOTE   If you're dealing with an IMAP account (which includes Mac.com accounts), you'll have the additional option of turning on or off Store Deleted Messages on the Server. If you turn off this option, messages that are marked as deleted will be removed from the server immediately, even if they haven't been fully erased yet in your version of Mail.

If you've turned off the Move Deleted Mail option, you can change Mail's behavior so that deleted messages also remain in your message window. To do that, choose View ➢ Show Deleted Messages. As you're working again in the viewer window, you delete a message by selecting it in the message list and clicking the Delete button in the button bar. Alternatively, you can press the Delete key on the keyboard after selecting a message; you can also select more than one message by holding down the F key, if desired, before invoking the Delete command. Once a message has been deleted, it will continue to appear in the message list, but it will be grayed:

●	●	From	Subject	Date Received	▲
		bubbajax@mac.com	Watch the big game?	Today	10:01 PM
		Todd Stauffer	Checking in	Today	10:27 PM

To undelete a message, select the message and choose Edit ➢ Undelete. (You also can press Shift+⌘+Delete while the message is selected.) The message will reappear in the message list, now it will be ungrayed.

If you'd like to permanently remove messages that have been marked as deleted, you can choose Mailbox ➢ Erase Deleted Messages and choose the account (or choose In All Accounts). You can also press ⌘K to erase deleted message in all your accounts at once. You'll be asked to confirm that removing the message is what you want to do. Click OK, and the messages will be removed from the Trash.

NOTE   If you have more than one account and those accounts are set up to move deleted items to the Trash, you may have more than one Trash mailbox. Click the disclosure triangle next to the Trash icon, and you'll be able to access each Trash mailbox individually.

REBUILD THE MAILBOX

Mail offers a special command that enables you to rebuild a mailbox that's seen a lot of activity. Because each mailbox is based on a single database file, that database file can experience corruption or fragmented entries over time. If you experience trouble, or if accessing the mailbox has slowed down considerably, the Mailbox ➤ Rebuild command can recover lost or damaged messages. You'll sometimes find that rebuilding the mailbox will return deleted messages to an undeleted state as well as make the mailbox more efficient and, in many cases, reduce the storage space it requires.

WARNING   It's a good idea to have a backup of your Mail folder (inside your personal folder) before performing a rebuild operation, in case something goes wrong during the rebuild process. Of course, it's a good idea to always have a backup of your mail and other important files, as detailed in Chapter 26, "Hard Disk Care, File Security, and Maintenance."

Viewing by Thread

In recent versions, Mail has added the ability to display messages in a *threaded* view. Threading essentially enables you to look at a series of back-and-forth e-mails as related to one another, grouping them closely so that you can see the entire conversation.

To turn on threading, choosing View ➤ Organize by Thread. A new column appears at the far left of the message list, where you'll see disclosure triangles for any messages that have been grouped into a thread. Click the triangle, and you'll see the series of e-mails in that thread.

What you're seeing is a discussion thread. The topmost entry (the one right next to the disclosure triangle) is actually just an informational entry—if you click it, you'll see a list of the entries in the thread.

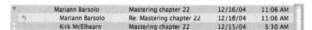

The rest of the entries under the first one are the e-mail messages that have been grouped together. This is basically a matter of convenience—it allows you to see the previous messages that you've received on the same topic. This can be particularly helpful if you have a number of different people involved in the same e-mail "conversation," as Mail is able to group those messages and allow you to follow the "thread" more easily.

NOTE   Mail has two other threading-related commands: View ➤ Expand All Threads and View ➤ Collapse All Threads, which you'll find handy when you want to tidy up your message list.

Using Multiple Mailboxes

Once you've gotten more than a few messages in your Inbox(es), you'll be ready to create new mailbox folders for storing your mail. Mail allows you to create multiple mailboxes, open them to see their messages, and move messages between different mailboxes to organize them. Most of this is done through the mailbox list.

TIP   Is the terminology confusing enough? Most other e-mail applications would call these "folders," not mailboxes. They're simply designed for organizing and filing the received mail you want to keep.

The mailbox list is the center of mailbox management. Through this interface, you'll create mailbox folders, move mail between them, and delete messages. To open the mailbox list—if it's not already showing—select View ➤ Show Mailboxes from the menu or click the Mailbox icon on the button bar. The mailbox list appears on the left side of the Mail viewer window (see Figure 12.5).

FIGURE 12.5

The mailbox list, at the left of the window, enables you to view, open, and manage your mailbox folders.

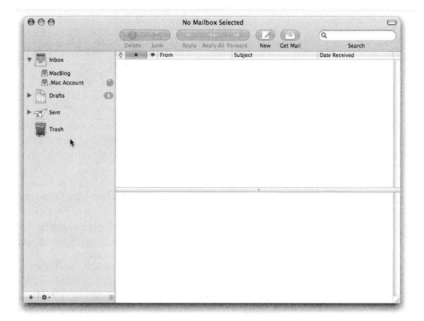

In addition to the mailboxes discussed earlier—In, Out, Drafts, Sent, and Trash—you can create your own. To create a new mailbox, select Mailbox ➤ New or click the small plus (+) icon at the bottom of the mailbox list. The New Mailbox dialog box appears.

NOTE   If you're using both POP and IMAP (or Mac.com) e-mail accounts, you'll see a Location menu in this dialog box. Select where you want the new mailbox to be stored: On My Mac (the folder is created physically on the local computer) or the name of the remote account (the folder is created on the Mac.com or IMAP server computer). If you don't choose On My Mac, you'll be creating a folder that resides on the distant e-mail server.

Enter a name for your mailbox (such as **Friends**) and then click OK. The new mailbox appears in the mailbox list.

NOTE   You can create mailboxes within mailboxes if you like, for better organization. You create the "child" mailbox the same way, but first select the mailbox that will be the "parent." Then, choose Mailbox ➤ New. Enter a name for the child folder. (If you selected the "Business" mailbox as a parent, then you might name the child "Meetings" where you'll store messages about your business meetings. To create more parent mailboxes, simply select On My Mac or the icon for your Mac.com account before invoking Mailbox ➤ New.

Once you've created a new mailbox, you can select the new mailbox in the mailbox list, and you'll see the viewer window change to show the contents of that mailbox. You can then read, manage, and search through mail in that mailbox, just as you can with the Inbox. Of course, you'll need some messages in that box first.

NOTE   Again, if you have more than one account type, the folder may appear under another icon. If you chose to place the folder on your Mac, it will appear directly in the mailbox list. If the folder is for a remote server (IMAP or Mac.com), it will appear under its own icon, such as me@mac.com if that's what you've named that account in the Accounts pane of Mail Preferences.

To transfer messages, switch to an Inbox (or switch to another mailbox where you have messages). Then, in the message list, select a message you'd like to transfer. (You can use the ⌘ key while selecting multiple messages in the message list.) With message(s) selected, choose Message ➤ Move To and then select the mailbox to which you'd like to transfer the message(s). You also can drag and drop messages from the viewer window to a particular mailbox when the mailbox list is open. Simply select the message (or multiple messages) and use the mouse to drag it (or them) to the destination mailbox in the mailbox list.

TIP   The Move To command is shadowed by a Copy To command, which can be used to make a copy of an e-mail message and place it in a particular mailbox. (We suppose sometimes two are better than one.)

To delete a mailbox, select it in the mailbox list and then select Mailbox ➤ Delete. The mailbox disappears, along with any messages in that mailbox, so make sure that's really what you want to do. (You should move the messages to another mailbox first if you want to save the messages but delete the mailbox.) You can rename mailboxes with a similar command: Mailbox ➤ Rename.

TIP   Want another way to transfer items? Hold down the Control key, point the mouse at a message, and click the mouse button. (If you have a two-button USB mouse, you can use the right mouse button instead of holding down Control.) You'll see a context menu. Select Move To and the mailbox to which you'd like to transfer that message. This method also will work if you have highlighted multiple messages (using ⌘+click) and you perform the Control+click maneuver on any of the highlighted messages.

Rules and Automatic Filing

Does your In mailbox fill up in a hurry? One way to deal with that is to tell Mail that you'd like certain incoming messages—for instance, those from a particular person or with a particular keyword in the subject line—to be filed automatically in one of your personal mailboxes. You can do that—and automate other behaviors—fairly easily.

To implement automatic filing, you need to create a *rule*. A rule is a simple test applied to each incoming message. It follows the form "if *part of the message* contains *a keyword,* then transfer the message *here.*" You can have multiple rules, and each message will be tested against each rule in turn. When a message meets the criteria of one of the rules, then the message is transferred automatically to one of your personal mailboxes. If the message gets by all the rules, it's left in your In mailbox. If a message meets the criteria of two or more rules, it will be moved according to the first rule it matches.

NOTE Filing messages is just one thing that can be done with Mail's rules. Messages can also be replied to automatically, a sound can be played, or the message can be deleted, marked as read, and so on. Dig into the rules to see how powerful they can be.

You'll create the rules in the Rules section of the Mail Preferences window. Select Mail ➢ Preferences, and the Mail Preferences window appears. Click the Rules icon. Then you'll see the Rules window, where you can set up the automatic behaviors (see Figure 12.6).

NOTE You'll notice that Mail already has a rule or two, including a self-serving rule that highlights e-mail messages from Apple. You can select one of Apple's rules and click Edit to get a sense of how rules work.

FIGURE 12.6

The Rules section of Mail Preferences enables you to set up rules for filing incoming e-mail automatically.

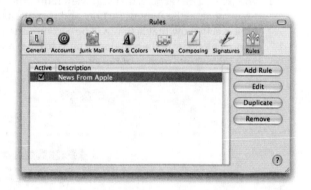

Here's how to set up a rule:

1. Click the Add Rule button to create your first rule. A dialog sheet appears with the rule's default name highlighted so that you can type your own name for the rule, if desired.

2. Set up the rule using the menus and text boxes. To begin, choose Any or All from the pull-down menu at the top of the criteria section.

3. Next, use the first menu on the criterion line to select the e-mail header field that you'd like to search (such as To, From, or Subject). After that, in the second menu, choose how you'd like to search that header field.

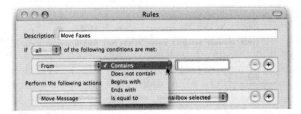

4. Enter a keyword (or even a series of letters) against which the selected header will be compared. If you enter the word *upgrade,* for instance, only messages that contain (or begin with, end with, and so on) that word in the selected header field will be processed. If you'd like additional criteria for this rule, click the plus (+) button and repeat steps 3 and 4.

NOTE   You've got to be as exact as you can when you enter a keyword. Enter *upgrade,* for instance, and you'll get messages that have *upgrade* in the selected field, as well as permutations such as *upgrades, upgraded,* and so on. However, if you select Contains from the second menu and then enter *up,* you may or may not get what you bargain for—you'll get resulting messages that include words as diverse as *supper, upright,* and *cupboard.*

5. Now, choose the actions that you want if the criteria specified are matched from the first pull-down menu in the Actions section, and then use the corresponding entry elements to determine exactly how that action will be accomplished. (For some actions there will be no other entry elements; for others you may need to enter an e-mail address or a message or select additional items from menus or buttons.)

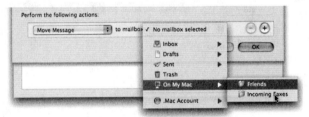

6. Click OK in the dialog sheet.

That's it—the rule is now active. You're returned to the Rules screen in Mail Preferences, where you can create a new rule, if desired. You also can drag the rule that you just created to another part of the rule list if you'd like to change that rule's order; the higher the rule, the sooner it's applied to each incoming mail message.

If you'd like to remove the rule, you can select it in the rule list and click the Remove button. The rule is removed instantly. If you'd like to turn the rule off (so that it isn't used to process incoming e-mail) but not delete it, click the check mark in the Active column next to the Description in the rule list. Without the check mark, that rule is off and won't process incoming e-mail.

Creating a Smart Mailbox

New in Mac OS X 10.4 and higher is the Smart Mailbox, a feature that combines the regular mailbox and the rules that we've discussed in the past two sections. In fact, a smart mailbox actually represents a saved *search*—you set some search criteria and then, when you select the smart mailbox, that search is conducted and the results are shown.

To create a smart mailbox, choose Mailbox ➤ New Smart Mailbox from the menu or click the small action menu button at the bottom of the mailbox list and then choose New Smart Mailbox. A dialog sheet similar to the Rules interface will appear.

Give your mailbox a name in the Smart Mailbox Name entry box, and then use the menus to build the criteria for this smart mailbox. From the Contains Messages Which Match menu, choose whether you want to match any of the criteria or all of them. Then, use the menus to choose the portion of the e-mail that the smart folder should look to match, then the way it will be matched and the keywords for the match.

If you'd like to add another criterion, click the plus (+) icon next to the first criterion line; if you're just searching based on the one keyword, click OK to create the smart mailbox. Note that you can also turn on or off the option to include messages from the Trash or Sent folders.

When you click the smart mailbox in the mailbox list, you'll see the results of that search appear in the main viewer area (see Figure 12.7). Remember that these messages haven't been *moved* to the mailbox; the smart mailbox is actually just a handy way to quickly sort through the messages that are stored elsewhere in Mail.

Handling Junk Mail

Built into Mail is a nice feature that started in Mac OS X 10.2—the capability to detect and deal with junk mail automatically. The feature isn't exactly magic, but it can be interesting if you're sick of annoying solicitations and unwelcome messages in your In mailbox.

The Junk Mail feature works in phases. If you allow it to remain activated after you first begin using Mail, it will go through a "training" phase in which it tries to learn what e-mail messages you consider to be junk and what messages you want to continue to receive as normal messages. This learning phase can be activated by launching Mail Preferences and clicking the Junk Mail icon. On the Junk Mail screen, if the option "Leave It in My Inbox, but Indicate It Is Junk Mail" is selected, then Mail is in training on Junk Mail.

FIGURE 12.7
Choose a smart mailbox
to see the results of its
criteria-based search.

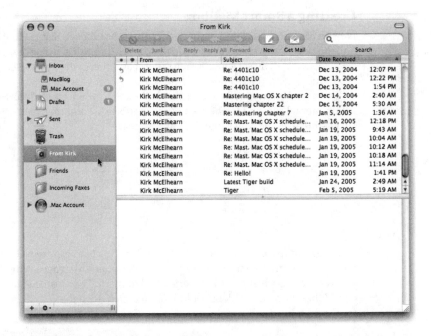

During the training phase, it's up to you to let Mail know when it's getting things right. If you notice a message that's marked as junk but is not supposed to be, select it and choose the Mark Not Junk button in the toolbar. If the message is open, you can click the Not Junk button in the open window.

If the message is junk but Mail didn't catch it, select it and click the Junk icon in the toolbar or in the message window.

Once you feel you've trained Mail well, you can switch to the automatic mode. Open Mail Preferences, click Junk Mail, and then activate the Move It to the Junk Mailbox option. Mail will create a special mailbox called Junk, where e-mail that Mail identifies as junk will be moved automatically. You can then comb through it and make sure it's all junk and delete it if desired.

TIP To dig deeper into the criteria that define mail as junk mail, click the Advanced button on the Junk Mail screen in Preferences. The Advanced settings work almost exactly like Rules do, as described earlier in the section "Rules and Automatic Filing."

Bouncing a Message

Hand in hand with the Junk Mail feature comes the capability to bounce a message from your In mailbox. Bouncing a message returns it to the sender in such a way as to make it appear that your ISP bounced the message because your e-mail address no longer exists. This is sometimes a good way to fool junk mailers (or others) into believing that your e-mail address is no good and should be removed from future mailings. To bounce a message, select it and choose Message ➤ Bounce. The message is returned to the sender complete with a "postmaster" address and a bounce message that appears to be legitimate. (You should avoid sending the bounce to personal contacts if you don't want them to think you've changed e-mail addresses or met with some untimely doom.)

Searching Mailboxes

By default, you'll come across two different ways to search within Mail—you can search for a word in the body of a particular message, or you can search within a mailbox (or within all mailboxes) for a particular message. The Find Text command, accessed via Edit ➤ Find ➤ Find , enables you to search for text within a particular e-mail message while you're reading or composing that message.

When you're composing or replying to a message, this works like the Find and Replace feature in most Mac OS X applications: enter a term in the Find entry box of the Find Panel, then click Next to find the next occurrence of that term. You also can enter a term in the Replace With entry box (assuming you're searching a message that you're composing) and click Replace to replace the found term with the Replace With term.

The other search feature, accessed through the small Search Mailbox entry box in the Mail toolbar, enables you to search the message headers or contents in a particular mailbox or in all mailboxes. You begin by entering a keyword in the small search box. You'll immediately begin to see results appear.

If you'd like to tweak the search so that you only see items that match your keyword in the To section of an e-mail, for instance, or only in the current mailbox, then you can click the small buttons that appear in the row above the results—you'll see buttons for From, To, and Subject, as well as options to select All Mailboxes or the one that is currently selected.

Your search term should be something fairly unique, such as a keyword that would be in the subject of the message or part of the name (or e-mail address) of the person who sent you the message you're seeking. As you type, the list of messages will slowly dwindle until, hopefully, you're viewing one or a few of the messages you want to see.

It's nice to be able to whittle down the messages in your Inbox mailbox by name or subject quickly, but what if you want to search more deeply into your stored e-mail? You can use the Search Mailbox entry box to search *within* messages in the currently selected mailbox (including the In mailbox or one of your personal mailboxes) and to display any messages that include the keyword you type.

To search the full text of messages (including the headers) in a selected mailbox, all you need to do is select Entire Message after typing in the Search In entry box. You'll want to have entered a word or phrase that you'd like to search for in your messages—something fairly uncommon that's likely to be found in only a limited number of messages. Avoid articles (a, an, the), prepositions (of, for, over), and other very common words.

TIP The Mail application searches for words similar to those you enter, so you'll get best results if you enter the simplest form of the word. For instance, entering *sleep* will find results that include *sleepy*, *sleepiness*, and so on.

You'll notice that the results of your search are altered automatically as you type different words or change the options in the menu. The results appear in the message list, ranked in order of *relevance*. Mail weighs the number of appearances of your keyword (and their proximity, if you enter more than one), coming up with a relevance ranking. Messages with higher ranks are shown toward the top of the list (see Figure 12.8).

FIGURE 12.8
When you're searching a mailbox, the listing includes a relevance rank for each message.

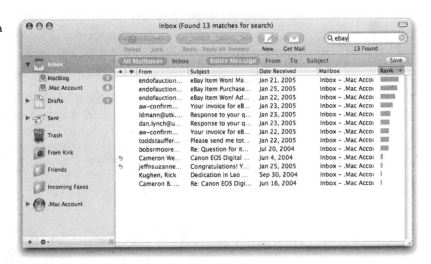

Done looking at search results? Click the small × icon in the entry box to clear the keywords and view the current mailboxes' full contents again.

Advanced Sending and Attachments

Earlier, we covered the basics of sending, receiving, and replying to messages. In Mail, these basics are similar to almost any other Mac- or Windows-based e-mail program.

In this section, though, you'll take a closer look at the message-composition window, getting deeper into the options you have for composing and sending messages. In addition, you'll look at the process of attaching files—documents or file archives—to your e-mail messages so that you can transmit them over the Internet.

The Composition Window

Whether you're replying to a received message or composing a new one, the composition window offers some sophisticated options. Earlier in this chapter, you saw how to address messages for your users in the To and Cc lines of the composition window. The composition window can do more than that, however, enabling you to create more advanced, colorful, and better-spelled messages. Figure 12.9 shows this window.

FIGURE 12.9
The composition window

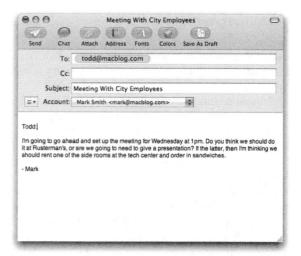

Mail's composition window is really pretty straightforward. The buttons across the top enable you to send the message, chat with your recipient, attach a file, access the Address Book, change fonts and colors, and save the e-mail as a draft.

Notice that in the body of the text, by default, misspelled words (or those that the Mac OS X dictionary doesn't recognize) appear underlined in red as you type. You'll likely find this feature helpful, but you can turn it off by selecting Edit ➤ Spelling ➤ Check Spelling ➤ Never. (You still can use the other spelling tools, discussed later in this section.)

TIP   The option Edit ➤ Spelling ➤ Check Spelling ➤ When You Click Send is a pretty cool one, as it waits until you're done composing and then pops up the spell-checking interface after you've decided to click the Send button. You can then check spelling before the e-mail heads out to its recipient.

WORKING WITH THE ADDRESS BOOK

The Address Book is a separate application that's included with Mac OS X. It's covered in more depth in Chapter 16, including its features that enable you to use it with Mail. It's worth noting here, however, how the Address Book may affect your work in the composition window.

The first thing you may notice is the *autocomplete* feature in Mail, where addresses that have been stored in the Address Book will automatically be completed as you type the first few letters of a name or e-mail address in a To, Cc, or other header line. For instance, typing **Ste** might cause the address Steve Jobs <steve@apple.com> to fill in on that header line automatically. If that's the address you want to enter, press Tab to move to the next entry box; if it's not the address you want, keep typing to finish the address you started. Once you get used to this feature, you'll find it very handy for often-typed addresses.

You also can open the Address Book quickly to add names to your header entry boxes. Choose Window ➢ Address Panel to quickly gain access to your Address Book contacts. Locate a person you'd like to add to your message, then drag and drop that person's icon from the Address Book window to one of the entry boxes (To, Cc, or Bcc if you'd added a Bcc line) to add that address to your message.

BLIND COURTESY COPY

As discussed earlier, entering an address on the Cc line in the composition window doesn't really cause the message to be sent differently than to a To recipient. The courtesy copy suggests "for your information," and all recipients see the Cc entry. Ideally, Cc recipients need not respond to the message.

A blind courtesy copy (Bcc) is different. Bcc recipients receive a copy of the message, but other recipients won't see any e-mail addresses you place in the Bcc field; in fact, your regular recipients won't even know the message has been sent to the Bcc recipients. Although it may seem impolite to send messages secretly, it can be useful in a number of circumstances.

In an organizational setting, you may want to send a blind courtesy copy of a message to a colleague or your supervisor. For instance, if you're sending a reply to a customer and you'd like your manager to see the message, you can include the manager's e-mail address in the Bcc line. That way, the manager sees the message, but the customer doesn't know that the manager has seen your reply.

The Bcc line can be important for privacy. Any address entered in the Bcc line is kept private, so you can use the Bcc line to send a message to multiple recipients without revealing their e-mail addresses to one another. For instance, if you're sending the same e-mail to multiple customers (or to a group of friends to invite them to a party), you can enter each of their addresses (or an entire Address Book *group*, as discussed in Chapter 16) on the Bcc line so as not to reveal their e-mail addresses to the rest of your recipients.

NOTE　When a recipient replies to your message, none of your Bcc recipients will appear in his e-mail program, even if he invokes a Reply to All command. Only To and Cc recipients are responded to when a Reply to All command is used.

To add a Bcc line to your message in the composition window, choose View ➢ Bcc Address Field from the menu or press Option+⌘B. (In Mac OS X 10.4, there's also a small menu next to the Account line in a composition window, where you can choose to add a Bcc Address or Reply To field.) A Bcc line appears, where you can enter e-mail addresses for your blind courtesy copy recipients.

REPLY TO

In some cases, you may want to send your e-mail messages with a different Reply To address so that recipients' responses will go to a secondary location. Although you set the Reply To address whenever you create an e-mail account (it's in the e-mail Address entry box), you can change the Reply To address on an individual basis when you're sending a message. From the composition window, select Edit ➢ Add Reply to Header to add a Reply To line (or choose Reply to Address Field from the small menu next to the Account entry box), then enter the e-mail address you'd like your users to see in their From header lines.

Mail Format

By default, e-mail messages in Mail are sent as Rich Text messages, meaning the messages can include special formatting, fonts, colors, and other elements that you generally have at your disposal when you're using other applications, such as word processors. Although Rich Text makes for more interesting-looking messages, those messages can't be displayed correctly by some e-mail programs and computing platforms.

Mail also has the capability to create messages in plain text, and you can switch between Rich Text and plain text as desired. Rich Text, in Mail, refers to the MIME format, whereas plain text means ASCII. (MIME means Multipurpose Internet Mail Extension, which is a standard system for augmenting e-mail messages with Rich Text and formatting, as well as attachments. ASCII is the standard computer-independent standard for exchanging basic text characters.) To change the format in which a current message will be sent, select Format ➢ Make Plain Text or Format ➢ Make Rich Text (as appropriate).

TIP   If you want your new messages to be in plain text by default, you can set that in the Preferences panel. Choose Preferences from the Mail menu and then click the Composing icon. You can choose the default message format—Plain Text or Rich Text—from the Default Message Format menu. You also can choose some other behavior, such as turning on the option Use the Same Message Format As Original in the When Replying to Messages section.

CHANGE FONT STYLE

Only a Rich Text e-mail can have different fonts styles in it, so if you opt to change the font, using the Format ➢ Style menu, you'll be asked if you want to change your e-mail to Rich Text if it's not already in that mode. Or, if you know you'll be styling text, you can set the mail type to Rich Text if you haven't already done so. Then you can select text and use the Format ➢ Style command menu to change the text to bold, italic, underlined, and so forth.

For more options, choose Format ➢ Show Fonts, press ⌘T or click the Fonts button in the toolbar on the composition window. This brings up the Font panel (which should be familiar if you've read

Chapter 4, "Using Applications"). You also can click the Fonts button in the composition window's toolbar to open the Font panel.

You can change the font either before or after typing. To change the font before typing, simply open the Font panel, select a font, and begin typing in the composition window.

You also can highlight text that has already been typed and select a new font in the Font panel. As soon as you make your choice, the change is made.

> **WARNING** Because not all computers have the same fonts, your message may not appear in your recipients' e-mail applications with the same font you selected. If you're sending to other Mac OS X users, they should be able to see the message as you intend. For other users, you should avoid special fonts and use only very common fonts such as Helvetica, Arial, and Times.

CHANGE COLORS

When editing a Rich Text e-mail, you can change the color of the text by opening the Colors panel and choosing Format ➢ Show Colors (or by clicking the Colors button in the composition window's toolbar). As with fonts, you can either choose a color first and then type your text or highlight text and choose the color.

Actually, the Colors panel offers many of the standard color tools built into Mac OS X (and discussed in more detail in Chapter 4). Basic use is simple:

1. Highlight the text for which you want to change the color, unless you're simply going to turn on a color for any new text you type.

2. Click in the Color Wheel area to choose a color.

3. Click the Color panel's Close button. The chosen color is applied to the selection (if no text was selected, the color is activated so that new words are typed in that color).

FORMAT TEXT

Aside from font and color, you also can change the alignment of elements in the message. Select a paragraph (or simply place the insertion point within a paragraph), choose Format ➢ Alignment, and then select an alignment command—Align Left, Center, Align Right, or Justify.

CHECK SPELLING

As noted, spelling is automatically checked as you type. (If you've turned off the feature, you can select Edit ➢ Spelling ➢ Check Spelling to have the misspelled words highlighted in the window or choose Edit ➢ Spelling ➢ Check Spelling ➢ As You Type to turn the feature back on.) When you find a misspelled word that you don't know how to spell correctly, you may need to consult the Spelling panel. To open the Spelling panel, select Edit ➢ Spelling ➢ Spelling. The panel appears.

When opened, the Spelling panel will select the first misspelled word and display suggested new spellings in the Guess list. If you see the word you meant to type, select it from the list and click Correct. If you'd like to correct the word yourself, you can type its replacement in the text area next to the Correct button and then click the Correct button to change the spelling in your message. If the word is correctly spelled, you may want to teach it to Mail so that Mail won't mark the word as misspelled in the future. Click the Learn button at the bottom of the Spelling panel.

When you've made the correction, or if you simply want to ignore this word, click Find Next. The Spelling panel will move on to the next word it believes is misspelled. When no more words are found, Mail thinks that your message is correctly spelled. As with other common application panels, the Spelling panel is discussed in more depth in Chapter 4.

ADDING A SIGNATURE

It's common with Internet e-mail to include a signature block at the end of your e-mail messages, usually including your name, e-mail address, and associated website. You also might include a favorite quote, information about your business, or a little bit of bragging about your current job title, projects, or accomplishments. With Mail, you can create a standard signature that's attached to all your messages, or you can set up multiple signatures if you'd like to switch between them. (For example, I have signatures that include my phone and fax number that I send to people who need that information, but my other signatures include just my website for when I'm not interested in revealing that information.)

To set up a signature, you'll open the Mail Preferences dialog box (Mail ➤ Preferences) and select the Signatures icon. You'll see a list of your current accounts, an empty list of signatures and some plus and minus buttons at the bottom of the column. (See Figure 12.10.)

To create a new signature, select the account that you want to associate with this signature (or choose All Signatures if you'd like to be able to use this signature with more than one account) and click the plus (+) button. Type a name for the signature, then edit it in the rightmost panel. When you're done editing, you can click elsewhere in the window to make your changes.

NOTE The Always Match My Default Message Font option can be turned off if you would prefer to set your own fonts and colors and use those for your signature in Rich Text messages that you send.

You can then use the Choose Signature menu to determine which will be the default signature for the selected e-mail account. Once chosen, that signature will be added to all e-mail messages you send out for that account.

NOTE The Select Signature menu offers two other options: In Random Order and In Sequential Order. If you've created multiple signatures simply for the sake of variety, choose one of these options to get a different signature with each message.

FIGURE 12.10
Creating a new signature

With a signature defined, you'll see a new menu in the composition window. This menu enables you to choose a signature (or change from the default signature) whenever you're editing a message.

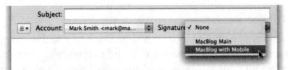

To edit a signature, simply select the name of the signature in the list and then edit it in the right pane. To remove a signature, select it in the signature list and click the minus (–) button. When you've finished creating and editing signatures, close the Mail Preferences window.

TIP Turn on the option Place Signature above Quoted Text if you'd like your signature to appear directly beneath your answer in a reply instead of at the bottom of the entire message. This is handy when you are replying to a message and want to include your signature; by default, Mail puts your signature at the bottom of the message, where your recipient might miss it.

Sending Attachments

As you've seen so far, e-mail is designed primarily for sending text messages back and forth between users. If you plan to transfer other types of files, you can use a variety of approaches including FTP or File Sharing, as discussed in Chapter 17, "Accessing Network Volumes." iChat can also be used to transfer files, as can iDisk or Homepage, discussed in Chapter 11.

However, it is certainly possible and common to transfer files via e-mail, and often it can be a convenient way to get files to a specific individual. You do that by *attaching* a file to your e-mail message before sending it. Unfortunately, by default, the Internet e-mail protocols are really not designed to transfer files; rather, they are designed primarily to transfer plain-text documents. In order to be transferred, attached files must be *encoded*, a process that changes a binary file into a text, or ASCII, file. The file is then added to the e-mail message and sent along as though the entire e-mail message were just regular text. Once the message arrives at its destination, the receiving mail client needs to decode the attachment and turn it back into a binary file. In most cases, this is done easily by the client application.

Mail encodes messages using the base-64 format, which is generally compatible with most other platforms (Microsoft Windows, Mac OS 9) and e-mail programs. Although other formats exist (including BinHex and uuencode, among others), Mail doesn't support them.

TIP Often it's advisable to compress a file before sending it as an attachment. File compression is discussed in Chapter 11.

When you're ready to attach a file to an outgoing message, click the Attach button in the composition window or choose File ➢ Attach File. An Open dialog sheet appears in the window, enabling you to locate the file you'd like to attach. Find it, select it, and click Open. You'll then see a small document icon at the bottom of the message you're composing. That indicates that the document is attached, ready to be sent. (If the document is a recognized image, you'll see the image appear in the composition window, instead of an icon.) When you send the message, the attachment will go along for the ride.

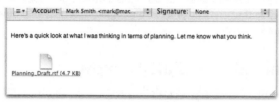

NOTE Don't see an icon? If you attach an image file that Mail can recognize, the actual image (or movie) appears in the window instead of an icon. You can play back compatible audio files, as well.

To remove the attachment, you can either highlight it in the message area and press the Delete key or choose Message ➢ Remove Attachments.

NOTE It's often important to send file attachments complete with a filename extension (such as .doc or .rtf) so that your recipient's computer knows what type of document it is receiving. This is particularly true for documents that you're sending to non-Mac platforms. In the Attachment dialog box, you also have the option of sending Windows-friendly attachments, which is useful for sending to Windows users who have trouble with your attachments.

A cool new feature in Mail its ability to automatically resize an image that you attach to an e-mail message. After attaching an image, at the bottom of the Composition window you'll see the size of the e-mail indicated and you'll see a menu; use the menu to change the size of the image if you feel that the e-mail is too large to send to your recipient. (Hover over the sizes and you'll see the exact size in pixels that the image will be changed to.)

Want to attach other e-mail messages to your message? Although you can forward messages using the Forward button in the viewer window's toolbar, there's a more convenient way to attach multiple e-mail messages to a message you're creating in the composition window. First, return to the viewer window and select one or more messages in the message list. Click the composition window to make it active and then choose Edit ➢ Append Selected Messages. The messages will appear at the bottom of your composition window, enabling you to send them quickly.

Receiving Attachments

Receiving attached files is even easier than sending them. When you open a message that includes an attachment, you'll see a document icon, usually at the bottom of the message. That icon represents the attached document. Simply click the icon's name (it's in blue text, much like a web link) to launch the document. You also can drag the icon to a Finder window or to the desktop to save it.

NOTE In the Viewing pane of Mail Preferences, you can turn off an option (Display Remote Images in HTML Messages) that automatically downloads images or embedded HTML objects. Doing so puts another step in the receiving process, but it guards against attachments that could be objectionable or pose a security risk.

Creating and Editing Mail Accounts

The basic account information taken by Mail when you first launch the program is adequate for many needs, but you can customize quite a bit in Mail, including setting up additional e-mail accounts. To see the options available to you, select Mail ➤ Preferences. You'll see the Mail Preferences window, where you can choose the Accounts icon to show the Accounts screen (see Figure 12.11).

On the Accounts screen, you'll see a list of e-mail accounts that have been created on the left side. That list should include any Internet or Mac.com accounts that you've set up with Mail or the Internet pane of the System Preferences application.

FIGURE 12.11
The Mail Preferences window displaying account options

General Options

Click the General icon and you'll see global options for automatic or manual e-mail checking. If you have a dial-up Internet connection or you don't want Mail to check your e-mail account(s) automatically for some other reason, select Manually from the Check for New Mail menu. Your e-mail will then be checked only when you invoke the Get Mail command.

If you want e-mail to be checked automatically, you can choose a frequency from the Check for New Mail menu—Every Minute, Every 5 Minutes, Every Hour, and so on.

Also, you can use the New Mail Sound menu to select a sound from the standard OS X alert sounds if you'd like one played whenever new mail arrives in your Inbox.

Creating or Editing an Account

The processes for creating and editing accounts are very similar. To create a new account or edit an existing account, open Mail Preferences (Mail ➤ Preferences) and select the Accounts icon. For a new account (so that you can access more than one Internet e-mail account from within Mail), click the Add button (+) at the bottom of the list of accounts. To edit an existing account, select the name of the account you want to edit and proceed to make changes on the right side of the window.

On the Account Information tab, you'll have access to the basic e-mail account settings that Mail asks for when you first launch the application. (For a new account, these items will be blank.) You can enter or change the name of the account in the Description entry box, which can be whatever you want—it's just Mail's designation for the account. You also can enter or change the type of account (using the Account Type pop-up menu), as well as the hostname of your mail server, your e-mail account username, and your password.

Click the Mailbox Behaviors tab, and you'll see options that enable you to decide how the Sent, Junk, and Trash mailboxes will work for this particular account. You have two sets of options. First, if you're setting up a POP or IMAP account, you'll simply decide if and when items are erased from the Sent, Junk, and Trash mailboxes. You can set a certain time period, such One Day Old, One Week Old, One Month Old, or Never to have these items deleted.

TIP Although you might want to keep the mail you send for later reference, you might also see the advantage of automatically deleting items in the Trash and Junk mailboxes after a specified time period, if you use those features. Note that you can also set them to delete items when you quit Mail, but if you often use the Sleep function in Mac OS X instead of quitting applications and shutting down, bear in mind that you may end up leaving Mail open for weeks at a time.

If you're setting up an IMAP or Mac.com account, you'll have additional options on this tab. In essence, those options enable you to decide whether the Drafts, Sent, Junk, and Trash mailboxes should be stored on the IMAP server or on your local computer. If you tend to use several different computers to access your e-mail (for instance, in a computer lab setting), you may want to store your special mailboxes on the server so that you can access them from anywhere. If you tend to use just one computer for all of your filing, and you'd like to avoid storing items on the IMAP server, you can turn off options such as Store Draft Messages on the Server or Store Junk Messages on the Server.

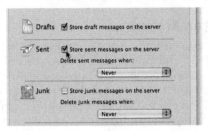

Click the Advanced tab, and you'll see a series of additional options that you can alter, if desired. The options available depend on the type of account you're creating. For a POP account, you can set the following options:

Enable This Account   When turned on, this account is active in Mail.

Include When Automatically Checking for New Mail   This option is interesting. If you've set Mail to check for new messages automatically (see the earlier section "General Options"), turning off this option means that mail is checked only when its In mailbox is selected in the mailbox list and you click the Get Mail button. If you've set Mail to check new accounts manually, however, you cannot check for new mail in this account at all if this option is turned off. If you don't seem to be receiving mail, make sure you haven't unchecked this option.

Remove Copy from Server after Retrieving a Message   When this option is turned on, messages that you download into Mail are deleted from the server according to the time limit chosen in the menu (Right Away, After One Day, After One Week, and so on). If this option is off, the messages are left on the server. If you subsequently retrieve your mail from a different e-mail application, those messages can be downloaded again. Click the Remove Now button whenever you want to clear messages off the server.

TIP   There's also a When Moved From Inbox option that will delete items from the server when you move them from your Inbox in Mail, either by filing them in another mailbox or deleting them. This one is an interesting option if you'd like your server account to reflect your Inbox contents for easy access.

Prompt Me to Skip Messages Over __ KB   When you enter a number in this entry box, Mail will ask you if you want to skip any messages larger than the number of kilobytes indicated. (For instance, if you enter 50, any messages over 50KB will result in a dialog box asking if you want to skip the message.) The option can be helpful if you want to decide when to download larger messages and messages with attachments.

Account Directory   Click the Choose button if you'd like to choose a different Mail folder on your hard disk. (By default, your Mail accounts are stored in your personal ~/Library/Mail folder, but you can change that here, in some cases.)

Port __   If you connect to your mail server using a nonstandard port, you can enter that port number here. If the account will accept an SSL connection (for a secure transfer of e-mail messages between the client and server), then turn on the SSL check box. SSL tends to slow down operations slightly, but it can be a benefit for the security conscious.

Authentication If your e-mail account offers an encrypted authentication option such as Kerberos or MD5, you should specify that option here. This causes your password to be sent to the server in an encrypted sequence, which is more secure than sending the password in clear text (unencrypted).

If you're setting up an IMAP account (or a Mac.com account, which uses IMAP), you'll see a slightly different list of options:

Enable This Account When turned on, this account is active in Mail.

Include When Automatically Checking for New Mail This causes a list of e-mail messages to be retrieved whenever you launch Mail or whenever Mail automatically checks for new mail.

Compact Mailboxes Automatically With an IMAP account, messages that you choose to delete aren't deleted from the server immediately (unless you specify that they should be on the Special Mailboxes tab). Instead, they're marked for deletion and then deleted when you compact a particular mailbox. This option enables you to do away with messages marked for deletion automatically every time you close Mail.

Account Directory Click the Choose button if you'd like to choose a different Mail folder on your hard disk.

Keep Copies of Messages for Offline Viewing Use the pull-down menu to select whether or not messages will be stored on your Mac when you check for mail (All Messages and Their Attachments or All Messages But Omit Attachments), when you read the message (Only Messages That I've Read), or never (Don't Keep Copies of Any Messages). If you'd prefer that your e-mail not be saved to the local Mac (usually for security purposes, particularly if you access your account from multiple computers in a computer lab or similar environment), make sure Don't Keep Copies of Any Messages has been selected.

Automatically Synchronize Changed Mailboxes Special to IMAP accounts is the ability to have your Mac automatically synchonize itself with the online account, which causes all mailboxes to be kept in synch on both the server and on your own Mac. (This can be very handy, but it's also something that you might want to consult your server administrator about, if only because this can lead to a lot of stored e-mail on the server which your administrator may not appreciate.)

IMAP Path Prefix This entry is available for you to specify a path that Mail can use in conjunction with mailbox names in order to find them on the remote server's drive. In most cases, you won't put anything here unless your system administrator or ISP's instructions recommend it.

Port __ If you connect to your mail server using a nonstandard port, you can enter that port number here.

Authentication If your e-mail account offers an encrypted authentication option such as Kerberos or MD5, you should specify that option here. As with POP accounts, this causes your password to be sent to the server in an encrypted sequence, which is more secure than sending the password in clear text.

When you're done configuring the account, click the Close box in the Mail Preferences dialog box if you've finished setting options. You'll be asked if you want to save changes; click Save if you're happy with the changes, and you want Mail to start working with them. If you created a new account, you'll also see that account listed under the In icon the mailbox list back in the main viewer window. You can access a new account just as you did your first account.

NOTE Once you've added more than one account in Mail, you'll see a new option in the composition window—an Account menu. You can use this menu to choose the account from which you want to send the message. By default, replies that you create are sent from the account they were initially sent *to*, but you can change that by using the Account menu when you're composing the reply.

E-Mail Security and Virus Avoidance

Issues of security with e-mail tend to boil down to two issues—keeping others from gaining access to your e-mail account and avoiding the proliferation or execution of viruses or other malicious code. You can take some proactive and defensive steps in each case, which we'll explore in this section.

E-Mail Security

E-mail accounts tend to be surprisingly insecure, given the overall desire for security that people express when it comes to other Internet services, such as the Web. In many cases, typical e-mail applications and servers exchange passwords and messages in plain text, unencrypted, and without the basic security methods used for such things as credit card payments over the Web. Part of the logic for that lax approach has been that e-mail is much more *distributed* than the Web; whereas hackers, for instance, can target an e-commerce server computer directly and hope for significant results such as credit card numbers or passwords, targeting a single e-mail transaction in order to grab a password is a less-interesting prospect (so the logic goes). However, the argument for better security in the e-mail arena is winning out, and more and more ISPs and organizations are considering e-mail security an important component of securing business or personal transactions.

What does that mean for us as users? If you're looking to secure your own e-mail account, there are a couple of steps you can take, including asking questions of your ISP and, if the answers aren't good, looking for another ISP. More and more ISPs are beginning to offer options to security-conscious consumers—fortunately, Apple is right in line with new security options in Mail. Here are some considerations:

How Secure Is Your Password? As with any other password, your e-mail password should be as secure as possible, using non-dictionary words mixed with numbers—ideally, a nonsensical stream of letters and numbers. (Note that many e-mail servers will recognize only the first eight characters of a password, so those characters should be the most creative.) Remember that many mail servers are case sensitive, so you should use that to your advantage when creating a password. If you can, you should change your e-mail password on a regular basis, and you should use a password that is different from your ISP login password and your Mac OS X login.

How Are Your Username and Password Transmitted? Many, if not most, e-mail accounts use clear text to transfer the username and password to the e-mail server, and this transfer can take place many, many times over the course of a day. A more secure method is to use an encrypted authentication method for logging into your e-mail server. You'll need to ask your ISP if it offers encryption, then you'll need to dig into the Advanced Settings tab in your account's setup dialog box to enable encrypted logins via the Authentication menu. This single step, however, should secure your password's transmission against any potential snooping.

NOTE   If your ISP uses APOP for authenticated POP, then all you need to do is set the Authentication type to Password, which is the default on the Advanced tab for an account you're configuring on the Account screen of Mail Preferences. If your ISP supports a different type of secure login, you'll need to choose that from the Authentication menu instead.

How Is E-Mail Transmitted to Your Client Application?   Perhaps not as widespread, but gaining popularity is the use of SSL (Secure Sockets Layer) technology for establishing the connection to a mail server. This is the same security used for secure web transactions, enabling the entire transfer process to be encrypted so that even if e-mail transmissions between you and your e-mail server are intercepted, they can't be read easily without breaking a code. Again, you'll need to ask your ISP if this capability is offered and then configure the Advanced tab of your account (in Mail) by turning on the Use SSL option.

Should You Encrypt Messages Yourself?   The final level of security is to encrypt the body of messages. Even if you use SSL for your connection to your mail server, a typical e-mail message still bounces from server to server on the Internet without any secure mechanism to keep the message from being intercepted and read. Generally, this isn't a problem because others probably don't care what your e-mail messages say, and there are billions of messages bouncing around all the time. Still, if you desire more secure communications, you need to encrypt the body of the message. Usually, this is done with a process called *public key encryption*, in which you use your recipient's public key code to encrypt the message so that it can be read only by that recipient when she plugs in her private key passphrase. For this to work, you need to know the recipient's public key, which you can exchange via e-mail or learn from a public key server. (Many people interested in receiving encrypted messages will publish their public keys as part of their e-mail signatures.)

NOTE   The public/private key system can also be used to "sign" an e-mail message, using the key to verify the identity of the sender via that sender's private passphrase.

The most widely used method of encrypting personal messages is Pretty Good Privacy (PGP). Commercial versions of PGP are sold by PGP (`www.pgp.com`), which offers PGP Mail and PGP Disk (among other encryption tools) for Macintosh. Their products aren't cheap, but "personal" versions are offered for a reasonable price if security is a strong issue for you. (The tools secure both encrypted e-mail and encrypted disks, if you're interested.)

Also, open-source development of PGP tools has continued, and various projects such as Open-PGP and its Mac incarnation, GNU Privacy Guard (GnuPG), offer open-source PGP encryption solutions. GnuPG is available for Mac OS X (`http://macgpg.sourceforge.net/`) in the form of downloadable binaries and source code that can be compiled and installed manually.

Although GnuPG is a command-line tool, a graphical front end—GPGKeys—is also available, as well as a number of other tools (the GPGFileTool, GPGPreferences, and GPGDropThing, among others) that need to be installed for the best experience. Also available is GPGMail (`www.sente.ch/software/GPGMail/`), which can be used to integrate the encryption features into Mail. (It actually hacks into Mail, so you'll want to consider carefully if it's compatible with the current version and worth the risk.) Also, GPG Tools (`www.tomsci.com/gpgtools/`) can be used to add such features as decryption capabilities via the Services menu in Mac OS X.

TIP   The site `http://macgpg.sourceforge.net/` also tracks links to AppleScripts and plug-ins that can be used with other e-mail applications, such as Entourage and Eudora.

Installation and use of the tools can take a bit of effort because there are a number of packages to download and work with. (Consult Chapter 23, "Command-Line and Application Magic," for a discussion of installing Darwin-based applications, and read the FAQ and documents that come with GnuPG carefully.) Once they are installed, however, you can use the GUI applications to create encryption keys, encrypt text, and copy the encrypted text into an e-mail message and send it. If you install GPGMail, it will add a PGP menu command to the Message menu in Mail, which can then be used to encrypt messages you're sending and decrypt messages from others.

NOTE   Again, read the Mac GPG FAQ that comes with these various installations to learn how to install and work with Mac GPG. Doing so isn't for the faint-of-heart, but it isn't rocket science, either. Once it is installed and you are educated, you should be able to send and receive encrypted messages without too much trouble.

Avoiding E-Mail Viruses

These days, viruses tend to be distributed more and more often via e-mail and the Internet than via other mechanisms, if only because people are using broadband connections to swap files and e-mail attachments instead of physical disks and removable media. At the same time, the move to Mac OS X has actually opened up the Mac user to more virus and malicious code infections. Mac OS X is based on a Unix variant, and Unix viruses are more prevalent than viruses written for the Classic Mac OS. (The lack of market share for the Classic Mac OS worked in its favor for many security issues because it wasn't seen as a potential target by malicious coders as often as Unix and Microsoft Windows.) With Mac OS X and the modern Internet, it's becoming increasingly important to watch your e-mail closely—especially the attachments—to avoid picking up a virus or activating other malicious code.

NOTE   For definitions and more in-depth explanations of viruses, worms, and other malicious code, see Chapter 26.

So far, no one has come up with a way to infect an e-mail message with a virus, partly because e-mail messages are always ASCII (plain text) documents. (Perhaps some messages with malicious *scripts* embedded in them, aimed at Windows users, would technically qualify.) Virus authors have created the next best thing, though—e-mail *attachment* viruses. Viruses that travel via e-mail, including some that have received a great deal of news attention, work by attaching themselves to an e-mail message. Then, when the attachment is double-clicked by a recipient, the virus generally does two things. First, if it's in a compatible e-mail application, the virus sends itself to everyone in the user's e-mail address book. Then it does whatever else it was designed to do: delete files, change settings, and so on.

Viruses can do these things because Microsoft built scripting commands into Outlook Express, Microsoft Outlook, and Microsoft Entourage that the virus authors exploit. The scripting is (ideally) designed to help automate tasks in the same way that AppleScript helps automate tasks in the Mac OS. Unfortunately, a few security holes in the design of Microsoft's scripting make it fairly easy to exploit for less-laudable purposes. Fortunately (for Mac users, at least), most virus authors write their viruses to damage Microsoft Windows computers because there are many more of them to infect. Still, Mac-specific strains of these viruses have popped up in the past and, using Microsoft applications on a Mac, can replicate the viruses and send them to others.

The solution is to avoid launching an attachment that you're not familiar with; this is especially true if the attachment seems very enticing (using target words such as *love, free,* or *money*). Also, remember that an attachment from a friend isn't necessarily a good thing; many of these viruses are designed to appear to be from your friends and colleagues, which is why viruses exploit the address book feature in the affected e-mail programs. Instead, you should launch and work with only attachments that you specifically expect to receive. When in doubt, contact the person who sent you the message (by phone, if possible) and confirm that he meant to send the attachment. If not, that's a good sign that you should delete the attachment and let that person know that a virus may be at work on his computer.

NOTE   Some virus checkers can check e-mail attachments for viruses as they appear and warn you of trouble. (Norton AntiVirus has the capability, but .Mac's Virex doesn't.) If you have the option, this is good to turn on; if not, remember to check your questionable attachments before launching them.

What's Next?

In this chapter, you learned about Mac OS X's Mail application. You saw the basics of creating an e-mail account, retrieving e-mail, replying, and composing new messages. You also saw how to dig deeper into the Mail application in order to manage your messages with mailboxes, deal with junk mail, automate the filing of messages, format Rich Text messages, and work with attachments. You also learned about some of the issues involving e-mail security and virus protection when it comes to e-mail.

In Part 3, you'll learn more about Apple's multimedia capabilities, including a look at QuickTime's capability to play back video on-screen and over the Internet, as well as Mac OS X's support for digital video technology. You'll be introduced to some of Apple's iApps (iMovie, iTunes, iPhoto). You'll also examine digital image technologies, computer sound, and MP3 music, as well as the speech recognition and handwriting recognition technologies that are built into Mac OS X.

Part 3

Audio, Video, and Your Personal Information

In this section, you will learn how to:

- ◆ View streaming video using QuickTime
- ◆ Manipulate files using QuickTime Pro
- ◆ Play DVDs
- ◆ Listen to music with iTunes
- ◆ Connect to the iPod
- ◆ Work with digital images using Preview and iPhoto
- ◆ Manage your addresses and appointments

Chapter 13

Video Playback and Editing

One of the true advantages of the Mac OS is the level at which QuickTime technology is integrated into the operating system. QuickTime is a far-reaching multimedia technology that makes a number of fun and useful tasks possible, including the playback, translation, and editing of QuickTime movies. QuickTime is more than skin deep, however: it not only incorporates obvious tools such as the QuickTime Player application (which is what enables you to view QuickTime movies on your desktop), it also works at the programming interface level, making it possible for application developers to include quite a few QuickTime capabilities in their programs, utilities, and games.

In this chapter, we'll take a look at QuickTime 7, the latest version included with Mac OS X 10.4. We'll examine it first from a user's perspective—watching and playing back movies and compatible files—as well as from a technology perspective, including a discussion of QuickTime's capability to translate between various file formats. Then, later in the chapter, you'll see the capabilities that the QuickTime Player offers for editing and exporting movie files, especially after you've upgraded to the QuickTime Pro version. Also, you'll see how QuickTime integrates with iMovie, which is included with many Mac OS X installations, enabling you to export movies directly into the Quick-Time file format.

In this chapter:

◆ The Many Facets of QuickTime

◆ The QuickTime Player

◆ QuickTime (and Other Digital Media) on the Internet

◆ Advanced Topics with QuickTime Pro

◆ QuickTime Preferences

◆ Playing DVD Movies

The Many Facets of QuickTime

Apple calls QuickTime a "software architecture," suggesting that QuickTime is much more than what it might seem at first glance—a movie player application. Indeed, QuickTime is a major technical pillar within Mac OS X, responsible for a lot of Mac OS X's inherent capability to deal with multimedia. At its essence, QuickTime enables the Mac OS and its applications to work with *time-based data*—by which we mean data that changes over time. That's usually audio or video data. Like the flipbook animations you may have sketched for yourself on the edge of each page in your notebook or textbook,

QuickTime can display a series of images or sound samples quickly enough to give the illusion of continuous playback.

Of course, QuickTime is much more sophisticated than a flipbook. QuickTime movies can have a number of different *tracks*, so that audio, video, and even text or still graphics can have a time-based relationship to one another. QuickTime movies are generally highly compressed data files, with different *codecs* (compressor/decompressors) being used for different parts of the playback. QuickTime ties all this together with a special file format—the QuickTime Movie format—that enables you to distribute time-based data to other computer users. Here's a quick look at the different elements that constitute QuickTime:

The QuickTime Movie File Format   The QuickTime Movie file format enables you to deal with movie or audio "documents" just as you might deal with Microsoft Word or AppleWorks documents. QuickTime Movie documents often have the filename extension .mov or .qt. Note also that "movie" is something of a misnomer because a QuickTime movie can contain audio data, text tracks, sprites (animated elements), or other non-"movie" data.

QuickTime Translation Capabilities   QuickTime technology gives the QuickTime Player or other QuickTime-enabled applications the capability to translate to and from a number of different video and audio formats, including popular formats for Microsoft Windows and other computing platforms. That makes it easier for programmers to create digital media applications that "play nice" with a variety of file types.

The QuickTime APIs   QuickTime is an underlying technology that's part of Mac OS X, so it isn't just the QuickTime Player that can play back, edit, or translate to and from the QuickTime Movie format. QuickTime provides *application programming interfaces (APIs)* that make it possible for third-party application authors to include these capabilities in their own programs. All sorts of applications can work with the QuickTime system software in any way the developer sees fit. As you're working with Mac applications, you may come across similar QuickTime interfaces and commands (such as the QuickTime Export dialog box or the QuickTime playback controls) in different applications such as the Finder (see Figure 13.1). Likewise, applications such as iMovie integrate directly with QuickTime, using the familiar dialog boxes to import and export edited video to QuickTime movies.

QuickTime Movies

To users, QuickTime movies seem pretty straightforward. You double-click or otherwise launch a QuickTime movie, an audio file, or some other compatible document, and the QuickTime Player launches or activates. Then, that media file appears in its own window in the QuickTime Player. There you can play it, fast-forward through it, pause it, and so forth. The fact is, though, that there's quite a bit of magic that goes on behind the scenes with QuickTime.

First, QuickTime is doing something that's fairly close to impossible: playing full-motion video by placing one image after another (the *frames* of the video) on the screen up to 30 times per second, while synchronizing a soundtrack and (depending on the movie) other types of data as well. The reason that's nearly impossible is that individual, full-color image files can take up lots of storage space—multiple megabytes in some cases. Macs are pretty sophisticated, but it's still a stretch to ask them to load and process 30MB to 40MB of data per second, especially if you're also asking them to do anything else, such as respond to user input, check your e-mail in the background, and so on.

FIGURE 13.1
Because QuickTime is a technology that's part of Mac OS X, even Finder windows can play back QuickTime movies.

Yet QuickTime seems capable of doing this, thanks to a few tricks. Most QuickTime movies are actually quite heavily compressed using the codecs mentioned earlier. The codecs enable a Quick-Time movie to store and process much less data than might seem necessary at first. That's because the codecs toss out a lot of redundant information; for instance, if the sky is blue, you don't need to store each blue pixel when a simple instruction such as "paint the next 300 pixels blue" would suffice. Such compression schemes are called *lossy* schemes because the more you compress, the more image quality you lose, often in the form of *artifacts*, or glitches, in the image playback. (For instance, since a blue sky in an image is likely not to be uniformly blue, the more this sort of compression takes place, the more detail is lost.) Audio portions of a QuickTime movie also can be compressed.

Besides compressing each image, QuickTime movies also save storage space and processing time by changing only those parts of the image that need to be changed. Each movie has multiple *keyframes*, which are special frames of the movie that are fully updated every second or so. Then each nonkey-frame image is used to update the changes between it and the previous keyframe. For instance, in a QuickTime movie showing a person talking, perhaps only the areas around the person's mouth and eyes need to be updated as he speaks, at least until another keyframe comes along in a fraction of a second. If that's the case, the QuickTime movie can store only those changes between frames, instead of all the data that would comprise each individual frame. With less data per frame to store, the movie file is smaller, and it plays back smoother because there's less data to process.

Finally, another trick employed by QuickTime cuts down on the amount of data needed for a movie by fooling the eye a bit. Although television generally uses about 30 frames per second to show motion (actually, NTSC, the North American standard, uses 29.97 frames per second, and the European and Asian PAL standard uses 25 frames per second), that many frames per second (*fps*, or the *frame rate*) isn't always necessary. Theatrical films, for instance, show 24fps; for CD-ROM or Internet-based video, you can often get away with as few as 12fps and still show acceptable video quality and fairly smooth motion. With fewer frames stored, QuickTime files are smaller, and QuickTime doesn't have to work as hard to render the motion on-screen.

Besides all this video magic, the QuickTime Movie format is capable of storing audio data, text data, and other elements (such as animated graphics and even Macromedia Flash buttons and animations that can react to mouse clicks), all of which can be held together by that common QuickTime Movie file format. As a result, QuickTime movies can be all sorts of things besides just movies or videos. They can be interactive, they can be sound-only "movies" without a video component, and they can even include different tracks in various languages, with text-based subtitles or even different chapters that you can move between. The QuickTime file format is versatile enough to deal with pretty much everything that's considered *multimedia* in today's computing environment. And the file format is only one aspect of QuickTime.

What Can QuickTime Play?

So QuickTime can deal with QuickTime Movie files—that much is evident. But a big advantage of the application is that its underlying technology also makes it possible for a Macintosh to work with a variety of other file formats that fit under the general heading "multimedia." That technology includes the capability to translate between file formats common to Microsoft Windows, Unix, and other computing platforms. What's more, these translations don't have to take place within the QuickTime Player—application developers are free to add these translation capabilities to third-party applications.

Besides video and soundtracks, QuickTime movies can incorporate text tracks, animated elements, and even clickable controls, thanks to Macromedia Flash support. QuickTime can also play back QuickTime VR (virtual reality) scenes, which are special panoramic or 3D image movies that you can rotate or move around in (see the section "Playing QuickTime VR Movies," later in this chapter).

That covers the native formats. Here's a quick look at some of the other video file formats that QuickTime can play back and translate:

AVI (.avi)   Audio Video Interleaved (AVI) is a popular digital movie format used on Microsoft Windows computers. QuickTime can also work with the OpenDML extensions to the AVI format.

OMF   Avid Technology, a developer of high-end video editing applications and hardware, created the Open Media Format specification for exchanging high-end video data. QuickTime supports that format, so Mac applications can exchange data with Avid and similar systems.

MPEG (.mpg or .mpeg)   The Moving Picture Experts Group (MPEG) format (actually MPEG-1) is popular for CD-based and Internet-based movies. You can load an MPEG-1 file into the QuickTime Player and play it back or even translate it to QuickTime Movie format. MPEG-2 is the standard for DVD movies, and it can't be played back in the QuickTime Player. (You can, however, pay extra to add the capability, via the QuickTime MPEG-2 Playback Component, available at http:// www.apple.com/quicktime/mpeg2/ on Apple's site. Likewise, other applications can be used to translate between the QuickTime format and MPEG-2.) You can, however, play back MPEG-4, the new standard for streaming video that Apple supports in QuickTime. (In fact, MPEG-4 was based, in part, on QuickTime technology.)

NOTE   In QuickTime 7, Apple has updated MPEG-4 to support the H.264 codec, which offers a reported four-fold increase in quality and frame size for downloadable, highly compressed movies.

3GPP   The 3GPP (Third Generation Partnership Project) standard is the agreed-upon standard for distributing multimedia data on wireless networks, as in portable phones and personal digital assistants. 3GPP movies are highly compressed and based on the MPEG-4 standard, which means the latest versions of QuickTime (and the applications based on QuickTime) can export to 3GPP fairly easily. The QuickTime Player can play back 3GPP content natively.

DV Stream (.dv)   Digital camcorders store images in a computer file format rather than on analog tape in VHS or Betamax format. This computer file is a digital video file (DV or DV Stream), which QuickTime can launch and play back directly. If you work with iMovie or other Apple movie-editing software, you may find yourself exporting DV Stream files using the QuickTime Pro Player for some editing and then reimporting the DV Stream file into iMovie or Final Cut Pro. One word of caution: DV Stream files are *huge*, requiring up to 3.5MB of storage space per second of video.

QuickTime can handle more than just video formats, however. It can also launch, play back, and translate between many different audio file formats, such as these:

AAC   Advanced Audio Coding (AAC) is the audio component of MPEG-4 video and a more efficient rival for the dominant music codec, MP3. AAC is gaining popularity for playback over the Internet and as part of high-quality multimedia movies. It's also a strong audio codec for use over wireless networks (for example, for audio distributed to wireless phones and personal digital assistants) and will likely become increasingly common for all sorts of digital audio storage and playback.

MPEG-3 (.mp3)   An enduringly popular audio file format for storing and selling digital music is the MPEG Level 3 format, also called MP3. This format offers a high level of compression while still maintaining almost CD-quality sound, resulting in files that require only about 1MB per minute of playback. These features have made MP3s popular for Internet downloads and swaps, and that popularity has encouraged Apple to include the capability to play back MP3s in the QuickTime Player.

AIFF (.aif or .aiff)   The Audio Interchange File Format (AIFF) has been an Apple standard for a number of years and is still very popular for recording and playing back sounds and music.

WAV (.wav)   WAV (short for *wavetable*) is a common format on the Microsoft Windows platform, used much the same way as AIFF—for recording small sound files, sound effects, and occasionally longer sound bites.

AU (.au)   AU (short for *audio*) is a common Unix-based audio format, originally developed by Sun Microsystems.

Sound Designer II   Many Mac-based sound-editing applications can work with the file format that was once the most popular among them: Sound Designer II. The QuickTime Player and applications based on QuickTime technology can work with such files, too.

MIDI (.mid or .midi)   Musical Instrument Digital Interface (MIDI) is a special case. A MIDI file is actually a set of instructions to MIDI-capable musical instruments—it's not a digital audio format as much as it's a special format all its own. Still, QuickTime includes a MIDI Musical Instruments library that enables QuickTime to play MIDI files directly and save MIDI information as a QuickTime movie.

TIP   QuickTime uses a built-in music synthesizer library for playing back MIDI files on your Mac—it's decent, but you have other options. If you've installed a third-party MIDI playback device or library, you can choose QuickTime Player ➢ Preferences ➢ QuickTime Preferences and then click the Music category. On the Music Preferences screen, you can choose a new Synthesizer for MIDI playback; click that synthesizer's row in the Default column to make it the default.

Want more? QuickTime can also translate between various still image formats. (This capability isn't built directly into the QuickTime Player, but it's available to other graphical applications that are based on QuickTime technology. For instance, Preview, the image-viewing application installed with Mac OS X, can translate between these different image formats.) The possible formats include TIFF, PICT, PDF, Windows Bitmap (BMP), Adobe Photoshop, Portable Network Graphics (PNG), JPEG, and GIF files. QuickTime can even work with Macromedia Flash data and import and export some data as FLC animation documents.

As mentioned, all these capabilities are found in QuickTime technology, where application developers can get at the APIs and make the tools available to users. One such application is the QuickTime Player (particularly the Pro version), which is described in the following section.

NOTE In real-world applications, QuickTime technology really does offer benefits. For instance, many QuickTime-enabled applications can make on-the-fly translations between image formats—drag a TIFF or PICT image to your QuickTime-enabled web page design applications or translate it easily to a web-friendly JPEG or PNG format. That's possible because the developer can tap into the tools that QuickTime makes available to the programmer. It's an advantage that not everyone knows is going on behind the scenes, but it's exactly what makes QuickTime such an important underlying technology.

The QuickTime Player

Mac OS X includes the QuickTime Player, an application designed not only as a showcase for QuickTime technology but as a practical little application in its own right. The QuickTime Player can be used to play back just about any type of QuickTime-compatible file you can throw at it, including audio, movie, and text-only documents and files. If you've got something that you think is time based, and you're trying to "play" it, the QuickTime Player is where you should start.

NOTE We'll cover this in more depth later in the chapter, but a big part of the QuickTime experience is revealed when you sign up and pay for a QuickTime Pro license from Apple, currently about $30. You order that license online and then enter a registration code in the QuickTime pane of System Preferences. When you do, a number of new features are revealed in QuickTime, including the ability to play files at full screen, to edit portions of the video, and, in QuickTime 7, to record video clips directly to a QuickTime movie. So, we'll touch on some of those features here before digging completely into the QuickTime Pro section later in the chapter.

Playing QuickTime Movies

You can open a QuickTime-compatible file in any of the standard ways: double-click the file, drag and drop the file onto a QuickTime Player icon (or the Player's icon on the Dock), or use the File ➤ Open File command in the QuickTime Player's menu. Note that some files—images, audio files, and non-QuickTime video files—won't always open directly in the QuickTime Player when you double-click them. (They may be associated with other applications, as discussed in Chapter 4, "Using Applications.") If that's the case, drag and drop the file onto the QuickTime Player icon or use the File ➤ Open command.

Once you have a file open in the QuickTime Player, you'll see the QuickTime Player interface. This interface is the same whether you're dealing with audio or video (remember, QuickTime documents are collectively called "movies" even if they don't have a video track). The Player includes a number of controls that should be fairly familiar—they're based on the typical controls found on a VCR or cassette player (see Figure 13.2).

To select one of the controls, you simply click the button with the mouse; for Review and Fast Forward *while* the movie is playing, you need to click and hold down the mouse button. To select a volume level, click and drag the small Volume slider.

You can also use the keyboard to control some commands with the QuickTime Player:

◆ Press the spacebar to toggle between Play and Pause.

◆ Press the left and right arrows to move back one frame or forward one frame, respectively.

◆ To play the movie backward, hold down the Shift key and double-click the movie image. Keep holding the shift key for as long as you want the playback to continue.

◆ Press Option+left to move to the beginning of the movie (or of the selected portion of the movie); press Option+right to move to the end of the movie (or of the selection).

◆ Press the up and down arrows to change the volume level, and press Option+up to jump to full volume or Option+down to jump to mute.

TIP   If you have the QuickTime Pro upgrade, you can also use ⌘F to enter full-screen display, Esc to exit full-screen, ⌘+0 to view the movie at half size, ⌘+1 for actual size and ⌘+2 for double size.

FIGURE 13.2
The QuickTime Player offers the same controls for audio and video playback.

If you'd like to go directly to a particular part of your QuickTime movie, you can drag the small *playhead* around on the *scrubber bar*, which is the small scrolling area that shows you where you are currently while you're playing your movie. You can also simply click on the scrubber bar to place the playhead.

You can move the playhead to a new position to move immediately to a different part of the movie. If you do so while the movie is playing, the QuickTime Player won't miss a beat—it'll pick up and continue playing from that point.

As in many Mac OS X windows, you can drag the bottom-right corner (the resize area) of a Quick-Time movie window to change the size of the window. Because it's a movie, you'll also notice that the size of the video track (if you have one) changes as you drag the window's size. By default, the video image will maintain its current *aspect ratio*, meaning that the ratio of its width to its height will stay the same. If you'd like to distort that ratio so that the image is exactly the same size as the window that you drag to create, hold down the Shift key while you drag the resize area.

TIP   If you drag the image out of proportion and want it to snap back, select View ➤ Actual Size from the QuickTime Player's menu or just resize the window again without holding down the Shift modifier.

While you're viewing a QuickTime movie with a video track, you also have a few basic options for changing the size of the video. Select the View menu, and you'll see Actual Size, Double Size, and Full Screen options. Although a movie that's originally small usually won't look good if it fills the screen (it becomes very *pixelated* with details that are difficult to make out), you can double some Internet- or CD-based QuickTime movies and have them look pretty good on your Mac's screen.

The QuickTime Player also has some hidden sound and video controls that you can access by selecting Window ➤ Show AV Controls. The controls will appear in a separate window, enabling you to set Balance, Bass, and Treble responses, as well as make some choices about how the video plays back.

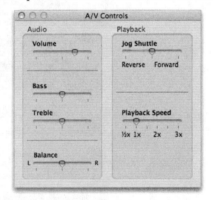

QuickTime Player Preferences

In the preferences (QuickTime Player ➤ Preferences), you'll find options that govern how QuickTime movies play back.

At the top of the dialog box are options that control the automatic behavior of the QuickTime Player, including Automatically Play Movies When Opened and Open Movies in New Players, an option that opens each newly double-clicked movie in a new Player window. (Opening additional players can be particularly useful when editing QuickTime movies, which is discussed in the section "Editing in QuickTime Pro Player," later in this chapter.)

You can also choose some Sound options. You can turn off Play Sound in Front-Most Player Only if you'd like to hear more than one movie's sound at once (or if you'd like to listen to one movie even while you're moving others around on the screen). Turn off the Play Sound When Application Is in the

Background option if you want to hear a movie's audio only when the QuickTime Player is in the foreground. If you like, you can turn off the Content Guide movie that appears by default whenever you open the QuickTime Player. Finally, the preferences include an option that enables you to pause movies when you log out using the Fast User Switching option discussed in Chapter 5, "Personalizing Mac OS X."

The QuickTime Controller

You won't always be playing QuickTime movies in the QuickTime Player. Often you'll find yourself playing the movies in Finder windows to preview them or playing them in other applications where you've embedded the QuickTime movie in a document. You may even find yourself controlling a QuickTime movie that's playing over the Internet in a web browser window. In those cases, you'll see the somewhat simpler controller (compared to the QuickTime Player), shown in Figure 13.3.

FIGURE 13.3
The QuickTime
controller within other
applications, such as the
Finder's Info window,
offers simpler controls.

You may encounter another special case as well. In some documents and applications, you won't even see the simple controller. Instead, you'll see a *poster frame* (a single image from the movie, often the first frame), along with a small QuickTime icon in the bottom-left corner.

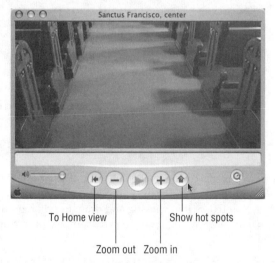

Click the movie once, and it should begin playing. If it doesn't, that may be because it's set to play automatically when the application enters a particular mode. For instance, in presentation applications such as Microsoft PowerPoint, QuickTime movies can be set to play automatically when a particular slide is displayed. (Remember, QuickTime movies can be audio only, meaning that a

PowerPoint presentation, for example, could be narrated using a voice recording saved as a Quick-Time Movie file.)

NOTE Not all poster frames have a QuickTime movie icon, but one that doesn't generally has text in the frame identifying it as a QuickTime movie and inviting you to click the frame to begin playback. This is especially true of the movie trailers that Apple makes available on the Web at www.quicktime.com.

Playing QuickTime VR Movies

A QuickTime VR movie is a slightly different animal—actually two animals. A QuickTime VR movie can take one of two forms: a 360-degree panoramic view that you can maneuver with the mouse or a 3D view of an individual object that you can manipulate to see from all sides. QuickTime VR is a particularly popular technology with real estate agents, who use the scrolling panoramas to show entire rooms in houses that are for sale, and car manufacturers, who use 3D VR movies to show a car from all sides.

When you launch a QuickTime VR movie, you'll see a slightly different QuickTime Player window with different controls for manipulating the movie. Because you don't play a VR movie linearly, the Play button is grayed. Instead, you'll see buttons for zooming in and out, for returning to the home view of the movie, and for revealing *hot points*—points that can be clicked within the virtual reality scene. (A hot point can be clicked to move to a new scene—sort of like a 3D action adventure game—or to view more information or even a web page about the clicked item.) Figure 13.4 shows the unique controls used for QuickTime VR movies.

FIGURE 13.4
The QuickTime Player
controls change when
you view VR movies.
(VR example courtesy of
Ray Broussard, www.
photographicvr.com)

Along with the new controls come new behaviors for the mouse. If you click and drag within the scene, you'll move it; either you'll move the panorama or you'll rotate the 3D object, depending on what you're viewing. You'll note that clicking and dragging changes the mouse pointer to either an eight-way pointer or a fist, depending on the type of movie you're viewing. You can also use keyboard keys and modifiers:

- ◆ Zoom in and out by pressing the Shift and Control keys, respectively.

- ◆ Use the arrow keys to move around in the scene.

- ◆ If you're viewing a panorama and the pointer turns into a forward-pointing arrow, you've found a hot spot. Click the mouse button to load the associated movie or web document.

Registering QuickTime Pro

There is one dirty little secret about the QuickTime Player that you should know: it's keeping stuff from you. Specifically, it's disabling a number of commands, ranging from additional viewing options to commands that enable you to save and translate between different file formats. Why? Apple wants you to pay for those privileges. For $29.95 (at the time of this writing), you can register QuickTime with Apple, which results in a registration code. Simply visit www.apple.com/quicktime/ and look for the registration link (or click the Register On-Line button in the Registration dialog sheet that you can access from the QuickTime pane of System Preferences).

NOTE   Even if you already have a QuickTime Pro registration key for an earlier version of Quick-Time, you'll need to pay again for a QuickTime Pro 7 registration key. With version 7, Apple has decided to charge all users again to upgrade.

Once you have a registration code, enter that number (along with your name and the name of your organization, if applicable) in the Registration window within the QuickTime Player (from the Application menu, select QuickTime Player ➢ Registration). That actually opens the QuickTime pane of System Preferences, which you can do directly, as well. On the Register tab, enter your name and the registration code you received from Apple.

After you've entered the requisite information, click the OK button. If your registration is accepted, you'll have the QuickTime Pro Player with all of its additional capabilities, including these:

◆ The capability to save, import, and export movies in various formats, including the ability to save movies from the Internet (in many cases)

◆ Additional movie sizes in the View menu, including the Present Movie command, which blanks the rest of the screen and shows the movie at the largest size possible

◆ The View ➢ Loop Back and Forth command, which enables you to play a movie forward then backward repeatedly

◆ Additional options in the View menu, including the ability to set a poster frame (the frame of the movie that's used as its main image and icon)

- The capability to select a portion of the movie by holding down the Shift key and dragging along the scrubber bar (also, the ability to play only that selection using the View ➤ Play Selection Only command

- Enabled editing and special-effects commands, including the capability to cut, copy, paste, enable, disable, or delete tracks selectively within an individual movie file

- The capability to create and edit MPEG-4 content

- The capability to create "media skins" that can be used to change the look and feel of the QuickTime Player window

- The ability to record audio and video via a digital camera that's connected to your Mac

- Additional Automator workflow commands that enable you to perform a number of automatic tasks using QuickTime technology

You'll see more on the editing features of QuickTime movies later in this chapter. First, though, let's move on to some additional freebie capabilities: viewing streaming QuickTime movies over the Internet.

NOTE   Apple has instructions for creating media skins on its website at `www.apple.com/quicktime/tools_tips/tutorials/mediaskins/` if you'd like to dig into changing the look of the QuickTime player. You can also download and use a number of AppleScripts that Apple has created for working with QuickTime and the QuickTime Player from `www.apple.com/applescript/quicktime/`.

QuickTime (and Other Digital Media) on the Internet

As discussed in Chapter 11, "The Web, Online Security, .Mac, Sherlock, and iChat," Apple's Safari features a QuickTime plug-in that enables you to view QuickTime movies that are embedded in web pages. (Other third-party browsers, such as Netscape and OmniWeb, can also utilize the QuickTime plug-in.) This trick makes it possible for a basic QuickTime interface to appear right there in the browser window, where you can play, pause, review, and fast-forward a movie that's downloaded from a remote Internet server.

Beyond that capability, still other cool tricks are made possible by QuickTime's Internet awareness. One such feature is called *streaming*—the capability to display a QuickTime movie while the data for that movie is still being downloaded to your Mac. With a quick enough Internet connection, you can watch live events (either QuickTime or MPEG-4 based) or view saved QuickTime movies almost immediately upon clicking the link. This differs from embedded and downloaded movies, where generally you must wait for the entire movie (or almost the entire movie) to download to your Mac before you can see it displayed.

Streaming has become very popular in a number of different forums, from political websites to sites that play back movie trailers and short films, such as iFilm.com (`www.ifilm.com`). Apple has perfected the art of the streaming video tradeshow keynote speech, and you'll find CEO Steve Jobs' speeches available at `www.apple.com/quicktime/`. More and more television network websites are making streaming video available. Streaming video isn't a distant vision—it's actually beginning to become fairly common, thanks in part to MPEG-4 and QuickTime.

NOTE   One thing that does require the upgrade to QuickTime Pro is the capability to save some Internet-based QuickTime movies to your local disk. If you've upgraded, you can hold down the Control key while clicking an embedded QuickTime movie and choose Save As QuickTime Movie from the context menu. You'll then be able to give the movie a name and save it to disk for repeated viewing. (Note that some servers will use special commands to disable this feature, and you won't be able to save live, streaming movies.)

Streaming QuickTime

You can view a streaming QuickTime movie in one of two ways: in the simple QuickTime controls of an embedded streaming movie on a web page or in the QuickTime Player itself. Generally, you won't have much control over which way you view—it's up to the web developer who created the page where the movie is hosted. Click a link to a streaming movie, and either it will appear on the page or the QuickTime Player will be launched, in which case the movie will appear in a new QuickTime Player window.

TIP   One Internet viewing feature that requires QuickTime Pro, QuickTime Streaming Server comes with Mac OS X Server and can be installed for free on Mac OS X—see `www.apple.com/quicktime/products/qtss/` on Apple's website. (There's also an open-source version that Apple has released that has been turned into freeware ports to Mac OS 9 as well as to some open source operating systems.)

How do you know that you are watching (or listening to, if the stream is audio only) a streaming QuickTime movie? You'll know because you'll see special messages in the scrubber bar area of the window. First you'll see the Negotiating message, which means the QuickTime Player is determining what protocols and how much data your Internet connection can handle, which in turn determines the size and quality of the image. (The Connection Speed setting in QuickTime Preferences can affect this, as discussed at the end of this section.) Then you'll see the Waiting For Media message, which shows you how much QuickTime data is being stored temporarily on your hard disk so that the playback can be as smooth and "skip"-free as possible.

There are two basic types of streaming video: stored video and live *webcasts*. You can't use the Review and Fast Forward buttons while viewing either type of streaming movie. With stored video, however, you can move the playhead around on the scrubber bar to start viewing the movie at a different point. When you do this, the Player is forced to reconnect to the server and renegotiate the connection, so it may take a few seconds before you see the video.

NOTE   Mac-native streaming movies can be in one of two formats: QuickTime and MPEG-4. From the user's perspective, there's not too much difference in how you watch the streams—you tend to use your eyes and ears. As far as initiating the stream, you'll see some pages on the Internet that have links to both MPEG-4 and QuickTime (and perhaps other formats) so as to be as compatible as possible with computers out there. Since your Mac is MPEG-4 compatible (by virtue of the fact that it's running Mac OS X), it's probably the best choice for overall video and audio quality.

With live webcasts, you generally can't move around in the streaming video at all, because you're watching the event as it's happening. With some webcasts, though, you can click the Pause button, which is really like pressing the power button on a TV. When you subsequently click the Play button, the webcast will pick up at the current moment in the webcast, as if you had turned a TV back on again.

Streaming movies act differently from regular web-based movies because the QuickTime Player is actually connecting to a different type of Internet server. Instead of connecting to a web server, it's accessing a special type of QuickTime movie (called a *hinted* movie) that has been stored on a Quick-Time Streaming Server. The file is then accessed using a different Internet protocol, the Real-Time Transport Protocol (RTP). So, URLs to streaming QuickTime movies begin with `rtp://`. In fact, the QuickTime Player includes a File ➤ Open URL command that brings up an entry box where you can enter a URL for the streaming movie.

If the movie isn't a streaming movie, it can still be accessed directly via the File ➤ Open URL command, but with a conventional URL such as `http://www.ourcomp.com/movies/mymovie.mov`. (Note that some streaming movies can use the `http://` protocol, depending on the server.) In that case, the movie will be downloaded to your Mac as usual and played back in the QuickTime Player window.

You can set certain preferences for the way streaming movies are sent to your Mac. Select Quick-Time Player ➤ QuickTime Preferences, and then select the Streaming tab. In the QuickTime pane of the System Preferences application, click the Connection tab. Then use the Streaming Speed menu to tell QuickTime Player what sort of connection you have to the Internet. This enables it to configure an optimum data stream automatically whenever possible. (QuickTime 7 has an Automatic setting that works in almost all instances.)

The Enable Instant-On check box can be used to toggle the instant-on feature, which causes Quick-Time movies to be playing without a delay; you should turn this off (or change the amount of delay before streams begin) if you notice that you often have trouble with the quality of your streaming media playback.

Other Movie Formats

Occasionally, you'll encounter a movie format on the Internet that isn't directly supported by the QuickTime Player—or, at least, when you click a link, it won't launch in the QuickTime Player. This is particularly true of other streaming formats, such as those used by the Windows Media Player and Real Networks' RealPlayer. To view those streaming media types, you'll need to download their individual player applications.

At the time of this writing, Microsoft has made a Windows Media Player application available for Mac OS X (`www.microsoft.com/mac/`), but it doesn't support embedded Windows Media streams, only those that will launch the player as a helper application. Real Networks has released a version of its player (`www.real.com/mac/`) that enables you to view Real Media streams—look for the link to the free player if you're not interested in the subscription service. (Chapter 11 has more specifics on setting up your web browser to work with helper applications.)

Advanced Topics with QuickTime Pro

In the section "Registering QuickTime Pro," earlier in this chapter, you saw some of the benefits that come from paying to register and upgrade your version of QuickTime. Although some of those features are additional options for playing and saving movies, the real benefits are found in some considerably more sophisticated tools that enable you to use the QuickTime Player as a QuickTime file translator and a movie editor of sorts. In this section, we'll cover some of those capabilities in more depth.

Translating File Formats

QuickTime technology enables application developers to offer quite a few different translation capabilities between movie formats, audio formats, and even still-image formats. The free QuickTime Player doesn't give much access to these capabilities, but once you've upgraded to QuickTime Pro, you can access more of them. They break down into import and export features.

By default, most of the movie formats that QuickTime can deal with will simply open up in the player. If you have trouble associating a movie with the QuickTime Player, try dragging the movie's icon to the Player's icon, or use the File ➤ Open command from within the QuickTime Player and locate the movie using the Open dialog box.

SHARING FILES

To save the movie from a non-QuickTime movie file format (whether or not it includes a video track) as a QuickTime Movie file, choose File ➤ Save and use the standard Save dialog box to select a folder and give the file a name.

Before you click Save in the Save dialog box, you'll need to choose either Save as a Self-Contained Movie or Save as a Reference Movie. The Save as a Reference Movie option creates a QuickTime movie that doesn't necessarily include all of the translated movie's data in the new movie file. In other words, you'll still need to have the original movie file available on your disk—in fact, the original often needs to be in the same location. Because all of the translated movie data is included in the newly created QuickTime Movie file, the Save as a Self-Contained Movie option is the better choice if you plan to place the QuickTime Movie file on a removable disk or network volume or if you intend to transmit the movie over the Internet.

Once you've made your choice, click Save.

EXPORTING FILES

You use the Save command to save any sort of imported or edited movie as a QuickTime Movie file. But what if you want to save a QuickTime movie in some other multimedia file format? In that case, you need to export. With the movie that you'd like to export open, choose File ➤ Export from the menu.

NOTE Actually, there are two reasons to export your movie. The first is to get the movie into a different file format. You can export QuickTime movie data as a Windows-friendly AVI movie, for instance, or you can export an MP3 audio file as an AIFF file for easy editing in Macintosh sound editors. Second, you can export data from a QuickTime Movie file to another QuickTime Movie file. This might seem redundant, but performing this export gives you the opportunity to make some advanced choices—you can select a different codec and quality levels via the Options button discussed in this section.

You may notice that the dialog box, shown in Figure 13.5, looks a little different from the standard Save dialog box. The Save Exported File As dialog box includes some additional menus as well as an Options button.

In the Export menu, choose how you'd like the movie to be exported. You'll find two basic types of options: Movie To and Sound To. If you're exporting a QuickTime movie that has both video and audio components, you'll see both types of options. If your movie has only a soundtrack, you'll see only Sound To options; if your movie has only a video track, you'll see only Movie To options. The Movie To options include a number of file formats—both video formats and still-image formats—that were discussed in the section "What Can QuickTime Play?" earlier in this chapter; likewise, the Sound To options include many of the audio file formats discussed in that section. You'll notice that not *all* of the file formats discussed there are shown in these options; that's because QuickTime can read, import, and play back more formats than it can export to. For more export options, you generally need to turn to a third-party application such as Discreet's Cleaner series of applications. (Discreet's web address is www.discreet.com.)

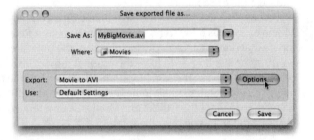

After you've chosen an option in the Export menu, you select from the Use menu *how* the movie will be exported. The options you see in the Use menu depend on the type of export you're performing. If you're exporting a movie that includes video to the AVI format, you'll see a few preset options for the compression and frame rate for that particular movie.

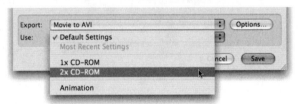

If you export the audio within your movie to an audio file format, you'll see options in the Use menu for selecting the quality of the sound file, such as 44.1 kHz 16-Bit Stereo (CD quality) or 11.025 kHz 16-Bit Mono (approximately AM radio quality). Make your selection in the Use menu, and then click Save to save the exported file.

Before you click the Save button, however, you may want to dig even deeper into the compression settings. The Options button gives you access to the advanced settings that are possible for audio and video compression and quality levels. You'll need to know a little something about codecs and other settings in order to make sense of these options. (That's why the Use menu is there; it offers simpler preset codec and quality settings.)

After you click the Options button, the particular Movie Settings dialog box you see depends on the type of file you're exporting to. If you're exporting video and audio to a movie format, you'll see a Movie Settings dialog box that includes controls for both video and sound settings. Select either the Video Settings button or the Sound Settings button to dig deeper into those settings (see Figure 13.6, which shows the QuickTime-specific options). Note that if you've chosen to export to QuickTime Movie format, you can also choose Prepare for Internet Streaming. (If you're exporting to other formats, you won't see that option.)

NOTE For some video formats, you'll see some additional buttons in QuickTime 7, such as Filter and Size. Click those to dig deeper into the effects and scaling options that you can set for your exported video.

FIGURE 13.6
Select Options when exporting to a movie format, and you can then select both the Video and Sound Settings buttons to set quality levels.

If you're exporting directly to a still-image format, clicking Options brings up the Compression Settings dialog box. Here you can select the type of compressor to use for the image you're creating. For most still images, you'll use a compressor that matches the image file format, such as TIFF for TIFF files and JPEG for JPEG files, with the exception of Picture, which can also use JPEG compression. You may also find other settings such as a color depth menu and a Quality slider. The higher the quality, the larger the exported image file will be.

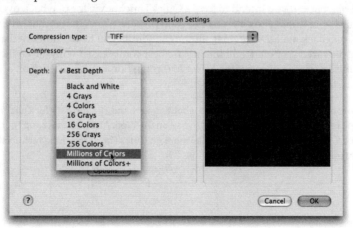

TIP   The Compression Settings dialog box is also what you'll see if you've chosen Options for exporting to a movie file format and then clicked the Video Settings button (shown in Figure 13.6). For video, however, you'll often have additional options in the Motion section, including the number of frames per second and the data rate for the movie.

If you're exporting directly to an audio file format, you'll see the Sound Settings dialog box. Here you can choose a compressor (codec) for the audio file, along with a *sample rate* (the kHz number that contributes to sound quality), a *size* (either 8-bit or 16-bit), and whether the sound should be exported as mono or as stereo.

TIP   This Sound Settings dialog box is also what you'll see if you've chosen Options for exporting to a movie file format, such as QuickTime file format, and then clicked the Settings button (shown in Figure 13.6) in the Sound section of the Options dialog.

What do you select for all these settings? Unfortunately, getting deep into which codec to use for which circumstance—and how to optimize the settings in each case—is a bit outside the scope of this book. For QuickTime movies, the H.264 and Sorensen codecs are recommended for hard-disk and CD-ROM playback; if you intend to save a QuickTime movie for playback over the Internet, the Use menu in the Export dialog box offers some good presets. (Don't forget that MPEG-4 movies are a great choice for playback over the Internet, although it limits you to an audience that has relatively recent playback software.) As noted, still images are best compressed with the codec that matches the file format, for example, TIFF codec for TIFF file format. For a quick discussion of audio quality, see the "Understanding Audio Quality" sidebar.

TIP   Apple offers additional information about codecs and file formats for QuickTime "authors" at www.apple.com/quicktime/tools_tips/ on the Web. Also, see www.apple.com/quicktime/products/qtss/ on Apple's website for more on QuickTime streaming technology and the QuickTime Streaming Server.

UNDERSTANDING AUDIO QUALITY

While video quality is a function of codecs, frame rate, and keyframes, audio quality is measured by different standards. The key factors for audio quality are the sample rate (measured in kilohertz), the sample size (either 8-bit or 16-bit), and the number of channels (mono or stereo).

When a computer stores a digital sound file, it does so by creating thousands of *samples* per second of that sound. Unlike a cassette tape or similar analog device, a computer can't simply record the analog source; instead, it takes samples of the sound and records them digitally. The more samples per second, the truer the reproduction of the sound is. But more samples means a larger computer file, so there's some balancing to be done.

A digital recording at CD quality has a sample rate of 44.1kHz, or 44,100 samples per second. FM radio quality is about 22kHz, and AM radio quality is about 11kHz. Much lower than that, and the sound file approaches the quality of a typical telephone call.

The next indicator of audio quality is the *sample size*, which is usually either 8-bit or 16-bit, meaning that either 256 numbers or 65,536 numbers can be used to represent the sample. Sixteen-bit is much preferred in this case because the human ear can distinguish more than 256 sounds; in an 8-bit sample, a lot of the quality of the sound is lost by rounding down the sound to those 256 numbers. An 8-bit sound file requires a lot less storage space, but it's an extreme compromise.

Finally, the *channel depth*, or number of channels used, means simply that you can select mono or stereo sound for your exported sound files. Mono takes up less space; stereo, of course, offers better sound quality.

Editing in QuickTime Pro Player

Once you've upgraded to QuickTime Pro, you'll find that you're free not only to save and export your movies but to edit them as well. Using the scrubber bar and playhead, you can select portions of your QuickTime movies and copy and paste them between other movies. You can also enable and disable tracks within movies and paste one track over another, if desired.

TIP With a movie open in QuickTime Player, select Window ➤ Show Movie Properties or press ⌘ +J to see the Movie Properties palette. You'll find a number of property settings you can play with, including some that let you adjust the volume and quality settings and even perform a special effect or two. Note also that you may need to convert your videos to QuickTime or MPEG-4 format in order to edit them.

SELECTING MOVIE PORTIONS

You begin editing in QuickTime Player by selecting part of a movie that you'd like to copy or cut from the current movie. You can do this in a few different ways. One way is to place the playhead on the scrubber bar at the point in the movie where you'd like to begin the selection. Hold down the Shift key and drag the playhead to the end point of your selection. You can also position the movie at the starting position, then Shift+click to select the end point of the selection. When you've done that, a portion of your movie will be grayed (selected) in the scrubber bar.

TIP   Hold down the Shift key while pressing the left and right arrows to fine-tune your selection with the playhead.

You can also make a selection (or change an existing one) by dragging the small selection triangles that appear beneath the scrubber bar. The triangles represent the "in" and "out" points on your selection, so you can drag them around to make a more exact choice.

Once you've made a selection, you might want to clear it so that you can try again. To do that, select Edit ➢ Select None or press ⌘+B. Notice also that you can select the entire movie by choosing Edit ➢ Select All or pressing ⌘+A.

EDITING COMMANDS

With a portion of your movie selected, you're ready to issue a command. Using the Edit menu, you can choose Edit ➢ Copy to place that selection on the Mac's Clipboard or Edit ➢ Cut to place the selection on the Clipboard and remove it from the current movie. Then you can move to another Quick-Time movie window, place the playhead, and select Edit ➢ Paste to paste the selection into the target movie (see Figure 13.7).

NOTE   Remember that you can opt to have QuickTime open new movies in their own Player windows automatically, which is convenient for editing work. Select QuickTime Player ➢ Preferences and on the General tab turn on the Open Movies in New Players option in the Player Preferences dialog box.

As you might guess, it's best to copy and paste between movies that are the same size (in width and height). If you paste together movies of different sizes, you'll end up forcing portions of the movie to play with larger borders than those clips require, so that the largest of the clips can be accommodated in the Player window.

Besides Copy and Paste, you can use some other special commands in the Edit menu to do some editing. Select a portion of your movie and do the following to perform some interesting edits:

◆ Select Edit ➢ Delete to delete that selection from the movie.

◆ Choose Edit ➢ Trim to Selection to crop the selection. (Only the selected clip will remain, and the rest of the movie will be cleared out.)

FIGURE 13.7
Copy a portion from the
first movie and paste it
into the second.

◆ The Edit ➢ Add to Movie command adds the copied material to the second movie as another
track, beginning at the point where the playhead has been placed in the target movie. This is
particularly useful for adding other *types* of tracks to a movie; for instance, you could copy
music from an audio-only movie and then use the Edit ➢ Add to Movie command to add that
audio as a soundtrack in the second movie.

◆ The Edit ➢ Add to Selection and Scale command is similar, except that it makes the track it creates exactly as long as the selection in the target movie. For example, if you copy four seconds
of audio from one movie and select two seconds of the target movie and click Edit ➢ Add to
Selection and Scale, QuickTime will squeeze the audio down to two seconds. Of course, sound
played at double time isn't terribly useful, so the Add to Selection and Scale command normally is used for adding still images. Select an image that has the same dimensions as your
movie, copy it, and then choose Edit ➢ Add to Selection and Scale to add it to your movie.
(Note that when you add images in this way, you're not replacing part of the existing movie—
for instance, you will still hear the audio portion of the target movie while you're viewing the
still image.)

Recording QuickTime Movies

Built into QuickTime 7 is the ability to record QuickTime movies, both video and audio, directly to
your hard disk. If you'd like the option of quickly recording small clips using a digital video camera
connected to your Mac (or even a webcam-style camera like the Apple iSight), then you can pop open
QuickTime Player and make that recording happen. Likewise, you can record using the microphone
built into your Mac or you can attach a microphone and record using it.

To record video, choose File ➢ New Movie Recording in the QuickTime Player. When you do, the
Movie Recording window will appear and, if you don't have a valid recording device connected,
you'll see a dialog sheet appear and tell you that. Click OK to dismiss the window.

If you do have a recording device—either a digital camcorder connected via FireWire or a Mac-compatible webcam—then you'll see that image appear in the window. When you're ready to record, click the Record button and then talk, move around, or point the camera at things. When you're done, click the Record button again or press the spacebar. That stops the recording and you'll have a file (by default it's on your desktop) called movie.mov. You can then choose Save As, Export, or even Share to get that file another name and in another format, if desired. (Share is discussed next.)

Audio is similar, except that when you choose File ➤ New Audio Recording you get a slightly different QuickTime Player window; this one has an audio level indicator to let you know that your Mac can hear you.

Sharing QuickTime Movies

One final fun feature of QuickTime Pro is the Share command, which enables you to export your movie to QuickTime formats in ideal sizes and compression rates for various output options that enable you to share the movie via the Internet.

Choose File ➤ Share, and you'll see the Share dialog sheet, where you can name your movie and choose its destination and size.

These options let you quickly set up a movie for export so that it can be sent through e-mail or posted to your .Mac account on the Web. As you can see from the illustration, you're shown an approximate size for the final movie file, which can be helpful for determining if it's going to be the right size for your needs.

QuickTime Preferences

Throughout this chapter, you've seen the preferences you can set in the QuickTime Player application, and you've seen how to enter registration information for QuickTime Pro. QuickTime also stores another set of preferences in the System Preferences application.

Launch System Preferences and select the QuickTime icon to open the QuickTime pane. There you'll see a number of tabs for setting QuickTime preferences, including Plug-In, Connection, Music, Media Keys, and Update. You've already seen the Connection options (in the section "Streaming QuickTime"), but you may find some of the others interesting as well.

Register

The Register screen is used to enter information about yourself and to enter your QuickTime Pro registration code once you've purchased the registration update.

Browser

On the Browser screen, you'll see options for the QuickTime web browser plug-in—the software that makes it possible to view QuickTime movies in a web browser window. Place a check mark next to any of the options that you'd like to turn on.

Play Movies Automatically   This option causes movies to be played as they're downloaded to your web browser, without requiring you to click the Play button in the QuickTime controller.

Save Movies in Disk Cache   When this option is turned on, some movies will be stored in your Internet browser's cache when viewed. That means that returning to the movie might be easy; since it's already stored on your hard disk, the movie should play more quickly than the first time around. QuickTime movies tend to be large files, however, so you may want this option turned off to prevent your web browser's cache from filling with the movie (and, hence, very little else).

Update

On the Update tab, you can choose to update QuickTime manually by clicking the Update button, or to turn on the option Check for Updates Automatically, which will cause QuickTime to look for updates whenever it accesses the Internet for some other reason. You can also click the Install New 3rd-Party QuickTime Software if you'd like to see what options are available for updating with non-Apple QuickTime components.

Streaming

On the Connection screen, you can use the Streaming Speed menu to tell your Mac how you connect to the Internet, so that QuickTime can request the proper size movie files (generally, these are streaming files) to ensure that playback on your Mac is smooth and quality is as high as possible. (The faster your connection to the Internet, the higher the quality of the stream that can be sustained by the connection.) The entry Automatic is usually good enough; QuickTime 7 has been updated to do a much better job of detecting this speed.

NOTE   If you choose a modem-based connection from the Connection Speed menu, QuickTime will turn off the Instant On option, as it requires a connection speed of 112Kbps or higher.

The Connection screen also gives you access to the Instant On option which, when enabled, allows QuickTime movies to begin playback immediately if the transport speeds allow it.

Advanced

Default Synthesizer   On this menu, you can select a MIDI synthesizer to make it the default. This is useful only if you've installed additional MIDI synthesizers that you'd prefer to use instead of QuickTime Music Synthesizer.

Transport Setup This menu is used to select the protocol that you plan to use for connecting to streaming movies; the Automatic mode generally works well, but if you're behind certain types of firewalls and you have trouble accessing streaming movies, you may need to change this setting. Sometimes selecting Custom and then changing the Transport Protocol to HTTP can help when you're having trouble accessing streaming movies.

Enable Kiosk Mode When this option is turned on, it isn't possible to Control+click a movie to see a context menu that enables you to save the movie.

Media Keys Media keys are special codes that you can use to access movies, sound files, and other multimedia files that require confirmation of your identity. Some QuickTime movies can include "secured" tracks that require a special key for playback, generally in exchange for having paid for the movie or song.

TIP If you notice that the QuickTime plug-in seems to be displaying or playing media types that you'd prefer it didn't, click the MIME Settings button on the Plug-In tab. You can then select or deselect the types of files the QuickTime plug-in will attempt to handle.

Playing DVD Movies

Would you like to watch DVD movies on your Mac? Launch the DVD Player application in the main Applications folder. If you have a DVD-compatible optical drive in your Mac, you'll see a small window and controller (see Figure 13.8).

FIGURE 13.8
The controller features hidden controls that you double-click from the side of the DVD Player control.

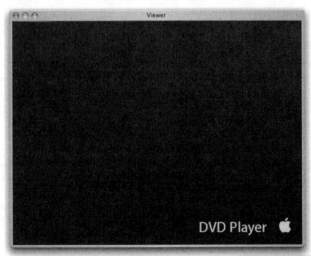

Insert a DVD movie and the fun begins. (With most movies, you can actually insert the DVD first and the player will appear.) You can use the controller as you would the buttons on the front of a home entertainment DVD player—the Play/Pause, Stop, Forward, and Reverse controls are all self-explanatory. The round dial-like area is used to move around on the screen and make choices (view outtakes, see extra material, set options, and so on). In many movies, you can ignore the dial and simply select items with the mouse. The Eject and Title buttons are also self-explanatory. The Menu button takes you to the DVD's main menu.

NOTE Aside from playing DVD movies that are actually on a disc, DVD Player can also play back DVD movie *folders* that reside on your hard disk. (For instance, Apple's DVD Studio Pro creates such folders.) Simply select File ➤ Open VIDEO_TS Folder and locate the DVD movie folder you want to open in the Open dialog box.

Double-click the two lines at the right of the controller (or click and drag on the "drawer"), and you'll see the extra controls that enable you to choose different language soundtracks, subtitles, slow motion, step (frame-by-frame) playback, and for movies that support them, different camera angles. Point your mouse at a button and hover over it for a second to see that button's label.

When playing back a movie, you can use the Video menu to change the size of the playback window to Half size, Normal size, or Maximum size. For best viewing, choose Full Screen to see the movie play without a background or other distractions. In most cases, the controller will disappear 10 seconds after your last command (unless you leave the mouse hovering over the controls), and you can enjoy the movie. Just move the mouse pointer to bring the controller back. To see the menus, move the mouse pointer to the top of the screen.

The controller itself can be changed; choose Controls ➤ Use Vertical Controller or Controls ➤ Use Horizontal Controller to choose the one that you'd like to use. Likewise, you can simply hide the controller (Window ➤ Hide Controller) and use the commands in the Controls menu or their keyboard equivalents to watch the movie. You may also appreciate the Window ➤ Video Zoom and Window ➤ Video Color commands that give you on-screen controllers for how the video plays back. Window ➤ Audio Equalizer can be handy for getting the sound just right. Window ➤ Bookmarks can be an interesting way to manage a DVD, because it allows you to return to a specific moment on the disc, regardless of where the disc's author but the chapter breaks.

Finally, don't forget to check out the preferences (DVD Player ➤ Preferences) for a number of different options that you can set for the player and the way the application responds to an inserted disc.

NOTE Some DVDs have web links embedded in them. In order to click those links, you'll first need to open DVD Player's Preferences, click the Disc Setup tab, and turn on the option Enable DVD@ccess Web Links.

What's Next?

In this chapter, you saw how to work and play with QuickTime, both in the QuickTime Player and in other applications. You learned what types of multimedia files can be imported and played back by the QuickTime Player and other QuickTime-enabled applications. You also saw how to work with streaming Internet movies. Next, you learned the power of the QuickTime Pro edition, which enables you to import, export, and edit QuickTime movies. You also learned about the integration between QuickTime and iMovie, including iMovie's ability to export movie projects as QuickTime files.

Finally, you saw some of the QuickTime preference settings in the System Preferences application and you were introduced to the DVD Player for the playback of DVD movies.

In the next chapter, we'll move on to some of the other applications bundled with the Mac OS that enable you to work with digital audio, CDs, and the iPod. Plus, you'll get a look at some of the technologies that enable you to use speech commands to communicate with your Mac.

Chapter 14

Audio, iTunes, and the iPod

As part of Apple's "digital hub," music takes center stage. Apple has evolved into much more than a mere computer company to become the leading purveyor of digital music players. The iPod has changed Apple's perspective on computing and consumer electronics, and playing and managing music has become one of its main focuses for hardware and software.

Mac OS X is a great platform for music; iTunes depends on QuickTime, Apple's multimedia software, to play music and convert music files from many formats. In addition, iTunes is easy to use and offers just about every feature you'd want from a music management program. As digital music becomes the norm, the tools you use to manage your music files become essential.

Mac OS X also includes an implementation of Apple's PlainTalk technology, which enables Text to Speech and Speech Recognition capabilities—at least on a limited basis. Not too many Mac OS X applications support speech technology, but it is something you can play with and find out if it works well for you. In Mac OS X 10.4, Apple has taken this speech technology to a new level to provide assisted access for people with visual impairments and reduced mobility. This new technology, called VoiceOver, helps such people use a Mac more easily.

In this chapter:

- ◆ Digital Music Files and CDs

- ◆ Using iTunes

- ◆ Managing Music

- ◆ Burning Audio CDs

- ◆ Using an iPod

- ◆ Working with Speech

- ◆ VoiceOver Assistive Technology

Digital Music Files and CDs

In just the past few years, digital music has become commonplace. While you have been able to convert your CDs to MP3 files for several years, it's Apple's iPod and iTunes that have helped spur the burgeoning music download industry. After all, when you want to listen to music, what counts most is the music itself, not the plastic disc or jewel box that, until recently, contained the tunes. Sure, many people still want CDs with nice covers and liner notes, but what remains important is getting the music you want and listening to it easily.

Digital music sales are far from overtaking CD sales, and probably won't do so for many years; you'll be buying CDs for a long time. Also, audiophiles and fans of classical and jazz music still shun digital music downloads because they don't offer the same quality as CDs (or so they think). But the flexibility and speed of buying music online makes it a tempting choice for many people.

Whether you buy music on CDs or online, there are many reasons to want to play back and work with music on your Mac. You may simply be listening to tunes while you're getting work done, and there are some sophisticated ways to improve that experience. You may have an iPod or other music player and want to synch your music to that device. And you may want to mix your music into custom playlists and burn CDs to listen to in other places, or export audio for use in QuickTime movies or iMovie projects.

Music Compression Technology

Since recorded music is just bits and bytes, it's not complicated to put music into computer files and manipulate it on a Mac. In addition, compression formats allow music files to be shrunk to take up much less space. The first popular compression format was MP3 (which is short for MPEG-1 Audio Layer 3), which is both a file format and a special compression scheme that results in high-quality audio files, almost indistinguishable in sound quality from CD audio, but generally about to one-tenth the size. A compressed MP3 file is only 3 megabytes for a three-minute song, while CD audio is generally about 30–40 megabytes for the same amount of music. This makes MP3 files easy to transmit across the Internet, which is exactly why they've ushered in a mini-revolution of sorts, including peer-to-peer sharing and other schemes (legal and otherwise) that have made MP3 audio popular.

Apple jumped on this bandwagon by releasing iTunes, which can play CDs and MP3 files, as well as its native format called AAC (Advanced Audio Coding, which is part of the MPEG-4 standard). These files are even higher quality than MP3 at the same *bit rate*, or level of compression. By default, iTunes encodes digital music in the AAC format, but you can also encode music files in MP3, AIFF (the Mac uncompressed audio standard), WAV (the Windows uncompressed audio standard) and Apple Lossless sound files.

It's important to understand this last format, Apple Lossless, and how it relates to other compression formats. When software compresses music in MP3 or AAC format, it uses *lossy* compression. By eliminating non-essential information, this compression makes the resulting files very small compared to the original. Lossless compression, however, loses nothing, as its name suggests. While files compressed with a lossless compression scheme are about half the size of the original (or about 300MB per hour) they provide the *exact* same music as the original. When you decompress a lossless file, you have the same information as the original. This is attractive to audiophiles and professional musicians, who don't want their music to lose any of its nuances.

TIP   These are not the only compression formats available for music files. Another popular format is Ogg Vorbis (www.vorbis.com), which you can listen to with iTunes if you install the appropriate plug-in. As for lossless compression schemes, two formats are used: SHN, or Shorten (www.etree.org/shncom.html), and FLAC, or Free Lossless Audio Codec (flac.sourceforge.net). Both of these lossless formats are used by fans to compress music of bands that allow taping and trading of their music.

WARNING   One result of the ease with which the Mac OS works with music files is to make it a lot easier to duplicate and use copyrighted audio material. When you're working with CD tracks and music files, try to keep copyright law in mind—you can use songs you've bought on CD for your own private use, but you should avoid distributing copies of songs over the Internet, via CD, or elsewhere if you aren't licensed to do so. Consult an attorney if you want specific advice—generally, though, it's best to err on the side of caution and try to get permission when you're copying (and using or presenting) other people's music.

Audio Files and CDs via QuickTime

Because QuickTime is a technology layer in Mac OS X (and not just a player application, as discussed in Chapter 13, "Video Playback and Editing"), its built-in capability to play back audio, as well as video, is incorporated in the Finder. In other words, you can play a song file quickly by locating it in a Finder window's column view, as shown in Figure 14.1. This is true for both digital music files and CD tracks, as well as for other digital sound formats that QuickTime supports, such as AU and AIFF files.

FIGURE 14.1
You can play back
sound files directly in
the Finder.

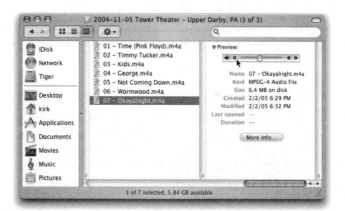

If the Finder can play these files, then the QuickTime Player will definitely have no trouble with them. To play a sound file in the QuickTime Player, drag the sound file from the Finder to either the QuickTime Player icon in the Dock or the QuickTime Player icon in the Finder. Likewise, you can launch the QuickTime Player first and then use the File ➤ Open Movie in New Player command to locate a CD track or an MP3 file. Once it is loaded, you can play back that file just as if it were any sort of QuickTime movie. If you have QuickTime Pro, you can save the audio as a QuickTime movie or export it to AIFF or WAV (Windows Audio or Wave) format.

NOTE   By combining two different playback methods—for example, playback in the QuickTime Player and playback in a Finder window—you can play two tracks from the same audio CD at the same time. Why you'd want to do so is beyond me, unless you have friends who need to be impressed.

QuickTime support means other applications automatically support digital music and CD tracks, too. For instance, in iMovie HD (and in earlier versions of iMovie) you can import both CD tracks and digital music files by selecting File ➤ Import File from the iMovie menu bar. In the Import File dialog sheet, locate the MP3 or AAC file and click Import. Once imported, the song appears on one of the audio tracks in your movie's Timeline interface (it will pop up where you last placed the playhead).

Even cooler is the built-in Audio panel in iMovie HD that lets you import CD or digital music files from within the iMovie HD interface. Click the Audio button under the iMovie shelf (on the right side of the interface), and you'll see the Audio panel appear. At the top of the panel, choose where you'd like to get the audio from the pop-up menu—choose Audio CD, iTunes Library, or one of your iTunes playlists. (You also have the option of choosing some sound effects that Apple makes available with iMovie.) Then you can play parts of a track and record as much as you want using the VCR-like controls, or you can simply drag a track from the Effects panel down to the Timeline to add the entire track to your movie immediately.

TIP   In iMovie HD, you can drag audio files—if they're in QuickTime-compatible file formats—to the Timeline from the desktop or a Finder window to add them without going through any sort of import process.

Using iTunes

Apple's iTunes is without a doubt the best tool for managing and listening to music on the Mac. (And it is, so far, the only Windows application Apple has ever released, not counting the QuickTime engine.) Apple has written iTunes in the spirit of some of its other consumer offerings, such as iMovie and iPhoto, to help you accomplish music-related tasks using a friendly, simple interface. iTunes enables you to create libraries of music, arrange your songs into custom playlists, and generally turn your Mac into a capable little stereo system.

iTunes comes with Mac OS X; in fact, it's the only "digital hub" application that is part of the operating system. Other tools, such as iPhoto and iMovie, which were part of previous versions of Mac OS X, are now only available as part of the iLife package (though iTunes, for some reason, is also included in that package). If you buy a new Mac, you'll get a copy of iLife with it for free; otherwise you'll have to purchase it if you want to use iPhoto, iMovie, iDVD, and GarageBand.

NOTE   Once installed, iTunes is updated by Apple automatically via the Software Update pane, so if you use Software Update, you should get regular updates to iTunes. If you don't use Software Update, you can check www.apple.com/itunes/ periodically for new versions, which tend to be released in order to support new CD/DVD drives and external MP3 devices, such as Apple's iPod and other third-party MP3 players.

To start working with iTunes, click its icon in the Dock or double-click its icon in the Applications folder to launch it. The first time you launch the application, the iTunes Setup Assistant appears, asking you some basic questions about whether you would like to use iTunes for Internet playback (for playing audio streams that you access via the Web) and whether iTunes should connect automatically to the Internet when it wants to access online information. (For instance, iTunes can look up the name and playlist of your CDs using a standard online database, so that it can accurately report the artist and names of the songs on most audio CDs.)

When you've made those decisions, the Assistant will ask if you would like iTunes to search for MP3 and AAC files on your hard disk. If you select this option and click Next, the iTunes interface will appear, and the application will begin searching the local volume for any MP3 files to which you have access and add them to its library.

iTunes then asks if you want to go to the iTunes Music Store, or simply to your iTunes Library. Click Done to complete this setup process. If you chose to go to the iTunes Music Store, you'll see the interface for the music store (see the section "Using the iTunes Music Store" later in this chapter). If not, iTunes will show your library, displaying any music files it has found in the main iTunes window (including, in some cases, sound files from other applications such as sounds stored in a game application's folder). By default, all MP3 and AAC files are listed in the iTunes Library, which can be selected in the Source list on the left side of the iTunes window. If you click the Browse icon at the upper-right of the iTunes window, you'll see three columns display, showing all your music sorted by genre, artist, and album (see Figure 14.2). If you prefer, you can organize music files in other ways, as you'll learn in the next sections.

Playing Songs

Once iTunes has added your song files into the Library, you can begin playing them immediately. To play a song, simply double-click it in the Library listing. You'll see a small speaker icon next to the song's entry, and you'll hear the song begin to play through your speakers. With the song playing, you can use the controls at the top-left corner of the window to control the playback.

FIGURE 14.2
In Browse mode, the iTunes Library displays all your music, grouped by genre, artist, and album.

The following image shows the iTunes player as it looks when you've collapsed it by (perhaps counter-intuitively) clicking the Zoom (or Maximize) button at the top of its window.

These controls work much like those on an actual CD player:

◆ Click the Rewind button once to move to the previous song. If the current song has already played for more than a few seconds, clicking Rewind will restart the song at the beginning. If that happens, click it again to move to the previous song in the Library.

◆ While the song is playing, click and hold the Rewind button to move backward in the current song.

◆ Click the Forward button once to move to the next song.

◆ While a song is playing, click and hold the Forward button to move forward within the current song.

◆ Click the Pause button to pause playback.

The slider below these controls changes the volume of the playback. You also can use the slider in the information area (where the song's title is shown at the top of the iTunes window) to move forward and backward within a song.

TIP The Controls menu duplicates many of the playback controls with menu commands. In many cases, there also are keyboard shortcuts for controlling song playback, which you can see next to each command in the Controls menu. Plus, you can execute some commands in iTunes by clicking and holding the mouse button on the iTunes icon in the Dock and then selecting items from the pop-up menu.

PLAYING AUDIO CDS

If you would like to play songs from an audio CD, insert the CD in your Mac's CD (or DVD) drive. The audio CD should be recognized, and, after a few seconds, the songs will be displayed in the iTunes window. You'll also see a CD icon in the Source list of the iTunes window (beneath the Radio Tuner icon). If you've opted to allow iTunes to access the Internet, it will attempt to access an online database (the CDDB) to learn the name of the CD and the names of the songs on its playlist (see Figure 14.3).

NOTE CDDB (www.gracenote.com) is a database of CD names and track and artist info that is made available to software developers such as Apple for inclusion in their CD-playing applications. Your Internet connection must be active before a CDDB lookup can be performed.

FIGURE 14.3
iTunes has recognized an audio CD and displays information about its contents.

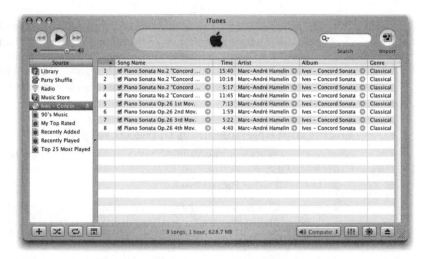

The controls for playing an audio CD are the same as those for playing songs in the Library. To eject a CD, click the small Eject button next to the CD in the iTunes Source list.

TIP   Select a CD and choose Edit ➢ View Options to view a dialog box where you can decide what information should be shown in the iTunes window about this particular CD.

MANAGING PLAYBACK

Whether you're playing songs from the Library or from a CD, you can use three other CD player–like commands to manage the way songs are played:

◆ Controls ➢ Shuffle plays the songs in random order.

◆ Controls ➢ Repeat All causes the entire playlist or CD to be repeated indefinitely.

◆ Controls ➢ Repeat One causes the currently selected song to be repeated indefinitely.

You'll also find buttons for these commands on the bottom-left side of the iTunes window, next to the Add Playlist button. Click the Shuffle button (on the left) to play songs in random order. Click the Repeat button once to play the entire CD or playlist (or Library, if that is what is selected) continuously; click it again to play only the currently selected song continuously.

TIP　iTunes has a fun little feature called the Visualizer, which changes the iTunes window into sort of a psychedelic light show synchronized to your music. To turn on the effect, click the small eight-point, star-shaped icon in the bottom-right corner of the iTunes window or select Visualizer ➤ Turn Visualizer On. (You can also press ⌘T.) As a song plays back, the graphics follow it for an interesting effect. Select Visualizer ➤ Full Screen if you'd like the entire display filled with the effects. This is great for parties.

Adding and Deleting Songs in the Library

After you have iTunes up and running, you may want to add new music files to the Library or delete files from the list.

You can add music files in two ways:

- Insert a CD and then click the Import button to *rip*, or import the contents of the CD to your iTunes Library. (See the section "Importing from a CD" later in this chapter for more information about this.)

- Select File ➤ Add to Library and, in the Choose Object dialog box, locate either a song file or a folder of song files that you would like to add; then select Choose. The songs will be added to your Library.

- Drag a song file or a folder of song files to the iTunes window. Drop the file or folder, and the song(s) will be added to the Library.

By default, iTunes copies the music file to your personal `Music` folder when it is added to your iTunes Library. It does not have to work like that—if you choose iTunes ➤ Preferences and then select the Advanced icon, you can turn off the option Copy Files to iTunes Music Folder When Adding to Library. This is good if you want to store your music in a different location; if you have a lot of music, you may want to store it on a second drive or partition. If you do, you can use the iTunes Music Folder Location setting to change the location of your music.

NOTE　Want to know where a particular song's file is located on your disk(s)? Select it in iTunes and then choose File ➤ Show Song File from the menu. That song's folder will be opened in a window in the Finder, and the file will be highlighted.

To delete a song from the Library, select it in the song list and press the Delete key on your keyboard. You'll see a dialog box asking you to confirm the deletion; click Yes if you really want to delete the song. If the music file is stored in your iTunes `Music` folder, then you'll see a dialog box that asks if you want to move the file to the Trash. If you don't, click No; if you do want to move the file to the Trash, click Yes.

If you've removed a file from your Library, but iTunes didn't delete it and you want to add it again, you'll need to drag the song to the iTunes window or use the File ➤ Add to Library command.

Using the iTunes Music Store

iTunes is more than just a tool for organizing and playing your music. It's also a gateway to Apple's iTunes Music Store. You don't have to use the iTunes Music Store; in fact, if you don't plan to do so, you can turn off its icon in the Source list by selecting iTunes ➤ Preferences and clicking the Store tab. Uncheck Show iTunes Music Store, and you'll never be tempted again.

However, if you do want to buy music from the iTunes Music Store, this is pretty simple (some might say too simple). Click the Music Store icon to display the main page of the music store (see Figure 14.4). You'll need to create an account to purchase music; click the Sign In button and then click Create New Account. You'll have to enter the usual information: name, address, credit card information, and so on.

FIGURE 14.4

The main page of the iTunes Music Store

The iTunes Music Store displays and functions like a website, even though you access it within iTunes. Songs, albums, and artists displayed are links that take you to specific pages, where you can click Buy Album or Buy Song links to purchase music. It's a good idea to use a shopping cart with the iTunes Music Store so you don't get carried away. You can turn this option on in the Store preferences by checking Buy Using a Shopping Cart. This adds a Shopping Cart to the Source list, just below the Music Store icon, and changes the links for songs and albums to Add Song or Add Album. When you've decided what you want to buy, click the Shopping Cart icon to make your purchase.

NOTE   Those little gray arrows you see next to artists, songs, and albums take you to the iTunes Music Store. Clicking one of those arrow icons searches for the name on the store, though you may find that some of them take you nowhere (if the artist, for example, has no music available on the iTunes Music Store). You can remove these icons from the General tab of the iTunes preferences; deselect Show Links to Music Store.

When you buy music from the iTunes Music Store, you download it to your iTunes Library. The first time you do this, iTunes adds a Purchased Music playlist below the Music Store icon in the Source list. As your songs download, they are added to this playlist. You can then organize them and listen to them any way you want. (See the section "Creating Playlists" later in this chapter.)

NOTE You only get to download your iTunes Music Store purchases once. Make sure you back up your music as soon as possible. (See Chapter 26, "Hard Disk Care, File Security, and Maintenance," for more on backing up your files.) If you lose your music files, you won't be able to download them again. However, if you have problems with your Internet connection during download, don't fret. When your connection is straightened out, select Advanced ➤ Check for Purchased Music to check with the iTunes Music Store server and restart any downloads that haven't completed.

Sorting, Searching, and Browsing

Whether you're viewing your Library or a CD list, you can sort the song list by clicking the headings at the top of the list: Song Name, Time, Artist, and so on. Note that the wider the iTunes window is, the more information you can see about individual songs, including the artist, album name, and genre.

You can also use the small Search field to search for a particular song, either in the Library or on a selected CD or playlist. To search, simply click in the Search entry box and begin typing your search text. You'll notice that iTunes begins finding matches as you type each letter, so you don't need to press Return after you've finished typing your keyword. In fact, you don't even need to finish your typing.

iTunes will attempt to find all entries that match the search text you enter. For instance, if you enter **blue** as your keyword, you'll see not only entries that are in the blues genre, but also any that have "blue" as part of the name of the song or album (or the artist, if that's relevant). If you prefer, you can limit the search by clicking the small magnifying glass icon to choose exactly what you want to search (artists, albums, composers, or songs).

You'll likely find that searching is more useful once you've amassed a large collection of music files in your Library. If you do have such a collection, you may also find that Browse mode is useful. With the Library icon selected (you can't browse a CD), click the Browse icon in the top-right corner of the iTunes window. You'll see the iTunes window reconfigure to help you dig through your collection of music files by genre, artist, and album. If you don't like this display, click the Browse button again to return the window to its upright and locked position.

You can't change much about this mode, but you can choose to not display the Genre section if you wish. In the General tab of the iTunes preferences, uncheck Show Genre when Browsing to do this.

Creating Playlists

Some people like to listen to entire albums, and others like to mix and match their music to fit their moods. iTunes gives you both of these possibilities. (It even lets you allow chance to rule your listening; see the next two sections for more information about smart playlists and the Party Shuffle playlist.) If you have a fairly sizable collection of songs in your Library, you may find that you're interested in playing only subsets of those songs at different times. You might want to organize some of the songs for lazy afternoons and others for all-nighters of coding, studying, or trying to keep the baby quiet. Playlists are also useful if you intend to use iTunes with an iPod or if you're interested in creating mix CDs from your music files.

Whatever your plan, you can accomplish it most easily by arranging the songs in your Library into playlists.

There are two ways to create a new playlist:

◆ Click the Add Playlist button at the bottom-left side of the iTunes window. (It's the leftmost icon—the plus (+) symbol—next to the Shuffle and Continue buttons.) You also can select File ➢ New Playlist. This creates an empty playlist.

◆ Select songs in the Library first (you can use Shift+click to select a range of songs or ⌘click to select multiple, noncontiguous songs) and then choose File ➢ New Playlist from Selection or press Shift+⌘N to invoke the command. This creates a playlist that includes all the songs in your selection.

When the new playlist appears in the Source list on the left side of the iTunes window, it's immediately highlighted so that you can type in a name for it. Give your playlist a name and press Return.

Now you can add songs to the playlist simply by dragging them from the Library's song list to the playlist's entry in the Source list on the left side of the iTunes window. This enables you to organize the songs however you would like—by artist, by mood, and so on. The same songs can be added to multiple playlists if you want; a song remains in the Library no matter how many playlists you add it to.

The songs in your playlist will play in the order they display. If you click one of the headers (such as Song Name or Album), this sorts the songs in alphabetical order according to that criterion. To organize the songs in a different order, click the left-most header, the one over the track numbers. You can then drag songs into the order you want.

To play from a playlist, simply select the playlist from the Source list. Just as with a CD, the song list will change to display only the songs you've added to that playlist. Use the controls or the Shuffle and Continue buttons to play the songs on your playlist.

To remove a song from a playlist, select it and press the Delete key. (A dialog box will appear asking you to confirm that you want to delete the song.) It will be removed only from the playlist; it remains in the Library.

To delete a playlist, highlight the playlist in the Source list and then press the Delete key. If the playlist has songs in it, you'll see an alert box asking you to confirm that you want to delete the playlist. Click Yes if you're sure that is what you want to do. The playlist is deleted, although, as mentioned, the songs will remain in the Library.

NOTE You can select a playlist in the Source menu and choose Edit ➢ View Options to change the information that iTunes shows about that particular playlist, including items such as the sample rate of each music file, the size, date, kind of file, and so forth. Also, you can export playlists as plain-text documents for use in other applications such as spreadsheets, databases, or other sound applications. Choose a playlist in the Source list and then choose File ➢ Export Song List. Use the Save dialog box to name the file and choose a location and then click Save.

CREATING SMART PLAYLISTS

You've certainly noticed that iTunes contains a bunch of preset playlists; these appear with gear icons (unlike the music note icons that appear when you add normal playlists), indicating that they are *smart playlists*. If you recall in Chapter 3, "The Finder," Mac OS X lets you create smart folders, or folders that search your files and display only those files that match the criteria you select. Smart playlists work the same way; you choose which criteria you want to match, and the smart playlists fill themselves with all the songs that fit your choices.

You can get an idea how this works by looking at the smart playlists that are set up by default in iTunes. Click the Recently Played playlist and then select File ➢ Edit Smart Playlist. (You can also hold down the Option key and click the playlist's name to edit it.) This displays the Smart Playlist dialog and shows how the playlist is set up.

As you can see in this example, the condition selected is simple: `Last Played is in the last 2 weeks`. You can change this, if you want, to a different time; say you want the Recently Played playlist to contain songs you've listened to only in the last few days. Click the menu that shows `weeks` and select `days`. Then enter a number of days in the field before the menu.

You can choose to limit the playlist to a number of songs, minutes, hours, MB, or GB (click the menu that displays `songs` to select this). You can match only checked songs; if you uncheck the boxes to the left of any of your songs, they won't show up in this playlist. And you can use Live Updating, which means that as songs get played, the playlist updates automatically.

Smart playlists get better when you create your own. Hold down the Option key and click the plus (+) icon below the Source list to create a new smart playlist. Figure 14.5 shows a simple example. For this playlist, we selected two criteria and told the playlist to match all of the conditions selected: `Album contains Live` and `Genre is Jazz`. We limited the playlist to `2 hours` and set it to select songs at random.

FIGURE 14.5

A simple smart playlist

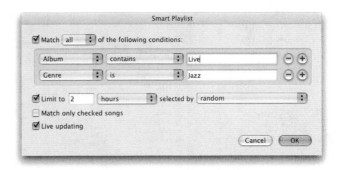

To get the most out of smart playlists, you need to fiddle with them and see what results they offer. Each criteria offers nearly two dozen choices (including album, artist, genre, last played, time, year, and more), and you can select songs that match your criteria by rating, when they have been played, when they have been added, and how often you've played them. Smart playlists are limited only by your imagination, so if you want to use iTunes to get the most out of your music, try as many different ways as you can think of.

THE PARTY SHUFFLE PLAYLIST

The Party Shuffle playlist is a special playlist that selects songs at random from a source that you choose. If you click the Party Shuffle icon in the Source list, you'll see a display of songs. These songs come from your entire Library, by default, but you can narrow this down by selecting a specific playlist from the Source menu at the bottom of the window.

> **NOTE**   Here's a good use of smart playlists: Create a playlist for each of your favorite genres. Just add the Genre is [*name of genre*] criterion to a smart playlist, and it will always contain all the music in your Library that is tagged as belonging to that genre. You can then select these genre playlists as sources for the Party Shuffle, allowing you to fine-tune the Party Shuffle playlist to fit the style of music you want to hear.

By default, the Party Shuffle playlist displays 5 recently played songs and 15 upcoming songs, so you can see what you've just heard (in case you're curious) and see what's cued up to come. You can change these settings in the Display menus if you want to see more or fewer songs. Figure 14.6 shows you an example of the Party Shuffle in action.

When you first select the Party Shuffle, or when you select a new source, iTunes changes its contents. If you like what you see, just click the Play button. If not, you can change the selection by clicking the Refresh button at the top left of the iTunes window. You can also delete individual songs if you want; just select a song and press the Delete key to remove it from the Party Shuffle.

The Party Shuffle gets even better when you use it as a waiting list for the music you want to hear. You can drag any song, artist, album, or even genre from your Library to the Party Shuffle icon to add that music to the end of the Party Shuffle list. This is a good way to choose the music you want to listen to during a party, or even during your workday. If you want to add a specific song while browsing your library, hold down the Control key and click a song (or click the right button of your mouse), and a contextual menu displays. This offers two choices for the Party Shuffle: Play Next in Party Shuffle, which cues the song up right after the current song, and Add to Party Shuffle, which adds the song to the end of the Party Shuffle list. If you select multiple songs, you can also add them to the Party Shuffle in this way.

FIGURE 14.6
A selection of music in the Party Shuffle playlist

SHARING AND STREAMING MUSIC FROM ITUNES

You use iTunes to listen to music on your computer, and you use it to organize music that you put on an iPod, if you have one (see the section "iTunes and the iPod" later in this chapter for more on the iPod). But you can also use iTunes to share your music with another iTunes user on a local network, to listen to other user's music, and to stream music to your stereo, if you have an AirPort Express and a wireless network.

Sharing Music

iTunes uses Apple's Bonjour technology to discover other iTunes clients on a local network that have music sharing turned on. If this is the case, and if you have your copy of iTunes set to share and look for shared music, you can both provide your library to others on your network and listen to their music.

To activate these functions, open the iTunes preferences (iTunes ➤ Preferences) and click the Sharing tab. Check Look for Shared Music to display shared libraries in your iTunes Source list; check Share My Music to allow others to tune in to your library. When you check this option, you can then decide whether you want to share your entire library or only selected playlists. You can name your library; by default, this is [*your name*]'s Music, but you can put anything you want in the Shared Name field. You can also choose to require a password (check this option at the bottom of the window and enter a password), and you can view which users are connected at any time.

When iTunes discovers any shared libraries, it displays them in the Source list just below the Music Store icon (if this is set to display), showing the name the other user has set for their music library.

To access the shared library, click it in the Source list. iTunes displays a message that it is loading the library in its info window, and then it displays the contents of the library. Click the disclosure triangle next to the library's name to display its playlists or browse the library by clicking the Browse button at the top right of the iTunes window.

You can listen to any of the music on the remote library, but you can only listen to music purchased from the iTunes Music Store if your Mac is also authorized for the same account. If you're at home, you'll probably authorize all your computers for this. (The first time you try to play music purchased at the iTunes Music Store you'll be asked for a username and password for the appropriate account.) You cannot, however, play any content purchased from Audible.com via a shared library (though you can play audiobooks purchased from the iTunes Music Store.)

When you're finished listening to music from the shared library, you can disconnect from the library by clicking the Eject icon next to its name.

Streaming Music Using AirTunes

If you have an Apple AirPort Express wireless base station and a wireless network, or an AirPort card in your Mac, you can use iTunes' AirTunes feature to stream music from iTunes on your Mac to your AirPort Express, connected to a stereo or to self-powered speakers anywhere within the range of your wireless network. The AirPort Express has a 3.5mm analog/optical audio jack; you can plug in a cable to connect to your stereo, or you can plug self-powered speakers into this jack.

NOTE   See Chapter 18, "Building a Network and Sharing Files," for more on the AirPort Express.

If you have an AirPort Express base station set up for AirTunes, iTunes detects it automatically. To stream music to the base station, select its name from the pop-up menu that displays at the bottom of the iTunes window.

You can stream music to any AirPort Express base station that's within range, but remember that you can only control your music from the Mac that's running iTunes and streaming the music.

CD Burning in iTunes

In addition to managing and playing your music, iTunes lets you burn an audio CD from your music files using either an internal drive or one of many external models supported by the software. (See `www.apple.com/support/itunes/` for a list of compatible drives.) You can also create MP3 CDs or DVDs, or data CDs or DVDs. (The former contain MP3 files that you can play on some compatible CD players; the latter copy the selected music files as they are on your Mac, so you can back up your music.)

Begin by creating a playlist of the songs you want to place on the disc, as discussed in the previous section. Note that, at the bottom of the iTunes window on each playlist, iTunes keeps track of the number of songs, the amount of time they take, and their approximate size in megabytes when a playlist is selected. A typical audio CD can handle 74 minutes of audio, so try to keep your playlist under that number.

NOTE   When burning an audio CD, iTunes by default adds two seconds between each song. This is not reflected in the total time shown in a playlist, so take it into account when you're adding up the final tally and you get close to 74 minutes. Also, you can change the gap length; open iTunes Preferences and click the Burning icon.

With your playlist complete, click the Burn button in the top-right corner of the iTunes window. From there, iTunes will walk you through the burning process. Depending on the speed of your disc burner, it can take several minutes to burn an audio CD. When you're done, you should be able to play the CD in a typical home or car CD player (particularly if you use CD-R media; CD-RW media will often fail to play on consumer players).

As we mentioned earlier, you can burn three types of discs with iTunes: an audio CD, an MP3 CD or DVD, or a data CD or DVD. An audio CD is playable in most consumer CD players but is limited to 74 minutes worth of audio. An MP3 CD can be played back in any computer that has an MP3 player, as well as in most DVD players. The MP3 CD created is a hybrid CD, using both HFS+ and ISO 9660 formats so that the CD can be played in either a Mac or PC. When you create an MP3 CD, iTunes converts your music files from their original format to MP3 (at least for those that are not already MP3 files). Finally, a data CD or DVD simply copies the actual files to the disc, in their current formats. Use this to back up your music, especially any music you have purchased from the iTunes Music store. To choose which type of disc you want to burn, select iTunes ➤ Preferences and click the CD Burning tab in the iTunes Preferences dialog box.

NOTE   Having trouble completing the burn? iTunes has a Burning icon in its Preferences dialog box that you can use to lower the speed of the burning process, which might make your drive a little more reliable. Apple notes in its Knowledge Base that some CD-R media are designed for a particular burning speed, so you may need to change the setting to reflect that speed on the CD Burning tab.

Importing from a CD

Playing a CD certainly is easy with iTunes, but it's a bit more limited than working with song files in the Library. After all, once you take the CD out of your Mac, you won't have access to the songs. Also, you can't mix the songs on a CD with the songs in your Library to create a custom playlist that includes both.

The solution is to import songs from audio CDs into your Library. The import process reads the songs from the CD and turns them into AAC files (by default—you can also choose to have the songs turned into MP3s, AIFF, WAV, or Apple Lossless files). Then you will be able to browse them in the Library, add them to playlists, copy them to your iPod, and listen to them when the audio CD isn't in your CD-ROM drive, or burn a song to your own "personal mix" CDs.

NOTE   As when copying any commercial music, you should use iTunes for creating music files only for the music that you already own or have otherwise licensed. Ideally, that means using only CDs that you've purchased and plan to keep.

IMPORTING SONGS

You can import individual songs from a CD, or you can import an entire CD to the iTunes Library. To import a single song, simply drag that song's title from the CD's song list to the Library icon in the Source list on the left side of the iTunes window. You can drag multiple songs if you first select them by Shift+clicking or ⌘clicking. When you drag a song (or songs), you'll see a small orange icon next to the selected song. You'll also see the top indicator change to show the song that's being imported and the time remaining for the import process to finish.

NOTE   iTunes can play songs as they're imported, but it can import songs faster than it can play them, so the import process may finish before the song finishes playing. Likewise, iTunes imports more quickly when a song isn't playing, so if the import process is your first priority, stop the play-back (of either the CD or other song files in iTunes) while songs are being imported.

When a song finishes importing, the small orange icon will change to a green check mark to indicate that the song has been imported. It's now a file, and you'll find it in the iTunes Library.

To import an entire CD of songs into your Library, just click the Import button at the top-right side of the iTunes window. (You can also drag the CD's icon from its place in the Source list to the Library icon.) iTunes will begin importing all the songs from that CD into your Library. When it's finished, you'll hear a tone and see a small green check mark next to each song on the CD.

IMPORTING PREFERENCES

By default, iTunes imports songs as AAC files at a high quality (128 kbps) setting. You can change this in the iTunes Preferences dialog box. Select iTunes ➢ Preferences and then click the Importing tab in the Preferences dialog box (see Figure 14.7).

In the Import Using pop-up menu, you can select the type of file that should be created when you import: AAC, MP3, AIFF, WAV, or Apple Lossless. In the Configuration menu, select the quality level for the songs. Be aware that the higher the quality, the larger the resulting song file will be. The Play Songs While Importing option at the bottom of the dialog box is checked by default. You can turn it off if you would prefer to have the songs imported in silence (and often more quickly).

FIGURE 14.7

The iTunes Preferences dialog box lets you change how songs are imported.

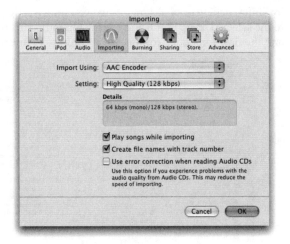

NOTE Apple Lossless compression, as its name suggests, compresses music files without losing *any* of the original data on CDs. Other types of compression, such as MP3 and AAC, are *lossy* compression; they eliminate some of the data to compress the files, and when you play them back, you don't get exactly the same sound as your original CDs (though at normal bit rates, most people can't tell the difference). If you want to have the best possible sound for your music, you can use Apple Lossless compression, but at the expense of disk space. While AAC or MP3 files at 128kbps take up about one-tenth of the space of original music files, Apple Lossless only compresses music to about half its size. It's a tradeoff, but one that audiophiles may want to make.

RETRIEVING IMPORTED SONGS

Once a song is imported, you may want to do something other than play it back in the Library or add it to a playlist—you may want access to the song file (AAC, MP3, or otherwise) itself. Music files are generally only a few megabytes in size, making it possible to upload them to your iDisk for access from other Macs or send them to a friend through e-mail (after considering the copyright implications of doing so!). To work directly with the MP3 or AAC file, you'll need to find it.

By default, iTunes stores ripped song files in the iTunes Music folder, which is inside an iTunes folder that is created in your personal Music folder (that is, ~/Music/iTunes/iTunes Music). There you'll find the AAC, MP3, or other types of song files that are created whenever you rip songs from a CD. (Note that the songs may be in their own subfolders, sometimes named for the artist or album.) The songs are regular files that can be copied, attached to e-mail messages, or moved (although you may need to reimport them into the Library if you move them).

If you would prefer to use a different folder—such as a Shared folder where multiple users can access the music files—you can change that setting in the iTunes Preferences dialog box. Select iTunes ➤ Preferences and then click the Advanced icon.

Click the Change button in the iTunes Music Folder Location area and then select the folder you would like to use for your music files in the Choose A Folder dialog box that appears.

Listening to Internet Radio

If you're connected to the Internet (and have a fairly speedy connection), you may enjoy iTunes' Radio feature, which enables you to listen to Internet radio stations. The tuner works by streaming audio from Internet sites and then playing it back as it arrives at your Mac. Note that this can affect other Internet operations (surfing in a web browser or downloading e-mail), but shouldn't be much of a problem for high-speed and broadband connections.

To listen to an Internet radio station, make sure that your Internet connection is active and then select the Radio icon in the Source list on the left side of the iTunes window. You'll see a list of music genres. Click the arrow next to a genre that you would like to explore. When you see a show that interests you, double-click it to begin listening to that show (see Figure 14.8).

FIGURE 14.8

Listening to an Internet radio show

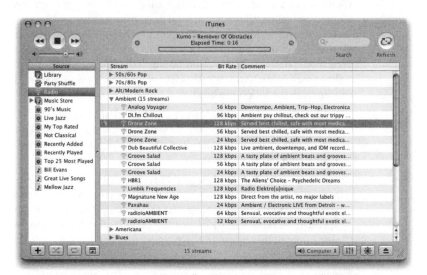

If you have a modem connection, you'll get your best results if you select a stream that is about the same speed as your modem connection, such as 56Kbps. If you have a broadband Internet connection, you can choose the highest-quality connections available; some connections are 128Kbps or more. Some radio stations available through iTunes radio have two or more connection options; select the lower-speed connection if you're having trouble listening to the show. Lower-speed connections also mean lower quality.

You can't record or save songs that you hear on Internet radio stations, but you can save the stations for quick access by dragging them to a playlist in the Source list. Save a list of your favorite stations, and you won't need to hunt them down each time.

TIP   If you note that iTunes often pauses while playing back music, you may want to try increasing the streaming buffer—the amount of music that is downloaded to your Mac before it begins trying to play continuously. Select iTunes ➢ Preferences and click the Advanced icon. Select Large from the Streaming Buffer Size menu.

iTunes and the iPod

Apple's portable digital music player, the iPod, has become an icon. Its ubiquity is almost surprising, making Apple one of the world's best-known brands. Apple has a rich line of iPods, ranging from the iPod shuffle, a tiny flash-memory–based device, to the mid-sized iPod mini, to the larger iPod and iPod photo, which offer capacity of up to 15,000 songs. (At press time, the largest-capacity iPod has a 60GB hard disk; this will certainly increase soon.) But Apple has taken this beyond music with the iPod photo, capable of showing photos on its color screen or on a TV—Apple has pushed the limits of this kind of device.

The iPod was designed from the beginning to work with iTunes for all of its music management. In fact, iTunes is, in a way, the control panel for your iPod. If you use automatic synching between iTunes and the iPod, your music is copied exactly as it is organized in iTunes—all your songs and albums, as well as all your playlists.

If you're planning to use an iPod, it's best to bear in mind that your iTunes library is also your iPod library. The easiest way to work with this is to let your iPod synch automatically; after you connect your iPod, select iTunes ➤ Preferences and then click the iPod tab (or click the iPod icon at the bottom right of the iTunes window). This lets you choose how iTunes and the iPod work together. You can choose from the following modes:

Automatically Update All Songs and Playlists In this mode, iTunes mirrors its entire library on the iPod. Each time you connect the iPod, iTunes updates its contents, adding new songs and playlists, deleting songs and playlists you have removed from the iTunes Library, and synching play counts and last played dates.

Automatically Update Selected Playlists Only If your iTunes library contains more music than your iPod can hold, this is a good choice. If you check this option, you can then choose from the playlists you've created. Note that this only updates playlists, not other music in your library. So if you go this route, think of creating playlists for all the music you want on your iPod, even if you just lump all this music in one playlist; you can still access it on the iPod by genre, artist, album, and so on.

Manually Manage Songs and Playlists This mode tells iTunes to do nothing other than add the iPod to its Source list when you connect it. You then drag songs, playlists, albums, artists, or entire genres from the iTunes library to the iPod icon to copy the music. If you only use part of your iPod's capacity for music (perhaps using it for contacts and file storage, as discussed in Chapter 25, "Peripherals, Internal Upgrades, and Disks"), you may prefer the manual approach.

Working with Speech

Mac OS X includes the capability to speak text aloud and to recognize, in a limited way, voice commands. While this technology certainly isn't yet up to science-fiction standards, if you would like to toy with your Mac's capability to speak and be spoken to, it's there for the testing.

The speech technologies are divided into two distinct areas: Text to Speech and Speech Recognition. Text to Speech technology enables your Mac to speak text aloud—whether that speech occurs in Apple's applications, third-party applications, or Mac OS X itself. For example, you may find commands in some applications that enable you to select text and have it spoken aloud. Speech Recognition refers to the Mac's capability to listen for and recognize certain commands that you speak into the Mac's microphone.

Tiger adds a new feature called VoiceOver, which takes Text to Speech technology to a new level of functionality. VoiceOver is a fully integrated screen-reader technology that reads the text of all kinds of documents and that also describes the workspace for visually impaired users so they can access all the features of Mac OS X.

Using Text to Speech

To configure Text to Speech capabilities, launch the System Preferences application and open the Speech pane. On the Text to Speech tab, you'll see options to turn on spoken phrases and alert text and for choosing the voice that you want your Mac to use for speaking. You can also use the small slider to select the rate at which that voice speaks. To test your selections, click the Play button.

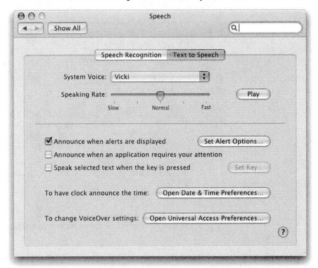

After you've chosen a voice, you can decide which speech options you want to use. You can have your Mac announce the text of alerts when they are displayed; if you check this option you can adjust how the system speaks. Click Set Alert Options, where you can choose a different voice for alerts, a text that will be spoken before the alert, and the delay after which the alert is spoken. You can have your Mac announce when an application requires your attention, and you can set a hotkey to tell your Mac to speak selected text.

This preference pane also contains buttons to set the clock to announce the time at set intervals, such as every hour, and to access VoiceOver settings. (See the section "Using VoiceOver" later in this chapter for more information about VoiceOver.)

Using Speech Recognition Technology

Speech Recognition technology is the flip side of Mac OS X's Spoken User Interface technology—it listens to your voice commands. To use Speech Recognition, you need to have a microphone attached to your Mac, or a microphone that's built into your Mac; all current Macs, except the Mac mini, have built-in microphones. If you have an older Mac, you may need a PlainTalk microphone—this is a special microphone designed by Apple. Alternatively, if your Mac doesn't have a PlainTalk microphone port or other line-in audio jack, you may need to buy a USB microphone.

NOTE Speech Recognition automatically notes what microphone(s) you have plugged in. You then can choose which microphone it should listen to using the Microphone menu on the Listening tab of the Speech pane in System Preferences.

With your microphone plugged in, you're ready to dig into the Speech Recognition settings. Launch the System Preferences application and select the Speech pane. On the Speech Recognition tab, you begin by clicking the On radio button to turn on Speakable Items (see Figure 14.9).

FIGURE 14.9
Use the Speech Recognition tab in the Speech pane to turn on Speakable Items.

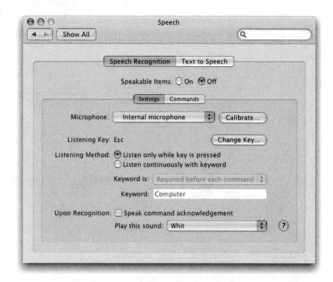

After you turn on Speakable Items, you'll see the small Speakable Items disc appear on your desktop.

This is the interface to Speakable Items. When you hold down the Escape key, Speakable Items will begin listening to the microphone. You can then speak commands. You'll see the small color bars on the disc light up to let you know that you are being heard. If a command is recognized, you'll hear a small tone, and the command will be put into action.

TIP It's recommended that you hold down the Escape key for a full second, then speak the command, and then wait another second before releasing the Escape key. For other hints, click the Helpful Tips button on the On/Off tab of the Speech Recognition tab.

The Speakable Items commands are stored in the Speakable Items folder, which you can open by clicking the Open Speakable Items Folder button on the Commands tab of the Speech Recognition tab. (It's in the Library inside your personal folder at ~/Library/Speech/Speakable Items/ on your disk.) If you have additional Speakable Items you would like to add to your Mac (perhaps from a third-party source), you can install them in this folder.

NOTE   Speakable Items don't have to be special files—they can be normal aliases to applications or even AppleScripts that perform tasks. As long as the item has a unique name and is launchable, you can add it to the `Speakable Items` folder.

While you're working with the Speakable Items interface, you may find it handy to have the Speech Commands window open. You can open it by clicking the small arrow at the bottom of the Speakable Items disc and selecting Open Speech Commands Window. You can then use the Speech Commands window to see when a command is recognized (recognized commands appear at the top of the window) as well as to see the currently installed commands.

NOTE   Speech commands can be specific to the Finder or to individual applications (such as Mail), or they can be general Speakable Items commands that work anywhere. Note that the Speech Commands window has small disclosure triangles next to each major topic area, so you can see the different commands that are available. When you change applications, that application will often show up in the Speech Commands window.

If you're not pleased with the hold-down-Escape system of speaking to your Mac, you can change that. On the Speech Recognition tab, you can change the listening key by clicking the Change Key button. In the dialog box that appears, you can press another key that should take the Escape key's place; then click OK.

You also can change what the listening key does. You can choose to have your Mac listen continuously, waiting for a keyword, such as "computer" or your computer's name, to prompt the speech recognition system that you are issuing a command. For instance, if you name the computer Hal and select the Required before Each Command setting, you'll need to say, "Hal, what time is it?" and "Hal, get my mail," and so on in order to invoke your voice commands.

All in all, Speakable Items can be somewhat hit-and-miss. You'll find that the better your microphone, the better the overall recognition will be. Built-in microphones tend to offer the worst recognition, although recent Macintosh models with quiet internal fans or no-fan operation seem to work fairly well with the built-in microphone. If you can get an external microphone—particularly a USB microphone that's designed for speech—you may have better luck. We tested with all three types and found that a USB headset-style microphone designed specifically for Speech Recognition offered somewhat better results.

TIP   If you're having trouble getting Speech Recognition to work at all, make sure your microphone volume is set optimally. On the Listening tab in the Speech Recognition options, click the Volume button next to the Microphone menu. You'll see a dialog box that helps you select the appropriate volume setting for your microphone. When the volume is set correctly, your Mac may be much better at recognizing your speech.

If you're intent on experimenting with Speakable Items, you may want to try it out using the Chess application that's included with Mac OS X. That application is capable of receiving voice commands for playing the game, such as "Knight B1 to C3." In our experience, it doesn't work very often, but you might have fun with it for 10 minutes or so. (Or, if you figure it out and get Speech Recognition to work well, more power to you!)

TIP   Other companies have created speech-recognition solutions that are more robust than Apple's built-in Speakable Items (although Speakable Items may continue to improve with age). In particular, third parties tend to focus on *dictation*. MacSpeech (www.macspeech.com) offers Mac OS X products such as iListen, which is a full-featured dictation and command-control voice application.

Using VoiceOver

As we mentioned at the beginning of this chapter, VoiceOver is a system designed to help visually impaired users work with Mac OS X. The name VoiceOver is a bit of a misnomer, since this technology includes more than just speech: VoiceOver also provides display functions to make it easier to interact with the Mac OS X interface, as well as full keyboard control, so that users with limited mobility can use only the keyboard and still access the full array of Mac OS X functions.

You access VoiceOver options from the Universal Access preference pane, which also provides other options for people who need assistance with seeing, hearing, and using the keyboard or mouse. (Chapter 5, "Personalizing Mac OS X," discusses the Universal Access preference pane.) To configure VoiceOver, click the Seeing tab of the Universal Access preference pane, check the On radio button to activate VoiceOver, and then click Open VoiceOver Utility. This utility is where you configure the many VoiceOver options.

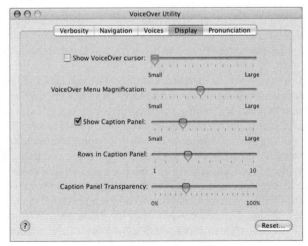

VoiceOver lets you set options for

◆ Verbosity (how the Mac speaks)

◆ Navigation (how the Mac tracks cursor movement and text selection and how the VoiceOver cursor works)

◆ Voices (setting voices to use for different elements)

◆ Display (whether to use the VoiceOver cursor, menu magnification, and caption panel options)

◆ Pronunciation (where you can set specific pronunciations for abbreviations and acronyms)

For more about using VoiceOver, select the Help menu in the VoiceOver Utility; there is comprehensive help on all the available functions and options.

What's Next?

In this chapter, you learned about some of the multimedia features that are built into Mac OS X. For managing and playing music, Mac OS X users can use the QuickTime Player, the Finder, or iTunes. iTunes is a great program that enables you to turn audio CDs into audio files that you can organize in playlists, make your own CDs, and synch your music with an iPod

We also looked at Mac OS X's speech technologies that, while included with Mac OS X, haven't quite caught on yet. (In fact, similar technologies have been in the Mac OS since the early 1990s, but they may yet catch fire.) If you would like to experience talking to and listening to your Mac, you can. Finally, we described VoiceOver, a new technology that provides visually impaired users with a system that enables them to get full access to Mac OS X and its applications.

In the next chapter, you'll learn a little more about digital photos and images. We'll also look at a variety of applications you can use with those images, and the Mac's built-in support for digital still cameras.

Chapter 15

Working with Digital Images

The Mac OS—again thanks to that QuickTime layer—is a whiz with digital images, along with movies and sound. Digital images are files made up of pixels (called *bitmapped* images) that describe, for the most part, photographic imagery or computer-based drawings. These files can be cropped, altered, edited, added to, pasted together, and used in any variety of ways. Clearly, working with digital images is one of the strengths and benefits of using a Mac, and the Mac's built-in image capabilities are what make it so popular among graphic artists.

Aside from the QuickTime underpinnings, which make it possible to view, edit, and translate between a variety of image formats, Mac OS X includes some pretty cool graphics applications.

If you purchase a new Mac, you also receive iPhoto, which is a great consumer application with a few professional-level aspects—notably, its capability to help you organize a disk full of image files as thumbnail images, tweak them, and arrange them or even publish them on the Internet. However, Apple is no longer including iPhoto with Mac OS X upgrade purchases.

Also included with Mac OS X is Preview, which is the main application for viewing image files in Mac OS X, and Image Capture, which is designed to help you retrieve image files from a digital camera. Mac OS X also includes Grab, an interesting little application that enables you to create images of your desktop, applications, and windows.

Along with the included applications and iPhoto, we'll also discuss briefly some third-party applications for working with images, including Snapz Pro, a high-end screenshot application, and GraphicConverter, a shareware option for editing and translating image files.

In this chapter:

- ◆ Digital Images Explained

- ◆ Viewing and Translating: Preview

- ◆ Screenshots: Grab

- ◆ Image Capture

- ◆ Image Command and Control: iPhoto

Digital Images Explained

Like digital movies, which are discussed in Chapter 13, "Video Playback and Editing," digital images have their own file formats, compression schemes, and even filename conventions. In fact, digital movies and digital images are close cousins, as a digital photo can be thought of as a digital movie that doesn't move (and vice versa). In some cases, they even share compression and file format technologies.

Digital images are files that describe series of pixels—their color and sometimes their opacity—that, when placed side by side, eventually make up an image. These files are created by a variety of devices and applications—digital cameras, still captures from movie files, input from scanners, and drawings in photo or animation software. Likewise, once created or input, digital images can be used for a variety of applications, from creating brochures to publishing web pages to insertion in other media files, such as digital movies or animations.

NOTE   "Drawing" applications, such as Adobe Illustrator or the Drawing module in AppleWorks, can be used to create *vector* graphics instead of bitmapped graphics. Vector graphics are graphics files that define discrete objects such as lines, circles, and squares and allow those objects to be moved around in the file; they're also *scalable*, meaning they can be enlarged without losing image detail. Bitmapped images are those where each pixel is described either mathematically or by storing a specific value—color, intensity, and so on. Bitmapped images tend not to be scalable, losing image quality when you make them larger. Drawing applications usually create vector graphics, although they generally can save their work to bitmapped image formats—the type we're discussing here. Often, that's what you'll do if you need to use a vector drawing in another application—you'll export it as a TIFF, JPEG, or similar bitmapped graphics file and then place it in your word processor, layout program, or similar.

File Formats

Just to complicate things a bit, digital images come in a variety of formats. Often, a particular file format is best suited to a certain range of uses—for instance, GIF and JPEG image files are useful on the Web, while TIFF formats often are better for images that you plan to print or use in printed materials such as brochures or magazine pages. To begin, let's take a quick look at some of those graphics formats. It's worth mentioning that the QuickTime layer in Mac OS X can enable applications to work directly with all these formats:

TIFF (Tagged Image File Format: `.tif` or `.tiff`)   TIFF is a very common bitmapped image file format and is popular for its high level of quality. It doesn't compress as completely as some other formats do, meaning TIFF files are often larger than other formats when describing the same sort of image. TIFF is often used for the highest-quality, no-compression setting on scanners and digital cameras.

JPEG (Joint Photographic Experts Group: `.jpg` or `.jpeg`)   JPEG is a high-quality image format that also compresses well, enabling photographic images to be stored in smaller files. The JPEG compression scheme is a *lossy* scheme, meaning that the more you compress the file, the more image quality you lose. (Most image editing applications will let you choose a compression percentage or a slider value to determine how much image quality loss you're willing to tolerate.) JPEG is commonly used on the Web for photographic images, and it's often the file format that digital cameras use for compressed images taken on a lower quality setting, so that you can get more images on a memory card.

PICT (Macintosh Picture: `.pct` or `.pict`)   This is the original Macintosh image format, and it has served well for many years. It's actually a *meta-drawing* format, in that it can be either a vector drawing or a bitmapped image. When you are storing a PICT bitmap, it can be uncompressed or use JPEG compression. Most QuickTime-enabled applications can handle PICT, but it's not the "default" image format in Mac OS X the way it was in Mac OS 9. It's also not commonly used on other computing platforms, so you'll rarely want to send an attached PICT to a PC-using friend or colleague, for instance.

GIF (CompuServe Graphic Interchange Format: `.gif`)   The GIF format is an interesting beast: one of the more popular image formats on the Web or elsewhere, it includes patented technology owned by CompuServe (now owned by AOL), which requires small royalties from applications that use the GIF format. The GIF format is better for digitally "drawn" images than it is for photographic ones, and it tends to look good at lower color depths (256 colors, for instance). It's commonly used for drawn elements on web pages (graphs, buttons, and elaborate text fonts) because it creates a highly compressed file. Its main claim to fame (in the GIF89a version) is the fact that a single color of a GIF file can be made *transparent*, which is how images often appear to be floating on a web page. The image format also supports the capability to display simple animations, which is common for web-based advertising, for instance.

PNG (Portable Network Graphic: `.png`)   The PNG file format is largely a response to the GIF licensing issues—it's a nonproprietary format designed primarily for the Web. It offers features similar to GIF, including transparency and good compressibility. It's a relatively new image format, however, so not all applications—and more to the point, not all web browsers—can work with it. Fortunately, any QuickTime-enabled Mac OS X applications (and all Mac OS X–native web browsers) can deal with PNG.

Along with these file formats, QuickTime can also import and export BMP (Windows bitmap) images, SGI (Silicon Graphics workstations) images, TGA (Targa bitmap) graphics, QuickTime Images, Photoshop format, and MacPaint files. That means that any application that's QuickTime enabled has the option of importing, displaying, or otherwise working with these file formats.

NOTE   Remember that QuickTime's support of these image formats means they can be displayed in Finder Columns view, in the Get Info window, and anywhere that QuickTime movies can be displayed (as discussed in Chapter 13).

Outside of the QuickTime repertoire of image formats, other formats can pop up from time to time. The PCX format is still commonly used by some Windows-based graphics applications. Likewise, the EPS (Encapsulated PostScript) file format often is used in professional printing and as a standard of sorts for many Unix and Unix-like operating systems.

Another important consideration is PDF, which technically isn't a graphics format, and it isn't something for which QuickTime provides compatibility. Instead, PDF support is built into Mac OS X via its Quartz graphics layer, the portion of the operating system that's responsible for the screen display and for aspects of the printing subsystem. PDF files are special documents that can include both text and images. The text is designed to retain its original formatting by embedding font information in the document. In fact, the entire PDF system is designed for electronic publishing so that documents can look as close to the original as possible without requiring that the same applications and fonts are installed on different computers. PDF is important in Mac OS X; in fact, starting with version 10.2, the default file format for screenshots is PDF, and the option to save documents directly to PDF is an important feature of the modern Mac OS.

Compression, Color Depth, and Resolution

As with digital movies, the process of compressing a digital image is an important part of determining how it will look and how useful it will be to you. While not all images are compressed—indeed, some formats are designed not to compress—being able to compress an image and make it smaller is an important option. For instance, a TIFF image might be good for transferring a high-quality, large, uncompressed image from a digital camera to a page-layout application and then printing that page layout to a high-quality printer. That same TIFF, however—perhaps tens of megabytes in size—would perform poorly on the Internet, where even a large image (one that dominates a web page) shouldn't take up more than a few hundred kilobytes in storage space *at most*. Images that are mixed with text and headings on a typical web page often are 25KB to 50KB or smaller.

How do you transform the high-end image for publishing—one that takes 10MB or more of storage space—and compress it into a 50KB image suitable for the Web? Aside from the actual dimensions of the image—the smaller the image's dimensions (width and height) are, the less storage space it takes up—you need to consider four factors: file format, compression, color depth, and resolution.

FILE FORMAT

The file format can dictate both the medium that you can use the image in and the types of compression and settings available. For instance, GIF and PNG offer support for a transparency; JPEG offers heavy compression and is one of the standard file formats for the Web. If you're sending a high-quality image to a PC user, you might consider the TIFF format; for serious publishing and some other uses on Unix machines, you might use the EPS format.

The file format may also dictate the types of compression you can use. PICT and JPEG file formats both can support the JPEG compression scheme, which can compress an image to as little as five percent of its original size, but which also can also result in substantial quality loss when set for extremely high compression. GIF and PNG have their own compression schemes; TIFF can be uncompressed, or it can use the LZW or CCITT scheme, among others. With JPEG compression, you also often can choose a *level* of compression, giving you a bit more choice than in other cases.

NOTE Explaining all of the compression schemes is a little outside the scope of this book. Suffice it to say that for personal and web use you'll generally want to choose the JPEG file format, with JPEG compression, when you're dealing with photographic files, you want smaller files, and you don't mind losing some quality. For the highest-quality images, choose TIFF; LZW isn't a lossy scheme, so you can use it to get the size of TIFF files down somewhat. (Unlike JPEG, TIFF images don't lose quality when they're compressed. The only concern with LZW compression is that it may not be compatible with all graphics applications.) For drawn images or images that are mostly computer-created text—particularly if they'll be placed on web pages—choose GIF or PNG.

COLOR DEPTH

Color depth refers to the number of available colors used to create an image—in other words, the image's *palette*. Standard color depths are 256 (good for drawn graphics and textual graphics, but not photos), "thousands" of colors (often 32,768), or millions of colors (often 16.7 million). The number of colors in each palette is dictated by binary math. A 256-color image is an 8-bit image, thousands is 16-bit, millions is considered 32-bit (actually, 24-bit with an 8-bit *alpha* channel, which is used to determine how the other three color channels will blend).

SIZE

By size, we're talking about the dimensions of the image in pixels. A 1600-pixel × 1200-pixel image requires a larger file (all things, such as compression settings, being equal) than does a 640-pixel × 480-pixel image. You can change the size of an image by *scaling* it in an image-editing program or by *cropping* it, cutting out parts of it to make it smaller.

RESOLUTION

Finally, the resolution of an image has a lot to do with both its file size and its suitability to a variety of tasks, particularly when you're dealing with an electronic image acquired using a scanner, when often you can choose the resolution you'd like for your scanned image. The typical resolution for an image that looks good when printed is 200 or more dots per inch (dpi). On a computer screen or when an image is designed for use with video-editing software, an image should generally be 72 to 75dpi. An image file destined for the Web, for instance, can save quite a bit of file space by tossing out all those extra dots, but a printed image needs those dots to create a quality print.

NOTE This discussion of resolution is less relevant if you're working with images from a digital camera, where the real key is the size of the image (in terms of raw pixels) and not the resolution, which is usually already 72dpi. If you have an image from a digital camera, and you'd like it to take up less storage space, the solution is to crop it or resize the image so that its pixel dimensions are smaller (640 × 480 versus 1600 × 1200, for instance).

This information wouldn't be important if you weren't supposed to do something with it—you are. Applications included with Mac OS X, as well as iPhoto, can be used to crop images or change their color depths. Third-party applications, such as GraphicConverter, can be used to translate between image formats, change image characteristics, and so forth. We'll look at those applications in the following sections.

Viewing and Translating: Preview

Preview is Mac OS X's built-in viewer application, designed to display image files and Portable Document Format (PDF) files. Double-click a compatible image file, and Preview will launch automatically and display the image, as shown in Figure 15.1. (Preview can display a ton of different formats. The official list includes TIFF, PICT, JPEG, GIF, PNG, Windows BMP, MacPaint, Photoshop, Quick-Time Image, SGI, TGA, and PDF documents.) If you want to launch Preview directly, you'll find it in the Applications folder.

NOTE As you might expect, if you've specified a different application for certain graphics file formats, that application will launch instead of Preview. See Chapter 4, "Using Applications," for details on specifying document associations.

In Preview, you can launch multiple Preview-associated images at once by double-clicking them or dragging them to the Preview icon on the Dock or elsewhere in the Finder. When you do, they will be arranged in the Thumbnails drawer shown in Figure 15.1.

In Mac OS X 10.4, a new feature enables you to view those multiple images in a slideshow by choosing View ➤ Sideshow. When you do, the screen will go to black momentarily, and then each image will appear with a dark border for about three seconds. Press the spacebar to see controls for the slideshow, which you can then choose with the mouse.

FIGURE 15.1
Displaying an image in
Preview

Viewing an Image

Preview is a simple program in terms of the commands it offers, but it's good at what it does. Preview offers a few controls, both on the toolbar and in the View menu, that you can use while you're viewing an image, including these:

View ➢ Actual Size (⌘O)   Select this command to return the image to its full actual size, even if that size is larger than the screen can show. (This command is particularly useful if you've previously used one of the other Display commands to change the size of the image.)

View ➢ Zoom In (⌘+)   Zoom in on the image so that more detail can be seen.

View ➢ Zoom Out (⌘–)   Zoom out from the image to show more of it at once. (If an image doesn't fill the screen and you choose Zoom Out, you'll effectively make the image appear smaller.)

View ➢ Zoom to Fit   This causes the image to zoom to a level that fills the current size of the window as exactly as possible.

View ➢ Zoom to Selection (⌘*)   If you've drawn a selection box on the screen, you can use this command to zoom so that the area inside the selection box fills the Preview window.

Tools ➢ Rotate Left (⌘L) and Tools ➢ Rotate Right (⌘R)   These commands cause the image to be rotated 90 degrees in the selected direction.

Tools ➢ Flip Horizontal and Tools ➢ Flip Vertical   These commands cause the image to be flipped horizontally (creating a mirror image) or vertically (creating an upside-down image).

View ➢ Drawer (⌘T)   Opens and closes the Thumbnails drawer.

Remember, too, that the Preview application is used to display PDF documents, which often can be made easier to read by changing the zoom level. Other commands exist in Preview for dealing with PDF documents, which unlike most image files, sometimes consist of multiple pages. For instance, the commands Go ➤ Next (⌘→) and Go ➤ Previous (⌘←) are used to move back and forth within a PDF file. The Page number box on the toolbar can be used to go directly to a particular page of a PDF, as can the thumbnails in the Thumbnails drawer.

You can use the File ➤ Save As command to save an image file to another location. If you'd like to save the image in a different file format, use File ➤ Export, as discussed in the next section.

Preview in Mac OS X 10.4 and higher offers some interesting preference options. In Preview ➤ Preferences, you can use the General tab to change the size of the thumbnails that appear in the drawer, and you can change the background that surrounds each image in the Preview window. On the Images tab, you can make a variety of decisions about how images are displayed and scaled. On the PDF tab, you'll see options that dictate how PDF documents are displayed. On the Bookmark tab, you can manage the bookmarks that you create for your PDF documents. On the Color tab, you can make some sophisticated choices about the ColorSync information that Preview uses for displaying and working with images.

Translating an Image

One task that Preview is particularly handy for is translating an existing image into another file format, if you'd like—again, this is a capability that Apple could easily provide in Preview because it relies on the underlying QuickTime layer. To translate an image, simply select File ➤ Save As. A dialog sheet appears:

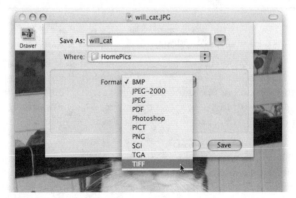

From here, exporting is straightforward:

1. Start by giving the image a name and selecting a location for it from the Where menu. (Like any Save dialog sheet, you can click the disclosure triangle button next to the Save As box to reveal the Columns-like interface for choosing a destination folder.)

2. Select the file format to which you want to export this image from the Format menu. When you select the format, you'll notice that the name you've given the file will automatically be appended with a suitable filename extension. Filename extensions are important for any Mac document, but they're particularly important for graphic files because those files, in most cases, adhere to completely cross-platform standards, and other operating systems (Windows, Unix, Linux) rely on the filename extension to identify the files.

3. At this point, you may see additional choices depending on the format you've chosen. For instance, if you choose to save to JPEG format, for instance, you'll see a slide that enables you to choose the quality level; lower quality means a smaller image file that looks worse; higher quality means an image file that takes up more storage space, but looks better.

4. Click Save.

NOTE Preview also is used by the Mac OS as the main mechanism for previewing documents before you print them. This capability, coupled with Mac OS X's built-in support for PDF, makes it possible to create PDF documents from nearly any Mac OS X application via a detour to Preview and its File ➤ Save As PDF command. See Chapter 7, "Printing and Faxing in Mac OS X," and Chapter 8, "PDFs, Fonts, and Color," for more details on using Preview for printing and for PDF creation, as well as for coverage of Adobe Acrobat, another PDF viewer that's included with Mac OS X.

BEYOND 'SAVE AS': GRAPHICCONVERTER

GraphicConverter by Lemkesoft (www.lemkesoft.com) easily is one of the most accomplished shareware applications ever released for the Macintosh, if not for any computer platform. Still available (native for Mac OS X) via the Web for around $30 as try-before-you-buy software, it's in the arsenal of many seasoned Mac users, whether they're graphics professionals or not.

The name tells you one part of GraphicConverter's capabilities—it can translate between file types, going beyond even the capabilities of QuickTime. GraphicConverter can import upward of 160 graphic formats and export to 45, often translating an entire folder at a time. Using a batch mode, you can automate the process, turning tens or hundreds of images into a new file format—often with many other settings changed, too, without intervention on your part.

GraphicConverter does more than its name suggests, however—it also has built-in cropping, photo-editing, and manipulation tools, making it a poor man's Photoshop of sorts. You can use GraphicConverter to change color depths, resolution, and dimensions and to apply some basic filters and effects, such as Sharpen Edges or color permutations. GraphicConverter also can be used to add text to existing images or create images that are only text, shapes, and color; if you're a true freehand (or mouse-hand) artist, you can draw with some of its tools.

Although it certainly isn't a replacement for big-name applications such as Macromedia Freehand or Adobe Photoshop, it is a good first place to look for advanced image manipulation, going beyond the capabilities of both Preview and iPhoto for importing/exporting and altering your digital images. If it happens to be all you need in an image-editing package, you'll save hundreds of dollars!

Screenshots: Grab

Grab is another included Apple application, enabling you to take *screenshots*—pictures of the current state of your Mac's open windows—and save those screenshots as image files. In essence, a screenshot is just a picture of the screen, saved as a standard image file document. In fact, Grab is one of the programs we used to produce the screenshots you see as figures and graphics in this book. (The other is Snapz Pro, which is discussed later in a sidebar.)

Mac OS X also has a screenshot capability built into the OS that doesn't require Grab. At almost any time, you can press ⌘Shift+3 to take a shot of the entire desktop or ⌘Shift+4 to bring up a "target" icon, draw a box, and create a screenshot of the enclosed portion of the screen. (In this mode, you can press the spacebar to switch to a camera icon, which enables you to take screenshots of a particular object, such as a window or dialog box). When the screenshot is taken, you'll hear a sound similar to a camera's shutter (assuming you've got the volume turned up). The image file then will appear on your desktop, named `Picture 1` (with the number going up every time you add another screenshot). Interestingly, in Mac OS X version 10.4 and higher, the default format for a screenshot is now PNG—not PDF, as it was from 10.2 through 10.3, and not TIFF, as it was from 10.0 to 10.2. Aside from the little problem that Apple seems to have with making up its mind regarding format, things are the same. Double-click the image to view it in Preview. (Note that you can enable and edit the screenshot keyboard commands in the Keyboard & Mouse pane of System Preferences.)

You can use screenshots for a variety of purposes. They can be useful when you need to show something to a technical support person (or to book authors when you're asking questions in e-mail). You can use a screenshot to teach others how to use a particular application or setting. You can take a screenshot of a web page to help you remember how it looked at a given time (after all, web pages can change quickly). You can even take a screenshot of the high score you've achieved in a game so that you can brag to friends.

Whenever you need to take a screenshot, just start up Grab, which you'll find in the `Utilities` subfolder of the `Applications` folder. When you launch Grab, you won't immediately see any windows—just menu items. Grab offers four different commands that you can use to take a screenshot; all these commands are found in the Capture menu:

Selection Select Capture ➤ Selection, and Grab will display a pointer that you can use to draw a rectangle around the on-screen item that you'd like to capture as an image file. The selection mouse pointer also includes a small box that shows you the *x*- and *y*-coordinates of the mouse pointer and the size of the selection as you drag, just in case that's helpful. After you've dragged a rectangle around the item you want to capture, release the mouse button; the image will appear in Grab.

Window Select Capture ➤ Window, and Grab will enable you to capture a single window that appears on-screen (other than the Screen Grab window). Just click the window (it can be any type: a document window, a dialog box, an alert, or a palette), and Grab will create an image of only that window.

Screen Choose Capture ➤ Screen, and Grab will take a screenshot of the entire screen immediately after you click outside the Screen Grab window.

Timed Screen Select Capture ➤ Timed Screen, and Grab will enable you to take a screenshot of the entire screen, but with a twist: you'll have 10 seconds after you click the Start Timer button in the Timed Screen Grab window to arrange things on-screen before the screenshot is snapped. This option gives you the capability to select a particular window, highlight items, open menus, and perform other tasks, within the time allotted, in order to accomplish more "active" screenshots.

In each case, selecting a screenshot command doesn't immediately cause the screenshot to be taken. Instead, you'll first see the Grab dialog box, giving you instructions according to the command that you choose. (Each dialog box has a slightly different name, such as Timed Screen Grab or Selection Grab, depending on the command.) For instance, the Selection Grab dialog box offers a Cancel button so that you can cancel the selection grab, while the Timed Screen Grab dialog box offers both a Cancel button and a Start Timer button, which you click to begin the timer.

Once you've successfully taken the screenshot, you'll be switched back to the Grab application, where a document window will appear, complete with the screenshot you just took (see Figure 15.2). Now you can choose to save the document or discard it. To save it, select File ➢ Save. In the Save As dialog sheet, find the folder where you'd like to save the image, give the image a name, and click Save. (You don't need to add a filename extension because `.tiff` is added for you. Grab saves all screenshots as TIFF image files.) If you don't want to save the screenshot, click the image's Close box and then select Don't Save from the Close dialog sheet that appears.

Want to view a Grab image after it's been saved? Double-click its icon in a Finder window, and it should launch Preview and display itself. If not, you can also drag a screen image document to the Preview icon (in the `Applications` folder) to display it in the Preview application.

One feature you might want control over as you take screenshots is the way the mouse pointer appears on-screen. By default, Grab doesn't display the mouse pointer in screenshots. Select Grab ➢ Preferences, though, and you can customize how the mouse pointer will look (or whether it will appear at all).

FIGURE 15.2
Don't let this image confuse you. We used Grab to create this screenshot of a Finder window.

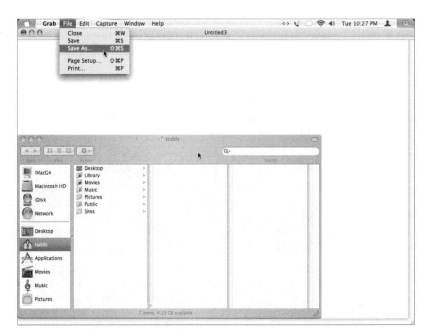

Select the blank button if you don't want a mouse pointer to appear on-screen at all; otherwise, select the button that corresponds to the pointer that you'd like to see on-screen when the screenshot is taken. (Note that you can force Grab to change the mouse pointer to any of these options, even if the mouse pointer wouldn't normally look this way at the time the screenshot is taken.)

Also note that you can turn the sounds on and off in the Preferences window, just in case you decide you don't want to hear Grab's shutter sound every time a screenshot is taken.

NOTE In Grab, select Edit ➢ Inspector to see a small inspector window that shows detail of the active screenshot document (if there is one).

SNAPZ PRO X: SCREENSHOTS FOR DOLLARS

Most people can get along with Grab, the Mac OS's built-in screenshot key commands, or a combination of both. When you really need to get serious about a screenshot—as we were forced to do for many of the more complex shots in this book—only a third-party tool will do.

Enter Ambrosia Software's shareware offering, Snapz Pro (www.ambrosiaSW.com/utilities/snapzprox/). Their Mac OS X version enables you to take screenshots of open menus and items in transition and even select a particular object, such as a dialog sheet or a menu command, instead of simply a region on the screen. (That's when we really appreciate it for book building.)

Snapz Pro can save to a variety of image formats; it can place the image in a particular folder, sequentially name them, change color settings, or even add a border. Plus, a special version of the software has the capability to create a QuickTime movie from your screen—a great way to teach tutorials on using software products. Snapz Pro costs about $30 for the basic version and about $70 if it includes QuickTime-capture capability.

Image Capture

You can download images from many digital cameras quickly to your Mac via a USB connection using Mac OS X's built-in Image Capture. You may prefer to use iPhoto (which is no longer bundled with Mac OS X), but note that iPhoto doesn't immediately download images to your hard disk for easy access in other applications—instead, the images are brought into iPhoto, where a few more steps are needed to export them to the disk and access the image files directly.

The Image Capture software is a simpler beast, enabling you to manage the images on your digital camera (or your scanner, if it's compatible) quickly and selectively. As an added bonus, it also features the capability to process those images automatically as they're downloaded if you turn on the Automatic Task feature and select a task from the pop-up menu.

NOTE Image Capture is compatible with a limited number of digital cameras and devices, although Apple often updates the Mac OS X to increase that number. The web page tends to change from version to version, so start at www.apple.com/macosx/ to locate information about devices that are compatible with Image Capture.

To begin using Image Capture, launch it from the Applications folder. Then, plug your digital camera into an available USB port on your Mac, your keyboard, or your USB hub. (If you happen to have a FireWire-based camera, congratulations. Image Capture can work with some FireWire-enabled models, too.)

If your camera is compatible with Image Capture, it should be recognized automatically. You can then make other choices in the window (see Figure 15.3). For instance, in the Download To menu, you can either choose to use the `Pictures`, `Movies`, and `Music` folders in your home folder (which should simply place the images in your `Pictures` folder, unless the camera happens to be able to record movies or sound) or, also in the Download To menu, choose Other and use the dialog sheet to choose a folder for the images.

NOTE Choose Image Capture ➢ Preferences and, in the Camera Preferences menu, you can choose what will happen when you plug your camera into a USB port on the Mac in the future. For instance, you may want to have iPhoto launch automatically (which is the default setting, and it's why you may very well have seen iPhoto launch when you connected your camera to your Mac, if you have iPhoto installed). You can also choose to have Image Capture launch, you can choose a different application (select Other), or you can choose to have nothing happen at all when you plug in the camera. You can set a similar behavior using the check box that automatically opens the scanner window with Image Capture is launched.

FIGURE 15.3
Image Capture has recognized a camera attached via USB.

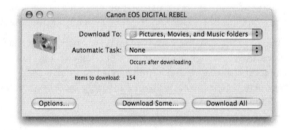

With a camera connected and your download folder selected, click the Download All button to begin downloading immediately all images from the camera to the selected folder. If you'd prefer to choose the images to be downloaded, click Download Some and then select the specific images you want to download in the Download Some window that appears. (See Figure 15.4; note that the window isn't named explicitly.) Use the Shift key while clicking to select a contiguous row of photos. Use the ⌘ key while clicking to add noncontiguous photos to your selection. When you're done, click Download.

TIP You can use the Download Some window to perform a neat trick—you can rotate an image before you download it to disk. Select an image in the window, and click one of the curly arrow icons at the top of the toolbar; clicking either will rotate the image in the direction of the arrow. When it's aligned the way you like, click Download. Note that the Download Some window can be changed by selecting View ➢ As List, and you can edit the toolbar using View ➢ Customize Toolbar.

A dialog sheet will appear, showing you the progress of the download; when it's done, your selected download folder (`Pictures` or otherwise) will be opened in the Finder. You can then work with the images; double-click them to view them (or translate them) using Preview.

FIGURE 15.4

If you choose Download Some, you can select the images you want to download.

NOTE   Image Capture won't overwrite an image (or another image with the same name) if it already exists in the target folder you've chosen in Image Capture; you'll need to move the image, rename it, or select a different folder for the download.

Image Capture can do more than just import the images and place them in a folder; in fact, it has some fairly interesting options for digital camera lovers. In the main Image Capture window, before clicking Download Some or Download All, you can choose an item from the Automatic Task menu. (This menu also appears in the Download Some window.) In that menu, you'll find a number of commands that enable you to format the images in different dimensions, as standard photo print settings (3×5, 5×7).

Another choice in the Automatic Task window is Build a Web Page. This takes the images that you download and automatically creates a web page (also stored in the Pictures folder, or the folder that you choose, inside a subfolder called webpage). The web page is no-frills, but it's useful for getting those images quickly on the Web. The web page displays thumbnails of the images, which can then be clicked to view the full-size images. Now, to add the image gallery to your website, all you have to do is copy the index folder to your web server computer. For instance, if you use .Mac, you could copy the index folder to your Sites folder on your iDisk; the web page created would then be available at http://homepage.mac.com/*yourname*/webpage/*index.html*, where *yourname* is your .Mac account name. It also wouldn't hurt to rename the webpage folder something else (such as myphotos or holiday2003), then copy it to Sites on your iDisk (or to another web server computer).

NOTE   Image Capture can be used to share a camera or scanner—or to access a shared camera or scanner—over a network connection. To share a camera or scanner, choose Image Capture ➤ Preferences and click the Sharing tab. There you can turn on the Share My Devices option, give them a name and, if desired, a password. If you want to use devices that are shared by another Mac, turn on the Look for Shared Devices option on this dialog tab. (Click OK when you're done with the dialog.) You can then choose Devices ➤ Browse Shared Devices in Image Capture to look through and choose shared devices on your network.

Image Command and Control: iPhoto

NOTE Apple did not include iPhoto 5 for those upgrading to Mac OS X 10.4. Users who purchase a new Mac may still receive iPhoto. We will still cover some of the more appealing aspects of iPhoto, but if you want the most up-to-date version, you will have to purchase an iPhoto upgrade separately.

iPhoto is a great application designed to make it easier for consumers to work with digital cameras and image files, following Apple's model of an easy-to-use yet surprisingly powerful application. In fact, it's a close relative to both iMovie and iTunes, borrowing interface similarities from both (see Figure 15.5).

FIGURE 15.5
iPhoto is similar to other Apple applications (the "iApps"), particularly iTunes and its approach to file management.

TIP The higher your screen's resolution setting, the easier it will be to work with iPhoto. At 800 × 600, working with iPhoto is very difficult. At 1024 × 768 or higher, things get a little better.

iPhoto is not, however, a replacement for an application such as Adobe Photoshop or even a lower-cost version such as Adobe Photoshop Elements, GraphicConverter, or PixelNhance Those applications enable you to really dig and alter, manipulate, and otherwise shape your photos. With powerful filters, airbrush-like tools, and support for sophisticated text, those applications are true image-editing packages.

iPhoto isn't a true image-editing application, although it does enable you to crop images and make some tweaks to an image's appearance. (Each iPhoto version seems to add another tool or two.) However, iPhoto does excel at interacting with digital cameras and organizing image files and your hard disk. It also has some special output options, including the capability to print images in various configurations and publish them to the Internet.

Importing Photos

Like the much simpler Image Capture application, iPhoto can interact with your digital camera and import images into its interface. As with iTunes, you also can use iPhoto to import images that are already stored on your hard disk. In fact, iPhoto can scour your hard disk for image files, which it then can import automatically into the Photo Library. Once imported, the image files can be organized into photo "albums" for easier access and printing.

First, though, you need to get images into iPhoto. One way to do that is by connecting a digital camera to your Mac, via either USB or FireWire, and then launching iPhoto. In fact, iPhoto may launch automatically when you connect the camera.

Once connected, if your camera is recognized, you'll see the iPhoto screen change to show a camera icon and the number of photos that have been found on it. If you'd like to leave the images on the camera after they're imported, turn off the option Delete Items From Camera After Importing. Otherwise, to import the images, click the Import button. (In an alert box that pops up, you're given a chance to confirm whether or not you'd like to delete the originals.) As the images are imported, you'll see an indicator bar grow across the bottom of the display, and the Import button will change to Stop so that you can stop the import process if needed.

Once the import is complete, the photos will appear on-screen. You can double-click an image to see it in its own window.

NOTE Each time you import images, you create a new "roll" in the Library; each roll is supposed to be a little like a roll of film that you would have processed at the drug store. The rolls are just one way that images can be organized and managed in the Library. You can also choose a different sort order; select View ➢ Sort Photos and then the method you'd prefer to use if you don't want to view your photos sorted by film roll.

The other way to import images into iPhoto is to use the File ➢ Add to Library command. This enables you to import an image file directly from your hard disk, network volumes, or removable media. When you select one in the Import dialog box and click Open, iPhoto will automatically bring those images into the iPhoto library.

WARNING iPhoto will import every image file on a particular disk if you select that disk and click Open. It's not very good at dealing with thousands of images in its library, however, because it can bog down under the burden. It's best to import only a few images at a time—keep each import in the tens or hundreds of images, not thousands. When the library has a few thousand images in it, scrolling and viewing can be difficult, particularly with a less-powerful Mac. The later the version of iPhoto and the more recent the Mac model, the less of a problem this is.

Organizing in iPhoto

iPhoto's greatest strength is its capability to help you manage hundreds of digital images that you've imported from your digital camera or from your connected disks. iPhoto stores all of your images in the Photo Library, which you can browse or search through easily. You can also create *photo albums*, which are roughly analogous to playlists in iTunes. In each photo album, you can gather different collections of your images that can then be used for on-screen slide shows, turned into a web page, or exported as image files.

PHOTO LIBRARY

Click the Library icon in the albums list and you'll see the images in your Library. You can scroll through them or use the slider at the bottom right of the window to change the size of each image. At the bottom of the album list, you can click the information button ("i") to display an information pane, where information about the selected image is shown. In that pane, you can edit the title of the image. Click it again, and you'll see an area to enter comments about an image.

While you're viewing images in the Library, you also can rotate them if necessary. Select an image and then click the rotate button (it's just to the right of the information button). Each time you click the button, it rotates another 90 degrees. (You also can select an image and choose Edit ➤ Rotate and then choose Clockwise or Counter Clockwise.)

TIP In the View menu in iPhoto are four commands: Titles, Keywords, Film Rolls, and My Rating. You can select from among them to change the amount of information that's shown in the iPhoto Library.

To delete an image from the Library, select it and choose Photos ➤ Move to Trash or press ⌘Delete. When you do that, images are moved to the trashcan that appears in the left-side listing of photo albums. The images aren't deleted yet—they can still be recovered. If you're sure you want to get rid of those photos and recover the available disk space, choose iPhoto ➤ Empty Trash.

NOTE By "trash," iPhoto isn't referring to the Trash icon in the Dock. Instead, iPhoto has its own Trash item on the Source list. Click it to see the photos that have been placed in the iPhoto trash. If desired, you can drag them out of there or you can select them and choose Photos ➤ Restore to Photo Library if you'd like them put back where they were stored originally.

PHOTO ALBUMS

Ready to add a photo album? It's a good idea to create a photo album whenever you want to use a collection of the images you've stored in iPhoto for some particular purpose. After you've arranged the images in a photo album, you can export them, print them, and so on. It's a convenient way to deal with them.

To create a new photo album, click the New Album button (the + button), choose File ➢ New Album, or press ⌘N. In the dialog box that appears, give the photo album a name. Click OK, and the album will appear in the Album list. Then you can drag images to it from the Photo Library to add them to the album. When you do so, the photos aren't moved from the Library, and they aren't moved on your disk; like a playlist in iTunes or aliases in the Finder, each album is just an alternative listing of images.

With a photo album created, you can work with that subset of images, dragging them around on the screen to change their order or using the information area (again, by clicking the "i" icon at the bottom of the albums list) to rename the images. Next, you can decide whether you're going to edit the images or simply move on to the book-editing and sharing options discussed in later sections.

TIP   While you're in the Organize mode, you have a number of options available to you for doing fun stuff with your images. Select an image or group of images and then click one of the icons at the bottom of the screen to set that icon's task into motion. For instance, to create a slideshow, select a number of photos and then click the Slideshow icon. To send photos via e-mail, select a photo or photos and then click the Email icon. You can do the same thing with the Order Prints, Book and HomePage icons, which all use Apple services via the Internet. Finally, you can select a photo and click the Desktop icon to make it your desktop background.

You can also delete a photo album without deleting the images in it. Simply select the name of the album and choose Photos ➢ Delete Album. The album will be removed, but your images remain in the Photo Library.

TIP   iPhoto 5 and higher offers Smart Albums, which use Spotlight-style searching technology to create dynamic photo albums that are, essentially, regularly updated search results. Choose File ➢ New Smart Album from the iPhoto menu, and then choose a search phrase that you'd like to use for the smart album. It can be based on the filename, the date of the image, comments that have been typed about the image, or other criteria. You can also combine those factors to create an album of images with "work" in the title that were taken in your most recent five rolls, for instance.

Burn CDs

Photo albums are handy for one other thing—you can burn them to recordable discs using iPhoto. To burn photos to a CD-R , CD-RW, DVD-R, or DVD-RW disc (if you have a drive that's capable of doing so), highlight the photo album (or albums) that you'd like to burn to CD, and then click the Burn button. You'll be asked to enter a new, blank disc. Once the disc has been inserted, it will appear in the information area, complete with the number of photos to be burned and the amount of space they will take up. (In this example, we're only taking up a small portion of the available space on the DVD -R that's been inserted.)

If everything looks like it will fit, and you've selected the photos you want to burn, click the Burn icon again. You'll see the Burn Disc dialog box; if it says what you expect, then click the Burn button. Next, you'll see a Progress dialog box and then a Burning dialog box showing you how the burn is going. When disc burning is complete, the disc will be ejected automatically.

TIP   You can burn data CDs and DVDs this way, but if your Mac has a SuperDrive, you can also burn your images to a DVD that could be played back on a consumer DVD player and a television. This is a clever way to send photos to grandma or to an important client. To get your images from iPhoto to iDVD, select a photo album or your library and choose Share ➤ Send to iDVD. There you can edit the interface for your DVD, create a slideshow, add music, and do quite a bit to build an entertaining slideshow production.

EXPORT TO QUICKTIME

One other iPhoto feature is worth specifically mentioning here—you can export images for use in other computing applications, which is probably something you'll want to do fairly often, particularly if you use iPhoto as the main interface to your digital camera. Again, this export capability is based on QuickTime technology.

Select one or more images, then choose Share ➤ Export from the menu. From the Export dialog box, you can perform three types of exports—a file export, a web page export, or an export as a QuickTime movie.

Select one of the three tabs and then make choices. (For a web page, for instance, choose a title for the page and the maximum sizes for the thumbnails and full images.) When your choices are made, click Export. A dialog sheet will appear in which you can choose a destination for the exported files.

Editing in iPhoto

As we've mentioned, iPhoto isn't really an image-editing application in the same vein as Photoshop, so its editing tools are limited. You can constrain an image to a certain size, crop an image, eliminate the "red-eye" effect that some camera flashes create, retouch an image, "enhance" it, or make an image black and white. All of that is done in the Editing screen.

With either an individual photo selected in the Photo Library or a photo album selected in the album list, click the Edit button. You'll see the editing tools appear at the bottom of the screen.

Here's what they do:

Constrain Drag a box on the image, and then select a size from this menu if you'd like your image reshaped to certain dimensions. The box will snap to that size, and you can crop the image. This is particularly important if you plan to use iPhoto to order prints of your images.

Crop The crop tool enables you to trim the excess margins from an image and change it to focus on a smaller portion of the image. To use crop, you first drag a box on the image area—start in the top-left corner of the area you want to keep, and click and hold the mouse button while dragging to the bottom-right corner of the area you want to keep. That frames your cropping area. Next, click Crop. The image will change so that the area outside your cropping area is discarded.

NOTE You can choose Edit ➢ Undo to undo a cropping command immediately after it has been performed. iPhoto supports multiple Undo commands. You can also choose Edit ➢ Revert to Original if you're working on an image in a photo album, because iPhoto leaves the original image untouched in the Photo Library.

Enhance Click this button to improve the colors in your photo. Each time you click, you essentially bump up the saturation of the image. Once you've clicked the Enhance button, press the Control key to compare it to the old image levels. If you don't like what you see in the new one, just select Edit ➢ Undo to return to the old levels.

Red-Eye This tool is designed to "auto-magically" take the red-eye effect out of your subject's eyes. Drag a box around your subject's eyes and then click the Red-Eye button. In most cases, the red effect will simply disappear.

Retouch Click the Retouch tool, and then move the cursor onto a blemish on your image. Hold down the mouse button and use short, small strokes to blend the blemish into the background. After retouching, you can press the Control key to compare your work to the older version. (Holding down the Option key while retouching makes the effect a little more dramatic.)

Black and White This one is obvious—it turns the image to black and white (actually, it will be *grayscale*, with many shades of gray), as if it were taken with black-and-white film. If you'd like to try the effect, just click the button. You can choose Edit ➢ Undo to return the image to color.

Sepia Similar to Black and White, this tool turns the image to a slightly brown and white that makes the image appear aged.

Adjust Choose this option, and you'll see a dialog window that enables you to change the brightness and contrast levels in the image, as well as the saturation, color temperature, and a number of other options that can tweak the images considerably.

To move to the next image in your Library or in your selected photo album, click the right arrow button; you can use the left arrow button to return to earlier images. Note also that the top of the window shows thumbnails of the images in your library or the selected photo album, making them easier to get access.

Click the Done button to return to the main iPhoto interface; you can also click the Library icon or one of your photo albums in the Source list.

What's Next?

In this chapter, you saw the different image file formats that Apple's QuickTime layer can support, along with a few others that you'll come across from time to time. You also learned some of the basics of image-related technology, such as compression and resolution issues. From there, you saw a number of Mac OS X's included tools for working with images, including Grab, Preview, and Image Capture. Finally, you were introduced to iPhoto, where you saw the basics of its capability to organize, edit, and output images in a variety of ways.

In the next chapter, you'll take the first steps into Macintosh file sharing and networking—how to connect and sign on to network server volumes, as well as how to troubleshoot those connections.

## Chapter 16

Managing Contacts, Appointments, and Personal Info

Mac OS X comes bundled with quite a few applications, some of which are designed to work with remote data (such as Safari for web browsing), others that are designed for you to communicate (such as Mail for e-mail and iChat for text, audio, and video chats). But Mac OS X also comes with a handful of programs that help you organize your life: your contacts, appointments, to dos, and personal info.

In this chapter we'll cover the following applications: Address Book, which you use to organize contact information; iCal, which manages calendars and to dos; and Keychain Access, which stores your passwords and other private information. We'll also look at iSync and .Mac synchronization, which let you synchronize this information to other devices (with iSync) or to .Mac's servers, so you can use it on other computers.

In this chapter:

◆ Address Book

◆ iCal

◆ iSync and .Mac Synchronization

◆ Keychain Access: Securing Passwords and Private Data

Address Book

Address Book might seem a bit redundant if you use Microsoft Entourage, Palm Desktop, or another application to manage people and addresses. If you don't have one of those applications, you'll find that Address Book is a useful accessory application, and it has a hidden strength—integration with the Mail application.

NOTE Although using Address Book doesn't require that you use (or understand) Mail, it doesn't hurt, particularly since Address Book is designed to work so closely with Mail. See Chapter 12, "Managing E-Mail," for more on Mail.

In fact, the Address Book is intended to be a central repository for people-related data on your Mac—going so far as to be well integrated with some of Apple's other applications such as iCal (a calendar/schedule management application) and iSync (for synchronizing data with other devices). This new push to make Address Book a central part of the Mac computing experience may take a while because Microsoft Entourage, Palm Desktop, and their ilk are much more powerful. However, it's possible that those other tools will integrate with Address Book in the future, and Apple's own applications—iCal, Mail, and others—will definitely be useful in conjunction with Address Book.

Address Book is located, by default, in the main `Applications` folder, and its icon is preinstalled on the Dock. Locate and double-click the Address Book icon to launch the program (or single-click the Dock icon). Once it's launched, you'll see the main Address Book window, as shown in Figure 16.1.

FIGURE 16.1
The main Address Book interface

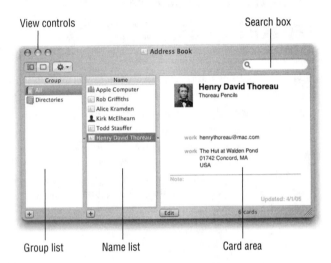

You'll notice right off that Address Book is similar in design to many of Apple's other programs, such as iPhoto and iTunes. It offers a simplified interface that works, in some ways, similarly to the Finder window's Column view. Actually, that's only one of the view options—you also can select a card-only view, which enables you to view Address Book as if it were a series of business cards or perhaps like a Rolodex.

To change the view, either select View ➤ Cards and Columns or View ➤ Card Only or click the small buttons that appear at the top of the Address Book window.

Like Mail and the Finder, Address Book has a Search entry box that can be used to locate particular individuals quickly in the Name listing area. The Search entry box can be used to focus the Address Book database on the entries that have certain text in the name, the company name, the phone number, and so on. Enter text such as **212**, for instance, to see entries that have those characters in them somewhere—in most cases the results would be New York phone numbers, although you also might get someone who happens to have 212 in their address or postal code. Still, it's a great way to whittle down the list to something manageable when you have a lot of entries.

NOTE Address Book uses Spotlight to search for contacts—this makes it fast and efficient. You can also search for your contacts from the Spotlight menu or window. Address Book entries display in the Contacts group in the Spotlight menu and window. When you find the one you want, double-click it to open Address Book with that card visible.

Adding and Editing Cards

You can add address cards in one of three ways:

◆ From within Address Book

◆ In Mail, by selecting an e-mail message and choosing Message ➢ Add Sender to Address Book

◆ In Mail, by Control+clicking an e-mail address in a message header and selecting Add to Address Book from the contextual menu

If you add a person via Mail, only the name and e-mail address are stored for that person in Address Book—you'll have to select the entry in the Name list and click Edit in the status bar (or select Edit ➢ Edit Card) to add other information.

You have two ways to create a new card in Address Book: In Columns view, click the button with a plus (+) sign or select File ➢ New Card. When you do that, a new entry will appear in the Name list (if you're viewing the Address Book via its Columns interface), and the Card area will now be editable (see Figure 16.2).

FIGURE 16.2
Editing a newly added card

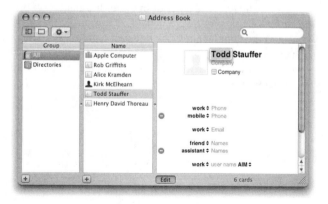

TIP   At the top of the Card pane, next to the name, is a small box. You can drag an image file (from the desktop or from a Finder window) to that box in order to add a picture of the person. You can also double-click that box to choose an image or crop one you've added, and if you have a video camera like an iSight connected to your Mac, you can make a "video snapshot" of your contact.

As you're editing, you can change the label for some of the fields—those that have small up and down arrows next to them. Click the arrows to reveal a menu where you can choose different labels for a particular entry—if you want to change the Work phone entry to Mobile or Home, for instance.

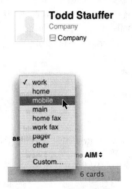

You can add fields to the card, too. Choose Card ➤ Add Field and choose from the menu that appears so that you can add one of the fields listed. Note also that the Card menu is useful for selecting from a variety of custom settings for the way your card appears, including swapping the positioning of names or, by selecting This is a Company, determining whether the card is for a person or contact information for a company.

You can choose Card ➤ Make This My Card to mark the card as your personal information; this enables you to select Card ➤ Go to My Card in the future. It's also useful under other circumstances when you use the Address Book in conjunction with other applications.

If the default card still doesn't offer the elements you'd like, you can edit it in another way. In the Address Book window, click the Edit button at the bottom of the Card pane. Plus (+) signs will appear next to the item labels. Click one of the plus sign buttons to add another field for a particular entry type. For instance, if you click the plus sign next to an address, you'll get another block of address fields that you can edit and use. The same is true for adding additional phone number fields or e-mail fields.

When you're done editing the card, click the Edit button again to return it to the Card View mode.

TIP   The Note field can be edited whether or not you're in Edit mode—it's designed so that you can quickly switch to an existing card and add a note without changing modes. Just click in the field and begin typing.

Deleting Cards

To delete a card from your address book, select the person in the Name list (in the main Address Book window) and choose Edit ≻ Delete Card. This will delete the card immediately without a warning, so be sure this is what you want to do. If you realize you've made an error, choose Edit ≻ Undo Delete Record, and the card will be reinstated.

You also can select a person (or group) in the list and press the Delete key on the keyboard. This will cause a dialog sheet to ask if you're sure you want to delete the person. Click Delete to proceed or Cancel to return to the window without deleting the person.

TIP The Address Book files are located in a folder called `AddressBook`, in the `Application Support` folder inside your personal `Library` folder. It's a good idea to back up this folder occasionally. Don't move items out of the folder, however, because doing so may affect Address Book's ability to track your contacts in the future.

Creating a Group

A group is used primarily to put individual recipients together so that you can send e-mail messages to an entire group at once, rather than having to type in individual addresses. Address Book gives you two ways to create a group. The first way is to select each person you want to add to the group in the Address Book people list. Then choose File ≻ New Group from Selection. You'll see a new group appear in the Group pane of the Address Book window, enabling you to edit its name—type a name and press Return (see Figure 16.3). The selected names will already be added to that group.

FIGURE 16.3

The new group is created and ready to be named.

The second way is to choose File ≻ New Group or click the plus button beneath the Group list pane; when you do either, a blank group will appear in the Group list. You can name the group (type a name and press Return) and then drag people from the people list to this group entry to add them. The group will then be available in Mail's New Message window. You can start typing the first few letters of the group's name in the To, Cc, or Bcc fields to add the group's addresses to the message.

TIP In Mail, it's best to add a group on the Bcc line so that every recipient of the message isn't shown every e-mail address in the group. This ensures the group's privacy while avoiding an annoying situation in which each recipient has to scroll through a long list of e-mail addresses before they can read your message. See Chapter 12 for more on Mail.

If you have more than one e-mail address for some of the entries in your group, you can choose Edit ≻ Edit Distribution List to view the list of entries so that you can choose the correct e-mail address for those with multiple addresses stored. To choose one over the other, simply click it once in the list—it will be bolded.

Click OK to close the distribution list and save your selection.

To delete a group, select it in the Group list and press the Delete button, and then answer Delete in the dialog sheet that appears to warn you about deleting the group. Note that the e-mail addresses and other data in that group are not deleted—they're still stored as cards in Address Book. Only that particular group is deleted, not the people it contains.

To delete a group immediately without a warning, select it in the Group list and then choose the Edit ➤ Delete Group command.

Importing Contacts

If you have a list of contacts from another application that you'd like to import into the Address Book application, you can do that in four different ways:

◆ Using the LDIF standard

◆ Using the vCards standard

◆ In a tab-delimited text file

◆ From a comma-separated-values (CSV) file

You'll need to import from applications that can *export* via those standards, although more and more do.

NOTE Address Book automatically imports contacts from a previous version of Address Book if you install Mac OS X version 10.4 (or higher) over a previous version of Mac OS X. If you don't see all of your contacts, particularly the "temporary contacts" used in earlier versions of Address Book, open Mail and choose Window ➤ Previous Recipients. From there you can add recently accessed e-mail addresses to your Address Book.

LDIF (the LDAP Interchange Format) is reasonably common in Mac applications and, in fact, may be the only option you're given. If you're interested in exporting your entire address book database from one application to another, look for an Export or Export Contacts option in that application. Then, if you're given the choice, export the contacts as an LDIF file. If not, use either tab-separated or

CSV files; these are plain-text files, where the fields in your contact list are separated either by tabs or by commas. Address Book spots these separators and lets you import the fields, even choosing which field corresponds to which Address Book field.

NOTE   If your e-mail or contact application won't export to one of the formats mentioned in this section, you can check for a translator or script that can import items from other applications. Start at www.apple.com/downloads/macosx/ and search for Mail Import Scripts or similar keywords.

Once you have the contacts exported from your previous application, choose File ➢ Import and select either vCards, LDIF, or Text File from the Import submenu. Use the Open dialog to locate the file and click the Open button. You'll see Address Book work to import the contacts, if it's able to. Scroll through the Name list to see if names appear to have been added correctly.

LDIF is the best option for exporting entire Address Book databases; if you're looking to import just one or a few Address Book entries, you'll likely use vCard, which is a nice, standard way to send people your information as an e-mail attachment, for instance. (Eventually it may become common-place for people to trade their vCard Address Book information the way they trade paper business cards today.)

If you receive a vCard as an e-mail attachment, or if you're working with an application that can export contacts as vCards, then you have another way to add contacts to Address Book. Simply double-click the vCard file, and that contact is added. You can also drag one or more vCards to the Address Book window. (As a bonus, all the vCard fields are recognized by Address Book, so there's no need to retype a person's info.) You can create vCards yourself, as well, simply by dragging a person's listing (ideally, yours) from the Address Book window to your desktop.

Henry David Thoreau

The vCard can then be sent to others as an attachment, making it easier for them to add you (or the person whose vCard you e-mail them) to their own address book applications, even if they aren't using Mac OS X or Address Book.

iCal

Apple's calendar/to do list management application, iCal, lets you organize your events, set reminders, and even share calendars with other users. iCal is designed so each user can have their own calendar and you can view multiple calendars: these could be calendars for different employees in a company, or calendars for different family members. With iCal, you can manage your events while viewing other people's schedules to ensure that they don't conflict.

The principle behind iCal is that each calendar is distinct yet can be overlapped with others. For example, you can have separate calendars for work, personal events, holidays, your favorite team's schedule, and other specific uses, such as your tennis reservations or club meetings.

Changing Calendar View

You can view your calendars in three different ways, according to the scope or detail you want to see. You have a choice between Day, Week, and Month view. You switch from one to another by clicking one of the view buttons at the bottom of the iCal window:

You can also move to the next or previous day, week, or month by clicking one of the arrow buttons.

When you're in Day or Week view, you may need to scroll to see all the hours in your calendar; iCal displays times outside those you set as your working day shaded to show that they are not working hours. To adjust the hours in your working day, select iCal ➤ Preferences, and in the Day section of this dialog, set a start and end time.

Showing and Hiding Calendars

If you have several calendars, you may not want them all displayed all the time. For example, if you have a calendar for your favorite sports team, you may find it gets in the way, especially if they play a lot of games, such as baseball, basketball, or hockey teams. Each calendar has a check box next to it in the Calendars list, allowing you to show or hide the calendar. Just click this box to change its view. If it is checked, the calendar is visible; if not, it is hidden.

This way, you can record your appointments and events in your own calendar and then display, say, your co-worker's or children's calendars to see if there are any conflicts.

TIP   Want to find more calendars, such as sports team schedules, TV schedules, movie releases, holidays in different states and countries, or tour calendars for your favorite band? Go to `http://icalshare.com`, where you can subscribe to hundreds of different calendars in dozens of categories. (See the later section, "Sharing Calendars," for more on sharing and subscribing to calendars.)

Adding Events to Calendars

When you first open iCal, two calendars are present: Home and Work. You can use these calendars, or you can add your own (see the section "Creating and Deleting Calendars" later in this chapter). To add a new event to an existing calendar, click the calendar you want to use in the Calendars list and then double-click the day or time of your event. You'll see a new event displayed, appropriately called New Event:

Just click the name of the event and type a new name. After you create a new event, you can display the Info drawer to enter more detailed information about the event, such as the time and any additional notes. Click the Info button (the i icon) at the bottom of the iCal window to display this drawer.

Some sections in this Info drawer have arrows that, when clicked, display pop-up menus offering additional options. For example, click Repeat to select from several repeat choices, such as Every Day, Every Week, Every Month, Every Year, and Custom. Then you can create a repeating event—such as a weekly or monthly appointment or meeting—once, and its information will repeat on your calendar at the frequency you choose.

You can also move an event from one calendar to another by clicking the Calendar arrows in the Info drawer and selecting a different calendar.

Click the Info button again to hide the Info drawer.

Setting Alarms

In addition to recording your events, iCal can alert you when an event is approaching in several ways:

- Display a visual alert
- Display an alert with sound
- Display an e-mail message
- Open a file
- Run an AppleScript

With the Info drawer visible, click the arrows next to Alarm and then select one of its choices. Another line will display below the alarm choice, where you can select, for example, the amount of time before the event you want the alert message to display, the e-mail address you want the alert sent to, or the file you want opened.

Creating and Deleting Calendars

You can create as many iCal calendars as you like, and you can even subscribe to shared calendars to access other people's events, as described in the next section. To create a calendar, just click the plus (+) button below the Calendars list. A new calendar displays, called Untitled. Type a name for it, and when this calendar is selected in the list, you can create events within it. You can also show and hide it, as necessary, as mentioned previously.

To delete a calendar, just click it in the Calendars list to select it and press the Delete key on your keyboard. If the calendar has no events or To Do items, it will be deleted immediately; if it has any of these items, iCal will display an alert asking if you're sure you want to delete it.

Sharing Calendars

While iCal is great for organizing your own life, its real power lies in its ability to share calendars with others, so you can organize events within your company, family, or school. When you have access to other people's calendars, you'll know when your events conflict with theirs, and you'll also be able to schedule events and appointments according to their availability.

You can share calendars in two ways, depending on how you or others work with iCal. The first way is to export the calendar as a file. To do this, click the calendar you want to share in the Calendars list and then select File ➤ Export. Save the file wherever you want. You can send this file to anyone by e-mail or over a network, and all they have to do is double-click it: iCal imports its events and To Do items into an existing calendar or creates a new calendar. This is a good way to share calendars for fixed events, such as sports schedules, school schedules, or vacations.

When you share a calendar like this, however, it's a snapshot of the calendar at a certain time. If you make changes to your calendar, you'll need to export it again and resend it to your friends or colleagues.

The second way to share calendars uses the Internet and a .Mac subscription to keep every user's copy of the calendar up to date. (See later in this chapter for more on synching calendars with .Mac.) Sharing a calendar like this involves two steps: *publishing* and *subscribing*. When you share your calendar so others can access it, you publish it; when you access another shared calendar, you subscribe to it.

NOTE   If you start sharing calendars, you may end up with quite a few calendars in your list. Or if you subscribe to a lot of calendars, such as for sports team schedules or TV schedules, you'll quickly find your overall view to be a bit confusing. Select File ➤ New Calendar Group to create a sort of "calendar folder" and then drag calendars into this group. Name it if you want and then use the group's check box to turn on or off the views for all the calendars, or click the disclosure triangle to view or hide individual calendars that belong to the group.

To publish a calendar, click it in the Calendars list to select it and then select Calendar ➤ Publish. You can select several options from the sheet that displays. If you want your changes to be made automatically, check Publish Changes Automatically. You can also choose to publish titles and notes, alarms, and To Do items.

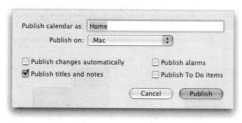

You must also have a .Mac account or use another WebDAV server. If you use the latter, select Private Server from the Publish On pop-up menu and then provide its URL, username, and password.

When you have selected your options for the calendar, click Publish. After the calendar has been published, you'll see a dialog that shows two URLs for the calendar: the first, in the form `webcal:/ /ical.mac.com/`*username*`/calender.ics`, is the URL that others can use to subscribe to your calendar, if they use iCal. The second, in the form `http://ical.mac.com/`*username*`/calendar`, is a web URL that allows any user to view your calendar on a web page, whether they use iCal or not. This is great when you need to share a calendar with people who cannot access a shared iCal calendar (in a company or school, for example), or even for people using other platforms, such as Windows or Linux. Your calendar will be updated according to the options you set when publishing it, and if you chose to publish changes automatically, this web page will always reflect the current version of your calendar.

If you click Send Mail in the URL dialog, your e-mail program will open with a new message containing these two URLs; the recipients of this e-mail simply click the URLs to access your calendar. If they click the `webcal://ical.mac.com/`*username*`/calender.ics` URL, their copy of iCal will open and subscribe to the calendar; if they click the web page URL, their web browser will open and take them to the web page.

NOTE   iCal now lets you create a special birthday calendar that contains the birthdays for all your contacts in Address Book (if you have entered their birthdays). Just go to iCal's General preferences and check Show Birthdays Calendar. The Birthdays Calendar updates automatically when you add birthday information to your contacts in Address Book.

Subscribing to Calendars

The easiest way to subscribe to a calendar is by clicking that URL. You can also subscribe to a calendar by selecting Calendar ➢ Subscribe and entering a URL manually. When you subscribe in this way, you can choose several options:

◆ To refresh the calendar automatically, and at what frequency

◆ To remove alarms

◆ To remove To Do items

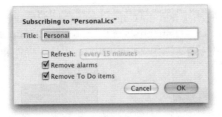

For calendars you subscribe to by clicking URLs, you can access these options by selecting the calendar in the Calendars list and then clicking the Info button.

Working with To Do Items

In addition to organizing your events and appointments, iCal can manage To Do items, helping you organize the tasks you need to do and reminding you to do them. You can set To Do items in any calendars you have created (but not in calendars you subscribe to) and also set their priorities, due dates, alarms, and more.

To see your To Do items, you display the To Do items list by selecting View ➢ Show To Dos. To hide them again, select View ➢ Hide To Dos. (You can also click the pushpin button at the bottom of the iCal window to show and hide To Do items.)

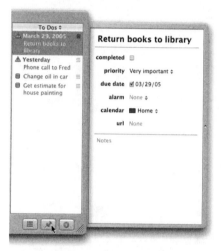

The To Do list gives you several options to help you organize your tasks; you can access these options by clicking the Info button at the bottom of the iCal window, which displays the Info drawer.

To create a new To Do item, select File ➢ New To Do or press ⌘K. Type the name of the new To Do item; you can enter notes in the Info drawer, but it's best that the To Do item be sufficiently clear. To set any options, such as alarms, priorities, or due dates, use the Info drawer.

NOTE   What if you have set up a To Do item and want to change it to an event? Or if you want to move an appointment from a calendar to your To Do list? Piece of cake. Just drag a To Do item to a calendar or an event to the To Do list and then make any changes you want in the Info drawer. This won't delete the original, so if you want to remove the original, you'll need to do that manually.

You can sort your To Do items by due date, priority, title, calendar, or manually. To change the sort order, click the To Dos header above the To Do item list and select one of these options. By default, this is set to Manually; you can drag your To Do items in the order you want.

When you have completed a To Do item, just put a check mark in its check box. Completed To Do items are hidden one day after you have checked them; you can change this in iCal's preferences.

When you hide a calendar, the To Do items it contains are hidden as well; you need to make sure, when checking your To Do items, that all your calendars are displayed.

NOTE   You can search for items in any of your calendars—this includes events, To Do items, notes, locations, and more. Type a search string in the Search field at the bottom of the iCal window. To refine your search and look only in specific items, click the triangle and choose your search criteria.

Printing Calendars and To Do Lists

It's great to be able to view your calendars on your Mac, or on the Web (see Chapter 11, "The Web, Online Security, .Mac, Sherlock, and iChat," for more on using .Mac to view calendars), but it's even better to be able to take them with you on paper. Yes, that old-fashioned print technology that needs no battery and never crashes is sometimes the best way to work. Printing calendars and to do lists to take on the road or to put on the refrigerator or bulletin board is a good way to have them handy.

iCal gives you several printing options. Select File ➤ Print to see what your options are.

You can choose from the following:

View Choose from Day, Week, Month, or List view.

Paper Select a paper size. This can be standard letter or A4 paper, or special paper sizes to fit in organizers.

Time Range Choose the time range you want to cover. This setting depends on the View option you chose; if you choose Week, for example, the time range will let you select from a specific week or date to a number of weeks ahead.

Calendars Check the calendars you want to print; uncheck those you don't want to print.

Options Choose from a number of options, such as whether you want to include all-day events, whether due dates are printed with To Do items, text size, and more.

When you've decided what you want to print, click Continue to go to the standard print dialog. If you've chosen a special paper size, make sure to insert the necessary paper in your printer.

iSync

As part of Mac OS X's personal information tools, iSync exists to allow you to extend the reach of the data you store on your Mac. You can synchronize that data with the various devices you carry on our belts, in pockets, or in purses—iPods, mobile phones, and personal digital assistants, among other items. iSync makes sure the contacts and calendar items on your "walking around" technology are up to date—if those devices are compatible with iSync and your Mac. iSync can do more than that, too, by using your .Mac account to synchronize items between your iDisk and your local Mac, if you so desire.

We'll begin with devices. When you launch iSync, you just see the basic iSync window:

Connect a device (an iPod, a Palm PDA, or turn on your Bluetooth phone if you have one and Bluetooth is set up) and then select Devices ➤ Add Device. iSync scans your Mac's connectors and displays any devices it finds.

Double-click the device to add it to iSync, which displays synchronization options for the device. What options are at your disposal depend on the device. For most handheld devices—phones, iPods, and so on—you'll be making selections that help you determine how you're going to synchronize your Address Book contacts and iCal events and appointments.

To synch the device, just click the Sync Devices button. Depending on how much data you have and the type of device, this may take a couple of minutes. When you're finished, disconnect the device and access your personal data using its menus and commands.

You can also synchronize certain data with your .Mac account. This allows you to access your Safari-based web bookmarks, your Address Book contacts, and your iCal calendars from anywhere that you can get Internet access. Once synchronized, you can log in to .Mac via any web browser and view your contacts, calendar, or bookmarks. To set up .Mac synching, go to the .Mac pane of the System Preferences. (The .Mac icon in iSync is there simply for those who were used to finding .Mac synchronization in the iSync application; if you click it, it merely displays a message about using the .Mac preferences pane.)

So to set up .Mac synching, go to the System Preferences, click the .Mac icon, and then click the Sync tab. This tab lets you turn on and configure synching for six different types of data. When you synch this data, some of it is available online when you log on to the .Mac website, and other data is available to synch to other Macs.

First, choose whether you want to synchronize your data with .Mac by checking the Synchronize with .Mac check box. If you do this, you can then choose a synchronization frequency from the pop-up menu: Manually means your data only synchs when you choose to do so; Automatically means that it synchs whenever your Mac detects changes and when you have a network connection. You can also choose Every Hour, Every Day, or Every Week. At the bottom of the window you can check Show Status in Menu Bar; this displays a synchronization icon in the menu bar, which turns when synching is occurring and lets you choose from this icon's menu to synch right away or open the .Mac synchronization preferences.

You can synchronize six different types of data:

Bookmarks Synch your Safari bookmarks to .Mac so you can use them from any web browser when logged onto .Mac, or so you can synch them to another Mac.

Calendars Synch your iCal calendars to .Mac to access them online or to synch them to another Mac.

Contacts This is your Address Book contact list. Synch this for online access, or to synch to another Mac.

Keychains   Synch your keychains and passwords they store to another Mac so you can access them.

Mail Accounts   If you synch these to another Mac, you can access your e-mail without having to set up your accounts.

Mail Rules, Signatures, and Smart Mailboxes   Synch these to another Mac, and you'll be able to run Mail exactly as it is on your first Mac. (For more on Mail, see Chapter 12.)

As you can see in this list, some of this data gets synched to the .Mac server so you can access it online, and other data gets synched to another Mac. For the former, synching lets you use this data online from any web browser, even from a computer running Windows. (See Chapter 11 for more on using this data with .Mac.) The latter is designed to help ensure that two Macs, such as a desktop computer and a laptop, have the same data.

To synch one Mac with another, both computers must be registered. Computers can only synch if they are set up to work with the same .Mac account in the .Mac preferences. When you check Synchronize with .Mac on one Mac, this turns on synchronization and registers the computer with the .Mac server. (If one of your computers is using an earlier version of Mac OS X, you'll need to set this up in the iSync application.) When you click the Advanced tab of the .Mac preferences, you'll see which computers are set up for .Mac synching. You can select one of your computers and click Unregister to remove if from your synch list; in this case, .Mac won't retrieve any data from it nor send any data to it.

NOTE   Other applications can use .Mac synchronization to store data as well. Generally, programs synch their preferences, or in the case of programs that manage personal data such as calendars, tasks, or contacts, they synch their database. If you have another program that uses .Mac synching, check its Help to find out how to set up this synching.

Keychain Access: Securing Passwords and Private Data

Keychain Access is a utility application used to manage your personal keychain. A *keychain* is a special database, protected by a single password, that's used to store a group of usernames and passwords. It's a convenient way, for instance, to store passwords that you use for secure websites and remote servers—or even passwords such as your bank PIN number and other information you'd like to store securely on your Mac.

The name "keychain" is meant to be an evocative metaphor for what's going on here, but Apple could have called it a "password database" or something similar to make its function more clear. It's essentially a repository for snippets of personal information, such as login names and passwords that, in turn, are protected by a single password.

Once you've entered these other passwords in Keychain Access, all you have to remember is your main keychain password. When you enter that password, you "unlock" your keychain, which means you can then view the stored account names and passwords.

The other trick with your keychain is that items can be accessed automatically in some cases. For instance, some applications can access the keychain directly, with your permission, and learn your username and password information for a particular resource, such as an Internet site or a networking volume.

NOTE   See Chapter 11 to learn more about accessing Internet sites via your keychain and Chapter 17, "Accessing Network Volumes," for a discussion of accessing network volumes with it.

By default, a keychain is created for you when your Mac OS X account is initially created, and that keychain has the same password as your login password. When you first launch Keychain Access by double-clicking its icon in the `Utilities` folder inside your main `Applications` folder, you'll see a list of all the items your keychain contains, as shown in Figure 16.4.

FIGURE 16.4
The keychain window

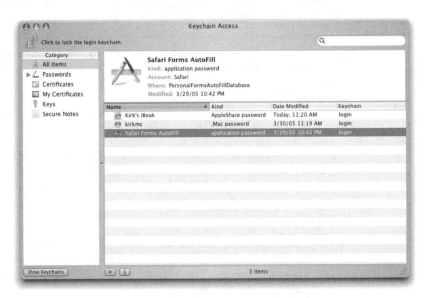

You may also see items that have already been added to the keychain—for instance, when you opt to save an e-mail account password in Mail, that account password is saved in your keychain. (This is also true of other native Mac OS X e-mail applications such as Microsoft Entourage.) Likewise, if you've signed up for .Mac service, you may see that password on your keychain. You'll find passwords that you've saved when accessing network volumes, and if you've turned on Safari's AutoFill feature, you'll find an entry for that as well.

NOTE If an administrative user has changed your login password, you may find that your keychain password is different from your current login password. (When you change your own login password, Mac OS X will optionally change your keychain password, too. If an administrator changes your login password, however, your keychain password won't change automatically.) If that's the case, and you've never changed your keychain password in the past, then you need to use your original login password to access your keychain. You should then change it to your current login password, as discussed in the next section.

Changing Your Keychain Password

As mentioned, your keychain password by default is the same as your Mac OS login password. If you're concerned about security, you should change it immediately, and you should use the advice in Chapter 11 (in the section "Securing Passwords") to create an effective password. After all, this may end up being a pretty important password, because it's guarding all of your other passwords and account information.

To change your keychain's password, follow these steps:

1. Click the Show Keychains button at the bottom left of the Keychain access window. This displays all your keychains at the top of the Categories list. (Your login keychain is the one used by default.) Click the keychain whose password you want to change to select it.

2. Choose Edit ➤ Change Password for Keychain *Keychain Name*. (*Keychain Name* is replaced in the command with the actual name assigned, such as login.)

3. In the Change Keychain Password dialog box, enter your current password in the top entry box, type the new password in the middle entry box, and enter it again in the Verify entry box to ensure that you've typed it correctly. You can also click the Details disclosure triangle if you'd like to see the details of where the keychain file is stored and what application is currently accessing it. (This might be handy for ensuring that you're changing the correct keychain's password.)

4. To see how secure your password is, click the key button in this dialog box; this displays the Password Assistant. As you type your new password, the Password Assistant shows you the quality of your password and gives you hints as to why it's not secure enough.

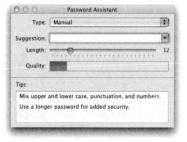

5. Click OK in the dialog box to change the password. Next, click Save to close the Keychain Settings dialog.

NOTE   If the password isn't at least six characters long, an alert will pop up telling you that the password is not secure and asking you to type a longer one. In fact, even though your original password might be shorter than six characters, you won't be allowed to set a different one that is not at least six characters long.

Adding to Your Keychain

Want to add an item to your keychain? There are two basic ways to store passwords on your keychain. The first way is via another part of the Mac OS, such as the Connect to Server window discussed in Chapter 17. You may also find commands in some third-party Internet applications, such as some popular FTP applications. (Fetch, discussed in Chapter 17, can add passwords to the keychain.) Using a command from within those applications, you may be able to add usernames and passwords to your keychain automatically.

The other way to add items is completely manual in nature. When you add an item this way, you're really just creating a record of the resource, username, and password. This is pretty flexible for storing any sort of password that you'd like to keep secure; you can even enter your bank's ATM PIN or the combination for your gym locker if you like. The whole point is that you can store these little bits of information, but the information can be accessed only by someone who knows your master keychain password.

In the main keychain window, click the Password button or choose File ≻ New Password Item. You'll see the New Password Item sheet, shown in Figure 16.5.

FIGURE 16.5

The New Password Item window

In the New Password Item window, you can manually enter a name, account name, and password that you'd like to store in your keychain. For instance, you can enter a website's name or URL, an account name, and a password. Or you could enter **Bank ATM** as the name, skip the Account entry box (or enter your bank account number, if you'd like) and enter a password. In some respects, it doesn't really matter. If you happen to enter a URL as the name and a valid user account and password, you may be able to sign into the Internet site automatically. In many cases, though, what you enter here is really just personal information that you'd like to secure with your keychain password.

NOTE If you enter a complete URL in the Name entry box, you'll create an Internet password item, which can be used to access and log in to that Internet site automatically (under certain circumstances). To create an Internet password item, remember to type the correct protocol as part of the URL, as in http://www.mcelhearn.com instead of simply www.mcelhearn.com.

When you've finished entering details for a particular password item, click the Add button. You'll see the item in the main keychain window.

TIP   If you turn on the option Show Typing, as shown in Figure 16.5, you can see the password as you're typing it in the Password entry box. Otherwise, you'll see dots instead of the characters you're typing.

Accessing a Password Item

Can't remember a particular username or password? If you've stored it as an item on your keychain, you can access that password item and retrieve both the account name and the password. Begin by opening and unlocking your keychain (that is, launch Keychain Access and enter your keychain password if prompted). With your keychain's main window open, you should be able to click any of the entries to see information about it in the information pane in the lower part of the window. If you have a lot of passwords, you may find it easier to click the disclosure triangle next to Passwords and then click one of the groups that displays such as

◆ AppleShare, for network passwords

◆ Application, for passwords stored by specific programs

◆ Internet, for specific Internet passwords

If you double-click one of these password items, you'll see your account name and some other information about this item. You can view the password itself by clicking the Show Password check box. You may be asked to enter your keychain password first; the password will appear immediately in a small entry box.

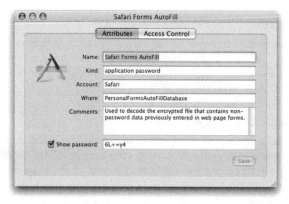

In some cases, you won't see the password dialog box immediately; instead, you'll see the Confirm Access to Keychain dialog box. This is just another checkpoint that pops up in the Mac OS to confirm that an application is authorized to access your keychain automatically.

NOTE This happens in other places, too, such as the Connect to Server window and some Internet applications that attempt to access the keychain. Whenever something tries to access the keychain that hasn't in the past, this dialog box will appear, and it will continue to appear in the future if you click Deny or Allow Once.

Click the Allow Once button if you'd like Keychain Access to decrypt the password and display it only one time; click Always Allow if you'd prefer the password to be visible whenever you click the View Password button for the item. Click Deny if you don't want to allow Keychain Access to access your keychain. (You're not likely to choose this now, but you may encounter it in another application that you do want to deny access to your keychain.)

NOTE You can decide whether or not a particular keychain item will warn you when an attempt is made to access it. Choose the Access Control tab in the info pane when you're viewing the item in question. There you can check the option Allow All Applications to This Item, which will allow Keychain Access to bypass the Confirm Access to Keychain dialog box. (If you don't want to bypass the dialog box for this item, turn on Confirm before Allowing Access; if you want to ask for the keychain password before allowing access, turn on the Ask for Keychain Password check box as well.) If you'd like to specify the applications that can access this item without a dialog box, use the Add and Remove buttons to add applications that can access this item without the warning.

Removing an Item

To remove an item from your keychain, highlight that item in the main keychain window and click the Delete button. You'll see an alert box asking if you really want to remove the item. If so, click Delete. (If you have second thoughts, click Cancel.) Once you click Delete, the item is removed, and there's no getting it back. (You'll need to re-create it.)

Lock and Unlock Your Keychain

Whenever you plan to leave your Mac idle or whenever you feel that it's important to secure your passwords, you should lock your keychain. Locking the keychain simply forces you to enter your main keychain password again to access the individual keychain items. You can lock your keychain immediately by clicking the Lock button in the main keychain window or by selecting File ➤ Lock Keychain *Keychain Name* or File ➤ Lock All Keychains. (In the Lock command, *Keychain Name* is replaced by the current keychain's name, as in File ➤ Lock Keychain mychain.)

WARNING   Keychain Access presents an interesting security problem. By default, your keychain is always unlocked whenever you're logged in to your Mac (assuming your keychain password and Mac OS X account password are the same). That means that anyone who gains access to your account can also see those prized passwords that you've hidden in your keychain. Knowing this, it's important to be vigilant about locking your keychain either manually or automatically by using one of features detailed in this section.

If you lock the keychain but leave it open, you'll see the Lock toolbar icon change to Unlock:

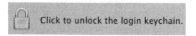

To unlock the keychain, click the Unlock button and enter your keychain password in the alert box that appears. Click OK, and your keychain is unlocked once again.

NOTE   Your keychain is automatically locked when you log out of your user account on the Mac and at certain other times, such as when you shut down the Mac.

Each keychain can also accept some individual settings that govern automatic behavior; in other words, you can tell your keychain to lock itself. Select Edit ➤ Change Settings for Keychain *Keychain Name* from the Keychain Access menu. (*Keychain Name* is replaced in the actual command with the name of the current keychain, as in Edit ➤ Change Settings for Keychain mychain.) The Change Keychain Settings dialog box appears:

This dialog box offers two options for automatically locking your keychain:

◆   In the Lock after ___ Minutes of Inactivity option, you can select the number of minutes the keychain should stay open (without any activity) before it becomes locked again.

◆   In the Lock When Sleeping option, you can choose to have your keychain lock itself automatically whenever the Mac sleeps—whether that sleep setting happens automatically or results from you actively putting the Mac into Sleep mode.

WARNING   Closing Keychain Access doesn't necessarily lock any unlocked keychains. If you have an automatic setting active (such as Lock after 5 Minutes of Inactivity), that setting will still be in effect if Keychain Access is closed. Otherwise, you need to lock your keychains explicitly before quitting Keychain Access.

You'll also notice that this dialog lets you choose to synchronize the keychain with .Mac. Clicking the .Mac button in this dialog opens the .Mac preference pane, discussed earlier in this chapter.

Managing Multiple Keychains

Whenever a user account is created on your Mac, that user also gets his own keychain; there's no need for you to create individual keychains for different users of your Mac.

However, you may decide to create additional keychains that help you manage your own passwords and user account names. For instance, you might have one keychain that enables you to access network volumes and secure websites and another keychain to hold your bank and credit card PINs. The advantage of this system is that anyone who does happen to gain access to one of your keychains won't necessarily get access to all of them (especially if you use a different password for each keychain).

To create an additional keychain, choose File ➤ New Keychain. A small New Keychain dialog box appears; enter a name for the keychain and click Create or press Return.

Next, enter a password (twice, pressing the Tab key between each and typing it the same way each time) and click OK or press Return. If your passwords are typed correctly, you'll see another new keychain window in which you can manage the new keychain.

You can lock an individual keychain by clicking the Lock button in its window. You can lock all keychains at once by choosing File ➤ Lock All Keychains. As noted, each keychain has its own Change Settings for Keychain *Keychain Name* command to determine if and when it locks automatically.

If you have multiple keychains, you can choose a different default keychain, if desired. (The default keychain is used to store password items that are generated by other applications or utilities, such as the Connect to Server window or a keychain-enabled web browser.) To change the default, switch to that keychain's main window and select File ➤ Make Keychain *Keychain Name* Default, where *Keychain Name* is the actual name of the selected keychain.

What's Next?

This chapter introduced you to some of Mac OS X's included applications for managing personal information—Address Book, iCal, iSync, and Keychain Access, which can be used for password management and security. In the next chapter, you'll be introduced to networks and accessing network volumes, including file sharing, FTP, and other common ways to share and access files.

Part 4

Networking, Connectivity, and Portables

In this section, you will learn how to:

- ◆ Access network volumes
- ◆ Build a network
- ◆ Share files
- ◆ Get the most out of your iBook or PowerBook
- ◆ Add portable peripherals
- ◆ Integrate Mac OS X with other platforms

## Chapter 17

Accessing Network Volumes

If your Mac is connected to a network, you can access remote disks and volumes via a number of different protocols, including Apple File Protocol, which is common if you're using Mac OS X Server or AppleShare IP on your server computer; the SMB protocol (for accessing disks served by Microsoft Windows computers); and Network File System (NFS), which is a common protocol when you want to connect to a Unix computer and share files. Once you have established a connection to one or more of these types of server, you'll be able to see the contents of those remote disk drives (or at least the folders and items to which you have been granted access) and share files on those remote servers.

In this chapter, we'll discuss getting connected to remote volumes over a network connection. This chapter assumes you're already connected to a network—for instance, in an office environment—or that you intend to connect to remote servers over an Internet connection that you configured in Chapter 10, "Configuring Internet Access." If you need to set up your network and configure it for file sharing services, you should consult Chapter 18, "Building a Network and Sharing Files."

In this chapter:

◆ Are You Set Up for Networking?

◆ Accessing Remote File Services

◆ Understanding Remote Login

◆ Accessing FTP Sites

Are You Set Up for Networking?

In many cases, particularly in organization and corporate settings, someone else is responsible for your Mac's network connection. To share files with other computers, you'll need to have either an Ethernet or an AirPort (wireless) connection established and configured. If you have such a connection established, you should be able to find out in a number of ways.

NOTE   If you plan to connect to remote servers over the Internet and not to other Macs on a local network, you should already be configured as long as you have an active Internet connection, as discussed in Chapter 10. As a rule, if you can access items in your web browser, you should be able to access remote networking servers.

Of course, the first way to find out if your Mac is connected to a network is to ask. If you have other computers in your office, and wiring or special networking hubs connect them, there's a good chance they're connected for networking. If they aren't cabled or otherwise configured to talk to one another, you'll want to move on to Chapter 18 to establish the network before you can sign on to a remote server.

Checking the Connection

When you first access the Network pane in the System Preferences application, you'll see the Network Status window, which shows you what is currently going on with your Mac's networking connections, as shown in Figure 17.1.

FIGURE 17.1
The Network Status screen is handy for a quick check of your network connection.

As you can see from the figure, this is a friendly window that gives you a good idea of what's going on with your Mac's recognized networking connections. This is the first place you can go to get a sense of how your Mac is connected to a network and how you should go about making that connection happen if you don't see one that's available. If you would like to dig deeper into one of those connection types, you can either double-click it in this window or choose that connection from the Show menu. To return to the Network Status window, choose Network Status from the Show menu.

NOTE If you don't see a connection that you expect to see, it might be because it isn't active; choose Network Port Configurations from the Show menu and make sure that port is turned on. If it is, but it still doesn't appear in the Network Status window, it's possible that the port isn't configured or isn't detected. For instance, Built-in Ethernet may not show up on some Macs when an Ethernet cable is not plugged into that Mac.

Turning on Ethernet

Many desktop Macs will be connected to a network via Ethernet, which connects you to a networking *hub* or *switch* using a special cable. Since all Macs that support Mac OS X have Ethernet built in, and Ethernet is faster than most other networking options, it's the best choice if you don't plan to move your Mac around much (assuming it's convenient to stretch an Ethernet cable to that Mac). To check for an Ethernet connection, you can open the System Preferences application and click the Network icon to open the Network pane. In the Show menu, choose Built-in Ethernet or double-click Built-in

Ethernet on the Network status screen. You'll see the Ethernet configuration contacts, as shown in Figure 17.2.

If your Ethernet connection is configured manually on the TCP/IP tab as shown in the window, there's a very good chance that your Mac has been set up for networking. There's also a good chance that it's been set up if any of the other options (Using DHCP, Using BootP) is chosen in the Configure IPv4 menu, and you have a router address shown in that panel.

FIGURE 17.2
Viewing your Ethernet
configuration

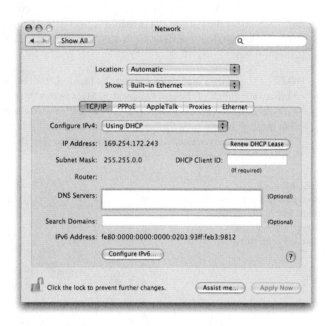

It's less likely that you have a network configured if, on the Network Status screen, you see that your IP address has been *self-assigned*. (It's still possible, particularly on a small network at home or in a small business. Such networks can self-configure, making it possible for you to access the other Macs without any special configuration in the Network pane. See Chapter 18 for details.) Likewise, if you don't have an IP address assigned at all, that may be a sign that you're not connected via Ethernet.

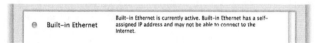

NOTE   In past versions of Mac OS X, it was possible to use AppleTalk as the protocol for File Sharing as well as for printer services. In Mac OS X 10.4, however, accessing AppleShare servers over the AppleTalk protocol is no longer supported. If you need to do that (to access a much older Classic Mac, for instance) the solution is to run an application like Shareway IP on the older Mac, which gives it the capability to access File Sharing services over TCP/IP instead of via AppleTalk. Apple-Talk is still an option in the Network pane when you're configuring Ethernet or AirPort, but it's only used for printing and for locating older AppleShare servers—those older servers, ultimately, must be updated to support TCP/IP if you're going to be successful at sharing.

TURNING ON AIRPORT

If your Mac doesn't connect to other computers via Ethernet, it may have an AirPort wireless networking connection built in, particularly (but not exclusively) if it's an iBook or PowerBook. There are two ways to tell. In the Network pane, you'll see AirPort in the Show menu if you have an AirPort card installed. (AirPort compatibility requires that a special card be installed in your Mac; all modern Macs are compatible and offer a slot for upgrading with an AirPort card.) If the AirPort configuration on the TCP/IP tab shows signs of life, it means that your connection is up and running. If you don't see numbers for the entries, it's possible your AirPort connection is turned off. Check the AirPort tab; if the By Default, Join menu is grayed out (cannot be accessed) then there's a chance the AirPort is turned off (see Figure 17.3).

NOTE   The truth is that AirPort is popular for all sorts of Macs, not just laptops. In Todd's magazine office, about half of the current desktop Macs (a few iMacs and a Power Macintosh G4, as well as iBooks and PowerBooks) use AirPort to share files with the others on the network, as well as to get an Internet connection. AirPort is not just about portable computing; it's also about getting computers on the network when it isn't convenient to stretch an Ethernet connection across the room or to another floor in your building.

FIGURE 17.3
No access to the By Default, Join menu on the AirPort pane suggests that AirPort is turned off.

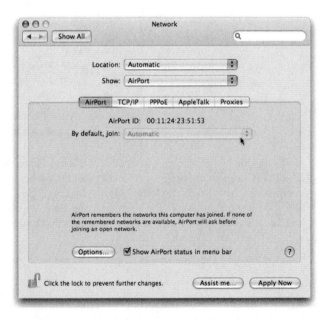

You can turn on your AirPort connection in one of two places—in the Internet Connect application (located in your /Applications/Utilities/ folder) or from the AirPort menu bar icon, if you see one on your Mac's menu bar. If you see that menu, open it and, if Turn AirPort On is an option, select it. This is how you actually turn on the AirPort card in your Mac so it can attempt to locate a wireless network in the vicinity.

Once AirPort is turned on (or if AirPort is already turned on), and you're near an AirPort Base Station or a similar "WiFi" router, you'll see the name of a network, such as is shown here. (If there are multiple available networks, you'll see each of them listed.) Choose the network that you want to connect to in the menu.

NOTE Some AirPort networks are "closed" networks, for security reasons, meaning their names won't show up when an AirPort-enabled Mac attempts to discover them. In that case, you'll want to select Other from the menu and type in the name of the network.

Once you've chosen the network, you may be asked for the network's password—you'll need to know what it is and enter it in the dialog box before you can access that AirPort network. (Ask the system administrator for the password if you don't know it.) In some cases, you may not be asked for a password; this is a less secure network, but it may be a choice the administrator makes, particularly if the network is in a public place such as a trade show office, coffee shop, or anywhere that allows many different wireless computers to connect. If you connect to the AirPort Base Station successfully, you'll probably see your TCP/IP tab change from blanks to filled-in addresses (particularly if you're set to Using DHCP).

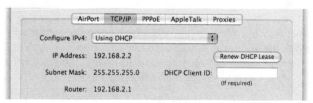

If you've successfully located a router in the AirPort menu and then you see that the IP address has been provided by the DHCP server, it means that a link has been established to your network router, which suggests that you're ready to access remote servers.

TIP You can also use AirPort for computer-to-computer networks when you simply want to share files between two Macs that are AirPort capable; see Chapter 18 for details.

If you get through this process and it doesn't appear that you have an Ethernet or AirPort connection working, you may need to set up your network—see Chapter 18 for a much more in-depth discussion and for some troubleshooting tips. You may simply need to discuss the options with your system administrator to find out exactly how you should connect to your local network.

Checking for Servers

Once you have your network connection up and running, the next step is to check if your Mac sees any computers or servers on the network that it can attempt to access.

Servers that can be auto-detected by the Mac—particularly those on your local network—are found in the Network folder on your Mac, where you can access them by double-clicking them in a Finder window. In the Finder, choose Go ➤ Network or click the Network icon in the Sidebar of a Finder window. If you're connected to a network, you should see icons for the various servers and file-sharing Macs that are available on that network.

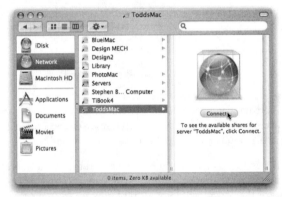

If you see the names of various servers in this folder, there's a good chance that you're connected to a network. If no servers appear to be accessible via the Finder window's Network icon, and you know that you have an active Ethernet or AirPort connection, it's possible that no Macs or PCs on your network have Personal File Sharing enabled.

If this doesn't sound right (if you expect to see file-sharing servers, for instance), you should consult with your system administrator or head to Chapter 18 and check the configuration of your file-sharing Macs.

There's another way to connect to servers—the Connect to Server window. In older versions of Mac OS X, this was the main way you located network resources; starting in Mac OS X 10.3, Apple integrated the Network icon's auto-search capabilities into the Finder. To launch the Connect to Server window choose Go ➤ Connect to Server in the Finder.

Connect to Server is still useful in a few specific instances. You can use it if you want to contact a server over the Internet using a protocol other than web protocols; for instance, Mac OS X has the built-in ability to connect to FTP servers for read-only access. (That means you can copy files from FTP servers but not to them; we'll discuss that later in this chapter.) Connect to Server can also be used for Apple file sharing over the Internet or for other types of network connections. Via the Recent Servers menu that appears in the window, you can even use Connect to Server to access servers to which you have recently connected. (It looks like a clock face.)

Throughout the rest of the chapter we'll look at times when you can use the Network icon versus times when it's appropriate to use Connect to Server or the Internet Connect application to establish different types of network connections.

Accessing Remote File Services

There are five different types of servers that your Mac is designed to log in to actively using the Connect to Server window. (A sixth type, Unix-style NFS sharing, is a more permanent connection, as discussed later in this chapter.) Those five types are the following:

♦   An Apple File Protocol (AFP) connection. This is the standard connection to another Mac that is running file sharing or to a Mac OS X server or AppleShare IP server computer.

♦   A remote AFP connection—a file-sharing connection that occurs over the Internet.

♦   An SMB connection, or one to a Windows PC that is running its own version of file sharing.

♦   A WebDAV connection, which is a remote networking connection to a special type of web server computer.

♦   An FTP (File Transfer Protocol) server computer, a remote computer designed primarily for making files available for others to download.

These connection types are similar, but each has its nuances, which we'll cover in the following sections.

Connecting to AFP Servers

You can use two basic methods to connect to servers that are using the Apple File Protocol. First, you can use the Network icon in the Finder to locate local servers that your Mac automatically recognizes. Second, you can use the Connect to Server window to connect to a server that doesn't appear in your Network folder; this would include any server that you're going to access by directly entering that server's IP address or network address. (We'll cover that in the next section.)

NOTE   Once you've gained access to the server, by either of these approaches, you can log in to it with either a guest account or a username and password. Once you've successfully logged in to the remote Mac, the folder or disk that you're accessing will appear on your desktop.

If your goal is to connect to another computer on your local network, and that computer has already been configured for file sharing, then you should find that those file-sharing servers on your local network are automatically discovered for you. That means you can easily locate servers. Here's how:

1. In a Finder window, click the Network icon in the Sidebar.

2. Locate a server that you want to access, and double-click it or click the word Connect that appears beneath it.

3. You'll now see the Connect To dialog box where you can enter the username and password you want to use to access the remote volume. You must have a valid user account and password on the remote system to access the remote volume successfully with appropriate user privileges. If you don't, you can select the Guest radio button to access the remote server as a guest. If the remote server doesn't accept guests, the Guest radio button will be grayed out (not selectable). Once you've entered a name and password or selected Guest access, click the Connect button.

Once connected, you'll see a listing of the volumes and folders to which you have access privileges. In the case of an administrator account, generally you'll see the main volume of the remote Mac listed, along with mounted removable disks and your home folder. For more limited accounts, you'll see only your account's home folder and the names of other users, representing their Public folders. To access a volume, select it and click OK; you also can double-click the name of a volume.

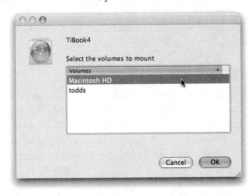

TIP You can select more than one volume by holding down the ⌘ key while clicking additional volume names. Then click OK to mount all of them.

Once you've successfully logged in, the remote volume(s) will appear in the Sidebar in your Finder windows, as well as in Open and Save dialog boxes. You may also see the volumes on your Desktop if your Mac has been configured to display them via Finder Preferences. Figure 17.4 shows a Finder window's Sidebar with two volumes mounted and displayed in Finder windows, including the user's remote home folder (in the figure, the home folder is `todds`).

FIGURE 17.4
Two remote volumes have been mounted and accessed.

When you're done working with one of the volumes, you can click the small eject icon next to its entry in the sidebar. This will eject the volume and remove it from the Finder window; you'll now have to log back in to that remote server in order to access that volume again.

WHAT CAN YOU ACCESS WHEN YOU'RE LOGGED IN?

It's worth noting that when you access another user's `Public` folder, you have read access, but not write access, to any items in that folder. In other words, you can't save files directly to that user's `Public` folder. However, you can save files to the `Drop Box` folder that appears in each `Public` folder. The `Drop Box` folder offers you write access, but it doesn't give you read access, as a security precaution. If you have a file that you'd like to share with the user, copy it to that user's `Drop Box`.

If you've signed in with a valid user account, you have full access to your own home folder on that remote machine. You can copy files to and from your home folder, your `Documents` folder, or your `Public` folder, as desired.

Connecting to AFP Servers via URL

The Connect to Server window enables you not only to choose servers on your local network but also to log in to remote AFP servers—even those that you're accessing over the Internet—by entering the server's URL directly. You do that in the Server Address box at the top of the Connect to Server window. (Remember, AFP is the protocol used for Personal File Sharing.)

You also could enter a numerical IP address or a text URL for any AFP server with an address available on the Internet, including, of course, your own Mac if you're accessing it from the road. For AFP servers, you begin the URL with `afp://` followed by the IP address or hostname and domain name.

Once you've clicked Connect, the process is the same as if you were logging in to a local server. The server will be found, and you'll be asked to enter a username and password or choose Guest. With that accomplished, you'll see the volumes you're allowed to access; select them and they'll appear in the Finder.

Connecting to WebDAV Servers

Along with signing in to AFP servers, you can use the Connect to Server window to log in to some web servers and gain access to their root folders (where the web files are stored) if you have an account that has the proper permissions to do so. In general, you can access only specific types of web servers that offer WebDAV (Web-based Distributed Authoring and Versioning) services. Put succinctly, WebDAV is a type of web server that improves on the HTTP model by giving both read and write access to authorized users.

In most cases, you'll need to enter an IP address manually to access a WebDAV server. Enter it in the Address entry box, starting with `http://` and finishing with the WebDAV server's IP address or hostname and domain. Then click Connect.

The WebDAV server will be mounted on your desktop, where you can access it like a regular file-sharing server. If that server also happens to be an actual web server (such as the `Site` folder in your .Mac iDisk, if you have one), WebDAV enables you to change files directly on it as if it were a remote volume, and those changes are reflected immediately on the Web. That's the main reason for the WebDAV standard—to cut out the need to use an FTP application to access a web server computer and to enable you to edit files directly on the remote web server from your desktop.

NOTE Your iDisk can be accessed via either a WebDAV connection or an AFP connection. See Chapter 11, "The Web, Online Security, .Mac, Sherlock, and iChat," for details.

Connecting via Alias

Mac OS X offers another way to shortcut the steps required to log in to a server: you can create an alias of a mounted server volume. (While it's available on the desktop, select the volume's icon and choose File ➢ Make Alias, or select the icon and press ⌘D+L. Note that this doesn't work with the volume in the Sidebar of a Finder window; you need to use Finder ➤ Preferences to show volumes on the desktop if they aren't shown there automatically.) After you've disconnected from the server and want to access it again, you can double-click the alias you've created. You then will see a login window that lets you bypass the Connect to Server window completely.

Login Options and Security

If you've logged in to a few remote servers by now, you may have noticed that the Connect To dialog box (where you generally enter your username and password after selecting a remote server) includes options in the window and an Options menu, which can be accessed by clicking the small action button at the bottom-left of the window. It enables you to set a few preferences for how your password is sent, for adding the password to your keychain, and for changing your password on the remote server, as long as you know the current password.

NOTE   If you decide to change your password, you'll need to enter the correct username in the Connect To window before you click the Options button.

Here are the options you can consider in the Connect to Server window:

Remember Password to Keychain   Turn on this option (it's a check box under the Password entry box) if you'd like the password for this connection to be added to your keychain. In the future, your password will be entered automatically in the Connect window (as long as your keychain is available and open). Also, if you access a particular volume on that server by double-clicking an alias or selecting a Favorite, you won't be asked for your password at all—the volume will mount immediately. See Chapter 11 for more on keychains and the Keychain Access application.

Allow Sending Password in Clear Text   With this option on, your Mac is able to send an unencrypted password to connect to a remote server. If security is paramount, you should turn this off; however, some servers may not be able to accept encrypted passwords.

Warn When Sending Password in Clear Text   If the Allow Clear Text Password option is on, you can turn on this option so that an alert dialog box appears when a password is sent unencrypted.

Allow Secure Connections Using SSH   Turning on this option enables you to use SSH encryption to maintain a secure connection to this particular server. This is ideal for connections to remote AFP networks running Mac OS X 10.2 (or Mac OS X 10.2 Server) or higher.

Warn When Connection Does Not Support SSH   When you have the Allow Secure Connections Using SSH option active, this secondary option is also active; if checked, you'll be told when you're connecting to a server that doesn't support SSH security.

Click the Save Preferences button if you've made changes that you want to save.

The action menu also gives you the opportunity to change your password on the remote server when you choose the Change Password command. In the interest of security, it's a good idea to change your password on a regular basis.

To change your password, remember that you first must have entered your username correctly in the Connect window. Then, after clicking the task menu button and choosing Change Password, you'll see the Change Password dialog sheet. Enter your current password in the Old Password entry box. Then enter the new password in the New Password and Confirm Password entry boxes, typing them exactly the same each time. Finally, click OK.

Connecting to SMB Servers

If you have Windows-based PCs that have file sharing active on your network, or if you have access to Windows-based network servers that don't offer Apple File Protocol services as an option, you can access those servers using the SMB protocol, which is built into Mac OS X. You also can connect to other computers that have SMB file sharing active, including some Unix- or Linux-based PCs. Mac OS X 10.2 (and higher) enable you to connect to SMB servers by selecting them in the Connect to Server window. There are two approaches. In recent versions of Mac OS X, you can access SMB volumes via the Network icon in the Finder. In other cases, you'll need to use the Connect to Server command.

NOTE You also can connect to your Mac from Windows if you have Mac OS X 10.2 or higher installed and you turn on Windows File Sharing, which is discussed in Chapter 20, "Mac OS X and Other Platforms."

Before you connect, you'll need to have at least one *share point* defined in Windows. From within Windows, you designate a share point by right-clicking a folder or disk and then choosing Sharing and Security from the menu that appears. (In some cases, the folder that you share may need to be dragged to the main `Shared Documents` folder first.) In the Properties window, turn on the Share This Folder on the Network option and enter a name (for best compatibility, don't use spaces or nontext characters). You also can choose how the share point can be accessed. If it's read only, then anyone who has access to this PC can access this share point and copy items from it—they simply can't change anything on the disk or copy items to it. If you'd like to allow full access (read and write), turn on the Allow Network Users to Change My Files option and enter a password—anyone who connects to this PC will need to know the password in order to have full access to the share point.

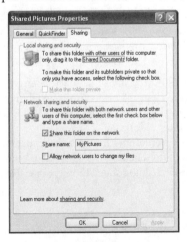

With the share point set up, you're ready to connect to the server from your Mac. You have two different approaches you can take:

◆ In the first approach, you select the Network icon in the Finder and then chose the name of the Network Neighborhood for your Windows computer. When you locate the server, double-click its icon to gain access.

◆ Alternatively, you can open the Connect to Server window and enter a direct IP address to the Windows-based PC in the Address entry box at the bottom of the Connect to Server window. Use the format smb://192.168.1.45 or smb://win01.yourco.com/, substituting the correct IP address or hostname and server name for that PC. (You also can enter the name of the share point you want to access after entering the server's address, as in smb://192.168.1.45/ CDISK/, if you'd like to skip the SMB Mount dialog box.)

In either case, next you'll see a dialog box that asks you which SMB mount you'd like to connect to; select it in the menu (there may be only one) and click OK.

Now you'll see the Authentication dialog box; enter a username for the remote connection (it doesn't matter what the username is) and enter the password for the share point that was created in Windows. (Remember that the password dictates which type of access you have; if the share point is set up for Read Only access exclusively, then no password is required in this box.)

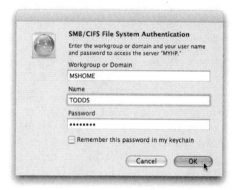

Click OK, and if the password is correct, you'll see the share point mounted on your desktop just as if it were any other shared server. Now you can access files and folders on the remote Windows share point using the Finder.

Disconnecting from Shared Volumes

How ever you managed to log in to a remote server volume or folder, logging out is easy. First, you should close any documents or applications accessed on the remote server. Next, if the volume is on your desktop, drag the remote server's icon from your Mac's desktop to the Trash icon in the Dock. You'll notice that the Trash icon changes to the Eject icon; release the mouse button to drop the server icon on the Eject icon. Your Mac will no longer be connected to the server.

Alternatively, you can select a server icon that's either on the desktop or in a Finder window (for example, when you're viewing the Network folder in a Finder window) and select File ≻ Eject from the Finder's menu. In the Finder window Sidebar, you can click the eject button next to a network volume for the same effect. Finally, you can Control+click (or Right-click, if you have a two-button mouse) on a remote server volume and select Eject from the context menu.

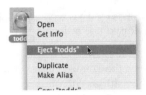

VIRTUAL PRIVATE NETWORKS

A Virtual Private Network (VPN) can be handy. It allows you to create a secure file-sharing network connection via the Internet so that you can connect, for instance, with your office LAN or even a home network. Mac OS X can connect to some servers via the Internet using either *PPTP* (Point-to-Point Tunneling Protocol) or *L2TP over IPSec* (Layer Two Tunneling Protocol over IP Security) to create a secure file-sharing connection over the Internet. Both protocols are used often with Windows servers and networks, although other types of networks use it as well. PPTP is the older of the two standards, but it's still common.

To launch a VPN connection, open Internet Connect (in the Applications folder) and click the VPN button. You'll be asked what type of VPN you want to create—make your choice and click Continue. Now enter a server address, a username, and password for the connection and click Connect. You'll also disconnect via this window in Internet Connect or via the VPN menu bar icon. (To create multiple configurations that you can switch between quickly, choose Edit Configurations from the Configuration menu.)

If you've logged in to more than one volume on a given server using the Connect to Server window, ejecting only one of those volumes doesn't log you off the server completely—if you return to the Network icon and access that server again, you won't be asked to authenticate by entering your password—you'll simply be shown a list of available volumes. To log out of a server completely, you need to eject all the volumes you've mounted from that server. When that's accomplished, you'll need to log in to the server again before you can remount any of its volumes.

Working with NFS Servers

So far we've dealt exclusively with the type of server that you log in to and out of whenever you feel the need to share files. Using AFP and/or various Internet protocols, you mount these servers on your desktop, open them up, do your business, close them, and drag them to the Trash or click their Eject buttons.

Mac OS X supports another approach using the Network File System (NFS) that is one way to mount server volumes in Unix and Unix-like operating systems. Creating the network mounts is a task for a system administrator because it can get a bit complicated, and it isn't a standard service offered by Mac OS X. (Other Unix operating systems offer NFS sharing, as does Mac OS X Server.) Accessing an NFS server volume couldn't be simpler. All you have to do is access the Network item at the Computer level of your Mac's folder hierarchy. Then select Servers, and you'll see all mounted NFS servers. Select a server, and you'll see a listing of the volumes for that server.

These servers act pretty much as if they were an extension of your Mac's hard disk—in fact, the Macintosh interface is designed to make them appear to be just that. Instead of logging in to and out of the server volumes using the Connect to Server window, they're always there (unless there's a problem with the server computer). Logging in to your Mac with your Mac OS X username and password grants you access and determines your privileges.

Like local folders, you can have a range of permissions on NFS volumes, from read-only to read/write to write-only. Your network administrator determines the permissions and exactly which volumes or folders will show up. The Mac looks for the NFS network mounts whenever it is restarted and, for all practical purposes, the mounts are permanent. The icons don't appear and disappear; if a server happens to be down for maintenance, you'll see an error message when you attempt to access it.

Understanding Remote Login

Telnet and SSH are standard protocols for *terminal emulation*, a method by which an application can pretend to be a command-line terminal, like those used to access mainframes and minicomputers in large-scale computer centers. Unlike a desktop computer or a personal computer (such as a Macintosh), terminals are screens and keyboards that don't do their own processing. Instead, they're used to connect to a remote computer, where the processing, storage, and other "computing" takes place. For this reason, such terminals are often called "dumb terminals."

NOTE We refer to both Telnet and SSH because SSH can be considered a secure implementation of Telnet (or at least what Telnet has come to mean to people). In Mac OS X 10.1 and higher, the Remote Login service requires that you use SSH for secure connections; however, you may still find yourself using a Telnet client to access other servers.

Of course, your Mac is not just a dumb terminal. For that reason, the Terminal application is used to *emulate* a terminal for the purpose of connecting to other computers and accessing them as though your Mac were a dumb terminal. In practice, the Terminal application is used for three different tasks: accessing *your own* Mac using a command-line interface, accessing remote Macs using a command-line FTP application, and accessing remote Macs using a command-line Telnet or SSH application.

When you're using Telnet or SSH, you sign in to the remote computer using a username and password. Then, just as with Mac OS X, you'll have access to your home folder on the remote computer, as well as certain command-line applications that are accessible on that remote computer. In fact, there's a whole underbelly of command-line applications that are installed with any Unix variant— even Mac OS X, via its version of FreeBSD—that you can access using Telnet.

Telnet isn't limited to other computers running Mac OS X. You can use the Terminal application and the `telnet` command to access any Unix or Unix-like computer for which you have a user account and password. That might include university computers, your ISP's web server computer, or any number of command line–based public servers and bulletin board systems (BBSs). All you have to know is the correct Telnet address.

In summary, both Telnet/SSH and FTP (File Transfer Protocol, discussed later in this chapter) are command-line applications that you can use from within the Terminal application to access remote computers. With Telnet/SSH, you're logging in to the remote computer to access command-line applications or manage files. In the case of FTP, you're logging in to the remote computer to transfer files between the remote computer and your own.

NOTE Chapter 18 covers turning on Remote Access so that others can connect to your Mac.

Accessing Computers Remotely

Got another Mac or other computer you'd like to log in to using Telnet or SSH? You can accomplish that easily using the Terminal application that's built into Mac OS X. As mentioned, Terminal is a multipurpose application designed to give you access to Mac OS X's command line. Once you've launched Terminal, you then can access the Telnet or SSH application and use it to log in to remote access servers.

This also works for any Unix-style operating system on which you have a username and password. The process is a little different for accessing remote Telnet and SSH servers (such as, for instance, an automated library catalog), as discussed in the section "Accessing Telnet Applications," later in this chapter.

NOTE Even if you've enabled the Root account on your Mac (as discussed in Chapter 28, "Solving System-Level Problems"), you can't log in to your Mac via Telnet or SSH using that Root account. However, you can use an administrator account and the sudo command to gain root privileges.

LOGGING IN USING SSH

For connecting between Macs—for instance, for transferring files or accessing command-line applications—SSH is more common these days than Telnet, which is useful more for cross-platform settings and for accessing online Telnet servers and applications. An SSH connection can go a little differently because it requires a bit more security. For the most part, the steps are the same, but you may need to jump through additional hoops to get signed in correctly. Here are the steps:

1. Launch the Terminal application. You should find it in the main Applications folder inside the Utilities folder. Once it is launched, you'll see the main prompt, which should look something like this.

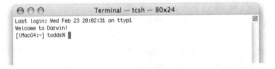

2. With the Terminal open, type **ssh *username@xxx.xxx.xxx.xxx*** (where *xxx* represents the remote SSH server's IP address) or **ssh *username@hostname.domain.tlx***, where *tlx* is the three-letter extension for the host's domain—com, net, org. (An example is ssh bluemac.mac-upgrade.com). Press Return after entering the address. Note in this image that you don't have to enter the username portion of the ssh command if your remote username is the same as your current Mac account name.

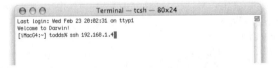

TIP In current versions of Mac OS X, you can enter the computer's name and .local to reach a Mac on your current network, as in ssh RyansiBook.local.

3. In some cases, as shown below, the next message you see may begin, "The authenticity of host…" and continue with a warning message. If you're sure that the host you're connecting to is valid (for instance, if you're connecting to a Mac on your local network), you can enter **yes** at the prompt and press Return. The machine then will be remembered as valid when you log into it in the future.

WARNING   Once you've established a connection to a particular IP address, SSH will alert you when the IP address and identification key don't match in the future and disallow login. For instance, if your computers are set up for DHCP, often they'll change IP addresses. If at some point in the future you attempt to access Mac B at the same IP address at which you once accessed Mac A, the connection will fail. The easy solution is to configure your local network connection manually, in the Network pane of System Preferences; the harder solution is to change the entry in the known_ hosts file (using a text editor), found in the hidden folder .ssh in your home folder.

4. Now, enter your password on the remote machine and press Return.

NOTE   On Unix and Unix-like (Linux, FreeBSD) systems, usernames and passwords are case sensitive.

If the password is accepted, you'll see the welcome message; if not, you'll be asked to enter it two more times before the connection will drop.

Once you're logged in, you'll see the command-line prompt. Now you can access the remote Mac by typing commands at the prompt and pressing Return. Of course, you'll need to know what some of those commands are before you can accomplish very much.

```
todds@192.168.2.4's password:
Last login: Mon Feb 21 10:52:00 2005
Welcome to Darwin!
[TiBook4:~] todds%
```

NOTE   In the Terminal, type **man ssh** and press Return to learn more about the different authentication methods and arguments you can use to alter SSH's behavior. Trust me—they can get complicated.

Basic Remote Access Commands

The commands you'll use in a remote access session, whether Telnet or SSH, are similar to the commands used at any Mac's command line, including your own. For a more complete overview, you can consult Chapter 22, "Terminal and the Command Line," which includes details about accessing your Mac via the Terminal application.

These commands are all typed commands, which you'll enter at a prompt, followed by pressing the Return key. When you press the Return key, the command is executed.

NOTE Telnet and SSH applications generally support a subset of all the commands that are available in a Darwin command-line session. You can experiment with other commands, as discussed in Chapter 22, but here we'll just cover the basic commands used to get around in a Telnet or SSH session.

As an example, when you first log in to a remote Mac, you'll be taken to your home folder on that Mac. This is the same folder where, if you had logged in to the remote Mac physically using the Mac OS X prompt, you would have found your personal `Documents`, `Library`, and other folders. They look a little different from the command line, but they're the same folders. To see them immediately, type the letters **ls** and press Return.

The `ls` command is the "list" command, which enables you to list the contents of a folder. In the example above, you're seeing a mix of subfolders and documents.

When you use the basic `ls` command, though, it can be a bit tough to tell exactly which listed items are folders and which are files. One way around this is to add a special *argument* that modifies the `ls` command: `ls -l`. Type that at a prompt and press Return. The result should look something like this:

Now it's a little easier to tell the types of files apart. Thanks to the argument, the list now shows quite a bit of information about the files and folders, including a giveaway: the letter d that appears in the leftmost column for the listed items. The d stands for *directory*, which is the standard way Unix-like operating systems refer to folders. (The use of "directory" is important to note because many of the commands, which often are abbreviations, will make more sense in this context.) When you see items listed that have a - (hyphen) instead of a d, those are regular files.

Many commands accept path statements as arguments. You may have noticed, for instance, that by default you're able to see only the listing of your home folder when you access a remote Mac via Telnet or SSH.

To work with the contents of another folder, you'll need to change to that folder. You do that by entering the `cd` (change directory) command, followed by the directory to which you'd like to change. For example, you could enter **cd Documents** and then press Return. As a result, the prompt would change to indicate that you've moved to the new directory.

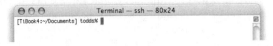

The portion of the prompt that shows ~/Documents indicates that you're now in the Documents folder that's a subfolder of your home folder. If you invoke the ls command, you'll see a listing of that Documents folder. (You also can use ls with a path statement, such as ls ~/Documents, if you'd like a listing of a folder without first changing to that folder.)

NOTE As you may have read in Chapter 3, "The Finder," the tilde (~) is a shortcut character used to represent your home folder. You can use that character (press Shift+`, which is the key immediately above your Tab key) in Telnet/SSH commands, such as cd ~, to change to your remote home folder. Also noted in Chapter 3 is the leading slash character (/). When used alone or at the beginning of a path statement, the slash represents the root folder on the remote disk.

As we've discussed elsewhere, the folders on a Mac OS X machine are part of a hierarchy of folders that can be represented as their names separated by slashes, such as /Users/Documents. Using this hierarchy and format, you can change directly to a completely different folder on your Mac, as long as you enter the path correctly. For example, you can change immediately to the main Applications folder by entering **cd /Applications** and pressing Return. That causes you to change to the root folder, then the subfolder Applications. The prompt should now indicate that you're in that subfolder.

TIP A special directory command also can be used with cd: two periods (..). Type **cd ..** and press Return to change to the parent folder of the current folder. For instance, if you're currently in the folder /Documents/Memos, then typing **cd ..** and pressing Return will take you to the /Documents folder.

You'll find that many of the most common command-line commands can be used while you're accessing a remote computer. They include the following.

mkdir Make a directory (a subfolder) within the current directory (folder). Enter **mkdir Memos** within the Documents folder, for instance, to create a subfolder called Memos.

TIP Unix and Unix-like operating systems weren't designed with the idea that folder names would include spaces, but it's fairly common with Mac OS X. To enter a folder name with a space at the command line, you have to jump through an odd hoop. Use a backslash character (\) before typing the space, as in mkdir New\ Folder. This will create a folder called New Folder, with the space properly placed. In some cases you also can use quotes, as in mkdir "New Folder" and cd "New Folder", to refer to a folder name that includes spaces. (This won't always work because some non-Mac systems prefer the backslash character.)

mv Move a file to another location. For instance, mv Memo.rtf ~/Documents/Memos would move the file Memo.rtf to the Memos subfolder of the Documents folder in my home folder.

cp Copy a file. For instance, cp Memo.rtf MemoCopy.rtf would create a copy of Memo.rtf called MemoCopy.rtf. Or cp Memo.rtf ~/Documents/Memos would create a copy of Memo.rtf and place it, with the same name, in the Memos folder. Alternatively, cp Memo.rtf ~/Documents/Memos/MemoCopy.rtf would copy the file to the Memos subfolder but also rename the file as MemoCopy.rtf. In all cases, the original stays the way it was—this is like the duplicate command in the Finder. (Be careful about how this command works; if you mistype the name of a destination folder—for instance, Memo instead of Memos in the above examples—the command will assume that you want to copy the file's contents to a *new* file with that accidental name. A file is copied to a folder only if the folder already exists.)

TIP   You can use an asterisk (*) as a wildcard character with many commands in a Telnet session. Among other things, this enables you to copy more than one file at a time. For instance, the command cp * ~/Documents/Memos would copy all the files in the current folder to the Memos folder. You also can use the wildcard in other ways, such as to view only the files and folders that start with certain letters in a particular folder. For example, type **ls doc*** and press Return to see a listing of files and subfolders that start with doc in the current folder.

rm   Remove a file. For example, rm Memo.rtf would delete that file if it's in the current folder.

rmdir   Delete an empty directory (folder). Once you've used the rm command to clear out a folder, you can use rmdir to remove the directory (folder) from existence. For example, rm ~Documents/Memos will remove the subfolder Memos if it's empty.

man   Display a manual ("man") page. This is a special command that's used to give you help regarding commands in Unix-like operating systems. Type **man rmdir** and press Return, for instance, to see the man page regarding the rmdir command.

more   Display a text file. Using the more command not only displays the file but shows the More bar at the bottom of each screen of text. Press the spacebar to advance to the next screen. An example is more text.txt if the file text.txt is in the current folder.

Other command-line commands work as well—for instance, the chmod and chgrp commands for altering file privileges will work in remote sessions, assuming your remote user account has the correct privileges for altering files. This can be useful if, for example, you're creating shell scripts on the remote computer (see Chapter 23, "Command-Line and Applications Magic,") or you need to change privileges on a remote web server so that others can view files properly (see Chapter 24, "Web Serving, FTP Serving, and Net Security," for more on web server files and privileges).

What about running actual programs? To launch a program, you can simply type the path to its name and press Return. If it's in the current directory, you still need a path, as in **./myscript.sh**. If you're launching an application that's not in the current directory (folder), you can type a full path statement to the program, such as ~**/bin/myprog**, and press Return.

However, only command-line applications will launch correctly while you're accessing a Mac via Telnet or SSH; graphical applications (those that use the standard Mac OS X Aqua interface) can't be launched. There's a set of typical programs that ships with Unix-like applications that you can access from the command line, such as mail, grep, finger, Emacs, and Pico. Simply typing their names at any prompt can launch most of those programs.

As an example, you could send an e-mail message from the remote account. Type **mail e-mail_ address**, where e-mail_address is the address to which you want to send the message. You'll be prompted for a subject; type one and press Return. Now, type the body of your message. When you're done, press Control+D on a blank line. If the remote computer is set up to send e-mail using Sendmail (most Mac OS X machines aren't set up by default, but other Unix machines may be), the message is sent.

Logging Out

If you're connected to a remote machine via Telnet or SSH, you can log out in most cases by typing **logout** or **exit** and pressing Return. You'll be returned to your original prompt in the Terminal application—you'll be back on your own Mac's disk, probably viewing your local home folder (as opposed to the remote folders you just left).

In some cases, you may be returned to the Telnet prompt when you exit the remote application. (You can also access the Telnet prompt without connecting to a remote server by simply typing `telnet` and pressing Return at a command-line prompt.) If you encounter the Telnet prompt, you can either enter `quit` and press Return or enter `open` *`hostname.domain.tlx`* to open a new Telnet connection to a remote host.

Graphical Telnet

Interested in accessing Telnet servers from the Mac OS X Aqua interface? It's easy enough—a few programmers have created graphical Telnet clients you can use for Telnet or SSH connections. Here's a quick look at some options:

MacTelnet (`www.mactelnet.com/`)   This is a full-featured Telnet client that uses scripts and macros to make your time spent using Telnet more efficient. You can handle multiple sessions, connect to SSH and other services, and manage Telnet connections efficiently if you tend to use Telnet frequently.

TelnetLauncher (`www.pidog.com/`)   This shareware program (free to try) offers a convenient way for you to create and manage bookmarks to Telnet and SSH servers. When you access one of the bookmarks, a session is launched in a new Terminal window.

TermXL (`http://homepage.mac.com/jrrouet/jerp/`)   TermXL (shareware) offers some functionality similar to TelnetLauncher, enabling you to save parameters for many different Telnet/SSH connections and then launch those connections in Terminal at any time. TermXL offers an extensive Dock menu and supports the Mac OS X Services menu, including a New Terminal command for quickly launching a new Terminal window.

Accessing Telnet Applications

Not all remote access connections are designed simply for managing files and running remote programs. Some are designed specifically for running a particular program, such as a database lookup application or an information server of some kind. In those cases, you may still log in with a username and password, if you have them, or you may log in as an anonymous user.

You'll begin the session the same way you begin any Telnet session: at a prompt in the Terminal window, enter **Telnet** *`hostname.domain.tlx`*, which can be either an IP address or a hostname and domain name combination, where *`tlx`* is the three-letter extension such as `com`, `net`, or `org`. (In most cases, you'll use Telnet to access a public server, particularly if you don't have a user account on that server. If the server supports SSH, however, you can use it at the command line instead.) Press Return, and the Telnet program will attempt to access the remote server. Once it's found the server, you should see a login prompt. If you don't have an account for accessing the application, you'll likely be prompted with the correct username for entering the system; otherwise, you'll need to contact that server's administrator for assistance.

TIP   Sometimes you're asked for a terminal type when logging into a Telnet application. Choose VT100.

When you've successfully logged in, you likely won't see a command-line prompt—in most cases you'll navigate menus by typing numbers that represent commands and pressing Return (see Figure 17.5). Most Telnet applications offer a help feature of some sort. You can usually access the help feature by typing **help** or **?** and pressing Return.

FIGURE 17.5

Here's a menu from the New York Public Library's Telnet application (nyplgate.nypl.org, login is leo).

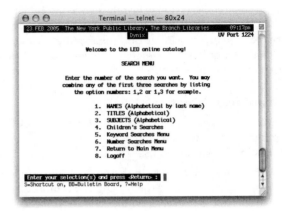

Most Telnet applications also have an `exit` or `logout` command; try typing either of those commands and pressing Return if you need to leave the session. (If typing a command doesn't work, you may have to find a numbered "logout" command.)

Sometimes a Telnet application will hang or otherwise appear to be stuck. If that's the case, you can try sending an escape character to the remote computer, which often will reset it and return you to some predetermined menu. (It may log you out of the application and server immediately.) To send an escape character, press Ctrl+C or select Control ➤ Send Break from the Terminal's menu.

NOTE The Terminal application window has a scroll bar and scroll arrows, which enable you to return to previous screens that you've seen during the Terminal window's session. Before you assume that a command prompt is missing, make sure you haven't accidentally scrolled back a bit in your session.

Most of the Telnet applications we come across these days are library catalogs, although government offices, universities, and some companies and other organizations use them extensively. In any case, you often may find it useful to save the text of a Telnet session as a file for later review or for printing. You can do that by selecting File ➤ Save Text As and using the Save dialog box to save a text file record of your session. You also can use the File ➤ Print command to print your current session. When you select that command, you can select the Terminal command from the unnamed pop-up menu, where you can choose among special options, and then print as usual.

Accessing FTP Sites

File Transfer Protocol (FTP) is one of the major mechanisms, along with the Web's HTTP protocol, for transferring files over the Internet. In fact, FTP often is preferred over HTTP when it comes to moving large files, for both reliability and speed.

To use FTP for transferring files, you need two things. First, you need a program that's capable of connecting to an FTP server. Second, you need a valid FTP server to connect to. Fortunately, both of those are easy to come across.

Using the Finder

In Mac OS X 10.3 and above, the Finder can be used to connect to an FTP server, view that server's public contents, and download files. It cannot be used to upload files—that's something for which you'll rely on a third-party application, which we will discuss later in this section.

TIP Actually, there is an FTP client built into the Darwin layer of Mac OS X, but it's not a graphical client. FTP can be accessed from within the Terminal window in Mac OS X. See the section "FTP via the Terminal" later in this chapter.

To access an FTP server from within the Finder, simply choose Go ➢ Connect to Server. In the Connect to Server window, enter the URL or IP address for a valid FTP server, remembering that you must begin the address with the `ftp://` protocol identifier.

Once the server is accessed, you'll be asked to enter your username and password. Once you successfully log in, the icon for that FTP server will appear on your desktop in the Finder (in 10.3 and higher), and you'll be able to access the remote FTP server as if it were a disk connected to your Mac.

NOTE What's interesting about using an FTP server on your Mac's desktop is that it doesn't act like an FTP server—all of the arcane commands are done in the background. You can copy files from the FTP server just as you would with any network drive in the Finder.

Third-Party FTP Clients

As mentioned, FTP isn't only about downloading files—you can also upload files to FTP servers when appropriate. For example, the ISP that serves one of Todd's websites is located across the country, so he regularly logs in to his web server computer via Transmit, an application that's designed to access an FTP server and send or receive files. He can then access the web folder, upload new files for displaying web content, and rename or delete others.

A number of FTP clients exist for the Mac OS, including the venerable Fetch (`www.fetchsoftworks.com`), a popular Mac application for many years that has recently been updated for Mac OS X. Other FTP clients include the popular Interarchy (previously Anarchy) from Stairways Software (www.interarchy.com), Transmit (www.panic.com), Vicomsoft FTP (www.ftpclient.com), and Captain FTP (http://captain-ftp.xdsnet.de/).

FTP clients enable you to log in to remote FTP servers using your username and password; then they work a little like the Finder to help you maneuver the remote filesystem. (In Fetch, for instance, choose File ➤ New Connection to open the New Connection dialog box, where you'll be able to input a host server address along with your username and password. See Figure 17.6.) Once you find the file you want to download, select the Get File command within any FTP client (or in a graphical client such as Fetch, drag and drop the file from the FTP client's window to the desktop or a Finder window).

FIGURE 17.6
Signing in to an FTP site with a user account and password using Fetch

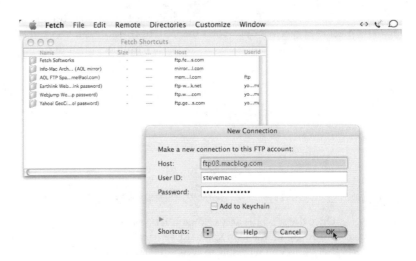

If you're uploading files, you generally can do so by locating the destination folder on the remote server, selecting the file you want to send, and using the Put File command to upload that file. In some FTP clients, it's even easier—just drag and drop the file from your desktop or a Finder window to the remote directory. The file will be uploaded (you'll probably see a progress indicator in the FTP window or in a dialog box).

File Encoding and Compression

FTP is a binary file transfer protocol, meaning that, unlike with e-mail attachments, you aren't required to encode a file before you send it using an FTP program. That doesn't mean encoding isn't a good idea, at least in some cases. The process of encoding files enables them to preserve any important OS-specific features in the files; this is particularly important for dual-fork files created in Mac OS 9 and earlier. You'll find that your FTP application (if you're using a graphical client such as Fetch or Interarchy) can encode such Mac files in the MacBinary format before you send them.

If you're sending files from a Mac OS X machine to another or to a Unix-based server, there's less concern for encoding. That said, you'll often want to *archive* files—turning multiple files or folders into a single archive file for easy transfer—and *compress* files to make them smaller for quicker transfer. You can decompress most archives using either the Finder or the utility program StuffIt Expander, which is included with Mac OS X. If you're sending files via FTP, however, you may want to create your own compressed archives. You can do that in two ways—using the Finder's built-in ability to deal with Zip files or using DropStuff, a program available from the same people who produce StuffIt Expander, Aladdin Systems (`www.allume.com/mac/index.html`).

FINDER ZIP

If you use the Finder, you'll create your archive in the popular Zip format, which is historically a format that's more common on Microsoft Windows computers. However, with Mac OS X 10.3 and higher, Apple has incorporated the ability to create compressed Zip archives. To archive a file using the Finder, simply select it and choose File ➤ Create Archive, or Control+click the file and choose Create Archive from the context menu.

A file with the same name as that file but with the filename extension `.zip` will appear on the desktop or in the same folder as the original file. In most cases, the archive will be smaller in file size than the original.

You can also create an archive from a folder (by highlighting it and choosing File ➤ Create Archive), or you can select multiple files, then use the File ➤ Create Archive command to put them all together in a compressed archive that the Finder will name `Archive.zip`.

DROPSTUFF

Drag a file, a group of files, or a folder to the DropStuff icon. DropStuff launches and begins creating an archive, a single file that includes all the files you've dropped on the application. It also compresses that archive in the StuffIt format, making it smaller for quicker transfer via FTP. (StuffIt is the "traditional" Mac format, and it's handy for sending files to other Mac users.) When it is completed, you'll have a new archive (called `archive.sit`) that includes all the files and folders you dropped on DropStuff. You can now send that file via FTP.

NOTE DropStuff is shareware, which means that it works when you download it, but you're expected to register the software by paying a fee if you find it useful. Allume Systems (`www.allume.com`) currently charges about $50 for the registration code.

To decompress the file, your recipient will need StuffIt Expander or a similar program that can handle the StuffIt format. StuffIt Expander is preinstalled on most Macs up until Mac OS X 10.4, when it was discontinued. However, it's still available for free from www.allume.com. Programs to decompress StuffIt archives, such as Windows Stuffit Expander from Allume, also exist for Microsoft Windows–based computers, although StuffIt is not the most popular archive format on Windows machines.

NOTE   For sending to non-Mac Unix-based computers, you'll probably want to use a different format: *tar* (usually *GNUTAR*, with a .tar extension) for creating the archive and Unix-style *zip* (GNUZIP, with a .zip or .z extension) for compressing the archive. Mac OS X includes Terminal-based tools for creating Unix archives, as discussed in Chapter 23. You also can use the popular OpenUp (www.stepwise.com/Software/OpenUp/) and ColdCompress (www.stepwise.com/Software/ColdCompress/) tools to work with these Unix-style compression and archiving formats. StuffIt Standard can also create Tar, Zip and similar formats.

FTP via the Terminal

Another of Mac OS X's included command-line applications is an FTP client that you can use to transfer files to and from your Mac. The FTP client works a little like accessing a remote volume via Telnet or SSH, although you're never really *on* the remote server as you are with Remote Login. Instead, you're able to access listings from the remote server while downloading them back to your home folder (and subfolders) on your local Mac.

For you to access the remote computer, it must have an FTP server running. Depending on the type of server, you also may need to have a username and password to access the computer; this is particularly true if you're transferring files between machines on your local network or between yourself and a corporate or organizational FTP server.

Another type of FTP server, called a *public FTP* server or *anonymous FTP* server, doesn't require a user account and password. Instead, you enter the word **anonymous** as your username, and traditionally you enter your e-mail address as your password. (Most anonymous FTP servers don't actually require that you enter your e-mail address as a password, but it's considered a common courtesy.) Entering your e-mail address as a password stores the e-mail address in the FTP server's logs so that the Mac's administrators can look up users if necessary when there's a problem or concern.

Anonymous FTP servers abound—you'll find that they're still very popular and common for trading shareware and freeware applications, as well as a variety of other purposes. To get started, you can check out Apple's own anonymous FTP servers at mirrors.apple.com. First, though, you'll need to know how to log in to a remote FTP server.

LOGGING IN

Logging in to a remote FTP server is very similar to logging in via Telnet or SSH, with one particular difference: you should use the Terminal application first to switch to the folder where you plan to store your downloaded files before you launch the FTP client application. At the command prompt, you can use the cd command to change to a different directory (folder). For instance, to change to a folder called downloads that you've created in your home folder, type **cd ~/downloads** and press Return. (It is possible to change your local folder while you're connected via FTP, but it's easier if you start by changing to the folder where you'd like to store downloaded files or where you have files you'd like to upload.)

NOTE   At the main prompt in the Terminal, you also can use the commands discussed previously in "Basic Remote Access Commands" on your own folders. You can create directories, remove them, and so on. This also is discussed at length in Chapter 23.

Once you've set your local working directory to the correct folder, you're ready to log in to the remote FTP server. Type **ftp *remote_server***, where *remote_server* is either the IP address or the hostname and domain name of the FTP server to which you'd like to connect. Then press Return. The

FTP command-line application is launched and will attempt to connect to the remote server. If the server is found, you're ready to log in. Here's a typical prompt from a remote Mac OS X FTP server.

At the Name prompt, enter your username or **anonymous** if the remote server supports anonymous access, and press Return. (If the name shown as part of the prompt is also the username you want to use on the remote FTP server, you can simply press Return.) You'll then see the Password prompt; enter your password and press Return. (If you're logging in anonymously, either enter your e-mail address at the Password prompt and press Return or simply press Return.)

Now you'll see a message welcoming you to the system. If it's a public server, it may be a rather long message, detailing the rules, hours, and limitations of the system. As shown here, the message can be a simple "logged in" message, too. You'll be presented with the FTP> prompt. This is your indicator that you're signed in to the remote server and ready to begin transferring files.

Basic FTP Commands

At the FTP> prompt, you can use the familiar Unix-like commands that work during Telnet sessions, such as ls (for listing the contents of remote directories) and cd (to change to a new remote directory). If you have the correct privileges, you also can use mkdir to create remote directories.

Other commands differ, however; some are similar to Telnet/SSH commands, and others specifically enable you to take special advantage of the FTP program's capabilities to transfer files to and from your Mac.

For instance, two commands right up top are important to understand: ascii and binary. These commands put FTP in certain *modes* that determine how files are transferred. If you're transferring text files or files that have been encoded using a text-encoding format (such as BinHex, MacBinary, uuencode, or base64/MIME encoding), you can type **ascii** and press Return to place FTP in ASCII mode.

TIP   Common filename extensions for textual files include .txt, .htm, .html, .hqx, .uu, .mime, and .mim.

Binary mode is used to transfer nontext files; binary files are those that use 1s and 0s to represent computer data. This includes any sort of program, document, or archive that's compressed using StuffIt or Zip formats. If you're transferring a Word document, a PDF document, an image file, a QuickTime movie—anything that isn't in plain text—you may need to type **binary** at the FTP> prompt and press Return to put the server in binary mode.

Here's a look at those and the other FTP commands:

ascii   Sets the file transfer type to ASCII for transferring text-based files.

binary   Sets the file transfer type to support binary file transfer.

bye Ends the FTP session and closes the FTP program. You're returned to the main shell prompt in Terminal.

close Ends the FTP session with the remote server, but leaves you at the FTP> prompt. You can then use the open command to open a connection to a new remote server.

delete Deletes a file on the remote machine. For example, delete memo.rtf will delete the file memo.rtf on the remote server (assuming you have the file privileges to do so).

dir Displays a listing of the contents of the specified folder on the remote server. (By itself, it lists the contents of the currently selected folder; you also can type **dir path**, such as dir /users/todds/documents, to see the contents of a folder that isn't currently selected on the remote server.) Note that dir is a special FTP command that displays a content listing in whatever way the remote server thinks is appropriate, so the listing can vary from one server OS to another.

get This is the command to download a file from the remote server to your Mac. Type **get full_filename** and press Return to retrieve a particular file, such as get memo.rtf if memo.rtf is in the currently selected folder. (If it's not, use the cd command to change to that folder.) You also can type **get path/filename** to download a file that isn't in the current folder, such as get /users/sjobs/documents/memo.rtf. This will download the file according to the current type setting (binary or ASCII), so make sure you change the type setting before transferring the file, if necessary.

TIP Again, the common use of spaces in Mac OS X filenames can rear its ugly head here. In many cases you should be able to use quotes with the get command (such as get "My File.txt") when dealing with filenames that have spaces. You also can use the escape character, as in get My\ File.txt, and press Return.

lcd Changes the selected folder on your local machine. If the command is used by itself, you're changed automatically to your home folder. Otherwise, include a path statement, such as lcd ~/sjobs/documents, and press Return.

lpwd Displays the current folder on your local machine.

mget This is a "multiple get" command that enables you to download more than one file at a time. You specify the multiple files using wildcard characters. For instance, type **mget doc*** to attempt to download all files and folders that start with doc. You can use mget * to download all files in the currently selected remote folder. You'll then see a prompt that lets you step through which files you'd like to download by typing a **y** or **n** next to each (and pressing Return after each). You also can type **a** and press Return to download all matching files. (A similar command, mdelete, can be used to delete multiple files on the remote server if you have the file privileges.)

TIP You can type **prompt** and press Return to toggle the level of prompting that FTP uses with your commands. If you toggle prompts off, mget will automatically retrieve all files that match the wildcard items you type (and mput will upload all matching files).

mput This is the "multiple put" command. As with mget, you can use wildcards with mput to upload multiple files to the remote server at once (see put). For example, mput * would upload all files in your current local folder to the currently selected remote folder.

newer This command is identical to get except that it compares the modification date of the remote file to the date of the same file on your own Mac. If the file doesn't exist in your local Mac's currently selected folder, or if it does exist but it's older, the file is downloaded from the remote server. If the file exists on your local Mac but its modification date is more recent, the download doesn't occur.

open Opens a new FTP remote connection. This works only from the FTP> prompt after you've issued the close command (or if you've launched FTP by simply typing ftp and pressing Return). To open a new server, type **open *server_address***, where *server_address* is the IP address or the hostname and domain of the remote server; then press Return.

progress This toggles on an active progress bar to show you the progress of downloads. (It also doesn't always work.)

put Uploads the specified file from your local Mac to the currently selected folder on the remote server. For example, type **put memo.rtf** and press Return to upload that file to the remote server. You also can specify a path, as in put ~/documents/memos/memo.rtf, to upload a file from a par-ticular folder on your local Mac to the remote server. Remember that put uses the current setting for type (ASCII or binary), so you'll need to set it appropriately.

pwd Displays the name of the currently selected folder on the remote machine.

quit Works just like bye, signing off from the remote server and closing FTP.

size Displays the size of a file on the remote server. For example, type **size memo.rtf** to see the size of that file.

That's most of them. You can see a quick listing of FTP commands by typing **help** or **?** and press-ing Return at the FTP> prompt. At a shell prompt (not the FTP> prompt), you can type **man ftp** and press Return to see the man page on the FTP application, including additional commands and differ-ent ways you can use FTP and special arguments to alter the way FTP works.

To sign out of FTP, simply type **bye** or **quit** at any FTP> prompt and press Return. That's it—you're returned to the main shell prompt in Terminal.

What's Next?

In this chapter, you learned how to determine if your Mac has been configured for network access and saw how to connect to remote servers, whether they are Apple File Protocol servers, WebDAV serv-ers, SMB-based file-sharing servers, or mounted NFS volumes. You also saw how to access other Macs and computers using Telnet and SSH for remote access, as well as how to transfer files using FTP. In Chapter 18, you'll learn how to create a network, configure your Mac(s) to access the network, and turn on file sharing.

Building a Network and Sharing Files

If you've got more than one Mac in your home, office, or organization, chances are that you'd like to connect them to each other in order to share files—as well as share printers and other resources. Fortunately, that's easy to do in Mac OS X. Mac OS X enables you to access individual Macs using Personal File Sharing, which places a folder or hard disk from a remote computer directly on your desktop to be accessed via the Finder.

The process of building a network begins with deciding what type of networking hardware to use to connect your computers (even if those connections are wireless). When you've chosen the hardware, you'll need to choose a networking protocol (AppleTalk or TCP/IP) and configure the hardware to use that protocol. Finally, you'll turn on Personal File Sharing, thereby turning your Mac into a server. Once it's a server, you'll need to configure user accounts and manage those users' access to your hard disks.

In this chapter, you'll see how to create a *local area network* (LAN) for sharing files and other resources such as printers. (A LAN is differentiated from a *wide area network*, or WAN, in that a WAN is a group of more than one LAN. The Internet is an example of a WAN.) The chapter includes a discussion of the technologies behind networking as well as a look at the various protocols and standards for networking. We'll also take a look at how to make it all work, including wired, wireless, and even Internet connections for your LAN.

In this chapter:

◆ Putting Together a Network

◆ Personal File Sharing

◆ Internet and Personal File Sharing Together

◆ AirPort computer-to-computer Networks

Putting Together a Network

The term *network* refers to two or more computers (or other devices, such as printers) that communicate via some form of cabling or wireless solution. For Macs that support Mac OS X, that connection is either Ethernet cabling or AirPort wireless connections. (All modern Macs have Ethernet support built in, whereas AirPort is an add-on for the latest models of iMac, Power Macintosh, iBook, and PowerBook.)

Once they are connected, the computers use a common protocol to communicate—in the case of Mac OS X, it's the Transmission Control Protocol/Internet Protocol (TCP/IP) or the AppleTalk protocol. The protocol routes data between the computers in an orderly way, making sure packets of data leaving one Mac arrive at the other. Although TCP/IP is commonly thought of as the protocol used on the Internet, it's not used exclusively for web browsing and e-mail. In fact, it's the basis of all networking between Unix-based computers, which includes Mac OS X, thanks to its FreeBSD-based underpinnings. AppleTalk is an older and less efficient protocol, but it's popular for compatibility with older Macs, as well as for accessing older laser printers and for slightly more secure local networking (under certain circumstances).

Once a protocol has been established, services can be made available via that protocol. The most common service for a typical office network is file sharing, which, in the case of the Mac OS, generally uses a technology called Apple File Protocol (AFP). AFP is a service that can be used with either TCP/IP or AppleTalk. When used with TCP/IP, the service makes it possible for Mac OS X and earlier Mac versions to share files via the protocol commonly called *AppleShare over IP*. As with earlier versions of the Mac OS, you can log directly into a Mac that has Personal File Sharing active, mounting its disk (or a volume that represents a shared folder on that Mac's disk) directly on your desktop or in a Finder window.

NOTE   You can also use NFS (Network File Services) over TCP/IP to create permanent network connections between Mac OS X machines or between Mac OS X and Unix machines. The remote volume would then be permanently available in the /Network/Servers folder on your Mac, as discussed in Chapter 17, "Accessing Network Volumes."

Aside from Personal File Sharing, you can use two services generally associated with the Internet, FTP (File Transfer Protocol, used for transferring files) and HTTP (Hypertext Transport Protocol, used for serving web pages and files), to share files and information. These are covered in more depth in Chapter 11, "The Web, Online Security, .Mac, Sherlock, and iChat," and Chapter 24, "Web Serving, FTP Serving, and Net Security," but it's worth noting here that you can use them between local machines just as easily as you can use them over the Internet.

WHAT ABOUT SHARING WITH WINDOWS?

This chapter focuses on using AFP—a protocol common in the Macintosh world. That leaves a big chunk of the computing world out of this equation—computers using Microsoft Windows. How do you share files with Windows users? You have a few options:

SMB   Mac OS X offers direct support for the Server Message Block (SMB) protocol that Windows uses for networking. You can connect to Windows servers, and Windows machines can connect to your Mac for Personal File Sharing. Although doing this really isn't much different from using Personal File Sharing, using SMB and sharing with Windows is covered separately in Chapter 20.

Windows Services for Macintosh   The Server version of Windows includes an option to turn on Apple Filing Services over TCP/IP, which makes the Windows server look like it's a standard AFP server. If you have a Windows server on your LAN, you should be able to access it directly from your Mac, as described in Chapter 17, "Accessing Network Volumes."

Dave from Thursby Software   Dave (www.thursby.com) is a third-party solution that enables your Mac to sign in to Windows machines for file sharing. Thursby also offers a product called ADmit-Mac 2, which enables a Mac client to access a Microsoft Windows Server 2003–based network.

PC MacLAN from Computer Associates   PC MacLAN (www.ca.com) is another third-party utility that enables a Windows computer to log in to a Mac OS 9 or Mac OS X computer or server that has Personal File Sharing enabled.

NOTE Want still more protocols? Mac OS X supports networking between connected Macs and Windows-based PCs using the SMB protocol—the open version of Microsoft Windows networking—more so than in previous versions of Mac OS X. See Chapter 20, "Mac OS X and Other Platforms," for more details on networking between Macs and Windows machines.

We'll take a close look at all these elements and how they work together to build a network.

Ethernet Connections

By far the most common method used to connect computers in a network is Ethernet. In the past, Macs also have been connected via other types of cabling, including LocalTalk and token ring standards. These days, all Macs come with Ethernet built into the computer, including all models that are compatible with Mac OS X. All Macs also use the *unshielded twisted-pair* (UTP) standard of Ethernet cable, not the older, obsolete 10Base-2 (or *coaxial*) standard.

Twisted-pair cabling can be used between Macs that support three different Ethernet speed standards: 10Base-T, 100Base-T, and Gigabit Ethernet. All three standards can use the same type of UTP cable (called UTP *Category 5* cable or just *Cat 5*) to make the connection. UTP Category 5 cable resembles the telephone cable you'd use to connect a telephone to a wall jack, but Ethernet cable is thicker, with a larger connector (RJ-45) on each end. The cable works with all Ethernet port speeds, so you can use it to connect your Macs regardless of whether they support 100Base-T or Gigabit Ethernet. (The earliest Mac OS X–compatible models are limited to 10Base-T; they're still compatible, just slower.)

In most cases, you can't simply connect Macs to one another directly using standard Cat 5 cable. Instead, you need to use an Ethernet *hub*, which is a special device designed to act as a central connecting point for all the Macs in your LAN. The cost of a hub ranges from as low as $50 to many hundreds of dollars, depending on how many connections the hub supports and whether or not it's *managed*—that is, whether it actively moves data from one port to another. (Unmanaged hubs simply replicate data from one Mac on all the ports, which is less efficient.)

Each length of UTP cabling is connected between a port on the hub and the Ethernet port on the side (or back) of the Mac. Once two or more Macs are connected to the hub, you're ready to configure the TCP/IP protocol and enable the Macs to communicate.

NOTE You can connect only *two* Macs (or two devices, such as a Mac and an Ethernet-capable printer) using a special cable called a *crossover cable*. It is Cat 5 Ethernet cable, but the wires inside are crossed to create the appropriate connection for sharing data. The cabling isn't ideal for long-term networking, but if you're simply connecting two Macs to share data quickly or you're connecting a single Mac to an Ethernet-based printer, a crossover cable will work fine. The software configuration is the same; you simply don't need a hub. However, the latest Mac models (including most PowerBook G4, iBook G4, Mac mini, and any G5-based desktop Mac) *don't* require a crossover cable for connecting directly to another Ethernet-based device. Instead, you can connect directly to those Macs using standard Cat 5 cable; the port will automatically detect that it's not using a hub and make it so that the connection is still available.

AirPort Connections

Mac OS X supports another type of network "cabling," if we can stretch the term a bit. AirPort is a wireless technology, enabling Macs to share data without requiring them to be cabled together; instead, data is transferred via a wireless radio connection. AirPort is actually Apple's name for a technology otherwise known as the *IEEE 802.11b* or *WiFi* standard.

Other manufacturers have cards and devices that are compatible with the IEEE 802.11b standard as well, making it possible for you to upgrade other non-AirPort-capable Macs with third-party cards and upgrades. Older PowerBooks, which can accept PC Card–based IEEE 802.11b–compatible expansion cards, are prime candidates for such an upgrade. All PowerBooks made in 2000 or later support AirPort.

In AirPort's original implementation, AirPort-enabled Macs can share data with Macs that are up to 150 feet (46 meters) away, assuming those Macs have AirPort capabilities installed and activated. In most Macs, you first need to install a special AirPort card, if the Mac can support it.

All recent Macs support what Apple calls AirPort Extreme—devices that follow the IEEE 802.11g standard, which is backward compatible with IEEE 802.11b but much faster (up to 56Mbps). Using AirPort Extreme to its utmost requires an AirPort Extreme Base Station (or another 802.11g-compatible wireless router), but a Mac that has AirPort Extreme is compatible with older WiFi and 802.11b networks.

The following Mac models support AirPort:

iMacs (and eMacs)   The iMac DV series introduced in 1999 can accept an AirPort card, as can all iMac DV, DV SE, and DV+ models made since then. Since early 2001, all iMac models have been updated to accept an AirPort add-on card; the iMac G4, most eMacs, and the iMac G5 support AirPort Extreme.

iBooks   All iBook models can accept an AirPort card; the iBook G4 and later support AirPort Extreme.

PowerBooks   The PowerBook G3 2000 (FireWire) and all PowerBook G4 models include a slot for an AirPort card; some earlier PowerBook G3 models can accept an IEEE 802.11b PC card expansion device, although you may need to look for a PC card that is specifically compatible with Mac OS X.

Mac mini   Mac mini models have AirPort Extreme support as an option.

Power Macintosh   The Power Macintosh G5, G4, G4 Cube, and later models can accept an AirPort card, with the latest models supporting AirPort Extreme. However, the Power Macintosh G4 (PCI Graphics) model, offered for a limited time in the fall of 1999, doesn't support AirPort.

If you're working with a Mac that has an AirPort card installed, the next step is to consider how that Mac will be connected to the network. Like Ethernet connections, AirPort connections generally work with a hub, although the hub doesn't have to be a special hardware device. Any Mac running Mac OS X can act as a hub for other wireless Macs. For instance, an iMac DV could act as a hub for other wireless Macs, including the ability to share an Internet connection with the connected Macs, if it's running Mac OS X 10.2 or higher. (That said, having a dedicated base station is considerably more efficient.) We'll discuss this sort of network later in the section "AirPort computer-to-computer Networks."

Hardware hubs are ideal for AirPort connections, particularly the AirPort Base Station and AirPort Express models from Apple. These hardware devices offer an Ethernet port as well as AirPort capabilities and a built-in modem (on many models), making it not only a wireless hub (connecting multiple wireless Macs) but also a wireless-to-wired hub, making it possible for both Ethernet-based and AirPort-based Macs to communicate with one another.

Hubs are also available from a number of other manufacturers, including hubs that offer a combination of wired and wireless ports, more advanced firewalls, and so on.

Network Status

Introduced back in Chapter 10, "Configuring Internet Access," the Network Status screen is a handy feature of the Network pane in System Preferences. Network Status reports to you the networking (and potential networking) ports that it finds and then tells you if those ports are active, how they're configured, and if they appear to have Internet access. This allows you, at a glance, to get a sense of how your Mac is connected to other computers and what ports your Mac has automatically recognized (see Figure 18.1).

FIGURE 18.1
The Network Status screen in the Network pane of System Preferences

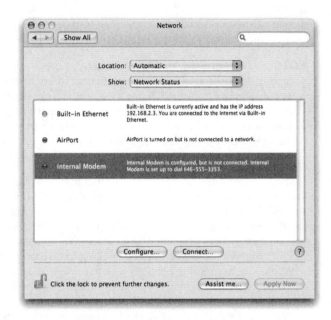

You can get to the Network Status screen by choosing Network Status from the Show menu; to edit a particular network port, double-click its listing on the Network Status screen or select it and click Configure. (For instance, to change settings for Built-in Ethernet, double-click it on the Network Status screen.)

TCP/IP and AppleTalk Protocols

Mac OS X allows file sharing over both TCP/IP and AppleTalk protocols, although AppleTalk is recommended only for backward compatibility because it's slower and a bit less flexible. However, it remains an option in Mac OS X. Both protocols can be used over either Ethernet or AirPort connections, so how your Macs connect doesn't really influence the protocol they use.

TCP/IP is the basis of most networking between Mac OS X machines (and between Mac OS X machines and other computers) primarily because it's the basis of all networking between Unix machines. In fact, TCP/IP serves as the foundation of the Internet for pretty much the same reason—Unix machines were the early basis of the Internet (and remain largely so today). If the Internet had begun as a huge global network consisting completely of Macs, it might have been based on Apple-Talk instead (although certain efficiencies of TCP/IP also help make it the obvious choice of the Internet).

AppleTalk was the main networking protocol for Macs since the beginning of the Mac in the mid-1980s, and it remains perhaps the most popular protocol for Macs running Mac OS 9 and earlier (especially for smaller networks). The Mac OS had begun to migrate away from AppleTalk, however, because TCP/IP is more efficient and faster, even for Apple's traditional Personal File Sharing capabilities. Mac OS 9, for instance, includes Personal File Sharing over IP capabilities, which makes it possible to share files between Mac OS 9 (and Mac OS X) machines using the TCP/IP protocol instead of AppleTalk.

If you plan to do some file sharing between your Macs, you have some decisions to make. If you want to stick with TCP/IP, you can simply configure it on all of your Macs (as discussed in the next section, "Configuring TCP/IP") and then turn on Personal File Sharing. In Mac OS X, Personal File Sharing automatically uses the TCP/IP network if it's available. In most cases, this is the best solution.

NOTE   When you install Mac OS X (or when you start a new Mac with Mac OS X preinstalled), the Startup Assistant asks for TCP/IP configuration information. So it's possible that your Mac is already properly configured. If that's the case, you can skip the "Configuring TCP/IP" section that follows and move on to later sections regarding starting up Personal File Sharing and managing users. (In other cases, your Macs may auto-configure themselves for network access.) If your network settings weren't configured properly at installation time or you've added a new network interface, you'll need to configure TCP/IP.

If you want to use AppleTalk for sharing files with Macs running earlier versions of the Classic Mac OS, you can do that as well. Although you might decide to do this because you're also using AppleTalk for printing, we'd recommend that you use AppleTalk only when TCP/IP is impractical. Usually that's because your Mac exists on a large network that's already using the AppleTalk protocol, or you're networking with older Classic Mac OS–based machines that don't support AFP over TCP/IP. In those cases, you might be willing to take the performance hit and go with AppleTalk.

AppleTalk has another plus: it's easy to configure. To use AppleTalk, you'll simply activate it in the Network pane of System Preferences by selecting a port and enabling AppleTalk for that port. For instance, if you're using Ethernet for connecting your Mac to your network, select the Ethernet port in the Show menu, choose the AppleTalk tab, and turn on the option Make AppleTalk Active (shown in Figure 18.2). If you're using AirPort for your networking, choose it in the Show menu, and you'll see that it has its own AppleTalk tab.

NOTE   AppleTalk can be turned on for only one port at a time, so if you have both Ethernet and AirPort ports configured, for instance, you'll have to choose one or the other for AppleTalk connections.

If necessary, you can choose an AppleTalk zone on this screen by choosing that zone from the AppleTalk Zone menu. You also can choose to configure the AppleTalk Node ID and Network ID manually, if necessary, by selecting Manually in the Configure menu. Enter the Node ID and Network ID numbers in the boxes that appear.

NOTE   AppleTalk zones are created by servers or routers that designate different parts of a large AppleTalk-based network. For instance, your computer might belong to the EnglishDept zone, while other computers and printers belong to the ComputerLab zone. If your AppleTalk network has been divided into zones, you can pick the one that's appropriate for your Mac in the AppleTalk Zone menu.

Once AppleTalk is active, you can use it for file sharing, as discussed in Chapter 17.

FIGURE 18.2
Enabling AppleTalk for
an Ethernet port

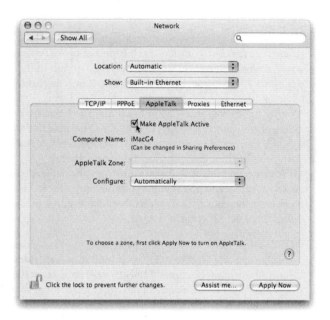

Remember, though, that if you don't have any other Macs on your local network that are (a) configured for AppleTalk and (b) have Personal File Sharing turned on, you won't see any available servers when you attempt to access them by selecting the Network icon in a Finder window.

NOTE   It can be tough to remember that Mac OS X Personal File Sharing using Apple File Protocol (AFP) and AppleTalk are different—particularly for old Mac hands who have grown used to generically labeling all Mac networking "AppleTalk." AFP is a sharing protocol (akin to Windows' SMB and Unix's NFS) while AppleTalk is a networking protocol, like TCP/IP. If you turn on AppleTalk networking but don't configure your Ethernet or AirPort port for a TCP/IP networking, you'll be able to access a Mac that has Personal File Sharing active *only* if that remote Mac also has AppleTalk configured. If you configure both AppleTalk and TCP/IP as networking protocols for a particular port, then you can access another Mac that has Personal File Sharing turned on whether you're connected to that Mac via AppleTalk or TCP/IP protocol network.

Configuring TCP/IP

To configure TCP/IP, you (may) need to know a little about your network. First, you need to decide what type of network interface(s) you have and, from that, how your network addresses are assigned. Next, you'll need to determine what factor, if any, the Internet will play in your TCP/IP configuration. Then you may need to know some specifics concerning your network, including arcana such as the IP address, subnet mask, and other necessary evils.

NOTE   Before you configure TCP/IP, you'll need to either log in to Mac OS X using an administrator (Admin) account or click the padlock in the Network pane and enter an Admin account name and password. You can't alter the Network configuration without an administrator's password.

SELECTING THE PORT

If you have more than one networking port in your Mac, you need to begin by selecting the appropriate port for configuration. Each Ethernet or AirPort card that's installed in your Mac constitutes a *port*, so for each networking port you can assign individual TCP/IP addresses. (The Network pane also is used to set up your modem, if you have one, for TCP/IP access. That's discussed in Chapter 10.)

Why have more than one networking port? You may want to use different ports at different times—for instance, any AirPort-capable Mac also has an Ethernet port built in. With two ports configured, you could switch back and forth between types of networks, for instance, when you take your portable Mac from one location to another.

You also might want to have more than one network port to access two different networks at once. As an example, you might want your desktop Mac to access an Ethernet network and an AirPort network simultaneously, in order to share data with a portable Mac via AirPort while connecting to a wired LAN via Ethernet.

NOTE If you have an AirPort-capable Mac, you'll be choosing between multiple ports because all AirPort-capable Macs have Ethernet built in as well. (Most have modems, too.) If you want to use only AirPort, you can turn off the Ethernet port, as detailed in the section "Network Port Configurations," later in this chapter. (You can configure it at some later time, if desired, to connect to an Ethernet network.)

You select the port that you're going to configure using the Show menu in the Network pane. (This menu, above all the tabs, is where you can select from Ethernet and, if installed, Modem and AirPort options.) Note, as shown in Figure 18.3, that the options change according to the type of port you're configuring; AirPort options are slightly different from Ethernet options.

FIGURE 18.3
The TCP/IP tab for an Ethernet connection

NOTE   In most cases, Ethernet and AirPort hardware devices are automatically recognized by the Mac and displayed in the Show menu. If you don't see a card that you believe is correctly installed, see Chapter 25, "Peripherals, Internal Upgrades, and Disks," for details on installing cards and driver software. Also, see the section "Network Port Configurations," later in this chapter, because the particular port in question may have been turned off.

To begin configuring a networking port, you should select it in the Show menu. Once it's selected, make sure you've clicked the TCP/IP tab. Now you're ready to enter TCP/IP information.

SELECTING THE TYPE OF CONFIGURATION

If you don't know much about TCP/IP setup, that might be okay. You might not need to dig into the arcana of IP addressing. In some cases, you'll simply select a configuration method and leave it at that. In other cases, though, you'll have to enter all the addresses manually. Mac OS X gives you a few different choices, including Manually, Using DHCP, and Using BootP.

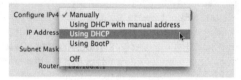

Here's a look at each choice for addressing:

Manually   Select Manually if you intend to give the Mac a fixed IP address and if you otherwise need to specify the particulars of your network setup, as directed by your network administrator. If you select Manually, you'll need to enter the IP Address, subnet mask, and so on. (See the section "Configuring TCP/IP Manually," later in this chapter.)

Using DHCP with Manual IP Address   With this option, your Mac will use a DHCP server to retrieve all TCP/IP settings except the IP address, which you can enter manually. This is a nice compromise when you have a DHCP server available, but you want to make sure this Mac always has the same IP address (for instance, when you want to make Internet services such as web sharing available from this Mac).

TIP   If you don't have a DHCP server or router, DHCP can still be valuable. As long as you're not worried about Internet access using the selected Ethernet port, you can use DHCP to create a local network automatically. Select Using DHCP on all your Macs that are connected by Ethernet. Then, after a short delay while the Macs look for and fail to find a DHCP server, addresses will be assigned automatically, making it possible for you to share files between the Macs using Personal File Sharing. Note also that DHCP is the most-often-used choice for AirPort networks that include an AirPort Base Station. (If you *are* worried about Internet access on your LAN, you need to configure a router or configure your Mac as an Internet Sharing host, as discussed later, in the section "Internet and Personal File Sharing Together.")

Using DHCP   The Dynamic Host Configuration Protocol is the more popular way to configure TCP/IP automatically these days, especially on networks of personal computers. Server computers (such as Macs running Mac OS X Server) or special router devices that include DHCP server functions can manage DHCP. If you have a DHCP server or router on your network, select Using DHCP from the Configure menu. The server will automatically configure your Mac.

Using BootP   If your network offers a special BootP (Bootstrap Protocol) server, you can use it to configure your Mac's TCP/IP settings automatically. Select Using BootP from the Configure menu, and you won't need to enter any other addresses or information. Note, however, that if you don't have a BootP server on your local network, your TCP/IP configuration will not be completed correctly. BootP is especially common if you're using Mac OS X Server on your LAN.

WHAT IS BONJOUR?

Bonjour (previously called *Rendezvous*) is Apple's implementation of the ZeroConf (www.zeroconf.com/) standard, which makes it possible for computers on a TCP/IP-based network to find network services automatically. If your Mac is connected to such a network (and most typical networks these days use TCP/IP) then you'll also be able to take advantage of Bonjour's seemingly magic capabilities.

Bonjour's value becomes apparent when you have an application or device that recognizes it. Bonjour-compatible printers, for instance, can be discovered on a local network by your copy of Printer Setup without interference on your part. Bonjour-aware applications such as iChat AV will find resources on your network automatically, such as the automatic discovery of other Bonjour users when you launch iChat AV on a local network. Beyond that, Bonjour does something else that is interesting—it gives your Mac a local name, instead of just a number. It's Bonjour technology that enables you to access the personal Web pages of other Mac users on your network by accessing the Bonjour menu in your Safari bookmarks bar.

The upshot of all of this is that Bonjour likely will make networking configuration quite a bit less involved, and over time, the memory of manually configuring network services will grow dimmer and dimmer, at least for certain users and administrators. Ironically, the future likely will hold less of a spotlight on Bonjour because it may fade into the background as TCP/IP networks begin to work and seem to be "plug-and-play." In some later revision of this book, the technology may make this chapter a lot shorter, after Bonjour is built into many devices and applications.

Now, if you've selected an automatic type of TCP/IP configuration (and you don't need to specify DNS addresses, which are discussed in the following section), you can click the Apply Now button in the Network pane to apply the changes to your TCP/IP settings. You can then close the System Preferences application and, with any luck, begin using your new network settings immediately. (In most cases, changes to network settings are immediate.)

NOTE   Mac OS X supports IPv6, a version of IP (Internet Protocol) that allows for longer addresses. (Because the Internet is increasing in size, a larger pool of potential addresses is important.) Currently, only a few institutions are using IPv6, and most of those are configured automatically. If you need to manually configure an IPv6 address, click the Configure IPv6 button at the bottom of the TCP/IP tab.

CONFIGURING DNS

Both the automatic and manual approaches to TCP/IP settings optionally give you the opportunity to enter Domain Name Service (DNS) information for your Mac. Whether you need DNS entries depends on how your LAN is configured; when in doubt, consult your network administrator. In general, DNS settings aren't required for local networking, but they may be required if you plan to use a single networking port for both local networking and Internet access. Also, on larger networks, you may use a domain name server to resolve the names of your individual machines, in which case a DNS entry may be required. Here are the settings:

DNS Servers   These IP addresses are those of DNS computers, which translate text names (for example, www.macblog.com) into numerical IP addresses. DNS servers are designed so that they automatically update when a domain name is moved or added somewhere on the Internet. Web browsers and other Internet applications reference the DNS servers most often to determine the proper IP address associated with an Internet domain name entered by the user.

Search Domains   Enter local domain names in this entry box so that Internet applications don't have to request information from a DNS server. In most cases, these local domain names are those that are assigned to your local network. On Todd's network, he might enter **macblog.com** in the Search Domains entry box. Then, if he types **imacx** into the address box in a web browser (or if someone else on his network types it), TCP/IP will first look in Search Domains and attempt to access imacx.macblog.com.

CONFIGURING TCP/IP MANUALLY

If you've selected Manually from the TCP/IP tab's Configure menu, you'll need to dig into each of the TCP/IP settings and enter them by hand. (As you type, you can press the Tab key to move to the next entry box.) Here's a look at the different addresses:

IP Address   The IP address is the unique address number, in the format *xxx.xxx.xxx.xxx* (four parts of *up to* three digits, but without leading zeros, so that 192.168.1.2 is a valid IP address but entering it as 192.168.001.002 isn't necessary—if you enter an address like this, it will be reduced to the first form. An IP address is assigned to a particular node (networked device, whether a computer or other device) on a TCP/IP network. The exact nature of the IP address depends on the type of network you're creating. For instance, if your Mac has a direct connection to the Internet (without a router or firewall), you must have a unique IP address so that you can be differentiated from other servers on the Internet. But the Internet isn't the only type of TCP/IP network—you can have a private IP network for small groups of computers, if desired.

TIP   If you're selecting the IP address on your own, and you're creating a small private network, you should use the common private IP address ranges. Use the format 192.168.1.*x* within the range 192.168.1.2 through 192.168.1.254. Note that the 1 address and the 255 address are generally reserved. (If you need more IP addresses than this, you can use the entire range of 192.168.*x.x*, but you would then need a subnet mask of 255.255.0.0.)

Subnet Mask   The subnet mask is a special number used to help your Mac understand what *class* of network you're operating on. In most cases (home, small office, or direct Internet connection), you're operating on a class C network, which means, essentially, that only the last of the four numbers in a given IP address differentiates the machines on your network. (For example, on a class C network, only the numbers 2 and 254 in the addresses 192.168.1.2 and 192.168.1.254 are significant for differentiating between the two local Macs.)

The subnet mask uses the number 255 to indicate that a portion of the IP address isn't relevant and 0 to indicate that it is. Most small networks use the subnet mask 255.255.255.0 to indicate that the last number in the Mac's IP address is the one that's relevant to the local network. (For instance, if you have a Mac that has the IP address 192.168.1.3, and the subnet mask is 255.255.255.0, the Mac knows that all devices with an address 192.168.1.x are in the local network. If the subnet mask is 255.255.0.0, then the local network includes machines with an address 192.168.x.x.) The likelihood is that you'll use 255.255.255.0 unless you're told differently by your Internet service provider or your organization's network administrator.

Router   The router address is the IP address of the routing device that provides access to any larger networks to which the LAN might be connected. For instance, if your LAN is connected to the Internet via an Internet router, the IP address for that router is entered here. If you don't have such a router, you don't need a particular number here—the .1 address of the current subnet (for example, 192.168.1.1) will suffice.

After you enter all the settings, you can click the Apply Now button in the Network pane to make them your current TCP/IP settings. Your changes should take place immediately—in almost all cases, no restart is required.

NOTE   Before you finish with a manual TCP/IP configuration, you will probably also want to configure DNS manually, as discussed in the previous section, "Configuring DNS."

Configuring AirPort

So far we've looked mostly at configuring an Ethernet port for a direct connection to your LAN. How is an AirPort port configured differently? Usually, it isn't. If you want the AirPort-enabled Mac to have the same IP address all the time—and you don't frequently move between different AirPort networks—you can select AirPort in the Show menu of the Network pane and then select Manually from the Configure menu on the TCP/IP tab. From there, follow the instructions in the previous section, "Configuring TCP/IP Manually."

More often, however, you'll configure AirPort by selecting Using DHCP from the Configure menu on the TCP/IP tab of the Network pane. This is particularly true if you're using an AirPort Base Station or a similar wireless hub or router. It's also the most convenient configuration if you tend to move from one AirPort network to another. By relying on the DHCP server that's built into most wireless routers (such as the AirPort Base Station), your Mac can receive its TCP/IP configuration automatically whenever necessary.

NOTE   For the most part, using AirPort for a day-to-day networking connection requires a wireless router of some kind, either the AirPort Base Station or a compatible wireless networking device. (Configuring an AirPort Base Station is discussed in Chapter 25.) For occasional connections, however, two AirPort-enabled Macs can connect together and share files. See the section "AirPort computer-to-computer Networks," later in this chapter, for details.

If you've been configuring TCP/IP for an AirPort connection, you have another step before you're ready to begin sharing files. With AirPort selected in the Show menu of the Network pane, select the AirPort tab (see Figure 18.4). In the By Default, Join menu you have two choices—Automatic or Preferred Networks:

Automatic   If you tend to use your Mac on multiple networks or in an area served by more than one base station, select this option.

Preferred Networks   This is the best choice for a Mac that is often in a location that's served by more than one base station, but you want this Mac to access only a particular one, or you at least want your Mac to try first for a particular base station.) In the list, you'll see stations which your Mac has recently accessed; you can drag base stations around in that list to change the order in which your Mac attempts to access them. To remove a base station from the list, highlight it and click the minus (-) button; you can also select a base station and click Edit to change its name or security settings.

NOTE   Choosing the Preferred Networks option is required if you want to automatically connect your Mac to a "closed" network, which is one that doesn't make its name available for discovery by unauthorized computers. The base station or router can be set so that its network is closed. In that case, users have to know the network is there and type in the name of the network and access password manually.

FIGURE 18.4
The AirPort tab appears when you're configuring an AirPort connection in the Network pane.

Aside from these options, you have a few others that you can enable by clicking the Options button. At the top of the dialog sheet that appears, you can choose how your Mac will behave when none of your recent networks (in the case of Automatic) or preferred networks (in the case of a Preferred Networks setting) are found. The options ask you if you'd like to join an open network, automatically join an open network, or if you'd like your Mac to keep looking for recent/preferred networks.

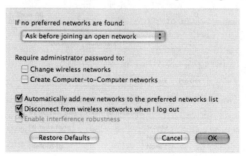

TIP   This is basically a security caution so that you don't end up surfing on an open wireless network unintentionally. You might like the option Ask Before Joining an Open Network, because a dialog box will pop up when you're in an Internet café, for instance, but it'll work normally when you're on your home or office network.

The next set of options enables you to decide whether an administrator's password is required for changing wireless networks and/or creative computer-to-computer networks. You might not want to require a password to change wireless networks. (Doing so might be a good idea if you're not sure whether you trust all the users on your Mac, such as in a lab setting.) However, requiring one for a computer-to-computer network is a good idea—if only to keep your Mac from being accessible via an ad-hoc AirPort network without some sort of authorization.

NOTES ON AIRPORT SECURITY

Although it sounds like issues involving metal detectors and passports, this "AirPort security" is focused on wireless networking (and bad puns). Enabling AirPort networking between your Macs can have a few security implications that you may want to consider.

Because of AirPort's wireless nature, the biggest security risk is the potential that an unauthorized computer in your immediate vicinity can gain access to your AirPort network. (Soon after the release of AirPort technology, there were reports, perhaps apocryphal, of "drive-by hackings" in and around Silicon Valley.) To keep that from being a problem, the first step is to secure your network with a password and, if desired, to encrypt the transmissions between Macs and your AirPort Base Station. Setting up the passwords for your AirPort Base Station is described in Chapter 25; entering passwords and accessing AirPort networks is discussed in Chapter 17. Impress upon your users the need to keep the AirPort password private, because there is only one password per network.

As we've alluded to, you can create a closed network with the Apple Base Station and some third-party routers. A closed network requires that the user know the name of the network and its password before being allowed to access it—the network isn't *discoverable*, so outside users won't know it's there and, hence, won't try to access it.

Also, you can limit access to specific computers with the Apple Base Station and certain routers. You do that by adding the AirPort ID number for each authorized computer in the base station or router's setup software. Then, only those computers can access the network wirelessly.

Aside from closing networks, enabling passwords and encrypting transmissions, you can take other precautions just in case an unauthorized machine does gain access to your Mac via AirPort. Those include some standard considerations for network security: turn on only the network services that are necessary (Personal File Sharing, for instance); ensure that all of your users have good passwords (as detailed in Chapter 9, "Being the Administrator: Permissions, Settings, and Adding Users"); and make sure your users know that the contents of their Public folders could be viewed by others, and others could potentially put items in their Drop Box folders, as discussed later, in the section "User Access via Personal File Sharing."

The other security issue involves others accessing your AirPort network via the Internet (assuming your AirPort router is also connected to an Internet connection). In most cases, your AirPort Base Station or WiFi router should include firewall capabilities, including network address translation and more sophisticated port-blocking schemes. Get to know those schemes (again, the Base Station is discussed in Chapter 25, and Internet/LAN issues are discussed later in this chapter) and turn on those features to keep others from gaining access to your AirPort network via the Internet.

NOTE Creating a computer-to-computer network is discussed later in this chapter, and using the AirPort menu icon to change AirPort networks and turn the AirPort card on and off is discussed in Chapter 17.

The final set of options is fairly straightforward. You can check the first one to have your Mac automatically add new networks to your preferred network list. You can use the second option to automatically disconnect from wireless networks when you log out (by default, you remain connected so that another user account can access the AirPort connection). The third option, Enable Interference Robustness, is designed for AirPort Extreme connections; you can turn it on if an appliance, such as a microwave oven, seems to cause interference for your AirPort connection. According to Apple, this isn't an option for earlier AirPort cards because they have the feature always on. Note also that it increases reliability of the connection but reduces the speed.

NOTE Creating a computer-to-computer network is discussed later in this chapter, and using the AirPort menu icon to change AirPort networks and turn the AirPort card on and off is discussed in Chapter 17.

Network Port Configurations

The Network pane offers advanced settings that you may want to dig into at some time, particularly if you find yourself configuring multiple ports for your Mac and using a variety of different connections. Choose Network Port Configurations from the Show menu in the Network pane, and you'll see the Network pane, shown in Figure 18.5.

The Network Port Configurations options enable you to do three things: you can turn ports on and off, you can create multiple configurations for a particular port, and you can set port priority.

FIGURE 18.5
The Network Port Configurations options of the Network pane

To turn a particular port on or off, click the check box next to that port's listing. Without a check in the check box, the port is off; it won't appear in the Show menu until it's turned on again. (Turning off a port that you don't use can speed up your startup time somewhat.)

To create another configuration, select the port you'd like to duplicate and click the Duplicate button. You can then give the new port configuration a name in the dialog sheet that appears. Click OK, and that new port will appear in the list. That entry will also appear in the Show menu, enabling you to configure it as desired. You also can create a completely new port by clicking New and then entering a name and choosing the port from the Port menu in the dialog sheet that appears. You'll have a new port configuration that starts out with blank settings. Select it in the Configure menu and configure away. To delete a port configuration, select it in the list and click the Delete button.

If you have multiple ports listed, you can change the priority of those ports by dragging them up and down in the list. For instance, if Built-in Ethernet is the first priority, your Mac will attempt to access the network via Ethernet; if it fails and AirPort is the second option, it will attempt to connect via AirPort. This is a good approach for portable Macs, which can look for the highest-speed (Ethernet) connection first and then look for the next most appropriate port (AirPort) if the first doesn't connect.

TIP Port priority works for Internet access as well as for network access, so you can change the priority if you'd like your Internet connections to attempt the different ports in a particular order. (Changing port settings for Internet access is discussed in more detail in Chapter 10.)

When you've finished making changes to the configurations and priority, click Apply Now in the Network pane. Then select one of the configurations from the Show menu to alter that configuration, if desired.

TIP Although these Port Configuration settings are handy, they're generally useful only in limited circumstances, where your Mac has more than one static network connection to choose from. If you find that you're often switching your networking connections because you're moving your Mac from place to place (for instance, from your office to your home, where the networking or Internet connections are different), then you may want to use the Location Manager for those changes. The Location Manager is discussed in Chapter 19, "PowerBooks, iBooks, and Mac OS X."

Personal File Sharing

With TCP/IP or AppleTalk configured, the next step in your network configuration is to determine whether you want Personal File Sharing turned on. Turning on Personal File Sharing enables users at Macintosh computers running Mac OS X or earlier to access portions of your Mac's hard disk (and other connected disks) by mounting those volumes on their desktops.

A network that employs this sort of file-sharing approach is called a *peer-to-peer* network because each computer is a potential server. If you want a file from Julie's computer, you log in to that computer and enter your password; you then gain access and begin transferring files. If Julie wants access to your computer, she gains access in the same way, assuming that you've turned on Personal File Sharing.

NOTE The other type of network besides a peer-to-peer network is a *client/server network*. With client/server networks, a central server computer is the only (or primary) repository for shared files. In some cases, you'll still log in to the server, especially if it uses AFP. (For instance, a Mac OS X Server computer can be used as a central AFP server for a group of Macs, with each running Mac OS 8, Mac OS 9, or Mac OS X.) In other cases, particularly Unix-style NFS mounts (discussed in Chapter 17), the network volumes are always available to your Mac, without requiring that you log in.

User Access via Personal File Sharing

When you have Personal File Sharing enabled, a remote user can log in through the Connect to Server window or the Network icon (in Mac OS X 10.3 and higher) discussed in Chapter 17. For regular access, the remote user must have a valid account on your Mac—the same type of user account you saw how to create in Chapter 10. If a valid account doesn't exist, the user can still access your server as a guest, with access only to the Public folders on your Mac.

NOTE Mac users don't have to have Mac OS X to access File Sharing on your Mac—a user with a Mac running Mac OS 8.1 or higher can sign in to your Mac if Personal File Sharing is enabled. In versions prior to Mac OS 9, the user may need to enter your server's IP address in the Chooser by selecting AppleShare and clicking Server IP Address.

Once logged in, users can select volumes or folders that will then appear on their desktops. The users can then read from and save to your disk. What the user sees depends on the type of permissions granted to the user's account. With an Admin account, the user can see and access:

◆ That user's own home folder

◆ Most of the Mac OS X startup disk, including other users' Public folders

◆ Any other attached hard disks or removable disks

If the user has a normal user account, the only items that will be accessible to that user will be:

◆ That user's home folder

◆ The Public folders of all users on the computer

Note that regular users are a bit more limited than with earlier versions of the Classic Mac OS, which enabled them to access virtually any portion of the Mac they wanted.

NOTE If you're familiar with the Classic Mac OS, you'll notice that Mac OS X lacks the capability to limit sharing to certain folders or certain groups and users. In this sense, file sharing in Mac OS X is simpler but a little less powerful. If you'd like to add other folders or volumes for sharing (and control the permissions more closely), you can use a third-party "donation-ware" utility called Share-Points (www.hornware.com/sharepoints/). SharePoints is a powerful program, enabling you to perform tasks such as creating new File Sharing–only users, turning off the sharing of particular users' Public folders, and configuring preferences that govern the built-in File Sharing server.

Guest users don't require a username or password and are given access only to Public folders. With Mac OS X, security is paramount, so regular and guest users are limited to accessing Public folders during remote connections.

Turning On Personal File Sharing

If you think you'd like to turn on Personal File Sharing, it's easy enough to do. Here's how:

1. Open the System Preferences application.

2. Select the Sharing icon.

3. In the Sharing pane, unlock the administrator's padlock, if necessary. (You can't change the Personal File Sharing state without an administrator's password, but it may be unlocked if you're signed in to an administrator's account.)

4. Make sure the Services tab is selected, and then click to place a check mark next to the Personal File Sharing option.

SECURITY ISSUES WITH PERSONAL FILE SHARING

Any time you decide to make your Mac available for remote connections and file sharing, you're introducing a possible security risk. After all, a remote user may be able to guess or crack a valid username and password on your Mac, thereby gaining access to your files. Here are a few security issues to ponder:

◆ Think carefully before turning on Personal File Sharing on any Mac with a publicly available IP address—that is, any Mac with a static (or otherwise *direct*) IP address on the Internet that isn't situated behind a firewall. Although it's convenient to access remote volumes across the Internet, you should take into account that anyone might be able to access the files on your Mac. See Chapter 10 for more on securing your Macs from others on the Internet.

◆ Mac OS X allows guest access by default—it can't be turned off. That means anyone can access the Mac via its guest account, giving an unauthorized user (for instance, one that accesses your Mac over the Internet if you don't heed the previous warning) the opportunity to access Public folders. You should warn your users—those who have accounts on your Mac—that others might be able to access items in their Public folders and not to place sensitive files in them. Also, users should be warned that an unauthorized user conceivably could put items in their Drop Box folder—even a virus, worm, or other damaging application or document. (You can turn off the sharing of Public folders using Share-Points, which might be a good solution if you're willing to put in the effort.)

◆ Turning on Personal File Sharing in Mac OS X may give some users (particularly Admin accounts) unfettered access to any external volumes (such as an external disk drive) that are attached to your Mac. In general, this shouldn't be a problem—you should trust your users with Admin accounts. If it *is* a problem, consider assigning those users regular accounts (you can turn off Admin status in the Users pane of System Preferences). Also, you can use the Get Info command in the Finder to change the privileges for sensitive folders on those external volumes. (See Chapter 9 for more information.)

That's it. You'll see a message indicating that Personal File Sharing is starting up. Once it meets with success, you'll see the message change to Personal File Sharing On, and the button under it will read Stop (see Figure 18.6).

TIP   As noted in the sidebar "Security Issues with Personal File Sharing," when you turn on Personal File Sharing, your Mac can be accessed over the Internet as well as locally. Assuming your Mac isn't guarded by a router or firewall and you have an active Internet connection with a publicly available IP address, you should be able to read your IP address in the Sharing pane and tell others that address. If they have Macs (or Apple Filing Services client applications for other platforms), they should be able to log in to your Mac over the Internet.

FIGURE 18.6

After you enable Personal File Sharing, the Sharing pane will indicate that Personal File Sharing is on.

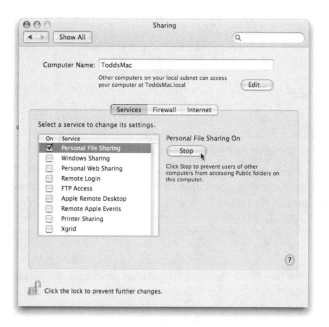

NOTE   What about all those other services listed in the Sharing pane? Windows Personal File Sharing is covered in Chapter 20, web sharing and FTP in Chapter 24, remote login in Chapter 17, remote Apple events in Chapter 21, "Automator and AppleScript," and printer sharing in Chapter 7, "Printing and Faxing in Mac OS X."

Naming Your Mac

If you have TCP/IP configured, remote users will be able access your Mac for file sharing using its IP address in the Connect to Server window (or for earlier Macs, in the Network Browser or Chooser). You'd probably also prefer to give your Mac a unique name that users can see in their Connect to Server or Network Browser window. (And you'll need a name if you're using AppleTalk.) To rename your Mac, enter a name in the Computer Name entry box in the Sharing pane.

Once you rename your Mac, you'll notice that Mac OS X automatically gives your Mac a *local hostname*, which is shown in the text "Other computers on your local subnet can reach your computer at *local hostname.*"

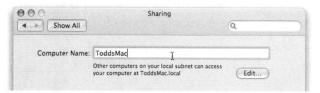

The local hostname name is used much the same way as the computer name, except in a TCP/IP context. For instance, if you have Web Sharing turned on for a particular Mac, you can access that Mac via its local hostname name in a web browser by entering something such as `http://iMacG4.local/` in the browser's Address entry box. (In essence, it serves as a substitute for that Mac's raw IP address on your local network.) If you'd like to change that name, click the Edit button and change the local hostname in the dialog sheet that appears.

TIP The Sharing pane also shows you the correct IP address for accessing your Mac at the bottom of the pane, so you'll know what IP number to give out to remote users if you need to. That address can be used to access your Mac remotely if it has a direct IP address on the Internet (see Chapter 17).

Turning Off Personal File Sharing

Turning off Personal File Sharing is about as easy as turning it on. In the Sharing pane, click the Stop button that appears under the message Personal File Sharing On, or click to remove the check mark next to Personal File Sharing in the Services list. That begins the process of turning off Personal File Sharing. If no users are currently connected, you'll see the button change to Start and the section head change to Personal File Sharing Off, indicating that remote users can't access Personal File Sharing anymore.

If users are currently connected to your Mac via Personal File Sharing, you'll see another dialog box (see Figure 18.7) where you can enter the number of minutes that Personal File Sharing should wait before disconnecting users. In the text area, you can enter a message that remote users will see. If you enter **0** in the Minutes entry box and click OK, users will be disconnected immediately, and they will see a message stating that the server unexpectedly closed down. Otherwise, users will see a warning message when you click OK, telling them how many more minutes they have. Then they'll be disconnected automatically once the time is up.

FIGURE 18.7
If you shut down Personal File Sharing while users are connected, you're given a chance to warn them.

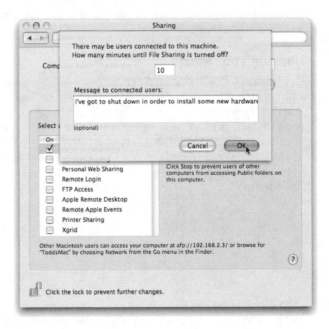

NOTE If you simply log out of your account on your Mac, users can continue to access the Mac via Personal File Sharing. If you restart or shut down the Mac, however, remote users will receive an error message and will no longer be able to access items on your Mac. Once your Mac is up and running again, they'll be able to log in once more.

Personal File Sharing over IP (Mac OS 9)

Mac OS 9–based Macs also can share files with Mac OS X machines. The Mac OS 9 machine must have a valid TCP/IP configuration that makes it part of the same subnet as the Mac OS X machine or an AppleTalk configuration in the same AppleTalk zone (if applicable), connected via Ethernet or AirPort. Of course, you also can access the Mac OS 9 machine via a fixed IP address on the Internet if it is so configured.

If all the stipulations are met, you can configure the Mac OS 9–based machine to share its files. In the Personal File Sharing control panel (Apple menu ➢ Control Panels ➢ Personal File Sharing), turn on the Enable Personal File Sharing Clients to Connect over TCP/IP option if you're using TCP/IP as your protocol (turning on the option isn't necessary if you're using AppleTalk) and then click the Start button to start up Personal File Sharing on the Mac OS 9 machine (see Figure 18.8). Once Personal File Sharing has started, you'll be able to connect to this Mac using a valid username (if you have an account in the Mac OS 9 machine's Users control panel) or as a guest.

FIGURE 18.8
The Personal File Sharing control panel in Mac OS 9 lets you share files with other Macs.

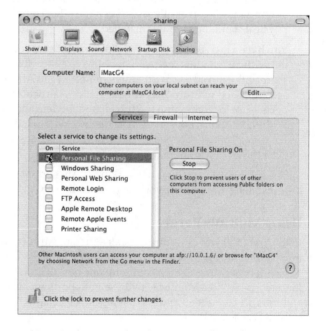

Internet and Personal File Sharing Together

The fact that the same protocol—TCP/IP—can be used for both Personal File Sharing, as discussed in this chapter, and Internet connections, as discussed in Chapter 10, can cause some interesting dilemmas to crop up. In order to share files and access the Internet at the same time, you may need to get a bit creative with your solutions. Here are a few possible scenarios, followed by a few possible solutions:

You have one networking port (Ethernet), and you need both Internet and file sharing access via that port.   You have a few different options. If you can use AppleTalk for your file sharing and TCP/IP for Internet access, then you're okay. If you need to use TCP/IP for both, then you need to either add a second networking port (literally add another Ethernet card) for the Internet connection or install a router on your network.

You have an Internet connection you want to share with others on your network.   If you have a cable or DSL modem connection (or even a modem connection) that you'd like to share with others, you can do that using Apple's Internet Sharing capability. The only caveat: your Mac still needs two networking ports. If you're using a modem for the Internet connection, you can route the Internet data to others on your network through your Ethernet port. If you're using Ethernet for the Internet connection, you'll need to use AirPort for your networking, or you'll need another Ethernet port via an expansion card. If you don't want to use your Mac as the router (you want to be able to turn it off or otherwise keep the other computers from relying on it), then you'll want a physical stand-alone router installed.

You have a mixed network of AirPort and Ethernet connections, and you want to share the Internet with all.   In this case, you might have a broadband or modem connection that you'd like to share with a mixed bag of Ethernet-connected and AirPort-connected machines. That's most easily accomplished with an AirPort Base Station, particularly the later models that offer two Ethernet ports—one for connecting to a broadband modem and the other for connecting to an Ethernet hub. With those connections made and the Internet routed properly, your entire network can benefit. For a small network (three or four wired connections and one to 10 AirPort connections), you can get a third-party combination hub/router.

The solutions to any dual-networking (LAN and Internet) situation involve one of three scenarios—installing a second networking port, adding an AirPort Base Station, or adding a physical router.

Using Multiple Ports

In the first case, you can simply install either an AirPort card or a third-party Ethernet card in order to expand your Mac's networking capabilities. Doing so adds another entry to your Show menu in the Network pane. You can then configure one port to access your LAN and another port to access your Internet connection. Your Mac will use both ports seamlessly, enabling you to access your LAN and Internet connection at the same time. (See Chapter 25 for help on installing additional internal upgrade cards.)

But what about that second case—using those two ports to share Internet access with the rest of your LAN? You can enable Apple's built-in Internet Sharing system, which enables you to use your Mac to connect to the Internet and share that connection with others on your network. If you have a modem, for instance, then you can connect via modem and share that Internet connection with other computers connected via Ethernet or AirPort.

If you have a broadband connection, however, the caveat is that you should have two networking ports to make this work. (You're able to turn on Internet Sharing if you have only Built-in Ethernet, but we can't really come up with a good reason to do so.) If you're using your one Built-in Ethernet port for the broadband connection, you'll need to install another networking port in your Mac in order to share the Internet connection with your LAN. Adding another Ethernet port (via an expansion card of some sort) will be necessary if you want to use Ethernet for both your LAN and Internet connections. Once the Ethernet expansion card is installed, you'll see it in the Show menu of the Network pane.

You can also use Internet Sharing to route an Internet connection *from* Built-in Ethernet *to* an AirPort connection, which makes sense if you don't have an AirPort Base Station or wireless router. A stand-alone router is a better solution, but if you need to share a wireless connection with only one or two Macs, you can use Internet sharing.

Once you have the proper connections in place, turning on Internet Sharing is easy. Open the Sharing pane of System Preferences and choose the Internet tab. In the Share Your Connection From menu, choose the port where your Mac gets its Internet connection. Then, in the To Computers Using box, place a check mark next to the port where you'll be sharing the Internet connection. Now, click the Start button under Internet Sharing to begin the sharing process.

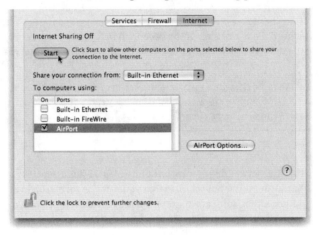

WARNING   Some ISPs (particularly for cable and DSL modems) may technically require that you pay for each computer on your LAN that receives Internet access, and they may enforce that policy strictly. If you intend to share a single broadband connection with multiple computers, check with your ISP to see if an Internet router is considered within the rules or if the ISP charges extra for or has other rules governing the use of such a device. This is true for both an Internet Sharing setup and using a physical router, discussed in the next section.

Using a Router

The steps in the previous section enable you to use two Ethernet ports (or an Ethernet port and an AirPort connection) to gain access to both Internet data and a local LAN. But what if you need Internet access for your entire LAN? The solution in that case is an Internet router. Such a device sits between your Internet connection and your Ethernet hub, moving data from the broadband device to your entire network. Some routers are also integrated Ethernet hubs, enabling you to connect multiple computers directly to the router. The router then forwards IP data from the Internet connection (usually a broadband modem) to your entire LAN.

THE AIRPORT BASE STATION

The AirPort Base Station device, offered by Apple, is a hybrid router and wireless hub for AirPort-based networks. If you don't need Internet access, you can use the Base Station simply to connect multiple AirPort-based Macs in a wireless network. You also can opt to use the Base Station as an Ethernet-to-AirPort router by connecting an Ethernet cable between one of the Base Station's Ethernet ports and the *uplink* port on an Ethernet hub or switch. (Apple has released three Base Station models if you include the AirPort Extreme model; the more recent models offer two Ethernet ports specifically for this purpose. Apple has also released the AirPort Express, which doesn't include an Ethernet port for routing to wired networks. It's designed to offer AirPort-only access.) In that way, the Base Station can be used to make both AirPort and Ethernet-based Macs appear on the same TCP/IP network, so that files can be shared among them all.

Finally, the Base Station also can be used as a router for Internet access. By connecting a broadband modem to (one of) the Base Station's Ethernet port(s), you can give Internet access to all of your AirPort-based Macs. If you have the 2.0 version of the Base Station (which features two Ethernet ports), you also can connect it to the uplink port on your Ethernet hub and share the Internet connection with your wired network as well.

Mac OS X 10.1 and higher include the software needed to configure and manage an AirPort Base Station, which is covered in Chapter 25. For more information on AirPort and the AirPort Base Station and for software updates, see www.apple.com/airport/ on the Web.

NOTE Again, the Internet Sharing feature built into Mac OS X is essentially a *software router*, which is similar to a hardware router but requires that your Mac be turned on in order to route IP packets to other computers. Other software routers, such as IPNetShareX (www.sustworks.com), offer similar functionality with more choices and more of a user interface.

Besides simply forwarding IP data, routers can offer security settings, enabling you to create a firewall between your network and the Internet. One scheme, *network address translation* (NAT), is common to most of today's consumer Internet routers. NAT translates your public IP address into private addresses on your LAN, making it much more difficult for outsiders on the Internet to access one of your Macs directly. Some routers also offer "virtual server" features, which automatically reroute server requests to a particular computer on your LAN while denying other requests. Some even offer access control features, which enable you to deny your own users access to particular websites or domains. (See Chapter 11 for more discussion of firewalls and Internet security.)

You configure the router as specified in its documentation; then, with it connected to the same Ethernet hub to which your other Macs are also connected, you can configure the Macs to access that router. Most hardware routers are platform independent, so they'll work with Macs, PCs, Unix machines, and most any other computer. Figure 18.9 shows an example of a router configuration screen; note that it's being accessed via a web browser.

Configuring your router is beyond the scope of this book, so follow the instructions that came with your router. Once the router is set up, however, there are two ways to configure your Macs to access the router and, hence, the Internet:

◆ Most routers act as DHCP servers, assigning IP addresses to the Macs on your LAN. If you've set up your router to serve DHCP, you can simply select Configure ➢ Using DHCP in the TCP/IP tab of each Mac's Ethernet port that you want to be configured automatically.

FIGURE 18.9
The XRouter Pro from MacSense (www.macsense.com) offers a web-based configuration for options such as DHCP serving, PPPoE setup, and firewall options.

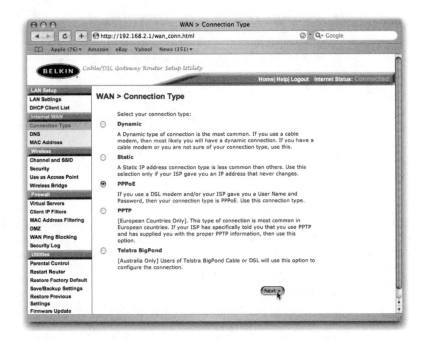

◆ With most routers, you also can assign fixed IP addresses in the private range to your Macs. If you elect to do this (by selecting Configure ➢ Manually in the TCP/IP tab), you'll need to enter the router's IP address in the Router entry box. You also might need to configure a domain name server address (or addresses) to access Internet sites successfully.

In either case, once you've finished setting your TCP/IP addresses and options, close System Preferences and restart your Mac. When you sign back in, your LAN-based Macs should have access to the Internet through the router.

AirPort Computer-to-Computer Networks

Before this chapter ends, one other quick network configuration possibility needs to be discussed—the computer-to-computer network using AirPort. This enables you to use AirPort to quickly create a small network so that you can turn on Personal File Sharing and move files between two or a few Macs without requiring an AirPort Base Station. In a computer-to-computer connection, one Mac creates a network, and the other(s) accesses that network as if it were an AirPort Base Station network. The steps include the following:

1. In the AirPort menu bar menu, or via the Network menu on the AirPort tab in Internet Connect, select the Create Network command on the host Mac to create an AirPort network that the other Mac can access. You'll see a dialog box that prompts you to enter a name and choose a channel. If you'd like to add a password, click Show Options, then turn on the Enable Encryption option. That allows you to specify a password and a confirmation of the password. You can also choose the type of encryption key to use for the network connection. With those choices made, click OK.

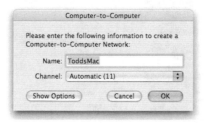

2. With the network created, you'll probably want to make sure Personal File Sharing is enabled on the host Mac.

3. Now, other AirPort-enabled Macs within the wireless area should be able to see and access that network via their AirPort menu bar items, Internet Connect, or the AirPort application in Mac OS 9. If you see the network appear in one of those places, select that network and, if necessary, enter a password.

4. With the AirPort network established, use the Connect to Server window or the Network icon to access the host Mac's Personal File Sharing services, as discussed in Chapter 17. Also, note that the menu bar item icon changes slightly for a computer-to-computer network.

5. Access files on the host Mac, the same way you would if you were accessing any other remote Mac on your local network. Again, for more details, see Chapter 17.

TIP   Need to cancel a computer-to-computer network? It goes away automatically the next time you sign in to a regular Base Station network, or you can choose Disconnect from Current Network from the AirPort menu bar icon menu.

What's Next?

In this chapter, you learned how to configure your Mac for network access via Ethernet or AirPort connections. You also saw how to turn on Personal File Sharing so that remote users can connect to your Mac, and you read some of the security implications involved in doing that. You also learned how to get Internet access and network access to work together on the same computer or network, as well as how to create a computer-to-computer network using AirPort technology. In the next chapter, we'll cover issues that primarily concern portable computers running Mac OS X, including file synchronization, synchronizing files between a portable and a desktop Mac, and saving energy.

## Chapter 19

PowerBooks, iBooks, and Mac OS X

If you use Mac OS X with a portable Macintosh, you'll find that you have a few special tasks, tools, and techniques to consider. Mac OS X supports Apple's portables well—in some ways, it's as good as or better than any version of the Mac OS that Apple has ever written for portables. In some other ways (such as DVD playback support for older PowerBooks), Mac OS X falls down a bit. Overall, however, you'll find it's great for late-model PowerBooks and iBooks.

In this chapter, we'll discuss topics that are useful to both portable and desktop Macs but that affect PowerBooks and iBooks differently—for instance, we'll discuss networking your portable and using the Location Manager. You'll also learn about some tools that are designed specifically to make portable Macs more useful, including FireWire Target Disk Mode and the use of multiple displays via mirroring or, in some cases, to extend your desktop.

Finally, we'll discuss the Energy Saver settings and some suggestions for getting your portable's battery to last as long as possible.

In this chapter:

◆ Using the Location Menu

◆ PC Cards, IrDA, and External Displays

◆ Target Disk Mode

◆ Saving Battery Life

Using the Location Menu

The technology involved in networking a portable computer for an Internet connection, a local area network connection, or both isn't really any different from the technology used for desktop computers. If there's any difference, it's that you're likely to move your portable Macintosh around a bit more, and so you want a bit more flexibility for your connections.

Multihoming versus Locations

One way to achieve more flexibility in your connections is to use Mac OS X's native capability to take advantage of multihoming, as discussed in Chapters 10, "Configuring Internet Access," and 18, "Building a Network and Sharing Files." In the Network pane, you can set up multiple configurations for accessing a network connection and then allow the Mac OS X to determine which connection is working at that time.

NOTE   As a reminder, you manage multiple ports (see Figure 19.1) by selecting Network Port Configurations from the Show menu in the Network pane of System Preferences.

For instance, if you're interested in accessing the Internet from your portable, you could set up three different ports and arrange them according to priority. First, the Mac OS will check for an Ethernet-based connection, followed by an AirPort-based connection. If neither of those can connect, the Mac will attempt a modem-based connection. That's how Figure 19.1 is configured.

FIGURE 19.1
Setting up multihoming for an Internet connection

This is a useful approach to configuring a network connection, but it's probably a strategy best suited to a desktop Mac. For a portable, you might find that you're better off using the Location menu to create different configurations that can be switched whenever you move the Mac. That's what the Location menu does—in essence, it enables you to save multiple configurations for your Network pane and switch between them manually.

For instance, if you use your Mac in both your office and home, you may need to configure it differently for network and Internet access at each location. At the office, perhaps you use an Ethernet-based connection for your Internet and LAN access; at home, perhaps you have an AirPort-based network connection for the Internet and your desktop Macs. When traveling, you might want to use a modem-based Internet connection, with different phone numbers programmed for different cities and locales.

Adding Locations

The solution is to use the Location menu to create different sets of network port configurations, called—surprisingly enough—*locations*. By creating different locations, you can have different settings for your ports and switch between them easily. Here's how:

1. To create a location, select the Location menu at the top of the Network pane and choose New Location.

2. In the dialog sheet that appears, type a name for this location, then click OK.

3. The Location menu will indicate the new location, and you'll notice that all of your port settings are blank—ready for you to fill in information for the new location.

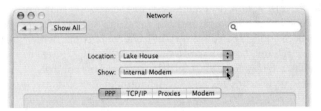

4. Now, select a port in the Show menu and configure it as desired for this location. For instance, if you're creating the Home location, and you're setting up your built-in Ethernet port for your DSL connection, you'll probably dig into the PPPoE tab. If, on the other hand, you're setting up a location you've named JavaGrinder (for when you visit the local coffee shop that has a wireless connection), then you would concentrate on the AirPort settings.

Once everything is configured, you can use the Location menu to add more locations, or you can switch between them using the Location menu. You can quickly change between entire sets of Network settings without altering or retyping constantly.

Realize that a new location isn't just about TCP/IP settings; each location can have different AppleTalk, PPP, and proxy settings—and anything else you can set in the Network pane. The individual locations don't have to vary dramatically; you could create Dallas and Houston locations, for instance, in which all of the port settings are the same, and the only difference is the local phone number on the PPP tab for your modem. The menu is there to make things more convenient, enabling you to switch quickly between saved configurations.

There's another trick to creating locations: you don't even have to open the Network pane to switch between them! Open the Apple menu and select Location, and you'll see all of your locations appear in the menu.

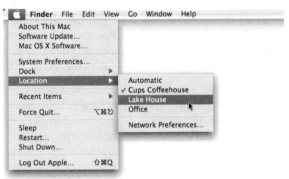

Whenever you move your portable Mac (or whenever you want to change to a different set of network settings), you can simply select a new location in the Apple menu, and your network settings will change immediately.

PC Cards, IrDA, and External Displays

PowerBooks don't offer just portability and integrated LCD displays; they also tend to offer a port or two that isn't found on Apple's desktop models. In particular, PowerBooks support expansion cards that follow the *PC card* standard—credit card–size electronics that can enhance your PowerBook's capabilities for networking, storage, and other reasons.

Some PowerBook models can also support IrDA connections, which are wireless communications via the infrared port found on the back of some PowerBook G3 (FireWire) and PowerBook G4 models. (Infrared is the same technology used for television remote controls.) In some configurations, this port can be used for synchronizing with Palm handheld devices or networking via an IrDA-equipped mobile phone.

NOTE   Although some earlier PowerBook models have an IrDA port, Apple's documentation suggests that only PowerBooks that include FireWire ports and IrDA are supported in Mac OS X. (The FireWire ports don't have anything to do with IrDA—it's just that those are the models supported.)

Finally, many portables make it easy to connect the Mac to an additional external display, either mirroring the Mac's display to the second screen or actually increasing your screen "real estate" so that you can use both screens for your applications and documents.

In this section we'll look at technologies for adding items to your PowerBook and Mac OS X's support for them.

Using PC Card Upgrades

PC card is the name of the standard that was once called *PCMCIA*. The term describes a type of upgrade card that can slide in and out of a PC card slot, one or two of which are built into most Power-Book models. (In fact, a PC card slot is one of the features that differentiate PowerBooks and iBooks.) PC card slots can be Type I (the thinnest), Type II (most common), or Type III. Type III cards are not accommodated by all PC card slots—often, a PowerBook can accept either two Type I/II cards or a single Type III card. (Type III cards are often *microdrives*, or tiny hard disks.) The one-inch-thick Pow-erBook G4, for instance, offers support for only Type I and Type II, not Type III cards.

NOTE   When discussing PC card technology, it is important to mention another technology that enables a PC card to work as an interface port—*Cardbus*. A Cardbus-enabled PowerBook can accept a PC card that adds bus-level services, such as support for FireWire and USB ports. All PowerBook models that are compatible with Mac OS X support the Cardbus standard.

PC card upgrades aren't used quite as often as they once were, particularly with Macs. In past years, the cards were often used to add modem and Ethernet capabilities to PowerBooks, which now have those technologies built in. But PC cards are still useful in a variety of ways, often to add newer technologies to PowerBooks that lack them, such as FireWire, additional USB or USB 2 ports for PowerBooks that don't have a particular port (or *enough* of a particular port). PC Cards can also be used to add Ethernet or wireless network connections for PowerBooks that aren't equipped with Air-Port (or when you want to use a different wireless technology, such as some mobile-phone options).

For the most part, PC cards need to have Mac OS X–compatible drivers before you can use them. You'll need to download the driver (or insert your installation CD for the device) and install it. In some cases, you may need to restart your PowerBook before you can use the device—PC cards often are enabled by kernel extensions, which are very low-level system code.

WARNING   Because you're adding kernel extensions, it's also possible that you'll affect the stability of your Mac's kernel and hence the Mac OS's overall stability. Read the instructions for your device carefully and take precautions—back up important files and install your PC card device only when you have enough time to do some troubleshooting.

How PC card upgrades manifest themselves depends in part on the type of card you're trying to use. If you have a PC card that's used for storage (for instance, one that enables you to plug a digital camera's CompactFlash or SmartMedia card directly into your PowerBook), that card will more than likely display an icon directly on your desktop. The PC card, if recognized, will mount just as if it were a removable disk or volume. You then can copy items to and from it as you might with any mounted volume.

If the PC card is designed for networking, it will likely appear only in System Preferences, either in its own pane or in the Networking pane. In some cases, you'll first configure the card using its own System Preferences pane, then you'll switch to the Network pane to set up TCP/IP and other settings for the card.

NOTE   Have a WaveLAN or similar wireless PC card from Lucent or Orinoco? They're designed to add AirPort-compatible wireless networking to older PowerBooks, so they're definitely popular. Unfortunately, neither Apple nor Lucent has released Mac OS X drivers, and there's no indication that they will soon. The solution? An open-source driver has been developed and is available at http://wirelessdriver.sourceforge.net/. We've installed it with success, but we definitely recommend that you back up and have some time available just in case the installation goes badly. Another option, this one commercial, is IOXperts (www.ioxperts.com/80211b_X.html), which offers both Mac OS 9 and Mac OS X drivers for supported cards and PowerBooks.

PC card support can be spotty in Mac OS X, with the occasional crash apparently still the fault of the operating system. (Because PC card drivers are often kernel drivers, crashes can cause kernel panics, which usually bring your Mac to a halt, requiring a restart and losing data.) How well your PC card functions will ultimately depend on whether the device's manufacturer has written a good Mac OS X driver and otherwise supported it for Mac OS X.

Working with IrDA

Mac OS X offers limited support for the IrDA port, with Apple officially recommending that you use AirPort (IEEE 802.11b) or Bluetooth technology for wireless networking instead of IrDA because IrDA is less reliable and good for only short distances. Support for a network connection is available only on early PowerBook G4 models, for instance, which can be used for some limited infrared network connections (via the *IrComm* protocol).

NOTE   Apple notes in its support knowledge base that some third-party USB-based IrDA connectors can also be used for IrComm networking. Apple has moved away from IrDA for its own Mac models—with PowerBook G4 models introduced in April 2002 dropping the port. More recently, Apple has moved to include Bluetooth technology in some of its portables. Bluetooth makes it possible to access peripherals wirelessly. You can also use Bluetooth for wireless Internet connections using compatible mobile phones (see Chapter 25, "Peripherals, Internal Upgrades, and Disks," for more on Bluetooth).

In addition, any FireWire-based PowerBook can use its IrDA port for a connection to a Palm-compatible handheld computer, making it possible for you to synchronize your Palm Desktop software and the handheld device wirelessly. The same PowerBooks can support an IrDA modem-based connection, which enables you to connect to the Internet using one of a number of popular mobile phones as your modem.

For a Palm connection, you'll need to set up HotSync from within the Palm Desktop application and make sure that the IR port is selected. In Palm Desktop, choose HotSync ➢ Setup. In the HotSync Software Setup dialog box, make sure HotSync is turned on, and then click the Connection Settings tab. On that tab, enable IR Port by placing a check in its check box.

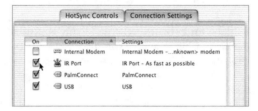

Now, align the Palm handheld's IR port with the IrDA port in the back of the PowerBook and initiate the sync from the handheld.

NOTE   Palm Desktop 4 is not able to install applications via an IR connection, so you may need to disable application installation from the Conduit Settings dialog box (HotSync ➢ Conduit Settings). Double-click the Install conduit to view its settings in a dialog sheet; choose Do Nothing to disable those installations until you're able to use a direct-connect HotSync cradle.

For IrDA modem connections, you'll find that the compatible PowerBook models have an additional entry in the Show menu of the Network pane of System Preferences. Choose IrDA Modem Port from the menu, and you'll see options similar to those for a modem-based Internet connection, as discussed in Chapter 10. Most likely you'll need to configure TCP/IP for a PPP connection and then configure the PPP tab with instructions from your mobile phone's service company or ISP. Note in particular that the IrDA Modem tab enables you to choose the particular modem script for your IrDA-capable mobile phone, as well as the option to display IrDA status in the menu bar.

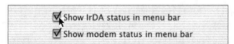

You can initiate your IrDA modem connection from the IrDA Modem menu bar item or via the Internet Connect application, where you'll also find status information for the connection, just as with a phone line–based modem connection.

Adding Another Display

All Mac OS X–compatible PowerBooks and many later iBooks offer an external video port of some kind that can be used to display the Mac's desktop on an external monitor or device. In some cases, that port is a full-sized VGA port, compatible with the bulk of CRTs and many LCD-based displays on the market. If that's the case, connecting to such a monitor is as easy as connecting its cable to the Mac's VGA or DVI port. (This is the case for all PowerBook G3 and G4 models at the time this is being written. It's also true of the "slot-loading" iMac models that shipped between 2000 and 2002.)

The iBook, the flat-panel iMac, and the eMac all ship with a small mini-VGA port, which requires a special adapter from Apple. That adapter can be used to connect the external monitor's standard VGA cable to the mini-VGA port.

On most of the Mac models that support a second display (including the iBook, iMac, and many PowerBook G3 models), connecting an external display simply mirrors the display onto the external screen. In other words, what you see on your Mac's display is the same thing that will be shown on the external display.

On the PowerBook G4 and some PowerBook G3 models, you have the choice of extending your desktop when you attach an external monitor. You'll make that decision in the Displays pane of System Preferences.

For any external display, the first step generally is to shut down the Mac or put it into Sleep mode. (That's not the case on the latest "aluminum" PowerBook models from Apple, where the video port is "hot swappable" and it's actually recommended that your PowerBook and display be powered on when they're connected. If you have a late-model PowerBook G4, check its user manual for details.) Displays generally aren't recognized if plugged in while the Mac is active. Next, connect the monitor to the Mac's external VGA port, using an adapter if necessary. Then, start up the Mac again or wake it from Sleep.

TIP On some PowerBooks, you can force the Mac to look for and recognize an external display by pressing ⌘F2. The PowerBook G4 17-inch model uses the F7 key to switch between dual-monitor and mirror display modes.

After you've started up your Mac, you'll likely want to launch the Displays pane of System Preferences. There, you'll be able to choose the color depth and resolution that look best for both your built-in and external displays. In most cases, your external display will be more capable than your Mac's built-in display, so you should set the resolution at the ideal setting for the iBook's or PowerBook's LCD display. The external display should be able to mirror that.

NOTE Some PowerBook models also have an S-Video port that can be used to mirror or, in some cases, extend the desktop to a television or a video recorder.

If you're working with a PowerBook that supports extending the desktop to the external display, you'll see additional options when you launch the Displays pane. First you'll see an Arrangement tab, which can be used to arrange the displays for extending the desktop. Turn off the Mirror Displays option and drag the representations of the displays to arrange exactly how the desktop will be enlarged (see Figure 19.2).

When you turn off the Mirror Displays option, a second thing happens—the second monitor shows a dialog box with display settings. Now you can set the resolution and color depth on each display independently.

NOTE Want to work on an external display with your PowerBook's clamshell closed? You can. Begin by putting the PowerBook to sleep by closing its clamshell. Next, plug in your display as well as an external keyboard and mouse. Now, press a key on the keyboard to wake the PowerBook up. Note that this is not recommended for iBooks. Also the procedure for the PowerBook G4 17-inch is the opposite—connect the display to the PowerBook while it's still active, then close the clamshell to put it to sleep. Wake it with the external keyboard and it will use just the external display.

FIGURE 19.2
On the Arrangement tab
in the Displays pane, you
can change the arrange-
ment of your expanded
desktop.

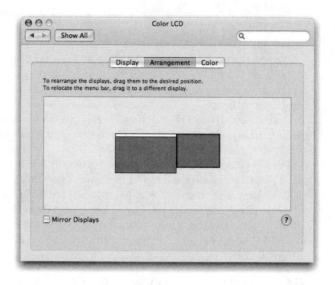

Target Disk Mode

One of the special problems that sometimes crop up when you use a portable Macintosh is the need to synchronize files with your desktop Macintosh in order to be productive with both computers. Of course, one solution to that problem is to use a PowerBook or iBook exclusively—that way, whenever you travel, all of your files and applications can come with you. Another solution is a local network, as discussed in Chapter 18, which enables you to share files between two or more Macs with ease, while making it possible to use both your portable and desktop at the same time or allow others to use one or the other of them.

TIP   You can get a number of freeware and shareware applications that are designed to help you syn-chronize files between computers. For instance, FolderSynchronizer (www.softobe.com) is designed for that specific purpose. Chapter 26, "Hard Disk Care, File Security, and Maintenence," discusses a number of other different backup software options that can help you synchronize fold-ers on two different hard disks. Doing so might be the perfect solution for keeping a PowerBook or iBook synchronized with your desktop Mac.

For many, a PowerBook or iBook is primarily a second computer, designed for travel, vacation, or work away from the office. In that case, you might want to dig into Mac OS X's capability to mount a PowerBook or iBook on the desktop of another Macintosh, thus enabling you to treat the portable Mac exactly as if it were an external hard disk connected via FireWire. This is a great convenience for the user of both a portable and a desktop. It's useful in other situations, too, such as sharing data on your portable with others—even other portables. Also, it is faster than any other solution, working at FireWire speeds instead of the slower rates offered by most Ethernet networks and all AirPort con-nections.

Initiating Target Disk Mode requires two things: First, you'll need a PowerBook or iBook equipped with a FireWire port—any model that includes FireWire is capable of FireWire Target Disk Mode. Second, you'll need a 6-pin-to-6-pin FireWire cable that you can stretch between the two.

NOTE   According to Apple, any FireWire-equipped Mac—including those with FireWire on an upgrade card—can be a host for a Target Disk Mode connection. The computer that will be the target (the one that will appear as a disk on the host's desktop) must be a Macintosh model that Apple shipped with internal FireWire capabilities, including iMac and Power Macintosh G3/G4 models as well as iBook and PowerBook models.

Here are the steps for FireWire Target Disk Mode:

1. Shut down the PowerBook, iBook, or other FireWire-equipped Mac that will be the target. (That's the computer that you want to appear on the host computer's desktop.) If the Mac is a portable, plug it into a wall socket.

2. Unplug all FireWire devices from both Macs.

3. Connect the FireWire cable to one of the FireWire ports on each of the Macs.

4. Switch to the Finder on the host Mac.

5. Power up the target Mac and immediately hold down the T key after hearing the startup tone. Keep holding it down until you see the FireWire symbol appear on the target Mac as a screen-saver or you see the target Mac's hard disk appear in the Finder with a FireWire icon.

NOTE   In Mac OS X 10.4, you can restart your Mac in Target Disk Mode without holding down the T key. Simply open the Startup Disk pane of System Preferences and click the Restart in Target Disk Mode button. You'll be asked to confirm, and then your Mac will restart. When you see the FireWire icon on-screen, you're ready to connect to another Mac via FireWire and start transferring files.

Now you can copy items to and from the target Mac's disk in order to synchronize files between the two. In fact, you should take special care, because FireWire Target Disk Mode gives you access to the target computer's disk without regard to Mac OS X's privileges. In other words, you're able to copy and delete just about anything, almost as if you'd booted into Mac OS 9. You should be as careful with Target Disk Mode as you would be with an Admin or Root account on your Mac.

NOTE   The fact that your Mac's file security privileges can be bypassed so easily by someone with a FireWire cable and another Mac might be a bit disturbing. To combat this possibility, Apple offers the powerful (and somewhat dangerous) Open Firmware password-protection scheme. You can disable Target Disk Mode and other boot-up scenarios, requiring a password to reenable them. See Chapter 26 for details.

Once you've finished moving files between the two disks, you can eject the target disk from within the Finder by highlighting it and choosing File ➤ Eject or by pressing ⌘E. Then you can press the Power button on the target Mac to shut it down. Unplug the FireWire cable and press the Power button on the target Mac to start it up again normally.

Saving Battery Life

Although any Mac user might be interested in saving energy when using a Mac, the PowerBook or iBook owner has a particular interest because the more energy saved, the longer a portable's batteries will last. If you often find yourself using a portable Mac while away from a wall socket, you might want to dig into your energy settings—and make a few other adjustments—to extend your Mac's battery life.

TIP   It can take some battery power to start up your PowerBook or iBook from having been shut down, so it's best to use Sleep mode when you're on battery power. If you do need to start up, here's a neat trick—hold down the F3 key to start up your PowerBook G4 or iBook without making the startup tone (great for planes).

First, though, consider the following, which will help you extend the battery life of your portable Mac:

Get More RAM   The more RAM you have in your Mac, the less it will need to access the swap file on the hard disk. The *swap file* is used to place inactive memory contents—applications and documents—on the disk temporarily in order to enable you to switch to a different application or document and use it in active RAM. Because accessing the hard disk requires more energy than accessing RAM, avoiding this disk means a longer battery life. The corollary to this rule is to use fewer applications when you're running on battery and avoid saving often (if you're comfortable with the risk of data loss).

Avoid PC Cards and AirPort   Eject PC cards, which can use up quite a bit of energy, and when possible turn off your AirPort card when you're running on battery and you're not accessing a wireless network. The AirPort card can be turned off via the AirPort menu bar icon or via the Internet Connect application.

Avoid AppleTalk and Classic   Holdover technologies from yesteryear—particularly the AppleTalk protocol and the Classic environment—should be turned off and avoided if at all possible while you're running on battery. (You can use TCP/IP on Ethernet or AirPort, for instance, without running AppleTalk.) Classic in particular should be avoided when at all possible. It's a resource hog, and since it's a full-fledged operating system, it tends to launch extensions and support applications that will write to the disk or otherwise use power unnecessarily.

Avoid External Devices   Unplug USB hubs, FireWire devices, and any other devices that require power from your Mac, particularly if you're not actively using them. Also, if you can, avoid using the internal CD/DVD drive in your portable—it requires quite a bit of power.

Aside from these ideas, you can save battery power by lowering the brightness of your display in the Displays pane of System Preferences and by choosing conservative settings in the Energy Saver pane of System Preferences. In particular, you can choose very short idle-before-sleep times (as short as five minutes) for your hard disk and display, the two items that require the most power in a portable.

NOTE   On the Options tab of the Energy Saver pane in System Preferences, you'll find a special option for portable Macs, Show Battery Status in Menu Bar. Turn it on if you'd like quick access to a battery status menu, which includes a battery life indicator. Energy Saver is discussed more generally in Chapter 9, "Being the Administrator: Permissions, Settings, and Adding Users."

TIP   In Mac OS X 10.4, you can use the Dashboard and a freeware third-party widget called Battery-Status (`www.emeraldion.it/software/widgets/batterystatus/`) to monitor your remaining time when on battery power. It's a cute little add-on that changes color to tell you at a glance when power is getting low.

What's Next?

In this chapter, you saw some of the special settings and options available to PowerBook users, including additional ports and connections, additional displays, FireWire Target Disk Mode, and special energy-saving considerations. In the next chapter, you'll learn about using Mac OS X with other computing platforms—such as Microsoft Windows and Unix—in terms of both sharing data and using alternative applications.

## Chapter 20

Mac OS X and Other Platforms

No computer exists in a vacuum anymore, particularly because of the ubiquity of the Internet. That's not the only reason, though. The Mac's continued existence as a viable computing platform is owed, to some extent, to its compatibility with the dominant operating system—Microsoft Windows. A Mac user can deal easily with the bulk of documents that can be sent from a Windows machine, and that same Mac user can create documents that can be read and edited in Windows applications. Mac OS X can even be upgraded with software to run Windows applications, and Mac OS X 10.2 (and higher) has the built-in capability to read Windows-formatted media and even to offer file sharing to Windows-based users. This level of compatibility makes it possible for computing platforms to coexist, while still giving Mac users the flexibility of using Mac OS X and taking advantage of its uniqueness.

Mac OS X's cross-compatibility extends, in many ways, to Unix and Unix-like platforms. After all, Mac OS X is based on a Unix variant, so it ought to be able to work with some Unix applications and documents. For instance, in this chapter you'll see how Mac OS X can be augmented (using free or commercial software) so that it can run not just the command-line Darwin applications (discussed in Chapter 23, "Command-Line Applications and Magic") but also X Window applications—the graphical Unix applications similar to Mac applications.

Speaking of "similar to Mac applications," this chapter also discusses Java applications—the fourth style of application that the Mac OS is designed to run. While there may not be an overwhelming number of stand-alone Java applications that have been targeted at the Mac OS, they do exist, and some of them are compelling and interesting to use.

Finally, there are some workarounds to consider when you need to deal with multiple platforms and you're not sure of the solution. At the end of this chapter, we'll discuss a few scenarios and how to take advantage of Mac OS X and its tools to share files successfully.

In this chapter:

◆ Mac OS X, Windows, and Unix-Style Operating Systems

◆ Document and Media Compatibility

◆ Using Mac OS X File Sharing with Windows Computers

◆ Running Windows Applications

◆ Running Java Applications

◆ Running X Window Applications

◆ Cross-Platform TCP/IP Solutions

Mac OS X, Windows, and Unix-Style Operating Systems

Although you're probably aware that Mac OS X differs somewhat from other operating systems on the market today, it may not be abundantly clear as to exactly how it differs. Other than the marketing reasons to differentiate products, there are a few basic technological differences that you can point to between the Mac, Windows, and Unix operating systems. While these differences don't encompass the full breadth of features and options that make each product unique, they're a head start on answering the question of why we have different computing platforms. Here's a look at some of the technological differences:

Mac OS, Windows, and Unix-style operating systems use different filesystem formats for media. When you format a disk—either a hard disk or a removable—for native use in the Mac OS, most of the time you'll format that disk using the Mac OS Extended (Journaled) format. (Mac OS X offers the option of formatting disks in the Unix File System format, but there can be drawbacks to doing so.) The filesystem dictates, ultimately, how files are stored, cataloged, and read back into the computer when necessary. Each operating system has a dominant filesystem—various versions of Windows use the 32-bit File Allocation Table (FAT32) format or New Technology File System (NTFS), while Unix uses the Unix File System (UFS) format. While there's occasional cross compatibility (for instance, many Linux variants can run from a FAT32–formatted disk and Mac OS X can actually run from a UFS partition), these basic formats define some fundamental differences, making it a challenge to place a removable disk in the drive of a computer that uses a different operating system.

NOTE While the filesystem may be different, that doesn't mean *file formats*—that is, the format of individual computer files—can't be compatible. As you'll see later in this chapter, it's a simple matter to transfer files from one computing platform to another and use them successfully.

Different operating systems offer different application programming interfaces (APIs). Put more simply, operating systems generally run applications that have been written specifically for them. For instance, even though Microsoft Word is available for both Mac OS X and Microsoft Windows XP, those are really two versions of Word, written separately, with a version of the application targeting each operating system. That's because the internal commands for such things as opening files, saving files, and printing files are different on different operating systems. The way in which a program communicates with the OS—the API—varies from one operating system to another. You must have an application designed specifically for Mac OS X in order to run it natively within Mac OS X. However, there are many ways to run other types of applications—the Classic environment can run Classic Mac OS applications, certain types of Unix applications can be recompiled (or *ported*, which is generally a rewrite on an existing application for a new operating system) to run in Mac OS X, and Mac OS X can run certain types of Java applications as if they were native. Plus, if you need to run a Microsoft Windows application that hasn't been ported to the Mac, you may still have an option—a Windows emulation application, which can be used to run Windows applications simultaneously with Mac OS X applications.

Each operating system offers different signature technologies. This is similar to the previous point, but worth noting separately. For instance, Mac OS X offers technologies such as a Quick-Time layer for multimedia manipulation and playback, Quartz for a rendering and printing engine, and OpenGL for 3D display. Unix-like operating systems often include OpenGL support, but some use Display PostScript or an open-source PostScript-like description language for printing and screen display. Microsoft Windows has proprietary technologies—DirectX for 3D,

Windows Media for multimedia, and so on. While some technologies are accessible across platforms—Windows can play back QuickTime movies if QuickTime for Windows has been installed—the native technologies will influence the way in which native applications are written. A Windows game that supports DirectX, for instance, may need a more significant rewrite in order to be Mac-compatible than does a Unix graphics application that supports OpenGL.

Operating systems support different hardware. At a fundamental level, an operating system has to translate all programming instructions and requests into commands that the hardware—the CPU, memory, and disk controllers—can understand. To do that, the operating system has to be familiar with the hardware and address it using a specific machine language. That means the Mac OS can't simply be installed and run on an Intel-compatible personal computer, because the Mac OS is written specifically for the PowerPC processor manufactured by Motorola and IBM. That relationship means, in most cases, that applications need to be *recompiled* when they're ported to a new operating system—the software's language compiler must rewrite it in code that the new processor can understand. Sometimes this is a simple step, as with some open-source applications originally written for Unix and recompiled for Mac OS X's Darwin layer. In other cases, it can require tweaking, testing, and rewriting so that differences in the processors and hardware interfaces can be accounted for.

As we said, those are some basic differences, but not all of them. From the user's perspective, however, these four issues are what dictate the "compatibility" problems that can sometimes make using Mac OS X seem more difficult than it needs to be. In most cases, each of those differences also has a solution or workaround you can employ in order to improve your compatibility with other operating systems. Those solutions, in a nutshell, include these:

Disk and File Formats Mac OS X has the built-in capability to read disks that use Windows or Unix formats, including removable media. Likewise, it's possible to save files in universally recognized file formats that can be easily read and edited on different computers.

Application Compatibility In many cases, applications that are available for Macintosh have direct counterparts for Windows, and those analogs can generally read one another's files. If it's important that you run a certain application, you may be able to use a Java version of the application. Also, if the application is written only for Windows, a Windows emulation program may be able to run it in Mac OS X. If you need to run a Unix application, you may be able to find a Mac OS X–compatible version or recompile one fairly simply.

NOTE Working with Windows and emulation applications is covered in this chapter; X Window Darwin applications also are covered here. Dealing with ported or recompiled Unix applications is discussed in Chapter 23.

Technology Compatibility This isn't always as easy to solve, but it's usually a developer issue (for instance, when a programmer has to port an application from Windows to Mac OS X) and not an end-user problem. When it does crop up from a user standpoint is generally when you're dealing with multimedia—you want to play back a Windows Media item in Mac OS X or a QuickTime movie in Windows. Fortunately, players are available for Mac OS X that play back multimedia that prevails on other platforms—see Chapter 13, "Video Playback and Editing," for details.

We'll look at these solutions—along with some networking and file-sharing solutions for cross-platform environments—throughout the rest of this chapter.

Document and Media Compatibility

For most Mac users, the most vital level of compatibility is being able to read documents received from Windows or Unix users. In most cases, you'll succeed with relative ease. In fact, many Mac users get through their entire day working happily with documents and removable media exchanged with colleagues, and no one ever knows or cares that they're using a Mac instead of a Windows PC.

Sharing Documents

Probably the most important thing to realize is that the document format isn't reliant on the computer platform. For instance, there's little about a Microsoft Word document that's saved on a Mac that makes it inherently a Mac file as opposed to something that could be used on a Windows computer. What's most important about a Word document that's created on a Mac is simply that the Windows user to whom you send the file has a compatible version of Microsoft Word for her own computer. It's up to Word to read the file formats that its various versions create, not the operating system itself.

For the most complete document compatibility, you need to look to the applications you're using and not the operating system. If you're talking about a proprietary format such as a Windows document created in Microsoft Word or Excel, the solution generally is to use the Mac version of the same program or a program that's compatible with the file format in question. (Certain versions of open-source and third-party office applications can read the basic formatting of a Word document. In fact, even AppleWorks ships with this capability.)

If you're interested in more general compatibility, you might consider using file formats that are considered to be more universal. Graphics file formats generally are cross-platform—save a GIF, JPEG, PNG, TIFF, or similar file, and you should be able to open it and, with the right application, edit or manipulate it on another computer, regardless of platform. The same is generally true of RTF (Rich Text Format) documents, which offer basic formatted text documents that can be read on multiple platforms. PDF files can usually be viewed and printed on different computers, even if they often can't be edited without an application that's devoted to the task.

If there's a caveat to this cross-compatibility, it's simply the slightly different ways that operating systems know what type of file they're dealing with. In most operating systems, the general solution is to put an accurate filename extension on the end of a document's name, so that Microsoft Word documents have `.doc` on the end, Rich Text documents have `.rtf`, and image files end in an extension such as `.tif`, `.gif`, or `.jpg`. (When in doubt, use a three-letter extension, as opposed to the more Mac-centric four letters such as `.tiff`, `.jpeg`, or `.pict`.)

TIP One helpful approach, if you use your Mac with documents that you send to or receive from users of other platforms, is to get used to seeing filename extension on the ends of filenames. You might consider always viewing filename extensions in the Finder. Select Finder ➢ Preferences and turn on the Always Show File Extensions option.

Another special case is an issue that crops up when dealing with "plain text" documents. Each native operating system can have a slightly different approach to how text documents are saved, centered on the special character used to create a linefeed (a new line) within the document. The Classic Mac OS uses one approach, Windows uses another, and Unix tends to use a third. In Mac OS X, how linefeeds are handled can depend somewhat on the application you're using. In most cases, this won't be a problem—it usually crops up when you're dealing with scripting or programming issues, and occasionally when you're developing for the Web or receiving complicated text documents via e-mail. The best solution is to get an application that works well with different approaches to linefeeds and carriage returns, such as TextWrangler and BBEdit (www.barebones.com); see Figure 20.1.

FIGURE 20.1
TextWrangler is a share-
ware application that
can be used to translate
between different
approaches to text
linefeeds.

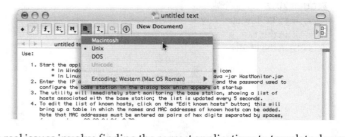

Beyond these basics, the real issues involve finding the correct applications to translate documents that you otherwise can't load into your applications. DataViz (www.dataviz.com) offers some of the more popular tools, including MacLinkPlus, which can translate many documents into formats commonly compatible with popular Mac applications such as AppleWorks. The company also offers Conversions Plus, which makes it possible to convert Mac-formatted documents on a Windows-based computer.

TextEdit in Mac OS X 10.3 and higher can open, edit, and save in Microsoft Word format, although it can't handle terribly advanced Word formatting. (Basic documents work well.) If you need more than that, icWord (www.icword.com) can translate and display Microsoft Word documents if you don't have Word; icExcel (www.icexcel.com) can do the same for Microsoft Excel documents. VINC (www.recosoft.com/products/vinc/index.htm) is a Mac OS X application that can display and translate various word processing and graphics formats.

TIP   Having trouble with an e-mail attachment? Occasionally attachments are sent using encoding that your Mac (or your e-mail application) doesn't recognize (or somehow missed). Often, such a file will spring to life after it's been dragged to StuffIt Expander (located, by default, in the Utilities folder inside your Applications folder or available at www.stuffit.com).

Sharing Media

Most removable media that you'll encounter that isn't in a Mac format is likely in a Windows (FAT or FAT32) format. That's because even Linux and other PC-based Unix-derived OS versions will generally offer FAT32 (or older FAT) compatibility, in part because they recognize the same need for compatibility with the dominant standard (Windows) that the Mac community does. Plus, most of today's removable disks support either Mac or Windows directly, so media needs to be in a compatible format for it to work correctly.

If you have a removable disk (or a writable CD or DVD) that's been formatted for use with a Windows PC, most likely you can simply place it in your drive and view its contents. Note also that some discs (almost always data CDs) can be formatted for both Windows and Mac simultaneously and will display the Mac-formatted partition by default. (For instance, this is the format used by many national ISPs, such as America Online, for their free startup disks.) If you insert a PC disk and you have the proper drivers installed for your removable drive (as you likely do, if it works with Mac media), the disk should be accessible in the Finder like any other (see Figure 20.2). Once a PC disk is mounted, if it's writable, you can copy files to that disk, and they'll be readable on a PC.

NOTE   Reading a Mac disk on a Windows computer is a different story—for that, you'll generally need a third-party utility. For instance, MacDrive (www.mediafour.com/products/macdrive/) and MacOpener (www.dataviz.com/products/macopener/index.html) are competing products designed to make Mac-formatted disks available to Windows users.

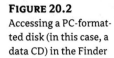

FIGURE 20.2

Accessing a PC-formatted disk (in this case, a data CD) in the Finder

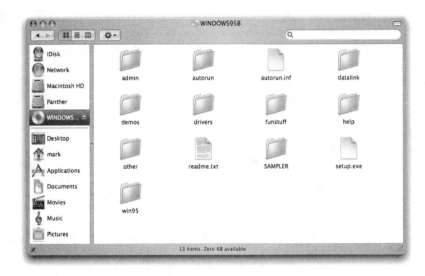

Using Mac OS X File Sharing with Windows Computers

Another level of compatibility that Mac OS X gives you is improved integration with Windows networking. For many years, networking between Macs and Windows computers has been tough, thanks to the proprietary ways in which both have accomplished their connections. But, as was discussed in Chapter 17, "Accessing Network Volumes," Mac OS X version 10.1 and higher have added the capability of connecting to Server Message Block (SMB) file-sharing servers, including the latest versions of Windows' personal file sharing. Mac OS X also has the capability of serving SMB file sharing, making it possible for Windows clients to log in to your Mac.

Turning on Windows Sharing

Turning on SMB sharing is easy enough—simply launch System Preferences, access the Sharing pane, make sure the Services tab is selected, and click to place a check in the box next to Windows Sharing (see Figure 20.3).

NOTE   SMB servers, including your Mac with the Windows Sharing option turned on, can be accessed by a URL using the smb protocol plus the name of the user who has turned on Windows file sharing, such as smb://192.168.1.3/rogerb/. Without the proper path to a user, the connection will fail. (Note that, from a Windows machine, you may need to reverse the slashes, as in \\192.168.1.3\rogerb, depending on the application you're using.)

In some cases, you may be asked to enable user accounts so that they can be used with Windows Sharing. To do that, click the Enable Accounts button, and then click to place a check mark next to the accounts that you would like to be able to access on this Mac from a Windows computer. You'll then have to enter the password for that user. When you're done enabling users, click Done—you can return to this dialog later to enable other users as necessary.

FIGURE 20.3

Turn on Windows Sharing in the Sharing pane of System Preferences.

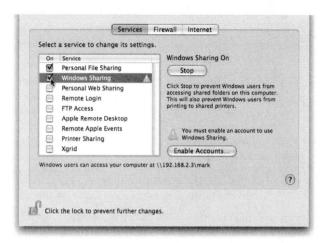

Aside from the fact that user accounts need to be enabled, users are managed the same way they're managed for local logins and for Personal File Sharing—you create them in the Accounts pane of System Preferences, where you can assign them to be regular users or administrators. You should then set any privileges for folders that need to be made accessible or inaccessible to remote users. (See Chapter 9, "Being the Administrator: Permissions, Settings, and Adding Users," for details.)

Setting Up the Windows Client

Setting up Windows to access your Mac is similar to setting up a Windows machine to access another Windows machine. If you have a version of Windows prior to Windows XP, there are a number of steps—you'll want to consult the instructions that came with your PC or with Windows.

Windows XP makes connecting to network resources a bit easier than earlier versions, so you may find that you don't have to go through nearly as many steps. Here is a quick look at getting Windows XP to talk to a Mac that has Windows Sharing active:

1. Make sure that your Windows XP–based PC is connected to your local network via Ethernet or a WiFi connection.

2. Ensure that the Windows XP machine is configured for TCP/IP access and that it's on the same subnet (with a valid IP address) as the Mac that you'll be using as a server. If your Mac uses DHCP to retrieve its IP address from a router, for instance, then configure the Windows XP computer to do the same. You can configure an Ethernet connection in Windows XP by choosing Start ➤ Control Panel and choosing Network Connections and then clicking Set Up or Change Your Home or Small Office Network. This launches the Network Setup Wizard, which walks you through configuring your network port on the Windows XP machine.

NOTE WORKGROUP is the default name for a workgroup that your Mac connects to, so you should enter that for your Windows XP machine unless you've changed it on the Mac. You can change your Mac's workgroup name by opening the Directory Access program in the Utilities folder, double-clicking SMB in the list, typing the new workgroup name, and clicking OK.

3. When your Windows XP machine is configured to connect via the network, the next step is to create a network connection to the Mac. You do that from My Network Places, which you can access in the See Also section of the Network and Internet Connections control panel or by choosing Start ➢ My Network Places.

4. In My Network Places, you'll need to create a new connection. Choose Add a Network Place, and the Add Network Place Wizard will appear. You'll use this wizard to create a connection to the Mac that has Windows Networking available, and you'll use the address that is listed in the Sharing pane of System Preferences on that Mac—at the bottom of the Services tab, when you select Windows Sharing, you should see "Windows users can access your computer at" and the URL that they can use.

5. Continue the wizard until the new network place has been added; you can now access it in the My Network Places window, making it an easy matter to connect to the Mac and share files with it.

If you don't want to create the permanent new network place icon, you can also access a server by skipping steps 4 and 5 above and, instead, choosing View Workgroup Computers. When you see the Mac, double-click it and enter a username and password to log in. When you connect in this way, you will also be able to attach the Windows machine to any shared printers that are connected to your Mac. You should find the setup fairly straightforward.

THIRD-PARTY SOLUTIONS FOR WINDOWS CONNECTIVITY

Until Mac OS X 10.2, which was the first to include Windows Sharing, that capability was reserved for third-party solutions. Many of those solutions continue to exist, and some offer benefits beyond the built-in Windows Sharing, including better compatibility, support for printer sharing, and more.

A program called Dave, made by Thursby Software (www.thursby.com), has a long history of enabling Mac and PC clients to share files and printers between one another. In essence, Dave is used to make the Mac a full client on the Windows network, giving it the capability to serve and be served by a variety of Windows versions. (Thursby also makes AdmitMac, an application that enables a Mac client to be managed on a Windows NT network as it if were a full-fledged Windows PC.)

PC MacLAN by Computer Associates (www.ca.com) works differently than Dave does—it's installed on the Windows computer, enabling a Microsoft Windows PC to act like a fully capable AFP over TCP/IP client as well as giving the Windows computer access to AppleShare-compatible printers.

PC-Mac-Net Fileshare is a program by Lava Software (www.lavasoftware.com) that's designed to help create very secure connections between Windows and Mac machines. The software uses 448-bit encryption and is particularly suited to Internet-based file sharing because it doesn't use the typical protocols (that is, you don't turn on file sharing or Windows Sharing to use it), and the software shares only a single folder's contents with the remote user. In fact, it has as much of a relationship to FTP as it does to file sharing, and it can be used in a very similar way, but with more secure connections and password negotiation.

Running Windows Applications

If simply sharing files and media with Windows users isn't enough, you may need to run a Windows-only application. Although many applications have Macintosh analogs of their Windows counterparts—and, in some cases, a shareware or competitive commercial option can stand in for a Windows application that doesn't offer a Macintosh alternative—sometimes you simply have no alternative but to use a Windows program. That's just a fact of life, given the size of the Windows market versus the size of the Macintosh market.

If that's the case for you, there's a fairly simple solution. Microsoft (`www.microsoft.com/mac`) offers an application called Virtual PC (formerly offered by Connectix Corporation), which enables you to launch a Windows-compatible environment and run Windows applications in a window on your Macintosh desktop. Virtual PC emulates the hardware of a Wintel computer, causing applications to believe they're running on a computer that's using an Intel-compatible processor and the types of peripherals that a Windows application would likely encounter.

Once you have Virtual PC running in Mac OS X, you can then use it to access PC-formatted CD-ROMs or other removable media—the software will read disks connected to your Mac as if they were connected to a PC. Then, install and run the Windows application you need to work with—it will be configured within Virtual PC. Virtual PC can communicate with your Mac's network connections, printers, and so forth, so in nearly all cases it's a complete (if slower) solution for running the occasional Windows application on your Mac.

There's another solution to the issue of running Windows applications on your Mac desktop, but it's a bit different. Timbuktu, from Netopia (`www.netopia.com`), is both file-transfer and remote-control software—it enables you to log on to and *control* another computer from your Mac. The computer that you take control of can be either a Macintosh computer or a Windows computer. It's another solution for working with Windows computers. If you have a Windows computer connected to your Mac via a network connection, you can use Timbuktu to log in to that Windows computer and launch an application. The Timbuktu window can be used to control the remote application, see its results, and so on, almost exactly as if you were sitting at the remote computer's keyboard and display (see Figure 20.4).

FIGURE 20.4
Timbuktu lets you control a remote computer—PC or Mac.

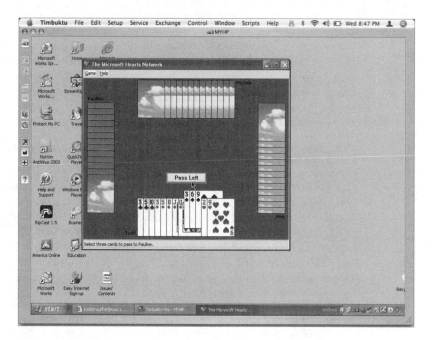

Running Java Applications

When Apple announced Mac OS X, it also announced its intention to give Mac OS X one of the best implementations of Java available on a desktop operating system. Java, by the way, is really two separate things. First, it's a fairly popular computer language. In fact, it's one option that programmers have for creating native Cocoa applications in Mac OS X. Java also can be used to create native Microsoft Windows or Unix applications.

Java is also a technology, which can be a bit confusing. As a technology, Java is designed to make computer applications *platform-independent*, meaning ideally that the same application can run on different operating systems. When you run a Java application that hasn't been compiled to be a native program, Mac OS X launches a *virtual machine* that enables the platform-independent Java application to run. Other operating systems have their own virtual machines (if the OS doesn't offer Java support, it can usually be installed), enabling the same Java application to run on those computing platforms with a minimum of difference and without being ported or recompiled. The virtual machine is an emulator of sorts—something along the lines of a universal computer. The virtual machine runs on top of the operating system, translating Java commands into commands that the native operating system understands. That's what makes it possible for a Java application to look a lot like a native application, including gaining access to native dialogs such as the Open and Print dialogs. Yet the same Java application can run on multiple platforms.

On the other hand, Java applications generally don't take full advantage of the operating system the way native applications can. Java applications have less flexibility in their design and can take advantage of fewer of the unique technologies in Mac OS X, specifically because of Java's cross-platform goal. If the program isn't written in a more generic way, it won't look the same on multiple platforms and may not be able to offer the same functionality.

Working with a platform-independent Java application is pretty simple. First, you have to find a Java application, which might be the toughest part. While many Java applications are one-trick ponies (items such as calculators or games), some productivity applications have been written in Java. For instance, Donohoe Digital (www.donohoedigital.com) offers games software written in Java, including DD Tournament Poker, shown in Figure 20.5. Note that few Java applications have a full set of menu items in the menu bar—there's often a single menu (named for the application) for hiding, showing, and quitting the application. Most commands will take place within the application, which may even have a second set of menu commands in the application window.

TIP   Java.com (http://java.com/en/) is a great site to explore Java applications and applets if you're interested in playing with Java or finding a useful Java tool.

Even though a platform-independent Java application can run on top of multiple operating systems, the easiest Java application to work with is one that's been created as a Mac OS X application bundle, if only so that the application knows how to launch itself once you've got it on your hard disk. If you're downloading items, look for a Mac OS X version of the Java application in question. Once you've downloaded and decompressed it, you should be able to double-click the application's icon to launch it. Note that Java applications generally don't support drag-and-drop and some other Mac-centric behaviors for launching documents and items.

NOTE   Some Java application developers use a tool called InstallAnywhere, which can be used to install a Mac OS X version dynamically—usually directly from a website. It's an interesting tool, and more to the point, it does a great job of creating a double-clickable Java application.

FIGURE 20.5

DD Tournament Poker looks like a native Mac OS X game, but it's designed to run in nearly any OS that supports Java.

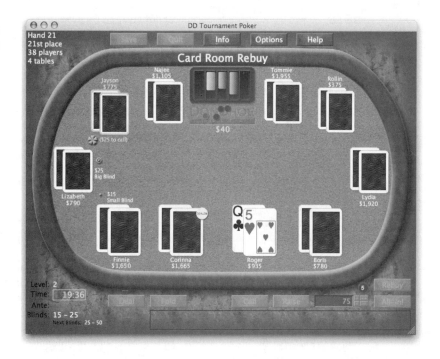

Java applications are sometimes specifically compiled and packaged for Mac OS X, and those are the easiest to run. But Mac OS X can also run three other types of Java programs—.jar applications, Java Web Start applications, and Java applets.

You should be able to double-click JAR files in the Finder to launch them, and they will work pretty much like a Java application that has been bundled for Mac OS X, like the one shown back in Figure 20.5.

Web Start applications use a special technology that makes it possible to launch a full-fledged application by clicking a link on a web page. When that happens, Java Web Start (an application in the Utilities folder) launches and manages your interaction with the program. If you end up using a Web Start application a few times, Java Web Start will ask you if you would like to turn it into an application icon, which you can then access via the Finder as you would a typical application. (Visit http://developer.apple.com/java/javawebstart/ for more info and a demonstration.)

What if you have a Java applet that hasn't been designed to run directly in Mac OS X? You may still have an option. With Mac OS X, Apple includes the Applet Launcher utility, which can be used to launch Java applications that are still in their raw .class format. When you encounter such an applet, you can generally launch it by first starting up the Applet Launcher, then clicking Open and using the Open dialog box to locate the main .html document that's used to display that applet.

NOTE   If the distribution didn't include an HTML document (most will), you may need to dig into the ReadMe file and see how to create your own HTML document that includes the <applet> or <object> code to embed the Java applet in a web page.

Once selected and launched, the Java applet should appear in its own window with the Applet Launcher application. You can quit the applet by choosing its internal Quit command, if it has one, or you can use the Applet ➢ Stop and Applet ➢ Close commands in Applet Launcher.

NOTE If you know a little something about Java and you want to tweak the Java plug-in (which lets you view Java applets in web browser windows), you can launch Java Plugin Settings, a small application in the `Java` folder inside the main `Applications` folder.

Running X Window Applications

Want to add yet another type of application to your arsenal? X Window technology is the basis of most graphical applications that run on Unix-derived operating systems, and a number of applications are available that run within the X Window environment. You can use some freeware, shareware, or commercial tools to add X Window applications to your Mac.

NOTE It might seem more natural to say "X Windows" because of Microsoft Windows, but the technology's actual name uses the singular "X Window."

Unlike Microsoft Windows, X Window isn't a complete operating system. Instead, it is a *window server*, which simply means it provides the graphical front end for applications that want to use it. (It also means that it can serve the interface across a network connection to another computer, making X Window similar to Apple's Remote Desktop or Netopia's Timbuktu, described earlier.) Because Mac OS X ultimately is based on Unix-like FreeBSD, it isn't too much of a stretch to see the X Window environment ported to Mac OS X. What's a little more of a stretch is to see X Window applications appear side-by-side with Aqua applications, but it can be done—and it has been, by Apple.

Although some third-party and open source options also exist, the easiest way to get up and running with X Window applications is with Apple's own X11 implementation (see Figure 20.6). X11 comes with Mac OS X, although it may be an optional install, depending on your version, so check your installation CDs or DVD if you don't see the X11 icon in the Utilities folder inside your Applications folder.

FIGURE 20.6

Apple's X11 implementation (shown running OpenOffice) integrates well with Mac OS X's Aqua appearance.

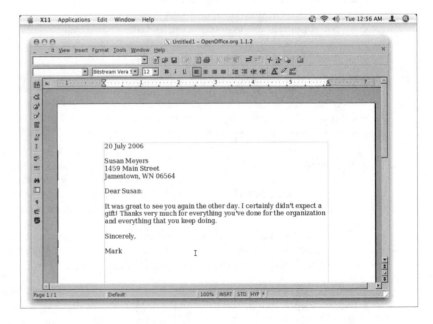

TIP   Other options aside from Apple's implementation include Xtools from Tenon Systems (www.tenon.com) and XDarwin (www.xdarwin.org).

Once you have X11 or another X Window environment up and running, you'll need applications to work with it. As mentioned, applications still need to be ported to Darwin before they'll run in the X Window environment. You should look for X Window applications that have been ported to Darwin. One of the most popular, The GIMP (GNU Image Manipulation Program), is a strong competitor for Adobe Photoshop, but it's an open-source project contributed to by many individual programmers and available (at least, as source code) for free. MacGIMP (www.macgimp.org) is a port of The GIMP to Darwin and runs under the X11 and XDarwin installation, among others. Currently, MacGIMP must be purchased for about $30.

The GNU-Darwin (http://gnu-darwin.sourceforge.net) distribution is another interesting place to find open-source X Window applications, including a free version of The GIMP for Darwin. In addition, you'll find other productivity applications. AbiWord is a Microsoft Word clone capable of emulating many of Word's features as well as reading and writing to Microsoft Word format documents. You'll find links to other popular open-source productivity applications on that site, including Gnumeric (a spreadsheet application), GnomePIM (an address book and calendar), and ImageMagick presentation software. Alternatively, OpenOffice.org is working on OpenOffice for Darwin (as well as a native version for Mac OS X), which features a suite of productivity applications (http://porting.openoffice.org/mac/).

Downloading and properly installing some open-source solutions can be a headache, which is why some alternative systems are available for getting Darwin applications up and running for Mac OS X. Fink (http://fink.sourceforge.net, also discussed in Chapter 23) is one fairly easy mechanism for keeping your Darwin installations up to date. Once you have your applications installed, generally you'll launch them by typing the name of the application in an X Window terminal window and pressing Return.

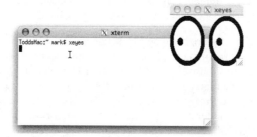

Once you've launched an application, X11 allows you to begin working with it just as you would any Mac application; in other X Window implementations, the approach depends on the default window manager. In XDarwin, the window manager requires you to click and drag (or just click and release the mouse button) on the desktop in order to create the new window. With the application's window(s) created, you should be able to begin working in the application, just as you would most any Mac OS X native (or Classic Mac) program.

NOTE   For more on installing and troubleshooting installed Darwin applications, see Chapter 23.

Cross-Platform TCP/IP Solutions

So far you've seen some dedicated solutions to the problem of sharing files with non-Mac platforms and running nonnative applications from within Mac OS X. Before we move on, however, you might want to consider some of the other alternatives that are built into Mac OS X and can make surviving in a cross-platform environment a bit easier. We'll cover these quickly because the majority of them are discussed more thoroughly in other chapters.

What we're talking about here are solutions that use TCP/IP as their main networking protocol, offering services on top of TCP/IP for file sharing or networking. While it may seem obvious that one can use web sharing for sharing HTML documents on the Internet, it might not be as clear that Mac OS X also supports using these services over a local network, and that doing so can be perhaps the most convenient way to share files on different computing platforms.

WARNING   Some of these are less secure than they should be, so they're not recommended for Macs that have a static IP address or are otherwise directly addressable on the Internet. If your Mac is behind a firewall or your LAN isn't connected to the Internet, these solutions should be secure enough.

Here are a few alternatives to consider for sharing files and working with different platforms:

Share Files via Web Sharing   Turn on Personal Web Sharing, and others can access your Mac directly at its IP address (such as `http://192.168.1.4`) or a named domain address. Also, others can access your personal `Sites` folder by using your name and the tilde symbol (`http://192.168.1.4/~sue/`). Note that if you create a folder in your `Sites` folder (or in the main `/Library/WebServer/Documents/` folder) that doesn't include an `index.html` document, a listing of that folder will be displayed by default. Users will be able to click a file to download it to their computers (see Figure 20.7).

TIP   And don't forget the Bonjour feature in Safari, which enables you to automatically access web pages served by any local Macs that have Web Sharing enabled.

Share Files via FTP   Again, because FTP sends passwords and commands in clear text, it's generally considered not secure enough for transactions that occur over the Internet. However, on a closed network or one situated behind a firewall, FTP is a great way to transfer files from one computer to another, particularly if those computers are of different platforms. In Mac OS X, use the Sharing pane of System Preferences to enable FTP serving. If you're interested in accessing others via FTP, you can use the Finder, a graphical FTP client or the Darwin command-line version of FTP. Both are discussed in more detail in Chapter 17, "Accessing Network Volumes."

Allow Remote Login   Finally, if you're working largely with Unix-derived computers, you may find it useful to log in to those computers using SSH, which Apple calls *remote login*. SSH lets you log in to your user account on the remote computer, enabling you to run command-line programs remotely and access files. In tandem with X Window, you even can launch remote X Window applications in machines that are based on a Unix-derived OS. That makes it possible for you to run graphical applications from a different machine, giving you the capability to control multiple computers at once. Again, Remote Login is discussed in Chapter 17.

FIGURE 20.7

A folder listing can be used to make files available for download via a web browser.

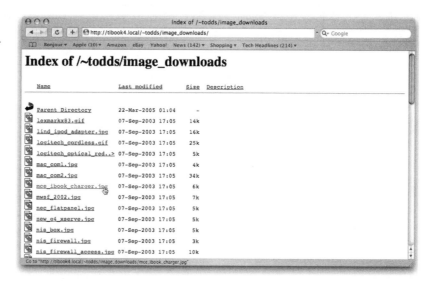

What's Next?

In this chapter, you saw the myriad ways in which Mac OS X is similar to other operating systems. You also saw the differences and how to bridge some of those gaps. Mac OS X can access media and work with files created on other computing platforms, and it can be made to share files over a network with those platforms as well.

With some additional software, Mac OS X can even be made to launch and run Windows, Unix, or X Window applications side-by-side with native programs. Plus, Java applications can be launched directly in Mac OS X or, failing that, run from the Java Applet Runner that's included with the OS, giving you the capability to work with cross-platform Java applications in Mac OS X as well as other operating systems. Finally, if you'd simply like to use the most common solutions on your local network, you can use standard TCP/IP network services—web serving, FTP, and SSH—to offer file sharing and remote access to client computers on your network.

In Part 5, we'll move on to some advanced topics, including AppleScript, working with the command line, installing command-line applications, creating Unix-style shell scripts, and managing Mac OS X's built-in and add-on Internet services. This will include an in-depth look at the Apache web server and various technologies you can use to enhance it.

Part 5

Advanced Mac OS X Topics

In this section, you will learn how to

◆ Understand AppleScript
◆ Use Darwin applications
◆ Work with the command line
◆ Serve files on the Web securely
◆ Manage an FTP server
◆ Add Internet and Network Services

## Chapter 21

Automator and AppleScript

With Mac OS X 10.4, the Mac OS now offers two distinct ways that you can automate tasks in the Finder and your applications: Automator and AppleScript.

One of the most distinct carryovers from early Mac OS versions to Mac OS X is AppleScript, Apple's unique approach to automating tasks within the Finder and other AppleScript-aware applications. AppleScript is a technology that enables you to create scripts, or even small applications, that automate tasks on your Mac.

Automator is new in Mac OS X 10.4, offering a different—some might say easier—approach to automating tasks on your Mac. With Automator, you create *workflows* that move data from one Macintosh application to the next. Certain applications are Automator-enabled, meaning you can use Automator to perform a command from that applications. By building a workflow of these automated tasks, you can get some pretty complex repetitive tasks done automatically.

In this chapter:

◆ Using Automator

◆ Understanding AppleScript

◆ First Script: Recording and Saving

◆ Creating Original Scripts

◆ Scripting Concepts

◆ Commands in AppleScript

Using Automator

AppleScript is extremely sophisticated and relatively easy to pick up and learn, particularly if you have any programming experience or a desire to gain some. But AppleScript isn't for everyone—in fact, a lot of people don't use it much at all. That's one reason that Automator was created for Mac OS X 10.4. Automator makes it possible for you to use prebuilt modules (some written in Apple-Script, others written in more advanced computer languages) called *actions*, which are provided by Apple and application developers. Those actions can then be pieced together into a workflow, which simply strings a series of actions together. You don't have to know anything about AppleScript to make Automator work; all you really need to do is be willing to experiment a bit with Automator and follow along to get a sense of *how* you accomplish things using the utility.

Automator Interface

To get started, locate and launch Automator, which you'll find in your main Applications folder. When you do, you'll see the main Automator window, shown in Figure 21.1. As you can see, Automator's initial interface is similar to many of the iLife applications and other programs that Apple has written, complete with a brushed-metal interface.

FIGURE 21.1

Automator looks a lot like other Mac applications, but it's designed to help you work with them more automatically.

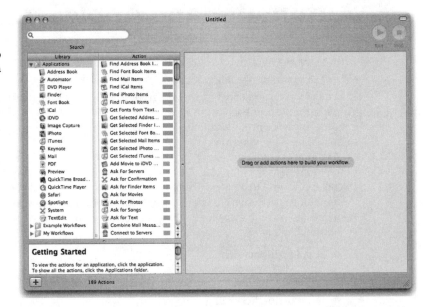

The first column in the interface is the Library column, where different collections of actions are stored. Most of these collections are related to a different application (each application has its own listing available under the Applications entry), although other collections are possible. (For instance, by default Apple provides an Example Workflows collection.) You can create your own collections by clicking the plus icon (+) at the bottom of the Automator window and entering a name for the collection. Then, drag items to that collection or choose File ➤ Import Actions to locate and import new actions that you've downloaded from the Internet.

NOTE Apple's website for Automator (www.apple.com/automator/) provides links to sites that offer third-party actions and workflows; www.automatorworld.com is an early leader in Automator ideas and downloads.

The second column, Action, is where you'll see the available actions when you select a particular collection or application in the Library column. If you click on a single application, you'll see just the actions that relate to that application. If you click a collection, you'll see all of the actions within that collection's contents. So, if you click the Applications entry in the Library, suffice it to say that you'll see a lot of actions.

At the bottom of those two columns, you'll see the information area, which pops up with information about a particular action whenever you click one. The information area is handy not just because it tells you about the action that you selected, but because it also tells you the Input and Result of the action. This is handy because it helps you build your workflow by placing actions in the proper order.

Sample Workflow

With that introduction to the interface, you're left with one pane of the Automator window to consider—the workflow area. Off to the right is where you'll drag each action; as you keep adding actions, you build toward your final workflow. Here's an example:

1. Select TextEdit from the Library (you may have to click the disclosure triangle next to Applications to see TextEdit) and from the Action column drag the action New Text File to the workflow area.

2. In the New Text File item, you can specify a name for the text file and its location.

3. Select Safari in the Library, and then drag the action Get Current Webpage from Safari to the workflow area.

4. Drag Get Text from Webpage to the workflow area. You'll notice the small triangle linking the Get Current Webpage from Safari entry to the Get Text from Webpage entry.

5. Click TextEdit in the Library again, and then drag Set Contents of TextEdit Document to the workflow area. In the action's entry item, you can choose either Appending (meaning text is added to the document) or Replacing (meaning text replaces any already in the document) from the By menu.

That's a complete workflow, as shown in Figure 21.2.

FIGURE 21.2
Here's a sample Automator workflow that retrieves text from a page in Safari and pastes the text into a TextEdit document.

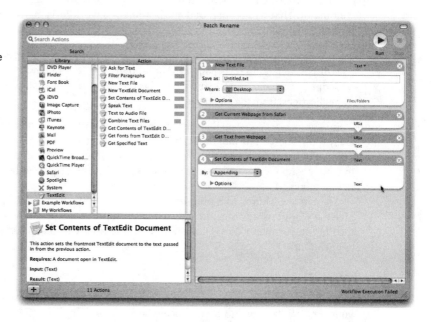

To test your workflow, open Safari and then access a web page within Safari (it's best if it's a relatively simple web page, such as one that's designed to be "printer friendly.") Then, switch to Automator and click the Run icon. You'll see a small indicator appear in each action, showing that it's running and then, if successful, showing a small green check mark icon. At the end of this sample workflow, you should be able to switch to TextEdit and see the document, complete with text from the web page that was open in Safari.

Saving and Launching Workflows

If you come up with a workflow that you like, you can save it and use it again. Choose File ➤ Save As from the Automator menu. A dialog sheet will appear. Give your workflow a name, and choose the type of file you want to save from the File Format window. If you save the file as a workflow, you'll be able to reopen it in Automator and make changes to it or run it from within the Automator interface. If you save your workflow as an application, it will become a double-clickable version of the workflow, enabling you to launch the workflow and have it perform its tasks without also launching Automator.

When you launch an Automator application, you'll see an indicator appear in the menu bar that shows you the progress of the workflow as it occurs.

What if you need to edit a workflow that you've saved as an application? Simply drag the application's icon to the Automator icon (in the Finder or in the Dock) or choose File ➤ Open from within Automator. That will reopen that application as a workflow, giving you the ability to edit the workflow and make choices.

TIP One handy place to put workflow applications that you use often is on the Script Menu, which is discussed later in this chapter in the section "The Script Menu" under "Understanding Apple-Script." The menu enables you to quickly access AppleScript applications (and, hence, Automator applications) from the menu bar.

In Automator, you can also save a workflow as a plug-in, which stores the Automator workflow as an application while making it immediately available as an add-on command for a particular application. For instance, if you store a workflow as a plug-in for the Finder, it will appear as a command in Finder contextual menus; store it as a plug-in for the Script Menu and it will appear automatically in that menu.

To save a workflow as a plug-in, choose File ➤ Save as Plug-In. In the dialog sheet that appears, give the workflow a name and choose the application you want the workflow associated with from the Plug-In For menu. Now, you should be able to access this workflow from within the selected application.

Workflows Ideas

You may not have enough ideas for workflows at the outset. The key is to observe how you spend your time computing and then notice when you're doing something repetitive (or when you know you're going to need to do something repetitive). At this point, you should consider whether or not an Automator workflow might be beneficial.

Here, though, are a few thoughts on how Automator workflows work and some tips that might encourage you to think of ways that Automator can help you turn over some repetitive tasks to a workflow:

◆ **Learn the actions.** Select any action and read about it in the info pane to get a sense of not only what it does but what sort of input and output it can work with. This is invaluable when you're trying to figure out the order that items should be in for your workflow.

◆ **Work with files.** You may find that you want to begin many of your workflows by opening a file. Use the Finder actions for that, particularly the Open Finder Items action (if you want to specify them in the workflow) or the Ask for Finder Items action (if you want to specify the files at the time that the workflow is run. In general, Get is used to gather items specified *in* the workflow, Ask will pop up a dialog box for the user to choose items, and Open is used to gather items that are fed from another application via the workflow.

TIP   The Finder has a special command in its contextual menu that enables you to choose items in the Finder first and then create a workflow that specifically uses those files. (First, highlight files in the Finder, then Control+click one of the files. Choose Automator ➤ Create Workflow.) That's handy if you need to rename a batch of files, crop a set of image files, or any of a number of similar tasks. (You can also drag and drop files or folders from the Finder to the Automator window, which will immediately create a Get Specified Finder Items icon in your workflow.)

◆ **Copy files before altering them.** It's often a good idea to use Copy Finder Items to make a copy of those items before you do anything drastic to them.

◆ **Use item searches.** Don't forget that the Spotlight can be used to search and locate all sorts of items, including files, e-mail messages, iPhoto items, iCal appointments, and so on.

◆ **Manipulate text.** TextEdit is handy for manipulating text, including speaking the text aloud using Text-to-Speech technology and turning text into an audio file.

◆ **Dig into samples.** The Example Workflows will help you get a sense of how to build workflows that do interesting things, as will workflows that you download from Apple or third-party Automator sites such as Automator World (`www.automatorworld.com`). Open those workflows and study them for ideas and techniques.

◆ **Think** *repetition* **and** *multiple steps*. Do you find yourself doing the same thing over and over again in the Finder or other applications? Or do you need to perform the same task on multiple items? Those are exactly the sort of problems that Automator is designed to handle. Repetitive tasks are things like renaming items, resizing photos, sorting and moving mail messages, opening and accessing Internet sites, and copying and pasting text from one file to another. Multiple-step tasks are things like reformatting images and sending them as e-mail attachments or opening web pages, copying text from them, pasting that text into TextEdit, saving the file, and printing it. All of those tasks are ripe for having workflows created and used.

> **NOTE** If you use pro-level creative applications such as Photoshop, InDesign, and Final Cut Pro, you're likely to have to pay for Automator workflows, but some of them may well be worth the cost. Automator can be very handy for helping you manage tasks in those applications and getting those applications to work automatically with others on your Mac.

Understanding AppleScript

AppleScript is a programming language that's built into Mac OS X. It's considered a *human-readable* language, meaning that you can figure out what it's doing most of the time simply by reading the commands. AppleScript uses a technology called Apple Events, which are messages passed between Mac applications, to enable you to send commands to one or more applications from within a script. That script then gets information about the settings for various objects within the application, and if you wish, changes those settings, invokes commands, or otherwise automates some processes.

Applications must be written to support Apple Events. Most applications understand at least a few events, such as open, quit, and print. Other applications support the standard suite of recommended Apple Events such as cut, copy, save, count, and delete. Still others take AppleScript very seriously, offering application-specific events such as a command that launches a URL in Safari or one that creates a new message in Mail.

Using Apple Events, you can send commands from the script to applications to get them to do things automatically and, in some cases, together. For example, an AppleScript script could do these things:

◆ Rename, move, delete, or otherwise alter all (or some) of the files or folders in a particular folder.

◆ Copy text from one application and automatically send it as an e-mail message to a predetermined recipient using an e-mail application.

◆ Launch a series of applications (such as your web browser, e-mail application, and address book application) and have them launch commands (open a particular website or check for e-mail) automatically.

◆ Gather files with specified attributes into a particular folder.

Beyond these examples, AppleScript can be implemented by an application developer to pretty much any extent that the developer desires. You can do very specific things in some applications that support AppleScript, such as Mail, Sherlock, and Microsoft Word.

As you'll see later in this chapter, most of what you're doing with AppleScript is telling applications (including system applications such as the Finder) to do particular things, in a particular order, and sometimes many times in a row. The more redundant the task, the better.

> **NOTE** AppleScript Studio (www.apple.com/applescript/studio/) enables the seasoned AppleScript author to take things even further. Not only can you create complex scripts, you can use the AppleScript language to create fully capable graphical applications, complete with a point-and-click interface. If you're serious about AppleScript, you should look into AppleScript Studio.

Mac OS X includes a Script Menu, which you can add to your menu bar, enabling you to quickly run a number of scripts that Apple has packaged with Mac OS X. These scripts are a great way to get started using AppleScript, even if you don't want to create your own. In addition, many applications include support for AppleScript, including not just Apple's own applications (iTunes, iPhoto, and others) but also third-party applications. While you may not be interested in scripting or programming on your own, you will still find a use for AppleScript.

The heart of AppleScript scripting is the Script Editor, which you can use to record actions—such as clicking icons, opening and moving windows, and selecting menu items—creating scripts without actually writing code. You also can use the Script Editor to write your own original AppleScript scripts. And you can use the Script Editor to view any AppleScript-capable application's dictionary, where you'll find listings and explanations of the AppleScript commands and objects available in that application.

Once you've explored the Script Editor, you'll be ready to learn some of the basics of AppleScript. AppleScript is an English-like language that offers a fairly easy-to-grasp syntax. After you've gotten to know the basics of AppleScript, you'll find that it can be easy to master new concepts and put them to use.

NOTE If you've spent some time with AppleScript in the past, we recommend that you launch the Help Viewer and choose the AppleScript Help module from the Help Center. There you'll see some good information regarding new features in AppleScript. We also recommend visiting www.apple.com/applescript/ on the Web for more information, documentation, and some good beginner tutorials covering AppleScript.

The Script Menu

For some Mac users, what's really cool about AppleScript is that you don't even have to write the scripts yourself. Instead, you can install and run scripts without worrying about their proper syntax and construction. In fact, dozens of scripts are included with Mac OS X for you to play with.

In the Applications folder, open the AppleScript folder. There you'll see the AppleScript Utility, which is new in Mac OS X 10.4. This application can be used to manage AppleScript, including setting up Folder Actions (script items that attach to folders in the Finder and react to changes in that folder), enabling GUI Scripting (which allows you to use AppleScript to automate the Mac interface more directly), and the Show Script Menu. Turn on that option and you'll see the Script Menu appear in your Mac's main menu bar.

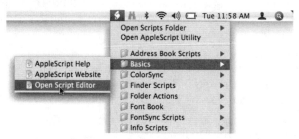

Click the Script icon, and a menu appears. The Script Menu works by looking in the /Library/ Scripts folder for any AppleScripts that you, the Mac OS X installer, or any third-party installers have placed there. In the AppleScript folder, you'll also find an alias to the /Library/Scripts folder, called Example Scripts.

NOTE In the AppleScript Utility you can opt to turn off the Library scripts, if desired, so that only those that you add yourself are displayed in the Script Menu. This includes plug-in workflows that you create via Automator.

The Script Menu also looks in your personal `Scripts` folder, which is stored at `~/Library/Scripts/`, and adds any additional scripts it finds. Whatever scripts you place in this folder will appear on the Script Menu. You also can add folders inside the `Scripts` folder, and they will become submenus in the Script Menu. The Open Scripts Folder command is on the menu to give you quick access to that folder. To add your own scripts to the Script Menu, open that folder and copy scripts to it, creating subfolders if you like. When you install scripts there, they show up in the Script menu the next time you click it.

Now you can run some scripts, just to get a sense of how AppleScript works. To run a script, select its name from one of the submenus. Several types of scripts are found among the example scripts, including these:

Finder Scripts Among the example scripts, those in the Finder Scripts menu are designed to work directly on items in the Finder. In most cases, you need to have a Finder window open or one item (or more) selected in a Finder window before these scripts will work correctly. The Finder scripts can perform a number of interesting tasks, most of which automatically rename (or alter the name of) batches of selected items, such as the Add to File Names or Add to Folder Names script.

Navigation Scripts There are only a few navigation scripts, but they all open new windows at specific locations: your `Applications`, `Documents`, `Favorites`, or `Home` folders. Or, using the Open Special Folder script, you can select from several commonly used folders, such as the `Utilities`, `Public`, or `Scripting Additions` folders.

AppleScript Scripts and Code Snippets These scripts are designed to work completely within AppleScript—they don't act on outside applications. In the Info Scripts menu, you'll find Current Date & Time, which simply uses some built-in AppleScript commands to get those items and return them to you. Other scripts (under Script Editor Scripts) are really just portions of sample code that the intrepid script author can use to get started on advanced scripts. In the FontSync Scripts menu, you'll find two scripts that enable you to create and match FontSync profiles, as discussed in Chapter 8, "PDFs, Fonts, and Color." In the Internet Services menu, the two sample scripts (temperature and stock quote) access sites on the Internet and return their results in a dialog box. You can also select About Internet Services Scripts from this menu to see a little bit about the Internet services that are being accessed.

Application Scripts In some of the other menus, you'll find examples of the types of scripts you may want to write (or download or purchase) and use—code that automatically tells applications what to do. The example scripts include scripts that send commands and exchange information with Mail, Sherlock, and even the Script Editor application.

As you can see, these scripts are a fairly decent representation of some of the tasks that can be accomplished with AppleScript. For instance, AppleScript scripts can perform functions on their own with built-in commands from AppleScript itself—functions such as retrieving the date and time or enabling the user to enter data via a dialog box.

Scripts can also send commands to objects in the Finder, meaning that you can do everything from moving windows to copying files, renaming files, and (yes) deleting files. For instance, the script Add to File Names in the Finder Scripts menu simplifies the task of adding filename extensions to a folder full of files that don't have them.

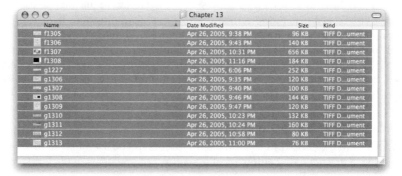

When Add to File Names is launched, a dialog box appears. In it, enter the filename extension you'd like to add (including a period, because this script takes things very literally).

Now, click the Suffix button to add the filename extension to each filename in the folder. (Note also that you could choose Prefix, if desired, to add `proj1` to the beginning of each file's name, for instance.) The script goes into action, appending the suffix to each file in the folder. The result is this:

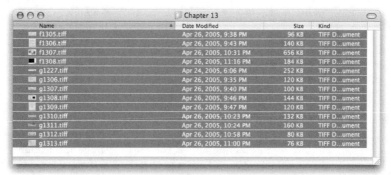

In addition, scripts can send commands to applications, as long as they accept them. While most applications will accept four basic commands (open, print, quit, and run), others are designed specifically to accept a wide range of commands from AppleScript scripts. As you'll see, each application can have its own AppleScript dictionary full of commands and objects that it will understand and respond to from a script.

If you're not much of a programmer and don't want to learn, you can focus on simply adding scripts and workflows to help automate certain tasks on your Mac. If they're compiled scripts (not applications), you can store them in your personal `Scripts` folder and use the Script Menu to access them. If the scripts are applets, you can store them anywhere and launch them like any other application. You'll also find that many applications have their own script folders and AppleScript menus, as discussed in the next section. If you add scripts for such an application to that application's script subfolder, you'll be able to access scripts from within the application.

Want to download more scripts? Using the Script Menu, select URLs and then select AppleScript Related Sites. Select one of those URL scripts to launch automatically and access the website in Internet Explorer. You'll also often find extra AppleScript scripts that can be downloaded from Apple's site (`www.apple.com/applescript`). Scripts that support your applications may be found at the application publisher's website.

Using Scripts with Applications

As you saw with the Script Menu, AppleScript scripts can be used in conjunction with full-blown applications to do something automatically, such as rename items in the Finder or launch an e-mail application in Apple Mail. In fact, many applications are designed to work well with AppleScript. As you'll see later in this chapter, you can create your own scripts that automate the behavior of applications in many different ways.

Without any scripting knowledge, you can access scripts that will perform automatic tasks using your applications. For instance, Apple engineers often write scripts and make them available on Apple's website for use with Apple's applications, such as iTunes and iPhoto. Visit `www.apple.com/applescript/iphoto/` on the Web, for instance, and you can download quite a few scripts that work in conjunction with iPhoto to perform tasks beyond the applications' capabilities, such as sending iPhoto images via e-mail or creating a QuickTime slide show that includes audio.

Beyond scripts that are designed simply to work with an application, you'll sometimes find applications that actually integrate scripting into the application itself. For instance, Microsoft's Entourage, its e-mail and PIM program included with Microsoft Office, has a special AppleScript menu that enables you to access AppleScripts from within the application.

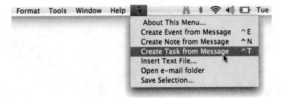

Scripts for this menu are stored inside your /Documents/`Microsoft User Data` folder, in a special folder called `Entourage Script Menu Items`. Many of these scripts act on items that are highlighted in the document window, while others simply act on the Entourage application itself. You can download additional scripts for Entourage and other applications at `http://scriptbuilders.net`.

iTunes offers the same capability—in fact, if you download scripts from Apple and install them, iTunes will automatically add the AppleScript menu to its menu bar. Simply visit `www.apple.com/applescript/itunes/index.html` and download the iTunes scripts for Mac OS X. Then, create a folder called `Scripts` inside the `iTunes` folder that's inside your personal `Library` folder (`~/Library/iTunes/`) and copy the scripts to that folder. The next time you launch iTunes, the new AppleScript menu will appear.

You'll find that a number of applications support scripts in this way, from editing applications to high-end desktop publishing applications. The point is to make AppleScript as integrated as possible with an application—so much so that launching an AppleScript is almost as simple as selecting any other menu command.

Using Folder Actions

Folder Actions are an extension of AppleScript's capabilities that allow you to "attach" scripts to folders, so the scripts are launched when any of the following events occur:

- ◆ A folder is opened.

- ◆ A folder window is closed.

- ◆ A folder window is moved.

- ◆ Items are placed in a folder.

- ◆ Items are removed from a folder.

The idea behind Folder Actions is to alert you or carry out an action—such as copy a file or send a file to another user—when one or more of these events has happened. You can attach a script to any folder you want, once you have turned on Folder Actions, and use a script included with Mac OS X or write your own.

To use Folder Actions, you first need to turn them on, or enable them. There are two ways to do this: (1) hold down the Control key and click your mouse anywhere on the desktop or in a Finder window, then select Enable Folder Actions from the context menu, or (2) double-click the Folder Actions Setup application (which is actually an AppleScript application) found in the `AppleScript` folder in your `Applications` folder.

Once you have enabled Folder Actions, you can attach a Folder Action script to any folders you want. As an example, one good place to do this is the `Drop Box` folder inside your `Public` folder (which is in your home folder). This folder can serve as a receptacle for files any user wants to transfer to you over a network. All users are allowed to write to this folder, even though it is in your home folder. To find out when users put files there, you can set up a Folder Action script that alerts you when there are new files. To do this, move to your `Public` folder, then hold down the Control key (or click your right mouse button, if you have a two-button mouse) and click on the `Drop Box` folder. From the contextual menu that displays, select Attach a Folder Action. (You'll only see this command if you've enabled Folder Actions as discussed previously.) A dialog box will appear enabling you to choose a Folder Action script.

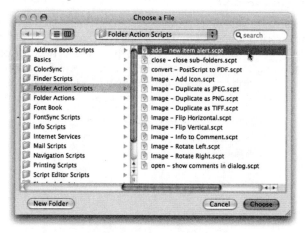

This opens a dialog box that lets you select from the existing Folder Action scripts in your `AppleScript` folder. Select Add - New Item Alert. This script checks the folder every few seconds to see if its contents have changed. If items are added, the script displays a dialog box, telling you that there are new items and asking if you want to view them.

If you want to see the new item(s), click Yes, and the folder in question opens. If not, click No, and the dialog box goes away. If you do nothing for 30 seconds, the dialog box will go away on its own. This, however, is not very practical, because you might miss this dialog box if you are away from your computer for a minute. You can easily change the amount of time after which the dialog box goes away, the *time-out* period, by editing the script.

This script is found in `/Applications/AppleScript/Example Scripts/Folder Action Scripts`. If you double-click the script file, the Script Editor opens, and you can make changes to it. To change the time-out, look for the first line of the script after the comments—you can tell this is the script because some of the keywords are in color and in bold. Here's the line to look for:

```
property dialog_timeout : 30 -- set the amount of time before dialogs auto-answer.
```

As you can see, the time-out is set for 30 seconds. You can change that to any amount you want by changing the number of seconds; for example, to make sure you never miss any new files, change it to 3600, which is one hour. Save the script by selecting File ➢ Save, and the new value will be used.

You can make other changes to this script or any of the Folder Action scripts, or you can write your own scripts and attach them to any folder. See "Creating Original Scripts" later in this chapter for more on creating your own scripts.

CONFIGURING FOLDER ACTIONS

Once you have started using Folder Actions, you may want to configure them, turn them on or off, or add and remove scripts to specific folders. While you can do this from the contextual menu for each individual folder, you'll find it difficult to recall which folders have scripts attached to them.

There's a small AppleScript application called Folder Actions Setup in the `AppleScript` folder; you can also open this application from any context menu by selecting Configure Folder Actions. This application shows you a list of folders you have attached scripts to and which scripts you have attached.

This application has a simple interface, but you can do a lot with it:

◆ You can turn Folder Actions on or off by checking or unchecking Enable Folder Actions.

◆ You can turn Folder Actions on or off for any folder by checking or unchecking the On box next to its name in the folder list.

◆ You can turn any script attached to a folder on or off by checking or unchecking the On box next to its name in the script list.

◆ You can display any folder by selecting it in the list and clicking Show Folder.

◆ You can add folders to the list by clicking the plus button (+) and remove folders by clicking the minus button (–).

◆ You can attach scripts to any folder by clicking the plus button (+) and remove scripts by clicking the minus button (–). You can attach as many scripts as you want to any folder.

◆ You can edit scripts by selecting them and clicking Edit Script; the selected script opens in Script Editor.

If you plan to use Folder Actions for more than just one or two folders, this application is your control center, enabling you to manage all your folders and their scripts from one central location.

Scripts As Applications

The Script Menu runs compiled scripts that you've placed in a special folder in your home hierarchy. Likewise, individual applications can enable you to run scripts from the application's menu bar. But AppleScript code can also be distributed as an application (or an *applet*, a term that's meant to suggest "small application"). These AppleScript applications work pretty much like any other applications: you can double-click them, they have menus (although usually with very few options), and in some cases you can even drag and drop files on the script applications. AppleScript applets (on the left) have slightly different icons from the basic scripts (on the right).

Such applications can be handy because you can put them on your desktop or in the Dock; you can even add them to your Login Items list in the Login pane in System Preferences and have the applets launch automatically when you log in to your Mac. Script applications also can be designed to stay open as background processes, enabling them to monitor the time or date, for instance, and to execute when something in particular happens. Later in this chapter, you'll see how to save scripts as applications.

AppleScript applets can come in another form—*droplets*: a type of script that's designed to accept dragged-and-dropped files as input. For instance, some of the applets made available by Apple for use with iTunes are activated when you drag a compatible sound file to the AppleScript and drop it. Then, the script goes into action, using that dragged file as the input it needs to perform a task. In this example, dragging a file on the droplet will "shred" the file by deleting it and overwriting the deleted data.

Droplets usually quit after they've run and accomplished their tasks. If you double-click a droplet, you'll see either an About box, telling you what the script does, or a prompt asking you to select a file or program to process. If you see an About box, click OK in the box and the droplet will quit. If you see a dialog box, you can select a file or program to run the script.

First Script: Recording and Saving

If the first level of AppleScript commitment is running scripts from the Script Menu in applications or as double-clickable applets, the second level isn't much tougher. The Script Editor—an application included with Mac OS X for the express purpose of creating and editing scripts—has a fun little function you can play with called Record. You turn on the Record function and then switch to applications and perform tasks that you'd like to script. When you switch back to the Script Editor, you'll see the scripting steps there in the Script Editor window (see Figure 21.3).

One of the major benefits of recording a script is that it can give you some idea of the commands that are available within an application (such as the Finder), as well as how that application prefers to receive instructions. As noted previously, many AppleScript scripts are geared toward individual applications. When you record an application scripting itself, you may be able to gain a bit of insight into how it likes to be scripted.

FIGURE 21.3

Here's the Script Editor recording the steps I'm taking with the Finder to open and arrange some windows for copying.

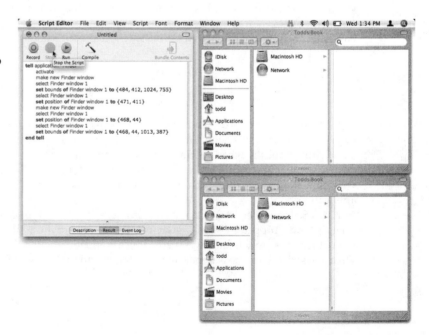

Not all applications are *recordable* applications that send AppleScript commands to the Script Editor while it's in Record mode. That doesn't necessarily mean that the application isn't *scriptable;* an application can offer very sophisticated AppleScript support without offering recordability. If you find that an application doesn't seem to record script commands well, you can check for an AppleScript dictionary that's related to that application, as discussed in the section "Application Commands," later in this chapter.

Recording Actions As a Script

In order to record the actions you perform in an application and turn those steps into a script, you need to do two things. First, you need to launch the Script Editor, which is located in the `AppleScript` folder inside your `Applications` folder. Second, you need to be working with a recordable application. If the application isn't recordable, you'll know soon enough because you'll get little-to-no response from your actions in the Script Editor. In some cases, the Script Editor still will record a few commands from nonrecordable applications (such as closing or moving windows), but it won't know how to record commands with more detail.

Now you're ready to begin recording. Here's how:

1. Launch the Script Editor and the application(s) you want to work with. (In most cases, you don't want to record them being launched.) The best place to start recording actions is in the Finder, so if you use it, you won't need to launch it.

2. Click the Record button in the Script Editor or select Controls ➢ Record.

3. Switch to the application(s) you're recording and perform actions that you'd like the Script Editor to record.

NOTE If you hear a beep after you take the first action, the Script Editor may need your attention. It may need to know what application you've just selected if it can't figure it out on its own. It will let you know that by displaying the Choose Application dialog box. Highlight the application in the Choose Application dialog box and click Select. Next, return to the recordable application and begin performing actions.

4. Switch back to the Script Editor and click Stop when you're done.

When you click Stop, you'll notice that an `end tell` command appears in the window. Now you can click the Run button to run the script again and see if it works as you had hoped.

When you record scripts, the Script Editor rarely gets the whole thing right the first time, but watching the recording process can be handy for creating a basic structure from which to work. For instance, in the example shown in Figure 21.3, I had to go back and tweak in the command and make a new Finder window toward the beginning of the script because the Script Editor didn't record that initially. (When I switched to the Finder, a window was created automatically and the Script Editor didn't catch it.) So, if you run into errors, try to think creatively about solutions to recording glitches—it can be kind of fun.

Saving Your Scripts

After you've recorded your first script (and later, when you're creating scripts from scratch), it's important to save the script. To do this, select File ➢ Save. You'll see the Save dialog box, shown in Figure 21.4, where you'll make choices about the type of script or applet you want to create from the Format menu.

FIGURE 21.4
The Save dialog box in
the Script Editor

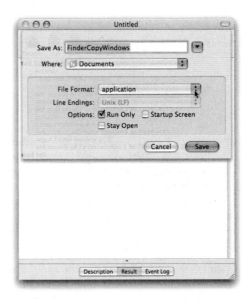

The Save dialog box is fairly standard, but you should note that the Format menu gives you some interesting options for saving:

Script A *script* must be run from within the Script Editor, the Script Menu, or an application that includes the capability to launch scripts. This is a full-fledged (and ideally, working) script, but you can't just double-click it in a Finder window. (If you do, you'll launch the Script Editor, not the script.)

Application With this option, you're creating an AppleScript applet or droplet that launches as a native Mac OS X application.

Script Bundle A *Script Bundle* is a special type of script that is built in a similar way to Mac OS X application packages. Developers can add additional scripts, resources, localization files, and more to a Script Bundle, enhancing and extending the script's operations.

Application Bundle An *Application Bundle* is like a Script Bundle, but it is a double-clickable applet.

Text Save as a plain-text file when you're in the middle of editing the script and it doesn't yet work. You also can edit these files in text editors other than the Script Editor. If you save a script as a text file, you can select from four options telling Script Editor what type of line breaks to use:

UNIX (LF) This uses a line feed character (ASCII character 10) to mark line endings.

MAC (CR) This uses a carriage return character (ASCII character 13) to mark line endings.

WINDOWS (CRLF) This uses a combination of a carriage return character and a line feed character to mark line endings.

Preserve Line Endings This retains the file's current line endings.

Choosing the Application or Application Bundle options gives you three more check boxes to consider. Select Stay Open if this script is designed to launch and then wait as a background process for other things to happen. Such scripts are more complex (and outside the scope of this book). Turn on Startup Screen if you'd prefer that the applet show a startup, or "splash," screen when it launches. If you leave this option on, the startup screen will appear when the applet is launched:

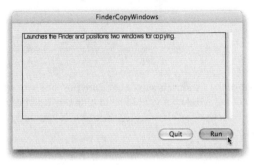

TIP   The startup screen for an applet includes any comment text you've typed in the bottom of that script's window after clicking the Description tab in the Script Editor.

If you select Run Only, you'll save the application as a noneditable file. You can run the application, but you won't be able to make any changes to it. This is useful if you are planning to distribute scripts to other users and you don't want to take the chance that, out of curiosity, they try to fiddle with them in the Script Editor.

If you save a file as a Script or Script Bundle, the only option available is Run Only.

Creating Original Scripts

Now that you've seen how to record a script, perhaps you've learned a little about how the Finder and other applications like to be scripted. Next, you're ready to create your own script from the bottom up.

To begin, launch Script Editor and choose File ➤ New Script. A new script window appears. At any time, you can decide to save the script, giving it a name and choosing whether it will be saved as text or a compiled script. You can then save your changes as you improve the script.

Let's start with a script that's considered an old standard in the programming universe: the Hello World script. It's customary whenever you learn a new language to first create a quick program or script to say "Hello World." In the case of AppleScript, this script is easy.

Entering the Script

Begin by clicking the Description tab at the bottom of the Script Editor window and entering some information about the script. It may seem like a silly thing to worry about for a short script, but it's worthwhile to *document* your scripts as much as you can—including information about who you are, why the script was written, and what it's supposed to do.

TIP The bottom part of the window is separated from the code section by a divider, which you can drag to the bottom of the window if you'd like to hide the description and see more code in your script's window. This section can also display the result of your script or the Event Log, if you click the appropriate tabs.

In the script below, you'll see a couple of special commands that AppleScript installations generally offer through something called *scripting additions,* which we'll discuss later.

```
display dialog "Hello World."
say "Hello World."
```

Simply type those lines into the Script Editor window, pressing Return after each line. Now you can click the Run button to see (and hear) the result. You'll notice that the font of the text in the Script Editor window changed immediately after you clicked Run. That's because the Script Editor recognized the text as valid after putting it through a quick check system.

In fact, at any time before you run the script you can initiate that check yourself to make sure you're formatting something correctly. (That way, you can check the syntax quickly without having to execute the script over and over again.) Click the Compile button in the Script Editor window, or press the Enter key, to have the Script Editor check your syntax and convert it into AppleScript commands. If it's happy with what you've typed, it will change the font of the text (and may even make some words boldface). If the Script Editor doesn't like something you've scripted, it may return an error message.

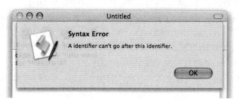

When you receive such a message, you'll have to dig back into the script and see what you may have mistyped or what commands you're using incorrectly. Usually, the Script Editor highlights the first place where it finds an error.

NOTE Whenever you click the Compile button or the Run button, your script is automatically reformatted in a way that makes it acceptable to the AppleScript compiler and easy to read. You can change this formatting by selecting Script Editor ➤ Preferences, clicking the Formatting tab, and then changing the defaults. You should also note that, even if the compiler accepts the words and constructs you've used, your script *might* not work correctly.

Adding Comments to the Script

While you're entering commands, you have another option that's important to take advantage of: you can add *comments* to the script. Comments are useful for reminding yourself of what you're doing in longer scripts; likewise, comments can be used to tell future readers of your script what the script (or portions of it) was meant to do. Though some people feel that AppleScript is easy enough to read on its own, that isn't always the case. Sometimes the comments are very important.

You can add comments to your script in two ways. The first way is to add the comment text at the end of a command line within the script. You do that by adding two hyphens, or dashes (--), before typing the comment:

```
display dialog "Hello World." -- pops up a dialog box
```

You can also use the double hyphen approach to place a comment on its own line:

```
-- The following displays and speaks "Hello World."
display dialog "Hello World." -- dialog box
say "Hello World." -- spoken
```

In all these cases, the double hyphens simply tell the AppleScript compiler (the engine that's turning your commands into reality) to ignore anything that comes after them on that single line of text. In fact, you'll note that once you've clicked either Run or Compile, the comments will be changed to italic, and a space will be added in front of the double hyphens if you didn't already type a space there. That indicates that the text has been recognized as a comment. (Note, incidentally, that you don't have to type a space after the hyphens, as in my examples, although I recommend it for easier reading.)

Do you have longer comments to add? Another way to enter them (particularly if they are paragraph-length) is to place the comments between a combination of parentheses and asterisks:

```
(*
This script is designed to display a dialog box. Once the user has clicked OK to
dismiss the dialog box, the computer will speak the same text aloud, using Apple's
Text-to-Speech technology. The Text-to-Speech voice can be selected in the Speech
pane of System Preferences, and the audio volume must be above 0 for the speech to
be heard.
*)
display dialog "Hello World."
say "Hello World."
```

Formatting Issues

The Script Editor is good at reformatting your script—whenever you click either the Run or Compile button—so the script is more readable. For instance, the Script Editor, by default, changes the color of words that are recognized as AppleScript language keywords to blue and bold, assigns blue to application-specific commands, puts variables and subroutines into green, changes comments to italics, and makes references purple; it leaves other words in a plain style. In fact, the formatting doesn't matter much to the compiler; you can even select Edit ➤ AppleScript Formatting to change the default way that scripts are auto-formatted, changing not only the colors and fonts used, but also the size (which can make your scripts easier to read).

If you're familiar with AppleScript in its previous incarnations, you may recall having to enter a special character to break long lines: you needed to press Option+Return in the middle of a command line to insert a *soft break*, represented by the *continuation symbol* (··). This is no longer the case in Mac OS X 10.3 and higher: with the new version of Script Editor, line breaks are automatically added in the display—but not in the actual code—and the Script Editor changes its display as you resize it, breaking lines so they fit in its window.

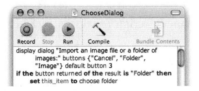

Checking Results

Another element of the Script Editor that's useful to know about is the Result pane. The Result pane is designed to show the resulting values from calculations and assignments as they occur during your script. In practical applications, most of what you'll see in the Result pane will be the final result of your script, since the script will usually execute too quickly for you to see any results that occur as it runs.

Still, the Result pane can be useful for giving you a sense of what your script is doing and what values it's dealing with. Whenever you run a script that returns a result, the Result pane displays at the bottom of the window, unless you have hidden this part of the window by moving the divider. You can always switch to this pane by clicking the Result tab. So, when you run a script, you can see the final assigned or computed result (see Figure 21.5).

As your scripts get more complicated, the results that you see will get more complicated as well. While you're learning to script, you may find it helpful to leave the Result pane visible to see what results, if any, are being recognized and returned when the script runs.

FIGURE 21.5
Scripts that compute or assign values will return a result in the Result pane.

Using the Event Log

The Script Editor also offers an *Event Log*, a log that records certain events that take place while an AppleScript is running. You can use this log to debug complex scripts. To view this log, click the Event Log tab at the bottom of the Script Editor window. This pane doesn't always display events; it depends on your script, its events, and whether you tell it to log certain events.

Using the Event Log is beyond the scope of this book, but you can learn more about AppleScript in general, and the Event Log in particular, by reading the AppleScript documentation at Apple's Developer website: `http://developer.apple.com/documentation/AppleScript/`.

Scripting Concepts

AppleScript is *object oriented*, which means that it's designed primarily to deal with objects and their properties. In the real world, the main items you deal with are objects (e.g., a chair, a room, or a house). Those objects are composed of *elements*—a room might have a wall, a window, and a light switch (among other elements). Those objects and elements can have *properties*—a light switch is in the "on" position, and a wall has certain width and height dimensions.

Within the AppleScript world, many of the main items that you work with in applications or the Finder can be considered objects. That includes folders, files, windows, disks, and documents, among others. A window can have many elements—a title bar, a Close button, a scroll bar. The objects and elements can both have properties: a file has a modification date, and a window has a title.

Objects, References, and Properties

In AppleScript, objects can have both properties and *containers*. Containers are important for dealing with items in the Finder as well as in other applications.

For instance, if you're dealing with folders located on your hard disk, the container might be obvious, as in this command:

```
tell application "Finder"
open the folder "Users" in the startup disk
end tell
```

The Users folder has a container, the startup disk. The relationship between objects and their containers can be more complicated:

```
tell application "Finder"
open the folder "Backup" in the
    folder "Documents" in the folder "ralphie"
    in the folder "Users" in the startup disk
end tell
```

When you're creating one of these long paths, you can truncate it a bit by using colons to divide portions of the path:

```
tell application "Finder"
open the folder "Users:ralphie:Documents:Backup"
    in the startup disk
end tell
```

For other disks, all you need to do is name them:

```
tell application "Finder"
open the folder "Documents:CD Movies" in the disk
   "Firewire HD"
end tell
```

NOTE   It's important to note that even though Mac OS X uses the Unix convention of using slashes (/) as path separators, AppleScript still uses colons. If you need to get a file or folder path from an external location to use in an AppleScript, you will need to replace the colons with slashes.

You'll come across many other types of objects as you explore the scriptable parts of both the Finder and other AppleScript-aware applications. As you'll see in the section "Application Commands," later in this chapter, your applications can have their own objects—windows, documents, etc.—that you address in a similar manner.

That's how you dig down through the containers to an object. What do you do once you get there? What's often more important in scripting is the fact that an object has properties. These are the attributes of the object—its height, weight, and shoe size. Using AppleScript, a fair number of the commands you'll give will be to learn, compare, and change the attributes of objects, both in the Finder and in applications. For example:

```
tell application "Finder"
   get owner of startup disk
   set bounds of window 1 to {20, 60, 700, 500}
end tell
```

In this example, we're getting the value of the startup disk's owner property (if you have the Result window open, you'll likely see root as the result, which corresponds to the Root account) and assigning (setting) a value to the bounds property (the on-screen position) of a window.

That's a good deal of what you'll be doing in AppleScript—learning and setting the properties of objects. One way you'll do that, though, is through another special type of entity—the variable.

Working with Variables

When you're working with an object's properties in a script, often you'll want to assign the value of a particular property to a temporary holding area. You'll find this useful for any number of reasons, not the least of which is convenience. These temporary holding areas are called *variables,* which are named areas of memory where AppleScript lets you temporarily store values. Here are two examples:

```
set x to 10
set myDisk to name of startup disk
```

Both statements use the AppleScript set command to set a value to a variable. In the first instance, the variable is named x; in the second, it's named myDisk. (For the record, the second command won't work unless you use a tell statement to send the command to the Finder. See the section "Apple-Script Commands," later in this chapter.)

These variable names represent the customary way in which AppleScript variables are named. If you need a quick variable for a number or numeric evaluation, it's fairly common to use a simple letter such as x or i. If you're creating a more permanent variable for use later in your script, it's common to give it a compound name that suggests that variable's purpose. Examples might be `myCounter`, `docFolder`, and `fileCount`.

NOTE How you name your variables doesn't actually matter—the suggestions here are just following AppleScript custom. There's a good reason for the custom, though: using these types of variables can improve the readability of your script (e.g., `fileCount` makes more sense than `xyz`). Also, a compound or one-letter approach is more likely to keep you from accidentally using an AppleScript command as a variable name, which will confuse the AppleScript compiler and create an error in your script.

If you're used to almost any other type of programming or scripting, you may be surprised at the flexibility of variables in AppleScript. Any variable can hold pretty much any sort of value, regardless of the variable's *type*. In other words, there's nothing special you have to do to create a variable that can hold a number, as opposed to a variable that can hold text or even a list. They're basically the same. Here are a few ways you can set variables:

```
set x to 1.5
set y to 5 + 6 -- evaluates to 11
set firstName to "John"
set filePath to {Users:Shared:Memos:Memo1.rtf}
```

You can see here a few of the various types of values that AppleScript can work with, including integers, strings (text between straight quotation marks), real numbers (numbers with decimal places), and file paths. You can also set variables to Boolean values (true or false) as well as to lists of other value types, which are placed between braces (curly brackets) and separated by commas, such as in these examples:

```
set classList to {"Julie", "Tom", "Eric"}
set numList to {1, 3, 5, 7, 9, 11, 343}
```

You'll find that this listing approach to variables is also useful for such things as storing all the values in a particular folder to a single variable:

```
set fileList to name of every item in folder "Documents"
    in disk "Firewire 40GB"
```

One more note on variable type: you sometimes may find it necessary to change one type of value (an integer, a string, or a decimal number) into another type of value. In AppleScript, you do that with a system called *coercion*, which simply causes a variable to be of the new type (if possible). You do that using the `as` keyword:

```
set x to 5
set numText to x as string -- assigns value as a string
```

Now `numText` has the value 5, but it's considered a string, not an integer (so that you could concatenate it to another string, for instance). Other `as` options include `as real` (decimal number), `as integer`, and `as list`.

Finally, it's interesting to know that there's another important variable that's built into AppleScript: `result`. Immediately after performing some sort of operation or command, you may have seen that the result of that operation can appear in the Result pane of the Script Editor's window.

Whatever is placed in that Result pane is also placed in the `result` variable. It's not a good idea to rely on the `result` variable, because it changes after each new assignment and after many commands. Still, it's possible to do something like this:

```
get 5 + 5
set numTotal to result
```

The `get` command adds 5 and 5, assigning the result, 10, to the special `result` variable. Then, the `set` command assigns the current value of `result` to the named variable `numTotal`, making `numTotal`'s value 10.

Loops and Conditionals

Hand in hand with variables come *loops* and *conditionals,* which are simply ways to control the flow of your script from one command to the next. Sometimes, you'll want a particular command to be executed only if a certain criterion has been met. That's a conditional. Other times, you'll want a particular command (or group of commands) to execute a certain number of times or until something else happens. That's a loop.

AppleScript allows you to accomplish this type of flow control with two different statements: the `if then` statement and the `repeat` statement. `If then` statements are used to evaluate conditionals; `repeat` statements are used for looping.

IF THEN COMPARISONS

An example of an `if then` statement follows.

```
tell application "Finder"
    set numItems to the number of
    items in the folder "Desktop Junk"
        if numItems > 10 then display dialog
        "Time to clean out the Junk folder."
end tell
```

Note that the `if then` construct always includes a portion that needs to be evaluated as either true or false (Boolean). In this example, that portion is `numItems > 10`, where `numItems` is a variable that was created immediately before the `if then` statement.

NOTE   In the previous example, AppleScript will look for the folder Desktop Junk on the current desktop. (The current user's desktop is the first place a script will look for a folder if you don't specify any other containers such as the startup disk or a named disk.) If you want the script to look in a different folder, include a full path to that folder, as discussed in the section "Objects, References, and Properties," earlier in this chapter.

Other types of comparisons are possible, too, such as these:

```
if x > 5
if x <= 4
if numItems is equal to 5
if totalFolders is greater than numFolders
```

The common comparison operators include =, ≠, >, <, >=, and <=. (You can produce the ≠ symbol by pressing the Option and = keys together.) If you'd prefer to use actual words as your comparison operators, you can experiment a little with the text that AppleScript recognizes (it recognizes quite a few variations beyond those outlined here), including `equals`, `does not equal`, `is greater than`, `is less than`, `is greater than or equal to`, `is less than or equal to`, and so on.

You'll find that it's also possible to compare other items; for instance, you can use certain operators to determine whether a list or string variable contains a particular item or bit of text:

```
if (fileList contains ".txt") then New
if (myString starts with "Hello") then New
```

Containment operators include: `contains`, `doesn't contain`, `starts with`, or `ends with`, among others.

An `if` statement that has more than one command as part of the statement needs to have an `end if` at the end of the string of commands so that the script knows what commands to avoid if the comparison is false. Here's an example:

```
set x to 3
if x is less than 5
    set lessTrue to 1
    display dialog "It's lower than five."
end if
```

In the example, if x happened to be higher than 5, neither the `set` nor the `display dialog` command line would be executed, because the script would immediately skip to the `end if` and move on to the rest of the script.

Any `if` statement can also have an `else` statement as part of it. The `else` statement is used to specify what the script should do in case the condition isn't true. Here's an example:

```
tell application "Finder"
    set numItems to the number of
    items in the folder "Desktop Junk"
        if numItems = 0 then display dialog
        "There are no items in the Junk folder."
        else display dialog "The Junk folder has items in it."
        end if
end tell
```

Note that incorporating an `else` statement also means that you need to include the `end if` statement to complete the `if then else` construct.

REPEAT STATEMENTS

A `repeat` statement is used to perform tasks repeatedly until some condition is met. You can use the same kinds of comparisons in `repeat` statements as in `if then` statements, although you don't have to, depending on how you create the `repeat` loop. For instance, you can use the `repeat exit repeat` construct to leave an endless loop, as in this example:

```
set x = 0
repeat
```

```
    set x = x + 1
    if x = 10 then exit repeat
end repeat
```

In its current form, this script doesn't do much good; but in other ways, it can. For instance, you could use this construct for a fun little script that asks the user to specify the correct number:

```
repeat
    display dialog "Enter a number between 1 and 50:"
    default answer ""
    set numChosen to text returned of result
    if numChosen = "10" then exit repeat
end repeat
```

You can see through the additional commands how the `exit repeat` command is used when the desired value is entered.

TIP The `default answer` attribute is used in conjunction with the `display dialog` command to cause the dialog box to show an entry box for text. See the section "Scripting Additions," later in this chapter, for more details.

Other `repeat` constructs work differently. For instance, you can have a certain loop repeat a certain number of times using the `repeat x times` construct:

```
set x to 0
repeat 10 times
set x to x + 1
end repeat
display dialog "Total equals: " & x & "."
```

In this case, the `repeat` loop will continue until the number of times has been exhausted. (You also can use an `exit repeat` command if you need to have the loop end before the specified number of loops is completed.) Another `repeat` construct is `repeat until`, which you can use as sort of a combination of an `if then` and a `repeat`, because you're using a condition:

```
set x to 0
repeat until (x=5)
set x to x + 1
end repeat
```

In `repeat until`, the loop continues as long as the condition is false. The `repeat while` command is similar, but the loop continues as long as the condition is true.

Commands in AppleScript

Now that you've seen some of the basics of AppleScript programming, as well as how to record, create, and save your AppleScript scripts, it's time to explore the commands that AppleScript has to offer. The best way to learn AppleScript is a combination of looking at the various AppleScript dictionaries (discussed in the section "Application Commands," later in this chapter) and opening up other prewritten scripts or recorded scripts to get a sense of how they work. In this section, then, we'll focus on how to find the various commands you'll have at your disposal.

AppleScript works on four different levels. Some (in fact, very few) commands are built right into AppleScript itself. The second group of commands comes from applications themselves, where the bulk of new and interesting commands are found. The third group of commands comes from scripting additions, which are special AppleScript add-ons that add important and very useful commands to the AppleScript vocabulary. Finally, there's an additional group of commands that come from Mac OS X's Unix foundation, which you can run through AppleScript scripts.

AppleScript Commands

AppleScript commands are very basic commands that are used with other commands and constructs to learn property values and to set new property values to objects. These commands can be used for some basic programming and mathematical tasks. Built-in AppleScript commands include `activate`, `copy`, `count`, `get`, `launch`, `run`, and `set`.

The `activate`, `launch`, and `run` commands all have to do with starting up applications; `run` and `launch` are similar, and `activate` generally is used to make an application come to the front, as in these two examples:

```
activate application "Finder"
tell application "Finder"
    activate
end tell
```

The `get`, `set`, and `copy` commands are special within AppleScript because they're used for learning and changing the values of object properties. You've already seen some of them in action, as in these examples:

```
get bounds of window 1
set bounds of window 1 to {20, 50, 600, 700}
copy {20, 50, 500, 700} to bounds of window 1
```

Perhaps one of the most important commands in AppleScript isn't technically a command, but rather a statement. The `tell` statement is used to focus a script on a particular application, such as the Finder. It's a *statement* because it has a beginning and an end, between which you place commands that you want AppleScript to pass on to the targeted application. For instance, the following line has AppleScript contact the Finder, load the Finder's AppleScript dictionary (in which the Finder's AppleScript commands are stored), and prepare to send commands to the Finder:

```
tell application "Finder"
```

The commands then follow, with a trailing `end tell` command to close the `tell` statement:

```
tell application "Finder"
    open folder "Applications" of the startup disk
end tell
```

You can have repeated `tell` statements, if desired, that enable you to have a script work with two different applications:

```
tell application "Finder"
   open folder "Applications" of the startup disk
end tell
tell application "Internet Explorer"
   activate
   OpenURL "http://www.macblog.com/"
end tell
```

For the record, you don't need the `end tell` statement if you keep the entire `tell` construct on a single line:

```
tell application "Finder" open folder "Applications" on the startup disk
```

Clearly, it's important to have the `end tell` if you have more than one command's worth of instructions for the application.

TIP A `tell` statement can be used to send commands to a Classic application, even if the script itself is compiled as a Mac OS X applet.

Application Commands

The second type of AppleScript commands are those that are built into Mac OS applications themselves. Most applications that are AppleScript-aware include a few different sets of commands. The Required Suite of commands is the group of commands that any Macintosh application needs to adhere to: run, open, print, and quit. It's not a long list, but you can be fairly confident that any native Macintosh application that launches and runs on your Mac will respond to one or more of those four Apple Events, such as in this example:

```
tell application "TextEdit"
   print window 1
   quit saving yes
end tell
```

In this example, the print command will open a Print dialog box in which the user can make additional choices before printing. Once the print job has been sent to the printer, the application will receive the quit command along with the saving yes option, which means the application will quit and automatically save changes in any open documents.

Beyond these basic commands, applications are free to add their own commands for you to use in scripts; in fact, most of your scripting will use application-specific commands. In order to use them, though, you'll need to know them. Although a particular application's manual might include such information, the easiest way to see the commands available to you is through the Script Editor's Open Dictionary command. If an application is AppleScript aware, it will have a special AppleScript dictionary that's part of it. Using the Open Dictionary command, you can view that dictionary and, hence, the commands in it.

To view an application's dictionary, select File ➢ Open Dictionary. This displays a window showing all the available dictionaries on your computer. You'll see three types of items listed here:

Applications   Mac OS X applications, either Cocoa or Carbon.

Classic Applications   Mac OS 9 or earlier applications.

Scripting Additions   Special files that add commands and functions to AppleScript. These are described in the next section, "Scripting Additions."

In the Open Dictionary dialog box, locate the application you'd like to use with your script. Select that application and click Open. (If you don't see the application in question, you can try to locate it by clicking the Browse button in the Open Dictionary dialog box and locating the application using a typical Open dialog box.) The dictionary appears in its own window in the Script Editor, as shown in Figure 21.6.

FIGURE 21.6

An application's Apple-Script dictionary

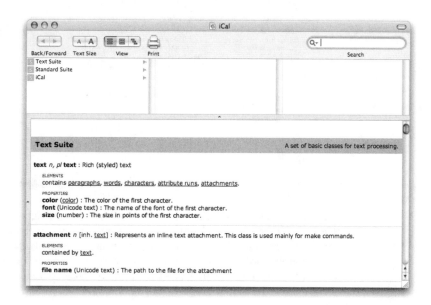

The dictionary for an application is written by the application's developer, so it can vary in exactly how comprehensive, useful, or understandable it is. In most cases, you'll need to take a little time to understand how items are presented in the dictionary; after that, some additional experimentation often will be needed before you'll get the true sense of the application's scriptability.

That said, you'll notice some constants in almost any AppleScript dictionary. The dictionary is there basically to show you what items the application considers to be scriptable classes and elements, what properties those items have, and what commands the application will recognize in a `tell` statement. Putting those things together (classes, properties, and commands) along with standard AppleScript commands, you can begin to build a script to control that application.

NOTE   Don't let the word "class" throw you off in this context. It just means a collection of elements and properties—the stuff in an application to which you can apply commands.

How do you use the dictionary? Simply click an item on the left side of the window, expanding the list by clicking disclosure triangles if necessary, and the definition of that item will appear on the right. Here's a look at the way the left side is organized:

Suites   In most cases, the classes, properties, and commands are stored in suites of related items. By selecting the name of one of the suites listed down the left side of the window, you can see all the items that are considered part of that suite. Sometimes seeing the whole suite can give you an idea of how the elements interact.

Commands   Commands appear on the second column when you select a suite; commands have an uppercase C icon. Select a command, and you'll see a quick reference to how that command is supposed to be structured. In most cases, the commands are meant to act on the objects that are also in the suite.

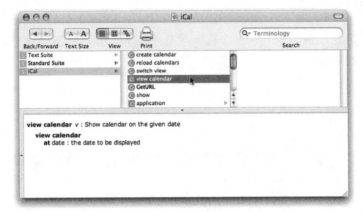

Classes   The classes in a given suite have a lowercase "c" icon. Select a class, and you'll see the elements and properties related to that class. Often you can change those properties through a script (as mentioned, that's one main reason to create a script). As part of the class entry, you'll see the properties and the type of data that each property expects. Properties that can't accept changes from a script have (r/o) after them, meaning that they're read-only. In that case, you can only retrieve the value of that property, not set it. Still, that can be very useful in a script.

The first area where you might find the dictionary particularly useful is where most people start scripting—the Finder. The Finder has its own dictionary, which can be selected the same way other applications' dictionaries are selected, via the Script Editor. Opening the Finder's dictionary can be pretty revealing—the Finder offers a number of suites, including commands that affect your Mac, Finder items, folders, files, windows, and other classes and elements. Spend a little time exploring the Finder dictionary, and you'll see some amazing options for scripting the Finder. Experiment!

Scripting Additions

The third group of commands comes from *scripting additions*, which are special command libraries that can be added to a Macintosh to expand AppleScript's capabilities. These are compiled add-ons for AppleScript—usually written in C or C++—that extend AppleScript by giving you access to different commands. Scripting additions can be installed on your Mac and used for a variety of purposes to extend the usefulness of scripts that you create. Some of them help you build advanced interfaces (dialog boxes and windows) for your scripts, and others add commands that enable you to access network resources, retrieve items from databases, manipulate data stored in lists, activate Unix commands, and so on. In most cases, you'll use scripting additions only for scripts you don't intend to distribute to others, because you can't assume those other folks will have the same scripting extensions that you do. You can always share any freely available scripting additions, however, and if you're adept at AppleScript, you can write a script to install them in the necessary folder on other users' Macs.

There's a special case—Apple's own Standard Additions, which are included with all Macs. These commands are safe to use on any Mac having a compatible version of AppleScript, including Mac OS 9 and Mac OS X. In fact, you've already seen some of the Standard Additions commands, such as `display dialog` and `say`. Others offer even more powerful features, such as `choose file`, which enables you to get input from the user via an Open dialog box.

When Apple engineers decide to add commands to new implementations of AppleScript, they generally do so by adding commands to the Standard Additions scripting extension. These are commands that can be used throughout your scripts to perform special tasks that aren't built into AppleScript and aren't included with most applications. In fact, you don't have to put these commands between `tell` statements (that's true of any scripting extension command).

You can view the Standard Additions the same way you view other applications' AppleScript commands: open the dictionary. Using the Script Editor's File ➤ Open Dictionary command, locate the file `Standard Additions`. Open it, and you'll see the Standard Additions dictionary (see Figure 21.7).

FIGURE 21.7
The Standard Additions dictionary shows these powerful commands.

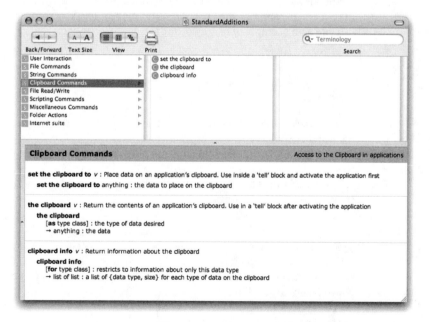

As far as other scripting additions go, you'll need to check out AppleScript-related websites in order to obtain native Mac OS X scripting additions files. Scripting additions from Mac OS 9 cannot be installed in Mac OS X—you'll need native (or, in some cases, hybrid) versions. Once you've downloaded a scripting additions file, you can install it in a folder called `Scripting Additions` in the main `Library` folder if you have an administrator account. (If the `Scripting Additions` folder doesn't exist, you can create it.) If you don't have an administrator account, you can create a folder called `Scripting Additions` in your personal `Library` folder and store the scripting additions file there—but remember that other users on your Mac won't be able to use any scripts that you create using commands from that scripting additions file.

Once `Scripting Additions` is created and you've installed a scripting additions file (they generally have the filename extension `.osax`), the Script Editor should be able to find it whenever you access the File ➤ Open Dictionary command. You can then open the new scripting additions dictionary in the Open Dictionary dialog box to see the new commands it offers.

TIP   Don't forget the URLs menu in Script Menu, where you'll find links to some popular AppleScript websites. Check them out for news on third-party scripting additions for Mac OS X. Also, `http://osaxen.com/` is a site dedicated to AppleScript scripting additions.

Shell Commands

Another type of command you can use in AppleScript is the *shell command*, which extends your range of possibilities almost infinitely. Shell commands are normally accessed from the Mac OS X Terminal. Since Mac OS X is built on a Unix foundation, you can run hundreds of built-in commands from the Terminal; you can also combine these commands in shell scripts. AppleScript, through the `do script with command` and `do shell script` commands, lets you combine these two types of commands.

Here's an example of using `do script with command`:

```
tell application "Terminal"
    activate
    do script with command "top"
end tell
```

This displays the `top` command in a new Terminal window, opening the Terminal if it is not running, and creating a new window with that command. You can run any command that you ordinarily access from the Terminal in this manner (see Chapter 22, "Terminal and the Command Line," for more on using the command line).

The `do shell script` command works a bit differently. You can specify either a shell script or a single command as follows:

```
do shell script "ls -l"
```

The difference is that the `do shell script` doesn't need to use the Terminal—it patches directly into the Unix underpinnings of Mac OS X. Because Terminal isn't activated, however, running the command in the previous example returns the contents of the current user's home folder to the Result pane of the Script Editor.

You can learn more about the `do shell script` command at `http://developer.apple.com/technotes/tn2002/tn2065.html`, as well as in the Standard Additions scripting dictionary under Miscellaneous Commands. And you can find information on `do script with command` at `www.apple.com/applescript/terminal/`.

What's Next?

In this chapter you learned a bit about AppleScript, the built-in programming language for Mac OS X. You saw how to launch AppleScript scripts, how to record them, and how to save scripts as text, compiled scripts, or applications. You also saw the basics of the AppleScript language, and you saw how to learn the commands that are available to you from AppleScript, your applications, and scripting additions.

In Chapter 22, you'll learn how to work at the Darwin command line—Mac OS X's Unix underbelly, accessible via the Terminal. You'll see what Darwin is and why you might be interested, and you'll learn the basics of working at the command line, including an introduction to shell scripting.

Terminal and the Command Line

While you generally only see the flashier part of Mac OS X—the sleek brushed-metal windows, the colorful icons, the Dock, and the menus—Tiger is really just a graphical layer built on top of a Unix-based operating system. Known as Darwin, the Unix foundation of Mac OS X is a rock-solid version of the venerable FreeBSD operating system. Available for free as an independent operating system, Darwin is *open source*, which means that the code used to create the system is accessible and changeable by anyone with the requisite know-how.

All of Mac OS X's graphical programs and tools, including applications such as Sherlock and Explorer, run on top of this Unix foundation; Darwin is always there, working silently in the background. You can directly access this part of Mac OS X using Terminal, the text-only command-line program that Apple provides with Mac OS X. While this Spartan interface may seem threatening to users familiar with windows and icons, it offers a great deal of flexibility and power. Apple has put a lot of work into making sure you don't have to use the command line directly so that you can stay in the more-familiar graphical areas of the OS. But there's a great deal of power "under the hood," if you're interested in exploring a bit, and becoming familiar with the command line can be useful should you ever need to go beyond the basics or perform troubleshooting operations on your Mac.

In this chapter:

◆ Why Use Terminal?

◆ Using Terminal

◆ Using the Command Line: A Quick Tour

◆ Unix Philosophy

◆ Useful Shell Tricks: `bash` and `tcsh`

◆ Terminal Preferences

◆ Unix Filesystem Differences

Why Use Terminal?

Most Mac users are more than happy to be able to point and click. You point to a file or menu, and then you click or double-click to activate it. In fact, in the early days of the Mac, this ease of use is what attracted people to the platform. To many, the idea of typing commands in an austere text window may seem a heresy; yet since the advent of Mac OS X, more and more Mac users have started dabbling with the seemingly esoteric command line.

Mac OS X is the easiest-to-use Unix-based operating system ever; yet most users never realize what's under the hood. If you want to go further and discover how to streamline some of your work and get more control over your Mac, using the command line is the best place to start.

In many cases, working on the command line can save you time. For instance, if you accidentally download a bunch of MP3s into your Documents folder, you could quickly make a new folder in your home folder by typing the command **mkdir ~/mp3** and pressing Return. Then, one more typed command, **mv ~/Documents/*.mp3 ~/mp3**, would move all those MP3 files to the new folder. Once you get used to the command line (assuming you *do* get used to the command line), you may never want to go back.

Additionally, the *shell* you use (a shell is a command-line interpreter, the program that reads the commands you type and returns the results of those commands) offers a great deal of power for automating tasks. Wildcards and loops (see the section "Shell Scripting and Behavior" in Chapter 23, "Command-Line Applications and Magic") turn many time-consuming operations on the Mac into single commands or simple combinations. Another major benefit of shell scripts is that they don't require physical proximity. Unix systems are designed to be usable and manageable from anywhere on the Internet. This offers a great deal of power, from the ability to access home files from work to full-featured remote troubleshooting, without additional software.

There are some rough edges in Mac OS X. If you have a permissions problem, or if Apple hasn't yet provided a graphical tool to manage something you need to do, you may appreciate the capability to log in to Terminal, use the sudo (*substitute user do*) command to gain root access, and fix the problem directly. (Some of these workarounds are suggested in Chapter 28, "Solving System-Level Problems," and Chapter 29, "Typical Problems and Solutions," as well as elsewhere in this book.) Apple has done a great job of insulating the Aqua experience from the underlying nuts and bolts, but the command line still offers some capabilities that aren't yet mature on the graphical side.

Finally, with the command line, you can work with free open-source programs such as the following:

Apache This is the world's most popular web server (already included with Mac OS X and discussed in Chapter 24, "Web Serving and Net Security").

analog A powerful, flexible program to analyze web logs, telling you who's been accessing your Apache websites, analog generates an HTML document that can be displayed in any web browser.

Ghostscript A tool for interpreting, displaying, and printing PostScript files. Ghostscript can also work with PDF files and convert files between PostScript and PDF formats.

LaTeX LaTeX is a high-quality typesetting system, designed for the production of technical and scientific documentation. LaTeX is the de facto standard for the communication and publication of scientific documents.

Samba Samba is a full-featured Windows file server and client that lets a Unix/Darwin/Mac OS X computer participate in a Windows network just like a Windows computer. (For more information on Samba, see Chapter 24.)

mrtg This is a charting program that monitors and graphs network activity.

The command line therefore lets you accomplish many tasks that you would otherwise not be able to do. In some cases, the command line gives you access to the innards of Mac OS X; in others, it lets you run programs that offer you much more power and flexibility than graphical programs. But in all cases, learning the command line helps you have more control over your Mac. While you certainly won't use the command line all the time, it's good to know how to use it for specific tasks to save time and get your work done more efficiently.

Using Terminal

To access the command line on a Mac OS X system, first log in to Mac OS X, just as you would to use Mac OS X normally. Then go to the Utilities folder inside the main Applications folder, find the Terminal icon, and double-click it to launch Terminal.

When you open Terminal, you'll see a simple window containing a *prompt* and a cursor. The standard prompt is something like this: Kirks-iMac:~ kirk$. This is your computer's name (which you can change in the Sharing pane of the System Preferences), followed by the current working directory. (In this example, it's ~, a shortcut for your home directory, followed by your username, followed by $). As you type commands, they'll appear after the prompt, and once you press Return, the system's responses will follow your commands. When execution is complete, the system will show another prompt so that you'll know you can type another command.

NOTE When Apple released Mac OS X 10.3 (Panther), they made a big change to the default Terminal behavior. In early versions of Mac OS X, the default shell was tcsh; starting with Panther, the default shell became bash. Users who upgraded from previous versions of Mac OS X would still see tcsh; Apple assumed that users may have gotten familiar with this shell and had their own custom settings, so Apple only changed this shell for new accounts created under Panther. With Tiger, Apple continues to use bash as the default shell. For this reason, we'll only look at using bash in this and the following chapter.

Figure 22.1 shows what a Terminal window looks like. In this figure, note that two commands have been issued: the pwd command, which displays the current working directory, and the ls -l command, which displays a "long list" of the files in the current directory. In each case, you type the command and then press Return.

FIGURE 22.1

A Terminal window showing some simple commands and their output. Note the prompt Kirks-iMac:~ kirk$ followed by typed commands.

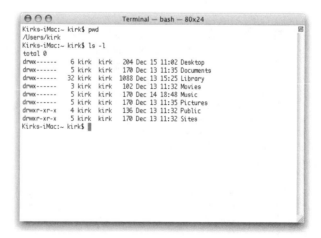

Quitting Terminal

To leave Terminal, type **exit** and press Return to log out of the Terminal session and then close the window (if Terminal doesn't automatically close it for you when the session is ended). If you're using other programs with their own command-line interfaces, such as Telnet, SSH, and FTP, you may have to exit multiple times to get all the way out. You also can use the File ➤ Close command, the Terminal ➤ Quit Terminal command, or their standard keyboard shortcuts (⌘W and ⌘Q), but be careful not to break a connection without logging out first. Doing so could abruptly shut down any programs or processes that you've started from Terminal, possibly causing problems to files. This is unlikely, but it's still good practice to log out before closing shell windows.

Using the Command Line: A Quick Tour

Terminal is the application that you'll use (most of the time) to access the command-line layer of Mac OS X. Whenever you access the command line via Terminal, you do so through a shell. The shell is responsible for displaying the command-line prompt, accepting your input, and returning results. It's the user interface for working with the command line. As you'll see later in this chapter, you can change your shell and even program it to perform commands automatically.

If you aren't familiar with shells and shell commands, try following these steps to get a feel for some basic commands and how the command line works. More explanation of these commands appears in the sections that follow. For now, though, you can perform this quick run-through.

First, open Terminal and make sure a Terminal window is open. (If one isn't open, select File ➤ New Shell.) If you've already got a Terminal window open and have typed commands, close it and open a new window; this ensures that you see the same things we explain after you type these commands. After each command, press Return.

pwd Just to make sure you know where you are, type this command (which stands for *print working directory*). The shell will return the full path of that directory, or /Users/[your user name]. This command is like a "You are here" spot on a map; you can always type it to find out where you are in your filesystem.

NOTE It's conventional in Unix-based environments to use the term *directories* to refer to what the Mac OS calls "folders." We'll use that convention here, because many commands (such as pwd and cd) have "directory" as part of their name or definition. Just remember that the terms *directory* and *folder* refer to the same thing.

ls This command shows (lists) the contents of a directory. If you've just started a Terminal session, you'll see the contents of your home directory:

```
Desktop      Library     Music      Public
Documents    Movies      Pictures   Sites
```

ls -al This command displays more information about the items in the current directory (the -1 option), along with some additional items that don't show up when you use the normal ls command (the -a option; note that you can put two options together following a single hyphen):

```
total 40
drwxr-xr-x  13 kirk   kirk       442 Dec 14 17:33 .
drwxrwxr-t  10 root   admin      340 Dec 13 15:36 ..
-rw-r--r--   1 kirk   kirk         3 Dec 13 11:32 .CFUserTextEncoding
-rw-r--r--   1 kirk   kirk     12292 Dec 15 10:00 .DS_Store
drwx------   5 kirk   kirk       170 Dec 15 09:39 .Trash
drwx------   5 kirk   kirk       170 Dec 15 10:00 Desktop
drwx------   5 kirk   kirk       170 Dec 13 11:35 Documents
drwx------  32 kirk   kirk      1088 Dec 13 15:25 Library
drwx------   3 kirk   kirk       102 Dec 13 11:32 Movies
drwx------   5 kirk   kirk       170 Dec 14 18:48 Music
drwx------   5 kirk   kirk       170 Dec 13 11:35 Pictures
drwxr-xr-x   4 kirk   kirk       136 Dec 13 11:32 Public
drwxr-xr-x   5 kirk   kirk       170 Dec 13 11:32 Sites
```

cd Documents   This moves you into your Documents directory.

ls   Now this command lists the contents of your Documents directory. (There may not be anything here yet, particularly if you've just installed Mac OS X.)

cd ..   This command moves you up one level. This is a useful shortcut; when you've moved into a directory (such as Documents, as in this example) you can get back to its parent directory by typing just a few characters. You can even type ../.. to move up two levels in the filesystem.

mkdir Test   This creates a new directory called Test in the current working directory.

ls   Now the ls command will display a list of all the directories, including the new directory Test that you just created.

rmdir Test   This command removes, or deletes, the directory Test that you just created.

cd /Users   This takes you to the /Users directory of your Mac; this is where Mac OS X stores all the users' home folders. If you have more than one user on your Mac, you can type **ls** to see a list of these home folders. (Even if you are the only user on your Mac, you'll see your home folder plus an additional Shared directory.)

Notice that this command contains a slash before the name of the directory; this means it is an *absolute* file path. The / is the *root* of your filesystem, or the top point. So typing **cd /Users** tells the shell to look for a Users directory at the very top of the filesystem. If you had typed the same command without the slash, as earlier with cd Documents, the shell only looks in the current working directory.

That's all it takes to move through your folder hierarchy using typed commands. Next, we'll move on to explain some of those commands and see what else can be accomplished.

Useful Terminal Tips

You can resize Terminal windows just like other Mac windows. When resizing, you'll see that the title bar shows two numbers separated by an ×; these are the width and height of the window in characters.

It's often convenient to make Terminal windows wider for certain commands so that you can see more text without wrapping, or taller to see more text without scrolling.

Terminal supports the standard Edit ➤ Copy and Edit ➤ Paste commands to move text into and out of the Mac clipboard. You can drag an item from a Finder window into Terminal—the path to the dragged item is appended to whatever you've typed at the command line—and you can drag text out of Terminal windows to create text clippings.

Terminal's Edit ➤ Find ➤ Find command opens a dialog box where you can enter a keyword to search for in the window buffer (the area you can scroll back through to see a history of your actions). Once you've entered a keyword, you can use the Edit ➤ Find ➤ Find Next (⌘G) and Edit ➤ Find ➤ Find Previous (⌘Shift+G) commands to search again. When you close the window, though, its buffer is lost unless you save it first. The File ➤ Save Text As and File ➤ Save Selected Text As commands also enable you to save the whole session or selection as a text file. This is useful for keeping track of what you've done or for recording interesting program output. The File ➤ Save command can be used to store the positions and settings of one or more open windows. By checking the Open This File When Terminal Starts Up check box, you can save your preferred layout for future use.

Keyboard shortcuts for scrolling are plentiful: Press ⌘↑ and ⌘↓ to scroll up and down by line, press Page Up or Page Down to scroll by screen, and press Home or End to go to the top or bottom of the window buffer.

Terminal can use any installed font, but monospaced fonts such as Monaco and Courier generally work best. To change fonts, select Terminal ➤ Window Settings. In the Terminal Inspector window, choose Display from the drop-down menu. Click the Set Font button to change the font used in the Terminal window.

Terminal is a minimalist program; its purpose is to be a window or portal of sorts that enables you to work on the command line, not to be interesting itself. Terminal's features are focused on connecting the shell with the rest of your system and on being unobtrusive.

Terminal will happily open multiple windows for you; this is often useful for reading directory listings or documentation with the man command (Unix's basic help tool) in one window, while acting on this information in another. It's also often convenient to dedicate one window to the local shell and use other windows for commands that work on other machines, such as telnet, ssh, and ftp, or on other users, perhaps using sudo.

To switch between windows, press ⌘*number*, where *number* is the number of the window—you'll find this number in the Window menu—or press ⌘← and ⌘→, also the standard Command+`, will cycle through open windows in numerical order.

Working on the Command Line

To use Terminal, you'll probably want to memorize a few commands. (You could conceivably post the commands on a sticky note next to your monitor, but you'll find that they become natural the more you use the command line.) Basic Terminal commands include

- ◆ pwd (print working directory) to tell you where you are

- ◆ cd (change directory) to move around

- ◆ ls to list the files in a directory

- ◆ exit to log out (finish using Terminal and disconnect)

Working with Terminal, you have access to hundreds of commands, including telnet and ftp, as described in Chapter 17, "Accessing Network Volumes." Because Terminal gives you access to standard Unix-based commands included with Mac OS X, a large number of reference books for these commands are available, including Kirk McElhearn's *The Mac OS X Command Line: Unix Under the Hood*, published by Sybex, which looks specifically at using the command line in a Mac OS X context.

As a general rule, whenever you type something at a shell prompt, the first word you type on the line is a command, and the rest of the line consists of arguments and options. Most commands, including `telnet` and `ftp`, are actually names of programs. When you type such a command, the shell finds the program you've named and starts it—like double-clicking a program in the Finder.

NOTE If you've worked with Unix-based operating systems in the past, you may already be aware of their *case sensitivity*, meaning their interpretation of an uppercase and lowercase letter as two distinct characters. (For instance, on many Unix systems, the file `MyFile` and `myFile` could both be saved in the same folder, which you couldn't do on a Mac.) With Mac OS X, you generally don't have to worry about case sensitivity because it's installed on a Mac filesystem (HFS+). If you happen to be using a UFS-formatted volume for your Mac OS X installation, then case sensitivity will be an issue. (See the section "Case Sensitivity" later in this chapter and Appendix A, "Getting Installed and Set Up," for details.)

To give these programs additional information, you can add *arguments* after the command's name. Any arguments you type are passed on to the program, which then tries to figure out exactly what you wanted from the arguments. For example, if you type `ls /`, the `ls` program displays the contents of /, which is the system's root directory, the top level of the filesystem.

Programs also take options, which modify the processing of arguments and normally start with a hyphen (-). For instance, typing `ls -l /` displays a longer listing because of the `-l` option.

To find a program's location on your hard disk from just its name, use the `which` command, which accepts a command name as its argument and responds by showing you its location, called a *path*. For more on paths, see the section "Unix Filesystem Differences" later in this chapter.

As mentioned earlier, the program that accepts your typing and invokes other commands is called the shell. It's similar to the Finder in Mac OS X in that its main purpose is to control other programs. Like the Finder, shells have commands built into them for managing files and folders. Many of the simplest and most-used commands, such as `cd` and `ls`, are *builtins*. To see a list of builtins, use the `help` command. Figure 22.2 shows the response to the `help` command from the default shell, which is named `bash`. (If you use the `tcsh` shell, the `builtins` command gives you the same information.)

FIGURE 22.2

The output from bash's help command

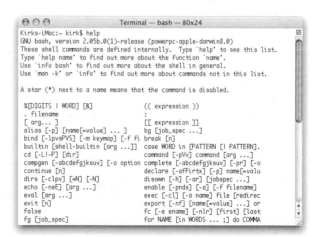

WARNING Some builtins are different from shell to shell. In particular, the csh-style (such as tcsh) and sh-style (such as bash) shells use different loop keywords and syntax to set variables. More information is available in the sections "Terminal Preferences" later in this chapter and "Shell Scripting and Behavior" in Chapter 23.

Some Basic Commands

Mac OS X includes commands to help you navigate around your Mac (and in some cases, other computers on a network), as well as commands that let you manage files. You can move and copy files and directories, get information about them, list them, and delete them. In fact, these commands together constitute something comparable to the Mac Finder. Here are a few basic commands, including some you've already seen:

pwd Print working directory. pwd shows you where you are.

cd Change directory. cd moves to the specified directory (see the later section "Unix Filesystem Differences"). If you type **cd** with no arguments and then press Return, it takes you to your personal home directory. An example with arguments is cd /Applications, which would move you to the main Applications directory on your startup disk. If you type **cd ..**, this moves you to the parent directory of the current working directory. And if you type **cd -**, you move back to the previous directory, wherever it is on your filesystem.

ls List files and directories. This command offers extensive options, which you can see by reading its manual page (type **man ls** and press Return).

cat Display one or more files. cat is a simple command; it spits out the whole file on-screen, and if you provide multiple files, it displays them all consecutively. Example: cat file.txt.

more Display a file on-screen, pausing after each screen of text. Press the spacebar to page through the file and press Q to stop. Additionally, if you type a slash (/) followed by some text and then press Return, more will search for the text you've typed. The more command is much more convenient than cat for reading long files. Example: more Walden.txt (see Figure 22.3).

FIGURE 22.3
Here's an example of the more command in action, which is useful for reading multiple screens of text.

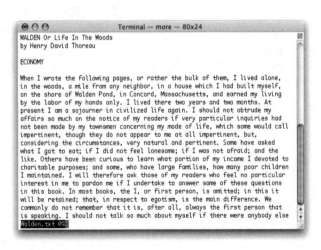

man   View online documentation (the manual) for a command. man requires an argument—the command to read about. man is based on more (or sometimes on its more powerful cousin, less), and it includes more's commands for paging through the file. The man command is one of the most useful when you're getting to know the command line. Each command's manual page explains the basics of a command, the options available, the arguments you can or must use, and often examples of using the command. Examples:

- ◆   man ftp shows information about the FTP program.

- ◆   man man shows information about the man command itself.

cp   Copy files. To copy directories and all files inside them, use cp -R (recursive). If the last argument is a directory, copies of the files specified by the other arguments are created in that directory. If not, the first argument is copied to the path specified by the second argument. Examples:

- ◆   cp *.txt ~/Documents/. This command copies all files that end in .txt to the Documents folder inside your home folder.

- ◆   cp readme.txt info.txt. This copies the contents of the file readme.txt to a file called info.txt, essentially making a copy of the file with a new name.

TIP   The first cp example uses the asterisk (*) as a *wildcard*; this means simply that the shell fills in any results that match the rest of the filename as entered. For *.txt, all files that end in .txt would be selected, such as readme.txt, notes.txt, and memo.txt. Similarly, * alone would select all the files in the current directory. Wildcards can be used with many commands, such as ls *.txt or ls mem* (which would return memo.txt, memory, and so on).

mv   Move or rename files and directories. This command uses source and destination arguments, like cp. Example: mv storytext.rtf ~/web.

WARNING   If the second argument for mv (or cp, for that matter) isn't a valid directory (for example, mv memo.rtf memos, where memos is not a valid directory name), the file will be "moved" into a *file* named by that second argument. If a file with that name already exists (if there is already a file called memos), it will normally be replaced with the file you're moving (memo.rtf) without warning. You can always add the -i (interactive) option to get a warning before overwriting files.

rm   Remove files and directories. Be careful with this one! Examples:

- ◆   rm memo.rtf

- ◆   rm *.rtf

To delete a folder that contains files, you use the -R flag for "recursive" deletion as in rm -R ~/Downloads/. Use rm -i (the interactive option) to have the command ask for confirmation for each file you remove. Using the rm command is not like moving files to the Trash, where you can recover them in case of error. The rm command deletes files *immediately*. We recommend using this option studiously; if you accidentally remove files with this command, you can't get them back.

mkdir   Make a directory. Examples:

- ◆   mkdir Movies

- ◆   mkdir ~/Documents/Movies/

rmdir Remove a directory. The `rmdir` command works only on empty directories, because `rm -R directory` removes a directory and all its contents. (Again, be careful!) Example: `rmdir ~/Documents/Movies/`.

exit Log out. (Many programs use `exit`; some use `quit`.)

Try using these basic commands to explore your Mac's filesystem a bit, as well as to create and alter files and folders in your home folder hierarchy. You'll find that getting used to some of the commands—particularly in conjunction with wildcards—can make certain operations easier, such as moving or deleting many files at once.

More Commands

After you've familiarized yourself with the basic commands, try these. A bit more involved, the following commands enable you to customize your environment, selectively extract information from files, find files, examine volumes, and do a bit of account management.

alias `alias` enables you to create your own commands. With no arguments, `alias` shows you aliases that have already been defined; with one argument, `alias` shows what the specified `alias` is defined to do; with two arguments, `alias` defines the first argument as a private command to execute the full command line specified by the second argument. Figure 22.4 shows the creation of an alias, the use of that alias, and then a listing of aliases.

FIGURE 22.4
Defining an alias, using that alias, and listing all defined aliases

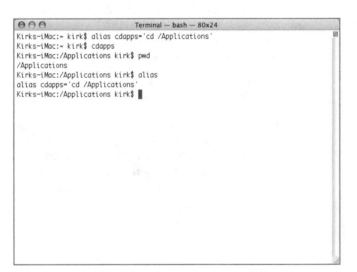

WARNING The `alias` command works slightly differently under other shells such as `tcsh`. See `man tcsh` for more on using aliases with this shell.

head Display the first few lines of a file. The syntax is `head -10` *myfile*, where *myfile* is the name of the file, and the number (after the hyphen) specifies how many lines to display.

tail Display the last few lines of a file. Its syntax is very similar to that of `head`. The `tail` command is particularly useful for displaying recent events in log files, many of which reside in the directory `/var/log`.

grep   grep is a powerful and flexible search command. In the simplest case, grep searches a single file for a specified string. It also can search multiple files, search for lines that don't match the search string, search with or without case sensitivity, and do wildcard searches. grep's syntax is complicated, but it is explained by man grep; it may be familiar to you if you've used other programs that support grep syntax, such as the popular Macintosh text editor BBEdit.

locate   locate is a simple tool for finding files. Unix has a powerful and confusing find command to search for specified files; the locate command uses a database and works very quickly, much like Spotlight does in the GUI. Just provide part or all of a file path as an argument, and locate will list all files on the system that match. Be careful with locate, though; it can return a lot of matches, especially if your search string matches a directory containing many files. The command locate *searchstring* | more passes the output from locate to the program for the more command, letting you page through the results and quit when you're done. Pipes (|) are discussed in the section "Shell Scripting and Behavior" in Chapter 23.

WARNING   The locate command uses a database that's automatically updated every week. This means that it won't find files added since the last update, and if you don't leave Mac OS X running overnight, the database won't get updated. For more on scheduled tasks, use man cron, man crontab, more /etc/crontab, and more /etc/weekly. Since this database is not created when you install Mac OS X, you may want to do this yourself. If you have an administrator account, run sudo periodic weekly, which does weekly maintenance tasks, including the creation of a locate database. You can run this command again any time you want to update this database. See Chapter 23 for more information about crontab editing.

df -H   Show all mounted disks and how much space they have free in kilobytes, megabytes, and gigabytes.

du -h   Show disk usage for the specified item(s) and each item inside any directories.

sudo   Using sudo, users with administrator accounts can execute commands as though they had logged in as someone else (normally root). When you use sudo, you'll be asked for your own password, and sudo will then run the rest of the command as root. See the section "Unix Philosophy" later in this chapter, for more on when to use root access. In the default configuration of Mac OS X, only administrators can use sudo.

TIP   One interesting command available in Mac OS X that is not found on other Unix systems is open. This curious command acts like the command-line equivalent of a double-click. If you want to open a file in the Finder, but do so from Terminal, use open *filename*. This tells the Finder to open the file as it would if you had double-clicked the file. You can also open a directory in this way: open ~/Documents, for example, opens your Documents folder in a new Finder window. And open . opens the current working directory; this lets you, for example, open a normally hidden directory to edit a file in a GUI text editor, copy the file in the Finder, or perform other operations in the Finder.

Advanced Commands

The following commands are a bit more involved and powerful. (In fact, they're all programs instead of shell builtins.) They enable you to manage files and archives and connect to other machines. You may be familiar with these capabilities from Macintosh programs with similar capabilities.

telnet   Log in to another computer. The telnet command normally is used with a single argument—the hostname of the computer to connect to. This command is not used very much any more, since it is inherently insecure. See Chapter17 for more information about this command.

ftp   Connect to another computer to transfer files. Like `telnet`, `ftp` typically takes a hostname as an argument. See Chapter 17 for more on `ftp`.

ssh   Establish an encrypted connection to another computer. The `ssh` command is basically a secure version of `telnet`, but it can also be used to provide encryption capabilities to other programs. You should use `ssh` instead of `telnet` whenever possible, and `scp` or `sftp` instead of `ftp`. These two commands are part of the `ssh` package, replacing `rcp` and `ftp`, respectively, with secure commands that take advantage of `ssh` encryption. The `ssh` tools are also discussed in Chapter 17.

nano   Edit the specified file. (`nano` is a version of `pico`; if you are familiar with Pico, you can still just type `pico` in Terminal; this is a hard link to `nano`.) The `nano` command is a simple Unix text editor with all the basic features. It's roughly comparable to TextEdit in that it's fine for simple writing or editing tasks but is much less powerful than other programs such as BBEdit and the notoriously complicated Emacs editing environment. One of the good things about `nano` is that it always shows basic Ctrl+*key* shortcuts at the bottom of the screen, which makes it much easier to use than Emacs or Vi. Text editors are discussed in a bit more detail in Chapter 23.

tar   Tape archive command. This is a complex but powerful tool for combining multiple files into a single archive (like StuffIt, but without compression). To "untar" an archive, first copy it into its own subdirectory, and then `cd` into that subdirectory and use `tar -xf archive.tar` to unpack the contents into the subdirectory (where `archive.tar` represents the name of the archive to unpack).

gzip   GNU compression program. The `gzip` command compresses individual files, but be forewarned that it removes the original. The Mac OS X `tar` command includes a very useful `-z` option to compress or uncompress archives with `gzip`. TAR archives are also called "tarballs," and when compressed, they usually have either `.tgz` or `.tar.gz` as a suffix. To uncompress a tarball, use the command `tar -xzf archive.tgz`. The `tar` and `gzip` commands are important for two main reasons. First, they are standards for compressing and uncompressing Unix freeware and shareware software that you'll find on the Internet. Second, as command-line utilities, they can be controlled remotely; you can log in to another computer, "tar up" a directory you want, and FTP the tarball to your own Mac—or "untar" a tarball on a remote system. This is important when you work with more than one machine. The command to uncompress a gzipped file is `gunzip`.

TIP   The combination of `tar` and `gzip` can be very convenient for creating archives of important files quickly. For instance, you could type `tar -czf backup.tgz ~/Documents` to create a compressed archive of your `Documents` folder. You could then copy that archive to a remote server or external disk as a backup.

Unix Philosophy

Unix has been around much longer than the Mac OS, and like the Mac, it has a rich history and some basic philosophy that's common among its users. Here are some of the highlights, to help you understand the concepts and attitudes behind the command line:

Programming is good for you.   Unix was originally a research project and software development environment. The creators were all programmers who believed programming was good mental exercise. This is part of the reason so many good compilers and software development tools exist for Unix and why the shell is fundamentally a programming environment, unlike the Finder or Windows Explorer.

The shell is an interpreter.   Each shell can run interactively to process commands one at a time or as an interpreter to process files of commands, called *scripts*. This makes programming the same as daily use, which encourages people to program.

The shell is a launcher.   The shell has lots of built-in commands, but it's fundamentally an interface that enables you to run other programs. Builtins have been added where appropriate to facilitate use of these external programs and to manage shell features (such as command-line editing and the command history).

Wasted time is bad.   The original Unix machines were much slower than current systems, and as you may have noticed, command-line computing requires a lot of typing. As a result, and with the realization that Unix users use the same commands over and over, the developers abbreviated many command, file, and directory names. Thus "list" became `ls`, "user" became `usr`, and "temporary space" became `tmp`. Although it's a bit harder to learn the abbreviations, with serious use, the time saved becomes significant.

Don't assume high-end hardware.   Many early Unix systems were used primarily through paper-based terminals—there were no graphics and not even backspacing! As a result, the most basic tools are line based. Vi (the "visual interactive editor") and Sed (the "stream editor," a find-and-replace tool) are derived from Ed, a line-based editor. Ed required the user to specify one line to be edited at a time. While Unix systems now assume that terminals have cursor control, and line printer support isn't a major issue, Unix has retained support for very basic interfaces. This provides great power without requiring much bandwidth or a complicated interface.

Root is unrestricted and dangerous.   Unix administrators have both a personal account and a separate Root account. Personal accounts are for general day-to-day use, and the Root account is used for system management. Root has few or no restrictions on its capabilities, which means that it's easy to destroy a system as root, and root access must be protected from malicious users.

Simple tools can be connected for complex tasks.   The pipe (|) enables several simpler programs to be chained together to perform complex actions. The simple tools are easier to use and maintain than custom programs written for each task, and shell scripting gives them great power and flexibility.

Don't second-guess the user.   The Mac OS includes lots of warnings—before erasing a disk, after a crash, before overwriting files, before emptying the Trash, and so on. Unix systems have fewer warnings. As a result, it's easier to destroy files irrevocably or (as root) to damage your system. Be careful not to misspell filenames and avoid mistyping any commands that remove or move files, because it's easy to `rm` a file you need or to `cp` one file over another one you want, inadvertently replacing the second file.

Computers are good; networks are great.   One of the reasons the Internet is based largely on Unix programs and technologies is that Unix has long been network friendly, and Unix users have understood that networked computers are much more useful than isolated ones. Mac OS X's fundamental orientation toward TCP/IP, options such as Personal Web Sharing (based on Apache), and the inclusion of Software Update show progress in this direction, as Unix systems historically have made much heavier use of networks.

Everything is a file.   Files are used to represent disks, directories, data streams, and even running programs under Unix. This improves consistency and flexibility, since the same commands apply to "regular" files, directories, devices, input and output, and other filesystem objects.

Useful Shell Tricks: *bash* and *tcsh*

The oldest Unix shell in active use is sh. There are several later shells, such as bash, that attempt to be backward compatible, meaning that anything that works in sh should work in its descendants. The other major family of shells is derived from csh (the "C shell"), and its descendants, including tcsh, are generally backward compatible with the original csh syntax.

As we mentioned earlier in this chapter, Mac OS X uses bash as its default shell but used tcsh in earlier Mac OS X versions (through 10.2). If you create a new installation, the system gives you bash as your shell; if you upgrade an old installation and had used tcsh, that will remain as your shell. And if you create new accounts under Mac OS X 10.4, you'll get bash.

Proponents debate the merits of each shell vigorously, but what is best for you is what you are most familiar or most comfortable with. If you come from a Linux background, where bash is more common, you'll be right at home using bash on Mac OS X—there's no difference. But if your background was on other Unix systems, with csh or tcsh, you can stick with one of those shells. To find out more about the differences between these shells and other shells, read the frequently asked questions document "UNIX Shell Differences and How to Change Your Shell" (www.faqs.org/faqs/unix-faq/shell/shell-differences/), which, while somewhat out of date, covers the main differences between the principal shells.

The easiest way to change shells is to use the chsh command: type **chsh -s tcsh [*username*]** and press Return. You can change this for your account, or, if you are an administrator, change it for any user's account. Another way to work with a different shell is to simply type the new shell's name at a Terminal prompt and then press Enter, or set a specific shell to run as a command in the Terminal preferences window. See the next section, "Terminal Preferences," for more on Terminal preferences.

Most of their functions are similar, though, and unless you get into shell scripting, you won't need to worry too much. Setting aliases and shell variables are a bit different, and as you can see right away, the shell prompts are different. But overall, for interactive work (you issue commands and read or act on the results), the differences are moot.

Because the shells and the command line are the primary interface to Unix-based systems, a lot of work has gone into making shells such as bash and tcsh powerful, fast, and convenient. You can see the complete reference for the tcsh shell by typing the command **man tcsh**, and for the bash shell by typing **man bash**, at a command prompt and pressing Return. Some highlights are these:

◆ *Command-line editing* enables you to make changes, such as fixing typos and changing arguments, using the arrow keys and Delete key on your keyboard. There also are several keyboard shortcuts to facilitate editing:

　◆ Ctrl+A moves the cursor to the beginning of the line.

　◆ Ctrl+E moves it to the end.

　◆ Ctrl+U clears everything back to the beginning of the line.

These conventions are the same in bash and tcsh, and they are available in many different programs. bash has two powerful advantages for advanced editing: It offers editing modes that use commands similar to the main Unix text editors (emacs and vi), and it lets you edit commands in your command history (see the next bullet).

◆ The *command history* stores your most recent commands; by default, bash stores the last 500 commands and tcsh stores the last 100 commands. You can use the up arrow to view previous commands and the down arrow to move forward (back toward more recent commands). Once you find the desired command, you can press Return to execute it again, as though you had typed it from the keyboard, or you can edit the command to do something slightly different. To see saved commands, use the history built-in command. This lists all saved commands, along with the time of day they were executed (tcsh only) and an identifying number for each line. You can use these command numbers to invoke saved commands rather than press the up arrow dozens of times. For example, an exclamation point followed by the number 50 (!50) would repeat command number 50 from the history. An exclamation point followed by letters repeats the most recent command that started with those letters—for example, !ft would repeat the last ftp command. Figure 22.5 shows part of a history listing, with command numbers.

FIGURE 22.5
The end of a history listing

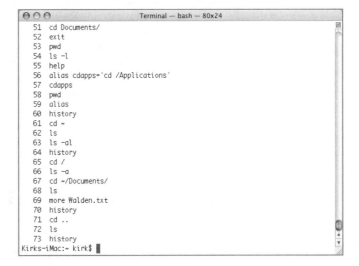

- bash and tcsh offer *filename completion*. This is a tremendous time-saver. When you type the beginning of a word and press the Tab key, either of these shells will look for complete words you might have started. If they find a single match, they fill in the rest; if they find multiple matches, they fill in the rest until the names diverge from the characters you typed; if they don't know which match is desired, they list the possible matches. Automatic completion works with commands (first word on the line), files and directories (one directory level at a time), and variables.

- Both the bash and tcsh shells use several special characters in addition to the space. Sometimes it's necessary to use one of these characters as itself instead of for its special function; this is called "escaping" or "protecting" characters. To tell tcsh to ignore the special meaning of such a character, precede it with a backslash (\). In some cases, double straight quotes (") and single straight quotes (') work as well, but a backslash is the most reliable.

Terminal Preferences

The Terminal ➤ Window Settings menu command provides a great deal of flexibility. This brings up the Terminal Inspector, which enables you to change quite a few settings. Choose Display from the menu in the Terminal Inspector, and you'll see the Set Font button (toward the middle), which you can click to change the font used in Terminal windows. The default is Monaco Regular 10.0, which fits four windows on a 1024 × 768 display with minimal overlap. If you spend a lot of time in Terminal, you will probably find such a layout to be very useful; additional windows might be logged in to another computer, displaying documentation, or logged in to another account. However, if you have poor eyesight, you will find it more practical to increase the font size—you can open as many windows as you need and switch among them using Terminal's Window menu.

NOTE   You also can choose Font ➢ Show Fonts to see the Fonts palette for changing the current font family or style.

Choose Window from the Terminal Inspector's menu, and you'll see Dimension boxes that enable you to set the size of new windows by entering their width in Columns and Rows. 80 × 24 is the standard width and height for a Terminal window. Since it's easy to resize windows after opening them, you probably won't need to change these settings.

Figure 22.6 shows the layout of Terminal's window settings. Note the menu at the top, which you can use to see different groupings of options. When you finish making changes, click the window's Close button.

FIGURE 22.6
The Window panel of
the Terminal Inspector
dialog box

TIP   The Active Process Name option in the Window pane of Terminal Inspector is an interesting one—it shows the current process in the title bar of the Terminal window, making it possible to tell at a glance what application or process is running in that window.

Unix Filesystem Differences

Mac OS X is basically a Unix-like system with lots of enhancements to make it suitable as the foundation for an advanced graphical operating system. Unix systems have several differences that are important when working on the command line. You won't need to know any of these if you only work in the Finder, but once you fire up Terminal, you'll need to bear in mind that these differences are important.

As noted earlier, one basic but minor difference is in terminology: What Mac OS calls "folders," Unix calls "directories." They're the same thing, but the terminology is different.

File Paths

The Mac filesystem, HFS+, allows any characters except colons in filenames. Colons (:) are not allowed because they're *delimiters*—they separate directories in paths. If you type a colon when naming a file or folder in Mac OS 9's Finder, the Finder inserts a dash instead. The HFS+ path Macintosh HD:System Folder:Preferences:Interarchy: refers to a folder named Interarchy inside a folder named Preferences, inside System Folder, on the disk Macintosh HD.

In Unix filesystems, the slash (/) is the delimiter, so the preceding path would appear as System Folder/Preferences/Interarchy/. The slash at the beginning means that this is an *absolute* path— expressed in terms of the root (top level) of the filesystem. Paths that *don't* start with a slash are *relative*—expressed in terms of the current working directory. (You can always find out what this is by typing the pwd command.) When you open a new Terminal window, the current working directory is set to your home directory—normally something like /Users/kirk/ or /Users/todd/. This means that if you type **ls Documents** when logged in as user kirk, you get back a listing of /Users/kirk/Documents. In contrast, typing **ls /Documents** would attempt to list a directory named Documents in the root directory on your disk.

Unix has several other useful filename conventions you should know about. Since spaces normally separate arguments, but filenames can contain spaces, we need a way to "protect" spaces. Without such protection, ls System Folder would try to list two items—System and Folder.

There are two ways to protect or escape actual spaces in pathnames and elsewhere on command lines. One way is to put a backslash before the space, and the other is to put quotes around the whole path. Thus, both ls System\ Folder and ls 'System Folder' list a single folder named System Folder in the current directory.

Fortunately, bash and tcsh can handle spaces in filenames, so if you type part of a filename that contains spaces and then use filename completion with the Tab key, they escape the spaces for you (see the section "Useful Shell Tricks: bash and tcsh" earlier in this chapter, for more on filename completion).

The dot-slash combination (./) refers to the current directory; this is useful for being clear about where a file is and for running programs not in your path (see the next section). The dot-dot-slash combination (../) refers to the parent of the current directory; it's essential for navigating around software packages that use multiple directories (see the section "Aliases versus Links" later in this chapter for more on ./ and ../).

The tilde (~) is used to refer to user home directories, so ~kirk/Documents represents the Documents folder inside user kirk's home directory, wherever that may be on the system. It's more common to use paths such as ~/Documents, which means *my* Documents folder (equivalent to /Users/kirk/Documents/ if you're logged in as user kirk).

NOTE If you have a file that's visible in a Finder window and you want its path, you can drag the file's icon to the Terminal, and the file's path will be inserted at the cursor.

Shells also perform something called *wildcard expansion*, which can save a lot of typing. If you put an asterisk (*) in a path, the shell replaces that path with all the filenames that match the specified pattern. This is very convenient for interactive use, as in ls *.jpg to list all files that end in .jpg or rm doc*.* to remove all files that start with the letters doc.

Wildcard expansion is also important for shell scripting because it enables scripts to specify files to process at runtime selectively and intelligently, even if those files don't exist when the script is written.

The other wildcard is the question mark (?), which matches any single character but only one character. (For instance, rm *.ex? would delete all files that end in .exe, .ext and .exs, but not just .ex.)

The *PATH* Variable

Mac OS X maintains an invisible database of all available application programs and what types of files they can handle, so when you double-click a Microsoft Word document, it automatically opens in Word. Unix systems, including the Unix layer of Mac OS X, use an older mechanism called the *PATH variable*.

In Mac OS X, the ls program is installed as /bin/ls, the more program is /usr/bin/more, and so on, with different programs stored in different directories and subdirectories all over your hard disk. Obviously, typing full paths for every command would be inconvenient, so each shell maintains a PATH variable containing places to look for programs. For a typical user, the predefined PATH variable might be the following list of directories, separated by colons:

```
/bin:/sbin/:/usr/bin:/usr/sbin
```

When you type **ls** and press Return, your shell goes through the directories specified in your PATH in the order specified, looking for a program named ls, and then executes it.

NOTE   Actually, it's a bit more complicated. The csh and tcsh shells scan the contents of the directories in your PATH variable ahead of time and remember it, so they don't have to scan each time you type a command. Because of this, if you add a new program and want it to be accessible immediately, you must use the rehash command to make your shell "notice" the new program. The bash shell uses a hash table as well, but does not have a built-in rehash command. Its hash table works as a kind of cache that makes finding commands quicker, but you don't need to tell it anything when you add new commands. However, if you move a command that you have already run in the current session to a different directory, you'll need to run hash -r to tell bash to *forget* the location of that program.

To view your own PATH variable, type **echo $PATH** at the shell prompt and press Return. If you want to execute a command or program not in your path (if you're testing it, for example), type its full path. First, make sure you have execute (x) permission on the program file (discussed in the next section). If the command or program is in the current working directory, use the dot-slash combination (./) to launch it, as in ./myscript.

If you'd like to add a new directory to your PATH variable, type **PATH=$PATH**":*newdir*" and press Return in bash, or type **setenv PATH $PATH:*newdir*** and press Return in tcsh, where *newdir* is the full path to the new directory. For instance, if user todd decided to create a new bin directory in his home directory (for storing his own shell scripts and, perhaps, replacement commands he'd prefer to use instead of the installed commands), he could use PATH=$PATH":/Users/todd/bin/" in bash, or setenv PATH $PATH/Users/todd/bin in tcsh, to add the new bin directory to the beginning of his PATH statement, making it possible to execute commands and programs stored there simply by typing the program's name.

NOTE   Unix systems don't deal with file types and creators (or even suffixes) at the most basic level; that's left to users and graphical add-on layers such as Mac OS X and file manager applications. Although you can name programs and documents anything you like, file suffixes are useful for exchanging files with others and quickly identifying your own files—so you may find yourself using .mp3, .txt, and .sh (for sh shell scripts), even though the shell itself doesn't care what you call your files.

Permissions and Ownership

Another difference between Mac OS and Unix systems is in permissions. In Mac OS 9, folders have permissions only if File Sharing is turned on, and then only for remote users. In Unix (along with Mac OS X), every file and directory always has permissions. To see permissions, use ls -l, which generates a long listing. Figure 22.7 shows such a listing.

FIGURE 22.7

Long listing of a sample directory showing permissions and ownership

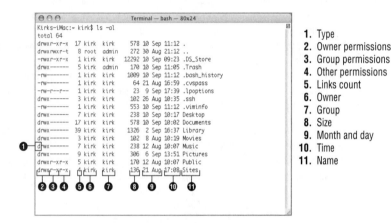

1. Type
2. Owner permissions
3. Group permissions
4. Other permissions
5. Links count
6. Owner
7. Group
8. Size
9. Month and day
10. Time
11. Name

NOTE   As with folders and directories, the Mac OS and Unix-like systems use different words when they refer to privileges (Mac OS) and permissions (Unix). They are essentially the same, with the exception that Unix offers an "execute" permission, which Mac OS X (in the Show Info window of the Finder) ignores.

In long listings, the first character represents the type of the item:

◆   A hyphen (-) for regular files

◆   d for directories

◆   l for symbolic links (See the next section, "Aliases versus Links.")

The next three characters are the owner's permissions:

◆   r—The owner can read the file.

◆   w—The owner can write the file.

◆   x—The owner can execute the file.

If one of these permission characters is a hyphen (-), it means that category of user doesn't have that particular permission. There are additional permissions and letters listed under man chmod.

The second group of three characters represents the same three permissions for members of the file's group, and the last group of three characters shows permissions for everybody else.

The second column, after the 10-character permission column, is the link count—normally 1 for files and 2 or more for directories. (See the sections "Aliases versus Links" and "Invisible Items" for more information on link counts). The third column identifies the owner of the file, and the fourth column is the file's group. The fifth column is the file's size in bytes; for directories, this doesn't include files inside the directory.

After that come two columns for the month and day the file was last modified, and the next column shows either the modification time (if within the past year) or the modification year (if older than the past year). The last column is the file's name.

WARNING When you install Mac OS X, the installation process automatically sets up appropriate permissions for the Mac OS X partition. It does *not* set permissions for other volumes (partitions and disks). As a result, any other users to whom you give access to your system are likely to have much more access than they should to any other volumes on your Mac. Be very careful when creating other user accounts on your system; you should definitely review ownership and permissions on all your partitions using the command ls -l /Volumes, or from the Info window in the Finder, before you create user accounts. (You can set some external disks to recognize permissions/privileges as discussed in Chapter 29.)

The system considers *any* file for which you have execute permission a valid command or program, so be careful not to make files executable if they aren't programs or scripts. If you want to protect a file from being accidentally corrupted or deleted, you can turn off your own write permission. Assuming you have write permission to the file's parent directory, you can give yourself write permission again later if you need to change the file.

If your system has any other users, you should give some thought as to who (if anyone) should have permissions to see or change your files and directories—primarily inside your home directory, but also in any other directories you control.

The capability to ls or cd into a directory is governed by the directory's x permission. Creating new files within a directory is controlled by the parent directory's w permission. For instance, you can create a file inside the Documents folder only if you have w permission—write permission—for that folder.

Besides ls -l, there are three main commands for managing file permissions: chmod, chown, and chgrp.

chmod Change permissions on files and directories. This command has two main modes of use—numeric and symbolic—and it can be very complicated. For starters, you can use commands of the symbolic form chmod **u+w** *filename*. The first argument has three parts. The first part indicates whose permissions will change; the options are u, g, o, and a, representing user (owner), group, other, and all three, respectively. The second part is either + or -, for adding or removing the permission. The third part is r, w, or x, for read, write, or execute, respectively.

The second argument is the file (or directory) to change; additional filenames may follow as additional arguments. For instance, chmod a+w textfile.txt would add *write* permissions for *all* users for this file.

You'll also see that you can use numbers to choose different levels of permissions; for instance, chmod 755 ~/Sites would assign read, write, and execute permissions for the owner and read and write permissions for the group and everyone. The three-digit number sets the owner, group, and user permissions, respectively, ranging from 1 (no permissions) to 7 (read, write, and execute permissions). Table 22.1 shows some common numbers used to set permissions.

TABLE 22.1:   Some Common Number Arguments for *chmod*

NUMBER	WHAT IT MEANS
444	File is read-only.
644	File can be read by anyone, written to by owner, but not executed.
664	File can be read by anyone and written to by owner or group.
755	File is readable and executable by anyone but writable only by owner.
775	File is readable and executable by anyone but writable only by group and owner.
777	File can be read, written to, and executed by anyone.

chown   Change the ownership of a file or directory. The first argument is the new owner (or *owner:group*, to change both the owner and the group), followed by the file(s) to change. For example, consider this scenario: You've created a new folder in a public Documents folder for a user named thoreau. Depending on circumstances, you might have that folder owned by that user so that he can alter it as desired: chown thoreau /Shared/Documents/thoreau.

Likewise, you could easily change the ownership of an individual file so that it can be moved, deleted, or otherwise managed by that user, as in this example: chown thoreau /Public/ memo2.doc.

NOTE   In most cases, you'll need to use the sudo command to change the owner of a file or directory unless you're logged in to the Root account. Thus, the preceding example would actually read: sudo chown thoreau /Public/memo2.doc. You'd then be prompted for an administrator's password in order to perform the change.

chgrp   Change the group associated with a file or directory, similarly to chown. Here's an example: chgrp authors index.html.

All three of these commands support -R as an option (before the arguments). This option makes these commands recursive, meaning that if you use them on a directory, they also will process all the directory's files and subdirectories and all their files and subdirectories, for instance,

```
chmod -R 777 /Library/WebServer/Documents/
```

Be careful when changing execution permissions recursively, because it's easy to scramble directory permissions accidentally this way.

Aliases versus Links

Mac OS aliases are similar to Unix links, but there are subtle differences in how they work. A Mac *alias* is a special file that provides information referring to another file or folder. Unix systems use *hard links* and *symbolic links* (also called *symlinks*) instead of aliases. The shell and command-line tools don't recognize or resolve aliases (they're visible but useless from the command line), but the Mac OS X Finder treats symbolic links as aliases and resolves them normally. Classic applications don't understand symbolic links, but if you double-click or drop them in a Finder window, the original file is opened just as with an alias.

One of the main differences between aliases and symbolic links is that aliases are based on file IDs, so if you move or rename the file that an alias points to, the alias still points to the file (as long as it remains on the same disk). Symbolic links, however, are based on file paths, so if you move the destination file, the link fails until you put it back or put a different file in the original location. Both methods have advantages; aliases are more robust but can cause trouble when there's a newer version of a file but the alias to the old version still works.

Another issue concerns the handling of directories. If you double-click a directory alias in the Mac OS, the Finder jumps to the new location. If you move into a directory symlink, the system may show your path as inside the symlink or inside the linked-to directory. This can be confusing, so be careful.

Aliases and symlinks are similar ways of accomplishing the same thing. Hard links, though, are different. With hard links, a filesystem object can have multiple valid names or paths, all independent and equally "real." By contrast, with symlinks or aliases, there's a single original and one or more references to that original. With hard links, two or more paths point to the same file. Deleting a hard link just removes one of the valid paths to an object; when the last link is deleted, the item itself is removed. The link counts shown in the second column of ls -1 listings increase as hard links are added and decrease as they're removed.

WARNING Shells use the alias command to define shell shortcut commands. This isn't the same as the Mac OS alias described here (and discussed in depth in Chapter 3, "The Finder"). Be careful to avoid confusion around the different meanings. The alias command is described in the earlier section, "More Commands."

File Forks

Mac files can have two forks: the data and resource forks. *Data forks* contain fundamental information such as text, Word documents, Photoshop images, and so on. *Resource forks,* if present, contain Mac-specific information: fonts, icons, system sounds, and such.

As cross-platform programs and data exchange between Macs and other computers have become prevalent, emphasis has gradually shifted away from resource forks because they're useless on other platforms. To simplify all this and make compatibility easier, Apple now encourages developers to store resource information in data forks. With a data-fork–only file, MacBinary, AppleDouble, and AppleSingle (all ways of maintaining a Mac file's resource fork when storing the file on a foreign filesystem) encodings are unnecessary.

The UFS filesystem supported by Mac OS X doesn't support forks directly; when you store a file with a resource fork on a UFS volume, Mac OS X actually creates two files. The data fork is stored under the specified filename, and the resource fork is stored in the same directory with a ._ prefix, which prevents the resource fork from showing up normally. (See the section "Invisible Items" later in this chapter, for more on how this is handled.)

Since HFS+ supports forks, Mac OS X stores both forks under the specified name on HFS+ volumes. On either UFS or HFS+, the Aqua side of Mac OS X handles all the fork magic invisibly. Unfortunately, the standard Unix commands under Darwin don't understand forks, so resource forks on HFS+ volumes aren't easily accessible from the command line or through Unix-based servers such as Apache or FTPD. Most Mac OS X applications create single-fork files, but if you work with files created in Classic applications, keep in mind that you may have trouble if you work with those files at the command line.

TIP   If you need to work with resource forks from the command line, you can append /rsrc to a filename to refer to the resource fork—for example, ls -l MyProgram/rsrc. To copy Mac files with forks intact, use CpMac (/Developer/Tools/CpMac). Note that in order to work with CpMac, you must have the optional developer tools installed using the Developer Tools CD that ships with Mac OS X. Another command that can preserve resource forks is ditto, which is part of the basic BSD installation.

Case Sensitivity

HFS+ is a case-insensitive, case-preserving filesystem. This means that if you save a file named myfile.txt and then save another file named MyFile.txt in the same directory, you get a warning, and the newer file replaces the older one. However, when you look at the file, you'll see the name you specified.

Unix filesystems are normally case sensitive, meaning that a single directory can simultaneously contain distinct files with names that are spelled the same but capitalized differently. On HFS+, if you try to open myfile.txt, but the file is actually named MYFILE.txt, there's no problem—the system understands that the names are equivalent, and MYFILE.txt opens. Under Unix, since these are distinct filenames, you get an error message instead.

Because HFS+ is case preserving, Unix programs generally run fine on HFS+ filesystems. Some programs may be confused by the case insensitivity, though. One example is filename completion in tcsh. Because tcsh assumes that myfile.txt and MYFILE.txt are distinct filenames (even though both are actually names for the same file under HFS+), if you miscapitalize the beginning of a file path, tcsh doesn't understand which file you're referring to and can't complete the path for you.

Invisible Items

Under Unix, files whose names start with a period are special. Most commands ignore them, and these "dot files" often contain special administrative information.

In addition to its main path or name, such as /Users/kirk, every directory contains two additional items:

- A directory called . that's a hard link to the directory itself (yes, this is recursive)
- ..—a hard link to its parent directory

In other words, /Users/kirk/ and /Users/kirk/. are the same directory, as are /Users/kirk/Documents/.. and /Users/kirk/Library/... (In fact, they are *all* the same directory.)

Since these additional directory entries are usually more confusing than useful, ls generally doesn't display them, but its -a option shows invisible items, including these special directory entries. This also is why link counts (see the "Permissions and Ownership" section, earlier in this chapter) for directories are greater than one; directories always have at least two valid paths or hard links.

TIP The links are useful when you want to move *up* in hierarchies, as in cd .. or cd ../; both will move you to the parent of the current folder.

HFS+ filesystems have an invisibility *bit*, or setting, for each file and folder. Apple makes many of the standard Unix directories invisible in Mac OS X, so that the Aqua environment looks simpler and more familiar to Mac users. If you look inside your Mac OS X system disk in a Finder window, you'll see much less than if you type ls -l / in a Terminal window, because most of the standard Unix directories are invisible from the Mac side.

In addition, if you begin the name of a file or directory with a period, this file is invisible not only in the Aqua layer of Mac OS X but also when you run the basic ls command in Terminal. You may recall earlier in this chapter when you saw the ls -al command; the -a option displays *all* files, including those whose names begin with periods.

Thus, to view or edit many Unix-based configuration files using a Mac OS X (or Classic) application, you may need to use a Unix-based tool such as more or pico or copy the files into a visible directory from the command line, edit them, and then put them back.

See Chapter 23 for more on pico and other command-line text editors.

What's Next?

In this chapter, you learned quite a bit about the Terminal application and how to access the underlying Unix command line. You saw reasons to learn the command line, basic and advanced commands, command-line applications, and basic Unix philosophy. You also learned about the different shells that are available, including tricks for the default bash shell and commands that, once you're used to them, can be used to perform quick tasks such as working with large numbers of files at once. (You were also introduced to some concepts and commands that will be useful for troubleshooting Mac OS X later, particularly as discussed in Chapters 28 and 29.) In addition, this chapter examined some of the differences between Darwin and the Aqua environment.

In the next chapter, you'll take a look at some of the ways you can work with an application on the command line, including the use of text editors, the installation of a third-party command-line application, and a look at creating your own shell scripts.

Chapter 23

Command-Line Applications and Magic

In Chapter 22, "Terminal and the Command Line," you learned some of the basics of the command line, including its syntax, philosophy, and quite a few of the built-in commands and programs. In this chapter, we'd like to look a little more closely at some of the programs and utilities you'll find useful on the command line, as well as how to install and manage even more utilities and applications. If you're really interested in finding ways to be productive at the Mac command line, this chapter will help.

In this chapter:

◆ Common Command-Line Programs

◆ Shell Scripting and Behavior

◆ Installing Command-Line Programs

Common Command-Line Programs

As you saw in Chapter 22, the Unix layer of Mac OS X comes with both useful *built-in* shell commands and external programs that can be run as commands from the command line. You saw others in Chapter 17, "Accessing Network Volumes," for instance, where SSH and FTP were covered. Later in this book, in Chapter 28, "Solving System-Level Problems," and Chapter 29, "Typical Problems and Solutions," you'll be introduced to some other interesting command-line programs for tracking down and fixing trouble.

In this section, we'd like to focus on some other perennial favorites of the command-line universe—text editing, event scheduling, and file archiving. We'll look closely at nano and cron, and touch on some others along the way.

Types of Darwin Programs

The Unix layer of Mac OS X has several types of programs you can use, just like the Mac OS. It's worth defining them here so that you can decide what to install on your own system.

First, there are command-line applications, such as cat, ls, tar, analog, and many of the other commands discussed in Chapter 22. These generally are controlled by command-line options or configuration files.

Interactive programs such as more, FTP, SSH, nano, and `tcsh` or `bash` (when used as interactive shells) have their own text-based interfaces available while the programs are running. These interfaces enable such programs to be more complex.

Some programs are actually libraries—pieces of code that may not do anything by themselves but can be used by other programs to perform useful functions; examples are `libm`, `zlib` (a compression library), and `libgd` (a graphics-generation library). You probably won't need to install any libraries unless they're required by other software you're installing; for example, `mrtg`, a network utilization program, requires `zlib` and `libgd` to function.

Stand-alone daemons (also called *servers*) run continuously, waiting to respond to requests from other programs. Apache is such a server—it constantly waits for requests from web browsers. Even when idle, it keeps running, waiting for new requests to handle.

Unix has another type of daemon, though, that has no direct counterpart on the Mac. The servers for telnet, FTP, and Finger (`telnetd`, `ftpd`, and `fingerd`, respectively) only run when connections are open. These daemons are controlled by `launchd`, the "super server," which runs all the time, awaiting requests for any of the services it manages. When `launchd` receives such a request, it starts a copy of the appropriate daemon and passes the connection over to the new copy. This is much more flexible and efficient than keeping all those programs running all the time, because one `launchd` manages all the ports for all its subsidiary services, potentially starting hundreds of services as needed. The cost is performance; having `launchd` receive each web request, start an Apache process, and then pass control over would cause a significant delay, so Apache normally keeps several idle processes waiting for new requests and completely eschews `launchd`.

Text Editors

Editing text is an important part of working at the command line. Even if you don't intend to do any scripting or programming, often you'll find that understanding a text editor on the Darwin command line is handy for editing configuration files and creating special preferences files required by some of the applications that operate on Darwin's level, such as Internet servers. While these files can generally be edited in a graphical text editor (TextEdit is fine for this, although a third-party editor such as BBEdit or its cousin TextWrangler [www.barebones.com] is often a better idea), being able to edit and manipulate these files on the command line may prove to be a valuable time-saving skill in the future.

Mac OS X ships with some familiar text editors on the command line, including the venerable Ed (for line-by-line editing, which you don't want to do), Vi (an early screen-based editor), Emacs (a popular, heavily used, and extended screen-based editor), and nano, a simple editor that offers a lot of the basic features you'll likely want to use on the command line. In this section we'll look at nano in some detail.

NOTE   In Mac OS X 10.4, Pico has been replaced by nano, a clone of Pico with some enhancements. All of Pico's features and commands are present in nano, so if you're familiar with Pico, you can continue using nano in the same way. You can access this either by using the Pico command or the nano command; the former is simply a link to nano, so you don't have to change your habits if you're used to using Pico.

You'll generally launch nano by typing both the name of the application and the file that you want to create or edit, depending on the circumstances. (Note that not all files you work with in nano will have `.txt` filename extensions; many configuration and preference files don't, for instance.) Here's an example:

```
nano newfile.txt
```

If the filename you type exists, nano will load that document, which will appear in the window ready to edit. If the file doesn't exist, you'll see a blank screen.

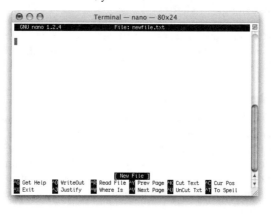

WARNING   nano allows you to open files to which you do not have write access (only read access), and it allows you to attempt to edit a file and save it in a directory where you don't have write access. That can be frustrating when you get to the end of an editing session and realize you can't save the file or that you have to save it in a different directory. The solution is to think about the current working directory and, if you need to override your current account's access to a file or directory, use sudo, as in sudo nano configfile.

Now you can type your entry. As with any standard text editor, text will wrap itself when it reaches the end of the line—add returns only at the end of paragraphs.

As you're typing, you can use the commands at the bottom of the nano interface to perform various tasks. The shortcuts all specify the ^ key, which is the Control key; so, you type Control+G for Get Help or Control+K for Cut Text. The Cut Text command works by cutting the current line; press Control+U to "uncut" the text, or paste it. (You can choose Control+U multiple times to paste the text repeatedly.)

Scrolling through a document, particularly a long one, gets easier when you learn the keyboard commands. Control+V is used for the next page, and Control+Y is used for the previous page. You also can use Control+A to go to the beginning of a line and Control+E to go to the end of it; Control+P goes to the previous line, and Control+N goes to the next line.

nano's Where Is (Find) feature can be handy, particularly if you're using nano to edit a long configuration file, such as the Apache's web server's configuration file (see Chapter 24, "Web Serving, FTP Serving, and Net Security"). Press Control+W, and the status line toward the bottom of the screen changes to Search:. Enter the word or portion of a word that you'd like to search for and press Return. The cursor will move to the first instance of the word or fragment that you entered. To search for the next instance, press Control+W again and notice that your most recent search word is in brackets; press Return again to continue the search.

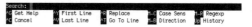

When you're done working with a file, you can press Control+O to save the changes you've made to a file. You also can press Control+X, which is the exit command, but it asks if you'd like to save your changes first before exiting.

TIP   Use Control+G while in nano or type **man nano** at the command line to learn more about it. To find out the differences between Pico and nano, check the nano homepage: www.nano-editor.org/overview.html.

Scheduled Tasks and cron

The cron utility is familiar to most Unix users. cron schedules tasks that happen in the background on your Mac, such as rotating log files and updating certain system files. By default, for instance, cron is set to run in the early morning hours on most Macs, performing those important housecleaning tasks.

You can alter the way cron performs those default tasks, or you can add other tasks that you'd like to see done automatically. In fact, you can use cron to schedule just about any task that can be accomplished from the command line—most of the time that means scheduling shell scripts, which are discussed later in this chapter.

The cron command is actually a daemon that is launched when you start up your Mac and runs until you shut it down. It usually just sits there, checking the clock and waiting until a specific time rolls around, when it will launch items as specified in the system crontab file stored at /etc/crontab as well as individual crontab files it has stored for your user account.

EDIT THE SYSTEM *CRONTAB*

For starters, you can edit the main crontab file if you'd like to change anything about the currently scheduled tasks, such as having the background maintenance tasks that Apple scheduled for early morning happen during the afternoon or over lunch. To do that, type **sudo nano /etc/crontab** and press Return.

TIP   Before editing a configuration file, it's a good idea to make a backup so that you can restore the system crontab from backup if you mess something up. To create a backup, type **cp /etc/crontab ~/crontab.bak** and press Return *before* you launch the file for editing in nano. That places a backup of the file in your home directory.

As explained in Chapter 22, sudo is used to execute a command as the superuser (root). You'll need to enter your administrator's password at the password prompt and press Return before nano will launch. When the file appears in nano for editing, you'll see something such as in Figure 23.1.

If you're familiar with previous versions of Mac OS X, you'll expect to see the periodic command in the /etc/crontab file. As you can see in Figure 23.1, the /etc/crontab file is empty; there are no jobs scheduled, either daily, weekly, or monthly, as the periodic command was. In Mac OS X 10.4, the new launchd (or launch daemon) not only launches network services and other daemons, but it also handles atrun and periodic jobs. You can see how these jobs are set by checking the files in /System/Library/LaunchDaemons. This folder contains a group of .plist files which describe, in XML, how the specific tasks are to run. When your Mac starts up, launchd reads all the files in this directory and sets the jobs to run at the scheduled times and on the scheduled days.

FIGURE 23.1

Editing the system crontab file

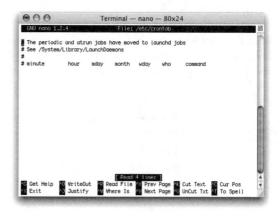

If you look at one of these files, you'll see how they are similar to the way these same tasks ran from the crontab file. For example, the com.apple.periodic-weekly.plist file contains the following:

```
<dict>
    <key>Hour</key>
    <integer>3</integer>
    <key>Minute</key>
    <integer>15</integer>
    <key>Weekday</key>
    <integer>6</integer>
</dict>
```

This is similar to the way the crontab file is organized, with integers set for the hour, minute and weekday. You can alter the times these scripts run by simply changing these values. The next time you restart your Mac, launchd reads the files and records the scheduled times.

NOTE What do these scripts do? Daily, your Mac will launch the periodic daily script(s), which attempts to clean up various log files and delete temporary files that haven't been used in a few days. Weekly, your Mac will run the periodic weekly script, which rotates log files (saves backups and starts new ones) and rebuilds system databases such as those used for the locate (find file) command at the command line. Monthly, the periodic monthly script runs some more cleanup commands and generates special reports.

While the crontab file no longer runs these periodic jobs, you can still use it if you want to schedule your own system tasks. Notice that the crontab file is arranged in a table of sorts, with headers for minutes, hours, mdays (days of the month), months, wdays (days of the week), who (the user account that runs the command), and command. You can add information below these headers to run specific scripts or commands when you want.

It's relatively simple to edit this file; all you need to do is add data to the table in /etc/crontab. Say you want to run a script every day to back up your web server logs; let's call this script log_backup. Enter the time in the first two columns: with 30 under minute and 12 under hour, the job will run at 12:30 pm every day. (Note that the actual layout of the columns is unimportant. Each value must be separated by one or more spaces; one space is sufficient, but you'll find it easier to read the file if you keep the values aligned.) Under mday, month and wday, enter *; this means that these values don't apply, which, in this case, means that the job runs every day. If you were to add a wday value, such as 1, the job would only run on Monday (the first day of the week). If you added a value under month, the job would only run in a specific month. Here's what the edited /etc/crontab file looks like:

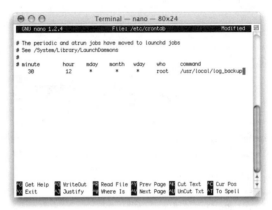

CREATE YOUR OWN *CRONTAB*

If you'd like to set scripts or applications to run at a certain time of day, week, or month, you can create your own crontab. With a crontab, you can cause a command or script to be run automatically whenever it works for you—even an Aqua application can be launched, or an AppleScript, if desired. However, cron jobs only run when you are logged into your account, so if you want a task to run no matter which user is logged in—or even if no users are logged in but your Mac is running, then use the /etc/crontab file to set these jobs. However, any cron jobs that start GUI applications will only work if a user is logged in.

NOTE We're going to use a made-up script name for the example, but later in this chapter you'll learn about creating scripts in some detail.

Unfortunately, editing the crontab for your account isn't quite as easy as editing the system crontab. That's because you need to use a special program to create the crontab called crontab. It's actually fairly easy to use crontab—it creates (or loads) your crontab and passes it to your favorite text editor, where you can enter the specifics of when you want a particular script to run. The crontab command doesn't have a default text editor as far as it's concerned—instead, it looks at an environment variable to know what text editor you want to use. (Sort of the equivalent of your default web browser setting in the Internet pane of System Preferences.) The default text editor is Vi, so you might want to type **export EDITOR=nano**, if you use bash, or **setenv EDITOR nano**, if you use tcsh, and press Return. That sets your EDITOR environment variable to the nano editor.

Now, you're ready to edit your crontab. You'll use the crontab program with an -e argument, as in: crontab -e. (The -e means edit; -l means list, or display, the crontab; and -r means remove it. If you need to edit another user's crontab, you can use the -u argument, as in crontab -u tony -e.) Press Return, and a Nano screen appears.

NOTE See other stuff on your `crontab`? If you haven't edited it personally, then maybe you've installed a disk utility application such as Norton SystemWorks, which uses your `crontab` to automate its own tasks. Just add your row after all the others. Also, note that editing your `crontab` doesn't require `sudo`.

On that screen, you need to enter a row that tells `cron` what script or program you want to execute and when you want it to happen, along the lines of:

```
minute hour mday month wday command
```

TIP If you're planning to use your `crontab` file to schedule many tasks or scripts, you might find it helpful to type the preceding line into the file, as a comment (preceded by #). This helps make sure you put the right data in the right columns.

For example, if at 2:30 P.M. every day, you want to execute the script `myscript` stored in your home directory in a subdirectory called scripts, you would use this:

```
30 14 * * * ~/scripts/myscript
```

For 1:00 A.M. on Wednesday of every week, it'd be

```
00 1 * * 3 ~/scripts/myscript
```

In nano, enter the schedule line that corresponds to the time, date, and name of the item that you want to run and then press Return. Now, press Control+X to exit nano; press Y and then press Return to save the file. When nano exits, you'll see a message from `crontab` telling you the changes have been made. Your script will now run automatically.

Shell scripting is covered later in this chapter, but it's worth noting that you can use your `crontab` to launch an AppleScript or Aqua application, too. Instead of putting a script name on your `crontab` row, add the command `open /pathto/application` as in `open /Applications/TextEdit.app`. You could set an AppleScript, if you save it as an application, to run automatically from your `crontab`:

At the appointed time (9:45 P.M. in the example), this script will run—as would any script or application that's plugged into a row in your `crontab`. You could even have an AppleScript pop up once a day to remind you to take your vitamins! (See Chapter 21, "Automator and AppleScript," for more on AppleScript.)

Shell Scripting and Behavior

Shell scripting offers two major advantages over AppleScript. The first is that shell scripts can be more flexible than AppleScript because shell scripts work without requiring additional features in the target program. Programmers have to add AppleScript capabilities to applications, and many applications, other than Apple's programs, have little or no scripting support. By contrast, shell scripts have as much flexibility as a person typing commands does. In the Unix world, almost anything can be controlled from the command line or a script, and graphical interfaces, as a rule, are purely optional.

The second major advantage of shell scripting is familiarity. Many advanced Mac users have never used AppleScript, and you can't figure it out from the everyday experience of using a Mac normally. However, if you get used to the command line, shell scripts use the same commands and facilities that you use all the time when typing commands at a shell prompt—there's not much new to learn. As a result, anyone who has spent some time working at the command line has almost all the knowledge necessary to write scripts. All you need to know is how to put together the script file and how to get it to perform all those commands that, after a few months, you've begun to memorize (if not dream about).

Although this section can't give you much more than a brief overview of shell scripting and some advanced command-line controls, you'll see that shell scripting is fairly easy to pick up. Then, in the future, when you're working at the command line and think to yourself, "I wish I could automate this tedious process," maybe you'll realize that you can, with a quick script.

Shell Scripts

A *shell script* is a series of commands, just as you'd type them at the prompt, saved in a file. There are two main differences. First, shell scripts contain blank lines and comments. Any line starting with a pound sign (#) is ignored by the shell, except the first line—and the first line itself is the other difference.

Each script starts with a line specifying the path to the shell for which the script is written, often called a *shebang*. Because different shells have different syntax and features, to work properly, a script must be executed by the shell it's written for. Since sh is the oldest shell in active use and the most widely available, most scripts are written for it. Scripts intended for sh on Mac OS X should start with #!/bin/sh. Some downloaded scripts specify the wrong location for the shell, so this is a good thing to check if a new script doesn't work.

WARNING Remember that each shell has a slightly different syntax. In this section, when you're writing scripts, you'll need to use sh syntax, which is the same as for bash. If you're using the tcsh shell in Terminal, this means there are some changes, though minor, in the way you type commands. Shells derived from sh, including bash, use sh syntax for loop control and setting variables and have their own set of builtins, but csh-descended shells, including tcsh, use a different syntax and slightly different builtins. See the man pages (man bash and man tcsh) for details.

Unix shells are also called "interpreters" because they interpret and execute commands and scripts. Generally, the term *shell* refers to interactive use, and *interpreter* is used for script processing. The same program performs both functions, though.

NOTE Some newer shells have sh compatibility modes, which disable new features so that they can be used in place of the "real" sh. Under Darwin, /bin/sh is actually the same file as /bin/zsh, using a hard link. Under Red Hat Linux, /bin/sh is a symbolic link to /bin/bash; when bash is invoked with the name sh, it runs in compatibility mode.

Scripts use the same commands and syntax as the command line, which means that writing scripts is easy to pick up once you're familiar with the command line. If you want to put two different commands on a single line, you can separate them with a semicolon. This is equivalent to typing the first command, pressing Return, and then typing the second and pressing Return, but it's more compact and sometimes more convenient.

Figure 23.2 shows an example of a script that was mentioned earlier; `/etc/monthly` is the script called by the system `crontab` to run every month and do automated maintenance—mostly log file management. In `/etc/monthly`, you'll see many of the same commands you've used yourself at the command line. This script starts with a specification of the interpreter, comments, variables, a pipe (|), and several standard commands (see the section "Pipes: Connecting Programs" later in this chapter).

FIGURE 23.2

`/etc/monthly`, a script that runs on the first of every month, shown via the `more` command

```
#!/bin/sh -
#
#       @(#)monthly    8.1 (Berkeley) 6/9/93
#

PATH=/bin:/usr/bin:/sbin:/usr/sbin
host=`hostname -s`

echo ""
echo "Doing login accounting:"
if type sort>/dev/null; then
    ac -p | sort -nr +1
else
    ac -p
fi

echo ""
printf %s "Rotating log files:"
cd /var/log
for i in wtmp install.log; do
    if [ -f "${i}" ]; then
        printf %s " $i"
        if [ -x /usr/bin/gzip ]; then gzext=".gz"; else gzext=""; fi
        if [ -f "${i}.3${gzext}" ]; then mv -f "${i}.3${gzext}" "${i}.4${gzext}"; fi
        if [ -f "${i}.2${gzext}" ]; then mv -f "${i}.2${gzext}" "${i}.3${gzext}"; fi
        if [ -f "${i}.1${gzext}" ]; then mv -f "${i}.1${gzext}" "${i}.2${gzext}"; fi
        if [ -f "${i}.0${gzext}" ]; then mv -f "${i}.0${gzext}" "${i}.1${gzext}"; fi
        if [ -f "${i}" ]; then mv -f "${i}" "${i}.0" && if [ -x /usr/bin/gzip ]; then gzip
 -9 "${i}.0"; fi; fi
        touch "${i}" && chmod 644 "${i}" && chown root:admin "${i}"
    fi
done
if [ -f /var/run/syslog.pid ]; then kill -HUP $(cat /var/run/syslog.pid | head -1); fi
echo ""

echo ""
printf %s "Rotating fax log files:"
cd /var/log/fax
for i in *.log; do
    if [ -f "${i}" ]; then
```

Creating a Script

To create a script, simply create a text file that has a shebang and scripting commands and then give yourself execute permission for that file. You can create the script in a regular text editor in Mac OS X, if you like, or you can use a command-line editor such as Emacs or Vi. In this example, we'll use nano.

If you use a Mac OS–based text editor such as BBEdit, you'll need to make sure your saved files use Unix-style line breaks; that's because Unix systems use different characters to identify line endings than does the Mac OS, and the Mac-style endings will confuse interpreters. In BBEdit and other programs that support Mac and Unix-style line endings, this is controlled through the Save or Save As dialog box.

Here's how to create a basic script entirely on the command line:

1. Make the directory `~/bin` with `mkdir ~/bin` (if it doesn't already exist). This is a special directory in your home directory that you'll use for scripts you create.

2. At the prompt, type **cd ~/bin** to enter the directory and then press Return.

3. Type **nano *myscript*** and press Return. (Replace ***myscript*** with the name you'd like to give the script in this step and in steps 6 and 7.)

4. Type the script. In this example, the script will simply use the echo command to return text to the screen.

5. Type **exit** as the last line of your script, then press Control+X. The status line at the bottom of the screen asks if you'd like to save your changes. Press Y and then Return to save your work.

6. You'll be back at the command line. Type **chmod u+x** *myscript*. Now you have execute permission for that script. Without this step, it's just a text file that lists some commands; with this step, it's a script that can be processed.

7. Type *./myscript* at the command line, and your new script will run. (The period and slash are used to specify that the script should be executed.)

```
Kirks-iMac:~ kirk$ ./myscript
Hello World!
This is my first script.
Kirks-iMac:~ kirk$ ▊
```

In the next few sections, you'll find information on some more advanced shell features that are particularly useful for scripts.

TIP Want to be able to execute a script without the dot-slash combo? You need to add the ~/bin directory to your PATH statement, as discussed in Chapter 22. At a command-line prompt, type **PATH=$PATH**":~/**bin**" and press Return in bash, or type **setenv PATH** ~/**bin**:**$PATH** and press Return in tcsh. That adds the ~/bin directory to your path so that you can type the script name directly to execute it.

Filters: Standard Input, Standard Output, and Standard Error

Filters are a key concept in Unix-based operating systems. A *filter* is a program that takes input, processes it in some way, and emits processed output. Many command-line utilities, including grep, head, tail, and tar, can be used in this way. These utilities can accept input in any of three ways: text typed by the user, file(s) specified on the command line, and *standard input* (also called stdin). Output is to the screen or to *standard output* (stdout). By chaining one program's output to another's input, it's possible to do very complex processing using simple component programs. In addition to input and output, there's a third stream: *standard error* (`stderr`).

File Redirection

To make a program read a file from standard input, use the < (less than) character. This isn't terribly important for interactive use because most of the standard commands also accept filenames as arguments, but it becomes useful in scripts; it enables you to control input and output of your own scripts without adding code to do argument processing or file management directly.

To make a program record its output in a file, use the > (greater than) character. An example using both < and > is `grep 212 < phonebook.txt > ny-pb.txt`. This would copy all the lines containing 212 from the file `phonebook.txt` into the file `ny-pb.txt`.

Pipes: Connecting Programs

Unix gains much of its power and flexibility from the capability to chain simpler programs together to perform processing that's more complex than any of the programs can do alone. To make one program's output go to another's input, use the pipe character (|). This is useful for programs that generate lots of output; results might be sent to `more`, `grep`, `head`, or `tail` to get just the relevant bits. A simple example is `ls -l | more`, which sends the output from `ls -l` to the `more` program as input.

You can use more complex *pipelines* to create long chains of commands and to process data through multiple steps. Pipes often start with commands that provide large amounts of data, such as `cat` (to bring files into a pipe) and `man`. The highly flexible commands `sort` and `grep`, with their many options, often go in the middle to extract or prioritize the relevant bits; and `more`, `head`, and `tail` often go at the ends of pipes, to facilitate reading the output. Another useful command for pipes is `tee`, which copies its input into one or more files and passes it along to `stdout` for additional processing.

Internal and Environment Variables

Shells, including `tcsh` and `bash`, work with two different kinds of variables: *internal variables* and *environment variables*. Environment variables are important because they are passed to other programs launched from the shell. To see all the current internal variables, use the `set` builtin with no arguments (type **set** and press Return); use `setenv` to see the current environment variables. To set variables for `tcsh`, use `set` or `setenv` with one or more arguments of the form *variablename=value*, as in this example:

```
set foo="Hello World"
```

For `bash` (and hence for scripts using `bash` or `sh`), the `set` command isn't required, so you would use this:

```
foo="Hello World"
```

But for environment variables, you have to use the `export` command:

```
export EDITOR=nano
```

Once a value is assigned to a variable, you'll use that value via *variable substitution*. When the shell sees a variable name starting with a dollar sign ($), it replaces the whole word with the variable's value before processing the command. In a script, it might look like this:

```
#!/bin/sh
foo="Hello World"
echo $foo
exit
```

As you can see, to send a single variable's value to standard output (usually the screen), you can use the echo command.

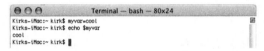

NOTE   To use a literal dollar sign in a command, you need to *escape* it with a backslash. The backslash protects special characters from being immediately interpreted, so that they can be passed along to the next program intact. For example, echo \$foo would avoid variable substitution and would return $foo regardless of what the variable foo was set to.

Want your script to be able to accept values from the user when it's launched and then assign those values to variables? You can use a couple of special variables to receive *command-line arguments* within a script (such as *myscript somefile*). The variable $# is used to determine the number of arguments the user entered, while $*n*, where *n* is an integer, is used to refer to a particular argument, such as $1 for the first argument or $0 for the script's name. $* is used to display all of the arguments. Here's an example:

```
#!/bin/sh
# This script demonstrates argument variables.
echo "You typed $# arguments."
echo "This script is $0"
echo "The first argument is $1"
echo "A list of the arguments is: $*"
exit
```

Getting argument variables this way enables you to create your own shell commands. For instance, you could create a script called lsize that uses the argument variables to perform ls -lS | more so that a long listing, sorted by size, is piped to the more command:

```
#!/bin/sh
# lsize: long listing sorted by size, using more.
ls -lS $* | more
exit
```

Save the script as ~/bin/lsize (with the proper permissions), and you'll be able to list long directories easily, sorted by size, with the help of the more command, as in lsize ~/Documents.

Flow Control

When a program finishes running, it returns an exit status. This is 0 if the program succeeded or a positive or negative number if it failed. (Depending on the program, the number might provide more information about the failure. Check the program's man page.) This exit status is stored in the variable status. Many programs also send error messages to standard error, which normally appears on the screen—so the errors show up in your Terminal window. Many programs also record error messages in log files (use ls /var/log to see the standard log files).

NOTE Be careful with the status variable, because commands (including echo $status) will change its value to their *own* exit status after they finish. The trick is that if you need to use status more than once, you must first copy it into another variable, and you can then use the copy as much as you want.

The basic *conditional test* in tcsh is if. It can be used on the command line in conjunction with a command, using the return value to determine what to do next. The syntax is if *test command*—if *test* returns true (0), then *command* is executed. To run a command and use its status value as the conditional, the command must be surrounded by braces (curly brackets, { }) and spaces.

Here's an example of a couple of tests that use the popular grep tool to see if a particular pattern is matched. The user root does appear in /etc/passwd, so that test is successful, and the conditional command runs and says Matched!. But gates isn't present, so that test fails, and the echo command is never executed.

Watch the spacing in this example if you're following along. You need a space on both sides between the curly brackets and text.

```
[Kirks-iMac:~] kirk% if { grep -q root /etc/passwd } echo Matched!
Matched!
[Kirks-iMac:~] kirk% if { grep -q gates /etc/passwd } echo Matched!
[Kirks-iMac:~] kirk%
```

The grep command's -q option puts it into Quiet mode: It returns status but doesn't list matches on standard output (normally the screen).

With bash, the conditional test is a bit different. bash requires that you construct an if; then; fi statement (fi is used to indicate the end of an if statement), so the equivalent of the preceding example under bash is the following:

```
$ if grep -q root /etc/passwd ; then echo Matched! ; fi
```

In addition to normal shell commands, tests may use special dedicated comparison operators. Tests using these operators must be enclosed in *square brackets*, and *each* bracket must be preceded and followed by a space, as in this example: if [$# -lt 1]. Note that normal commands used as conditionals must be enclosed in braces, but tests using the comparison operators in Table 23.1 use square brackets—and the spacing is crucial.

When you're scripting, often you'll use conditional tests to determine whether something is true. Conditional tests, like programs, return exit status of 0 for true or any other number for false. Table 23.1 shows some common conditionals. (There are others, and they can become rather complex, especially if you're dealing directly with the tcsh shell. See man test, man bash, and man tcsh for details.)

TABLE 23.1: Some Comparison Operators

OPERATOR	TEST
-eq	equal to
-ne	not equal to
-lt	less than
-gt	greater than
-le	less than or equal to
-ge	greater than or equal to

If you want more, the if structure can be more elaborate—and it is perhaps familiar to you if you've done other programming:

```
if [ test ]
    then command
elif [ test ]
    then command
else command
fi
```

Note that everything between the first then line and fi is optional, including the elif line, its then line, and the else line.

Here's an example that elaborates on some ideas you've already seen—it lists directories but uses a test:

```
#!/bin/sh
# Return sorted listing of specified directory
if [ $# -lt 1 ]
then
    echo "This script requires one or more arguments."
    exit -1
fi
ls -lS $* | more
exit
```

Now, if the user doesn't enter any arguments, the error message is returned, and the script aborts, returning –1 to signify failure, so it can be used by another script that needs to know if this one succeeded.

And that's just one way to test! You can also use `while`, `for`, and `case`. See "Flow-Control Constructs" in the `sh` man page for more on conditionals and loops.

NOTE   Want to learn more about shell scripting? Try Sybex's *Linux System Administration*, *Second Edition*.

Installing Command-Line Programs

You can install command-line applications in a number of ways. The easier methods involve simply decompressing an archive that includes an application that has already been compiled to run on the command line in Mac OS X. But the easiest way isn't always the most interesting, because there are lots of great programs available as Unix source code that aren't packaged for Mac OS X—although there are more every day. If you'd like to automate the installation of command-line programs, you can use an interesting system called Fink, which is designed to do the installing for you. We'll cover all three types of installations in the following sections.

Binary Installation Example: analog

When you download a *binary* of a Darwin application, what you're getting is the actual, precompiled application. Once installed, it will be ready to work with immediately, just like the vast majority of applications that you download and work with for Mac OS X's graphical Aqua environment. In this example, you'll see the simple download and installation of analog.

The analog program is a fast and free web traffic analyzer. It reads server logs from web servers such as the Apache server built into Mac OS X, analyzes them, and generates HTML reports showing traffic levels broken down in several ways. The analog program is a pure command-line program—its configuration is stored in `analog.cfg`, and optional additional configuration files are provided at the command line when starting the program. You can find analog in source form, as a precompiled Darwin/Mac OS X binary package, and as a Carbon or Classic application with a minimal Aqua interface, from `www.analog.cx/download.html`.

To get the Mac OS X binary distribution, head to `www.hmug.org/Analog.html` and download the file listed. It will be named something like `analog-6.0-1-osx3.tar.gz`, although the name may vary as new versions are compiled. The location may change, too, so check back at `www.analog.cx` for the latest Mac OS X binaries if it turns out someone else compiles them in the future.

The Darwin binary distribution of analog uses a very simple installation procedure: After downloading and unpacking the tarball, you need to run the installation script from the command line:

1. The tarball was most likely decompressed on your desktop after it was downloaded. Using Terminal, change the directory to that directory (it may be named slightly differently) on your desktop:

   ```
   cd ~/desktop/analog-6.0
   ```

2. Now run the installation script:

   ```
   sudo ./install.sh
   ```

That's all it takes. You should see results in the Terminal window—folders are created, files are copied and linked, and so forth.

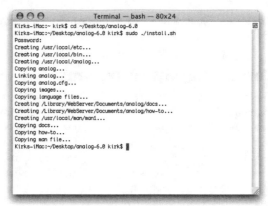

In the case of analog, you may need to edit the configuration file, located at /usr/local/etc/analog.cfg. If you want to edit the file, you can use nano for this (you might consider making a backup of the file first, as shown):

```
cp /usr/local/etc/analog.cfg ~/analog.bak
sudo nano /usr/local/etc/analog.cfg
```

In the nano interface, you need change the configuration file in one particular place. Look for this entry:

```
LOGFILE /var/log/httpd/access_log.*
```

Delete the period and asterisk so analog can read your current log file. (If you happen to know you need a special log file entry, you can change it here, but you shouldn't because analog knows how to access Apache's log file, and you're working with Apache.) Make any other changes you need to make and then press Control+X to exit, pressing Return to save the file first.

To launch analog, all you need to do is run the program by entering its name and file path:

```
/usr/local/analog/analog > /Library/WebServer/Documents/Report.html
```

Enter that command and press Return. After a moment, a new file called Report.html will appear in your /Library/WebServer/Documents folder. It's an HTML document, which you can view in a web browser to see the statistics for your Apache installation (see Figure 23.3).

Whenever you want to update the stats, just launch analog again and redirect output to the Report.html file, and it will be replaced. Or you can create a small script, name it myanalog or something similar, and you'll have some easier typing. Or how about adding this to your system crontab, and it'll check Apache's stats automatically on a regular basis!

Compiling Code for Command-Line Applications

Unix and Unix-based systems normally include compilers and software development tools. This is partially because Unix was designed as a programming environment, and also because so much software is available in source form for Unix systems, including excellent free tools.

FIGURE 23.3
Viewing the statistics as
compiled by analog

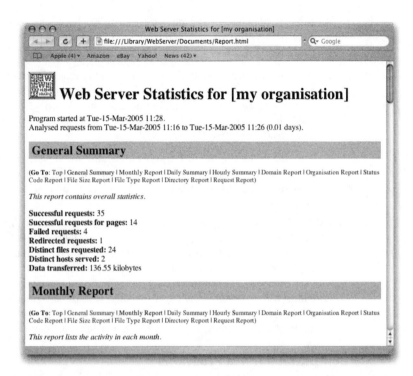

MacOS X, however, with its user-friendly Aqua focus, doesn't contain these tools as part of its base installation. Instead, Apple includes them on the Developer Tools CD, included with your Mac OS X installation CDs. Because these tools are open-source as part of the Darwin project, they should always be freely available, but exactly how they're distributed may change over time.

Carbon and Cocoa programs tend to follow their Mac OS (and NeXTStep) heritage and be pre-compiled so that users can just install them without any need for compilers. Unix programs, however, often are available only in source form. Supporting Mac OS X/Darwin for a Unix program may consist of making sure that the default compilation and installation procedure works, rather than pre-compiling and packaging the software, as you might expect for a Carbon application. To install Unix programs from source, then, you'll need to have the Developer Tools installed.

Here's the process for compiling freely available source code into a Darwin application:

NOTE This is one standard procedure; application authors often use slightly different steps. Check for instructions in README or INSTALL files included with the software or on the software's website.

1. Download the file (using NCFTP, FTP, WGET, or a graphical FTP client or web browser). The filename is likely to be something like `package.src.tgz`.

2. Use tar to unarchive (and decompress) the file. To continue the previous example, type **tar -xzf package.src.tgz** and press Return.

3. Change to the directory created by the unarchiving process. Type **cd package** and press Return.

4. If the archive has a `configure` script, run it. This script inspects the system environment and determines how to compile the included source code. To run `configure`, type **`./configure`** and press Return.

5. Next is the `make` command. This command reads its instructions from `./Makefile`—another file included with the program source code—and compiles and installs software. With no arguments, `make` generally just compiles. Any additional arguments desired may be defined in the `Makefile`, to compile or delete files or to install files to appropriate places on the system. Type **make** and press Return.

6. The final `make` command finishes the installation by copying files to their intended locations and possibly creating symlinks in standard directories to the actual executable programs, so files are effectively included in the PATH. Type **sudo make install** and press Return.

WARNING   OK—here comes another `sudo`/root warning. In Unix, regular users usually have permission to make changes only within their own home directories. In order to install software for general use, you'll need to install using `sudo`, which asks for your administrative password and then runs the rest of the command with elevated permissions. As a rule, you should be very careful with any new software, but this is even more important when you're using `sudo`. Whether you're compiling source code or installing binary files, consider how much you trust the author or packager of the software, as well as your own knowledge of Unix. If you're concerned, don't use `sudo` to install; just install the program inside your home directory for private use.

Compiling Darwin Programs

Aside from the general `./configure`, `make`, and `make install` steps outlined in the preceding section, there is no universal method for compiling and installing Unix programs from source. With each program, you'll have to read the included documentation (generally in a README or INSTALL file or on the program's website). There are a few useful tidbits to keep in mind, though, when compiling software for Darwin and Mac OS X:

◆ Mac OS X's command-line environment is basically the same as the stand-alone Darwin open-source operating system, so Unix programs written for Unix or Darwin normally run on Mac OS X as well. However, because Mac OS X has many features not in Darwin, most Mac OS X programs can't run in Darwin.

◆ Darwin is based on FreeBSD, which in turn is based on BSD Unix. This means that generic Unix software should work as well, possibly with minor tweaking to accommodate Darwin idiosyncrasies. Developers often build these workarounds into their installation procedures so that the next version compiles and installs without any manual intervention.

◆ Apple includes a great deal of software in Mac OS X, so don't compile new software without checking first to see if it's already present. Among the major packages that Apple installs are OpenSSH, Perl, Java 2, Emacs, and nano.

◆ If you're stuck, try online Mac OS X and Darwin resources. There are strong online communities for both Mac OS X and Darwin, and you may find instructions or help on a website or mailing list.

TIP Some good starting points for Mac OS X/Darwin tips and discussions are www.macosx-hints.com and the X-Unix mailing list at www.themacintoshguy.com/lists/X-Unix.html.

Explore Fink

Our last option for the installation of Darwin applications is a very appealing one. Called Fink (http://fink.sourceforge.net), it's a system for automating the installation and configuration of open-source software for Darwin. Fink tracks a number of open-source programs and components, and once it's installed on your Mac, it knows how to install those applications and update them. If you think you're really interested in digging in and working with Unix- and Linux-style open-source programs, Fink is the way to make that happen.

NOTE In fact, Fink is about more than just command-line programs—you can use it to install the X11 environment discussed in Chapter 20, "Mac OS X and Other Platforms," and various graphical Unix-based applications and tools as well.

On the Fink site, you'll find Quick Start instructions for installing the application, creating important folders, and editing configuration files. You'll download and install a regular Mac OS X package file (using graphical tools, shown in Figure 23.4), and then you'll switch to the Terminal.

FIGURE 23.4
Installing Fink

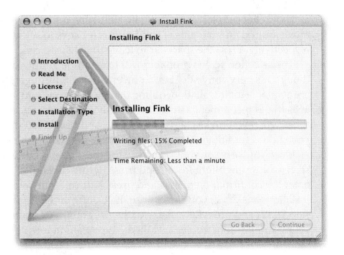

WARNING For exact configuration steps, check the site for the latest instructions at http://fink.sourceforge.net/download/index.php to ensure that nothing has changed. You'll also want to read the Fink User's Guide to get a sense of the different commands and options you have for installing files.

Once you've installed and configured Fink, you're ready to launch the standard Fink interface—type **sudo dselect** and press Return. Enter your password (if you're asked for one—it may have been only a short while since you last entered it), and you'll see the dselect menu. Here is where you'll manage Fink:

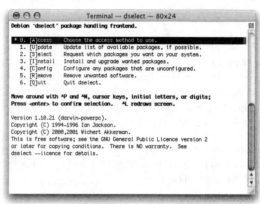

Use the arrow keys on your keyboard to move up and down to select an entry and then press Return to make the selection. Begin by selecting Update and pressing Return; your list of packages will be updated.

Next, choose Select. You'll see the Help screen first—read it carefully. You'll use the arrow keys to move around and the plus (+) and minus (–) keys to select or deselect a package for installation, respectively. Press the spacebar to leave the Help screen.

The selection screen probably will take a little getting used to—it's not terribly Mac-like, even though it's very convenient and powerful. Scroll through the list to get a sense of the packages that are available for installation, noting that the first time you install Fink, there may be a number of packages that it recommends installing. Make your choices according to the recommendations. (Sometimes when you make choices, you'll see another screen that lists the dependencies for that choice; you should turn them off only if you know that you don't need the file or files in question.)

Once you've made your choices using the plus and minus keys, press Return to go back to the main screen. Now, highlight Install and press Return. Read the instructions and, if everything looks good, enter the confirmation phrase and press Return. Your selected packages will be installed. When the installation is done, you can choose the Config and Remove items in the dselect interface, and then select Quit and press Return to exit the program. You should now be able to run some of those open-source applications you've installed—type their names at the command-line prompt to see if they'll launch.

TIP To launch an application in the background (so that you can get back to the command-line prompt), type its name and the & sign, as in **xterm &**, and press Return.

If you want to use a graphical application to manage, download, and install programs, you can use the Fink Commander application, which is included on the Fink installation disk image. Fink Commander provides a full list of files available to Fink and helps you install binaries and install programs from the source code.

There's a lot more to learn about Fink, but you'll need to do that exploration on your own. In the Fink disk image, you'll find the file documentation.html that you can view in a web browser to learn more about this tool. This includes a look at some of the different types of tools and packages you can download, a specific discussion of X11 (for graphical Unix-based programs), and a fuller explanation of what Fink is doing in the background (mostly it's just installing the latest versions of certain Darwin binaries from its server, in a very sophisticated way) and different ways it can do it.

What's Next?

This chapter began with an explanation of the different programs you'll find available via Darwin, the command-line layer of Mac OS X, and how you can access them. It looked in particular at nano, a simple but useful command-line text editor, followed by a discussion of cron, a scheduling utility.

The chapter then moved on to a discussion of creating your own shell scripts, including the concepts behind shell scripting as well as a hands-on look at how to create a script, where to save it, and how to make it executable. You also learned some basic shell scripting techniques, such as using pipes and flow control and dealing with external arguments and variables.

After the shell-scripting discussion, you learned how to download and install additional command-line applications, including prebuilt binary installations, compiling from source code, and using the Fink package manager to install the latest versions of popular command-line packages.

In Chapter 24, we'll move on to an in-depth look at Mac OS X's built-in Apache and FTP servers, including information and advice on configuration and extended Apache, accessing the logs, and keeping your servers secure.

Chapter 24

Web Serving, FTP Serving, and Net Security

In previous chapters, you saw how to get on the Internet and access various types of servers and content. What about creating and serving some of that content yourself? Mac OS X comes with some serious and sophisticated built-in servers that enable you to do just that. What's more, the servers are surprisingly easy to start up and work with online.

Mac OS X includes web and FTP server capabilities. Turning them on and off is simple: like other server functions, you access these in the Sharing pane of the System Preferences application. Managing these servers isn't much more difficult; you'll need to assign some permissions and locate the correct folders, but it's not much more difficult than any other administrative task. You'll also find special log files that enable you to see who is accessing your Mac via these Internet protocol servers.

The fact that these servers are built on top of the Darwin underpinnings of Mac OS X, however, makes them more powerful than they might seem at first. The web server in Mac OS X is a version of the well-known Apache web server, the most popular on the Internet. What that means is that it's possible—and fairly easy—for you to customize the servers with performance tweaks and additional features and settings.

But if a more robust server solution is important to you, your organization, or your business, you should consider Mac OS X Server, the version of Mac OS X that Apple sells bundled with a variety of tools and utilities for managing a workgroup of Macs that need access to a variety of networked services. Mac OS X Server manages file sharing, printer sharing, Internet services, network installations, and more.

What's interesting about Mac OS X Server is that it includes a lot of open-source solutions that you can add back into the regular version of Mac OS X if you'd like to go beyond its built-in capabilities. You won't get the full functionality of Mac OS X Server, but there's a lot that you can do. A number of third-party applications are available that enable you to augment Mac OS X's capability to serve files remotely. Those capabilities include free (and sometimes open-source) add-ons such as Apple's QuickTime Streaming Server and additional components for the Apache web server that can enable you to run special web applications.

In this chapter, we'll also discuss the security of using those servers, which is an important consideration for almost any Mac OS X user. Once you've made your security decisions, if you have a Mac with a direct Internet connection—or if you'd like to create an intranet for file and information sharing between your Macs—you're ready to turn on your Internet servers and get started. We'll also look at a few server add-ons, telling you what they do and how to install them. We'll tell you about using PHP and MySQL, and we'll show you how to use a free open-source tool to easily configure Samba.

In this chapter:

◆ Serving the Web

◆ Serving FTP

◆ Net Server Security Considerations

◆ Augmenting Apache: PHP and MySQL

Serving the Web

As mentioned, Mac OS X includes a built-in web server based on the popular and venerable Apache web server, an open-source web server application that's available for most Unix and Unix-like operating systems (along with others). Apache is the most popular web server application available, and its inclusion in the Mac OS is a boon for basic web authors or advanced developers of web applications. Compared to the Classic Mac OS, Mac OS X's FreeBSD underpinnings and reliance on Apache makes it possible for you to take advantage of all sorts of scripting, server-side processing, and other dynamic add-ons that you can download and tweak to improve your websites. The combination makes Mac OS X a very robust platform for web serving. Best of all is the fact that Apache has been integrated into the Aqua interface and made easy to turn on and off, so that any user can take advantage of the web server.

What Is a Web Server?

A *web server* is an application designed to respond to requests made by remote client applications (usually web browser applications) by sending documents to those clients using the Hypertext Transfer Protocol (HTTP). The client applications make the request by asking for a particular URL, which includes both the web server computer's IP (or domain name–based) address and a path to the particular document that the web browser would like to see. As you saw in Chapter 11, "The Web, Online Security, .Mac, Sherlock, and iChat," such URLs can be input manually by the user or they can result from the clicking of a hyperlink. In most cases, the web server reacts to a request for a file from the web browser by doing one of three things:

◆ The server will send an HTML document to the client application (including any other items, such as images and embedded multimedia files that are also part of that request).

◆ The server will process a request for an unrecognized file, which will generally result in that file being downloaded by the client application. For instance, this would work if the user clicked a link to a StuffIt archive, which would then be downloaded to the user instead of being displayed in that user's browser.

◆ The server will process an HTML form request by passing important data to a script or program through the Common Gateway Interface (CGI). Once the data is passed to a CGI script, the server will wait for a response from that script, usually in the form of an automatically generated HTML document.

That, in a nutshell, is what a web server does. Mac OS X provides for all of these possibilities, enabling you to turn on the web server and add files (HTML, image, and other downloadable files) that can be served by the web server to remote clients. Mac OS X also offers a special folder for CGI scripts, which you can create and store so that they may be accessed by an HTML request to process form data or to otherwise interact with the user.

Web Serving Schemes

Now that you know what a web server does, you may wonder why you should care. One reason may be obvious—you want to serve files on the World Wide Web. There are other reasons. Let's take a quick look at some of them:

Serving on the Web   This is the most obvious reason to use the web server built into Mac OS X. If you have a direct connection to the Internet and a static IP address, you can turn your Mac into a web server. (Even if you *don't* have a static IP address, you can turn your Mac into a web server temporarily, if necessary, and let people access it only for the duration of a single Internet connection.) This enables you to serve HTML documents and other files to anyone with web access.

Serving an Intranet   If you have a LAN, you may want to use the web server to disseminate files and other information. An *intranet* is a private network that uses web servers and other Internet-protocol servers to create an "internal Internet" of sorts. An intranet is a great means for updating your medium-to-large organization on regular news items, as well as a way to distribute web-based forms (human resources, mailings, important documents) and offer feedback (people can e-mail the CEO or access a chat room or bulletin board). You can serve that intranet easily using the built-in web server features.

Testing   Many individuals and small businesses find it inconvenient to use an internal computer as a dedicated web server because the equipment and high-speed access are expensive and the security issues can be daunting. Instead, you might use a co-location or shared-server solution for your websites. Having Apache built into Mac OS X, however, gives you the opportunity to run a web server that can be used to test your website's pages and scripts before they're uploaded and made available to the general public. For instance, if you plan to implement a sophisticated shopping cart or content management application, testing it thoroughly on your own Mac before uploading it to your server is probably a good idea.

Cross-Platform File Sharing   If you need to share files on a LAN with Windows-based or Unix/Linux-based PCs—and you find the Mac OS's built-in support for Windows or Unix connections inconvenient or unreliable—you can solve the problem using a web server. Just turn on the web server, place the files you want to share in the Web Documents directory, and access the web server from the PCs. Now you should be able to download the files easily. (You also can use FTP to solve this problem, as discussed later in this chapter, which could prove even easier.)

Which of the above you're capable of doing can depend in some cases on the type of connection you have to the Internet. For instance, if your LAN doesn't have an Internet connection at all, then only users on your local network will be able to see your web server—and they'll do that by entering the local IP address for your Mac in their web browsers, as in http://192.168.1.4. That would apply both to Mac users and to users of other types of computers, as long as they have access to your local IP subnet. This would also be the case if you were testing a site locally.

TIP   To see the output of a web server that's running on the same computer as your web browser, you can enter http://localhost/ or a full path such as http://localhost/products/download.html as the URL.

If you'd like to make your web server's output available on the Internet itself, your Mac will need a publicly available IP address. This will usually be a fixed IP address provided by your ISP. Once you have that IP address, users anywhere on the Internet will be able to enter that IP address in their web browsers to access your Mac's web server. If the address is fixed, those users will always know how to access your Mac.

You can serve web pages using a dynamic IP address, but it's considerably less convenient—you'll have to tell users the address for your web server every time you sign on to the Internet. (Your current IP address is shown at the bottom of the Sharing pane in System Preferences, whenever you turn on File Sharing, Web Sharing, or FTP. You can copy this text to send it to users, or even click the link to test it.) This makes it possible to serve web pages over modem and dial-up DSL connections. (Ideally, you'd want to limit this to single-session sharing where you call a friend or colleague and say, "Head to my IP address and download the file," or a similar scenario.)

NOTE Actually, if you're stuck with a dynamic IP address but you'd really like to use your Mac as a server, there is a way that can be done. Service companies on the Internet can forward requests for your domain name (such as www.yourname.com) to a dynamic IP address. Look for those that offer a Mac-compatible client; the client has to report your IP address to the service whenever it changes. See http://directory.google.com/Top/Computers/Software/Internet/Servers/Address_ Management/Dynamic_DNS_Services/ for a listing.

Of course, the ideal approach for a public web server is an actual domain name address that your users can easily remember, such as www.yourname.com. Getting such a domain name requires three things:

◆ You need to register the domain name with a domain name registration service such as Register.com, Network Solutions (www.networksolutions.com), or any of a host of others (many of which, such as GoDaddy.com, are much cheaper). Your ISP also can register a new domain name for you.

◆ In most cases, you need a static IP address for your Mac. If you don't have a fixed IP address, conceivably you can use a special registration service to forward web requests to your dynamic IP address, as discussed in the previous Note.

◆ Once you have the registered name and a static IP, you need to point that name at your IP address. Generally, you can do this by requesting that your ISP create a new Domain Name Service (DNS) record, then transferring the domain name from your registrar's DNS computers to your ISP's.

For most of these things, you'll consult your ISP. The ISP can register your domain name, if necessary, and create a DNS record that associates your fixed IP address with that particular domain name. Once the DNS record has had a chance to replicate itself to DNS computers around the Internet (this usually takes 24 to 72 hours), users anywhere will be able to access your Mac by name.

Turning on the Web Server

If you've decided you want to turn on the web server in Mac OS X, doing so is fairly simple. If you plan to use your Mac as a public server on the Internet, you'll first need to set up Internet access for at least one of your networking ports; see Chapter 10, "Configuring Internet Access." If you're going to use the server only for local network access, you can simply configure a networking port as discussed in Chapter 18, "Building a Network and Sharing Files." If your Mac sits all by its lonesome, and you're simply turning on the web server so that you can test your web programming efforts locally, you don't have to do anything special.

WARNING   Just to be clear: If you turn on the web server and your Mac connects directly to the Internet at any time (by modem, cable, DSL, or other broadband connection that isn't behind a firewall), that web server is then accessible via the Internet. If you decide you're going to turn on your web server and keep it on, please remember that it's a security risk that you should mitigate by activating the internal firewall and taking other precautions, such as turning off other servers and using a physical firewall/router, if applicable.

Once you get around to making the decision, actually turning on the server is a simple matter:

1. Launch System Preferences.

2. Open the Sharing pane.

3. Click the padlock icon and sign in as an administrator (if necessary).

4. Click the Services tab.

5. Place a check mark next to Personal Web Sharing.

That's it—you don't even have to restart the Mac for the setting to take effect. You've turned on the web server. (Figure 24.1 shows the Sharing pane.) It will remain on until you shut down the Mac (or turn off the server); if you shut down the Mac while the web server is still on, the server will be restarted the next time you start up the Mac.

FIGURE 24.1
Turning on the web server

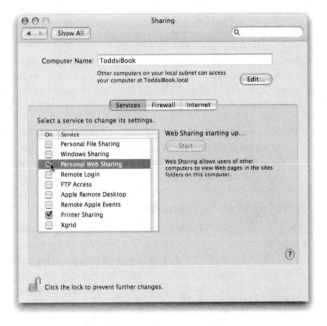

To turn off the web server, just click the Stop button under the Personal Web Sharing On heading or click to remove the check mark next to its entry in the list of services. There's no need to restart the Mac—the server is turned on and off immediately.

At the top of the Sharing pane, you'll see the Computer Name box, where your Mac's current name is displayed. Beneath that you'll see a sentence telling you the name others can use to connect to your Mac if you're connected to your local network.

You can even click one of the links with the web page address to check and make sure everything works.

If you'd like Internet users to see your main website and you have a direct connection to the Internet, tell them to enter your Mac's IP address in their web browsers. You can find that number at the bottom of your Sharing pane when you're connected to the Internet.

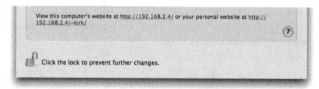

If you have a DNS record assigned to your Mac's fixed IP address, as discussed in the previous section, then Internet-based users should be able to access your web server by entering your domain name address. If your Mac sits behind a firewall or router with NAT capabilities, and your router is correctly configured, you should tell remote users to access the public IP address that's been assigned to the router; their requests will be rerouted to your Mac, and the documents will be served.

NOTE   If you don't see an IP address and you use a dial-up connection to the Internet, you may need to sign on to the Internet first. Then you should see the IP address that you can give to your web-based visitors if you want them to be able to access your Mac (until you shut the Internet connection back down).

Serving Web Documents

Once you've got the web server up and running, you may want to test it. You can do that from the same Mac or from another Mac, depending on the type of access that's available. If your Mac has a fixed IP address on the Internet, you can access it by entering that IP address in any web browser that's also connected to the Internet. If your network (or your particular computer) has its own domain, you can access the server by entering its server name (such as `mac12`) and domain name (`ourbigcompany.com`) together (`http://mac12.ourbigcompany.com`).

If your web server isn't connected to the Internet (or if you're connecting to it from behind a firewall on a private IP network), you can enter the server's private IP address either from your own Mac or from another Mac on your local network. (You also can use your Mac's local scheme, as in `http://ToddsiBook.local` to reach the machine.) The result, if all goes well, will be the Apache default document, downloaded to your client Mac from the web server (see Figure 24.2).

FIGURE 24.2

The default page served to a remote Mac by the Mac's built-in web server

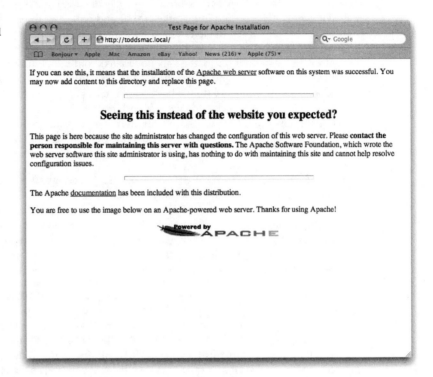

NOTE   If your server computer's name isn't www, you don't need to use www as part of the server name. For example, if your Mac's name is suesmac, and your domain is yourname.com, accessing it via suesmac.yourname.com (not www.suesmac.yourname.com) would cause the default web page on the server to load if Web Sharing is enabled. For this to work, your Mac's static IP address would need to have a DNS record for that domain name, and your Mac would need a hostname assigned to it.

This default page is somewhat informative, telling you not only what type of server is being used to serve your web documents (Apache), but also providing links that explain more about the server application. For instance, the page offers hyperlinks to Apache documentation, FAQs, and related websites. It also offers a *badge*, or small image, that you can use on your own website to advertise that you're using Apache. You can add that image to your own pages if you want.

TIP   A couple of additional badges can be found in the /Library/WebServer/Documents folder, including GIF images called PoweredByMacOSX.gif and PoweredByMacOSXLarge.gif. You can use these images to proclaim your loyalty to Mac OS X on your pages.

Of course, you probably don't want to display this default Apache page forever. (It's boring.) Web pages are stored in the Documents folder inside the WebServer folder that's inside the main Library folder on your startup disk. (The full path is /Library/WebServer/Documents, and we'll refer to it as the Web Documents folder for simplicity's sake.) To replace the default index page, you'll need to create and store a new index.html file in the Web Documents folder. Once you copy that file to the Web Documents folder—naming it index.html and replacing the current index.html—your new index page will be served to visitors who access your web server.

Apache has an interesting capability built in—it can automatically serve localized language pages to visitors. In the default setup, the Web Documents folder includes quite a few index files, such as index.html.fr (French) and index.html.es (Spanish). You can replace these files with your own translations if you want, and they'll be served to users using localized browser applications. Likewise, you can create other documents and end them with two-letter language codes for the same effect (for instance, product1.html.it for an Italian translation of a document called product1.html). However, if you have only one file named index.html, it will override any other localized file and will be used by default.

NOTE   If you delete the index.html files in the Web Documents folder, as you're likely to do when you customize it, you should make sure you add at least an index.html or index.html.en (if English is your default language) immediately. If you don't, you'll cause the server to display the directory of files in your Web Documents folder, enabling the remote user to see and download all files in that directory. If that isn't your intention, then remember that it's important to keep an index.html document in your Web Documents folder at all times. Otherwise, you're free to delete the default pages that are stored in the Web Documents folder and replace them with your own.

You can add subfolders to your Web Documents folder, which are then accessed as part of the URL. For instance, if you add a subfolder called files inside the Web Documents folder, that folder would be accessed using a URL such as http://192.168.1.4/files/ or http://www.yourname.com/files/. If that subfolder has a document in it called index.html, that document will be sent to the user's web browser automatically when a URL pointing to the folder is accessed. Other files can be accessed directly, such as http://www.yourname.com/files/listing.html or http://www.yourname.com/files/download.sit, and then either displayed in the web browser (if they're HTML files or browser-compatible image files) or downloaded to the remote computer.

By default, you must have an Admin-level account to create folders within the Web Documents folder. You should note, however, that if you create a subfolder within that folder, it will likely have different permissions than the Web Documents folder itself: instead of being writable by all Admin users, it may have write status assigned only to you, the owner.

In most cases, you'll probably want to change the permissions on any subfolders that you create in the Web Documents folder so that the Admin group has write access as well. (You don't have to do this if you want to be the only user who can add files to this folder.) Here's how:

1. Select the subfolder and choose File ➢ Get Info or press ⌘I.

2. In the Info window, select the Ownership & Permissions disclosure triangle.

3. Click the Details disclosure triangle to access permissions.

4. Using the Access menu, select Read & Write permissions for the admin group (see Figure 24.3).

You'll also need to have Read Only permissions assigned for Others, but you should be very careful not to set Read & Write permissions for Others. If you do, others on the Internet who access your site could conceivably delete files or upload files to your server, which you definitely want to avoid, because those files could be viruses, worms, or others of malicious intent.

FIGURE 24.3
Changing the permissions level for a subfolder within the Web Documents folder

Adding CGI Scripts

As mentioned earlier, one of the interesting capabilities of the web server is that it can be extended somewhat to provide a level of interactivity via the *Common Gateway Interface*. CGI is a method by which applications can be run on the web server so that your server can respond in real time to data and other input provided by the user. This can range from a CGI script designed to send HTML form data as an e-mail (see Figure 24.4) to an entire web shopping application written so that user feedback (for instance, the user clicks a "buy" link on the page) results in a personalized response (that item is added to the user's virtual shopping cart).

FIGURE 24.4
One use of CGI scripts is to gather data from a simple form and send it to a back-end application or e-mail it to a particular address.

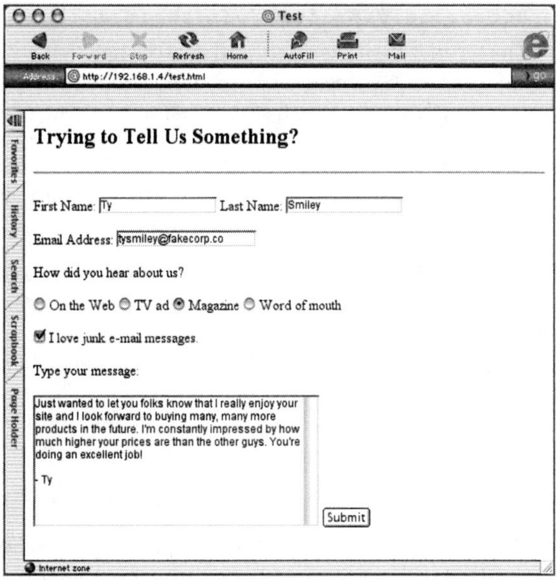

The built-in Apache web server, by default, can support CGI scripts and applications. *CGI scripts* are small programs that are used to accept data entered by users into HTML forms, process that data, and return dynamic HTML documents to the user in response. CGI scripts (also called just "CGIs") are used for everything from accessing databases of web documents to accepting web-based e-commerce orders or tallying votes in an online poll. In Mac OS X, you can write CGIs in any number of languages, including Perl, AppleScript, C, Objective C, Java, and others. (Scripts often will be saved with a filename extension that tells you the language used, as in `scriptname.pl` for a Perl script. However, generally you can save any script without a filename extension or with the generic extension `.cgi`, which is usually required anyway if you've enabled scripts to be executed outside the special CGI folder.)

NOTE   If you're creating a script in Perl and saving it to the `CGI-Executables` folder, you'll need to remember two things. First, you'll need to set execute permissions for that script, as detailed later in this section (as well as in Chapter 23, "Command-Line Applications and Magic"). Second, you'll need to save the Perl script using a text editor that supports Unix linefeeds for text documents; if you save the script using Mac or PC linefeeds, the script probably won't execute correctly. One popular text editor that does support Unix linefeeds from the Aqua environment (as opposed to from within Terminal) is BBEdit, from BareBones Software (`www.barebones.com/`). There is also a simpler version of the program called TextWrangler that you can download and use for free.

Writing the script is up to you—it's outside the scope of this book. Once you've written the script so that it properly handles data from the web server (or once you've downloaded a compatible third-party script), you can store the script in the `CGI-Executables` folder found inside the `WebServer` folder on your Mac. The `CGI-Executables` folder is mapped to the standard URL path `/cgi-bin/` (you don't use `CGI-Executables` in the URLs that you create). For instance, if you've stored a CGI script called `count` within the `CGI-Executables` folder and your server is accessible at `http://192.168.1.3`, you can access that CGI with this URL:

`http://192.168.1.3/cgi-bin/count`

If your Mac has a domain name, URLs should be accessible via that name, such as this:

`http://www.yoursite.com/cgi-bin/count`

The script is then executed, and if so designed, it will return HTML feedback to the browser. As an example, Mac OS X includes in the `CGI-Executables` folder a script called `test-cgi` that you can access directly on your own server just to make sure the CGI feature is functioning appropriately.

NOTE   You can configure Apache to allow CGI scripts to be stored and launched from within your `/Library/WebServer/Documents` folder hierarchy, if desired. To enable this, see the section "Tweaking Apache," later in this chapter.

Before a script in your `CGI-Executables` folder will execute correctly, however, you need to change the permissions for that file. Interestingly, Mac OS X doesn't really offer a graphical tool for enabling this permission—partly because what we're worried about here is the Unix-style *execute* permission, which is something that Mac OS X's File Sharing (and, hence, the Finder's Info window) doesn't let you change.

In any case, you're going to need to dig into the Terminal application to get CGI scripts working correctly. Here's how:

1. Locate and launch the Terminal application.

2. At the command line, type **cd /Library/WebServer/CGI-Executables** and press Return. That will make the `CGI-Executables` folder the current working directory.

3. Now, you're going to need to change the permissions for each CGI script that you want to make active. You'll do this using the chmod command described in Chapter 22, "Terminal and the Command Line." If you aren't logged in to the Root account, however, you'll also need to use the sudo command (which enables you to assume a different user account for a single command) in order to execute the chmod command. Here's what the command looks like for changing the permissions associated with the CGI script printenv:

```
sudo chmod 755 printenv
```

4. After typing this command, press Return. You'll see a password prompt—enter your Admin account password. If the password is correct, the command is executed. Proper permissions have been set, and you should be able to access the CGI script. (In your web browser, try http://localhost/cgi-bin/printenv to see if it works on your own Mac. If your Mac has a hostname other than localhost, enter it instead of localhost in the URL. You also can enter your IP address, if desired, as in http://192.168.1.3/cgi-bin/printenv.)

The 755 argument tells chmod to assign read and execute permissions for the Group and Others, but without giving them write permissions. This is the proper privilege level for a CGI script. Note that you'll need to perform this modification for any script you place in the CGI-Executables folder, replacing printenv in the command with whatever names you give the CGI scripts you place in the folder.

WARNING One issue to note when dealing with CGIs in Mac OS X is that it's fairly important to make sure you don't change the access privilege settings on the CGI-Executables folder itself unless you're sure of what you're doing. That's because changing the write permissions so that others can write to the folder is a security risk. (You don't want unauthorized users to be able to add executable scripts to your server, because they could be viruses, worms, or other malevolent bits of code. In fact, you may not even want any other Admin users to add scripts to the folder, because those scripts may have security holes in them as well.)

User Sites

By default, Mac OS X enables individual users to have a personal website via Web Sharing. As a user, you can place HTML documents in your Sites folder, making them accessible by simply appending *~username*/ to the URL of your web server, using the short username that's assigned to you. For instance, if my web server's IP address were 192.168.1.3, the URL http://192.168.1.3/~todd/ would cause the page index.html to be loaded from Todd's Sites folder. By default, that page looks like Figure 24.5. Scroll down the page to see Apple's discussion of turning on the web server and making pages available on an intranet or the Internet.

If your Mac's web server is accessible via a domain name address, such as www.yourname.com, then user sites can be accessed with an address such as http://www.yourname.com/~todd/. Users are able to place new pages in their Sites folder and create subfolders within the Sites folder. As a user, by default you can't store CGI scripts in a subfolder of your Sites folder, although you can link to CGI scripts stored in the CGI-Executables folder using a full URL such as http://www.yourname.com/cgi-bin/myscript or a relative URL such as ../cgi-bin/myscript.

Again, subfolders must have the correct permissions if they are to be accessible by other users. The subfolder should have read-only access assigned for both the Admin group and Others. Don't assign write permissions; doing so may enable visitors to copy and delete files in your folders.

WARNING   You also should avoid placing aliases or symbolic links in your Sites folder, because those links may enable a user to gain access to other locations on your Mac.

FIGURE 24.5

The default page for an individual Mac OS X user's site

Examining the Logs

Apache keeps logs of activity involving the web server, including an access log that tracks how often pages and files are accessed and an error log that tracks problems the server has had with requests from web browsers or other client software. These logs are somewhat hidden in the /private/var/log/httpd folder, which you can't access directly in a Finder window. The easiest way to view logs is to use the Console application. When you open this application and click the Logs button in its toolbar, you'll see a list of logs you can view. These are organized by location, so you'll see the two main log files, console.log and system.log, followed by ~/Library/Logs, /Library/Logs, and /var/log. Click the disclosure triangles to see the contents of these directories and then click one of the logs to view its contents. You can even view logs that have been backed up and archived (these have a .gz extension); the Console decompresses them on the fly to display their contents.

In the `/var/log/httpd` entry, you'll find two log files, `access_log` and `error_log`. The `access_log` keeps track of every "hit" that your web server receives, while the `error_log` makes a note of every problem that the web server encounters.

TIP   The error log can be particularly useful if you're working with CGI scripts or altering the Apache configuration file, as discussed in the next few sections. Check the error log whenever something goes wrong (such as a script that won't execute when tested), and it may give you a sense of where you need to look for the problem.

You can either examine these logs in Console or save a copy of these log files to another location. Select File ➤ Save a Copy As, preferably in your home folder hierarchy, if you want to analyze the website traffic and problems that have been logged to those files more closely.

Viewing the error log directly can be somewhat informative, but you may quickly find that viewing the access log directly in Console doesn't do you much good. Instead, it's generally more useful to use a special application to view the access log. Third-party applications are available that can process the log and return more meaningful statistics to you, generally via an automatically generated HTML document. The result gives you a summary of access to your site and a better idea of some relevant statistics, such as which pages were accessed the most and on which days of the week or month.

TIP   One of the more popular tools, analog, is currently available as a Carbon application that will run in both the Classic Mac OS and Mac OS X. See `http://summary.net/soft/analog.html` for details and downloading. A command-line version of analog can be downloaded and installed fairly easily, as discussed in Chapter 23. The analog tool will read the Apache access log and then output an HTML document, which you can view in a web browser to learn more about your site's visitor statistics.

Another important step in dealing with your Apache logs is to *rotate* them occasionally. By default, logs are rotated automatically, but you may occasionally find that a log file has become very large and that you'd like to start over again with a fresh file.

NOTE   Generally, these log files will rotate automatically, unless you make a habit of turning off your Mac most evenings after you're done working with it. If that's the case, you might also want to run an application called MacJanitor (`http://personalpages.tds.net/~brian_hill/mac-janitor.html`) that rotates files via a friendlier interface. Or, if you're comfortable on the command line, you can run the `periodic` command, which takes care of this. There are three ways to run this command: one runs daily maintenance tasks, another weekly tasks, and the third monthly tasks. To run the daily tasks, you must be an administrator, and run `sudo periodic daily`. To run all three sets of tasks, run `sudo periodic daily weekly monthly`.

Rotating the logs is essentially a process whereby you remove the current log file(s), ideally by moving them to another folder on your Mac, then restart the server so that the log files are re-created and begun again. Depending on how busy your web server is, the log files can grow to many megabytes—even gigabytes—in size. So it's a good idea to rotate them on a regular basis—or at least check occasionally to make sure they're being rotated as they should. Here's how:

1. Log in to your Mac so that you have the proper permissions to move and delete the log files. (This will usually require a root login, unless you intend to use the `sudo` command in the Terminal.)

2. Launch System Preferences, open the Sharing pane, and click the Stop button under Web Sharing to turn off the web server.

3. Open the /private/var/log/httpd folder and move the files access_log and error_log to another folder on your Mac. (If this duplicates the files instead of moving them, you also should delete the original log files by dragging them to the Trash. Double-check the copied files and make sure they were successfully duplicated, however, before deleting the originals, or you'll lose that log data for future analysis.)

4. In System Preferences, turn Web Sharing back on.

As a result of turning the web server back on, it's started up, and new log files are created in the /private/var/log/httpd folder. Those new log files begin with the first entry and, once again, will slowly grow as new access and error messages are added. You'll need to check in occasionally and rotate them regularly, depending on how busy your web server gets.

The Apache Configuration File

If you decide to dig deeper into the customization of Apache, you'll do so in the Apache configuration file. This is the file read by Mac OS X's file server whenever it starts up, receiving its preferences and settings. It has a decidedly "Unixy" flavor, but you'll get used to it after a little experience.

TIP   You can read about the Apache configuration file in numerous Apache and Unix-oriented books and at websites dedicated to discussing Apache and how it can be configured (for instance, www.apache.org). For a Mac-specific Apache discussion, we've found www.macosxhints.com to be a great place to find interesting tweaks and tricks, including such things as tweaking Apache for speed and for password-protecting documents and subfolders on your websites. Also, you can access Apache documentation that's preinstalled on your Mac by pointing your web browser to http://localhost/manual/.

The Apache configuration file is stored in the folder /private/etc/httpd, and it's named httpd.conf. Unless you're logged in to the Root account, you can't point and click to this folder in the Finder; instead, you'll need to open a Terminal window and use the cd command to access the folder. (With an Admin account, you also can use the Go ➢ Go to Folder command in the Finder and enter **/private/etc/httpd** or just **/etc/httpd** in the Go to Folder dialog sheet.)

NOTE   While these files are technically located in a hierarchy that starts with the folder /private, it's not necessary to type **/private**, because the /etc and /var folders have hard links on your system that point to /private/etc and /private/var. So, while we'll often mention that something is in the /private hierarchy, know that you can usually get away with not typing it in the Finder Go To Folder command, for instance.

WARNING   Once you've located it, you should copy the httpd.conf file to another folder on your hard disk (probably somewhere in your home folder) before attempting to alter it. This gives you a chance to look at it and play with it without potentially messing up the working version.

Drag the httpd.conf file (more appropriately, your copy of it) to the TextEdit icon or another graphical text editor that's capable of saving documents with Unix linefeeds. Or, in Terminal, change to the relevant directory and use pico httpd.conf to edit the file in the pico editor.

The configuration file is well documented, and you'll likely find that you'll get a sense of what some things do just by reading through it. You absolutely should avoid changing things in the file that you don't understand (particularly if you plan to implement this configuration file at some point). In most cases, working within the configuration file involves adding and removing the # sign in front of commands to enable or disable them. The # sign is the *comment* character for the log files (as it is in shell and Perl scripting), so placing the # sign in front of a configuration line effectively turns off that line. If there's no sign in front of a setting, it's activated.

```
# the order below without expert advice.
#
# Example:
# LoadModule foo_module libexec/mod_foo.so
#LoadModule vhost_alias_module libexec/httpd/mod_vhost_alias.so
#LoadModule env_module          libexec/httpd/mod_env.so
LoadModule config_log_module  libexec/httpd/mod_log_config.so
#LoadModule mime_magic_module  libexec/httpd/mod_mime_magic.so
LoadModule mime_module         libexec/httpd/mod_mime.so
LoadModule negotiation_module libexec/httpd/mod_negotiation.so
```

The other thing you'll often do in the configuration file, if you're customizing things, is change values. Some of the configuration lines in the file have a range of numerical values, while others have simpler Boolean values of On or Off. In most cases, the commented description that precedes a configuration line should make the range or type of acceptable values clear.

Once you've edited the configuration file, you can save it. To replace the current Apache configuration file, you'll need to either log in to the Root account (if enabled) or use the sudo command at the Terminal command line to copy the file to /private/etc/httpd. Here's how:

1. Open the Sharing pane of System Preferences, select Personal Web Sharing in the list of services, and click Stop under Personal Web Sharing On to stop the web server.

2. In /private/etc/httpd, rename the current httpd.conf file to httpd.conf.myback or something similar. It's important to do this so that you can recover the current, working httpd.conf file if necessary. (At the command line, if you're not in the Root account, type **cd /private/ etc/httpd** and press Return; then type **sudo mv httpd.conf httpd.conf.myback** and press Return again. You may be asked for your password—enter it and press Return.)

3. Copy your altered copy of httpd.conf to /private/etc/httpd/httpd.conf (making sure to name it httpd.conf exactly).

4. Restart the web server by opening the Sharing pane and going to the Services tab. Click to place a check mark next to Personal Web Sharing in the Services listing.

That's it. Apache will restart, read the new httpd.conf file, and start up with your new settings and preferences intact. To make sure everything went well, you can take a look at the Apache error_ log file discussed in the section "Examining the Logs," earlier in this chapter.

NOTE   The default Apache configuration is stored in a file called httpd.conf.default. If you ever need to revert Apache's configuration to its original (for instance, if you mess up the configuration file you're customizing), you can simply shut down Web Sharing, copy this file to apache.conf (sudo cp apache.conf.default apache.conf), and turn Web Sharing back on.

Tweaking Apache

Once you've figured out how to dig into the Apache configuration file, you may find that you're ready to perform a tweak or two that you can use to alter the way Apache works. In this section, let's take a look at some of the basic Apache configuration file changes you can use to implement popular web serving technologies and techniques.

NOTE As noted in the previous section, you should always turn off Web Sharing and back up the Apache configuration file before working with it and then remember to restart Web Sharing whenever you want to test the new file. (Ideally, you shouldn't test on a server that's currently serving pages on the Internet.) Also, consult the Apache documentation (http://localhost/manual/) for more options and possibilities for tweaking your server. Once you've worked through the samples in this section, the rest of the Apache documentation should make sense to you.

ALLOW CGI SCRIPTS OUTSIDE *CGI-BIN*

If you'd like to be able to store your CGI scripts outside of the CGI-Executables directory (and, hence, without the cgi-bin/ requirement for the URL), you can alter the Apache configuration file to allow that. With the file open for editing, search for the following entry:

```
<Directory "/Library/WebServer/Documents">
#
# This may also be "None", "All", or any combination of "Indexes",
# "Includes", "FollowSymLinks", "ExecCGI", or "MultiViews".
#
# Note that "MultiViews" must be named *explicitly* --- "Options All"
# doesn't give it to you.
#
    Options Indexes FollowSymLinks MultiViews
```

On the last line, we're interested in adding the option ExecCGI, which tells Apache that we want to be able to execute CGI scripts within this folder hierarchy. (You'll be able to execute CGI scripts inside the Documents folder as well as inside subfolders of the Documents folder.) The final line should look like this:

```
Options Indexes FollowSymLinks MultiViews ExecCGI
```

Next, you need to find the line:

```
#AddHandler cgi-script .cgi
```

When you locate that line, delete the leading # symbol so that it's no longer a commented-out command. Now, if desired, you can change or add to the filename extensions that will be recognized as a CGI script:

```
AddHandler cgi-script .cgi .pl
```

With those changes made, save the file, copy the changed configuration file to /private/etc/httpd/, and stop File Sharing as discussed in the previous section, "The Apache Configuration File." When you restart File Sharing, Apache will read the new settings and should enable you to execute CGI scripts from within the regular HTML folders of your site, as long as they're saved using the correct filename extensions.

NOTE   Scripts stored in your main HTML folders also need to have the correct permissions settings, just as do scripts stored in the `CGI-Executables` folder (see the earlier section "Adding CGI Scripts" for details.)

This approach is a bit broad, however, because it enables CGI scripts in every directory that the server can access, including all the subfolders of `/Library/WebServer/Documents/`. You might consider allowing CGI scripts only in your user's folders, but not everywhere else. You can do that, too. In the Apache configuration file, you'll find an entry that looks like this:

```
# Control access to UserDir directories.  The following is an example
# for a site where these directories are restricted to read-only.
#
#<Directory /Users/*/Sites>
#    AllowOverride FileInfo AuthConfig Limit
#    Options MultiViews Indexes SymLinksIfOwnerMatch IncludesNoExec
#    <Limit GET POST OPTIONS PROPFIND>
#        Order allow,deny
#        Allow from all
#    </Limit>
#    <LimitExcept GET POST OPTIONS PROPFIND>
#        Order deny,allow
#        Deny from all
#    </LimitExcept>
#</Directory>
```

What you're going to do is uncomment these lines (or copy them and place the copy in the document, uncommented, immediately after these lines), and then simplify them quite a bit. What's shown is a sample entry that doesn't do exactly what we're trying to do. The result will look quite a bit simpler:

```
<Directory /Users/*/Sites>
AllowOverride None
Options ExecCGI
</Directory>
```

The idea here is to enable the `ExecCGI` option for the `Sites` folders found in your users' home folders. Once the configuration file is updated and Web Sharing is restarted, those users can add and execute their own CGI scripts (with filename extensions according to the `AddHandler` entry discussed previously). You could also change this option only for a particular user by opening that user's file in the folder `/private/etc/httpd/users/`. There you'll see files for each user (for example, `todd.conf`) that can be changed individually—for CGIs, you'd add `ExecCGI` to the `Options` entry.

WARNING   Allowing execution of CGIs outside of the `CGI-Executables` folder generally is considered a security risk, although a slight one. Allowing your users to work with CGI scripts in their own folders can be an even greater security risk, particularly if those users aren't terribly knowledgeable. Turn on these options only if you're fairly certain that they won't affect your server's security.

CHANGE THE DEFAULT PAGE NAME AND BLOCK INDEXES

Among a host of other tweaks you can perform simply by editing the Apache configuration file, you may want to change the name of the default page that's served when a user accesses a directory on your server. Likewise, you may want to activate or block the capability of your visitors to see a listing of a particular directory if that default page isn't present.

By default, Apache will serve the page `index.html` if it exists in the directory that a user attempts to access. For instance, accessing `http://10.0.1.201/products/` should cause the `index.html` page that's stored in the `products` folder inside the main `/Library/Documents` folder on your server. (That is, it will attempt to load `http://10.0.1.201/products/index.html`.) What happens if that `index.html` file isn't there? By default, a directory listing will be displayed (see Figure 24.6).

FIGURE 24.6

By default, Apache will list the contents of a folder that doesn't have an `index.html` document.

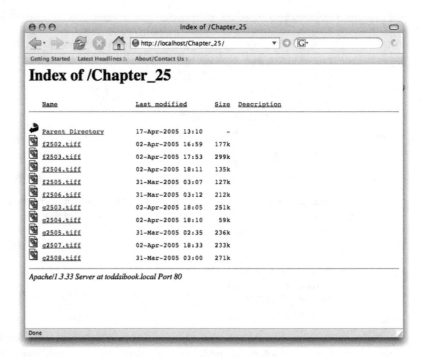

First things first—let's change the default page name. To do that, you can dig into the Apache configuration file and locate this entry:

```
#
# DirectoryIndex: Name of the file or
# files to use as a prewritten HTML
# directory index. Separate multiple entries with spaces.
#
<IfModule mod_dir.c>
    DirectoryIndex index.html
</IfModule>
```

That entry needs to change to reflect the new default filename that you'd like to use for the directory index page.

```
#
# DirectoryIndex: Name of the file or
# files to use as a prewritten HTML
# directory index. Separate multiple entries with spaces.
#
<IfModule mod_dir.c>
    DirectoryIndex default.html
</IfModule>
```

Note that you can separate more than one filename with a space, and Apache will try each:

```
#
# DirectoryIndex: Name of the file or
# files to use as a prewritten HTML
# directory index. Separate multiple entries with spaces.
#
<IfModule mod_dir.c>
    DirectoryIndex index.html default.html
</IfModule>
```

If a folder has either index.html or default.html in it, that document will be displayed instead of a basic directory listing. That doesn't cover you in every circumstance, though. If the whole point is simply to keep the user from being able to see the directory contents (which might be considered a security risk), you can simply turn off that capability completely. To do that, locate the following in the Apache configuration file:

```
#
# This should be changed to whatever you set DocumentRoot to.
#
<Directory "/Library/WebServer/Documents">
#
# This may also be "None", "All", or any combination of "Indexes",
# "Includes", "FollowSymLinks", "ExecCGI", or "MultiViews".
#
# Note that "MultiViews" must be named *explicitly* --- "Options All"
# doesn't give it to you.
#
    Options Indexes FollowSymLinks MultiViews
```

The last line is the one we're worried about. The option Indexes is telling Apache to display a file listing when a directory that doesn't have a valid default page is accessed. The solution is to remove Indexes from the line:

```
Options FollowSymLinks MultiViews
```

That's it. Save, copy, restart, and test to see that file listing attempts now result in error messages, as seen in Figure 24.7.

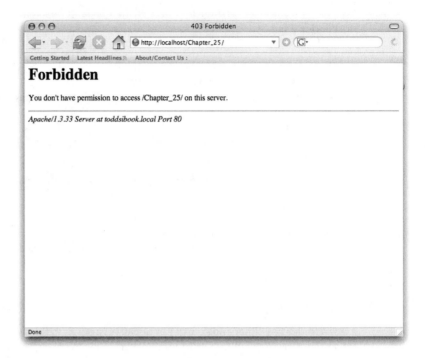

ADD SERVER-SIDE INCLUDES

Another common desire among website authors is the capability to use *server-side includes (SSIs)* in their pages. Server-side includes are special commands that the Apache server can process when it's displaying the web document, inserting dynamic content—anything from the current date or time to another HTML document—so that, for instance, you can use one central document as a navigation bar on all of your web documents.

Using SSIs is a bit outside the scope of this book, although you'll find that Apache's online documentation (`http://localhost/manual/howto/ssi.html`) does a pretty good job of explaining things. In this section, though, we'll look at the two steps necessary to enable SSIs.

First, you need to enable SSI processing for a particular directory or directories. The easiest way to do that is to enable SSIs for the main `/Library/WebServer/Documents` folder by locating the following section of the Apache configuration file:

```
#
# This should be changed to whatever you set DocumentRoot to.
#
<Directory "/Library/WebServer/Documents">
#
# This may also be "None", "All", or any combination of "Indexes",
# "Includes", "FollowSymLinks", "ExecCGI", or "MultiViews".
#
```

```
# Note that "MultiViews" must be named *explicitly* --- "Options All"
# doesn't give it to you.
#
Options Indexes FollowSymLinks MultiViews
```

This last line needs to be updated with the option `Includes`:

```
Options Indexes FollowSymLinks MultiViews Includes
```

Next, you need to enable the SSI processor for a particular filename extension. Generally, that extension is `.shtml`, meaning the server will automatically grab any document with an `.shtml` extension, look through it for server-side include commands, and if any are found, process them. Search the Apache configuration file for the following:

```
#
# To use server-parsed HTML files
#
#AddType text/html .shtml
#AddHandler server-parsed .shtml
```

To activate SSIs, simply uncomment those last two lines. Any file that has an `.shtml` filename extension will be processed by Apache, and its SSI commands will be active. For instance, Figure 24.8 shows the result of a document (saved with the name `index.shtml`) that has the following HTML and SSI commands:

```
This document last modified <!--#flastmod file="index.shtml" --><br />
The following is output from the test-cgi script:<br />
<!--#include virtual="/cgi-bin/test-cgi">
```

FIGURE 24.8
Here's the output, showing SSI commands working correctly.

Serving FTP

Mac OS X features a built-in *File Transfer Protocol (FTP)* server, which enables it to share files using the Unix-standard method of logging in to and out of individual computers. In a way, FTP is very similar to Apple File Protocol (AFP), in that it enables you to use a username and password to log in to a remote computer and copy files to and from that remote computer, according to the file permissions you have on the remote computer.

One real difference is that FTP is a multiplatform standard that's commonly used over the Internet as well as on a LAN; although AFP can be used in the same way, it's used primarily for Mac-to-Mac connections on a LAN or over the Internet. Although you can use a third-party FTP application (such as those discussed in Chapter 17, "Accessing Network Volumes") or Mac OS X's built-in Terminal (discussed in Chapters 17 and 22) to access remote FTP servers, you can also mount FTP volumes directly on the Finder desktop.

Turning FTP On and Off

As for turning your own Mac into an FTP server, the decision is up to you (assuming you have administrator or root access to your Mac). Once the server is enabled, anyone with an account on your Mac can access it using an FTP client application. Once users have gained access, they can read and write files according to their file permissions, exactly as if they were physically sitting at your Mac. (Users cannot execute applications on your Mac, however—that's reserved for telnet or SSH access, which is discussed in Chapter 17.)

The process of turning on FTP access is simple:

1. Open the System Preferences application.

2. If necessary, launch the Network pane and configure your Mac for TCP/IP and, if appropriate, Internet access (see Chapters 10 and 18).

3. If TCP/IP access is configured, open the Sharing pane.

4. Click the padlock icon and sign in as an administrator (if necessary).

5. Click the Services tab.

6. Click to place a check mark in the On column next to FTP Access.

FTP access is turned on immediately; if you have no further business in the System Preferences application, you can close it. You needn't even restart your Mac—once FTP access is activated, the Mac can be accessed immediately by remote FTP client applications.

NOTE   Other Sharing settings aren't relevant to FTP access, even though the File Sharing and Personal Web Sharing options also appear in the Sharing pane. If FTP access is turned on, files can be accessed by remote users (according to their file permissions), regardless of the File Sharing state. Note that file and folder permissions are relevant, however.

Once FTP is turned on, remote users, including your own account, can access this Mac using an FTP client elsewhere on your LAN. If your Mac is connected to the Internet and has a fixed IP address, you can use an FTP client to log in to it from anywhere on the Internet. Just launch the FTP application and enter your Mac's IP address or, if appropriate, the machine name, domain name, and three-letter domain extension. (Chapter 17 discusses FTP clients in more detail.)

One account isn't allowed to access the Mac remotely: the Root account, if it's enabled. You can't sign in as root via an FTP client—which is a good thing, because it means that no one can have root's file permissions and access the Mac from a distance. If it's you who is logged in to your Mac, however, don't forget to sign out of your FTP application whenever you leave it unattended, just to make sure that unauthorized users can't get even limited access to your Mac remotely.

To turn off the FTP server, simply reopen the Sharing pane, log in as an administrator via the padlock icon (if necessary), and click to remove the check mark next to FTP Access. When you uncheck the server, it's turned off immediately, and further access by remote FTP applications is denied.

FTP Security

Turning on FTP access is a potential security risk because it opens up your Mac to remote access over a network, via either your LAN or the Internet (or both) if your Mac is networked to other computers. By default, Mac OS X's FTP server doesn't allow anonymous or guest access via FTP, so the risk is limited to the possibility that a remote user will crack the password of an existing user account. As always, encourage your users (and yourself) to use difficult-to-guess passwords.

Also, if you have a fixed IP address and your Mac isn't guarded by a firewall or similar router protection, consider carefully whether it's appropriate to turn on FTP access. Mac OS X's built-in firewall, discussed in the section "Net Server Security Considerations," later in this chapter, is one option to keep a minimum level of security active.

WARNING   You should make sure that you haven't created a user called ftp in the Users pane of System Preferences, because creating such a user could allow anonymous FTP access to your Mac. Mac OS X 10.4 doesn't allow you to create such a user from the Accounts pane of System Preferences, although you could conceivably do so using the NetInfo Manager application.

FTP usernames and passwords sent to your Mac from a regular FTP application are sent in *clear text*, meaning they aren't encrypted and could be read easily if they were intercepted. If that happened, you'd likely be compromising actual user account passwords, because the same passwords used with user accounts are used for FTP. Mac OS X also supports a more secure method of FTP, called *SFTP (secure FTP)*; you activate SFTP by turning on Remote Login in the Sharing pane of System Preferences. Check Apple's website and technical information for updates. If security is important to you, it's best not to enable FTP at all. Instead, see the discussion in Chapter 18 regarding other IP-based networking options.

TIP   If you'd like to go beyond the built-in offerings, you can look into some third-party FTP solutions. For instance, Secure FTP Wrapper (http://www.glub.com/products/ftpswrap/) offers an option that enables you to "wrap" your FTP transactions in a secure layer, thus encrypting data that generally would be transmitted in plain text.

Accessing FTP Logs

The FTP logs, like the Web Sharing logs, are stored away in the `/private/var/log/` folder on your hard disk, and you can view the FTP log using Console, in the same way you view other logs. Just open Console, click the `/var/log` disclosure triangle, and click `ftp.log`. You'll see the FTP log appear in the Console window.

In the Console window, you can view the log file, which shows you successful and unsuccessful attempts to access your Mac via FTP. (If you plan to work with the file other than simply viewing it, you probably should save a copy to a folder within your home folder, where you can analyze it with third-party applications and so on.)

Net Server Security Considerations

Whenever your Mac has *any* IP address on the Internet, you've created a security risk, particularly if you have servers, including Web Sharing, enabled. That risk is lessened when the IP address is dynamic; if you sign on to and off the Internet and regularly get a different IP address from your ISP, you're less likely to run into any trouble.

With a fixed address, particularly if your Mac has an "always-on" connection to the Internet, you need to be especially security conscious. Whether or not your Mac has a domain name associated with it, that fixed address makes your Mac an enticing target for hackers, crackers, or any other malicious beings on the Internet, including automated *sniffer* applications that troll the Web looking for machines that are on the Internet.

We don't recommend running a web server with a fixed IP address from your personal computer—at least, not without a firewall of some sort in place. A *firewall* (or an Internet router with Network Address Translation and a "virtual server" function) is designed to block all requests from the Internet other than those requesting web pages. This is possible because web requests generally come in on a particular Internet *port* (port 80), enabling the firewall or router to block other types of access. Firewalls also can be configured for other, more-specific types of access blocking, including blocking of certain types of requests and attacks or blocking access from certain IP address ranges and domains.

The firewall built into Mac OS X was introduced in Chapter 10, but it's important to note here its relationship to Web Sharing and FTP Access. When activated, the firewall automatically blocks all traffic to your Mac until you activate a server, such as File Sharing or Web Sharing. When you do that, that service's ports are automatically opened up by the firewall, enabling access to that server.

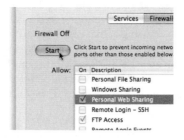

Although it's hard to call this a foolproof system, it is a good start. If you're working with any built-in server, you should turn on the firewall (click the Start button on the Firewall tab of the Sharing pane) and allow it to manage traffic. That, at least, is a useful first line of defense for the "sometimes a server" Macintosh.

Of course, there are third-party options, including firewalls built into physical Internet routers that use *Network Address Translation (NAT)*. This increases security by intercepting web requests that are sent to your public IP address and rerouting them to the private IP address of the Mac you've specified as the web server. That makes it so that the server computer itself isn't directly accessible to Internet users, because the static IP address made public by your network isn't the same as the address for the specific Mac you're using as a web or FTP server. This can help a bit to cut down on attempts to break directly into the web server. You can also consider an optional software firewall, which can help if you have a Mac that is directly connected to the Internet, you want to use it as a server, and you don't want to invest in additional hardware. See Chapter 10 for more on software firewalls.

If you opt to use your personal Mac as a public web server, you should—at the very least—turn on the included firewall. We'd also recommend that you turn off other servers, such as File Sharing, FTP, and remote login. (File Sharing is particularly important, because having it turned on while your Mac is connected via static IP to the Internet makes the default guest account available to anyone on the Internet!) If you choose not to turn these other services off, then keep in mind that other Internet users may be able to access the servers in ways that you don't intend and conceivably could gain access to your Mac and its files and applications. (They also may be able to gain access to other computers on your local network, if you have one.) That means you need to be vigilant about user accounts, passwords, and permissions on your Mac so that anyone who *does* gain access can't do any major harm.

Finally, consider using the most secure method for any connection—use secure FTP where possible or skip FTP and use File Sharing or another encrypted method for password authentication and data transfer. (You can enable secure FTP by turning on Remote Login in the Sharing preferences. Secure FTP uses a different protocol—the SSH, or secure shell, protocol—to make an encrypted FTP connection. If you want to only use SFTP, you *don't* need to turn on FTP Access in this preference pane; Remote Login is sufficient.) While it's generally unlikely that your data will be compromised, it's best to take the most secure route possible, particularly if your personal or professional business depends on it.

Augmenting Apache: PHP and MySQL

In this section, we'd like to focus on some solutions that may concern you if you're trying to install (or write and implement) web applications using Mac OS X. Many different interesting and exciting web applications can be downloaded and installed relatively easily, from discussion forums and shopping carts to full web logging and content management solutions. Although some of them may work with minimal configuration in Mac OS X, for many of them you'll have to dig in and do a little more customization—in particular, you'll find that you need to do some manual configuration if you want to use PHP (PHP Hypertext Protocol), and you'll need to download and install MySQL if your software calls for it.

Configuring PHP

If you have a web application that requires PHP as its scripting language, or if you'd simply like to implement PHP code within your web documents, you can do so by enabling PHP within Apache on Mac OS X. It's already there under the hood, but Apache by default isn't configured to process PHP code inside web documents. However, that can be changed.

NOTE Before editing the Apache configuration file, back it up and turn off Web Sharing, as discussed earlier this chapter.

To turn on PHP, you'll need to edit the Apache `config` file (`private/etc/httpd/httpd.conf`). You'll edit a few different lines in order to turn on PHP. First, you need to locate this line:

```
#LoadModule php4_module libexec/httpd/libphp4.so
```

When you've found the line, delete the comment sign (#) that appears in front of it so that it's no longer commented out and will be recognized by Apache when it's started back up.

In the next series of entries, locate this line:

```
#AddModule mod_php4.c
```

Now, save the file (copy it back to `/etc/httpd/` if necessary) and, if you'd like to test PHP to make sure it's working, restart Web Sharing. (Mac OS X probably won't allow you to save the document directly to the `/etc/httpd/` folder, but you can copy it in the Finder and choose to authenticate if you have an administrator's account.)

In a text document, create a file called `phpinfo.php` and add just this one line to the file:

```
<?php phpinfo() ?>
```

Save the file and place it either in the `/Library/WebServer/Documents` folder or in your `Sites` folder inside your home folder. Then, for the moment of truth, access that document in your web browser, using either `http://localhost/phpinfo.php` or `http://localhost.com/~yourname/phpinfo.php`, depending on where you put the file. If it works, you'll see something like Figure 24.9.

FIGURE 24.9
If PHP has been successfully enabled, you'll see the phpinfo() screen when accessing the test document.

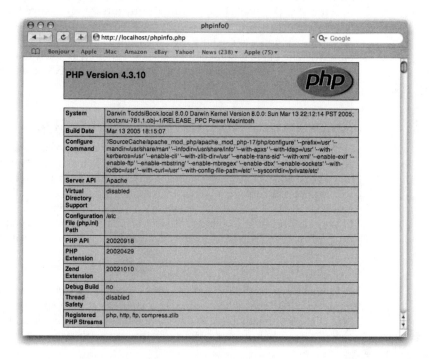

Installing MySQL

MySQL is a back-end Internet database solution that a lot of popular off-the-shelf web applications use. You can use it, too, to create and manage web applications. MySQL is an open-source implementation of IBM's original Structured Query Language (SQL). Its popularity on the Web certainly has been enhanced by its standard-bearing and open-source nature, although other databases are available for use on the Web as well.

If you want to install MySQL for use with Apache in Mac OS X, you'll need to download and install MySQL. The easiest way to do that is to head to www.entropy.ch/software/macosx/mysql/, where programmer Mark Liyanage has been keeping up with MySQL releases and offering instructions on installation. Download the latest version (check for Mac OS X 10.4 compatibility) and follow the instructions on that page because they may change from time to time and with different releases. All you'll really be doing is expanding the archive, installing MySQL, and then assigning ownership of the MySQL files to the special mysql user account (which is already created in Mac OS X 10.4). Then you launch the server and test it.

NOTE A number of third-party tools are available for managing your MySQL database on Mac OS X, including MacSQL (www.rtlabs.com/macsql/), SQL Boss (www.sqlboss.com/), and SQL Grinder (www.advenio.com/sqlgrinder/).

COMMERCIAL OPTIONS: COMMUNIGATE AND ITOOLS

If you're interested in extending Mac OS X even further into the world of Internet services and Unix-like functionality, you may want to consider a commercial application. Out of the gate, a few different companies have provided Mac OS X versions of popular server applications and add-ons, most notably Tenon Intersystems (www.tenon.com), which makes iTools, and Stalker Software (www.stalker.com), publishers of Communigate Pro.

Communigate Pro is a server application that focuses on adding complex mail-serving capabilities to your Mac. If you'd like your Mac OS X Server computer to act as a mail server for a local network, Communigate Pro offers those tools. Following are some of the features:

◆ POP3 server for Internet e-mail addresses

◆ IMAP server for "live" e-mail accounts

◆ Web-based e-mail retrieval for accessing e-mail accounts when the user is away from the computer

◆ Mailing list management, enabling groups to communicate via group mailing lists (often called "listservs")

◆ SMTP server for managing outgoing e-mail

◆ Hooks for antispam and antivirus applications

Communigate Pro generally is offered as a limited-license download from the Stalker Software website, so you can try the software before purchasing it.

Tenon's iTools is a suite of Internet applications, including a mail-server application and tools to augment Mac OS X's built-in FTP and Apache web servers. The tools include these:

◆ Secure Sockets Layer 3.0 (SSL) support for secure web transactions

◆ A web-based interface for configuring and customizing Apache for better performance

◆ Virtual host support, enabling a single Mac to host both multiple web addresses and multiple FTP addresses, so that remote users can directly access their own web server spaces

◆ Caching HTML files to improve web performance

◆ DNS support for your local network

◆ A built-in search engine for adding searches to your website

◆ An e-mail server that includes POP, IMAP, SMTP, and web-based e-mail options

iTools—carrying a retail price of about $350 at the time of this writing—isn't cheap. (Like Communigate, there's a free demo of iTools that you can download from Tenon's website.) Still, it's a nice add-on for hosting and managing professional-level websites, including FTP and e-mail service, from a single Mac OS X server. In fact, the tools are ideal for companies, other organizations, or even small Internet presence providers that want to offer web hosting to multiple clients.

iTools requires a Mac that has a static IP address and a broadband connection to the Internet. You'll also need to have the Mac properly configured with a domain name and hostname. Once you've installed iTools and logged in with a new username and password (these are unique to iTools and not based on your Mac OS X account name), you'll be able to configure the additional capabilities from within a web browser window.

What's Next?

In this chapter, you saw how to activate the web server that's built into Mac OS X, as well as how to manage that server's logs and add CGI scripts to augment the server's functionality. In addition, you saw how to edit the Apache configuration file and perform a few frequently necessary tweaks to the basic configuration. You also learned how to enable the FTP server and check its log file, and you saw an overview of the basic issues of server security.

In Part 6, "Hardware, Troubleshooting, and Maintenance," we'll move on to working with hardware, keeping system software up to date, and troubleshooting Mac OS X, its applications, and even its folders and files.

Part 6

Hardware, Troubleshooting, and Maintenance

In this section, you will learn how to:

- ◆ **Install and troubleshoot internal and external devices**
- ◆ **Partition and initialize hard disks**
- ◆ **Back up and maintain your files and disks**
- ◆ **Troubleshoot applications and the Classic environment**
- ◆ **Troubleshoot the Mac OS X system and Internet connections**
- ◆ **Solve common problems encountered with Mac OS X**

## Chapter 25

Peripherals, Internal Upgrades, and Disks

Over the course of Mac OS X's relatively short history, hardware compatibility has been a moving target. With early versions of the OS, a lot of devices that had worked in Mac OS 9 didn't work in Mac OS X. As the OS matured, so did its ability to work with legacy hardware. Of course, hardware compatibility often relies on a device's manufacturer to write a software driver, and many of those manufacturers have decided not to release Mac OS X drivers for legacy devices.

So, for many older devices, you'll need to find a third-party driver, find a workaround, or look for a new device. With Mac OS X 10.4, that's about where things stand—it will be the rare legacy peripheral that gets a new driver these days, unless it's offered by a third party.

And, in the meantime, the world of Macintosh is now replete with new peripheral technologies such as Bluetooth wireless connections, AirPort, USB 2.0, FireWire 800, and others that are playing a huge role in the Apple landscape. Mac OS X 10.4 has been designed to embrace those technologies and to improve the user experience with peripherals using technologies such as Bonjour, which can automatically locate and configure compatible peripherals and devices.

In this chapter, we'll take a look at some of the issues involved in getting Mac OS X to work with both new and existing peripherals. You'll also learn how to use Apple System Profiler to troubleshoot peripherals and Apple's Disk Utility application to partition and format hard disks. We'll end with a look at Mac OS X's Software Update feature, which you can (and should) use to update components of the operating system automatically.

In this chapter:

◆ Adding External Devices

◆ Adding Internal Devices

◆ Troubleshooting Hardware with System Profiler

◆ Using Software Update

Adding External Devices

Few of us can get by without adding external devices to our Macs—even if they mar the clean lines of your ideal Mac setup with cables and connectors, there's a good chance you'll come up with a reason to attach a printer, scanner, digital camera, iPod, or other device to your Mac.

If you're lucky, you'll find a driver for your device built into Mac OS X. On the other hand, you may be forced to rely on the manufacturer of a problematic drive to release a driver update—assuming that the manufacturer has the interest and resources to develop a Mac OS X–compatible driver. In the case of peripherals that have been purchased in the past few years, manufacturer updates are fairly likely. For older peripherals, you may need to hope for a third-party solution.

Drivers for hardware sometimes come in the form of a kernel extension (with a `.kext` filename extension), which is stored in the `System/Library/Extensions` folder on your hard disk. You'll need a special installer (and an administrator account) to install kernel extensions; then you'll need to restart the Mac. You should rarely, if ever, need to install a kernel extension by hand. However, you can do this by activating the Root account (see Chapter 28, "Solving System-Level Problems") and copying the kernel extension into the `System/Library/Extensions` folder.

NOTE If you need to remove an extension, you should check the Readme file associated with the extension's installer—the package installer for your driver may have an option to remove the extension. If you can't find any instructions, you can try the following as a last resort: Boot into Mac OS 9 or connect your Mac to another Mac in Target Disk Mode and remove the `.kext` driver file from `System/Library/Extensions`. In some cases, you may also need to remove the associated `.pkg` file from the `/Library/Receipts/` folder. Next, restart your computer in Mac OS X. (Target Disk Mode is discussed in Chapter 19, "PowerBooks, iBooks, and Mac OS X.")

Not every hardware device requires an extension—some require either support from the Mac OS itself or at least support from within applications. For instance, some external CD-RW drives may not be supported by Mac OS X directly for burning CDs from the Finder or iTunes, but they may still be accessible using the software that came with the device. In other cases, you'll find that third-party drivers or utility applications may be able to make an external scanner or input device usable, even if the manufacturer doesn't offer direct (or reliable) Mac OS X compatibility.

Here, we'll take a look at some specific categories of external devices, including external disks, CD-R and CD-RW drives, USB devices, keyboards, mice, modems, serial devices, and Bluetooth wireless devices. Also discussed is how to work with a connected iPod and how to configure an AirPort Base Station.

NOTE One thing to remember if you're having trouble with an external device is that there may be an internal culprit as well. If you're using a PCI adapter card for SCSI, USB, or FireWire connections, remember that the adapter card also may require an update. See the "Adding Internal Devices" section later in this chapter for details.

External Disks

External disks—both hard disks and removable drives—vary widely in their capability to work with Mac OS X. Mac OS X has the built-in capability to deal with some models of external USB, FireWire, and SCSI hard disks without requiring any additional drivers. Whether an external disk works depends in part on how the drive's interface with the Mac has been implemented.

NOTE Mac OS X 10.4 supports USB 2.0 and FireWire 800, the latest updates to those popular external connection technologies. In order to use such devices, your Mac will need to have the compatible ports built in—only the latest models do.

Users of external SCSI hard disks and removable drives report reasonably few problems working with them in Mac OS X. Iomega Zip and Jaz drives are supported by generic drivers that ship with

Mac OS X. Some other SCSI removable drives may require driver updates. (For instance, Castlewood Systems, makers of the Castlewood Orb drive, hasn't yet made Mac OS X drivers available for its line of high-capacity SCSI and USB removable drives, and it doesn't appear likely that the company will.) As always, SCSI isn't *hot swappable*—you need to shut down the Mac before altering your SCSI chain of external devices. (A hot-swappable device is one that can be plugged, unplugged, and recognized by the computer while is running.) Also note that the Apple Ultra Wide SCSI PCI card in the Power Macintosh G3 (beige) model can require a firmware update before it works correctly, which may also affect your capability to work with external SCSI drives.

One issue that can crop up in odd ways with Mac OS X is "SCSI voodoo," a common term for the ways in which SCSI configuration sometimes does not seem to make much sense. If you're dealing with an external SCSI device and you believe it should work, you can try shutting down your Mac, removing all external SCSI devices but the one you're troubleshooting, and then restarting Mac OS X. If that doesn't work, shut down your Mac again, try a different SCSI ID number for the device (usually via a switch on the back of the device), and restart. If that fails, shut down, try a different termination setting for the device, and start up again, and so on. If you're able to get the device to function, then you can attempt to rebuild your SCSI chain from there.

USB and FireWire disks should be hot swappable, so you can attach them to the Mac while it's running. If you plug in a USB or FireWire hard disk and it isn't recognized by your Mac, you may want to try restarting. (You also should ensure that the drive is properly plugged in, the power is turned on, and the USB or FireWire cable is attached correctly.)

TIP   Sometimes, Mac OS X can have trouble starting up with an external FireWire device attached, so you may want to start up Mac OS X before attaching the FireWire drive, and then attach it after the Finder has appeared and any startup applications or utilities have finished launching. Bring the Finder to the front and then connect the FireWire cable first to your Mac, then to the drive. It may help under some circumstances if you connect external devices while the Classic environment is not running.

If the drive requires a special driver to be installed in order for the drive to be recognized, you may need to get that driver from the manufacturer. In Mac OS 9, for instance, some external drives require a "shim" of sorts for the drive to be recognized as a true USB or FireWire drive. Such drives may have more trouble working in Mac OS X. Others mount automatically on the desktop or in the Finder window's Sidebar. Note the small eject icon, which you can click to eject the disk before disconnecting it—always a good idea to avoid data loss.

It's also possible that you will have problems with any external drive (USB, FireWire, or SCSI) that was formatted with a third-party formatting utility. If that's the case, your solution is either to obtain an update to the formatting software or to reformat the disk using Apple's Disk Utility (assuming Disk Utility can recognize the drive). Of course, this isn't a terribly appealing solution because you'll lose all of the data currently on that drive. (You can avoid data loss by backing up the drive fully, but that can be quite a task with a large hard disk.) See Chapter 26, "Hard Disk Care, File Security, and Maintenance" for more on partitioning and formatting hard disks.

NOTE If you use a PCI-based interface card to add SCSI, USB, or FireWire ports to your Mac, having the latest drivers for that card can be incredibly important for the operation of your external drives. See the section "Internal PCI Cards," later in this chapter, for more details.

CD-R and CD-RW Drives

To work correctly, an external CD-R or CD-RW drive (we'll refer to both as CD-RW drives, for simplicity's sake) needs two things: a CD driver to recognize and mount media that has already been created and an application that can recognize the drive well enough to burn data to recordable CDs. In some cases, the CD-RW drive also may need updated firmware from the manufacturer before it's fully compatible with Mac OS X.

As Mac OS X has matured, quite a few CD-RW drives have been added to the official list of those supported by Apple's built-in CD driver, so you may find that you're able to hook up your external CD-RW drive and get a disc to appear on the desktop relatively easily. Since the earlier days of Mac OS X 10.0, Apple has introduced support for many CD-RW drives and has boosted iTunes disc-burning capabilities significantly. As was noted in Chapter 3, "The Finder," it's relatively easy to create and burn CDs of your data using just the Finder and a compatible CD-RW drive.

NOTE So what drives are compatible? The most complete list is kept at www.apple.com/macosx/ upgrade/storage.html. For compatibility with iTunes, check www.apple.com/itunes/ burn.html where you can find drives that are compatible with all of Apple's CD-burning tools, such as the Finder, Disk Utility, and iTunes.

Aside from Mac OS X's Disc Burner and iTunes support, other options for burning CDs include Roxio's Toast (www.roxio.com, formerly Adaptec Toast) and Charismac's Discribe (www.charismac.com). You'll find in some cases that these applications are actually able to support more drives than Mac OS X does natively, and the software often will offer additional features, such as the capability to create CDs in multiple formats and to write video data to DVD media or special multimedia capabilities, such as Roxio Toast Titanium's capability to encode and write QuickTime-formatted movies to media in VideoCD format. You'll find these tools useful if your burning needs go beyond simple audio and data CD formats.

CD-RW and DVD-RW media can be not only written to but erased as well. This might seem a bit counterintuitive—while earlier Mac OS versions had an Erase command in the Finder, Apple has moved that command to the Disk Utility application, which must be launched before you can erase any sort of disk. See Chapter 26 for more on using Disk Utility to erase media.

USB and FireWire Issues

You'll generally find that your USB-based hard drive will either work or not—if not, you may need to reformat it (particularly if it was originally formatted with a third-party utility), install an newer disk driver for the disk itself, or otherwise install software from the manufacturer that makes the USB drive work with Mac OS X.

With USB and FireWire hard disks and removable drives, it's important to eject the disk properly before unplugging it, even though Apple supports these technologies as hot swappable. In the Finder, select an external disk that you no longer want to use—even a hard disk icon—and either drag it to the Trash icon in the Dock or select ⌘E to eject it. You can also eject a connected hard disk by either selecting it in a Finder window and choosing File ➢ Eject or Control+clicking (or right-clicking) the drive and choosing Eject. (In the Mac OS X 10.3 and 10.4 Finder, you can use the Action menu to eject a disk as well.)

Once the disk's icon(s) have been removed from the desktop or the Finder window Sidebar, it then should be safe to unplug it from the Mac. Apple notes one situation where unplugging an external disk results in the Mac not being able to properly go into low-power Sleep mode on its own in Mac OS X version 10.1 and higher—if you notice that behavior, the solution is to restart the Mac.

TIP   You may find that unplugging USB and FireWire devices helps when you can't seem to get the Mac to start up correctly. While conflicts are less common with USB and FireWire devices than they are with SCSI devices, they can still pop up every now and then.

Occasionally you'll find that USB hubs—the devices used to enable you to plug in multiple USB devices—can be the root causes of trouble. If you have problems with a particular device that's plugged in to a hub (and this includes your Mac's USB-enabled keyboard), it can be a good idea to plug it directly into a USB port on your Mac instead, to see if that fixes the problem.

Floppy Drives

Mac OS X 10.4 doesn't support any Mac models that shipped with an internal floppy drive, so using an internal drive isn't an option. Some (but not all) external USB floppy drives work with Mac OS X, however, so if you have an external model (or plan to purchase one to deal with floppy disks), you may have luck using it.

NOTE   Apple produced two distinctly different Power Macintosh G3 models. The Power Macintosh G3 (beige) computers were early, cream- or beige-colored models. They came in both desktop and minitower forms and included a floppy disk drive, an external SCSI port, and an Apple Desktop Bus (ADB) connector for keyboards and mice as well as serial ports for modems and printers. The Power Macintosh G3 (blue-and-white) computers are one of the early "candy-colored" professional Mac models. These models came only in a minitower design, and they included USB and FireWire ports instead of serial and SCSI ports.

One solution to working with data from floppy disks is to use a Mac that has a floppy drive and the ability to boot into Mac OS 9 and use Mac OS 9's version of the Disk Copy application to create a disk image of the floppy, which you can then mount in Mac OS X.

To create a disk image, first boot into Mac OS 9, and then follow these steps:

1. Insert the floppy disk from which you want to create an image.

2. Launch Disk Copy, which is likely found in the Utilities folder of your Applications (Mac OS 9) folder, assuming that you installed Mac OS X over Mac OS 9. (If not, you may simply have a Utilities folder on the root level of your Mac OS 9 startup disk.)

3. From the Disk Copy menu, select Image ➢ Create Image from Disk.

4. In the Select the Source Disk dialog box, locate the disk you want to copy.

5. In the Save Disk Image As dialog box, give the disk image a name in the Name entry box.

6. Select a format from the Format menu (likely Read-Only Compressed, unless you want the option of writing to the image; in that case, choose Read/Write). The Size menu should already have the size of the disk you're planning to create, but you can create a larger one if desired (particularly for a Read/Write image).

7. Click Save to create the disk image.

Now you have a disk image that can be double-clicked from within Mac OS X and mounted on your desktop like any other removable disk, thus giving you access to the contents of your floppies.

TIP   Need to take the "floppy" image with you? One solution is to create a CD-RW that includes a number of disk images, which you can then access using any other computer running Mac OS X (or, for that matter, any older Mac OS version).

Other USB-based floppy disk drives can require third-party drivers, and those drivers aren't always forthcoming. Even floppy drives that are supported in Mac OS X reportedly can be very slow. According to folks posting in Apple's discussion groups, there isn't a whole lot that can be done about it. Generally, it's best to work with Mac-formatted 1.4MB disks, although these drives can read and write to DOS-formatted media as well.

Input Devices

Mac OS X has built-in drivers for dealing with most USB keyboards and mice, giving them basic capabilities. If your keyboard offers special capabilities such as special "launcher" keys or other keys that can be custom configured, you'll need a special Mac OS X driver before you'll get full functionality.

Mice with two buttons are automatically supported by Mac OS X. (In fact, mice with more than two buttons are also supported, but only two buttons will work without a third-party driver.) One button will operate as usual, and the second button will be mapped to the Control+click combination, so that you can bring up context menus without holding down a key while clicking. You'll find that mice with scroll wheels aren't supported by all Mac OS X applications, but many of them do allow you to scroll in a window using the wheel. Most Microsoft applications support the scroll wheel, as do the Finder, Apple Mail, and many others.

NOTE   If you own a configurable USB-based mouse, check with the mouse's manufacturer to see if an updated driver is available for that mouse's extra features. Kensington Technology Group (www.kensington.com), for instance, has released its MouseWorks software for Mac OS X. This software is used to configure programmable buttons for some of the company's mousing products. Check your mouse manufacturer's website for updates and details. If your manufacturer doesn't have a Mac OS X solution, you should look into USB Overdrive (www.usboverdrive.com), a shareware driver that can be used to customize many types of input devices, including mice.

Mac OS X also works with Apple Desktop Bus (ADB) keyboards and mice that are plugged into Mac models that support ADB, including Power Macintosh G3 (beige) and most Power Macintosh G3 (blue-and-white) models. ADB keyboards generally are fully functional, although you sometimes may have trouble with some boot-key sequences (such as holding down the Option key during restart to bring up the boot picker screen).

WARNING   Mac OS X 10.3 dropped support for a number of Macs, including all of those that don't have USB built in. (That includes the Power Macintosh G3 beige models and early PowerBook G3s that have been supported by Mac OS X in the past.) Interestingly, that doesn't mean that ADB doesn't work at all—it will work in the special circumstance of the Power Macintosh G3 blue-and-white model. The "built-in USB" requirement is actually just a shorthand to refer to Macs that are based on the "New World architecture" and that are otherwise technically capable of running Mac OS X.

NOTE   Scanners can be a special case—most of the time, you'll need a driver from the manufacturer to make a scanner work in Mac OS X, and even then it sometimes can be iffy. If your scanner company offers Mac OS X drivers but no scanning software, you may be able to use the TWAIN Acquire commands in graphics software such as Adobe Photoshop, Adobe Elements, or Lemkesoft Graphic-Converter. If it looks as if your scanner company has no intention of releasing drivers, you still may have luck with VueScan (www.hamrick.com/vsm.html), which is stand-alone scanning software that for many scanner models doesn't require a manufacturer's driver.

Modems

You configure a modem through the Network pane of the System Preferences application. If your modem is recognized, you should be able to select it from the Show menu in the Network pane or by double-clicking it on the Network Status screen. Note that the recognized device won't necessarily have the correct name, so you may need to figure out which device is which if you have more than one.

Mac OS X should work with all internal Apple modems that shipped with Mac OS X–compatible Macs. Most external USB modems should be recognized and usable in Mac OS X, although standard modems (56Kbps models) seem to install more successfully than ISDN and other specialized modems. If you have a specialized modem that doesn't appear in the Show menu of the Network pane, try restarting your Mac while the modem is attached. You also can try plugging the USB modem directly into a USB port on the side or back of your Mac instead of into your keyboard, monitor, or an external USB hub. If restarting and replugging doesn't work, you may need to obtain a driver from the modem manufacturer. (Note that this doesn't apply to DSL or cable modems, which usually connect to the Mac via Ethernet, not USB.)

NOTE   Once an external modem (or similar USB device) has been recognized, it will remain as an entry in the Network pane, even if you unplug the device. If you're not careful, you may find yourself configuring a modem or networking device that isn't connected. If you've successfully connected in the past and you're suddenly having trouble, don't forget to make sure that the modem is plugged into a USB port on your Mac. You can disable or delete ports from the Network pane menu by choosing Configure ➢ Advanced, as discussed in Chapter 10, "Configuring Internet Access."

Once the modem is recognized, you should be able to configure it by selecting that device in the Show menu, and then clicking the Modem tab in the Network pane. In the Modem menu, you'll see entries for a variety of manufacturers' modems. These correspond to special modem script files, which are stored in the Modem Scripts folder inside the Library folder on your Mac's startup disk. If you need to add a modem script for your modem (if your modem's manufacturer makes one available), you can copy it to the Modem Scripts folder.

TIP   Modem script files are the same in Mac OS X as they were in Mac OS 9 and earlier. If you have a modem script file that you've used with an earlier Mac OS version, you should be able to copy that script file to the Modem Scripts folder inside the Library folder on your startup disk. Then your modem should appear in the Modem menu on the Modem tab in the Network pane.

Serial Devices and Adapters

Mac OS X 10.3 and Mac OS X 10.4 don't support Macs that include serial ports. If you have a serial device that you would like to use with your Mac, you still might have an option. USB-to-serial adapters are available (in fact, they've been a mainstay for many Mac users in the past few years), and some of those manufacturers are offering Mac OS X drivers, with Keyspan (www.keyspan.com) leading the pack. Users have reported success in connecting some serial devices to their Macs via a USB-to-serial adapter. Note that two components are necessary for this to work: a Mac OS X driver for the USB-to-serial adapter and software that recognizes the adapted device.

Once you have the adapter's driver installed (the drivers we've seen are kernel extensions, which require an administrator's password to install), you should be able to access the serial device as if it were a USB device. Then, if you have the application necessary to work with that device, you may be able to access it. This can be a fairly big *if*, because most applications designed to work with serial devices aren't going to be Mac OS X–native applications. You may be stuck in the Classic environment, where USB connections are shaky at best. If you can't seem to use the device from within Mac OS X, your only solution may be to boot into Mac OS 9 and use it from there.

AirPort Base Station

The AirPort Base Station and AirPort Express are Apple's wireless routers designed to transmit wireless network data to AirPort-enabled Macs. Mac OS X includes complete versions of key AirPort software components that enable you to manage your AirPort Base Station and the associated wireless network. These components include the AirPort Setup Assistant, the AirPort Administrator, and the AirPort menu bar item, all of which are described in this section.

NOTE   AirPort Base Stations have firmware that can be updated by Apple, and some updates are advised for Base Stations that will be used with current versions of Mac OS X—to increase compatibility with Apple's Bonjour technology, for instance. For more, visit www.info.apple.com/usen/airport/ and check for firmware and other software updaters.

AirPort Setup Assistant

The AirPort Setup Assistant has the primary task of helping you configure an AirPort Base Station—Apple's hardware router and hub for a wireless network. With an AirPort Base Station, you can enable one or more AirPort-based Macs to access a network wirelessly, both for file sharing and for Internet access.

NOTE If you don't have a hardware Base Station, you can still use one Mac to share data with other Macs via AirPort wireless connection. You do that using the Internet Sharing feature as discussed in Chapter 18, "Building a Network and Sharing Files."

If you have an AirPort card in your Mac and an AirPort Base Station or AirPort Express in the general vicinity (plugged in and powered on), you can launch the AirPort Setup Assistant to start configuring the AirPort Base Station (it's located in the Utilities folder inside the Applications folder).

NOTE Mac OS X 10.4 supports two different Assistants, one designed for the "Snow" and "Graphite" Base Stations and one designed for more recent Base Station Extreme and AirPort Express models. Launch the Assistant that's appropriate to your device. If you don't see the one you need, you should be able to download it from www.apple.com/support/.

The AirPort Setup Assistant walks you through the steps of connecting your Mac to the Base Station, determining how the Base Station will connect to the Internet, how you'll secure the Base Station so that only those authorized to use it have access to it, and so on. The Setup Assistant can even be used with later models, particularly the AirPort Express device, to connect to existing wireless networks so that you can share USB printers on that network or so that you can extend the reach of your existing wireless network using the new device as a signal repeater.

Regardless of the device you have or the steps you're taking, the AirPort Setup Assistant should be fairly easy to follow along and make decisions. Potentially, the most confusing part is setting up the device so that it can connect to the Internet. Generally, those choices are the same as if you were connecting your Mac directly to the Internet, so you can use the instructions in Chapter 10 and any materials that your ISP makes available to you.

Once you're done with the AirPort Setup Assistant, don't forget that you can launch it again to reconfigure your Base Station or AirPort Express device, if desired.

TIP With an AirPort Express device configured and connected to your stereo receiver, you can configure iTunes to send music over the wireless connection to the AirPort Express device and, then, to your stereo. You do that using a selector menu that appears at the bottom of the iTunes interface when an AirPort Express has been configured. By default it says "Computer," but you can click and change that to the name of your AirPort Express device if you'd like to send music to it.

AirPort Admin Utility

This utility offers the next step in functionality beyond the AirPort Setup Assistant; here you can dig in and make some important decisions about your Base Station's configuration. To begin, open the AirPort Admin Utility (it's in the Utilities folder inside the main Applications folder), select the Base Station you want to configure, and then click the Configure button. You'll be asked for the administrative password for this Base Station. Enter it and then click OK.

When the AirPort Admin Utility appears, you'll see the main configuration screen with tabs at the top of it that enable you to configure your Base Station or AirPort Express device with many more options than the AirPort Setup Assistant allows. Figure 25.1, for instance, shows the first tab, AirPort.

FIGURE 25.1
The AirPort tab enables you to name the Base Station and the network, configure a closed network, and change low-level settings.

Here's a quick look at what each tab offers:

AirPort　On this tab, you can give your Base Station a name and enter contact and location information. You can change the password for both the Base Station (for administration) and the network. You also can make a number of network-related tweaks, including changing the channel used for communication, setting a particular station density (for situations where you have multiple Base Stations), and changing the mode (whether the device will support 802.11b, 802.11g, or a combination of speeds). You also can enable or disable security and change the Wireless Mode of your device from creating a wireless network to connecting to an existing network or turning off wireless completely.

Internet　On this tab you can manually enter, tweak, or change the settings for your Base Station's Internet connection.

Network　On this tab, you can further customize the way in which the Base Station acts as a wireless hub. Specify whether or not the Base Station should distribute IP addresses (acting as a DHCP server) and how it should go about doing that for wireless clients—if you have an all-AirPort network, then you can share a single IP address; if you have a mix of AirPort and Ethernet machines, you may find it's helpful to share a range of IP addresses.

TIP   Enabling PPP dial-in allows a Base Station to answer incoming phone calls and allow the calling computer to connect via PPP; the result is a phone-based connection to your network and to the Internet via your network. You can also turn on the Enable AOL Parental Controls option if your Base Station connects to the Internet via AOL. When you use the AOL browser, parental controls (which limit or filter aspects of the Internet) will be respected.

Port Mapping   On this more advanced tab, you can specify the URL to which you'd like a public port (for example, the web server port of 80) to be mapped. When the Base Station receives outside requests, it will route those requests to the IP address of the computer that will be a server for that port.

Access Control   What if you'd like only certain AirPort-based Macs to have access to the Internet via your AirPort device? You can control that access on this tab. Click Add and then enter the AirPort ID and the name for a particular Mac. (The AirPort ID can be found on the AirPort tab in the Network pane of System Preferences; the name can be anything you want it to be.) Click OK, and that machine is recognized among those allowed to access the Internet via this Base Station. Only those on the list are allowed, but if none are on the list, any AirPort-enabled computer with the correct password can sign on. You also use this tab to configure your Base Station to work with RADIUS servers, which are designed to authenticate users on networks that use multiple wireless Base Stations.

WDS   If you have an AirPort Extreme Base Station or an AirPort Express device, this tab can be used to connect your base stations to others to form a Wireless Distribution System. You can choose to make this base station a main base station or a remote base station within your distributed network. (Remote base stations share the main base station's Internet connection.)

Music   If you have an AirPort Express device, you can turn on Enable AirTunes for this Base Station if you'd like to be able to send music wirelessly to a stereo receiver that's connected to this AirPort Express. You can then give Express a name for use by iTunes and, if you like, you can restrict AirTunes so that it can only be played back via AirTunes if you have the appropriate password.

Obviously, that's only a quick overview of what can be done. The AirPort Help (under the Help menu) will give you some sense of what can be accomplished. For more help and discussion, check out both www.apple.com/airport and www.apple.com/support/airport/index.html on the Web.

Bluetooth Wireless Devices

Mac OS X supports the Bluetooth wireless standard, which is simply a short-range, lower-bandwidth wireless connectivity solution for peripherals and external devices. While AirPort (and the IEEE-802.11 standard it's based on, called *WiFi* in the PC industry) is designed for Internet and file sharing access between computers, Bluetooth is designed for closer, less data-intense connections such as those used to update PDAs and cell phones from your desktop or to connect your Mac to a wireless keyboard. Ultimately, the point with Bluetooth is simply to replace USB or similar serial cables that can clutter your desktop.

Some current Mac models include Bluetooth capabilities built in, but for older Macs, Bluetooth support requires an external USB-to-Bluetooth adapter. Plug in the adapter; if it is properly recognized, you'll gain access to the Bluetooth connection available in a number of places—the Network pane, iSync, and the Bluetooth utilities found in the Utilities folder inside your Applications folder.

How you set up Bluetooth depends on what you want to do with it. Bluetooth offers three basic capabilities as of this writing—peripheral connections, data synchronization, and Internet connections, usually via a Bluetooth-capable mobile phone. Again, if you think of Bluetooth as "wireless USB," then all of these capabilities make sense. But how you set them up can vary a bit:

1. To set up a Bluetooth device so it can talk to your Mac, start in the Bluetooth pane of System Preferences.

2. Click the Devices tab and, if you don't see the device you're looking for, click the Set Up New Device button to launch the Bluetooth Setup Assisant.

3. Click Continue from the Introduction screen, and you're shown some options for the type of device to which you'd like to connect.

4. Choose one of those devices, and you'll see a screen that allows you to select the device if it's in the vicinity and "discoverable" (see Figure 25.2).

FIGURE 25.2
The Bluetooth Setup
Assistant enables
us to set up a Bluetooth-
enabled headset.

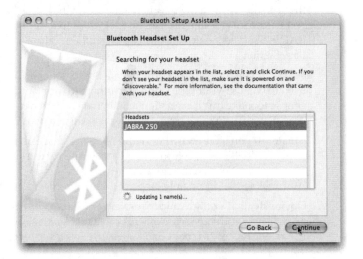

Click Continue, and you'll be guided through the next steps for setup—with a mobile phone, for instance, you'll enter a passkey, which you then enter on the phone, just to make sure that you've established a connection to the correct phone. (You don't want to accidentally change a bunch of phonebook information in Bob's phone in the next cubicle.) Other devices are likely to have a built-in passkey that the device can recognize. (On the Jabra headset we're setting up, for instance, the passkey is simply 0000.) After that, you may see a screen that enables you to configure the device's capabilities—if it's a phone or similar device, for instance, you can determine if you'll use iSync or Address Book or even use the phone for an Internet connection.

Once you've gotten your device connected, you can move on to using it with iSync (see the upcoming section, "iSync") or whatever applications work to synchronize data or otherwise allow you to use your Bluetooth devices—the device is now *paired* to your Mac and ready for action.

Want to use Bluetooth to transfer files? That can be handy if you need to send a file to a phone, PDA, or even another laptop computer that doesn't have any other type of wireless or compatible connection. Launch the Bluetooth File Exchange application in your Utilities folder and follow the on-screen instructions; you'll select a file and then select the device to which you want to send that file. (You can also drop a file's icon on the Bluetooth File Exchange icon to set things in motion.)

TIP   If you have trouble getting your connection to work via the Bluetooth Setup Assistant, you may be able to get it to work via the Sharing tab in the Bluetooth pane of System Preferences, which enables you to set up a "virtual" serial port that's paired with the Bluetooth device. You can then configure that serial port (in the Network pane, for instance) as you might a serial modem, etc. (It'll take some finagling, but this is how some intrepid souls have gotten their Macs to connect to the Internet over a Bluetooth mobile phone that wasn't supported as directly as some models are in Mac OS X.)

iPod as a Hard Disk

If you have an iPod, you've likely managed its audio files using iTunes on your Mac, and perhaps you've used iSync to manage contacts and iCal events (if not, see the next section). One of the wonderfully simple things about the iPod is the fact that it's also a hard disk (in fact, it's *basically* a hard disk with some music-playing and contact-storing circuitry), and as such, you can actually use it for storing files, backing up important documents, and transporting them with you.

Plug your iPod into your Mac, and you'll see its icon appear on the desktop (if your Finder preferences are set to allow that) and in the Sidebar of your Finder windows. When you access your iDisk in the Finder, you'll see that it works just like any other external FireWire hard disk.

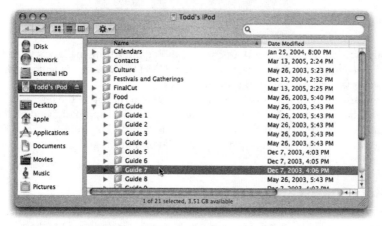

NOTE   Your Mac may automatically switch to iTunes when you plug in the iPod, but you should be able to switch back to the Finder to access the iPod for direct storage as a hard disk. If you try to switch to the Finder and you still can't access the iPod as a disk, you'll want to check a preference setting in iTunes. On the main iTunes interface window, click the small iPod icon at the bottom-right side of the window. In the iPod Preferences window, you can choose how the iPod is updated, whether or not iTunes should be opened automatically when the iPod is attached, and whether or not to Enable FireWire Disk Use.

As with any external disk, you can drag items to your iPod and they're stored there—you'll see the amount of available space in the status bar at the bottom of the Finder window. You can also add contacts to your iPod manually by dragging VCard contact documents to the Contacts folder that's accessible when you view your iPod as a disk. When you're done working with it, eject the disk (click the small eject icon next to its name in the Sidebar, select and choose File ➤ Eject, select and press ⌘E, or drag the iPod's icon to the Trash). Once ejected, it's safe to disconnect the iPod from your Mac.

iSync

As Mac OS X has begun to incorporate more tools such as the Address Book and iCal, it has become important to enable Mac users to synchronize that data with the various devices we carry on our belts, in pockets, or in purses—iPods, mobile phones, and personal digital assistants, among other items. So Apple developed iSync, which can do that—make sure the contacts and calendar items on your "walking around" technology are up-to-date—if those devices are compatible with iSync and your Mac.

NOTE   In early versions of Mac OS X, iSync was also used to synchronize items between your .Mac account and your Mac's; that same synchronizing feature is now handled by the Sync tab of the .Mac pane in System Preferences. See Chapter 16, "Managing Contacts, Appointments, and Your Personal Info," for more.

Launch iSync, and you'll see graphical representations of the devices that it encounters and recognizes.

In this example, we see a FireWire-connected iPod appearing in iSync's window. If you don't see a device that you know to be connected, you can select Devices ➤ Add Device and use the Add Device window to scan and locate the additional devices.

To synchronize data with a device, simply select it at the top of the iSync window. You'll see the options available for that device. What options are at your disposal depend on the device. For most handheld devices—phones, iPods, and so on—you'll be making selections that help you determine how you're going to synchronize your Address Book contacts and iCal events and appointments, as shown in Figure 25.3.

Monitors, Video Cards, and Performance

Quartz Extreme is technology built into Mac OS X (versions 10.2 and higher) that offers an improvement to the Mac OS X's underlying graphics engine that is designed to take advantage of the combination of the G4 processor's AltiVec instruction set and advanced video cards (with 16MB or more RAM). These include the following models that have shipped in Macs: any AGP-based ATI Radeon card, the NVIDIA GeForce2 MX, GeForce3, GeForce4 MX, and GeForce4 Ti. If you don't have one of these cards but you do have an upgradable Power Macintosh (or Power Macintosh G4 Cube), you'll see some significant benefits by adding such a card.

For Macs that can't support such a card and that are based on ATI Rage–based graphics accelerators, you may find that some QuickTime movies, games, and other highly graphical applications that rely on OpenGL actually seem a bit *slower* in Mac OS X 10.4. If so, Apple recommends that you set your display(s) to Thousands of colors instead of Millions—open the Displays pane in System Preferences to change color settings.

FIGURE 25.3
When synching with an
iPod, you can choose to
synch Contacts, iCal cal-
endars, and so on.

TIP Apple recommends an interesting way to figure out if you have Quartz Extreme support. Open System Preferences and launch the Desktop & Screen Saver pane. On the Desktop tab, choose one of the picture options (your Picture folder, the Desktop pictures, or an Album from iPhoto). Turn on the Change Picture option and choose Every Five Seconds from the menu. Now, watch your desktop. If the pictures fade in and out, you have Quartz Extreme support.

Adding Internal Devices

If you have a Power Macintosh model (as opposed to an iMac, iBook, or PowerBook), you might want to install internal hardware such as additional hard disks or PCI cards. For other Macs, you may want to add an AirPort card (if your Mac supports AirPort) internally. You also can add RAM to your Mac.

Internal components that shipped with your Mac should work fine with Mac OS X. If you've added secondary hard drives or if you've installed PCI cards, you may find that you need to do some tweaking to get Mac OS X to work correctly.

Internal Hard Disks

In most cases, you shouldn't have trouble with internal hard disks that are installed in your Power Macintosh. Mac OS X can't be installed on an ATA/IDE drive that is configured as a "slave," although it can see and work with such drives. (A similar problem can affect an internal CD or DVD drive that's been set as a slave—in particular, you can't launch the Mac OS X installation CD from such a drive, even if it doesn't give you many other problems.)

As with external hard disks, you may need to update the hard disk driver software for a hard disk if it was formatted with a third-party utility such as Lacie's Silverlining (www.lacie.com) or FWB's Hard Disk Toolkit (www.fwb.com). If you can't get an update to the hard disk driver, your best solution may be to reformat the disk using Mac OS X's Disk Utility, discussed in Chapter 26.

NOTE Mac OS X 10.4 prefers to work with Mac OS Extended (Journaling) format for hard disks, and it requires that journaling be turned on for features such as FileVault. If you're working with a drive that's formatted with a third-party utility, you may need to reformat it using Apple's Disk Utility or read carefully to make sure that the third-party utility is compatible with journaling and Mac OS X 10.4.

If you're working with internal SCSI drives, you may encounter a bit more trouble. First, you need to make sure that your SCSI adapter card is compatible with Mac OS X (assuming that you're using a SCSI adapter card, which is the only way SCSI drives are supported in Power Mac G3 and G4 models). You may need to install a driver to access the drive, although Apple has incorporated SCSI drivers for many popular cards into the OS release. Adaptec (www.adaptec.com), one of the most popular vendors of Mac SCSI cards, has released drivers for many of its SCSI cards, and the company tends only to post drivers that you need.

If you believe your SCSI card is compatible or you've updated the driver and you're still having trouble, you may be encountering SCSI voodoo (discussed in the "External Disks" section, earlier in this chapter). Try removing any external SCSI devices and restarting your Mac. If that doesn't work, you may need to check (or experiment with) the termination of the internal drives and make sure that you don't have any snagged or poorly connected cables inside the machine.

NOTE Other hard disk issues are noted in Appendix A, "Getting Installed and Set Up," including a problem where you may not be able to install Mac OS X onto a hard disk if its first (or only) partition is larger than 8GB.

Internal PCI Cards

In general, a PCI card needs a driver to work properly. If the PCI card in question originally shipped with your Mac, then the driver is most likely installed with Mac OS X. For instance, most video cards and SCSI cards sold as part of various Mac models have drivers that are built in and support Mac OS X. Your first step is to install Mac OS X (or, if Mac OS X is already installed, then install the card) and try out the card. It's likely that some internal PCI cards will work, particularly if they find generic drivers within Mac OS X that make them effective. For instance, many popular video cards that are Mac-compatible are automatically recognized by the Mac OS without requiring further configuration.

If you've added third-party video, Ethernet, video-capture, audio, or other PCI cards, you'll need Mac OS X drivers in many cases. Apple offers driver updates on its Mac OS X download site (www.apple.com/downloads/macosx/drivers/), which is one place to start looking. You also should consult the manufacturer of the device to see if the company is offering a Mac OS X driver.

If you have an immediate problem with a PCI card, it will likely be with a third-party Ethernet or SCSI card, many of which require drivers to work with Mac OS X, or with a specialized PCI card, such as a video-capture card. Makers of PCI cards that add FireWire and USB ports to Macs seem to be having luck with Mac OS X compatibility, including Sonnet Technologies (www.sonnettech.com) and Promax (www.promax.com). Both of them have Mac OS X-compatible drivers available for download. The newer the card, the more likely it is to "just work" either with the base Mac OS X installation or with the software installer that comes with the card. Again, check the manufacturer's site for upgrades and updates.

RAM

RAM is solid state—it either works or it doesn't. It doesn't require special driver software either, although it does need to be recognized correctly by the Mac. Most Macs have guides to RAM installation in their user's manual.

To check whether the RAM you installed is being recognized properly, choose the About This Mac command in the Apple menu to see if the total amount of RAM is being reported accurately. You also can consult the System Profiler (in the main Utilities folder), discussed in the next section, to see if RAM is being recognized properly.

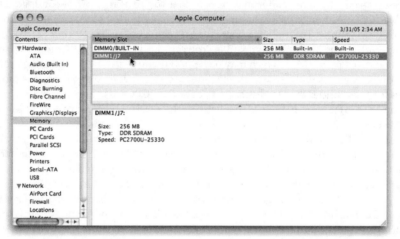

If you think you've installed RAM that isn't being recognized, you should shut down your Mac, reopen its case, and ensure that the RAM is properly aligned and seated in its slot. If that doesn't appear to be the problem, you may have a firmware issue. On the weekend of Mac OS X's debut, Apple posted firmware updates that caused trouble with some types of RAM suddenly being unrecognized. Visit www.apple.com/support/downloads.html and download the most recent firmware update for your Mac model. Run the installer to make sure your firmware is up-to-date.

NOTE   In some cases, RAM that has worked in your Mac model in the past may suddenly stop working after you've installed a firmware update. This is a known issue; Apple has reworked the firmware so that RAM that is "out of spec" for Apple systems is disabled, preventing it from causing trouble in Mac OS X. (Mac OS X, apparently, is more finicky about installed RAM than is Mac OS 9.) If you install a firmware update and suddenly note that you have less RAM, contact the RAM vendor to see if there is a solution for the problem.

Troubleshooting Hardware with System Profiler

Mac OS X includes System Profiler, a great utility for learning more about your Mac in general, but particularly useful when you're having trouble with hardware. System Profiler can tell you exactly what the Mac OS is recognizing about your hardware, making it easier for you to determine where the problem might be if you can't seem to get a particular piece of hardware to work correctly. If System Profiler is able to show you the device, you know that it's installed properly. You then can determine whether there is a driver associated with the device. If not, you will need an updated driver or application to deal with that peripheral.

NOTE System Profiler should be located in the `Utilities` folder inside your main `Applications` folder.

You'll find that you can select the different hardware items that interest you in order to get information about them—if you don't see the hardware items, click the disclosure triangle next to Hardware. Now you can click one of the items below Hardware—Memory, ATA, FireWire—to learn more about each item.

Hardware

Click the Hardware item itself, and you'll get an overview of the type of Mac, processor, bus speed, and processor speed. This information may be helpful if you're using a processor upgrade inside your Mac with Mac OS X. Although processor upgrades are unsupported by Apple, several third-party companies, including Sonnet Technologies (`www.sonnettech.com`) and XLR8 (`www.xlr8.com`), have declared their upgrades to be Mac OS X compatible. You can check System Profiler to see what CPU speeds are being registered by the Mac, which may be helpful if you're troubleshooting the processor upgrade.

If you have issues with a particular PCI upgrade card, your video card, or a modem, you'll find entries for those under the Hardware item; click the PCI Cards entry to get information about the cards and video circuitry in your Mac. Click Graphics/Displays to learn about the graphics cards that are attached to your Mac and the displays attached to those cards.

The ATA, SCSI, USB, and FireWire screens are useful for troubleshooting other internal and external peripherals, including all sorts of external devices and drives. Using the information on these, you can determine whether certain devices are being recognized and whether they seem to have a particular driver associated with them. If you find a problematic FireWire device, for instance, but it's listed when you select FireWire, then you know that the connection is being made, the cable is probably good, and the device is operational. That means you're probably encountering a driver issue—either you need a driver or the current driver isn't performing correctly.

USB

Select USB, and at the top of the USB screen, you'll see the USB devices that have been recognized by the Mac. Clicking a disclosure triangle next to a particular device can tell you more about the device, the driver that is associated with it, and other information such as the device's power consumption.

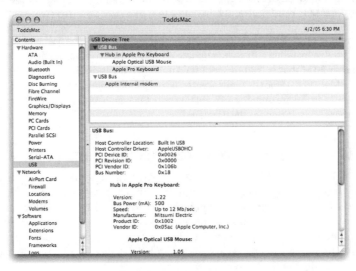

In this example, two USB buses are shown, because the iMac G4 version used for the example has two separate USB buses. No external devices are on one bus, although the Apple Internal Modem is recognized on that bus. On the other bus, two USB devices have been recognized: the Apple USB Keyboard and USB Mouse. The typical Mac keyboard is a passive hub, enabling you to connect the mouse and one other USB device. That connected device won't receive any bus-based power, however, so devices that require bus power must be plugged into a port on the Mac or an active USB hub.

FireWire

If you have FireWire ports and FireWire devices attached to the Mac, the FireWire entry will be next. Select the disclosure triangle next to a FireWire device to see information about it.

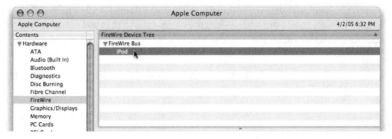

In this example, the device recognized is an iPod. Missing from the list is any indication of any secondary devices, such as an external FireWire CD-RW drive that's currently attached to the Mac. The drive definitely will need a third-party driver simply to be recognized; likewise, it'll probably need a third-party application for burning CDs. (Note for the record that some CD-RW drives don't show up if they don't have a disc in them, blank or not.)

ATA OR SCSI

Finally, choose either ATA or SCSI (or variants such as Serial-ATA or Parallel SCSI), and you'll see information about all internal disk volumes, including hard disk partitions and internal removable media.

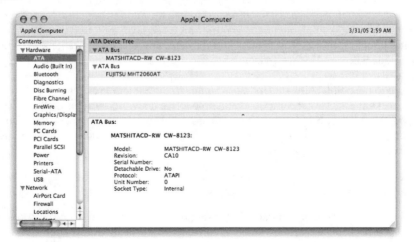

In this example, you see entries for my internal hard disk and the built-in CD-RW drive. Each entry for the hard disk's volumes (it's also divided into two partitions) includes information about the volume's format, capacity, and various tidbits about the drive's name and location in the Darwin layer—such as its mount point and how it can be accessed on the command line. This screen can be useful for learning whether or not a particular volume is being recognized, how it's formatted, and in the case of multiple partitions, the physical hard disk on which a particular partition is located.

TIP Want to dig even deeper? Select the Extensions item under Software in System Profiler to see all of the kernel extensions (and thus, many of the drivers) that are installed on your Mac. If you've recently installed a driver that you don't believe is working, you can search through this list to see if it was properly installed and seems to be functioning. You also can use this list to see if a particular device *seems* to have support. For instance, you'll find drivers for specific vendors (ATTO, NVIDIA, ATI, Sony, Adaptec, and so on) and devices that might mean that you can plug in a particular third-party device and use it successfully with Mac OS X.

TIP As mentioned in Chapter 28, the Logs item can be a handy way to look at some of the entries that Mac OS X logs when things go wrong.

Network

The Network screen shows, at a glance, information about all of your attached networking ports, including Ethernet, AirPort, and other networking interfaces that are recognized and configured for your Mac. This can be useful if you're wondering whether, for example, an Ethernet PCI adapter or an internal AirPort card is being recognized. You also can learn the Ethernet adapter's MAC address (a number such as 00.00.00.AA.0F.AA, which System Profiler calls simply the *Ethernet Address*), which you may need to know for some broadband modem setup or to track down which of your Ethernet devices (if you have more than one) is experiencing trouble.

Using Software Update

Software Update is an important tool for keeping your Mac running as efficiently and effectively as possible. Although Apple has had Software Update technology built into Mac OS versions for a few years, the Mac OS X implementation is the strongest so far. You'll find that Apple offers frequent updates to both the Mac OS in general and the company's own applications—iTunes, iMovie, and others—via Software Update. In fact, it has become the primary mechanism for Apple's software update distribution.

More to the point, Software Update is a pane in the System Preferences application. It automatically checks special server computers at Apple to see if any updates for the Mac OS or other Apple software have been posted. If so, the update is downloaded to your Mac so that you can install it. To use Software Update at any time, open System Preferences, select the Software Update pane, and click the Check Now button (see Figure 25.4).

NOTE You can skip the System Preferences application and have Software Update check immediately for available updates by choosing Apple menu ➢ Software Update.

It's important to check Software Update regularly or schedule it to check automatically, particularly if you have an "always-on" Internet connection. Apple distributes new updates to Mac OS X whenever they're needed and completed by the engineering team, thus getting the latest possible version to Mac users quickly. Instead of waiting for a CD to arrive or heading to Apple's website to download an update, you can use Software Update to retrieve new updates immediately and install them painlessly.

FIGURE 25.4
Click the Check Now button in the Software Update application to check for updates from Apple.

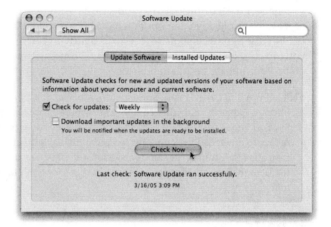

When Software Update locates a new update, you'll see the Install Software window (see Figure 25.5), which enables you to select the software updates that you'd like to install. After making your selections, click the Install button; you'll be asked to enter an Admin username and password. Although any user can check for new updates, Software Update requires an Admin password to download and install them. Once you're authenticated, the download and installation begin.

FIGURE 25.5
When Software Update locates an update, you'll see the Install Software window.

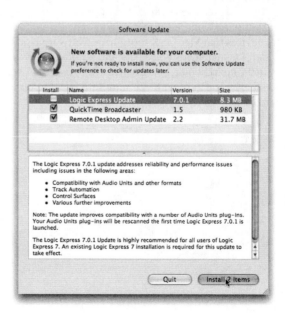

You can configure the Software Update application so that it checks for software automatically at regular intervals. If you're interested in having Software Update adhere to a schedule, you first may need to authenticate yourself as an administrator. (This will happen automatically in most cases.) Next, turn on the Check for Updates option. Then you can select how often you want to check for updates from the Check for Updates pop-up menu: Daily, Weekly, or Monthly.

Finally, note the other tab that appears in the Software Update pane; the Installed Updates tab can be used to see quickly what updates have been installed on this Mac so that you can check whenever you're curious or when you believe an update has been installed but you're not sure. It's also a record you can check in case you suspect that the wrong update has been installed and you need to track down your update installation history.

TIP If you don't want to use Software Update, you don't have to use it. The updates to the Mac OS, Internet Explorer, and other components generally are made available simultaneously on Apple's Support site at www.apple.com/support/downloads/ on the Web. In fact, you may have good reason to download your updates instead of using Software Update, particularly if you have more than one Mac running the same version of Mac OS X. The downloaded files can be archived, burned to CD, or made available over a network so that they don't have to be downloaded to each computer individually.

What's Next?

In this chapter, you learned some of the specific problems encountered when adding hardware under Mac OS X. We discussed the types of hardware that are supported by Mac OS X, as well as hardware that requires a workaround or third-party drivers. Also discussed were internal upgrades such as hard disks, expansion cards, and RAM and how you can get those upgrades working from within Mac OS X.

This chapter also covered two utilities that are useful for dealing with hardware: System Profiler and Software Update. System Profiler can be used to examine and troubleshoot the internal and external devices that Mac OS X recognizes. Software Update is Apple's mechanism for making Mac OS X updates available for you easily and automatically almost as soon as they're made available.

In the next chapter, you'll learn how to use Mac OS X's built-in tools to manage your hard disk, and you'll examine tools and techniques for backing up your Mac, avoiding viruses, and securing your hard disk.

Chapter 26

Hard Disk Care, File Security, and Maintenance

One of the keys to a happy Mac OS X system is regular maintenance. In most cases, maintenance means protecting yourself from viruses, checking for software updates, and managing your hard disk. Many of these tasks can be automated easily, so you'll rarely need to dive into the System folder or get your hands dirty with other parts of Mac OS X.

Perhaps the most important part of preventive care is backing up your hard disk. There are many backup solutions, including Apple's Backup utility, available to .Mac members (see Chapter 11, "The Web, Online Security, .Mac, Sherlock, and iChat," for more on .Mac), and third-party tools. Any strategy—even a manual strategy or one automated by AppleScript—is better than none. Fortunately, because of Mac OS X's hierarchical nature, creating a backup strategy is fairly straightforward, especially when it comes to securing important documents and data files created by your users.

Beyond backup, Mac OS X has built-in applications for basic disk functions, including the Disk Utility program, which works as a diagnostic utility, a tool for formatting and partitioning your hard disk, and a program for creating and managing disk images. Along with these tools, third-party utilities can be added to the mix to keep your disks in good shape and virus free.

In this chapter, we'll discuss all of these approaches to maintaining a Mac OS X system, including formatting and maintaining disks, recovering files, and backing up to keep your Mac OS X system up and running well as you work with it.

In this chapter:

◆ Using Disk Utility

◆ Disk Images and Encryption

◆ Disk Maintenance and Repair

◆ Backing Up Your Mac

◆ Securing Data and Password-Protecting Your Disks

◆ Virus Detection and Avoidance

Using Disk Utility

Mac OS X includes an application called Disk Utility, which provides a full range of disk repair, formatting and partitioning tools, and functions to create and work with disk images. Disk Utility can come in handy when you're dealing with new hard disks—internal or external—that you've added to your Mac. You can use Disk Utility to partition your disk, which erases and reformats it in the process. You can also use Disk Utility to erase all of the data from a disk and give it a new filesystem format simply and quickly. Disk Utility includes First Aid functions that help you repair problems with your disks' filesystems. And Disk Utility is also the way you erase rewritable optical disks (CDs and DVDs).

In the Utilities folder inside your Mac's main Applications folder, you'll find Disk Utility. The interface uses tabs at the top of its windows to separate the different tasks, with the disks that your Mac recognizes appearing in the left column (see Figure 26.1). Note that the list includes even disks that are connected to your Mac, but are not mounted. That means that unless a disk is physically disconnected (or the physical connection is broken), you should be able to use Disk Utility to work with it, even if it's nonfunctioning.

Disks appear with their individual volumes underneath them—in many cases you'll need to select a volume in order to perform a task. For instance, in the info section at the bottom of the window in Figure 26.1, you see information about an entire disk. Selecting a volume shows you information about that volume only. The other tasks you can accomplish via the tabs that run along the top of the Disk Utility window are running First Aid, erasing a disk or volume, partitioning a disk, creating a software-based RAID (Redundant Array of Inexpensive Disks) for speed or data integrity, and restoring software to a disk or volume using a presaved disk image.

FIGURE 26.1
With Disk Utility, you select a disk or volume on the left and a tab at the top.

NOTE   What's a volume versus a disk? In practical terms, sometimes they're the same thing. A disk can be partitioned into one or more volumes, each of which appears to be a separate disk (or, at least, a separate icon) on your desktop or in a Finder window. Because more than one disk-like entity can be created by dividing up a single disk, it's more accurate to call each disk icon a "volume." As you'll see in this chapter, partitioning is reasonably simple to do and something you may want to try.

You also can access a few commands outside of the tabs. Select a volume on the left side of the window and click the Mount button to mount the volume on the desktop; click Unmount to remove a hard disk from the desktop (even an internal volume, but not your current startup volume); clicking Eject removes a removable disk from the desktop. You'll occasionally find it useful to mount and unmount volumes in this way for diagnostic reasons or after a disk has been accidentally ejected or unmounted via the Finder or Terminal.

Disk First Aid

One of Disk Utility's tabs is the First Aid tab, which you can select in order to test and fix certain problems with a volume's directory information. As the name suggests, this is a first line of defense when you're having disk problems, as well as a task you should perform on a fairly regular basis to keep your Mac in good shape. Larger problems, however, need to be tackled by a third-party disk doctor application. (A few are discussed in the section "Disk Maintenance and Repair" later in this chapter.)

NOTE   If you need to repair the startup disk, you should begin by booting your Mac from the Mac OS X CD-ROM. When the Installer appears, choose Open Disk Utility from the Tools menu. Then you can use the First Aid tab to repair the startup disk.

First Aid can verify all the different types of disks (Mac OS Standard, Mac OS Extended, UFS, CD-ROM, and so on) that you might attach to your Mac. Occasionally one of the files used to track your applications and documents gets corrupted or includes an entry that doesn't match what's actually on the disk; Disk Utility's First Aid tab can verify the integrity of those files, and if necessary, catch and correct minor errors.

To use First Aid, open Disk Utility and select the First Aid tab. On the left, you'll see all the volumes that are currently connected to your Mac, including hard disks and removable disks. Select the volume that you would like to check and then click Verify Disk or click Repair Disk if the Repair Disk button is available. Clicking Repair Disk causes any errors to be fixed immediately if First Aid is capable. This is usually preferable, but the Repair Disk button sometimes will be dimmed because either the disk can't be altered (such as a CD) or it's the current startup disk (such as your main hard disk). Once you've clicked either Verify Disk or Repair Disk, First Aid starts checking the drive (see Figure 26.2).

NOTE   If you have *disk images* that are mounted on the desktop, you may see them in the First Aid window as well. These generally don't need to be verified by First Aid.

While First Aid is scanning the disk, it will report any errors and whether or not it was able to fix them. If it was unable to fix them, you may need to run a third-party disk doctor application as described in the next section. If First Aid finds errors on your startup disk, you may need to restart your Mac using the Mac OS X CD-ROM. Then you can run First Aid from the CD and attempt to repair items on your main hard disk. (Because you started up from the CD, First Aid will be able to fix the startup hard disk. Then you can restart your Mac once again from its main hard disk.)

FIGURE 26.2
First Aid is verifying
the disk.

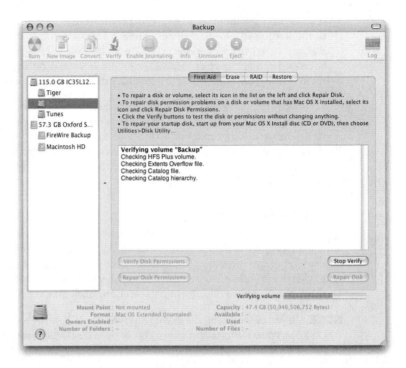

You'll notice on the First Aid tab a pair of buttons marked Verify Disk Permissions and Repair Disk Permissions. As we discuss in Chapter 29, "Typical Problems and Solutions," permissions are assigned to every file on your hard disk, and sometimes they can become corrupted, causing difficulties in launching applications, accessing files, and more. It's a good idea to repair the permissions on your startup volume from time to time. (You can use this function on any other volumes that have Mac OS X installed as well.) Disk Utility checks a special database and compares every file it finds, correcting the permissions of any files that differ. Curiously, you'll find that Disk Utility repairs permissions—sometimes a lot of them—every time you run it. But this action has proven to solve many problems with Mac OS X, and it is worth trying if you have a problem and can't find what's causing it. You might also want to repair permissions after any major system update, since that, too, seems to help Mac OS X run more smoothly.

Erasing a Disk

Disk Utility can be used to erase an entire disk quickly—also called *formatting* the disk or *initializing* it. This is useful if you no longer need any of the data on a particular disk or you want to change the filesystem that the disk uses.

NOTE   Erasing individual partitions will not erase the entire disk that the partition is part of. Once a disk has been partitioned, each partition is a separate *volume*, which can be erased without affecting other partitions on the same physical drive. (See the next section, "Partitioning a Disk.")

Disk Utility is also the accepted way to erase CD-RW/DVD-RW discs—reusable CD/DVD media—that have been created using the Finder, iTunes, or other CD-creation software. If you don't use proprietary software for your removable disks, you also can erase them using Disk Utility.

To erase a disk, launch the Disk Utility program and select the Erase tab (see Figure 26.3). Next, select the disk (or volume) you want to erase on the left and then choose a type of Volume Format for the disk—usually Mac OS Extended or Mac OS Extended (Journaled)—and give the volume its new name. If the disk will be used for booting into Mac OS 9, you should turn on the Install Mac OS 9 Disk Driver option and click Erase. (If you're erasing a CD-RW or DVD-R, you don't need to select a format type or give it a name, because recordable discs are simply erased, not formatted.)

FIGURE 26.3

The Erase tab in Disk Utility

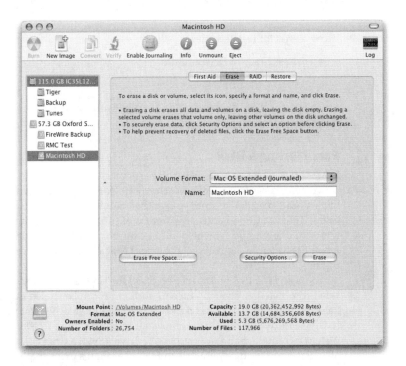

When you've made your selections, click Erase to proceed. You'll see an alert sheet asking you to confirm your decision; click Erase once again. You'll see the message "Erasing Disk" in the First Aid message area, and the formatting process will continue.

WARNING   When you click Erase, the erase process begins immediately. All of the data on the selected volume will be lost (and recoverable only possibly with some third-party disk utilities). Before clicking, double- and triple-check to make sure that you've selected the right volume and that you really want to erase every file on that volume.

If you want to securely erase your data, click the Security Options button before clicking Erase. This presents four options:

Don't Erase Data   This simply erases your disk's volume directory information. It's possible that, with disk recovery software, someone could recover your files. This is the fastest way to erase a disk, but the least secure.

Zero Out Data   This writes zeros to all sectors of the disk, overwriting your data rather than just deleting the disk's catalogue.

7-Pass Erase This writes random data over your entire disk seven times. This is much more secure than simply zeroing data. This takes seven times as long as the Zero Out Data operation.

35-Pass Erase This writes random data over your entire disk 35 times. It is virtually impossible to recover files after this has been done. This takes 35 times as long as the Zero Out Data operation.

You can also choose to erase your disk's free space; this operation is useful if you want to securely erase the parts of your disk that no longer contain files. Clicking Erase Free Space displays a sheet with three options:

◆ Zero Out Deleted Files

◆ 7-Pass Erase of Deleted Files

◆ 35-Pass Erase of Deleted Files

These options perform the same procedure as those which erase the entire disk, but only on your disk's free space.

Partitioning a Disk

In Mac OS X, partitioning a disk isn't particularly necessary. However, you may find disk partitioning convenient, because it enables you to create, for example, a startup partition and a backup partition, or a separate partition to store your music, movies, or pictures if you have a lot of media files. You can install different OS versions on different partitions while minimizing the chance that they will interfere with one another. You also might want to partition your drives if you would like to use two different filesystems—Unix File System and Mac OS Extended Format, for instance—on the same physical hard drive.

You also might want to partition disks for simple efficiency. For instance, a partition that is dedicated completely to scratch video or audio files can be erased quickly and completely after a project has been properly saved and backed up and you're ready to move on. Using the Erase tab command in Disk Utility, you're able to remove all the data you're finished with and start over with a completely reformatted and defragmented drive. (Such a drive allows files to be written *contiguously* or all together on the disk, which is much faster than a drive that's filled with snippets of files here and there.) This works well with partitions for multimedia work, file sharing, web serving, gaming, document files, or other data. Having two different volumes on the same disk offers a level of convenience in these situations.

What is inconvenient about partitioning a drive is the fact that the partitioning process will destroy all of the data on that drive *in all partitions*. Therefore, it's important that you partition a drive when you first add it to your Mac, or after you've backed up all of your important data and are willing to erase everything. In other words, it takes some commitment.

You can't partition disks that can't be written to, such as CD-ROMs or DVDs. Likewise, there's very little reason to partition removable media, because they are generally not large enough to warrant two volumes. (In almost all cases, you'll want each partition that you create to be at least a few gigabytes in size, so the overall disk should be many gigabytes before you consider partitioning it.)

NOTE If you need to partition your startup disk, you can start up your Mac using the Mac OS X CD-ROM and launch Disk Utility. Doing so will erase all data from the startup disk, meaning that you'll need to reinstall Mac OS X (and any documents, applications, and utilities you've created or installed) after creating the partitions.

To partition a disk, launch Disk Utility and select the drive in the list at the left of the window. Next, click the Partition tab in the Disk Utility window. The interface changes to the Partition tools, as shown in Figure 26.4.

FIGURE 26.4

The Partition tools in Disk Utility

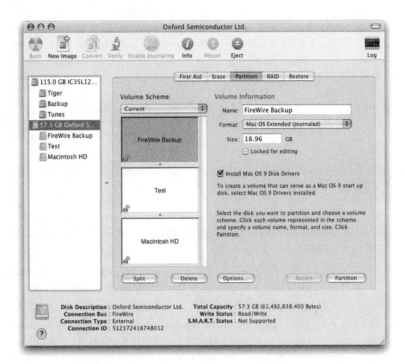

Select the disk (not just a volume) you want to partition on the left side of the Disk Utility window. Here are the other steps toward partitioning:

1. If this disk has never been partitioned or if you want a different number of partitions than it currently has, select the number of partitions you want to create from the Volume Scheme menu. You'll see the Volumes area change to represent that number of partitions.

2. Select one of the partitions in the Volumes area.

3. In the Volume Information area, click in the Name entry box and type a name for the volume.

4. From the Format menu, select the type of filesystem you want this partition to use. Mac OS Extended (Journaled) is recommended unless you have good reason to use Unix File System. Mac OS Standard isn't recommended unless you're dealing with removable media that needs to be compatible with Mac models running system software older than Mac OS 8.1.

5. Choose a size for the partitions. You can do this one of two ways. First, you can drag the small resize bar that sits between two partitions to change the percentage of the drive that is dedicated to a particular volume (see Figure 26.5). Alternatively, you can select a volume in the Volumes area (by clicking its area) and enter a precise size for that volume in the Size entry box that's in the Volume Information area.

FIGURE 26.5

You can drag in the Volumes area to resize your partitions.

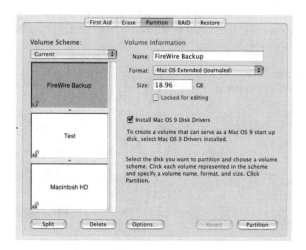

TIP You can use the Split button to further split a particular partition. Select a partition in the Volumes area and click the Split button. You also can delete a partition by selecting it and clicking Delete.

6. To lock the volume into a particular size or name (so that you can't accidentally resize it), either click the padlock icon in the Volumes area or turn on the Locked for Editing option in the Volume Information area.

7. If this volume will be used to start up in Mac OS 9, or if it is an external drive that will be connected to a Mac running Mac OS 9, turn on the Install Mac OS 9 Disk Drivers option. (Under most circumstances, it doesn't hurt to install them anyway.)

8. If you change your mind and want to revert the partition scheme to the original settings, click the Revert button. Otherwise, if you're ready to go forward with the partitioning (and initialization) process, click the Partition button.

9. You'll see an alert sheet appear from the title bar of the Disk Utility window. If you're absolutely sure that you want to go forward with the partitioning—you'll lose *all* data currently on the drive—click Partition. Otherwise, click Cancel.

WARNING Just for the record, we'll warn you again. You'll erase all of the files currently on your disk when you proceed with partitioning and initialization.

Once you click Partition, Disk Utility will spring into action. First, it unmounts the disk from the desktop, and then it partitions the disk and replaces it with the number of volumes you created. The volumes are formatted, and then they're ready for use.

NOTE   As we've mentioned in this section, Disk Utility erases your disk when you partition it. There are several Mac utilities that allow you to create partitions on the fly, adding, deleting, and resizing partitions without erasing the entire disk. Coriolis System's iPartition (www.`coriolis-systems.com`) is one such program, and it also has the added advantage of formatting disks in literally dozens of filesystems, so you can set up and partition external hard disks to use with just about any platform.

Disk Images and Encryption

A *disk image file* is a data file that's capable of looking and working as though it were a removable disk, as long as it's *mounted*. Disk image files are useful because they're (usually) compressed (similar to Zip archive files, for instance), but they work in a way that's familiar to most Mac users—just like a removable disk. You can use Disk Utility to create and mount disk image files.

Even experienced Mac users can sometimes take a while to understand the concept of a disk image, so we'll restate it: in essence, a disk image is a computer file that, when double-clicked, mounts a "virtual volume" that acts just as if it were a removable disk. Using the removable disk metaphor simply makes it easy to drag and drop files from that compressed archive to other parts of your hard disk so that you can work with those files. Furthermore, the files can be worked with directly from the mounted disk image, which sets this approach apart from other file-archiving methods.

Disk images can be compressed, allowing you to both organize your files in a virtual volume and save space at the same time. When you mount a compressed disk image, you can see and work with the files it contains. These files are only expanded when you open them (if you work with them while they are on the disk image), or when you copy them to another disk. It's simply a way of extending the Mac's Finder metaphor to the concept of the file archive.

While disk images were originally designed to serve as master copies of floppy disks, they have gone much further in recent years. You can create disk images of different sizes, or you can create disk images that can vary in size. For instance, a disk image can be made to duplicate a data CD's capacity of 740MB or so. Then, once you've filled the disk image, you can create a recordable CD from it—an interesting solution for backing up and archiving files. You can even password-protect a disk image, which will then be encrypted, making it impossible to read without the password.

The first place you'll probably encounter disk images is when installing some applications, updates, or drivers—particularly those distributed by Apple, which likes to use disk images for distribution. Once you get used to the metaphor, you may want to create some disk images, so we'll discuss that in this section as well.

NOTE   Why create disk images? The compression makes them take up less space on your hard disk (or on other media such as a CD-RW disc or a removable one), so you can use disk images for backing up existing files. You also can use disk images for sending projects to other Mac users—again, the compression and the convenience of the disk metaphor are nice for sharing items. Also, the fact that disk images can be encrypted—as discussed in the section "Creating Disk Images" later in this chapter—means that you can use a disk image for password-protecting sensitive or private information on your business or home Mac.

While you can mount and unmount disk images in the Finder, Disk Utility creates and manages disk images, and you'll use either the New Image or Convert buttons on the Disk Utility toolbar to do so, although some other functions for working with disk images are found in the Images menu.

Mounting Disk Images

Disk image filenames generally end with a .dmg extension. To mount a disk image, just double-click the image file. You'll see the disk image mount in the Finder window sidebar, as well as on the desktop as though it were a CD-ROM or similar removable disk.

Click the mounted disk image in the sidebar to view its contents. You can then work with its files or drag the files stored on the disk image to folders on your own disks. (Some disk images open their own window when they mount; you therefore can just switch to that window to access their files. This is often the case with disk images containing software installers that you may download.)

NOTE The volume does not appear on the desktop if you have the ability to show CDs, DVDs, and iPods turned off in Finder's Preferences dialog box (Finder ➤ Preferences).

When you've finished working with the mounted disk image, you can unmount it by clicking the eject arrow next to its icon in the Finder window sidebar or by selecting its icon and then choosing File ➤ Eject. You also can drag mounted disk images to the Trash to unmount them. (Note that dragging the disk image *file*—generally it's a document icon that looks like a piece of paper with a small hard disk picture drawn on it—to the Trash will place that file in the Trash for future deletion, so be sure that's what you want to do.) You can also select the disk image in Disk Utility and click the Eject button to remove it.

Many, but not all, disk images you download are read-only. Occasionally you may work with a disk image that offers some additional space for you to store files within the image file, but in most cases you can only read files from a disk image, not save files to one. That's one reason disk images are used primarily as archive files for installers and to transfer applications across the Internet. Of course, you can create your own disk images, which can be written to, as discussed next.

Creating Disk Images

You can use Disk Utility to create your own disk images—one of the most common reasons for doing this is to replicate a particular type of removable media—a floppy disk, a CD-R, or a Zip disk, for instance. You can create a disk image that's the exact size of a CD, which you can use for storing items that you'll later burn to a blank CD-ROM. You can also use Disk Utility to create a file from existing removable disks, for which other users may not have the necessary hardware, making it easy to share that data with Macs that don't have the requisite removable drive.

TIP We mentioned in the preceding paragraph the idea of creating a disk image that is standard size for a recordable CD or DVD. Disk Utility can burn a disk image directly to a recordable CD or DVD without any additional software. All it requires is a compatible disc recorder (either one built into a Macintosh or a supported third-party drive). Burning CDs is discussed later in this chapter, and third-party CD/DVD burners are discussed in Chapter 25, "Peripherals, Internal Upgrades, and Disks."

Disk Utility enables you to create images in a number of different ways. First, you can create a blank image that has no files—good for building your own image from the ground up. Second, you can also create an image from an existing source, such as a folder, a CD, or an existing removable disk. Third, you can convert an existing image into another type of image—for instance, you can convert a read-only image into an image that allows you to add your own files.

With any of these methods, you'll generally have a few choices to make. In some cases, you'll need to choose a size for the image—Disk Utility has some built-in sizes that you can choose for convenience, although you're free to choose almost any size you'd like. You may also need to choose a format for the image, whether it's a read/write image or one that resizes itself when necessary. Finally, you'll make a decision about whether or not the image should be password-protected and encrypted.

CREATING A NEW IMAGE

To create a new disk image, click the New Image button in the Disk Utility toolbar. The new disk image dialog sheet appears, where you'll make some choices about your new image. (Make sure you haven't selected a drive or volume when you click the New Image button; if you do, this creates a disk image from the selected volume.)

This sheet offers a number of different settings, so let's look at each individually:

Save As At the top of the dialog are some standard Save dialog controls. It's important to note that this will be the name of the disk image file, not the mounted disk image volume. Type a typical filename—the extension will be added automatically.

Where Choose a location where you'd like your image file to be saved. As with a standard Save dialog, you can use the disclosure triangle to reveal the Save dialog additional controls, which include a sidebar and columns-based interface for locating the folder where you'd like to save the file.

Size   Use this pop-up menu either to select one of the default sizes or to specify a custom size. Disk Copy offers a number of common sizes in the menu, including those that correspond to common data CD sizes and common recordable DVD sizes.

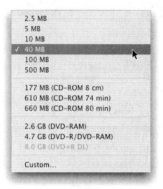

You can also specify a custom size by selecting Custom from the Size menu and then entering a number and choosing the units—sectors, kilobytes (KB), or megabytes (MB)—in the dialog sheet that appears. If you don't have enough space available in the selected location for any of the sizes—such as the DVD sizes at the bottom of the menu—these will appear dimmed. Once you've made your choices, click OK.

Encryption   Use this menu to decide whether or not the disk image should be password-protected and encrypted. If so, select the Encryption method from the menu. By default, you'll likely see only one method, AES-128, which is a strong encryption method that comes with Mac OS X. If other levels or schemes of encryption have been installed on your Mac, you may see those options here. If you want to encrypt this disk image, select a scheme; otherwise, leave the selection blank.

NOTE   Support for AES encryption is provided by the Mac OS at a low level, meaning other applications can also access this support and add AES encryption to their functionality. AES comes via a special plug-in that's stored in the CoreServices folder inside the System folder's Library folder.

Format   In the Format menu, you can choose from two disk image formats: Read/Write Disk Image, which creates a disk image that you can copy files to, or Sparse Disk Image, which is a kind of resizable disk image file. With a Sparse Disk Image, you give it a maximum size. An empty Sparse Disk Image is much smaller than its maximum size, and it grows as you add files to it.

With your choices made, click the Create button to create the disk image. Disk Utility will display a progress bar as the disk image is created. What happens next depends on whether or not you're attempting to create an encrypted disk image. If you are, then a dialog box will ask you to type and verify a password for this disk image. Carefully select and type your password in the boxes provided. If you'd like the password added to your keychain, leave the check box selected; if you'd like to enter the password any time you attempt to mount this disk image, uncheck the Remember Password (Add to Keychain) option. Finally, click OK to move on.

WARNING   If you forget your password, you won't be able to access the contents of this disk image, so make sure it's something you'll remember.

If your password has been correctly entered twice (or if you aren't creating an encrypted image), Disk Copy will move on and create and format the disk image using the selected disk format, just as if you were preparing a new removable or hard disk for use. Then the disk image will be mounted. When it's done, you'll see the new disk image in the disk list at the left side of the Disk Utility window, and the new disk image will be accessible via the Finder. It's ready for use, as discussed in the section "Working with the Disk Image's Volume" later in this chapter.

CREATING AN IMAGE FROM A SOURCE

Another convenient option in Disk Utility is the ability to take an existing disk volume—a hard drive, a removable disk, a CD, a data DVD, and so on—and turn it into a disk image. It is an exact replica, right down to hidden files and the file format (Mac OS Extended, Unix File System, and so on) of the disk.

NOTE   Creating an exact copy of a commercial disk may be enticing, and it may even be legal, particularly if you create that copy solely for archival use. However, you should read your licensing agreement carefully before making copies of commercial software, particularly for use on multiple computers—doing so could constitute software piracy.

To create a copy of an existing disk or volume, select a volume or disk in the disk list in Disk Utility and click the New Image button. Disk Utility displays the same sheet as discussed in the section "Creating a New Image," with the name of the disk already entered in the Save As field. (Note that the name shown here is not the name you see in the Finder, but is the internal name for the disk, such as `disk0s16`.)

In this sheet, you'll name the image, choose a format, and decide whether or not to encrypt the image. Although these controls work similarly to those described in the previous section, one item is different. The Image Format menu doesn't ask you about Mac OS Extended or similar formats because Disk Utility will use the original volume's format information. Instead, the Image Format menu is where you can specify whether the disk will be read-only (you can copy *from* but not *to* the mounted image volume), read/write, or compressed, which is also read-only. The fourth option, DVD/CD Master, is used to create a disc that, once burned to a recordable disc, will have all of the same functionality as the original disc.

NOTE   Choosing DVD/CD Master creates the disk image so that it will launch a special `.cdr` volume. This is the same type of volume used with the disc burner software that's built into the Finder. Once mounted, it can be used with the Burn Disc command in the Finder to create a recordable CD or DVD.

With your choices in the Convert Image dialog made, click Save, and Disk Utility will begin to create the disk image. If you've chosen to encrypt it, you'll see the password dialog described earlier, in the section "Creating a New Image." Otherwise, the Disk Utility window will report that it's preparing the image, reading data from the existing source, and creating the image. Finally, you'll end with a success message, and the new image will be mounted.

CREATING A DISK IMAGE FOR BACKUP AND RESTORATION

One reason to use Disk Utility to create disk images is to create a disk image that you can use as a backup of your files which you can restore to a blank volume. You can also use this type of disk image to create a set of applications and or files that you can then install on a series of computers, in a company, a school, or a lab.

To do this, select the source volume and then create a disk image from that volume as described earlier. After you have created the disk image file, select it in Disk Utility and then select Images ➤ Scan Image for Restore. This creates a checksum, a sort of digital verification code that allows Disk Utility to ensure that the data is restored correctly. See later in this chapter for more on restoring files from disk images with Disk Utility.

CONVERTING (AND COMPRESSING) AN IMAGE

What if you want to work with an existing disk image? You can convert that image into a new one with different characteristics, if desired. For instance, you can convert an existing read-only image into a read/write image so that you can save data to it. Likewise, you can convert an image to a compressed format or to an encrypted disk image file.

To convert an image, follow these steps:

1. Mount a disk image in the Finder. This disk image also shows up in Disk Utility's Source list.

2. Select the disk image in Disk Utility and then click the Convert button.

3. In the sheet that displays, enter a name for the new disk image and choose a location for it.

4. Make selections in the Image Format and Encryption menus as discussed in the earlier section, "Creating an Image from a Source."

5. Click Save, and if you've chosen to create an encrypted disk image, you'll see the password dialog discussed in the section "Creating a New Image." Otherwise, the Disk Utility window will report progress on the conversion. In the end, the new volume will be mounted and accessible in the Finder.

WORKING WITH THE DISK IMAGE'S VOLUME

Once a disk image has been created, you'll be able to work with it just like any other disk. If it isn't already mounted, simply double-click the image file, and Mac OS X will mount the image. It will then be available in the Finder. If the image mounts a read-only volume, you'll be able to copy files from it; if it's a read/write volume, you can also copy files to it as long as it has available space. Note also that changes to the volume are made immediately—it functions as a virtual disk.

As with any disk image, you can click the eject icon next to the disk image in the Finder window sidebar, or you can select the disk image in the Finder and choose File ➤ Eject to eject it so that it's no longer mounted. (The disk image file will still be available on your hard disk, ready to double-click and mount again.) Likewise, you can Control+click a disk image to access the Eject command, and you can drag the disk image volume to the Trash to unmount it. (Again, remember that the disk image *volume* is a mount/unmount item, while the disk image *file* is a regular computer file. Dragging the actual file to the Trash will delete it.)

Burning a Disk Image to CD or DVD

Disk Utility, through its disk image tools, offers the ability to burn recordable CDs and DVDs. As mentioned in Chapter 3, "The Finder," burning recordable discs has been well integrated into Mac OS X; this is another spot where it pops up, using Disk Utility.

Here's how to do that:

1. Begin by creating disk images that will be used to create the CD or DVD; in the new image sheet you can select some standard CD or DVD image sizes in the Size menu.

2. Fill up the disk image with files you'd like to burn to the CD or DVD. When you're done, unmount the image by dragging its mounted image icon to the Trash.

3. When you create a disk image, it is added to the list at the left of the Disk Utility window. If your disk image is not in that list, you can drag it there from a Finder window or from the Desktop. (You won't be able to select the mounted disk image, only the disk image file. Also, if the disk image is mounted, the burn will fail.) To burn the CD or DVD, select that image you want to burn and click the Burn button, or choose Image ➤ Burn from the menu to select a disk image that's not in the list.

4. You'll be prompted to insert a disc, and your CD/DVD drive will open automatically on some Mac models.

5. In the Burn dialog, click the disclosure triangle to select from Burn Options. You can choose to turn on Leave Disk Appendable if your data won't fill the disc completely and you'd like to make a multisession disc, burning more data at another time. You can choose a speed manually if your CD-RW/DVD-R drive recommends a particular burning speed. You can also choose from several additional options:

   ◆ Verify Burned Data, to have Disk Utility verify the disc after burning it

   ◆ Eject Disc, to have it ejected after burning

   ◆ Mount on Desktop, to have the disk mounted after burning

6. Click Burn. You'll see a dialog with the status of the burn. It begins by initializing the disc, followed by writing data to the disc. The writing process can take several minutes, depending on the speed of your drive and the size of the disk.

When the process is done, Disk Utility will report whether or not it was successful; in many cases, your drive will open automatically to give you the newly burned disc. Now you can access it again by slipping it into your CD/DVD drive; it should mount on the desktop, ready for use.

NOTE   See more on burning CDs and DVDs in Chapter 3 (which covers burning discs in the Finder) and Chapter 25 (which covers third-party drives and software).

RESTORING VOLUMES FROM DISK IMAGES

As you saw earlier in this chapter, you can create a disk image of an entire volume to use as a backup. Using Disk Utility's Restore function, you can load this backup onto a volume, restoring it completely. This can be useful for two reasons. The first is to make a regular backup of your Mac OS X startup volume. Since you cannot merely copy this volume to another disk as a backup—there are many files you are not allowed to copy—this disk image can save you time if you ever have serious system problems; you won't have to reinstall the entire system, your applications, fonts, and drivers. The second reason is if you are a system administrator and want to load the same configuration onto several Macs. If you create a disk image of the configuration you want to use and then use the restore function to load it on your computers, you'll avoid having to go through the installation process for each Mac.

Once you have created a disk image for restore, you can load this disk image onto any volume using Disk Utility. Open Disk Utility and click the Restore tab. To load a disk image, either drag it to the Source field or click Image to find it on your computer or network; you can even enter a URL for a disk image shared over the Web. Then drag a volume from the disk list in Disk Utility into the Destination field. (To restore data to a disk, the disk must not be mounted. If it is, select the disk and then click the Unmount button in the Disk Utility toolbar to unmount it.)

You can choose to Erase Destination, which erases the destination volume, or Skip Checksum, if you don't want Disk Utility to verify the restoration. Click Restore to restore the data from your disk image to the selected destination. This may take a while, depending on how much data is on the disk image and whether it is local or accessed over a network.

Disk Maintenance and Repair

A modern computer works with a lot of files. For instance, as Kirk wrote the section on Disk Utility earlier in this chapter, he checked the info for his Mac OS X startup volume and saw that it had more than 149,000 files stored on it. What with web browser cache files, tens or hundreds of e-mail messages a day, a few thousand tracks in an iTunes music library, fonts, system files, and an entire Unix underbelly beneath your Mac's glossy veneer, your disks have a lot of work to do.

The more a disk works, the more susceptible it is to errors, whether they're small problems in the way the files are recorded and details are maintained or larger problems with the way files are stored. In order to keep your Mac humming along nicely, it's important to maintain the disks. This maintenance is done in a two-step process: First Aid, discussed earlier, and disk "doctoring."

Disk Doctors

When Disk Utility's First Aid can't help with a problem, you need to turn to a disk doctor application. Common disk doctor applications include Norton Utilities (www.symantec.com), Alsoft DiskWarrior (www.alsoft.com), Micromat Drive 10, and TechTool Pro (www.micromat.com). Each has its strengths: Drive 10 is focused on the physical characteristics and performance of a drive as well as its files, TechTool Pro checks both your hard drives and other hardware elements on your Mac, Disk-Warrior rewrites disk directories, and Norton Utilities does a little of all the above, as well as defragment disks and recover lost files.

TIP   If you have any disk doctor utilities that were released before Mac OS X 10.3, you should update them before using them with Mac OS X 10.4, particularly if you have the "journaling" feature enabled for your drive(s). Utilities that were not written to work with journaling will not function correctly with journaled volumes, and may actually cause additional problems.

If you're having trouble with a drive that suddenly fails to be bootable, sometimes your best bet is to run Alsoft DiskWarrior (see Figure 26.6) if you have access to it. DiskWarrior is available directly from the company and in stores as well. In the case of a catastrophic disk failure (particularly a disk that won't mount or won't allow you to start up from it), DiskWarrior should be run immediately to attempt to rebuild the disk's directory; this often is a better solution than reconstructing it or attempting to recover individual files from the disk. Sometimes if you run another disk doctor application first, you hurt DiskWarrior's capability to do its magic. Most of the time you'll start up from the DiskWarrior CD and then run the application. (That's also the only way you can run the tool on your startup disk.)

FIGURE 26.6
Alsoft DiskWarrior is the tool of choice for fixing disk catalog problems.

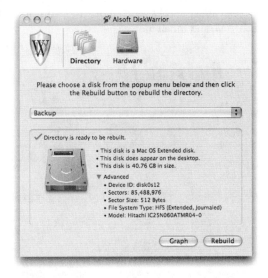

DiskWarrior is simple to use. Once it is launched, you select a volume and then click the Rebuild button. DiskWarrior will attempt to rebuild the disk's directory. If this is possible, your disk should function correctly, or at least you'll be able to access your files. If you ever do have serious disk failure and use DiskWarrior to repair the disk, you should back up your files and reformat the disk afterward, just in case. Use the DiskWarrior hardware check function (click the Hardware icon) to check the status of your drive.

TIP You also can use DiskWarrior in a maintenance mode; click the Update button to update Disk-Warrior's copy of the disk directory as a backup. Updating this record can make recovery easier and more successful in the future.

Norton Utilities 8 is a native Mac OS X suite that is divided into different, smaller applications such as Norton Disk Doctor and UnErase, each of which can be used separately, depending on the circumstances. If you're having trouble with a volume that can be seen and mounted but that has errors or corruption, Norton Disk Doctor is likely to be your first choice.

Norton Disk Doctor checks your disk's directory entries, partitions, files, and the actual media, doing a more thorough job than Disk First Aid. Disk Doctor needs to be up-to-date, however, so make sure you update the application whenever possible.

NOTE Norton Disk Doctor comes both as a stand-alone application and packed in the SystemWorks bundle, which also includes Norton AntiVirus and third-party tools such as Aladdin Spring Cleaning and even Retrospect Express backup software. It's a good deal if you happen to need all of those utilities and haven't yet bought them separately.

Micromat's Drive 10 is similar to Disk Doctor and has been native to Mac OS X for longer. It offers quite a few tests for the physical media as well as for directory structure and file recovery. Drive 10's battery of tests is interesting to watch and keep up with, and it offers recovery backup tools as well. Drive 10 prides itself on being fully aware of the unique Unix-like file structures at play in Mac OS X.

If you've got an AppleCare guarantee contract for your Mac, you may have a CD containing Micromat's TechTool Deluxe, which is a slightly different tool than Drive 10 from the same company. TechTool Deluxe checks much more than your hard drive: it verifies your processor, system RAM, video RAM, and much more.

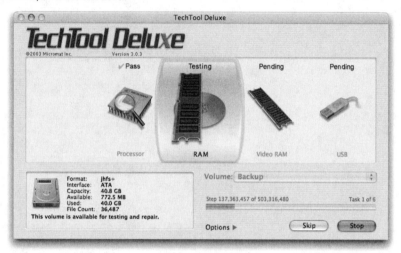

Whatever the name of your disk doctor utility, its function is to find fairly serious problems with individual files and folders, compare them with the disk's database, and fix those anomalies. That will help the Mac run more efficiently and make sure that corruption isn't creeping into your files, causing trouble with saved files or causing crashes within applications.

Most disk doctor utilities work best if you reboot your Mac from the recovery CD-ROM itself. Among other things, this will enable you to make low-level repairs to your main startup disk. You can restart from the CD-ROM in one of three ways:

◆ Insert the CD-ROM and select it from the Startup Disk pane within the System Preferences application.

◆ Insert the CD-ROM, restart your Mac, and immediately after you hear the Mac startup chime, hold down the C key on the keyboard until the Mac begins to start up from the CD-ROM.

◆ Insert the CD-ROM, restart your Mac, and immediately after the startup chime, hold down the Option key. You'll see a special screen that enables you to select the CD-ROM (among other options) as the startup disk. Select it and click the right-arrow icon to begin the startup process.

Once you've finished running the program, you may have the option of launching the Startup Disk application or control panel from the CD, selecting your main startup disk, and then restarting. If that doesn't work, you can hold down the Option key once again after the startup chime and then use the special startup screen to select your main Mac OS X startup disk.

Catching Problems Before They Happen

Besides fixing disks, many disk doctor programs have utilities that can stay in the background, always watching for problems with the disk (or checking periodically when you're not actively using the computer). Other programs offer additional tools that save information about your disk while it's still in good shape, making it easy to recover the disk later if something has gone wrong. In fact, three of the tools profiled in the previous section (all but TechTool Deluxe) offer this capability. Norton's FileSaver, in addition, can track deleted files and make them easier to recover if and when the Trash is accidentally emptied.

It's important to try and stave off any disk failure before it happens. Most new hard disks have a feature called S.M.A.R.T., which is an acronym for Self-Monitoring, Analysis, and Reporting Technology. Disk Utility shows you the S.M.A.R.T. status at the bottom of its window when you select a disk (and not a volume) that uses S.M.A.R.T. If it says S.M.A.R.T. Status: Verified, then your hard disk is in good shape. If, however, it says About to Fail in red letters, it's time to back up your hard disk and replace it.

Alsoft's DiskWarrior lets you turn on a setting to have the program check your hard disk's S.M.A.R.T. status hourly, daily, or weekly. DiskWarrior can display an alert, send you an e-mail, or run an AppleScript if your disk shows signs of problems. You can always check in Disk Utility; in fact, it's a good idea to add this to your regular maintenance routine.

NOTE Mac OS X includes a command-line utility, called *fsck*, that can be used to clean up the underlying filesystem. You must enter single-user mode to use fsck, along with a few other requirements. Single-user mode and using fsck are covered in Chapter 28, "Solving System-Level Problems."

Backing Up Your Mac

Although Mac OS X is a fairly stable and problem-free environment for computing, the fact is that bad things happen. It's important to perform some occasional maintenance tasks on any computer, regardless of the operating system, if only to ensure that your important files are always backed up and that the computer hasn't encountered any data corruption or other such errors that could cause harm to data. For any computer connected to a network or the Internet, protection against viruses is always a concern.

NOTE See the section "Virus Detection and Avoidance" later in this chapter, as well as the virus discussion in Chapter 12, "Managing E-Mail," for more on avoiding and combating viruses.

Your first line of defense against all these problems is a good backup. If you work with your Macintosh for a living—or if you use it at home or in the home office for managing money, taxes, and investments—then it's likely that your data is worth more to you than the computer itself. Personally, we would rather have a CD or removable disk with our important data on it than an entire roomful of Macs, because we really hate to rewrite book chapters and articles that we've already written. And we'd hate to have to reenter all of last year's checkbook data.

The solution is to create a *backup*, which simply means that you copy important files to some form of secondary media on a regular basis. The secondary media should be something that isn't fixed—that is, you don't just copy files to another hard disk in your office, but rather to a disk or tape of some sort that you can store in another location. Ideally, this means using *removable media* that enable you to transport the media and swap in new media whenever necessary. (Copying to another hard disk is certainly better than performing no backup at all, but removable media is better.)

The same basic process also enables you to create archives of your important data, meaning backup disks that are dropped out of the rotation. An archive is a copy of your documents and other files that represent a particular moment in time—for instance, it's a snapshot of how your documents and other files were on, say, March 15. If for some reason you need to recover a file that was deleted after that date, that became corrupted after that date, or that was changed and saved after that date, you can still get to the March 15 version. That's the first advantage in having an archive.

The second advantage is that the archive lets you avoid backing up files (or you can even opt to delete files) that don't change subsequent to that archive. That speeds up the backup process while requiring less disk space on the backup media.

In addition to having your backup data safe, a proper backup routine can help guard against problems such as data corruption and virus attacks. In fact, the most clever backup schemes will help you not only recover lost or corrupted files but actually retrieve earlier copies of files if you ever need to revert to a former version of a document. Perhaps most importantly, a smart backup scheme makes you—if you're the system administrator—look like a hero.

What You Need for Backing Up

To back up your Mac effectively, you'll need an external removable drive that's compatible with Mac OS X. The drive should support media that can store enough space in one setting to make the backup process worthwhile. With today's modern hard disks, that means the removable drive should probably be capable of storing a good amount of data. DVD writers are an excellent choice for large-scale backup tasks, especially if you use your Mac in a creative environment to produce large graphics or multimedia documents. Since you can use rewritable DVDs, you can work with a set of discs to back up your files, each time overwriting the oldest disc.

NOTE Again, you can use an internal or external hard disk for backup, but you should realize that it isn't as redundant a system—the best backup disks or tapes are those that you can store in a different location from your computer, ideally in someplace fireproof and physically secure.

For a professional-level backup solution, you may want to use a tape drive. Travan tape drives are inexpensive solutions; DLT (digital linear tape) and DAT (digital audio tape) are faster but more expensive. A tape drive is often called a *near-line solution* because the disk itself doesn't mount on your desktop (or in the Computer view of a Finder window). In order to access the tape, you have to use a special program; you can't simply copy your files to the tape. Tape is also linear, so you have to fast-forward or rewind through a tape to find a particular file. Still, it's a good solution for backing up many, many gigabytes of data on a regular basis.

Another solution is to use an external FireWire drive enclosure that allows you to insert and remove hard disks in cartridges. In this way you can buy a single enclosure and use several drives as "removable" cartridges. This allows you to use much larger capacity devices than most available removable media. Or you could simply use external FireWire drives that you move from a storage location to your workplace.

If you have an iPod, you can also use that as a backup device. This is less secure than many other solutions, but it's a good way to back up your current projects when you leave the office, or to transfer files from home to office.

Along with hardware, you'll likely want to use software to help you back up your files. For very infrequent backups, it's possible simply to drag and drop items from your Mac's disk to the removable disk; this isn't the most advised course of action, but it's *something*. You can even use the Finder to search for recently changed files if you're following a manual backup routine.

Backup software, however, enables you to automate the process, creating schedules for your backups as well as game plans for rotating your backup media and creating archives that you drop out of your rotation and store in a secure location. Backup software ranges from personal editions to network editions that back up an entire network at once.

A few different backup solutions are available as native Mac OS X applications. Dantz (www.dantz.com) offers the most sophisticated offerings in its Retrospect line of backup tools, including Retrospect 6.0 and Retrospect Express (which comes in the Norton SystemWorks bundle). The advantages of these tools include the capability to compress the backed-up files, encrypt the backup (if desired), and split the resulting files over multiple disks (or discs) without forcing you to do any math or drag-and-drop wizardry. Retrospect also will perform backup tasks automatically if you tell it to, and it can schedule different types of rotations. Dantz offers network-based tools as well for backing up entire organizations and computer labs.

If you have a .Mac account, Apple provides its Backup program, which gives you a simple, though limited tool for backing up your data. With Backup, you can back up selected types of data—such as your Address Book contacts, iCal calendars, and specific types of files—by checking items in a list. You can also add any files or folders you want to this list, and back up everything to your iDisk, an external FireWire hard drive, a CD or DVD (if you have an Apple drive or a supported third-party drive), or even to an iPod.

With Backup, you can select from common types of files in its list window, or you can add your own files, folders, or volumes by clicking the Add (+) button at the bottom of the window and selecting items.

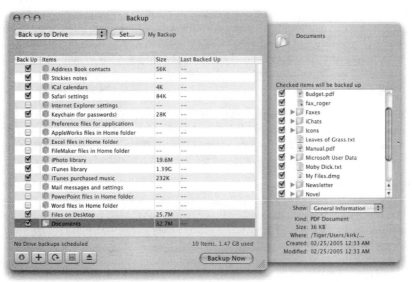

If you click the Info button when an item in the Items list is selected, a drawer opens, and you can check or uncheck any of that item's contents to select them for backup. When you have decided what to back up and selected a destination, click Backup Now.

You can also set Backup to run automatically and back up your files without your intervention. Click the Schedule button at the bottom of the window (the one that looks like a calendar) and choose the frequency, either daily or weekly, and the time of day.

Another good program is Intego Personal Backup (`www.intego.com`), which lets you automate backups to local disks, network disks, and even an iDisk, if you have a .Mac account. In fact, one good reason to use .Mac is to have this remote backup for small amounts of files. A .Mac iDisk gives you 250MB of space (which you divide among your e-mail and storage space), which, for most people, is more than enough for their irreplaceable files, though you can purchase more space if needed. See Chapter 11 for more on using .Mac and Chapter 3 for more on using an iDisk with the Finder.

TIP Along with Retrospect are a number of shareware and freeware tools that are useful for backing up an individual Mac. See the section "Personal Backup" later in this chapter for details.

What to Back Up

One important consideration is exactly what needs to be backed up. On most Macs, it may be less than you think—which is good, because you likely have a hard disk that's quite a bit larger than the disks your removable drive supports. You'll probably want to avoid backing up your entire hard disk every few days.

For the most part, you don't need to back up your applications, as long as you have access to the original CD-ROM or other disks used for distribution. If you've downloaded applications or application updaters from the Internet, those should be backed up (or, more to the point, archived and stored somewhere safe).

You probably don't need to back up most system files, especially those that you haven't touched since you installed the Mac OS. (Ideally, you won't need to touch much of anything in the System folder, because it's supposed to be changed only by Apple's official installer programs.) However, you can make a point of backing up any additional installers that you've used to augment your system—for example, any peripheral drivers, downloads from Apple, or other system-level tools you've used to upgrade your Mac over time. If you ever should need to reinstall Mac OS X, you'll be able to start from the Mac OS X CD and then add the other drivers and use the Software Update feature to retrieve updates.

NOTE If you're a system administrator for a number of Macs, however, you may find it more convenient to download and archive Mac OS X system updates individually, so that you won't have to sit through the software update process every time you restore a Mac to a CD version of the Mac OS X. Those updates can be downloaded individually at `www.apple.com/support/downloads/` on the Web.

If you have administrative responsibilities for your Mac (or if you're the only user), you'll want to back up the Mac's main `Library` folder hierarchy, where you're more likely to have system-related files that change frequently. Remember that drivers, fonts, web pages, and other common files are stored in the main `Library` hierarchy; if you have overall responsibility for the Mac, it's a good idea to back up those files.

NOTE If you're the type who likes to tweak, it's important to remember to back up any files that you plan to change manually, especially configuration files such as those used by Apache (see Chapter 24, "Web Serving, FTP Serving, and Net Security") and other low-level servers, applications, and tools. At the command line, the `/etc` hierarchy is where you'll find many of the configuration files for your Mac that you may have altered, thus making it a good candidate for backup. If you've worked at all in the Root account, remember that the Root account's home folder is `/private/var/root`. (See Chapter 28 for more on the Root account and Chapter 22, "Terminal and the Command Line," for more on the command line.)

In fact, most of the files you'll want to back up will be in the Users hierarchy. Since most Mac users have little choice but to store files in their home folders, it's much easier for you, as an administrator, to back up those folders. As an administrator, you'll probably opt to back up the entire Users folder and all its subfolders. Doing so not only creates a backup of all users' personal files but also the Shared folder, where users may be exchanging files with one another.

TIP File privileges can make backing up the Users hierarchy from a regular Admin account tricky at best. If you have a graphical backup application, it may allow you to authenticate so the backup program can read and copy other users' files. (This is true of Dantz Retrospect, for instance, which can be set to require an administrative login every time the application is launched manually.) Otherwise, you might consider enabling the Root account and logging in as root so that you can copy the Users folder to another disk or disks. Note also that Admin accounts have greater file privileges when logged in from a remote Mac, so you can log in (via Apple File Protocol or FTP) and back up the Users folder to another Mac that way.

Even if you're backing up only personal files, it may be tempting to focus solely on the Documents folder inside the home folder. This is probably a mistake, however, since important files are often stored in the Desktop folder inside the home folder, particularly recent downloads and any document folders that have been created or dragged to the desktop. Likewise, the Library folder in each home folder is an important repository of preference files, fonts, Internet plug-ins, and other items that may have been installed by that user. Also, within each user's Library folder is a Mail folder, which you should back up (and even archive) regularly in order to restore e-mail in case of a disk failure or other problem. Even the Public and Sites folders may be important if the user has shared files or a personal website.

The best plan is to back up your entire home folder if you're backing up your own files or the entire Users hierarchy if you have administrator responsibilities. Although that may sound like a lot of files, a system of rotation and incremental backups, as discussed next, should make creating regular, useful backups fairly painless.

Backup: Rotating and Archiving

Correctly backing up your Mac means following a routine. That routine may be helped by your backup software, particularly if you pay good money for it. Part of that routine is regular *rotation* and archiving. By rotating your backup media, you ensure against two problems: bad media and corrupt files. If you're regularly rotating different disks to back up, and one disk goes bad, the other can be used to recover files. Also, if a file becomes corrupt on one disk, a proper rotation and archiving scheme might enable you to recover an earlier version of that file.

TIP If you're interested in working at the command line in the Terminal application, you can use a combination of rsync (which synchronizes files in remote directories) and cron, a scheduling program, to automate the backing up of files. Use the man command (man rsync and man cron) to learn more about them, and see Chapter 22 and Chapter 23, "Command-Line Applications and Magic," for more on the command line and Terminal.

A proper rotation of media also can enable you to make use of *incremental backups,* meaning that you can back up only those files that have changed since a recent backup. Incremental backups are convenient because they require less time than a complete backup. For example, if I perform an incremental backup to a disk I created last Wednesday, only the files that have changed since Wednesday need to be included on the disk. But an incremental approach is only part of the solution. If you consistently make incremental updates to the same disk, you risk data loss if that one disk fails. You rotate media to avoid the possibility that a single media failure will leave you without your data.

Here's a typical rotation scheme:

1. Begin with three fresh removable disks or tapes.

2. On Monday, perform a full backup to disk A.

3. On Wednesday, perform a full backup to disk B.

4. On Friday, perform a full backup to disk C.

5. On the subsequent Monday, perform a full backup to a new disk—disk D. Disk A, used on the previous Monday, can become an archive—stored offsite or in a fireproof box, safe, safety deposit box, or something similar.

6. On Wednesday, perform an incremental backup to disk B. All data changed or added since the previous Wednesday will be added to this backup. This backup should take place more quickly than the previous backup.

7. On Friday, perform an incremental backup to disk C. All data changed or added since the previous Friday will be added to this backup.

8. On the next Monday, perform an incremental backup to disk D.

9. On Wednesday, perform a full backup to a new disk—disk E. Drop disk B out of the rotation and store it as an archive.

The process continues rotating from there. Note that this isn't the only solution; you might opt to use two disks for your rotation, or you may decide to drop out an archive less often—for example, every few weeks or once a month instead of once a week.

For a high-end corporate rotation, you'll probably opt to back up every day and rotate even more frequently. For a fairly bulletproof small business or organizational rotation, the approach outlined in this section is hard to beat. For instance, if the Mac (or the network or network server, if that's what you're backing up) fails on Tuesday, you have a recent backup from Monday, a backup from the previous Friday, and an archive that's less than a week old. Likewise, other archives are made every 10 days or so, so you can revert to a previous version of a file if necessary. Disks are used as archives fairly quickly to help ensure that they don't get worn out or begin to fail.

WARNING Even with a good rotation scheme, it's still important to test your backup disks or tapes on a regular basis, especially if you, your mission, or your organization is relying on those disks to secure your data.

Personal Backup

You may not always desire a high-end backup system using software and rotation plans. In some cases, you might not even be the administrator of your Mac, and your only desire is to back up your own personal files. In that case, regularly copying folders from your Mac to a removable disk is the best course of action. Of course, any backup strategy is improved by backup software so that you can perform incremental backups and rotation.

TIP One solution if you don't want to buy software is to use Find to locate files that have been created or updated since your last backup. This can be helpful because it enables you to perform a sort of manual incremental backup. Incremental backups are best done with add-on software, but you can use Find and the Finder to approximate it. Using Find, you can create a custom search that locates files that have a "date modified" since a particular date. (See Chapter 6, "Getting Help and Searching Your Files," for details.)

For simple, personal backup rotation, you might opt to back up using two different disks, performing the backup once a week:

1. In the first week, create a full backup to disk A of all the files and folders you want to safeguard.

2. In the second week, create a full backup to disk B.

3. In the third week, create an incremental backup to disk A.

4. In the fourth week, create an incremental backup to disk B.

5. In the fifth week, increment disk A.

6. In the sixth week, increment disk B.

7. After the sixth week's backup to disk B, turn disk A into an archive disk (store it somewhere safe). In the seventh week, create a full backup to disk C.

8. Keep rotating until the eleventh week. When you've made that incremental backup to disk C, turn disk B into an archive disk. In the twelfth week, create a new backup to disk D.

And so on. With a rotation like this, you're never more than one week out from a complete backup, and at all times you have an archive that's only a few weeks old. Also, you're still rotating disks so that they don't get too old and worn before you retire them as archives. You get longer life out of each disk.

NOTE Retrospect Express is suited to exactly this sort of rotation—in fact, it's one of the built-in options, called an EasyScript, on the Automate tab.

You may find that a shareware solution is a convenient way to back up your personal files to removable media quickly. One such utility is FoldersSynchronizer X, a shareware application from a company called Softobe (www.softobe.com). FoldersSynchronizer X offers a number of options to help you automate synchronizing or backing up folders in one location to folders in another location. (Synchronizing will make each of two folders an exact mirror image of the other, so that changes in either folder are duplicated in the other. Backing up makes the target folder identical to the source folder, but not vice versa.)

Another shareware program , Synk 4 (www.decimus.net/synk/), is also useful for quickly synchronizing two folders for personal backup.

A free option is SilverKeeper (www.silverkeeper.com) from LaCie, a manufacturer of upgrade drives for Macs (including externals and internals, removables, and so forth). SilverKeeper performs a basic backup, synchronize, or restore between two folders on different media. It supports multiple sets (you can specify different sets of source and destination folders) as well as scheduling the backup for a particular day of the week and time of day.

Securing Data and Password-Protecting Your Disks

We've looked at security in many different chapters in this book, including securing your Internet connection, e-mail, and your passwords for various resources. In this section, I'd like to focus on securing the data that's actually on your Mac, in particular by password-protecting data. Those are two different issues—encrypting on the disk and securing your Mac against unauthorized access.

Encrypted Volumes

In previous Mac OS versions, tools such as PGP (Pretty Good Privacy) encryption could be used on the desktop to create entire encrypted folders or volumes whose files could only be accessed by password. Mac OS X doesn't have a tool that can encrypt an entire volume, though FileVault lets you encrypt your home folder; see Chapter 5, "Personalizing Mac OS X." Another way to protect files by encrypting them is to make an encrypted disk image, as described earlier in this chapter. By creating an encrypted disk image, you can store sensitive files on the virtual "disk" volume and then close that volume when you're done working with it. The next time you need to work with files on that volume, double-click it to mount it. You'll be asked for your password (or your keychain will be accessed).

Disk images offer the additional possibility of being compressed, so the image's file actually takes up less space on your hard disk when stored. That also makes it a bit easier to archive, because you can simply drag the disk image file to an external disk and store it away both encrypted and compressed. Also, if you use FileVault to encrypt your home folder, that encryption is only in place when files are actually in that folder—if you back them up, move them elsewhere on your hard disk or to another volume, or send them to anyone else, they are no longer encrypted.

Password-Protecting Disks

One of the biggest loopholes in Mac OS X security is the fact that an individual can bypass the Login screen (and, thus, Mac OS X's privilege-based file security) simply by restarting the Mac using a CD-ROM or by holding down the Option key to select a different startup disk. There are other ways, too, including booting into single-user mode or using Target Disk mode to access your Mac on an external FireWire disk. The problem with allowing all of these options is that they all generally open up your Mac to different privileges than you've set in the filesystem—Mac OS 9, Target Disk mode, and others give unfettered access to the disk, regardless of privilege settings.

There is a way around this, however, using something called an Open Firmware password. Open Firmware is the low-level operating system that's used to bootstrap a Mac and get it started before control is handed off to the Mac OS. At that level, it's possible to use a password to keep keyboard commands and other reboot approaches from succeeding without a password.

Does this low-level password sound like a good idea? Here are the steps for implementing your Open Firmware password:

1. Make sure that you have the latest version of your Mac's firmware installed. (Visit `www.apple.com/support/downloads/` to look for firmware updates.)

2. Download the Open Firmware Password utility from `http://docs.info.apple.com/article.html?artnum=120095` on the Web.

3. Install the Open Firmware Password utility (drag it to your `Applications` folder) and double-click it to launch it.

4. Click the Change button to change the Open Firmware password. On the next screen, turn on the Require Password to Change Open Firmware Settings box and then enter a password in the Password entry box. Type it again in the Verify box and click OK.

5. When you click OK, you may be asked to enter an administrator's name and password. Do so and click OK.

The Open Firmware Password utility should report that the password changes have been made. Now, whenever you attempt to restart the Mac using a different startup disk or while holding down a startup keyboard combination, you'll be asked for a password. Enter the Open Firmware password you specified and click the right-facing arrow to move on with the startup process.

Virus Detection and Avoidance

A *virus* is a program designed to replicate itself as much and as often as possible. Viruses aren't always designed to cause data loss or other problems, but they generally end up causing trouble of some kind, whether maliciously or not. Viruses can vary in their intent from popping up messages on your screen to destroying low-level information on your disk drive in order to render it unusable. Poorly written viruses may not set out to be malicious, but they may still crash your applications, the Classic environment, or your entire Mac OS X environment.

Worms and Trojan horses are often lumped in the general category of "viruses," although technically they aren't the same things. A *Trojan horse* is a program that masquerades as something else—a malicious program disguised as something you might want to double-click and play with. (They often have "love," "free," or "money" in their names.) A *worm* is actually more similar to a virus; it can replicate itself and use system memory, but it can't attach itself to another program. Instead, it needs to be run on its own (often as a Trojan horse).

Mac OS X presents some interesting issues when it comes to viruses. The majority of computer viruses are written for Microsoft Windows computers, with far fewer written for Macs. Mac OS X, then, would ideally have very few viruses written for it. However, Mac OS X installations often will use the HFS+ hard disk format that's common to both older versions of the Mac OS and Mac OS X, meaning that some earlier Mac viruses can still infect the computer. Because you're likely to use some files created on older Macs, and the Classic environment is still there, the potential to be affected by Classic viruses still exists. Plus, Mac OS X is built on top of FreeBSD (as part of the Darwin underpinnings), meaning that it's also possible for Mac OS X to contract viruses and other malicious programs that are common to FreeBSD and similar operating systems.

Some Mac OS X applications are also susceptible to *macro* viruses—those that rely on built-in scripting behavior in certain applications. Common culprits are Microsoft applications, such as Microsoft Word and Excel, which are incredibly popular and also happen to have built-in scripting mechanisms that virus authors exploit. Likewise, e-mail attachment viruses can be written that take advantage of AppleScript integration with e-mail programs, such as MacSimpsons, which used Outlook Express and Entourage on the Mac to send itself to everyone in infected address books. So far, these viruses generally haven't caused damage to Macs and the Mac OS. However, they can be replicated by the Mac versions of Microsoft programs, so you should be aware of them.

Avoiding Viruses

How do you get a virus? Like human viruses, computer viruses generally require contact with the outside world. Computer viruses are small programs that attach themselves to other programs or documents and then spread when those programs are shared, whether it's via the Internet, a local area network, or a removable disk.

To avoid viruses, the most reliable solution is to not share files with others. That includes downloading files from online sources, working with attachments, and even copying files from CD-ROMs that are distributed with your favorite Macintosh magazines. In most cases, though, that's impractical, so you need to take some preventive steps:

◆ Never launch an attached document or application that you've received by e-mail—even from a friend or colleague—unless you fully expected to receive the attachment.

◆ Download files and applications from the most reputable sources possible. Major download sites (Apple, MacUpdate.com, and VersionTracker.com, for example) make a point of checking files for viruses before they are posted. (That's not a guarantee, but it helps.) Check other sites for indications that the owners scan for viruses and take other steps to avoid malicious code.

◆ Pay close attention to warnings you receive from applications immediately after launching documents. This is particularly true of Microsoft applications, which now attempt to detect attached macros before allowing a document to appear in the application. If you don't believe a particular document is supposed to contain a macro (or if you're not sure), cancel the loading of that document and contact the document's author to see if it's supposed to have a macro.

◆ Avoid using removable media from noncommercial sources. Don't swap programs, utilities, and documents with friends via Zip disks, CDs, or other removable disks. Of course, this is of limited effectiveness, because even commercial CDs can accidentally distribute viruses.

◆ Don't perform day-to-day tasks while logged in to the Root account, if it has been enabled. If you happen to set off a virus while you're logged in as Root, you may be giving that virus much more free reign over the files on your Mac, thanks to the Root account's privileges. Instead, do your application work in a regular account (one without Admin privileges is even better) when you're doing anything other than system maintenance and management. In fact, not enabling the Root account is a solid safeguard against many possible attacks.

WHAT ISN'T A VIRUS?

Internet hoaxes may be just about as popular as viruses when it comes to malicious little ways that some people like to have "fun." Some e-mail hoaxes are just stories or urban legends—the one about the cookie recipe, the "Forward this message for money" e-mails, or pretty much any dire problem whose solution is to forward the current message to as many people as possible.

Other e-mail hoaxes are virus alerts from supposedly credible sources. In most cases these cause no more harm than prompting naïve or cautious users to forward the message to everyone they know, alert the IT department, and take an early lunch just in case the building comes crashing down.

The fact is, most of these hoaxes are fairly easy to spot. The regular text of an e-mail message can't transmit a virus (only an attachment can), so simply reading a virus-infected e-mail can't cause it to spread. (This may change someday when someone exploits a security hole in an e-mail program's scripting implementation, but it hasn't happened yet.)

Finally, breathless e-mail messages warning of viruses will pretty much never be released by Microsoft, the U.S. government, or any major, official-sounding body—especially if that group's name is misspelled in the warning. If you'd like to check an official source, try HoaxBusters (hoaxbusters.ciac.org), a service of the Computer Incident Advisory Capability, which is a part of the U.S. Department of Energy. There you'll find a roundup of common hoaxes and suspected hoaxes, and you can learn what's real, what's not, and what may have been real three years ago and is still circulating as junk mail.

And the number one way to avoid viruses? Catch them before they enter your system. Buy and use a virus protection program, as discussed in the next section.

Identifying and Removing Viruses

You won't always know immediately when your Mac has contracted a virus; after all, part of the point of a virus is that it replicates beneath the surface before causing any damage. Still, there are "viral symptoms" that you can look out for on your Mac:

♦ Files that suddenly appear or disappear, folders that move on their own, or files and folders whose size or modification date has changed could indicate trouble. If an entire folder or hierarchy appears to disappear or to be deleted, you should immediately suspect a malicious program.

♦ Trouble opening or saving documents, particularly in Microsoft applications, or documents that once saved cannot be opened again for editing are possible symptoms. Also, if commands disappear or menus move in Microsoft applications (and the behavior is not expected macro behavior), you may have a macro virus.

◆ Dialog boxes that appear on their own, particularly with odd, malicious, or nonsensical text, could indicate some sort of infection. This is particularly true if the dialog box appears immediately after something else has changed, such as starting up your Mac, installing an application, or inserting a removable disk into the Mac or an attached drive.

◆ Any other automatic behavior—such as colors or screen resolution changing, the mouse pointer disappearing or moving on its own, or anything else that seems to happen without your input—could suggest a malicious or prank application. These behaviors are tougher to pin down, however, because some applications change screen resolutions and an errant driver could cause problems with the mouse pointer. Still, it's a good time to run a virus-checking application.

None of these is a surefire sign of virus infection. Still, if you note one of them and suspect foul play, the first thing you should do is stop working with other applications and documents. You want to avoid allowing the virus to spread to other files. This is especially true of macro viruses; once you have an infected Microsoft Word or Excel document, the Normal template in your Office application is infected. Documents that you subsequently create or open to edit might also be infected.

If you note odd disk activity, files disappearing as you watch, unfriendly dialog boxes flashing on the screen, or similar problems, you should shut down your Mac. If you can't get the Shut Down command to work—and you suspect a damaging virus—pull the plug.

The next solution is to get an antivirus software package as soon as you can. There are several antivirus programs for Mac OS X, including Intego VirusBarrier, Norton AntiVirus, and Virex, which is included with a .Mac subscription. Norton AntiVirus and Intego VirusBarrier are certainly viable candidates, and both are capable of checking your volumes for the latest viruses based on definitions they can automatically download to update themselves. You can then isolate files that are infected (or that appear to be infected) and, in some cases, clean the virus from the file. (In other cases, you may need to delete the infected file.) Virex is a little less feature-rich, but it's a good choice nonetheless, particularly for home and small-office use.

WARNING You may need to log in as an administrator or authenticate your antivirus application so that it has the correct permissions for accessing files and scanning them for viruses. See your antivirus application's instructions for details.

What do you do if you find an infected file? If you need the data from the file, you may be able to save it, depending on the type of virus; your antivirus application may have the capability to inoculate the file and remove the virus. If so, you can recover the file. (If it's a text-based file, you might be able to load it into TextEdit or a similar program and retrieve portions of the file.) Most of the time, though, the safest course of action with an infected file is to inoculate it with your antivirus program (if possible) and then delete it.

Also, most antivirus applications have a regular schedule on which their virus definitions are updated. These applications make updater files or libraries available, which you can download from the antivirus application's website. (The capability to download the updaters also may be built into the application.) You should make a point of updating your antivirus application whenever possible so that you can be assured of catching the very latest viruses if they've infected your files or disks.

WARNING Some users automatically think the best solution for a virus infection is to simply format the hard disk and reinstall the Mac OS. While this may be appropriate in some cases, you're better off running an antivirus application before doing any reinstallation. Some viruses (especially those that attack the boot sector of a disk) can survive a reformat and still be there to cause problems. Other viruses may have already infected files that you've backed up; if you add those files back to your reinstalled system, you'll simply infect it again.

What's Next?

In this chapter, you saw some of the maintenance tasks associated with keeping your Mac's files and disks up and running. Those tasks include backing up your Mac, fixing disks, and detecting viruses. Once you know the basics of each, the whole thing comes together as part of a maintenance routine that should help to keep your Mac OS X system "healthy" and running smoothly. You also saw how to work with disk images and how to use them to store and protect files by encrypting them.

In Chapter 27, "Fixing Applications and Managing Classic," you'll see some troubleshooting tips and instructions for dealing with applications that crash or encounter errors. You'll also see a discussion of troubleshooting Classic applications.

Chapter 27

Fixing Applications and Managing Classic

Although Mac OS X is a relatively "bullet-proof" operating system, that doesn't necessarily mean you won't encounter *crashes*, which simply are problems with applications that cause them to stop running. After all, applications in Mac OS X are pretty much free to crash all they want; bugs and corruption, the main causes of application crashes, can still occur.

So you should be ready. Application crashes are much less likely to affect your entire Mac OS X session; in most cases, you can continue computing after an application crash without a restart. Still, you'll want to look into some strategies for dealing with crashes when they occur. Afterward, you'll want to troubleshoot to see why applications are crashing and what you can do to stop it.

If you work with Classic applications, you'll find that some of the limitations of earlier versions of the Mac OS are still around in the Classic environment. Classic applications not only are able to crash themselves, but they also can affect other Classic applications that are running at the same time—indeed, a crashing application can affect the entire Classic environment. If you're having trouble with Classic applications, you'll want to troubleshoot those applications separately. We'll cover that later in this chapter.

In this chapter:

- ◆ Understanding Crashes and Errors
- ◆ Recovering from Crashes and Hangs
- ◆ Using Force Quit
- ◆ Diagnosing Application Troubles
- ◆ Troubleshooting Classic Applications

Understanding Crashes and Errors

Mac OS X native applications—those written in Cocoa or Carbon—are likely to crash for three different reasons: bugs, conflicts, or corruption. *Bugs* are problems with the way an application is written—usually a mistake or oversight by the programmer. A *conflict* occurs when an application and a Mac OS component have trouble communicating; although this (ideally) occurs less frequently in Mac OS X than it did in earlier Mac OS versions, it's still a possibility. For instance, a kernel extension—a low-level driver that is used by Mac OS X to interface with hardware devices—can sometimes cause instability due to conflicts with other parts of the operating system. Applications that use shared libraries (files that hold programming code that each application has access to) can sometimes conflict with one another, resulting in crashes and other problems.

Corruption happens when files contain errors in their data. This corruption can occur in the application file itself, but it's more likely to occur within the documents and preferences files that the application attempts to work with. For instance, a corrupt font, stored somewhere in your Mac's font folders, can cause an application to crash or encounter other trouble when the application attempts to work with that font. Many applications are designed to create and edit text or image documents, and errors can creep into those files in a number of different ways. When such errors are encountered by an application, the application may respond with an error message or something more drastic, such as a crash.

More to the point, though, is the issue of what actually constitutes a crash and what you can do about it. In general, you'll encounter a few different types of crashes and similar problems with applications in Mac OS X, each of which may have a different approach for rectifying it. These are as follows:

Error message If you encounter an error message but the application continues to function, that most likely means that the application has recovered and will continue to work properly. (Of course, if the error message told you something specific was wrong, you should correct that, if possible.) To be safe, you should save changes to any documents in which you're currently working. You also should consider quitting and restarting the application, particularly if you suspect that the application has encountered corruption—for example, if it reported an error with a document it attempted to open or a preference setting it tried to write.

Crash with error message In this case, an application crashes, and you see an alert message from that application; sometimes the alert message is helpful, but at other times it's less so. Sometimes an alert message can give you a hint that the problem is a bug, because the application has encountered a problem with an internal process and crashed. Error messages occasionally come from the application itself, but you're more likely to see standard Mac OS error messages:

Crash without message Sometimes you'll experience an application that crashes and simply disappears; this is often the result of the program encountering corruption, because some programs have a tendency to just give up when they're fed erroneous data. This is especially true if you've just opened a new document, or the application is accessing a settings or preferences file.

Hang A *hang* occurs when the application appears to stop responding. Often the spinning beachball mouse pointer will appear when you're trying to work with the hung application. In most cases, a hang is the result of a bug in the application: either the application has entered an *endless loop,* or it has encountered corruption and doesn't know how to deal with the problem gracefully.

Freeze A *freeze* is something you're much less likely to encounter in Mac OS X, but it happens from time to time. A freeze is like a hang, but you can't switch to other applications; in fact, you may not even be able to move the mouse pointer or get any response from the keyboard. In some cases, a freeze requires a *hard restart* of the Mac, but there are some steps you can take before that to make sure. Some types of freezes, called *kernel panics*, display a multilingual dialog on your screen telling you to hold down the power button to restart. See Chapter 29, "Typical Problems and Solutions," for more on kernel panics.

NOTE   Often, any sort of crash, freeze, or hang will result in lost changes in any documents that you haven't recently saved. The best defense against lost work is to save often and, if possible, to turn on auto-save and auto-recovery features in your individual applications.

Recovering from Crashes and Hangs

If you encounter a crash, there isn't much you have to do to recover—you'll usually be returned to the Finder or another open application after the crash. You can then relaunch the offending application (if you want to) or continue to work with other applications. You may want to troubleshoot the application following the crash; see the section "Diagnosing Application Troubles," later in this chapter.

NOTE   One other key to fixing a problematic application is to make a note of crashing behavior, including what you may have done immediately before the crash occurred. Whenever you're experiencing recurring crashes, jot down the circumstances on a pad of paper or in a Mac OS sticky note to help you remember the steps. Then you can use the discussion in "Diagnosing Application Troubles" to determine why the crash is occurring. Also, for a more advanced approach, see the discussion of Crash Reporter in Chapter 29.

If you have a hang or freeze on your hands, you'll need to take additional steps to determine what the problem is and resolve it. In most cases, you should be able to stop the offending application and recover to the Finder; sometimes, you may even be able to save data.

Of course, the steps you take with an unresponsive application depend on whether or not you have unsaved changes in the application. If you need to recover unsaved data, then you're probably willing to take some additional steps. The first step is to wait—sometimes applications can take many minutes before they'll recover from an internal issue and become available again for interaction. During this time, avoid pressing keys or the mouse button repeatedly; that will simply fill the input buffer and force the application to deal with all those presses if it comes out of its loop.

Waiting can be useful if your problem really isn't a problem. Say, for example, you have a network volume mounted on your Mac, and you put your Mac to sleep. This is not necessarily bad, because Mac OS X knows to look for that volume when you wake up your Mac. If the computer that houses that network volume is off or asleep when you wake up your Mac, however, your Mac may take a couple of minutes looking for it before telling you that the volume couldn't be found.

If waiting doesn't seem to be working, here are some other steps you should take if you encounter an unresponsive application in which you want to save data:

1. *Switch to another application.* Using either the Dock or the ⌘Tab keyboard combination, try switching to another application. (You also can try clicking the Mac's desktop to switch to the Finder.) If you switch successfully, you'll know that the Mac OS itself isn't responsible for the hang. If you can't seem to switch, then either you have a problem with your entire Mac, or you have a physical problem with an input device.

TIP   Look for clues that your problem is simply a busy background application. In certain versions of Safari, for instance, a large number of updating tabbed windows can seem to slow down response times in Safari and in other windows and applications.

2. *Check your keyboard and mouse connections.* If you've kicked or pulled your mouse or keyboard cable out of its port on your Mac, all of a sudden the mouse pointer or keyboard will stop responding. It may seem like you're encountering a software problem, when in fact the problem is physical. Plug your mouse or keyboard back into the appropriate port and see if your applications are responding correctly.

3. *Save the document.* Press ⌘S. If this saves the document, you may be able to keep working (the application may have sprung back to life), or maybe a particular thread of the application is hung. Once saved, though, you may be able to force-quit the application (see the following section, "Using Force Quit") without worrying about the document.

4. *Move the window or switch to another window.* Sometimes an application pops up a dialog box or error message that inadvertently becomes hidden behind other windows. If you can't seem to get the application to work correctly (particularly if you hear beeps whenever you click the mouse button on a document window), try moving or minimizing the frontmost window to see if another window or dialog box is behind it. The dialog box may be halting other operations in the application.

5. *Quit other applications.* If you have other applications open—particularly if you have *many* other applications open—you should close one or more of them. Doing so may free up system memory for the hanging application, just in case that application has encountered trouble because your Mac's system memory is being taken up by too many open applications at once.

6. *Quit the application.* If you can't save your document (or if you don't have a particular document with changes), you can try accessing the application's Quit command via its application menu or by pressing ⌘Q. Do this only once, though; if you aren't successful, continue to wait for a little while.

7. *Log out.* Another solution to a hung application is to attempt to log out and see if the application will quit and enable you to save the document.

If none of these steps works, you may have encountered an application that is truly hung. (If you've succeeded in switching to other applications, you can be fairly certain that the Mac OS itself isn't frozen.) The next step in dealing with a hung application, unfortunately, will cause you to lose unsaved data: Force Quit.

NOTE   If it appears that the Mac itself has hung (you can't move the mouse pointer or you can't seem to switch to other applications), you'll need to move on to some lower-level recovery options, discussed in Chapter 28, "Solving System-Level Problems."

Using Force Quit

The Force Quit command enables you to do just that—force an application to quit. Under almost all circumstances, an errant application will receive the Force Quit command and dutifully shut down. The command tells Mac OS X to stop running the underlying application *processes*. This step cuts the application off from the other side, so to speak, causing it to quit. However, it does not cause any unsaved changes in that application's open windows to be saved.

To force-quit an application, you launch the Force Quit Applications window. You can do this in one of three ways:

◆ Pull down the Apple menu and select Force Quit.

◆ Switch to another application (by using the Dock, pressing ⌘Tab, or clicking the desktop background) and select Force Quit from the Apple menu.

◆ Press ⌘Option+Esc.

Any of these three options (whichever one will work for you) will bring up the Force Quit Applications window.

TIP The Force Quit Applications window can be used to switch between open applications as well—simply double-click one of the applications in the list. This might come in handy on the off chance that the Dock is the application that has crashed or frozen.

In the Force Quit Applications window, select the application that you want to stop from running and then click Force Quit. You'll see a dialog sheet asking if you're sure you want to force the application to quit. If you're sure, click the Force Quit button in the dialog sheet. The application should be forced to close without attempting to save any changed data; it will disappear from the screen (if any windows are open), and its application icon will no longer be on the Dock. (If the application has its icon on the Dock permanently, the icon won't disappear; instead, the running indicator will no longer appear under the icon.)

NOTE If you select the Finder in the Force Quit Applications window, you'll notice that the Force Quit button will change to Relaunch; you can relaunch the Finder if it seems to be having trouble. In many cases, it will recover without further problems—you can continue computing after the relaunch.

The Force Quit Applications window stays floating over all other windows so that you can force any other applications to quit, if desired. If you're done with the Force Quit Applications window, click its Close button to dismiss it.

WARNING Generally, restarting your Mac by pressing the power button or plugging and unplugging the Mac from your surge protector or wall plug is not recommended. Instead, if Force Quit doesn't seem to be able to stop an application, check Chapter 29 for other tips on restarting the Mac in an emergency.

What do you do if Force Quit doesn't work? At that point, it's time to put on your system administrator's hat and dig into some of the more complex tools for troubleshooting and recovery. See Chapter 28 for tips on managing and killing processes as the administrator. There are ways to stop problem applications using the Process Viewer application as well as the Terminal command line that can sometimes be more effective than the Force Quit Applications window.

Diagnosing Application Troubles

Once you've gotten past the initial problems with your application and recovered or forced the application to quit, you can dig in and begin to figure out the root cause of the problem.

The first step in diagnosing problems is to note the symptoms. The key to this is probably to keep a notebook next to your computer when you begin to experience repeated trouble. Note the exact circumstances of a crash: what you were doing, what files or documents you were working with, and what button you clicked or other action you took. If you're experiencing chronic crashing in your applications, simply noting when and how the trouble occurs may help you begin to uncover the source.

The second step is to determine whether or not the error is reproducible. This can be the most important factor in helping you diagnose trouble. As you log symptoms, you may begin to see a pattern with that application—for example, it crashes every time it loads a particular document, it hangs when accessing a certain website, or it disappears from the screen without warning whenever you print. You should try to reproduce the circumstances within which the crash occurs. Go back through the steps you've logged and see if the problem happens again. If it does, you'll get a better sense of the type of problem you're having and what the solution may be. If it doesn't, you may need to continue logging symptoms until you get another idea for reproducing the problem.

Once you've successfully noted the symptoms and reproduced the problem, you can move on to deciding why the problem is occurring—whether the symptoms seem to suggest a bug, a corruption, or a conflict—and then taking some steps to resolve the problem.

Diagnosis: Bug

If you notice that a crash occurs every time you try to access a particular command in your application, that's a sign that you're dealing with a bug. Bugs can be generally characterized as "the application doing something wrong." Note that this can be different from trouble with a particular *document* or preference *setting*; if you can focus in on a problematic document, the issue might be corruption. If the problem happens in many different documents, or when you access a particular command or sequence of commands in the application, it's possible you're dealing with a bug.

The solution for most bugs is to either update the offending application or figure out how to work around the problem. If your application came with a Readme file or similar document in its installation folder or on its installation CD, read that document to see if any "known issues" are discussed. Sometimes application developers are already aware of the bugs and have offered ways to work around them.

You also should consult the application developer's website to see if an update has been made available that addresses the bug. If not, you should look to see if the website offers troubleshooting or workaround advice for dealing with the bug. If you still don't find any information, you may want to report the bug to the software manufacturer's technical support staff; the company may have a workaround they can tell you about. Even if they can't solve the problem immediately, they'll appreciate the information to help them track down the problem.

If the application's developer isn't particularly helpful, your solution likely will be simply to stop using the application or stop using the feature that's buggy. Just to be sure, though, check the next sections to make sure you aren't really encountering corruption or conflicts.

Diagnosis: Corruption

Corruption sometimes can be easy to diagnose, particularly if you notice problems when you're opening a particular document or set of documents. However, most applications often are also writing data to their preferences files, loading and working with fonts, and accessing underlying parts of the Mac OS. Others have internal documents that they store and constantly retrieve information from (such as e-mail or address book databases and cache files in an Internet browser). Any type of document file that is left open often and is constantly read from or written to is susceptible to corruption. This is especially true if an application crashes while working with a particular file, or if the Mac itself hangs, loses power, or shuts down abruptly.

Tracking down corruption requires that you carefully note and document the circumstances of each crash. If you notice that a particular document seems to cause the crash, that document is likely corrupt. If that's the case, you should stop using the document and see if crashing persists. If that document is the culprit, you might want to attempt to recover the data from the document if you can, or run a disk doctor utility to see if the file can be fixed. Otherwise, stop using it.

PREFERENCES FILES

You'll sometimes find corruption in the preferences files that applications create and store in your Preferences folder, which is located in the /Library/Preferences/ hierarchy in your home folder on your hard disk (see Figure 27.1). If you notice that your application crashes when you access its Preferences command, or that it crashes when you launch or quit the application, it's possible that you've run into some corruption.

If you suspect that an application's preferences file is corrupt, you should begin by quitting the application. Next, drag the file out of the Preferences folder and place it in another folder, perhaps a subfolder of your Documents folder. (Or you could drag the file to your desktop for temporary safekeeping.)

Now, launch the application and test it again. In most cases, applications aren't adversely affected by the absence of a preferences file; the application will simply create a new one. (Of course, you may need to reset some preferences if you've customized them.) If the same crashing continues, the preferences file may not have been the culprit; if you feel you need to, you can return the original file to the Preferences folder. (If you're okay with the newly created preferences file, there's no need to return the old one.)

Once you've fully tested the suspected preferences file and you're sure you no longer need it, you can toss it in the Trash.

FIGURE 27.1

Every time you launch a new application, a preferences file is created in your personal /Library/ Preferences folder.

> **NOTE** Not all applications follow the convention, but Mac OS X uses a special method for naming preferences files. The name follows the pattern domain_type.domain.application.plist. This is intended to be useful to the user because it gives you some hints for locating the website of the software publisher responsible for a particular preferences file, as in com.apple.clock.plist or com.microsoft.explorer.plist. Also, note that many preferences files are simply plain-text or, in some cases, XML (Extensible Markup Language) files. Although it isn't a great idea to play with your preferences files, if you're the intrepid type you may find interesting information within a preferences file by opening it (or, better yet, duplicating the file and opening the duplicate) in a text editor. Shareware and freeware utilities such as Marcel Bresink's PrefEdit (www.bresink.de/osx/) also can help you peek into and edit your preferences files.

DATABASE CORRUPTION

Along with documents and preferences files, other important files may sometimes become corrupt. For instance, if your application is based on a large database (such as Mac OS X's Mail application), portions of that database can become corrupt (or simply fragmented, thanks to repeated deletions or changes) and eventually cause problems. For this type of application, you'll probably need to look for a solution within the application. Most applications that are based on databases also have a built-in way to rebuild those databases. (For instance, Mail has the Mailbox ➤ Rebuild Mailbox command, which can be used to increase the speed and reliability of a particular mailbox's database.)

INTERNET CACHE CORRUPTION

Another area of trouble can be crashing within Internet applications. Web browsers and some other Internet applications rely on cache, history, and similar files that are written to and read from repeatedly. If you notice that your web browser is crashing often, you may want to test the different files in which the browser stores links and data. Internet Explorer, for instance, stores important files in a folder called `Explorer` in your `~/Library/Preferences` folder; there you'll find a number of files, including those where History and Favorites links are stored. By default, Internet Explorer also stores cached pages and images in a database file called `IE Cache.waf` that's stored in the folder `MS Internet Cache`, which is inside your `~/Library/Caches` folder.

NOTE   Safari is a little less likely to crash due to a corrupt cache file because Safari stores many small cache files in its cache folder (`~/Library/Caches/Safari/`). The Safari preferences file is in your preferences folder (`~/Library/Preferences/`), and a Safari folder is right there in your personal Library folder, where you'll find history and bookmark files.

When you have trouble with a web browser, you should shut down the browser and toss the cache file(s) in the Trash or delete the cache from the browser. In Apple's Safari, for example, you can select Empty Cache from the Safari menu to do this. Deleting the cache means that some pages you've visited recently will need to be completely downloaded again the next time you attempt to access them, but otherwise it's no great loss. Restart the browser and see if the problem disappears.

If it's still there, or if you notice that you have trouble specifically when you attempt to access your history or bookmarks files (Favorites in Internet Explorer), you can quit the browser again and move those files to a new folder. It's possible that one of them has been corrupted and is causing the browser to choke on bad data, resulting in an error or crash. In Safari, you can select History ➢ Clear History to delete your history file.

If you're having trouble with a number of different Internet applications, your main Internet preferences file might be corrupted. Troubleshoot the file `com.apple.internetconfig.plist` by removing it from your `Preferences` folder (place it in another folder) and retesting your Internet applications. If that solves the problem, you should delete the file and reset preferences in the Internet pane of the System Preferences application.

FONT CORRUPTION

If you notice trouble with your application as it starts up or when you select a particular font, that font may be corrupt. You also might encounter trouble when you're printing a particular document that contains a corrupt font. If you're experiencing crashes when attempting to print from a number of different applications, you should consider whether a particular font is being used in all of those applications. If so, remove the font from its folder (check the `Fonts` folder inside the Mac OS 9 `System Folder`, the `/Library/Fonts/` folder, or your personal `~/Library/Fonts/` folder, depending on where the font is installed) and check to see if the crashing continues. If the problem seems solved, you'll need to either avoid using the font or reinstall it.

NOTE   Trouble when printing from multiple applications could also suggest a problematic printer driver. If you don't find a corrupt font as the culprit, you might visit your printer manufacturer's website to see if troubleshooting information or a new printer driver has been made available.

You can also use font utilities to track down a corrupt font. As noted in Chapter 30, two such utilities are Font Reserve from DiamondSoft (`www.fontreserve.com`) and FontDoctor X from Morrison SoftDesign (`www.morrisonsoftdesign.com`).

Diagnosis: Conflict

Conflicts between the Mac OS and your applications aren't as likely in Mac OS X as they are in earlier versions of the Mac OS, mainly because Mac OS X acts as a barrier between your applications and the driver software you install. As you'll see in the next section, "Troubleshooting Classic Applications," previous versions of the Mac OS are capable of accepting *extensions*, which can alter the capabilities of the Mac OS but can also prove problematic with some applications. Mac OS X doesn't support extensions in this way.

If you suddenly begin having trouble with an application after you've installed new system software, new driver software, or a hardware device, that may indicate a conflict—many times these will manifest themselves as kernel panics, which are discussed in more detail in Chapter 29. In that case, the best plan is to attempt to uninstall the device or software. Once it's uninstalled, if the application works correctly again, you may have found the culprit. At that point, though, you may have to decide which is more important—the application or the component you just installed.

If you notice that crashes occur with specific applications when they interact with specific system software, that may suggest a conflict. For instance, if you notice crashing when an application attempts to access system dialog boxes (Print, Save, Open) or underlying technology like ColorSync, QuickTime, or graphics acceleration routines, you may have a conflict. This is particularly true if you're working with a newer version of the system software than the application was originally tested against, or if you've recently updated the Mac OS via the Software Update pane in the System Preferences application. (See Chapter 25, "Peripherals, Internal Upgrades, and Disks," for details on using Software Update.)

What can you do? Aside from not using one or the other of the items that are in conflict, your best approach may be to check the Readme files, websites, and documentation of each application and device that's involved. You may find that you're dealing with a known issue or a conflict that previously has been reported and identified. In that case, you may find a fix for the problem or a workaround of some kind. If not, you should contact customer service for one or more of the devices and let them know what problems you're having.

Troubleshooting Classic Applications

Aside from outward appearances—Classic applications look a little different from native applications—the most significant difference is that Classic applications don't offer the same robust defenses against crashes and conflicts that Mac OS X applications do. Although any application can crash, in Mac OS X such crashes are far less likely to affect other applications that are running at that time. In the Classic environment, however, the crashing of a Classic application can easily affect others—or even the entire Classic environment itself, which also can freeze or crash. In this section, we'll take a look at troubleshooting some of the issues that can specifically affect Classic applications.

Recovering from Crashes and Freezes

If a Classic environment application crashes or freezes, you can begin by troubleshooting the problem in the same way that you troubleshoot crashes and freezes with native Mac OS X applications. If you receive an error message in a dialog box during a crash, it may point you in the right direction. If you don't get an error, and the application simply disappears, you have less indication.

If a freeze or hang occurs, you'll want to take the same steps you use in combating a freeze or hang in a native application. In particular, you should wait a few minutes, check to see if you can switch to other applications, and make sure you aren't experiencing a problem with an unplugged keyboard or an errant peripheral device.

If you've encountered a problem that you believe requires you to force the application to quit, the solution is the same: simply press ⌘Option+Esc, which should bring up the Force Quit Applications window. (If that doesn't bring up the window, try switching to the Finder first via the Dock or the Classic application switcher menu over on the right side of the menu bar.) Select the Classic application and click Force Quit. The application should stop running.

Now, once a crash or Force Quit has taken place, it's important to restart any *other* running Classic applications, along with the Classic environment itself. That's because of the shared nature of the Classic environment's memory space (Classic applications can overwrite portions of each other's memory, causing problems), as well as the fact that, once a Classic application has crashed, the Classic environment is simply less stable.

Here are the steps to take after you've used Force Quit to stop a crashed or hung Classic application:

1. Immediately save changes to any other documents that are open in Classic applications, and then quit those applications.

2. Open the System Preferences application and select the Classic pane (see Figure 27.2).

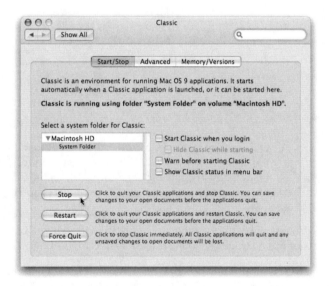

3. On the Start/Stop tab of the Classic pane, you have a number of options for managing the Classic environment, including these:

Start/Stop If you see the Stop button, that means that Classic is currently running. You can click the Stop button at any time to shut down the Classic environment. This is similar to selecting the Shut Down command in the Finder except that it will shut down only the Classic environment, not your entire Mac. It also will shut down any Classic applications that are running, and it will ask you to save changes in any documents that are currently open and unsaved. (If you see Start, it means the Classic is not running; click the button to start the Classic environment.)

Restart You can select the Restart button if you'd like to shut down and then restart the Classic environment. This is a good idea if you've had a Classic application crash or encountered memory errors. In fact, it's a good idea to restart the Classic environment periodically before trouble strikes, especially if you've been running many Classic applications or if the Classic environment has been running for a few days.

Force Quit   If you can't get the Classic environment to shut down or restart, you may need to force it to quit. You can do that by clicking the Force Quit button. This will kill the Classic environment processes, and any unsaved document changes will be lost. Also, if Classic won't quit and won't allow your Mac to shut down or restart, a Force Quit will allow you to shut down your entire system.

NOTE   As you can see in Figure 27.2, the Classic preference pane includes a Show Classic Status in Menu Bar check box. If you mark this check box, a Classic menu extra is added to your menu bar at the top of the screen. This menu extra shows whether Classic is running (it is gray with an orange 9 if Classic is running, and all gray if it is off) and lets you start and stop the Classic environment from its menu. You can also access items in your Classic Apple Menu from this menu. If you use Classic a lot, this menu extra will save you time.

4. Once you've made your choice, close the System Preferences window and continue computing, using native applications. If you like, you can restart any Classic applications from the Finder, or you can launch and troubleshoot the Classic environment as detailed in the section "Managing Classic Conflicts," later in this chapter.

After you've recovered from the problem and restarted the Classic environment, you should take some time to troubleshoot the application itself if you can. Check the sections earlier in this chapter for tips on troubleshooting bugs in native applications. The same ideas apply to Classic applications.

NOTE   For troubleshooting corruption in Classic applications, you'll find that the process is the same, but the location of some system-level files is different. For instance, if you suspect that the preferences file for a Classic application is the culprit, you may need to look in the Preferences folder of the System folder that you use for your Classic environment. Likewise, fonts for the Classic environment are stored in the Fonts folder inside Classic's System folder; if you suspect font corruption, you'll need to head to that Fonts folder to remove those fonts for troubleshooting.

Memory Issues

In the Classic environment, memory is handled differently than it is in the native Mac OS X environment. With native applications, Mac OS X is able to allocate memory dynamically, meaning that memory is given to applications as they need it. With Classic applications, memory can be allocated dynamically to the Classic environment as a whole, but individual applications are allocated memory in a more primitive, fixed way. If you're having trouble with an application that runs out of memory (or if you notice that crashing occurs when the application is asked to open a large number of documents or deal with a computing-intensive task), you may need to change the application's memory allocation.

MEMORY ALLOCATION

Memory allocation is managed through the Info window in the Finder. Here's how:

1. Quit the Classic application whose memory allocation you'd like to alter.

2. Locate the application's icon in the Finder.

3. Select the application's icon, and choose File ➤ Get Info or select ⌘I. This brings up the Info window.

4. In the Info window, click the disclosure triangle next to Memory. You'll see three items listed: Suggested Size, Minimum Size, and Preferred Size (see Figure 27.3).

FIGURE 27.3

In the Info window, you can set your minimum and preferred memory sizes.

The numbers in the Info window represent the amount of RAM, in bytes, that the Classic environment attempts to allocate to the application when it launches. If the Classic environment doesn't have at least the minimum amount available, you'll see an error message telling you that the application can't be launched. If the Classic environment has more than the minimum available, it will give the application as much memory as it can, up to the preferred size.

If you suspect that the application is crashing often and chronically due to memory problems, particularly if the application has trouble even starting up and warns of a memory problem, it's possible that the application's Minimum Size is too low. Click in the Minimum Size entry box and edit the amount of RAM allocated. You don't want to set Minimum Size too high; consider bumping it up one megabyte (approximately 1,024KB) or so.

NOTE Although a megabyte of RAM is technically 1,024KB, and you often see RAM minimums expressed as multiples of that number (for instance, 8,192 or 10,240), setting the preferred and minimum sizes at those levels isn't mandatory; you can enter 8,000 or 10,000 if you want.

You should set the preferred memory size to *at least* the suggested size, which is the recommendation built into the application by the application developers. If you notice that the application still runs into frequent memory errors, or you can't seem to open as many documents as you want, you can set Preferred Size higher by a few megabytes. Note that some applications, particularly graphics and multimedia applications, work particularly well with a large Preferred Size setting.

Remember, though, that the amount of RAM that's allocated to one application will take away from the amount of RAM that can be allocated to another application, whether it's a Classic or native Mac OS X application. This means that setting a particularly high preferred memory number can affect your ability to run other applications while that memory hog is running.

VIEWING CLASSIC MEMORY USE

If you'd like to get a visual sense of how memory is being used in the Classic environment, you can do that via the Classic pane of System Preferences. Launch the Classic pane and select the Memory/ Versions tab. This enables you to view each of the active Classic application processes, including their memory allocations and the amount of that memory allocation that's actually being used (see Figure 27.4). If you're familiar with Mac OS 9 and earlier, you may recognize this as similar to the information you get by selecting Apple ➢ About This Mac when viewing the Finder.

FIGURE 27.4
Viewing the allocation and use of memory in Classic applications

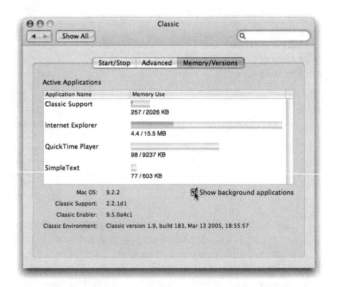

This information can give you some ideas for troubleshooting applications in Classic. For instance, if you notice a problematic application that seems to be using the bulk of its allocated memory (as indicated by the first of the two numbers in each application's Memory Use column, as well as by how full the progress bar appears), then you know one solution may be to increase that application's memory allocation. Likewise, if you notice that quite a few Classic applications are running with larger memory allocations than necessary, you might opt to quit some of them and lower their memory allocations (slightly) to avoid problems; or you might just opt to close some of the applications to clear up more memory for other Classic applications. The more Classic applications you have open, the slower and less stable the Classic environment, as a whole, may become.

Turning on the Show Background Applications check box can help you troubleshoot in another way, by showing you items that are launching and running in the background during your Classic sessions. These may be extensions of faceless applications that you need or find useful when booting into Mac OS 9 but that cause problems in the Classic environment. If you find one or more background processes (other than Classic Support) running, and you're having trouble in Classic, you might want to troubleshoot those items.

TIP See the section "Testing for Extension Conflicts," later in this chapter, for ideas on how to test for conflicts and create multiple extension sets.

MEMORY FRAGMENTATION

The Classic environment can run into another memory-related problem: memory fragmentation. When a number of Classic applications are started, quit, and then others are started—while the Classic environment runs continuously—those applications can leave *fragments* of memory behind, making it more difficult for the Classic environment to allocate RAM effectively. If you notice memory errors with your Classic applications that just don't seem to make sense (for instance, you can't launch a Classic application even though you have no or very few other applications running), you may need to restart the Classic environment. Restarting clears out Classic memory and enables it to begin allocating with a fresh block of available memory.

NOTE In general, you'll have trouble working with the Classic environment and Classic applications if you have less than 256MB or so of RAM installed in your Mac. Although Mac OS X and native applications can get by with less, the RAM requirements of launching both the Classic environment and a few Classic applications can double the amount of RAM required for decent performance on your Mac. If you plan to work regularly with Classic applications, you should upgrade your Mac to *at least* 512MB and, ideally, to as much as you can afford or your Mac will support.

Managing Classic Conflicts

As mentioned before, earlier Mac OS versions and applications are much more apt to encounter conflicts than is Mac OS X. The Classic environment, because it's based on Mac OS 9, is more susceptible to conflicts between it and Classic applications. If you find yourself having trouble with Classic applications, a conflict may be one issue to consider, after you've ruled out bugs and corruption.

In the Classic environment, conflicts can occur between two different applications; if you notice crashing or freezing, you should also note whether the problems occur when a particular pair or group of applications are open. If that's the case, you can test to see if the conflict is reproducible. First, launch each application that you suspect separately and test for bugs or crashing behavior. If you find none, then launch both (or all) applications together and reproduce the steps that caused the crash. If the crash can be reproduced every time (or if it happens with some frequency), you may have your conflict. You'll need to consult the applications' developers to see if they've developed a fix or workaround.

Most of the time, however, conflicts occur between *extensions* to the Classic environment and applications. These extensions, created by either Apple or third parties, augment the capabilities of the basic Classic environment by *patching* portions of it with new bits of code. (If you've worked with Mac OS 9 or earlier, you're probably very familiar with extensions.)

If you're having trouble with a Classic application, and it doesn't appear to be a bug, corruption, or conflict with another Classic application, it may be a conflict with an extension to the Classic environment.

NOTE Extension Overload is a handy application for learning more about extensions, control panels, and their potential conflicts in the Classic environment. Visit www.xoverload.com/extensionoverload/ for details and to download the application.

Testing for Extension Conflicts

Testing for extension conflicts in Mac OS 9 or the Classic environment can be tiresome. You first have to determine if an extension (or group of extensions) is causing the problem. Then you have to determine *which* extension or group of extensions is causing the problem. Finally, you have to decide what to do about the fact that an extension or group of extensions is causing the problem.

TIP Some conflicts are known issues. Consult the Readme file or customer support of the publisher of the crashing application to see if any extension conflicts have been identified. If so, and if you have the extension loaded, you may be able to stop the crashing immediately by disabling the extension.

There's a method to this madness of extension troubleshooting. Generally, you begin by turning off all extensions and launching the Classic environment. You then test the application to see if it has a problem. If it doesn't, you can move on to the next step. In the next step, you enable only the extensions that are native to the Classic environment, to see if the application is in conflict with a "built-in" extension—one that Apple includes or has updated. If there's no trouble with built-in extensions, the final step is to enable third-party extensions and determine which of those are causing the conflict.

Fortunately, the Mac OS has tools available for troubleshooting extension conflicts. Launch the System Preferences application and open the Classic pane. Click the Advanced tab, and you'll see some options that enable you to troubleshoot conflicts (see Figure 27.5).

FIGURE 27.5
The Advanced tab of the Classic pane offers options for troubleshooting conflicts.

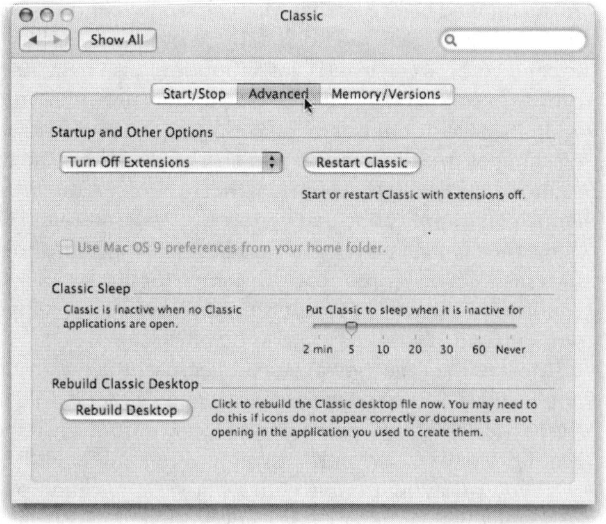

NOTE   The Advanced tab offers two other options. You can choose an amount of time before the Classic environment should go to sleep; this causes Classic to use very few system resources but makes it less responsive when you first access a Classic application. Second, you can use the Rebuild Desktop button to rebuild the desktop file used by Classic (and Mac OS 9) to manage files. Rebuilding can be useful if you're having trouble with document associations, aliases, or odd-looking icons.

From the Startup and Other Options pop-up menu, you have two choices for testing extensions:

Turn Off Extensions   If you choose this option and click Start Classic (or Restart Classic, if the environment is already running), the Classic environment will launch with no extensions active. You then can test your application again to see if the application isn't really conflicting with an extension but rather encountering a bug or corruption. If you start up Classic with extensions turned off and your application encounters the same trouble as before, you probably aren't seeing a conflict.

NOTE   If the application is now encountering *different* trouble after you've disabled extensions, the problem may be that the application requires one or more extensions to function properly. If that's the case, you'll need to enable at least the required extensions (consult the application's documentation) and then test again.

Open Extensions Manager   Select this option and click Start Classic. The Classic environment will start up and display the Extensions Manager (see Figure 27.6). You'll find the tools for activating sets of extensions or individual extensions in the Extensions Manager.

NOTE   These two Startup Options apply only when you start Classic from the Advanced tab by clicking the Restart Classic button; if you subsequently start from the Start/Stop tab or by launching a Classic application, extensions will load normally, and the Extensions Manager will not appear. (That's why there's no "normal" or default setting in the Startup and Other Options menu, just in case you were looking for one.)

For instance, if you've determined that the application doesn't have problems when no extensions are enabled, you can select the Mac OS X Classic Base option from the Selected Set pop-up menu, and then click the Continue button to enable Classic to continue the start-up procedure. (Depending on your Mac OS version, the option may be named for the actual version of Mac OS 9 you have installed, as in Mac OS 9.2.2 Base.) Once Classic is started, you can test to see if the conflict occurs. If it doesn't, then you've eliminated the possibility of a conflict with Apple's base set of extensions.

TIP   Actually, you have a third choice in the Advanced Options pop-up menu: Use Key Combination. If you'd like to start the Classic environment so that it believes certain keys are being held down (for instance, the Shift key to bypass all extensions or any keystroke combinations recognized by third-party extensions), select the Use Key Combination option, and then press up to five keys. Press the Clear Keys button to reset the key combination.

From here, you can use the Extensions Manager to enable individual extensions, in addition to the Base set. You then systematically restart the Mac and add to the extensions until you locate the conflict. Here's how:

1. Enable the Mac OS X Classic Base set, then place a check mark next to a few of the third-party extensions. (If you have a particular extension or set of extensions that you suspect as being the problem, you can enable those first.) The first time you do this, you'll be asked to create a new set of extensions. Name the set and click Save.

FIGURE 27.6
In the Extensions Manager, you can enable and disable extensions by clicking the check boxes next to them.

NOTE You can arrange items in the Extensions Manager in alphabetical order, by type of extension, or by package. You may find package order the most useful if you have some idea of what might be causing the conflict (for instance, if you suspect a particular manufacturer's extensions). Otherwise, enabling the control panels first and then the extensions, alphabetically, may be the best approach.

2. Click the Continue button. When the Classic environment finishes starting, launch the application and test it.

3. If you don't encounter trouble, restart Classic again with the Open Extensions Manager command, and then add three to five more extensions to your new set. Continue into the Classic environment and test your application. Keep doing this until you encounter trouble.

4. Once you encounter trouble, restart Classic with the Open Extensions Manager option once again; then, in the Extensions Manager, *disable* all but the first extension in your most recently added set of extensions. Continue into the environment and test the application.

5. Repeat step 4 but enable additional extensions each time until you find the extension that caused the problem.

FASTER CLASSIC STARTUP: MANAGE EXTENSIONS

If you use the Classic environment only on a limited basis or just for a few applications, you might find it useful to customize the number of extensions that are enabled in the Extensions Manager. If you choose a limited number of extensions, the Classic environment will launch more quickly and, once launched, it will require less overall system RAM.

The easy way to accomplish this is to launch Classic from the Advanced tab in the Classic pane of System Preferences, with the Open Extensions Manager option turned on. When the Extensions Manager appears, choose Mac OS X Classic Base.

Note that the first time you attempt to click one of these items to enable it, you'll be asked to create a new set. In the alert box, click Duplicate Set, give the set a name in the dialog box that appears (perhaps "Fast Classic" or something similar), and click OK. Now you can enable those important Classic extensions. Then, continue into the Classic environment by clicking Continue in the Extensions Manager. The launch should take between 15 and 45 seconds—faster than the typical startup time by a minute or more.

If you're feeling intrepid, you can dig in and disable other extensions as well, depending on what tasks you tend to attempt in Classic. (Note that this is absolutely not necessary and could cause stability problems.) Again, with the Fast Classic set you created in the Selected Set menu, begin turning off items. Turn off some of the items in the Control Panels folder, for instance, if you don't use the Appearance, Control Strip, and similar control panels.

If you don't use games or other 3D applications, you can turn off ATI extensions; if you don't print from Classic, you can turn off the various printer drivers (other than the LaserWriter 8 and PrintingLib) as well as the Desktop Print Spooler, the Desktop Print Monitor, and the regular PrintMonitor. In any case, you can turn off DVD extensions, since they aren't used in the Classic environment anyway. Note that the Classic environment requires all of the following in order to launch without complaint:

◆ General Controls and Startup Disk (in Control Panels)

◆ Apple Guide, AppleShare, CarbonLib, Classic RAVE, Classic Support UI, File Sharing Library, LaserWriter 8, Network Setup Extension, Open Transport, Open Transport ASLM Modules, OpenTpt Remote Access, PrintingLib, and QuickDraw 3D RAVE (all in Extensions)

◆ Classic Support UI (in the System folder)

When you're finished configuring, you can click the Continue button to launch the Classic environment; it should happen very quickly. The next time you launch Classic or a Classic application, it should seem like only a slight pause before the Classic application appears.

If there's a downside to this tweak, it's that you'll run into many applications that won't run without associated extensions or control panels. If that's the case, you'll have to relaunch Extensions Manager and enable the necessary components (such as certain fonts and QuickTime extensions that are required just to run Internet Explorer)—and they may not be particularly easy to figure out.

One other thing: If you boot into Mac OS 9 using the same System Folder that you use for Classic, you should hold down the spacebar while Mac OS 9 starts up. You'll see the Extensions Manager again, enabling you to select a different set of extensions in the Selected Set menu—preferably one you've created specifically for booting into the full Mac OS 9 operating system. In this case, you probably will want many or most of your extensions enabled so that you can get the most out of your sessions in the Mac OS 9 environment.

Now you may have isolated your conflict. If you notice that removing the extension from your startup set causes the trouble to stop with the problematic application, that extension may be all you need to worry about. Try to determine where the extension came from, and contact that software publisher to see if an update, workaround, or any other information is available. (Sometimes the order of an item's loading can prevent it from causing a conflict; try putting a space in the extensions name to have it load at the beginning of the process.)

NOTE   If you plan to boot your Mac into Mac OS 9, you might also want to consider the possibility of using two different extension sets—one for Mac OS 9 and one for the Classic environment. See the next sidebar, "Faster Classic Startup: Manage Extensions," for details. (Note that not all Macs can boot into Mac OS 9. Most Macs made after the beginning of 2003 are designed to boot only into Mac OS X.)

NOTING PROBLEM EXTENSIONS

In the Classic window, extensions are represented by small icons that crawl along the bottom of the screen, appearing as they're loaded by the Classic environment.

If an extension appears with an X through it, it means that the extension isn't loading correctly. In the Extensions Manager, you can disable that extension to make sure it doesn't try to load in the future, which could cause instability. Note, however, that the extension may be necessary for booting into Mac OS 9. In that case, it's a good idea to use the Extensions Manager to create two different sets of extensions—those for loading with the Classic environment and those that should be loaded when you're booting directly into Mac OS 9. You then can use the Extensions Manager to switch between the two sets, depending on which is appropriate.

TIP   To launch the Extensions Manager when you're booting into Mac OS 9, hold down the spacebar as the Mac is starting up until you see the Extensions Manager window. Then you can change the set you want to use by choosing it in the Selected Set pop-up menu.

What's Next?

In this chapter, you saw some of the problems that can affect applications in Mac OS X and how to troubleshoot them. Included was a discussion of recovering from crashes and hangs and forcing applications to quit when necessary. You also saw how to troubleshoot bugs, corruption, and conflicts. In the second half of the chapter, you saw how to troubleshoot the Classic environment, as well as conflicts and problems encountered by Classic applications.

In the next chapter, you'll learn some of the tools and techniques for troubleshooting at the system level within Mac OS X itself, including some tips for troubleshooting problems with performance and making use of Apple's special utility applications to solve problems.

Chapter 28

Solving System-Level Problems

Not that you'd know it from the hype, but sometime, somewhere, Mac OS X might not perform the way you want it to perform. Although Apple has been working diligently to improve Mac OS X for years since its initial release, there's always trouble when a new version emerges. The way Mac OS X behaved under laboratory conditions may not be the way it will behave for every user. Each user has a particular combination of software, hardware, and usage patterns.

However, there's good news. Thanks to Mac OS X's protected memory and file-level permissions, Mac OS X will probably crash less often than earlier versions of the Mac OS, so you should spend much less time troubleshooting Mac OS X. The bad news is that fallible humans make software, and operating systems are made by legions of humans.

If you're a convert from Mac OS 9, any experience you have from troubleshooting the Classic Mac OS generally will still be relevant for Mac OS X, and users with some experience in Unix or Linux will find at least some issues that are familiar. You still will need to know the expected behavior and recognize deviations from it. You still will need to gather information, isolate a problem, and try some solutions, depending on the symptom. In Mac OS X, though, the tools and techniques you use to perform these troubleshooting tasks will be different. In this chapter, we'll take a look at some of those tools and techniques, specifically in terms of troubleshooting at the system level. In Chapter 29, "Typical Problems and Solutions," you'll find answers to specific problems and troubleshooting issues in Mac OS X.

NOTE   Portions of this chapter and Chapter 29 were contributed by Dan Nolen, a technical writer and consultant based in Austin, Texas, who wrote the original troubleshooting chapter for the first edition of *Mastering Mac OS X*. Dan can be reached through his website at http://macmastery.com.

In this chapter:

- ◆ Dealing with Problems
- ◆ Finding the Cause of the Problem
- ◆ Mac OS X Diagnostic Utilities
- ◆ Performance Troubleshooting Tools
- ◆ Much Ado About Root
- ◆ NetInfo Manager
- ◆ Other Places for Help

Dealing with Problems

If you're reading this chapter to prepare for when something goes wrong, you're ahead of the game. There are things you can do (or avoid doing) right now to stay out of trouble. If you're reading this after running into problems, check out this section, but you'll probably want to focus on the tools discussed later in this chapter and the detailed solutions to specific problems outlined in Chapter 29.

> **TIP**   You can conduct some Mac OS X diagnosis and troubleshooting at the Terminal command line. If you aren't yet familiar with Terminal (or the Unix command line), you should read Chapter 22, "Terminal and the Command Line," to get a sense of how to work with the command line in Mac OS X.

Before Problems Occur

The most important step you can take to avoid serious problems is to back up your data regularly. You should do so anyway, even if you aren't installing an entirely new operating system. You have insurance on your home and car and perhaps even on your business. It only makes sense to have at least a little insurance on your Mac by backing up. (See Chapter 26, "Hard Disk Care, File Security, and Maintenance," for more on creating a backup strategy.)

Another key bit of advice, particularly for experienced Mac OS 9 (and earlier) troubleshooters, is to avoid fiddling with the files in Mac OS X's System folder hierarchy. In Mac OS 9 and earlier, troubleshooting system software problems was cumbersome and time consuming because both Apple and non-Apple components belonged together in the System Folder. Even if you knew what programs installed which items in every System Folder subfolder, picking out the bits after a clean install was tedious. That said, it wasn't unheard of for users to spend time moving items around in the System Folder.

In Mac OS X, the files and folders that are installed in the System hierarchy are not meant to be altered by a user via the Finder. If you're used to earlier Mac OS versions, think of the System folder in Mac OS X as similar to the System *file* in earlier Mac OS versions. If you alter the contents of the System folder, the Mac might fail to start up correctly. On the bright side, the mostly Apple-only nature of the System folder means that, at worst, you simply replace the Mac OS X System folder to bring your Mac back online after a severe problem. The only non-Apple components that might need to go in the System folder are third-party drivers (and some low-level utilities), in the form of kernel extensions. In that case, the drivers should come with an installer that puts them there for you; you shouldn't drag the files into the System folder yourself.

Know Your System

Another safety measure you should take is to learn about the underlying Mac OS X filesystem. Before you perform any system-level troubleshooting, you should be somewhat familiar with the hidden files and folders in Mac OS X, particular for command-line troubleshooting. In this section, you'll learn some fundamentals of the Mac OS X system.

HIDDEN FILES AND DIRECTORIES

Aside from the folders you see and work with in the Finder, Mac OS X also has a number of hidden directories that generally are visible only from the command line (in a Terminal window) and, in some cases, visible only while you're logged in to an Admin account.

NOTE   As discussed in Chapter 22, it's common to refer to *folders* in the Mac OS and *directories* when you're discussing the underlying Unix directory structure. Remember that they refer to the same basic concept, but Unix commands in Terminal often use a d (as in cd for change directory) for directory-related commands.

Here's a quick look at some of the directories that might appear at the root level of your hard disk (/) if you are in Terminal:

/bin   This directory is short for *binaries*. System-level command-line scripts and compiled programs are stored here. Most of the folder contents have names that can be typed in a Terminal window. At the command line, you also can type `man command` (where `command` is the command you want to learn about) and press Return. (See Chapter 22 for details.)

/cores   This directory appears at the root level of your hard disk, but it's really a link to the /private/cores directory. The directory is for *core dumps*, a snapshot of memory saved to disk during a crash. A core dump is useful only if you're developing software, so it's turned off by default.

/dev   The /dev directory contains the files that act as an interface to your devices, including the drives, keyboard, mouse, display, ports, and so on. You can look at these files, but we don't advise altering them.

/etc   The /etc directory appears at the root level, but it's actually a link to the /private/etc directory, which contains miscellaneous configuration and startup files. Many of these files aren't really used in Mac OS X unless the computer starts in single-user mode (described later in this chapter). You can inspect most of the miscellaneous configuration and startup files while in TextEdit or by using the command-line command more.

/private   This directory contains the real folders of several of the traditional Unix-like folders mentioned here, such as cores.

/sbin   This directory contains the system binaries, including many of the processes that run the system. It is similar to /bin.

/tmp   This directory is really a link to the /private/tmp directory, which holds temporary files. The contents of this directory are deleted at startup, so don't put anything here you care about. This is like Mac OS 9's hidden Temporary Items folder.

/usr   The /usr directory contains user-level items for a command-line user. Here you'll find less important commands and utilities and also pieces for command-line programming.

/var   This directory is really a link to the /private/var directory. It contains some of Mac OS X's log files, the NetInfo databases, root's home directory, and other important items accessible for Unix system administration.

THE *LIBRARY* FOLDERS

Mac OS X logically divides the filesystem into four distinct domains, based on their function and scope. (The *filesystem* is the collective name for all the volumes available to the computer, including the boot volume, other local fixed and removable drives, and network volumes.) The four domains are User, Local, Network, and System. You'll notice that most of the domains correspond to folders you'll see in the Finder window.

The Library folders in the User domain (~/Library or, for instance, /Users/stevej/Library) are for files that should be available only for the logged-in user. Preference files, for example, belong in each individual user's Library folder. What one user has in the Dock should be (and is) specific to that user and should not be changed by another user's (normal) use of the computer. The folders named for each user, which contain the user's personal documents, are stored in the Users folder on your startup disk.

The Local domain (which includes the root-level /Library and /Applications folders) is for files that should be available to everyone on the computer but that are not required for the computer to run and are not considered part of the core operating system. Fonts, screensaver modules, printer modules, and many other such items go in the root-level Library folder on your startup disk. Similarly, the Applications folder is in the Local domain. Only an administrator-level user can modify items in this domain. (In the case of only one system user, that user is the administrator.)

The Network domain is for applications, resources, and other items shared among all users on a network. This information normally is stored on a file server, and the most common use is on a network that includes a NetInfo server. In general, however, most users will simply use the Network icon for quick access to File Sharing servers—click the Network icon in your Sidebar to see those servers.

NOTE Mac OS X 10.4 no longer shows empty Network folders in configurations where you don't have a central network server à la Mac OS X Server. If you do have such a network, you may see a Library folder in the Network domain where fonts, preferences, and other important tidbits are stored for network use.

The System domain (everything inside the /System folder that you see on your startup disk when viewing in a Finder window) is for system software installed by Apple and is only on the boot volume. As noted previously, unlike for Mac OS 9 and earlier, users are not meant to modify this folder. (In fact, in Mac OS X 10.3 and higher, you have to be working in an administrator's account and you have to authenticate yourself in order to make changes within /System. In versions prior to 10.3, you have to be in the root account.) Long-time Mac users may take a while to get used to the idea that the System domain simply is not meant for user or even administrator changes. Instead, most non-core items will be installed in the Local domain, generally in the /Library folder (when viewed in the Terminal window) or by accessing the root-level Library folder on your startup disk.

WHAT'S IN /SYSTEM/LIBRARY?

The /System/Library hierarchy is supposed to be the exclusive domain of Apple's installers. An administrator-level account is required to delete the files and folders in the /System/Library hierarchy, and you must authenticate before doing so. Normally, it should not be necessary to alter any files there, so that's not too much of a concern.

Likewise, it should almost never be necessary to add files to these folders except by using an installer that puts them there automatically (such as drivers for a device). If you have a configuration file, plug-in, or similar system-level file you want to add to your Mac, you'll almost certainly use one of the other Library folders. Which Library folder you use depends on the domain into which you're installing the file. If the file should be installed for all users of your Mac, install it in the main /Library folder. For items that will affect only a specific user's Mac experience, files should be installed in the Users/*current_user*/Library folder (where *current_user* is the home folder of the specific user).

There are exceptions to any rule, of course, and you can troubleshoot the /System/Library folder—or, in fact, the entire /System hierarchy—from the command line (using the sudo command) or, in some cases, from Mac OS 9, where file privileges don't stop you from altering items. It's generally a last resort, however—only in the rarest of cases will it make much sense for you to dig around in those folders.

Finding the Cause of the Problem

The first step in finding the cause of a problem is to take a careful look at the symptoms of that problem—knowing exactly what's going wrong is important to finding ways to fix it. Once you've got a good idea of the symptoms, you can start to look for causes of those symptoms and apply some diagnostic tools to see if you can isolate the root cause. Once you've figured out the cause, you can move on to solutions—most of those are provided by utility software or information databases such as the Knowledge Base maintained by Apple at its website.

Symptoms: Gather Information

If you've determined that you have a problem, you need to gather information about the symptoms. First, you may want to consult Chapter 27, "Fixing Applications and Managing Classic," if the problem you're having is with a particular application or document—your problem may not be at the system level at all. If you believe you have a system-level problem, answer the following questions:

Is the symptom reproducible on that computer?   If not, then troubleshooting may be a big waste of time. If the time lost by encountering and recovering from the situation is less than the time and effort you would spend troubleshooting, it may not be worth it.

Is the symptom reproducible on another computer with the same version of Mac OS X?   If so, it may be a bug. If it is a bug, all you can do is report it to Apple's support staff and work around it while you wait for the fix. The odds of two separate computers developing the same problem at the same time are low enough that you can be fairly confident that a system-level problem on both is not specific to your computer and, therefore, not something you can fix.

NOTE   To report bugs to Apple, either call in, if you're within your complimentary support period (check the documentation that came with Mac OS X), or post the bug on Apple's discussion boards (`http://discussions.info.apple.com/`). (You can also go to `www.apple.com/macosx/ feedback` if you'd like to vent to Apple about a particular problem.) When reporting a problem to a technical support person, you should tell the service representative the corrective steps you took, the results, and exact error messages or steps to reproduce the issue. You also should try to determine whether the error happens with more than one computer (if you can) and more than one application and whether it's a problem that's isolated to Classic applications or the Classic environment.

When did the symptom start?   Note whether anything in particular happened before the problem appeared, particularly if anything *automatic* seemed to take place. If you noted trouble with the interaction of your applications or if the computer went into Sleep mode or did something similar before trouble struck, that may help you find the cause.

What was the last action you took?   This is the corollary to the above question—did the problem occur after you did something? Did you install a new application, try a new feature, install a peripheral device, or undertake some particular task before the problem occurred?

As you can see, tracking a problem can require some testing and observation. Sometimes it can be handy to keep a notepad next to your Mac and make a note when a crash or other problem occurs, noting the most recent action, the symptoms, the applications that were running, whether or not Classic was active, and so on. Even if you aren't able to get a full sense of the problem immediately, after it occurs a few times you may start to see a pattern emerging that can help you troubleshoot.

Checking the Logs

Mac OS X does not always display a message in the Finder or elsewhere when something has gone wrong. However, a *log file*, a plain-text document in which information about a particular activity is saved, can provide useful information for determining the cause, extent, and duration of a problem. Mac OS X logs information to a number of such files. Checking these files periodically, whether or not you encounter trouble, is a good idea.

CONSOLE

A good early troubleshooting step is to look in the Console. The Console is an application that displays the contents of the file /Library/Logs/Console/*<uid>*/console.log (where *<uid>* stands for your short name ID on this Mac),which is created every time you log in. If you can't reproduce a problem easily, you should check the Console before you log out or restart. You also might find it useful to leave the Console application running in the background. Applications can send several types of messages to the file read by Console, including, warning, status, and debugging messages.

TIP You can use the Mark icon in Console to add a time-stamped line to the log—that way you can scroll back in the log at some point in the future and see what happened after your mark. You might find that handy for troubleshooting.

To launch the Console, you can double-click its icon in the Utilities folder of the Applications folder. Then, as you work in the Mac OS, actions and problems are logged constantly in the Console window.

Console can be used to open a variety of different log files. Choose File ➤ Open System Log to view the system log, where you'll find a log of the Mac's very low-level activity, such as waking from sleep and turning on and off network protocols. Choose File ➤ Open Quickly, and you'll gain access to tons of other logs that are stored in various parts of the Mac's underlying filesystem. Probably most handy are the crash logs, found at File ➤ Open Quickly ➤ ~/Library/Logs/CrashReporter (for your personal applications that crash) and File ➤ Open Quickly ➤ /Library/Logs/CrashReporter for a log of crashes that happen to system-wide applications. Click the Logs button in the Console window and you'll also be able to access various log files quickly and easily (see Figure 28.1).

READING LOG ENTRIES

The format of the messages in the Console window will usually be as follows:

```
Date   Time   Hostname or Application   [Process ID]:   Process name   Message
```

Not every message will include all the variables. Here's a quick look at what the items in a log entry mean:

Date and Time These variables can help you target the timing of a problem. You might have to compare these variables against a time stamp in other log files.

Hostname This shows the name of your computer, as reported by the Domain Name Services (DNS), but without the domain. If an IP address in the DNS server is 1.2.3.4, and it represents foo.bar.com, foo will be displayed as the hostname. If you move a log file to another machine later, you'll have some idea of where the log file came from. However, if the hostname is listed as `localhost`, and you have a real domain name, you might infer that network services or DNS was down. (In many cases, stand-alone Macs won't have a domain name, so `localhost` is correct in those situations.)

NOTE   In some logs, the hostname entry is the name of the process (or application) in question.

FIGURE 28.1

You can use Console to view a variety of log files.

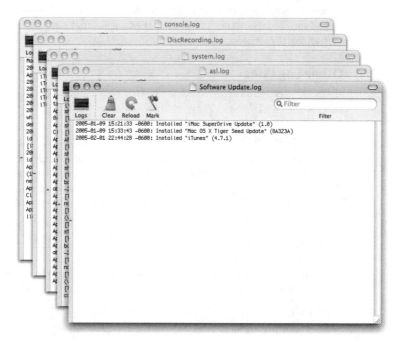

Process ID (PID)   The value of PID is the unique number of the process (program) that generated the log entry. When the computer starts, the first process is 0, and each subsequent process is the next higher number. Generally, the larger the number, the longer the computer has been running without restarting. More to the point, you can tell the order in which processes have been launched, and you can see if a particular process seems to be quitting and relaunching on its own, perhaps in response to an error. If you quit a program and start it up again, it gets a new process ID.

Process Name   This is more useful than PID—exactly how much more depends on the process. If you know what the process does, it is most helpful. (For instance, if the process is System Preferences or NetInfo, you can infer that something might be wrong with a configuration setting that you can access from one of those applications.) Even if the process name isn't familiar, the text that comes after it might be useful.

NOTE   A *process* is another name for an application program. Just as in Mac OS 9 and earlier, many processes run in the background without a user interface.

Message   The Message field contains the substantive information. Remember, the messages can be warnings, errors, or just notes.

Many log entries will mean very little to you. They often are useful only to programmers trouble-shooting their applications. But you may pick up on certain malfunctions—for instance, your network settings may be reported as inaccurate, applications may have trouble completing a task, or many errors may occur within a particular process. The Console log at least may give you a hint for locating the problem.

NOTE   It's worth noting that not every log entry is an error message, and even the error messages aren't always worth getting worked up about. If you're having trouble at the system level, however, and you see a related error message in the Console, that's one more bit of information you'll have for tracking the problem.

Other Log Files

As mentioned, you can open additional log files using Console's File ➢ Open Quickly command. In this section, we'll look at a few of them.

THE /VAR/LOG FILES

The /var/log folder can be accessed using the command Open Quickly ➢ /var/log in the Console. Here you'll find log files for background applications and servers, such as FTP, Web, and other items that work in the background like the CUPS printing system and the system log.

Which log files do what? Here's a quick look at the log files found in the /var/log folder:

ftp.log   This file shows connections and successful and failed logins.

httpd/access_log   The access_log file is the standard Apache access log in the httpd directory. If you are using Mac OS X Personal Web Sharing (which is powered by the industrial-strength, open-source Apache web server), the file will contain the information about each "hit" to your website. For more on Personal Web Sharing and Apache, see Chapter 24.

httpd/error_log   This log is the standard Apache web server error log in the httpd directory.

lookupd.log   This optional log file can be configured for the lookupd background process to use. Messages about lookupd are stored in system.log if you don't set a custom log in NetInfo Manager. (The lookupd background process is designed to be running at all times so that it can speed up requests to the NetInfo database to locate a particular resource.)

lpr.log   Messages found here are about LPR (IP-based) printing, mostly from the lpd (line printer daemon) process. You are using only lpr and lpd if you have set up a printer with the LPR Printers Using IP option in Print Center. If you are using a USB or AppleTalk printer, this log file will probably not be used.

mail.log   Messages from command-line mail programs such as Sendmail, the command-line mail-sending program, are contained here. The file is not used by the Mail application that comes with Mac OS X. It's really useful only if you are sending or checking mail on the command line or if you're using Apple's built-in Sendmail server. The log would report problems mailing automated reports.

netinfo.log   This log file stores messages about processes relating to NetInfo, mostly lookupd and nibindd.

secure.log   The file logs messages relating to security. Failed logins from `login` and messages from `/System/Library/CoreServices/SecurityServer` are stored here. The log might be of value if you believe users are trying to access your Mac without a proper username and password or if you'd simply like to see who attempts to log in. Because of the sensitive information that this file might contain, it cannot be opened in the Console. Only the root user can read it (or an administrator using the `sudo` command at a command line prompt).

system.log   This is one of the important log files, containing much information. After `console.log`, `system.log` is most likely to be helpful when you're troubleshooting a problem. Most of the information shown at startup is logged here. Some of the information stored in other log files is also duplicated in `system.log`. If you're worried about redundant information that appears in other log files, double-check the times when each message is logged.

wtmp   This file stores information about who has logged in to the computer recently. It is not a text file and cannot be read by a normal application; you can read it with the Terminal command `last`. That command lists the user, terminal, originating host (if remote), time logged out, time logged in, and whether the user is still logged in or was disconnected by a crash. Unless you allow many people to log in to your computer, `wtmp` probably will not be that useful. This file also shows when the computer was rebooted or shut down, although such messages are also duplicated in `/var/log/system.log`.

LOGS FOLDER

Want more logs? You'll find log files about AppleFileService (also known as Personal File Sharing) and Directory Services (which includes LDAP, NetInfo, and Kerberos) in the `Logs` folder inside the main `Library` folder (`/Library/Logs`) as well as in your home folder's `Log` folder (`~/Library/Logs`). You'll find these log files for the Apple-specific services particularly useful when you're encountering local networking problems. (Again, you can access them using the Console's File ➢ Open Quickly command.) We'll describe the files here:

AppleFileServiceError.log   The file shows when File Sharing was started. It logs a warning that AppleTalk is not active. (Regrettably, System Preferences does not display an alert to warn you.)

DirectoryService.server.log   This file reports whether Directory Service plug-ins (NetInfo, LDAP, Kerberos) have loaded.

DirectoryService.error.log   Errors with the Directory Service plug-ins are reported here.

Likewise, you'll find a `CrashReporter` folder here in the `/Library/Logs` and `~/Library/Logs` folders. In those folders, log files appear and are updated when applications or system components crash or encounter reportable errors.

/SBIN/DMESG

In the Terminal window, type **/sbin/dmesg** and press Return to display the system-message buffer, which contains information about Ethernet, FireWire, and PPP, among other protocols. Some messages here are similar to what is displayed as your Mac starts up. You can read the message (use the `more` application, if desired, as in `/sbin/dmesg | more`) to see many of the basic settings your Mac is using for startup configuration. For instance, you may see messages in this log that tell you certain drivers have failed to load or are unloaded by the Mac OS, perhaps because the devices that they drive aren't found due to faulty installation.

Mac OS X Diagnostic Utilities

If the log files don't provide an answer for you—or if they've pointed you in a direction that you'd like to test further—your next step might be to fire up one of Mac OS X's troubleshooting utilities. In this section, you'll see the System Profiler and the Network Utility, two utility applications that may help you track down problems.

Troubleshooting with System Profiler

System Profiler is a good tool for gathering information about many different subsystems of your computer, which is particularly useful in Mac OS X if you are not yet familiar with the operating system. If you have a device that you can't use under Mac OS X, System Profiler can help you see whether the device is recognized by the system itself, even if a particular application program does not recognize it. The graphical version of the System Profiler is discussed in Chapter 25, "Peripherals, Internal Upgrades, and Disks."

One feature not discussed in other chapters is System Profiler's capability to display the contents of certain log files. Click the Logs entry in System Profiler, and you'll see a number of logs listed. Select any log to see its contents (see Figure 28.2). This provides another convenient way to access certain log files that you may prefer over the Console.

You can access a nongraphical version of System Profiler from the command line, whether via single-user mode or in the Terminal. Type **system_profiler | more** and press Return. (If you've read Chapter 22 or you're familiar with the Unix command line, you'll notice that the contents are being fed to more so that only one screen of text appears at a time. Press the spacebar to move to the next screen.) If you'd like to output System Profiler's findings to a text report, type **system_profiler >** **/Users/***user_name***/Desktop/profile.txt** and press Return. The report will be placed in the file profile.txt on the desktop of the user specified in *user_name*. Change the user folder and report filename as you desire.

FIGURE 28.2

The Logs entry in System Profiler gives you quick access to some of Mac OS X's troubleshooting logs.

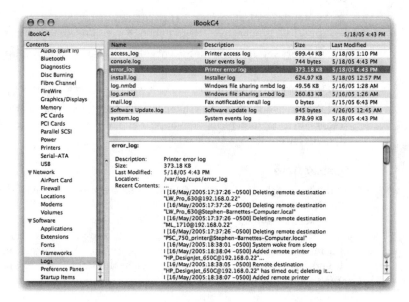

NOTE The full path to this utility is /usr/sbin/system_profiler, in case you have trouble accessing it.

System Profiler can be useful in troubleshooting because you can see what devices are on each hardware bus. In some cases, you can see very specific information about the ROM and firmware versions of your devices. In one place, System Profiler shows a summary of all your networking connections and volumes; that's not possible elsewhere in Mac OS X. The command-line version of System Profiler in Mac OS X shows more general, device, and volume information than the graphical Mac OS X version.

Test with Network Utility

Mac OS X ships will a full-fledged utility called Network Utility for testing networking and internetworking connections. With Network Utility, you can get basic information about your network connections easily, test your Mac and other devices, trace the path between you and servers you're interested in, and even look up information about other servers on the Internet. Figure 28.3 shows the Network Utility interface. In this section, we'll look at each of the tabs in the Network Utility interface.

FIGURE 28.3
Network Utility enables you to test and trouble-shoot a variety of TCP/IP networking problems.

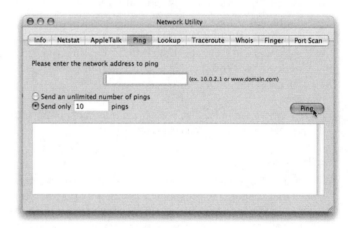

INFO

On the Info tab, you'll find general information and statistics about your connection and your network hardware:

Hardware Address This is your Ethernet chip's Media Access Controller (MAC) address. A unique 48-bit number identifies each Ethernet chip; the number normally is written as six pairs of hexadecimal numbers. A hexadecimal number has 16 possible values (0–9 and a–f) instead of 10 (0–9). The first three pairs uniquely identify the vendor of the chip. For more information on which vendors have which codes, see http://standards.ieee.org/regauth/oui/index.shtml.

IP Address The series of four numbers that represent this Mac's unique address either on the Internet or on your LAN if your network receives Internet access via a router.

Link Speed *Link* is simply a physical connection to another device. The speed will normally be 10MB, 100MB, or 1GB (as negotiated with the switch, hub, router, or other machine). If you have an AirPort wireless networking card, your speeds may be a little different at 1MB, 2.5MB, 5MB, 11MB, 20MB, 26MB, and so on up to 54MB.

Link Status   The value shows whether the connection is currently active or inactive.

Vendor   The vendor listed is the company that manufactured the network interface.

Model   Here, the model name of the network interface (according to the manufacturer) is shown.

Sent Packets   Sent Packets shows how many pieces (packets) of information have been sent.

Send Errors   Errors are rare but possible. You should be concerned only if the Send Errors number is constantly climbing. You'll probably have other problems before you notice the relatively high number. The Send Errors variable measures an error known as *dropped frames*.

Received (Recv) Packets   Received Packets shows you how many pieces (packets) of information have been received.

Receive (Recv) Errors   Here also, errors are reasonably rare but possible. You should be concerned only if the number shown is constantly climbing. If you notice problems with your networking applications, you also might check this number to see if you're encountering receive errors. The Receive Errors value also represents dropped frames.

Collisions   A collision occurs when two computers are talking at the same time. Computers on a network take turns communicating with each other. If two computers talk at once, that's a collision. You will see proportionally more collisions on networks with more computers or with heavy network use. You should be concerned only if the number is high (as in more collisions than sent packets).

TIP   At the command line, you can get information similar to what is displayed on the Info tab by typing `ifconfig -a` and pressing Return.

NETSTAT

Netstat gives you information about the way network information is routed through your computer. Such information will probably be useful only for troubleshooting multiple, simultaneous connections to a network. For example, if you have a connection to your ISP over AirPort and also a connection to a local Ethernet LAN, then Netstat may come in handy. If needed, you can give this information to a network administrator or to an ISP technician who requires specific, detailed information about your problem.

TIP   At the command line, type `man netstat` and press Return for more information on using a command-line version of Netstat.

APPLETALK

If you're having trouble with your AppleTalk network, you can click the AppleTalk tab to get a variety of information about the port that you're using for AppleTalk as well as the network to which it's connected. Most of this requires an AppleTalk expert to decipher, but it can be handy if you're feeling stumped about whether or not your Mac is connecting via AppleTalk. The last option, Lookup Specified AppleTalk Entity, can be used to access another machine on your LAN by name (as in "TiBook4" or "Rob's Computer") to see if it seems to be accessible from yours.

PING

On the Ping tab, you can test whether your computer can communicate using TCP/IP at the most basic level. Ping sends a special kind of message (an ICMP `Echo_Request` packet) to the hostname or IP address you specify. If a computer responds, you can infer that the computer is active on the network and responding at least on some level and that the physical connection between your two computers is good.

Ping is useful when testing for basic TCP/IP connectivity. Suppose you've just added a Mac to your network, and you want to know if the connection is working. Enter the IP address of another machine on the network and get a response. If you're testing to see if an Internet connection is working, you could enter `www.apple.com` or another address. You can even ping yourself (that is, your own IP address) to make sure round-trip communication exists between the TCP/IP networking part of Mac OS X and your networking hardware.

Because pinging yourself almost always works, you should start with pinging something else. What you ping depends on what you're testing. If you can't get to a certain website with your browser, you can try pinging the same website or another machine in that site. For example, if `www.apple.com` doesn't come up in your web browser, but you can send and receive e-mail, your own network configuration is probably functional. You might ping `www.apple.com` or `ftp.apple.com` to see if anything in the `apple.com` domain responds (see Figure 28.4). The connection from your ISP might be down, or Apple may have trouble with its servers (however unlikely that might be).

If you're like us, you tend to test Internet connections by launching a web browser and seeing if it'll work. Ping can be helpful for testing connections that seem to be giving you "weird" trouble. If, for instance, you can ping a distant IP number (such as `17.112.152.32` for Apple), but the URL isn't working (such as `www.apple.com`), you could infer that your Domain Name Services (DNS) server is down. Ping is useful for determining that you do, in fact, have a good connection so that you can move on to troubleshooting the services that operate on top of that connection. (Ping can be blocked by firewalls, however, so you may sometimes be unable to ping a server that you can connect to over the Web.)

TIP Type **man ping** in a Terminal window for more information on the command-line equivalent of Ping.

FIGURE 28.4

Using Ping to test your connection to a remote (in this case, Apple's) web server

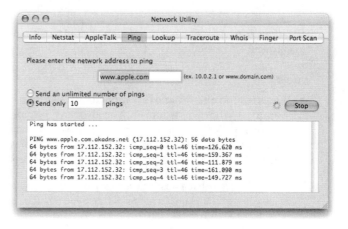

LOOKUP

The Lookup tab is a convenient little tool—it enables you to convert a TCP/IP hostname to its IP address and back. If you need to test whether you have incorrect DNS information or your DNS server went down, you can use the Lookup tab from another computer to get an IP address from the hostname (as in www.apple.com). Then try the IP address to the computer you're troubleshooting with the Ping command or in a web browser (if it is the IP address of a web server).

Also, if you want to see if a particular IP address has a hostname associated with it, you can type in the IP address and get back a name. However, not all IP addresses have a corresponding hostname. Some ISPs have a generic hostname that includes the IP address; for example, cs6668170-19.austin.rr.com would be the same as 66.68.170.19. Remember, a DNS server translates an easier-to-remember name (like www.apple.com) into an easy-to-compute number.

On the Lookup tab, notice that you also have a number of different options for the type of information that you can look up in the Select the Information to Lookup menu.

TRACEROUTE

As the name suggests, this tab offers a tool that traces the route your packets take between your computer and any other computer. You can use Traceroute whenever local network services work (the previous commands, such as Ping and Lookup, are successful for machines on your network), but multiple remote services are unavailable. For example, if your local mail server works at your ISP, but neither www.apple.com nor www.yahoo.com responds, then Traceroute might help you figure out where the problem is. (Again, traceroute requests can be blocked by some firewalls.)

Here's how to use Traceroute:

1. Enter the computer name (hostname) or IP address of the machine to which you want to map the route.

2. Click the Trace button. The results will be displayed.

3. The results are displayed in the following format:

```
Hostname (IP address of hostname); maximum, average, minimum
    millisecond times
```

TIP Type **man traceroute** in a Terminal window for more information on the command-line equivalent of Traceroute.

WHOIS

The Whois tab contains the whois command; it looks up records in the database of the domain name registrars to see who owns a domain. You also can type part of a domain name and see what domains contain that part. Besides simple ownership questions, whois can give you an administrative contact for a domain when a website you expected to be up is unavailable. If you find that you're being harassed by traffic from a certain domain, you can look up the owner of the domain to complain.

TIP One technique that harassers use to avoid getting caught is to fake (or *spoof*) another domain. If you are going to complain, be polite, because you might be contacting another victim.

Here's how to use `whois`:

1. Click the Whois tab.

2. Type the domain or IP address in question.

3. Change the Whois server, if desired.

4. Click the Whois button. The information about who the domain is registered to will be displayed.

TIP Type `man whois` in a Terminal window for more information about the command-line equivalent of `whois`.

FINGER

The Finger tab shows information about user(s) logged in to a machine. It also displays a file named `.plan` in the user's home directory.

WARNING Many server administrators turn off the Finger server process (technically, the `fingerd` daemon) on their servers because they consider it a security hole. If crackers can determine the names of people logged in to a machine, they only have to guess passwords, not names and passwords. (In Mac OS X, `fingerd` is disabled by default.) Also, people who put extensive info in their `.plan` file make the *social engineering* approach to cracking easier. This approach is used by someone who calls a company and, through charm and guile, gets a representative to reveal information about internal systems or operations that can be used later for cracking.

You can use Finger when you want to see if a specific person is logged into a specific machine or to see what users are logged in to a specific machine. Here's how:

1. Type a user in the entry box to the left of the @ symbol.

2. Type a domain in the entry box to the right of the @ symbol.

3. Click the Finger button.

Any information available from the host domain will be returned.

TIP Type `man finger` in a Terminal window for more information about the command-line equivalent of Finger.

PORT SCAN

The Port Scan tab has a utility that scans the TCP ports (not the physical ports on the outside of your computer) that are open (listening for connections) on a machine. An Internet server often will use different port numbers to receive different types of clients—for instance, the same computer can accept web, FTP, Telnet, and other clients, all by using different port numbers for each type of connection. Port 80, for example, is the port generally used by web servers.

NOTE The port address can be specified in a URL. If you enter `http://www.servername.com:79/` in a web browser, your request will likely fail, whereas `http://www.servername.com:80/` accesses the proper port.

If a web server on a remote computer has a problem, and you want to see if that machine supports AFP, FTP, SMB (Server Message Block, discussed in Chapters 17, "Accessing Network Volumes," and 20, "Mac OS X and Other Platforms"), or some other connection, Port Scan can be useful. It also can be useful for finding out what services are running on your own computer.

WARNING Using Port Scan on a machine you don't own may trigger an alert if that machine is monitoring for such behavior. Be aware that some crackers use Port Scan to look for ways to break into a machine. You may be presumed to be a cracker, so let that guide your behavior. Your network administrator or Internet service provider may have rules against scanning, so check before you scan anyone other than yourself or a local network that you administer.

You can scan yourself by entering `localhost` or `127.0.0.1` as the address to scan. This reserved address, called a *loopback address,* always refers to the machine you're on.

The list of well-known ports for TCP and UDP is in a document called RFC 1700 (`www.freesoft.org/CIE/RFC/1700/4.htm`). You can see some of the most common ports in the file `/etc/services` in Mac OS X or most Unix-like operating systems. To reveal this file in the Finder, choose Go to Folder from the Go menu. In the dialog sheet that pops down, type **/private/etc/** and press the Return key.

Performance Troubleshooting Tools

You can attack problems in Mac OS X a few different ways. For some problems, it may be easiest to stop and start again, if you can. Quit and restart the application, log out and back in again, or just restart the computer. Restarting won't fix anything, but if the problem is sufficiently intermittent, it may be the most efficient way to handle the situation.

If a particular program keeps the computer from responding in a timely manner or at all, you may need to force applications or parts of the operating system to quit. Of course, you'll have to identify the offending component first.

To minimize problems caused by bugs in software, you should always install software updates for Mac OS X, whether you use the Software Update pane of System Preferences or you download individual updates from `http://www.apple.com/support/downloads/` on the Web.

CLASSIC TROUBLESHOOTING THAT DOESN'T APPLY TO MAC OS X

If you're an old hand with Mac OS 9 or earlier, understand that some types of troubleshooting are obsolete in Mac OS X—that is, troubleshooting that doesn't take place in the Classic environment. Here are some obsolete troubleshooting steps (note that many of them that *are* still appropriate for Classic are discussed in Chapter 27):

Extension Conflicts Troubleshooting extensions for Mac OS 9 and earlier are necessary when a carelessly programmed or malicious extension has changed the way part of the system software works and resulted in a side effect. For the most part, Mac OS X has abandoned third-party operating system extensions. You still may have to troubleshoot extensions in the Classic environment, but that should be increasingly less frequent.

Rebuilding the Desktop You don't have to rebuild the desktop for Mac OS X. You still can rebuild the desktop for Mac OS 9 in the Classic pane of System Preferences, as discussed in Chapter 27.

Adjusting Memory Allocation/Virtual Memory   In Mac OS X, the kernel allocates any available memory that is asked for by an application. Applications do not have to reserve the amount of memory they need up front. Also, Mac OS X users no longer are expected to toggle virtual memory on and off or adjust its settings. Again, Classic applications still can benefit from manually allocating memory. A few applications, such as Photoshop and Microsoft VirtualPC, will allow you to limit the amount of memory they use and you'll want to tweak those settings occasionally. As a general rule, though, this is very rare in Mac OS X.

Replacing Missing Ancillary Application Files   Most Mac OS X applications are delivered as packages. That is, they come in a special package folder with a name ending in . app; the folder (which looks like a regular application icon in the Finder) contains versions for different languages or different platforms (such as OS X and Mac OS 9). You can just drag-copy applications in the Finder, and all the supporting files should just come along for the ride. Gone are the days of digging around in the System Folder and guessing which programs install what files.

Performance Problems

In general, the newest hardware will run better because of faster processors, processor speeds, bus speeds, hard disks, more and faster memory, caches, and video hardware. If you think you're encountering some severe performance issues, you can take several steps to find the problem:

Measure Performance   Processes using most of the CPU usually will cause a slowdown. The symptom usually will be the spinning rainbow optical-disc cursor. A single application can become unresponsive because of bugs or other limitations in the way it was written. You can test for that by clicking on another application's window or moving the mouse toward or over the Dock (if the hiding or magnification option is on). If other applications pop up and seem to perform well, you know that the performance issues are confined to the problematic application. If you have the CPU Monitor visible, it may be full before you even notice a slowdown. (See the section "Measuring Performance," later in this chapter, for more on performance-monitoring tools.)

Identify the Culprit   Common culprits for performance slowdowns are the Classic environment and Apple File Server (the background process for Personal File Sharing). Depending on your use patterns and software, you may find other culprits.

NOTE   File Sharing, Web Sharing, USB Printer Sharing, and other networking services can put a load on your Mac, particularly if you have a number of people accessing your Mac at once. Don't forget to consider those as a possibility when you're looking for a process that's affecting your Mac's performance.

Get More Memory   If you have only a minimal amount of RAM installed in your Mac, you will notice seriously downgraded performance. (With Mac OS X 10.4, 256MB is the recommended minimum and 512MB is a recommended minimum for decent performance.) When the computer runs out of available system memory, it allocates available hard drive space to store unused items it transfers from memory. Hard disk access is much slower than RAM, so when RAM is used up, you will feel the pain when virtual memory kicks in. Because no (easy) way exists for the user to control virtual memory in Mac OS X, the best you can do is to have enough real memory so that virtual memory will rarely be used.

Report Problems Every new operating system version comes with some bugs and other problems, and the same is true of new applications versions and other updates. When you can, report your problems to the application vendors to see if they can help out or, at least, take your bug report into consideration when they do more programming and development.

Troubleshoot the Spinning Cursor

If you notice the cursor spinning continuously, be patient. First, troubleshoot for application problems, as discussed in Chapter 27. If the problem doesn't seem to be application specific (for instance, the cursor spins even before the Finder appears at startup), you might need to consider what the OS is trying to accomplish. Here are some thoughts:

◆ If you can hear nearly constant clicking from your hard drive, you know something is going on. When you don't have enough RAM, and virtual memory needs to rearrange RAM contents, you may hear the drive *thrashing*. Generally, the solution is to run fewer applications, disable any network services (such as the web server or AFP server), and as soon as you can, install more RAM.

◆ If you're seeing the spinning cursor while your network activity lights are active on a network card, transceiver, hub, switch, or router, there may be a networking issue, particularly if you don't have a large network copy operation (or something similar) going on at the time. You may be having trouble with a name server, Directory Services, or a bootstrap (BootP or DHCP) server on your network. Also consider the possibility that someone else has logged in to your Mac and is performing a large network operation, if you have File Sharing turned on.

◆ If you are using Network File Services (NFS) disks (if you don't know, your network administrator will), and the servers are *hard-mounted*, then any time the server has problems, you will too. If you're using NFS and the remote drive has become unavailable, it can be quite some time before your Mac allows you to work in the Finder again. You may need to ensure that the remote server is back online and restart your Mac before you can work without delay in the Finder.

In Mac OS X, the spinning cursor does not necessarily mean that the whole operating system is unresponsive; usually, it's just one particular program (or the whole Classic environment). Again, consult Chapters 27 and 29 for more on troubleshooting apparent hangs and freezes.

NOTE The spinning cursor problem gets better with each iteration of Mac OS X, as more code becomes fully native (particularly the Finder and important parts of the OS) and optimized. Of course, it won't ever go away, but patience, vigilant updating, and RAM are the best cures.

Measuring Performance

Mac OS X offers two essential tools for measuring your Mac's performance. Activity Monitor is the main graphical tool—it enables you to learn all sorts of things about your Mac, including which applications and background processes are running, how system memory is being used, what sort of activity your CPU is experiencing, and other performance statistics such as how much disk and network activity your Mac is experiencing. You can launch Activity Monitor by double-clicking its icon in the Utilities folder inside the main Applications folder on your hard disk.

At the command line, Mac OS X offers top, which enables you to see some of the same information that you can see in Activity Monitor. The top tool works with kill, another command-line program, which you can use to stop errant processes and, often, recover from frozen applications or similar problems. This can be particularly handy if you're accessing your Mac using Terminal (or a similar program) from a remote computer.

NOTE If you're familiar with earlier versions than version 10.3 of Mac OS X, the functions of CPU Monitor and Process Viewer have been rolled together into Activity Monitor.

MONITOR CPU ACTIVITY

Through Activity Monitor, you can keep an eye on how busy your computer is. You do this by activating the CPU Monitor, which can appear in a number of different ways. Choose Window ➤ Show Floating CPU Window ➤ Vertically or Horizontally, and you'll see a graphical representation of CPU activity appear at the bottom-left corner of your screen. If you'd prefer to have the CPU Monitor float in a small palette window, choose Monitor ➤ Show CPU Usage.

You can also use the Activity Monitor icon in the Dock to show CPU activity by selecting View ➤ Dock Icon ➤ Show CPU Usage. That turns the Dock icon into a small representation of the CPU usage monitor.

If the CPU usage monitor updates too slowly (in whatever configuration you've chosen), select View ➤ Update Frequency and then the frequency that you'd like to try. Be warned, though—the more frequently it checks, the more CPU time the CPU Monitor itself requires!

So what is the CPU Monitor telling you? It's showing you how much activity it's registering at a given moment in time. Realize, however, that even when CPU Monitor shows full, you don't necessarily have a performance problem. The first test should be the responsiveness of your computer. If the computer is responsive, it doesn't matter if CPU Monitor spikes to the top somewhat. If your computer is sluggish and CPU Monitor is pegged at the top, you might need to look into things further.

VIEW AND MANAGE PROCESSES

When the computer becomes less responsive, you can dig further into Activity Monitor. Activity Monitor does a few important things. First, it lets you see what applications may be monopolizing CPU time and, perhaps, determine what process may be causing trouble. Second, it gives you a window into the background processes that are running on your Mac—the faceless programs that are running even though they don't appear on the Dock. Knowing what background processes are running could help you troubleshoot a potential conflict or recognize that you have something installed or running that you weren't aware of or had forgotten about. Third, it enables you to quickly see how system memory (and other assets) are being used.

Here's how to use Activity Monitor to manage processes:

1. If Activity Monitor is active, but you don't see the Activity Monitor window, choose Monitor ➤ Show Activity Monitor.

2. Click the % CPU column heading. Doing so will sort the list by percentage of the processor(s) used (see Figure 28.5).

TIP Just as with CPU Monitor, you can change the frequency of Activity Monitor updates by selecting View ➤ Update Frequency and then selecting a frequency.

3. It's interesting to watch the Activity Monitor change frequently, but note that Activity Monitor itself uses more of the processor when you sample every second—which may defeat your purpose. Be sure to quit Activity Monitor when you've determined which processes are monopolizing the processor.

FIGURE 28.5
Here's Activity Monitor, sorted so processes that are taking up the most CPU time are listed first.

4. With the list sorted by percentage of CPU time, you should be able to find the process that's monopolizing the processor. If it is a program running under your account name (as opposed to something that the OS is running), see if you can quit it normally by switching to it and using the application's Quit command. If you see no change in overall performance, try quitting other programs that don't need to be open.

TIP You can select a process in the list and choose Process ➤ Inspect to learn more about it. A dialog box appears with information about the process, its memory usage, and any files that it has open (including system files and open ports that it is accessing).

5. If the culprit is not a program you're running, you may need to log out and log back in. All the user processes that are running will quit, but not the administrator (system) processes.

6. If step 5 doesn't work, you have to restart your computer to get all the system processes to start from scratch.

Occasionally, you will have a process that you cannot stop from within the program or by using the Force Quit window (discussed in Chapter 27). Sometimes, such a process even can prevent you from restarting. Restarting may be something you want to avoid at all costs. Activity Monitor may be the only way to quit the program without going into the Terminal.

To quit a process, select it in Activity Monitor and choose View ≻ Quit Process. (You can also click the Quit Process button in the toolbar.) You will get a dialog sheet asking if you want to Quit or Force Quit. The former is a request, and the latter is a demand. Always try Quit before Force Quit.

WARNING If you kill the ATSServer or Window Manager process, Mac OS X will quit all your graphical applications without giving you a chance to save any unsaved work. You should avoid quitting anything with which you are unfamiliar.

Just because a process uses a lot of CPU time doesn't mean that it uses a lot of memory (and vice versa). The Real Memory column can show you if a particular process is using quite a bit of memory.

A program can have a bug called a *memory leak*, which is when an application takes memory but does not properly release it after it is done using it. The symptom is that over time, the process's memory use can grow to an unusually large amount of RAM. Generally, you can simply restart an application (or a particular process) to reset its memory partition. If you find that the process has a pattern of leaking memory, be sure to report it to the developer.

When using Activity Monitor, note the following:

◆ You can use the Processes menu to choose which processes you want to view; by default, you'll see My Processes, but you can change that via the menu.

◆ You can double-click a process to get in-depth information about it along with commands that enable you to quit it.

◆ Processes running because of something you did are (mostly) running as the user you are logged in as (the user's short name). Processes running whether or not you are logged in will be running as root. They don't quit when you log out. Note that if you have Web Sharing turned on, you will see one or more copies of httpd running as the user www, a special user allowed only to run the web server.

◆ Running more than one instance of the same process usually is not a problem. Some processes are used within other programs. For every Terminal window you have open or for every remote user connected with Telnet or SSH, you'll see a copy of tcsh (or whatever your shell is set to). For every log you have open in the Console, you'll see a copy of tail. Other processes have one copy that launches a second copy. The first one watches the second one. If the second one has a problem, the first one can relaunch it.

◆ The TruBlueEnvironment process is the heart of the Classic environment. If you ever need to force Classic to quit from Activity Monitor, TruBlueEnvironment is the process you need to kill. (Note that the Force Quit window from the Apple menu shows Classic Environment instead of TruBlueEnvironment and also shows each individual Classic application, which Activity Monitor doesn't. Killing TruBlueEnvironment instantly kills any open Classic applications, so kill it wisely.)

◆ You can't quit any process owned by another user, even if you're the administrator. You also cannot quit two important processes launched by the system when you first log in (and are running as yourself). If you try to quit pbs or loginwindow, you may see an error message such as WARNING: Quitting pbs Will Log You Out.

VIEW SYSTEM RESOURCES

The new Activity Monitor offers some goodies down at the bottom of its screen—the tabs enable you to see different sets of information that may help you get an overall sense of how much activity your Mac is handling, and if you're having performance problems, you may be able to look here to track down those problems. Here is a quick look at them:

CPU This tab shows you not only CPU activity, but what type of processes compose that activity—are they user processes, system processes, idle processes, or "nice" processes? (Nice processes are those that are willing to run less when the system is busy and wait for slowdowns before taking up processor time.) You can also see how many processes and threads are running.

System Memory This tab can be pretty useful, as it gives you a sense of how your Mac is making use of its system memory (see Figure 28.6). If you have a limited amount of RAM, and you're getting close to its capacity even with relatively few applications running, that is a good sign that you need to run fewer applications or buy more RAM. The pie graph can be particularly handy for getting a quick sense of how much your Mac is taxing its system memory. (Actually, system memory will fill up fairly quickly if you launch more than a few applications. You'll really start to see slowdowns, however, when the Page Outs number becomes excessive. If you learn to check this tab in Activity Monitor, you may start to get a sense of when your Mac is taxed.)

FIGURE 28.6

Click the System Memory tab to get a visual representation of your Mac's memory usage.

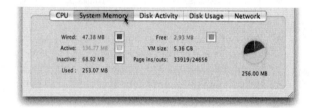

Disk Activity Click this tab to see your Mac's disk in action and to get a sense of how much data it is reading and writing at any given time.

Disk Usage This tab offers handy tools for quickly seeing how much space you have free on your disks (choosing their names from the menu).

Network This last tab gives you a visual representation of the amount of data that is being sent and received by your Mac.

While these aren't exactly diagnostic tools in the sense that they specifically help you track down problems, you may find it handy to use Activity Monitor when you feel like you have performance problems you can't explain. You can quickly glance at the tabs at the bottom like the gauges in a car—visually sweeping them to see if anything looks out of whack. If you see an odd number, such as disk space or system memory nearly used up, then you'll have a better idea of your next step toward relieving the performance bottleneck.

TOP AND KILL

If you ever need to check the performance of all processes running on your computer from the command line, use top. The top tool basically is a command-line version of Activity Monitor. Having such functionality from the command line is handy when you have to kill a process, a particular application—or the whole Mac OS X Aqua interface—is hung up, and you want do everything possible to avoid losing unsaved info.

To use **top**, simply open a Terminal window (or log in remotely using Telnet or SSH), type **top -ocpu** and press Return. (In versions prior to Mac OS X 10.3, you can type just **top -u** and press Return.) This will give you a listing of your most active processes, with the one using most of the processor at the top. The list will refresh itself every second. Though the list has 11 columns of information, the first three are the most relevant. (See Figure 28.7.)

FIGURE 28.7

top is the command line's version of Activity Monitor.

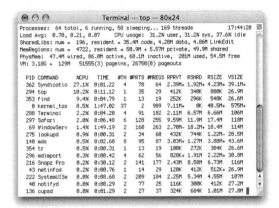

TIP   When top is running, you can drag the Terminal window so that it displays more information, and top will refresh itself, showing more processes (if it has more to show).

In order, the first three columns show the process ID (described earlier in this chapter), the name of the process (or "command"), and the percentage of the CPU it's using. Using the same criteria as with Activity Monitor, decide what process you want to quit.

TIP   top and kill are particularly useful for logging in to a Mac (that appears to be frozen, for instance) via remote access—Telnet or SSH—from another Mac and then testing to see if a problem application is monopolizing CPU time.

If you are not able to quit a process from the Finder or Force Quit window, you can force a process to quit on the command line using kill as follows:

1.   Write down the process ID of the process you want to quit.

2.   Type **q** to cancel top.

3.   Type **kill** *process_ID*, inserting the process ID you just wrote down.

4.   If the process you want to kill is not a program you started, you will need to type this command with sudo in front of it: **sudo kill** *process_id*. Remember, when you type sudo followed by a command, you will be prompted for your Admin password.

5.   If the regular kill command doesn't work, you can try substituting kill −9 instead of kill in the commands in step 4. The −9 attribute is the equivalent of Force Quit.

WARNING   The sudo kill version of the kill command will kill just about any process. Killing processes that are required by Mac OS X can have severe and immediate effects. If you kill the ATSServer, pbs, loginwindow, or WindowServer process (and possibly others), Mac OS X will quit all of your graphical applications without giving you a chance to save any unsaved work.

If you'd rather avoid command-line procedures, simply force the computer to restart if it doesn't catch up with itself after a reasonable time (a few minutes) and appears to remain frozen. This is less than ideal (it's always better to kill a process than it is to reboot or restart a frozen Mac).

For more information, type **man top** or **man kill** in the Terminal.

Much Ado About Root

The Root account is a special user account on a Unix-based system that has special privileges, allowing it to read or write any file and accomplish a number of tasks without interference. By default, it's disabled in Mac OS X, because it can be a security risk and nearly any important task can be accomplished using a typical administrator's account. The account can be turned on, however, if you have a compelling reason to do so.

Do You Actually Need to Be Root?

Some users falsely believe that they must be logged in to the Root account to be able to see hidden files and folders. For simplicity's sake, the Finder hides certain items from all users, even Root. (Note that this also is true in Mac OS 9 and earlier.) However, for any user, you can force Finder to show all files. In the Terminal, type **defaults write com.apple.finder AppleShowAllFiles true**. The command will take effect the next time you log in (or you can just relaunch the Finder using the Force Quit command in the Apple menu).

If you don't want to clutter up your Finder window with the hidden folders showing all the time, you can view a hidden directory's contents when needed. To show a hidden directory in the Finder, use the Go to Folder command in the Finder's Go menu. For example, to show the hidden directory /var/log/, type **/var/log/** in the Go to Folder box and press Return. (The method works only if you know the name of the folder.)

Users might believe they need the Root account to access the /System/Library hierarchy. Although that was true in earlier Mac OS X versions, it is not true in Mac OS X 10.3 and higher, which allows an Admin user to make changes in this hierarchy. That said, you most likely shouldn't be changing or adding *anything* in the Library subfolder of the System folder. In general, items that you think should go in the System/Library folder hierarchy actually belong in the root-level Library in subfolders of the same name. If those folders do not exist, you can create them. Their contents will be scanned and included. (For experts in Mac OS 9 and earlier: Imagine never having to sort through the hundreds of files Apple installs to find one or two items of which you don't have a backup copy!)

Finally, you may need root access to get at certain hidden folders in the Finder, such as some folders in the /var hierarchy. There is a workaround for that, too—use the Terminal. But if you prefer the Finder, enabling Root is an option.

Alternatives to the Root Account

One way you can get around logging in to the Root account is by giving yourself temporary root privileges at the command line. To execute a single command as root, type **sudo *command*** and press Return at the command line in a Terminal window. The computer will prompt you for the administrator's password. `sudo command` performs the `command` as root and brings you right back to your user prompt. The method here is best when you have only one or two commands to type.

To get a command-line prompt where you don't have to type this before every command, type **sudo -s** and the Admin password when prompted in a Terminal window and press Return. This gives you a new shell, where you're logged in as root until you close the window or type **exit**.

WARNING   The fact that you recently authenticated as the superuser (root) using sudo will be remembered for five minutes. If you type more than one sudo command in that time, commands after the first one won't prompt you for your password. If that bothers you, just type **sudo -k** and press Return.

Enabling (or Reenabling) the Root Account

When the Root account is disabled (including by default when you install Mac OS X), you can't log in as root at the login window or connect via SSH (Secure Shell). Normally, this isn't a big deal because of the alternatives just discussed. Even if you reenable the Root account, you still won't be able to log in to the Root account using Telnet, FTP, or AFP without additional steps. However, if you have to delete files or folders that no other user has permissions to delete *and* you don't want to use the command line, your only option short of booting into Mac OS 9 or reformatting is to reenable the Root account and log in as Root. You can enable the Root account as follows:

1. Open NetInfo Manager from the Utilities submenu of the `Applications` folder.

2. Choose Security ➤ Authenticate, then type in an Admin password (and Admin name, if needed). Unlike most other places in Mac OS X, NetInfo Manager does not automatically authenticate you even though you're the Admin user.

3. Select Security ➤ Enable Root User. If this is the first time you have set up the Root account, you will be warned that the Root password is blank, and you'll be forced to change it to a nonblank password. You should now be able to log in from the login window or SSH (but not Telnet, AFP, or FTP).

If you change your mind or want to undo the process when you're done rooting around, select Security ➤ Disable Root User. Having the Root account enabled while connected to the Internet is considered a security risk, so we'd recommend disabling it immediately after you've accomplished whatever you needed to get done in that account.

NetInfo Manager

The previous section introduced a utility that this book hasn't really mentioned much to this point—the NetInfo Manager. There's fairly good reason that NetInfo Manager isn't mentioned in detail. For the vast majority of users of Mac OS X, it isn't necessary to know anything about NetInfo Manager, and for the people who do need to know a little something about it, it's generally something that's a fix-and-forget issue—you set up NetInfo Manager, get it working, and then don't worry about it. For the sake of completeness, however, let's define the NetInfo Manager, and we'll look at a tweak or two that you can accomplish with its help.

NetInfo is a system that NeXT, Inc., invented for NeXTStep and, later, OpenStep, the operating systems upon which Mac OS X is based. (NeXT, Inc. is the company formerly owned by Steve Jobs and sold to Apple in 1997.) NetInfo is similar to NIS, another standard created by Sun Microsystems, and both have relatively similar goals. NetInfo is a network-enabled database that can store information about all sorts of resources that are connected with a network of computers. Users, printers, machines, groups—all sorts of info about your "net."

For home users—and, indeed, many corporate and organizational users—NetInfo isn't something you'll have to dig into. It is there, however, and can be useful to the average user in two situations. First, it can be useful for implementing some Unix-style networking capabilities, including the capability to create and share NFS mounts (in conjunction with third-party utilities if desired). NetInfo also can enable you to change a user's information beyond what can be accomplished in the Accounts pane.

Second, NetInfo can be used for some low-level user management. By logging in to NetInfo, you can alter characteristics about your users, including a user's home folder, short name, and other characteristics. This can be helpful, particularly if you're in charge of a fairly sizable network or laboratory of computers.

NOTE   Before you can work with the NetInfo settings, you need to authenticate as an administrative user. Either click the padlock in the NetInfo window or choose Security ➢ Authenticate. In the dialog box that appears, input an administrator's username and password.

WARNING   It really isn't necessary for most users to mess with NetInfo, and one false move can ruin your Mac OS X installation, requiring a reinstall. Think carefully and back up the database if you decide to experiment.

NetInfo can be particularly useful for changing a user's information directly, including items that can't be altered via the Accounts pane of System Preferences. Remember that messing with the NetInfo database is dangerous—if you mess up a user account, you may have trouble fixing it.

Launch NetInfo Manager and authenticate. In the main window, select the slash (/) in the first column. Next, scroll in the second column until you see the entry users, and then click it once. Now, click a user to see his information (see Figure 28.8).

FIGURE 28.8
Selecting a user in
NetInfo Manager

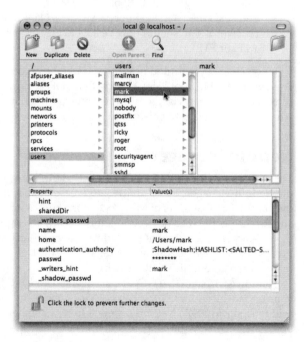

Now you're free to edit items about this user. For instance, you could enter a password hint in the `hint` entry, change the user's `realname` entry (to correct a misspelling, for instance), or even type a new path and filename for the user's picture that appears in the login window.

WARNING   Don't change the user's password in the `passwd` entry box. Because of the encoding method NetInfo uses to store passwords securely, they can't be altered directly from within NetInfo. Use the Accounts pane of System Preferences or, failing that, start up from a Mac OS X installation disc and choose Reset Password from the Installer menu.

Of course, those also are items that can be changed in the Accounts pane. Some things that can't be changed there, however, are the user's home folder (in the `home` variable) or the user's short name (in the `name` variable). Being able to change one or both of these gives you an interesting capability— you can assign a user a home folder that isn't the same as his short name or vice-versa. All that matters is the setting in this user record—they don't have to match.

To alter a setting, simply double-click the Values column within that entry item's row. Now you can make your change. Press Return when you're done (see Figure 28.9).

If you're done making changes, choose Domain ➤ Save Changes. You'll be asked to confirm the changes. Now you can quit NetInfo Manager and restart the Mac so that changes can be made.

FIGURE 28.9
Altering a value in
NetInfo

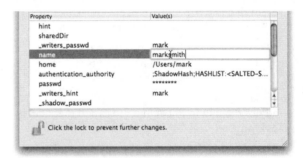

Other Places for Help

Tons of Internet sites are available for discussing and working with Mac OS X—some folks have truly become experts on the subject. If you're looking for advice beyond what you find in this book—particularly if you're looking to take it to the next level of tips, tricks, and hacks or customizations, the Web is the right place to look.

Here are some resources on the Web that you can use to learn more about Mac OS X troubleshooting:

Apple Support Site and Knowledge Base   Apple's Knowledge Base is part of its support site, where you can find tons of documents, downloads, and hints and tricks that Apple has put together to help you keep up your Mac. The support site (at the time of this writing) has been streamlined quite a bit, and it's a pleasure to deal with in most cases. Visit `www.apple.com/support/` and select an item to learn more about it, or enter keywords in the Search Support entry box to search the Knowledge Base or other documents.

TIP Apple has a special keyword, `kmosx`, that's used to represent Mac OS X. Enter keywords such as `kmosx drivers` or `kmosx panic` to search only for Knowledge Base articles that are relevant to Mac OS X.

Apple Discussion Boards Though Apple moderates the discussion boards, you are as likely to get answers from another helpful person as from Apple. Nevertheless, Apple employees have been known to read messages at this site to keep a pulse on user sentiment. Just stay on the topic and be constructive. If you make inflammatory posts, expect them to disappear like Houdini in a witness protection program. (You can find the discussion boards at `http://discussions.info.apple.com`.) You'll find a lot of good answers here, and the search mechanism is good, too.

Apple Mac OS X Feedback Page Apple has a feedback page for Mac OS X so that a customer can get something off his chest while feeling like the "mothership" is listening. Apple does not want you to report bug here, but if you have some feedback about Mac OS X, this is probably the most direct way to get it into Apple's ear without waiting on hold. You can find the Mac OS X feedback page at `www.apple.com/macosx/feedback/`.

MacFixIt.com This is a popular site for researching issues with the Mac OS and with non-Apple products. It includes daily reports, extensive discussion between users and moderators regarding Mac OS X, and it includes other troubleshooting topics (hardware, peripherals). The MacFixIt Mac OS X forum is at `www.macfixitforums.com`.

Macosxhints.com This one may have been first on the scene, and it takes a user-generated approach to its content, offering hints and tricks that the online community tests and talks about. The site is at `www.macosxhints.com`.

OSXFAQ.com Featuring the popular Bob "Dr. Mac" Levitus, this site offers regular hints and advice ranging from beginner to expert (a lot fall in the intermediate range). The site is at `www.osxfaq.com`.

MasteringMacOSX.com This list wouldn't be complete without some self-promotion, right? Check out our site for updates to this book as well as news, advice, and information on Mac OS X, including public forums for asking questions.

What's Next?

In this chapter, you saw the many approaches you can take to troubleshooting Mac OS X at the system level. Mac OS X is a very robust operating system, which will hopefully translate into fewer OS-level troubles than in previous versions of the Mac OS. When trouble does strike, the steps to correct the trouble can be more confusing in some ways than with past versions. Using a combination of graphical and command-line tools, however, you can get your Mac up and running in most cases.

In Chapter 29, we'll discuss some specific problems you might encounter with Mac OS X and how to fix them. There you'll find a quick guide to dealing with trouble as it's happening—then you can refer back to this chapter to learn more about the tools and techniques of troubleshooting.

Typical Problems and Solutions

Chapter 28, "Solving System-Level Problems," covered some of the general issues and suggestions involving Mac OS X troubleshooting, including the tools you use to troubleshoot your Mac and get it up and running again. In this chapter, we'd like to focus on some quick-reference solutions you can use immediately when you're having a problem—if necessary, you can cross-reference with Chapters 28 and 27, "Fixing Applications and Managing Classic," to learn more about the tools and techniques for troubleshooting and solving problems.

In particular, this chapter will focus on the most basic problems you're likely to encounter at some point in day-to-day work with Mac OS X. Those problems include trouble starting up Mac OS X, trouble with native applications, problems with file and folder permissions, password problems, and what to do when severe problems like freezes or kernel panics occur.

In this chapter:

◆ Startup Trouble

◆ Quits, Freezes, and Panics

◆ Problems with Permissions

◆ Fixing File and Directory Corruption

◆ Troubleshooting with the Mac OS X Installer

◆ Users and Passwords

Startup Trouble

A few different problems can crop up with the Mac OS at startup time. Before you get too far, however, consider whether the cause of the problem could be hardware. First, check to make sure your Mac is plugged in and getting power, your display is turned on, and your keyboard and mouse are properly attached. If you've recently added any external hardware, it's a good idea to turn it off and unplug it. Also consider removing any drivers you may have installed for new hardware devices; these can sometimes cause problems.

If you've eliminated (for the most part) the possibility that there's something wrong with your hardware, you should consider it a software issue. This section covers a few steps you can take to get your Mac to start up, depending on the nature of the problem.

Can't Boot into the Correct OS

Sometimes a startup problem is as simple as having a wrong setting in the Startup Disk pane of System Preferences. System Preferences enables you to set the Startup Disk pane's startup volume and then close System Preferences, forgetting that you've set your Mac to a new startup disk.

NOTE In most cases, unless you're still using Mac OS 9 on a Mac that supports it, you won't have a choice of operating systems. Exceptions are those who may have installed Tiger on two different partitions for testing software, or those who may have installed a Linux or Unix system on another partition.

On all recent Macs, you can hold down the Option key at startup to bring up a list of volumes to boot from. The list is sometimes called the Boot Picker, System Picker, or Startup Manager. When the screen appears, you'll see icons representing each possible startup disk—select one and click the right-facing arrow icon to begin the boot process. Be aware that using the Startup Manager is a one-time change and will not change which OS you will boot into the next time. To make a lasting change, use Startup Disk. (Remember that most Macs built in 2003 and later don't allow you to boot into Mac OS 9, although you can still use Boot Picker to switch between versions of Mac OS X.) If the Startup Manager won't let you choose the correct operating system, you have another choice: Using the Mac OS X installation disc that came with your Mac or a later disc, you can start up into the Mac OS X Installer. (Insert the disc, restart your Mac, and hold down the C key on your keyboard.) When the Installer appears, mouse up to the menu bar and choose Utilities ➤ Change Startup Disk. That gives you a Choose Startup Disk window that looks similar to the Startup Disk pane in System Preferences. Choose your startup disk and then click Restart.

Mac OS X Won't Start Up

If your Mac won't start up at all, you may have a more serious problem on your hands. Your Mac can communicate two fundamental problems to you, depending on the small icons it blinks on-screen soon after the startup chime.

BLINKING QUESTION MARK

The first is an icon with a folder and a blinking question mark. This generally means that the Mac can't find a valid startup folder on a local hard disk. In fact, the first step in troubleshooting this problem is to wait a while—sometimes over two minutes. If your Mac has been inadvertently set to start up from a network server, and you don't have a NetBoot server available, you'll see a flashing "world" icon; eventually it will give up and start up from the hard disk. Even if your Mac hasn't been set for a NetBoot server, it may have been set to a startup disk that's no longer available (such as a FireWire volume). After a moment, it should time out and begin looking for a valid OS. When it finds one, the blinking icon will disappear and be replaced by the happy Mac or Apple logo.

If that doesn't work, your next option is to press the Option key; while the blinking question mark is on-screen, pressing the Option key moves you to the Startup Manager screen. There, as detailed previously in the section "Can't Boot into the Correct OS," you can choose a different OS for a volume from which to start.

If neither of those steps works, try inserting a disc from which the Mac can start up: use either a Mac OS X Installer disc, or a third-party startup disc from Norton Utilities, Micromat, Alsoft, or another utility vendor. If you boot from the Mac OS X Installer disc, choose Installer ➤ Open Disk Utility to launch Disk Utility. Then use its Disk First Aid and other tools to test the hard disk or disk volume with which you're having trouble.

Finally, if none of these work in fixing Mac OS X, you may need to take additional steps, perhaps including reinstalling Mac OS X. See the section "Troubleshooting with the Mac OS X Installer" later in this chapter.

BROKEN FOLDER OR UNIVERSAL "NO" ICON

If your Mac won't start up and a *broken folder* icon *or* an icon that looks like the universal symbol for "No" (as in No Trespassing or No Smoking) appears on-screen, this has a very specific meaning. Your Mac is telling you that something is wrong with the system-level files that Mac OS X requires to start up and run. These include a number of hidden files (at least, they're hidden in Mac OS X), including an important file hidden on the root level of your hard disk—mach_kernel. The mach_kernel file is usually a hidden file in Mac OS X, but various utilities can reveal it on purpose, and some applications will reveal it accidentally.

NOTE   Another symptom—a kernel panic immediately after startup—can also suggest that important system files are corrupt or missing.

File or Folder Problems

Apple has a list of items that, according to its Support Knowledge Base, can cause this problem if they have been moved or deleted:

◆   mach_kernel

◆   The Applications folder

◆   The automount folder

◆   The Library folder

◆   The System folder

◆   The Users folder

If these files or folders are corrupt or deleted, or if other important files in the /System hierarchy are altered inappropriately, the Mac will be unable to start up in Mac OS X, and you'll see the broken folder icon. If one of these items is deleted, Apple's recommendation is that you completely reinstall Mac OS X. If you have a Mac OS X installation disc that installs *exactly* the same version (or a later version) of Mac OS X that's running on your Mac (for instance, you have Mac OS X version 10.4.0 installed, and you have the Mac OS X version 10.4 installation disc), then you can run the installation disc to repair or replace the missing items (see the section "Troubleshooting with the Mac OS X Installer" for details.)

If you have a Mac OS X installation disc that installs a version of Mac OS X that's *earlier* than your current version (you've updated to 10.4.1 via the System Update feature, for instance, but you have only the 10.4 disc), then you'll need to back up your important files and then use the Mac OS X installation disc to erase the current installation and install a new copy of the OS.

TIP   Actually, the installer can archive your current installation and install another copy of Mac OS X on your disk if you'd like (and if you have enough hard disk space). That enables you to install a fresh copy of Mac OS X and still be able to access older files. See Appendix A, "Getting Installed and Set Up," for more on installation options.

If you're daring enough—or if you'd prefer to try to fix the problem without all the installation headaches—there is one option you can attempt. If you believe the problem is with the mach_kernel file, you can replace it either from a backup of your hard disk (if you have one) or from a Mac OS X disc that is the same version as your Mac OS X installation.

WARNING Just for the sake of clarity, let us say this again—you should copy the mach_kernel file from one disk to another only if it's from an installation or distribution that is exactly the same version as the Mac OS X version you have installed. If you know they're not the same version, the better solution is to reinstall the Mac OS.

There are three ways to restore the mach_kernel file.

First, if your Mac can start up in Mac OS 9, take these steps:

1. Start up in Mac OS 9 and mount the Mac OS X installation disc on your desktop.

2. Double-click the installation disc's icon. (You won't find the correct file in the window that opens automatically when the installation disc is inserted.)

3. Locate the file or files on that installation disc and then copy them to your Mac's hard disk at the root level.

4. Choose your Mac OS X startup volume from the Startup Disk control panel and then restart your Mac.

If your Mac now manages to start up in Mac OS X, you've likely fixed the problem. Otherwise, you may need to resort to reinstalling completely.

TIP You can actually back up your mach_kernel and other low-level files before problems occur so that you could replace them if you had to. While this might be overkill for a home computer, it might not be a bad idea in an office or computer lab environment where having the option of restoring your Mac from backup media might help recover the Mac more quickly.

Second, if you have another Mac available and you're used to working with Terminal, follow these steps:

1. Start up the "sick" Mac in Target mode. To do this, connect the two Macs with a FireWire cable and then start up the healthy Mac. Next, start up the sick Mac. As soon as you hear the startup chime, press the T key. You'll see a FireWire icon on screen.

2. On the healthy Mac, you'll see the sick Mac's hard drive mount on the desktop. Open Terminal and issue the following commands:

```
cd /
ls
```

You'll see a list of files that are at the root level of your Mac's hard drive.

3. Enter the following command to copy the mach_kernel file from the healthy Mac to the sick Mac:

```
sudo cp /Volumes/[your_startup_volume]/mach_kernel
➥/Volumes/[the_sick_Mac_startup_volume]/
```

If your startup volume is named Tiger and your sick Mac's startup volume is Tiger2, you'd enter the command as follows:

```
sudo cp /Volumes/Tiger/mach_kernel/Volumes/Tiger2/
```

You'll be prompted to enter an administrator's password; do so and then press Enter. This copies the file.

4. You can now attempt to restart your Mac.

Third, if you have only one Mac, take these steps:

1. Start up your Mac from the Mac OS X installation disc as described earlier.

2. When the Installer is running, select the Utilities menu and then select Terminal.

3. Issue the command described in the previous section, using the installation disc as the startup volume and your startup disk as the sick Mac startup volume.

4. Quit Terminal and then quit the Installer. A sheet will display asking if you want to restart your Mac. It's a good idea to click Startup Disk and select your sick Mac's startup volume. If you cannot select it, try restarting your Mac and holding down the Option key to select it.

System Files Not a Problem

There are some steps you can take if you're seeing the broken folder icon but you don't believe there's anything wrong with your system files. Here are a few suggestions from Apple's Knowledge Base:

♦ You can start up via a Mac OS X installation disc and run the Disk First Aid feature within Disk Utility to ensure that files or folders on your hard disk aren't experiencing some sort of corruption.

♦ Restart your Mac and clear PRAM and NVRAM by immediately holding down the Option+⌘P+R keys until you've heard the startup chime at least twice. That may clear up the problem. As the Mac starts up, see if it gets past the blinking question mark and locates a valid System folder. (See Chapter 28 for details.)

♦ Start up using a Mac OS X installation disc and checking to make sure a valid volume has been selected. Choose Utilities ≻ Startup Disk to choose a startup volume. Changing your startup disk setting may fix the problem. Restart the Mac and see if the broken folder icon is gone.

Common Startup Issues

When you start up a Mac running Mac OS X, it goes through a fairly long startup routine before it's ready for you to log in (whether manually or automatically) and access the Finder. During this process, a number of things happen—the Mac's hardware performs some minor diagnostics tests, the Mac confirms that it has a valid operating system on the disk, and then Mac OS X begins starting up. First, it loads the necessary fundamental operating system components, and then it turns on protocols and services and activates drivers for accessing hardware.

KEY COMMANDS AT STARTUP

You can take a few active steps to learn more information about your Mac as it starts up. Obviously, doing so is most helpful if you're actually experiencing trouble during startup, but it also can be helpful if certain underlying components, such as servers, networking, printing, or peripherals, don't seem to be working correctly. You take these steps by holding down keyboard combinations immediately after your Mac has restarted and you've heard the startup chime. You can try the following:

Boot in Verbose mode   While your Mac starts up, hold down the keyboard combination ⌘V. *Verbose mode* displays detailed text messages about each step of the booting process. You'll want to use Verbose mode any time your computer is not getting to the login window, so you can see where it's stopping. You can also use Verbose mode if there is a long delay during startup. You might use it if you are looking for a specific piece of information. The information displayed in Verbose mode is not stored in any one place. Some of it is stored in `system.log`, and some of it is stored in the system message buffer. Some of it is not captured at all.

Boot in single-user mode   Hold down ⌘S while your Mac starts up, and you'll boot into *single-user mode*. With that mode, you can start the computer part of the way so that you can gather information or fix the problems that keep it from starting the rest of the way. Single-user mode does not have a graphical user interface, networking, and multiple users. However, if you ever have to perform major command-line surgery, single-user mode gives you an option for recovery and repair. To make changes to files on your Mac's main volume, you'll need to mount it by typing the command **/sbin/mount -uw /** and pressing Return.

NOTE   If you have severe directory damage, the Mac OS may drop you into single-user mode automatically and display a message to that effect. Such an occurrence should be rare. If it does happen, read the section "Fixing File and Directory Corruption" later in this chapter.

Boot with kernel extensions off   If your Mac is crashing or freezing at some point in the middle of the startup process (usually on the Mac OS X screen the Starting Mac OS X message displays), your problem may be a kernel extension. You can boot in Safe mode, which disables third-party kernel extensions, by holding down the Shift key immediately after hearing the startup chime. This also causes the Mac to run the fsck disk verification and repair program; at the end of this process, the Login screen displays with the words "Safe Boot". Note that booting in this mode turns off automatic login. See the section "Getting Past a Kernel Panic" later in this chapter, for more information.

Boot into Mac OS X   If your Mac is set to boot into Mac OS 9 (or another Mac OS X installation elsewhere on the drives attached to your Mac), you can hold down the X key immediately after the startup chime to force your Mac to start up from the main Mac OS X installation on your root hard disk.

NOTE   If you're having trouble getting keyboard combinations to work correctly when starting up Mac OS X, it's possible that your Mac has an Open Firmware password set. See Chapter 26, "Hard Disk Care, File Security, and Maintenence," for details on working with an Open Firmware password.

Startup Stalls

As your Mac starts up, it offers messages regarding the services it's launching or the drive extensions it's loading. If you notice that your Mac stalls on one of those items, it may give you a clue as to the problem, particularly if startup doesn't resume. In most cases, it will. Mac OS X generally will begin exhibiting problems on startup only when something has changed recently—trouble with an external peripheral, a network connection, or after you've installed new software and restarted your Mac.

Starting up in Verbose mode (described earlier in this chapter) helps you spot where the problem occurs. You can see the various system messages as Mac OS X starts up system services, and if your Mac stops displaying messages, it's likely that the problem is related to the specific service or driver that it is attempting to launch.

If the computer stalls when network services start, disconnect the Ethernet cable. Network operations may then time out faster and allow the startup process to continue. If you see your Mac stall with other network-related messages (such as those involving web servers or a time server), it's possible your Mac's primary form of Internet access is down—particularly if your Mac receives Internet access via its Ethernet port, either over a broadband connection or a LAN-based connection. In most such cases, the startup process should continue after a moment or two.

If your Mac stalls when looking for external disks, you may have a FireWire or similar external drive to blame—try unplugging the device to see if startup continues. In fact, that's good general advice for startup stalls—try unplugging all third-party devices (your keyboard and mouse shouldn't be a problem) and then wait to see if the startup process revives. If it doesn't, you eventually might opt to hard-reset your Mac, but you should wait as long as possible before doing so, because any hard reset has the potential to corrupt files and cause trouble.

Login Trouble

If you're having trouble at login, you can use one of a few techniques to get around the trouble and get your Mac up and running again, depending on when the trouble occurs.

BLUE SCREEN

If after normal startup messages you have a blue screen with an alternating spinning wheel and cursor, you may have a font problem. The ATSServer process scans your font directories on startup, including the Fonts folder of your Mac OS 9 System Folder if you have one. If the ATSServer doesn't like a font there, that font could be causing the symptom.

As a workaround, you can boot into another installation of Mac OS X either from a hard drive or a disc and move or rename the Fonts folder. (You'll have to rename this folder using Terminal from the Mac OS X Installer if you don't have another Mac OS X installation on another drive.) After taking care of the Fonts folder, try rebooting back into Mac OS X.

If the problem persists, just troubleshoot your fonts and put the Fonts folder back. Another solution (and an easier one) is to run a font-maintenance application that includes font-fixing or font-corruption tools.

If that doesn't work, you can take a more general troubleshooting step for startup problems—try deleting the file /Library/Preferences/com.apple.loginwindow.plist. That deletes the preferences file that governs the login window's behavior; it may have become corrupted and is blocking the login window's appearance. Once it's deleted (you can also rename it or simply move it from the Preferences folder if you want to hang on to it), restart the Mac in Mac OS X and see if your problem is solved.

TIP   If you're comfortable using single-user mode (as described earlier, you hold down ⌘S as your Mac starts up), you might find this easier than starting up from a Mac OS X installation disc. In fact, if you happen to be on the road with a PowerBook or iBook, you may not have your installation disc with you. Start up in single-user mode and then make the changes described—move the Fonts folder and/or delete the preference file—using the Mac OS X command line. If you're unfamiliar with the command line, consult Chapter 22, "Terminal and the Command Line," for details.

FINDER CRASHING ON LOGIN

The Finder, by design, is the first application to start when you turn on your computer, and it enables you to start other programs. If you suspect that the Finder is damaged and you need to attempt repairs instead of reinstalling, you can tell Mac OS X to start some other program by default. From any command-line prompt (that includes the Terminal or single-user mode), type the following:

```
defaults write com.apple.loginwindow Finder
   ➥/Applications/Utilities/Terminal.app
```

This command sets Terminal as the default application instead of the Finder the next time you log in. (For other applications, substitute the full path to the application after the Finder entry.) To change it back, enter this command:

```
defaults write com.apple.loginwindow Finder
   ➥/System/Library/CoreServices/Finder.app
```

When you once again log out and log in, the Finder will be active again.

STOP AUTO-LOGIN IN SINGLE-USER MODE

If your computer is set to log in automatically but you have a crashing Finder, you won't be able to try any of the troubleshooting steps for Finder crashing at login. However, you can force it to display the login window at startup; just press and hold the Shift key after the progress window finishes displaying. This lets you log in as a different user. If you only have one user account, you'll have to do some command-line work to get there, booting in Single User mode. Note that many techniques used by logging in as >console (discussed next) or used remotely with Telnet or SSH can be performed in single-user mode as well.

To force the computer to display the login window, do the following:

1. Start up in single-user mode by restarting the Mac (if appropriate) and holding down ⌘S until your Mac boots into a command-line interface.

2. Mount your Mac's root hard disk with the command /sbin/mount -uw / and press Return.

3. Type

```
nicl -raw /var/db/netinfo/local.nidb delete /localconfig/autologin
```

and press Return.

WARNING   If you're trying to force the computer to display the login window over the network instead of in single-user mode, replace nicl -raw with sudo nicl. The first version of this command could damage your NetInfo database if you run it outside of single-user mode.

LOG IN AS *>CONSOLE*

Is the Finder or Dock crashing? Another way to get to the command line in Mac OS X (as if you didn't already have enough ways) is to type **>console** in the User field in the login window and press Return. Doing so will shut down all graphical parts of Mac OS X and give you a text-only login prompt.

NOTE   Whether or not you can do this depends on how your login window is configured, particularly in Mac OS X 10.3 and higher. In the Accounts pane of System Preferences, click the Login Options button, and from the Display Login Window As radio buttons, choose Name and Password. Otherwise, you can't enter the >console command.

If the problem is caused by the Finder or Dock (two programs that always start up when you log in), you can move aside the preferences files for those two programs. The files are com.apple.finder.plist and com.apple.dock.plist, respectively, and are located in your home directory in ~/Library/Preferences/.

Assuming you're already logged in at the command line, here's how to reset the preference files:

1. Type

   ```
   mv ~/Library/Preferences/com.apple.dock.plist
   ➥~/Library/Preferences/com.apple.dock.plist.old
   ```

   and press Return. To move the Finder's preference file, just substitute com.apple.finder.plist in place of com.apple.dock.plist.

2. Type **exit** to log out of the text-only mode.

3. Log in as the user having the problem. If the problem is fixed, you can continue computing. If not, the preferences files weren't the problem—you should restore them by typing the command in step 1 again with the paths reversed, as in

   ```
   mv ~/Library/Preferences/com.apple.dock.plist.old
   ➥~/Library/Preferences/com.apple.dock.plist
   ```

STOPPING A LOGIN ITEM

If your problems aren't caused by the Finder but rather by a program that's set to launch when you log in, you can stop the program temporarily by holding down the Shift key immediately after entering your name and password and clicking Log In on the login window. Once you've started up in the Finder, use the Accounts pane of System Preferences to access your startup items and stop the offending login item from starting next time (see Figure 29.1).

You may find that Shift doesn't work and that you need to reset login items from a command line. (Again, this could be the Terminal or a >console login, or you could be in single-user mode.) Once you've logged in as the user who is having trouble (because login items are user-specific), type

```
rm ~/Library/Preferences/loginwindow.plist
```

FIGURE 29.1

Open the Accounts pane of System Preferences, select your username, and click Login Items to remove or troubleshoot login items.

This one command will delete the loginwidow.plist file. Now you'll be able to log in to your Mac and troubleshoot the login items (refer back to Figure 29.1) to see which is the problem. (The easiest way to do that would probably be to add them back one at a time and test each. Remember that you can simply log out and log back in to test a login item—you don't have to restart your Mac.) See Chapter 27 for some ideas on how to troubleshoot Mac OS X applications.

Quits, Freezes, and Panics

After a few years of experience with Mac OS X, we can now say that it's much more stable than the Classic Mac OS ever was—our daily-work machines encounter fewer than one problem a week, and that one problem is almost always an application that quits unexpectedly, not a hard freeze or other system-related problem.

The Classic Mac OS could "freeze up"—literally make it impossible for you to move the mouse point or select any command—with some regularity, depending on a number of factors, including the type and quality of applications you ran. (And by quality I don't mean expensive—Microsoft's pricey Office applications regularly could freeze a machine as often as any cheap shareware offering.)

With Mac OS X, the entire Mac OS will freeze very rarely, and almost always as a result of something that's reasonably easy to pin down. Using the Classic environment or playing full-screen, high-graphics games can contribute to a freezing problem, but otherwise it should be very rare.

We've seen more kernel panics than freezes during our time spent with Mac OS X, although again, they're often fairly easy to attribute. Most kernel panics are the result of a problem with a new driver installed to support a hardware device or a new low-level kernel extension that performs some utility function. We'll discuss those later in this section. To start, let's focus on the problems you're more likely to encounter. First, we'll look at applications quitting, and then we'll move on to freezes and panics.

Sluggishness or Spinning Cursor

If your Mac appears to freeze for a few moments at a time—that is, you can't accomplish anything because the Mac won't respond or you have a spinning cursor—then something is taking up your CPU's time. That sort of interference can come from a number of different places, and some of the ways to keep it from happening are more like workarounds instead of solutions. (In many cases, the solution is to update to a version of the offending software that no longer has errors.)

NOTE Many users are surprised to find how well their Mac runs with more RAM. In Mac OS X, having more RAM is a significant boost compared to Mac OS 9, because Mac OS X uses RAM more efficiently and automatically. If you encounter sluggishness running more than one or a few applications, consider upgrading your Mac with additional RAM before you take more drastic measures.

Here are some typical causes of sluggishness and what you can do about them:

Repair permissions On the First Aid tab of Disk Utility is the option to repair permissions. It's a good idea to run this task fairly regularly. With Mac OS X, the OS will occasionally encounter files and folders that have permissions set incorrectly. When the OS has to deal with such files and folders, it can slow down considerably as it fails and looks for solutions. It's recommended that you run Repair Permissions using the latest version of the Mac OS that you have installed. If you have a later update on your hard disk than on your disc, run Disk Utility directly from the Utilities folder inside your Applications folder.

Suspect kernel extensions While most applications don't install kernel extensions, some do—particularly low-level utility applications. (That includes disk-fixing utilities, some virus checkers, and peripheral utilities such as printer drivers.) Those extensions can cause problems and slowdowns. If you have a utility program installed, make sure it's up-to-date. If you believe it's causing trouble, consider whether you need to continue using it. Most applications have an uninstall option that can remove kernel extensions. Todd has encountered problems with both Norton SystemWorks and driver software for Hewlett-Packard and Lexmark printers that were fixed either by uninstalling the software or updating to a newer version.

Turn off background processes Sluggishness can be the result of items running in the background that you don't always think about, including items in your Login Items list (in the Accounts pane of System Preferences) as well as servers that you have turned on in the Sharing pane. Turn off File Sharing, Windows Sharing, Printer Sharing, and others to see if that helps speed up your Mac. The Classic environment can contribute to sluggishness throughout the Mac OS—when you're not using a particular Classic application, you should shut down Classic (or use the Advanced tab in the Classic pane in System Preferences to *sleep* Classic) until it's needed again.

Mac OS X Is Frozen

If you've completed the troubleshooting steps in Chapter 27 for an application that seems to be unresponsive, and you've concluded that the Mac OS itself is frozen (you can't access any other applications, can't access the Dock, and can't bring up the Force Quit Applications box), you still may have another option. It may be that the Aqua interface is frozen or encountering trouble, while the underlying system can still be accessed. If your Mac is connected to a network and has remote access enabled, you can attempt to access it using SSH at the command line or a secure Telnet application.

NOTE See Chapter 17, "Accessing Network Volumes," if you're unfamiliar with remote access options.

From another Mac OS X machine on the network, launch Terminal. Then use Telnet or SSH to log in to the problem Mac using an administrator account on that Mac. Once logged in, run the `top` command; this displays a list of all running processes on the Mac you're connected to. If you see one process that uses a lot of CPU time, this could be causing your Mac to hang. The `top` command displays a half-dozen lines at the top of the Terminal window, showing some general system information, and then lists all active processes and data about them. Here's an example of part of the `top` command display:

```
PID COMMAND      %CPU
205 VShieldChe  84.8%
```

In this case, a component of the Virex anti-virus program was using 84.8 percent of the CPU time, slowing down operations on one Mac. You can shut down this process using the command line by entering this command:

```
sudo kill -9 [PID]
```

where *PID* is the number you see in the left-most column. Type the command and press Return and then type your administrator password when prompted.

If your Mac's not being slowed down by a single process, you can enter the command **sudo halt** at the command line and press Return. You'll be prompted for your password again. Enter it. If the command succeeds, you'll see a message stating that the problem Mac is being shut down—you'll also be logged out of the remote Mac.

If the command doesn't shut down the frozen Mac, your only choice is to hard-reset the Mac. How you do that depends on your Mac model—press the Power button on the front of the Mac for 5 to 10 seconds, press the reset button (on some Power Macintosh models), or press Ctrl+⌘Power on the keyboard (or Ctrl+⌘Eject on newer keyboards). After a hard reset, it's a good idea to run Disk First Aid or `fsck`, as discussed in the section "Fixing File and Directory Corruption" later in this chapter.

Getting Past a Kernel Panic

What is a *kernel panic*? According to Apple's TIL article number 106227 (`http://docs.info.apple.com/article.html?artnum=106227`), "A kernel panic is a type of error that occurs when the core (kernel) of an operating system receives an instruction in an unexpected format or that it fails to handle properly." When a kernel panic occurs, you will see a message of white text on a black background drawn on top of whatever was on the screen at the time. This message, in several languages, tells you that you need to restart your computer and that you should hold down the Power button for several seconds or press the Restart button.

A kernel panic is the most severe software problem you can have in Mac OS X (although your saved data is usually safe). The machine will be unusable at that point until it's restarted, and aside from restarting or resetting the Mac, you can do nothing to get past a kernel panic.

If you think you know what caused the kernel panic, try to avoid it. The cause might be related to your hardware (video cards or accelerator cards). Try detaching an external device to see if you can cause the kernel panic to recur. Also, if you were doing several device-level operations at once, try doing them one at a time. For example, if you were waking up a PowerBook from Sleep while ejecting a PC card, hot-swapping a device into a media bay, and attaching a string of six FireWire devices, you tested the limits of how much the system can keep track of at once.

TIP During a kernel panic, note the steps that led up to the problem, because developers and tech-support staffers find them valuable for troubleshooting. Note the complete error message and report it to Apple or another appropriate developer. It can be particularly helpful to look for a message that includes .kext (as in a recent error Todd got with com.symantec.kext.NPC), because that may be the offending kernel extension. Not all panics are the result of a kernel extension, but the name may give you a sense of the particular extension and sometimes the author of that extension.

If you've recently installed a kernel extension (such as driver software for a peripheral or utility application) and encountered a kernel panic while starting up, the extension may be buggy or corrupt. The solution is to boot into Safe mode and, when your Mac reaches the Finder, remove the extension by uninstalling the software. (Most installer applications have an uninstall option.) Safe mode is a special startup mode that loads only the kernel extensions absolutely required to start the computer. You can see video on your screen, mount the hard drive, and have basic mouse and keyboard functionality.

To invoke Safe mode, restart your Mac. After hearing the startup chime, hold down the Shift key; the Login window displays, showing the words Safe Boot.

Safe mode in Mac OS X is useful only if you have installed non-Apple software kernel extensions. Although the non-Apple extensions use the same key for turning off extensions in Mac OS 9 and earlier, you'll find that Safe mode is used considerably less often in Mac OS X because kernel extensions do not compromise stability like Mac OS 9 system extensions do.

As mentioned, the easiest way to remove an offending extension or utility program is to run its installer and then choose the Uninstall option. If you don't have an uninstaller, the easiest way to fix a kernel extension problem is to manually delete the appropriate folder from /System/Library/Extensions. (You can do this if you have an Admin account in Mac OS X 10.3 or later.)

WARNING We recommend you delete kernel extensions only if you're absolutely sure you've found the offender and you're sure that you've located the correct kernel extension file. Otherwise, you should troubleshoot in other ways—run the installer and choose Uninstall, or contact the manufacturer of the device or program you suspect is causing the problem to see if they're aware of the problem or can offer any solutions.

Problems with Permissions

Probably one of the top-ranking problems for users of Mac OS X who have migrated from either the Classic Mac OS or from Microsoft Windows is the issue of privileges or permissions. (Both words mean the same thing, but Apple didn't change to using "permissions" in dialog boxes and their documentation until Mac OS X version 10.2.) In a multiuser (and ultimately Unix-based) operating system, permissions are important—they determine who can see what documents, who can launch what applications and utilities, and who has control over the system-level settings. They also can cause some fairly serious headaches, particularly for those of us who consider ourselves regular end users, not system administrators.

That said, permissions problems can be fixed. If you're having trouble manipulating files, accessing external volumes, or getting applications to launch, you may have a permissions problem. You'll probably be able to solve it.

Fixing Problems with File/Folder Permissions

Because Mac OS X is a multiuser operating system to the core, you can't turn off multiple users even if you're the only person working on your Mac. It's difficult to say how permissions problems will manifest themselves. When an action—such as copying, moving, or deleting an item in the Finder—is disallowed, you may have a permissions problem.

ERRORS OF PERMISSION

Some other problems that don't appear to be related to permissions (judging by their dialog box messages) may be. Apple notes that errors of type –192 or type –108 may be related to problematic privileges or permissions, as can some errors that affect the capability of your Mac to print or start up the Classic environment.

Apple offers a utility called Repair Permissions in Mac OS X versions 10.2 and above, which is part of the Disk Utility application. In Mac OS X 10.4, launch Disk Utility, select your startup disk, click the First Aid tab, and choose Repair Disk Permissions.

To act on a file or folder, the action must be permitted at the user, group, or global level. The possible permissions are read, write, and execute (run an application or script, or open a folder). If you're an Admin user, you are automatically in the Admin group. Any user on the computer is automatically in a group with their name. When the Finder's Get Info window shows system as the owner of a particular file or folder, that is a less scary term for root. You will see both an Unknown user and an Unknown group.

The Finder lets you change permissions only for files that you own. However, if you change permissions on files and folders while logged in to the Root account in the Finder or the Terminal using the sudo command, you can cause quite a bit of trouble. You shouldn't experiment with changing the permissions of anything as root unless you're prepared to reinstall programs or undo changes. Of course, permissions that need to be changed can be using these same tools, so they're double-edged swords.

NOTE   An Admin user can change permissions in quite a few places simply using the Get Info window and its tools in the Finder. See Chapter 5, "Personalizing Mac OS X," and Chapter 9, "Being the Administrator: Permissions, Settings, and Adding Users," for more discussion on regular permission management.

Fixing Permissions via the Terminal

Consider this example: You're cleaning out the /Users/Shared folder on your Mac and realize that some of the files can't be deleted because the Finder reports that you're not the owner of those files. One solution is to ask the owners of those individual files to log in when they can and delete the files; another solution is to log in as root and use your superpowers to delete the files in the Finder. Of course, there are good reasons to avoid the Root account, as detailed in Chapter 28.

If you're willing, the easiest solution is probably to either change permissions for the files or delete them directly from the command line using the Terminal utility. Launch Terminal and use the sudo command to delete items in the Shared folder. For instance, to delete *every* file in the Shared folder, you could enter

```
sudo rm /Users/Shared/*
```

Press Return and then enter your Admin password and press Return again. You'll have executed the rm command as if you were root—in other words, with the power to delete any file, regardless of ownership. If you want to delete an individual file, simply specify its name:

```
sudo rm /Users/Shared/file1.txt
```

The rm command deletes only the files on this level of the Shared folder, not any subfolders. You'd need to use the powerful -r tag (for instance, rm -r /Users/Shared/* to *recursively* delete all files in the Shared folder), but it's dangerous to use (you're deleting *all* subfolders and files), so be careful with it.

You have another option. You could change the ownership of the files in question to your own account, enabling you to delete the file, change it, or otherwise do as you please. That's accomplished with the chown command, as discussed in Chapter 23, "Command-Line and Application Magic:"

```
sudo chown thoreau /Users/Shared/*
```

This command would change the ownership of all files (and folders) in the Shared folder to the user short-named thoreau. Now, that user (or, you, if you use your own account's short name) has ownership of the files and folders in question. As with rm, you can use chown with individual files, as in

```
sudo chown stevej /Users/Shared/file1.txt
```

The Terminal offers an opportunity to deal with another annoying instance—the Trash that can't be emptied because of file permissions problems. You can solve that fairly easily, as well, because the Trash folder is a hidden folder. At the command line, enter the following command:

```
sudo rm -r ~/.Trash/*
```

When you press Return, you may be asked for your Admin password. Enter it and press Return again. Trash is emptied. (In some cases, you may be asked to confirm some of your deletions, but it's rare. If you can, use the -f flag—as in rm -rf ~/.Trash/*—to avoid being asked for confirmation.) You may notice it takes a moment for the Trash icon in the Dock to catch up and refresh to its empty state, but eventually it will.

Ignore Ownership on This Volume

Buried in the Get Info window is an option that crops up when you're viewing the information for a disk or other volume and you disclose the Ownership and Permissions panel: Ignore Ownership on This Volume. This small option is available for you in two different instances and for fairly different reasons.

First, more commonly, you may want to turn on the Ignore Ownership option when you're working with an external hard disk or similar removable device—particularly if you want to use that hard disk with other computers. In most cases, your Mac will automatically ignore file ownership and permissions on typical removable disks, based on the assumption that the removable disk doesn't require the security of a fixed disk, and that anyone who is physically using your Mac, regardless of their Admin status, should have access to a removable disk that's in the drive.

For an external hard disk, however, Mac OS X doesn't make this same assumption. Instead, it assumes that you don't necessarily move the drive around often and that you want it to store information about permissions so that you can protect files and folders from other users or otherwise manage who has access to what on that drive. Figure 29.2 shows a FireWire drive's Info window, which has the Ignore Ownership option.

FIGURE 29.2

Because an external hard disk's permissions aren't automatically ignored, you'll see an option in its Info window.

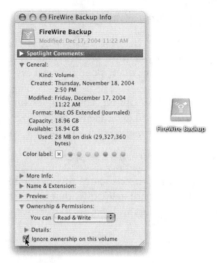

The Ignore Ownership option is there for you to turn on if you'd prefer that the external disk *not* track user permissions issues—in other words, that it be treated as a standard removable disk. That's the easy way to make sure you can use the disk on a variety of different computers, perhaps for backup or installation purposes or to move the disk from one Mac (in your office, for instance) to another (in your home).

NOTE The other situation where this option can be handy is less common. If you regularly work with the external volume connected to your Mac, and you have Ignore Ownership (or Ignore Permissions in older Mac OS X versions) turned off, it's likely that files have been stored with their full ownership and permissions settings. Apple notes a specific circumstance in its Knowledge Base where this can be a problem—if you've just completely reinstalled Mac OS X. (Apple's note on this covers versions prior to Mac OS X 10.2, but you may still encounter this issue in later versions.) Even if after the reinstall you create a user with the same name as the user account you used previously, a new Mac OS X installation can make it difficult to use an external disk—the external disk won't recognize the new user accounts as the owners of the files on that disk. The solution: Turn on Ignore Permission or Ignore Ownership for that external disk and then restart the Mac. Now you should be able to access files on that drive.

Fixing File and Directory Corruption

What is *corruption*? In short, corruption is unexpected information or information in an unexpected format. For example, in Mac OS 9, because the memory a program was using could be modified "behind its back" when a program saved its memory to disk, that information would not necessarily be the information that should have been saved. The result was corrupted information on disk.

Directory Corruption

Just as in Mac OS 9, incorrect information about hard drive contents can exist on your hard drive in Mac OS X. The incorrect information can result from a freeze, a power outage, or some other forced reboot.

As a program makes changes to a file in memory, the changes normally are saved often but not immediately. If the Mac OS X does not shut down properly, it checks the directory structure on the boot volume when it starts up (using fsck, the command-line File System Check command).

NOTE Since Mac OS X added *journaling*, a method by which disks store a log of their actions, directory damage has become much less common. Apple describes journaling as follows: "When you enable journaling on a disk, a continuous record of changes to files on the disk is maintained in the journal. If your computer stops because of a power failure or some other issue, the journal is used to restore the disk to a known-good state when the server restarts." While directory damage may occur, it is much less frequent than with volumes that don't use journaling. You can check your hard disks in Disk Utility to see if journaling is turned on (the format will be Mac OS Extended (Journaled)—this is the case by default for new Macs and if you reformat a hard disk). If not, select the volume and click the Enable Journaling button in the Disk Utility toolbar.

If the directory structure is really damaged, it's rare—but possible—for Mac OS X to stop its startup process and drop you into single-user mode, displaying a command-line interface instead of the typical login window or Finder. If that happens, you should follow the instructions that appear on-screen. You'll type **/sbin/fsck -fy** (or **/sbin/fsck -y** if the volume is not journaled) and press Return to run fsck. The information displayed about what fsck is checking and fixing will be very similar to what you see in Disk Utility in Mac OS X. When the check and any repair are done, you can just type **reboot** to restart your Mac and test to see if it will start up all the way to the login window or Finder.

If the problem can't be fixed by fsck, you may need to use other disk repair utilities such as Symantec's Norton Disk Doctor or Alsoft's DiskWarrior. (See Chapter 26 for more information about these utilities.)

WARNING To work on your Mac's startup disk with Disk Utility, you'll need to boot from the Mac OS X installation disc to run the Mac OS X Disk Utility and make repairs. (Select it from the Utilities menu in the Installer.) Otherwise, problems reported might not really exist, and Disk Utility won't be able to repair your main startup disk unless it's run from the CD. Also, avoid older, third-party utilities that may not have been updated since before Mac OS X 10.3; they won't be able to correctly work with journaled volumes.

If none of your disk utilities can repair the directory damage, your only option is to back up what you can and to reformat the hard disk. If your data is so valuable that reformatting (and hence losing some of that data) is not an option, your option may be to have the drive looked at by an Apple-authorized dealer or service center or by a drive-recovery company such as DriveSavers (www.drivesavers.com). Bringing in the big guns can be costly, but it might be worth it, particularly if your data is worth more than the cost of service to recover it.

File and Font Corruption

When files or fonts are corrupted, an application can begin to behave erratically. Likewise, an application can appear to crash for little reason if its preferences file becomes corrupt or, in the case of applications such as an e-mail program, if the underlying database upon which the application is based encounters corruption.

The easiest way to fix a single corrupted file is to replace it. If a file is auto-generated, such as a preference file in ~/Library/Preferences, you can simply move or rename it, and a new one will be created the next time that file is needed. It might be necessary to relaunch the application or even to log out or restart the computer. Avoid the temptation to delete the suspect file until it's clear that file was causing the problem.

Even then, it's worth keeping the file if you plan to contact Apple or another software vendor. The representative might ask for an auto-generated file. If the representative can't reproduce the problem, your file will be the only record of what happened.

The easiest way to stay on top of corruption is to run a disk doctor utility on a regular basis. If you make a point of running First Aid (part of Disk Utility) monthly or so—depending on how much you use your Mac—then you may stay out of harm's way a bit easier. Even better is running a good third-party disk utility—such as those discussed in Chapter 26—on a regular basis.

Fortunately, file corruption generally won't go much beyond causing an application to crash or quit unexpectedly. Because every file and folder in Mac OS X has permissions assigned, and just about every program you run has the same permissions as you do (that is, the same permissions that your user account has) in the Finder, any problems should be limited to files you could corrupt manually in an administrator account. The kernel prevents unauthorized access to memory or files. Any program that tries to access a file it doesn't have permissions to modify will fail and probably display a permissions-related error message. The kernel will force any application to quit if it tries to touch memory other than its own.

A specific class of files—fonts—can cause some interesting problems when they become corrupt. As noted earlier in this chapter, font corruption can cause trouble as Mac OS X attempts to start up. Likewise, some applications will scan the various fonts folders on your Mac to cache the fonts for later access; if the application encounters a corrupt font during this scan, it may quit unexpectedly or otherwise crash. Likewise, applications can encounter a corrupt font when it's selected in the Font Panel or another font-chooser interface element. And font corruption can crop up when you're saving, loading, or printing a document that has a corrupt font.

NOTE If you suspect font corruption might be the cause of your problem, you can toss or replace the font in question—if you can figure out which one it is. If you can't, another solution is to purchase and use a font utility application that can track down font problems. Try Font Reserve from Extensis (www.fontreserve.com) or FontDoctor X from Morrison SoftDesign (www.morrisonsoft-design.com), both of which are capable of finding and repairing font corruption in Mac OS X.

Troubleshooting with the Mac OS X Installer

With a caveat, the Mac OS X Installer can be quite useful in fixing most operating system problems. When reinstalling the OS, the Installer looks at special files called *receipts* in the main Library folder and compares the files listed there to the files it has to install. If the file has been moved, renamed, modified, or corrupted, it will be replaced under most conditions.

WARNING The caveat is this: You should never run the Mac OS X Installer in an attempt to fix a version of Mac OS X that has been updated beyond the version that's on the installation disc. If you have Mac OS X version 10.4 on disc, and you've updated your installation to Mac OS X 10.4.1 (via Software Update), running the Installer from the disc may not be useful for troubleshooting.

Unless you select the Erase option in the Installer—which erases the target disk and starts over with a new installation—the Installer will not alter your data files. Reinstalling OS X is the easiest way to correct widespread OS file corruption. Also, if you have no interest in command-line tools and workarounds, rerunning the Installer is your best troubleshooting fix when you've run out of GUI options. Reinstalling is overkill for fixing permissions problems, but if using Repair Disk Permissions on the First Aid tab of Disk Utility doesn't fix a permissions problem, the command line is currently the only other way to fix them.

When you're reinstalling over an existing Mac OS X installation, the Installer doesn't replace everything it installed before. To retain files that most users would not want reset to their default state, the Installer checks a list of certain files that it treats specially. This checking can make a reinstallation take up to twice as long as a first-time installation. The file (the list) is called `default.hints` and is located in `/System/Library/PrivateFrameworks/Installa.framework/Resources/`.

You can open `default.hints` in TextEdit and inspect its contents. (If you do so, copy the file to your home folder first so that you don't accidentally overwrite it. If you're signed in to the Root account, make sure you *copy*—as opposed to *move*—the file.) The list is self-explanatory about what files would be replaced and why. Most notably, your user and group information, stored in the Net-Info database (`/private/var/db/netinfo/local.nidb`), will not be replaced. When you restart after the reinstall, the computer won't restart the Setup Assistant and so on. Most files on the list are traditional Unix files that are hidden by default.

Users and Passwords

If you have multiple users on your Mac or on a group of Macs, you know that those users can be loads of trouble. Not only the people themselves—who can forget their passwords, move files around, and mess things up—but the user accounts can be trouble, too. This section looks at some of those problems and how to fix them.

NOTE   If users are a *security* problem—that is, for some reason you don't want them to be able to access and reconfigure the Mac when they have physical access to it—you need to do more than set permissions and manage their passwords. In that case, you might want to consider setting an Open Firmware password, as discussed in Chapter 26.

Problems with User Accounts

If your user account information becomes confused or corrupted—particularly if you've been attempting to alter it using NetInfo Manager—you will not be able to fix it by reinstalling Mac OS X. User account information is stored in the NetInfo database. The NetInfo database is not installed by the installer but is created when the computer starts up for the first time. The NetInfo database is first created without any users that can log in. (If it created an account and logged you in with some default password, that would be a big security hole.) To create all of the information needed to log in, you should rerun the Setup Assistant.

If you get into a situation that requires you to re-create the NetInfo database (by typing **root** as the name of the user in the Setup Assistant, for example), you have to force the computer to create a new NetInfo database and force it to rerun the Setup Assistant. To do this, take the following steps:

1. Boot the computer in single-user mode.

2. If the computer was not shut down cleanly, run `fsck` (described in the section "Fixing File and Directory Corruption" earlier in this chapter).

3. Make sure to mount the filesystem as specified by typing **mount -uw /** and pressing Return, so you can make changes to the disk. At this point, you are using the powerful Root account, so be careful what you type.

4. Type

   mv /var/db/netinfo/local.nidb /var/db/netinfo/local.nidb.old

   This will rename your NetInfo database that contains your user and group information.

5. Type

   rm /var/db/.AppleSetupDone

   to force the Setup Assistant to run again.

6. Type **exit** to continue booting. You should now boot into the Setup Assistant. Proceed normally through the Setup Assistant to create a new user.

Resetting Passwords

If you forget your password and can't log in, the password must be reset. For security reasons, you can't recover a lost password—passwords can only be replaced. You have three password-replacement methods:

◆ The easiest way to reset the password of a regular (non-administrator) user is to have the administrator reset the password in the Accounts pane of the System Preferences application. As the administrator, reset the user's password to something of your choosing and tell the user what it is. Once logged in, regular users can reset their own passwords (and should be encouraged to) in the My Account pane of the System Preferences application, but they can't replace a forgotten password without an administrator's help.

◆ If the system has more than one administrator, a second administrator's account can be used to reset the first administrator's account in the Accounts pane of the System Preferences application. If no other administrators are available, you must use the Root account (if active) or the Mac OS X installation disc, discussed next.

◆ The easy way to change an administrator account is to boot from the Mac OS X installation disc. After you pick your language, choose Utilities ➤ Reset Password. Keep in mind that anyone with a Mac OS X installation disc can reset your passwords, so it's important to keep your Mac OS X installation disc in a secure place. If the security problem worries you, secure your system physically. (That is, put it in a locked room and lock it to the furniture using the connector built onto the machine. Again, you can also use the Open Firmware Password system discussed in Chapter 26.)

As a last resort, follow these steps if you don't have the Mac OS X installation disc and you need to reset the administrator's password:

1. Restart the computer.

2. After you hear the startup chime but before you see the spinning rainbow wheel cursor or Apple icon, press ⌘S. Your computer will start in single-user mode. You'll know you've pressed the keys properly if you see scrolling text messages. If you see the spinning rainbow wheel cursor, you were too late—restart and try again. If you press the keys too early (before the chime), you'll see a normal graphical startup, which you'll also see after the spinning cursor if you were too late.

3. If you successfully started in single-user mode, the computer will start part of the way and then give you the prompt `localhost: / root#` or something similar that's followed by the pound (#) sign.

4. At this point, you are root with no other users and no networking; the hard drive is mounted as read-only. Don't be surprised if you see messages such as

   ```
   kmod_destroy: com.appledriver.AppleCore99PE (id 16), deallocating
   ➥8 pages starting at 0x721f000.
   ```

   Such messages, though scary-looking, are innocuous; they are sent from the kernel as it conserves memory by unloading drivers for hardware that does not exist on the machine.

5. If the computer previously was not shut down properly, type **/sbin/fsck -fy** (or **/sbin/fsck -y** if the volume is not journald) and press Return. The `fsck` program in the /`sbin` directory will run.

6. In order to make changes to the hard drive, you have to mount the drive so that it can be written on. Type

   ```
   /sbin/mount -uw /
   ```

   and press Return to mount the hard drive to be written on at the root level.

7. Type

   ```
   /usr/bin/nicl -raw /var/db/netinfo/local.nidb -create
   ➥/users/username passwd
   ```

   but replace *username* with the user's short name. Press Return. This sets the user's password to blank. The `nicl` command allows you to edit the NetInfo database of settings for the machine. You are editing it in Raw mode, without the help of daemons (which aren't running now anyway).

WARNING Do not use `nicl` with the `-raw` tag on a computer that is booted all the way up and running with the NetInfo daemons (server processes) `netinfod` and `lookupd` running. Modifying a database in Raw mode when NetInfo is running can cause corruption of the NetInfo database, where all your user and group information is stored. For more information about `nicl`, type **man nicl** in a Terminal window.

8. Type **exit** and press Return to allow the computer to continue starting up.

9. Log in as the user whose password you just reset. (You won't need to enter a password in the login window.)

10. Open the System Preferences application from the Apple menu.

11. Click Show All if needed.

12. Click the Password pane's icon.

13. Change the password for the user (remember, it's currently set to blank), following the on-screen instructions.

The user's password is reset, and that user will be able to log in successfully with the new password.

What's Next?

In this chapter, you saw the many approaches you can take to troubleshoot Mac OS X at the system level. Mac OS X is a very robust operating system, which will hopefully translate into fewer OS-level troubles than in previous versions of the Mac OS. When trouble does strike, the steps to correct the trouble can be more confusing in some ways than with past versions. Using a combination of graphical and command-line tools, however, you can get your Mac up and running in most cases.

In the appendices, you'll learn how to install Mac OS X, you'll consult a guide for migrating from Mac OS 9 to Mac OS X, and you'll learn about some of the applications included with Mac OS X.

Part 7

Appendices

Appendix A

Getting Installed and Set Up

If Mac OS X isn't yet installed on your Mac, you'll want to do a little planning before you get started. First, consider how you're going to set up your hard disk to accommodate Mac OS X. If you still have a Mac that can start up in Mac OS 9, and you need to use older applications occasionally that don't function correctly in the Classic Environment, you may want to run both Mac OS X and Mac OS 9, allowing you to dual-boot between the two of them. To use Mac OS X in a dual-boot environment, you may decide to partition your disk.

In this appendix, you'll take a look at the requirements for Mac OS X. Then you'll learn how to plan your Mac OS X installation, including how to initialize and partition your hard disk, if necessary. Finally, you'll learn how to run the Installer and set up Mac OS X for the first time.

In this appendix:

◆ Reviewing Mac OS X Requirements

◆ Preparing to Install Mac OS X

◆ Installing Mac OS X

◆ Dual-Booting

Reviewing Mac OS X Requirements

Before you install Mac OS X, you should know its requirements. On the Mac OS X CD, you'll find a PDF document called READ BEFORE YOU INSTALL.pdf. You can open this file and examine its contents using Preview or Adobe Acrobat Reader. You can also read this ReadMe file on the third screen of the Mac OS X Installer.

Mac OS X requires 256MB of RAM (according to Apple). At least 512MB of RAM is recommended if you plan to run many programs at the same time and use the Classic environment extensively. For designers, video editors, and anyone using high-end graphical applications that deal with large files, at least 1GB is recommended.

In addition to the minimum of 256MB of RAM, Mac OS X requires the following:

◆ A PowerPC G3, G4, or G5 processor

◆ A DVD drive or CD drive (While Apple says in its system requirements that you need a DVD drive, and Tiger is indeed supplied on DVD, you can exchange your DVD for a set of CDs if you don't have a DVD drive. Go to www.apple.com/macosx/upgrade/ for information on the Media Exchange Program.)

◆ Built-in FireWire

You can't install Mac OS X on an external Universal Serial Bus (USB) hard disk, although you should be able to use most such disks for data and application files once Mac OS X is booted up. You can, however, install Mac OS X on an external FireWire hard disk, if you have one that is bootable. (Most recent models of FireWire hard disks are bootable.)

Apple's requirement that your Mac have built-in FireWire is a way of saying that certain G3 Macs, which do not have this, are not compatible with Tiger. The lack of FireWire itself is not the deal-breaker, but models that don't have FireWire also lack certain other technologies.

NOTE If you have an older Mac, not officially supported by Mac OS X, and you absolutely want to try to run Mac OS X on it, check out XPostFacto (http://eshop.macsales.com/OSXCenter/ XPostFacto), a free tool that lets you install Mac OS X on many legacy Macs. This is not for the faint of heart, and you do this entirely at your own risk, but it does work on many older Macs, such as the 7300, 7500, 7600, 8500, 8600, 9500, and 9600, as well as some clones that were based on these systems.

Mac OS X uses either the Unix File System (UFS) or HFS+ (Journaled) format as the disk format for its volumes; the default for new volumes is HFS+ (Journaled), but you can install Mac OS X over a previous installation on a plain HFS+ volume. Earlier Mac OS versions use the HFS (Hierarchical File System) or HFS+ format, also called Mac OS Standard and Mac OS Extended, respectively. Although Mac OS X can read and write data to a Mac OS Standard volume, it can't be installed on one. It must be installed on either a Mac OS Extended or UFS volume. If you plan to boot your Mac from Mac OS 9, you must format the volume as Mac OS Extended. See the Read Before You Install.pdf document for more information on specific third-party hardware compatibility.

Preparing to Install Mac OS X

Before you install Mac OS X, consider carefully how you want to install it and complete some preparatory steps, as follows:

◆ Decide whether you want to use the Classic environment and if you would like to be able to dual-boot between Mac OS X and Mac OS 9. (This is only possible on Macs built before 2003 and some models sold after January 1, 2003.)

◆ Back up all the important files on your hard disk.

◆ Partition your disk into multiple volumes and initialize those volumes.

NOTE Some Mac models—particularly PowerBook G3 Series models, "beige" Power Macintosh G3, and early (233–266MHz) tray-loading iMacs—require that you install Mac OS X on the first 8GB of your hard drive. If your drive is bigger than 8GB, you must create a partition that is no more than 8GB to install Mac OS X. In certain cases, you may need to repartition your disk to work with Mac OS X. (This is applicable only to ATA/IDE drives; if you have an internal SCSI drive and a compatible SCSI interface in your Power Mac G3, you should be able to install Mac OS X on it without trouble.)

◆ If necessary, install or update to the latest version of Mac OS 9. The latest, and last, version is Mac OS 9.2.2.

◆ Update your Mac's firmware, if necessary, as well as the firmware for any of your internal cards and other devices, particularly if the device's manufacturer has a special firmware update that supports Mac OS X. If the Mac OS X Installer displays a message saying that you need to do this, go to www.apple.com/support/downloads and find an updater for your Mac model.

◆ If you have a third-party video card in your Power Macintosh G3 or G4, Apple warns that you may need to remove it (and use only an Apple-supplied video card to attach to your monitor) before installing Mac OS X. The best plan is to check the video card manufacturer's website to determine if that card is supported in Mac OS X and if it needs any sort of driver or firmware update.

NOTE If you have a version of Mac OS X prior to 10.1 installed, you can't upgrade it directly to Mac OS X 10.4; you need to either upgrade your current version to 10.1 or initiate a clean installation of Mac OS X 10.4, as discussed in the section "Running the Mac OS X Installer," later in this appendix.

Making the Classic Mac Decision

While most readers installing Mac OS X 10.4 have already been working with a previous version of Mac OS X, there are still some people who are updating a Mac that has been running Mac OS 9. In this case, one of the main considerations before installing Mac OS X is whether you want to use the Classic environment and whether you want to be able to dual-boot between Mac OS X and Mac OS 9. If you have both operating systems installed on your Mac, you'll have the option of booting the Mac in either of those operating systems, depending on the task you're trying to accomplish. If you install only Mac OS X on your Mac, you won't have the option of booting into Mac OS 9, and you won't be able to run Classic applications within the Classic environment.

NOTE Mac OS 9 needs to be installed for you to dual-boot between Mac OS 9 and Mac OS X and use the Classic environment. You aren't required to install Mac OS 9—Mac OS X will run fine without it as long as you're willing to forgo the ability to run Classic applications. In early 2003, Apple began shipping Macs that won't dual-boot into Mac OS 9, although they will still run Classic applications. If you're installing Mac OS 9 from scratch, you'll need to install version 9.1 or later from existing CDs and then update to the latest Mac OS 9 version by downloading it from www.info.apple.com/support/downloads.html or by using the Software Update control panel in Mac OS 9. If you already have Mac OS 9 installed and updated, you can go ahead and install Mac OS X 10.4 over Mac OS 9 (or later).

If you opt to dual-boot or run Classic, you have another decision to make: whether to install Mac OS X and Mac OS 9 on separate volumes or disks. If you have more than one disk drive installed in your Mac, you may be able to install Mac OS 9 on one and Mac OS X on another. Even if you have only one hard disk in your Mac, you can opt to partition your disk, thus dividing it into multiple volumes. Each volume acts more or less as a separate disk. You can initialize volumes using different file systems, for instance, and each can have a different name.

NOTE Remember, with the 2003 models and later, you may not be able to dual-boot at all, so this discussion may not be a consideration.

Partitioning a disk is a bit tricky, though, because it requires you to erase the entire disk, thus losing any data that's currently stored on the disk. If you can fully back up your important files, however, partitioning your disk and installing Mac OS 9 and Mac OS X can have some advantages.

Here's a summary of the installation options:

Mac OS X and Mac OS 9 on the same disk   You can install Mac OS X on the same disk as an existing installation of Mac OS 9. This is the easiest way to install Mac OS X, because it probably won't require you to do any low-level reinitializing of the hard disk. This requires that the disk already be formatted in the Mac OS Extended format.

Mac OS X and Mac OS 9 on different disks or partitions   You can install Mac OS X on a separate disk or on a different partition of your main hard disk from Mac OS 9. Then, you can still dual-boot between the two operating systems, and you can use the Mac OS 9 installation for the Classic environment in Mac OS X. The advantages include the fact that the Mac OS X partition or disk can be formatted as a UFS volume (if you have a good reason to do this, such as integrating your Mac into a Unix environment more easily), and the Mac OS 9 volume can be formatted as Mac OS Extended.

Mac OS X and Mac OS 9 on the same disk *and* Mac OS 9 on a second disk   You can install Mac OS 9 or lower on a separate disk or partition and then install Mac OS 9 *and* Mac OS X on another disk or partition. This has the advantage of enabling you to dual-boot into a fully customized version of Mac OS 9 or lower, while using a "clean" version of Mac OS 9 for the Classic environment within Mac OS X.

Apple has designed Mac OS X to coexist on the same Mac OS Extended partition as a previous installation of Mac OS 9. Mac OS X's Installer recognizes the Mac OS 9.1 installation and properly install its files *over* that installation, moving some of the Mac OS 9 files to different folders, such as the Applications (Mac OS 9) folder that the Installer creates. Using one partition is certainly possible, and it still allows you to dual-boot between Mac OS 9 and Mac OS X. If you like to boot into a specially configured version of Mac OS 9, you may want to use two Mac OS 9 installations installed on separate partitions—one for dual-boot and one for the Classic environment.

NOTE   Why is customization of Mac OS 9 an issue? The Classic environment works best with a Mac OS 9 installation that includes very few third-party extensions, control panels, and drivers. However, for some dual-boot uses, you may need those important extensions and other add-ons. If that's the case, two installations of Mac OS 9 may make sense. (Or, alternatively, you could just avoid the Classic environment whenever possible.) That way, Mac OS X won't attempt to launch the heavily configured Mac OS 9 installation as the Classic environment, which could cause trouble or incompatibilities.

Backing Up Files

Before you install Mac OS X, you may want to use a backup utility on your Mac to make sure you create a complete backup. Ideally, you should always have a current backup of your important data files, and the best backups are on removable media that you can store in another location. (Online backup can work quite well for securing your important data, too.) For the purpose of this installation, though, you can simply copy your files to an external hard disk, a removable disk, or other media you have available. Mac OS X will be able to read those disks after installation, and you'll be able to copy applications and documents back to your Mac OS X machine for future use. Chapter 26, "Hard Disk Care, File Security, and Maintenance," discusses backup utilities.

Partitioning and Initializing

As noted earlier, you can install Mac OS X in one of two basic ways: on the same volume as an existing Mac OS 9 installation or on a separate volume. If you plan to install Mac OS X on a separate volume, you may need to create that volume by partitioning your existing hard disk into two or more volumes.

WARNING Partitioning a disk always requires initialization of the partitions after they've been set up. The initialization process, by definition, means that data on the disk will be erased and that each partition will subsequently appear as a separate volume (a separate disk icon in the Finder). If you have important data on that disk that you haven't backed up and tested, avoid partitioning and initializing that disk until you've performed the backup.

There are two ways to partition your drive, and each is equally effective—you can run Drive Setup from the Mac OS 9 CD or Disk Utility from the Mac OS X CD. We'll cover using Mac OS X's installation disc in this section.

If you have a Mac OS X installation disc available, start up from that CD by placing the CD in your Mac's CD/DVD drive and then restarting the Mac. Immediately after you hear the startup chime, hold down the C key until the Mac begins starting up from the disc.

Then, when the Installer appears, select the language you want to use and then click the arrow button. After the Installer displays, choose Utilities ➢ Disk Utility to launch Disk Utility. Click the Partition tab to see the controls for partitioning your hard disk. In the Disk Utility window, you'll see a list of drives you can select to initialize and partition. To set up a disk, select it in the list on the left side of the window. (You need to select an actual disk, not a volume that's on one of the disks.) Then you'll see the partition information for that disk (see Figure A.1).

NOTE If your hard disk is already partitioned, you don't need to run Disk Utility. You simply can back up the data on the target volume and then use the Erase command under the Special menu in the Finder to erase the volume you want to use for Mac OS X. You then can move on to the section "Installing or Updating to Mac OS 9," later in this appendix.

NOTE You can install Mac OS X on a secondary hard disk if you have one installed inside your Mac or attached via a FireWire port or an external SCSI bus. (That said, installing Mac OS X on an external SCSI disk isn't a recommended setup, and there are some compatibility problems with SCSI controllers and Mac OS X.) You can't install Mac OS X on removable disks or external hard disks connected to your Mac via USB ports, and some older FireWire drives are not bootable.

On the Partition tab, choose how many partitions you want on this disk after it's initialized. If you plan to use this disk for both a Mac OS 9 (or earlier) version and Mac OS X, you'll want at least two different partitions. You can have more if you like, as long as the volume you plan to use for Mac OS X has at least 3GB of available disk space and ideally 5GB or more. (Don't forget that you'll probably want a good deal more space than this so that you can store documents, new applications, and downloaded files on the Mac OS X partition.) If you plan to install the Mac OS X Developer Tools, count on an additional 1GB for these files.

FIGURE A.1
The Partition tab of Disk Utility enables you to select and visually partition your hard disks.

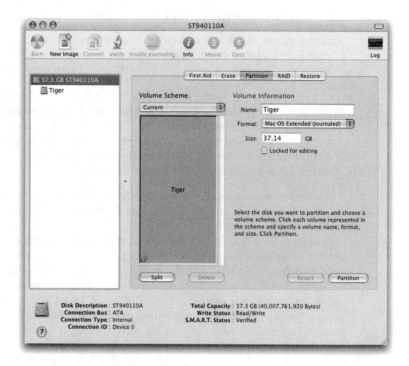

You can change the size of the partitions in two ways:

◆ Between each partition in the Volume Scheme area, you'll see a line with a small drag box; click and drag that box to change the size of the partitions.

◆ Click a partition in the Volume Scheme area and enter a numerical size for it in the Size entry box.

NOTE If you plan to have two partitions for dual-booting on an IDE drive, your best bet is to install Mac OS 9 on the first partition and Mac OS X on the second partition. Be sure to plan the size of your partitions accordingly.

You should also choose the formatting type for each partition by selecting the partition in the Volume Scheme area and choosing the type of format for that volume from the Format menu. For the Mac OS 9 partition, you should choose Mac OS Extended. For the Mac OS X partition, you'll need to format using Mac OS X Extended (Journaled) or UFS. Mac OS X Extended (Journaled) is recommended for most installations because journaling provides additional disk security. Use UFS only if you have good reason to, perhaps because you want to run specific Unix applications or use your Mac as a file server on a network containing Unix or Linux systems.

Once you have your partitions set the way you want them, click the Partition button to begin the formatting process. You'll see one more dialog box appear to confirm your decisions, and then the initialization takes place. This erases all of the data on the selected drive (including all volumes on that drive) and creates the new partitions on that disk.

WARNING   Last warning! Don't initialize your disk without creating backups of important data. All the data on the selected disk will be erased. If you erase a disk accidentally, immediately stop working with it until you can run Norton Utilities, Alsoft DiskWarrior, or a similar disk doctor recovery application. That way you *may* recover some of your data.

When Disk Utility is finished initializing, you'll see any Mac OS Extended partitions appear on the desktop as separate disk icons. (UFS partitions aren't recognized by Mac OS 9.) You can quit Disk Utility by choosing Quit from its File menu.

Updating Your Firmware

Another necessary task for some Mac OS 9 and Mac OS X installations (particularly on some of the earlier Mac models that Mac OS X supports) is the need to update your Mac's *firmware*. Firmware is an internal, rewritable snippet of code that is used to help the Macintosh when it's first powering up and recognizing its components. As time goes on, Apple often makes slight changes and fixes to the firmware code that can then be used to update your Mac to be fully compatible with new technologies such as Mac OS X.

If the Installer tells you that you need to update your firmware, visit `www.apple.com/support/downloads` in your web browser and search for firmware updates for your Mac model.

WARNING   Firmware updates available from Apple's website for iMac and Power Macintosh G4 (and G4 Cube) models since early 2001 carry a special caveat: The updates can disable some third-party RAM modules. Apple has stated that the firmware update disables modules that aren't fully compatible with your Mac and Mac OS X, causing crashes and freezes. If you find you've installed the firmware update and suddenly your Mac seems to have less RAM available, the firmware update may have disabled a RAM module that it considered faulty.

Updating firmware is fairly painless. You launch the updater—double-click the updater's icon, whether it's on the Mac OS X installation CD-ROM or on a disk image that you've downloaded from Apple's website—and then follow the instructions provided in the ReadMe document included with the updater. In some cases, with older Mac models, you may need to boot into Mac OS 9 to run the firmware updater. If you've just formatted your Mac's hard disk, and you have no version of the Mac OS on it, you'll need to install Mac OS 9 or Mac OS X first because you can't start up from the Mac OS X CD and install the firmware update. You must start up from your hard disk.

If your firmware is up to date, you'll see a dialog box telling you so. If not, follow the on-screen instructions for the update. In most cases, the updater will tell you to shut down your Mac and then hold down the programmer's button on the back or side of your Mac while you press the Power button. (This depends on your Mac model; some work slightly differently.) Finally, you'll hear a long tone, which is your cue to release the buttons. Your Mac should start up. In many cases (depending on your Mac model), you'll see a status bar and a success message. You also might see a blinking question mark before your Mac finds its startup disk—that's normal.

As part of the firmware update process, PRAM (Parameter RAM, a small portion of RAM reserved for system-level settings and the Mac's clock) is also reset, so you may need to reset your Startup Disk, Date & Time, Monitor, AppleTalk, and other control panels.

NOTE   As mentioned earlier, visit the websites of the manufacturers of any third-party peripherals you have attached to your Mac. Many of them likely will have both firmware updates and driver software updates designed to make their products compatible with Mac OS X. This is particularly true of internal PCI adapter cards, but it can extend to external devices as well.

Installing or Updating Mac OS 9

If you've opted to partition and initialize your hard disk, your next step will be to install Mac OS 9 on one or both of those partitions if you wish. If all the applications you're going to use run natively in Mac OS X, you're better off not installing Mac OS 9 at all. The only reason to install OS 9 now is if you need to run older programs that have not been updated to run under OS X. Before you can make the leap to stand-alone Mac OS X, however, there are some issues to consider as this overall transition continues:

◆ Some Classic applications simply work better when you dual-boot into Mac OS 9.

◆ Even if you don't plan to dual-boot, Mac OS 9 is required for the Classic environment in Mac OS X, and you may find *some* reason to run a Classic application at some point.

With Mac OS X 10.4, a Mac OS 9 installation CD is no longer included, so you'll need to use an existing Mac OS 9.1 or higher CD (if you have one) to install Mac OS 9. To start up from the CD, place the Mac OS 9.1 or higher CD in your CD/DVD drive and restart your Mac. Immediately after hearing the startup chime, hold down the C key on your keyboard. After a moment, you'll see the Mac OS 9 startup screen, and you should hear the CD/DVD drive whirring away. (If you've just partitioned or initialized your hard disk, you probably already booted from the Mac OS 9.1 or higher CD.)

TIP If you don't have a Mac OS 9 installation CD, you probably don't need to install Mac OS 9 and run Classic. Apple provides Mac OS 9 installation packages on an installation disc included with all new Macs, so if you want to use Classic and don't have an OS 9 installation disc, use that disc to install Mac OS 9.

When the desktop appears, you should see the Mac OS 9.1 (or higher) CD window. Locate the Install Mac OS 9 icon and double-click it to launch the Installer. Now, you'll walk through the steps of the Mac OS 9.1 Installer:

1. The first screen is the Welcome screen. Click Continue to move to the next screen.

2. On the Select Destination screen, select from the pop-up menu the volume onto which you want to install Mac OS 9 and then click Continue.

3. You see the Important Information screen, which includes the contents of the Before You Install file on the Mac OS 9.1 (or higher) CD. Read through it to see if it addresses any particular issues that relate to your Mac, such as incompatibilities or warnings regarding firmware and other updates. When you're ready, click Continue.

4. The Software License Agreement screen appears. Page through the license agreement (you should read the whole thing, although we know you won't). When you're finished, click the Continue button. A dialog box appears, asking if you agree with the license agreement; if you do, click Agree. If you click Disagree, the Installer application quits.

5. Finally, you arrive at the Install Software screen, shown in Figure A.2. Here you have two choices. You can click Start to begin a standard installation on the specified volume (check to make sure the specified volume is correct), or you can choose Customize if you would like to customize the Mac OS 9 installation (and you know what you're doing).

FIGURE A.2
The Install Software
screen

When you click Start, the Installer will begin the installation process by scanning the hard disk and noting any errors. In most cases, it will fix minor errors, but occasionally it will encounter one that it can't fix. If that happens, you'll need to either run a disk repair program or reinitialize the disk before installation.

When the disk has been checked, the Installer goes about installing (or updating) the System Folder on the target disk. After 15 to 20 minutes, Mac OS 9 should be installed. You can now restart into Mac OS 9, if desired, and complete the Setup and Internet Assistants. Those settings will be used whenever you boot into Mac OS 9 in the future.

Finally, you should use the Software Update control panel (Apple menu ➢ Control Panels ➢ Software Update) to update Mac OS 9 to the latest version available from Apple's servers. If the Software Update tool won't work for you, head to www.apple.com/support/downloads.html to locate and download the latest Mac OS 9 updates. You should work with the latest Mac OS 9 version possible in order to have the best dual-boot and Classic environment experience.

Installing Mac OS X

With your drive partitioned and initialized, your firmware updated, and Mac OS 9 installed (if desired), you're ready to install Mac OS X. First, you run the Installer program, and then you set up Mac OS X using the Setup Assistant. To complete the Setup Assistant, you'll need to know some things about your network access, such as information provided to you by your Internet service provider (ISP) regarding dial-up account settings, phone numbers, and your e-mail accounts. Also, if you use NetBoot, you'll need to have information about the NetBoot server on your network.

Running the Mac OS X Installer

To install Mac OS X, you must boot your Mac from the Mac OS X installation disc. Insert the disc in your CD/DVD drive and restart your Mac, holding down the C key on your keyboard. When Mac OS X starts up from the disc (it can take a while), you should see the Installer application. (You can also mount the disc in your existing Mac OS X or Mac OS 9 installation and then double-click the Mac OS X Install icon. Doing so will automatically restart your Mac.) If you're upgrading from a previous version of Mac OS X, just insert the installation disc and double-click the Mac OS X Install icon. You'll be asked to enter an administrator's password before the Mac restarts. (If you don't have this password, you'll need to get an administrator to enter it.)

NOTE If you can't seem to get your Mac to start up from the installation disc, or if you subsequently have trouble getting the Installer to work correctly, it's possible that you have a drive's ATA status set incorrectly. (This would be particularly likely if you've installed additional hard drives or CD/DVD disc drives in your Mac.) See the Apple Knowledge Base article number 106728 (`http://docs.info.apple.com/article.html?artnum=106728`) for details.

Now, you're ready to install Mac OS X, as follows:

1. On the Language screen, select the language you want to use for Mac OS X's main language and click the arrow button to continue.

2. The next screen is the Welcome screen. Click the Continue button after reading the welcome message, which includes information about Mac OS X such as computer models supported, information about software updates, and limitations of the current release.

3. The Software License screen appears. Read through the license and then click Continue. In the dialog sheet that appears, click Agree if you agree with the license agreement. (If you click Disagree, you won't move on in the Installer.)

4. On the Select a Destination screen, select the hard disk where you want to install Mac OS X. With your selection made, click Continue.

NOTE On the Select a Destination screen, you can click the Options button for three additional possibilities, depending on whether or not Mac OS X is already installed on the destination drive that you've selected. If you're upgrading from a previous edition of Mac OS X and want to install this new version *over* the existing installation, choose Upgrade Mac OS X (that's the default choice). If you'd like to install the new version but don't want to use the existing installation as a base for an upgrade, choose Archive and Install. (This will keep your old installation on a compressed disk image, but install a fresh copy of Mac OS X for day-to-day use.) You also can choose Preserve Users and Network Settings so that you don't have to go through the Setup Assistant again. (This option is a good idea if you're having trouble with the stability of the operating system or believe you may encounter trouble with a hardware driver when you move to the new version.) Finally, you may also want to choose the Erase and Install option, using the pop-up menu to select the disk format you would like to use. Use this option only if you're planning to initialize the target volume—it will be erased, so it shouldn't have important data on it. (If you're installing over Mac OS 9, you shouldn't select this option, since you cannot choose Mac OS Extended format for your hard disk.)

5. The Easy Install screen appears. If you want to customize the installation, click the Customize button and use the check boxes to determine which portions of the installation you want to install. (This is a good idea, because you can deselect the various language packages that you don't need, as well as other software packages like printer drivers that can take up a lot of disk space. Show the Language Translation entries by clicking the disclosure triangle, then look through the languages. Click to remove the check box next to any of the languages you don't speak—or just turn off all Localized Languages—but leave everything else turned on.) Otherwise, click the Install button to begin the installation. Do the same for the Printer Drivers entries. Together, the Language Translation and Printer Drivers installations take up about 2GB of disk space, so not installing the ones you don't need is a good idea.

The Installer will check your hard disk and then begin installing components. After about 20 to 30 minutes, the installation will finish. The Installer will restart your Mac and launch the Setup Assistant automatically.

Using the Setup Assistant

The Setup Assistant walks you through the process of configuring your Mac for the first time with Mac OS X. You'll choose a number of settings, including an administrative password, the time and date, and information about your network and Internet connection. You'll also be able to create user accounts for users on this Mac OS X system. Follow these steps to configure Mac OS X with the Setup Assistant:

1. The first screen you see welcomes you to Mac OS X, with an animation and fairly loud music, and then a second screen welcomes you to the Assistant. Select the name of the country you're in and then click the Continue button. (If you don't see the correct country, check the Show All option.)

NOTE The Assistant includes both Continue and Go Back buttons. If at any point you want to go back one or more screens within the Assistant, click the Go Back button. You then can change settings and move forward again with the Continue button.

2. The Do You Already Own a Mac screen lets you use the Mac OS X Migration Assistant to copy your data if this is not a new Mac. You have three options: you can transfer information from another Mac, you can transfer information from another partition on this Mac, or you can choose to not transfer any information. The first two options allow you to run a clean install on your Mac, yet still recover all your files and settings from another Mac or another partition.

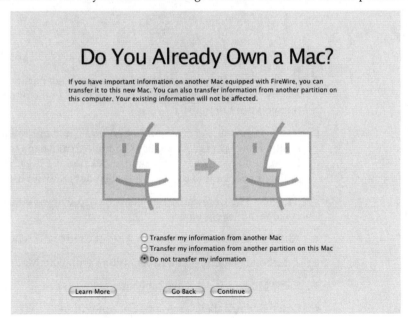

A. If you choose to transfer information from another Mac, check this option and then click Continue. You'll see instructions telling you how to connect your Mac to another Mac using a FireWire cable and then restart your old Mac. The Transfer Your Information screen lets you choose what is copied from your old Mac. You can copy user accounts, network and other settings, applications, and files and folders. Check the items you want to copy (if you only want to copy certain user accounts, check the disclosure triangle next to Users and select those you want to copy). Click Transfer to start transferring the data. This may take several minutes, depending on how much data you are transferring.

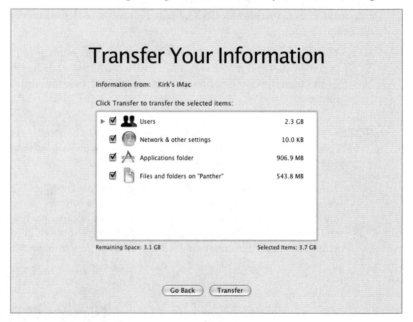

B. If you choose to transfer information from another partition on your Mac, check this option and then click Continue. Proceed as described in the previous step, selecting the information you want to transfer.

C. If you do not transfer any information, you'll move ahead through the Setup Assistant and create a new user account. Click Continue to move to the next screen, then select the keyboard layout you want to use, and click Continue. Again, you can turn on the Show All option if you want to use a keyboard layout that isn't listed.

3. The How Do You Connect screen lets you choose how you'll be connecting to the Internet. Choose one of the following:

◆ AirPort Wireless, if you have an AirPort Card and a wireless network

◆ Telephone Modem, if you're connecting with your Mac's modem

◆ Cable Modem, if you have cable Internet access

◆ DSL modem, if that's your mode of connection

◆ Local Network (Ethernet), if your Mac is connected by Ethernet

◆ My Computer Does Not Connect to the Internet, if you won't be using your Mac for network access

If your Mac is already connected to a network (via Ethernet or AirPort), the Setup Assistant will most likely skip this screen, though if you have an AirPort card, it will ask you to select a wireless network.

4. Depending on the type of connection method you choose, the next screen will ask you to enter the necessary information for your network. This could be simply a telephone number, username, and password for a dial-up connection, or standard network information, such as the type of connection (DHCP, PPP, BootP) and the DNS Host or other information. If you are not sure about what to enter in this screen, contact your ISP or your administrator or simply go back to the How Do You Connect screen and choose My Computer Does Not Connect to the Internet. In this case, you can configure your network access later using the Network pane of the System Preferences.

5. If you've set up your Mac for network access, the next screen asks you to enter your Apple ID. This is an ID you use on Apple's websites, from their .Mac service to the iTunes Music Store and Apple's support pages. If you already have an Apple ID, enter it here, with your password. (If you already have a .Mac account, this ID is your mac.com e-mail address.) If you don't have one, click Continue to move to the next screen; you'll create an Apple ID later.

6. On the Registration Information screen, enter your personal information. The Assistant requires that you enter a name, address, city, state, ZIP code, and phone number. If you would like to read Apple's privacy policy, click the Privacy button. Finally, click Continue.

7. On the next screen, answer the survey questions, select Yes or No regarding whether Apple can send you e-mail newsletters and offers, and then click the Continue button.

8. On the Create Your Account screen, you can create the first user (and administrator) account for your Mac. Enter your full name in the Name entry box and then enter a shorter, one-word username in the Short Name entry box. You'll see your name and short name already there, but you can change them if you want. You may especially want to change the short name, which is, by default, your first name and last name in one word, in lowercase letters, and which is therefore not very short. Next, enter a password in the Password entry box and enter the same password in the Verify box so that the Assistant can ensure you have typed the password correctly. Then, enter a short hint that will help you remember your password (but that isn't easy for others to guess). Finally, select a picture that will be displayed on the login screen. (You can change this later in System Preferences if you want to use a real picture of yourself.) Click the Continue button, and your account is created.

NOTE The best passwords are nonsensical to anyone but you, preferably composed of both numbers and letters without spaces. All passwords in Mac OS X are case sensitive, so you need to remember exactly how you enter passwords, including uppercase letters and numbers that you use.

9. If you didn't enter an Apple ID, the next screen tells you about the .Mac subscription service. If you've purchased a .Mac subscription in a box, you'll be able to enter the activation key after clicking Continue. If you already have a .Mac subscription, you can check I'm Already a .Mac

Member; in this case, the next screen asks for your .Mac member name and password. You can also choose to purchase .Mac online right away, or to not purchase it at all. If you choose this option, the next screen offers to set you up with a free 60-day trial subscription.

NOTE .Mac is Apple's special online subscription service that gives you access to special applications—iDisk, Mac.com e-mail, HomePage, online backup, and antivirus, along with lots of free software and other perks. They're discussed in more detail in Chapter 11, "The Web, Online Security, .Mac, Sherlock, and iChat."

10. The next screen, Your .Mac Membership, lets you create a free trial .Mac account (60 days, currently). Enter a username to use for your .Mac account (it does not need to be the same as your Mac OS X account username) and then type the password you will use for .Mac twice. Next, enter a password question and password answer that the .Mac server can use to confirm your identity if you need to ask for your password in the future. Use a question and answer that you'll remember but that isn't easily guessed and that has nothing to do with your actual password. Something such as "What is my favorite color?" or "Who was my childhood dog?" and the appropriate answer will work well. Finally, select your birth month and year (again, for confirmation when you need to retrieve your .Mac password) and click Continue. You don't have to do all this; you can always sign up for this trial subscription later from the .Mac preference pane in System Preferences. Click Continue to move ahead.

That should be it. You'll see a final congratulatory screen. Click Go, and your Mac should finish booting into Mac OS X. Your desktop appears, ready for action.

NOTE After you have completed the Setup Assistant and your desktop has appeared, you may find that Software Update launches automatically. If your Mac is connected to the Internet, and Software Update finds updates, you can opt to download them so that Mac OS X and its components can be updated immediately to the latest version. Software Update is discussed in Chapter 25, "Peripherals, Internal Upgrades, and Disks."

TROUBLE SELECTING VOLUMES

If you have trouble selecting volumes in the Installer, see if any of the following explanations help. For more on these and other possible problems, check Apple's Support site at www.apple.com/support/ or call Apple's 800 support number for help.

VOLUMES SHOW RED EXCLAMATION POINTS

◆ If all your volumes show red exclamation points, and the Mac OS X Installer tells you that you can't install Mac OS X on any of your volumes, try quitting the Installer and restarting.

◆ If you have several volumes and only one of them shows an exclamation point, this could mean that it's formatted in a manner that OS X cannot use. You may need to erase the volume (after backing up your data) and reformat it using Disk Utility.

VOLUMES ARE DIMMED IN THE INSTALLER

◆ If the volume you want to install onto is dimmed in the Installer, that volume is not able to contain Mac OS X. Possible reasons include volumes formatted as Mac OS Standard Format (HFS), locked volumes (such as a CD-ROM), or USB hard drives, which Mac OS X doesn't support.

◆ On older PowerBook G3 (Wallstreet) models, tray-loading iMac models, and Power Macintosh G3 (beige) models, Mac OS X can be installed only on a partition that is entirely contained within the first 8GB of the drive. If your disk is larger than 8GB, you'll need to partition it, but be careful that the first partition is smaller than 8GB. If you have a 12GB drive whose first partition is 10GB and second partition is 2GB, you won't be able to install Mac OS X on either of them. Both volumes will be gray in the Mac OS X Installer. If you have the same drive with an 8GB partition and a 4GB partition, you can install Mac OS X only on the first partition.

◆ The Mac OS X installation cannot install to some UFS volumes that were created with Drive Setup 1.9.1 (the version included with some Mac OS 9.0 installations). If you expect to see a UFS volume and don't, you'll need to reformat the volume with the version of Drive Setup on the Mac OS 9.1 or later CD or Drive Utility from the Mac OS X installation CD.

NO VOLUMES ARE VISIBLE IN THE INSTALLER

If you don't see any volumes in the Installer, you will get a warning about not having Mac OS 9 installed, just before the screen where your volumes would appear. The most likely cause of this is that your Open Firmware settings are messed up. (Open Firmware is a low-level set of instructions that the operating system uses for communicating with the Mac's hardware.) Resetting Open Firmware may fix this problem. To reset Open Firmware, take these steps:

1. Restart the computer (press F⌘Option+O+F). When you've done this correctly, you will see a white screen that says Open Firmware.

2. Type **reset-nvram** and press Return.

3. Type **reset-all** and press Return.

The computer should restart. After you hear the startup chime, hold down the C key to get the computer to start up from the CD. If Open Firmware was the problem, you now should see your volumes.

A PARTICULAR DISK DOESN'T APPEAR IN THE INSTALLER

This is most likely due to a configuration problem, according to Apple. If the disk is an ATA drive, it may be set to slave mode, which can be a problem if it's the only ATA disk that's installed. You'll need to open up your Mac and check the jumper settings on the drive to reset it to master mode—see the Apple Knowledge Base article number 106442 (`http://docs.info.apple.com/article.html?artnum=106442`) for details.

Dual-Booting

If you've installed Mac OS 9 and Mac OS X on the same disk, or if you've installed Mac OS X and an earlier Mac OS version on separate volumes, you now have the option of booting into different Mac operating system versions whenever you find it necessary. How you choose a volume depends on the OS you're currently using.

If you're in Mac OS X, you can switch to another OS version by opening the System Preferences application and selecting the Startup Disk pane. Mac OS X scans your volumes for valid System folders. Once they've appeared, select the system you would like to use the next time you restart the Mac. (Note that you need to have an administrator's account or password to change the startup disk.)

After you've selected the startup disk, click the Restart button if you want to restart right away, or close the System Preferences application if you want to change startup disks for the next time you restart. When you restart your Mac (by selecting Restart from the Apple menu), it should start up using the System folder you selected.

If you're in Mac OS 9.1, you can decide to boot into a different OS by opening the Startup Disk control panel, which shows you each disk that is connected to the Mac. You can then click the disclosure triangle next to a disk to see the operating systems that are available for startup on that disk. Select the OS you want to use the next time the Mac is restarted. Then click the Restart button to restart the Mac into the selected OS.

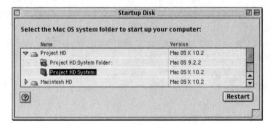

If you're currently using an earlier Mac OS version, its Startup Disk control panel may not recognize Mac OS X partitions. In that case, you have two options:

◆ You can use the Startup Disk control panel in that version to select a Mac OS 9.1 or higher System Folder; then, once you're in Mac OS 9.1 or higher, you can use *its* Startup Disk control panel to restart again in Mac OS X.

◆ You can restart your Mac (Special ➤ Restart) and then hold down the Option key after hearing the startup chime. Next, you should see the startup picker screen. Select the volume you want to use for startup (most likely the volume with a small OS X icon) and then click the right-facing arrow to continue with the startup process.

Either way, your Mac should restart in Mac OS X.

Appendix B

The Classic Mac User's Migration Guide

With Mac OS X seeing regular and increasingly impressive updates, the inevitability of a migration to Mac OS X for most Mac users is a given. If your hardware can support Mac OS X, it's an increasingly good idea to choose to move up to Mac OS X and leave the Classic Mac OS (Mac OS 9 and earlier) behind—or, at the very least, leave it as a secondary option on your dual-boot Mac setup. The Classic Mac OS is certainly good for many things, not the least of which is running applications that have trouble in Mac OS X's Classic environment and troubleshooting certain issues that are more difficult to handle from within Mac OS X. The latest applications and innovations will continue to happen for Mac OS X, so many users will find it important to switch over the next few months and years.

In this appendix, we'll work from the assumption that you're a user who is familiar with the Classic Mac OS and you now find yourself trying to translate that familiarity to Mac OS X. Whether you're moving to Mac OS X of your own free will or you're being "forced" over to Mac OS X in an organizational setting, the move can be unsettling because Mac OS X has both a visual similarity to Mac OS 9 and some stunning differences. We'll explore these similarities and differences in this appendix—we hope you'll find that this quick primer helps you turn those Mac OS 9 skills into an understanding of Mac OS fairly quickly.

NOTE In the Classic Mac OS, most important operating system–level files are stored is the System Folder. In Mac OS X, the folder is just called System, but we'll sometimes refer to it as the System folder—"folder" is lowercase. If you have Mac OS 9 and X installed on the same disk, you'll find both folders on that disk.

In this appendix:

- The Finder and Apple Menu
- Launching, Switching, and Minimizing
- Your Documents and Preferences
- Control Panels versus System Preferences
- The Control Strip versus Menu Bar Icons
- Networking
- Printing
- System Extensions versus Login Items and Kernel Extensions

The Finder and Apple Menu

Mac OS X's Finder is similar to and yet notably different from the Classic Mac OS's Finder. We'll detail the differences in this section.

The Finder Window

Clearly the most important change is the Finder window, which offers the new Columns view. The Classic Mac OS has no analog for the Columns view, although Mac OS X enables you to use two views that are familiar to Classic Mac users—List view (Figure B.1) and Icon view (Figure B.2). To place a window in one of these two views, either click their buttons in a Finder window's toolbar or choose View ➢ As List or View ➢ As Icons.

NOTE   Mac OS X has no View As Buttons option.

Once you've put a Finder window in one of these two views, you'll find that it still behaves differently in that double-clicking a folder in either view causes that folder to open in the same window instead of a new window as it does in the Classic Mac OS. One solution to this problem is to click the Toolbar button in the top-right corner of the window. When the icon toolbar isn't showing, Finder windows act as they do in the Classic Mac OS. When the toolbar is showing, the window acts more like a web browser. You can open a new window by holding down the ⌘ key while double-clicking a folder; hold down the Option key while double-clicking a folder icon, and the previous window will also disappear.

If you'd like the Finder always to open a new folder in a new window, choose Finder ➢ Preferences and turn on the Always Open Folders in a New Window option.

In Mac OS 9, you can choose Edit ➢ Preferences in the Finder and set some options including Simple Finder and Grid-Spacing, which have no counterparts in Mac OS X. However, in Mac OS X you can choose a different size for the icons in an Icons view via the View ➢ Show View Options command.

Mac OS X's Finder includes the spring-loaded folders capability that Mac OS 9 offered—when you hover over a folder icon while dragging another icon, that folder will "spring open" after a moment, enabling you to dig through folders without releasing a dragged item. Like Mac OS 9, this capability can be turned on and off in Finder Preferences in Mac OS X; choose Finder ➢ Preferences and use the check box next to Spring-Loaded Folders and Windows, along with the slider to determine the length of the delay before a folder pops open.

FIGURE B.1

The List view in
Mac OS X

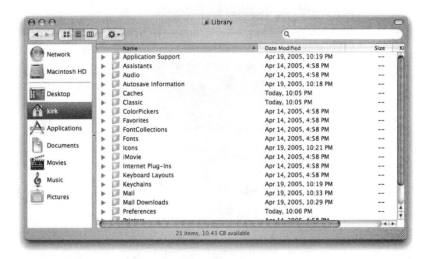

FIGURE B.2

The Icon view in
Mac OS X

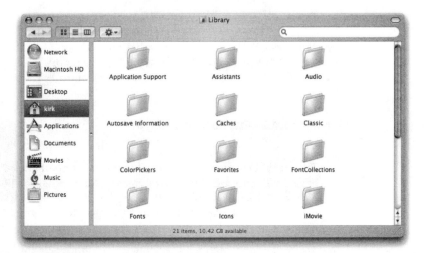

NOTE   In Finder Preferences dialog, on the Advanced tab, there's another option that might seem a
bit odd to you if you're a recent Classic Mac OS convert—the Show All File Extension option. Mac OS
X, unlike the Classic Mac OS, relies more heavily on filename extensions (three or four letters at the
end of a file's name, such as .tif, .html, or .doc) to determine whether a file is a document or an
application. If the file is a document, the Mac OS often uses the extension to determine what type
of document it is and what application created it (or should be used to edit it). See Chapter 4, "Using
Applications," for more on the peculiarities of Mac OS X's new approach to filename extensions.

Where's the Special Menu?

Mac OS X has done away with the Special menu, on the theory that it makes more sense for the Classic Mac's Special commands—particularly Sleep, Restart, and Shut Down—to be on the Apple menu, where they're accessible from any application.

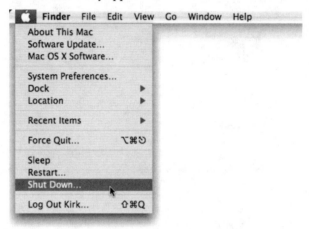

The Burn Disc, Eject, and Move to Trash commands found on many Mac OS 9 Special menus have moved to the File menu in the Mac OS X Finder. The Empty Trash command is found in the Finder menu itself (Finder ➤ Empty Trash). You can also Control+click the Trash to see the Empty Trash command.

Missing File Menu Commands

A number of commands found in the Finder's File menu in Mac OS 9 are missing in Mac OS X:

- The Encrypt command in Mac OS 9 has no counterpart in Mac OS X because Mac OS X doesn't have the file encryption tool that ships with Mac OS 9. If you need desktop encryption, you can look into Disk Utility, discussed in Chapter 26, "Hard Disk Care, File Security, and Maintenance," which enables you to create encrypted disk images. Also, you can encrypt your entire home folder using FileVault, as described in Chapter 5, "Personalizing Mac OS X."

- The Finder in Mac OS X doesn't have the built-in capability to print a window, so the Page Setup command found in Mac OS 9 is lacking in Mac OS X. (You can, however, choose a document in the Finder and select File➤ Print or press ⌘+P to print that document. In most cases, it will be launched first using its associated application.)

- Mac OS X has no Put Away command, which is used in Mac OS 9 to return a recently moved item back to its previous location. Mac OS X adds an Edit ➤ Undo command, but this helps only if you're immediately putting back a file that you mistakenly moved; the Put Away command in Mac OS 9 could be used to return an item to its previous location quite some time after it was originally moved.

◆ In Mac OS X 10.3, the ability to assign a label to folders returned, but the Label command changed somewhat. To give a folder a color label, select the folder in the Finder and then open the File menu. At the bottom of the File menu are the various color labels as colorful dots—select one to assign that label. The label names can be changed by choosing the Labels icon in the Finder Preferences window.

The Desktop

The desktop in Mac OS X isn't radically different from Mac OS 9. Perhaps the most jarring difference is the lack of a Trash icon on the desktop. Trash has moved to the Dock in Mac OS X (where, at least in terms of the whole "desk" metaphor, it does make a little more sense to put the trash.)

In Mac OS X, the desktop need not display all attached disks and hard drives if you'd prefer not to see them. Turning them on and off is an option accessed via Finder ➤ Preferences (click the General icon if it's not selected). Viewing the disk icons is not optional in the Classic Mac OS.

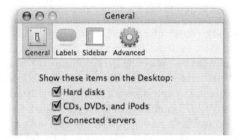

As in Mac OS 9, choosing View Options when the desktop is selected in Mac OS X lets you make choices for managing the icons on the desktop. Unlike the Classic Mac OS, you can change the text size and choose an exact icon size from this preferences dialog. You also can have an icon's label appear either beneath it or on the icon's right side.

The Apple Menu

The Apple menu in Mac OS X isn't completely different from Mac OS 9's, but it's close. No longer a quick-launcher like the Classic Apple menu, Mac OS X's version is for accessing a few system-level commands. You can access System Preferences, change the positioning or behavior of the Dock, choose a location, and select one of four options for changing the state of Mac OS X—Sleep, Shut Down, Restart, or Log Out.

Perhaps the most significant thing that you *can't* do with Mac OS X's Apple menu is this: you can't alter it. Unlike the Classic Apple menu, which has a corresponding Apple Menu Items folder in the System Folder, where aliases and applications can be stored, the Mac OS X Apple menu can't be customized. In fact, the only dynamic menu in the Mac OS X Apple menu is the Recent menu, which replaces the Recent Applications and Recent Documents menus in the Classic Apple menu.

TIP　The Appearance pane of System Preferences is used to determine how many items appear in the Recent menu.

Favorites, while available up until Mac OS X 10.2, are no longer supported by default in Mac OS X 10.3 and higher, so there's no way to add to them. Instead, the Mac OS encourages you to add folders to your Sidebar for quick access, as discussed in Chapter 3, "The Finder." Those items are added to Open and Save dialog boxes as well, much in the same way that Favorites were used.

You may look in the Classic Apple menu for anything else, such as Desk Accessories, Sherlock, Stickies, and Calculator. Many have replacements in Mac OS X 10.4 that are accessible via the Dashboard feature. By default, you access the Dashboard by pressing F12 (see Chapter 4 for more on Dashboard). Other utility applications available via the Classic Apple menu—such as Classic's Remote Access (Internet Connect in Mac OS X)—have new analogs available in Mac OS X and found in the `Applications` or `Utilities` folder.

NOTE   Although Mac OS X includes Sherlock, it is not used for searching your local disks anymore, as it was in the Classic Mac OS. Instead, Mac OS X 10.4 introduced the Spotlight feature, which you access by clicking the small blue magnifying glass in the top-right corner of the operating system. Also, you can use the Search box in any Finder window to quickly locate files.

The Chooser is replaced by the Printer Setup Utility, discussed later in this appendix. The Control Panels menu has been replaced by System Preferences, although the individual panes can't be accessed directly as control panels could be—selecting the Apple menu ➢ System Preferences command simply launches the whole System Preferences application, not an individual pane. In the past, each control panel was separate. (For more, see the section "Control Panels versus System Preferences," later in this chapter.)

Although the Classic Mac OS enables you to create a quick-launch menu by adding a folder of aliases to your `Apple Menu Items` folder, you'll find you can't do that in Mac OS X. However, you can drag folders to the Dock in Mac OS X, where, when you click and hold your mouse button (or Control+click) on that folder icon in the Dock, a menu pops up, giving you quick access to those items (see Figure B.3). It's arguably a little less convenient, but it offers similar functionality.

FIGURE B.3

Similar to using the Apple menu in the Classic Mac OS X, you can add a folder alias to the Dock in Mac OS X for quick access to its contents.

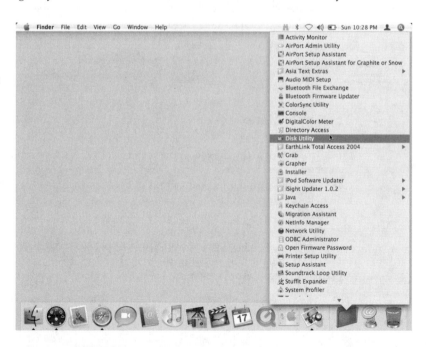

TIP Want to use your Apple menu in more traditional ways? Try a third-party add-on program. FruitMenu (www.unsanity.com), once it's installed, enables you to add menus to the Apple menu by placing aliases in the Fruit Items folder inside your Library folder.

Launching, Switching, and Minimizing

In Mac OS 9, you launch applications from the Finder or by selecting them in the Apple menu or in the Launcher window if you have the Launcher configured. Mac OS X replaces both the Apple menu's and the Launcher's functionality with the Dock. In fact, the Dock is a convenient launcher. What can be a bit more confusing about it, however, is the fact that it doubles as an application *switcher*, as well—a role filled in the Classic Mac OS by the Application menu.

Launching: The Launcher

Mac OS X offers the Dock as a rough equivalent of the Launcher that is available for single-click launches of applications (and documents) in the Classic Mac OS. In some ways they are similar—you can add an item to either the Dock or the Launcher simply by dragging its icon from the Finder and dropping it on the Dock or the Launcher. You can single-click items in each to launch them, or you can drag and drop documents from the Finder onto an icon in either (an icon on the Dock is the equivalent of a button icon in the Launcher). The Launcher, however, could be separated into different sections (or panes), where an entirely new set of icons could be organized and accessed by topic. Mac OS X has no equivalent of Mac OS 9's Launcher.

Also, unlike Mac OS 9, the Dock (although it's easily edited using drag-and-drop) cannot be edited by accessing a system-level folder. By contrast, the Launcher could be altered by adding or removing aliases (and folders) in the Launcher Items folder, found inside the System folder.

TIP A number of third-party Launcher substitutes are available—try Launcher from Brian Hill (http://personalpages.tds.net/~brian_hill/launcher.html).

Switching: The Application Menu

The Application menu in the Classic Mac OS and the Dock in Mac OS X are different paradigms, but they accomplish the same thing—you can switch between active applications by selecting a different application in the Dock, just as you could in the Application menu. You also can press ⌘Tab or ⌘Shift+Tab to cycle through running applications forward and backward, respectively.

TIP For a neat trick, notice that ⌘Tab will switch you back and forth between two different applications when used correctly. For instance, suppose you're working in Word, and you switch to Safari. Simply press ⌘Tab, and you're switched back to Word. Do a little work and press ⌘Tab, and you're switched back to Safari. It's a handy way to move between applications without mousing around.

NOTE Here's something else that seems odd if you're a Classic Mac OS convert: Mac OS X switches to a background application when you click one of its windows, just as in the Classic Mac OS. However, it doesn't bring *all* of that application's windows forward. For instance, if you click one of Internet Explorer's windows in the Classic Mac OS, all IE windows come to the foreground along with IE's menu bar. In Mac OS X, only the window you click will come to the foreground. This isn't the case if you click the application's icon in the Dock or switch to it by pressing ⌘Tab.

The Dock offers one particular advantage over the Application menu in the Classic Mac OS—icons in the Dock offer much easier drag-and-drop targets. Not only can you drag a document to an application icon in the Dock and have both the application and document launch, but you can also drag and drop a document on an *active* application's icon in the Dock and that document will be launched in that already-running application.

NOTE If you've ever "torn off" the Classic Application menu and used the floating palette of application icons for switching or drag-and-drop targets, you should be able to adjust to the Dock fairly quickly.

Just to confuse things a bit further, Mac OS X actually has something called the "application menu"—it's on the left side, instead of the right, and it's not used for application switching, although it does have the same Hide and Show commands that are found in the Classic Application menu. On top of that, Apple has standardized Mac applications in such a way that commands that deal directly with an application from within that application—the Quit and Preferences commands, for instance—are always to be found in the application menu. This makes sense once you get used to it.

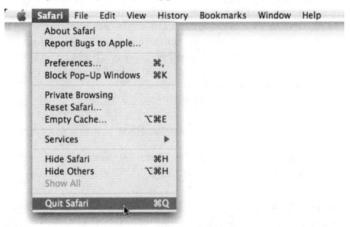

TIP Do you want some of that Classic-style application switcher functionality back? One interesting option is MaxMenus (www.proteron.com/maxmenus/), which doesn't really duplicate the look of the old Application switch menu. However, it can offer you the same ability to quickly switch between applications using a menu command. Plus, it offers much more, including the ability to customize launcher menus and add keystroke commands to your menu items.

Minimizing Windows

In the Classic Mac OS, you don't minimize windows the way you can in Mac OS X—the Classic Mac OS had a feature called Windowshade. When you click the special Windowshade control in a Classic Mac OS window—or, under certain circumstance, when you double-click the title bar of a window—the window portion of the window disappears, leaving only the title bar. While this approach seemed odd to some, others found it convenient because it enabled you to see quickly the contents of a window behind the current window. (Mac OS X offers this feature in its Stickies program, but that's the only place it works other than for Classic applications.)

In Mac OS X, the default behavior when you click the minimize button is to have the window minimize to the Dock. That also gets it out of the way so that you can see background windows, but it requires you to mouse down to the Dock and click the item again in order to expand it back to regular size.

Mac OS X also features Exposé, which can substitute for Windowshade in the sense that it enables you to see windows that are stacked upon one another. By default, you can press F9 to see all open windows minimized on-screen for quick perusal, or you can press F11 to see and access the desktop behind all of your open windows. Get used to Exposé, and you may never really miss Windowshade.

TIP   If you still miss Windowshade, there are third-party solutions. Windowshade X, also available from Unsanity (www.unsanity.com), is ideal if you're a Windowshade aficionado.

Your Documents and Preferences

In the past, the Classic Mac OS generally hasn't had a specific place where documents needed to be stored on your hard disk. Because earlier Mac OS versions were built as single-user systems, there was no structure for multiple users to store documents and preferences. Mac OS X changes that.

The Documents Folder(s)

Mac OS 9 has support for multiple users, but documents and preferences aren't stored in exactly the same way. Even as a single-user system, however, Mac OS 9 creates a Documents folder on the main level of the hard disk, where it's recommended that you store your documents. If you enable Multiple Users in Mac OS 9, the Mac will create a Users folder, and your individual files will be stored inside it.

In Mac OS X, this multiuser approach is *always* the case. You will always have a personal home folder with a Documents folder inside it, where you are encouraged to store your personal documents. You also can place documents in the other folders inside your home folder, including the folders specially designed to work with Personal Web Sharing (Sites) and File Sharing (Public). If you're an Administrative user (or if you're the only user on your Mac), you're free to store documents in a folder other than your personal Documents folder. In fact, if you've installed Mac OS 9 along with Mac OS X, you'll likely find a Documents folder on the root level of your hard disk. You can use that folder, although it is a bit less secure if you use your Mac in a file-sharing or multiuser environment. For convenience, or if you plan to use your Mac with multiple users, however, it's recommended that you stick to saving documents to your home folder and its subfolders.

Preferences

It's good to know where your application's preference files are stored, if only because you'll often find that tossing out an application's preference file is part of a troubleshooting routine for a crashing application. The Preferences folder also is where some applications will put application support files, such as web browser cache files, user information, and other items that the application might want to store or track.

Mac OS 9 and Mac OS X put their application's preference files in slightly different places. In the Classic Mac OS, preference files are stored in the Preferences folder inside the System Folder. Even on a multiuser system, Mac OS 9 will mirror your preference files in the Preferences folder inside the System Folder, so you can still access them in that location.

In Mac OS X, each individual user can have a different set of preferences stored. As a user, that means that you need your own Preferences folder, which is found inside your personal Library folder (such as `~/Library/Preferences/`). Apple encourages authors developing native Mac OS X applications to name their preference files a certain way, which is supposed to make it easier for a user to know what software author created a particular preference file. The files follow the format `com.apple.applicationname.plist`, where the first two parts are the Internet domain name of the company that created the application that created the preference file.

You'll also find subfolders in the `Preferences` folder, where some applications will store multiple files. (For instance, the `Explorer` folder is where Microsoft will store various files that Internet Explorer uses, such as a download cache and a Favorites—bookmarks—file.)

In Mac OS X, applications also have the option of using a folder in your personal `Library` called `Application Support` (`~/Library/Application Support/`), which is meant to give application developers a more specific location for support files that don't really qualify as preference files. Some developers use this folder, and some don't.

Control Panels versus System Preferences

In the Classic Mac OS, configuring system-wide preferences is done via *control panels*, which are individual windows that launch when accessed via the Apple menu ➤ Control Panels command. These control panels offer options for configuring many of the same (or similar) items found in Mac OS X, which are configured using the System Preferences application. In fact, System Preferences can be thought of as a repository for all the control panels (Apple now calls them *panes*) that Mac OS X needs. Even third-party panes are installed in System Preferences. Compost (`http://acutus.ca`), which can be used to manage the Trash more effectively, is shown here.

Individual Control Panels

Wondering what System Preferences pane manages the same functionality that you used to access in control panels? Not all control panels have equivalent panes in System Preferences. Some, such as Remote Access, have applications that perform similar duties in Mac OS X—such as Internet Connect. Others offered functionality in Mac OS 9 that's not available—or is radically different in Mac OS X. Table B.1 gives you a sense of what's where when it comes to configuring the Mac OS.

TABLE B.1: Mac OS 9 Control Panels and Their Mac OS X Counterparts

MAC OS 9 CONTROL PANEL	COUNTERPART IN MAC OS X
Appearance	Appearance and Desktop & Screen Saver panes
Apple Menu Items	None
AppleTalk	AppleTalk tab on the port's screen in the Network pane

TABLE B.1:   Mac OS 9 Control Panels and Their Mac OS X Counterparts *(CONTINUED)*

MAC OS 9 CONTROL PANEL	COUNTERPART IN MAC OS X
ColorSync	ColorSync Utility in the Utilities folder
Control Strip	Menu bar icons (turned on/off throughout System Preference panes and utility applications)
Date & Time	Date & Time pane
DialAssist	None
Easy Access	Universal Access pane
Energy Saver	Energy Saver pane
Extensions Manager	None (Startup Items are found on a tab for each user in the Accounts pane)
File Exchange	None
File Sharing	Sharing pane
General Controls	Appearance pane
Internet	None (.Mac features on the .Mac pane)
Keyboard	Keyboard & Mouse and International panes
Memory	None
Modem	Modem tab in Network pane
Monitors	Displays pane
Mouse	Keyboard & Mouse pane
Multiple Users	Accounts pane
Numbers	International pane
QuickTime Settings	QuickTime pane
Remote Access	Internet Connect application
Software Update	Software Update pane
Sound	Sound pane
Speech	Speech pane
Startup Disk	Startup Disk pane

TABLE B.1:   Mac OS 9 Control Panels and Their Mac OS X Counterparts *(CONTINUED)*

MAC OS 9 CONTROL PANEL	COUNTERPART IN MAC OS X
TCP/IP	TCP/IP tab in Network preferences
Text	International pane
USB Printer Sharing	Sharing pane
Web Sharing	Sharing pane

Overall, Mac OS X doesn't let you tweak the interface quite as much as Mac OS 9 does. You'll find that the functionality of the Appearance control panel in Mac OS 9 really isn't completely duplicated by the Appearance and Desktop & Screen Saver panes in Mac OS X, but what options there are in Mac OS X are found in those two panes. (Earlier Mac OS X versions had a General pane that was basically identical to Appearance.)

Probably the biggest difference between the two OSs in terms of configuration—aside from the System Preferences interface itself—is the lumping together of networking technologies (AppleTalk, TCP/IP, and Modem control panels) into the single Network pane in Mac OS X. Also, connecting to the Internet (for network types that need to request a connection explicitly, such as modem and PPPoE connections) is now out of the bailiwick of a control panel and is handled by the Internet Connect application. (AirPort connections and some remote network connections are also handled by the Internet Connect application.)

In general, though, Classic Mac users should transition fairly quickly to the System Preferences application, which offers the advantages of a central location for nearly all system-wide settings.

NOTE   Another significant difference, of course, is the fact that some System Preferences items can only be accessed if you authenticate yourself using an administrator's password. (The Classic Mac OS doesn't require a password for any settings unless Multiple Users is turned on in Mac OS 9.) See Chapter 9, "Being the Administrator: Permissions, Settings, and Adding Users," for more on administrator accounts.

Accessing Individual Preference Panes

We mentioned earlier in this appendix that you don't access System Preference panes individually in the Apple menu as you do the Control Panel menu. That's true. However, it doesn't mean you can't access individual preference panes. Because they're stored in the PreferencePanes folder inside the Library folder that's inside the main System folder (/System/Library/PreferencePanes/), you can access the panes individually by simply dragging that folder to the Dock. Then, click and hold the mouse on the folder's Dock icon (or Control+click the folder icon), and you'll be able to access a list of every preference pane that's installed (see Figure B.4).

FIGURE B.4

Here's how you can access preference panes in a manner that's somewhat similar to the Control Panel menu in the Classic Mac OS

The Control Strip versus Menu Bar Icons

Mac OS 9 features the Control Strip, an innovative, optional little doohickey for quickly accessing a number of settings such as system volume, Internet access, and so on. In Mac OS X, there isn't a feature that supports as many little control items as the Control Strip can handle in Mac OS 9, but turning on or installing *menu bar icons* can have a similar effect on the Control Strip. The icons can be turned on in a number of panes within System Preferences. Third-party menu bar icons can be installed as well. (See Chapter 2, "The Fundamentals of Mac OS X," and Chapter 5 for more on menu bar icons.)

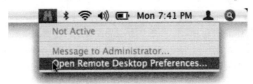

Networking

Mac OS X has a very different networking infrastructure—one that in many ways is more advanced than networking in the Classic Mac OS. Some of the differences were mentioned in the previous section—instead of the TCP/IP, AppleTalk, and Modem control panels, Mac OS X puts all of those controls in the Network pane of System Preferences. Likewise, Web Sharing and File Sharing control panels' functionality is found in the Sharing pane of System Preferences, and Mac OS X adds to those capabilities a number of other networking services, such as remote access, FTP serving, Windows file sharing, and more.

Technologically, one of the more significant differences is the fact that you can have TCP/IP active on more than one port at once. That's part of the reason for the switch to a Network pane from all of those control panels—in the Classic Mac OS, you focused on the protocol when configuring a Mac for network access because each protocol could be active over only one port at a time. Under those circumstances, it makes sense to open the TCP/IP control panel—for instance, when you want to change from a modem-based connection to an Ethernet-based connection.

In Mac OS X, multiple ports can use TCP/IP as their protocol at the same time. (AppleTalk is still limited to one port per computer.) You use the Network pane to configure TCP/IP for each individual networking port, as well as to turn on and off or prioritize ports, and thus the Mac knows which port to try first when it needs to communicate via TCP/IP. (See Chapters 10, "Configuring Internet Access," and 18, "Building a Network and Sharing Files," for more on networking in Mac OS X.)

Another significant difference is the fact that Mac OS X does not support remote AppleTalk connections as the Classic Mac OS does. (For instance, in Mac OS 9, you can use the Remote Access control panel to dial your modem, connect to another Mac that's set up to receive incoming calls, and create a remote AppleTalk connection.) Instead, Mac OS X relies on TCP/IP for remote connections over the Internet and then enables you to use file sharing over an IP connection to share files between Macs.

NOTE   Need a direct-dialed remote access solution? One option is Timbuktu, from Netopia (www.netopia.com/software/products/tb2/mac/index.html). It's discussed in more detail in Chapter 20, "Mac OS X and Other Platforms." You can also dial into some AirPort Base Stations and access your network that way.

The fact that Mac OS X uses the Internet Connect application for dialing your modem may take a little getting used to, particularly if you're a fan of the Remote Access control panel. Internet Connect also can be used for PPPoE connections (common for a DSL-based broadband connection), which can be a real boon for Mac OS 9 users, who generally have to use a third-party PPPoE dialer to achieve such a connection.

Finally, connecting to remote servers (including other Macs running Personal File Sharing) is a little different in Mac OS X than it is in Mac OS 9. Instead of using the Network Browser or the Chooser, you use the Network icon in a Finder window in Mac OS X (see Figure B.5) and the Go ➤ Connect to Server menu command for accessing servers via URL. The Connect to Server window (see Figure B.6) has an Address box where you can type a URL to connect directly to a server, if it's available. (In Network Browser, you use the Shortcuts menu to select the entry Connect to Server, and then you can enter a URL. Also, you can enter a URL directly in the Chooser if you've selected the AppleShare icon.)

FIGURE B.5
The Network icon makes connected servers appear directly in the Finder in Mac OS X.

FIGURE B.6
The Connect to Server window replaces Remote Access and the Chooser.

Printing

Mac OS X's controls for printing are completely different, with the Chooser in the Classic Mac OS replaced by the Printer Setup Utility, which, unlike the Chooser, is an application. (It's also buried in the `Utilities` folder inside the main `Applications` folder on your Mac.) The Printer Setup Utility takes a slightly different approach—whereas the Chooser asks you to select a driver for a printer before the printer is located, the Printer Setup Utility asks you to choose the method by which the printer is connected to the Mac (AppleTalk, TCP/IP, USB, and so on). Then the printer is detected, and you choose a driver for it (see Chapter 7, "Printing and Faxing in Mac OS X").

Once your printer is connected, detected, and configured, the Printer Proxy (an icon that shows that printer's queue) will pop up in the Dock—a task that's done by the PrintMonitor in the Classic Mac OS. The Printer Proxy icon in the Dock also does something that the Desktop Printer icon in the Classic Mac OS doesn't do—it uses an animated icon to show you the current page number of the document that's being printed.

In both Mac OS X and the Classic Mac OS, you can have a Desktop Printer—an icon that sits on your desktop and gives you quick access to a print queue window for your printer. The print queue window enables you to stop and start the printer's queue as well as manage and delete individual print jobs (see Figure B.7).

FIGURE B.7

A printer queue in Mac OS X works much like its Desktop Printer counterpart in the Classic Mac OS.

System Extensions versus Login Items and Kernel Extensions

Perhaps no one topic makes it more clear that Mac OS X and the Classic Mac are fundamentally different operating systems than the issue of *extensions*. In the Classic Mac OS, extensions are an incredibly important component of the operating system, which relies on those extensions for many of its capabilities, ranging from networking and Internet access to printing, scripting support, and even the look and feel of the operating system. In Mac OS X, by contrast, most everything is a part of the overall operating system, not an "extension" to it, and the operating system itself really isn't extensible in the same way.

NOTE   Of course, Classic extensions are still a part of life for some Mac OS X users—those using the Classic environment for older applications. See Chapter 27, "Fixing Applications and Managing Classic," for details on managing Classic's extensions.

Kernel Extensions

What Mac OS X calls an *extension* is really a driver—only one type among many of the types of extensions that the Classic Mac OS would use. Furthermore, those drivers are of a special type. They're kernel extensions, which patch or extend the low-level kernel that Mac OS X uses to communicate between the operating system and hardware. You'll find that you need relatively few kernel extensions. (You'll also find that they need to be written well or they can really mess up the stability of your Mac.)

Kernel extensions in Mac OS X are stored in the /System/Library/Extensions folder (the files have a .kext filename extension) and must be installed by the Package Installer after it's been authenticated by an Admin user. Then, you'll generally need to restart the Mac before the kernel extension is put to use. Unlike the Classic Mac OS, you won't select different groupings of extensions for different purposes—to take up less RAM for gaming, for instance. Likewise, Mac OS X doesn't have an Extensions Manager application for its extensions.

These extensions can cause trouble—just as can Classic extensions. If they give you trouble, however, they can be disabled by holding down the Shift key as you start up. If necessary, they can be removed. (See Chapters 25, "Peripherals, Internal Upgrades, and Disks," and 29, "Typical Problems and Solutions," for more details on kernel extensions.)

Login Items versus Startup Items

In the Classic Mac OS, you can specify Startup Items (usually applications, documents, or server connections that you want to launch every time your Mac restarts) by placing them in the Startup Items folder found inside the Classic Mac OS's System Folder. In Mac OS X, you have a similar option—you can specify items that launch automatically right after you log in to your user account. These items are configured in the Accounts pane in System Preferences by selecting your account name and then the Login Items tab.

Is a Startup or Login Item giving you trouble? These items can be bypassed in the same way—in the Classic Mac you hold down the Shift key right before the Finder launches (and immediately after the extensions icons disappear from the startup screen) and keep holding it until the desktop appears and is active. In Mac OS X, you hold down the Shift key immediately after you log in to your account. (If your Mac logs in automatically, you hold down the Shift key beginning immediately after the Mac OS X startup screen disappears.) You keep holding it down until the desktop appears—the Login Items are disabled.

In this appendix, you learned some of the differences between the Classic Mac OS and Mac OS X, including how to work around some of the oddities in each OS's user interface, preferences, networking, and other system-level components.

Mac OS X Applications

Throughout this book, we've looked closely at many of the applications and utilities included with Mac OS X. While many of these programs are designed to help you with particular tasks covered in other parts of this book, Mac OS X also includes a number of other programs, many of which have limited scope or only perform simple tasks. These include utilities for checking up on your Mac, tools for working with notes and numbers, and features that are of limited use, such as handwriting recognition.

In this appendix:

◆ System Profiler

◆ TextEdit: Read, Create, and Edit Text Documents

◆ Accessories and Extras

◆ Stickies

◆ Preview

◆ Handwriting Recognition

System Profiler

System Profiler is a utility designed to tell you some important, low-level statistics about your Mac, including the processor and memory installed in your Mac, the peripheral devices that are attached, and the applications that are installed. You'll find that System Profiler is a useful utility to access when you want to know something in particular about your Mac.

System Profiler is located in the Utilities folder inside the Applications folder. Double-click it in a Finder window to launch the application. Once it's launched, you'll see the System Profiler window, as shown in Figure C.1.

System Profiler has a familiar layout, with the left pane showing categories of information you can select and the right pane displaying information about your selection. Click one of the following items in the Contents list to view its information:

Hardware   The Hardware section contains subheadings that tell you about your Mac and its processor. You'll find low-level information about the Mac, such as the internal ROM (read-only memory) chip version number and other important information. You'll also find out about the rest of your hardware, such as USB, PCI, SCSI, ATA, FireWire, BlueTooth, and other system buses or ports that connect devices to your Mac, both internally and externally.

FIGURE C.1

The System Profiler window

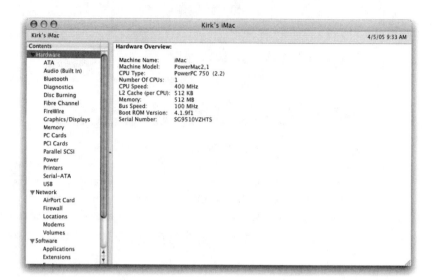

Network   The Network section gives you information about any network ports this Mac has. It shows your IP address, your subnet mask, and your Ethernet address. It also provides information about your AirPort card (if you have one), your firewall (if you use the built-in firewall), locations, modems, and volumes.

Software   In this section, you'll find a Software Overview showing information about Mac OS X and the startup disk, and a listing of applications that the Apple System Profiler finds on all attached and mounted storage volumes. You can click any application's name to see information about that application in the pane at the bottom of the window.

The Extensions subsection shows the kernel extensions (mainly device drivers) that are installed. The Frameworks subsection (only visible if you select View ➤ Extended Report) shows some of the low-level system components that are installed on your Mac, including the name and version number. The Logs subsection lets you view system logs, and the Preference Panes and Startup Items subsections list these items.

The Apple System Profiler has one other significant capability: It can generate a report (for viewing or printing) that includes this information. Select File ➤ Print, and a report is generated; set up your printer and click Print to send the report to your printer. You may, however, not want to print out all this information; to change the level of detail this program presents, select the View menu and choose Mini Profile, Basic Profile, or Full Profile (the default). You'll be able to see if the shorter profiles are sufficient for your needs.

You also can save the report and e-mail it as an attachment, which might be requested if you ever call a customer support hotline to discuss problems with your Mac or its software. Just choose File ➤ Save, and, in the Save dialog sheet, you can choose from different file formats—Apple System Profiler 4.0 (XML) format, Rich Text, or Plain Text. (Plain Text is probably best for sending to others.) Then click Save in the dialog sheet. After you've e-mailed the report to the technical service representative, the rep will know more about your Mac and what's installed on it, perhaps offering better solutions to your problems.

NOTE   Command-line mavens may find it useful to know that there is a command that you can use in Terminal to generate the same type of report: `system_profiler`. This command offers the same options: it can display a report in Terminal, save it in XML format, and offers three different levels of detail.

TextEdit: Read, Create, and Edit Text Documents

TextEdit is Mac OS X's text editor, but it's much more than that. It's both a plain-text and a Rich Text editor, meaning it can be used for a variety of functions ranging from basic text editing—editing configuration files, HTML (Hypertext Markup Language) documents, and other plain-text documents— all the way up to basic word processing functions. In addition, TextEdit can read and write Word (`.doc`) documents. Apple has been adding new features and functions to TextEdit with each version of Mac OS X, and Tiger sees the addition of tables and lists, multiple, vertical, and non-contiguous selections, clickable hyperlinks, and page breaks. TextEdit is not a full-featured word processor, but some users will find its features sufficient for many of their documents.

NOTE   Do you really need a word processor? If you work in a collaborative environment, you probably do. Or if you need complex formatting features, columns, automatic tables of contents, and other layout features, you won't be able to do without a word processor such as Microsoft Word or Apple's Pages (part of the iWork suite). However, many people write simple documents and don't need any fancy frills. TextEdit is fast and easy to use, and it could do the job for you. Kirk likes to use text editors whenever possible, and has two personal favorites. BBEdit (`www.barebones.com`) is the granddaddy of text editors for the Mac. It is the most powerful text editor out there, with syntax coloring, built-in shell worksheets, FTP browsers, and hundreds of other features. (The free TextWrangler, also by Bare Bones, has a simpler subset of these features.) Smultron (`http://smultron.sourceforge.net`) is an astounding "little" text editor. This free open-source program has a unique interface, syntax coloring, excellent management of multiple documents in a project, a great find function, and more. If all you need is text, any of these editors will meet your needs. If you need basic formatting, TextEdit goes the extra distance. In any case, you might be able to do without that complex word processor.

To launch TextEdit, you can either double-click a plain-text or Rich Text document or double-click the TextEdit icon in the main `Applications` folder.

Most of the time, Rich Text documents have an `.rtf` filename extension, and plain-text documents have either no filename extension or a `.txt` filename extension. If you double-click a Rich Text document, you'll be able to view and edit it in Rich Text; if you double-click a plain-text document, you can view and edit that document in plain-text mode.

Creating a Rich Text Document

If you launch TextEdit from its application icon, it opens a blank window that by default enables you to create a Rich Text document. Type in the window, remembering that you don't need to press Return at the end of each line—press it only at the end of a paragraph. As you're typing, you can use the Format ➤ Font menu to change the look of your fonts (including the Format ➤ Font ➤ Show Fonts command to launch the Font panel). Figure C.2 shows a Rich Text document in progress.

FIGURE C.2
Creating a Rich Text document

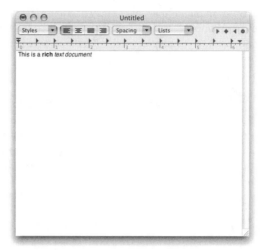

TIP   You can drag and drop images into TextEdit documents from Finder windows or from some other open document windows. When you drag the image to the TextEdit window, the mouse pointer adds a small plus (+) sign. Point to place the image and release the mouse button—the image is added *inline*, meaning text won't wrap around it.

When you're editing a Rich Text document, you're free to change font sizes, font faces, and other settings at any point, including within a single sentence. You can also use the Format ➢ Text submenu of commands to align paragraphs of text:

Format ➢ Text ➢ Align Left   Aligns all text at the left margin of the page.

Format ➢ Text ➢ Center   Centers text on the page.

Format ➢ Text ➢ Align Right   Aligns all text at the right margin of the page.

Format ➢ Text ➢ Justify   Aligns text on both sides, so that there are no jagged left or right edges. This makes the page look similar to a newspaper column.

TextEdit also includes the Format ➢ Text ➢ Show Ruler command, which displays a ruler in the top of the document window. (When you create a new document, the ruler is shown by default.) This ruler can be used to set tab positions, change alignment, and change the spacing between individual lines of text. The commands Format ➢ Text ➢ Copy Ruler and Format ➢ Text ➢ Paste Ruler can be used to copy and paste ruler settings between different documents.

In a Rich Text document, you can also choose Format ➢ Allow Hyphenation, which enables Text-Edit to hyphenate larger words at the ends of lines of text to keep the page from becoming unbalanced by large gaps at the right margin. (If you have your paragraphs justified, it's particularly important to turn on hyphenation to prevent TextEdit from stretching the spaces between words on some lines of text.)

TextEdit also offers the Format ➢ Wrap to Page option, which causes the document to be viewed as if it were on the printed page. When selected, this option changes to Format ➢ Wrap to Window, which is the default behavior. The wrap to page approach is best when you're creating documents that you plan to print.

When you save a Rich Text document, you need to save it as either an RTF (Rich Text Format) file or as RTFD (RTF that supports graphics). You don't have to do anything special to do that; simply choose File ➢ Save or File ➢ Save As and give your document a name in the Save As entry box. It will be saved with the filename extension .rtf if the document contains only text or .rtfd if the document includes images.

TextEdit also allows you to format text in tables and lists. The Format ➢ Text submenu lets you choose table and list formatting; this is also where you can choose to add hyperlinks to your documents. To add a table to a document, select Format ➢ Text ➢ Table and then choose the formatting options for your table. The Table inspector lets you select the size of the table in rows and column, the alignment, the borders, and the cell background.

To apply list formatting, select the lines of text you want to use as a list and then click the Lists menu in the TextEdit toolbar. You can choose from bulleted lists, numbered lists, and several other formats, including capital letters, lowercase letters, Roman numerals, and more.

To set a hyperlink, select the text you want to display for the link, then select Format ➢ Text ➢ Link. Enter the URL for the link and then click OK. You'll see that the link is in blue text and underlined; you can click this link in the TextEdit document to go to the web page it points to.

USING TEXTEDIT WITH WORD DOCUMENTS

TextEdit can read Word (.doc) files and save files in Word format. You can open any Word file in TextEdit, either from the Open menu item or by dragging the document on the TextEdit icon. However, you won't be able to see everything in TextEdit that you can see in Word documents. You'll lose graphics, tables, and any advanced formatting features, but you will at least be able to read the text.

To save a TextEdit file as a Word document, you must start from a Rich Text document. Choose File ➢ Save or File ➢ Save As, give your document a name in the Save As entry box, and then select Word Format in the File Format pop-up menu. Any formatting you apply in TextEdit will be visible in Word if you save documents this way.

If your document contains graphics, you won't be able to save it as a Word document; TextEdit offers no choices when saving such documents and saves them in RTFD format.

Creating a Plain-Text Document

When you're working with plain-text documents, you have fewer options than with Rich Text. You can't add images, for instance, and you don't have as much freedom with fonts and alignment. (You can select a font, but all text in a document must be the same font and size, and you can't change the alignment or line spacing of text.)

NOTE "Plain text" is how you'll often see text files referred to within Mac OS X. Plain text is also commonly known as ASCII text because it refers to a set of characters laid out in the American Standard Code for Information Interchange. ASCII documents, unlike any other type, are generally readable by any computer, even if the computer runs a command-line MS-DOS or Unix operating system without the capability of displaying Rich Text or other graphical documents.

Still, it's important to be able to work with plain-text documents, because these documents are the heart of a number of machine-readable technologies. For instance, many configuration and preferences files, such as those found in your personal `Library` folder in your home folder, are plain-text files and must be maintained as plain text in order for the Mac to be able to read and use them. Likewise, files such as HTML documents—those readable by web browsers—must be saved as plain text via TextEdit. If you inadvertently save such a document as Rich Text, it will be useless as a configuration file or HTML document.

By default, new documents in TextEdit are Rich Text documents. You can change that by selecting Format ➢ Make Plain Text or by pressing Shift+⌘T on your keyboard. This causes the document to switch to plain-text mode; certain formatting options will be disabled in TextEdit, and when you save the document, it will be saved as plain text. In fact, you can use the Format ➢ Make Plain Text command even if you've already begun editing in Rich Text mode. Figure C.3 shows the document that was created for Figure C.2, switched to plain-text format.

FIGURE C.3

A plain-text document

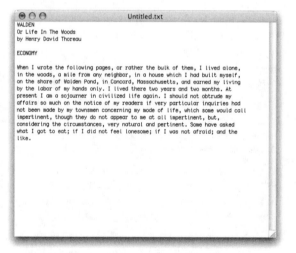

NOTE   In Figure C.3, the document appears in an Untitled window. Whenever you switch from plain-text format to Rich Text format (or vice versa), TextEdit will place the altered document in an Untitled window so that you can save the document in its new format. A plain-text document can't be saved with an `.rtf` filename extension, because it will be confused by applications as a Rich Text document.

Most of the time, when you work with configuration files and other plain-text documents, you'll find it useful to set the document so that it wraps to the window (Format ➤ Wrap to Window) and so that there is no hyphenation (Format ➤ Do Not Allow Hyphenation).

NOTE   If you don't see these commands (if you instead see Format ➤ Wrap to Page and Format ➤ Allow Hyphenation), it means they're already set correctly.

When you save a plain-text document, TextEdit doesn't forcibly append `.txt` to the document's name (it will recommend it in the Save dialog sheet), although this is generally a good idea. Even Mac OS X applications will react better if the `.txt` extension is part of a plain-text document's name. If the document is something other than a plain-text file (a configuration file or an HTML document), give it an appropriate filename extension so that it's recognized. For instance, an HTML document should have the filename extension `.htm` or `.html`, Mac OS X preference files often have the extension `.plist`, and many configuration files have no filename extension.

Accessories and Extras

Mac OS X ships with a number of other, smaller applications and utilities that generally perform a single function or otherwise aren't as complicated as those discussed earlier in this appendix. Mac OS X doesn't really have a formal name for them, but "accessory applications" will do fine; these are bonus applications that can be used to customize your Mac or otherwise make the time spent with your Mac more useful.

In this section, we'll look briefly at some of these applications to give you a sense of what they are and what they're capable of. Some of them are pretty self-explanatory, but if you've gone spelunking in your `Applications` folder (and in the `Utilities` folder inside your `Applications` folder) and wonder what everything is (or where else in the book to find information on it), check out the quick descriptions in this section.

Activity Monitor

Located in the `Utilities` folder inside your `Applications` folder, Activity Monitor is a graphical tool that lets you see what programs are running on your Mac. You'll notice, if you look at its display, that there are many programs that you didn't launch; this is normal. Mac OS X runs many background processes, sometimes called *daemons*, for a number of its tasks and services.

You'll probably never need to use Activity Monitor unless you're troubleshooting a system problem. One way it's useful is to see the % CPU column. This shows what percentage of CPU or processor time each program or process is using. If you find that your Mac starts running slowly, check Activity Monitor to see if there's a particular program that is hogging the processor. If so, and that program is not doing much work, there may be a problem with the program in question.

You saw in Chapter 27, "Fixing Applications and Managing Classic," how you can force-quit a program that you're running. With Activity Monitor, however, you can also force-quit other users' programs if several user sessions are active with Fast User Switching. Select Other User Processes from the Show menu and then select the program you need to quit. Click the Quit Process button in the toolbar; you'll be asked for your administrator's password. Enter this password and click OK to quit the program. Bear in mind that the other user's program may have open files, and by force-quitting they may lose unsaved data.

Calculator

Mac OS X comes with a Calculator accessory application in the main `Applications` folder (see Figure C.4) that can be used for both basic arithmetic and more complex scientific calculations. By default, Calculator is found in the main `Applications` folder.

FIGURE C.4
To access the more complicated features, select View ➤ Scientific.

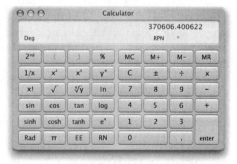

In addition to advanced scientific functions, the View menu lets you select Programmer, which provides conversions between decimal, hexadecimal, and octal numbers, lets you find Unicode character equivalents, and more. If you select View ➤ RPN, you can use the calculator as a reverse Polish notation calculator; those familiar with this way of calculating will know what to do.

The Calculator application is designed to work well with the number pad on an extended Mac keyboard, with all functions mapping exactly to the keypad.

TIP   Late-model PowerBooks and iBooks offer numeric keypad capabilities when you press the Fn key while pressing keys on the right side of the keyboard that represent the numeric keypad (look at the small numbers on the U, I, and O keys, for instance). If you don't press the Fn key, you'll end up typing letters and punctuation.

The Calculator can add, subtract, multiply, and divide in the basic mode, or it can perform scientific functions in the Advanced mode. Select View ➤ Show Paper Tape to see a separate window appear showing recent calculations. To clear the display, click the C button or press Clear on your Mac's numeric keypad.

You can also use Calculator to convert a wide range of values. Select Area, Speed, Weight, or another type of value from the Convert menu and then select the units you want to convert from and to.

Since Mac OS X now includes a simple calculator as a Dashboard widget (see Chapter 4, "Using Applications,"), you may not need to use Calculator for basic math; there's also a unit conversion widget, so you may not bother using Calculator for that either. However, Calculator's scientific and programmer modes are very powerful, and they provide the features of the most expensive portable calculators on your Mac.

NOTE   If you need to do graphs with your calculations, Apple provides Grapher in the Utilities folder. This is a high-powered graphic calculator, with a breathtaking 3D display.

Chess

Just as the name suggests, Chess is Mac OS X's version of the classic board game. (Actually, it's a *port*—a reprogramming and recompilation—of the GNU Chess application, which is an open-source application that can run on a variety of Unix and Unix-like operating systems.) Double-click the Chess application in the `Applications` folder to begin playing by moving your pieces on the board. You can begin a new game by choosing Game ➤ New Game. If you don't finish playing, you can save a game by choosing Game ➤ Save Game—in the Save dialog box, choose a folder for the game, give it a name, and then click Save. Later, you can open it using Game ➤ Open Game.

NOTE Kirk would like to see a go game, in addition to chess. Go, also known by its Chinese name wei-qi or its Korean name baduk, is a very old board game played with black and white stones. Unlike chess, where the goal is to kill the king, you win a go game by surrounding the most territory with your stones. Unfortunately, go is so complex that it's impossible to create software of any quality; unlike chess, which involves brute-force searches and databases, go is almost infinite in its possibilities. You can, however, play go over the Internet for free. One place to check out the game is KGS (the Kiseido Go Server; `http://kgs.kiseido.com`). You can download a Java client that works perfectly with Mac OS X and play against people around the world.

In the Moves menu, you'll find my favorite command—Moves ➤ Show Hint. It will give you a suggestion for your next move by highlighting a piece on the board and then highlighting the square to which you should move the piece. Other commands in the Moves menu let you see the most recent move and take back your most recent move (using ⌘Z, which is commonly the keyboard shortcut for Undo commands).

Chess also has voice commands enabled by default, using Mac OS X's Speech Recognition technology. In my experience, it doesn't work terribly well, but it's something to play with. See Chapter 14, "Audio, iTunes, and the iPod," for more detail on Speech Recognition, including more on Chess's implementation of the technology.

TIP Choose Chess ➤ Preferences to see the Preferences dialog box, where you can turn off Speech Recognition or choose how you'd like to play in the Game menu. (This is discussed more in Chapter 14 in the section "Working with Speech.") You can also choose how difficult you'd like the game play to be using the Level slider.

ColorSync Utility

The ColorSync program, located in the `Utilities` subfolder of the `Applications` folder, is designed to perform recovery operations on a corrupt ColorSync document, as well as to view information about ColorSync profiles and devices that are being managed on your Mac. See Chapter 8, "PDFs, Fonts, and Color," for information about ColorSync.

Console

Another program in the `Utilities` subfolder, Console, is designed to access certain log files that are generated by Mac OS X—specifically, by its Unix layer. Console can be used for troubleshooting and for checking logs generated by Mac OS X's built-in web server and other programs, as well as the Mac OS X system. See Chapter 22, "Terminal and the Command Line," and Chapter 28, "Solving System-Level Problems," for details on Console.

Grab

Grab is an application that enables you to take a picture of your Mac's desktop—a *screen shot*—and save the screen shot as an image file. Grab is covered in detail in Chapter 15, "Working with Digital Images."

NOTE   In Mac OS X version 10.2 and 10.3, Apple used the PDF format for screen shots. In Tiger, Apple has changed this to the PNG format.

Image Capture

This sample application works with certain models of still digital cameras and scanners to download images from these devices to your Mac via a USB connection. It also features the capability to process those images automatically as they're downloaded if you turn on the Automatic Task feature and select a task from the pop-up menu. If you have a compatible digital camera, see Chapter 15 for details on using Image Capture, along with other included applications such as iPhoto.

Keyboard Viewer

Keyboard Viewer is something of a one-trick pony—it's a small tool designed to help you determine what combination of keystrokes is necessary to cause a particular character to appear on-screen. Keyboard Viewer can be used to view most of the nonstandard characters available in any of the fonts on your Mac.

Keyboard Viewer is not an independent application; you need to tweak your preferences to be able to access it. To provide access to Keyboard Viewer, open the System Preferences, click the International pane, and click the Input Menu tab. You'll see a list of keyboards and palettes with check boxes next to them. Check Keyboard Viewer—and, while you're at it, check Character Palette—and then quit the preferences.

These settings display a menu extra in your menu bar—it's a small icon showing a flag for your default keyboard (or a combination of letters for some keyboards, such as Dvorak.) Click this icon, and you can select Keyboard Viewer.

Once the application is launched, you'll see the main Keyboard Viewer window; it's simply a miniature version of your Mac's keyboard. Every time you press a key, that key's representation in the Keyboard Viewer window is highlighted at that same moment.

Keyboard Viewer is useful for finding where nonstandard characters are located. When you press one or more of the modifier keys on your keyboard—Control, Option, Shift, or ⌘ (Command)—you'll see that the Keyboard Viewer window changes to show you what characters are available when you're pressing these modifier keys. In the next example, the Option key is held down. (Note that the image will be slightly different if you're using a PowerBook or an iBook.)

You may notice that some of the keys are outlined; on Keyboard Viewer, these keys show in orange. They are a special type of keys called *dead keys*. These keys add diacritics (accents, tildes, macrons, etc.) to other characters. You press a dead key combination first, and then you type a character that can be modified by that particular combination. For instance, in most fonts you can enter Option+N to create a tilde and then type the character *n* on its own. The result: ñ.

Keyboard Viewer not only shows you what's possible when you're pressing modifier keys, it also shows what's possible within each of the different fonts installed on your Mac. Keyboard Viewer lets you choose which font you want to display on its keys by selecting from any of the fonts installed on your computer; click the Font pop-up menu, select a font, and for fonts with multiple styles, select a style. Select any font from the Font menu, and you'll see Keyboard Viewer change slightly so that it represents that font. When you press the modifier keys, you'll see the extra characters that are available from within that font.

You can use what you've learned from Keyboard Viewer (for instance, that pressing Shift+ Option+K when the font Lucida Grande Regular, or certain other fonts, is active results in a small Apple logo) as you're typing in other applications. If you want to just enter one or two characters in a document, your best bet is to use the Character Palette (which I suggest you check in the International preferences), which was described in Chapter 4. But if you often need to use accented characters, Keyboard Viewer will help you figure out which key combinations to use so you can type them more quickly.

Stickies

If you've used an earlier Mac OS version, you're probably familiar with Stickies, an application that enables you to type quick notes into "sticky note" windows. You can leave these notes displayed on your screen to help you remember things or to keep track of small blocks of text (see Figure C.5).

FIGURE C.5
The Stickies application lets you jot down quick notes and leave them on-screen.

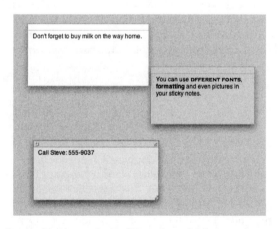

Once you've launched Stickies (located in the main `Applications` folder), you can use the File ➢ New Note command to create a new note on the screen. Then drag the resize control in the bottom-right corner of the note window to change its size. You can customize the color of the note by selecting a color from the Color menu. As you type, you can also use standard font controls to change the look and feel of the fonts in your note.

TIP Highlight some text that's formatted in a way that pleases you and then choose Note ➤ Use As Default from the Stickies menu bar. All new notes will have the same font settings when you begin typing them.

You can add an image to your note by dragging and dropping the image file onto an open note window.

To save changes in all your notes, select File ➤ Save All.

When you close a sticky note (by choosing File ➤ Close or by clicking the note's Close box), you're really deleting it. Stickies will display an alert box that asks if you'd like to save the note. If you click Save, you'll see the Export dialog box, where you can enter a name, select a folder, and choose the format for the saved version (plain text, Rich Text format, or RTFD, which is Rich Text that can include images). Once you've made your choice, click Save.

You don't have to close sticky notes to get them out of the way—Stickies offers a special way of dealing with overlapping notes. Double-click any note's title bar and something interesting happens: the note collapses to show only the title bar. This is familiar to users of previous Mac OS versions, which offered *window shade* controls instead of Mac OS X's minimize-to-Dock feature. Stickies holds onto that window shade feature and augments it by using the first line of your note as the title that appears in the collapsed note's title bar, as shown here:

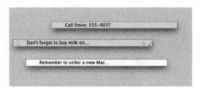

To reveal a note, just double-click the title bar.

Stickies offers some other standard text application features, such as an Edit ➤ Spelling ➤ Check Spelling command. Also note that Stickies offers you the capability to print the frontmost note (File ➤ Print Active Note) or all notes (File ➤ Print All Notes). When you choose Print All Notes, notes are printed so that they fill an entire piece of paper instead of printing to separate pages.

TIP If you still happen to have sticky notes from pre–OS X versions of Mac OS, you can import them into the latest version of Stickies. Choose File ➤ Import Classic Stickies and then locate the Classic Stickies document file (called Stickies File) in the Open dialog box. By default, Mac OS 9 stores Stickies files in the Preferences folder inside the System folder.

Handwriting Recognition

Mac OS X includes Inkwell, an OS-level technology for handwriting recognition. Inkwell enables you to use a graphics tablet and pen to write input (a regular mouse will not work), which is then translated into computer text. Using Inkwell, either you can write directly in applications or you can write first on the InkPad window, have it translated to text, and paste it into other documents.

Although Inkwell certainly is sophisticated technology, it doesn't appear to be as sophisticated as handwriting recognition can be—it appears to have trouble with cursive writing, for instance, something that Apple's previous handwriting technology, designed for the Newton handheld computer, was capable of recognizing.

Handwriting technology is handy, so to speak; whether its inclusion in Mac OS X portends some future development (a tablet-based Mac or a move to some form of personal digital assistant) is speculation. It's in the operating system, and you can work with it now if you have a graphics tablet.

NOTE   A *graphics tablet* is an input device that responds to the pressure of a pen-like instrument as you write or draw on the surface of the pad. Popular Mac OS X–compatible graphics pads are made by Wacom Technology (www.wacom.com). Note that you may need to download current drivers to work with Inkwell technology in Mac OS X.

If you have a graphics pad, you can turn on the Inkwell technology by accessing the Ink pane of System Preferences. At the top of that pane, you'll see a simple option to turn on Handwriting Recognition: click the On radio button. When Inkwell is turned on, you'll see the InkPad window (which is titled simply Ink). In the InkPad window, you can use your graphics tablet to begin writing words. As you write, the words will be recognized and turned into computer text.

In the InkPad window, you can click the Clear button to clear the current text or the Send button to send text to the application that's in the foreground, such as TextEdit or another text application. (The InkPad window is a floating palette, so it will always appear over the active window.) As you write, you'll also find that you can use certain gestures for important items such as tabs, backspaces, and returns. You can see the gestures by choosing the Gestures tab in the Ink pane of System Preferences. (You can also turn the gestures on and off on that tab.)

TIP   Unless you're experienced in working with a graphics tablet, you may find that it doesn't offer enough resistance for you to write well. Here's a trick to help you get used to working with a tablet: Put a piece of paper over it. You'll get just the right amount of drag—about the same as when you write with a pencil and paper—and most tablets will work fine with a piece of paper between the pen and tablet.

In addition, the InkPad window gives you the option of sending drawn text to the frontmost application, as well. Choose the Star icon at the bottom of the InkPad window, and you'll see a grid; you can draw on that grid (or write text that won't be translated) and then use the Send button to send a graphical image of your work to the target application (see Figure C.6).

FIGURE C.6
Adding graphical images to documents using the InkPad window—just draw and click Send.

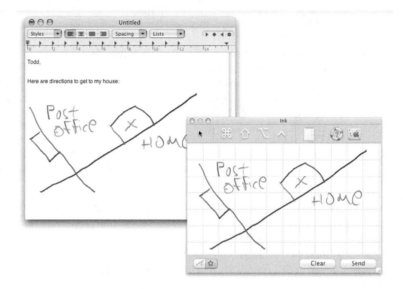

NOTE   The InkPad's toolbar includes icons that look like Apple's special keyboard keys such as ⌘; you can select one of those and then write letters, such as Q or S, to invoke keyboard shortcut commands. In my experience, they work only when you have the Write Anywhere option turned on and you write the command letter over the window in question; more on Write Anywhere in this section.

The Ink pane gives you access to a number of options. On the Settings tab, you can choose whether Inkwell will respond only to written gestures in the InkPad or if you can write anywhere on the screen. With Write Anywhere turned on, a sheet of paper seems to appear under your pen's pointer when you begin writing; the writing is interpreted by the computer and immediately placed in the active application. (As noted, this also is how keyboard commands can be invoked with the modifier icons in the InkPad window.)

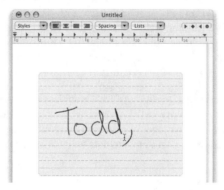

On the Settings tab, you also can tell Inkwell how far apart you generally write. Change this if you see spaces between the letters in your words or no spaces between the words as they're interpreted. You also can choose a font and a sound to be used in the InkPad. Click the Options button, and you'll see a dialog sheet that lets you alter some other Inkwell behaviors, such as how long it waits before recognizing your text (set this longer if you write slowly and Inkwell is always getting ahead of you) and other preferences.

TIP On the Word List tab, you can add words that you write frequently but which aren't recognized well. This might be a good place to put your last name, business name, technical terms, or something else that you type frequently but that Inkwell doesn't properly recognize.

The InkPad window can get in the way sometimes, so note that you can use its Maximize button to change its size, even though you can't minimize it to the Dock. To close it, you'll need to turn off Inkwell by clicking the Off radio button in the Ink pane of System Preferences.

What's Next?

Congratulations, you've reached the end of the book! There's nothing left but the index, which you'll find very helpful when you want to dip back into the book and look up something specific. We wish you all the best with Mac OS X Tiger, and we hope you'll find lots of useful information, explanations, and tips in this book.

Index

Note to the Reader: Throughout this index **boldfaced** page numbers indicate primary discussions of a topic. *Italicized* page numbers indicate illustrations.

Features

Designers, writers, musicians, business leaders & our technical expert team offer their own personal interpretation of things that only the Mac system can deliver. 200 pages of news, insights, trends and the largest Macintosh buyer's guide including over 5,000 Mac products and services.

MacDirectory

SUBSCRIBE ONLINE NOW AT MACDIRECTORY.COM

Subscribe

For faster delivery, subscribe online:
macdirectory.com/mw.html
One year subscription for $32 or two years for $64. Please send check to:
MacDirectory Subscription Department
326 A Street, 2C, Boston MA 02110